YEARBOOK OF INTERNATIONAL HUMANITARIAN LAW

YEARBOOK OF INTERNATIONAL HUMANITARIAN LAW

H. FISCHER
General Editor

AVRIL MCDONALD
Managing Editor

VOLUME 5

2002

T·M·C·ASSER PRESS

Published by T.M.C.ASSER PRESS,
P.O. Box 16163, 2500 BD The Hague, The Netherlands
www.asserpress.nl

T.M.C.ASSER PRESS English language books are distributed exclusively by:

Cambridge University Press, The Edinburgh Building, Shaftesbury Road,
Cambridge CB2 2RU, UK,
or
for customers in the USA, Canada and Mexico:
Cambridge University Press, 100 Brook Hill Drive, West Nyack, NY 10994-2133, USA

www.cambridge.org

Cover photograph: Tuzla. Little girl holding the photo
of a family member who went missing during the war.
© CICR/PELLEGRINI, Paolo / Courtesy of the ICRC

ISBN 90-6704-189-0
ISBN 978-90-6704-189-8
ISSN 1389-1359

**T.M.C. Asser Instituut – Institute for Private and Public International Law, International
Commercial Arbitration and European Law**
Institute Address: R.J. Schimmelpennincklaan 20-22, The Hague, The Netherlands; Mailing Address: P.O. Box 30461, 2500 GL The Hague, The Netherlands; Tel.: (31-70)3420300; Fax: (31-70)3420359; Internet: www.asser.nl.
Over thirty years, the T.M.C. Asser Institute has developed into a leading scientific research institute in the field of international law. It covers private international law, public international law, including international humanitarian law, the law of the European Union, the law of international commercial arbitration and increasingly, also, international economic law and the law of international commerce.
Conducting scientific research, either fundamental or applied, in the aforementioned domains, is the main activity of the Institute. In addition, the Institute organizes congresses and postgraduate courses, undertakes contract-research and operates its own publishing house.
Because of its inter-university background, the Institute often cooperates with Dutch law faculties as well as with various national and foreign institutions. The Institute organizes *Asser College Europe*, a project in cooperation with East and Central European countries whereby research and educational projects are organized and implemented.

CORRESPONDENTS

The Yearbook of International Humanitarian Law *extends its sincere thanks and appreciation to its correspondents, without whose assistance the compilation of this volume would not have been possible:*

AFRICA
Dr Jose Doria, *Angola*
Mr Kamel Filali, *Algeria*
Mr Adel Maged, *Egypt*
Dr Phenyo Keising Rakate, *South Africa*
Dr Kinthure Kindiki, *Kenya*
Professor Khadija Elmadmad, *Morocco*
Dr Abderrahim Kounda, *Morocco*
Mr Abdul Tejan-Cole, *Sierra Leone*
Dr Khoti Kamanga, *Tanzania*
Dr Emmanuel Kasimbazi, *Uganda*

ASIA-PACIFIC
Professor Tim McCormack, *Australia*
Mr David Boyle, *Cambodia*
Mr Nilenadra Kumar, *India*
Professor Hideyuki Kasutani, *Japan*
Professor Seigo Iwamoto, *Japan*
Ms Dana Zhandayeva, *Kazakhstan*
Ms Treasa Dunworth, *New Zealand*
Mr Sol Santos, *The Philippines*

EUROPE
Dr Thomas Desch, *Austria*
Mr Peter Kustor, *Austria*
Mr Munir Mammadov, *Azerbaijan*
Mr Oleg Starovoitov, *Belarus*
Professor Eric David, *Belgium*
Mr Jan Hladik, *Czech Republic/Slovakia*
Mr Peter Otken, *Denmark*
Mr Tanel Kerikmäe, *Estonia*
Mr Andres Parmas, *Estonia*
Mr Michael E. Hartmann, *Federal Republic of Yugoslavia*
Professor Miodrag Starčević, *Federal Republic of Yugoslavia*
Professor Paul Tavernier, *France*
Dr Sascha Rolf Lüder, *Germany*
Mr Gregor Schotten, *Germany*
Dr Maria Gavouneli, *Greece*
Dr Péter Kovács, *Hungary*
Professor Colm Campbell, *Ireland*
Dr Ray Murphy, *Ireland*
Dr Clara Bosco, *Italy*
Dr Giovanni Carlo Bruno, *Italy*
Dr Rosa Dinuzzi, *Italy*
Dr Valeria Eboli, *Italy*

Dr Ornella Ferrajolo, *Italy*
Dr Valentina della Fina, *Italy*
Professor Sergio Marchisio, *Italy*
Dr Fabio Raspadori, *Italy*
Dr Guilliano Salberini, *Italy*
Professor Gedimanas Mesonis, *Lithuania*
Mr Rytis Satkausas, *Lithuania*
Professor Nico Keijzer, *the Netherlands*
Dr Elies van Sliedregt, *the Netherlands*
Professor Elzbieta Mikos-Skuza, *Poland*
Professor Santiago Castellá, *Spain*
Professor Antoni Pigrau I Solé, *Spain*
Mr Ola Engdahl, *Sweden*
Ms Roberta Arnold, *Switzerland*
Mr Peter Hostettler, *Switzerland*
Dr Djura Inomzoda, *Tajikistan*
Mr A.P.V. Rogers, *United Kingdom*

MIDDLE EAST
Mr Mehrdad Molaei, *Iran*
Professor Djamchid Momtaz, *Iran*
Dr Yuval Shang, *Israel*
Dr Mustafa Mari, *Occupied Palestinian Territories*

NORTH AMERICA
Professor René Provost, *Canada*
Mr Joseph Rikhof, *Canada*
Professor William A. Schabas, *Canada*
Mr Burrus M. Carnahan, *USA*

CENTRAL AND SOUTH AMERICA
Professor José Alejandro Consigli, *Argentina*
Mr Gabriel Valladares, *Argentina*
Professor Carlos Dettleff Beros, *Chile*
Dr Sebastián Lopéz Escarcena, *Chili*
Professor Hernan Salinas Burgos, *Chile*
Professor Rafael A. Prieto Sanjuan, *Colombia*
Dr José A. Guevara, *Mexico*
Ms Fatima Andrada, *Paraguay*
Professor Alfonso Velázquez, *Paraguay*

CORRESPONDENTS-AT-LARGE
Dr Avril McDonald
Ms Maria Nybondas

TABLE OF CONTENTS

CORRESPONDENTS' REPORTS

Roberta Arnold, Clara Bosco, David Boyle, Giovanni Carlo Bruno, Burrus
M. Carnahan, Santiago Castellá, José Consigli, Anna Danieli, Eric David,
Valentina Della Fina, Thomas Desch, Rosa Dinuzzi, Treasa Dunworth,
Valeria Eboli, Khadija Elmadmad, Ola Engdahl, Ornella Ferrajolo, José
A. Guevara, Michael E. Hartmann, Jan Hladik, Peter Hostettler, Seigo
Iwamoto, Hideyuki Kasutani, Nico Keijzer, Phenyo Keiseng Rakate,
Abderrahim Kounda, Péter Kovács, Nilenadra Kumar, Peter Kustor,
Sebastián Lopéz Escarcena, Mustafa Mari, Tim McCormack, Avril
McDonald, Ray Murphy, Maria Nybondas, Peter Otken, Antoni Pigrau,
Rafael A. Prieto Sanjuán, René Provost, A.P.V. Rogers, Sascha Rolf
Lüder, Hernán Salinas Burgos, Rytis Satkauskas, Gregor Schotten, Yuval
Shany, Miodrag Starčević, Paul Tavernier, Gabriel Valladares, Dana
Zhandayeva

DOCUMENTATION

ABBREVIATIONS

Abl .	Amtsblatt
AC	Appeal Cases
ACTR	Australian Capital Territory Reports
AD	Annual Digest of Public International Law Cases
Adelaide LR	Adelaide Law Review
ADF	Australian Defence Force
AFDI	Annuaire français de droit international
African JI & CL	African Journal of International & Comparative Law
African YbIL	African Yearbook of International Law
Air Force LR	Air Force Law Review
AJIL	American Journal of International Law
Albany LR	Albany Law Review
All ER	All England Law Reports
ALR	Australian Law Reports
Amer. Univ. JIL & Pol.	American University Journal of International Law and Policy
Amer. Univ. ILJ	American University International Law Journal
Amer. Univ. ILR	American University International Law Review
AP	Additional Protocol
AP	Associated Press
APL(s)	Anti-personnel landmine(s)
ARABSAT	Arab Satellite Communications Organization
Arizona JI & CL	Arizona Journal of International and Comparative Law
ASEAN	Association of South East Asian Nations
ATCA	Alien Tort Claims Act (USA)
Australian YIL	Australian Yearbook of International Law
Austrian JPIL	Austrian Journal for Public International Law
Austrian Rev. Int. & Eur. L	Austrian Revue of International and European Law
AVM	Anti-vehicle landmine
Berkeley JIL	Berkeley Journal of International Law
B.O.	Boletín Oficial de la República Argentina
BGBl	Bundesgesetzblatt (Austria)
BGH	Bundesgerichtshof
BlbNR	Beilagen zu den Stenographischen Protokollen des National-rates
Boston Univ. ILJ	Boston University International Law Journal
Boston College Int. & Comp. LR	Boston College International and Comparative Law Review
BTF	Balkans Task Force
BverfGE	Bundesverfassungs Gesetzblatt
BYIL	British Yearbook of International Law
Calif. Western ILJ	California Western International Law Journal
Can. JL & Jur.	Canadian Journal of Law and Jurisprudence

Canadian YIL	The Canadian Yearbook of International Law
Case Western Reserve JIL	Case Western Reserve Journal of International Law
Catholic Univ. LR	Catholic University Law Review
CCW	Convention on certain Conventional Weapons
CD	Conference on Disarmament
CENTCOM	Central Command
CHR (UN)	Centre for Human Rights
CIA	Central Intelligence Agency
CICR	Comité International de la Croix Rouge
CID	Criminal Investigation Division
CIS	Commonwealth of Independent States
CIVPOL	Civilian Police
CLA	Chief Legal Advisor
CLJ	Criminal Law Journal
CLR	Commonwealth Law Reports
CMAC	Court Martial Appeal Court
Cmnd.	Command Paper
Colorado JI Environ. L & Pol.	The Colorado Journal of International Environmental Law and Policy
Colum. HRLR	Columbia Human Rights Law Review
Columbia JTL	Columbia Journal of Transnational Law
Cornell ILJ	Cornell International Law Journal
Cr. App. R	Criminal Appeals Reports
CRC	Convention on the Rights of the Child
Creighton LR	Creighton Law Review
Criminal LF	Criminal Law Forum
Criminal LR	Criminal Law Review
CSP	Conference of States Parties
CTBT	Comprehensive Test Ban Treaty
CTS	Commonwealth Treaty Series
CWC	Chemical Weapons Convention
Dalhousie LJ	Dalhousie Law Journal
Denver JIL & Pol.	Denver Journal of International Law and Policy
DLR	Dominian Law Reports
DMU	Detainee Management Unit
DoD	Department of Defense (USA)
Duke JC & IL	Duke Journal of Comparative & International Law
ECCAS	Economic Community of Central African States
ECHR Rep.	European Convention on Human Rights Reports
ECHR	European Convention on Human Rights
ECOMOG	ECOWAS Monitoring Group
ECOSOC	UN Economic and Social Council
ECOWAS	Economic Community of West African States
EHRR	European Human Rights Reports
Emory ILR	Emory International Law Review
EJIL	European Journal of International Law
ERW	Explosive Remnants of War

EU	European Union
Eur. Ct. HR	European Court of Human Rights
Eur. Comm. HR	European Commission of Human Rights
Eur. J. Crime, Crim. L & Crim. Jus.	European Journal of Crime, Criminal Law and Criminal Justice
Ex D	Exchequer Digest
F	Federal
F Supp.	Federal Supplement
FCJ	Federal Court of Justice (Canada)
FCR	Federal Court Reports
FDC	Force Detention Centre
FDTL	East Timorese Defence Force
Fed. Rep.	Federal Reporter
Finnish YIL	Finnish Yearbook of International Law
Fordham ILJ	Fordham International Law Journal
FRETILIN	Frente Revolucionaria Timor Lest Independence
FRY	Federal Republic of Yugoslavia
GA Res.	General Assembly Resolutions (UN)
GA	General Assembly (UN)
GAOR	General Assembly Official Records (UN)
GC	Geneva Conventions
German LJ	German Law Journal
Georgetown Int. Environ. LR	Georgetown International Environmental Law Review
Georgia JL & Comp. L	Georgia Journal of International and Comparative Law
GP	Gesetzgebungsperiode
GrCC	Greek Criminal Code
GU	Gazzetta Ufficiale (Italian Official Gazette)
GYIL	German Yearbook of International Law
Hague Recueil	Recueil des Cours (Collected Courses, Hague Academy of International Law)
Hague YIL	Hague Yearbook of International Law
Harvard ILJ	Harvard International Law Journal
HCJ	High Court of Justice
HRLJ	Human Rights Law Journal
HRQ	Human Rights Quarterly
I/A Court HR	Inter-American Court of Human Rights
I/A Comm. HR	Inter-American Commission on Human Rights
ICA	International Council on Archives
ICBL	International Campaign to Ban Landmines
ICBS	International Committee of the Blue Shield
ICC	International Criminal Court
ICCPR	International Covenant on Civil and Political Rights
ICCROM	International Centre for the Study of the Preservation and Restoration of Cultural Property
ICJ	International Court of Justice

ICJ Rep.	International Court of Justice Reports
ICLR	International Criminal Law Review
ICLQ	International and Comparative Law Quarterly
ICOM	International Council of Museums
ICOMOS	International Council on Monuments and Sites
ICRC	International Committee of the Red Cross
ICTR	International Criminal Tribunal for Rwanda
ICTY	International Criminal Tribunal for the Former Yugoslavia
IFLA	International Federation of Library Association and Institutions
IFOR	Implementation Force
IHL	International Humanitarian Law
IJ Est. & Coastal L	International Journal of Estuarine and Coastal Law
ILC Yearbook	Yearbook of the International Law Commission
ILM	International Legal Materials
ILR	International Law Reports
ILSA JI & CL ILSA	Journal of International and Comparative Law
IMT	International Military Tribunal (in Nuremberg)
IMTFE	International Military Tribunal for the Far East (in Tokyo)
Indian JIL	Indian Journal of International Law
INTELSAT	International Telecommunications Satellite Organization
Int. LF	International Law Forum
INTERFET	International Force in East Timor
IRA	Irish Republican Army
IRRC	International Review of the Red Cross
ISAF	International Security Assistance Force
Israel LR	Israel Law Review
Israel YB	Israel Yearbook
Israel YB HR	Israel Yearbook on Human Rights
J Armed Conflict L	Journal of Armed Conflict Law
JIL & Prac.	Journal of International Law and Practice
JPI	Judicial Police Inspectors
KFOR	Kosovo Force
LAS	League of Arab States
Leiden JIL	Leiden Journal of International Law
LNTS	League of Nations Treaty Series
LOAC	Law of Armed Conflicts
Loyola LA I & CLJ	Loyola of Los Angeles International and Comparative Law Journal
LQR	Law Quarterly Review
Maryland JIL & T	Maryland Journal of International Law and Trade
MCC	Military Criminal Code
Melbourne JIL	Melbourne Journal of International Law
Melbourne Univ. LR	Melbourne University Law Review
Mich. JIL	Michigan Journal of International Law
Mich. LR	Michigan Law Review
Mil. LR	Military Law Review

MLR	Modern Law Review
MNF	Multinational Force
Monash LR	Monash Law Review
Moscow JIL	Moscow Journal of International Law
MPYBUNL	Max Planck Yearbook of United Nations Law
MPYIL	Max Planck Yearbook of International Law
NATO	North Atlantic Treaty Organisation
NCOs	Non-Commissioned Officers
New England LR	New England Law Review
New York ILR	New York International Law Review
NGO	Non-Governmental Organisation
NILR	Netherlands International Law Review
NLR	Naval Law Review
Nordic JIL	Nordic Journal of International Law
Notre Dame JL	Notre Dame Journal of Law
Notre Dame JL Ethics & Pub. Policy	Notre Dame Law Journal of Law Ethics & Public Policy
NPC	New Penal Code
NQHR	Netherlands Quarterly of Human Rights
NY Univ. JIL & Pol.	New York University Journal of International Law and Politics
NY Univ. LR	New York University Law Review
NYIL	Netherlands Yearbook of International Law
NZLR	New Zealand Universities Law Review
ÖAD	Österreichische Außenpolitische Dokumentation
OAS	Organization of American States
OECS	Organization of Eastern Caribbean States
OIOS (UN)	Office of Internal Oversight Services
ONU	Organisation Nations Unies
ONUC	United Nations Force in the Congo
OPCW	Organisation for the Prohibition of Chemical Weapons
OSA	Operational Support Arrangement
OTP	Office of the Prosecutor (of the ICTR and/or ICTY)
Pace ILR	Pace International Law Review
Palestine YIL	Palestine Yearbook of International Law
PD	Probate Division, English Law Reports
Penn. State ILR	Pennsylvania State International Law Review
PKF	Peace Keeping Force
PMG	Peace Monitoring Group
POW	Prisoner of War
Proc. ASIL	Proceedings of the American Society of International Law
QB	Queen's Bench
RBDI	Revue Belge de droit international
RDI	Rivista di diritto internazionale

RDPC	Revue de droit pénal et de criminologie
Recueil des Cours	Collected Courses of the Hague Academy of International Law
RGDIP	Revue générale de droit international public
RIAA	Reports of International Arbitral Awards
RICR	Revue International de la Croix Rouge
RQDI	Revue Québécoise de Droit International
RSC	Rules of the Supreme Court
RSCDPC	Revue de science criminelle et de droit pénal compare
RV	Regierungsvorlage
SADC	South African Development Community
SASC	South African Security Council
SC (UN)	Security Council
SC Res.	Security Council Resolution
SCOR	Security Council Official Records
SCR	Supreme Court Reports
SCU	Serious Crimes Unit
SFOR	Stabilization Force
SFRY	Socialist Federal Republic of Yugoslavia
SIPRI	Stockholm International Peace Research Institute
SOFA	Status of Force Agreement
South African LR	South African Law Review
Sri Lanka JIL	Sri Lanka Journal of International Law
Stanford JIL	Stanford Journal of International Law
SZIER/RSDIE	Schweizerische Zeitschrift für internationales und europäisches Recht / Revue Suisse de droit international et de droit européen
Texas ILJ	Texas International Law Journal
Texas LR	Texas Law Review
TIAS	Treaties and other International Acts Series
Tilburg For. LR	Tilburg Foreign Law Review
TLPS	Timorese Police Force
Transn. L & Contemp. Probs.	Transnational Law and Contemporary Problems
TRC Report (South African)	Truth and Reconciliation Commission Report
Tulane JI & Comp, L	Tulane Journal of International and Comparative Law
UNAMET	United Nations Mission in East Timor
UNAMIR	United Nations Assistance Mission for Rwanda
UNCHR	United Nations Commission on Human Rights
UNCHS	United Nations Centre for Human Settlements
UNCIVPOL	United Nations Civilian Police
UNCTAD	United Nations Conference on Trade and Development
UN Doc.	United Nations Documents Series
UNDP	United Nations Development Programme
UNEF	United Nations Emergency Force (in the Sinai)
UNEP	United Nations Environment Programme

UNESCO	United Nations Educational, Scientific and Cultural Organisation
UNFICYP	United Nations Force in Cyprus
UN GAOR	United Nations General Assembly Official Records
UNGCI	United Nations Guards Contingent in Iraq
UNHCR	United Nations High Commissioner for Refugees
UNHFOR	United Nations Human Rights Field Office in Rwanda
UNICEF	United Nations (International) Children's (Emergency) Fund
UNIDIR	United Nations Institute for Disarmament Research
UNIFIL	United Nations Interim Force in Lebanon
UNIIMOG	United Nations Iran/Iraq Military Observer Group
UNIKOM	United Nations Iraq/Kuwait Observer Mission
UNITAF	United Nations Unified Task Force
UNITAF	United Nations Task Force (in Somalia)
Univ. Calif. Davis JIL & Pol.	University of California, Davis Journal of International Law and Policy
UNOMSIL	United Nations Observer Mission in Sierra Leone
UNOSOM	United Nations Operation in Somalia
UNPF	United Nations Peacekeeping Force
UNPROFOR	United Nations Protection Force (in Bosnia and Herzegovina)
UNSC	United Nations Security Council
UNTAC	United Nations Transitional Authority in Cambodia
UNTAET	United Nations Transitional Authority in East Timor
UNTS	United Nations Treaty Series
UNWCC	United Nations War Crimes Commission
USDOD	United States Department of Defense
Vanderbilt JTL	Vanderbilt Journal of Transnational Law
Vermont LR	Vermont Law Review
Virginia JIL	Virginia Journal of International Law
Virginia LR	Virginia Law Review
WCR	War Crimes Reports
WHO	World Health Organisation
Whittier LR	Whittier Law Review
Wisconsin ILJ	Wisconsin International Law Journal
WLR	Weekly Law Reports
Yale LJ	Yale Law Journal
Yale JIL	Yale Journal of International Law
Yb Eur. Conv. HR	Yearbook of the European Convention of Human Rights
Yb ILC	Yearbook of the International Law Commission
YIHL	Yearbook of International Humanitarian Law
Yug. Rev. IL	Yugoslav Review of International Law
ZaöRV	Zeitschrift für ausländisches öffentliches Recht und Völkerrecht
ZöR	Zeitschrift für öffentliches Recht (Austrian Journal of Public and International Law)

ARTICLES

ANGOLA: A CASE STUDY IN THE CHALLENGES OF ACHIEVING PEACE AND THE QUESTION OF AMNESTY OR PROSECUTION OF WAR CRIMES IN MIXED ARMED CONFLICTS[1]

José Doria[2]

1. © J. Doria 2004.

2. José Doria, LL.M (Moscow), Ph.D (Moscow), is a former Associate Professor (Chair of International Law) at the People's Friendship University of Russia (Moscow), currently with the Prosecution Division of the Office of the Prosecutor, UN International Criminal Tribunal for the Former Yugoslavia in The Hague. The views expressed herein are solely those of the author and do not necessarily reflect those of the Office of the Prosecutor or those of the United Nations.

1.   INTRODUCTION

On 22 February 2002, Jonas Malheiro Savimbi, who led the UNITA[3] rebel movement during the bloody armed conflict in Angola[4] and who had battled to take power by force since Angola's independence from Portugal in 1975, was killed in a gun battle with the Angolan Army.[5] During the Cold War, Savimbi was a proxy for the United States against the then-Marxist government of Angola. But after the end of the Cold War, he lost international support for rejecting peace efforts. He was accused of perpetuating a bloody internal conflict to advance his own interests and was exposed to international sanctions.[6] Meanwhile, the government of President José Eduardo dos Santos moved closer to the United States.[7]

The 27-year-long armed conflict is believed to have killed approximately one million people and driven four million others from their homes, creating a humanitarian crisis.[8] In addition, the conflict destroyed almost all of the country's infrastructure, and effectively disrupted every effort by the government to start the long desired national reconstruction after independence, and the building of prosperity for the nation's children.

Savimbi was viewed as the primary obstacle to peace, personifying the 'corrupting influence of ambition, mineral wealth, and the grinding brutality of war'.[9] His

---

3. 'UNITA' is the Portuguese acronym for 'National Union for the Total Independence of Angola' (União Nacional para a Independência Total de Angola). It was founded in 1966 by the late Mr Jonas Savimbi.

4. With a surface area of 1,246,700 sq. km (equal to the combined territory of France, Germany, Spain and Portugal), Angola is situated in the tropical zone of southwestern Africa. It shares borders with Congo (Brazzaville) to the north, with the Democratic Republic of Congo to the north and east, with Zambia in the East and with Namibia to the south. In the west, the Atlantic Ocean coast extends for 1,650 km. The land border stretches for 4,827 km. The population is estimated at 12 million, mainly of the Bantu ethno-linguistic group of Africa which is believed emigrated here from central Africa in the first millennium BC. The eight major Bantu ethno-linguistic subgroups living in Angola are: Bakongo, Ambunbu, Lunda-tchokwe, Ovimbundu, Nganguela, Herero, Nhaneka-Humbi and Ambo. One major non-Bantu ethno-linguistic group in Angola is the Khoisan. These groups settled here over the ages and founded Kingdoms, such as the Kongo, Pungo-Andongo, Lunda, Bailundo and others. The Portuguese first arrived in the territory that is now Angola in 1482, opening a period of trade relations with the various Angolan Kingdoms. These relations were strengthened with the arrival a century later in 1575 of another hundred Portuguese families to settle in what is nowadays Luanda (the capital city). See generally about the history of Portugal in Angola: G.J. Bender, *Angola under the Portuguese – The Myth and the Reality* (London, Heinemman 1978); D.L. Wheeler, R. Pélissier, *Angola* (London, Pall Mall Press 1971).

5. See Editorial, 'Jonas Savimbi morre em combate', *Jornal de Angola* (23 February 2002). See also M. Dynes, 'Hope for Peace in Angola After Savimbi Death Report', *The Times* (London) (23 February 2002).

6. See A. Blondin Beye, 'Le Processus de Rétablissement et de Maintien de la Paix en Angola', 5 *African YbIL* (1997) p. 3; See also F. Wahid Dahmane, 'Les mesures prises par le Conseil de Sécurité contre les entites non-étatiques', 11 *African JI &CL* (1999) p. 227.

7. In 1993, the United States recognised the government of Angola, 18 years after its independence. See M. Nash (Leich), 'Recognition of Governments – United States-Angola', 87 *AJIL* (1993) p. 595.

8. See Interim Report of the UN Secretary-General on the United Nations Mission in Angola, UN Doc. S/2002/1353 (2002).

9. Editorial, 'Death of a Warlord', *The Times* (London, 25 February 2002) at p. 46.

death finally paved the way for peace, and enabled the Angolan government and UNITA to sign the Luena Memorandum of Understanding on 4 April 2002.[10]

This agreement established an immediate ceasefire and called for UNITA's return to the peace process as laid down in the 1994 Lusaka Protocol.[11] Angolan legislation expressly states that no political party should be armed.[12] UNITA was, so far, the sole exception. This factor was one of the major obstacles to the peace process in Angola since the 1991 Bicesse Accords.[13] Therefore, the main provision of the Luena Memorandum of Understanding provides for the complete disbanding of UNITA's military wing.[14] Accordingly, UNITA quartered all its military personnel in established reception areas and handed its remaining arms over to the Angolan government. By 2 August 2002, this objective was achieved.[15] There were no more UNITA military forces in Angola, marking the effective end of a conflict that had lasted for more than a quarter of a century and the advent of a lasting peace in the country.

1.1   The aim and structure of this paper

A study of certain aspects of the transitional process in Angola is useful in particular for showing the difficulties facing countries trying to achieve lasting peace and reconciliation while at the same time deal with the question of justice for the victims of war crimes, and highlighting the difficult compromises that in reality are often reached. Particularly where the conflict is mixed, complex and long-lasting, as in the case of Angola, the overriding political objective may be to end foreign interference within the state's internal affairs, terminate hostilities and disarm and demobilise the rebel forces and incorporate them into civilian and political life. Under these circumstances, very often, the question of justice for the victims is only partly solved (perhaps, if at all, in terms of community-based compensation to the victims), but not in terms of prosecution of indigenous perpetrators of serious crimes. Prosecution is not only a lesser objective but its absence is considered an obvious condition *sine qua non* for achieving a lasting peace still dependant on other factors considered even more important than this (the cessation of foreign interference within the internal affairs of the country). Indeed as the Angolan experience shows, lasting peace in the country never was dependant upon the grant-

---

10. Memorandum de Entendimento Complementar ao Protocolo de Lusaka Para a Cessação das Hostilidades e Resolução das Demais Questões Militares Pendentes nos Termos do Protocolo de Lusaka, 4 Abril 2002 (hereinafter, Luena Memorandum) UN Doc. S/2002/483 (2002). For a detailed account of the Luena Memorandum see *infra* Section 5.

11. See Protocolo de Lusaka, 21 de Novembro de 1994 (hereinafter, Lusaka Protocol), UN Doc. S/1994/1441, annex (1994).

12. Lei dos Partidos Políticos, Lei No. 15/91, de 11 de Maio de 1991, Art. 5, Diário da República, I Série No. 20.

13. Acordos de Paz Para Angola, 31 de Maio de 1991 (hereinafter, Bicesse Accords), UN Doc. S/22609 (1991).

14. See Luena Memorandum, *supra* n. 10 (chapter II, 2, (f)).

15. See Interim Report of the UN Secretary-General on the United Nations Mission in Angola, *supra* n. 8.

ing of amnesty to the rebels. Over a period of 41 years of permanent fighting, UN-endorsed amnesties were granted in all four peace agreements but these concessions failed to stop war restarting. The Angolan case study shows that, at least in this case, it was the cessation of armed foreign intervention in the conflict (be it in the form of direct or indirect military intervention or complicity in diamond smuggling), rather than the grant of amnesty (albeit that one was granted as part of the Bicesse Accords, Luzaka Protocol and Luena Agreement) that proved to be the crucial factor for the achievement of a lasting peace. For this reason the paper will discuss both factors (internal and external) relevant to the achievement of a lasting peace in the country.

Regarding the internal processes, the paper discusses the negotiating process which led in 2002 to the signing of the lasting ceasefire and peace agreement, bringing about the definitive termination of the armed conflict in Angola. The factors considered decisive in enabling an agreement leading to an effective termination of this long-term mixed armed conflict are considered in detail. The place, scope, importance and legal foundations of amnesties and pardons in the context of internal armed conflicts, as factors considered in reaching lasting peace agreements, are reviewed, as are the questions of the legal obligation of states to prosecute war crimes committed in internal armed conflicts and the legal basis of international criminal responsibility for such crimes.

The paper also seeks to illustrate the complexity of regulation of internal armed conflicts which are fought not as genuine internal wars but as *proxy* wars in which superpowers and foreign armed forces are heavily involved, which makes difficult not only the characterisation of the conflict and application of the laws of war to it, but also the achievement of a lasting peace and successful termination of the armed conflict until such interference ceases. The question of justice to the victims in the international segment of the Angolan mixed conflict both in terms of prosecution of serious war crimes and compensation for the victims is reviewed.

The following structure will be adopted. The study will next deal briefly with the history of the Angolan mixed armed conflict, and the various peace agreements which fell apart (Section 2). Next is an analysis of the character of the various segments of the armed conflict in Angola, followed by an analysis of the application of the laws of war to them (Sections 3 and 4). Then the paper will deal properly with the legal problems of the post-war transitional period. It starts with an analysis of the Luena Memorandum, and why it succeeded where earlier peace agreements did not (Section 5), followed by a discussion of the question of criminal accountability or amnesty for persons who committed war crimes in the context of the internal armed conflict in Angola, and in this context, the circumstances and validity of criminal proceedings against UNITA rebel commander Savimbi on the one hand, and the adoption of the 2002 Amnesty Law to pardon the deeds of the rest of the rebels on the other (Section 6). This is succeeded by a discussion of the question of war reparations and criminal accountability of persons who committed serious war crimes and crimes against humanity in the international segment of the armed conflict involving South Africa (Section 7). The paper ends with some concluding remarks (Section 8).

2.   A BRIEF HISTORY OF THE ANGOLAN ARMED CONFLICTS AND THE FAILED PEACE PROCESSSES

In 1951, in an attempt to perpetuate the colonial domination of Angola, Portugal decided to change the administrative colonial status of Angola, upgrading it to that of an 'overseas province'. There followed a period of intense diplomatic efforts by Portugal in trying to ascertain its rights to Angola. Portugal argued that Angola was an integral part of it, and the Angolan people were all 'Portuguese citizens'.[16]

However, Portugal came under increasing UN pressure to cede independence. The UN, in reaching its conclusion that Angola was a non-self-governing territory, analysed, *inter alia*, the following factors: a) Administratively, the central authorities were in Lisbon and they alone were responsible for taking final decisions, without the people of Angola concerned being heard or represented; b) Economically, the overseas territories were not only less developed than metropolitan Portugal but also relegated by the structure and organisation of their economy to a secondary and subordinate position; c) Finally, regarding the contested issue of historic titles, the Portuguese possession of Angola derived from war and military conquest and these did not confer legitimate sovereignty.[17]

The UN position in favour of the decolonisation of all non-self governing territories, which came of age with the adoption of the 1960 UN Declaration on conceding independence to all colonial countries and peoples,[18] boosted the national liberation war efforts in Angola. On 4 February 1961, the Popular Movement for the Liberation of Angola (MPLA)[19] launched its first armed attack in Luanda, marking the beginning of the armed struggle against the colonial power in Angola.[20]

The Portuguese soldiers sent to quell the growing liberation struggle in Angola lacked enthusiasm for the war. In April 1974, Portuguese soldiers staged a successful coup ('the revolution of the carnations') to overthrow the Salazar and Caetano regime in Portugal. The new Portuguese revolutionary government under General Costa Gomes decided to grant independence to Angola and other African colonies.[21]

---

16. See F. Nogueira, *United Nations and Portugal, A study of anti-colonialism* (London, Sidgwick and Jackson 1963) at pp. 65-93.

17. Ibid., at pp. 74-75.

18. See UNGA Res. 1514 (XV), 14 December 1960 (UN Declaration on the granting of independence to all colonial countries and peoples).

19. MPLA (Movimento Popular de Libertação de Angola) was founded in 1956. Its President, and also the First President of Independent Angola, was the late Dr Agostinho Neto.

20. F.-W. Heimer, *The Decolonization Conflict in Angola, 1974-76, An Essay in Political Sociology*, (Geneva, Institut Universitaire de Hautes Etudes Internationales 1979) at p. 28.

21. Ibid., at pp. 39-46. See also R.A.H. Robinson, *Contemporary Portugal: a History* (London, George Allen and Unwin 1979); N. McQueen, *The Decolonization of Portuguese Africa: Metropolitan Revolution and the Dissolution of Empire* (London, Longman 1997); A. Humbaraci and N. Muchnik, *Portugal's African Wars: Angola, Guinea-Bissau, Mozambique* (New York, The Third Press 1974); John P. Cann, *Counterinsurgency in Africa, The Portuguese Way of War, 1961-1974* (Westport CT, Greenwood Press 1997); M. Smith-Morris, 'Angola-Recent History', *Africa South of the Sahara* (London, Europa Publications 1995).

Following armistice and ceasefire agreements between the Portuguese government and the fighting movements, the way was paved for direct negotiations of the terms of Angolan independence. As no single movement could claim to represent the aspirations of all of the Angolan people, three nationalist movements were recognised as their legitimate representatives and entered into an agreement with the new Portuguese government to end 500 years of Portuguese colonial rule: the MPLA, the National Front for the Liberation of Angola (FNLA)[22] and UNITA. The Alvor Agreement, signed on 15 January 1975[23] by Portugal with the three movements, was intended to provide a political and legal framework for a peaceful transference of power. A transitional government made up of the MPLA, FNLA, UNITA and Portugal was established under the Agreement to administer the country until independence, which date was set as 11 November 1975. The Agreement also provided for a general ceasefire and amnesty, and the formation of Unified Armed Forces made up of Portuguese and Angolan soldiers representing each of the three movements.

The Alvor Agreement, which had the objective of fostering mutual understanding among the three movements, soon broke down in August 1975, however, leading to a full-scale civil war among them.[24] The MPLA, a leftist movement, successfully seized power and declared the independence of the country in November 1975. FNLA, backed by Zairian troops and Western mercenaries[25] coming from the north, and UNITA/FNLA, backed by South African troops[26] coming from the south, attempted an assault on Luanda on the eve of independence. These

---

22. FNLA (Frente Popular de Libertação de Angola) was founded in 1962. Its President is Mr Holden Roberto.

23. Acordo entre o Estado Português e a Frente National de Libertação de Angola (FNLA), o Movimento Popular de Libertação de Angola (MPLA) e a União Nacional Para a Independência Total de Angola (UNITA) de 15 de Janiero de 1975 (hereinafter, Alvor Agreement). See Portuguese and English texts: *Angola, O Governo de Transição, Documentos e Personalidades* (Luanda, Livrangol 1975).

24. Commentators have expressed the view according to which failure by Portugal to insist in a 'power-sharing' principle (as the MPLA movement suggested), as opposed to the principle the 'winner takes all', in the post-election period of the Alvor Agreement is one of the major reasons for the fiasco of the Alvor independence process. As a result, having the most heavily and better prepared army and fearing for its fate after elections, FNLA (soon followed by UNITA) attempted instead of elections, a military solution to the conflict by attacking MPLA forces. MPLA resisted and expelled both movement forces from the Angolan major cities. The Portuguese Governor declared thereafter, in August 1975, the transitional government suspended until the date of elections on 11 November 1975. See Heimer, op. cit. n. 20, at pp. 60-61. See also W. Minter, *Apartheid's Contras, an inquiry into the roots of war in Angola and Mozambique* (London, Zed Books 1994) at pp. 19, 95.

25. On the involvement of mercenaries in the civil war in Angola in 1975-76, see J. Stockwell, *In Search of Enemies: a CIA story* (New York, Norton & Co. 1978). Stockwell was (by his own words) the CIA resident chief in Zaire of Special operations in Angola in 1975-1976. On early plans for American intervention in the Angolan conflict see M.A. El-Khawas and B. Thomas, eds., *The Kissinger Study of Southern Africa: National Security* Memorandum, (Westport CT, Lawrence Hill 1976) p. 39. See also, E. Harsch and T. Thomas, *Angola: The Hidden History of Washington's War* (New York, Pathfinder Press 1976). See about the trial of 13 of these mercenaries in Angola *infra* Section 7.

26. On the South African Intervention in Angola in 1975-1976, see 'Truth and Reconciliation Commission Report, 5 volumes' (Cape Town, Truth and Reconciliation Commission, 1998), Vol. 2 chapter 2, 'The State Outside South Africa between 1960 and 1990' (hereinafter TRC Report). See

forces were however repelled by the MPLA-based government with the assistance of Cuban troops[27] and Soviet weaponry.[28]

In the months that followed, the government of Angola was recognised by a majority of African and other states and admitted into the Organisation of African Unity (OAU[29]) and UN.[30]

While the FNLA defeat in 1975-1976 meant its total collapse, UNITA managed to avoid it and continue its bid for power, thanks to United States support[31] and a more solid rear base given by Apartheid South Africa, which feared its interests in illegally occupied Namibia would be jeopardised if the progress-oriented MPLA

---

also R. Hallett, 'The South African Intervention in Angola, 1975-76', 77 *African Affairs* (July 1978) pp. 347-386. See about the crimes of South African Army in Angola, *infra* Section 7.

27. About the Cuban and Soviet Intervention in Angola, see G. Garcia Marques, 'Operation Carlota', Nos. 101-2, 27 *New Left Review* (March-April 1977) p. 76 et seq.; W.J. Durch, 'The Cuban Military in Africa and the Middle East: From Algeria to Angola', 11 *Studies in Comparative Communism* (1978) p. 64 et seq.; J. Valenta, 'The Soviet-Cuban Intervention in Angola, 1975', 11 *Studies in Comparative Communism* (1978) p. 11 et seq.; B. Ponomarev, 'Invincibility of the Liberation Movement', *Socialism: Theory and Practice* (Moscow, Novosti Press Agency (Supplement) 1980); C. Stevens, 'The Soviet Union and Angola', 75 *African Affairs* (1976) p. 299.

28. See for a comprehensive overview of the dramatic events in 1974-1976 in Angola: P. Pezarat Correia, *Descolonização de Angola* (Luanda, Ler & Escrever 1991); Heimer, op. cit. n. 20; C. Legum and T. Hodges, *After Angola: The War over Southern Africa* (London, Rex Collings 1976); J.A. Marcum, *The Angolan Revolution, Volume II: Exile Politics and Guerrilla Warfare, 1962-1976,* (Cambridge MA, MIT 1978); F. Andersen Guimarães, *The Origins of the Angolan Civil War: Foreign Intervention and Domestic Political Conflict* (London, Macmillan 1998); H. Ekwe-Ekwe, *Conflict and Intervention in Africa, Nigeria, Angola, Zaire* (London, Macmillan 1990); V. Brittain, *Death of Dignity, Angola's Civil War* (London, Pluto Press 1998); W.M. James III, *A Political History of the Civil War in Angola 1974-1990* (New Brunswick NJ, Transaction Publishers 1992).

29. The OAU recognised the Angolan government on 11 February 1976, during its second meeting to discuss the situation in Angola. The first attempt in January 1976 to get OAU recognition of the new MPLA-led government of Angola ended in a draw: 22 to 22. The OAU member states in favour were: Guinea-Bissau; Mozambique; Cabo Verde; Sao Tome e Principe; Algeria; Congo (Brazzaville); Guinea Equatorial; Guinea; Madagascar; Somalia; Niger; Nigeria; Benin; Libya; Sudan; Tanzania; Mali, Ghana, Chad, Burundi, Mauritius, Comoros Islands. Those against recognition were: Egypt; Morocco; Tunisia; Botswana; Cameroon; Coté d'Ivoire; Gambia; Gabon; Burkina Fasso; Kenya; Liberia; Lesotho; Malawi; Mauritania; Rwanda; Central African Republic; Senegal; Sierra Leone; Swaziland; Togo; Zaire; Zambia. Thereafter, Ethiopia as the host country joined the group of those in favour, whereas Uganda holding the OAU presidency joined the group of those against recognition. Although later all these countries initially against came to recognise Angola, the support of some of them to UNITA rebels never ended. Not surprisingly, countries which were against recognition were also among the ones that violated the UN sanctions against UNITA in the 1990s (Togo, Burkina Faso, Coté d'Ivoire, Zambia, Zaire, Gabon, etc.). About the OAU split on recognition of the MPLA government see James, ibid., at pp. 73-76, 86. About the countries violating the UN sanctions against UNITA in the 1990s see 'Report of the Panel of Experts on Violations of Security Council Sanctions against UNITA', UN Doc. S/2000/203, 10 March 2000.

30. Angola was admitted to the UN on 1 December 1976, becoming its 146th member. See 'Angola's Foreign Minister', *New World Review* (January-February 1977) at pp. 18-21.

31. After the 1975-76 events in Angola, the US Congress blocked any support overt or covert to terrorist organisations fighting against the government in Angola. However in 1985 the Clark Amendment was repealed by the Congress and covert assistance to UNITA rebels resumed. An estimated $250 million worth of covert aid was sent to UNITA between 1986 and 1991 according to commentators. See A. Vines, *One Hand Tied: Angola and the UN* (CIIR briefing paper, June 1993) p. 4. See also James, op. cit. n. 28; Minter, op. cit. n. 24.

consolidated its power in Luanda.[32] South Africa did incorporate into its Army the three thousand-men Chipenda faction (which defected in 1974 from MPLA and joined FNLA), who retreated together with UNITA and South African forces into Namibia after the 1976 defeat (they later became the infamous South African Army 32 Battalion, which was used against the fellow Angolan Army),[33] but not the UNITA forces. South Africa reorganized UNITA, to be used as an independent destabilizing force against the Angolan government.[34] South Africa gave UNITA a sanctuary of its own in 'Jamba' situated in a 'buffer zone' illegally created by South Africa deep in the south of Angola, allegedly as a 'quarantine' area against SWAPO incursions into Namibia.[35] With this backing, UNITA guerrillas were able to continue challenging the Angolan government. At the same time, South Africa itself, although defeated in 1976, was to restart shortly thereafter its direct acts of aggression against Angola. The intensity of these acts had increased substantially by 1983, and turned into a permanent occupation of southern parts of Angola.[36]

Under constant pressure from the UN Security Council to withdraw its troops, South Africa was forced in February 1984 to sign an agreement with Angola (the Lusaka Accord) by which it promised to withdraw its troops and end support to UNITA's insurgency.[37] However, South Africa never actually intended to withdraw from Angola, and when in 1985 the Angolan government carried out a fully-fledged operation to destroy UNITA's insurgency, South Africa reversed its commitment under the Lusaka Accord and returned in full support of UNITA's rebels introducing thousands of its elite troops in the ground alongside them.[38]

The young Angolan government had no other choice but to call for the help of Cuba, with which it had a pact of collective self-defence,[39] to stand against the-

---

32. TRC Report, Vol. 2, *supra* n. 26, chapter 2, para. 11, at p. 45 (noting that: 'The South African government's initial objective, therefore, was to prevent the MPLA from taking power at independence. When this failed, the goal became its overthrow and replacement by a 'friendly' anti-communist government led by the National Union for the Total Independence of Angola (UNITA)).'

33. See James, op. cit. n. 28, at pp. 165-166.

34. O. Oye, 'Angola: Ideology and Pragmatism in Foreign Relations', 57 *International Affairs* (Winter 1980/81) at p. 263 (noting that: 'The South Africans have backed Jonas Savimbi not so much to further his aims, although this could be a reason, but, more importantly, because he compliments the Botha administration's objectives of destabilizing Angola, on the one hand, whilst making it difficult for PLAN (Peoples' Liberation Army of Namibia – the armed wing of SWAPO – JD) to have a totally safe rear, on the other.'). See also Robin, loc. cit. n. 26.

35. See Brittain, op. cit. n. 28, at p. 11.

36. Ibid. See also TRC Report, *supra* n. 26, chapter 2, para. 17, at p. 46 (noting that: 'Though the SADF's intervention failed to prevent the MPLA from taking power at independence in November 1975, and even though SADF forces were withdrawn in March 1976, South African military and political involvement in Angolan affairs continued for the next thirteen years ... South African forces were not entirely withdrawn; the SADF created an eighteen-km-wide demilitarized zone (DMZ) along a 1000 km stretch of the border, which it retained after termination of the invasion.') .

37. See for an account of the negotiation process, W. Kühne, *Südafrika und seine Nachbarn: Durchbruch zum Frieden? Zur Bedeutung der Vereinbarungen mit Mosambik und Angola vom Frühjar 1984* (Baden-Baden, Nomos Verlagsgesellschaft 1985).

38. See Minter, op. cit. n. 24, at pp. 42-48.

39. Two such Agreements were signed by the Angolan government with Cuba on 4 February 1982 and on 19 March 1984.

then better prepared South African troops. By 1987, major conventional battles were being fought in the south of Angola, with more than 100,000 troops in the theatre of war, and widespread air bombardment and the use of other heavy weaponry by South Africa on the one side and Angola/Cuba on the other.[40] Growing casualties among South Africans (both in military equipment (mainly combat air jets) and human resources), and the fierce resistance offered by the combined Angolan/Cuban forces in the besieged Angolan city of Cuito Cuanavale (also known as the 'Angolan Stalingrad') that South Africa tried in vain to take over a six-month period in 1987-1988, brought to an end the international segment of the armed conflict in Angola. This stalemate finally convinced South Africa that it had lost the ability to violate with impunity the territory of Angola[41] and that the game was up.[42]

It was against this background that diplomatic efforts were quickly intensified (with US mediation), with a view to the withdrawal of South African troops from Angola. In 1988 an Agreement was eventually reached according to which South Africa was to withdraw its troops from Angola and Namibia and end support to the UNITA insurgency, in exchange for Cuba's withdrawal from Angola.[43] This peace deal was part of a global process that was later not only to lead to the independence of Namibia but also the dismantling of Apartheid in South Africa itself and the first free and democratic elections in Angola in 1992.[44]

---

40. See J. Marcum, 'Retrenchment and Recalculation: South Africa and the Angola-Namibia Agreements', in O.E. Kahn, ed., *Disengagement from Southwest Africa: the Prospects for Peace in Angola and Namibia*, (New Brunswick NJ, Transaction Publishers 1988) pp. 131, at 133-236; P.S. Falk, 'Cuba and the Conflict in Angola and Namibia', in Kahn, ibid., at pp. 95-101; Minter, op. cit. n. 24, at p. 48.

41. See N. Mc Queen, 'Angola', in O. Furley and R. May, eds., *African Interventionist States* (Aldershot, Ashgate Publishing 2001) at p. 93 (noting that: 'one side effect of two decades of continuous conflict was that by mid-1990s the Luanda regime had acquired probably the largest and most heavily equipped armed force in Africa. An army of about 110,000 was supported by the most advanced artillery and armour to be produced in the eastern bloc before the collapse of the Soviet Union. The Angolan air force similarly equipped, remains immensely powerful, despite the end of the cold war and eastern bloc armament production which went with it.').

42. A. Vines, *Angola unravels, The rise and fall of the Lusaka Peace Process* (New York, Human Rights Watch 1999) at p. 14 (noting that: 'In 1987, a series of major battles in the south of Angola culminated in the siege of Cuito Cuanavale by South African and UNITA forces. Although this resulted in a military stalemate, the outcome was a psychological defeat for the South African Defence Forces (SADF), which came to believe they could not win militarily in Angola. This prompted a rethinking of South African military strategy.'). Also see I. Tvedten, 'U.S. Policy Towards Angola Since 1975', 30 *Journal of Modern African Studies* (1992) at p. 31 (noting that: 'It is generally agreed that the battle of Cuito Cuanavale in March 1988 marked the final attempt to secure a military solution to the Angolan conflict').

43. The entire package is comprised of the following acts: the New York Principles for a Peaceful Settlement in South-western Africa, 20 July 1988; The Geneva Understanding among the Republic of Angola and South Africa, 5 August 1988; The Brazzaville Protocol, 13 December 1988; The New York Agreement Among the People's Republic of Angola, the Republic of Cuba, and the Republic of South Africa, 22 December 1988. See UN Doc. S/22609 (1991).

44. See C.A. Crocker, 'Southern Africa: Eight years later', 68 *Foreign Affairs* (1989) pp. 144, at 147-155; C.W. Freeman, Jr. 'The Angola/Namibia Accords', 68 *Foreign Affairs* (1989) pp. 126, at 130-138. C.A Crocker was Assistant Secretary of State for African Affairs at the US Department of

According to an Understanding in Geneva, a ceasefire was established between Angola and South Africa on 5 August 1988, and by 1 September 1988 South Africa completely withdrew unilaterally its troops from Angola. When this commitment was fulfilled, the parties proceeded to negotiate the complete withdrawal of South African troops from Namibia and its independence in the terms of the UN SC resolution 435/28 adopted on 29 September 1978, and the complete withdrawal of the Cuban troops from Angola.[45] According to the Brazzaville Protocol signed on 13 December 1988 and the New York Agreements signed on 22 December 1988, South Africa committed itself to withdraw its troops and grant independence to Namibia by November 1989, whereas Angola and Cuba committed themselves to withdraw and did in fact withdraw the Cuban contingents from Angola by July 1991.

In a meeting held in Luanda on 16 May 1989 with the heads of state of Congo, Gabon, Mozambique, Sao Tome e Principe, Zaire, Zambia and Zimbabwe, the president of Angola put forward a comprehensive plan of national reconciliation in Angola, which provided for an end to the armed conflict, an amnesty to the rebels and the reintegration of UNITA forces and cadres in the Angolan government and Army. However, the plan did not contemplate Jonas Savimbi, the rebel leader. The Angolan government, finding the UNITA leader too odious to the Angolan people, proposed that Jonas Savimbi instead accept an offer of exile abroad at least for a period of time, until the Angolan people, having forgotten his inglorious deeds, would be willing to forgive him.[46]

Savimbi was invited to attend a Summit of 18 heads of state of Angola, Botswana, Burundi, Cameroon, Cape Verde, Chad, Congo, Gabon, Guinea-Bissau, Morocco, Mozambique, Niger, Rwanda, Sao Tome e Principe, Tanzania, Zambia and Zimbabwe, convened in Gbadolite (Zaire) on 22 June 1989, to serve as witnesses of his acceptance of the plan proposed by the Angolan government for peace and national reconciliation in Angola.[47] However, Savimbi later denied having accepted external exile and this aspect of the undertaking was not in writing. Two months later, eight of the African leaders present in Gbadolite (those who had convened the initial meeting in Luanda), confirmed in a meeting thereafter that Savimbi had indeed accepted before the 18 heads of state a 'temporary and voluntary retirement' in exchange for amnesty and national reconciliation. Savimbi rejected this interpretation and declared the armistice to be over.[48] It became clear that his agreement was part of his strategy to get promoted and rehabilitated (after

State, 1981-89; C.W. Freeman, Jr. was principal Deputy Assistant Secretary of State for African Affairs at the US Department of State, 1986-1989.

45. For an earlier analysis of legal issues involved in the linkage of granting independence to illegally occupied Namibia by South Africa, with the ending of the legitimate presence of Cuban troops in Angola, see L.B. Francis, 'Some Legal Implications of Linking Independence for Namibia to a Withdrawal of Cuban Forces from Angola', 26 *The Indian JIL* (1986) p. 113.

46. See James, op. cit. n. 28, at pp. 243-245.

47. A declaration was adopted at the end of the summit: Declaração de Gbadolite, 22 de Junho de 1989. (hereinafter Gbadolite Declaration) See detailed account of the summit in James, op. cit. n. 28, at pp. 243-245 . See text of the Gbadolite Declaration, ibid. at pp. 280-282.

48. See James, op cit. n. 28, at pp. 243-245.

his alliance with Apartheid South Africa) in the eyes of the world as a valid interlocutory force in the country.[49] The Gbadolite Declaration was never implemented
and Savimbi restarted his terrorist acts against the civilian population, while the
entire continent considered what to do with him. Here again external factors were
crucial for Savimbi's change of position and continuation of terrorist actions.

The Angolan people had to wait for the end of the cold war to see UNITA rebels
finally agreeing to an end of the civil war. The 1991 Bicesse Peace Accords signed
in Portugal were a complex of agreements accepted by the government mostly to
the satisfaction of UNITA with the hope of bringing a definitive peace to the country and to see the supreme power in the country legitimised by the peoples' vote,
not by force. This comprehensive peace deal involved the establishment of a ceasefire, demobilisation not only of UNITA but also government troops, and creation
of Unified Armed Forces (FAA) in proportional terms, and the holding of general
free, direct, and multiparty elections in the country. The demobilisation process
and the elections were to be monitored by international peacekeeping forces and
international observers including the UN and a troika of observer states (US, Russia and Portugal). An amnesty was also accorded to the rebels.[50]

All the political aspects of the peace process were implemented with the exception of the one according to which Savimbi's UNITA should have respected the
laws in force and demilitarise itself prior to the realisation of free and democratic
elections.[51] This factor had a major consequence for the fiasco of the peace accords.

When the general elections were held, the MPLA in power won again the legislative elections, with the former President Dos Santos taking 49.6 percent of the
presidential vote and Savimbi 40 percent. The UN and the international observers
monitoring the elections recognised the results to be fair and just. Electoral law
required a second round if no one achieved 50 percent, but it was never to be held.
As soon as he realized he had lost, Savimbi took up arms. It became clear that his
adherence to the ceasefire had hinged on the belief that UNITA would win the
elections. Knowing the outcome, and with his army still intact, there was no reason
for him to continue to respect the ceasefire or to accept defeat. UNITA recalled all
its 11 high-ranking generals in the FAA and launched a nationwide operation to

---

49. James, sympathetic to Savimbi, writes: 'In 1975, the Alvor Agreement had placed UNITA as a
political partner to FNLA and MPLA. Now the Gbadolite Declaration gave new status to Savimbi. No
longer was he a South African 'puppet', but a leader of stature who commanded respect. For example,
Savimbi left Zaire in the company of President Joaquim Chissano of Mozambique.' James, op. cit. n.
28, at p. 244.

50. See M.J. Anstee, 'The experience in Angola, February 1992-June 1993', in J. Whitman and D.
Pocock, eds., *After Rwanda: the coordination of United Nations humanitarian assistance* (New York,
St. Martin's Press 1996) at pp. 161-178; Blondin Beye, loc. cit. n. 6. Margaret J. Anstee was Special
Representative of the UN Secretary-General in Angola to monitor the first multi-party elections in
1992. The late Alioune Blondin Beye was Special Representative of the UN Secretary-General in the
post election period, and it was under his mediation that the Lusaka Protocol was signed in November
1994.

51. See V. Krška, 'Peacekeeping in Angola (UNAVEM I and II)', 4 *International Peacekeeping*
(1997) pp. 75, at 87.

occupy cities and municipalities across the country and remove the government's local administrative structures.[52] The plan also contemplated the seizure of power in Luanda itself. After a three day battle in the capital, UNITA forces were repelled by the government but the UNITA siege of many other cities across the country started.[53]

There were several reasons for the military aspects not having been fully implemented, but among them, it is clear that the essential were two: 1) UNITA's lack of will to do so; as a fallback position in case it would lose the elections, it still contemplated attaining power by force of arms; and 2) the absence of any 'power-sharing' provisions in the peace accords for the post-election period. According to commentators, one of the major blows of the Bicesse legal and political framework for peace in Angola was indeed reliance on the principle 'the winner-takes all'. The assumption of those who 'advised' Savimbi to opt for this principle instead of the one of 'power-sharing' (proposed by MPLA once again) was that with the collapse of the Soviet Union and the end of cold war, Savimbi would 'easily' win in democratic elections, as he was the one identified with true democracy.[54] Savimbi himself was not that sure. These observers turned a blind eye to insistence by the government that demobilisation of troops should be completed before elections took place.[55] When the elections went against Savimbi, the shocking perspective of being left with 'nothing', after years of fighting in the bush, prompted him to restart war, hoping to take the power denied to him by the people's vote by force of arms. It would only be a small compromise for the government to accept now 'power-sharing' instead of the principle 'the winner-takes-all' enshrined in the Bicesse Accords by UNITA itself.[56]

Indeed, the government encouraged by the UN and the observer countries (US, Russia, and Portugal) continued its policy of showing flexibility, making one after another concession (now already by far beyond what it was required to accept according to the Bicesse Accords) in trying to accommodate as much as possible UNITA and Savimbi and bring a lasting peace to the country. As one observer recognises 'talks were held on the basis of MPLA making political concessions in return for UNITA making military concessions'.[57]

At the end of this peace marathon the government accepted once again the signing of a new peace Agreement (the Lusaka Protocol[58]), whose basic provisions included now a power-sharing at all levels, including embassies abroad (but rejected by UNITA before the elections in the Bicesse Accords). The government went even further and in addition offered Savimbi the post of vice-president (refused); under a special law, special privileges were offered to him as the leader of a

---

52. Ibid., at pp. 88-89.
53. Anstee, loc. cit. n. 50, at p. 165.
54. See Brittain, op. cit. n. 28, at p. 46. See also A.W. Pereira, 'The Neglected Tragedy: The Return to War in Angola, 1992-93', 32 *Journal of Modern African Studies* (1994) pp. 1-28.
55. See Brittain, ibid., at pp. 49-55.
56. Ibid., at pp. 56-68.
57. See J. Lewis, 'Angola 1995: The road to peace', XIII *International Relations* (1996) at p. 83.
58. *Lusaka Protocol, supra* n. 11.

major opposition party; and it even accepted his requirement that he be guarded by 400 bodyguards.[59] After a series of frustrating meetings in Namibia, Addis Ababa and finally Abidjan, UN-sponsored peace talks resumed on 15 November 1993 in Lusaka, under the mediation of Alioune Blondin Beye, which led to the signing on 21 November 1994 of the Lusaka Protocol.[60]

In exchange, the government only required that UNITA respect the core provisions of the Bicesse Accords, mainly that it allow state administration to extend to all corners of the country, and undergo complete demilitarisation and disarmament. The Lusaka Protocol provided for the return of the UNITA generals who left the FAA, but also, on UNITA insistence, the reformation of the FAA in proportionality terms once again.

New provisions were also introduced concerning a social and reintegration program for demobilised soldiers and repatriation of all mercenaries in Angola. The UN was called upon to oversee the implementation of the Lusaka Protocol.

However, Jonas Savimbi, desirous of acceding to supreme power by force of arms, once again blocked the realisation of even the Lusaka Protocol, favourable though it was to UNITA. Instead of demilitarisation, he opted once again for rearming.[61] By 1997, four years after the signing of the Lusaka Protocol, the government had fulfilled all its good will commitments, but UNITA continued to sabotage the entire peace process. It had not yet withdrawn from all the areas it occupied, and the administration of the state had not yet been extended nationwide.[62]

On the other hand, UNITA deputies were working in the national parliament (sworn in on 9 April 1997) and its ministers were working in the government of national unity (inaugurated on 11 April 1997), but only some of its generals and soldiers were serving in the Unified Armed Forces (8,000 out of an estimated 26,000 soldiers).[63] The majority of its soldiers and generals were still in the bush fighting the FAA, without having disarmed or demobilised.[64]

The international community could no longer understand Savimbi and he became isolated. Without open external funding, Savimbi decided to turn (again with external complicity) to the lucrative business of illicit diamond mining in order to supply his private army with bombs and bullets to continue terrorising innocent civilians.[65] He was then exposed to international sanctions by the United Nations.

---

59. Blondin Beye, loc. cit. n. 6, at pp. 17-19.

60. Krška, loc. cit. n. 51, at pp. 91, 92.

61. See N. Mc Queen, 'Peacekeeping by attrition: The United Nations in Angola', 36 *Journal of Modern African Studies* (1998) pp. 399, at 407-418.

62. See Secretary-General Report on Angola (UN Doc. S/1997/640 (1997)).

63. See McQueen, loc. cit. n. 61, at p. 412.

64. Under the Lusaka Protocol, UNITA was also obliged to quarter 62,500 soldiers, but over 22,686 deserted after having registered. By 11 December 1996, when the quartering process officially ended, UNITA claimed that a total of 41,796 UNITA soldiers had been demobilized. However, the UN found out later that most of those quartered had not been combat troops, but people *hors de combat* quartered to 'make up the numbers' or child soldiers. Thus, the UN found, for example, that 10,728 were war-disabled soldiers and 4,799 were child soldiers. See Vines, op. cit. n. 42, at pp. 32-35.

65. See for a comprehensive study of conflict diamonds, I.J. Tamm, 'Diamonds in Peace and War: Severing the Conflict Diamond Connection', World Peace Found. Report No. 30 (2002) p. 2.

The UN Security Council on several occasions considered indeed the situation in Angola to constitute a threat to international peace and security and was forced to impose an embargo regime on UNITA. In 1997, it strongly deplored UNITA's failure to comply with its obligations under the Bicesse Peace Accords and the Lusaka Protocol and with relevant Security Council resolutions, and demanded, *inter alia*, that UNITA should immediately implement its obligations under the Lusaka Protocol, including demilitarisation of all its forces, and condemned any attempts by UNITA to restore its military capabilities. It imposed an embargo on UNITA demanding *inter alia* that 'all states impose travel restrictions on all senior UNITA officials, including the cancellation of their travel documents, visas or resident permits, close all UNITA offices in their territories and prohibit flights of aircraft by or for UNITA'.[66]

Under pressure of the UN SC sanctions, UNITA was forced to sign on 9 January 1998 an understanding with the government to complete the implementation of the key outstanding elements of the Lusaka Protocol. This understanding provided, *inter alia*, for the extension of the state administration to all areas under UNITA control by the end of January of that year.[67] However, upon UNITA request, this deadline was successively extended up to 1 July 1998. When UNITA requested another extension, the UN lost its patience and imposed a new sanctions package covering the embargo on trafficking in illicit diamonds.[68] These measures had an impact on Savimbi's ability to continue to fuel his terrorist acts against the civilian population. And after another request for extension of a deadline set at 31 August 1998, the government also lost its patience this time, and suspended UNITA from the government of National Unity.[69] Subsequent to this, the UNITA members who had served in the government announced a split with Savimbi, launching a party called the 'Renovation Committee of UNITA'. The government stated that it would only negotiate with this new' UNITA and urged others to do the same.[70]

By December 1999, a major military offensive by the Angolan government reclaimed almost all the territory it had lost to the UNITA rebels during the previous years, putting Savimbi and his close allies on the run. In September 2000, the Angolan government offered a pardon to Jonas Savimbi 'if he were to ask for it and ask for the forgiveness of the Angolan people'.[71] In December 2000, the government granted amnesty to all those who desposed of their arms and intended to embrace the peace process, including Savimbi.[72]

The government announced that until such time as Savimbi accepted the government's offer and ceased his campaign of violence, the Angolan government

---

66. See UNSC Res. 1127, UN Doc. S/Res/1127 (1997), and UNSC res. 1135 (1997), UN Doc. S/Res/1135(1997).

67. Vines, op. cit. n. 42, at pp. 23-24.

68. See UNSC Res. 1173, UN Doc. S/Res/1173 (1998).

69. Vines, op. cit. n. 42, at p. 26.

70. Ibid., at pp. 26-27.

71. See 'Angola Government Offers Savimbi Pardon', *AfrolNews*, (2 September 1998) <www.afrol.com>.

72. See Lei de Amnistia No. 7/00, de 15 de Dezembro de 2000, Diário da República, I Série - No. 53.

would continue military actions to stabilise the situation, protect the citizens of the country against rebel atrocities, and re-establish state authority over all areas of Angola. In December 2001, the Angolan government suggested three possible scenarios for Savimbi: capture and justice as a war criminal, surrender and pardon, or death in combat.[73] Savimbi chose the last scenario. In February 2002, surrounded by government troops in the bush in the far eastern province of Moxico, and abandoned by his former allies, he refused to surrender. In a subsequent gun battle with the Angolan Army, he was killed together with his closest allies on 22 February 2002.

3.   THE LEGAL CHARACTERISATION OF THE ARMED CONFLICT(S) IN ANGOLA

In order to correctly apply the laws of war to the events reviewed in Angola, it is essential both to ascertain the exact nature of the conflict(s) in Angola and whether the relevant provisions bound Angola during the relevant period. Classification of the conflict(s) as an international armed conflict would mean in principle that the whole body of international humanitarian law, (i.e., the Hague Regulations of 1907,[74] the Geneva Conventions of 1949[75] and 1977 Additional Protocol I,[76] and relevant customary law) would apply. In the case of a non-international armed conflict, only the minimum rules contained in common Article 3 of the Geneva Conventions, 1977 Additional Protocol II[77] (depending on the circumstances) and relevant customary law would apply.

In defining what constitutes an armed conflict (international or non-international) controlling is the following ICTY *Tadić* jurisdiction decision:

'An armed conflict exists whenever there is a resort to armed force between States or protracted armed violence between governmental authorities and organized armed groups or between such groups within a State. International humanitarian law applies from the initiation of such armed conflicts and extends beyond the cessation of hostilities until a general conclusion of peace is reached; or, in the case of internal conflicts, a

73. See 'Savimbi Death a Chance for Angolan Peace', *AfrolNews*, (25 February 2002) <www.afrol.com>.

74. Convention (IV) Respecting the Laws and Customs of War on Land, and attached Regulations signed at The Hague, 18 October 1907, English translation with references in D. Schindler and J. Toman, *The Laws of Armed Conflicts*, 3rd edn. (Geneva, Institute Henry-Dunant 1988) at p. 69.

75. Convention (I) for the Amelioration of the Condition of the Wounded and Sick in Armed Forces in the Field; Convention (II) for the Amelioration of the Condition of Wounded, Sick and Shipwrecked Members of Armed Forces at Sea; Convention (III) Relative to the Treatment of Prisoners of War; Convention (IV) Relative to the Protection of Civilian Persons in Time of War; all four Conventions signed at Geneva, 12 August 1949; texts in Schindler and Toman, ibid., at pp. 373, 401, 423, 493.

76. Protocols Additional to the Geneva Conventions of 1949 (Protocol I), opened for signature 12 December 1977, reprinted in 16 *ILM* (1977) p. 1391 (hereinafter, AP I).

77. Protocols Additional to the Geneva Conventions of 1949 (Protocol II), opened for signature 12 December 1977, reprinted in 16 *ILM* (1977) p. 1442 (hereinafter, AP II).

peaceful settlement is achieved. Until that moment, international humanitarian law continues to apply in the whole territory of the warring States or, in the case of internal
conflicts, the whole territory under the control of a party, whether or not actual combat
takes place there.'[78]

International humanitarian law recognises today at least *four* different types of
armed conflicts, two of which were introduced by the 1977 Additional Protocols
and two of which are defined by the Geneva Conventions:

1. International armed conflicts according to Article 2 common to the 1949 Geneva Conventions and to Article 1(3), of Additional Protocol I (which is the classical case of armed conflict between two or more states);
2. Wars of national liberation according to Article 1(4) of Additional Protocol I
   (armed conflicts between a colonial power and people fighting for self-determination);
3. Non-international armed conflicts according to Article 1 of Additional Protocol II
   (conflicts between the state and dissident armed groups or other organised groups,
   which under a responsible command, control a part of the national territory such
   as to enable them to carry out sustained and concerted military attack; and
4. Non-international armed conflicts according to common Article 3 of the 1949
   Geneva Conventions (a conflict between a state and at least one rebel group or
   between such groups of sufficient intensity to qualify as an armed conflict).[79]

In addition, the existence of mixed types of armed conflicts and the difficulties of
their legal characterisation is broadly recognised. Such conflicts have been identified
by the ICTY case-law. In the *Tadić* Appeals judgement the Appeals Chamber ruled:

'It is indisputable that an armed conflict is international if it takes place between two or
more States. In addition, in case of an internal armed conflict breaking out on the territory of a State, it may become international (or, depending upon the circumstances, be
international in character alongside an internal armed conflict) if (i) another State intervenes in that conflict through its troops, or alternatively if (ii) some of the participants in
the internal armed conflict act on behalf of that other State'.[80]

3.1   The nature of the conflicts in Angola and the parties to the conflict(s)

Commentators have expressed the opinion, with which this author concurs, that at
least the early events in independent Angola have shown that there was an armed

---

78. *Prosecutor* v. *Duško Tadić*, Case No. IT-94-1-AR72, Decision on Defence Motion for Interlocutory Appeal on Jurisdiction, 2 October 1995, para. 70 (hereinafter, *Tadić* Jurisdiction Decision).

79. For a discussion of the four categories of armed conflicts, see D. Schindler, 'The Different
Types of Armed Conflicts According to the Geneva Conventions and Protocols', 163 *Recueil des
Cours* (1979) p. 117. See also M. Veugthey, 'Implementation and enforcement of Humanitarian law
and Human Rights Law in Non-International Armed Conflicts: the Role of the International Committee of the Red Cross', 33 *Amer. Univ. LR* (1983) pp. 83, at 88.

80. *The Prosecutor* v. *Duško Tadić*, Case No. IT-94-1-A, Appeal Judgement, 15 July 1999 (hereinafter *Tadić* Appeal Judgement) para. 84.

conflict and that it was of a mixed character, i.e., it contained elements of both an international armed conflict and those of a non-international armed conflict.[81]

In addition, the research shows that during the years before and since independence, the following foreign armed forces were active in Angola: 1) the Portuguese Armed Forces, as a colonial power until 1975; 2) Cuban Armed Forces, on the governmental side (since independence in 1975 until the 1988 New York Agreements); 3) South Africa Defence Forces, in support of UNITA/FNLA rebels (since independence in 1975 until the 1988 New York Agreements); 4) Zairian Armed Forces, in support of FNLA in 1975-1976; 5) foreign mercenaries, especially from 1975-1976 on the side of FNLA/UNITA rebels; 6) hiding Rwandan Hutus and Zairian pro-deposed Mobutu rebel forces on the UNITA rebels' side in the 1990s. In addition, not involved in the ongoing Angolan conflicts but based on the Angolan territory were 7) Namibian SWAPO forces and Zairian Katanguese forces.

This author's research shows that the following periods may be identified in the Angolan armed conflict(s):

i) The period from 1961 to independence in 1975 (an international armed conflict of the Additional Protocol I type two defined above – wars of national liberation – between the liberation movements and Portugal);

ii) The period from 1976 to 1986 (a mixed conflict, where an internal armed conflict between the Angolan government and rebels of a common Article 3 type was fought alongside the international conflict between Angola and South Africa. However, if evidence was to emerge that UNITA was under the overall control of South Africa, the entire conflict from 1975 to 1988 could then be deemed to be international for the purposes of imputing international responsibility for UNITA's crimes to the state of South Africa and in particular to its commanding staff, applying the *Tadić* Appeals Judgement test of 'overall control' and applicable law concerning criminal responsibility of multiple offenders.[82]);

iii)The periods 1975-1976 and 1987-1988 (a mixed conflict which became fully international in view of the extensive intervention of Zaire (1975-1976) and South Africa (in both periods) on the side of the rebels, to the point where it is more reasonable to say that the foreign forces and the rebels were one side of the conflict rather than two different sides and the government, using its legitimate right of collective self-defence, was forced to have recourse to Cuban assistance to repel the foreign invading forces together with their internal puppets);

iv)The period from 1988 to 2002 (a Protocol II internal armed conflict between the Angolan government and UNITA rebel forces).

---

81. See M. Bothe, 'Völkerrechtliche Aspekte des Angola-Konflikts', 37 *ZaöRV* (1977) pp. 590-598; M. Hess, *Die Anwendbarkeit des humanitären Völkerrechts, insbesondere in gemischten Konflikten* (Zürich, Schulthess Polygraphisher Verlag 1983) pp. 207, 211.

82. In the Indictment against Slobodan Milošević, the former President of the Federal Republic of Yugoslavia, he was charged with being a member of a joint criminal enterprise whose objective was to commit war crimes through rebel armed groups fighting an internal war in the neighbouring country of Bosnia and Herzegovina, which were under overall control of FRY. See the *Prosecutor* v. *Slobodan Milošević*, Indictment, Case No. IT-01-51-I, 22 November 2001; for the 'overall control' doctrine *Tadić* Appeal Judgement, *supra* n. 80 paras. 137; 117-145.

4.   APPLICATION OF THE LAWS OF WAR TO THE ARMED CONFLICTS IN ANGOLA

Angola is bound since 1984 by the 1949 Geneva Conventions and by the 1977 Additional Protocol I.[83] She is also bound by applicable rules of customary international humanitarian law. It can be argued that the following rules of international humanitarian law are applicable to the conflicts in Angola during the relevant periods as characterised above.

4.1   The conflicts of the period before independence (at least common Article 3 of the Geneva Conventions and relevant customary law applicable in any type of armed conflict)

Since Portugal was a party to the Geneva Conventions from 1961, the war of national liberation led by different nationalist movements in Angola until independence was at the very least covered by common Article 3, even though Portugal entered a reservation to the effect that it would not apply that article, based on the argument that it fails to define what is meant by a non-international armed conflict.[84] For the reasons stated below,[85] this reservation did not bind the other Parties, and in any event it could not have prevented the application of the article as a matter of customary law.[86]

Moreover, since 1965 the UN has adopted successive resolutions wherein it recognised the legitimate right of the Angolan people to fight for their self-determination and independence, which suggests that the UN recognised the conflict to be international in nature,[87] and therefore the entire body of the laws and customs of

---

83. Angola is also a party to the following treaties which may apply in event of an armed conflict: a) the 1925 Protocol for the Prohibition of the Use of Asphyxiating, Poisonous or Other Gases, and of Bacteriological Methods of Warfare, since 1990 (applies only in situations of international armed conflicts); b) the 1989 Convention on the Rights of the Child, since 1990 (applies in any type of armed conflict); c) the 1997 Convention on the Prohibition of the Use, Stockpiling, Production and Transfer of Anti-Personnel Mines and on their Destruction, since 2002 (applies in any type of armed conflict); d) the 1977 OAU Convention for the Elimination of Mercenarism in Africa, since 1979 (applies in any type of armed conflict); e) the 1989 International Convention against the Recruitment, Use, Financing and Training of Mercenaries, since 1990 (applies in any type of armed conflict); f) In addition Angola has signed and is presently in the process of ratification of the 1998 Rome Statute of the International Criminal Court (applies in any type of armed conflict).

84. At the moment of ratification of the Geneva Conventions in 1961, Portugal entered the following reservation: 'As there is no actual definition of what it meant by a conflict not of an international character, and as, in case this term is intended to refer solely to civil war, it is not clearly laid down at what moment an armed rebellion within a country should be considered as having become a civil war, Portugal reserves the right not to apply the provisions of Article 3, in so far as they may be contrary to the provisions of Portuguese law, in all territories subject to her sovereignty in any part of the world.' See <www.icrc.org/ihl.nsf/>.

85. See *infra* n. 96.

86. See *Case Concerning Military and Paramilitary Activities in and Against Nicaragua, (Nicaragua v. US)* (Merits), *ICJ Rep.* (1986) (hereinafter '*Nicaragua* case') p. 14, paras. 217-220.

87. For a discussion of the status of people fighting for self-determination as subjects of international law, and the applicability of the entire body of the laws of war to their fighting, see H.A. Wilson,

war could be said to be applicable to the conflict, *qua* customary law.[88] For example, in November 1968 the UNGA adopted resolution 2395 (Question of territories under Portuguese Administration) in which it 'called upon the government of Portugal in view of the armed conflict prevailing in the territories and the inhuman treatment of prisoners to ensure the application to that situation of the Geneva Convention relative to the treatment of prisoners of war of 12 August 1949'.[89]

4.2   The conflicts of the period after independence (the laws and customs of war, including the Geneva Conventions, their common Article 3 and relevant rules of customary law)

4.2.1   *The internal segment of the mixed conflict: the relationship between the Angolan government and the rebels*

As Angola became a party to the Geneva Conventions only from 1984, and has not yet acceded to Additional Protocol II, the relationship between the government and the rebels was governed from the beginning of the conflict in 1977 by common Article 3 *qua* customary law,[90] and other relevant customary law rules. From 1984 on, this relationship under common Article 3 of the Geneva Conventions became conventional.

There has been much discussion as to what really binds a rebel movement to common Article 3 or AP II[91] if it cannot be a party to such agreements, and is not even entitled to lodge a unilateral declaration of its acceptance.[92] Although the explanation that such movements are bound by force of the state's act of acceptance has not succeeded in convincing everyone,[93] it is still the position with which most scholars seem to conform.[94]

International Law and Use of Force by National Liberation Movements (Oxford, Clarendon Press 1988); G. Abi-Saab, *Wars of National Liberation and the Laws of War*, 3 *Annales d'Études internationales* (1972) p. 93.

88. UNGA Res. 2105 (XX) adopted 20 December 1965, stating that the UN 'recognises the legitimacy of the struggle by the peoples under colonial rule to exercise their right to self-determination and independence and invites all States to provide material and moral assistance to the national liberation movements in colonial territories'. See also UNGA Res. 2107(XX) adopted 20 December 1965; UNGA Res. 2189 (XXI) 13 December 1966; UNGA Res. 2326 (XXII) 16 December 1967; UNGA Res. 2446 (XXIII) 19 December 1968.

89. See UNGA Res 2395 (XXIII) 29 November 1968. See also UNGA Res. 2465 (XXIII) 20 December 1968; UNGA Res. 2548 (XXIV) 11 December 1969; UNGA Res.2674 (XXV) 9 December 1970.

90. See *Nicaragua* case, *supra* n. 86.

91. See for example P.H. Kooijmans, 'In the Shadowland Between Civil War and Civil Strife: Some Reflections on the Standard-Setting Process', in A.J.M. Delissen and G.J. Tanja, eds., *Humanitarian Law of Armed Conflict, Challenges Ahead, Essays in Honour of Frits Kalshoven*, (Dordrecht, Martinus Nijhoff Publishers 1991) pp. 225, at 228-235.

92. Such right is, however, accorded to the national liberation movements under Art. 96(3) of API.

93. See Kooijmans, loc. cit. n. 93.

94. See S. Junod, 'Additional Protocol II: History and Scope', 33 *Amer. Univ. LR* (1983) pp. 29, at 34, (noting that: 'Art. 3 and Protocol II are binding not only on the established government, but also on the insurgent party. They bind all parties to the conflict in their relation to each other. How an

To remedy this situation, however, the ICRC has taken the initiative to encourage and collect declarations of all parties agreeing to abide by the principles or the provisions of the Conventions, on a pragmatic basis. UNITA did provide the ICRC with a unilateral declaration of intent to abide by humanitarian law on 25 July 1980.[95] The government explicitly recognised that it was faced with an internal armed conflict in the country by 1989 at the latest, when it signed the Gbadolite declaration providing for a ceasefire with UNITA.[96] However the absence of such official recognition has never impeded the government from acting with due respect for the rules of war concerning humane treatment and fundamental guarantee to the rebels. The minimum humanitarian provisions of common Article 3 do not add anything to the already existing penal provisions in every country, and therefore they are commitments that any government is obliged to comply with anyway.[97] As common Article 3 does not confer on rebels any legal status, the only expectation and incentive that the rebels have to obey the laws of war (and provided that they really do so) is to be treated as political offenders not bandits, and to be amnestied at the end of hostilities.[98]

4.2.2 *The international segment of the mixed conflict: the relationship between the Angolan government/Cuban forces and South Africa/UNITA rebels and Zaire/FNLA rebels*

In at least two periods of the history of the Angolan mixed armed conflict (1975-1976, and 1987-1988), the intensity of the conflict and the direct involvement of foreign troops (of Zaire and South Africa) in the Angolan internal conflict were such that the government was forced to ask for assistance from Cuba, acting in legitimate right of collective self-defence to repel the foreign invading forces.

---

opposition party, which is not a High Contracting Party, can be bound by an international treaty, is a question that must be considered. In theory, the ratification of or adherence to an international treaty creates rights and obligations not only for the authorities in place, but also for the entire population of the territory of that state. Although this explanation, which is followed by the ICRC, has not always been considered doctrinally satisfactory, it has never really been formally contested.').

95. See 716 *RICR* (1980) p. 328. See for an account of the circumstances, Hess, *supra* n. 81, at p. 212.

96. There had been a bit of discussion as to whether common Article 3 applies automatically, when the objective conditions for existence of an armed conflict are in place, or, if it needs recognition by a state. However the *Tadić* Jurisdiction Decision definition of an armed conflict above clearly suggests that the test is purely objective (*protracted* armed violence and *organized* armed groups). This is however easy to argue, when we have an international institution adjudicating the facts. In most situations of internal violence, states are still reluctant to recognise such an armed conflict, even when the objective requirements are in place. For an interesting discussion of the implications of such a position, see W.A. Solf, 'The Status of Combatants in non-international armed conflicts', 33 *Amer. Univ. LR* (1983) pp. 53, at p. 59.

97. Ibid., at p. 64.

98. There is no obligation to do so under international humanitarian law, however, as killing members of the State Armed Forces, Police or other security forces by rebels even in combat situations is still a crime under national law, and international law does not override this rule, nor does it prohibit states from treating rebels as ordinary criminals in such circumstances. See Solf, loc. cit. n. 96, at pp. 58-60.

In the period 1975-1976, when Zairian troops in support of FNLA guerrillas attacked the government troops from the north, and South African troops invaded Angola from the south, the Geneva Conventions and the entire body of the laws and customs of war applied as customary law to this mixed conflict which has thus become totally international according to the *Tadić* test.[99]

During the period 1976-1988, South Africa acted as the sole foreign armed intervener in the Angolan armed conflict. After defeat in 1976, Zairian troops totally retreated from the Angolan soil, confining its support to Angolan rebels in terms of rear base logistical support. However South Africa continued in permanent occupation of southern parts of the Angolan soil and in the period 1987-1988 made an incursion involving thousands of troops, deep into the territory of Angola further north (holding a six-month siege of the Angolan city of Cuito Cuanavale) in support of UNITA rebels, thus becoming directly involved in the ongoing internal conflict. At this stage the separation between the Angola/South African conflict and Angolan government/UNITA rebels conflict became impossible. During this period, the entire mixed armed conflict in Angola became an international armed conflict according to the *Tadić* test, and therefore the entire body of the laws and customs of war including the Geneva Conventions applied to the conflict.

Provided there is no evidence that UNITA was operating under the overall control of South Africa, such that the *Tadić* Appeal Judgement overall control test would be applicable, the entire body of the laws and customs of war applied only to the relationship between the Angolan government and South Africa in the period before 1987.

Not all commentators agree with this characterisation of the conflicts in Angola however. For example, some commentators would differentiate in the conflict of the 1975-1976 period between the relationship Cuba/South Africa, states that were mutually bound by the Geneva Conventions and other laws of war, and Angola/South Africa, supposedly because Angola was not a party to the Geneva Conventions, and then advocate that only common Article 3 applied to this last relationship.[100] This author respectfully dissents. The problem is that even if the MPLA-led government was not yet recognised (or because it became a party to the Geneva Conventions only from 1984) the MPLA movement did not lose its right to fight for self-determination of the Angolan people, and in this case as already noted (with Portugal), the UN insisted that the entire body of IHL applied *qua* customary law to the conflict.[101]

Another commentator has divided the armed conflict between Angola and South Africa into two periods: the 1975-1976 period (an international armed conflict), and the period when the war was circumscribed to southern Angola (a non-international armed conflict to which common Art. 3 applied).[102] This author however

---

99. For the *Tadić* test see *supra* n. 80.

100. See Bothe, loc. cit. n. 81, at pp. 592, 596, 597; Hess, op. cit. n. 81, at pp. 210, 211.

101. Regarding the relevant UN resolutions concerning Portugal, see *supra* nn. 86, 89. See also *Nicaragua* case on the customary law status of the Geneva Conventions, *supra* n. 88.

102. See J. Dugard, 'South Africa's Truth and Reconciliation Process and International Humanitarian Law', 2 *YIHL* (1999) pp. 254, at 259.

respectfully dissents. The conflict between Angola and South Africa was at all times an international armed conflict, to which all the relevant laws and customs of war fully applied, *qua* customary law.[103] In addition, from 1984, when Angola became a party to the Geneva Conventions,[104] these conventions also applied as treaty law. The international character of an armed conflict does not depend upon the intensity of the conflict. Even an occupation which does not meet with resistance constitutes an international armed conflict according to the Geneva Conventions.[105]

5. THE END OF WAR I: THE 2002 LUENA MEMORANDUM OF UNDERSTANDING – A BLUEPRINT FOR NATIONAL PEACE AND RECONCILIATION

With the end of foreign support to the rebels in Angola and the UN international sanctions for rejecting peace efforts, the Angolan government was able to kill in combat the UNITA rebel commander Savimbi. These factors enabled the signing of a definitive ceasefire with the remnants of UNITA rebels.

5.1 A more forceful approach to peace

One distinguished commentator, Anja Miller, has argued that one of the causes of the initial fiasco of the peace process in Angola since the Bicesse Accords in 1991 was that 'Jonas Savimbi's UNITA rebels repeatedly acted as greedy or total spoilers'. And that this explained 'why the merger of UNITA with the government military was a complete failure in spite of a process that very closely resembled the one used successfully in Mozambique'.[106] This situation was aggravated by the way in which the international community dealt with Savimbi. Miller argues that 'the UN continually tried to appease UNITA and its leader in order to induce

---

103. See *Nicaragua* case, *supra* n. 88.

104. South Africa became a party to the Geneva Conventions in 1952 and to the Additional Protocols in 1995. See Dugard, loc. cit. n. 102, at p. 258.

105. Common Art. 2 of the Geneva Conventions states that the Conventions apply to 'any ... armed conflict between two or more of the High Contracting Parties, even if the state of war is not recognised by one of them ... and to all cases of partial or total occupation of the territory of a High Contracting Party, even if the said occupation meets with no armed resistance'. The ICRC has interpreted these provisions as meaning that 'any difference arising between the two States and leading to the intervention of armed forces is an armed conflict within the meaning of Art. 2, even if one of the parties denies the existence of a state of war. It makes no difference how long the conflict lasts, or how much slaughter takes place. The respect due to the human person as such is not measured by the number of victims.' See J. Pictet, ed., *Commentary on Geneva Convention IV* (Geneva, ICRC 1958) p. 20. This interpretation has been cited as authoritative by the ICTY in its various decisions. See for example *Prosecutor* v. *Duško Tadić*, Case No IT-94-1, Opinion and Judgement, 7 May 1997, paras. 118-119, 569, 607; *Prosecutor* v. *Zejnil Delalić et al.*, Case No. IT-96-21-T, Judgement, 16 November 1998 (hereinafter *Čelebići* Trial Judgement) para. 208.

106. A. Miller, 'Military Mergers: The Reintegration of Armed Forces After Civil Wars', *25-SUM Fletcher F. World Aff.* (2001) pp. 129, at 131-132.

them to demobilize and reintegrate with the government military. It should have treated Savimbi more forcefully after his many infractions against the peace accords became known.'[107]

5.1.1   Stedman's spoiler model

According to a model elaborated by Stephen John Stedman, rebels disrupting peace processes may be indeed divided into three groups of spoilers: a) limited spoilers (those who 'want certain concessions, but support the process as a whole'); b) greedy spoilers (those who 'will take all they can get up to a point of diminishing returns'); and c) total spoilers (those who 'feel they have no stake in the peace and want it to fail at all costs').[108]

To deal with 'total spoilers' rebels, both Stedman and Miller advocate 'using force or a "departing train" strategy of continuing the process without them'; for 'greedy spoilers', they advocate 'a long term strategy of socialization' establishing 'a set of norms for acceptable behaviour by internal parties who commit to peace' and then carefully 'calibrating the supply of carrots and sticks' to ensure that the spoiler abides by prescribed norms'; whereas the 'limited spoilers' can be induced to remain committed to the peace process when their 'reasonable demands' are met.'[109]

1. It appears that UNITA had all these facets over the years since the Bicesse Peace Accords for Angola in 1991. And that the Angolan government thus correctly used and was justified in using the appropriate remedies to quell the rebels. When the rebels behaved as 'total spoilers' the government used force and the strategy of 'departing train' (it cut off all contacts with Savimbi, and recognised a UNITA faction (UNITA-Renovada) as the legitimate interlocutor for the Lusaka Peace Process).
2. When thereafter UNITA turned to a 'greedy spoiler' model, the government set up a long term strategy of 'socialization' of those who were willing to abide by the strict requirements of the constitutional order in the country (with a package of incentives which included amnesty laws and others, many high-ranking officers of Savimbi's private army and his faction members started to desert into the hands of the government).
3. And finally when Savimbi was killed in combat and UNITA turned into a 'limited spoiler' model, the government showed interest to listen to and accommodate the former rebels 'reasonable demands' (within the framework of the Luena Memorandum Peace Process).

5.2   The Luena Memorandum negotiation process

On 13 March 2002, the government announced its 15-point plan for national reconciliation and lasting peace. The plan included a recognition of the validity of

---

107. Ibid.

108. S.J. Stedman, 'Spoiler Problems in Peace Processes', 22 *International Security* (1997) at pp. 9-15.

109. Ibid. See also Miller, loc. cit. n. 106.

the Lusaka peace process, an offer of immediate cessation of hostilities and general armistice (to start on 14 March 2002), the demilitarisation of UNITA, the full integration of UNITA into national political life, and its rebel soldiers into the Angolan army, or social reintegration, and a general amnesty.[110]

The definitive ceasefire negotiations, which aimed to resurrect the 1994 peace and power-sharing Lusaka Protocol along the lines delineated in the peace plan of the government, began on 15 March in the far eastern Angolan city of Luena and two weeks later led to the signing on 4 April 2002 of the Memorandum of Understanding[111] between the Angolan government and UNITA, bringing to an end the longest running civil war in Sub-Saharan Africa. As 'witnesses' to the Memorandum, the document was also signed by the Special Representative of the UN Secretary-General Ibrahim Gambari and the Ambassadors of Portugal, the United States and Russia, the so-called 'troika' of peace monitors set up under the Bicesse Accords and the UN-brokered Lusaka Protocol.

5.3 Main provisions of the Luena Memorandum

The 28-page Memorandum, with six annexes, is intended to be a supplement to the Lusaka Protocol and in particular to override its annexes three to five concerning the military and police issues. In its preamble the Memorandum states that it was adopted for the resolution of 'all the negative military factors which have been blocking the Lusaka Protocol, and consequently the building up of the necessary conditions for its definitive conclusion'.

While the objective of the Memorandum remained the same as the one in the Lusaka Protocol: ceasefire, disengagement, quartering, disarmament, demilitarisation and integration of UNITA troops in the FAA, this objective was to be achieved on the basis of a different cardinal set of principles.

The fundamental political principle from which all the remaining principles derived their force was that of confidence building. According to the memorandum, the peace process would only be lasting if all the seeds of suspicion among the parties were removed.[112]

5.3.1 *The principle 'the commanders first'*

According to this principle, the process of integration into the FAA would parallel the process of quartering and demobilisation, and second, the commanders were to be the first to be demobilised and integrated in the FAA and were the ones made

---

110. See 'Announcement of Cessation of all Offensive Military Operations', 13 March 2002, *Afrol-News* <www.afrol.com>.

111. See the Luena Memorandum, *supra* n. 10.

112. See Miller, loc. cit. n. 106, at p. 131 (noting that: 'Political will to integrate is a threshold problem without which no reconciliation is possible. The institutional arrangements created by peace accords should develop mechanisms that generate trust and increase cooperation between parties. However, as the examples of Angola and Bosnia demonstrate, political will cannot be manufactured from the outside. It is important to distinguish whether commitment to a peace agreement is sincere or merely a military tactic to buy time or rebuild military strength.').

responsible for the quartering, disarmament and demilitarisation of UNITA forces. These two principles are essential for a process of demobilisation based on confidence building. UNITA soldiers started moving to the quartering areas where they knew their commanders were already awaiting them but in their new role, as officers of the FAA. According to this principle, the Memorandum provided that the 12 UNITA generals who were the commanders of the UNITA military regions were now in FAA the ones responsible in each military region for the demilitarisation process of their former forces. Additionally, the internal organisation of the quartering areas was also the responsibility of the other UNITA officers. The FAA General Staff was responsible for logistical support to the process (Annex I.1.iii, 2.ii, 3.i).

5.3.2   *The principle 'no tails behind'*

According to this principle, the forces were to be demobilised and quartered together with their own families (a factor ignored in previous agreements, mainly the Bicesse Accords and the Lusaka Protocol). This is a very important principle, which radically marked the departure from previous agreements and showed the frank interest of UNITA to end the war, because UNITA used a system of guerrilla warfare which was based on the Maoist doctrine of self-reliance. Under these circumstances, families were supposed to follow their husbands and fathers-soldiers and help to feed them and carry military equipment. This system also ensured that soldiers would not be thinking about where the families were as they were constantly travelling from one combat position to another. Therefore, demobilisation could not be successful, if, as in previous agreements, the family was left behind in the bush. In previous failed attempts of demobilisation of UNITA, the situation was that these soldiers could easily leave the quartering areas, returning to their previous strategic positions where their family members waited. This had been one of the main blocking factors of earlier peace processes. To break this system and make the peace irrevocable, one had to make the families part of the demobilisation process. An estimated 50,000 demobilised UNITA forces were to be followed by 300,000 people or family members. The government had to find accommodation and logistical support for these people. The demilitarisation process should lead to the complete extinction of the UNITA armed wing. (Chapter II e) 3.11); Annex I.1.i, iii).

There were 41 quartering areas for UNITA soldiers and a similar number of quartering areas for the family members of UNITA forces. The government also registered more then 305,000 family members of UNITA soldiers. On 25 May 2003, the government closed the last quartering area. The process of quartering and demilitarisation of UNITA soldiers and their families had cost the Angolan government until then some US$ 150 million. However, the program of social-professional reinsertion of the demobilised UNITA soldiers had still to be carried out.[113]

---

113. See 'Nota do Governo sobre o encerramento das areas do acolhimento', ANGOP (Angola Press Agency) 20 June 2003. The government has been using a similar formula for the resolution of a short-lived strife in Cabinda, the far northern province of Angola, where two separatist groups have been terrorizing the civilian population in reclaiming from the government more autonomy for the

5.3.3   *The principle of 'availablility of vacant posts'*

This principle overrides the principle of proportionality in the formation of the FAA in both the Bicesse Accords and the Lusaka Protocol (and therefore also marks a radical departure from these previous agreements, thus showing the genuine and confident intention of UNITA to end war and embrace national reconciliation). After successive failed attempts to complete the formation of the FAA, and integration into the FAA of some UNITA soldiers and officers, it was only normal that the government could no longer be requested to demobilise part of its troops supposedly 'coming from the government', as the Unified Armed Forces were all now coming from the government (including former UNITA forces), and were non-partisan. According to this principle, from an estimated number of 50,000 troops needing to demilitarise, there were vacant posts for 5,000 men, including officers. To show confidence in the process, and absence of hidden intentions, UNITA also agreed to depart from its previous suspicious intention also to have police forces everywhere (according to a misconceived application of the principle of proportionality). Instead in the Memorandum, a different and radical approach was adopted. UNITA was to be represented in the national police, in an effort by the government to have as much as possible all the members of the commanding structure of UNITA involved in the process. For this reason some 40 former UNITA officers (excluded from the army due to lack of sufficient vacant positions) were also to be given commanding positions in the Police, after adequate formation in a frank spirit of national identity and reconciliation with the sole aim to serve the nation and its people (Chapter II(c,d); Annex 2; Annex 3).

5.3.4   *The principle 'no foreigners in the process'*

According to this principle, all the military aspects were to be solved by the Angolans themselves (starting from the monitoring of the ceasefire and ending with the demilitarisation and integration of UNITA forces into the FAA). This principle also departed from previous models (most sharply from the Lusaka model where verification and monitoring was to be carried out by UN peacekeepers, and slightly from the Bicesse model, where the UN had a limited monitoring mandate only over the Angolan monitoring joint commissions). In contradistinction, in the Luena Memorandum, the UN role was simply reduced to that of an observer. Again, the basic assumption was that if the process was to be lasting, confidence among Angolans had to be the leading spirit. (Chapter III,1.2,(a.3))

Apart from these principles, security concerns drove the parties to adopt a clear program of social-professional reintegration (to avoid banditry of unemployed former soldiers) which provides clearly that demilitarised troops are to be on the administrative registry of the FAA General Staff through the regional FAA

---

province. According to the Angolan Press Agency (ANGOP), the former members of these terrorist groups are now being integrated into the Army or demobilized for integration in the civil society. See 'Cabinda: Iniciou o programa de apoio aos ex-militares da FLEC', ANGOP, 29 November 2003.

commands in the settlement areas, and are to be given vocational training with a view to their speedy reinsertion into social life (Chapter II (e,f)). The process of social-professional reintegration will involve using the demilitarised soldiers in the following sectors: Service of National Reconstruction; Settlement Programs; and Reinsertion in the free labour market after vocational training (Annex 4).

It was also recognised that UNITA had foreign forces of Rwanda and Zaire alongside them. For these forces it was established that they would be quartered, disarmed and repatriated to their home country (Annex I/A).[114]

A detailed implementation timetable was set forth which was to last one year. (Chapter III (2)).

Annexes 5 and 6 refer to the fact that with the signing of the Luena Memorandum all the conditions were in place for the normal functioning of UNITA as a political party (it would have no more private armies), and that the security arrangements for UNITA leaders in the Lusaka Protocol would apply within the terms of the Memorandum. Two institutional bodies were established to oversee the coordination and management of this process: a) a Joint Military Commission (JMC) with the responsibility to promote and oversee the application of the Memorandum of Understanding; and b) a Technical Group (TG) with the responsibility to assist the JMC in the performance of its duties, including the drawing up of detailed timetables and definition of specific activities to be carried out to ensure the application of the provisions of the Memorandum of Understanding. The JMC was to be headed by a FAA general coming from UNITA forces, and a UNITA general as a member, and military representatives of the UN and the traditional observer states – Portugal, Russia and US – as observers. The JMC had the right to establish regional structures and working groups to oversee the implementation of the peace plan (Chapter III).

When on 2 August 2002 the military aspects of the peace plan were considered exhausted with the demilitarisation of all UNITA troops and the extinction of the military wing of UNITA, the Joint Commission created in the framework of the Lusaka Protocol was re-established on 26 August 2002, to solve the outstanding political issues, under the UN chairmanship.[115]

---

114. Six hundred and fifty eight foreign troops (from Democratic Republic of Congo and Rwanda) together with 253 of their dependents were found under to be with UNITA. Among them the former Chief of Staff of the Rwandan Army, General Augustin Bizimungu, whom the International War Crimes Tribunal in Rwanda sought for charges of genocide, figured prominently. He was arrested by the Angolan government on 2 August 2002, acting on the basis of an arrest warrant issued by the ICTR on 12 April 2002, and handed over by it to the Rwanda Tribunal in Arusha. See 'Interim Report of the Secretary-General', *supra* n. 8, para. 4. See also ICTR Press release 'Former Chief of Staff Pleads not guilty', ICTR/Info-9-2-321.Eng , <www.ictr.org/default.html>.

115. The government and UNITA on 26 August 2002 formally signed a new 'Memorandum of Commitment' to solve the outstanding political questions (within a 45-day timeframe) which included the following: 'national reconciliation including the social reintegration of UNITA ex-combatants; allocation of facilities for UNITA and residences for the Party leadership; submission of UNITA's nominees for positions in the government and public service; establishment of UNITA as a political party, and reinstating the status of the leader of the largest opposition party; review of the symbols of the Republic and the electoral process'. The Memorandum also provided for the re-establishment of the Lusaka Protocol Joint Commission under UN chairmanship. On 20 November 2002, the Joint

On 19 June 2003, the government announced that it had completed the process of selection and incorporation of the 5,000 UNITA soldiers to be included in the Army, concluding the military aspects of the Luena Memorandum. Among the troops incorporated into the FAA were 12 generals. Another four demobilised generals were in the reserve forces of the FAA General Staff, to be used if and when needed. Another 40 officers went to the Police. The government also announced that in the period since the demilitarisation process started on 21 April 2002 until November 2002, 87,000 UNITA soldiers were registered, although the initial UNITA estimate amounted to only 50,000.

The process that began with the signature of the 'Memorandum of Understanding' on 4 April 2002 has largely been carried out in accordance with the objectives agreed upon by the parties as regards the resolution of 'all outstanding military issues under the Lusaka Protocol'. It is clear that the strict timetable was made possible thanks to the genuine political will of both parties, to which attest the fact that throughout the process of demobilisation, not a single ceasefire violation was registered, and the quartering, demobilisation and disarmament of UNITA military forces proceeded orderly and *en masse*.

6.   THE END OF WAR II: ACCOUNTABILITY AND JUSTICE V. NATIONAL RECONCILIATION (THE AMNESTY AND FORGIVENESS TO THE REBELS)

Very often the problems faced by parties while negotiating the termination of an internal armed conflict are connected with ensuring a durable peace and national reconciliation after the war. Unfortunately, humankind has not yet seen a war without crimes. And one of the dilemmas faced by governments is whether they should prosecute war criminals according to the applicable provisions of the laws of war and national legislation or concede amnesty and pardon. These two are often an obvious condition imposed by rebel forces in exchange for peace. The Angolan conflict was not an exception, and almost all of the ceasefires and peace agreements signed since the very beginning envisaged the concession of amnesty to the rebel forces. The question is therefore whether such practice is consonant with the laws of war applicable to internal armed conflicts.

However, before discussion of the issue of the legality of amnesties and pardons and its application in the Angolan context (Sections 6.3 and 6.4), it is necessary to first address some preliminary questions, namely, whether international law has evolved to criminalize atrocities committed in internal conflicts and whether individuals can be held responsible for such crimes on the basis of command responsibility (Section 6.1), and whether atrocities amounting to war crimes were indeed committed within the context of the Angolan internal armed conflict, for which the perpe-

---

Commission determined that the main tasks of the Lusaka Protocol had been concluded, recommended that the UN SC lift all sanctions against UNITA, and decided to dissolve itself accordingly. See 'Interim Report of the Secretary-General on the United Nations Mission in Angola', *supra* n. 8, paras. 5-7, 17-21.

trators could be held accountable in particular UNITA rebel commander Savimbi, against whom the government had indeed started criminal proceedings (Section 6.2).

6.1   Problems concerning criminalization and prosecution of internal atrocities

6.1.1   *The issue of criminalization*

It is now settled in the international jurisprudence that violations of international humanitarian law in internal armed conflicts constitute war crimes entailing individual criminal responsibility.[116] In the *Čelebići* case, the Appeals Chamber of the International Criminal Tribunal for the former Yugoslavia came to the conclusion that a distinction should be made between the concepts of 'criminalisation' and 'jurisdiction', the former being 'the act of outlawing or making illegal certain behaviour'[117] whereas the latter relates to 'the judicial authority to prosecute those criminal acts'.[118] The fact that the obligations in common Article 3 and AP II are addressed foremost to governments 'is not dispositive of the penal responsibility of individuals, if individuals clearly must carry out that obligation'.[119] As the language of common Article 3 clearly prohibits fundamental offences such as murder, that means that such acts 'were intended to be criminalised in 1949, as they were clearly intended to be illegal within the international legal order'.[120]

This Appeals Chamber holding is of the utmost importance for countries like Angola, where the IHL conventions have not been appropriately transformed into national law,[121] although the Constitution holds that agreements duly ratified by Angola apply directly within the national legal system.[122] Even in such circumstances, countries will normally apply the rules of international agreements only if they are self-executing, i.e., if they contain provisions which are capable of being directly implemented into the national legal system because they create direct obligations for individuals.[123]

With its findings in the *Tadić* and *Čelebići* cases, the Appeals Chamber has factually confirmed that the laws and customs of war applicable to internal conflicts

---

116. See *Tadić* Jurisdiction Decision, *supra* n. 78, paras. 128-136; See *Prosecutor v. Zejnil Delalić, Zdravko Mucić (aka 'Pavo'), Hazim Delić and Esad Landžo (aka 'Zenga')*, Case No. IT-96-21-A, 20 February 2001, Appeal Judgement (hereinafter *Čelebići* Appeal Judgement), paras. 160-172 .

117. *Čelebići* Appeal Judgement, ibid., para. 163.

118. Ibid.

119. T. Meron, 'International criminalization of internal atrocities', *89 AJIL* (1995) pp. 554 at 562.

120. See *Čelebići* Appeal Judgement, *supra* n. 116, para. 163.

121. Angolan legislation has conferred jurisdiction on Angolan Courts to adjudicate cases of war crimes, and crimes against humanity since 1976. However, no material law defines these crimes and their constituent elements. See Lei dos Tribunais Populares Revolucionários, Lei No. 8/78, de 26 de Maio de 1978, (Art. 4), Diário da República I Série, No. 137 (1978); Lei do Sistema Unificado de Justiça, Lei No. 18/88, de 31 de Dezembro de 1988, (Art. 21, (b)), Diário da República I Série, No. 51 (1988).

122. See Lei Constitucional de Angola, Com Emendas de 22 de Agosto de 1992, Art. 21. An English translation can be found on the official website of Angola: <www.angola.org>.

123. See L. Henkin, 'Treaties in Constitutional Democracy', 10 *Michigan JIL* (1989) p. 425.

and (in particular common Article 3) can be directly implemented as they create direct obligations for individuals to abstain from violating the law in the conduct of hostilities.[124]

Therefore, as provisions of common Article 3 were not only in force for Angola but were capable of being implemented by national courts, the fact that they do not contain specific penal sanctions is of no importance since this question was specifically left for countries to regulate under the Geneva Conventions.[125]

6.1.2   *Command responsibility as a mode of individual criminal liability in internal armed conflicts*

Command or superior responsibility is a doctrine by which a person (civilian or military superior) in a position of authority may be held accountable for violations of the laws of war committed by subordinates. Therefore 'the purpose of command responsibility is to ensure that persons vested with *responsibility over others* fulfil their *duty* to ensure that their subordinates do not commit criminal acts'.[126]

To be applicable, the doctrine requires proof of the following elements: a) a superior was in a position of authority over the subordinate(s) who committed the crime (superior–subordinate relationship), b) the superior knew or had reason to know that a crime has been committed or was to be committed by his subordinate(s) (knowledge standard), and c) with that knowledge he failed to prevent or punish his subordinate(s) who committed the crime (failure to prevent or punish standard).[127]

The doctrine developed and gained consistency during WWII case-law as a rule of customary law and was given conventional form in the 1977 AP I (Arts. 87 and 86). Mainly because of its inclusion solely in API and not in APII, the defence in the ICTY *Hadžihasanović* case did challenge a Prosecution's position that command responsibility applied in any type of armed conflict, including to situations of non-international armed conflicts.[128]

Recent ICTY Appeal jurisprudence explicitly held that the doctrine also applies to non-international armed conflicts.[129] In coming to this conclusion, both the Trial and the Appeals Chambers in *Hadžihasanović* case relied on the principle of re-

---

124. See *Tadić* Jurisdiction Decision, *supra* n. 78, para. 128-136; *Čelebići* Appeal Judgement, *supra* n. 116, para. 163.

125. See *infra* section 6.3, about relevant legal issues concerning domestic prosecution of violations of the laws of internal armed conflicts.

126. *Prosecutor* v. *Enver Hadžihasanović, Mehmed Alagić, Amir Kubura*, Case No. IT-01-47-PT), 'Decision on Joint Challenge to Jurisdiction', 12 November 2002, para. 174 (hereinafter, *Hadžihasanović* Trial Decision).

127. *Čelebići* Trial Judgement, *supra* n. 105, para. 346.

128. See Joint Challenge to Jurisdiction Arising from the Amended Indictment, Written Submissions of Enver Hadžihasanović, 10 May 2002; Written Submission of Amir Kubura on Defence Challenges to Jurisdiction, 10 May 2002; Submissions of Mehmed Alagić on the Challenge to Jurisdiction Based on the Illegality of Applying Article 7(3) to Non-International Armed Conflict,' dated 9 May 2002, and filed on 10 May 2002.

129. The doctrine was applied before in the ICTY and ICTR contexts but without the question of legality being raised.

sponsible command, and its interrelation with the broader principle of individual criminal responsibility.[130] The Trial Chamber concluded that:

'the purpose behind the principle of responsible command and the principle of command responsibility is to promote and ensure the compliance with the rules of international humanitarian law. The commander must act responsibly and provide some kind of organisational structure, has to ensure that subordinates observe the rules of armed conflict, and must prevent violations of such norms or, if they already have taken place, ensure that adequate measures are taken.'[131]

In similar terms, the Appeals Chamber held that the 'basis of the commander's responsibility lies in his obligations as commander of troops making up an organised military force under his command, and not in the particular theatre (internal or international) in which the act was committed by a member of that military force'.[132] And that 'responsible command was an integral notion of the prohibition imposed by Article 3 common to the 1949 Geneva Conventions against the doing of certain things in the course of an internal armed conflict'.[133]

The Appeals Chamber then concluded that:

'wherever customary international law recognises that a war crime can be committed by a member of an organised military force, it also recognises that a commander can be penally sanctioned if he knew or had reason to know that his subordinate was about to commit a prohibited act or had done so and the commander failed to take the necessary and reasonable measures to prevent such an act or to punish the subordinate. Customary international law recognises that some war crimes can be committed by a member of an organised military force in the course of an internal armed conflict; it therefore also recognises that there can be command responsibility in respect of such crimes'.[134]

6.2   Violations of international humanitarian law in Angola

In the course of the internal armed conflict in Angola, many war crimes were reportedly committed. Most of these crimes, as was recognised by UNITA leaders[135]

---

130. *The Prosecutor* v. *Enver Hadžihasanović, Mehmed Alagić, Amir Kubura*, Case No. IT-01-47-PT, Decision on Interlocutory Appeal Challenging Jurisdiction in Relation to Command Responsibility case, 17 July 2003, paras. 21, 22 (hereinafter *Hadžihasanović* Appeal Decision).

131. *Hadžihasanović*, Trial Decision, *supra* n. 126, para. 66.

132. *Hadžihasanović*, Appeal Decision, *supra* n. 130, para. 20.

133. Ibid., para. 15.

134. Ibid., para. 18.

135. Addressing the Angolan people on 6 January 2003 in a radio message, Mr Camalata Numa, UNITA political affairs secretary and a former UNITA general, stated that: 'UNITA made the war and assumes responsibility for much of the errors produced during the armed conflict, because many lives were lost and nobody can pay for a life. And UNITA assumes responsibility for that many lives were lost as consequence of this war.' And that it was 'within this framework that UNITA comes forward before the people to beg for pardon because many lives were lost'. 'We assume responsibility for our errors. We ask for forgiveness for the period of war that in this country endured since 1975.' See

themselves, were committed by the UNITA rebel movement. The government entrusted with the mission of protecting the constitutional order in the country and the safety of the civilian population has fought over the years to end the insurgency, and re-establish normal life in the country. As anti-terrorist operations may involve the commission of acts which would be otherwise illegal under international human rights law, the government is interested in strictly obeying humanitarian law provisions (which are all non-derogable) on minimum human treatment to persons not taking part in hostilities.

For this reason, many acts considered by some human rights groups as violations of human rights law, or even war crimes supposedly committed by the Angolan government, are not such, either because they are covered by norms from which states may legitimately derogate under the applicable relevant international human rights law or because they are not yet part of the common core norms applicable in any type of armed conflict.[136]

International human rights instruments, in particular the UN International Covenant on Civil and Political Rights (Art. 4) contains the so-called derogation provisions which enable states to suspend most of their obligations on human rights, with the exception of the few considered fundamental, in cases of emergencies. The few non-derogable provisions include the obligation to respect the right to life, prohibition of torture, slavery, non-retroactivity of the penal law and freedom of conscience. Further, in the most serious emergency situations like armed conflicts, the non-derogable provisions are again limited by the provisions of international humanitarian law as the *lex specialis*. Therefore, whether killing, wounding, arresting or limiting the freedom of expression or movement of a person or taking alien property during an armed conflict is lawful or not will be determined by applying the relevant rules of international humanitarian law and not international human rights law.

Examples of permissible coercive acts in emergency situations (falling short of *unlawful* killing, or torture, or slavery) include arrests, limitation of the freedom of expression or movement and forced conscription into the Army (i.e., those acts blamed on the government). The argument that the government 'never declared a state of emergency' does not help in dealing with the facts in place, which clearly indicated that a serious emergency situation was indeed extant in Angola throughout the 27-year war.

Anyway, the absence of any declaration of emergency represents a violation of a procedure rule (the procedure to follow before such measures can be taken) not substantive law (no doubt that an emergency situation was *de facto* in place in Angola, which would require from any government in asserting its legitimate con-

---

'UNITA apologises for partaking in Angolan war', *AfrolNews* (8 January 2003) <www.afrol.com>, visited 10 January 2003.

136. Examples of acts supposedly committed by the government, which however do not constitute a violation of international law in any way are: parading 'prisoners of war' (regarding UNITA rebels, however, prisoner of war status is not recognised in internal armed conflicts); transfer of civilians from one place to another (permissible, however, for security reasons) etc. See Vines, op. cit. n. 42, at pp. 75-79.

stitutional mission of protecting the citizens and the public interest to take such measures as are allowed under international law). On the other hand, the absence of any declaration of a state of emergency speaks on the contrary: of the intention of the government to limit the abrogation of the rights of the citizens to the minimum possible and necessary (i.e., an exception rather than a rule), to protect the public interest and the interests of the majority of the citizens (something which would not happen had a declaration of emergency been enacted).

Moreover, the Angolan government and the rebels are not equal under national and international law in terms of which acts are legitimate. Whereas most of the acts of the Angolan government against the rebels would be legitimate in its fight against terrorism and armed rebellion (apart from any violations of the minimum non-derogable human rights provisions or violations of international humanitarian law), the same does not apply to rebels. As rebels do not enjoy any recognised legal status under international law, and still less under national law, acts committed by them may be a violation either of the domestic law or international humanitarian law. Human rights law provision on permissible derogations does not apply to them, since they are not state agents, although they could theoretically be the subject of human rights violations. However, in certain circumstances, international law allows (but does not oblige) states to consider strict adherence by the rebels to the rules of war and the so-called legitimate acts of combat (i.e., those in combat situations directed strictly to the opposing armed forces) for the purposes of granting amnesty.[137]

UNITA rebels have inflicted on the Angolan people untold suffering and pain, have destroyed the entire infrastructure of the country, and are solely responsible for the situation of instability and insecurity created in the country, in their inglorious goal of terrorising the civilian population and making the country ungovernable, and as the research shows often at the service of foreign interests. Among those atrocities certified and confirmed by UNITA itself are: hostage-taking in the period 1981-1985;[138] siege of cities in the period 1993-1999;[139] targeting of civilian population (killing, mutilation, looting, terrorization (indiscriminate shelling of cities the best example being the indiscriminate shelling of the city of Kuito in central Angolan Province of Bie)); use of child soldiers;[140] destruction of civilian objectives throughout the war; use of civilians as human shields, etc.[141]

---

137. Please note however that as the law is generally permissible, international jurisdictions (as the ICTY case-law shows) may adopt different approaches. See *infra* section 6.3 for a discussion about the duty or right of national states to prosecute violations of international humanitarian law in internal armed conflicts.

138. See James, op. cit. n. 28, at pp. 120-122.

139. See Vines, op. cit. n. 42, at pp. 59-62.

140. See *supra* n. 64.

141. See Human Rights Watch Reports from 1992 to 2002 <www.hrw.org>.

6.2.1   *Criminal proceedings against UNITA rebel commander Jonas Savimbi*

Faced with all these barbaric acts, the Angolan government had no other alternative but to call for accountability of Savimbi, as the person principally responsible. With a series of successive national and international steps starting from September 1998, the government sought to institute criminal proceedings against him.

The Southern African Development Community (SADC) branded Jonas Savimbi a war criminal and threw its support behind the 'new' UNITA on 3 September 1998.[142] On 27 October 1998, the National Assembly abrogated the law granting a special status to Jonas Savimbi for his failure to fulfil his party's obligations under the Protocol.[143] And on 27 January 1999, the National Assembly passed a resolution declaring Savimbi 'a war criminal and international terrorist', and called for legal proceedings leading to Savimbi and his direct collaborators being held accountable, in criminal and civil law, both nationally and internationally.[144] On 24 July 1999, the national police issued an arrest warrant for Savimbi on charges that included 'rebellion, sabotage, murder, and torture, kidnapping, robbery, and the use of explosives – including planting landmines at sites used by civilians.'[145] With Savimbi's death in combat in February 2002, all of these criminal proceedings have become void.

Based on the analysis *supra*, a sound argument can be made that the criminal proceedings against Savimbi reviewed here were lawful. However, a question is still open as to whether the government has discretion to prosecute or concede amnesty to suspected criminals in internal armed conflicts, i.e., was it justified for the Angolan government to seek prosecution of Savimbi but concede amnesty to the rest of the rebels, or not?

6.3   **Domestic prosecution of violations of the law of internal armed conflicts: a right or a duty?**

Although the national legislation of many states in transition (like in Angola) does not contain any specific provisions implementing international humanitarian law, the broad assumption has been that provisions of general criminal law of the states concerning unlawful homicide, offences against physical or sexual integrity or against property could be applied in situations where war crimes were committed.[146] Since states may within the framework of their constitutional order provide for legal exemption of criminal responsibility (such as amnesties and pardons), the question therefore is: could such laws apply also in situations where the relevant acts are not only prohibited under national law but also under international humanitarian law?

---

142. See Vines, op. cit. n. 42, at p. 26.
143. See UN Doc. S/1998/1110, 23 November 1998.
144. See text: 'Parliamentary Resolution Declaring Jonas Savimbi a War Criminal', 27 January 1999, <www.angola.org>. See also Vines, op. cit. n. 42, at p. 28.
145. Vines, ibid., at pp. 28, 29.
146. See Solf, loc. cit. n. 98, at pp. 56, 64.

This requires an answer to the following question: whether the law of internal armed conflicts imposes upon territorial states a mandatory duty to punish acts considered war crimes in internal conflicts? The opinion of states and commentators is divided. Some think it should be a duty, others that it is not.[147] This author's understanding is that most of those who advocate a mandatory duty to punish war crimes have generally in mind war crimes in international armed conflicts,[148] but that some others would have liked to extend the mandatory war crimes jurisdiction regime applicable in international armed conflicts to violations committed in internal armed conflicts. The most striking example was given by the now-repealed Belgian law on punishment of grave breaches of international humanitarian law,[149] which considered any act committed (by whomsoever and wherever) in violation not only of the Geneva Conventions and Additional Protocol I but also common Article 3 and Additional Protocol II to be a grave breach of international humanitarian law. However this approach is manifestly confusing at the very least. Because the Belgian law was based on conventional international law sources (Geneva Conventions and Additional Protocols), it is worth remembering by importing the concept of 'grave breaches' in those sources into national legislation that it is not a mere juxtaposition of terms. It has a certain *legal* meaning.

In particular the universal jurisdiction regime (whomsoever, wherever) (which Belgium was trying to assert by enacting such a law) is only attached to those violations of the Geneva Conventions and Additional Protocol I considered 'grave breaches'. And the regime pertaining to those acts is only applicable to international armed conflicts and even then only under certain conditions therein specified.

It has since been argued and this author agrees that normally the grave breaches regime (essentially its mandatory universal enforcement mechanism) under customary law should apply to all serious violations of the laws and customs of war in international armed conflicts.[150] However, no one has ever argued that the grave

---

147. For example Michael Scharf considers that such a duty exists only where a Convention specifically so provides (this is the case of the Geneva Conventions (in relation to grave breaches) and the Genocide and Torture Conventions) and that in other circumstances, like crimes against humanity or crimes committed in internal armed conflicts such a duty does not exist. See M. Scharf, 'The Letter of the Law: The Scope of the International Legal Obligation to Prosecute Human Rights Crimes', 59 *Law and Contemporary Problems* (1996) pp. 41 at 43. See also Solf, loc. cit. n. 98, at pp. 59, 60 (noting that 'none of the provisions of the Conventions relating to enforcement, therefore, including the prosecute- or-extradite provisions, apply to the norms of common article 3.').

148. See M. Cherif Bassiouni, 'Searching for peace and achieving Justice: The need for accountability', 59 *Law and Contemporary Problems* (1996) pp. 9, at 17 (stating that: 'Crimes against humanity, genocide, war crimes (under conventional and customary regulation of armed conflicts), and torture are international crimes that have risen to the level of *jus cogens*. As a consequence, the following duties arise: the obligation to prosecute or extradite; to provide legal assistance; to eliminate statutes of limitations; to eliminate immunities of superiors up to and including heads of states. Under international law, these obligations are to be considered as *obligatio ergo omnes*, the consequence of which is that impunity cannot be granted.').

149. Loi Belge relative a la repression des infractions graves aux conventions de Genève du 12 aôut 1949 aux protocoles I et II du 8 juin 1977, de 16 de juin de 1993, *Moniteur belge*, 4 aôut 1993, as amended by Loi du 10 février 1999, *Moniteur belge*, 23 mars 1999.

150. See Cherif Bassiouni, loc. cit. n. 148.

breaches regime enshrined in the Geneva Conventions and AP I is let alone implied (because explicitly it is not there) also for violations of common Article 3 or for violations of AP II. On the contrary, the ICTY jurisprudence in *Tadić* Jurisdiction Decision has ruled explicitly that the grave breaches regime (mainly because of the attached universal jurisdiction enforcement mechanism) is not extendable to violations of common Article 3.[151] No matter how interested we all are to see that accountability also comes to domestic perpetrators of atrocities, especially in these times when most of the conflicts are internal in character, this author doubts if forcefully pushing the boundaries of the law will help. As the *Congo* v. *Belgium* case shows,[152] the unilateralist approach adopted by some countries may only hurt developments in the right direction, especially now with the adoption of the 1998 Rome Statute of the International Criminal Court, which already imposes a restricted *aut dedere aut judicare* obligation upon member states (*vis-à-vis* the Court) in internal armed conflicts, although still within a conventional framework.

Under these circumstances, in this author's view, much closer to the truth are those who try to find foundations for such an obligation strictly within the existing framework of general international law. For example, there is growing consensus that in view of the fact that violations of the laws of internal armed conflicts have come to be considered war crimes, at least the jurisdictional penal provisions of the Geneva Conventions concerning violations other than the grave breaches probably should apply to violations of common Article 3 in internal armed conflicts.[153] The point of disagreement is the extent to which prosecution is not only a right but also a mandatory duty of the territorial state of jurisdiction, thus factually equating this non-grave breaches regime to that of the grave breaches of the Geneva Conventions.

We will analyse this and two other commonly alleged potential basis of such a duty of prosecution of war crimes in internal armed conflicts.

6.3.1   *The penal provisions of the Geneva Conventions as a potential basis of a duty to prosecute under international law*

All the four Geneva Conventions provide for a distinction between *grave breaches* and *other* violations of the Conventions (which at least theoretically would include violations of common Article 3, since it is also a part of those Conventions, although with a distinct material field of application – non-international armed conflicts) in terms of the enforcement measures which the countries are entitled to take in case of violations. In relation to *grave breaches* the requirements are strong and a universal jurisdiction regime is established (according to the principle *aut*

---

151. See *Tadić* Jurisdiction Decision, *supra* n. 78, paras. 80-81.

152. See *Case Concerning the Arrest Warrant of 11 April 2000* (*Democratic Republic of Congo* v. *Belgium*) ICJ, 14 February 2002.

153. See M. Bothe, 'War crimes in non-international armed conflicts', 24 *Israel YB HR* (1994) pp. 241, at 247-249.

dedere, aut judicare).[154] The same however does not follow from the language of the Geneva Conventions when at issue is 'suppression of *other* infractions':

> 'Each High Contracting Party *shall take measures necessary for the suppression* of all acts contrary to the provisions of the present Convention *other* than the grave breaches defined in the following Article.'[155]

The ICRC has noted the difference between the term '*suppression*' in the English text and '*faire cesser*' in the authoritative French text and commented in part that:

> 'The expression '*faire cesser*', employed in the French text, is open to various interpretations. In our opinion it covers *everything* a State can do *to prevent* the commission, or *the repetition* of acts contrary to the Convention.'[156]

Measures necessary for the 'suppression' clearly would indeed include the obligation to adopt the relevant legislation to impose penal sanctions for such violations in internal armed conflicts. But it seems difficult to argue that States Parties when adopting the Geneva Conventions envisaged that 'prosecution' would be the only way available to the states to cope with violations of common Article 3 of the Geneva Conventions. If that had been so, states would just have extended the grave breaches regime to apply to *any* violation of provisions of the Geneva Conventions, and most importantly to violations of common Article 3. However this was clearly never the intention.

Because states have no obligation as of law to hand over to other countries persons accused of such violations committed in internal armed conflicts, an argument that the law *requires* prosecution as the sole legal alternative in such situations does not seem defensible. In our view, even if a case can be made that these jurisdictional penal provisions of the Geneva Conventions require that a state should do something, it is clear that this 'something' includes not only prosecution, but also other measures the country finds appropriate in order 'to prevent the repetition' of violations of the laws in question.

Without prejudice to what the UN Security Council acting under Chapter VII may otherwise establish,[157] these 'necessary measures' that states are deemed to adopt under the provisions of international humanitarian law may include pardons and amnesties for past atrocities, if they best serve the interest of ensuring lasting peace, and therefore the effective prevention of recurrence of violations of the laws of war. Alternatively, this can be considered a duty from which derogation is permissible in the interests of ensuring lasting peace.

---

154. See First Geneva Convention, *supra* n. 75, Art. 49; Second Geneva Convention, *supra* n. 75, Art. 50; Third Geneva Convention, *supra* n. 75, Art. 129; Fourth Geneva Convention, *supra* n. 75, Art. 146.

155. Ibid.

156. J. Pictet, ed., *Commentary on I Geneva Convention Relative to the Protection of Civilian Persons in Time of War,* (Geneva, ICRC 1958) p. 367.

157. See *infra* nn. 165, 184.

6.3.2   *The general customary law principle of state responsibility as a potential legal basis of a duty to punish*

To ascertain that there is an obligation to punish, commentators also refer to the customary law principle of state responsibility. According to this principle, a state is obliged before other contracting parties to give some satisfaction in case of violations of the agreed conduct. This satisfaction would include the obligation to punish a concrete perpetrator of the violation, as the armed conflict cannot be considered a circumstance excluding the wrongfulness of the act. It is argued that international humanitarian law rules binding the state were specially adopted to apply in such situations, and the state responsibility in case is in relation to an obligation incumbent upon the state under this law.[158] Although this argument seems reasoned, the fact is that the scope of the state responsibility in this situation will also be subject to the limitations adopted in the same system of law, i.e., that there is a difference between violations considered as 'grave breaches' of the Geneva Conventions and those considered as 'other infractions'. The suppression of 'other infractions' of the Geneva Conventions like common Article 3 does not require, as we just saw above, that states have recourse to prosecutions as an irrevocable legal alternative, having in mind the objective of ensuring lasting peace and national reconciliation in post-conflict societies.

6.3.3   *International human rights law as a potential legal basis of a duty to punish*

Another argument put forward as the legal basis of a mandatory duty to punish is found in certain provisions of human rights law. It is argued that instruments such as the International Covenant on Civil and Political Rights (Art. 2) implies such a duty, as it obliges State Parties, through passage of legislation or other steps, to give effect to the rights recognised in the Covenant and to ensure that victims have an effective remedy, and that claims to such a remedy be determined by the competent authorities, be they judicial, administrative, legislative, or such other authorities as the legal system may provide, and that the remedy, when granted, be enforced by the competent authorities.

Based on similar provisions of the regional American Convention on Human Rights, (Arts. 1, 8 and 25),[159] victims of human rights abuses and human rights organisations challenged the blanket amnesty laws of Argentina and Uruguay before the Inter-American Commission on Human Rights. The Inter-American Commission found that those amnesty laws violated the victims' right to a fair hearing and to judicial protection, and the correlative obligation incumbent upon governments to investigate the crimes in question. Commentators note, however, that the decision was not taken as a binding statement of the law (only

---

158. See Bothe, loc. cit. n. 153, at p. 248.

159. American Convention on Human Rights, opened for signature 22 November 1969, *O.A.S.T.S.* No. 36, reprinted in 9 *ILM* (1970) p. 673 (entered into force 18 July 1978) (hereinafter, the American Convention).

the inter-American Court of Human Rights is empowered to do so), but as a recommendation to the states.[160] This is an indication in their opinion that even the Commission lawyers were not sure of the appropriateness and likeliness of a binding decision on this issue.[161] One argument against this approach is that although it is recognised that in situations of armed conflicts, human rights law continues to have effect, it is however superseded by international humanitarian law as the *lex specialis*.[162] Therefore, the differences in IHL between the legal regime of 'grave breaches' and 'other infractions' of Geneva Conventions, would again apply.

One should note, however, that there is a difference between, on the one hand, gross violations of human rights, such as genocide and crimes against humanity (legal provisions on these crimes are not superseded by rules of international humanitarian law), and other ordinary human rights violations in internal armed conflicts, on the other. As genocide and crimes against humanity are not dependent upon the circumstances of their commission (in peace or wartime), the duty to punish such crimes maintains in situations of armed conflicts.[163]

A mandatory obligation to punish violations of the law of internal armed conflicts could however be imposed upon a state by force of provisions of a conven-

---

160. See Bothe, loc. cit. n. 153 at pp. 248-249. Commentators also rely on the following three communications issued by the Human Rights Committee established to monitor compliance with the Covenant on Civil and Political Rights to find a 'duty to punish' in internal armed conflicts: a) Responding to a communication alleging torture in Zaire, the Committee commented that Zaire was 'under a duty to … conduct an inquiry into the circumstances of torture, to punish those found guilty of torture and to take steps to ensure that similar violations do not occur in the future'. b) In another case involving allegations of extra-legal executions in Surinam, the Committee requested the government 'to take effective steps … to investigate the killings … and to bring to justice any persons found to be responsible'. c) In response to a communication alleging forced disappearances in Uruguay, the Committee urged the government of Uruguay to take effective steps to bring to justice any persons found responsible. Michael Scharf rejects such reading, noting that: 'During the negotiations of the Covenant, the delegates specifically considered and rejected a proposal that would have required states to prosecute violators. To read in such a requirement on the basis of the Human Rights Committee's comments would be to contravene the understanding of the Conventions' drafters upon which the majority of Parties relied when ratifying the Convention.' Scharf, loc. cit. n. 149, at p. 49.

161. See R.O. Weiner, 'Trying to make ends meet: reconciling the law and practice of human rights amnesties', 26 *St Mary's LJ* (1995) at pp. 857 at p. 869.

162. See 'Legality of the Threat or Use of Nuclear Weapons', (Advisory Opinion) *ICJ Rep.* (1996) 226, para. 25 (8 July 1996).

163. For the crimes of genocide and torture the relevant conventions specifically impose an obligation to punish (Art. VI of the Convention on the Prevention and Punishment of the Crime of Genocide, 9 December 1948, Art. II, (78 *UNTS* 277, 280), and Arts. IV, VII of the Convention Against Torture and Other Cruel, Inhuman or Degrading Treatment or Punishment, opened for signature 4 February 1985, reprinted in 23 *ILM* (1984) p. 1027. For crimes against humanity, most of the commentators support the view that customary law imposes an obligation to punish. See C.C. Joyner, 'Redressing Impunity for Human Rights Violations: The Universal Declaration and the Search for Accountability', 26 *Denver JIL & Pol.* (1998) pp. 591 at p. 613 (stating that: 'the duty to prosecute certain grave human rights violations, derived from international criminal law, clearly implies that criminal acts subject to such a duty cannot at least in principle be amnestied'). The cases of the former Yugoslavia and Rwanda are examples of situations where gross violations of human rights have prompted the international community to request that the perpetrators of these acts do not go unpunished, as the best way to ensure lasting peace in those countries.

tional instrument (to which it is a party) such as the 1998 Rome Statute of the International Criminal Court, or by force of a decision by the UN Security Council that prosecution of internal atrocities is the best way to bring about peace and security in a certain country or region. [164]

Based on this analysis, a sound argument may be advanced that prosecution of violations of the laws of internal armed conflicts is a right and not a mandatory duty imposed upon territorial states under international law, or alternatively, it is a duty from which derogation is permissible in the interest of ensuring a lasting peace. In making a decision about the necessary measures to prevent continuation of the armed conflict and therefore recurrence of violations of the laws of war, the territorial state is entitled to consider all the implications of the position taken. Such measures could include prosecution, but they are not limited to it. Depending upon the circumstances, a truth commission procedure, forgiveness or amnesty could be considered as a valid alternative in the interests of ensuring a lasting peace.[165]

There is support for the idea that this possibility is not excluded even under the ICC Statute.[166] During the ICC Statute negotiations, the question was raised concerning what to do in cases of declared amnesties; however it was simply dropped for lack of a compromise among states.[167] As the question of whether to prosecute or not is left at the discretion of the Prosecutor (under Art. 53(1)(c), (2)(c) of the

---

164. This approach, which finds support in the UN SC practice, is not disputed by anyone. It was supported by the International Court of Justice and by commentators. See *Arrest Warrant* case (*Congo v. Belgium*) *supra* n. 152, para. 61. See also Scharf, loc. cit. n. 147, at pp. 59-60 (noting that: 'The Security Council can, through a Chapter VII resolution, create binding obligations on states to bring individuals responsible for international crimes to justice. The Council, for example, adopted Res. 748, requiring Libya to surrender to the United States or the United Kingdom for prosecution the two Libyan officials charged with bombing Pan American Flight 103. A year later, the Council adopted Res. 837, calling for the arrest of Somali Warlord Mohamed Farrah Aidid, who was responsible for the murder of 24 UN peacekeepers. In addition, the Security Council resolutions establishing the Yugoslavia and Rwanda War Crimes Tribunals impose an obligation on all states that are members of the United Nations to cooperate fully with the Tribunal, including its orders of arrest.').

165. There are commentators who go so far as to admit that the amnesty alternative to prosecutions has even become a 'customary law right for democracies in transition', although it seems to be what the authors desire rather than already any law: See E.W. Schabacker, 'Reconciliation or Justice and Ashes: Amnesty and the Duty to Punish Human Rights Offences', 12 *New York ILR* (1999) at p. 54, stating that: 'Custom yields a different set of norms and rules in the cases of governments making the transition to democracy. From Latin America to Asia, Africa, and Eastern Europe, fledgling democracies have rejected prosecution and opted instead for reconciliation through a combination of truth and forgiveness. In these cases, the evidence of state practice and the goals of human rights protection create a rule of customary international law that allows governments to make this choice when necessary to preserve law and order.'

166. See S. Chesterman, 'No justice without peace? International Criminal Law and the decision to Prosecute', in S. Chesterman, ed., *Civilians in War* (London, Lynne Rienner Publishers 2001) pp. 145, at p. 157.

167. See Scharf, loc. cit. n. 149, at p. 41 (noting that: 'At the preparatory conference for the establishment of a permanent international criminal court in August 1997, the U.S. Delegation circulated a paper suggesting that the proposed permanent court should take into account such amnesties in the interest of international peace and national reconciliation when deciding whether to prosecute.').

ICC Statute), this suggests that he could consider situations of declared amnesties, if they are in the interest of justice as a reason not to initiate an investigation.

6.4   Conditional or blanket amnesties and the need of preserving justice in Angola

This section reviews the practice of states and the various options available to strike a balance between preserving justice and conceding pardons, and the solutions found in Angola in conceding a blanket amnesty to the rebels and programming other non-retributive means of preserving justice for the victims.

Commentators differentiate among the following three alternative forms of domestic responses to past human rights abuses, which depend on whether the victorious side is the former regime or a new regime: In case of a regime change the tendency is to apply either a *conditional* amnesty or lustration or both. In cases of a conflict ending up with the former rulers in power, the alternative adopted is a *blanket* amnesty to all those involved in the conflict, although truth commissions are also envisaged.

Most of the peace agreements signed at the conclusion of the armed conflicts since the 1960s have included a provision on amnesty: France-Algeria (1962); Pakistani-Bangladesh (1971); Portugal-Angola (1975); Chile (1978); Brazil (1979); Uruguay (1986); Argentina (1986); Nicaragua (1990); Honduras (1991); Cotê D'Ivoire (1992); El Salvador (1993); Mozambique (1993); Haiti (1994); Peru (1995); Guatemala (1996); Algeria (1999); Sierra Leone (1999) and others.[168]

The many wars that ravaged countries all over the world and the amnesties that followed stand in contrast with the number of official condemnations of such practice. Moreover, the international community not only does not condemn but also even at times tends to encourage such amnesties. This reinforces the rule that prosecution of violations of the law of internal armed conflicts should be considered only one of the alternative rights of the territorial state of jurisdiction. For example, there was no reaction to the decision of the new South African regime in 1994 not to prosecute Apartheid-era criminals but to establish a Truth and Reconciliation Commission. The US, Portugal and Russia encouraged the Angolan government to concede amnesty to the rebels within the framework of the Bicesse Peace Process which began in 1991. The UN also encouraged the Angolan government to concede amnesty to the rebels in the Lusaka Protocol in 1994 negotiated under its direct mediation.[169]

The normal justification for amnesties is the 'claim that criminal accountability undermines the transition to democracy and must therefore be limited in whole or

---

168. See D. Cassel, 'Lessons from the Americas: Guidelines for International Response to Amnesties for Atrocities', *59 Law and Contemporary Problems* (1996) pp. 197, 200-201; see also Chesterman, loc. cit. n. 166, at p. 154.

169. The UN has also in the past encouraged similar amnesty deals in other countries like El Salvador, Haiti, South Africa, Mozambique. See Scharf, loc. cit. n. 147, at p. 41. See also C. Stahn, 'United Nations peace-building, amnesties and alternative forms of justice: A change in practice?', 84 *IRRC* (2002) pp. 191-205.

in part'.[170] For example the Amnesty Law of Angola adopted in April 2002 grounds the law on the need to ensure the necessary 'legal and political environment to promote the realization of the goal of national reconciliation'.[171]

The South African Constitutional Court called attention to the difference in circumstances between an internal armed conflict and an international one to justify amnesties in internal conflicts stating that:

'It is one thing to allow officers of a hostile power which has invaded a foreign state to remain unpunished for gross violations of human rights perpetrated against others during the course of such conflict. It is another thing to compel such punishment in circumstances where such violations have substantially occurred in consequence of conflict between different formations within the same state in respect of the permissible political direction which that state should take with regard to the structures of the state and the parameters of its political policies and where it becomes necessary after the cessation of such conflict for the society traumatised by such a conflict to reconstruct itself. The erstwhile adversaries of such a conflict inhabit the same sovereign territory. They have to live with each other and work with each other and the state concerned is best equipped to determine what measures may be most conducive for the facilitation of such reconciliation and reconstruction.'[172]

Opponents have however questioned the legitimacy of blanket amnesties and their purported reconciliation objective. They ask, 'how can there not be something deeply unsatisfactory about a 'reconciliation' that lets murderers walk in the street and gives their justifications such prominence?'[173] In their opinion, programs of national healing and reconciliation must include mechanisms to reveal the truth. The South African commission is proposed as a model.[174]

This author agrees with the above position with the caveat that what should be followed is not necessarily the *format*, rather the *substance*. And the substance is that, those who are responsible for human rights violations, if given amnesty, must have the courage to come before the people to confess their crimes, and ask the people for forgiveness. Only this frank acknowledgement of the atrocities of the past, and the requested pardon can minimize the tortuous process of national healing and reconciliation. This does not need to happen within strictly established formal institutions, which may have the potential of creating, depending upon the circumstances, a sense of humiliation and impair genuine repentance. In addition, the *format* adopted will also inevitably depend upon the particular circumstances of the peace process, and the kind and external dimensions of the atrocities committed.

---

170. Chestermann, loc. cit. n. 166, at p. 156. See about the US position on this issue, *supra* n. 165.

171. Lei de Amnistia, Lei No. 4/02 de 4 de Abril de 2002, Diário da República, I Série - No. 27. See also 'Angola Rebels Granted Amnesty', BBC News, 2 April 2002, <www.bbc.com>.

172. '*Azanian Peoples Organization (AZAPO)* v. *President of the Republic of South Africa* (1996)', 4 *South African LR* (1997) pp. 671, at p. 683, para. 31.

173. See Schabacker, loc. cit. n. 165, at p. 51.

174. Ibid., at p. 53.

On the other hand, the process should not under normal circumstance stop there. Amnesty only replaces the alternative duty to punish, but the remedies due to the victims are not limited to punishment, forgiveness and amnesty. They should also involve compensation for the victims.[175] The government should make an effort to compensate the victims of rebel atrocities (even though it made every effort to protect them), if justice is to be completely done. Compensation does not necessarily mean financial reparations.[176] Depending upon the circumstances and the availability of means, compensation may be provided with a showing of genuine interest on the part of the government to develop short and long-term programs of national development and social protection of all the citizens and in particular the most disadvantaged victims of the war, the orphan children and the widows. This task is in the agenda for peace and reconciliation of the Angolan government enacted on 13 March 2002.

Indeed, while assistance from the international community is still lacking, the government has been doing what it can to advance this process of community-based compensation. Thus, the government has adopted and is implementing a comprehensive short-term development and settlement program called 'Aldeamentos em Angola', a nationwide 'strategy of combat against poverty', and is preparing a comprehensive long-term program of national reconstruction and development to be implemented by 2025. The Project 'Aldeamentos em Angola' will involve the creation of new agro-industrial complexes throughout Angola each benefiting more than 100 thousand displaced or demobilised families, with the cooperation of Israel and other countries.[177] Efforts are also underway to re-establish minimum supporting infrastructure in the country, the demining of the roads and of the countryside to enable the free movement of people nationwide. However the challenges are enormous and without external financial assistance, it will be impossible to achieve the short term goals of settlement of the more than four millions war displaced and war demobilised Angolans, and establish a minimum of normal life in the country, conditions so crucial for the ongoing process of national reconciliation and pacification of spirits.

6.4.1   *The Amnesty Law of Angola of 4 April 2002*

As noted above, the government's plan for national peace and reconciliation announced on 13 March 2002 recognised the principle of a general amnesty to all those who disarmed. Pursuant to this, an Amnesty Law was enacted on the same day as the Luena Memorandum, on 4 April 2002.[178] According to its Article 1,

---

175. See Bassiouni, loc. cit. n. 148, at p. 22, (noting that: 'Victim compensation is a necessity.'). See also B. Akinrinade, 'International Humanitarian Law and the Conflict in Sierra Leone', 15 *Notre Dame JL Ethics & Pub. Policy* (2001) pp. 391, at pp. 448-450.

176. See Bassiouni, ibid. (noting that: 'Monetary compensation should not be deemed the only outcome. Non-monetary forms of compensation should also be developed, particularly in societies where the economy is unable to sustain large monetary sums.').

177. See 'Conselho de Ministros Aprova Projecto Aldeamentos em Angola', Angop-Press Agency, 20 December 2003.

178. See Lei de Amnistia, Lei No. 4 /02, de 4 de Abril de 2002, *supra* n. 171.

amnesty is given to all those who committed crimes against the security of the state, within the framework of the Angolan internal armed conflict. The amnesty was valid for 45 days, from the date of the enactment of the law. In addition, the amnesty was also to cover all the crimes committed against the military service, in particular the crime of desertion. The special representative of the UN Secretary-General, who signed the Memorandum as a witness, made a hand-written disclaimer to the effect that the UN 'does not recognise amnesties for crimes against humanity and war crimes'.

The Memorandum is an addendum to implement the 1994 Lusaka Protocol, which was signed under the auspices of the UN and provided for amnesty. However the UN Secretary-General Representative did not make such a disclaimer while signing that mother agreement. The present amnesty law is the fifth to be adopted by the Parliament, within the framework of the peace process initiated by the Bicesse Accords and the Lusaka Protocol.[179] Therefore, the UN's disclaimer in the addendum may be considered to be intended to serve as a *carte blanche* to the government to prosecute whomever among the former UNITA rebels would be inclined to restart war in the country,[180] rather than a UN intention to impose on

---

179. See about the Amnesty Law of Angola adopted in 2000, J. Doria, 'Recent developments in Angola concerning IHL', 3 *YIHL* (2000) at p. 411.

180. A similar *right* in the way of a disclaimer by the UN Secretary-General's Representative appended to the Lomé Peace Agreement for Sierra Leone concerning amnesty provisions was also given to the government of Sierra Leone in 1999. When the rebels once again violated this peace agreement and resorted again to war, the government of Sierra Leone, based on this disclaimer, requested on 12 June 2000 UN assistance to establish a mixed international/national Special Court to try the responsible rebels. See Fifth Report of the UN Secretary-General on the United Nations Mission in Sierra Leone, UN Doc. S/2000/751 (2000), 31 July 2000, paras. 9, 10. Thereafter, the United Nations Security Council adopted Res. 1315/2000 on 14 August 2000 (UN Doc. S/RES/1315(2000) stating: 'Noting that the Heads of States and Governments of ECOWAS agreed at the 23rd Summit of the Organization in Abuja on 28 and 29 May 2000 to dispatch a regional investigation of *resumption of hostilities*', 'Recalling that the Special Representative of the Secretary-General *appended* to his signature of the Lomé Agreement *a statement* that the United Nations holds the understanding that the amnesty provisions of the Agreement shall not apply to international crimes of genocide, crimes against humanity, war crimes and other serious violations of international humanitarian law', 'Recognising that *in the particular circumstances* of Sierra Leone, a credible system of justice and accountability for the very serious crimes committed there would end impunity and would contribute to the process of national reconciliation and to the restoration and maintenance of peace', '*Taking note in this regard of the letter dated 12 June 2000 from the President of Sierra Leone* to the Secretary-General and the Suggested Framework attached to it', 'Recognising further the desire of the government of Sierra Leone for assistance from the United Nations in establishing a strong and credible court that will meet the objectives of bringing justice and ensuring lasting peace', '*Reiterating that the situation in Sierra Leone continues to constitute a threat to international peace* and security in the region', '1. *Requests the Secretary-General to negotiate an agreement* with the government of Sierra Leone to create an independent special court consistent with this resolution', '2. Recommends that the subject matter jurisdiction of the special court should include notably crimes against humanity, war crimes and other serious violations of international humanitarian law, *as well as crimes under relevant Sierra Leonean law* committed within the territory of Sierra Leone', '3. Recommends further that the special court should have personal jurisdiction over *persons who bear the greatest responsibility* for the commission of the crimes referred to in paragraph 2, including those *leaders* who, in committing such crimes, *have threatened* the establishment of and *implementation of the peace process* in Sierra Leone') [Emphasis added].

the Angolan government a mandatory duty to punish suspected war criminals at this stage.[181]

Such a duty, even if it was to be established, could only be imposed by the UN SC acting under Chapter VII.[182]

The UN Secretary-General in his Report about the mission in Angola only informs the UN SC that a disclaimer was made. However he did not recommend to the UN Security Council that prosecutions necessarily follow, to override the specific alternative measures already taken by the government in order to strike a balance between the need for justice on the one hand and national reconciliation in the Angolan context on the other.[183]

The UN Security Council for its part, in its most recent resolutions on Angola, has vigorously supported the peace process in Angola, and the program of national reconciliation and healing adopted and being implemented by the government, having even withdrawn the sanctions imposed against UNITA.[184]

There is nothing indicating that this UN Security Council support does not include the amnesty program – one of the key elements of the project of national reconciliation of the government.[185] Moreover, two of the permanent members of

---

181. The government did attempt to prosecute UNITA rebels in the past. However, such efforts met with a cold UN reaction. Thus, when in 24 July 1999 the Angolan government issued an arrest warrant against Savimbi for charges which included rebellion, sabotage, murder and torture, the UN Secretary-General Koffi Anan reacted negatively stating that the warrant was 'wrong' and that 'you make peace with enemies, and to make peace you have to have communications, either directly or through third parties'. See Vines, op. cit. n. 42, at p. 29.

182. Such was the case, for example, in the aftermath of the conflicts in the territories of the former Yugoslavia and Rwanda, when the UN SC adopted resolutions under Chapter VII imposing a duty on countries of the world to give effect to those resolutions. See UN SC Res. 827/1993 (UN Doc. S/RES/827(1993), stating that the UN SC: 'Determining that this situation continues to constitute a threat to international peace and security', 'Convinced that *in the particular circumstances* of the former Yugoslavia, the establishment as an ad hoc measure by the Council of an international tribunal and the prosecution of persons responsible for serious violations of international humanitarian law would enable this aim to be achieved and would contribute to the restoration and maintenance of peace', '...4. Decides *that all States shall cooperate fully* with the International Tribunal and its organs in accordance with present resolution and the Statute of the International Tribunal and that *consequently all States shall take any measures necessary under their domestic law to implement the provisions of the present resolution and the Statute*, including the obligation of States to comply with requests for assistance or orders issued by a Trial Chamber under article 29 of the Statute'. Also see UN SC Res. 955/1994 (UN Doc S/RES/955(1994), stating that the UN SC: 'Determining that this situation continues to constitute a threat to international peace and security', 'Convinced that *in the particular circumstances* of Rwanda, the prosecution of persons responsible for serious violations of international humanitarian law would enable this aim to be achieved and would contribute to the process of national reconciliation and to the restoration and maintenance of peace', '...2. Decides that *all States shall cooperate fully* with the international Tribunal and that *consequently all states shall take any measures necessary under their domestic law to implement provisions of the present resolution and the Statute*, including the obligation of States to comply with requests for assistance or orders issued by a Trial Chamber under Article 28 of the Statute and requests States to keep the Secretary-General informed of such measures.' [Emphasis added].

183. See UN Secretary-General Interim Report on Angola (2002), *supra* n. 8.

184. See UNSC Res. 1412 (2002), 17 May 2002 (UN Doc S/Res/1412 (2002)); UNSC Res. 1448 (2002); 9 December 2002 (UN Doc. S/Res/1448(2002)).

185. In its Res. 1432 (2002) of 15 August 2002, the UN Security Council welcomed 'the historic

the UN Security Council (the US and Russia) are observers of the peace process since the 1991 Bicesse Accords, and have encouraged since then this very amnesty program of the government as the most effective way to national reconciliation and healing in a country ravaged by almost a half century of war.

UNITA, cognisant of its responsibilities for the many crimes committed in the country and the situation of instability created over the 27-year war, has accepted its full responsibility for those acts, and has begged the pardon of the Angolan people.[186] This effectively closes the issue of the need for investigations and accountability in the Angolan internal armed conflict context. However the government has still accrued responsibilities concerning the victimised Angolan people by UNITA atrocities. A program of essentially community-based short-term compensation schemes is already being implemented. However the government needs assistance from all the international community to accomplish it.

7. THE END OF WAR III: THE ANGOLAN EXPERIENCE IN PROSECUTING WAR CRIMINALS AND THE ISSUE OF CRIMINAL RESPONSIBILITY AND REPARATIONS IN THE CONFLICT BETWEEN ANGOLA AND SOUTH AFRICA

In the Angolan context, the external factor was always the catalyzing force behind the ongoing armed conflict. Even when the direct intervention of South African troops on the ground ceased with the signing of the New York Agreements in 1988, and UNITA become isolated for refusing to accept the verdict of the people's vote, it was external complicity that helped UNITA to continue terrorising innocent civilians through diamond smuggling. It was not until the UN Security Council imposed a verified embargo on trafficking in diamonds smuggled from Angola that the government was able to effectively end the armed insurgency.

In the period between 1975 and 1988, foreign forces (mercenaries and regular troops from Zaire and South Africa) on the ground in Angola committed unaccounted war crimes.[187] While the presence of Zairian troops in Angola was short-lived (less than one year), South African direct military intervention and occupation of parts of Angola extended for more than ten years. It can be said that the foreign forces in Angola fought the war with total disregard for the laws of war, and were instrumental in the way in which UNITA rebels fought their own war in Angola. The process of the mercenaries in Angola and the work of the South African Truth and Reconciliation Commission revealed numerous evidence of such crimes committed in Angola. The question therefore is: should South African war

---

step' taken by the government of Angola and UNITA on 4 April 2002, in signing the Luena Memorandum of Understanding and emphasised 'the *importance of the full implementation* of the 'Acordos de Paz', the Lusaka Protocol, the Memorandum of Understanding Addendum of 4 April 2002, and the relevant United Nations Security Council resolutions in close cooperation with the United Nations and the Troika of Observers'. [Emphasis added]. See UN Doc. S/RES/1432(2002).

186. See *supra* n. 135.
187. See Stockwell, op. cit. n. 25.

criminals be held accountable for the crimes committed in Angola, and the Angolan victims fully compensated, having in mind that the South African war machine was for many years the direct driving force behind UNITA rebels, or not? If so, what is the applicable law?

Although from the analysis above it would appear that the Angolan government has lawful discretion in deciding whether or not to prosecute the rebels who committed atrocities during the internal armed conflict, the same cannot be said in relation to the crimes committed by the South African war machine. The laws of war are unambiguous in this respect. The customary law obligation of states to prosecute war crimes committed in international armed conflict is absolute, to which attests the principle *aut dedere aut judiciare* enshrined in the Geneva Conventions.

Before reviewing the factual and legal circumstances enabling Angola to exercise its duty to prosecute South African war criminals, and its right to war reparations for the atrocities committed in Angola against the civilian population and civilian objectives (sections 7.2, 7.3), this part will deal first with the experience of Angola in prosecuting the crime of mercenarism and its contribution to the development of the laws of war (7.1).

7.1   The trial of the mercenaries in Angola and development of the rules concerning mercenaries

The single trial of war criminals so far in Angola was also to be the first major such trial against mercenaries, and the most important in history[188] – the trial of 13 mercenaries[189] in Angola in 1976.[190]

During the 1975-1976 mixed armed conflict in Angola, on the side of the FNLA rebels coming from the North were not only Zairian regular troops but also hundreds of mercenaries, i.e., basically foreign individuals who had agreed to fight in Angola not as part of regular Armed Forces like the Zairian troops but in their individual capacity, driven by an exclusive profit purpose. During the combat that ensued, 13 such mercenaries retreating in disorder back to the territory of Zaire were taken captives by the Angolan armed forces. They were later to stand trial in Luanda in June 1976. The essential difficulties and originality of the process in Angola have to do with the fact that the trial was not based on existing treaty law but on customary law as it was in evidence in the practice of states prohibiting the

---

188. There were, however, other trials of mercenaries but of minor importance in terms of the number of accused. For example, the trial in Conakry of the mercenaries who invaded Guinea in 1970, the trial of Rolf Steiner in the Sudan in 1971, and the trial of mercenaries in Seychelles in 1981. See J.C. Zarate, 'The emergence of a new dog of war: Private international security companies, international law, and the new world disorder', 34 *Stanford JIL* (1998) pp. 75 at pp. 95, 96.

189. They were one Irish, nine British, and three Americans.

190. For a detailed account of this trial see W. Burchett and D. Roebuck, *The Whores of War: Mercenaries Today* (London, Longmans 1977); M.J. Hoover, 'The Laws of War and the Angolan Trial of Mercenaries: Death to the Dogs of War', 9 *Case Western Reserve JIL* (1977) p. 323; I.P. Blishchenko and J. Doria, *Precedents in international public and private law* (Moscow, MNIMP Publishing House 1999) (in Russian: *Pretsedenty v Mejdunarodnom Publytchnom y Tchastnom Prave*) pp. 280-285.

service of nationals in a private capacity for profit in armed conflicts abroad,[191] two cases,[192] and the pertinent OAU, UN SC and GA Resolutions, defining mercenaries as war criminals and demanding that States take action to prevent or punish them.[193]

By finding all the 13 accused guilty of the crime of mercenarism[194] in addition to other specific crimes, the trial in Luanda helped to identify elements of the crime of being a mercenary. The results of the process and decision of the Tribunal were used to adopt the definitions of mercenary in the 1977 OAU Convention for the Elimination of Mercenarism,[195] in Additional Protocol I (Art. 47), and in the 1989 UN Convention against the Recruitment, Use, Financing and Training of Mercenaries.[196] In the process in Angola, the accused were charged with the crime of being mercenaries, crimes against peace, and more specific crimes of 'murder; maltreatment; insults and harassment of members of the civilian population; murder of members of the Angolan Army and destruction of military equipment; murder of other mercenaries and FNLA soldiers; kidnapping of civilians and stealing of their property'; among others.[197] The court made a basic argument, that when a person is charged with the crime of being a mercenary which can be proved, it means that he becomes a common criminal (not a combatant), and therefore may be charged for whatever acts he commits under ordinary provisions of the penal code incriminating any such act, with the sole aggravating circumstance of the profit motive which prompts it.[198]

The absence of any legal standing under international law was patent in that the mercenaries were also condemned for crimes such as killing in combat members of the Angolan armed forces, and destruction of military equipment, which if they had a status of combatants, would constitute the so-called legitimate acts of combat exempting them from responsibility. However it is not disputed today that unlawful combatants may be prosecuted for their mere participation in hostilities, even if they respect all the rules of international humanitarian law, in addition to their responsibility for war crimes.[199] The trials in Luanda just confirm this.

---

191. See for a list of such countries and their detailed legislation in Burchett and Roebuck, op. cit. n. 190.

192. See trial of mercenaries in Guinea in 1970 and in Sudan in 1971, *supra* n. 190.

193. The Tribunal based its decision among others on the following UN resolutions: UNGA Res. 2395, UN GAOR, 23rd Sess. 1, Supp. 18, at 59 (UN Doc. A/7218 (1968)); UNGA Res. 2465, UN GAOR, 23rd Sess., Supp. 18, at 5 (UN Doc. A/7218 (1968)); UNGA Res. 2548, UNGAOR, 24th Sess., Supp. 30, at 5 (UN Doc. A/7630 (1969)); UNGA Res. 3103, UN GAOR, 28th Sess., Supp. 30, at 142 (UN Doc. A/9030 (1973)).

194. Nine were given sentences up to 30 years in prison, and four were sentenced to death. See Blishchenko and Doria, op. cit. n. 190, at p. 284.

195. OAU Doc. CM/433/Rev.L, Annex I (1972).

196. See UNGA Res. 44/34, UN GAOR 6th Comm., 44th Sess., 72nd plen. Mtg.; Annex, Agenda Item 144, UN Doc. A/44/766 (1989) reprinted in UN GAOR, 44th Sess., Supp. No. 49, at 306, UN Doc. A/44/49 (1990) (hereinafter, Convention against Mercenaries).

197. See full text of the indictment in Hoover, loc. cit. n. 190, at p. 352.

198. See the full text of the judgement, ibid., at p. 374.

199. See R.R. Baxter, 'So-called 'unprivileged belligerency': spies, guerrillas, and saboteurs', 28 *BYIL* (1951) at pp. 328 et seq. and 343 et seq.; Y. Dinstein, 'The distinction between unlawful comba-

Commentators have made two criticisms of the trials in Luanda, based on alle-gations of violation of the principle *nullum crimen sine lege*: A) that reliance on UN and OAU resolutions is erroneous as these resolutions did not confer on the Angolan Tribunal authority to find the accused guilty of the crime of being mer-cenaries, since these resolutions were not hard law.[200] This author submits that the criticism is based on a misconception: the Tribunal relied on these resolutions not as a source of material law, but as evidence of *opinion juris* of states. These resolu-tions and the case-laws together with the practice of various states which crimina-lized aspects of the act of mercenarism, such as a ban on private service abroad for profit without permission of the national state, have combined in the opinion of the Tribunal to establish in international criminal law, the crime of being mercenary as customary law. B) The Law on the Prevention and Repression of the Crime of Mercenarism, which specifically implemented this customary law into Angolan law, was adopted after the events took place in 1976.[201] This argument is in this author's view not convincing either, as according to the 1966 Covenant on Civil and Political Rights (Art. 15(2)), the principle *nullum crimen sine lege* is not vio-lated if the trial is based on a provision of customary or conventional international law which existed prior to the enactment of the Act.

7.1.1   The status of the Executive Outcomes foreign military advisers in Angola

By irony of destiny, the government of Angola, which boosted the issue of crim-inalization of the activity and use of mercenaries in armed conflicts, was also among the countries which have used private foreign military advisers for its bene-fit, in support of its war effort against the UNITA insurgency in 1992-1996. It has thus made a contribution to the refining of the definition of mercenary, as opposed to other legitimate private foreign forces acting on official duty for the govern-ments of the countries concerned.[202]

In 1992, the first free and democratic elections were held in Angola. Savimbi defeated in the elections decided to return to war.[203] While the government had disarmed its best troops according to the Bicesse Accords, Savimbi instead of dis-

---

tants and war criminals, in Y. Dinstein, ed., *International Law at a time of Perplexity* (Essays in honour of Shabtai Rosenne) (Dordrecht, Martinus Nijhoff 1989) p. 103 at p. 105; F. Kalshoven, 'The position of guerrilla fighters under the law of war', 11 *Revue de droit penal militaire et de droit de la guerre* (1972) at pp. 73 et seq.

200. See for example P. Cesner and A. Brant, 'Law of the Mercenary: An International Dilemma', 6 *Cap. Univ. LR* (1977) pp. 339, at p. 349.

201. See Zarate, loc. cit. n. 188, at p. 137 (text in fn. 148).

202. It should be noted, that many countries have foreign forces under their service, for example the 'British Gourka', or the 'French Foreign Legion', or even the former South African 32 battalion (Angolans), although there, the situation is slightly different since they are made formally part of the national Army (though still independent structures, in terms of national composition (as the units remain made up mainly of foreigners, sometimes apart from the commanding staff). See T. Garmon, 'Domesticating International Corporate Responsibility: Holding Private Military Firms Accountable under the Alien Tort Claims Act', 22 *Tulane JI & Comp. L* (2003) pp. 323, at 332, 333.

203. The next free and democratic elections in the country (a process interrupted by UNITA's war after the previous elections), are still to be announced. UNITA is rashly pushing again for immediate

arming was rearming. When full-scale violence resumed in 1992, UNITA was able very quickly to assert control of almost 80 percent of the territory of the country, while the government was disarmed. Under these circumstances, the government was forced to contract the services of a South African security company, Executive Outcomes, to help to assemble and quickly train the new Army, consisting of few former UNITA rebels and the few remaining non-demobilised government troops. Eventually these South African private advisers also helped in the process of co-ordination of defensive actions of the government forces, making an effective contribution to the reposition of the state authority over territory previously held illegally by the rebels after losing the elections.[204]

Executive Outcomes is a private security organisation composed of former commando forces, which by a strange twist of fate used to help Savimbi in his fight against the government, back in the Apartheid-era in the 1980s. Now on invitation of the government, they were much eager to help Angola since they knew the UNITA guerrillas' weak points. They used their knowledge of UNITA tactics to the advantage of the government forces and helped them to fight against UNITA rebels.[205] The question is: are they 'mercenaries' or not? The position of the Angolan government is: they are not. Although the government suggested that it was not viewing the South African Executive Outcomes military advisers as 'mercenaries', but lawful belligerents in Angola on official duty for the government vested with peoples' legitimacy, the inclusion by UNITA insistence of a provision in the old Lusaka Protocol to the effect that 'all mercenaries should be expatriated from Angola',[206] suggests that the parties had different interpretations of the notion of 'mercenary'. UNITA rebels obviously thought they were. Those who support this view have obviously only in mind the 'profit element' of the definition of mercenaries. This position in this author's opinion is only partly true as it refers only to one aspect of the concept of 'mercenary'. The conventional and case-law definition of mercenary calls for a number of criteria, which should be read together and not in isolation. There are at least three conventional acts codifying the status of mercenaries. Among them only 1977 AP I does not refer to the 'aim of the war effort' as a controlling element of the definition of mercenary, and yet it applies only to international armed conflicts.[207] This lack of the criteria of aim of war effort in the 1977

---

elections. Having in mind the experience of the past, not only demobilization but also complete social reintegration of the demobilized troops and reasonable settlement of the 4 million displaced Angolans is an imperative before normal elections can take place in the country, to avoid return to war again in case UNITA loses the elections. An optimal timeframe for elections would be September 2006, when the spectrum of war could reasonably be expected to be completely left behind, and the government together with all the international community to have essentially carried out the defying post-war period goals of social stabilization and pacification of spirits in the country. See 'UNITA exige eleicoes', ANGOP, 18 February 2003.

204. See A.J. Venter, 'Anguish in Angola', *Soldiers of Fortune* (December 1996) at p. 63.

205. The Executive Outcome military advisers had the same success in ending another insurrection movement in Sierra Leone. See Garmon, loc. cit. n. 202, at pp. 333, 334.

206. Lusaka Protocol (Annex 2, para. II(6)). See *supra* n. 11.

207. Under the 1977 Additional Protocol I (para. 2 of Art. 47), a mercenary is any person who: '(a) is specially recruited locally or abroad in order to fight in an armed conflict; (b) does, in fact, take direct part in the hostilities; (c) is motivated to take part in the hostilities essentially by the desire for

API was among the reasons of adoption of the UN Convention against the Recruitment, Use, Financing and Training of Mercenaries in 1989,[208] which reinstates the conditions of the 1977 OAU Convention.

The 1977 OAU Convention for the Elimination of Mercenarism provides the following definition of mercenary (Art. 1):

'Under the present Convention a 'mercenary' is classified as anyone who, not a national of the state against which his actions are directed, is employed, enrols or links himself willingly to a person, group or organisation whose aim is: (a) to overthrow by force of arms or by any other means the government of that Member State of the Organisation of African Unity; (b) to undermine the independence, territorial integrity or normal working of the institutions of the said State; (c) to block by any means the activities of any liberation movement recognised by the Organisation of African Unity.'

The 1989 UN Convention against the Recruitment, Use, Financing and Training of Mercenaries provides (Art. 1) that:

'1. A mercenary is any person who: (a) Is specially recruited locally or abroad in order to fight in an armed conflict; (b) Is motivated to take part in the hostilities essentially by the desire for private gain and, in fact, is promised, by or on behalf of a party to the conflict, material compensation substantially in excess of that promised or paid to combatants of similar rank and functions in the armed forces of that party; (c) Is neither a national of a party to the conflict nor a resident of territory controlled by a party to the conflict; (d) Is not a member of the armed forces of a party to the conflict; and (e) Has not been sent by a State which is not a party to the conflict on official duty as a member of its armed forces.'

But adds in addition a second controlling group of conditions:

'2. A mercenary is also any person who, in any other situation: (a) Is specially recruited locally or abroad for the purpose of participating in a concerted act of violence aimed at: (i) Overthrowing a government or otherwise undermining the constitutional order of a State; or (ii) Undermining the territorial integrity of a State; (b) Is motivated to take part therein essentially by the desire for significant private gain and is prompted by the promise or payment of material compensation; (c) Is neither a national nor a resident of the State against which such an act is directed; (d) Has not been sent by a State on official

---

private gain and, in fact, is promised, by or on behalf of a Party to the conflict, material compensation substantially in excess of that promised or paid to combatants of similar ranks and functions in the armed forces of that party; (d) is neither a national of a Party to the conflict nor a resident of territory controlled by a Party to the conflict; (e) is not a member of the armed forces of a Party to the conflict; and (f) has not been sent by a State which is not a Party to the conflict on official duty as a member of the armed forces.'

208. See M.-F. Major, Mercenaries and International Law, 22 *Georgia JI & Comp. L* (1992) pp. 103 at p. 114.

duty; and (e) Is not a member of the armed forces of the State on whose territory the act is undertaken.'

This author's understanding is that as these two Conventions clearly indicate the person must have been recruited for the purpose of participating in activity aimed at 'Overthrowing a government or otherwise undermining the constitutional order of a State', the concept of mercenary clearly was not applicable to the context of the Angolan events in 1993-1996, and therefore the use of private foreign military advisers in the war against the rebels by the government was not a violation of the laws of war.

7.2   Gross violations of the laws of war and human rights law by South Africa and the issue of individual criminal responsibility for crimes committed in Angola

There is no doubt that South Africa committed unaccounted atrocities in Angola. All these atrocities are well documented in a report of the Angolan government, the so-called 'white book' of crimes committed by Apartheid South Africa in Angola.[209] However, there is nothing better than the evidence of such atrocities by their direct perpetrators. The South African Truth and Reconciliation Commission found based on direct evidence of the masterminds that gross violations of human rights were indeed committed in Angola for which the South African political leadership and direct perpetrators are both held responsible. Concerning one of the incidents in Angola the South African TRC held:

'The commission finds that operation Reinder was a violation of the territorial sovereignty of the Republic of Angola and that it resulted in the commission of gross human rights violations against the civilian occupants of the Kassinga camp which entailed deliberate planning on the part of the following persons who are held accountable: Prime Minister BJ Vorster in his capacity as head of State; Minister of Defence PW Botha in his capacity as political head of the SADF; General Magnus Malan in his capacity as chief of the SADF; Lieutenant General Constand Viljoen and RH Rogers in their capacities as chiefs of the Army and Air Force respectively.'[210]

The scope and magnitude of the heinous atrocities committed by the Apartheid South African war machine in Angola against civilian objectives and the peaceful Angolan civilian population, especially children – its preferred target – can be seen from the following excerpts of the South African TRC Report:

'In addition to destroying Angolan towns in the south of the country, the SADF targeted economic installations in Angola, especially its petroleum facilities.'

---

209. See *Livre Blanc sur les Agressions du Régime Raciste d'Afrique du Sud contre La République Populaire d'Angola* (Luanda, Ler & Escrever 1987).
210. 'TRC Report' Vol. 2, *supra* n. 26, at p. 55.

'The environmental effects of the war on the South (of Angola) were devastating. Both forest lands and wildlife were destroyed. This rape of the environment was sanctioned by the SADF. In the early 1980s, covert front companies were established to facilitate trading in rare woods like teak and kiaat, and in ivory, skins and diamonds. A safari company was also set up through which the hunting of big game was regulated. Ostensibly, these activities were undertaken to raise secret funds for UNITA, but they led quickly to widespread and high-level corruption.'

'The effects of the war on Angolan civilians were devastating. UNICEF has estimated that, between 1980 and 1985, at least 100,000 Angolans died, mainly as a result of war-related famine. The cumulative effect of the battering of the economy and social infrastructure in the 1980-85 period produced an even greater escalation in the death rate after 1985. Between 1981 and 1988, again according to UNICEF, 333,000 Angolan children died of unnatural causes. The Angolan government estimated the economic cost of war damage to be US$12 billion in 1987 alone.'[211]

The South African TRC also found that the attack on *Kassinga* in Angola (a camp of Namibian refugees) in 1978, which led to gross violation of human rights against the civilian inhabitants of the camp, occurred through use of fragmentation bombs in the initial air campaign, and that it constituted 'an indiscriminate and disproportionate use of force'.[212] While the Commission did not specifically refer to these attacks as also being violations of international humanitarian law, clearly they do constitute such violations. Therefore not only the Geneva law on protection of victims was violated but also Hague law limiting the parties to a conflict in their choice of means and methods of conduct of hostilities.

The South African TRC found further that the South African government campaign in Angola between 1977 and 1988 more generally was aimed precisely at Angolan civilian objectives and peaceful Angolan civilians and 'led to gross violations of human rights on a vast scale' and constituted a 'systematic pattern of abuse' for which the Apartheid-era South African political and military leadership was also responsible.[213] This includes not only the specific acts committed by South African invading forces in violation of the laws of war but also those acts committed by UNITA rebels in the same period, if the evidence reveals that UNITA was under the overall control of South Africa.

The South African TRC rightly rejected a flawed allegation of the South African masterminds to the effect that the operation in Angola was in legitimate self-defence (as Angola gave sanctuary to Namibian Patriots fighting for independence of their country), as South Africa was itself in illegal occupation of Namibia.[214] Another incident reported concerned the abduction and illegal deportation of some

---

211. Ibid., at p. 80.
212. Ibid., at pp. 52-55.
213. Ibid., at pp. 60-61.
214. Ibid., at p. 53. In several occasions the UN SC has condemned the illegal occupation of Namibia by South Africa, the illegal use of the Namibian Territory as a springboard for acts of aggression

200 to 300 Namibian refugees from camps in Angola and their torture in Namibia until 1984.[215] The TRC concluded that all these crimes were of such serious gravity that their masterminds could not have qualified for amnesty and therefore recommended that they be prosecuted accordingly.[216]

It is clear that although the South African TRC qualified the atrocities committed in Angola as gross violations of human rights, they do not only qualify as serious crimes against humanity, given the Apartheid discriminatory policy, the widespread and systematic pattern of the atrocities and the civilian victims, but also as serious violations of the laws and customs of war as the atrocities were committed during the armed conflict between Angola and South Africa, and for which there is no statute of limitation.

7.2.1   Who has the right to prosecute suspected South African war criminals?

Under international law, jurisdiction in this case may be as a minimum asserted either by South Africa (following the nationality principle) or Angola (following the usual principle of territorial jurisdiction).[217] In addition, jurisdiction could also be asserted by any state of the world following the principle of universal mandatory jurisdiction for crimes against humanity, grave breaches of the Geneva Conventions and other serious violations of the laws and customs of war in international armed conflicts.

In similar situations when several states may assert jurisdiction over the same perpetrators, the general principle of law *ne bis in idem*, may have a barring effect over prosecutions in another country (under certain circumstances), unless prosecutions in the original country were intended to shield the perpetrators from responsibility.[218] Angola and South Africa are bound by a Protocol on Extradition, which provides for such a principle.[219] However, so far nothing has transpired from

---

against Angola and legitimized the Angola's support of Namibian Patriots. See for example UN SC Res. 428 (1978) of 6 May 1978; Res. 447 (1979) 28 March 1979; Res. 577 (1985) 6 December 1985.

215. Ibid., at pp. 67-68.

216. See also the ruling of the South African Constitutional Court on illegitimacy of pardons for perpetrators of war crimes in international armed conflicts, *supra* n. 172.

217. The jurisdiction of Namibia could in theory be asserted based either on the so-called protective principle (covers acts against a State's security interests committed by aliens abroad) or the so-called passive personality principle (covers acts against a State's nationals committed by aliens abroad). However an argument *a contrario* could be made since the victims although of Namibian origin had not yet a Namibian citizenship at the time the crimes were committed, but certainly such jurisdiction can be asserted under the principle of universal jurisdiction. In the *Eichmann* case, Israel asserted jurisdiction based on universal jurisdiction for crimes committed during WWII against Jewish people prior to existence of Israel. 'Attorney Gen. of Is. V. Eichmann', 36 *ILR* (1968) pp. 18, at pp. 273-276. See also A. Munkman, 'Eichmann Case: Summary', 36 *ILR* (1968) pp. 5, at 5-7.

218. Noting that the practice of states is not however uniform in recognizing a binding effect on this principle. In the absence of a specific treaty, countries tend to disregard it. See D.E. Lopez, 'Not twice for the same crime: How the dual sovereignty doctrine is used to circumvent *non bis in idem*', 33 *Vanderbilt JTL* (2000) p. 1263. See also J.E. Costa, 'Double jeopardy and *non bis in idem*: principles of fairness', 4 *Univ. Calif. Davis JIL & Pol.* (1998) p. 181.

219. See text of the Protocol on Extradition signed by Angola and South Africa within the framework of the Southern Africa Development Community (SADC) on 3 October 2002 at <www.sadc.int>.

South Africa to the effect that those direct or indirect perpetrators have already been prosecuted. Therefore, Angola can assert jurisdiction and request the extradition of those suspected perpetrators to Angola. In addition, Angola could enact an international arrest warrant against the suspects and request the cooperation of the countries of the world in their detention and extradition to Angola, wherever they find themselves.

The South African government and society must be interested to see those suspects stand trial, as this was one of the peremptory recommendations of the South African TRC. If the South African government lacks the political will to do so, Angola has the right and duty to do so, as the territory where those horrendous crimes were committed. In this connection it is important to note that the recent Amnesty law of Angola does not cover foreign perpetrators of war crimes in Angola, and it anyway refers only to the crimes committed within the framework of the Angolan internal armed conflict. This was at times a mixed conflict. But the incidents for which the South African political and military leadership is accountable were committed in the context of an international armed conflict between Angola and South Africa, for which the applicable human rights law and the laws and customs of war do not recognise amnesties. In addition, the argument fails also because the law stipulates that those interested in the amnesty should have presented themselves to the Angolan authorities within the period of 45 days. The suspected perpetrators in question never appeared before the Angolan government asking for forgiveness. The way is therefore open to the Angolan government to approach their South African counterpart requesting the extradition of those suspects specifically named in the Report of the South African Truth and Reconciliation Commission. The Truth Commission is also under a duty to forward to Angola all the evidentiary materials collected during its valuable work.[220]

7.2.2   War reparations for the crimes committed by South Africa in Angola

With the possible prosecution of the potential perpetrators of war crimes in Angola hiding in South Africa, the issue of responsibility of South Africa for the pain caused to the Angolan people is not exhausted.[221] Under international law, states are also materially responsible for the illegal acts of their combatants. Article 3 of the Hague Convention on land warfare of 1907, states:

'A belligerent party which violates the provisions (of the Regulations on Land Warfare annexed to the Convention) shall, if the case demands, be liable to pay compensation. It

---

220. South Africa and Angola are also bound in addition to the Protocol on Extradition by a Protocol on mutual legal assistance on criminal matters, since 3 October 2002, signed within the framework of the Southern Africa Development Community, which specially regulates cooperation of States Parties on matters of legal assistance in criminal matters. See text of the Protocol in <www.sadc.int>.

221. F. Kalshoven, 'State Responsibility for Warlike Acts of the Armed Forces', 40 *ICLQ* (1991) p. 827; See also A.V. Freeman, *Responsibility of States for Unlawful Acts of their Armed Forces* (Leiden, A. W. Sijthoff 1957); M. Sassòli, 'State Responsibility for Violations of International Humanitarian Law', 84 *IRRC* (2002) pp. 401-434.

shall be responsible for all acts committed by persons forming part of its armed forces.'[222]

Provisions of the Hague Regulations were undoubtedly part of the universal realm of the laws and customs of war which engaged any party to an international armed conflict at the time of the relevant events in Angola.[223]

There is no doubt that the victims of the atrocities of South African war machine should be compensated, in light of the relevant applicable rules of the laws and customs of war, and several UN Security Council resolutions to this effect.[224] This could be done by way of war reparations that the government of South Africa should pay to Angola.[225] This issue can be solved in a friendly manner, since an authoritative South African body has already ruled that the South African leadership was responsible for the many atrocities and destruction in Angola. However, should problems arise, the parties may agree to settle the contention by way of recourse either to the International Court of Justice (ICJ) or to an international arbitration, for example, the Permanent Court of Arbitration (PCA) in the Hague.

8.   CONCLUSIONS

Very briefly, here are some of the lessons of this case study:

1. The Angolan case shows that armed conflicts in developing countries are complex, and in most of the cases are a result of external manipulations rather then irreconcilable internal problems. Once the foreign support of UNITA ended, and Mr Savimbi was isolated, the government had no problem in creating the conditions for an immediate end to the 27-year long armed conflict. The external factor is a serious problem to take into account while negotiating the termination of internal armed conflicts in developing countries.

---

222. See Hague Convention (IV) Respecting the Laws and Customs of War on Land, *supra* n. 74.

223. See Report of the Secretary-General pursuant to para. 2 of the Security Council Res. 808 (1993) on the Establishment of the UN International Tribunal for the Former Yugoslavia, Doc. S/25704, 3 May 1993, para. 42 (noting that: 'The Nurnberg Tribunal recognised that many of the provisions in the Hague Regulations, although innovative at the time of their adoption were, by 1939, recognised by all civilized nations and were regarded as being declaratory of the laws and customs of war. The Nuremberg Tribunal also recognised that war crimes defined in Art. 6(b) of the Nuremberg Charter were already recognised as war crimes under international law, and covered in the Hague Regulations, for which guilty individuals were punishable.').

224. The UN SC has on several occasions demanded that South Africa fully pays compensation to Angola for its acts of wanton destruction and seizure of civilian objectives, and killing of innocent civilians in Angola in blatant violation of the laws of war. See UN SC Res. 387 (1976) 31 March; Res. 428 (1978) 6 May; Res. 447 (1979) 28 March; Res. 454 (1979) 2 November; Res. 475 (1980) 27 June; Res. 545 (1983) 20 December; Res. 546 (1984) 6 January; Res. 567 (1985) 20 June; Res. 571 (1985) 20 September; Res. 574 (1985) 7 October; Res. 577 (1985) 6 December; Res. 602 (1987) 25 November; Res. 606 (1987) 23 December.

225. See generally on war reparations, R. Dolzer, 'The Settlement of War-related claims: Does International Law Recognise a Victim's Private Right of Action? Lessons after 1945', 20 *Berkeley JIL* (2002) p. 296.

2. From the point of view of the laws of war, mixed armed conflicts create serious problems of application of the laws, starting from the issue of proper characterization of the armed conflict, the choice of the relevant applicable rules, the prospects for a lasting peace after the end of the war and the question of imputation of responsibility for crimes committed by internal actors in a mixed conflict. The experience of the *ad hoc* Tribunal for the former Yugoslavia shows that much depends on the degree of *control* exercised by a foreign country over rebels fighting in a *prima facie* internal armed conflict. At the same time, this problem also shows that the law needs development in order to fully correspond to the realities of our world. There is a need to limit to the maximum the discretion prevailing in the application of the laws of war in mixed conflicts, in which case preference should be given to the law of international armed conflicts, as the body of law offering the best protection to the victims of war.

3. On the other hand, as the case study shows, the dichotomy in the application of the laws of war in internal and in international armed conflicts limits the reach of the duty of states to prosecute war criminals in internal armed conflicts, still leaving to the states the option of conceding amnesties at the end of internal armed conflicts, even for war crimes. The adoption of the ICC Statute represents a limited step in the right direction but should be followed by adoption of a third additional protocol to the 1949 Geneva Conventions on the Protection of Victims of War recognising the unconditional absolute universal application of the rule *aut dedere aut judiciare* in the context of internal armed conflicts as well.

4. However, even when prosecution is not possible, the victims of war should be compensated. The scarcity of cash in developing countries like Angola means that in most of the cases compensation is community-based, rather than personal. After years of war and lost opportunities of development of a potentially the richest African nation, the Angolan people seem to prefer a lasting peace rather then a tortuous disturbance of wounds of the past. This resignation seems more obvious since all understand that the war was imposed on Angolans from outside, and was not a genuine internal product.

5. On the other side, Angolans show the same determination in their will to see that whoever came illegally from outside the country in wars of aggression to commit barbaric acts against innocent civilians in violation of peremptory norms of international humanitarian law is held fully accountable for that – an unconditional requirement of applicable rules of international law. These atrocities were of particular magnitude in the actions of the aggressor South African war machine. The victims of South African atrocities committed in the country should be fully honoured. The Angolan case represents a unique opportunity for doing so, as there is mutual understanding of both the most interested states, Angola and South Africa (as it follows from the authoritative Report of the South African Truth and Reconciliation Commission), as to the need to see that the perpetrators don't go unpunished and the victims and Angola are fully compensated.

DISENTANGLING LEGAL QUAGMIRES: THE LEGAL CHARACTERISATION OF THE ARMED CONFLICTS IN AFGHANISTAN SINCE 6/7 OCTOBER 2001 AND THE QUESTION OF PRISONER OF WAR STATUS[1]

Yutaka Arai-Takahashi[2]

---

1. © Y. Arai-Takahashi 2003.

2. Lecturer in International Law, Kent Law School, University of Kent, United Kingdom, and Deputy Director of LL.M. Programme, Brussels School of International Studies, Belgium. The author is grateful to Professor James Crawford for his helpful comments on earlier drafts, and for Professor Robyn Martin for corrections on my English expression.

1.   INTRODUCTION

The September 11 attacks and the ensuing military operations in Afghanistan have raised a multitude of complex and disturbing problems for the existing humanitarian normative order.[3] Much of the legal scholarship on recent events concerning Afghanistan has focused on the issues of the legal status of captured Taliban and Al Qaeda soldiers under humanitarian law,[4] their detention conditions at Guantána-

---

3. For the examination of the implications of both the September 11 attacks and the war against Afghanistan on humanitarian law, see in particular, Y. Dinstein, 'Humanitarian Law on the Conflict in Afghanistan', *American Society of International Law Proceedings* (2002) p. 23.

4. See *inter alia*, G.H. Aldrich, 'The Taliban, Al Qaeda, and the Determination of Illegal Combatants', 96 *AJIL* (2002) p. 891, Editorial Comments; R. Cryer, 'The Fine Art of Friendship: *Jus in Bello* in Afghanistan', 7 *Journal of Conflict and Security Law* (2002) p. 37; M.H. Hoffman, 'Terrorists are Unlawful Belligerents, not Unlawful Combatants: A Distinction with Implications for the Future of International Humanitarian Law', 34 *Case Western Reserve JIL* (2002) p. 227; H.-P. Gasser, 'Acts of

mo Bay in Cuba and the inadequacy of procedural safeguards for judicial proceedings of the proposed Military Commissions[5] under the US Presidential Order[6] and the Department of Defence Order.[7] This paper takes a somewhat different approach, looking first at the legal characterisation of the armed conflicts in Afghanistan since 6/7 October 2001 and particularly the internecine hostilities that have continued since the apparent end of the war, before examining the status of combatants and that of prisoners of war. Clarification of the nature of the armed conflicts and of the scope of application of the rules on prisoners of war is essential for disentangling the legal quagmire surrounding the controversy over the legal status of both Taliban and Al Qaeda soldiers under the *jus in bello*.

The analysis presented in this paper can be divided into five main areas. First, the paper seeks to delineate the legal nature and characteristics of armed conflicts that have been waged in Afghanistan since 6/7 October 2001.[8] The author argues that the Afghan 'war' can be considered as consisting of several armed conflicts, each of which has a distinct normative nature. The establishment of the transitional government, following the Agreement on Provisional Arrangements in Afghanistan pending the Reestablishment of Permanent Government Institutions (the Bonn Agreement) on 5 December 2001, constitutes a watershed for determining the legal nature of ongoing armed conflicts against Taliban and Al Qaeda remainders.

Second, on the basis of the preceding analysis, the paper attempts to provide clarity as to the criteria for prisoners of war under the Third Geneva Convention of 1949 and 1977 Additional Protocol I. In view of the non-ratification of the latter by the United States and Afghanistan, it is essential to explore the customary law status of relevant rules.

Third, examination focuses on special categories of captured soldiers, namely, the so-called 'unlawful combatants' or 'unprivileged belligerents', who do not benefit from the rights and privileges of prisoners of war.

Fourth, the analysis turns to the conditions under which a 'competent tribunal' may be established to determine the legal status of a captured soldier in accordance

---

Terror, Terrorism' and International Humanitarian Law', 84 *RICR/IRRC* (2002) p. 547; R.P. Masterton, 'Military Commissions and the War on Terrorism', 36 *International Lawyer* (2002) p. 1165; S.R. Ratner, 'Jus ad Bellum and Jus in Bello After September 11', 96 *AJIL* (2002) p. 905, Notes and Comments; and P. Rowe, 'Response to Terror: The New 'War'', 3 *Melbourne JIL* (2002) p. 301.

5. See *inter alia,* C.M. Evans, 'Terrorism on Trial: The President's Constitutional Authority to Order the Prosecution of Suspected Terrorists by Military Commission', 51 *Duke LJ* (2002) p. 1831; J. Fitzpatrick, 'Jurisdiction of Military Commissions and the Ambiguous War on Terrorism', 96 *AJIL* (2002) p. 345; H. Hongju Koh, 'The Case Against Military Commissions', 96 *AJIL* (2002) p. 337; M. J. Matheson, 'U.S. Military Commissions: One of Several Options', 96 *AJIL* (2002) p. 354; D.A. Mundis, 'The Use of Military Commissions to Prosecute Individuals Accused of Terrorist Acts', 96 *AJIL* (2002) p. 320; J. Steyn, 'Guantánamo Bay: The Legal Black Hole', 53 *ICLQ* (2004) p. 1; and R. Wedgwood, 'Al Qaeda, Terrorism, and Military Commissions', 96 *AJIL* (2002) p. 328.

6. President George W. Bush, Military Order of November 13, 2001, 'Detention, Treatment, and Trial of Certain Non-Citizens in the War Against Terrorism', 66 Fed. Register, 16 November 2001, p. 57,833. See also Federal Register website, <http://www.gpoaccess.gov>.

7. US Department of Defense, Military Commission Order No. 1 (21 March 2002), 41 *ILM* (2002) p. 725, available at< <http://defenselink.mil/news/Mar2002/d20020321ord.pdf>.

8. The official date of the coalition's initiation of the attack was 6 October 2001, but it was on the following day according to Afghan time.

with Article 5 of the 1949 Third Geneva Convention and Article 45(1) of Additional Protocol I.

Fifth, in view of the armed conflicts of a non-international character that exist in Afghanistan, the types of humanitarian rules applicable to internal armed conflict must be ascertained. Again, the absence of ratification of 1977 Additional Protocol II by both the United States and Afghanistan necessitates an evaluation of customary rules applicable to non-international armed conflict.

The investigations of this paper are strictly confined to the Afghan context in light of the five foregoing angles, excluding analysis of both the humanitarian rules governing the conduct of hostilities and the conditions of detainees at detention centres, most notably at Guantánamo Bay, and the procedural rules that should be observed for trials of military commissions. At a time when the fallout of the war against Iraq is keenly felt in terms of continuing guerrilla attacks carried out by Baathist remnants and other militant groups against the Anglo-American occupying forces, revisiting the still live Afghan theatre and closely examining the rights and privileges of captives through the juridical prism will enable us to gain useful lessons regarding both the potential effectiveness and limits of humanitarian rules.

2.   LEGAL CHARACTERISATION OF ARMED CONFLICTS IN AFGHANISTAN SINCE 6/7 OCTOBER 2001

2.1   General overview

From a strict legal point of view, the war that has been, or is being, waged in Afghanistan since the attack initiated by the US-led coalition forces on 6/7 October 2001 can be considered to consist of five separate conflicts, each of which is subject to a distinct normative regime.

Three types of armed conflicts in Afghanistan can be discerned in the period between 6/7 October and 5 December 2001. First, there was an international armed conflict between the US-led coalition and the Taliban government. Second, an 'armed conflict' between the coalition forces and Al Qaeda needs to be treated separately from the conflict between the coalition and the Taliban in view of the controversy over the humanitarian norms applicable to members of Al Qaeda, a transnational terrorist organisation. Third, an armed conflict was fought between the Northern Alliance and the Taliban government, which was *prima facie* an internal armed conflict but could be perceived as 'internationalised' by virtue of the close link between the Northern Alliance and the coalition member states.[9] Fourth, since the coming into existence of the Karzai government, the Taliban forces have been transformed into armed rebels or insurgents, to which Al Qaeda remnants are thinly aligned. The fighting between the newly established governmental forces and the anti-governmental 'coalition' forces of Islamic militants (consisting of the

---

9. Cf., T. Meron, 'Classification of Armed Conflict in the Former Yugoslavia: Nicaragua's Fallout', 92 *AJIL* (1998) p. 236.

Taliban and Al Qaeda remainders and supporters of a Mujaheddin warlord, Gul-buddin Hekmatyar) is classified as internal armed conflict, and not only the government but also insurgent troops are bound by customary law relating to internal strife. Fifth, there is a continuing armed conflict between the US-led coalition forces and the anti-government insurgents. Sixth, the armed hostilities between the International Security Assistance Force (ISAF) acting in self-defence and the anti-governmental rebels raises questions relating to the types of humanitarian rules applicable to multilateral troops acting in furtherance of a Security Council enforcement action.

2.2   The nature of hostilities prior to 5 December 2001

2.2.1   *Armed conflict between the coalition forces and the Taliban: international armed conflict*

It is incontrovertible that the armed conflict between the US-led coalition and the Taliban government was an international armed conflict, governed by international humanitarian rules based on 'Hague rules' and 1949 Geneva Conventions I, III and IV. While the applicability of 1977 Additional Protocol I to both the Taliban government and the US is hampered by their non-ratification of this treaty, some coalition states are parties to it. Further, many rules embodied in Protocol I have hardened into customary law[10] and are applicable to both the coalition forces and the Taliban government.

2.2.2   *'Armed conflict' between the anti-terrorism coalition forces and Al Qaeda*

The regulatory framework of traditional humanitarian law does not foresee a scenario such as the hostilities between the anti-terrorism coalition forces and Al Qaeda.[11] Al Qaeda is a transnational terrorist organisation which based its main operational camps in Afghan territory under the auspices of the Taliban government. Analysis of the applicability of humanitarian law to the conduct of warfare by the coalition forces and by Al Qaeda requires examining the threshold question as to whether there existed an 'armed conflict' between the coalition forces and Al Qaeda in the sense of humanitarian law. Despite the internationalisation of the conflict based on the military campaign carried out by UN-led coalition forces, it seems that, at first glance, international humanitarian law does not apply. Common Article 2(1) of the Geneva Conventions defines international armed conflict as 'all cases of declared war or of any other armed conflict which may arise between two or more of the High Contracting Parties'.

---

10. For analysis of customary humanitarian norms, see T. Meron, 'The Continuing Role of Custom in the Formation of International Humanitarian Law', 90 *AJIL* (1996) p. 238.

11. Fitzpatrick, loc. cit. n. 5, at p. 8.

Although loosely aligned with the Taliban regime, Al Qaeda is not an insurgent in a non-international armed conflict,[12] benefiting from the traditional practice of belligerent recognition, now in disuse. Nor can Al Qaeda be considered oppressed 'peoples' entitled to exercise the principle of self-determination against occupying or colonial forces within the meaning of Article 1(4) of Protocol I.

It might, however, be argued that the conflict between the coalition forces and Al Qaeda should be subsumed into the conflict between the coalition and the Afghan (Taliban) government. Such an argument can be made on the basis that Al Qaeda could be regarded as 'other militias and members of other volunteer corps … belonging to a Party to the conflict', namely Afghanistan, within the meaning of Article 4A(2) of the Third Geneva Convention, although the mere act of fighting in concert is not sufficient to meet the test of 'belonging'.[13] The remaining questions would be whether such belligerents are considered as 'belonging to a Party to the conflict' and if so, whether they acted in observance of the four established conditions under this provision, which are constitutive of the status of POWs.

2.2.3   *Armed conflict between the Northern Alliance and the Taliban government*

There existed an internal armed conflict fought between the Northern Alliance and the Taliban government. The Afghan Northern Alliance was the loosely formed anti-Taliban forces made up of disparate ethnic and religious groups (though mainly non-Pashtun ethnic groups), which was united for the sole aim of toppling the Taliban government. The Northern Alliance can be considered insurgents fighting against the Taliban government.

This conflict was *prima facie* an internal armed conflict. It is, however, arguable that this conflict can be classified as an 'internationalised non-international armed conflict',[14] in view of the close link between the Northern Alliance and the coalition member states (in particular, the United States). Internationalised non-international armed conflicts, which have occurred with intense frequency since 1945,

---

12. For examinations of non-international armed conflicts, see G. Abi-Saab, 'Non-International Armed Conflict' in UNESCO, ed., *International Dimensions of International Humanitarian Law* (Dordrecht, Martinus Nijhoff/Geneva, Henry Dunant Institute/Paris, UNESCO 1988) pp. 217, at p. 222; R.K. Goldman, 'International Humanitarian Law: Americas Watch's Experience in Monitoring Internal Armed Conflicts', 9 *Amer. Univ. JIL & Pol.* (1993) p. 49; T. Meron, 'Towards a Humanitarian Declaration of Internal Strife', 78 *AJIL* (1984) p. 859; T. Meron, 'Application of Humanitarian Law in Noninternational Armed Conflicts', 85 *American Society of International Law Proceedings* (1991) p. 83; T. Meron, 'International Criminalization of Internal Atrocities', 89 *AJIL* (1995) p. 554; and T. Meron and Allan Rosas, 'A Declaration of Minimum Humanitarian Standards', 85 *AJIL* (1991) p. 375.

13. Rowe, loc. cit. n. 4, p. 301.

14. See D. Schindler, 'The Different Types of Armed Conflicts According to the Geneva Conventions and Protocols', (1979-II) *Receuil des Cours* 121, at p. 150. For examination in specific context, see B. Akinrinade, 'International Humanitarian Law and the Conflict in Sierra Leone', 15 *Notre Dame Journal of Law, Ethics and Public Policy* (2001) p. 392; H.-P. Gasser, 'Internationalized Non-International Armed Conflicts: Case Studies of Afghanistan, Kampuchea, and Lebanon', 33 *Amer. Univ. LR* (1983) p. 145.

remain mired in confusion with respect to the applicable humanitarian rules. Where foreign troops intervene on behalf of a government fighting against rebels that are regarded as falling outside the oppressed people exercising self-determination in the sense of Article 1(4) of Protocol I, such intervention is governed by humanitarian rules on internal armed conflict, as it does not engender an armed conflict between two states.[15] On the other hand, where a foreign state intervenes in aid of rebels against a government, it is clear that this will bring into forth the whole array of rules on international humanitarian law. The artificial nature of the dichotomy between international and internal armed conflicts, however, has become increasingly contested in view of the growing recognition of human rights law. In the *Tadić* case, the Appeals Chamber of the International Criminal Tribunal for the former Yugoslavia (ICTY) acknowledged that '[i]f international law, while of course duly safeguarding the legitimate interests of States, must gradually turn to the protection of human beings, it is only natural that the … dichotomy should gradually lose its weight.'[16] Moir observes that the convergence of the two bodies of law (with respect to international and internal armed conflict) will eventually reach the stage where the focus of examinations should turn to the threshold question relating to whether or not there exists an armed conflict.[17]

Since Afghanistan is not a party to Additional Protocol II, the fighting between the Taliban and the Northern Alliance in Afghanistan is characterised as internal armed conflict, the humanitarian rules applicable to such conflict are, strictly speaking, limited to common Article 3 of the Geneva Conventions and customary rules. However, an argument might be made that the degree of control exercised by the United States over the conduct of the Northern Alliance was sufficiently close to impute the conduct of this anti-Taliban insurgent to the responsibility of the United States. According to this reasoning, the responsibility for the killing of a number of Taliban and Al Qaeda prisoners subsequent to the uprising at Qala-e Jhangi Fort near Mazar-e Sharif between 25 November and 1 December 2001,[18] as well as other incidents of grave concern,[19] might be attributed to the coalition states.

It might further be surmised that the satisfaction of the attribution test under the rubric of state responsibility would transform what is *prima facie* an internal armed

---

15. L. Moir, *The Law of Internal Armed Conflict* (Cambridge, Cambridge University Press 2002) at pp. 50-51. In relation to the Soviet intervention, obstensibly on the side of the Afghan government against Mujahidin groups, until its withdrawal in 1989, the ICRC described the conflict as internal: H. McCoubrey, *International Humanitarian Law* (Aldershot, Dartmouth 1990) p. 175.

16. *Prosecutor* v. *Tadić*, Case No. IT-94-1-AR72 (Appeal on Jurisdiction), 35 *ILM* (1996) p. 32, para. 97.

17. Moir, op. cit. n. 15, at pp. 51-52.

18. A. Roberts, 'Counter-terrorism, Armed Force and the Laws of War', 44 *Survival* (2002) pp. 7 at pp. 20-21.

19. There were numerous reports of dozens of Taliban fighters being asphyxiated in shipping containers transporting them to prison in Shibarghan, a northern city near Mazar-e-Sharif, after their surrender to the Northern Alliance. Reports also refer to beatings of the detainees in order to extract confession; C. Gall, 'A Nation challenged: Prisoners; Witnesses Say Many Taliban Died in Custody', *The New York Times* (11 December 2001) Section A, p. 1; and R. Caroll, 'Afghan jailers beat confessions from men', *The Guardian* (28 December 2001) p. 13.

conflict into an international one. The armed conflict between the Northern Alliance and the Taliban government till the latter was overthrown may be described as an 'internationalised non-international armed conflict', on the ground that the military operation of the Northern Alliance was closely supervised and even controlled by the United States. The statement made by Donald Rumsfeld, the US Defense Secretary, that the US enjoyed a 'relationship with all of those elements on the ground', in view of supply of food, ammunitions and of assistance with overhead targeting,[20] might indicate that the US exercised a degree of control ranging between an overall control and an effective control over conduct of the Northern Alliance. There was close military coordination between the coalition and the Northern Alliance, so that the coalition's air campaign was directed against specific Taliban strongholds on the ground at the request of the Northern Alliance. Without the coalition's effective contribution, it would be unimaginable that this anti-Taliban insurgent that exercised control only over one tenth of the territory at the inception could so swiftly advance and eject the Taliban government.[21]

Applying the test of 'effective control' that the International Court of Justice (ICJ) established in the *Nicaragua* case with respect to the assessment of state responsibility,[22] the Trial Chamber of the ICTY, in the *Tadić* case, ruled that the degree of authority wielded by a state over armed forces fighting on its behalf, which is sufficient to invite the application of international humanitarian law, must be 'effective control'. However, rejecting the view of the Trial Chamber, the Appeals Chamber held that the degree of control exerted over armed forces fighting against the same adversary must be set at a lower level of 'overall control'.[23] The degree of control is not so strong as to require specific orders to be issued for each military action,[24] but it must go beyond the mere coordination and cooperation between allies in political and military activities.[25] The Appeals Chamber expressed a caveat that where the controlling state in question was not an adjacent state with territorial ambitions with respect to the territories where the conflict occurred, the standard of evidence would be set at a high level. It added that 'more extensive and compelling evidence' revealing not merely the act of financing and equipping but also that of generally directing or helping plan, must be adduced to demonstrate that the conflict became internationalised.[26] Doubt may remain as to whether the test employed to examine the question of state responsibility can be

---

20. Rumsfeld, Press Briefing with General Pace, 30 November 2001, <http://www.defenselink.mil/news/Nov2001/briefings.html>.

21. See Cryer, loc. cit. n. 4, at pp. 44-47 and the BBC sources cited in n. 48.

22. *Case Concerning the Military and Paramilitary Activities in and against Nicaragua (Nicaragua v. USA)*, (1986) ICJ 14, at pp. 62, 64-65, paras. 109 and 115 (27 June 1986).

23. Case IT-94-I, *Prosecutor v. Tadić*, Judgment of 15 July 1999, paras. 145, 146 and 162. See also *Cyprus v. Turkey*, where the European Court of Human Rights ruled that Turkey's state responsibility under the European Convention on Human Rights could arise, with her 'effective overall control' over northern Cyprus suggesting her 'acquiescence or connivance' in acts of private individuals violating others' rights: Eur. Ct. H.R., Judgment of 10 May 2001, paras. 77 and 81.

24. Ibid., para. 145.

25. Ibid., para. 152.

26. Ibid., para. 138.

imported to the issue of identifying the international armed conflict as defined in common Article 2 of the Geneva Conventions.[27] The Appeals Chamber's approach is even more puzzling, in that the conditions under which irregulars such as organised resistance groups are regarded as 'belonging' to a party to the conflict within the meaning of common Articles 13(2)/13(2)/4A(2) of the 1949 First, Second and Third Geneva Conventions were mixed up with the conditions for the internationalisation of an internal armed conflict.[28]

In the context of Afghanistan, it may not be sustainable to argue that on the basis of the rationale used by the Appeals Chamber, the degree of control exercised by the coalition over the conduct of the Northern Alliance reached the overall control sufficient to internationalise the armed conflict between the latter and the Taliban. Considerable doubt remains concerning whether the stringent standard of evidence required for 'overall control' exercised by an external power other than a neighbouring state was met in the Afghan context. In that sense, as Cryer notes,[29] the Northern Alliance may not be considered to 'belong' to the coalition forces in the sense of the Appeals Chamber in the *Tadić* case, so that the violations of *jus in bello* by the Northern Alliance would not give rise to the responsibility of the coalition states. This construction can leave open the possibility that the armed conflict between the Taliban and the Northern Alliance was non-international.

2.3   The nature of hostilities after 5 December 2001

2.3.1   *The armed conflict between the Afghan government forces and the US-led coalition forces on one hand, and the anti-governmental insurgents on the other in the Post-Bonn Process*

Since 11 August 2003, more than 12,000 US troops in Afghanistan, together with troops from NATO member states, have been fighting as part of the ongoing *Enduring Freedom* operation against the Taliban and Al Qaeda remnants. These are in addition to about 5,500 ISAF soldiers stationed in and around Kabul.[30] The resurgence of the Taliban and the Al Qaeda groups, in loose collaboration with supporters of Gulbuddin Hekmatyar, a former prime minister, and regular armed attacks against US and Afghan governmental forces as well as some against aid workers, reveal the tenacious nature of the insurrectional forces and the remote prospect of the end of the hostilities in Afghanistan.[31] While NATO has assumed

---

27. J. Crawford, *The International Law Commission's Articles on State Responsibility – Introduction, Text and Commentaries* (Cambridge, Cambridge University Press 2002) at p. 112. See also the separate opinion of Judge Shahabudeen, Case IT-94-1, *Prosecutor* v. *Tadić*, paras. 145-146, 162.

28. R. Provost, *International Human Rights and Humanitarian Law* (Cambridge, Cambridge University Press 2002) at p. 92.

29. Cryer, loc. cit. n. 4, at p. 47.

30. See 'Afghan in trouble', *The Financial Times*, Editorial (6 June 2003) p. 20; P. Reeves, 'Afghan battle ends with death of 40 guerrillas', *The Independent* (6 June 2003) p. 13; and J. Dempsey, B. Benoit and G. Wiesmann, 'Nato expects to come under pressure to patrol outside Kabul', *The Financial Times* (11 August 2003) p. 6.

31. See E. MacAskill, 'Extra troops must fill vacuum beyond Kabul to quell warlords, warns

command of ISAF since 11 August 2003,[32] the US and British coalition forces have established 'Provincial Reconstruction Teams' (PRTs) as a backdoor effort to introduce an international military and civilian presence in remote areas where governmental control is weak.[33]

Since the coming into existence of the Interim Afghan government led by Hamid Karzai, the Taliban forces have been transformed into armed rebels or even insurgents, to which Al Qaeda remnants are thinly aligned. The fighting between the nascent governmental forces and the anti-government insurgents consisting of the Taliban and Al Qaeda remainders as well as of Mujahidin militants goes beyond the threshold of internal disturbances and tensions and it can be classified as internal armed conflict.[34] Moreover, the ongoing armed hostilities between the US-led coalition forces and the Taliban and Al Qaeda forces can be subsumed into the non-international armed conflict, since the involvement of the US troops is based on the express consent and invitation of the Kabul government. All the humanitarian rules germane to civil wars, namely, common Article 3 of the Geneva Conventions and customary rules, bind all the parties to this type of conflict. While both Afghanistan and the United States are not parties to Additional Protocol II, query is needed as to customary law status of many rules embodied in this Protocol.

With respect to customary law applicable to internal armed conflict, not only the government but also insurgent troops are bound by customary law relating to internal strife. In its 1999 Third Report on the Situation of Human Rights in Columbia, the Inter-American Commission on Human Rights stated that humanitarian law is binding on paramilitary groups.[35] In the *Tadić* case, the Appeals Chamber of the ICTY went so far as to suggest that Article 3 of the ICTY Statute (relating to violations of the laws or customs of war) encompasses all (serious) violations of international humanitarian law (both Geneva and Hague rules, except for grave breaches of the Geneva Conventions (as prescribed by Art. 2 of the Statute), genocide (Art. 4) and crimes against humanity (Art. 5)).[36] Concurring with Aldrich,[37] Meron criticises the Appeals Chamber's approach as over-inclusive, entailing the implication that both Hague law and the provisions of the Geneva Conventions (bar provisions on grave breaches) apply to both international and non-interna-

---

Musharraf', *The Guardian* (19 June 2003) p. 15; 'Kandahar berates Straw for a leftover life of gun law and broken promises', ibid. (2 July 2003) p. 13 and V. Burnett, 'UN forced to halt aid work in southern Afghanistan', *The Financial Times* (11 August 2003) p. 6.

32. Demsey et al., loc. cit. n. 30.

33. Reeves, loc. cit. n. 30; Burnett, loc. cit. n. 31. Since 6 January 2004, the German-led Kunduz Provincial Reconstruction Team (PRT) has been officially transferred from Coalition Forces Command to the ISAF.

34. Art. 1(2) of Additional Protocol II sets the minimum threshold of its applicability, providing that it 'shall not apply to situations of internal disturbances and tensions, such as riots, isolated and sporadic acts of violence and other acts of a similar nature, as not being armed conflicts'.

35. OAS Doc. OEA/Ser.L/V/II.102, Doc. 9 rev. 1, 26 February 1999, para. 13, available at <http://www.cidh.org/countryrep/Colom99en/table%20of%20contents.htm>.

36. *Prosecutor v. Tadić*, Case No. IT-94-1-AR72, Appeal on Jurisdiction, 2 October 1995, reprinted in 35 *ILM* (1996) p. 32 at pp. 49-50, 71, paras. 87-88, 137.

37. G.H. Aldrich, 'Jurisdiction of the International Criminal Tribunal for the Former Yugoslavia', 90 *AJIL* (1996) pp. 64 at 67-68.

tional armed conflicts.[38] In other words, the implication is that there are rules of customary humanitarian law applicable to internal armed conflict, the basis of which lies outside the framework of common Article 3 of the Geneva Conventions, Protocol II and Article 19 of the 1954 Hague Convention on Cultural Property.[39]

It might be questioned whether subsequent to the establishment of the Karzai government, the Taliban remnants, in collaboration with other anti-governmental militants and Al Qaeda can be regarded as 'peoples' fighting against an occupying power. For all the near universal antipathy toward the Taliban theocracy for its gross violations of human rights, especially those of women, such an argument cannot be brushed aside. It is not to belittle the Taliban's oppressive nature to hypothesise a scenario of unlawful occupation from a juridical perspective. Indeed, the situation in Afghanistan might be compared to the circumstances in Cambodia after the Vietnamese invasion, which ousted the Khmer Rouge in 1979. The continued fighting in Cambodia between the Vietnamese forces on one hand and the Khmer Rouge and other Khmer forces on the other did not cease even after the instalment of the Vietnamese-backed 'puppet regime' (the Hen Samrin government). It is possible to consider that the hostilities between the Vietnamese forces and the troops of the Khmer Rouge after the establishment of the Hen Samrin government were governed by the law of *international* armed conflicts, with the hostilities perceived as an extension of the conflict between the Vietnamese forces in alliance with the coalition of insurgents, the United Front (which later formed the Hen Samrin government) and the Khmer Rouge forces.[40]

The armed hostilities in Afghanistan between the US-led coalition forces and the anti-governmental forces might be regarded as a prolongation of the initial phase of the war, namely the international armed conflict between the coalition forces and the former Taliban government. This hypothesis is based on the assumptions that the Karzai government has been installed by the occupying power, namely, the US-led coalition forces, and that the government set up by the occupying power is debarred from obtaining a license for 'friendly presence' of its troops, by entering into an agreement between them. Such assumptions would mean that the relation between the US-led forces and the Afghan civilian population has been covered, uninterruptedly since 6/7 October 2001 onward, by rules on belligerent occupation under the Fourth Geneva Convention, so that the civilian population must not be deprived of 'the benefits from the present Convention by any change introduced … into the institutions or government' of the territory concerned.[41] A twist of this hypothesis would be to view the Taliban-led coalition as fighting against an 'alien occupation' within the meaning of Article 1(4) of Protocol I,[42] albeit that state

---

38. Meron, loc. cit. n. 10, at p. 243.
39. Moir, op. cit. n. 15, at pp. 188-189
40. Gasser, loc. cit. n. 14, at p. 154.
41. Art. 47 of the Fourth Geneva Convention 1949.
42. A. Cassese, *Self-Determination of Peoples – A Legal Reappraisal* (Cambridge, Cambridge University Press 1995) pp. 201-204.

practice has so far proved insufficient to warrant the argument that this provision has ripened into a customary international norm.[43]

However, the fundamental pitfall of drawing an analogy from the Cambodian case to the Afghan context is that, unlike the Hen Samrin government which did not receive the UN's recognition for geopolitical reasons, the Bonn process, and hence the Afghan Interim Authority led by Hamid Karzai, have been expressly endorsed by a series of Security Council resolutions passed under Chapter VII.[44] Security Council Resolution 1378, although not adopted under Chapter VII, even called on the Afghan people to exercise the right of self-determination to overthrow the Taliban regime. Surely, it may be argued that as a non-binding resolution, Resolution 1378 cannot be seen to yield 'constitutive' effects of delegitimizing the then Taliban government. However, there has been both in state practice and *opinio juris* a universal recognition that the Karzai government, which has the effective control over most of the Afghan territory and population, is the sole legitimate government representative of the Afghan people.[45]

2.3.2   'Armed conflict' between the International Security Assistance Force and the Taliban and Al Qaeda remnants

The International Security Assistance Force[46] is a peacekeeping force established under the Security Council's Chapter VII Resolution 1386 of 20 December 2001.[47] Its main objective is to assist the Afghan Interim Authority to maintain national security in Kabul and its surrounding areas, facilitate UN personnel to work in a secure environment and ensure that the war-torn society can initiate the process of national reconstruction.[48] The prospect of expanding peacekeepers to other cities depends on the outcome of the continued US military campaign against the Taliban and Al Qaeda remnants. Where ISAF troops exchange fire with the resurgent Taliban or Al Qaeda soldiers, or with any other warring factions, can such 'hostilities' be regarded as an 'armed conflict' susceptible to normative constraints of *jus in bello*?

ISAF is a multinational force under the unified command of the troop-contributing states that signed the joint Memorandum of Understanding in London on 10 January 2002.[49] As such, it is not under the UN Force Commander. It was initially

---

43. Ibid., at pp. 203-204.

44. See, *inter alia*, Resolution 1387, 20 December 2001, S/RES/1386 (2001); Resolution 1413, 23 May 2002, S/RES/1413 (2002); and Resolution 1444, 27 November 2002, S/RES/1444 (2002).

45. For discussions on the recognition of governments, see *Tinoco Concessions* Arbitration (*Great Britain* v. *Costa Rica*), (1923) 1 *RIAA* 369; and S. Talmon, *Recognition of Governments in International Law* (Oxford, Oxford University Press 1998).

46. So far, 18 mainly western countries (Austria, Belgium, Bulgaria, Great Britain, Denmark, Finland, France, Germany, Greece, Italy, the Netherlands, New Zealand, Norway, Portugal, Romania, Spain, Sweden, Turkey, France, Italy, Germany and Britain) have provided troops.

47. See also additional authorization derived from Security Council Resolution 1413, 23 May 2002, S/RES/1413 (2002); and Resolution 1444, 27 November 2002, S/RES/1444 (2002).

48. Resolution 1386 of 20 December 2001, operative para. 1.

49. The Memorandum, which was signed by Austria, Denmark, Finland, France, Germany, Greece,

under the British unified command for six months, followed by the command exercised by other troop-contributing states (Turkey and Germany/the Netherlands), and since August 2003 was handed over to NATO. Nevertheless, ISAF's mandate has been specifically provided by binding Chapter VII resolution, and it works closely with the United Nations and the Afghan interim government. The normative framework for its use of force follows the models of the multilateral forces against Iraq[50] and the involvement of the NATO member states in Yugoslavia[51] and UNITAF in Somalia.[52] In all these cases, the Security Council, with its renewed assertiveness after the end of the Cold War, has granted member states an express authorization to use force. Such a form of delegation of the Security Council's enforcement function to member states has been seen in Rwanda,[53] Haiti,[54] Albania,[55] the Central African Republic,[56] Kosovo,[57] East Timor[58] and Congo.[59]

The question as to whether, and if so what part of, humanitarian law applies to the conduct of UN and other multilateral forces acting pursuant to enforcement action of the Security Council is not only of academic but also practical importance.[60] Multinational forces can form part of the enforcement action pursuant to the Security Council's Chapter VII resolutions, or act as a humanitarian mission[61] based on non-binding Security Council resolutions outside the framework of

---

Italy, New Zealand, Netherlands, Norway, Portugal, Romania, Spain, Sweden, Turkey and the UK, formally initiated Operation Fingal: available at <http://www.operations.mod.uk/fingal/index.htm>.

50. See Security Council Resolution 678, 29 November 1990, S/RES/678 (1990).

51. The first such authorization was granted by Resolution 770 (1992).

52. For examinations of multinational forces, see Gray, op. cit. n. 66, at p. 187.

53. Resolution 929 of 22 June 1994, S/RES/929 (1994).

54. Resolution 940 of 31 July 1994, S/RES/940 (1994).

55. Resolution 1101 of 28 March 1997, S/RES/1101, operative para. 4 (compare reference to multinational forces for non-enforcement purposes under operative para. 2).

56. Resolution 1125 authorized member states, which contributed to the MISAB, the Inter-African Mission to Monitor the Implementation of the Bangui Agreements, (established in January 1997) to use force for secure the security of their personnel: Resolution 1125 of 6 August 1997, S/RES/1125 (1997).

57. Resolution 1244 was passed under Chapter VII, authorizing member states and relevant international organisations to create KFOR, to which NATO contributed.

58. Resolution 1264, adopted under Chapter VII, authorised the creation of a multinational force under a unified command structure assumed by Australia, INTERFET.

59. See the deployment of the Interim Emergency Multinational Force (IEMF) in Bunia, Congo in close coordination with the UN peacekeeping force, the MONUC: Resolution 1484 of 30 May 2003, S/RES/1484 (2003), operative, para. 1.

60. L. Doswald-Beck, 'Implementation of International Humanitarian Law in Future Wars', in M. N. Schmitt and L.C. Green, eds., *The Law of Armed Conflict: Into the Next Millennium* 71 *US Naval War College International Law Studies* (1998) pp. 39 at pp. 59-62; R.D. Glick, 'Lip Service to the Laws of War: Humanitarian Law and United Nations Armed Forces', 17 *Michigan JIL* (1995) p. 53; C. Greenwood, 'Protection of Peacekeepers: the Legal Regime', 7 *Duke JCIL* (1996) p. 185; P. Rowe, 'Maintaining Discipline in United Nations Peace Support Operations: the Legal Quagmire for Military Contingents', 5 *Journal of Conflict and Security Law* (2000) p. 45; and B.D. Tittemore, 'Belligerents in Blue Helmets: Applying International Humanitarian Law to United Nations Peace Operations', 33 *Stanford JIL* (1997) p. 61.

61. Doswald-Beck, ibid., at p. 60.

Chapter VII.[62] With respect to multilateral forces under the Chapter VII mandate, existing humanitarian law treaties do not recognise such forces as a party to the armed conflict. As compared with UN peacekeeping forces,[63] which are expected to be neutral forces rather than adversarial 'parties to a conflict',[64] there should be no obstacle to the idea of the multinational forces as a whole being recognised as a belligerent. In the context of UN peacekeeping forces, the UN model agreement between the United Nations and troop-contributing countries (TCCs) includes only a general reference to compliance with the laws of war.[65] The *Brahimi Report*[66] is confined to such general compliance with humanitarian law[67] and the recommendation to secure a clear chain of command for UN peacekeeping forces.[68]

A temporary solution to the lack of humanitarian law applicable to multinational forces as a whole is to surmise that each national contingent is bound by humanitarian treaties that its flag state has ratified. This means that there would be an ineluctable difference in the humanitarian laws applicable to national troops contributing to the ISAF. The fact that not all participating states are parties to specific humanitarian treaties gives rise to problems of 'interoperability'. Such problems can arise in relation both to a regional organisation such as NATO and the Organisation for Security and Cooperation in Europe (OSCE) and to ad hoc multilateral forces, such as the Economic Community of West African States (ECOWAS) Monitoring Group (ECOMOG) in Liberia in 1990.[69] In order to fill such legal loopholes, amending existing humanitarian law treaties or supplementing them through a protocol would be essential. With specific regard to the Afghan situation of armed hostilities between the anti-governmental rebels and the ISAF acting in self-defence, it is possible to foresee a scenario in which the ISAF's action exceeds the remit of self-defence by getting actively involved in the fight against the rebels. Such likelihood reinforces the argument that the ISAF as a whole should be bound by the humanitarian rules based on common Article 3 of Geneva Conventions and customary norms applicable to internal armed conflicts.

---

62. See for instance, Resolution 1101 of 28 March 1997, which relates to Albania: S/RES/1101 (1997), operative para. 2.

63. See Secretary-General's Bulletin: Observance by United Nations Forces of International Humanitarian Law, 38 *ILM* (1999) p. 1656.

64. Doswald-Beck, loc. cit. n. 60, at pp. 59-60; and Tittemore, loc. cit. n. 60, at p. 80.

65. Doswald-Beck, loc. cit. n. 60, at p. 60.

66. The Report of the Panel on UN Peace Operations of 21 August 2000 (The Brahimi Report), A/55/305, S/2000/809, available at <http://www.un.org/peace/reports/peace_operations/>; 39 *ILM* (2000) p. 1432. For the commentary on the report, see C. Gray, 'Peacekeeping after the Brahimi Report: is there a Crisis of Credibility for the UN?', 6 *Journal of Conflict and Security Law* (2001) pp. 267 at 281; and N. White, 'Commentary on the Report of the Panel on UN Peace Operations (The Brahimi Report)', 6 *Journal of Conflict and Security Law* (2001) p. 127.

67. A/55/305, S/2000/809, p. 17, para. 6.

68. Ibid., p. 61, para. 267.

69. Doswald-Beck, loc. cit. n. 60, at p. 60.

3.   CRITERIA FOR COMBATANTS UNDER HUMANITARIAN LAW

Having examined the nature of armed conflicts in Afghanistan and determined the applicable laws in each facet of the war, the next section explores the criteria for 'lawful combatants' under the 1949 Third Geneva Convention and 1977 Additional Protocol I. The analysis of Additional Protocol I is necessary to the extent that part of it may be considered as having attained the status of customary international law applicable to both parties. There is also brief appraisal of laws governing internal armed conflict, such as common Article 3 of the 1949 Geneva Conventions, Additional Protocol II, as well as customary rules.

3.1   Criteria for combatants under Article 4 of the Third Geneva Convention

3.1.1   *General overview*

The first two paragraphs of Article 4(A) of the Third Geneva Convention stipulate that:

> 'Prisoners of war, in the sense of the present Convention, are persons belonging to one of the following categories, who have fallen into the Power of the enemy:
> (1) Members of the armed forces of a Party to the conflict as well as members of militias or volunteer corps forming part of such armed forces.
> (2) Members of other militias and members of other volunteer corps, including those of organized resistance movements, belonging to a Party to the conflict and operating in or outside their own territory, even if this territory is occupied, provided that such militias or volunteer corps, including such organized resistance movements, fulfill the following conditions:
> (a) That of being commanded by a person responsible for his subordinates;
> (b) That of having a fixed distinctive sign recognizable at a distance;
> (c) That of carrying arms openly;
> (d) That of conducting their operations in accordance with the laws and customs of war.'

Article 4A(2) of the 1949 Third Geneva Convention reaffirms the four conditions laid down in Article 1 of the Hague Regulations,[70] subject to a minor linguistic change in the second condition concerning the distinct sign, such as uniform or outfit. The only marked change is that, in response to the crucial contribution made by organised resistance movements in Axis-occupied territories in Europe, it was felt necessary to extend, under Article 4A(2) of the Third Geneva Convention, the scope of combatants to cover organised resistance movements in occupied territories. The four criteria set out in Article 4A(2) of the Third Geneva Convention need to be cumulatively met. It is generally accepted that though the stringency

---

70. See also Arts. 1 and 2 of the Geneva Convention relative to the Treatment of Prisoners of War 1929, available at <http://www.icrc.org/IHL.nsf/>.

with which to interpret each of the criteria may vary, these criteria are 'constitutive' in nature for the purpose of claiming the qualification of POW status on the part of independent forces.[71]

3.1.2   *The four defined conditions*

3.1.2.1   Being commanded by a person responsible for his subordinates

With respect to the first condition, such a responsible leader may be civilian or military. This condition suggests the existence of an organisational structure that enforces discipline, with its essence being to provide 'reasonable assurance' that the other three conditions will be observed.[72]

3.1.2.2   Wearing of fixed distinctive signs

As regards the second condition, its main objective is two-fold: to protect the members of the armed forces of the occupying power by avoiding treacherous attacks; and to safeguard non-combatant civilians from adverse effects of war by preventing a perpetrator of a belligerent act from escaping into the general population.[73] The question of the types of 'fixed distinctive sign' remained unresolved when the identical terms were used in the two Hague Conventions and in the 1929 Geneva Prisoner-of-War Convention.[74] The ICRC's Commentary on the Third Geneva Convention explains that a variety of signs other than an arm-band can be used by partisans, including a cap, a coat, a shirt, an emblem or a coloured sign worn on the chest.[75] Another aspect of controversy concerns the interpretation of the phrase, 'recognizable at a distance'. Oppenheim/Lauterpacht proposed a more stringent requirement for a member of a resistance group than for members of the regular armed forces, stating that 'it is reasonable to expect that the silhouette of an irregular combatant standing against the skyline should be at once distinguishable from that of a peaceful inhabitant by the naked eye of ordinary individuals, at a distance at which the form of an individual can be determined'.[76] However, such a proposal does not seem compatible with the ensuing humanitarian trend to approximate resistance groups to the status of regular armed forces. The ICRC's position has been that the visibility of the 'distinctive sign' should be treated in a manner analogous to a uniform.[77]

---

71. H.S. Levie, *Prisoners of War in International Armed Conflict* Vol. 59 (Newport RI, US Naval War College International Law Studies 1978) at p. 53.

72. J.S. Pictet, ed., *Commentary on the Third Geneva Convention Relative to the Treatment of Prisoners of War* (hereinafter *Commentary, GCIII*) (Geneva, ICRC 1960) p. 59.

73. Levie, op. cit. n. 71, at pp. 46-47.

74. Ibid., at p. 47.

75. *Commentary, GCIII*, op. cit. n. 72, at p. 60.

76. L. Oppenheim, *International Law*, 7th edn., H. Lauterpacht, ed. Vol. II, (London, Longman 1952) p. 257, fn. 2. See also *Military Prosecutor* v. *Kassem* (1971) 42 *ILR*, at p. 478.

77. Levie, op. cit. n. 71, at p. 48. See also *Commentary, GCIII*, op. cit. n. 72, at p. 60.

3.1.2.3   Open carrying of arms

In relation to the third condition, the 'open' carrying of arms, this does not require 'visibility', so that a hand-grenade or a revolver can be placed in a pocket or under a coat.[78] However, a soldier concealing a sidearm or hand-grenade or dagger in the clothing is not held to this requirement.[79]

3.1.2.4   Compliance with the laws and customs of war

Among the four defined conditions, the fourth condition leaves many questions unanswered. It seems indisputable that in order to avail themselves of the entitlement to POW status, the irregular forces must ensure that their members comply with the laws and customs of war. The ICRC's Commentary is confined to the general statement that partisans are obliged to observe the Geneva Conventions 'to the fullest extent possible'.[80] It is not required that combatants both as a group and individually strictly observe all details of humanitarian law provisions[81] What remains unclear is whether this requirement is a constitutive condition for POW status or a general obligation for all combatants.[82] Rosas argues that the fourth condition of Article 4A(2) should be treated as a constitutive condition both for combatants and POWs in respect of independent forces.[83]

Moreover, it is contested whether this condition should be regarded as an individual or group requirement. While the question as to an individual or collective requirement can also arise in respect of the second requirement of wearing fixed distinctive signs and the third requirement of carrying arms openly, it has become the focus of examinations with regard to the requirement of observing *jus in bello*. Can an individual belligerent's scrupulous observance of the laws and customs of war reward him/her the POW status even if the group as a whole to which s/he belongs has openly disregarded such laws and customs? It is reasonable to argue, on the basis of the collective criterion, that where the great majority of an organised resistance movement comply with the laws and customs of war as a matter of official policy, this would satisfy the fourth condition, notwithstanding individual cases of violations and even of war crimes.[84] There is an implicit recognition under Article 4A(2) of the Third Geneva Convention that if non-fulfilment by

---

78. *Commentary, GCIII*, ibid., at p. 61.

79. Oppenheim, op. cit. n. 76 at p. 257, n. 3; Levie, op. cit. n. 71, at p. 50. See also *Military Prosecutor* v. *Kassem, supra* n. 76, at pp. 478-79.

80. *Commentary, GCIII*, op. cit. n. 72, at p. 61.

81. A. Rosas, *The Legal Status of Prisoners of War – A Study in International Humanitarian Law Applicable in Armed Conflicts* (Helsinki, Suomalainen Tiedeakatemia 1976) at pp. 362-363.

82. Ibid., at pp. 359-375.

83. Ibid., at p. 363.

84. Levie, op. cit. n. 71, at p. 52; and G.L. Neuman, 'Humanitarian Law and Counterterrorist Force', 14 *EJIL* (2003) pp. 283 at p. 294. See US Department of the Army, *The US Army Field Manual 27-10, the Law of Land Warfare* (1956), <http://www.adtdl.army.mil>, para. 64(d), which reads that '[t]his condition is fulfilled if most of the members of the body observe the laws and customs of war, notwithstanding the fact that the individual member concerned may have committed a war crime.'

members of the resistance movement is incidental, there is no collective violation that would deny the whole group the entitlement to POW status.[85] Yet the assertion may be made that since the observance of all the four conditions should be regarded as constitutive in nature, the converse is not the case, so that gross and systematic non-compliance by the organised resistance movement with most (as opposed to detailed) rules of humanitarian law deprives any of its members of POW status.[86] As will be explained below, however, the rule embodied in Article 44(2) of Protocol I, which accords the right to be a prisoner of war even to an individual soldier who has not honoured *jus in bello*, can be considered as transformed into customary law. There might be some scope to argue that while accepting the parallel existence of two sources of law on the same subject,[87] the emergence of such a customary norm has strengthened (if not overstretched) the normative effectiveness of Article 4A(2) of the Third Geneva Convention, allowing the meaning of this provision to be modified.[88] This would mean that while this provision is premised on a collective assumption, the systematic policy of a group riding roughshod over rules of humanitarian law should not detrimentally affect the right to be a prisoner of war of an individual member who has conscientiously observed such rules.

3.1.3   *Applicability of the four conditions to Article 4A(1) of the Third Geneva Convention*

There are two schools of interpretation regarding whether the four criteria for evaluating lawful combatants as laid down under Article 4A(2) of the Third Geneva Convention should apply to all categories of 'lawful combatants' enumerated in Article 4A(1). The first view is to hold that, consistent with the textual meaning and structural framework of Article 4A, only '[m]embers of other militias and members of other volunteer corps' under the chapeau of Article 4A(2) have to meet the four criteria set out in this paragraph. This means that members of the regular armed forces and members of militias or volunteer corps incorporated into the national army are *ipso facto* considered lawful combatants and, if captured, entitled to the status of a prisoner of war, without the need to determine whether their overall conduct has satisfied the four criteria laid down in the second para-

---

85. Rosas, op. cit. n. 81, at p. 337.

86. Levie, op. cit. n. 71, at pp. 52-53; and Rosas, ibid., at pp. 361 and 363. Neuman's position is close to such view, though he emphasizes the need to examine the structure of the group and the degree to which an individual member has participated in serious violations of humanitarian law: Neuman, op. cit. n. 84, at p. 294.

87. *Case concerning the Military and Paramilitary Activities in and against Nicaragua (Nicaragua v. US)*, Judgment of 27 June 1986, *ICJ Rep.* (1986) pp. 14, at 94, para. 176.

88. The possibility that the normative content of a treaty provision changes through the concurrent emergence of state practice and *opinio juris*, despite apparent contradiction with another treaty provision, is recognised by the European Court of Human Rights in *Öcalan* v. *Turkey* (the recognition that capital punishment may be considered as 'inhuman and degrading treatment' in breach of Art. 3, notwithstanding Art. 2 of the European Convention on Human Rights): Judgment of 12 March 2003, para. 198.

graph.[89] Lawful combatants must not be punished for the fact of having taken part in an armed conflict.

The second view considers that all participants in armed hostilities, including members of regular armed forces, must satisfy the four conditions set forth in Article 4A(2).[90] According to this view, customary international law prior to 1949 always required members of regular forces to adhere to these four conditions.[91] It can be contended that the application of the four conditions to members of the regular armed forces is implied in their definition under the Third Geneva Convention.[92] With the four defined conditions deemed as constitutive, the failure to meet any of them would justify the approach whereby the right to POW status, if not combatant status, could be removed. The support for the second view can be found in national jurisprudence. In *Mohamed Ali* v. *Public Prosecutor*,[93] the Judicial Committee of the Privy Council of the United Kingdom was asked in 1968 to adjudicate on the question whether the defendants belonging to the Indonesian Army, who landed in Singapore (then a part of Malaysia) and killed some civilians by explosives, could claim POW status. A state of armed conflict existed between Indonesia and Malaysia. Though the case concerned the defendants wearing civilian clothes when they set explosives, the Privy Council held that '[s]hould *regular* combatants fail to comply with these four conditions, they may in certain cases become unprivileged belligerents … mean[ing] that they would not be entitled to the status of prisoners of war upon their capture.'[94]

The ICRC's Commentary on the Third Geneva Convention states that there was an overall agreement at the 1949 Diplomatic Conference that it was superfluous to expressly lay down the four criteria, as mentioned under Article 4A(2), for members of regular armed forces under Article 4A(1).[95] While the Commentary sug-

---

89. Aldrich, loc. cit. n. 4, at p. 894 and Matheson, loc. cit. n. 5, at p. 355. Rowe seems to follow this reasoning, stating that since the Taliban fighters belonged to the armed forces of a party to the conflict, i.e., Afghanistan, they 'are likely to be prisoners of war', without referring to the four conditions under Article 4A(2) of the Third Geneva Convention: Rowe, loc. cit. n. 4, at p. 317.

90. See for instance, Y. Dinstein, 'The Distinction Between Unlawful Combatants and War Criminals', in Y. Dinstein, ed., *International Law at a Time of Perplexity – Essays in Honour of Shabtai Rosenne* (Dordrecht, Nijhoff 1989) pp. 103 at p. 105; H. Fischer, 'Protection of Prisoners of War', in D. Fleck, ed., *The Handbook of Humanitarian Law in Armed Conflicts* (Oxford, Oxford University Press 1995) Ch. 7, at p. 335 (the requirement of carrying arms openly as a 'constitutive element' both of combatant and of prisoners of war status); Levie, op. cit. n. 71, at pp. 36-37; W. T. Mallison and S. V. Mallison, 'The Juridical Status of Irregular Combatants Under the International Humanitarian Law of Armed Conflict', 9 *Case Western Reserve JIL* (1977) pp. 39, at 44-45, 48, and 61-62; and Wedgwood, loc. cit. n. 5, at p. 335.

91. For instance, Art. 3 of the *Oxford Manual* provides that '[e]very belligerent armed force is bound to conform to the laws of war.'

92. S.R. Ratner, 'Jus ad Bellum and Jus in Bello after September 11', 96 *AJIL* (2002) pp. 905, at p. 912.

93. 42 *ILR* (1971) p. 458.

94. Ibid., at p. 466 (emphasis in the original). See also *The Military Prosecutor* v. *Omar Mahmud Kassem and Others* (Israeli Military Court, 1969), where the Israeli Military Court agreed that the four conditions of Article 4A(2) must apply to regular forces as well, pp. 17, at 32. *Law and Courts in the Israel-Held Areas* 42 *ILR* (1971) pp. 470 at p. 479.

95. The Commentary states that the expression 'members of regular armed forces' denotes that

gests that the second strand of argument – that regular forces are also covered by the four conditions –may take the upper hand, further dissection of the nature of the conditions is needed. As suggested by Rosas' analysis,[96] it is submitted that the four defined conditions under Article 4A(2) are constitutive and collective conditions only for independent forces. In contrast, the same cannot *a priori* be said with respect to regular forces under Article 4A(1), and the four conditions can be regarded as declaratory and individual in respect of such forces.

3.2   Criteria for combatants under 1977 Additional Protocol I

3.2.1   *General overview*

Article 43(1) of Protocol I stipulates that:

> 'The armed forces of a Party to a conflict consist of all organized armed forces, groups and units which are under a command responsible to that Party for the conduct of its subordinates, even if that Party is represented by a government or an authority not recognized by an adverse Party. Such armed forces shall be subject to an internal disciplinary system which, *inter alia,* shall enforce compliance with the rules of international law applicable in armed conflict.'

Article 43 no longer employs the terms, militia and volunteer corps. Article 43(1), in contrast to Article 4A(1) of the Third Geneva Convention, makes it clear that all the participants, including members of armed forces, are required to be subject to some of the established conditions: they must be under a military command and governed by an internal disciplinary system capable of enforcing compliance with humanitarian rules. The second paragraph of Article 43 defines all the members of the armed forces, bar medical personnel and chaplains, as combatants in the sense that they have 'the right to participate directly in hostilities'.

The approach of Protocol I is to reconfirm the overlapping nature of the concept of combatants and that of POWs, with Article 44(1) providing that '[a]ny combatant, as defined in Article 43, who falls into the power of an adverse Party shall be a prisoner of war'. Article 44(3) entails an innovative aspect, expanding the concept of combatants to cover members of national liberation movements and guerrilla fighters, provided that they meet the even less stringent condition of distinction than those laid down in Article 4A(2) of the Third Geneva Convention. This provision was inserted in response to the growing demand of the socialist and newly independent countries in Africa and Asia for upgrading the status of national liberation movements (NLM) and guerrilla movements in the decolonisation

---

such forces 'have all the material characteristics and all the attributes of armed forces', ...[based on the conditions that] they wear uniform, they have an organized hierarchy and they know and respect the laws and customs of war': *Commentary, GCIII,* op. cit. n. 72, at 63. See also Mallison and Mallison, loc. cit. n. 90, at p. 48.

96. Rosas, loc. cit. n. 81, at pp. 328, and 371-372. See also pp. 340-341, 348-349, 354, 358, 363 and 367.

process and the Vietnam War. While the first sentence of Article 44(3) reiterates the requirement that members of such groups must distinguish themselves from civilians, the scope of application of this requirement becomes very narrowly defined in the second sentence.[97] The most widely accepted view among the delegates at the 1974-77 Geneva Conference was that the requirement of distinction as stipulated in Article 44(3) should equally apply to members of regular armed forces organised in accordance with Article 43.[98]

3.2.2 *The requirement of complying with the laws and customs of war*

Article 44(2) of Additional Protocol I, which reiterates the fourth condition as laid down under Article 4A(2) of the Third Geneva Convention, is not intended to be a prerequisite for combatant status, and even for POW status (unless otherwise provided in Article 44(3) and (4)). Article 44(2) makes it clear that the perpetration by an individual of violations of laws of war, including war crimes, does not affect his/her combatant and POW status. This does not have exculpatory effect on a combatant who has perpetrated war crimes or other violations of laws and customs of war, who remains punishable under national military law or international criminal law. As will be discussed below in relation to detainees belonging to the Taliban or Al Qaeda, there is ample scope for argument that the rule embodied in Article 44(2) of Protocol I can be considered as having attained the status of custom and that it is binding on non-contracting parties, such as the United States and Afghanistan.

The ICRC's Commentary on Protocol I in respect of Article 44(2) makes it clear that Protocol I has changed the previous rule derived from the Hague law and Article 4A(2) of the Third Geneva Convention. Article 44(2) adopts a *uniform* approach to participants in hostilities, irrespective of whether members of regular armed forces or those of independent forces (such as organised resistance movements and national liberation movements).

With respect to the requirement of complying with laws and customs of war, Article 44(2) retains a collective criterion, which is, however, accompanied by an express guarantee that a violation of laws and customs of war by an individual

---

97. The second sentence of Art. 44(3) reads that: 'Recognizing, however, that there are situations in armed conflicts where, owing to the nature of the hostilities an armed combatant cannot so distinguish himself, he shall retain his status as a combatant, provided that, in such situations, he carries his arms openly: (a) during each military engagement; and (b) during such time as he is visible to the adversary while he is engaged in a military deployment preceding the launching of an attack in which he is to participate. Acts which comply with the requirements of this paragraph shall not be considered as perfidious within the meaning of Article 37, paragraph 1(c).'

98. *Official Records of the Diplomatic Conference on the Reaffirmation and Development of International Humanitarian Law Applicable in Armed Conflicts, Geneva (1974-1977)*, (hereinafter *Official Records)*, Vol. XV (Bern, Federal Political Department 1978) p. 157; and Y. Sandoz, C. Swinarski and B. Zimmermann, eds., *Commentary on the Protocol Additional of 8 June 1977 to the Geneva Conventions of 12 August 1949, and relating to the Protection of Victims of International Armed Conflicts (Protocol I)* (hereinafter *Commentary, Protocol I)*, (Geneva, ICRC/Martinus Nijhoff 1987) at p. 535, para. 1719.

combatant does not disqualify him/her for POW status.[99] It may be argued that the humanitarian objective underlying Article 44(2) supports the argument that even systematic disregard for laws and customs of war by the group, whether regular armed forces or national liberation movements, should not warrant the decision to deprive an individual soldier abiding by such laws and customs of his/her POW status. This means that only where an individual member has followed the general policy of the group and systematically disregarded laws and customs of war, can such an individual lose his/her right to POW status. That the ICRC has consistently asserted that the legal status of each internee at Guantánamo Bay must be determined on an *individual* basis[100] reinforces such progressive construction.

3.2.3   *The requirement of carrying arms openly*

The requirement of distinction is assessed on an individual basis, so that the failure to carry arms openly when captured would deny a soldier the right to be POW, despite the overall compliance with this requirement by a group as a whole.[101] The remaining question is whether such a failure to distinguish from civilians would lead to the deprivation of the right to be a combatant as well. The wording of Article 44(4), which provides that a 'combatant' flouting the requirement of distinction as formulated under Article 44(3) is disabled from claiming only his/her right to POW status, might suggest that the combatant status is retained. In contrast, the ICRC's Commentary on Protocol I[102] and many other commentators[103] suggest that *all* the individuals captured while not meeting the requirement of carrying arms openly lose the right to a combatant as well and may be criminally prosecuted for their participation in hostilities.[104] The two views may not be set apart in practical terms. Even if the first view is accepted, this does not exonerate an individual from the offences based on the failure to distinguish him/herself from civilians, leaving the possibility of trial and punishment pursuant to military law and international criminal law. What is fundamentally at stake, as the representatives of a national liberation movement insisted at the Geneva Conference, is the recognition that a member of a national liberation movement, who face greater difficulty in abiding by the requirement of distinction, should receive no less privi-

---

99. *Commentary, Protocol I*, ibid., at pp. 525-526, paras. 1689-1690. Many Socialist countries attached reservations to Art. 85 to the effect that perpetrators of war crimes, when convicted, would be deprived of the POW status.

100. See ICRC, 'Guantánamo Bay: the work continues', 9 May 2003, Operational update, available at <http://www.icrc.org/Web/Eng/siteeng0.nsf/iwpList74/5C867C1D85AA2BE541256-C94006000EE>.

101. Provost, op. cit. n. 28, at p. 37.

102. *Commentary, Protocol I*, op. cit. n. 98, at p. 538, para. 1719.

103. Dinstein, loc. cit. n. 90, at pp. 105 and 111 and Provost, op. cit. n. 28, at p. 37.

104. This was also the position of the United Kingdom delegation during the Working Group's discussions at the Geneva Diplomatic Conference. According to the delegation, '[a]ny combatant who violated the rules in paragraph 3 ... lost his combatant status and was therefore to be treated as a person who did not have the right to engage in armed conflict even though he would be accorded rights equivalent to those contained in the third Geneva Convention of 1949.' *Official Records*, op. cit. n. 98, Vol. XV, p. 157, para. 14.

lege and benefit as a POW than members of regular armed forces at the captor's will.[105]

Protocol I introduces another innovative element of humanitarian considerations, obliging the contracting parties to offer those captured while not meeting the open arms requirement under the second sentence of Article 44(3) the 'protections equivalent in all respects to those accorded to prisoners of war' by the Third Geneva Convention and by Protocol I.[106] This protective status includes the due process guarantees 'equivalent to those accorded to prisoners of war by the Third Convention in the case where such a person is tried and punished for any offences he has committed'.[107] Even those who fall outside POW status can be assured of a series of specific minimum guarantees as laid down in Article 75 of Protocol I.

4.   CONTROVERSIAL CATEGORIES OF BELLIGERENTS

4.1   'Unprivileged belligerents': general overview

The question arises as to the legal status of those participants in hostilities who are not members of regular armed forces and who do not meet the necessary qualifications for lawful belligerents provided in Article 4 of the Third Geneva Convention and Article 44 of Protocol I. Examples of such persons include spies, guerrillas, partisans, saboteurs, mercenaries, 'war-traitors', *francs-tireurs*, terrorists and others.[108] The US military manuals interchangeably use the concepts, 'unlawful combatants',[109] 'unprivileged belligerents'[110] and 'illegal combatants',[111] to refer to such persons. While the terminology, 'unlawful combatant', does not entertain a long lineage, there were some earlier equivalents, such as 'irregular combatants' and 'marauders'.[112]

---

105. *Official Records,* ibid., Vol. VI, p. 148; and *Commentary, Protocol I, supra* n. 98, at p. 539, fn. 82.

106. Art. 44(4), first sentence.

107. Art. 44(4), second sentence.

108. R.R. Baxter, 'So-called "Unprivileged Belligerency": Spies, Guerrillas and Saboteurs', 28 *BYIL* (1951) p. 323. See also J. Klabbers, 'Rebel with a Cause? Terrorists and Humanitarian Law', 14 *EJIL* (2003) p. 299.

109. *US Army, Operational Law Handbook* (1997), JA 422, (Charlottesville, Virginia, International and Operational Law Department, The Judge Advocate General's School, US Army, 1997), <http://www.cdmha.org/toolkit/cdmha-rltk/PUBLICATIONS/oplaw-ja97.pdf>, p. 18-19.

110. *US Army, Operational Law Handbook* (2002), (Charlottesville, Virginia, International and Operational Law Department, The Judge Advocate General's School, US Army, 2002), <https://www.jagcnet.army.mil/JAGCNETInternet/Homepages/AC/CLAMO-Public.nsf/0/1af4860452f962-c085256a490049856f?OpenDocument>, Ch. 2, p. 6.

111. *US Navy, Commander's Handbook of the Law of Naval Operations, NWP 1-14M,* Department of the Navy, 1995, available at <http://www.nwc.navy.mil/ILD/NWP%201-14M.htm>, para. 12.7.1.

112. Hoffman, loc. cit. n. 4, at p. 228.

When discussing spies, guerrillas and saboteurs, the concept of 'unprivileged belligerents'[113] should be preferred to the expression 'unlawful combatants'.[114] Baxter has observed that

'armed and unarmed hostilities, wherever occurring [whether in occupied or unoccupied areas], committed by persons other than those entitled to be treated as prisoners of war or peaceful civilians merely deprive such individuals of a protection they might otherwise enjoy under international law and place them virtually at the power of the enemy'.[115]

It may be argued that Baxter's view augured the progressive construction of humanitarian law that characterised the Geneva Diplomatic Conference in 1977. Article 46 of Protocol I stipulates that those members of armed forces who are captured while engaging in espionage are treated as spies and bereft of the right to be treated as prisoners of war, without, however, alluding to the loss of the right to combatant status.

Capital punishment for unprivileged belligerents is not excluded under the 1949 Geneva Conventions, except for those in occupied territories as prescribed in Article 68 of the Fourth Geneva Convention. However, even those labelled as 'unprivileged belligerents or combatants' are entitled to the minimum guarantees without discrimination. Such minimum guarantees should correspond to the safeguards for participants in civil conflicts, as provided in common Article 3 of the Geneva Conventions.[116] They are deemed as having been grafted onto customary law. More detailed guarantees based on the rights to physical and mental integrity and due process are enumerated in Article 75 of Protocol I, which in itself should be considered as customary international law.[117]

4.2   The right to partake in hostilities

With respect to whether unprivileged belligerents have the right to partake in hostilities, two strands of argument can be presented. First, all such unprivileged belligerents lack the right to engage in warfare with immunity from any liability under national or international law.[118] Members of such groups can be punished for their

---

113. Baxter, loc. cit. n. 108. See also J. Stone, *Legal Controls of International Conflicts* (London, Stevens 1958) at p. 569.

114. Many jurists use the expression, 'unlawful combatants'. See, for instance, Dinstein, loc. cit. n. 90; and Knut Ipsen, 'Combatants and Non-Combatants', in Fleck, op. cit. n. 90, Ch. 3.

115. Baxter, loc. cit. n. 108, at p. 343.

116. Aldrich, loc. cit. n. 4, at p. 893.

117. C.J. Greenwood, 'Customary Law Status of the 1977 Geneva Protocols', in A.J.M. Delissen and G.J. Tanja, eds., *Humanitarian Law of Armed Conflict: Challenges Ahead: Essays in Honour of Frits Kalshoven*, (Dordrecht, Martinus Nijhoff 1991) pp. 93 at p. 103. The US government has also considered Art. 75 as part of the customary rules embodied in Protocol I: *US Army, Operational Law Handbook* (1997), op. cit. n. 109, p. 18-2; and *US Army, Operational Law Handbook* (2002), op. cit. n. 110, Ch. 2, p. 5.

118. Dinstein, op. cit. n. 90, at p. 111.

participation in hostilities and for any crimes, such as murder, assault, rape and looting, that may have been committed in that connection, on the basis of national law. Or, as in the event of a soldier who has killed an enemy soldier while wearing the adversary's uniform, the basis for prosecution can be either a war crime in international law (perfidy) or an ordinary crime in national law (murder).[119] The reasoning of the US Supreme Court in *Ex parte Quirin* conforms to this argument. In respect of German saboteurs who clandestinely landed in the United States, the Court, distinguishing lawful and unlawful combatant, ruled that upon capture, '[u]nlawful combatants… are subject to trial and punishment by military tribunals for acts which render their belligerency unlawful'.[120] Vulnerability of such persons to criminal prosecution for the mere involvement in hostilities is the sanction to deter their entry into armed conflicts.[121]

The second strand of argument is to deemphasise the distinction between the members of belligerents whose act of participating in hostilities is lawful and those whose such act itself should be deemed as unlawful. The thrust of the second argument is that susceptibility to punishment is not because their involvement in armed conflicts is regarded as unlawful but due to the danger that they pose to adverse parties. Baxter's seminal work in 1951 adopts this unitary approach, postulating that all the categories of unprivileged belligerents are, while being vulnerable to the forfeiture of their POW status and to punishment upon capture, not unlawful in terms of their participation in hostilities.[122] Such a unitary approach explains Baxter's criticism that the finding of the United States Supreme Court in *Ex parte Quirin,* that the saboteurs in question violated international law, was 'a fundamental confusion between acts punishable under international law and acts with respect to which international law affords no protection'.[123] The absence of legal protection prescribed by humanitarian law does not suggest that the act of participation in hostilities is unlawful. The result of a captured soldier being classified as an unprivileged belligerent is that s/he would be disentitled to POW status and subject to

---

119. Aldrich, loc. cit. n. 4, at p. 893; Dinstein, ibid., and G.I.A.D. Draper, *The Red Cross Convention*, (London, Stevens 1958) at p. 52. See also *US Army Field Manual, supra* n. 84, para. 73, 'Persons Committing Hostile Acts Not Entitled To Be Treated as Prisoners of War'.

120. *Ex parte Quirin*, 317 US 31.

121. Aldrich, loc. cit. n. 4, at pp. 893-894. Yet, Aldrich states that Al Qaeda personnel 'were combatants in hostilities and are not entitled to POW status', suggesting that they are at least entitled to the right to be combatant: ibid., at p. 893.

122. Baxter argues that: 'Since these qualities [disregard for and deliberate non-observance of the qualifications to be recognized as a prisoner of war] are those which most conspicuously inhere in espionage, resistance activities in occupied areas, guerrilla warfare, and private hostilities in arms, they afford grounds for believing that all these acts of warfare, whether or not involving the use of arms and whether performed by military persons or by civilians, are governed by a single legal principle.' Baxter, loc. cit. n. 108, at p. 342. Baxter applies the same reasoning to simple evaders, escaped prisoners of war captured or recaptured in civilian clothes, as well as military personnel captured while wearing civilian clothes under their uniforms: ibid., at pp. 340-341.

123. Ibid., at p. 340. In another context, Baxter states that '[t]he judicial determination which is necessary before a person may be treated as an unprivileged belligerent is … not a determination of guilt but of status only and, for the purposes of international law, it is sufficient to ascertain whether the conduct of the individual has been such as to deny him the status of the prisoner or of the peaceful civilian.' Ibid., at pp. 343-344.

the same rights and disabilities as the civilian population, albeit his/her conduct is considered relevant to assessment of penalty.[124] Such an unprivileged belligerent, who is not held either as a POW or as a peaceful civilian, can be tried under the municipal law of the capturing state for a war crime *stricti juris*, as in the case of killing of civilians, pillage or refusal to quarter.[125] However, persons arrested and captured in an occupied territory, as contrasted to those captured other than in an occupied territory, will benefit from favourable treatment under Articles 64, 65, 67 and 68 of the Fourth Geneva Convention.[126]

The practice of the United States during the Vietnam War[127] may be deemed as harmonious with the second position. The US Military Command in Vietnam during the Vietnam War adopted the policy of treating as POWs the captured members of Viet Cong main and local force personnel, and Viet Cong irregulars, despite considerable doubt as to whether members of these groups met the criteria set forth in Article 4A(2) of the Third Geneva Convention.[128] Members of the Viet Cong were not granted POW status but treated as equal to POWs, on the condition that when captured, they carried arms openly and engaged in combat or a belligerent act, 'other than an act of terrorism, sabotage, or spying'.[129] The US guidelines did not require that a participant in armed hostilities wear a uniform.[130] There was also a possibility of an Article 5 tribunal to determine the status of those captured whose status was in doubt.[131]

In relation to terrorists,[132] Baxter's comprehensive approach is again instrumental in bringing a measure of legal discipline and cohesion into their classification under humanitarian law. He discussed 'private hostilities in arms' on the equal footing to spies and guerrillas in view of their 'disregard for the qualifications for a prisoner of war status'. This, together with his argument that 'a single legal principle' should apply to these categories, suggest that members of a transnational terrorist organisation, such as Al Qaeda soldiers, be treated in the same vein as other unprivileged belligerents.[133] Baxter's unitary position can corroborate the lib-

---

124. Ibid., at p. 340.

125. Ibid., at p. 344.

126. Ibid. Art. 68 of the Fourth Geneva Convention forbids the application of capital punishment.

127. See Annex A, 'Criteria for Classification and Disposition of Detainees', part of Directive no. 381-46 of 27 December 1967; and Directive no. 20-5 of 15 March 1968, 'Inspections and Investigations: Prisoners of War – Determination of Eligibility'; both reprinted in C. Bevans, 'Contemporary Practice of the United States Relating to International Law', 62 *AJIL* (1968) pp. 754 at 765.

128. Gasser, loc. cit. n. 4, at p. 567.

129. Bevans, loc. cit. n. 127, at p. 767.

130. Gasser, loc. cit. n. 4, at p. 567.

131. Those found outside the status of lawful combatants and POWs were to be transferred to the South Vietnamese authorities. Ibid.

132. While acknowledging the obsolete nature of the term, 'belligerency', Hoffman describes terrorists as 'unlawful belligerents', who do not entertain the right to partake in armed hostilities, but perpetrate indiscriminate attack in peacetime (for certain political goals). The 'unlawful belligerents' would be distinguished from 'unlawful combatants', such as saboteurs, guerrillas and spies, who have such a license and direct attack *normally* against lawful military objectives, though by deceptive or treacherous means and methods: Hoffman, loc. cit. n. 4, at p. 229.

133. Baxter, loc. cit. n. 108, at pp. 342-343.

eral construction, based on the humanitarian object and purpose of the Geneva Conventions, that all those participating in armed conflicts should be described as 'combatants' and *prima facie* deemed as entitled to a POW status till their status is determined by a competent tribunal. The underlying rationale of this argument is that the question of their right to be considered as combatants in modern warfare has lost importance, with the focus of examination having shifted to the conditions of the POW status. As discussed above, such rationale underscores Article 44(4) of Additional Protocol I, according to which, while 'unprivileged belligerents' are stripped of the right to POW *status*, they can benefit from POW *treatment* in respect of due process guarantees.

4.3 The detaining power's own nationals

In relation to the status of a belligerent belonging to the nationality of the capturing state or that of its ally, examples of such genus include members of Viet Cong, who were South Vietnamese nationals, and the Taliban soldiers captured after the coming into existence of the new Karzai government, which is allied to the United States. One strand of argument is that a detaining power is not required to accord POW status to its own nationals.[134] Oppenheim/Lauterpacht explained that nationals of the capturing state falling into its power while serving in the armed forces of the adversary were disqualified from POW status in view of their traitorous act.[135] While this provided the underlying rationale for the decision of the United Kingdom Privy Council in the *Oie Hee Koi* case,[136] this decision became the subject of criticism. The argument made by Oppenheim/Lauterpacht entails a pernicious implication that traitorous citizens of a belligerent could be denied the protection of the Geneva Convention from the beginning of captivity, with no account taken of the complexity of nationality and of the sense of allegiance.[137] The proponents of the teleological construction based on the humanitarian objectives of the Geneva Conventions argue that international humanitarian law should apply to the nationals accused of treason as well, and that they should be granted POW status and all the safeguards as required under the Third Geneva Convention.[138] The facts that the definition of a prisoner of war in Article 4 does not contain reference to nationality and that there was some precedent for disregarding altogether the question of nationality, are cited to support their argument.[139]

---

134. See for instance, *US Army Field Manual*, *supra*, n. 84, <http://www.adtdl.army.mil>, para. 79.

135. Oppenheim, op. cit. n. 76, at p. 268.

136. *Oie Hee Koi* v. *Public Prosecutor* and connected appeals, Judicial Committee of the Privy Council, 4 December 1967, (1968) 9 *British International Law Cases (BILC)* pp. 250-254, and [1968] AC 829.

137. R.R. Baxter, 'The Privy Council on the Qualifications of Belligerents', 63 *AJIL* (1969) pp. 290 at 290-294. See also R.-J. Wilhelm, 'Peut-on modifier le statut des prisonniers de guerre?', 35 *RICR* (1953) pp. 681, 684 and 686.

138. S. Elman, 'Prisoners of War under the Geneva Convention', 18 *ICLQ* (1969) pp. 178 at 180-185.

139. Elman refers to the state practice of the United Kingdom during the Boer War, in which the

There are a few post-WWII US decisions that might provide succour to the second view. In *ex parte Quirin*, the US Supreme Court ruled that hostile acts against the Untied States by American citizens amounted to violations of the laws of war committed by 'enemy belligerents'.[140] In *Re Territo*, the application for a writ of habeas corpus by a US citizen that served the Italian army was denied on the basis that he was a prisoner of war.[141] However, Rosas has questioned the effect of these decisions on the basis that the express recognition of POW status was limited only in the case of *Territo*, and in that case the reasoning was adduced with a view to denying the petitioner a constitutional right available to US citizens. In that sense, it may be contended that these decisions cannot serve to alter the traditional premise that the detaining power is not required to offer POW status to its own nationals.[142] Nevertheless, Rosas concedes that the decisive factor should be 'material allegiance' rather than formal nationality, referring to the members of national liberation movements, and individual persons who have renounced their nationality many years before the outbreak of the war but without their former country (the detaining power) formally acknowledging this.[143] It must be recalled that the Appeals Chamber of the ICTY in the *Tadić* case ruled that what matters most was the sense of allegiance rather than mere nationality, enabling the grave breach regime under the Fourth Geneva Convention to apply to the atrocities committed by Serbs against Muslims and Croats in the so-called Republika Srpska.[144] This reasoning is equally applicable to the appraisal of the expression, 'fallen into the power of the enemy', under Article 4 of the Third Geneva Convention,[145] so that even nationals of a detaining power should not be excluded from POW status under the Third Geneva Convention while awaiting possible trials for treason.[146]

4.4   Judicial guarantees for detainees accused of war crimes

In the aftermath of World War II, national courts of several western allied powers were asked to determine whether detainees of Axis nationals accused of war crimes could plead minimum judicial guarantees underlying Articles 45 to 67 of the 1929 Geneva Convention. Such pleas were rejected on the ground that there was a well-established customary rule that those who have violated the laws of war cannot avail themselves of the protection that they afford, with the captured mem-

---

Irish prisoners who had taken the oath of allegiance to the South African Republic were treated as prisoners of war. Ibid., at pp. 181-182.

140. *Ex parte Quirin* (US Supreme Court, 1942), 37 *AJIL* (1943) p. 152. See also *Colepaugh* v. *Looney* (US Court of Appeals, Tenth Circuit, 1956), 23 *ILR* (1956) pp. 759-762.

141. *Re Territo* (US Court of Appeals, Ninth Circuit, 1946), (1946) 156 US FedR. (2d) 142.

142. Rosas, op. cit. n. 81, at pp. 385-386.

143. Ibid., at p. 387.

144. *Prosecutor* v. *Tadić*, Case No. IT-94-1-A, Appeals Judgment, 15 July 1999, para. 166.

145. Indeed in the *Oie Hee Koi* case, the counsel for the respondents made this point, arguing that '[i]t is not patriotism or national allegiance which predominates but political allegiance': *Oie Hee Koi* case, *supra* n. 136, 9 *BILC*, p. 242.

146. Even such nationals can benefit from basic guarantees equivalent to POWs under Art. 44(4), as well as Art. 75 of Protocol I.

bers of armed forces who have committed war crimes disentitled to claim the status of POWs.[147] The ICRC Commentary on the Third Geneva Convention criticises that national legislation did not corroborate this interpretation.[148] Indeed the ICRC took initiatives to insert a provision designed to afford minimum procedural guarantees for individual persons accused of war crimes in the course of any judicial proceedings. Such a move was prompted by the concern that it would be dangerous not to supply the accused with the guarantees embodied in a humanitarian law treaty. This trepidation was borne out by the fact that war crimes trials in many national courts were based on the use of special *ad hoc* legislation rather than on the regular penal legislation and that a number of the accused persons were deprived of the protection of the 1929 Geneva Prisoners of War Convention prior to the judicial pronouncement.[149] At the Geneva Conference of Government Experts in 1947, many Anglo-Saxon states were initially opposed to the idea of maintaining the judicial guarantees of the Convention for those accused of war crimes until after conviction. However, their position underwent a complete change, and in conformity with the ICRC's proposal, they advanced that such prisoners of war should continue to benefit from due process rights even after they had been judged. Since then opposition to this innovative approach waned,[150] and this principle is recapitulated in Article 44(2) of Protocol I.

Article 85 of the Convention has introduced an obligation to offer prisoners of war convicted of war crimes all the benefits accruing from the Convention. These benefits encompass 'all the safeguards which the Convention provides', including notification of the protecting power, assistance by a counsel, the right to be informed of the procedure to be followed, and to call witnesses and an interpreter, as well as the right of appeal.[151] While the application of Article 85 even in the post-conviction period may be objected to as controversial,[152] one can at least recognise that such an innovative move has been influenced by the development of human rights law. The marked significance attached to due process guarantees is demonstrated by the principle that the denial of the right to a fair trial may constitute a grave breach of the Convention as prescribed by Article 130.[153] The same rationale underpins the requirement, as laid down under Article 75(7)(b) of Protocol I, that

147. See *inter alia, Yamashita* Trial, the judgment of 4 February 1946 of the United State Supreme Court: *Law Reports of Trials of War Criminals*, Vol. 4, p. 1, (with one judge dissenting); and *Rauter* case, 12 January 1949, the Netherlands Special Court of Appeal, ibid., Vol. 14, p. 116.

148. *The Final Record of the Diplomatic Conference of Geneva of 1949*, Vol. II-A, pp. 570-571; and *Commentary, GCIII*, op. cit. n. 72, at p. 416.

149. Ibid., at p. 414.

150. Provost, op. cit. n. 28, at pp. 30-31.

151. *Commentary, GCIII*, op. cit. n. 72, at p. 423; and Ipsen, loc. cit. n. 114, at p. 94. Note that Art. 75(7)(b) of Protocol I provides such judicial guarantees for non-combatants accused of war crimes and crimes against humanity.

152. Dinstein, op. cit. n. 90, at p. 114. Note that in the *Kappler* case, the Supreme Military Tribunal in Italy ruled out the benefit of Art. 85 in relation to war criminals: *Kappler* Case, Supreme Military Tribunal, Italy, (1952), 49 *AJIL* (1955) pp. 96 at 97.

153. *Commentary, GCIII*, op. cit. n. 72, at p. 422.

even non-combatants accused of grave breaches of war crimes should be given the due process guarantees.[154]

The approach followed in respect of the POWs accused of war crimes does not appear consistent with the treatment of those persons who have committed perfidious attacks under civilian disguise, war crimes which are expressly proscribed under Article 37(1) of Protocol I and susceptible to the loss of POW status. A proposal submitted at the end of the 1976 session of the Geneva Diplomatic Conference by the Working Group of Committee III was that while losing both their POW status and combatant status, they should benefit from treatment equivalent to that provided for POWs in the Third Convention.[155] It may be seriously questioned how persons convicted of crimes against humanity or even genocide, the nature of which are considered more grave than war crimes of perfidy or war crimes in general,[156] should remain beneficiaries of POW treatment. However, there may be little practical difference in handling these two cases. According to Article 44(4) of Protocol I, persons convicted of perfidy by not distinguishing themselves from civilians can benefit from the rights and privileges akin to those afforded to POWs under the Third Geneva Convention. It should be recalled that the former socialist countries asserted that persons convicted of war crimes and crimes against humanity would forfeit their POW status and entered a reservation on this matter upon their ratification of the Convention. Yet, their assumption was that such convicted criminals would lose their entitlement to POW status only after they are convicted.[157] suggesting that even according to their view war criminals would retain combatant status.

5.   INTERNAL ARMED CONFLICT AND THE HUMANITARIAN RULES

An attempt to extend the status of 'lawful combatants' and that of a prisoner of war to those engaging in guerrillas and armed rebels against armed forces of a state has faced a stonewall of opposition by a large number of states. Such a move has been perceived to send a signal of recognising the legal status of members of such groups and even the status of disputed territory. Additional Protocol II responds to that apprehension of states by avoiding any reference to the terms, 'combatants' and 'prisoners of war'. Instead the approach of Protocol II is to capture the wide range of persons, with the field of application *ratione personae* covering all the

---

154. *Commentary, Protocol I,* op. cit. n. 98, at pp. 887-889, paras. 3131-3143.

155. Rosas, op. cit. n. 81, at p. 312.

156. M. Frulli, 'Are Crimes Against Humanity More Serious Than War Crimes?', 12 *EJIL* (2001) pp. 329 at p. 344. Contrast, however, *Prosecutor* v. *Kambanda* (Case No. ICTR 97-23-S, Judgment and Sentence, 4 September 1998, para. 14) in which crimes against humanity were recognised as more serious than violations of Art. 3 common to the four Geneva Conventions 1949, with *Prosecutor* v. *Tadić* (Case No. IT-94-1, Judgment in Sentencing Appeals, 26 January 2000, paras. 65-69), where the Appeals Chamber of the International Criminal Tribunal for the former Yugoslavia refused to distinguish between them in terms of seriousness.

157. *Commentary, GCIII,* op. cit. n. 72, at pp. 415-416.

persons 'affected by an armed conflict', within the meaning of Article 2(1).[158] While Article 4 provides a non-exhaustive list of proscribed acts against such protected persons in an unconditional manner,[159] Article 5 of Protocol II supplements Article 4, laying down concrete measures of obligations to safeguard the rights of the '[p]ersons whose liberty has been restricted', either by internment or detention. Such an expression denoting the protected persons has been chosen in lieu of specific terms such as 'prisoners' or 'detainees' in order to capture all the persons whose liberty has been circumscribed for reasons relating to the conflict.[160]

6.   TRIBUNALS FOR DETERMINING THE LEGAL STATUS OF PRISONERS

6.1   'Article 5 Tribunals'

The second sentence of Article 5 of the Third Geneva Convention provides that:

> 'Should any doubt arise as to whether persons, having committed a belligerent act and having fallen into the hands of the enemy, belong to any of the categories enumerated in Article 4, such persons shall enjoy the protection of the present Convention until such time as their status has been determined by a competent tribunal.'

This general requirement has been incorporated into national military manuals.[161] Article 5 does not spell out clear guidelines on the terms and conditions under which a 'competent tribunal' is constituted. Just as with limitations on the right to a fair and public hearing as embodied in Article 14 of the ICCPR, proceedings for determining the status of prisoners can be *in camera* to preserve national security. It might be argued that in contrast to the prevailing interpretation of Article 45(2) of Protocol I, which will be discussed below, such proceedings do not have to take place prior to a trial for an offence.[162]

The meaning of '[s]hould any doubt arise' in relation to the inclusion of captured persons in any of the six categories enumerated in Article 4 is not certain. It has been submitted that Article 5 sets out two criteria: procedural criterion and

---

158. According to the ICRC's Commentary on Protocol II, such persons include those 'who do not, or no longer take part in hostilities and enjoy the rules of protection laid down by the Protocol for their benefit' and who 'must ... conform to certain rules of conduct with respect to the adversary and the civilian population': *Official Records,* op. cit. n. 98, Vol. VIII, p. 210; and *Commentary, Protocol II,* op. cit. n. 34, para. 4485.

159. While implicitly connoting the ban on reprisals against protected persons, such an 'absolute' and non-derogable nature of the rule embodied in Art. 4 can signify its *jus cogens* status: *Commentary, Protocol II,* ibid., para. 4530 and n. 17.

160. *Commentary, Protocol II,* ibid., at p. 1384, para. 4564.

161. *US Army, Operational Law Handbook* (1997), JA 422, op. cit. n. 109, p. 18-19; *US Army, Operational Law Handbook* (2002), op. cit. n. 110, Ch. 2, p. 16; and *US Navy, Commander's Handbook of the Law of Naval Operations, NWP 1-14M,* op. cit. n. 111, paras. 11.7 and 12.7.1.

162. Roberts, loc. cit. n. 18, at p. 23.

factual criterion.[163] First, according to the factual criterion, 'doubt' relates simply to the question whether a person appertains to one of the six categories of 'lawful combatants' as laid down in Article 4A. This criterion coincides with the 'quasi-presumption' of POW status for all participants in hostilities.[164] Second, in contrast to the first, the procedural criterion means that 'doubt' arises only when a captured person claims POW status before or at the trial. The United States 1997 Army Regulation follows this position[165] The second position seems to reverse the pre-sumption, unless a claim for POW status is made. This is the view upheld by the UK Privy Council in the *Oie Hee Koi* case.[166]

A question remains as to the meaning of a 'competent tribunal' under Article 5 (2) of the Third Geneva Convention, especially with regard to its composition, competence and procedural rules. The reference to a 'competent tribunal' can also be seen in Article 14 of the International Covenant on Civil and Political Rights (ICCPR) and Article 8 of the American Convention on Human Rights (ACHR). The original draft provision of Article 5(2) at the Stockholm Conference in 1949 referred to the requirement that the legal status of an apprehended person be deter-mined by 'some responsible authority'.[167] Subsequently at the Geneva Conference it was proposed that the term 'responsible authority' be replaced by 'military tribu-nal' in order to provide safeguards against the danger that decisions on the right of a captive to benefit from POW status may be made even by a single non-commis-sioned officer.[168] However, the controversy over serious implications of bringing an apprehended person before a 'military tribunal' led to the further amendment that used the term, 'competent tribunal', leaving the scope of discretion to national authorities as to the type of tribunals (military, civil or administrative).[169] A captive found not entitled to POW status by a 'competent tribunal' might be left with no right to reassert such status before a judicial tribunal convened to examine whether his/her act arising out of hostilities is a lawful 'belligerent act' or an criminal of-fence.[170] The ICRC's Commentary on Protocol I states that such omission allows a captured person to run a 'double risk' of being accused of merely participating in the hostilities, which does not necessarily constitute an offence, and of being de-nied the same procedural guarantees as should be afforded to prisoners of war.[171]

---

163. Y. Naqvi, 'Doubtful Prisoner-of-War Status', 84 *RICR/IRRC* (2002) pp. 571 at pp. 574-577.

164. Ibid., at p. 576

165. *Army Regulation 190-8, Enemy Prisoners of War, Retained Personnel, Civilian Internees and Other Detainees*, (Washington D.C., Headquarters Departments of the Army, the Navy, the Air Force, and the Marine Corps 1997) <http://www.usapa.army.mil/pdffiles/r190%5F8.pdf>, para. 1-6(b).

166. *Public Prosecutor* v. *Oie Hee Koi, supra* n. 134, [1968] AC 829.

167. 'XVIth International Red Cross Conference, Draft revised or new Conventions', p. 54, as referred to in *Commentary, GCIII*, op. cit. n. 72, at p. 77.

168. *Final Record of the Diplomatic Conference of Geneva of 1949* (Federal Political Department, Bern) Vol. II-A, p. 388; and *Commentary GCIII*, ibid. Note, however, that upon the determination of his/her POW status, the captured person must be tried by a military court of the detaining power: Art. 84 of Geneva Convention III.

169. *Commentary, Protocol I*, op. cit. n. 98, at p. 551, para. 1745. See also Bothe et al., op. cit. n. 163, at p. 260; and Naqvi, loc. cit. n. 163, at p. 579.

170. Naqvi, ibid., at p. 580.

171. *Commentary, Protocol I*, op. cit. n. 98, at p. 554, para. 1751.

6.2   A 'competent tribunal' under Article 45 of Protocol I

Article 45(1) elaborates upon the succinct provision of Article 5 of the Geneva Convention III. A participant in hostilities who is captured by an adverse party must be presumed to be a prisoner of war, provided that:

(i) s/he claims the status of prisoner of war;
(ii) s/he appears to be entitled to such status; or
(iii) the Party on which s/he depends claims such status on his/her behalf by notification to the Detaining Power or to the Protecting Power.[172]

The effectiveness of the *prima facie* presumption not only of lawful combatant status but also of POW status is supported by the principle that in cases of doubt, a captured person remains entitled to the POW status 'until such time as his status has been determined by a competent tribunal'.[173]

Article 45(1) of Protocol I, which adopts a combined approach of both factual and procedural criteria, purports to elucidate the imprecise meaning of Article 5 of the Third Geneva Convention.[174] Contrary to the position of Article 5(2) of the Third Geneva Convention, the implication of Article 45 of the Protocol I is that with the presumption of POW status, it assigns onus of proof to a capturing state claiming that there is doubt as to the legal status of a captive.[175] While such a novel approach may cast doubt on the customary law status of Article 45(1) of Protocol I, it is possible to describe a norm prescribing the general presumption of POW status for all participants in hostilities as *evolving* into a customary rule.[176] As Naqvi notes,[177] the fact that for all the US non-ratification of Protocol I, the 1997 US Army Regulation recognises the right of a captured person, who does not appear to be a prisoner of war, to assert entitlement to POW status and to have this question determined before a competent tribunal, suggests that the US treats such a right as reflective of customary law. As discussed above, the practice of the United States during the Vietnam War has contributed to the progressive transformation of the presumptive status rule into a customary norm. While abandoning the initial approach that confined the application of POW status to the North Vietnamese regular forces, the United States decided to accord the privileged status to the Vietcong as well.[178]

Article 45(2) in Protocol I has somewhat remedied the deficiency concerning the absence of the right of a detained person who is not being held as a POW by a 'competent tribunal', to reassert such status before a judicial tribunal adjudicating

---

172. Art. 45(1), first sentence, Additional Protocol I.
173. Art. 45(1), second sentence, Additional Protocol I.
174. *Commentary, Protocol I,* op. cit. n. 98, at p. 544, para. 1726.
175. Ibid., at p. 456, para. 1730. See also Naqvi, loc. cit. n. 163, at p. 576.
176. Naqvi, ibid., at p. 592.
177. Ibid., at p. 593.
178. Mundis, loc. cit. n. 5, at p. 326.

on the legality of his/her acts of hostilities.[179] The 'judicial tribunal' in Article 45 (2) may differ from the 'competent tribunal' in Article 45(1).[180] The 'judicial tribunal' must re-examine the legal status of a captive who is tried for an offence arising out of the hostilities and who, though not held as a prisoner of war by a 'competent tribunal' under the first paragraph, claims such status.[181] The ICRC Commentary on Protocol I suggests that Article 45 of Protocol I adopts a 'two-tiered system'.[182] First, a 'competent tribunal' must be set up to determine POW status where substantial doubt can be cast on the general presumption. Second, as stated by the Rapporteur of Committee III when drafting Protocol I, in case a captive who is held to be not entitled to a prisoner of war status is charged with an offence arising out of hostilities, a 'judicial tribunal' must adjudicate *de novo* his/her legal status.[183] According to Article 45(2) of Protocol I, '[w]henever possible', the adjudication on legal status must precede the trial for an offence by a judicial tribunal,[184] as all procedural protections accorded to prisoners of war by the Third Geneva Convention hinge on such determinations. As the Commentary on Protocol I notes, in some instances such determinations, on whose outcome Article 44(4) depends, are possible only after examining the merits of the accusation in relation to the compliance with the requirements prescribed in Article 44(3), especially the requirement of carrying arms openly.[185] The judicial tribunal, which may or may not be the same one that tries the offence,[186] can be either civilian or military,[187] but it must provide all the necessary procedural guarantees pursuant to the Third or the Fourth Geneva Convention and, otherwise, in conformity with Article 75 of Protocol I.[188] If a captive is held to be a prisoner of war, Articles 84 and 102 of the Third Geneva Convention apply, with the consequence that s/he can be tried only by a military tribunal applying procedural guarantees as afforded by that Convention.[189]

---

179. *Official Records*, op. cit. n. 98, Vol. XV p. 433, CDDH/III/338; and *Commentary, Protocol I,* op. cit. n. 98, para. 1752.

180. Naqvi, loc. cit. n. 163, at p. 578.

181. *Official Records*, op. cit. n. 98, Vol. XV, p. 433, CDDH/III/338.

182. Naqvi, loc. cit. n. 163, at p. 579.

183. *Official Records,* op. cit. n. 98, Vol. XV, at 433, CDDH/III/338.

184. *Commentary, Protocol I,* op. cit. n. 98, para. 1755

185. Ibid., para. 1755.

186. *Official Records*, op. cit. n. 98, Vol. XV, at 433, CDDH/III/338.

187. *Commentary, Protocol I,* op. cit. n. 98, para. 1753.

188. Ibid., para. 1754

189. Ibid., para. 1753.

7.   THE LEGAL STATUS OF THE TALIBAN AND THE AL QAEDA
        DETAINEES

7.1   **The legal status of Taliban soldiers captured prior to 5 December
        2001**

The United States government initially treated both the Taliban and Al Qaeda soldiers as 'battlefield detainees' and 'unlawful combatants', refusing to apply the
Third Geneva Convention both to the Taliban and Al Qaeda.[190] However, on 7
February 2001, President Bush announced that the Third Geneva Convention, to
which both Afghanistan and the United States are parties, would apply to the
armed conflict between the Taliban and the United States, but not to the 'armed
conflict' between Al Qaeda and the United States.[191] To that extent, the Bush administration did not succumb to the dubious interpretation that the Taliban soldiers
were 'irregular armies' akin to those of warlords, who were not 'members of the
armed forces' within the meaning of Article 4A(1). Such an interpretation could
not have countered the objection that, although recognition was granted by only
three countries, the Taliban government exercised 'effective control' over most of
Afghanistan.[192]

Despite the pronouncement to apply the Third Geneva Convention to Taliban
soldiers, it was decided that since the Taliban soldiers did not meet some of the
four conditions of lawful combatants set out in Article 4A(2) of the Convention,
they would be stripped of the privilege to be treated as prisoners of war. According
to the Bush administration, the Taliban personnel failed to comply with the two
requirements of wearing a fixed distinctive sign recognisable at a distance and of
undertaking operations pursuant to the laws and customs of war.[193] The concern
that the Taliban (and Al Qaeda) captives would lose protective status was only
slightly assuaged by the subsequent announcement that they would nonetheless be
treated humanely, in accordance with the general principles of the Convention, and
that the United States would allow the ICRC access to each detainee.[194]

One policy-oriented explanation of the US intransigency over the legal status of
Taliban personnel is that they provided support to Al- Qaeda.[195] The thrust of such
argument is that offering sanctuary to Al Qaeda personnel was tantamount to a
violation of international law that can warrant the denial of POW status to the

---

190. White House Spokesman, Ari Fleischer, Press Briefing, 28 January 2002. Available at <http://
www.whitehouse.gov/news/releases/2002/01>.
191. White House Fact Sheet: Status of Detainees at Guantánamo, 7 February 2002, at <http://
usinfo.state.gov/topical/pol/terror/02020700.htm> or at <http://www.state.gov/p/sa/rls/fs/7910.htm>.
Reprinted in this volume at p. 662.
192. Aldrich, loc. cit. n. 4, at p. 894. See also the *Tinoco Concessions* Arbitration, *supra* n. 45, p.
369, which was grounded on the concept of effective control to meld the constitutive and declaratory
effects of recognition.
193. Aldrich, ibid., at p. 895.
194. White House Fact Sheet: Status of Detainees at Guantánamo (7 February 2002), *supra* n. 228.
195. Ibid.

Taliban.[196] However, while logistical support to Al Qaeda both in peace and in an armed conflict is contrary to international law, this does not, *ipso facto*, amount to a failure to abide by the requirements of the *jus in bello*.[197] Such argument also sits ill with the non-reciprocal nature of the obligations of the Geneva Conventions, as evidenced by common Article 1(1), which provides the duty to 'respect and to ensure respect' for the rules of the Geneva Convention '*in all circumstances*'.[198] There has also been a suggestion that the granting of POW status to the Taliban and Al Qaeda soldiers would frustrate an attempt to obtain vital intelligence information, as it would debar the US from questioning a POW on anything more than his or her name, rank, date of birth and personal or serial number.[199] However, such a concern must not affect the juridical exercise of determining the POW status of the captured Taliban soldiers.

The dearth of evidence, especially in relation to the failure of Taliban soldiers to distinguish themselves from civilians, makes it difficult to warrant the argument against the granting of POW status. It is questionable whether an assumption can be made that *all* units of the Taliban forces were indistinguishable. Further, an assumption that most Taliban soldiers might have breached the laws and customs of war would not justify measures to treat all of them in a blanket manner.[200] Such generalisation would create a slippery slope of abuse. It should be recalled that the decisions of North Korea during the Korean War and of North Vietnam during the Vietnam War to deny POW status to US soldiers was based on the argument that the United States was an aggressor state and that some of its personnel had committed war crimes.[201]

As explained before, it was the implicit understanding at the 1949 Diplomatic Conference that the four defined criteria as set out in Article 4A(2) must be fulfilled by members of the regular armed forces, militia and volunteer forces. The United States could, however, have followed the mode of interpretation that the four defined criteria under Article 4A(2) are only declaratory conditions for regular forces under Article 4A(1), so that all the captured Taliban members should be deemed as prisoners of war. Following this construction, the forcible transfer to and confinement of Taliban captives at Guantánamo Bay would run afoul of the requirement, as provided in Article 118 of the Third Geneva Convention, that prisoners of war must be released and repatriated upon the termination of active hostilities, except in case of pending criminal proceedings against them.[202] Be that as it may, the fact that, in harmony with the drafters' view, the United States has con-

---

196. Wedgwood, loc. cit. n. 5, at p. 895.
197. Aldrich, loc. cit. n. 4, at p. 895.
198. Emphasis added.
199. Roberts, loc. cit. n. 18, at p. 24.
200. Aldrich, loc. cit. n. 4, at p. 895.
201. Ibid., pp. 895-896. Such an argument implies that these two states regarded the requirement of complying with humanitarian law as constitutive of the entitlement to POW qualification. It should be noted that North Vietnam, together with other former Socialist countries, formed a reservation to Art. 85 of the Third Geneva Convention to the effect that perpetrators of war crimes, if convicted, would not be entitled to POW status.
202. Rowe, loc. cit. n. 4, at p. 317.

sidered the four criteria to cover regular forces as well does not justify its continuing failure to establish a 'competent tribunal' to determine the status of members of the Taliban. As will be discussed below, according to Article 5 of the Third Geneva Convention, until the 'doubt' over their legal status is fully resolved by a competent tribunal, members of regular armed forces like Taliban soldiers entertain the presumption that they are *ipso facto* deemed as entitled to the rights and privileges as POWs. The difficulty in interrogating those classified as POWs cannot be pleaded to warrant the denial of, or the limitation upon, the basic rights accorded to POWs. They can be compelled to disclose only limited information, and they cannot be confined except in cases of penal or disciplinary sanctions.[203] With respect to those Taliban soldiers who may be guilty of war crimes, they could be prosecuted while remaining POWs.[204]

In relation to the captured Taliban soldiers of foreign nationality, such as John Walker Lindh (the US citizen) and Aïrat Vakhitov (the Russian citizen),[205] it could be said that they were members of militia or volunteer corps forming part of the Taliban's regular armed forces, as governed by Article 4A(1). The incorporation of foreigners into the regular armed forces as fully integrated members does not impair the qualification for prisoners of war status.[206] As Cryer notes,[207] to deprive such foreign Taliban of POW status on the basis that they could be described as mercenaries – a highly unlikely event –could not counter two objections. First, Article 47 of Additional Protocol I, which stipulates that mercenaries are stripped of POW status, is not part of customary law. Second, the motivation of such foreigners was not based on substantial financial reward. The foreign Taliban soldiers should receive the same treatment as the Afghan Taliban soldiers, meaning that they must be granted POW status until a competent tribunal within the meaning of Article 5 of the Third Geneva Convention determines their legal status in light of the four criteria.

7.2   Taliban soldiers captured in the post-Bonn process

To the knowledge of the author, there is no reported case of a foreign Taliban soldier still operative in Afghanistan, so that the following analysis assumes that all the active Taliban members are Afghan nationals. With respect to the Taliban soldiers who have been captured by the US-led coalition forces or by the newly formed Afghan armed forces since the Bonn Agreement of 5 December 2001, it must be noted that the nature of ongoing armed conflict has shifted from international to internal armed conflict. This means that the international humanitarian law applicable to international armed conflicts and concerning POWs has ceased

---

203. Aldrich, loc. cit. n. 4, at p. 896.

204. Ibid.

205. See S. Shihab, 'Des "talibans" rusés détenus à Guantánamo refusent d'être extradés vers Moscou', *Le Monde* (14 August 2003) p. 4.

206. L.C. Green, *The Contemporary Law of Armed Conflict*, 2nd edn. (Manchester, Manchester University Press 2000) at p. 199.

207. Cryer, loc. cit. n. 4, at pp. 70-71.

to apply, with the result that only customary law applicable during internal armed conflicts, namely, common Article 3 of the Geneva Conventions, and customary parts of Protocol II apply to the new Afghan government and to their armed forces, as well as to resurgent Taliban rebels. The Taliban soldiers have been converted into insurgents who are aligned with the Al Qaeda and Mujaheddin fighters.

Since Afghanistan has become an ally of the United States, the Taliban remnants have not 'fallen into the power of the enemy' within the meaning of Article 4A *chapeau* of the Third Geneva Convention,[208] and are not deemed prisoners of war under that Convention. Note should also be taken of Article 87(2) of the Third Geneva Convention, according to which the courts and authorities of the detaining power must take into account 'the fact that the accused, not being a national of the detaining power, is not bound to it by any duty of allegiance, and that he is in its power as the result of circumstances independent of his own will'. The obligation to make allowance for the accused being a non-national can also be found in Article 100(3) of the Convention relating to the death sentence.[209]

Captured Taliban soldiers are entitled to minimum guarantees as laid down in common Article 3 of the Geneva Conventions and to customary humanitarian rules applicable to internal armed conflict, many of which may derive from Additional Protocol II. It must be noted that the rights and privileges as laid down in Article 5 of Protocol II go beyond the minimum guarantees as provided in Article 75 of Protocol I. A detaining power is enjoined to safeguard humane treatment, due process rights, as well as even economic, social and cultural rights. It is arguable that the rule embodied in Article 5 of Protocol II, which is distilled from the essence of the International Covenant on Civil and Political Rights and the International Covenant on Economic, Social and Cultural Rights, has reached the status of customary law.[210]

7.3   The legal status of Al Qaeda soldiers

7.3.1   *Preliminary observations*

Controversy over whether the Al Qaeda soldiers are regarded as belligerents or combatants entitled to the status of prisoners of war has had earlier equivalents.[211] Al Qaeda, which is not an insurgent entitled to the recognition of a belligerent status, lacks international legal personality. The strict juridical construction might lead to the conclusion that there existed no armed conflict between the coalition forces and the Al Qaeda between 6/7 October and 5 December 2001, so that the Al Qaeda members might be treated as 'international outlaws' or 'enemy combatants',

---

208. *Commentary, GCIII*, op. cit. n. 72, at pp. 50-51.

209. All these provisions may, however, suggest that the Third Geneva Convention is based on the assumption that prisoners of war owed no allegiance to the detaining power: Rosas, loc. cit. n. 81, at p. 384.

210. The ICRC's Commentary on Protocol II is silent on whether this provision has attained the status of customary law: *Commentary, Protocol II,* op. cit. n. 34, paras. 4564- 4596.

211. Baxter, loc. cit. n. 108, at pp. 323-45; and Levie, op. cit. n. 71, at pp. 76-84.

who would be disentitled to the benefits of humanitarian law. However, close appraisal needs to be made of the argument that the conflict between the coalition forces and Al Qaeda might be subsumed into the international armed conflict between the anti-terror coalition and the Taliban government.

Two modes of distinction need to be made for the purpose of appraising the legal status of members of Al-Qaeda. First, as with the Taliban soldiers, the demarcation point of 5 December 2001 proves crucial to elucidating their legal status. Second, analysis must focus on whether the nationality of Al Qaeda members, namely the distinction between Afghan nationals and non-Afghan nationals, may give rise to different outcomes in assessing their legal status.

7.3.2   *Al Qaeda members captured prior to 5 December 2001*

With regard to Al Qaeda members captured prior to 5 December 2001, query is needed as to whether Al Qaeda was an independent force analogous to 'other militia' or 'other volunteer corps' within the meaning of Article 4A(2) of the Third Geneva Convention. The Al Qaeda soldiers do not meet three of the four conditions as set out in Article 4A(2). They have failed to distinguish themselves openly from civilians by not wearing uniforms and a fixed distinctive sign and not carrying arms openly. They have also patently avowed to disregard the laws and customs of war. As members of a transnational criminal organisation, Al Qaeda soldiers are subject to trial and punishment under national criminal law.[212] In that sense, the Al Qaeda soldiers can be treated as 'unprivileged belligerents' under humanitarian law, who are entitled only to minimum guarantees as laid down in Article 75 of Protocol I. These guarantees include respect for physical and mental integrity and due process rights, which are deemed as ripening into customary humanitarian law. The Al Qaeda members are also beneficiaries of basic human rights, such as the freedom from torture or other form of maltreatment, the right to life, freedom from forced labour, and the freedom from *ex post facto* application of criminal law, all of which are designated as non-derogable even in time of war under international human rights law and as such considered as part of *jus cogens*.[213] In the realm of international criminal law, their tactic of feigning civilian, non-combatant status can be punished as a war crime of perfidy.[214]

Further, captured Al Qaeda soldiers can remain beneficiaries of the protections under the Geneva Civilian Convention.[215] Examinations are needed in respect of the contingency of the guarantees under the Fourth Geneva Convention upon the concept of nationality. In relation to the Al Qaeda soldiers of Afghan nationality, their participation in armed hostilities render them 'hostile civilians' in the sense of Article 5 of the Fourth Geneva Convention.[216] While activities hostile to the security of the belligerent state can exonerate it from ensuring rights and privileges of

---

212. Aldrich, loc. cit. n. 4, at pp. 893 and 898.
213. See Human Rights Committee, General Comment 29, CCPR/C/21/Rev.1/Add.11, para. 11.
214. See Gasser, loc. cit. n. 4, at pp. 557 et seq.
215. See Aldrich, loc. cit. n. 4, at p. 893, fn. 12.
216. See also Art. 51(3) of Additional Protocol I (which can be described as a customary rule); and

civilians as laid down under that Convention, the right to be treated humanely and the 'rights of fair and regular trial' are specifically classified as non-derogable under that provision. Nevertheless, the entitlement to such minimum guarantees does not mean the granting of immunity from prosecution for war crimes or other criminal conduct.[217]

The overwhelming majority of the Al Qaeda soldiers are non-Afghan nationals, who have not been sent by the states of their nationalities. As with foreign Taliban members, they are not mercenaries, since their motivation can be explained less by 'the desire of private gain' than by spiritual conviction, without any expectation of 'material compensation substantially in excess of that promised or paid to combatants of similar ranks and functions in the armed forces of that Party'.[218] Again, akin to the Taliban soldiers captured by the American forces in the post-Bonn situation, since these Al Qaeda captives are nationals of states with which the United States have had 'normal diplomatic representation', the strict legal construction of the concept of 'protected persons' under Article 4(1) and (2) of the Fourth Geneva Convention suggests that the Civilian Convention might not apply to them.[219] This means that while the Al Qaeda soldiers belonging to the nationality of the co-belligerent states which can exercise diplomatic protection against the United States, such as nationals of the United Kingdom and Saudi Arabia, preserve the status of foreign nationals,[220] they would be disentitled to the status of 'protected persons' under the Fourth Geneva Convention. Indeed, the ICRC's Commentary on the Fourth Geneva Convention envisions two classes of persons under this concept: first, enemy nationals found within the national territory of each of the Parties to the conflict; and second, the population of occupied territories, bar the nationals of the occupying power.[221] Those civilians placed outside the status of 'protected persons' can remain beneficiaries of the protective regime under Part II (Articles 13-26) of the Fourth Geneva Convention, which, according to Article 13, applies to 'the whole of the populations' of the belligerent states, 'without any adverse distinction based, in particular, on race, nationality, religion or political opinion'. However, they would be excluded from the most substantive protections as laid down in Part III (Articles 27-78), which are reserved only to 'protected persons'.

Art. 82 of the Instructions for the Government of Armies of the United States in the Field (Lieber Code).

217. Gasser, loc. cit. n. 4, at p. 568.

218. Art. 47(2) Additional Protocol I.

219. Rowe, loc. cit. n. 4 at p. 316 (though without distinction based on nationality or on the signature of the Bonn Agreement). See also the ICRC's Commentary on Geneva Convention IV, Art. 4, which states that:

'They [nationals of a co-belligerent State] are not considered to be protected persons so long as the State whose nationals they are has normal diplomatic representation in the belligerent State or with the Occupying Power. It is assumed in this provision that the nationals of co-belligerent States, that is to say, of allies, do not need protection under the Convention.'

J.S. Pictet, ed., *Commentary on the Fourth Geneva Convention Relative to the Protection of Civilian Persons in Time of War,* (hereinafter *Commentary, GCIV),* (Geneva, ICRC 1958) p. 48. Available at <http://www.icrc.org/IHL>.

220. Gasser, loc. cit. n. 4, at p. 568.

221. *Commentary, GCIV,* op. cit. n. 219, at p. 46.

The main criticism of such a rigidly formalistic view is that the subjective standard should also be used to assess nationality, taking into account the sense of allegiance held by individual persons in question. In the *Čelebići* case, a Trial Chamber of the ICTY was asked to decide whether the Bosnian Serb victims of the alleged offences could be considered 'protected persons' in relation to the detaining power, the Bosnian government. The Trial Chamber emphasized the need to construe the notion of nationality flexibly and to take into account an individual person's link to a specific ethnic group.[222] In the subsequent *Tadić* case, the Appeal Chambers of the ICTY reinforced this approach, ruling that the determination of individual persons' status as 'protected persons' must focus on whether or not they owe allegiance to a party to the conflict in whose hands they are, rather than on the formal link of nationality.[223] The Appeals Chamber confirmed this rationale in the *Čelebići* case.[224] Such 'creative interpretation' by the ICTY serves to expand the protective scope of the Geneva Conventions based on substantive links between an individual and a party to the conflict.[225] The line of reasoning that the Appeals Chamber of the ICTY adopted in the *Tadić* and *Čelebići* decisions needs to be imported into the appraisal of the nationality of Al Qaeda members. The non-Afghan Al Qaeda members should be treated in the same manner as Afghan comrades, namely as 'hostile civilians' within the meaning of Article 5 of the Fourth Geneva Convention.

7.3.3   Al Qaeda soldiers captured after 5 December 2001

Inquiry must be made with respect to the legal status of the Al Qaeda soldiers who have been captured after the initiation of Bonn process. It may be argued that the Al Qaeda remnants are considered as fully integrated into the Taliban-led insurgents in the post-Bonn process, so that they may be treated in the same manner as Taliban soldiers, irrespective of their different nationalities. As discussed above, the incorporation of aliens into a belligerent force is lawful, provided that such persons are fully integrated as members of that force.[226] The principle of non-discrimination based on nationality is embodied in Article 16 of the Third Geneva Convention. As with the Taliban soldiers, the Al Qaeda soldiers captured after the initiation of the Bonn process are considered entitled to minimum guarantees as stipulated in common Article 3 of the Geneva Conventions, as well as to customary law governing internal armed conflict, many of which may derive from Protocol II. In respect of Afghan nationals of Al Qaeda who have fallen into the hands of the fledging Afghan army, or who have been transferred to the Afghan interim government from the capturing US armed forces, they are treasonable, while en-

---

222. *Prosecutor v. Delalić, Mucić, Delić and Landžo* (the *Čelebići* case), Case No. IT-96-21-T, Judgment, 16 November 1998 at pp. 89-99, paras. 236-266, in particular paras. 251-266.

223. *Prosecutor v. Tadić*, Case No. IT-94-1-A, Appeals Judgment, 15 July 1999, paras. 165-168.

224. *Prosecutor v. Delalić, Mucić, Delić and Landžo* (the *Čelebići* case), Case No. IT-96-21-A, Appeals Judgment, 20 February 2001, paras. 51-106.

225. Provost, op. cit. n. 28, at pp. 39-40.

226. See Green, op. cit. n. 206, at p. 199.

titled to the minimum core of guarantees as outlined above. Members of Al Qaeda who are nationals of the belligerent or co-belligerent parties, such as citizens of the United States or the United Kingdom, are equally treasonable under the laws of the respective countries while benefiting from such guarantees.

7.4   The Article 5 Tribunal and the Taliban/Al Qaeda soldiers

With respect to Taliban soldiers captured prior to the establishment of the Karzai government, it must be questioned whether the persistent refusal of the US to grant POW status to any and all of them suggests that the US has had no doubt about their legal status. However effective and scrupulous it may be, the screening procedure for the captured Taliban soldiers before their transfer to Guantánamo Bay for the purpose of criminal investigation cannot be equated to an Article 5 tribunal under the Third Geneva Convention. This can be readily recognised by the denial of the right of access to court inherent in Article 5. The practice of the US with respect to the Taliban soldiers departs from the interpretation of Article 5 of the Third Geneva Convention, as provided in the *United States Army Field Manual 27-10, The Law of Land Warfare.* [227] According to this *Manual,*

> '[t]he foregoing provision [Article 5] applies to any person not appearing to be entitled to prisoner-of-war status who has committed a belligerent act or has engaged in hostile activities in aid of the armed forces and who asserts that he is entitled to treatment as a prisoner of war or concerning whom any other doubt of a like nature exists.' [228]

The US *Field Manual 27-10* requires an 'Article 5 tribunal' to be a 'board of not less than three officers acting according to such procedures as may be prescribed'. [229] As discussed above, wilful removal from a prisoner of war of the rights of fair and regular trial amounts to a grave breach of the Third Geneva Convention. [230]

As regards the relevant tribunal to determine the legal status of Al Qaeda soldiers under Article 5 of the Third Geneva Convention, their status is generally accepted as raising little doubt and they are presumed to be non-POWs, so that there may be no obligation to establish an Article 5 tribunal under the Third Geneva Convention. Yet, Article 45(1) of Protocol I requires that in case a captive claims such status, such a person must be given the entitlement to POW status till a competent tribunal determines his/her status. The onus of proof lies on the US authorities. The requirement and the rights prescribed under Article 45(1) and (2) of Protocol I have matured into customary law and as such are binding upon the United States. [231]

---

227. Aldrich, loc. cit. n. 4, at pp. 897-898.
228. *US Army Field Manual, supra* n. 84.
229. Ibid., para. 71(c).
230. Art. 130 of the Third Geneva Convention.
231. Aldrich, loc. cit. n. 4, at p. 898.

8.   CONCLUDING REMARKS

The continuing controversy over the treatment of Taliban and Al Qaeda soldiers at Guantánamo Bay in Cuba, especially the indefinite nature of their detention and the prospect of military trials, has attracted significant international publicity and widespread criticism. The ICRC expressed its concerns about the standard of treatment at Guantánamo Bay.[232] The ICRC has been involved in an on-site visit and interviewing of detainees since 18 January 2002.[233] In the meantime the Inter-American Commission on Human Rights indicated precautionary measures, urging the United States to adopt 'the urgent measures necessary' to have the legal status of each of the detainees determined by a competent tribunal and to furnish them with the legal protections commensurate with the 'minimum standards of non-derogable rights'.[234] In its letter dated 23 July 2002, the Inter-American Commission reiterated the importance of providing 'effective and fair mechanisms' for determining their legal status, and emphasized that both Article 5 of the Third Geneva Convention and Article XVIII of the 1948 American Declaration of the Rights and Duties of Man, which provides the right to access to court, must be given 'practical effect'.[235]

A report that the United States is preparing for the military trials of seven detainees, including two British citizens, who may be prosecuted on the basis of evidence obtained through plea bargains and may face executions,[236] has re-fuelled unrest and furore among governments around the world. The Parliament Assembly of the Council of Europe passed Resolution 1340 on 26 June 2003, calling on the United States to allow the status of each of more than 600 combatants and non-combatants in United States military custody, especially those held in Guantánamo Bay, to be determined on a case-by-case basis. Resolution 1340 also urged the member states of the Council of Europe whose citizens are held either in Afghanistan and Guantánamo Bay or elsewhere to seek diplomatic protection or extradition of those threatened with the death penalty.[237]

---

232. K. Sengupta, 'Campaign Against Terrorism: American Forces "May Be Breaking POW Convention"', *The Independent* (14 January 2002) at p. 9.

233. ICRC, 'First ICRC visit to Guantánamo Bay prison camp', Press Release 02/03, 18 January 2002.

234. Inter-American Commission on Human Rights, Detainees at Guantánamo Bay, Cuba, Request for Precautionary Measures (petitioned by the Center for Constitutional Rights), 41 *ILM* (2002) pp. 532, at 534. <http://www.photius.com/rogue_nations/Guantánamo.html>. See also Response of the United States to Request for Precautionary Measures – Detainees in Guantánamo Bay, Cuba (15 April 2002), 41 *ILM* (2002) p. 1015.

235. The Inter-American Commission of Human Rights, the letter dated 23 July 2002, as referred to, in *R. (Abbasi)* v. *The Secretary of State for Foreign and Commonwealth Affairs*, Court of Appeal, 6 November 2002 (2002) WL 31452052; [2002] EWCA Civ 1598, para. 21. The Abassi decision is reprinted in this volume at p. 604.

236. See for instance, J. Burns, J. Eaglesham, M. Huband and P. Spiegel, 'Blair may let US tribunal try UK al-Qaeda suspects', *The Financial Times* (10 July 2003) p. 1.

237. Resolution 1340, 26 June 2003, 'Rights of persons held in the custody of the United States in Afghanistan or Guantánamo Bay'.

Despite the clamours of the international community, the Bush administration has yet to establish a judicial procedure for clarifying the legal status of the detainees, making their indefinite detention arbitrary. Nor has it offered minimum due process guarantees, such as the right to contact legal counsel, in contravention to the Third Geneva Convention and international human rights law. There is also a denial of the right to contact their own consular representatives in violation of Article 36(1) of the Vienna Convention on Consular Relations.[238] The most disturbing of all may be the fact that among the detainees at Guantánamo Bay are a number of children, including even those who are between 13 and 15 years of age transferred from the Bagram Air Base in 2003.[239] Subjecting 'child soldiers' to the same harsh detention regime as adult detainees and to the possibility of capital punishment amounts to violations of the customary equivalent of Article 77 of Protocol I, which requires special safeguards for captured child soldiers, including the prohibition of the death penalty for children who were younger than 18 years at the time of the offence.[240] Such guarantees must be proffered irrespective of their POW status.[241] Military trials for children would also contravene Article 40 of the 1989 UN Convention on the Rights of the Child, which provides detailed guarantees for children in judicial proceedings.

While issues of the constitutional review of the detentions in Camp X-Ray exceeds the limit of this paper, it must be noted that the efforts to secure the US constitutional guarantees of *habeas corpus* and other due process rights before the US courts have so far been unsuccessful on jurisdictional grounds.[242] Nor has the attempt to stretch the concept of diplomatic protection to secure the rights of a detained person in another country borne fruit.[243]

It is incumbent on the Bush administration to put an end to the limbo status of the detainees at Guantánamo Bay by establishing a system of adjudication on the status of detainees and furnishing them with the rights and privileges as prisoners of war until their status is determined on an individual basis. Even those detainees

---

238. See *LaGrand Case* (*Germany* v. *United States*), Judgment of 27 June 2001; and the pending case of *Avena and Other Mexican Nationals* (*Mexico* v. *United States*), (2001) *ICJ Rep.* (forthcoming).

239. See Parliamentary Assembly of the Council of Europe, Resolution 1340, 26 June 2003, 'Rights of persons held in the custody of the United States in Afghanistan or Guantánamo Bay.'

240. Note that it is a war crime to conscript or enlist children under the age of 15 into the armed forces or employ them to actively participate in hostilities. See Arts. 8(2)(b)(xxvi) and 8(2)(e)(vii) of the Rome Statute of the International Criminal Court, which correspond to Art. 77(2) of Protocol I and Art. 4(3)(c) of Protocol II respectively. Cf., Arts 1 and 2 of the Optional Protocol to the Convention on the Rights of the Child on the Involvement of Children in Armed Conflicts (2002) (the lowest age for combatants is set at 18).

241. Paras. 3-5 of Art. 77, Protocol I.

242. See *Rasul et al.* v. *George Walker Bush et al.*, United States District Court, District of Columbia, 30 July 2002, 215 F.Supp.2d 55; *Al Odah et al.* v. *United States of America et al.*, United States Court of Appeals, District of Columbia Circuit, 11 March 2003, 321 F.3d 1134; and *Hamdi* v. *Donald Rumsfeld,* United States Court of Appeals, Fourth Circuit, 9 July 2003, 337 F.3d 335. These judgements are reprinted in this volume at pp. 626-628 and 691-700. Note that in the *Hamdi* case, which awaits the decision of the Supreme Court in relation to petitions for *certiorari*, no question of jurisdiction arises because he is detained on US territory and claims US citizenship. See also C. Dyer, 'Judges Condemn Camp X-Ray', *The Guardian* (11 October 2003).

243. *Abbasi* case, *supra* n. 272, para. 12.

who are found not to meet the criteria for prisoners of war must be accorded the minimum guarantees of humane treatment as required under the customary rule, which derives from Article 75 of Additional Protocol I. The proposed military commissions[244] are hardly compatible with the right of accused persons to an 'independent and impartial tribunal' under international human rights law. It is also hard to see such commissions meeting the requirement of providing a 'fair and regular trial' within the meaning of Article 130 of the Third Geneva Convention.[245] Detainees who will stand trial are entitled to a fair trial, and the principle of equal arms in defense must be given full effect so that they can exercise the right to a legal counsel of their own choice, the right to appeal, the right to cross-examine witnesses and the right not to incriminate themselves. Further, the subordination of detainees solely of non-US nationality to the 'offshore regime' at Guantánamo Bay, which does not benefit from the US constitutional guarantees such as the right of *habeas corpus*, and to the military commissions, squarely contravenes the requirement, as laid down in Article 102 of the Third Geneva Convention, that prisoners of war be treated in the same judicial procedures as in the case for members of the national armed forces.

The late Judge Baxter observed that '[a]s the current tendency of the law of war appears to be to extend the protection of prisoner-of-war status to an ever-increasing group, it is possible to envisage a day when the law will be so retailored as to place all belligerents, however garbed, in a protected status'.[246] His insightful prognosis of both the criteria for lawful combatancy and the expanding protective status in future warfare can be most aptly presented at the current juncture, when puddles of academic ink have been spilt over the continuing row about the qualifications of Al Qaeda and Taliban soldiers for POWs. While the unprecedented nature of atrocities committed by Al Qaeda in the September 11 attacks hardly needs any further comment here, it is axiomatic, however trite, to emphasise the importance of the path of the humanitarian rule of law, along which democracy's enduring fight against terror must proceed. The exigency arising from the fight against terrorism must not distract the international community from the spirit underlying the Martens clause and the yearning of humanity for reinforcing (rather than undermining) the edifice of humanitarian law, the bulwark against the retreat into barbarity.

---

244. For the procedural rules for the commissions, see US Department of Defense Military Commission Order No.1, Procedures for Trials by Military Commissions of Certain Non-United States Citizens in the War against Terrorism (2002) <http://www.defenselink.mil/news/Mar2002/d20020321ord.pdf>. Reprinted in this volume at p. 766.

245. See also common Art. 3(1)(d), which requires the State Parties to provide 'judicial guarantees which are recognized as indispensable by civilised people'.

246. Baxter, loc. cit. n. 108, at p. 343.

WHAT FUTURE FOR THE DOCTRINE OF BELLIGERENT REPRISALS?[1]

Shane Darcy[2]

1.   INTRODUCTION

Throughout its extensive history, the doctrine of belligerent reprisals has caused controversy and provoked debate, none more so than in the Twentieth Century, with its unprecedented developments in the codification of the laws of armed conflict. Belligerent reprisals are *prima facie* unlawful acts taken against a party to an armed conflict that is violating the law for the purpose of coercing that party to cease its unlawful conduct.[3] Owing to this law enforcement function, belligerent reprisals have historically been treated as lawful acts, provided that they have been carried out in observance of a number of established principles. The rules laid

---

1. © S. Darcy, 2004.

2. B.A., LL.M. The author is currently a doctoral fellow at the Irish Centre for Human Rights, National University of Ireland, Galway.

3. For the most comprehensive treatment of the subject of belligerent reprisals see F. Kalshoven, *Belligerent Reprisals* (Leiden, Sijthoff 1971).

down in international humanitarian law have increasingly limited the scope for taking reprisals by excluding certain categories of persons and objects from being the lawful targets of reprisal actions. While palpable disagreement exists regarding the customary status of the law pertaining to belligerent reprisals, more fundamental dispute arises in relation to the desirability of the actual institution of belligerent reprisals itself.

This article will set out and analyse the numerous arguments made by academic writers, judges, government representatives, military personnel and non-governmental organisations in relation to the doctrine of belligerent reprisals. The stances that have been taken both in favour of the abandonment and of the retention of reprisals as a means of enforcing the laws of armed conflict will be critically analysed. Such a discussion, it is hoped, may assist in a better understanding of the divisive nature of the issue of belligerent reprisals and will also contribute to the debate on whether this doctrine has a viable future in contemporary international humanitarian law. First, it is necessary to briefly specify the customary rules governing recourse to reprisals and to outline the conventional laws that have progressively restricted belligerents' power to resort to such measures.

2.   THE LAW OF BELLIGERENT REPRISALS[4]

Measures taken in the name of belligerent reprisals must conform to a number of established rules in order that their inherent unlawfulness may be removed.[5] Belligerent reprisals may only be carried out in response to a prior violation of the laws of armed conflict and for the declared purpose of bringing about an end to that unlawful conduct. Reprisals may only be ordered by a competent authority and any recourse thereto must adhere strictly to the principles of subsidiarity and proportionality. The Manual of the Law of Wars on Land,[6] adopted in 1880 by the Institute of International Law, enumerates these requirements in its articles dealing with belligerent reprisals:

'Art. 85. Reprisals are formally prohibited in case the injury complained of has been repaired.
Art. 86. In grave cases in which reprisals appear to be absolutely necessary, their nature and scope shall never exceed the measure of the infraction of the laws of war committed by the enemy. They can only be resorted to with the authorization of the commander in chief. They must conform in all cases to the laws of humanity and morality.'

---

4. For a fuller discussion see S. Darcy, 'The Evolution of the Law of Belligerent Reprisals', 175 *Mil. LR* (2003) p. 184.
5. See C. Greenwood, 'The Twilight of the Law of Belligerent Reprisals', 20 *NYIL* (1989) pp. 35, at pp. 39-49; Darcy, loc. cit. n. 4, at pp. 187-196.
6. *The Laws of War on Land* (Oxford, 9 September 1880) text reproduced in D. Schindler and J. Toman, eds., *The Laws of Armed Conflict: A Collection of Conventions, Resolutions and Other Documents* (Dordrecht, Martinus Nijhoff 1988) pp. 35-48 [hereinafter Oxford Manual].

These customary requirements governing the doctrine of belligerent reprisals are widely accepted. Differences of opinion begin to arise, however, in relation to the treaty law which prohibits certain categories of persons and objects from being subject to reprisals.

Prisoners of war were the first category of persons against whom reprisals were forbidden. This rule in the 1929 Convention Relative to the Treatment of Prisoners of War[7] was supplemented by a similar provision in the more widely accepted 1949 Geneva Convention III Relative to the Treatment of Prisoners of War.[8] The 1949 Geneva Conventions also introduced provisions prohibiting the taking of reprisals against new categories of persons and objects: the wounded, sick, personnel, buildings and equipment protected by Geneva Convention I for the Amelioration of the Condition of Wounded and Sick in Armed Forces in the Field,[9] the wounded, sick, shipwrecked, personnel, vessels and equipment protected by Geneva Convention II for the Amelioration of the Condition of Wounded, Sick and Shipwrecked Members of Armed Forces at Sea[10] and civilians and their property protected by Geneva Convention IV Relative to the Protection of Civilian Persons in Time of War.[11] The 1954 Hague Convention for the Protection of Cultural Property in the Event of Armed Conflict[12] introduced a prohibition against 'any act directed by way of reprisals against cultural property'.[13]

The categories of persons and objects given protection from reprisal actions were expanded considerably by the rules set down in the 1977 Protocol Additional to the Geneva Conventions of 12 August 1949, and relating to the Protection of Victims of International Armed Conflicts (Protocol I).[14] The unlawfulness of reprisals against the wounded, sick and shipwrecked was reaffirmed, the definition of those categories of persons was widened and a number of new objects and persons necessary for the protection of the wounded sick and shipwrecked were also deemed immune from reprisals.[15] Part IV of the Protocol introduced reprisal prohibitions against the civilian population or civilians,[16] civilian objects,[17] cultural objects and places of worship,[18] objects indispensable to the survival of the civilian

---

7. Signed at Geneva, 27 July 1929, Art. 2, para. 3, text reproduced in Schindler and Toman, op. cit. n. 6, at pp. 339-366.
8. Adopted 12 August 1949, entered into force 21 October 1950, 75 *UNTS* 135, Art. 13, para. 3.
9. Adopted 12 August 1949, entered into force 21 October 1950, 75 *UNTS* 31, Art. 46.
10. Adopted 12 August 1949, entered into force 21 October 1950, 75 *UNTS* 85, Art. 47.
11. Adopted 12 August 1949, entered into force 21 October 1950, 75 *UNTS* 287, Art. 33, para. 3. Protected persons are defined in Art. 4 as 'Persons protected by the Convention are those who, at a given moment and in any manner whatsoever, find themselves, in case of a conflict or occupation, in the hands of a Party to the conflict or Occupying Power of which they are not nationals.'
12. Adopted 14 May 1954, entered into force 7 August 1956, 249 *UNTS* 240.
13. Ibid., Art. 4, para. 4.
14. Adopted 8 June 1977, entered into force 7 December 1978, 1125 *UNTS* 3-608.
15. Ibid., Art. 20. For the expanded definition of those categories of persons and the new categories added see Art. 8.
16. Ibid., Art. 51, para. 6.
17. Ibid., Art. 52, para. 1.
18. Ibid., Art. 53.

population,[19] the natural environment[20] and works and installations containing dangerous forces (i.e., dams, dykes and nuclear electrical generating stations).[21] The 1977 Protocol Additional to the Geneva Conventions of 12 August 1949, relating to the Protection of Victims of Non-International Armed Conflicts (Protocol II) remained deliberately silent on the issue of belligerent reprisals.[22]

One further restriction on reprisals has been added since 1977. The 1980 Protocol on Prohibitions or Restrictions on the Use of Mines, Booby Traps and Other Devices[23] prohibits the directing of those weapons by way of reprisal against the civilian population or against individual civilians.[24] An amendment to this instrument in 1996 extended the applicability of its prohibitions to both international and non-international armed conflicts.[25]

The reprisal provisions of the 1929 Prisoners of War Convention and the 1949 Geneva Conventions are relatively undisputed and owing to the near-universal ratification of the latter, would seem to have crystallised into rules of customary international law. The provisions of Additional Protocol I dealing with reprisals have, however, proved problematic for some states: several States Parties have entered reservations or made declarations to those provisions,[26] while the United States, which has not ratified that instrument, points to the prohibitions on reprisals as one of the hindrances to its ratification.[27]

Considerable controversy exists on two main issues which merit a brief mention here: whether the treaty rules in Additional Protocol I have been transformed into custom, and to what extent reprisals are prohibited in internal armed conflicts. The International Criminal Tribunal for the Former Yugoslavia (ICTY) has recently held that 'the rule which states that reprisals against the civilian population as such, or individual civilians, are prohibited in all circumstances, even when confronted by wrongful behaviour of the other party, is an integral part of customary international law and must be respected in all armed

---

19. Ibid., Art. 54, para. 4.

20. Ibid., Art. 55, para. 2.

21. Ibid., Art. 56, para. 4.

22. Adopted 8 June 1977, entered into force 7 December 1978, 1125 *UNTS* 609. See S.E. Nahlik, 'Belligerent Reprisals as Seen in the Light of the Diplomatic Conference on Humanitarian Law, Geneva, 1974-1977' 42 *Law and Contemporary Practice* 2 (1978) pp. 36, at pp. 63-64.

23. Protocol II, annexed to the Convention on Prohibitions or Restrictions on the Use of Certain Conventional Weapons which may be deemed to be excessively Injurious or to have Indiscriminate Effects, adopted 10 October 1980, entered into force 2 December 1983, 1342 *UNTS* 137-255; reprinted in Schindler and Toman, op. cit. n. 6, at p. 179.

24. Ibid., Art. 2, para. 3.

25. Amended Protocol on Prohibitions or Restrictions on the Use of Mines, Booby Traps and Other Devices (Amended Protocol II), amended 3 May 1996, 35 *ILM* 1206, Art. 1, para. 3.

26. See declarations by Germany, Italy and Egypt and strong reservation by the United Kingdom, reprinted in A. Roberts and R. Guelff, eds., *Documents on the Laws of War*, 3rd edn. (Oxford, Oxford University Press 2000) pp. 504-507, 511. See also declaration made by France on 11 April 2001, French text available on the international humanitarian law treaty database of the ICRC website at: <http://www.icrc.org/ihl.nsf/db8c9c8d3ba9d16f41256739003e6371/d8041036b40ebc44c1256a34004897b2?OpenDocument>, para. 11.

27. See A.D. Sofaer, 'The Rationale for the United States Decision', 82 *AJIL* (1988) p. 784, at p. 785.

conflicts'.[28] In a subsequent case, the ICTY held that the rule in Additional Protocol I prohibiting reprisals against civilians is declaratory of customary international law, and thus binding on all states, including those which have not yet signed that instrument.[29] To highlight the divergence of views on these issues, it suffices to note that two eminent authorities on the laws of belligerent reprisals, Frits Kalshoven and Christopher Greenwood, have both written pieces roundly castigating these findings of the ICTY.[30] This article may go some way towards explaining why bodies such as the ICTY, the International Committee of the Red Cross (ICRC) and the United Nations seek to interpret the existing law in such a manner as to preclude reprisal measures, particularly against civilians, in almost all circumstances, and why, on the other hand, states such as Egypt, France, Germany, the United Kingdom and the United States are so eager to retain belligerent reprisals as a means of enforcing the rules of international humanitarian law.

3.   THE CASE FOR ABANDONING THE DOCTRINE OF BELLIGERENT REPRISALS

One early commentator on the laws of war described belligerent reprisals in a way which encapsulates the central dilemma of the doctrine. J.M. Spaight referred to reprisals as 'the very saddest of all the necessities of war'.[31] The doctrine allows for violations of the laws in place, yet such derogation is necessary if those laws are to be enforced. Many of the arguments made in favour of abandoning the doctrine stem from belligerent reprisals intrinsic unlawfulness, while proponents argue that the doctrine is indispensable if the laws of armed conflict are to be properly enforced. This section will look at the arguments made by those parties opposed to the doctrine.

The most common criticisms made of the doctrine of belligerent reprisals is that reprisal measures inflict suffering on innocent persons by relying on a principle of collective responsibility,[32] that they are of dubious effectiveness as a law enforce-

---

28. *Prosecutor* v. *Martić*, Case No. IT-95-11-R61, Decision, 8 March 1996, 108 *ILR* 39, paras. 16-17, p. 47. See also Resolution 2675 (XXV) on the Basic Principles for the Protection of Civilian Populations in Armed Conflicts adopted by the United Nations General Assembly on 9 December 1970, UN GAOR, 25th Sess., Supp., No. 28, UN Doc. A/8028, reprinted in Schindler and Toman, op. cit. n. 6, at pp. 267-268.

29. *Prosecutor* v. *Zoran Kupreskić et al.*, Case No. IT-95-16-T, Judgement, 14 January 2000, paras. 527-535.

30. F. Kalshoven, 'Two Recent Decisions of the Yugoslavia Tribunal', in L.C. Vohrah, ed., *Man's inhumanity to man: Essays on International Law in Honour of Antonio Cassese* (The Hague, Kluwer Law International 2003) pp. 481-509; C. Greenwood, 'Belligerent Reprisals in the Jurisprudence of the International Criminal Tribunal for the Former Yugoslavia', in H. Fischer, C. Kress and S. Rolf Lüder, eds., *International and National Prosecution of Crimes under International Law: Current Developments* (Berlin, Anro Spitz 2001) p. 539.

31. J.M. Spaight, *War Rights on Land* (London, MacMillan 1911) p. 462.

32. See for example Nahlik, loc. cit. n. 22, at pp. 54, 56; R. Bierzanek, 'Reprisals as a Means of Enforcing the Laws of Warfare: The Old and the New Law', in A. Cassese, ed., *The New International Law of Armed Conflict* (Napoli, Editoriale Scientifica 1979) p. 232, at p. 239; F. Kalshoven, 'Human

ment mechanism,[33] with a tendency to lead to counter-reprisals,[34] and that they offer an opportunity for belligerents to violate the laws of armed conflict[35] and are thus highly open to abuse.[36] Other arguments against the doctrine is that reprisals are often motivated by revenge,[37] that their use may contravene basic human rights,[38] that they are militarily uneconomical,[39] and that it is difficult for the customary requirements governing recourse to reprisals to be met in wartime conditions.[40] It is also pointed out that there are other means available for enforcing the rules of international humanitarian law.[41]

3.1   Striking innocents

An unlawful act taken for the purpose of putting an end to an enemy's lawbreaking will almost invariably strike at persons who are not in any way responsible for the initial violation. The Oxford Manual describes belligerent reprisals as 'an exception to the general rule of equity, that an innocent person ought not to suffer for the guilty'.[42] A review of the post-Second World War case-law concerning reprisals shows that it was prisoners of war and civilians unconnected to the original offences that bore the brunt of reprisal actions.[43] Belligerent reprisals by their very nature rely on a principle of collective responsibility, whereby an enemy's military, government and civilian population are treated as a single group, and measures directed at certain members of that collective will, in theory, coerce the actual guilty members of the group to cease in their unlawful conduct. One commentator views reprisals as resting on the principle of vicarious liability, whereby 'all enemy

---

Rights, the Law of Armed Conflict, and Reprisals', 11 *International Review of the Red Cross* (1971) p. 183, at p. 186.

33. See for example Kalshoven, loc. cit. n. 30, at p. 481; F. Kalshoven, 'Belligerent Reprisals Revisited', 21 *NYIL* (1990) p. 43, at p. 60; A.R. Albrecht, 'War Reprisals in the War Crimes Trials and in the Geneva Conventions of 1949', 47 *AJIL* (1953) p. 590, at p. 592.

34. See for example Greenwood, loc. cit. n. 5, at p. 36; Kalshoven, loc. cit. n. 33, at p. 78; M.L. Walzer, *Just and Unjust Wars* (New York, Basic Books 1992) 2nd edn., p. 215.

35. See for example Major M.C.C. Bristol III, 'The Laws of War and Belligerent Reprisals against Enemy Civilian Populations', 21 *Air Force JAG Law Review* (1979) p. 397, at p. 421; G. Best, *Law and War since 1945* (Oxford, Oxford University Press 1994) p. 311.

36. See for example Greenwood, loc. cit. n. 5, at p. 36; G.I.A.D. Draper, 'The Enforcement and Implementation of the Geneva Conventions of 1949 and the Additional Protocols of 1977', 163 *Hague Recueil II* (1978) pp. 9, at pp. 34-35; G. von Glahn *The Occupation of Enemy Territory: A Commentary on the Law and Practice of Belligerent Occupation* (Minneapolis, University of Minnesota Press 1957) p. 235.

37. R. Provost, 'Reciprocity in Human Rights and Humanitarian Law', 65 *BYIL* (1994) p. 383, at p. 415.

38. E. Kwakwa, 'Belligerent reprisals in the Law of Armed Conflict', 27 *Stanford JIL* (1990) p. 49, at p. 60.

39. M.S. McDougal and F.P. Feliciano, *Law and Minimum World Public Order: The Legal Regulation of International Coercion* (New Haven, Yale University Press 1961) p. 689.

40. Best, op. cit. n. 35, at p. 311.

41. *Prosecutor* v. *Zoran Kupreskić et al., supra* n. 29, para. 532.

42. Op. cit. n. 6, Art. 84.

43. See Kalshoven, op. cit. n. 3, at pp. 216-263.

nationals [are] held accountable for the actions of national decision-makers or individual combatants'.[44] The ICTY has stated on this issue that

> 'Reprisals typically are taken in situations where the individuals personally responsible for the breach are either unknown or out of reach. These retaliatory measures are aimed instead at other more vulnerable individuals or groups. They are individuals or groups who may not even have any degree of solidarity with the presumed authors of the initial violation; they may share with them only the links of nationality and allegiance to the same rulers.'[45]

The notion of collective responsibility upon which the taking of reprisals is based has become increasingly at odds with the rules and spirit of contemporary international humanitarian law. In addition to the existing treaty prohibitions of reprisals, this legal regime also provides a comprehensive prohibition of acts of collective punishment and repeatedly stresses the individual nature of penal responsibility.[46] A principle of collective responsibility serves to undermine the principle of distinction by which belligerents must always distinguish between combatants and non-combatants.[47] Frits Kalshoven further points out that such a notion of group responsibility is at variance with the entire concept of human rights, which stresses the rights of individuals 'as distinct from his position as a member of the collectivity'.[48] The infusion of human rights norms into the laws of armed conflict is acknowledged by René Provost, who has recognised '... a slow but profound transformation of humanitarian law under the pervasive influence of human rights, a transformation that underlies the fact that belligerent reprisals and individual rights are fundamentally inconsistent legal concepts'.[49] A principle of collective responsibility which allows innocent persons to suffer for the wrongs of others contravenes both humanitarian and human rights law.

---

44. Bristol, loc. cit. n. 35, at p. 411.

45. *Prosecutor* v. *Zoran Kupreskić et al., supra* n. 29, para. 528.

46. For example Art. 50 of the 1907 Hague Regulations, annexed to Convention IV Respecting the Laws and Customs of War on Land, signed at The Hague, 18 October 1907, states that '[n]o general penalty, pecuniary or otherwise, shall be inflicted upon the population on account of the acts of individuals for which they cannot be regarded as jointly and severally responsible'. Art. 33 of the Fourth Geneva Convention establishes that '[n]o protected person may be punished for an offence he or she has not personally committed'. Both Additional Protocols to the Geneva Conventions of 1949 contain a common provision which sets out that 'no one shall be convicted of an offence except on the basis of individual penal responsibility', Art. 75(4)(b) of Protocol I and Art. 6(2)(b) of Protocol II. On the customary status of the prohibition of collective punishment see S. Darcy, 'Punitive House Demolitions, the Prohibition of Collective Punishment, and the Supreme Court of Israel', 21 *Penn. State ILR* (2003) pp. 477, at pp. 488-491.

47. Kwakwa, loc. cit. n. 38, at p. 73. He asserts that this distinction is 'vital both to civil society and to basic human dignity', ibid., at p. 59.

48. Kalshoven, loc. cit. n. 32, at p. 186. See also Bierzanek, loc. cit. n. 32, at p. 244.

49. Provost, loc. cit. n. 37, at p. 427. The above-cited phrase was adopted almost verbatim by the ICTY in its discussion on belligerent reprisals in *Prosecutor* v. *Zoran Kupreskić et al., supra* n. 29, para. 529.

This 'inherent injustice' of reprisals[50] was a recurring theme during the debates on reprisals which took place during the Diplomatic Conference on the Reaffirmation and Development of International Humanitarian Law Applicable in Armed Conflicts held in Geneva, from 1974 to 1977.[51] The representative of the Ukrainian Soviet Socialist Republic pointed out that 'the placing of responsibility on some persons for acts committed by others was tantamount to applying the principle of objective incrimination, which was prohibited in criminal law'.[52] He went on to ask whether the Conference, from a moral point a view, could 'approve measures directed against the innocent and thus overlook the purposes for which it had been summoned'.[53] Another delegate stated that it would be 'unthinkable that an inhuman act should provoke a similar act involving innocent persons'.[54] For this reason and others, the end result of this Conference was that reprisal prohibitions were extended to previously unprotected persons, in particular to members of the enemy civilian population.

The argument that reprisals inflict suffering on innocent persons may also have resonance beyond the sphere of conventionally prohibited reprisals, i.e., permissible reprisals against enemy soldiers, through the use of prohibited weapons or the unlawful use of non-prohibited weapons. Soldiers who have done no more than engaged in the lawful wartime conduct of killing their opponents may, for example, be lawfully targeted by weapons which cause 'superfluous injury or unnecessary suffering',[55] on account of the unlawful conduct of some of their colleagues. It might be said, for arguments sake, that these targets of belligerent reprisals, like civilians and prisoners of war, are also innocent of any wrongdoing.

The victims of belligerent reprisals, in addition to being innocent of the unlawful activity in question, are usually not in a position to exercise control over those committing the actual violations.[56] One writer has contended that because an act of reprisal 'is intended to coerce, rather than to punish, it is, by its nature, directed toward the innocent not the guilty'.[57] Would it not make better sense to direct a coercive measure at the transgressor, rather than at persons who may only be connected to him by mere geography or nationality? Some commentators who accept that reprisals strike innocents, maintain, however, that certain categories of such

---

50. Ibid., at p. 399.

51. See for example *Official Records of the Diplomatic Conference on the Reaffirmation and Development of International Humanitarian Law Applicable in Armed Conflicts, Geneva (1974 – 1977)*, (Bern, Government of Switzerland, Federal Political Department 1978) Vol. XIV, at p. 114 (CDDH/III/SR.14); ibid., Vol. VI, at p. 166 (CDDH/SR.41), Vol. IX, at p. 75 (CDDH/I/SR.47) [hereinafter *Official Records*].

52. Ibid., Vol. IX, at p. 62 (CDDH/I/SR.46).

53. Ibid.

54. Ibid., Vol. IX, at p. 453 (CDDH/I/SR.73).

55. As prohibited by Art. 35, para. 2 of Additional Protocol I.

56. G.H. Aldrich, 'Prospects for United States Ratification of Additional Protocol I to the 1949 Geneva Conventions', 85 *AJIL* (1991) p. 1, at p. 16. See also G.B. Roberts, 'The New Rules for Waging War: The Case Against Ratification of Additional Protocol I', 26 *Virginia JIL* (1985) p. 109, at p. 143.

57. M.F. Noone, 'Applying Just War *Jus in Bello* Doctrine to Reprisals: An Afghan Hypothetical', 51 *Catholic Univ. LR* (2001) p. 27, at p. 29.

persons 'are not ... necessarily without influence over the future conduct of the war'.[58] The enemy's civilian population 'remains a "significant base of enemy power," providing political and economic support to the armed forces. Even children are not "precluded" from serving that power: they will grow up to be soldiers, munitions workers, and so on.'[59] So reprisal measures directed against such innocent persons may bring about the desired effect, although the opposite may also be true.

On this issue of reprisals striking at innocent persons, certain writers have attached even stronger caveats to their recognition of this argument. Edward Kwakwa maintains that the civilian population 'cannot always be regarded as entirely innocent of the acts of its political and military leadership'.[60] He offers the case of guerrilla warfare as a particular example, where it may not be possible to distinguish the policy of the military leadership from that of the civilian population.[61] While a civilian population may support the actions of its leadership, that should not give rise to an imposition of guilt or responsibility on the former for the unlawful actions of the latter. Françoise Hampson goes further, asserting that 'the objection that the victims of reprisals are innocent ... appears to be an oversimplification'.[62] Basing her argument on moral responsibility, she opines that individuals 'share in the responsibility of a community for the acts of that community', evidenced by the way 'some Germans, including some born since 1945, feel a sense of shame and obligation towards Jews'.[63] The writer concludes that individuals, as members of a community, 'may be the targets of reprisal action without violating the principle that the innocent should not be made the victims'.[64]

Such an argument relies on a concept of collective responsibility which has been shown to be variance with humanitarian and human rights law principles. The example of German feelings of shame for the Holocaust is misplaced, because although an individual may feel ashamed for the past or present actions of its military or leadership, that is not the same as saying that such an individual bears responsibility for those actions. Moreover, the moral responsibility of which Hampson speaks may not really have any bearing on the issue of belligerent reprisals. Reprisals are directed at innocent members of a particular collective, not because they are morally, legally or criminally responsible for the unlawful acts, but because they are members of the group and reprisals against them might coerce those responsible to abandon their unlawful conduct. The concept of collective responsibility underlying the doctrine of reprisals is based more on solidarity than on any attempt to ascribe actual responsibility to the entire group.[65]

---

58. Christopher Greenwood commenting on the enemy civilian population, see Greenwood, loc. cit. n. 5, at p. 61.

59. Walzer, op. cit. n. 34, at p. 214.

60. Kwakwa, loc. cit. n. 38, at fn. 106, p. 73.

61. Ibid.

62. F. Hampson, 'Belligerent reprisals and the 1977 protocols to the Geneva conventions of 1949', 37 *ICLQ* (1988) pp. 818, at pp. 840-841.

63. Ibid., at p. 839.

64. Ibid., at p. 840.

65. See Kalshoven, loc. cit. n. 32, at p. 186.

One objection to the doctrine of belligerent reprisals related to the argument that they inflict suffering on innocents is that reprisal measures amount to acts of collective punishment.[66] The authoritative commentary to the Additional Protocols views the prohibition of collective punishment in Additional Protocol II as being 'virtually equivalent to prohibiting "reprisals" against protected persons'.[67] The problem with this reasoning is that reprisals are not intended to be punitive, they are for the purpose of law enforcement.[68] An Italian Military Tribunal in the case of *Re Kappler* observed that '... it is well known that in practice the usage has become established to treat measures of collective punishment as reprisals, notwithstanding a clear distinction between the two institutions'.[69] It is clear, however, that in the past acts of a collective punishment were imposed as reprisals,[70] but to describe all reprisals as collective punishment is incorrect. Unfortunately, despite Additional Protocol II's prohibition of collective punishment 'at any time and in any place whatsoever',[71] the failure of states to accept the insertion of a prohibition on reprisals in that instrument means that the outlawing of collective punishment in internal armed conflicts may be circumscribed by way of a reprisal, provided that the customary requirements governing their use are met.

Some final subsidiary arguments stemming from the central objection that reprisals strike innocents are that belligerent reprisals are inhumane,[72] their employment would diminish a state's 'own standard of civilization'[73] and would have an adverse effect on neutral opinion,[74] while their prohibition against civilians would lead to an improvement in the level of treatment given to civilians in times of armed conflict.[75] Considering the previous discussion, it is not difficult to disagree with these contentions.

3.2   Ineffective as a sanction of the laws of armed conflict

Opponents of the doctrine of belligerent reprisals frequently assert that such measures are of doubtful effectiveness in enforcing the laws of armed conflict and that furthermore, they are likely to cause counter-reprisals and an escalation of levels of violence and law-breaking. Would a belligerent engaged in a course of violative activity respond to similar *prima facie* unlawful activity by ceasing its wrongful

---

66. See for example *Official Records,* Vol. IX, at p. 71 (CDDH/I/SR.47); Nahlik, loc. cit. n. 22, at p. 56.

67. Y. Sandoz et al., eds., *Commentary on the Additional Protocols of 8 June 1977 to the Geneva Conventions of 12 August 1949* (Geneva, International Committee of the Red Cross 1987) p. 1374.

68. See Provost, loc. cit. n. 37, at pp. 416-417.

69. *In re Kappler*, Italy, Military Tribunal of Rome, July 20, 1948. *ILR*, Vol. 15, Case No. 151, p. 471, at p. 477.

70. See generally J. Garner, 'Community Fines and Collective Responsibility', 11 *AJIL* (1917) p. 511.

71. Art. 4(2)(b).

72. Kalshoven, loc. cit. n. 32, at p. 189; Provost, loc. cit. n. 37, at p. 413.

73. Kalshoven, loc. cit. n. 33, at p. 79.

74. McDougal and Feliciano, op. cit. n. 39, at p. 689.

75. I. Detter, *The Law of War*, 2nd edn. (Cambridge, Cambridge University Press 2000) p. 302.

conduct, or by resorting to even further lawlessness? To answer such a question conclusively is impossible.[76] Nevertheless, history and the opinion of many learned writers would seem to point toward the ineffectiveness of the doctrine of reprisals as a law enforcement tool.

A delegate to the drafting of the Additional Protocols rejected a suggested proposal by France permitting reprisals, a stand based 'not on an emotional reflex but on the knowledge that in practice counter-measures never led to the observance of the law'.[77] A high-ranking member of the United States Air Force has maintained, in respect of reprisals against one category of persons at least, that '[h]istory has shown that reprisal attacks against enemy civilian populations have been largely ineffective as sanctions to enforce the laws of war'.[78] Frits Kalshoven, the foremost expert on the subject, would maintain that reprisals 'seldom if ever' are effective at coercing a belligerent to cease its unlawful activities.[79] Having reviewed extensively instances of actual and claimed reprisals in the World Wars and numerous other armed conflicts, he concludes that belligerent reprisals have 'lost virtually all credibility as sanctions of the law of war', the doctrine having become what he describes as 'a complete anachronism'.[80] In addition to this historical evidence, he maintains that any party that has deliberately set itself on a law-breaking course is likely to have calculated the risk of counterattack by way of retaliation or reprisal and will be undeterred when a reprisal is actually taken.[81]

The most commonly cited challenge to this ineffectiveness argument is that of the non-use of poison gas during the Second World War.[82] The United States President, Theodor Roosevelt, threatened to take harsh retaliation in kind if Germany were to use its stocks of poison gas. It is alleged that on account of this threat Germany refrained from using the gas.[83] The main shortcoming with this counter-argument is that this example deals only with the threat of retaliatory action.[84] Although other factors may have influenced Germany's decision not to use poison gas,[85] this example does not offer an insight into the effectiveness of reprisals

---

76. See Albrecht, loc. cit. n. 33, at p. 592.

77. Comments of the representative of Sweden, Mr. Bring, see *Official Records*, Vol. VI, at p. 210 (CDDH.SR.42).

78. Bristol, loc. cit. n. 35, at p. 427. At the time the article was published, Major Bristol was assigned as Chief, International Law Division, Office of the Staff Judge Advocate, Headquarters United States Air Forces Europe, Ramstein Air Base, Germany.

79. Kalshoven, loc. cit. n. 33, at p. 60.

80. Kalshoven, op. cit. n. 3, at p. 377.

81. F. Kalshoven, 'Remarks', *American Society of International Law, Proceedings of the 74th Annual Meeting* (1980) p. 202, at p. 205.

82. See for example H.H. Almond Jr., 'Reprisals: The Global Community is not yet ready to abandon them', *American Society of International Law, Proceedings of the 74th Annual Meeting* (1980) p. 202, at p. 211 (in response to remarks); Roberts, loc. cit. n. 56, at p. 143; Hampson, loc. cit. n. 62, at p. 841.

83. Roberts, loc. cit. n. 56, n. 186.

84. And it is doubtful whether such use by the United States would have amounted to a belligerent reprisal, see *infra*.

85. Roberts notes in an earlier footnote the contention that 'Germany refrained from using chemical weapons *partly* out of fear of Allied retaliation', loc. cit. n. 56, at n. 162 [emphasis added].

themselves. One can only speculate as to what would have happened had Germany used poison gas and the United States then acted upon its threat. Would this action have persuaded Germany to stop using the gas? Considering the atrocious record of that party during the conflict, it would seem doubtful at the very least.

The questionable effectiveness of belligerent reprisals as a law enforcement tool is underscored by their tendency to be met with further law-breaking and violence by the targeted state.[86] The recently published *Naval Commanders Handbook on the Law of Naval Operations* states that 'there is always a risk that [a reprisal] will trigger retaliatory escalation (counter-reprisals) by the enemy. The United States has historically been reluctant to resort to reprisal for just this reason'.[87] A party to a conflict that has violated the law and subsequently been the target of reprisal action may easily be provoked by the reprisal to commit further violations. Also, because the assessment of the unlawfulness of the initial violation is carried out unilaterally, what one side may see as a belligerent reprisal in response to an unlawful act, the other may see as being an original unlawful act which merits the taking of reprisal measures. This problem is particularly acute where there are different interpretations as to the law in force at the time.[88] The above-mentioned clash of opinion between the ICTY and leading experts on the law of belligerent reprisals indicates that this particular problem is certainly of contemporary relevance.

The propensity of reprisals to lead to counter-reprisals, which are themselves unlawful,[89] also has the potential of prolonging an armed conflict. The employment of belligerent reprisals may prolong hostilities by strengthening a targeted state's will to fight.[90] Undoubtedly, the employment of belligerent reprisals would be of significant value as a propaganda tool to the targeted state, serving to garner greater public support for the war effort. A civilian population, one that has perhaps itself been the target of reprisal measures, will foremost be struck by the cruelty and apparent unlawfulness of such actions and is unlikely to recognise or accept that such measures are undertaken for the purposes of enforcing the laws of armed conflict. It is doubtful that such a population would hesitate to support the resort to strong retaliation or possibly similar actions in the form of illegal counter-reprisals by its own military against the 'law-breaking enemy'. So while belligerent reprisals may be viewed as 'an obsolete and unsatisfactory means of enforcing the law of warfare' in and of themselves, their tendency to cause an escalation of unlawful conduct and levels of fighting, thus prolonging hostilities, serves to copper-fasten the argument that they are an ineffective sanction.

---

86. See for example Kalshoven, loc. cit. n. 33, at p. 78; Kwakwa, loc. cit. n. 38, at p. 72; Bierzanek, loc. cit. n. 32, at p. 244.

87. NWP 1-14M/MCWP 5-2.1/COMDTPUB P5800.1, (Official publication of the United States Navy, Marine Corps and Coast Guard), Art. 6.2.3.3 available at <http://www.nwc.navy.mil/ILD/ild_-publications.htm

88. See Kalshoven, op. cit. n. 3, at p. 41.

89. See Darcy, loc. cit. n. 4, at pp. 191-192.

90. McDougal and Feliciano, op. cit. n. 39, at p. 689.

3.3   Open to abuse

The doctrine of belligerent reprisals allows parties to an armed conflict to disregard certain rules governing the conduct of hostilities. As Frits Kalshoven points out, the doctrine provides warring parties with an 'opportunity to violate the laws of war with impunity'.[91] One of the foremost treatises on international law goes further, stating that belligerent reprisals 'instead of being a means of securing legitimate warfare may become an effective instrument of its wholesale and cynical violation in matters constituting the very basis of the law of war'.[92] That ruthless belligerents would seek the comfort of such a doctrine in order to legitimate their unlawful conduct is largely to be expected. As such the doctrine of reprisals is highly open to abuse and sits uncomfortably within the legal regime currently referred to as international humanitarian law.

'History', we are told, 'abounds in numberless examples of the most atrocious cruelties committed under the pretext of reprisals'.[93] Geoffrey Best points out that the theory of reprisals differs greatly from their practice and that more often than not they serve 'to justify or camouflage excesses than to check them'.[94] The danger for abuse of the reprisals doctrine lies in the fact that decisions on taking reprisals and whether the customary requirements for their use have been met are always made unilaterally. This inherent subjectivity allows considerable scope for abuse. A belligerent with a thirst for vengeance[95] is unlikely to observe the requirements of subsidiarity and proportionality in deciding how to respond to violations of the laws of armed conflict. Although more humane means of securing compliance may be available, an aggrieved party, supported by an angry public, is more likely to favour returning like with like. And once taken, the unilateral assessment as to what constitutes a proportionate reprisal again leaves the doctrine wide open to abuse. The *Einsatzgruppen* case concerned the killing of 2,100 persons in response to the deaths of 21 German soldiers; a manipulation of the proportionality requirement which highlighted 'the criminality of this savage and inhuman so-called reprisal'.[96]

At the Diplomatic Conference on the Reaffirmation and Development of International Humanitarian Law this problematic aspect of the reprisals doctrine was addressed by several delegates. The representative of the Ukrainian Soviet Socialist Republic again voiced his concern over belligerent reprisals, asserting that 'experience has shown that they carried with them a real danger of arbitrary action and

---

91. Kalshoven, op. cit. n. 3, at p. 367.

92. L. Oppenheim, in H. Lauterpacht, ed., *International Law: Disputes, War and Neutrality*, 7th edn. (London, Longman 1952) p. 565.

93. M. de Martens, *La Paix et la Guerre* p. 423 cited in Spaight, op. cit. n. 31, at pp. 462-463.

94. Best, op. cit. n. 35, at p. 311.

95. One commentator asserts that '[s]trong political and moral foundations exist for the view that reprisals are an instrument of revenge by a victim against the perpetrators of a breach of humanitarian law', see Provost, loc. cit. n. 37, at p. 415.

96. *United States* v. *Ohlendorf*, IV Trials of War Criminals before the Nuernberg Military Tribunals 1, (1950) pp. 493-494.

that it was sometimes impossible to limit the extent and scale of their uses'.[97] The representative of the United Kingdom recognised the potential for abuse, but argued that it was not logical to rule out this system of counter-measures 'because of possible abuses'.[98] The French proposal allowing for reprisals was seen by one delegate as 'an invitation to misuse and abuse',[99] and by another as allowing 'unlimited possibilities of violating the provisions of Protocol I'.[100] The representative of the Byelorussian Soviet Socialist Republic saw in this potential for abuse, a paving of the way for violations which could endanger the entire Protocol itself.[101] A delegate from Mexico is reported to have said that the French proposal could open the way to total anarchy.[102]

3.4   Difficult for customary requirements to be observed

Commensurate with the potential that the customary requirements governing recourse to reprisals might be ignored by an unscrupulous belligerent, it is also argued that there are real difficulties in meeting those requirements in times of armed conflict. For their successful functioning belligerent reprisals require 'information, self-restraint, goodwill, and ... time which are rarely available in real-war conditions'.[103] Observance of the principle of proportionality is singled out as being specifically problematic.[104]

Françoise Hampson points to the difficulty of assessing the existence of a prior violation attributable to the enemy state and to potential obstacles to meeting the rules of subsidiarity and proportionality.[105] Establishing the existence of a prior violation is done unilaterally, the shortcomings of which have already been discussed. Hampson raises the point that a victim state must 'distinguish between an unlawful act perpetrated as a matter of State policy and one which resulted from an individual soldier or group of soldiers running amuck'.[106] The latter scenario might not allow for the taking of reprisals, unless the state has failed to investigate or prosecute the offenders, and in the fog of war establishing a clear picture of what has transpired can prove problematic. Where the potential exists for the taking of reprisals against innocent civilians, this argument is quite compelling.

The potential difficulties associated with the principles of subsidiarity and proportionality may be more linked to the tendency of belligerents to abuse the doc-

---

97. *Official Records*, Vol. IX, at pp. 61-62 (CDDH/I/SR.46).
98. Ibid., at p. 74 (CDDH/I/SR.47).
99. *Official Records*, Vol. VI, at p. 210 (CDDH/SR.42).
100. *Official Records*, Vol. IX, at p. 74 (CDDH/I/SR.47).
101. Ibid., at p. 80.
102. See Nahlik, loc. cit. n. 22, at p. 58.
103. Best, op. cit. n. 35, at p. 311.
104. See for example Bristol, loc. cit. n. 35, at pp. 414-415; S.E. Nahlik, 'From Reprisals to Individual Penal Responsibility', in A.J.M. Delissen and G.J. Tanja, eds., *Humanitarian Law of Armed Conflict: Challenges Ahead: Essays in Honour of Frits Kalshoven* (Dordrecht, Martinus Nijhoff 1991) p. 165, at p. 173.
105. Hampson, loc. cit. n. 62, at pp. 822-824.
106. Ibid., at p. 822.

trine of reprisals rather than with actual wartime conditions, although allegations, denials and propaganda would obviously contribute to an exacerbation of an already fraught situation. Hampson argues that meeting the rule of subsidiarity would require a certain amount of time, which a belligerent is unlikely to give if its opponent is likely to 'strike again'.[107] If a victim state genuinely believes that it must take a reprisal immediately in order to compel the violating state to observe the law, then this is in conformity with the subsidiarity principle. Problems arise where this genuineness is lacking. While meeting the criterion of proportionality may also be hard, particularly where the response is not in kind,[108] it is the above-mentioned abuse of the principle that is the cause for most concern. A proportionate response, one devoid of 'obvious disproportionality',[109] should not prove trying for the sincere belligerent.

The preceding section has articulated the main assertions coming from the chorus of opposition to the doctrine of belligerent reprisals. It can be seen that several of these arguments are humanitarian based and influenced by international human rights law, while others, such as the contention that reprisals are ineffective sanctions and that their employment might thus be wasteful of military resources,[110] are clearly made with the realities of fighting battles and winning wars in mind. In more classical terms it has been asserted that resort to the doctrine of reprisals would violate the principle of chivalry: 'such is the nature of reprisals that there is no honour in their recognition of regulation but only in their repudiation'.[111] Those who favour the abandonment of the doctrine of belligerent reprisals have made logical and compelling arguments towards that end. The contentions of those who advocate retention of the doctrine are made with like coherency and conviction.

4.   THE CASE FOR RETAINING THE DOCTRINE OF BELLIGERENT REPRISALS

Proponents of the reprisals doctrine would argue first and foremost that reprisals are the only means available to a belligerent, faced with an opponent persistently violating the laws of armed conflict, of compelling that party to cease in its unlawful conduct.[112] It is also contended that reprisals serve as an effective means of deterring unlawful conduct[113] and that their prohibition could actually encourage violations[114] or even force the use of nuclear weapons.[115] Advocates of the doctrine

---

107. Ibid., at p. 823.
108. Ibid., at pp. 823-824.
109. Kalshoven, op. cit. n. 3, at p. 341.
110. See for example Bristol, loc. cit. n. 35, at p. 428.
111. Ibid., at p. 403.
112. See for example Almond, loc. cit. n. 82, at p. 211; Roberts, loc. cit. n. 56, at p. 143; Sofaer, loc. cit. n. 27, at p. 785.
113. See for example Hampson, loc. cit. n. 62, at p. 822; Sofaer, loc. cit. n. 27, at p. 785.
114. Bristol, loc. cit. n. 35, at p. 425.
115. Roberts, loc. cit. n. 56, at p. 143.

also assert that a party to an armed conflict which observes the rules could be placed at a military disadvantage *vis-à-vis* a violating party.[116] Additionally it is maintained that public opinion will not support abandonment of the doctrine.[117]

4.1   Only available sanction

The 1863 Lieber Code, one of the earliest attempts to codify rules governing the conduct of warfare, contains a number of provisions governing recourse to retaliatory measures.[118] Retaliation, 'as a means of protective retribution', is essential, as '[a] reckless enemy often leaves to his opponent no other means of securing himself against the repetition of barbarous outrage'.[119] Retaliation, in a modern manifestation as the doctrine of belligerent reprisals, is still viewed by many as one of the only means of properly enforcing the laws of armed conflict. France, as made it clear in its reservation to Additional Protocol I, views belligerent reprisals as 'indispensable for protecting its civilian population from serious, manifest and deliberate violations of the Geneva Conventions and this Protocol by the enemy'.[120] The United Kingdom also reserved the right to resort to reprisal measures in the face of 'serious and deliberate attacks' against the civilian population or protected objects.[121] The United States Joint Chiefs of Staff oppose ratification of Additional Protocol I because '[t]he total elimination of the right of reprisal, for example, would hamper the ability of the United States to respond to an enemy's intentional disregard of the limitations established in the Geneva Conventions of 1949 or Protocol I, for the purpose of deterring such disregard.'[122] The stances of these major military powers are reflective of the debates which took place at the Diplomatic Conference on the Reaffirmation and Development of International Humanitarian Law in Geneva.

The representative of France at that conference expressed his doubt as to 'whether the existing system of penal sanctions provided a true safeguard against violation of the Conventions'.[123] A sanctions mechanism should operate when the rule is broken, not after the event, particularly 'when that breach could cause a serious and perhaps decisive upset in the balance of forces'.[124] He also doubted whether appeals by the ICRC would be enough to put an end to unlawful conduct.[125] Belligerent reprisals were seen as 'the only measures which a Government can take to put a stop to [grave, manifest and deliberate] violations and safeguard

---

116. See for example Provost, loc. cit. n. 37, at p. 421; Greenwood, loc. cit. n. 5, at p. 59.

117. Nahlik, loc. cit. n. 104, at p. 173.

118. Instructions for the Government of Armies of the United States in the Field, Prepared by Francis Lieber, promulgated as General Orders No. 100 by President Lincoln, 24 April 1863; text reproduced in Schindler and Toman, op. cit. n. 6, at pp. 3-23.

119. Ibid., Arts. 27-28.

120. *Supra* n. 26 (author's translation of French text).

121. Roberts and Guelff, op. cit. n. 26, at p. 511.

122. Sofaer, loc. cit. n. 27, at p. 785.

123. *Official Records*, Vol. IX, at p. 58 (CDDH/I/SR.46).

124. Ibid.

125. Ibid., at p. 59.

the very survival of the nation in the exceptional circumstances that may arise'.[126] The French proposal legitimising reprisals as a means of enforcing international humanitarian law were viewed by the United Kingdom's representative as 'an attempt to make that law a living reality rather than a series of hopeful aspirations that had no effect in binding the parties at war'.[127] That representative found that '[e]xisting methods had proved inadequate' and that reprisals were 'a rational and legal response to an adversary's serious breaches'.[128]

Many academic writers would also argue for the indispensability of reprisals as a means of law enforcement, even while simultaneously recognising the shortcomings of the doctrine. McDougal and Feliciano accept that the reprisals are susceptible to 'perversion and abuse', but 'until a comprehensive, centralized, and effective sanctions process is achieved in the world arena, belligerents have to police one another and enforce the laws of war against each other'.[129] Another commentator notes that reprisals are not the most 'militarily effective means of controlling behaviour in warfare', but argues that there simply isn't anything else in place for that purpose.[130] Even writers with an aversion to the doctrine of belligerent reprisals can see the validity of this argument. Christopher Greenwood has accepted the ineffectiveness and escalating effect of reprisals but would contend that 'the removal of even an imperfect sanction creates problems unless something else is put in its place'.[131] Frits Kalshoven, one of the most ardent opponents of the doctrine, concedes that reprisals cannot be completely abolished until other means of law enforcement are put in their place.[132] As is obvious from these comments, it is the lack of alternatives that causes parties both sides of the debate to recognise the potential necessity of the doctrine.

The fact is, however, that resort to reprisals is not the only option available to a party that has been the victim of unlawful conduct. There are other legal and more humane means, although admittedly less immediate than reprisals, of seeking to bring about a change in an enemy's conduct. An aggrieved party can protest directly to the enemy, if communications are still in place. Other states might be petitioned and persuaded to isolate the enemy through the severing of diplomatic contact or the withdrawal of trade or other concessions. A complaint may be lodged with the United Nations, with condemnation by the General Assembly or Security Council having the potential to coerce a violator into observance of the law. A warning by a victim state of its intention to prosecute and punish offenders may also serve to bring about an end to unlawful conduct.[133] Recourse could be made to the system of Protecting Powers under Additional Protocol I[134] or to the

---

126. *Official Records*, Vol. IX, at p. 443 (CDDH/I/SR.73).
127. *Official Records*, Vol. IX, at p. 73 (CDDH/I/SR.47).
128. Ibid., at pp. 73-74.
129. McDougal and Feliciano, op. cit. n. 39, at pp. 681-682. See also Bristol, loc. cit. n. 35, at p. 404.
130. Almond, loc. cit, n. 82, at p. 211.
131. Greenwood, loc. cit. n. 5, at p. 56.
132. Kalshoven, op. cit. n. 3, at p. 375.
133. See von Glahn, op. cit. n. 36, at p. 235; Bierzanek, loc. cit. n. 32, at pp. 244-247.
134. Additional Protocol I, Art. 2, para. C and Art. 5.

International Fact-Finding Commission, which is authorised to inquire into allegations of grave breaches and to 'facilitate, through its good offices, the restoration of an attitude of respect for the Conventions and this Protocol'.[135] While there is obviously a temporal factor to be considered here – an unavoidable delay is inherent in several of these means – the threat to pursue any of these avenues can be made instantly and may then bring about the desired result. Those with an aversion to the above means may in any event retaliate with increased force against the military personnel or objects of the deviant enemy.

The effectiveness of the prosecution and punishment of war criminals as a means of law enforcement has been considerably augmented by recent developments. Not since the aftermath of the Second World War has there been such a commitment to trying persons suspected of committing violations of the laws of armed conflict. International courts and tribunals have been established to try those responsible for crimes committed in the Former Yugoslavia, Rwanda, Sierra Leone, East Timor and Cambodia. Probably the most significant and promising occurrence is the recent creation of the International Criminal Court, an organ with jurisdiction over war crimes. Admittedly the Court will only try those responsible for 'the most serious crimes of concern to the international community as a whole'[136] and it does not have jurisdiction over crimes committed by the citizens or on the territory of all states, only those which are party to its Statute. Nevertheless, in the five years since the adoption of the Rome Statute over 90 states have ratified that instrument, and a threat to petition the Prosecutor of the Court to take proceedings could be a very effective means of putting an end to unlawful conduct. It is interesting to note that the United States, while firmly wishing to retain its right to take reprisals in the absence of other means of law enforcement, is vehemently opposed to the viable alternative that is the International Criminal Court,[137] with its President George W. Bush having gone so far as to 'unsign' the Rome Statute.

While there may be other means of enforcement available, the most compelling counter-argument to the assertion that belligerent reprisals are the only option in the face of violations is that reprisals are ineffective as a sanction. Although they will certainly allow for an immediate response, that response is unlikely to bring about the desired result, and is in fact liable to lead to even further violations of the laws of armed conflict. By abandoning the doctrine of reprisals and embracing bodies such as the International Fact-Finding Commission and the International Criminal Court, those concerned about responding to large scale humanitarian law violations committed against them will put out the serious message that they will not respond with similar cruelty, nor that they will stand idly by, but that they will

---

135. Additional Protocol I, Art. 90, para. 2(c). On some potential problems associated with the Commission see Greenwood, loc. cit. n. 5, at p. 57; Kwakwa, loc. cit. n. 38, at p. 76-78.

136. Rome Statute of the International Criminal Court, (1998) UN Doc. A/CONF.183/9, adopted 17 July 1998, entered into force 1 July 2002, Art. 5, para. 1.

137. See for example D.J. Scheffer, 'The United States and the International Criminal Court', 93 *AJIL* (1999) p. 12; H.T. King and T.C. Theofrastous, 'From Nuremburg to Rome: A Step Backward for US Foreign Policy', 31 *Case Western Reserve JIL* (1999) p. 47.

rigorously pursue offenders by the more internationally acceptable and humane means available to them.

4.2   **Effective deterrent**

Proponents of the doctrine of belligerent reprisals would also argue that the threat of reprisals is a good means of deterring violations of international humanitarian law. One commentator would go so far as to argue that 'the primary policy served by reprisals is that of deterrence'.[138] It is believed by several writers that the availability of the countermeasure of reprisals can serve to dissuade belligerents from engaging in unlawful conduct in the first place.[139] This was a view shared by several of the delegates to the Diplomatic Conference leading to the adoption of the Additional Protocols.[140] Furthermore, to prohibit belligerent reprisals might actually encourage violations and more ruthless behaviour on the part of warring parties. Even more ominously, it is contended that removal of the sanction of reprisals has the potential to precipitate the use of nuclear weapons.[141]

Writing in 1949, A.R. Albrecht asked 'whether the prohibition of reprisals, rather than their use, does not to some extent weaken the efficacy of the laws of war by relieving potential war criminals from the fear of reprisals, although in no way diminishing the likelihood that they themselves will commit violations of the laws of war'.[142] He accepted that a prohibition would dispel some of the certainty surrounding the doctrine, but that the law would then be 'much less effective in fulfilling its function of providing minimum standards of conduct in war'.[143] More recently, Edward Kwakwa has speculated that the risk of reprisals is likely to deter states from breaching the law, while 'these nations would break the rules if reprisals were prohibited'.[144] Another commentator has asserted that the failure to legislate for the use of reprisals in Additional Protocol I 'condemned those victims [of armed conflicts] to arbitrary, unpredictable breaches of humanitarian law which might not otherwise have taken place'.[145] By prohibiting reprisals there is a likelihood that violence will 'escalate disastrously',[146] and that the ensuing fighting could lead to the unwelcome use of nuclear weapons.

Substantiating the claim that reprisals serve a deterrent purpose is a formidable task, as it requires proof that violations have not occurred. One might look again to the example of Germany refraining from using poison gas during the Second World War. Roosevelt promised 'full and swift retaliation in kind':

---

138. Almond, loc. cit. n. 82, at pp. 197, 200.

139. Kwakwa, loc. cit. n. 38, at p. 74; A. Roberts, 'The Laws of War: Problems of Implementation in Contemporary Conflicts', 6 *Duke J Comp. IL* (1995) p. 11, at p. 78.

140. See for example *Official Records*, Vol. VI, at p. 176 (CDDH.SR.41), ibid., Vol. IX, at p. 59 (CDDH/I/SR.46) and p. 93 (CDDH/I/SR.48).

141. Roberts, loc. cit. n. 56, at p. 143.

142. Albrecht, loc. cit. n. 33, at p. 613.

143. Ibid.

144. Kwakwa, loc. cit. n. 38, at p. 75.

145. Hampson, loc. cit. n. 62, at p. 843.

146. *Official Records*, Vol. IX, at p. 59 (CDDH/I/SR.46).

S. Darcy

'Any use of gas by any Axis power, therefore, will immediately be followed by the fullest possible retaliation upon munitions centers, seaports, and other military objectives throughout the whole extent of the territory of such Axis country'.[147]

Some would contend that this proves that the threat of reprisals serves a deterrent function.[148] Use of poison gas by Germany would have been in violation of the 1925 Protocol for the Prohibition of the Use of Asphyxiating, Poisonous or Other Gases, and of Bacteriological Methods of Warfare,[149] which it had ratified prior to the Second World War. The United States, on the other hand, had only signed the instrument prior to the war and was thus not bound by its provisions at that time. Roosevelt did not warn of reprisals, but rather threatened to forcefully retaliate in kind and it can only be speculated as to whether he would have threatened reprisals had the United States been a State Party to the Gas Protocol. It was the threat to use poison gas itself that probably deterred such use by Germany, rather than a threat to resort to the doctrine of belligerent reprisals.

It must be remembered that the purpose of reprisals is to put an end to existing unlawful activity – their utility as a deterrent is subsidiary to this central function. The doubt which exists as to the ability of the doctrine to fulfil its primary goal cannot be overcome by advocating some other unproven quality. In addition, if a reprisal threat were to be an effective deterrent it would have to be seen as a real threat and therefore a belligerent would have to be legally permitted and fully prepared to take such reprisal measures. To retain reprisals for the purpose of deterrence would thus imply their use, despite their dubious effectiveness as measures of law enforcement and the risk of escalating violence that such use would entail. The inhumanity involved in reprisal measures also serves to undermine the argument favouring their retention for deterrent purposes. While a threat to torture every man, woman and child of an enemy might also be a deterrent of unlawful acts, its use would be completely intolerable, being met with universal repugnance and violating a norm of *jus cogens*. It may be argued, finally, that the doctrine of belligerent reprisals is unlikely to be pivotal in the reasoning of would-be violators of the laws of armed conflict.

4.3   Military disadvantage

The argument is often made that abandonment of the doctrine of belligerent reprisals could be militarily disadvantageous for those parties which continue to observe the laws of armed conflict. Such criticism is raised chiefly in connection with the provisions of Additional Protocol I which add items such as historic monuments, works of art, places of worship, the natural environment and works, installations or military objectives containing dangerous forces to conventional

---

147. 8 State Department Bulletin (1943) at p. 507 cited in Kwakwa, loc. cit. n. 38, at p. 76.
148. Kwakwa, loc. cit. n. 38, at pp. 75-76; Hampson, loc. cit. n. 62, at pp. 841-842.
149. Signed at Geneva, 17 June 1925, entered into force, 8 February 1928; reprinted in Schindler and Toman, op. cit. n. 6, at p. 115. A list of ratifications and reservations are reproduced at ibid., at pp. 121-127.

law's list of prohibited reprisal targets. Prior to the adoption of that instrument, the French representative at the Diplomatic Conference voiced concern that such rules would place 'the combatant who respected the law in a position of inferiority to the combatant who violated it'.[150] Christopher Greenwood makes the argument that because the Protocol includes both Geneva and Hague-type rules, the observance of some of those will 'seriously restrict the options open to an army engaged in hostilities and will, in many cases, require such an army to sustain greater casualties than it would otherwise do in order to minimise the loss of civilian life'.[151] The intentional disregard of those rules could lead to a military advantage on the part of the lawbreaker and it would be 'unreasonable to forbid the victim of those violations to respond in kind unless other means of redress are available'.[152]

A total prohibition of reprisals is seen by one commentator as untenable, as it would give 'a significant military advantage to the aggressor side in a conflict'.[153] This particular comment is strange as it ignores the applicability of international humanitarian law irrespective of the legality of the resort to armed force, and it also implies that a party which violates the *jus ad bellum* is also prone to commit breaches of the *jus in bello*. Is a victim of aggression less likely to commit violations of the laws of armed conflict? More to the point, would observance of a prohibition of reprisals leave one at a military disadvantage? Hilaire McCoubrey pointed out that '[t]he humanitarian *jus in bello* imposes little or no restriction on the effective pursuit of military objectives, and the evidence of the 20th century by no means suggests that the most ruthless power must always emerge victorious'.[154] This comment refers to the law in its current state; were the reprisal prohibitions to be extended to *bona fide* military objectives, then this military disadvantage argument could well be valid. The question which arises is whether the new reprisal prohibitions in Additional Protocol I relate to objects of a military nature or whether their introduction was driven more by humanitarian concerns.

At the Diplomatic Conference the Swedish delegation contended that these new reprisal provisions were a development where 'humanitarian considerations are balanced in a very good way against military requirements'.[155] The most robust rejoinder to the assertion that these reprisal provisions offer a military advantage to those who violate the law was made by Frits Kalshoven.[156] He dismisses such contentions in relation to the articles protecting cultural objects, objects indispensable to the survival of the civilian population and the natural environment; these rules 'add little to existing general obligations or have been so phrased that military considerations are heeded to the maximum'.[157] Article 56, however, specifically protects works, installations or *military objectives* containing dangerous forces.

---

150. *Official Records*, Vol. IX, at p. 59 (CDDH/I/SR.46). See also ibid., at p. 93 (CDDH/I/SR.48).

151. Greenwood, loc. cit. n. 5, at p. 59.

152. Ibid., at p. 60.

153. Kwakwa, loc. cit. n. 38, at p. 76.

154. Hilaire McCoubrey, *International Humanitarian Law: Modern Developments in the Limitation of Warfare*, 2nd edn. (Aldershot, Ashgate-Dartmouth 1998) pp. 307-308.

155. *Official Records*, Vol. VI, at p. 199 (CDDH/SR.41)

156. Kalshoven, loc. cit. n. 33, at pp. 54-58.

157. Ibid., at p. 56.

Kalshoven points out that the prohibition on attacking a military objective containing dangerous forces applies only where it may cause 'severe losses among the civilian population';[158] a requirement that is only a 'little more exacting' than the general rule that belligerents refrain from attacking any military objective where civilian losses are 'excessive in relation to the concrete and direct military advantage anticipated'.[159] He would argue that the claim of significant military disadvantage is exaggerated and that these new rules 'may at times require some modest adjustment of military planning'.[160] He concludes that these new rules are fundamentally humanitarian in nature, 'purely for the protection of the civilian population'.[161]

While some would hold that the existing conventional reprisal prohibitions place an observant party at a military disadvantage, an objection made at the Diplomatic Conference was that the doctrine of belligerent reprisals actually constitutes a law of the strongest, that it tends to favour the militarily superior party.[162] The representative of the German Democratic Republic gave the following example:

'In a war between a country with an air force and a country without one, if the technically-developed country, in open and deliberate breach, launched air raids against the civilian population or civilian objects, the other party would be allowed to do the same – but would have no means of doing so. If, on the other hand, the party without an air force committed or was said to have committed such breaches, even if not directed against the civilian population, the other party could take that as an excuse for suspending the provisions concerning the protection of the civil population.'[163]

As Remigiusz Bierzanek points out armed conflicts are for the most part becoming asymmetrical affairs, with one party often compelled to resort to guerrilla warfare.[164] Some of the more recent major international armed conflicts, such as in Afghanistan and Iraq, would seem to corroborate this point. It is perhaps more than a coincidence then that many of the major military powers are the primary advocates for the retention of the doctrine of belligerent reprisals.

4.4   Public opinion

Finally, in support of the reprisals doctrine it is sometimes contended that public opinion will not agree to its abandonment. In particular, a civilian population which has been the target of unlawful acts by the enemy is likely to demand reciprocal treatment, as the British public did during the Second World War when the

---

158. Art. 56, para. 1.
159. Art. 57, para. 2(a)(iii).
160. Kalshoven, loc. cit. n. 33, at p. 57.
161. Ibid., at p. 58.
162. *Official Records*, Vol. IX, at p. 62 (CDDH/I/SR.46) and p. 79 (CDDH/I/SR.47).
163. Ibid., at p. 71 (CDDH/I/SR.47).
164. Bierzanek, loc. cit. n. 32, at p. 239.

Luftwaffe began bombing London and other towns in Britain.[165] Christopher Greenwood has said that some of the more recent laws concerning reprisals 'seek to impose upon governments a moral stance which public opinion will not sustain'.[166] Another writer contends that a government 'will rarely be able to resist the demand of its citizens for reprisals if its population has suffered unlawful attacks'.[167] It has also been asserted that reprisal actions may actually have a positive effect on the morale of the public of a state engaged in an armed conflict.[168]

It is a reasonable and well-heeded observation that public opinion will demand a response to unlawful acts directed against it. Such a demand is more likely driven by revenge however, than by a desire to see an end to unlawful conduct, that is to say, were another means such as the threat of punishment to prove effective, public opinion may not be sated unless its own state's response is in kind. Christopher Greenwood accepts the risks associated with responding to popular demands for revenge, but would consider that 'pressure of public opinion is one of the factors which may help to ensure respect for the law'.[169] Recent events show that governments can often be cynical when it comes to heeding public opinion, citing it when it is in their favour and ignoring it when it goes against them. The unprecedented public demonstrations prior to the current war in Iraq show that the British and United States Governments' actions, while being without a United Nations Security Council resolution and thus of highly questionable legality, were also in stark contrast to the majority of public opinion in those countries. States can and will resist demands of public opinion when they so desire. As Frits Kalshoven has stated 'it appears certain that in many (perhaps most) countries the population is an instrument in the hands of those in power, rather than the other way round'.[170]

5.   CONCLUDING COMMENTS

It would not seem unreasonable to make the claim that since the end of the Second World War there has been more diplomatic discussion and academic output on the subject of belligerent reprisals than there has been actual legitimate reliance on the doctrine by belligerents during the course of armed conflicts. This begs the question whether the doctrine of belligerent reprisals has any place in contemporary international humanitarian law. Has it become merely an interesting topic for legal scholars or does it remain a truly viable sanction of the laws of armed conflict?

This article has briefly highlighted the increasingly restrictive rules governing recourse to the doctrine and has sought to outline and analyse the principle arguments made in favour and against resort to reprisals. Over a decade ago, Christopher Greenwood wrote an article titled 'The Twilight of the Law of Belligerent

---

165. See Nahlik, loc. cit. n. 104, at p. 173.
166. Greenwood, loc. cit. n. 5, at p. 58.
167. Roberts, loc. cit. n. 56, at p. 145.
168. McDougal and Feliciano, op. cit. n. 39, at p. 689.
169. Greenwood, loc. cit. n. 5, at p. 58.
170. Kalshoven, loc. cit. n. 33, at p. 60. See also Almond, loc. cit. n. 82, at p. 202.

Reprisals',[171] and while certainly the treaty law pertaining to international armed conflicts has almost completely closed the door on the doctrine, the rules relating to reprisals in internal conflicts are still appallingly non-existent. Nonetheless, in the light of the above discussion, can it be argued that the doctrine of belligerent reprisals has a practical future in the laws of armed conflict? For the most part belligerent reprisals have *in practice* become a thing of the past, although debate on the issue continues apace and recourse to the doctrine is still theoretically possible.

As the above discussion will have revealed, it is impossible to sit on the fence in relation to the issue of belligerent reprisals and it is obvious which side of the debate the present writer falls on. Compelling arguments made from both a humanitarian and a military perspective convince one of the need to finally lay the doctrine to rest. Recourse to belligerent reprisals in the present day would fly in the face of the entire ethos of human rights, a movement which has propelled much of the modern development of international humanitarian law.

---

171. *Supra* n. 5.

DEVELOPMENTS IN THE LAW OF GENOCIDE[1]

William A. Schabas[2]

---

1. © W.A. Schabas, 2004.

2. Director of the Irish Centre for Human Rights, National University of Ireland, Galway; Professor of Human Rights.

Yearbook of International Humanitarian Law
Volume 5 - 2002 - pp. 131-165

1.   INTRODUCTION

Probably more has happened in the past five years to the Convention for the Prevention and Punishment of the Crime of Genocide than in the previous 50, that is,
in the half-century following its adoption by the United Nations General Assembly
on 9 December 1948.[3]

Indeed, for the first five decades of its existence, the Convention was
largely ignored by lawyers, viewed by most of them – as Georg Schwarzenberger famously remarked – to be 'unnecessary when applicable and inapplicable when necessary'.[4] Over the years there had been attempts to apply the
'g-word' to a wide range of atrocities and gross violations of human rights, including those of China in Tibet,[5] of Iraq against the Kurds,[6] of the United States in
Vietnam[7] as well as towards its African-American[8] and aboriginal populations,[9] of
Pakistan in Bangladesh,[10] the Khmer Rouge in Cambodia,[11] and Israel in

---

3. (1951) 78 *UNTS* 277. On the *Convention* generally, see W.A. Schabas, *Genocide in International Law* (Cambridge, Cambridge University Press 2000).

4. G. Schwarzenberger, *International Law*, Vol. I, 3rd edn. (London, Stevens & Sons 1957) p. 143.

5. In the 1959 United Nations General Assembly debate on Tibet, China was accused of committing genocide: UN Doc A/PV.812, para. 127 (El Salvador); UN Doc A/PV.831, para. 13 (Malaya),
para. 126 (Cuba); UN Doc A/PV.833, para. 8 (El Salvador), para. 28 (Netherlands). The charges were
sparked by a report from the International Commission of Jurists: *The Question of Tibet and the Rule
of Law* (Geneva, International Commission of Jurists 1959) pp. 68-71.

6. E.g., in June 1963, the Mongolian People's Republic requested that the United Nations General
Assembly include in its provisional agenda the item: 'The policy of genocide carried out by the government of the Republic of Iraq Against the Kurdish People'. See UN Doc A/5429 (1963).

7. See J.-P. Sartre, 'On Genocide', in R.A. Falk, G. Kolko and R.J. Lifton, eds., *Crimes of War*
(New York, Random House 1971) pp. 534-549. The charge is discussed by M.C. Bassiouni, 'United
States Involvement in Vietnam', 9 *Calif. Western ILJ* (1979) p. 274.

8. W.L. Patterson, ed., *We Charge Genocide! The Crime of Government Against the Negro People*
(New York, International Publishers 1961).

9. M.C. Bassiouni, 'Has the United States Committed Genocide Against the American Indian?', 9
Calif. Western ILJ (1979) p. 271.

10. India invoked Art. IX of the 1948 *Convention* as a basis of jurisdiction in a claim of genocide
directed against Pakistan *Trial of Pakistani Prisoners of War (Pakistan v. India), Interim Protection
Order of 13 July 1973*, ICJ Rep. (1973) p. 328. On the case, see L.J. Leblanc, 'The ICJ, the Genocide
Convention, and the United States', 6 *Wisconsin ILJ* (1987) pp. 43, 51; J.J. Paust and A.P. Blaustein,
'War Crimes Jurisdiction and Due Process: The Bangladesh Experience', 11 *Vanderbilt J Trans. L*
(1978) p. 1; C. Rousseau, 'Chronique des faits internationaux', 77 *Revue générale de droit interna-
tional public* (1972) pp. 544, 862; F.R. Teson, *Humanitarian Intervention, An Inquiry into Law and
Morality* (Dobbs Ferry NY, Transnational 1988) pp. 181, 187-188.

11. For example 'Situation of human rights in Cambodia', GA Res. 52/135, preamble. Cambodia
held a genocide show trial of Khmer Rouge leaders Pol Pot and Ieng Sary in 1979, but under an idiosyncratic definition of the crime that more closely resembles the concept of crimes against humanity. See H.
J. De Nike, J. Quigley and K.J. Robinson, *Genocide in Cambodia: Documents from the Trial of Pol Pot
and Ieng Sary* (Philadelphia PA, University of Pennsylvania Press 2001). The Committee of Experts
appointed by the Secretary-General in 1997 was reserved in its discussion of the subject, saying
'whether the Khmer Rouge committed genocide with respect to part of the Khmer national group turns
on complex interpretative issues, especially concerning the Khmer Rouge's intent with respect to its
non-minority-group victims'. 'Report of the Group of Experts for Cambodia established pursuant to
General Assembly resolution 52/135', UN Doc. A/53/850-S/1999/231, annex, para. 65.

Lebanon.[12] But in each of these cases, some interpretative flair was required in order to stretch the definition to fit the crimes, and the efforts were not always very convincing. In 1990 scholars Frank Chalk and Kurt Jonassohn wrote that 'the wording of the Convention is so restrictive that not one of the genocidal killings committed since its adoption is covered by it'.[13]

Of course, often the goal in using the term genocide was simply stigmatising specific atrocities, and no particular legal consequences were intended. From the standpoint of international law, the main interest in characterising acts as genocide was to unleash the provisions of the Genocide Convention. Article IX, which gives jurisdiction to the International Court of Justice, was of particular interest in this respect. The Convention established important legal principles that were simply inapplicable to the other core international crimes that served to enhance the protection of human rights, namely crimes against humanity and war crimes, at least as the law then stood. Article I of the Genocide Convention declares that genocide can be committed 'in time of peace or in time of war'. Until recently this could not be said with any certainty about crimes against humanity, and it is simply inapplicable, for obvious reasons, to war crimes. For international lawyers and human rights activists alike, a charge of genocide meant that the heavy artillery could be brought to bear.

The price to pay for such a powerful and innovative instrument – we should never forget that it was adopted in 1948, a day prior to the Universal Declaration of Human Rights, at the very beginning of the United Nations human rights system – was a relatively narrow definition of the crime itself. Over the years since the Convention's adoption, frustrated by the difficulties in fitting the facts of specific atrocities to the crime of genocide, many turned their attention to amending the definition, in the hope that this would give the Convention a broader scope and thereby enhance the protection of human rights. Historians and sociologists condemned the narrowness of the concept of 'legal genocide'. A number of alternatives were proposed. But by the 1990s, the categories of crimes against humanity and war crimes had evolved dramatically, extending to cover internal armed conflicts and, in the case of the former, peacetime as well.[14] This expansion in the scope of international criminal law reduced the onus on the crimes of genocide to cover a much broader range of serious human rights violations than had been in-

---

12. GA Res. 37/123 D. The Soviet Union was the first to launch the charge: UN Doc S/15419 (1982). See also the statements of Surinam: UN Doc S/15406 (1982); Madagascar: UN Doc A/37/489, Annex (1982); Mongolia: UN Doc A/37/480, Annex (1982); Vietnam: UN Doc A/37/489, Annex (1992); Pakistan: UN Doc A/37/502, Annex (1992). Many States argued that the term was being misused and abused, with a view to embarrassing Israel. See e.g., UN Doc A/37/PV.108, paras. 121, 164, 171, 178 and 197.

13. F. Chalk and K. Jonassohn, 'The Conceptual Framework', in F. Chalk and K. Jonassohn, eds., *The History and Sociology of Genocide* (New Haven, Yale University Press 1990) pp. 3-43, at p. 11. Also K. Jonassohn, 'What is Genocide?', in H. Fein, ed., *Genocide Watch* (New Haven, Yale University Press 1991) pp. 17-26; K. Jonassohn and K. Solveig Björnson, *Genocide and Gross Human Rights Violation* (Brunswick NJ, Transaction 1998) p. 1.

14. *Prosecutor* v. *Tadić* (Case No. IT-94-1-AR72), Decision on the Defence Motion for Interlocutory Appeal on Jurisdiction, 2 October 1995, paras. 71 et seq.

tended by the drafters of the Convention in 1948. When the Rome Statute of the International Criminal Court was adopted, in July 1998, there were only perfunctory efforts at modifying the definition of genocide, and these garnered no real support in any event.[15]

The flourishing of international criminal law in the final decade of the Twentieth Century also gave new dynamism to an instrument and to a legal category that had begun to show signs of atrophy. This revival began when charges started to circulate that genocide was being committed during the war in Bosnia and Herzegovina. In March 1993, Bosnia and Herzegovina invoked Article IX as the basis of a claim before the International Court of Justice that the Federal Republic of Yugoslavia was in breach of the Genocide Convention. The Court accepted jurisdiction, and said that 'there is a grave risk of acts of genocide being committed'.[16] A few weeks later, the Security Council established the International Criminal Tribunal for the former Yugoslavia (ICTY), with jurisdiction over genocide pursuant to Article 4 of its Statute.[17] The next year it did the same regarding Rwanda, where the case that genocide had been committed was much clearer and never really in dispute.[18] At more or less the same time, national courts began to express more interest in genocide prosecutions on the basis of universal jurisdiction,[19] something they had been hesitant to do in the past, with the notable exception of the *Eichmann* prosecution in Israel in the early-1960s.[20]

The International Court of Justice has yet to issue a final judgment in a genocide case, although there are now four applications on its docket, that rely upon Article IX of the Convention.[21] The International Criminal Tribunal for Rwanda issued its first convictions for genocide in 1998, and several of its guilty verdicts have now been upheld on appeal.[22] The record of the ICTY is rather more uneven; there have

---

15. See Schabas, op. cit. n. 3, at pp. 93-98.

16. Application of the Convention on the prevention and punishment of the crime of genocide (*Bosnia and Herzegovina* v. *Yugoslavia (Serbia and Montenegro)*), Requests for the Indication of Provisional Measures, 8 April 1993, 16 *ICJ Rep.* (1993) p. 18.

17. Statute of the International Criminal Tribunal for the former Yugoslavia, UN Doc. S/RES/827 (1993), annex.

18. Statute of the International Criminal Tribunal for Rwanda, UN Doc. S/RES/955 (1994), annex. In the preamble to the resolution, the Council 'Express[ed] once again its grave concern at the reports indicating that genocide and other systematic, widespread and flagrant violations of international humanitarian law have been committed in Rwanda.' There is no comparable reference to charges of genocide in the resolution establishing the Yugoslavia Tribunal.

19. E.g., *Duško Tadić*, BGH-Ermittlungsrichter [Federal Court of Justice, Germany], 13 February 1994, BGs 100/94; *Cvjetkovic*, Landesgericht Salzburg, 31 May 1995.

20. *A.-G. Israel* v. *Eichmann*, 36 *ILR* (1968) 5 (District Court, Jerusalem); *A.-G. Israel* v. *Eichmann*, 36 *ILR* (1968) 277 (Israel Supreme Court).

21. In addition, to the 1993 application of Bosnia and Herzegovina, see Legality of Use of Force (*Yugoslavia* v. *Belgium et al.*), Application, 29 April 1999; Application of the Convention on the Prevention and Punishment of the Crime of Genocide (*Croatia* v. *Yugoslavia*), Application, 2 July 1999; Armed Activities on the Territory of the Congo (New Application 2000) (*Democratic Republic of the Congo* v. *Rwanda*), Application, 10 July 2002.

22. *Prosecutor* v. *Akayesu* (Case No. ICTR-96-4-A), Judgment, 1 June 2001; *Kambanda* v. *Prosecutor* (ICTR 97-23-A), Judgment, 19 October 2000; *Serushago* v. *Prosecutor* (Case No. ICTR-98-39-A), Reasons for Judgment, 6 April 2000; *Prosecutor* v. *Kayishema and Ruzindana* (Case No. ICTR-

been two acquittals[23] and only one conviction,[24] although several genocide cases are pending, including the celebrated prosecution of Slobodan Milošević.[25] There have also been important rulings by national courts, and significant developments in state practice, some of it related to the implementation of the Rome Statute. These developments have breathed new life into the provisions of the 1948 Convention. This article attempts to provide an overview of some of the major legal developments concerning genocide that have taken place during the past decade.

2.   GROUPS PROTECTED

Probably no single aspect of the definition of genocide in the 1948 Convention has provoked more dissatisfaction than the scope of the groups protected. Article II of the Convention says that genocide consists of the intentional destruction of a 'national, ethnical, racial or religious group'. Critics have complained about the exclusion of political, social and economic groups,[26] as well as women,[27] homosexuals[28], the elderly[29] and the mentally disturbed.[30] Yet amendment has proven to be out of the question. When states were given an opportunity to revise the definition, at the Rome Conference in June-July 1998, they chose instead to reaffirm the text verbatim that had been adopted by the General Assembly of the United Nations some 50 years earlier.[31] This may be taken as evidence that states do

---

95-1-A), Judgment (Reasons), 1 June 2001; *Prosecutor v. Musema* (Case No. ICTR-96-13-A), Judgment, 16 November 2001.

23. *Prosecutor v. Jelisić* (Case No. IT-95-10-T), Judgment, 14 December 1999, appeal dismissed: *Prosecutor v. Jelisić* (Case No. IT-95-10-A), Judgment, 5 July 2001; *Prosecutor v. Sikirica et al.* (Case No. IT-95-8-T), Judgment on Defence Motions to Acquit, 3 September 2001.

24. *Prosecutor v. Krstić* (Case No. IT-98-33-T), Judgment, 2 August 2001.

25. Milošević has been indicted for genocide only with respect to the war in Bosnia and Herzegovina: *Prosecutor v. Milošević* (Case No. IT-01-51-I), Indictment, 22 November 2001.

26. Chalk and Jonassohn, op. cit. n. 13, at p. 11.

27. B. Whitaker, 'Revised and updated report on the question of the prevention and punishment of the crime of genocide', UN Doc. E/CN.4/Sub.2/1985/6, p. 16, para. 30; K.D. Askin, *War Crimes Against Women, Prosecution in International War Crimes Tribunals* (The Hague, Martinus Nijhoff 1997) pp. 342-344

28. B. Whitaker, ibid.; J.N. Porter, 'What is Genocide? Notes Toward a Definition', in J.N. Porter, ed., *Genocide and Human Rights, A Global Anthology* (Lanham MD, University Press of America 1982) pp. 2-33, p. 8.

29. M. Lippman, 'The Drafting of the 1948 Convention on the Prevention and Punishment of the Crime of Genocide', 3 *Boston UILJ* (1985) p. 62.

30. Ibid.

31. 'Report of the Preparatory Committee on the Establishment of an International Criminal Court,' UN Doc. A/51/22, Vol. I, para. 61: 'There was a suggestion to expand the definition of the crime of genocide contained in the Convention to encompass social and political groups. This suggestion was supported by some delegations who felt that any gap in the definition should be filled. However, other delegations expressed opposition to amending the definition contained in the Convention, which was binding on all States as a matter of customary law and which had been incorporated in the implementing legislation of the numerous States parties to the Convention. The view was expressed that the amendment of existing conventions was beyond the scope of the present exercise. Concern was also expressed that providing for different definitions of the crime of genocide in the statute could

not desire any evolution in the concept. This is in quite marked contrast to the dynamism of the definitions of crimes against humanity and war crimes.

Most states, when they introduce the crime of genocide into their national legis- lation, hold fast to the terms of Article II of the 1948 Convention, although there are some variations. The French Code *pénal*, for example, admits genocide in the case of intentional destruction of any group based upon an 'arbitrary criterion'.[32] In its legislation implementing the Rome Statute, Canada extends the definition of genocide to

> 'an act or omission committed with intent to destroy, in whole or in part, an identifiable group of persons, as such, that, at the time and in the place of its commission, constitutes genocide according to customary international law or conventional international law or by virtue of its being criminal according to the general principles of law recognized by the community of nations'.[33]

However, it goes on to establish a presumption that the provision in the Rome Statute, which corresponds to Article II of the Convention, corresponds to custom- ary international law.[34] When Spain enacted a crime of genocide in 1971, it defined it with reference to a 'national ethnic, social or religious group'. However, the legislation was changed in 1983 and Spain returned to the enumeration in Article II of the Convention. Portugal's 1982 penal code also included 'social groups' within the definition of genocide.[35] However, the code was revised in 1995 and Portugal reverted to the Convention definition.[36] Germany's recently adopted Code of Crimes against International Law adheres to the 1948 text. In other words, the deviations from the Convention definition are very much the exception rather than the rule. State practice, as reflected in national legislation, absolutely confirms the enduring recognition of the list of protected groups adopted by the United Nations General Assembly more than 50 years ago.

The first Trial Chamber decision of the ICTR, vexed by how to categorise the Rwandan Tutsi minority, ruled that the enumeration in the Convention definition of genocide should be interpreted so as to encompass any 'stable and permanent'

---

result in the International Court of Justice and the international criminal court rendering conflicting decisions with respect to the same situation under the two respective instruments. It was suggested that acts such as murder that could qualify as genocide when committed against one of the groups referred to in the Convention could also constitute crimes against humanity when committed against members of other groups, including social or political groups.' Egypt was the source of the proposal: H. von Hebel and D. Robinson, 'Crimes Within the Jurisdiction of the Court', in Roy S. Lee, ed., *The Inter- national Criminal Court, The Making of the Rome Statute, Issues, Negotiations, Results* (The Hague, Kluwer Law International 1999) p. 89.

32. Penal Code (France), *JO* 23 July 1992, Art. 211-1. See also the Belgian proposal to the Interna- tional Law Commission: 'Comments and observations of governments on the draft Code of Crimes Against the Peace and Security of Mankind adopted on first reading by the International law Commis- sion at its Forty-third Session', UN Doc. A/CN.4/448, pp. 35-36.

33. *Crimes Against Humanity and War Crimes Act*, S.C. 2000, c. 24, s. 4(2).

34. Ibid., s. 4(4).

35. Penal Code of 1982 [Portugal], Art. 189.

36. Decree-Law No. 48/95 of 15 March 1995. The provision is now Art. 239 of the Penal Code.

group.[37] The Tribunal was uncomfortable with the word 'ethnic' because it believed that the Tutsi could not be meaningfully distinguished, in terms of language and culture, from the majority Hutu population.[38] Political correctness may have led it to shy away from the archaic formulation 'racial group'. And the terms 'national' and 'religious' clearly did not fit. Confronted with the prospect that none of the four terms of the definition might apply to the Rwandan genocide, the Tribunal concluded that the Convention could still extend to certain other groups, although their precise definition was elusive. Pledging fidelity to the Convention's drafters, the *Akayesu* judgment declared:

'On reading through the travaux préparatoires of the Genocide Convention (Summary Records of the meetings of the Sixth Committee of the General Assembly, 21 September - 10 December 1948, Official Records of the General Assembly), it appears that the crime of genocide was allegedly perceived as targeting only 'stable' groups, constituted in a permanent fashion and membership of which is determined by birth, with the exclusion of the more 'mobile' groups which one joins through individual voluntary commitment, such as political and economic groups. Therefore, a common criterion in the four types of groups protected by the Genocide Convention is that membership in such groups would seem to be normally not challengeable by its members, who belong to it automatically, by birth, in a continuous and often irremediable manner.'

The Trial Chamber continued:

'Moreover, the Chamber considered whether the groups protected by the Genocide Convention, echoed in Article 2 of the Statute, should be limited to only the four groups expressly mentioned and whether they should not also include any group which is stable and permanent like the said four groups. In other words, the question that arises is whether it would be impossible to punish the physical destruction of a group as such under the Genocide Convention, if the said group, although stable and membership is by birth, does not meet the definition of any one of the four groups expressly protected by the Genocide Convention. In the opinion of the Chamber, it is particularly important to respect the intention of the drafters of the Genocide Convention, which according to the travaux préparatoires, was patently to ensure the protection of any stable and permanent group.'[39]

---

37. *Prosecutor* v. *Akayesu* (Case No. ICTR-96-4-T), Judgment, 2 September 1998. Other judges of the Tribunal have not endorsed this expansive interpretation, classifying the Tutsi as an 'ethnic group' within the literal definition of genocide: *Prosecutor* v. *Kayishema and Ruzindana* (Case No. ICTR-95-1-T), Judgment, 21 May 1999, para. 94.

38. Nevertheless, the Tribunal employed the 'ethnic' classification in applying the concept of 'crimes against humanity', finding Akayesu guilty of a 'widespread or systematic attack on the civilian population on ethnic grounds': *Prosecutor* v. *Akayesu*, ibid., para. 652.

39. Ibid., para. 515. But note that the same Trial Chamber, in a subsequent decision, *Prosecutor* v. *Rutaganda* (Case No. ICTR-96-3-T), Judgment, 6 December 1999, seemed to hedge its remarks somewhat: 'It appears from a reading of the *travaux préparatoires* of the Genocide Convention that certain groups, such as political and economic groups have been excluded from the protected groups, because they are considered to be 'mobile groups' which one joins through individual, political com-

Judges of the ICTY have viewed the import of the *travaux préparatoires* of the Genocide Convention rather differently. Using an historical analysis, and relying on provisions in similar human rights instruments, they have observed that the four categories protected by the Convention correspond in large measure to what other texts have designated 'national minorities'.

'National, ethnical, racial or religious group are not clearly defined in the Convention or elsewhere. In contrast, the preparatory work on the Convention and the work conducted by international bodies in relation to the protection of minorities show that the concepts of protected groups and national minorities partially overlap and are on occasion synonymous. European instruments on human rights use the term "national minorities", while universal instruments more commonly make reference to "ethnic, religious or linguistic minorities"; the two expressions appear to embrace the same goals. In a study conducted for the Sub-Commission on Prevention of Discrimination and Protection of Minorities in 1979, F. Capotorti commented that "the Sub-Commission on Prevention of Discrimination and Protection of Minorities decided, in 1950, to replace the word 'racial' by the word 'ethnic' in all references to minority groups described by their ethnic origin." The International Convention on the Elimination of All Forms of Racial Discrimination defines racial discrimination as "any distinction, exclusion, restriction or preference based on race, colour, descent, or national or ethnic origin." The preparatory work on the Genocide Convention also reflects that the term "ethnical" was added at a later stage in order to better define the type of groups protected by the Convention and ensure that the term "national" would not be understood as encompassing purely political groups.'[40]

Accordingly, '[t]he preparatory work of the Convention shows that setting out such a list was designed more to describe a single phenomenon, roughly corresponding to what were recognised, before the second word war, as 'national minorities', rather than to refer to several distinct prototypes of human groups.'[41]

Interesting, both interpretations rely upon the *travaux préparatoires*. Of the two, the better one is surely that of the ICTY in *Krstić*. It strikes an appropriate balance in interpreting the provision, avoiding the narrow positivism of an approach that focuses on individual definitions for the four categories. At the same time, it respects the intent of the drafters, orienting genocide prosecution to the genuine object and purpose of the Convention, which was to protect national minorities from attacks upon their right to existence. It is striking that the Trial Chamber of the ICTY, in *Krstić*, does not even allude to the case law of the ICTR on this point.[42]

---

mitment. That would seem to suggest *a contrario* that the Convention was presumably intended to cover relatively stable and permanent groups.' (reference omitted). Also *Prosecutor* v. *Musema* (ICTR-96-13-T), Judgment, 27 January 2000, para. 162.

40. *Prosecutor* v. *Krstić*, *supra* n. 24, para. 555 (references omitted).

41. Ibid., para. 556.

42. For a criticism of the approach of the International Criminal Tribunal for Rwanda to the protected groups, see W.A. Schabas, 'L'affaire *Akayesu*', in K. Boustany and D. Dormoy, eds., *Génocide (s)* (Brussels, Éditions Bruylant, Éditions de l'Université de Bruxelles 1999) pp. 111-130; W.A. Schabas, 'Prosecutor v. Akayesu, Commentary', in A. Klip and G. Sluiter, eds., *Annotated Leading Cases of International Criminal Tribunals, The International Criminal Tribunal for Rwanda 1994-1999*,

A related question is whether the group to be protected is determined according to objective or subjective criteria. The judgments of the ICTR are divided on this point, with some judges supporting the view that the group must have some objective existence,[43] others contending that it is the perpetrator who determines the existence and definition of the group irrespective of objective considerations.[44] The ICTY has favoured the subjective approach. In *Jelisić*, the Trial Chamber said:

'Although the objective determination of a religious group still remains possible, to attempt to define a national, ethnical or racial group today using objective and scientifically irreproachable criteria would be a perilous exercise whose result would not necessarily correspond to the perception of the persons concerned by such categorization. Therefore, it is more appropriate to evaluate the status of a national, ethnical or racial group from the point of view of those persons who wish to single that group out from the rest of the community. The Trial Chamber consequently elects to evaluate membership in a national, ethnical or racial group using a subjective criterion. It is the stigmatisation of a group as a distinct national, ethnical or racial unit by the community which allows it to be determined whether a targeted population constitutes a national, ethnical or racial group in the eyes of the alleged perpetrators.'[45]

These views were endorsed by a different Trial Chamber in *Krstić*.[46]

The subjective approach is appealing up to a point, especially because the perpetrator's intent is a decisive element in the crime of genocide. Probably its flaw is allowing, at least in theory, genocide to be committed against a group that does not have any real objective existence. To make an analogy with ordinary criminal law, many penal codes stigmatise patricide, that is, the killing of one's parents. But the murderer who kills an individual believing, erroneously, that he or she is killing a parent, is only a murderer, not a patricide. Should not the same reasoning apply to the crime genocide? Although quite helpful to an extent, the subjective approach flounders because law cannot permit the crime to be defined by the offender alone. It is necessary, therefore, to determine some objective existence for the four groups. This issue may not be of great practical significance, however. In the words of the former High Commissioner on National Minorities of the Organization for Security and Cooperation in Europe, Max van der Stoel: 'I know a minority when I see one.'[47]

Vol. 2 (Antwerp, Intersentia 2001) pp. 539-554. See also D.M. Amann, 'Prosecutor v. Akayesu', 93 *AJIL* (1999) p. 195.

43. *Prosecutor* v. *Rutaganda*, *supra* n. 39, para. 57.

44. *Prosecutor* v. *Kayishema and Ruzindana*, *supra* n. 37, para. 98.

45. *Prosecutor* v. *Jelisić*, *supra* n. 23, para. 70.

46. *Prosecutor* v. *Krstić*, *supra* n. 24, para. 557.

47. M. van der Stoel, 'Prevention of Minority Conflicts', in L.B. Sohn, ed., *The CSCE and the Turbulent New Europe* (Washington, Friedrich-Naumann-Stiftung 1993) pp. 147-154, at p. 148. His comment was inspired by United States Supreme Court Justice Potter Stewart who said the same thing about pornography: *Jacobellis* v. *Ohio*, 378 US 184, 197 (1963).

3.   THE MEANING OF 'IN WHOLE OR IN PART'

There has been much confusion about the requirement in the definition of genocide that the group be destroyed 'in whole or in part'. These terms appear in the *chapeau* of Article II of the Convention, and refer to the genocidal intent. Thus, the reference is not to the physical act, as if there must be some quantitative threshold where mass murder turns into genocide, but rather to the intent of the perpetrators. The actual result, in terms of quantity, will nevertheless be relevant in that it assists the trier of fact to draw conclusions about intent based on the behaviour of the offender. The greater the number of actual victims, the more plausible becomes the deduction that the perpetrators intended to destroy the group, in whole or in part.

This still does not resolve the problem of construing the meaning of the term 'in part'. Could it be genocide to target only a few persons for murder because of their membership in a particular ethnic group? A literal reading of the definition seems to support such an interpretation.[48] Nevertheless, this construction is rather too extreme, and inconsistent with the drafting history, as well as with the context and the object and purpose of the Genocide Convention.

Four different approaches to the scope of the term in part' have emerged. The first is the narrowest, and effectively insists that while the actual result may only be partial destruction, the intent must be to destroy the entire group. It was advanced by the Truman administration in its failed attempt to get congressional approval for ratification of the Genocide Convention. Members of the Senate were concerned that Article II might apply to the 'sporadic outbreaks against the Negro population'.[49] At the time, lynching of African-Americans was a not infrequent occurrence in the apartheid-like regime of the southern United States of America. Dean Rusk, then Deputy Under Secretary of State, testified before the Senate that the drafters of Article II meant to deal only with the intent to destroy the group as a whole, although the crime would be made out even if part of the group were actually destroyed. Rusk said: 'United Nations negotiators felt that it should not be necessary that an entire group be destroyed to constitute the crime of genocide, but rather that genocide meant the partial destruction of a group with the intent to

---

48. For an example, see L. Sadat Wexler and J. Paust, 'Preamble, Parts 1 & 2', 13*ter Nouvelles études pénales* (1998) p. 5.

49. According to a 1947 State Department internal memorandum prepared for those involved in negotiations on the draft *Genocide Convention*, 'The possibility exists that sporadic outbreaks against the Negro population in the United States may be brought to the attention of the United Nations, since the treaty, if ratified, would place this offence in the realm of international jurisdiction and remove the 'safeguard' of article 2(7) of the Charter. However, since the offence will not exist unless part of an overall plan to destroy a human group, and since the Federal Government would under the treaty acquire jurisdiction over such offences, no possibility can be foreseen of the United States being held in violation of the treaty': 'U.S. Commentary on Secretariat Draft Convention on Genocide, Memorandum, Sept. 10, 1947, Gross and Rusk to Lovett', National Archives, United States of America, 501. BD-Genocide, 1945-49. See also L.J. Leblanc, 'The Intent to Destroy Groups in the Genocide Convention', 78 *AJIL* (1984) p. 370, at p. 377.

destroy the entire group concerned.'[50] In somewhat the same spirit, Raphael Lemkin wrote to the Senate Committee in 1950 that 'the destruction in part must be of a substantial nature so as to affect the entirety'.[51] But this approach is not only not confirmed by the *travaux préparatoires*, it is also at variance with the words of article II themselves. As the International Law Commission noted in its 1996 report on the draft Code of Crimes: 'it is not necessary to achieve the final result of the destruction of a group in order for a crime of genocide to have been committed. It is enough to have committed any one of the acts listed in the article with the clear intention of bringing about the total or partial destruction of a protected group as such'.[52]

The second approach adds the adjective 'substantial' in order to modify 'part', and is the one that the United States eventually adopted when it ratified the Convention some 40 years later. The United States formulated a declaration affirming that the meaning of Article II is 'in whole or in substantial part'.[53] In its own domestic legislation, the United States defines 'substantial part' as 'a part of a group of such numerical significance that the destruction or loss of that part would cause the destruction of the group as a viable entity within the nation of which such group is a part'.[54] The International Law Commission considered that '[i]t is not necessary to intend to achieve the complete annihilation of a group from every corner of the globe. None the less the crime of genocide by its very nature requires the intent to destroy at least a substantial part of a particular group.'[55] One of the earliest academic commentators on the Convention, Nehemiah Robinson, wrote that genocide is aimed at destroying 'a multitude of persons of the same group', as long as the number is 'substantial'.[56] Similarly, the final draft statute considered by the Preparatory Committee of the International Criminal Court noted that '[t]he reference to 'intent to destroy, in whole or in part ... a group, as such' was under-

---

50. United States of America, *Hearing Before a Subcommittee Committee of the Committee on Foreign Relations, United States Senate, Jan. 23, 1950* (Washington, US Government Printing Office 1950) p. 12. According to A.J. Schweppe of the American Bar Association, Rusk 'mispoke', because the *Convention* clearly contemplates destruction of a group 'in part': ibid., 24 January 1950, p. 201. Discussed in Leblanc, ibid., p. 373.

51. Two Executive Sessions of the Senate Foreign Relations Committee, Historical Series 370 (1976). These views were not new to Lemkin, who had written, in 1947, that the definition of genocide was subordinated to the intent 'to destroy or to cripple permanently a human group'. See R. Lemkin, 'Genocide as a Crime in International Law', 41 *AJIL* (1947) p. 145, at p. 147.

52. 'Report of the International Law Commission on the work of its forty-eighth session, 6 May-26 July 1996', UN Doc. A/51/10, p. 126. Also 'Report of the Commission to the General Assembly on the work of its forty-first session', UN Doc A/CN.4/SER.A/1989/Add.1 (Part 2), p. 102, para. (6).

53. Lemkin had proposed the text of an 'understanding' that he invited the United States to file at the time of ratification: '[o]n the understanding that the Convention applies only to actions undertaken on a mass scale and not to individual acts even if some of these acts are committed in the course of riots or local disturbances'. Two Executive Sessions of the Senate Foreign Relations Committee, Historical Series 370 (1976).

54. Genocide Convention Implementation Act of 1987, sec. 1093(8).

55. 'Report of the International Law Commission on the work of its forty-eighth session, 6 May-26 July 1996', UN Doc. A/51/10, p. 125.

56. N. Robinson, *The Genocide Convention: A Commentary* (New York, Institute of Jewish Affairs 1960) p. 63.

stood to refer to the specific intention to destroy more than a small number of individuals who are members of a group.'[57] The ICTR, in *Kayishema and Ruzindana*, said 'that "in part" requires the intention to destroy a considerable number of individuals'.[58] According to the ICTY, genocide must involve the intent to destroy a 'substantial' part, although not necessarily a 'very important part'.[59] In another judgment, the Tribunal referred to a 'reasonably substantial' number relative to the group as a whole.[60]

A Trial Chamber of the ICTY has made the helpful observation that

> 'the intent to destroy a group, even if only in part, means seeking to destroy a distinct part of the group as opposed to an accumulation of isolated individuals within it. Although the perpetrators of genocide need not seek to destroy the entire group protected by the Convention, they must view the part of the group they wish to destroy as a distinct entity which must be eliminated as such. A campaign resulting in the killings, in different places spread over a broad geographical area, of a finite number of members of a protected group might not thus qualify as genocide, despite the high total number of casualties, because it would not show an intent by the perpetrators to target the very existence of the group as such.'[61]

In *Sikirica*, a Trial Chamber of the ICTY said it must be the group which is targeted, and not merely individuals within the group, adding that this is the meaning to be ascribed to the words 'as such' in the definition of genocide.[62]

A third approach takes more of a qualitative than a quantitative perspective, reading in the adjective 'significant'. In a sense, it is similar to the 'viable entity' formulation in the United States declaration, although it treats viability not as if there is some critical mass of a group in a numeric sense below which it cannot survive, but rather in terms of irreparable impact upon a group's chances of survival when a stratum of its population, generally political, social or economic, is liquidated. There is nothing to support this in the *travaux*, and the idea seems to have been launched by Benjamin Whitaker in his 1985 report. He wrote that the term 'in part' denotes 'a reasonably significant number, relative to the total of the group as a whole, or else a significant section of a group such as its leadership'.[63]

Citing the Whitaker report, the Commission of Experts established by the Security Council in 1992 to investigate violations of international humanitarian law in

---

57. 'Draft Statute for the International Criminal Court. Part. 2. Jurisdiction, Admissibility and Applicable Law', UN Doc. A/AC.249/1998/CRP.8, p. 2, n. 1.

58. *Prosecutor* v. *Kayishema and Ruzindana, supra* n. 37, para. 97. Cited in *Prosecutor* v. *Bagilishema* (Case No. ICTR-95-1A-T), Judgment, 7 June 2001, para. 64; *Prosecutor* v. *Krstić, supra* n. 24, para. 586.

59. *Prosecutor* v. *Jelisić* (Case No. IT-95-10-T), Judgment, 19 October 1999; also *Prosecutor* v. *Bagilishema, supra* n. 58, para. 64.

60. *Prosecutor* v. *Sikirica et al., supra* n. 23, para. 65.

61. *Prosecutor* v. *Krstić, supra* n. 24, para. 590. See also 'Report of the International Law Commission on the work of its forty-eighth session, 6 May-26 July 1996', UN Doc. A/51/10, p. 88.

62. *Prosecutor* v. *Sikirica et al., supra* n. 23, para. 89.

63. Whitaker, loc. cit. n. 27, at p. 16, para. 29.

the former Yugoslavia held that 'in part' had not only a quantitative but also a qualitative dimension. According to the Commission's chair, Professor M. Cherif Bassiouni, the definition in the Genocide Convention was deemed 'sufficiently pliable to encompass not only the targeting of an entire group, as stated in the convention, but also the targeting of certain segments of a given group, such as the Muslim elite or Muslim women'. The Commission of Experts gave several examples of such 'significant' portions of a group: political and administrative leaders, religious leaders, academics and intellectuals, business leaders, and others. 'Similarly, the extermination of a group's law enforcement and military personnel may be a significant section of a group in that it renders the group at large defence-less against other abuses of a similar or other nature, particularly if the leadership is being eliminated as well', the Commission noted.[64]

This approach was adopted by the Prosecutor of the ICTY, in indictments,[65] and subsequently endorsed by the judges themselves. According to the Trial Chamber in *Jelisić*, it might be possible to infer the requisite genocidal intent from the 'de-sired destruction of a more limited number of persons selected for the impact that their disappearance would have upon the survival of the group as such'.[66] How-ever, ultimately the Trial Chamber said it was not possible 'to conclude beyond all reasonable doubt that the choice of victims arose from a precise logic to destroy the most representative figures of the Muslim community in Brcko to the point of threatening the survival of that community'.[67] The same scenario of relatively small numbers of killings in concentration camps returned in *Sikirica*, but again, the judges could not discern any pattern in the camp killings that suggested the intent to destroy a 'significant' part of the local Muslim community so as to threat-en its survival. The victims were taxi drivers, schoolteachers, lawyers, pilots, butchers and café owners but not, apparently, community leaders. The Trial Cham-ber observed that 'they do not appear to have been persons with any special sig-nificance to their community, except to the extent that some of them were of military age, and therefore could be called up for military service'.[68]

The test, then, using the 'significant part' approach, would appear to be whether the destruction of a social strata threatens the group's survival as a whole. As the Commission of Experts noted, such an attack

'must be viewed in the context of the fate of what happened to the rest of the group. If a group suffers extermination of its leadership and in the wake of that loss, a large number of its members are killed or subjected to other heinous acts, for example deportation, the

---

64. 'Final Report of the Commission of Experts', UN Doc. S/1994/674, para. 94.

65. *Prosecutor v. Karadžić and Mladić* (Case Nos. IT-95-18-R61, IT-95-5-R61), Transcript of hearing of 27 June 1996, p. 15. The Prosecutor (Eric Ostberg) noted that he relied on the Whitaker report (see loc. cit. n. 27). Also *Prosecutor v. Jelisić and Cesić* (Case No. IT-95-10-I), Indictment, 21 July 1995, para. 17; *Prosecutor v. Jelisić and Cesić* (Case No. IT-95-10-I), Amended Indictment, 12 May 1998, para. 16; *Prosecutor v. Jelisić and Cesić* (Case No. IT-95-10-I), Second Amended Indict-ment, 19 October 1998, para. 14.

66. *Prosecutor v. Jelesić, supra* n. 23, para. 82.

67. Ibid., para. 93.

68. *Prosecutor v. Sikirica et al., supra* n. 23, para. 80.

cluster of violations ought to be considered in its entirety in order to interpret the provisions of the Convention in a spirit consistent with its purpose'.[69]

In *Jelisić*, the significant group was described as being composed of 'the most representative figures'.[70] In *Sikirica*, they were alleged to be community leaders.[71] In *Krstić* – the only one of the three to result in a conviction – the Trial Chamber seemed convinced by prosecution arguments whereby the men and boys of military age, who were the victims of the Srebrenica massacre of July 1995, were the 'significant part' of the Muslim community. This is not the same as the 'leadership', although the reasoning is similar, as is the 'decisive effect on the group's survival' criterion. The *Krstić* judgment explains:

> 'Granted, only the men of military age were systematically massacred, but it is significant that these massacres occurred at a time when the forcible transfer of the rest of the Bosnian Muslim population was well under way. The Bosnian Serb forces could not have failed to know, by the time they decided to kill all the men, that this selective destruction of the group would have a lasting impact upon the entire group. Their death precluded any effective attempt by the Bosnian Muslims to recapture the territory. Furthermore, the Bosnian Serb forces had to be aware of the catastrophic impact that the disappearance of two or three generations of men would have on the survival of a traditionally patriarchal society, an impact the Chamber has previously described in detail. The Bosnian Serb forces knew, by the time they decided to kill all of the military aged men, that the combination of those killings with the forcible transfer of the women, children and elderly would inevitably result in the physical disappearance of the Bosnian Muslim population at Srebrenica.'[72]

The 'significant part' approach inevitably leads to speculation about what the killing of one or another strata in a community will do to its survival. Perhaps killing the 'leaders' will do the trick. But somebody bent upon destroying a group might more logically focus on the children, or the women, as they ensure the group's survival in a biological sense. It becomes an invitation to value judgments about how important one or another segment of an ethnic group may be to the survival of the community. In *Krstić*, the Prosecutor had argued that 'what remains of the Srebrenica community survives in many cases only in the biological sense, nothing more. It's a community in despair; it's a community clinging to memories; it's a community that is lacking leadership; it's a community that's a shadow of what it once was'.[73]

It is important, not to confuse the concept of destruction of a 'substantial part' and that of a 'significant part'. The recent authorities that develop the 'significant part' interpretation use the phenomenon of selective killing of certain segments of

---

69. 'Final Report of the Commission of Experts', UN Doc. S/1994/674, para. 94.
70. *Prosecutor* v. *Jelisić, supra* n. 23, para. 93.
71. *Prosecutor* v. *Sikirica et al., supra* n. 23, para. 80.
72. *Prosecutor* v. *Krstić, supra* n. 24, para. 595.
73. Ibid., para. 592.

a group as evidence of intent to destroy the group as a whole, assuming it is predicated on a calculation that destruction of the 'significant' members of the group will irrevocably compromise the existence of what remains. The same reasoning does not apply to destruction of a 'substantial part', because it accepts the possibility that the perpetrators may only intend to destroy a part of the group. Of course, there is no reason why destruction of the leadership, that is, of a 'significant' part, could not provide proof of intent to destroy a 'substantial' part of a particular group.

The fourth interpretative approach to 'in whole or in part' focuses on the groups in a geographic sense. Thus, destroying all members of a group within a continent, or a country, or an administrative region or even a town, might satisfy the 'in part' requirement of Article II. The Turkish government targeted Armenians within its borders, not those of the Diaspora. The intentions of the Nazis may only have been to rid Europe of Jews; they were probably not ambitious enough, even in their heyday, to imagine this possibility on a world scale. Indications they were prepared to accept the departure of Jews from Europe for Palestine, even in the later stages of the war, can support such a claim. Similarly, in 1994 the Rwandan extremists do not appear to have given serious consideration to eliminating Tutsi populations beyond the country's borders. In all three 'classic' cases, then, an argument can be made that the intent was not to destroy the group as a whole, but rather a geographically delimited part of the group. According to Professor Bassiouni,

> 'Furthermore, a given group can be defined on the basis of its regional existence, as opposed to a broader and all-inclusive concept encompassing all the members of that group who may be in different regions or areas. For example, all Muslims in Bosnia-Herzegovina could be considered a protected group. One could also define the group as all Muslims in a given area of Bosnia-Herzegovina, such as Prijedor, if the intent of the perpetrator is the elimination of that narrower group ... For example, all Bosnians in Sarajevo, irrespective of ethnicity or religion, could constitute a protected group.'[74]

Surely, it is cases like these that are contemplated by the phrase 'in whole or in part' found in Article II of the Convention.

But if this approach seems plausible when applied to a single continent or to a country, can it also work with respect to much smaller units? A Chamber of the Yugoslavia Tribunal has noted that

> '[i]n view of the particular intent requirement, which is the essence of the crime of genocide, the relative proportionate scale of the actual or attempted physical destruction of a group, or a significant section thereof, should be considered in relation to the factual opportunity of the accused to destroy a group in a specific geographic area within the

---

74. M.C. Bassiouni, 'The Commission of Experts Established Pursuant to Security Council Resolution 780: Investigating Violations of International Humanitarian Law in the Former Yugoslavia', 5 *Crim. LF* (1994) pp. 279, at pp. 323-324.

sphere of his control, and not in relation to the entire population of the group in a wider geographic sense.'[75]

In *Jelisić*, another Trial Chamber of the same Tribunal agreed that genocide could be committed in a 'limited geographic zone'.[76] And in *Krstić*, the Tribunal held that 'the physical destruction may target only a part of the geographically limited part of the larger group because the perpetrators of the genocide regard the intended destruction as sufficient to annihilate the group as a distinct entity in the geographic area at issue'.[77] Actually, *Krstić* amounts to a hybrid of both the 'significant part' approach and the small geographic unit' approaches. Recent judgments of the Federal Constitutional Court of Germany and the Bavarian Appeals Chamber also confirm this interpretation.[78] Nehemiah Robinson wrote that the real point of the term 'in part' is to encompass genocide where it is directed against a part of a country, or a single town.[79]

The paradigm for this view is a 1982 resolution of the United Nations General Assembly declaring the massacre of a few hundred victims in the Palestinian refugee camps of Sabra and Shatila, located in the suburbs of Beirut, an 'act of genocide'.[80] The resolution was not unanimous, however, and a separate vote on the paragraph referring to genocide was approved by 98 to 19, with 23 abstentions, on a recorded vote.[81] Doubtless, many states used the term 'genocide' to express their outrage at the atrocity in a manner calculated to torment a state whose population had itself suffered so much as a result of the same crime. A General Assembly resolution could, in theory, be of considerable assistance in construing the scope of the words 'in whole or in part', as a form of authentic interpretation or merely an indication of *opinio juris* of states. Yet the circumstances surrounding the adoption of the Sabra and Shatila resolution, and the lack of unanimity, argue against drawing definitive conclusions.[82]

---

75. *Prosecutor* v. *Karadžić and Mladić* (Case Nos. IT-95-18-R61, IT-95-5-R61), Transcript of hearing of 27 June 1996, *supra* n. 65, p. 25.

76. *Prosecutor* v. *Jelisić*, *supra* n. 23, para. 83.

77. *Prosecutor* v. *Krstić*, *supra* n. 24, para. 590. Also *Prosecutor* v. *Sikirica et al.*, *supra* n. 23, para. 68.

78. *Nikolai Jorgić, Bundesverfassungsgericht* [Federal Constitutional Court], Fourth Chamber, Second Senate, 12 December 2000, 2 BvR 1290/99, para. 23; *Novislav Djajić, Bayerisches Oberstes Landesgericht,* 23 May 1997, 3 St 20/96, excerpted in *Neue Juristische Wochenschrift* (1998) p. 392. See C.J.M. Safferling, 'Public Prosecutor v. Djajic', 92 *AJIL* (1998) p. 528.

79. Robinson, op. cit. n. 56, p. 63.

80. GA Res. 37/123 D.

81. UN Doc A/37/PV.108, para. 151.

82. See *Prosecutor* v. *Jelisić, supra* n. 23, para. 83. Also A. Cassese, *Violence and Law in the Modern Age* (Princeton, New Jersey Princeton University Press 1988) pp. 82-84; A. Cassese, 'La Communauté internationale et le génocide', in *Le droit international au service de la paix, de la justice et du développement, Mélanges Michel Virally* (Paris, Pedone 1991) pp. 183-194, pp. 191-192. Four of six members of an international commission, chaired by Sean MacBride and established to investigate the massacre, concluded that the 'deliberate destruction of the national and cultural rights and identity of the Palestinian people amount[ed] to genocide': cited in L.A. Malone, 'Sharon v. Time, The Criminal Responsibility Under International Law for Civilian Massacres', 3 *Palestine YIL* (1986)

4.   'SPECIFIC INTENT' OR *DOLUS SPECIAL*

Judgments of the *ad hoc* Tribunals have helped to complicate the issue of genocidal intent by using the terms *dolus specialis*[83] and 'special intent'[84] to describe the particular mental element or *mens rea* of the crime of genocide, despite the fact that the mental element or *mens rea* is already set out within the definition itself. In *Kambanda*, a Trial Chamber of the ICTR observed: 'The crime of genocide is unique because of its element of dolus specialis (special intent) which requires that the crime be committed with the intent "to destroy in whole or in part, a national, ethnic, racial or religious group as such".'[85] In *Jelisić*, the Trial Chamber used the expression only once, in what is essentially a concluding paragraph of the December 14 judgment: 'The Trial Chamber therefore concludes that it has not been proved beyond all reasonable doubt that the accused was motivated by the dolus specialis of the crime of genocide.' In explanation, the Trial Chamber said that *Jelisić* 'killed arbitrarily rather than with the clear intention to destroy a group'.[86]

The issue was raised by the Office of the Prosecutor in the appeal of the *Jelisić* acquittal. For the Prosecutor, the concept of *dolus specialis* set too high a standard, and could not be equated with the common law concepts of 'specific intent' or 'special intent'.[87] The Appeals Chamber dealt with the matter rather laconically, saying simply that the Trial Chamber had used the term *dolus specialis* as if it meant 'specific intent'.[88] The Appeals Chamber employed 'specific intent' to describe 'the intent to destroy in whole or in part, a national, ethnical, racial or religious group, as such', or in other words the normative requirement set out in the *chapeau* of the definition of genocide.[89]

The definition requires that the accused commit one of five punishable acts, of which 'killing' sits at the top of the list and is arguably the most serious. Obviously the accused must have the intent to commit the act of 'killing'. In the common law system, 'killing' *simpliciter* (i.e., murder[90]) is a crime of 'specific intent', in that the accused may rebut a charge with evidence that he or she lacked the 'specific' intent to commit homicide, for example because of voluntary intoxication.[91] The result is acquittal for the crime of murder but conviction for the lesser and included crime of manslaughter or involuntary homicide, itself a crime of 'general intent'. But for

---

p. 41, at p. 70, fn. 169. Also W.T. Mallison and S.V. Mallison, *The Palestine Problem in International Law and World Order* (London, Longman 1986) pp. 387-440.

83. *Prosecutor* v. *Akayesu*, *supra* n. 37, paras. 121, 226, 227, 245, 268.

84. Ibid., paras. 226, 227, 238, 245, 246, 272, 296.

85. *Prosecutor* v. *Kambanda* (Case No. ICTR 97-23-S), Judgment and Sentence, para. 16. Also *Prosecutor* v. *Kayishema and Ruzindana*, *supra* n. 37, para. 91; *Prosecutor* v. *Rutaganda*, *supra* n. 39, para. 59.

86. *Prosecutor* v. *Jelisić*, *supra* n. 23, para. 108.

87. *Prosecutor* v. *Jelisić*, *supra* n. 23, Prosecution's Appeal Brief (Redacted Version), para. 4.22. Also *Prosecutor* v. *Sikirica et al.*, *supra* n. 23, para. 142.

88. *Prosecutor* v. *Jelisić* (Case No. IT-95-10-A), Judgment, 5 July 2001, para. 51.

89. Ibid., para. 45.

90. See *Prosecutor* v. *Kayishema and Ruzindana*, *supra* n. 22, para. 151.

91. *DPP* v. *Beard*, [1920] AC 479 (HL).

'killing' to constitute the crime of genocide, it must be accompanied by the 'intent to destroy, in whole or in part, a national, ethnical, racial or religious group as such'. This presumably is all that is meant by the *dolus specialis*, or the special intent, or the specific intent, of the crime of genocide.

Importation of enigmatic concepts like *dolus specialis* or 'specific intent' from national systems of criminal law may have unduly complicated matters. The *Sikirica* Trial Chamber criticised the Prosecutor for introducing a debate about theories of intent, noting that the matter should be resolved with reference to the text of the provision:

> 'The first rule of interpretation is to give words their ordinary meaning where the text is clear. Here, the meaning of intent is made plain in the chapeau to Article 4(2). Beyond saying that the very specific intent required must be established, particularly in the light of the potential for confusion between genocide and persecution, the Chamber does not consider it necessary to indulge in the exercise of choosing one of the three standards identified by the Prosecution. In the light, therefore, of the explanation that the provision itself gives as to the specific meaning of intent, it is unnecessary to have recourse to theories of intent.'[92]

In *Krstić,* evidence showed that the accused had participated in a 'joint criminal enterprise' involving the destruction of Bosnian Muslim men and boys of military age. Although he organised the evacuation of women, children and the elderly, he also participated in the subsequent operations, and these involved the summary executions. There was no evidence that he personally killed the Muslim men or boys, that he was present when they were killed, or that he ordered their killing. But as a participant in the overall military operation, the Trial Chamber considered it sufficient that Jelisić had knowledge that extermination was being carried out. But even here, there was no direct evidence of his knowledge of the mass killings. Nevertheless, 'General Krstić could only surmise that the original objective of ethnic cleansing by forcible transfer had turned into a lethal plan to destroy the male population of Srebrenica once and for all'.[93] Indeed, Krstić was commander, both *de facto* and *de jure*, of the Drina Corps, which 'rendered tangible and substantial assistance and technical support to the detention, killing and burial'[94] of the victims. The Trial Chamber seems to have presumed that General Krstić knew of the summary executions.

This *mens rea* falls considerably shy of the standard of *dolus specialis* in continental law systems. Nevertheless, it would appear consistent with the text of the definition, to the extent that General Krstić had knowledge of the plan to destroy the Bosnian Muslims of Srebrenica and participated actively in it. One interesting result of the *Krstić* Trial Chamber's analysis concerns the concept of command responsibility, which is set out in Article 7(3) of the Tribunal's Statute. Krstić

---

92. *Prosecutor* v. *Sikirica et al., supra* n. 23, para. 60.
93. *Prosecutor* v. *Krstić, supra* n. 24, para. 622.
94. Ibid., para. 624.

might have been convicted on this basis because genocide was committed by subordinates and he knew or had reason to know that they were about to commit genocide, or had done so and he failed to take the necessary and reasonable measures to prevent such acts or to punish the perpetrators. The Trial Chamber opted for what was apparently the more demanding route,[95] however, in effect presuming that General Krstić commanded his troops to participate in the massacres, although nowhere does it state this explicitly. Still, if he was convicted qua commander because his troops actually carried out what the Trial Chamber deemed to be genocidal acts, then it should have been because he gave the orders, and not because his troops carried out acts that he had reason to know about, which is the scenario contemplated by command responsibility. *Krstić* is a bold decision, based on circumstantial evidence and presumptions, but one more satisfying from the standpoint of criminal law theory than a discounted conviction relying only upon proof of negligence.

Accordingly, the issue of whether or not genocide can actually be convicted on the basis of command responsibility still remains to be decided. After all, the knowledge requirement of command responsibility ('had reason to know') is an objective negligence standard that manifestly falls short of the 'specific intent' required by the chapeau of the genocide provision. And yet the statutes of the ad hoc tribunals, as well as Article 28 of the Rome Statute, contemplate this apparently contradictory hypothesis, namely that a person who only 'had reason to know' may also have had the intent to destroy a protected group. The decisions on command responsibility in genocide indicate a profound judicial malaise with the entire concept. The Rwanda Tribunal acquitted Akayesu on the portions of the indictment concerning command responsibility because it found these to be ambiguous.[96] Similarly, in *Bagilishema*, the Tribunal acquitted the bourgmestre of the commune of Mabanza of genocide charges founded mainly upon the doctrine of command responsibility.[97] The ICTR convicted Omer Serushago of genocide pursuant to Article 6(3) of its Statute, in other words, on the basis of command responsibility, pursuant to his guilty plea. As the Tribunal explained, Omar Serushago was the *de facto* leader of the political militia known as the Interahamwe. The relevant portion of the judgment reads:

'28. It was submitted by the Prosecutor and admitted by the Defence, that Omar Serushago, in the commission of the crimes for which he has been found guilty, played a leading role and that he therefore incurs individual criminal responsibility under the provisions of Article 6(3) of the Statute. At the time of commission of the offences for which he is held responsible, Omar Serushago enjoyed definite authority in his region.

---

95. Ibid., para. 605.

96. *Prosecutor v. Akayesu*, supra n. 37, para. 689: 'Although the evidence supports a finding that a superior/subordinate relationship existed between the Accused and the Interahamwe who were at the bureau communal, the Tribunal notes that there is no allegation in the Indictment that the Interahamwe, who are referred to as 'armed local militia,' were subordinates of the Accused. This relationship is a fundamental element of the criminal offence set forth in Article 6(3)'.

97. *Prosecutor v. Bagilishema*, supra n. 58.

He participated in several meetings during which the fate of the Tutsi was decided.

29. He was a de facto leader of the Interahamwe in Gisenyi. Within the scope of the activities of these militiamen, he gave orders which were followed. Omar Serushago admitted that several victims were executed on his orders while he was manning a road-block erected near the border between Rwanda and the Democratic Republic of Congo. As stated supra, thirty-three persons were killed by people placed under his authority. The accused admitted that all these crimes were committed because their victims were Tutsi or because, being moderate Hutu, they were considered accomplices.'[98]

The ruling is equivocal, because to the extent Serushago commanded the Intera-hamwe and gave orders that were carried out, he was guilty as a principal offender or accomplice pursuant to Article 6(1) of the Statute, and not on the basis of command responsibility. Similarly, the Tribunal accepted the guilty plea of Jean Kambanda to an indictment for genocide containing elements of command responsibility. Kambanda was Prime Minister of Rwanda during the genocide, and there was uncontested evidence that he had actually participated in the orders to commit genocide.[99] Thus, as in *Serushago*, the command responsibility indictments were redundant and unnecessary. Similarly, Clement Kayishema was found guilty based on command responsibility, but only after the Tribunal had determined he had also planned, instigated, ordered, committee or otherwise aided and abetted in the planning, perpetration or execution of the crimes.[100] In *Musema*, the Trial Chamber held the accused responsible on the basis of command responsibility after noting that he was 'personally present at the attack sites' and that he 'nevertheless failed to take the necessary and reasonable measures to prevent the commission of said acts by his subordinates, but rather abetted in the commission of those acts, by his presence and personal participation'.[101] Thus, none of these decisions is a particularly convincing authority for a conviction of genocide on the basis of command responsibility in the pure sense. In all of them, the basis of guilt is much closer to traditional forms of complicity, or at any rate those contemplated by joint criminal enterprise liability. The real test of the command responsibility provisions will be a finding of guilt where, as in the classic case of Yamashita,[102] it is not proven beyond a reasonable doubt that the commander or superior had knowledge of genocide committed by subordinates.

---

98. *Prosecutor* v. *Serushago* (Case No. ICTR-98-39-S), Sentence, 5 February 1999.
99. *Prosecutor* v. *Kambanda*, *supra* n. 85.
100. *Prosecutor* v. *Kayishema and Ruzindana*, *supra* n. 37, para. 473.
101. *Prosecutor* v. *Musema*, *supra* n. 39, para. 894; also paras. 899, 905, 914, 924.
102. *United States of America* v. *Yamashita*, (1948) 4 LRTWC 1, pp. 36-37; *In re* Yamashita, 327 US 1 (1945).

5.   'INTENT TO DESTROY'

There are many ways to destroy a national, ethnic, racial or religious group, of which extermination camps like those at Auschwitz-Birkenau, Treblinka and Belzec are only one. It is also possible to destroy a group by prohibiting its language, or by eliminating its traditional economy, or by a multitude of means falling short of actual physical elimination whose consequence is loss of identity by a people. The *chapeau* to Article II of the Convention requires that a perpetrator of genocide have the 'intent to destroy' a protected group. But it does not specify the type of destruction. Obviously, this covers physical extermination. But does it also cover other means of destruction that ensure the disappearance of a group although by means that strike at its culture, its language and its economy rather than its physical or biological existence?

The drafters of the Genocide Convention meant to confine its scope to physical and biological genocide. At various stages in the process they debated whether to include 'cultural genocide' alongside physical and biological genocide. Advocates of a narrow approach argued that cultural genocide was more properly addressed under the rubric of minority rights in other human rights instruments, like the Universal Declaration of Human Rights, whose preparation was contemporaneous to that of the Convention.[103] They carried the day in the Sixth Committee of the General Assembly, which voted to exclude cultural genocide from the Convention.[104]

The initial draft of the Genocide Convention, prepared by the United Nations Secretariat in 1947, referred, in the chapeau of Article II, to acts committed 'with the purpose of destroying it in whole or in part, or of preventing its preservation or development'.[105] This phrase was followed by a list involving physical acts, such as killing, biological acts, such as sterilisation or compulsory abortion, and 'destroying the specific characteristics of the group' by such measures as prohibiting the national language.[106] The *chapeau* of the final text of the Convention uses the word 'destroy', but without reference to 'preventing preservation or development'. Moreover, it eliminates the reference to 'destroying the specific characteristics of the group'. The list of acts of genocide in Article II of the Convention is considerably shorter than what appears in the original Secretariat draft. One of them, forcibly transferring children, is all that remains of the cultural genocide provisions in the early version. And it was added as an exception to the general exclusion of

---

103. GA Res. 217 A (III), UN Doc A/810. But the minority rights clause in the draft declaration was dropped and did not appear in the final version: W.A. Schabas, 'Les droits des minorités: Une déclaration inachevée', in *Déclaration universelle des droits de l'homme 1948-98, Avenir d'un idéal commun* (Paris, La Documentation française 1999) pp. 223-242.

104. UN Doc. A/C.6/SR.83.

105. Raphael Lemkin himself, in the book that initially proposed the term 'genocide', attached great importance to its cultural aspects. See R. Lemkin, *Axis Rule in Occupied Europe, Analysis of Government, Proposals for Redress* (Washington, Carnegie Endowment for World Peace 1944) pp. 84-85.

106. UN Doc E/447, pp. 5-13.

cultural genocide, on a proposal from Greece, made long after the notion of cultural genocide had been definitively rejected.[107] Greece successfully argued that even states opposed to cultural genocide did not necessarily contest inclusion of forcible transfer of children.[108]

Yet if the *travaux* attest to the exclusion of cultural genocide, a literal reading of the text can certainly support an alternative interpretation. The Convention does not say that genocide is committed by one of the five prohibited acts, that is, that a perpetrator must intend to destroy a group by killing, causing serious bodily or mental harm, inflicting harsh conditions of life, imposing measures to prevent births and forcibly transferring children. The text of Article II says that genocide is perpetrated if one of those five acts is committed by a person with the intent to destroy the group. In other words, it can be argued that a person who intends to destroy a group by means that fall short of physical extermination, but who kills members of the group in so doing, or commits one of the other four prohibited acts, falls within the parameters of the definition of the crime.

This view is supported by recent rulings of the German courts, in cases involving prosecution related to the war in Bosnia and Herzegovina. According to one judgment, the 'intent to destroy' set out in the *chapeau* of Article II of the Convention need not be to destroy the group physically. It is sufficient to put the group in a situation likely to result in its destruction.[109] In a ruling issued in December 2000, the Federal Constitutional Court said that

> 'the statutory definition of genocide defends a supra-individual object of legal protection, i.e., the social existence of the group [...] the intent to destroy the group [...] extends beyond physical and biological extermination [...] The text of the law does not therefore compel the interpretation that the culprit's intent must be to exterminate physically at least a substantial number of the members of the group.'[110]

These words were cited with considerable sympathy the following August by a Trial Chamber of the ICTY when it held that the Srebrenica massacre of July 1995 could be described as genocide. Nevertheless, the Trial Chamber felt that such a progressive approach might offend the principle *nullum crimen sine lege*. It said that

> 'despite recent developments, customary international law limits the definition of genocide to those acts seeking the physical or biological destruction of all or part of the group. Hence, an enterprise attacking only the cultural or sociological characteristics of a human group in order to annihilate these elements which give to that group its own

---

107. UN Doc A/C.6/242.

108. UN Doc A/C.6/SR.82 (Vallindas, Greece).

109. *Kjuradj Kusljić, Bayerisches Oberstes Landesgericht*, 15 December 1999, 6 St 1/99, appeal dismissed: *Kjuradj Kusljić, Bundesgerichtshof* [Federal Court of Justice], 21 February 2001, BGH 3 Str 244/00.

110. *Nikolai Jorgić, supra* n. 78, para. (III)(4)(a)(aa).

identity distinct from the rest of the community would not fall under the definition of genocide'.[111]

The question to be asked is whether it is now desirable that the definition of genocide move from the *lex lata* articulated by the Trial Chamber in *Krstić* to the *lex ferenda* proposed by the German Constitutional Court in *Jorgić*.

This issue is of particular relevance to attempts to extend the prohibition of genocide so as to cover related attacks on minority groups that have, in recent years, been described as 'ethnic cleansing'.[112] There is no generally-accepted definition of the term 'ethnic cleansing', in a legal sense. Ad hoc Judge Elihu Lauterpacht of the International Court of Justice has described ethnic cleansing as 'the forced migration of civilians'.[113] The United Nations Commission on Human Rights has said that 'ethnic cleansing ... at a minimum entails deportations and forcible mass removal or expulsion of persons from their homes in flagrant violation of their human rights, and which is aimed at the dislocation or destruction or national ethnic racial or religious groups'.[114] In a 1998 resolution, the Sub-Commission on Prevention of Discrimination and Protection of Minorities described it as 'forcible displacement of populations within a country or across borders'.[115] Thus, ethnic cleansing falls short of physical destruction in the sense of extermination. But it may still result in the disappearance of the group. A minority may be forcibly displaced as a result of the terror that ensues from killing, or from some of the other acts enumerated in Article II of the Convention.

If the definition of genocide is extended to include acts that we now describe as 'ethnic cleansing', it becomes difficult to delimit the lower end of the concept. The net gets cast very widely. For example, when the Allies agreed in Article XIII of the 1945 Potsdam Protocol to the forced displacement of Germans from Poland and other parts of Eastern Europe, they almost certainly did not intend to annihilate the German people.[116] Nevertheless, this 'ethnic cleansing' was associated with a range of violent acts, including killings, that fit without difficulty within the paragraphs of Article II of the Genocide Convention. If an expansive interpretation of the crime of genocide is adopted, as proposed by the German Constitutional Court, then it is a short step to the conclusion that the Allies conspired to destroy a sub-

---

111. Cited in *Prosecutor* v. *Krstić*, *supra* n. 24, para. 580.

112. Apparently, the expression 'ethnic cleansing' first appeared in 1981 in Yugoslav media accounts of the establishment of 'ethnically clean territories' in Kosovo. D. Petrović, 'Ethnic Cleansing – An Attempt at Methodology', 5 *EJIL* (1994) p. 342, p. 343.

113. Application of the Convention on the prevention and punishment of the crime of genocide (Bosnia and Herzegovina v. Yugoslavia (Serbia and Montenegro)), Further requests for the Indication of Provisional Measures, 13 September 1993, (1993) *ICJ Rep.* p. 325, Separate Reasons of Judge *ad hoc* Lauterpacht, p. 431, para. 69.

114. 'The Situation of Human Rights in the Territory of the Former Yugoslavia', CHR Res. 1992/S-1/1, preamble.

115. 'Forced Population Transfer', S-CHR Res. 1998/27.

116. See for example A. De Zayas, 'International Law and Mass Population Transfers', 16 *Harvard ILJ* (1975) p. 207; A. De Zayas, *Nemesis at Potsdam; The Expulsion of the Germans from the East* (Lincoln NE, University of Nebraska Press 1989); Freiherr Von Braun, 'Germany's Eastern Border and Mass Expulsions', 58 *AJIL* (1964) pp. 747.

stantial or significant part of the German people in Pomerania, Bohemia and the other areas from which they were 'cleansed' in 1945 and 1946.

In *Krstić*, the Trial Chamber concluded that there was evidence of genocidal intent because the Bosnian Serbs had decided to kill all of the military aged men, combined with the forcible transfer of the women, children and elderly, something that 'would inevitably result in the physical disappearance of the Bosnian Muslim population at Srebrenica'. How can we make a meaningful legal distinction between the alleged 'genocide' in Srebrenica and the 'population transfers' in postwar Poland and Czechoslovakia? It may be preferable – this is as much question of policy as it is of law – to treat both of these gross human rights violations as a serious attack on the existence of national minorities in a given region that falls short of the crime of genocide as defined in the 1948 Convention.

A useful precedent in this respect remains the *Eichmann* decision of the District Court of Jerusalem. Until 1941, Nazi anti-Semitic policies had been directed towards convincing Jews in Germany to leave the country. Jews were required, of course, to pay a price for their freedom. Large numbers who attempted to leave were unable to find refuge because other 'civilised' states refused to admit them.[117] The Nazi policy, at the time, was one that we might today describe as 'ethnic cleansing'. Jews were incited to leave by various forms of persecution, including discriminatory laws and periodic outbursts of violence such as the *Kristalnacht* of 9-10 November 1938. After the war against the Soviet Union was underway, the Nazi policy became physical annihilation of the Jews of Europe, in whole or in part. No longer was emigration permitted, even if asylum was possible. At this point, the Nazi intent became unquestionably genocidal. The District Court of Jerusalem, in the *Eichmann* case, noted this evolution in Nazi policy, commenting that '[t]he implementation of the 'Final Solution', in the sense of total extermination, is to a certain extent connected with the cessation of emigration of Jews from territories under German influence'.[118] Until mid-1941, when the 'final solution' emerged, the Israeli court said that 'a doubt remains in our minds whether there was here that specific intention to exterminate', as required by the definition of genocide. The Court said it would deal with such inhuman acts as crimes against humanity rather than genocide. Eichmann was acquitted of genocide for acts prior to August 1941.[119]

6.   STATE PLAN OR POLICY

In *Jelisić*, the prosecution evidence indicated that over a two-week period the accused was the principal executioner in the Luka camp, in northwest Bosnia. He was shown to have systematically killed Muslim inmates, as well as some Croats. The victims were essentially all of the Muslim community leaders. Jelisić was

---

117. United States Holocaust Memorial Museum, *Historical Atlas of the Holocaust* (New York NY, Macmillan 1996) pp. 25-27.
118. *A.-G. Israel* v. *Eichmann* (1968) 36 ILR 5 (District Court, Jerusalem), para. 80.
119. Ibid., para. 244(1-3); also paras. 186-187.

charged with genocide as both an accomplice and as a principal perpetrator. Examining the evidence, the Trial Chamber, presided by Judge Claude Jorda, concluded that the Prosecutor had failed to prove the existence of any general or even regional plan to destroy in whole or in part the Bosnian Moslims. It said that Jelisić could in no way be an accomplice to genocide if in fact genocide was never committed by others. It said there was insufficient evidence of the perpetration of genocide in Bosnia in the sense of some planned or organised attack on the Moslem population.[120]

After dismissing the charge of complicity, the Trial Chamber turned to whether or not Jelisić could have committed genocide acting alone, as the principal perpetrator rather than as an accomplice. This Trial Chamber said it was 'theoretically possible' that an individual, acting alone, could commit the crime – a kind of Lee Harvey Oswald of genocide. In the end, Jelisić was also acquitted as a principal perpetrator. But the Trial Chamber's approach is authority for the proposition that genocide may be committed without any requirement of an organised plan or policy of a state or similar entity. According to the Trial Chamber:

'The murders committed by the accused are sufficient to establish the material element of the crime of genocide and it is a priori possible to conceive that the accused harboured the plan to exterminate an entire group without this intent having been supported by any organisation in which other individuals participated. In this respect, the preparatory work of the Convention of 1948 brings out that premeditation was not selected as a legal ingredient of the crime of genocide, after having been mentioned by the ad hoc committee at the draft stage, on the grounds that it seemed superfluous given the special intention already required by the text and that such precision would only make the burden of proof even greater. It ensues from this omission that the drafters of the Convention did not deem the existence of an organisation or a system serving a genocidal objective as a legal ingredient of the crime. In so doing, they did not discount the possibility of a lone individual seeking to destroy a group as such.'[121]

This pronouncement was endorsed on appeal:

'The Appeals Chamber is of the opinion that the existence of a plan or policy is not a legal ingredient of the crime. However, in the context of proving specific intent, the existence of a plan or policy may become an important factor in most cases. The evidence may be consistent with the existence of a plan or policy, or may even show such existence, and the existence of a plan or policy may facilitate proof of the crime.'[122]

---

120. *Prosecutor* v. *Jelisić, supra* n. 23, para. 98.

121. Ibid., para. 100.

122. Ibid., para. 48. The Appeals Chamber's *obiter dictum* was followed in *Prosecutor* v. *Sikirica et al., supra* n. 23, para. 62.

Referring to its ruling in *Jelisić*, the Appeals Chamber recently declared that there is also no plan or policy element for crimes against humanity.[123]

Certainly, nothing in the text of the definition of genocide explicitly identifies a plan or policy as an element of the crime of genocide. During drafting of the Convention in 1948, proposals to include an explicit requirement that genocide be planned by government were rejected.[124] Nevertheless, while exceptions cannot be ruled out, it is nearly impossible to imagine genocide that is not planned and organised either by the state itself or a state-like entity, or by some clique associated with it. Raphael Lemkin, the scholar who first proposed the concept of 'genocide' in his book *Axis Rule in Occupied Europe*, spoke regularly of a plan as if this was a *sine qua non* for the crime of genocide.[125] In *Kayishema and Ruzindana*, the Rwanda Tribunal wrote: 'although a specific plan to destroy does not constitute an element of genocide, it would appear that it is not easy to carry out a genocide without a plan or organisation'.[126] Furthermore, it said that 'the existence of such a plan would be strong evidence of the specific intent requirement for the crime of genocide'.[127] The Guatemalan truth commission, which examined charges of genocide with respect to atrocities committed during that country's civil war in the early-1980s, considered it necessary to demonstrate the existence of a plan to exterminate Mayan communities that obeyed a higher, strategically planned policy, manifested in actions which had a logical and coherent sequence.[128]

Other authorities have considered this issue in the context of discussion of the mental element, holding that the plan or circumstances of genocide must be known to the offender, thereby implicitly confirming that a plan or policy is a material element of the crime. The Israeli court found that Eichmann knew of the 'secret of the plan for extermination' only since mid-1941, and acquitted him of genocide prior to that date.[129] It did not, by the way, – unlike the ICTY in *Jelisić* – speculate as to whether he had as an individual nurtured genocidal intent in the absence of a state plan or policy. According to the commentary of the International Law Commission on its draft Code of Crimes Against the Peace and Security of Mankind:

'The extent of knowledge of the details of a plan or a policy to carry out the crime of genocide would vary depending on the position of the perpetrator in the governmental hierarchy or the military command structure. This does not mean that a subordinate who actually carries out the plan or policy cannot be held responsible for the crime of genocide simply because he did not possess the same degree of information concerning the

---

123. *Prosecutor* v. *Kunarac et al.* (Case No. IT-96-23 & IT-96-23/1-A), Judgment, 12 June 2002, fn. 114.

124. UN Doc E/AC.25/SR.4, pp. 3-6. Also *Kadić* v. *Karadžić*, 70 F.3d 232 (2nd Cir. 1995), cert. denied, 64 USLW 3832 (18 June 1996).

125. Lemkin, op. cit. n. 105, at p. 79.

126. *Prosecutor* v. *Kayishema and Ruzindana*, *supra* n. 37, para. 94.

127. Ibid., para. 276.

128. Guatemala: Memory of Silence, Report of the Commission for Historical Clarification, Conclusions and Recommendations, 'Conclusions,' para. 120, <http://www.hrdata.aaas.org/ceh/report/english/toc.html> (consulted 14 January 2003).

129. *A.-G. Israel* v. *Eichmann*, *supra* n. 118, para. 195.

overall plan or policy as his superiors. The definition of the crime of genocide requires a degree of knowledge of the ultimate objective of the criminal conduct rather than knowledge of every detail of a comprehensive plan or policy of genocide.'[130]

Although individual offenders need not participate in devising the plan, if they commit acts of genocide with knowledge of the plan, then the requirements of the Convention are met.[131]

The draft Elements of Crimes, adopted by the Assembly of States Parties of the International Criminal Court in September 2002, includes the following element of the crime of genocide: 'The conduct took place in the context of a manifest pattern of similar conduct directed against that group or was conduct that could itself effect such destruction.'[132] This is what the Elements deem to be 'contextual circumstances',[133] to distinguish such facts from the classic criminal law concept of material element or *actus reus*. The term 'circumstance' appears in Article 30 of the Rome Statute of the International Criminal Court, requiring as a component of the mens rea of crimes that an accused have 'awareness that a circumstance exists'.[134] Three additional provisions appear in the Elements that complete but also complicate the construction of this somewhat puzzling text about genocidal conduct. The term 'in the context of' is to include the initial acts in an emerging pattern, the term 'manifest' is deemed an objective qualification, and '[n]otwithstanding the normal requirement for a mental element provided for in article 30 [of the Rome Statute], and recognising that knowledge of the circumstances will usually be addressed in proving genocidal intent, the appropriate requirement, if any, for a mental element regarding this circumstance will need to be decided by the Court on a case-by-case basis'.[135] The Elements eschew the word 'plan' in favour of a 'manifest pattern of similar conduct', but any difference between the two expressions would appear to be entirely semantic. Alternatively, the context may be 'conduct that could itself effect such destruction'. These criteria should be enough to eliminate the Lee Harvey Oswald scenario, at least with respect to genocide prosecutions before the International Criminal Court.

---

130. 'Report of the International Law Commission on the work of its forty-eighth session, 6 May-26 July 1996', UN Doc. A/51/10, p. 90.

131. See for example, 'Proposal by Algeria, Bahrain, Comoros, Djibouti, Egypt, Jordan, Iraq, Kuwait, Lebanon, Libyan Arab Jamahiriya, Morocco, Oman, Palestine, Qatar, Saudi Arabia, the Sudan, the Syrian Arab Republic, Tunisia, United Arab Emirates and Yemen, Comments on the proposal submitted by the United States of America concerning terminology and the crime of genocide', UN Doc. PCNICC/1999/WGEC/DP.4, p. 4.

132. 'Report of the Preparatory Commission for the International Criminal Court, Addendum, Finalised draft text of the Elements of Crimes,' UN Doc. PCNICC/2000/INF/3/Add.2.

133. Ibid., p. 5.

134. 'Rome Statute of the International Criminal Court', UN Doc. A/CONF.183/9, Art. 30(3).

135. 'Report of the Preparatory Commission for the International Criminal Court, Addendum, Finalised draft text of the Elements of Crimes', *supra* n. 132, p. 6.

7.   IMMUNITIES

The *Pinochet* case, and since then the *Arrest Warrant* case, not to mention the shenanigans of the United States with respect to the Rome Statute, have all focussed the attention of international criminal lawyers on the subject of immunities. Article IV of the Genocide Convention addresses this issue, but only indirectly. It states: 'Persons committing genocide or any of the other acts enumerated in Article 3 shall be punished, whether they are constitutionally responsible rulers, public officials or private individuals.' It is worth comparing Article IV with Article 27 of the Rome Statute, which has two distinct paragraphs on irrelevance of official capacity. This first of them looks rather like Article IV, whereas the second speaks directly to the existence of immunities which may attach to official capacity. In other words, there is a distinction between a defence of official capacity and one of immunity. It would appear that Article IV deals with the former, and not the latter. The former serves to eliminate any defence of official capacity for the national of a given state when an accused is tried before the courts of that same state. The latter deals with a defence of immunity when a head of state, foreign minister or diplomat is tried before the courts of another state. Apparently, then, the Genocide Convention is silent in this second situation. Indeed, during the drafting it appears to have been assumed that Article IV would have no impact upon diplomatic immunities.[136]

During the extradition proceedings of Augusto Pinochet, Article IV was briefly considered by the English courts.[137] The United Kingdom authorities invoked article IV, saying the head of state defence had been excluded by customary international law and by the conventional codification of customary norms in such instruments as the Genocide Convention. But in the Divisional Court, the Lord Chief Justice observed that when the Convention was implemented in national law, Parliament had failed to incorporate Article IV, implying equivocation about the principle set out in that provision,[138] a view that was subsequently endorsed by dissenters Lord Slynn of Hadley[139] and Lord Lloyd of Berthwick.[140]

In the 24 March 1999 ruling of the House of Lords, Lord Phillips of Worth Matravers wrote that Article IV of the Convention was hardly even necessary, be-

---

136. UN Doc. E/AC.25/SR.9, p. 7.

137. Pinochet had been charged, *inter alia*, with genocide. The genocide provision in the Spanish penal code differs somewhat from that of the Convention, although the reasoning of the Spanish judges indicates reliance on more than an idiosyncratic definition of the crime. Case 173/98, Penal Chamber, Madrid, 5 November 1998. See R.J. Wilson, 'Prosecuting Pinochet in Spain', 6 *Human Rights Brief* (2000) Issue 3, pp. 3-4.

138. *R.* v. *Bartle, ex parte Pinochet*, Divisional Court, Queen's Bench Division, 28 October 1998, (1998) 37 ILM 1302, paras. 65, 68.

139. *R.* v. *Bow Street Stipendiary Magistrate and others, ex parte Pinochet Ugarte*, [1998] 4 All ER 897, [1998] 3 WLR 1456 (HL), pp. 911-912 (All ER).

140. *R.* v. *Bow Street Stipendiary Magistrate and others, ex parte Pinochet Ugarte (Amnesty International and others intervening)* (No. 3), [1999] 2 All ER 97, [1999] 2 WLR 825 (HL), pp. 189-190 (All ER).

cause customary law deprived heads of state of immunity in the case of such crimes:

> 'Had the Genocide Convention not contained this provision, an issue could have been raised as to whether the jurisdiction conferred by the Convention was subject to state immunity ratione materiae. Would international law have required a court to grant immunity to a defendant upon his demonstrating that he was acting in an official capacity? In my view it plainly would not. I do not reach that conclusion on the ground that assisting in genocide can never be a function of a state official. I reach that conclusion on the simple basis that no established rule of international law requires state immunity ratione materiae to be accorded in respect of prosecution for an international crime. International crimes and extra-territorial jurisdiction in relation to them are both new arrivals in the field of public international law. I do not believe that state immunity ratione materiae can co-exist with them. The exercise of extra-territorial jurisdiction overrides the principle that one state will not intervene in the internal affairs of another. It does so because, where international crime is concerned, that principle cannot prevail. An international crime is as offensive, if not more offensive, to the international community when committed under colour of office. Once extra-territorial jurisdiction is established, it makes no sense to exclude from it acts done in an official capacity.'[141]

But the International Court of Justice, in the *Arrest Warrant* case, appeared to see this issue slightly differently. The Court noted 'that in international law it is firmly established that, as also diplomatic and consular agents, certain holders of high-ranking office in a state, such as the Head of State, Head of Government and Minister for Foreign Affairs, enjoy immunities from jurisdiction in other States, both civil and criminal'.[142] The purpose of the immunity is functional, that is, to permit the official in question to fulfil his or her duties. The Court dismissed Belgium's argument that there was an exception to this principle in the case of war crimes and crimes against humanity (and, presumably, genocide).[143] The immunity comes to an end when the person leaves office 'in respect of acts committed prior or subsequent to his or her period of office, as well as in respect of acts committed during that period of office in a private capacity'.[144] As we have noted above, there is now precedent for the possibility that genocide can be committed without any plan or policy, and so it is theoretically possible that the crime could be carried out 'in a private capacity'. But not very likely.

---

141. Ibid.
142. Arrest Warrant of 11 April 2000 (*Democratic Republic of the Congo* v. *Belgium*), Judgment, 14 February 2002, para. 51.
143. Ibid., para. 58.
144. Ibid., para. 61.

8.   UNIVERSAL JURISDICTION

Article VI of the Genocide Convention establishes the jurisdictional basis for prosecutions:

> 'Persons charged with genocide or any of the other acts enumerated in article 3 shall be tried by a competent tribunal of the State in the territory of which the act was committed, or by such international penal tribunal as may have jurisdiction with respect to those Contracting Parties which shall have accepted its jurisdiction.'

This was an unfortunate compromise, because the very reason for the Convention was that the states where the crime took place failed to punish it, and there was no international penal tribunal, nor would there be one for more than four decades.

Article VI fell considerably short of the hopes of those who had promoted the Convention. The draft resolution on genocide submitted to the General Assembly in 1946 that launched the process leading to adoption of the Convention had lamented the fact that 'punishment of the very serious crime of genocide when committed in time of peace lies within the exclusive territorial jurisdiction of the judiciary of every state concerned, while crimes of a relatively lesser importance such as piracy, trade in women, children, drugs, obscene publications are declared as international crimes and have been made matters of international concern'.[145] The first draft of the convention, submitted by Saudi Arabia, proposed that the crime should attract universal jurisdiction: 'Acts of genocide shall be prosecuted and punished by any state regardless of the place of the commission of the offence or of the nationality of the offender, in conformity with the laws of the country prosecuting.'[146] Similarly, the Secretariat draft, prepared by John P. Humphrey and his colleagues in 1947 with the expert assistance of Lemkin, Henri Donnedieu de Vabres, and Vespasian V. Pella, stated: '[Universal Enforcement of Municipal Criminal Law] The High Contracting Parties pledge themselves to punish any offender under this Convention within any territory under their jurisdiction, irrespective of the nationality of the offender or of the place where the offence has been committed.'[147]

There was widespread opposition from several quarters. The United States of America said prosecution for crimes committed outside the territory of a state should be allowed only with the consent of the state upon whose territory genocide was committed.[148] Its delegate added that '[t]he principle of universal punishment was one of the most dangerous and unacceptable of principles'.[149] The Soviet Union was also opposed to any form of internationalised prosecution.[150] It argued

---

145. UN Doc. A/BUR/50.
146. UN Doc. A/C.6/86.
147. UN Doc. E/447, pp. 5-13, art. VII. Also UN Doc. E/AC.25/8.
148. UN Doc. E/623, Art. V; also UN Doc. E/AC.25/SR.8, p. 11; UN Doc. A/C.6/SR.100.
149. UN Doc. A/C.6/SR.100.
150. 'Basic Principles of a Convention on Genocide', UN Doc. E/AC.25/7, Principle IX.

that no exception should be made to the principle of territorial jurisdiction, saying this was the only approach compatible with respect for national sovereignty.[151] France, too, challenged enforcement based upon universal jurisdiction, but because it favoured the establishment of an international tribunal.[152] A proposal to incorporate universal jurisdiction in the convention, subject to a requirement that the state of territorial jurisdiction fail to prosecute (an early form of complementarity), was rejected by the Sixth Committee of the General Assembly, by a vote of 29 to six, with ten abstentions.[153]

Despite the terms of Article VI and the unequivocal message of the *travaux préparatoires*, there is now considerable judicial support for the view that genocide is a crime subject to universal jurisdiction,[154] no shortage of favourable academic opinion,[155] and a growing body of national practise, in the form of enabling legislation. However, since the recent ruling of the International Court of Justice in the *Arrest Warrant* case, uncertainty continues to shroud the question of the legality of universal jurisdiction for the crime of genocide.[156]

Universal jurisdiction is often held out as the magic bullet in the war on impunity, an effective answer to the inability or unwillingness of states where the crime takes place to bring perpetrators to book. It is interesting to note, however, that in Rwanda, which is the one unarguable case of genocide since adoption of the Convention, the national courts have reacted rather admirably. Rwanda's genocide prosecutions began in late-December 1996. Thousands have now been tried and convicted for their role in the atrocities of April-July 1994. In his report to the United Nations, prepared in early-2000, Special Representative Michel Moussalli said some 2,406 persons had been tried by the special genocide courts.[157] He added: 'There is much to applaud in this process.'[158] Even in January 2003, when Rwanda authorised the release of some

---

151. UN Doc. E/AC.25/SR.7, pp. 3-4.

152. Ibid., p. 9.

153. UN Doc. A/C.6/SR.100.

154. *A.-G. Israel* v. *Eichmann, supra* n. 118, paras. 20-38; *A.-G. Israel* v. *Eichmann,* (1968) 36 ILR 277 (Israel Supreme Court), para. 12; *Application of the Convention on the prevention and punishment of the crime of genocide (Bosnia and Herzegovina* v. *Yugoslavia (Serbia and Montenegro)), Further requests for the Indication of Provisional Measures,* 13 September 1993, *ICJ Rep.*(1993) p. 325, Separate Reasons of Judge *ad hoc* Lauterpacht; *Prosecutor* v. *Tadić, supra* n. 14, para. 62; *Nikola Jorgić, supra* n. 78.

155. E.g., T. Meron, 'International Criminalisation of Internal Atrocities', 89 *AJIL* (1995) pp. 554, at p. 569; International Law Association, Committee on International Human Rights Law and Practice, 'Final Report on the Exercise of Universal Jurisdiction in Respect of Gross Human Rights Offences', 2000, p. 5.

156. Arrest Warrant of 11 April 2000 (*Democratic Republic of the Congo* v. *Belgium*), Judgment, 15 February 2002. See especially Separate opinion of President Gilbert Guillaume, pp. 5-6; Individual opinion of Francisco Rezek; Declaration of Raymond Ranjeva.

157. 'Report on the situation of human rights in Rwanda submitted by the Special Representative, Mr. M. Moussalli, pursuant to Commission resolution 1999/20', UN Doc. E/CN.4/2000/41, para. 136. See also W.A. Schabas, 'The Rwanda Case: Sometimes it's Impossible', in M.C. Bassiouni, ed., *Post-Conflict Justice* (Ardsley NY, Transnational 2002) pp. 499-522. Also M.A. Drumbl, 'Punishment, Postgenocide: From Guilt to Shame to Civis in Rwanda', 75 *NY Univ. LR* (2000) pp. 1221-1326.

158. Ibid., para. 137.

40,000 genocide suspects who had been detained for several years, it insisted that it was in no way renouncing its intent to bring these people to justice. In contrast, with respect to the conflicts in the former Yugoslavia, there is evidence of only a few perfunctory genocide prosecutions: two in Bosnia and Herzegovina,[159] one in Kosovo,[160] and one in Croatia.[161]

As for genocide prosecutions pursuant to universal jurisdiction, with respect to Rwanda, or for that matter Cambodia, Chile, or Sabra and Shatilla, or the many places where the crime has been alleged, they recall Mark Twain's famous saying about the weather: 'everybody talks about it, but nobody does anything about it.' Perhaps the most stunning case is that of the Cambodian 'genocide'. When, in June 1997, the United States believed it would be able to arrest Khmer Rouge leader Pol Pot and deliver him to a state willing to prosecute, it failed to interest Canada, Spain, the Netherlands and Israel in the case.[162] Canada has also declined to prosecute a Rwandan genocide suspect, although it has been willing enough to accuse him of the crime and to attempt to expel him from the country.[163]

---

159. Sretko Damjanović and Borislav Herak were sentenced to death on 12 March 1993 for genocide by the District Military Court (*Okruzni Vojni Sud*) of Bosnia and Herzegovina, sitting in Sarajevo, pursuant to Article 141 of the Criminal Law of the Socialist Federal Republic of Yugoslavia which was incorporated into the laws of the Republic of Bosnia and Herzegovina in 1992. The verdict was upheld on 30 July 1993 by the Supreme Court (*Vrhovni Sud*), and on 29 December 1993, by a differently constituted Supreme Court sitting in third instance. See *Damjanović* v. *Federation of Bosnia and Herzegovina* (Case No. CH/96/30), 5 September 1997, Decisions on Admissibility and Merits 1996-1997, p. 147.

160. *Vucković*, Supreme Court of Kosovo, 31 August 2001, AP.156/2001. The brief submitted by the International Public Prosecutor, Michael Hartmann, to the Supreme Court took the view that there was insufficient evidence of genocidal intent and that the initial conviction could not stand: 'Opinion on appeals of genocide conviction of Miroslav Vuckovic', Office of the Public Prosecutor of Kosovo, 30 August 2001.

161. Available at <http://www.icrc.org/ihl-nat.nsf/> (consulted 3 January 2003). On 25 June 1997, the Osijek District Court convicted a Serb of genocide for participation in acts of 'ethnic cleansing' in the village of Branjina during the war in 1991. 'M.H.' was involved, with other local Serbs, in a local administration following occupation by the Yugoslav National Army. A number of criminal acts were imputed to him, but no killings. These included introducing identity cards, forcing Croats to join the Serb paramilitary units under threat of expulsion from the village if they refused, imposition of a curfew, destruction of property, forced labour, detention, taking of hostages, 'arming the gypsies and encouraging them to shoot against the Croat houses', looting and expulsion. He was sentenced to five years imprisonment for genocide pursuant to Article 119 of the Basic Criminal Law of the Republic of Croatia. The Court said that to establish genocide, it would be enough to establish that he committed only one act against a single victim, to the extent that his intent was to partly or entirely annihilate a protected group. It noted that M.H. participated in the realisation of plans to create a Greater Serbia, and to ethnically cleanse the village of Branjina.

162. E. Becker, 'U.S. Spearheading Effort to Bring Pol Pot to Trial', *New York Times* (23 June 1997) p. A1; 'Editorial: A Trial for Pol Pot', *New York Times* (24 June 1997) p. A18; A. DePalma, 'Canadians Surprised by Proposal to Extradite Pol Pot', *New York Times* (24 June 1997) p. A10; B. Crossette, 'Beijing Says it Won't Go Along with Creation of Pol Pot Tribunal', *New York Times* (25 June 1997) p. A6; 'U.S. To Press for Pol Pot Trial', *New York Times* (30 July 1997) p. A10.

163. See *Mugesera et al.* v. *Canada (Minister of Citizenship and Immigration)*, [2001] 4 FC 421 (TD). Also W.A. Schabas, 'L'affaire Mugesera', (1996) 7 *Revue universelle des droits de l'homme* 193; W.A. Schabas, 'Mugesera v. Minister of Citizenship and Immigration', 93 *AJIL* (1999) p. 529.

There are a few examples of universal jurisdiction-based prosecutions for the Rwandan genocide in Switzerland and Belgium. Swiss prosecutors indicted Fulgence Niyonteze, who had once been the bourgmestre of Mushubati commune. The prosecution did not initially charge Niyonteze with genocide, and failed in its attempt, some 16 days after the trial had begun, to amend the indictment accordingly. In dismissing the prosecutor's motion to amend, the court noted that Switzerland was not, at the time of the trial, a State Party to the 1948 Genocide Convention.[164] Belgian courts have also undertaken prosecutions relating to the Rwandan genocide, although under provisions of Geneva law and not the Convention.[165]

Since the *Eichmann* decision there has been a tendency to treat Article VI of the Genocide Convention as being merely permissive, and the German courts have followed this approach. In one ruling, the Higher Regional Court at Dusseldorf referred to 'the generally accepted non-exclusive interpretation of Article VI of the 1948 Genocide Convention' to support the first limitation upon universal jurisdiction, that is, that there be no prohibition of universal jurisdiction prosecutions under international law.[166] The Federal Constitutional Court affirmed the lower court rulings, and observed that a hypothetical norm of customary international law forbidding the application of universal jurisdiction would be contrary to the rule prohibiting genocide, which is a peremptory or *jus cogens* norm.[167]

Thus, there are some glimmerings of state practice, in the form of actual prosecutions, supporting the existence of universal jurisdiction in the case of genocide, and this despite the terms of Article VI and their *travaux préparatoires*. Evolving views favouring universal jurisdiction are also reflected in recent changes to national legislation in countries like Germany[168] and Canada.[169] that explicitly authorise universal jurisdiction for genocide. Ironically, the drafters of Article VI were concerned that national courts would not prosecute genocide

---

164. *Niyonteze*, Military.Court of Appeal 1A, 26 May 2000; *Niyonteze*, Military Court of Cassation, 27 April 2001. See L. Reydams, 'International Decisions, Niyonteze v. Public Prosecutor', 96 *AJIL* (2002) p. 231. Switzerland acceded to the *Convention* on 7 September 2000. Note that Switzerland has also cooperated with the International Criminal Tribunal for Rwanda in transferring genocide suspects for trial in Arusha: *Prosecutor* v. *Musema*, *supra* n. 39, paras. 17-18; *Musema*, *Tribunal federal* [Federal court], 28 April 1997, 1A.36/1997, ATF 123 II 175. Transcripts of interviews conducted by Swiss *juges d'instruction* were used as evidence before the International Tribunal for Rwanda: *Prosecutor* v . *Musema*, ibid., paras. 91-92.

165. See E. Gillet, 'Le génocide devant la justice', *Les temps modernes*, No. 583 (July-August 1995) at p. 228. See also Brussels Court of Appeal (*Ch. mis. acc.*), 17 May 1995, *Journal des Tribunaux* (1995) p. 542.

166. *Nikolai Jorgić, Oberlandesgericht Düsseldorf* [Higher Regional Court, Dusseldorf], 26 September 1997, IV - 26/96, appeal dismissed: *Nikolai Jorgić, Bundesgerichtshof* [Federal Court of Justice], 30 April 1999, 3 StR 215/98F.

167. Ibid.

168. See G. Werle and F. Jessberger, 'International Criminal Justice is Coming Home: The New German Code of Crimes Against International Law', 13 *Criminal LF* (2002) pp. 191-223; F. Jessberger, 'Prosecuting International Crimes in Domestic Courts: A Look Back Ahead', 12 *Finnish YIL* (2001) pp. 281-304.

169. *Crimes Against Humanity and War Crimes Act*, S.C. 2000, c. 24.

because of political considerations. But political considerations have proven to be just as relevant, probably more so, in explaining the paucity of genocide prosecutions pursuant to universal jurisdiction. States have shown no inclination to prosecute genocide on the basis of universal jurisdiction in the absence of a particular interest, be it pressure from domestic lobby groups or a lingering paternalism towards a former colony. In any event, it should be clear enough that the legal obstacles are rapidly eroding.

As for the political obstacles, it is to be hoped that the stigma of an admissibility determination by the International Criminal Court, in accordance with Articles 17 and 18 of the Rome Statute, will incite states to prosecute those genocide suspects who are found on their territory, even in the absence of any other nexus with the crime. No such obligation is set out explicitly in the Rome Statute, and the closest expression of any applicable norm appears in an ambiguous paragraph of the preamble: 'Recalling that it is the duty of every state to exercise its criminal jurisdiction over those responsible for international crimes.'

9.   CONCLUSION

After 50 years of what many feared might be more or less permanent obsolescence, interest in the Genocide Convention has revived in recent years. Judgments of the two *ad hoc* Tribunals have propelled the agenda, pronouncing upon such questions as the nature of the protected groups, the concept of 'in whole or in part', the specific intent requirement, and the possible extension of the definition to cover forms of cultural genocide often described as 'ethnic cleansing'. There is a growing body of national practice, mainly from Rwanda, where the rather summary judgments and the underdeveloped state of the justice system mean that while there is an important contribution to the struggle against impunity, there is not much meat to chew on from a theoretical standpoint. There is also some evidence of the exercise of universal jurisdiction, clouded by the ambiguity of the International Court of Justice in the *Arrest Warrant* case.

But while much has been written in the past five years or so, the big judgments still hover on the horizon. The Appeals Chamber of the ad hoc Tribunals has confirmed several of the Trial Chamber rulings in genocide cases, but it cannot be said that it has issued a defining judgment on the subject of genocide. The appeal in the *Krstić* case, expected to be issued in 2003, may well develop some of the important questions. Much of it will come down to the highly politicised issue of whether or not genocide was committed by Bosnian Serbs, with the complicity of the Belgrade government, during the war in Bosnia and Herzegovina. If the matter is important to the ongoing *Milošević* prosecution at the ICTY, it also lies very much at the heart of the Bosnian application against Yugoslavia before the International Court of Justice. The two courts – located barely a kilometre apart in The Hague – may be competing to see which one will be the first to adjudicate this

difficult and complex question.[170] That the two bodies might reach different conclusions on points of fact and law remains a distinct possibility.

---

170. The Appeals Chamber of the International Criminal Tribunal for the former Yugoslavia has already had occasion to rule that it has no hierarchical relationship with the International Court of Justice. *Prosecutor* v. *Delalić et al.* (Case No. IT-96-21-A), Judgment, 20 February 2001, para. 24. Also *Prosecutor* v. *Kvocka et al.* (Case No. IT-98-30/1-AR73.5), Decision on Interlocutory Appeal by the Accused Zoran Zigić against the Decision of Trial Chamber I dated 5 December 2000, 25 May 2001. But see *Semanza* v. *Prosecutor* (Case No. ICTR-97-20-A), Decision, 31 May 2000, Separate Opinion of Judge Shahabuddeen, para. 32.

ESTABLISHING THE RESPONSIBILITY OF THE KHMER ROUGE LEADERSHIP FOR INTERNATIONAL CRIMES[1]

David Boyle[2]

---

1. © D. Boyle 2003.

2. Solicitor admitted to the Bar of the NSW Supreme Court, Australia; instructor at the Paris Law Clinic in international criminal law, University of Paris I; Doctorate candidate, University of Paris II.

Yearbook of International Humanitarian Law
Volume 5 - 2002 - pp. 167-218

1.   INTRODUCTION

Dragged reluctantly into the debate over Khmer Rouge accountability, the United Nations Secretariat has spent the last five years attempting to find a mutually acceptable judicial structure to try the leaders of the former government of Cambodia for international crimes committed between 1975 and 1979.

In response to a request for aid from the Cambodian government in June 1997,[3] the UN originally came down in favour of establishing a third *ad hoc* International Criminal Tribunal. Taking that proposal as a starting point,[4] this paper documents the series of events leading the Organisation towards unwilling participation in potentially unjust domestic trials after Cambodia's refusal of the UN proposal. Each time the negotiations seemed to have broken down, the UN and Cambodia came under pressure from certain Member States to return to the negotiating table. Beset with its responsibility in supporting the Khmer Rouge after the Vietnamese invasion in 1979, the UN compromised successively concerning the nature of the court (part 3) and its structure (part 4). A consensus finally seemed to have been reached in July 2000, when a UN negotiating team left Phnom Penh with a draft Memorandum of Understanding concerning 'significant international co-operation' in trials before 'Extraordinary Chambers' of the Cambodian courts (the 'draft MOU').[5] However, the law finally promulgated on 10 August 2001 in order to set up these Chambers (the 'Tribunal Law')[6] was not entirely consistent with the terms

---

3. Royal Government of Cambodia, Letter to the UN Secretary-General dated 21 June 1997 from Prince Norodom Ranariddh and Hun Sen, text reproduced in the Report of the Group of Experts for Cambodia Pursuant to General Assembly Resolution 52/125, 18 February 1999, UN Doc. A/53/850, 16 March 1999, Annex, para. 5, unofficial copy available at <http://www.camnet.com.kh/ngoforum/un-report.htm.>

4. This paper does not relate in detail the evolving internal and international approaches to Khmer Rouge crimes leading up to the Cambodian request for UN aid, as they have already been recorded in an earlier volume of the Yearbook: see B. Rajagopal, 'The Pragmatics of Prosecuting the Khmer Rouge', 1 *YIHL* (1988) pp. 189 at 190 et seq.; see also D. Boyle, 'Quelle justice pour les Khmers rouges ?', 40 *Revue trimestrielle des droits de l'homme* (1999) pp. 773 at 774 et seq.

5. Unofficial copy available at <http://www.yale.edu/cgp/tribunal/mou_v3.htm.>

6. Cambodia, Law on the Establishment of the Extraordinary Chambers in the Courts of Cambodia for the Prosecution of Crimes Committed during the Period of Democratic Kampuchea (Kram NS/

of the draft MOU, the exact legal status of which then became a bone of contention (part 5). In the absence of progress on this and other contentious issues, the Secretary-General pulled the UN out of the negotiations in February 2002. However, the General Assembly renewed his mandate to negotiate on the basis of the Tribunal Law and, in March 2003; an amended agreement replacing the draft MOU was negotiated which went some way towards addressing the concerns of the Secretary-General (the '2003 Agreement').[7] The Agreement was formally signed by both parties in June 2003, but must be ratified by Cambodia and receive sufficient voluntary contributions before the Extraordinary Chambers become a reality (part 6).

The review of this process also provides the basis for comments regarding the extent to which the varying proposals could offer meaningful justice and contribute to national reconciliation in the Cambodian context. To this end, the paper first outlines the parameters against which the Cambodian experience will be analysed (part 2). Of course, informed comment on the likely operation of such an experiment in mixed justice requires a wide range of expertise, both in international law and international criminal law, and also in UN Charter law and Cambodian criminal law and procedure, and even constitutional principles. Clearly, given this challenge, some questions will remain unanswered. This paper aims, more modestly, to identify the questions which will have to be resolved by any court established to try the Khmer Rouge and analyse the capacity of the Extraordinary Chambers to provide real justice.

2.   THE AIMS OF INTERNATIONAL JUSTICE

The aims of international justice are globally the same as those of national justice: establishing the truth concerning acts which violate the social contract, punishing those responsible, preventing future occurrences and, less commonly, compensating the victims. Yet these aims take on new dimensions in the international context and their relative importance is not necessarily the same.[8] This results, in particular, from the fact that, in the aftermath of international crimes, it is more often a question of reinventing than preserving the social contract, often as part of a larger international post-conflict peace-building operation. Moreover, the concept of international crimes implies the existence of an international moral order, which

---

RKM/0801/12, 10 August 2001), official translation available at <http://www.ocm.gov.kh/krt> as promulgated (English translation 6 September 2001) pdf, unofficial copy also available at <http://www.ridi.org/boyle/kr_law_10-08-02.htm.>

7. Draft Agreement between the United Nations and the Royal Government of Cambodia concerning the prosecution under Cambodian Law of crimes committed during the period of Democratic Kampuchea, 17 March 2003, Report of the Secretary-General on Khmer Rouge trials, UN Doc. A/57/769, 31 March 2003.

8. For an analysis of the specificity of international courts, see H. Ascensio, 'La notion de juridiction internationale en question', in *La juridictionnalisation du droit international*, 36e Colloque de la Société française pour le droit international, Lille 13-14 September 2002 (forthcoming Paris, Pedone).

must also be preserved, which may lead to changes in the 'broader rules of international relations and legitimacy'.[9]

2.1   Establishing the truth

Given the nature of international crimes, 'truth' is often a political variable. In Cambodia, access to the truth concerning the Khmer Rouge has always been subordinated to political priorities. After having been swamped with information concerning the Khmer Rouge regime between 1979 and 1991, in order to justify the Vietnamese occupation, study of the period was dropped from school curricula after the UN intervention, purportedly to promote national reconciliation and avoid revenge.[10] Yet knowledge of the truth concerning such crimes is essential to successful national reconciliation, especially where victims disappear, never to be seen again by their family.[11] Before turning the page, it must first be read.

From this perspective, the means employed are less important than the result: access to credible information. Nevertheless, international involvement can contribute to this goal because, given the mass criminality involved, it will be difficult if not impossible to find qualified local personnel who are not associated in some way with either the victims or the perpetrators.

Exposing the truth concerning international crimes also serves the needs of the international community to condemn crimes which go beyond national borders to effect humanity as a whole. Clearly, international involvement in the process of determining the truth will better satisfy this perceived need to express universal opprobrium.[12]

It should be noted from the outset that the idea of establishing some form of quasi-judicial Truth and Reconciliation Commission has never been seriously discussed as a means of satisfying the seemingly contradictory needs for truth, reconciliation and justice in Cambodia.[13] A number of factors may help to explain this. On the one hand, while it is undeniable that court proceedings are not necessarily the best means of exposing the historical truth concerning past crimes,[14] in this case, serious historical studies of the Khmer Rouge period have already confirmed the criminal nature of their regime. This historical information is supplemented by plethoric evidence collated by the Documentation Center of Cambodia concerning the extent of the personal responsibility of the Khmer Rouge leader-

---

9. P. Akhavan, 'Beyond Impunity: Can International Criminal Justice Prevent Future Atrocities?', 95 *AJIL* (2001) p. 7.

10. E. Madra, 'Cambodia schools skip "killing fields"', Reuters 27 April 1999.

11. On the importance of 'Truth' in cases of 'disappearance' type crimes, see E. Malarino, 'Argentina: the Difficult Reconstruction of Truth', *Judicial Diplomacy* (September 2002).

12. On the 'expressive' function of international criminal justice, see D. Amann, 'Group Mentality, Expressivism, and Genocide', 1 *ICLR* (2002) pp. 117-131.

13. For a minor exception, see 'TRC: "Tutu will help Cambodia"', *Daily Mail and Guardian* (Johannesburg, South Africa) 18 January 1999.

14. See A. Lollini, 'La construction d'une mémoire collective en Afrique du Sud - La Commission vérité et réconciliation: « hypertrophie de la sentence » ou « hypertrophie de l'Histoire »?', 8 *L'Astrée, Revue de Droit pénal et des droits de l'homme* (1999) p. 25.

ship.[15] On the other hand, given the extreme gravity of the crimes thus brought to light, it appears clear that any acceptable solution must include criminal sanctions. Indeed, not only would a non-judicial solution fall short of the expectations of the victims (to the extent that their wishes are known[16]), and Cambodian[17] and international NGOs,[18] but any system proposing an amnesty in exchange for the truth would likely be in breach of Cambodia's international obligation to prevent and punish international crimes.[19] In any case, the rare declarations by potential accused make it clear that, while some are prepared to seek forgiveness for past 'mistakes', they generally refuse to admit any criminal intent, show little remorse and claim not to have been privy to policy decisions taken by Pol Pot.[20]

To cite but one example, it is widely accepted that, starting in 1976, Khmer Rouge policy towards 'reactionary elements' changed significantly, touching a wider population and increasing the pace of killings. However, opinions differ as to the exact reasons for this phenomenon: a paranoid yet real fear of infiltration by

---

15. This initiative grew out of a Yale University program run by Benedict Kiernan, funded through United States federal legislation, the Cambodia Genocide Justice Act, (11 USC 2656, Part D, sections 571-574), May 1994, available at <http://www.yale.edu/cgp>.

16. For a long time, commentators simply assumed that Cambodians wanted to see justice done. This certainly seems to be true of many *diaspora* Cambodians, many of whom fear to return to Cambodia to live until the Khmer Rouge have been tried. Some have even taken *partie civile* action under Belgian universal jurisdiction legislation. More recently, limited surveying undertaken in Cambodia shows more mitigated support: while a majority would like to see the Khmer Rouge brought to justice, they are not prepared to do so if there is a serious risk of renewed conflict: see e.g., *Justice and Cambodia: A Collective Inquiry*, Cambodian Genocide Program, Yale University, available at <http://www.yale.edu/cgp>; as well as 'Leaders of Civil Society speak out', A. Marcher and Y. Soeum, 'Khieu Samphan wants to go public', *Phnom Penh Post* (4-17 February 2000) Issue 9/3, and 'Truth, justice, reconciliation, peace: the KR 20 years after - Summary of Research Results', *Phnom Penh Post* (18 February-2 March 2000) Issue 9/4, available on subscription at <http://www.phnompenh post.com/>.

17. See e.g., NGO Forum on Cambodia, *Statement In Support of an International Tribunal* (Phnom Penh, 4 December 1998), available at <http://www.bigpond.com.kh/users/ngoforum/: 'A UN-sponsored tribunal could ... provide some useful tools for reflection and reconciliation among Cambodian people... A free and fair adjudication of the crimes committed by the Khmer Rouge is essential to resolving the heritage of suffering which is so pervasive in Cambodia today. Under Khmer Rouge rule the very fabric of Cambodian society was systematically destroyed ... Adjudication by an international tribunal would help to accelerate the resurrection of Cambodian society by serving to re-establish a sense of justice and personal accountability.'

18. Amnesty International, *Kingdom of Cambodia, Accountability for gross human rights violations: Open Letter to King Sihanouk and the National Assembly* (Report ASA 23/10/96, 11 September 1996), available at <http://www.amnesty.org/>: 'Amnesty International recognises and appreciates the need for national reconciliation in Cambodia. However, the organization believes that any conciliatory steps which are taken independent of an effort to identify and hold accountable those responsible for human rights violations in the past, may seriously jeopardise human rights protection in the future.'

19. On the treatment of this problem in the context of the South African Truth and Reconciliation Commission, see J. Dugard, 'Is the Truth and Reconciliation Process Compatible with International Law? An Unanswered Question', Cases and Comments: *Azapo v. President of the Republic of South Africa*, 13 *South African Journal on Human Rights* (1997) p. 258.

20. K.B. Richburg, 'A Small Apology to the Dead: For Nearly 2 Million Killed, "Let Bygones Be Bygones" ', *The Washington Post* (30 December 1998). Only Duch has indicated his willingness to testify concerning his role in the Tuol Sleng torture facility: see K. Johnson, 'Torture camp survivor willing to testify', *South China Morning Post* (16 March 2000).

counter-revolutionary forces, or a search for scapegoats to avoid admitting the fail-ure of the agrarian revolution and calm internal opposition. Furthermore, it is still uncertain who exactly was responsible for this change in policy. Elucidating the intentions behind these policies would not only help prevent ongoing stigmatisa-tion of traditional Cambodian scapegoats, such as the Vietnamese minority, but also influence the characterisation of the crimes in international law and the attri-bution of personal responsibilities. Only scrupulously impartial proceedings invol-ving direct testimony from those involved at high levels within the Khmer Rouge hierarchy would be able to shed light on such questions.[21]

2.2   **Punishment**

Although state instigation is generally not a constitutive element of international crimes, it is present in most cases. Yet the idea of establishing the international criminal responsibility of state representatives remained so entirely at odds with diplomatic practise before the 1990s that international lawyers still disagree whether there is any customary rule providing for jurisdictional immunity and, if so, whether there is an exception in the case of international crimes. The decision of the ICJ in the recent *Arrest Warrant* case held that questions of jurisdictional immunity do not arise before purely international courts,[22] but leaves open the question of the effect of domestic constitutional immunities in national trials. Un-surprisingly, most examples of national prosecution in such cases have involved *former* leaders, often many years afterwards.

Yet one of the aims of international justice must be to facilitate the exclusion from power of those who espouse criminal policies. In particular, the establishment of individual responsibility for the conception and implementation of such crimes can put an end to the collective 'demonization' of entire national, ethnic or politi-cal groups, thus preparing the reintegration into society of the innocent members.[23] If not, former leaders such as Slobodan Milošević will continue to portray them-selves as martyrs for their 'people'.

International courts find it difficult, however, to establish the responsibility of lower-level perpetrators of international crimes, often due to the sheer number of them, but also because of the difficulty in proving their specific intent to commit such crimes. The UN Security Council has instructed the two *ad hoc* International Tribunals that 'civilian, military and paramilitary leaders should be tried before them in preference to minor actors'.[24] This sort of selectivity is not necessarily

---

21. See S. Heder, 'Trial might shed light', *Phnom Penh Post* (10-23 December 1999) Issue 8/25, Letters to the editor, available at <http://www.phnompenhpost.com/TXT/letters/L825-2.htm.>

22. ICJ, *Case concerning the Arrest Warrant of 11 April 2000 (Democratic Republic of the Congo v. Belgium)*, Judgment, 14 February 2002, para. 61, available at <http://www.icj-cij.org; Art. 27(2) of the Rome Statute of the International Criminal Court expressly provides, that '[i]mmunities or special procedural rules which may attach to the official capacity of a person, whether under national or inter-national law, shall not bar the Court from exercising its jurisdiction over such a person' (UN Doc. A/CONF.183/9, 17 July 1998), available at <http://www.un.org/law/icc/.

23. See Akhavan, loc. cit. n. 9, at p. 21.

24. UN Doc. S/RES/1329, 30 November 2000, preamble.

contrary to the principle of systematic punishment as long as the international trials provide 'seeding' for domestic prosecutions. It even seems to create a logical division of tasks between the international community and the national population, allowing the latter to take some responsibility for dealing with their past. While this is a strong argument in favour of creating internationalised domestic tribunals, care must be taken to avoid such selectivity leading to *de facto* or *de jure* amnesty for perpetrators falling outside the jurisdiction of the internationalised court.

2.3   **Prevention**

Given the collective (and generally state-directed) reality of most international crimes, the question is whether international justice can prevent 'elite-induced mass violence', or at least prevent its recurrence in post-conflict situations. As compared with domestic justice, the means of prevention will be chosen based on their capacity to 'stigmatise and marginalise' such behaviour. 'Effective' police action may receive less priority than training in human rights principles for those who exercise public force and providing for effective judicial control over groups espousing criminal philosophies, including political parties. The aim is to make it clear that the international community will no longer accept 'international crimes committed as an instrument of statecraft and political control' as being of purely internal concern.[25] Such 'progressive entrenchment' of principles is arguably ineffective without a 'credible threat of punishment'.[26] Excluding power hungry leaders responsible for such crimes through the judicial process, rather than by political or military means, may also be less likely to perpetuate violent conflict or 'behind the scenes' continuation of control by the same individuals. Expeditious justice should also be more conducive to the eventual rehabilitation of offenders, especially when they are very young.[27]

In the absence of any permanent international criminal court, the preventive function of international justice has been weakened by the random or selective nature of repression, too heavily reliant on the political will of victor states, the Security Council or individual states willing to grant universal jurisdiction to their national courts.[28] Clearly, the establishment of two *ad hoc* international tribunals for the former Yugoslavia and Rwanda 'could not have been expected to instantly transform an entrenched culture of impunity into an abiding respect for the rule of law'.[29] The perception of selective justice, given the untried international crimes being committed elsewhere at the same time, even in neighbouring countries such as Burundi,[30] may even weaken such respect. Another problem affecting the pre-

---

25. ICTR, Trial Chamber, *Prosecutor* v. *Kambanda*, Case No. ICTR 97-23-S, Judgement and Sentence, 4 September 1998, para. 28, available at <http://www.ictr.org/.

26. See Akhavan, loc. cit. n. 9, at pp. 12-13.

27. Amann, loc. cit. n. 12, at pp. 115-116.

28. On the effects of randomness and selectivity, see Amann, ibid., at pp. 116-117.

29. Akhavan, loc. cit. n. 9, at p. 10.

30. Massacres of civilians, disappearances, torture, arbitrary arrest and massive population movements; see e.g., *Burundi, Between Hope and Fear*, Amnesty International (AI Index: AFR 16/007/01, March 2001), a summary of this and other Amnesty reports on Burundi is available at <http://www.

ventive force of international tribunals is that 'they tend to sit at a single location, perhaps countries away from defendants, witnesses, and directly affected members of the public', thus lessening local publicity for, and participation in the proceedings.[31] International decisions may be more likely to establish principles for posterity, as was the case at Nuremberg, but national proceedings are more likely to strengthen a post-conflict culture of justice for ordinary crimes, especially if the procedure adopted is transposable to the domestic court system afterwards.

One difference between international and internal accountability is that domestic trials often come many years after the crimes, except in cases of victor's justice (which may not respect internationally recognised principles[32]). Recent exercises in purely international justice, on the other hand, have responded to public perceptions of urgency. The existence of a current threat to international peace and security is even a prerequisite for UN Security Council action.[33] However, such urgent judicial activity should not be used as a substitute for concrete action to put an end to violations.

The Cambodian situation differs in one significant manner from those for which *ad hoc* International Tribunals were created (the former Yugoslavia and Rwanda) and those in which other internationalised domestic tribunals have been established (East Timor, Sierra Leone) or envisaged (Kosovo), due to the fact that the crimes in question ceased many years ago. Since then, the UN has made extraordinary efforts to strengthen respect for the Rule of Law in Cambodia through an unprecedented international peacekeeping operation, followed by the establishment of the first ever permanent national human rights watchdog, the UN Centre for Human Rights in Cambodia.[34] These major innovations were supported by wide-ranging associative, bilateral and regional initiatives. In particular, NGOs have placed constant pressure on the donor states grouped together in the Consultative Group on Cambodia[35] to put human rights in general and Khmer Rouge accountability in particular high on their reform agenda.[36] Empirical evidence suggests that the absence of Khmer Rouge accountability contributed significantly to the poor results of these efforts, having had a direct bearing on the prevailing atmosphere of impunity. Indeed, it is difficult to justify accountability for common crimes without a

---

amnesty.org/ailib/index.html; however, Burundi now having ratified the Rome Statute [AFP, 22 April 2003], such crimes may now be brought before the ICC.

31. Amann, loc. cit. n. 12, at p. 114.

32. This was certainly the case for the 1979 trial of the 'Pol Pot/Ieng Sary clique', see *infra* part 3.4.

33. See United Nations Charter, Chapter VII, esp. Art. 39.

34. For further information regarding the structure and mandate of the Human Rights Field Presence in Cambodia, see <http://www.unhchr.ch/html/menu2/5/cambodia.htm>; see also <http://www.un.org.kh/uncohchr/>.

35. Formerly, ICORC (International Committee for the Reconstruction of Cambodia).

36. See e.g., 'Human Rights Agenda for Cambodian Donors', *Human Rights Watch* (Press release 2000/05, New York, 23 May 2000), <http://www.hrw.org/press/2000/05/camb0523.htm>.

commitment to punishing those responsible for the gravest of all crimes committed in the past.[37]

Problems also arise when national reconciliation is not seen as a beneficial by-product but rather as the main aim of the judicial process. Limited prosecution in such conditions will only obtain 'illusory closure' through 'the ritual of legal process'.[38] Previous attempts to bring the Khmer Rouge to trial in Cambodia, in 1979 and 1994,[39] have had some success in putting an end to overt armed conflict by bringing former Khmer Rouge fighters 'into the fold' at the expense of the other aims of justice and have failed to achieve lasting reconciliation. The failure of the Royal Government's policy of reconciliation through amnesty, development and respect for human rights, just when the effective repression of international crimes was coming to fruition in the mid-1990s, has strengthened the hand of those who insist on the need for justice in Cambodia.

2.4   Reparation

Traditionally, reparation for victims was not a high priority in public prosecution of common crimes. If punishment of the offender was not sufficient for the victims, a private legal action might be available in order to seek compensation. However, perhaps because of the possibility of combining these two processes in civil law countries through the *partie civile* system, the victim is taking on increasing importance in some legal systems, and not only from a purely monetary point of view.[40] It is now being increasingly recognised that victims perceive crime as a breach of the equality underlying the social contract, which impedes their capacity to participate fully in public life. Especially in cases of crimes against humanity, the judicial process may provide the victims with 'a symbolic return to life' through which 'the victims hope that justice will "re-humanise" them'. One important means of satisfying this desire is to 'return the victims to a position of legal reciprocity' through 'restitution of their power to take action'.[41] It may even be that participation in the establishment of individual responsibility for mass crimes through testifying publicly may help survivors shrug off the weight of a perceived duty to bear witness for those who did not survive.[42]

---

37. Adhoc - Licadho - Human Rights Watch, *Impunity in Cambodia: How Human Rights Offenders Escape Justice* (HRW Report, Vol. 11/3(C), June 1999), available at <http://www.hrw.org/reports/1999/cambo2/>: 'Cambodia's culture of impunity starts with the fact that no Khmer Rouge leader has been called to account for crimes against humanity committed from 1975 to 1979.'

38. Akhavan, loc. cit. n. 9, at p. 10.

39. See *infra* part 3.4.3.

40. For France, see R. Vogler, 'Criminal Procedure in France', in J. Hatchard, B. Huber and R. Vogler, eds., *Comparative Criminal Procedure* (London, The British Institute of International and Comparative Law 1996) pp. 25-27; for the United States, see the Alien Tort Claims Act, 28 U.S.C.A. § 1350 (2001) and the Torture Victim Protection Act, 28 U.S.C.A. § 1350 note (2001).

41. A. Garapon, in A. Garapon et al., eds., *Et ce sera justice, Punir en démocratie* (Paris, Odile Jacob 2001) pp. 268-272.

42. Dr Reichmann, 'Sequelles psychologiques des rescapés', in *Khmers rouges: jugés ou impunis?*, Conference organised by the Comité des victimes des Khmers rouges, Paris, 23 March 2002 (forthcoming).

Despite this evolution in domestic legal systems, the two *ad hoc* International Tribunals make little provision for reparation. Both envisage, in addition to prison terms, 'the return of any property and proceeds acquired by criminal conduct, including by means of duress, to their rightful owners'.[43] As regards other forms of compensation to victims, however, the ICT Rules simply confirm that 'a victim or persons claiming through him may bring an action in a *national* court or other competent body to obtain compensation', pursuant to the relevant national legislation.[44]

In 1996, the UN Sub-Commission on Prevention of Discrimination and Protection of Minorities (the Sub-Commission) published a report on the right to reparation for victims of gross violations of human rights, which recognised the duty of states to ensure 'the right to a remedy against violations of human rights and humanitarian norms'. The available measures include restitution, compensation, rehabilitation, satisfaction and guarantees of non-repetition. The report also affirmed that '[r]eparation shall render justice by removing or redressing the consequences of the wrongful acts and by preventing and deterring violations.'[45] The International Criminal Court (ICC) has responded to this evolution by becoming the first international criminal court to make some direct financial provision for the needs of victims.

When international justice is only seen as a means of punishing criminal leaders or of excluding them from political life, it might be argued that it is incompatible with diplomatic or military efforts to end ongoing conflict. However, pursued in compliance with the above principles, it can encourage *restorative* justice, designed to regenerate the links binding diverse societies ravaged by international crime.[46] Seen in this light, international justice appears not only complementary to peacekeeping but also indispensable. In any case, only impartial justice and enforcement can achieve all of these objectives.

---

43. ICTY Statute, UN Doc. S/RES/827 (1993), 25 May 1993, Annex, Art. 24(3); ICTR Statute, UN Doc. S/RES/955 (1994), 8 November 1994, Art. 23(3). The Tribunals may exercise this power '[a]fter a judgment of conviction' containing a specific finding of 'unlawful taking of property by the accused'. ICTY, Rules of Procedure and Evidence (adopted 11 February 1994 as amended, UN Doc. IT/32/REV), available at: <http://www.un.org/icty/basic.htm>, Rule 105; ICTR Rules of Procedure and Evidence (adopted 5 July 1995 as amended), available at: <http://www.ictr.org>, Rule 105.

44. ICTY Rules, ibid., Rule 106(B); ICTR Rules, ibid. Rule 106(B) [emphasis added]. The only advantage is that under sub-rule (C), '[f]or the purposes of a claim made under Sub-rule (B) the judgement of the Tribunal shall be final and binding as to the criminal responsibility of the convicted person for such injury.'

45. UN Sub-Commission, *Revised set of basic principles and guidelines on the right to reparation for victims of gross violations of human rights and humanitarian law prepared by Mr. Theo van Boven pursuant to Sub-Commission decision 1995/117* (UN Doc. E/CN.4/Sub.2/1996/17, 24 May 1996), esp. paras. 4 and 7.

46. Garapon, loc. cit. n. 41.

3. THE NATURE OF THE JUDICIAL MECHANISM: COMPETING INTERESTS LEAD TO A MIXED CAMBODIAN COURT WITH INTERNATIONAL PARTICIPATION

There were international and internal antecedents to the Cambodian request for UN aid. On the one hand, after having supported the Khmer Rouge for many years, either actively or through 'a policy of silence',[47] in 1997 the UN formally recognised the fundamental relation between national reconciliation, the strengthening of democracy and the resolution of the question of individual criminal responsibility in Cambodia. This moral responsibility led the Human Rights Commission to declare that it would receive favourably any Cambodian request for aid in trying the Khmer Rouge.[48] On the other hand, it must be remembered that the June 1997 letter that set the whole process in motion[49] was a *joint* request by Prince Ranariddh and Hun Sen (the co-Prime Ministers, then representing the dominant Cambodian political forces), just before the former was ousted by the latter in a bloody coup. The antagonism between the two coalition partners had been exacerbated by the attempts of both sides to win over defectors from a deeply divided Khmer Rouge movement after the defection of the influential central committee member, Ieng Sary, in 1996 and the purging of its historical leader, Pol Pot, in June 1997. Internal power politics were thus a fundamental motor for the process from the start.

These competing moral and political interests must be kept in mind when analysing the exclusion of a third *ad hoc* international criminal tribunal and the subsequent negotiations for international participation in municipal trials.

3.1 The exclusion of a third *ad hoc* international criminal tribunal

The 1997 Cambodian letter requested the United Nations to provide the country with 'similar assistance' to that given to Rwanda and the former Yugoslavia, with a view to 'establishing the truth about this period [between 1975 and 1979] and bringing those responsible to justice'. They recognised that 'Cambodia does not have the resources or expertise to conduct this very important procedure'.[50]

Despite having co-signed the request for UN aid, which was apparently drafted for the government by the UN Centre for Human Rights in Cambodia,[51] Hun Sen subsequently opposed any proposal to create a third *ad hoc* international court.

---

47. T. Hammarberg, Special Representative of the UN Secretary-General for Cambodia, in UN Information Service, *Commission on Human Rights Starts Debate on Advisory Services and Technical Cooperation in Field of Human Rights* (UN Press Release HR/CN/928, Geneva, 22 April 1999) p. 9, available at <http://www.un.org/News/Press/docs/1999/19990422.hrcn928.html>.

48. UN Human Rights Commission, *Human Rights Situation in Cambodia* (UN Doc. E/CN.4/RES/1997/49, 11 April 1997), para. 12, available at <http://www.unhchr.ch/huridocda/huridoca.nsf/(Symbol)/ E.CN.4.RES.1997.49.en?Opendocument>.

49. Letter to the UN Secretary-General dated 21 June 1997, *supra* n. 3.

50. Ibid.

51. Rajagopal, loc. cit. n. 4, p. 192, fn. 11.

Moreover, a number of international factors also weighed heavily against this solution.

3.1.1   Systematic opposition from Hun Sen

The Cambodian request for assistance must be viewed in the context of extreme political tension between the two co-prime ministers before the 1997 coup. The UN did not even have time to respond to the Cambodian invitation before the coup. The resulting international isolation of Cambodia and the suspension of Cambodia's seat in the UN put an end to discussion of the issue at the time.

The organisation of free and fair elections was the international community's principal condition for renewed relations with the Cambodian government. Nevertheless, under the influence of the Secretary-General's Special Representative for Cambodia, Thomas Hammarberg, the issue of Khmer Rouge accountability took on increasing significance as a means of evaluating Hun Sen's resolve to promote the Rule of Law in Cambodia. In October 1997, the UN Secretary-General informed the General Assembly that '[t]he most serious human rights violators in Cambodia in recent history have been the members of the Khmer Rouge', that they were continuing to do so, and that '[n]o Khmer Rouge leader has been arrested or prosecuted by the Cambodian authorities.'[52] The Secretary-General was concerned that rehabilitated Khmer Rouge leaders might re-enter Cambodian political life without their individual criminal responsibility having been established, resulting in a new cycle of impunity in Cambodia. Consequently, he supported Thomas Hammarberg's request that the UN and its Member States 'respond positively and generously to the above-mentioned request, which is no less important after the violent events in July 1997'.[53] Accordingly, in December 1997, the UN General Assembly requested the Secretary-General to:

'examine the request by the Cambodian authorities for assistance in responding to past serious violations of Cambodian and international law, including the possibility of the appointment, by the Secretary-General, of a group of experts to evaluate the existing evidence and propose further measures, as a means of bringing about national reconciliation, strengthening democracy and addressing the issue of individual accountability'.[54]

Hun Sen only accepted the creation of the Group of Experts when the former UN High Commissioner for Human Rights, Mary Robinson, made it clear during a trip to Cambodia in January 1998, that the rapid recognition of his government depended on it.[55] The death of Pol Pot in April 1998, apparently of a heart attack,

---

52. Report of the Secretary-General: Situation of human rights in Cambodia (UN Doc. A/52/489, 17 October 1997), paras. 63-64.

53. Ibid., para. 67.

54. UN Doc. A/RES/52/135, 12 December 1997, para. 16.

55. Concerning this visit, see Human Rights Watch, *World Report 1999 - Cambodia*, available at <http://www.hrw.org/worldreport99/asia/cambodia.html>.

raised the possibility that international pressure would wane. On the contrary, interest in trying the remaining leaders redoubled and the Secretary-General finally set up the Group of Experts on 24 July 1998, two days before voting began in the Parliamentary Elections aimed at restoring democracy to Cambodia.

The Cambodian People's Party (CPP), led by Hun Sen, gained an absolute majority in the elections, but failed to reach the two-thirds majority necessary to form a government on its own under the 1993 Constitution.[56] The period after the elections was politically extremely tense. On the one hand, despite the grudging 'all clear' given by international observer groups,[57] Hun Sen's victory was contested by the other parties, in a climate of political violence.[58] On the other hand, disagreement over second-placed Prince Ranariddh's role in a new coalition arrangement resulted in a constitutional deadlock. Finally, on 11 November 1998, after significant international pressure on all parties,[59] a compromise was reached whereby Hun Sen became sole Prime Minister and Ranariddh was named President of the National Assembly.[60] The least that may be said is that Khmer Rouge accountability was not a priority at that time.

By the time the three members of the Group of Experts finally arrived in Cambodia for a two week visit in November 1998, the political situation had changed even more significantly in favour of Hun Sen. Not only did the creation of a new coalition government hold the promise of Cambodia reintegrating into the UN system,[61] but the Khmer Rouge insurgency was going through its final death throes.[62] Hun Sen, who had been using the threat of trials as a bargaining chip in negotiations for the surrender of the remaining Khmer Rouge leaders, personally informed

---

56. Arts. 11-12 of the Constitution of 24 September 1993, as amended by *Kram* [law] No. NS/KRM/0399-01, 8 March 1999, available at <http://www.bigpond.com.kh.>

57. The campaign period was relatively peaceful when compared with the previous 12 months, but was marred by a number of political killings and attacks, and a lack of free access to the electronic media for the opposition. The Joint International Observer Group (a UN-coordinated body of 37 countries) expressed its satisfaction with the election process on 27 July less than 48 hours after the polls had closed and well before the counting process was complete.

58. The crisis came to a head between 7 and 15 September 1998, when largely peaceful demonstrations organised by opposition leaders and Buddhist monks in front of the National Assembly in Phnom Penh were crushed by the authorities with excessive use of force. At least two people were killed by government security forces or their agents during the unrest, with another 24 deaths under investigation by the COHCHR: Amnesty International, Kingdom of Cambodia - Demonstrations Crushed with Excessive use of Force (AI Report - ASA 23/26/98, 22 September 1998), available at <http://www.amnesty.org/; see also, United Nations, Statement by Ambassador Thomas Hammarberg, Special Representative of the United Nations Secretary General for Human Rights in Cambodia, New York, 16 September 1998.

59. A Bill was even introduced into US Congress on 21 September 1998, just before the beginning of all-party talks aimed at setting up a new coalition, aimed at trying Hun Sen for crimes against humanity in relation to his suppression of the peaceful demonstrations after the elections.

60. However, because the President of the National Assembly acts as Head of State when the King is absent, it was also agreed to create a Senate, purely for the purpose of transferring this executive duty to its President.

61. The UN General Assembly's Credentials Committee accepted the representatives of the new coalition government on 7 December 1998.

62. The last forces surrendered or were captured in December 1998 (Ta Mok).

the Group of Experts that he now preferred internal trials.[63] A month later, in early-December 1998, the last major Khmer Rouge leaders, Khieu Samphan and Nuon Chea, surrendered and were feted in Phnom Penh without being arrested, apparently against a promise that there would be no international trial.[64] Only one hardline military leader, Ta Mok (and a handful of his followers) continued to fight near the Thai border (he was finally arrested on 8 March 1999). Having achieved both of his political objectives (legitimacy and the military reintegration of the Khmer Rouge), Hun Sen then implied that the question of accountability should be 'buried' to avoid rekindling the conflict.[65]

Faced with sustained public criticism and international indignation, however, Hun Sen backtracked. King Sihanouk also made it clear that he would not grant any more amnesties for Khmer Rouge leaders even if requested to do so by the government.[66] Accordingly, an *Aide Mémoire* on the question of Khmer Rouge accountability provided to the UN by Hun Sen in January 1999 recognised the need for trials, but insisted that 'justice and national reconciliation must be taken into account simultaneously, without intending to prioritize one over another'. While the *Aide Mémoire* formally left the question of the 'international' or 'mixed' nature of the court open, it clearly considered a mixed solution to be a more appropriate means of achieving the double purpose of the trials.[67] Above all, the Prime Minister based his refusal of an international solution on the need to respect Cambodian sovereignty and the desire to avoid any risk of renewed internal conflict.[68]

Despite, or perhaps because of the strong opposition from Hun Sen, the 1999 Report by the UN Group of Experts came down in favour of creating a third *ad hoc* tribunal.[69] However, a second Cambodian *Aide Mémoire*, sent to the UN in response to the Experts' Report, took a harder line, indicating that in order to promote 'peace and stability and national reconciliation', Ta Mok would be tried by the national judicial system 'under the Cambodian law in force'.[70] The implication was that the other leaders who gave themselves up would not be prosecuted at all and that no international participation was required.

---

63. 'Hun Sen Discusses Khmer Rouge Trial', Associated Press (3 December 1998).

64. C. Fontaine, 'Cambodia Premier Says No to Trial', Associated Press (28 December 1998).

65. H. Watkin, 'Irony not lost as Hun Sen "buries" the past', *South China Morning Post* (30 December 1998).

66. D. Brunnstrom, 'Sihanouk Won't Grant More Khmer Rouge Amnesties', Reuters, (30 December 1998).

67. Royal Government of Cambodia (RGC), 'An Analysis on Seeking a Formula for Bringing Top Khmer Rouge Leaders to Trial', *Aide mémoire* handed to the Special Representative for the Secretary-General, Thomas Hammarberg, Phnom Penh, 21 January 1999.

68. See e.g., N. Thaitawat et al., 'Hun Sen: Ieng Sary trial will bring war - Prosecution Means end of Royal Amnesty', *Bangkok Post* (10 January 2001).

69. Report of the UN Group of Experts, *supra* n. 3, para. 219(1).

70. RGC, *Aide mémoire* on the Report of the United Nations Group of Experts for Cambodia, 12 March 1999 (UN Doc. A /53/866, 18 March 1999, Annex). The 'law in force' referred to was undoubtedly the 1994 Law outlawing the Khmer Rouge.

3.1.2   *International obstacles*

Over and above Cambodian opposition to the establishment of a purely international tribunal, there were also international legal, political and financial factors weighing heavily against this solution.

On the legal side, the first Cambodian *Aide Mémoire* questioned the power of the Security Council to create an *ad hoc* tribunal for Cambodia. Hun Sen argued that an *ad hoc* international tribunal would not have jurisdiction to try the Khmer Rouge leaders *in absentia*. Given the difficulty he was then having mopping up the resistance strongholds in the Thai border region, he suggested that they be tried by '*contumace*' under French inspired domestic procedure.[71] While technically correct, this argument is weakened by the fact that the so-called Rule 61 proceedings available before the *ad hoc* International Criminal Tribunals allows the prosecution case to be presented in the absence of the accused, followed by the issue of an international arrest warrant carrying all the authority of a body created by the Security Council under Chapter VII of the UN Charter.[72] Furthermore, Thailand had indicated that it would respect its international responsibility to arrest any accused found on its territory.[73]

Nevertheless, the Khmer Rouge case does raise a problem with respect to the extent of the Security Council's general power to maintain international peace and security under Chapter VII of the UN Charter. Of course, Tribunal case law has confirmed the capacity of the Council to set up an *ad hoc* International Criminal Tribunal under Chapter VII.[74] However, in order to do so in this case, the Security Council would need to determine not only that the situation in Cambodia currently threatens international peace and security but also that the establishment of a tribunal would contribute to the maintenance of international peace. Although a continuing Khmer Rouge insurgency would clearly have a destabilising influence on its government, that risk cannot be compared with the major conflicts in the context of which the Security Council decided to create the tribunals for the former Yugoslavia and Rwanda, all the more so since the armed rebellion had all but collapsed.

Nevertheless, in May 1998, the US representative to the UN provided the members of the Security Council with a draft resolution based on Chapter VII of the Charter, supporting the establishment of an *ad hoc* tribunal to try the Khmer Rouge. The preamble of the draft reads as follows: 'Determining that *failure to try such persons* in light of the ongoing situation in Cambodia would constitute a threat to international peace and security.' Needless to say, such a resolution would have required the Security Council to accept a widened conception of its powers (true to the expectations of the founders of the United Nations), according to which

---

71. 'Hun Sen Discusses Khmer Rouge Trial', Associated Press (3 December 1998).

72. ICTY Rules, *supra* n. 43, Rule 61, 'Procedure in Case of Failure to Execute a Warrant'.

73. 'Cambodia "best suited" for trying Khmer Rouge', (Bangkok) *The Nation* (24 November 1998).

74. See *Prosecutor* v. *Duško Tadić Alias "Dule"*, (Case IT-94-1-T, 2 October 1995) Decision on Defence Motion for Interlocutory Appeal on Jurisdiction; and *Prosecutor* v. *Joseph Kanyabashi*, (Case ICTR-96-15-T, 18 June 1997) Decision on the Defence Motion on Jurisdiction.

massive human rights violations, as such, threaten international peace and security and justify Security Council intervention.

Even if such an extensive interpretation of its powers is legally conceivable, the Council would be unlikely to take the risk of characterising crimes committed over 20 years ago as a current threat to international peace, given the number of unresolved Cold War conflicts throughout the world. The Security Council is a political body composed of states, and the five permanent members have a right of veto. The United Kingdom, France and Russia appeared ready to support the American draft resolution in 1998. However, the fifth permanent member, China (formerly the principal supporter of the Khmer Rouge), seems likely to veto the establishment of an international tribunal as long as the Cambodian government opposes it.[75] Given the adverse effects on the pace of negotiations that seem to follow each Chinese official visit to Cambodia, the latter does not seem likely to make such a request as long as China opposes it.[76]

Finally, it should not be forgotten that the international community is becoming more and more wary of committing scarce financial resources to pure forms of international justice, increasingly giving priority to less expensive national[77] or hybrid solutions.[78]

Considering these drawbacks, the Group of Experts must have had very serious reservations concerning the other available options, given that it preferred the seemingly unreachable star of pure international justice.

3.2   The negotiations for international participation in national trials

The negotiations between the UN and Cambodia commenced, thus, with the two parties staking out diametrically opposed options. On 17 March 1999, Kofi Annan accepted the conclusions of the Group of Experts (provided to him and the Royal Government on 22 February 1999) and recommended the establishment of a third *ad hoc* international tribunal. Considering the hostility of China, three explanations are possible. It may be that, just as the Statute of the ICC was being finalised, the Organisation assumed sufficient international pressure could be brought to bear on Cambodia to bring it to accept this solution. Alternatively, it may have doubted that this would happen and either hoped that that the affair would be dropped, or simply chose to establish a strong negotiating position for the inevitable compromise to come.

Predictably, Hun Sen refused the UN's preferred solution, and a consensus solution avoiding Security Council action under Chapter VII became the only real alternative to impunity. Yet the UN Group of Experts had examined and rejected the

---

75. D. Brunnstrom, 'China declines comment on Khmer Rouge trial veto', Reuters (5 February 1999).

76. Y. Chhang, 'China's Advice Interferes with Sovereignty', *The Cambodia Daily* (30 June 1999).

77. E.g., the current move to transfer some ICTY cases to the Bosnian courts; see 'Delocalization of Cases: The Security Council Declares its Support', *Judicial Diplomacy* (24 July 2002).

78. This was a driving force, for example, behind the choice of a Special Court for Sierra Leone to be paid for out of voluntary contributions.

other available options.[79] Although technically feasible, these solutions would not benefit from the compulsory effect of Security Council resolutions. While the Group noted that the good faith cooperation of the Cambodian government would be more important than any theoretically compulsory resolution, it concluded that the chances of sustained internal support for the process were limited. Moreover, as Hun Sen claimed recently, Cambodia never formally requested UN aid to set up a *mixed* tribunal.[80] Thus, to some extent, the hybrid solution was imposed on *both* parties through international (and to a lesser extent local) pressure for continued negotiations.

Behind their apparently incompatible stands, both parties were in fact ready to make compromises. Nevertheless, a year of laborious negotiations was needed before an apparent agreement was reached in July 2000. Another year passed before Cambodia adopted the required legislation to give effect to this agreement.

3.2.1   *The laborious search for a compromise on a mixed Cambodian court with international participation*

The simplest option for the Cambodian government, and the most compatible with Cambodia's obligations under international criminal law, would have been to grant jurisdiction to the existing courts to try all international crimes committed in Cambodia, regardless of when they were committed, along the lines of the Belgian law adopted in 1999. However, given the poor state of the Cambodian legal system, the country needed not only the legitimacy but also the external judicial assistance coming with international participation. As for the UN, faced with Hun Sen's intransigence concerning the purely international option, the world body came under significant pressure to accept a compromise guaranteeing trials respecting due process. Both were thus obliged to envisage a 'mixed' solution involving international participation in the Cambodian courts.

The negotiations concerning the exact nature of this participation lasted until the end of 2000. The purported aim was to find a model that represents a balance between the exercise of truly independent and efficient justice, and respect for Cambodian sovereignty.[81] Behind the scenes, the struggle for control of the mechanism had begun. Many erroneously saw this as a competition for government or UN control of the process. If so, it was an unequal match, because the very concept of the UN controlling an internationalised tribunal is anathema. The UN participation was aimed at setting up a mechanism containing sufficient safeguards of the judicial independence of the tribunal from all outside influence, preferably guaranteed through UN administration.

---

79. Report of the UN Group of Experts, *supra* n. 3, paras. 185 et seq.

80. Nevertheless, the *Aide Mémoire, supra* n. 70, on the question of Khmer Rouge responsibility provided to the UN by Hun Sen in January 1999, before the Group of Experts handed down its report, mentions an 'international' or 'mixed' court.

81. J.-P. Getti and W. Schabas, *Violations des droits de l'homme au Cambodge: Justice et lutte contre l'impunité,* FIDH (Rapport No. 284, December 1999), available at <http://www.fidh.org/IMG/pdf/284camb.pdf>, para. 2.4, [our translation].

In August 1999, both parties circulated hybrid, but incompatible, proposals. Hun Sen supported a national court with external financing, supported by a small staff of international personnel. The UN also accepted a mechanism set up under Cambodian law, but proposed a Nuremberg-style joint trial of all suspects together, under which proceedings would be dominated by a majority of international personnel.[82] A week of negotiations between a team from the UN Department of Legal Affairs and the President of the Council of Ministers, Sok An, produced no visible results. The head of the UN team, Ralph Zacklin, stated that if Cambodia did not accept a number of basic conditions, the United Nations would not be able to support the process. In September 1999, Hun Sen renewed the request for help from the UN, either as a full participant or by simply providing aid in drafting the necessary legislation.[83] Finally, in October 1999, an American Senator, John Kerry, broke the deadlock with a US-backed proposal.[84] In order to ensure international control over the nature of the mechanism, he suggested following the procedure required by the United Nations, a binding bilateral agreement followed by national implementing legislation. As for the government's insistence on preserving its 'sovereignty', he proposed a structure including a majority of Cambodian judges, but with a 'super majority' needed for any decision, including at least one international judge.[85]

In spite of this significant breakthrough (reflected in Article 14 of the Tribunal Law), filling in the details, especially concerning the prosecutor, took until July 2000. On 20 December 1999, Hun Sen sent draft legislation to the UN, requesting a reply before Christmas. The UN Undersecretary-General for Legal Affairs, Hans Corell, replied on 23 December that, given the contents of the Cambodian draft, the United Nations would be forced to limit its participation to technical aid, as the proposal did not contain sufficient guarantees of impartiality.[86]

In January 2000, after a visit by the Japanese Prime Minister, Hun Sen agreed to reopen the question of international participation. On 5 January, Hans Corell met the Cambodian permanent representative to the United Nations, Ouch Borith, to provide detailed comments on the latest version of the law.[87] The following day, the Royal Government finalised the bill 'on the Establishment of the Extraordinary Chambers in the Courts of Cambodia for the Prosecution of Crimes Committed

---

82. Allied forces, Control Council Law No. 10 for Germany, 20 December 1945; on this proposal, see 'U.N. Should Insist on International Standards for Khmer Rouge Trial', *Human Rights Watch* (Press release, New York, 24 August 1999), available at: <http://www.hrw.org/press/1999/aug/camb0824.htm.>

83. J.-P. Getti, 'Comment juger les Khmers Rouges ?', 32 *La Lettre de la FIDH* (2000), 14 February 2000.

84. On US involvement in the negotiations, see A. Marcher, 'The American role in putting together a KR trial deal', Interview with US ambassador Kent Wiedemann, Issue 9/9, *Phnom Penh Post* (28 April-11 May 2000), available on subscription at <http://www.phnompenhpost.com/>.

85. See *infra* part 4.1.

86. 'Cambodia delays decision on genocide trial to Jan. 6', Kyodo News Service (24 December 1999).

87. F. Eckhard, Spokesman for the Secretary-General, Daily Press Briefing of Office of Spokesman for Secretary-General, United Nations, 6 January 2000.

during the Period of Democratic Kampuchea'.[88] It was tabled before the Cambo-dian National Assembly on 18 January 2000 and the UN received an official trans-lation the same day. This basic text would be revised on a number of occasions following further negotiations.

In February 2000, after Prince Ranariddh (who had been named President of the National Assembly under the new coalition arrangements), expressed frustration with United Nations silence on the matter, Hans Corell gave details of four main problems with the bill:

— the lack of independence of the international prosecutor and investigating judge;

— the absence of government guarantees of the arrest of the accused;

— ambiguity concerning amnesties; and

— the absence of rules concerning the qualified majority of foreign judges.[89]

Hun Sen retorted that the last three UN Secretaries-General should be held respon-sible for keeping the Khmer Rouge in Cambodia's seat throughout the 1980s. After this crisis, the negotiators did not meet again until 16 March, to discuss the pro-blems raised by Annan. Despite another week of tense, but 'constructive' discus-sions, there was still no agreement.[90]

On 29 April 2000, Senator John Kerry proposed a second compromise, concern-ing this time the prosecutors and investigating magistrates. The Prime Minister again gave his consent and, on 19 May 2000, formally requested the UN to reopen discussions along the lines set out by Kerry.[91] On 4 July 2000, Hans Corell re-turned to Phnom Penh for further discussions with Sok An. On 7 July 2000, they seemed to have come to a final agreement concerning the last details: organisation of the prosecution, funding for the trial, working languages, personnel security and the location of the Court. Mr Corell then presented a draft Memorandum of Under-standing to the Cambodian government ostensibly containing the final agreement between the parties concerning international participation in the trials (hereafter the 'draft MOU').[92]

3.2.2   Hold-ups in the Cambodian legislative process

According to its own terms, the draft MOU was not to be signed until the Cambo-dian Parliament had legislated to give effect to its terms. To that end, the Royal Government requested the Legal Commission of the Assembly to amend the bill to reflect the compromise reached by the parties. However, it appears that the gov-

---

88. K. Johnson, 'Cabinet gives nod to "killing fields" trials', *South China Morning Post* (7 January 2000).

89. H. Corell, Press Briefing by United Nations Legal Counsel, United Nations, NY, 8 February 2000; see also Puy Kea, 'Ieng Sary seen as key obstacle for Khmer Rouge trial', Kyodo News Service, 17 February 2000.

90. H. Corell, Head of the UN Delegation, *Statement to the Press*, Phnom Penh, 22 March 2000.

91. United Nations, Cambodia agree in writing on Khmer Rouge trial formula, Political Informa-tion Bulletin #1, 24 May 2000.

92. *Supra* n. 5; see also United Nations, Press Statement by H. Corell, Pochentong Airport, Phnom Penh, 7 July 2000.

ernment kept the exact terms of the Memorandum secret, not even providing a copy to the Legal Commission. This attitude was strongly criticised by the Forum of Cambodian NGOs, because it clearly prevented informed parliamentary and public debate concerning the nature of the court. Finally, a copy of the draft MOU was published unofficially by a Cambodian newspaper.[93]

Then nothing happened at all until the end of the year, when a third visit by an American Senator seems to have revived the lower house of Parliament, which met in plenary session on 14 December and placed the bill on its priority agenda. The bill was debated by the National Assembly from 29 December 2000 to 2 January 2001 and was adopted unanimously by all members present.[94] This unexpected eagerness revived hope that justice might finally be done. Once the law had passed the lower house of parliament, high level American diplomatic and commercial missions resumed, American development aid having been linked not only to a return to democracy but also to progress with the Court.[95]

Despite the unanimity of the Assembly, several aspects of the bill were raised for clarification during debate, especially the extent of the court's personal jurisdiction, statute of limitations problems, the right to choose an attorney and the death penalty. It also emerges from the record that, never having been officially informed of the contents of the draft MOU, the opposition parties were forced to accept government assurances as to the conformity of the two texts.[96]

On 9 January 2001, the UN formally expressed concern that the bill passed by the Assembly was inconsistent with the Memorandum.[97] However, the government did not forward the UN comments to the Senate before it debated and adopted the bill on 15 January 2001, also by all members present.

On 12 February 2000, the Cambodian Constitutional Council declared that the law complied with the 1993 Constitution. However, it requested that a technical problem relating to the death penalty be rectified. On 23 February, Hun Sen decided to return the law to the Council of Ministers for amendment, to specify that death sentences may not be handed down for the domestic crimes included in the court's jurisdiction. This decision has been interpreted in some areas as yet another time-wasting manoeuvre. Indeed, not only was it perfectly unnecessary to change the law in this respect, but several other more fundamental problems raised by the mixed model were not even raised by the Council.

Although a new parliamentary session began in May 2001, the Council of Ministers only approved the new formulation of the bill on 22 June. On 27 June, the UN Secretary-General reiterated Cambodia's responsibility rapidly to adopt a law

---

93. *Phnom Penh Post*, Issue No. 9/22 (27 October-9 November 2000), available on subscription at <http://www.phnompenhpost.com/>.

94. An unofficial translation of the bill adopted in January 2001 is available on the Cambodian National Assembly web-site at <http://www.cambodian-parliament.org/Legislative_Act_/legislative_act_.html>.

95. 'Gephardt-led U.S. delegation arrives in Cambodian capital', Associated Press (15 January 2001).

96. See D. Boyle, 'Trial in Cambodia, One More Step', *Judicial Diplomacy* (5 August 2001).

97. F. Eckhard, Daily Press Briefing by the Office of the Spokesman for the Secretary-General, United Nations, NY, 12 January 2001.

complying with the draft MOU. Hun Sen seized the opportunity of a visit by the Secretary-General's Special Representative for Human Rights, Peter Leuprecht, to denounce continued UN interference with the legislative process. The National Assembly finally debated the amended bill in July 2001. Criticising 'lies' by the Minister during the first passage of the bill, the leader of the opposition, Sam Rainsy, declared that his party would no longer support the law unless several amendments were made to bring it into line with the provisions of the draft MOU. The problems included the choice of attorneys, protection of witnesses and court staff and the persistent ambiguity concerning amnesties.

In the end, the National Assembly adopted the law on 11 July 2001 followed by the Senate on 23 July. Declared constitutional by the Council on 7 August, the Law on the Establishment of the Extraordinary Chambers in the Courts of Cambodia for the Prosecution of Crimes Committed during the Period of Democratic Kampuchea was promulgated by King Norodom Sihanouk on 10 August 2001 (the 'Tribunal Law').[98]

4.   THE STRUCTURE OF THE CAMBODIAN MIX

An official, if unsatisfactory,[99] translation of the Tribunal Law finally having been made public in 2002, the detailed structure of the Extraordinary Chambers envisaged in the Law may now be analysed with relative certainty.[100] Of course, the Tribunal Law must be read in the light of the 2003 Agreement, which takes precedence over the Law to the extent of any disparity.[101] Formally, the Extraordinary Chambers are established under Cambodian law. In reality, however, they will apply a hybrid legal system. In such an internationalised domestic tribunal, the competing forces outlined above play a much greater role in moulding the contours of the Chambers than for purely international tribunals. These forces explain the groundbreaking composition of the Chambers, the unique rules organising international participation, the mixture of domestic criminal procedure and international principles and the limitation of their jurisdiction to the crimes committed by the Khmer Rouge during their period in power.

4.1   The composition of the Extraordinary Chambers breaks new legal ground

Article 2 of the Tribunal Law provides for the establishment, in Phnom Penh, of Extraordinary Chambers within each level of the three-tiered Cambodian judicial hierarchy: the Phnom Penh Municipal Court at first instance, the Court of Appeal

---

98. *Supra* n. 6.

99. Certain important passages are translated differently in the French and English official translations.

100. The earlier non-official translation of the bill adopted in January 2001, *supra* n. 94, does not incorporate all of the changes introduced during the negotiations.

101. See *infra* part 6.

and the Supreme Court. [102] Thus excluding any role for the military courts, the Law provides the accused with appellate remedies, although there is no mention of any right to judicial review of the constitutionality of the law.[103]

Of particular note is the fact that the nature of the international participation varies between the judges and prosecution staff. The 'super majority' compromise on the judicial composition of the Extraordinary Chambers, set out in Chapters III and V of the Law, has remained basically unchanged since the original proposal by Senator Kerry in 1999. In response to sovereignty issues raised by the Royal Government, there will be a majority of Cambodian judges in each Chamber.[104] Furthermore, the presiding judge for each Chamber will be Cambodian. However, in order to guarantee effective international participation, a simple majority will not suffice for decisions. Article 14 of the Tribunal Law requires judges to 'attempt to achieve unanimity in their decisions'. If this is not possible, a qualified majority is required, involving the 'affirmative vote' of at least one international judge.[105]

This compromise provides a perfect example of the blending process characteristic of international criminal justice, which results from political compromise but also from the need to accommodate common law and civil law approaches to trial procedure. In this case, while the UN negotiators accepted the principle of unanimity inherited from the French judicial tradition, in return, they insisted on the inclusion of both majority and dissenting opinions in Chamber decisions, in cases where unanimity is impossible.[106] As compared with the laconic decisions typical of the civil law tradition, this helps to reinforce the expressive effect of the trials through the public enumeration of the crimes involved, as well as contributing to the growing body of international criminal case law.

Despite these failsafe measures, several potential loopholes have been uncovered in the 'super majority' system. Above all, whereas the qualified majority guarantees international protection of the rights of the defence, the international judges alone will not be able to ensure any convictions without the endorsement of at least two Cambodian judges. Although this may seem to be a major defect, given the Royal Government's partiality for certain potential accused, this problem is more likely to arise before these persons ever get to Court, when the prosecutor is deciding who to investigate. Furthermore, there has been some debate as to whether the super-majority rule applies only to final 'decisions' concerning culpability, or to all 'decisions' made by the Chambers, including interlocutory and procedural rulings.

---

102. The 2003 Agreement simplifies this structure, removing the intermediate appellate Chamber; see *infra* part 6.

103. While Art. 141 of the 1993 Cambodian Constitution (as amended, *supra* n. 56) provides for both *a priori* (before promulgation) and *a posteriori* (during litigation) constitutional review, it remains unclear whether the latter is available in cases where the law has already been declared constitutional before promulgation.

104. The Tribunal Law provided for three out of five judges at first instance; four out of seven appellate judges; and five out of nine before the Supreme Court; for the new system, see *infra* part 6.

105. This gave a voting formula of four out of five judges at first instance, five out of seven on appeal and six out of nine before the Supreme Court; for the new system, see *infra* part 6.

106. Draft MOU, *supra* n. 5, Art. 3(2), Tribunal Law, *supra* n. 6, Art. 14(2), 2003 Agreement, *supra* n. 7, Art. 4(2).

Clearly, if the Tribunal Law only subjects the former to international scrutiny, it may well be that trials never reach the conviction stage. As far as may be determined by reference to the original Khmer text, which is the official working language under the Tribunal Law, the term *seckdey samrec* covers *all* judicial decisions.[107]

The Tribunal Law reproduces the French-inspired division of the prosecution role between the 'prosecutor' and 'the investigating judge'.[108] Succinctly, the former is responsible for preparing indictments and pleading during the trial, whereas the latter is in charge of conducting an even-handed investigation of the alleged crimes in search of evidence for and against the accused. The system of international participation finally adopted for both of these roles differs significantly from that for the sitting judges, providing for the appointment of two 'co-investigating judges', as well as two 'co-prosecutors' for each level of the Chambers.[109] Accordingly, for each function, there will be a Cambodian and a foreign appointee with identical status and powers (Chapters VI and VII of the Law).

Interestingly, although the concept of international participation at the prosecution stage was accepted early on in the negotiations, two aspects caused major problems and were among the last to be resolved. First, it was necessary to reach agreement on the applicable legal system. The UN negotiators seemed eager to align the Chambers' criminal procedure to the common law-inspired system adopted by the *ad hoc* International Criminal Tribunals for the Former Yugoslavia and Rwanda, where the prosecutor performs both roles. Eventually, the Cambodian insistence on using their own system led to UN insistence on the inclusion of an international investigating judge.[110]

Once the Cambodian system had been chosen, the question of guaranteeing the independence of the international personnel became critical. According to the original Cambodian project, the co-prosecutors were required to work together and make all decisions by consensus. The UN feared that the Cambodian prosecutor would thus be able to prevent certain powerful suspects from being indicted. It was finally agreed, again through US mediation, that in the event of disagreement between the co-prosecutors, the prosecution shall continue unless one of them requests that the difference be settled by a 'Pre-Trial Chamber' composed of five

---

107. Translation provided by A. Daniel, Professor of Khmer at the Institut National des Langues et Civilisations Orientales, Paris. The precise term for the final decision concerning culpability is *Salkram* for the trial court and *saldeyka* for other courts.

108. For further details on the division of work under Cambodian Law, see S. Linton, 'Cambodia, East Timor and Sierra Leone: experiments in international justice', 12 *Criminal LF* (2001) pp. 185, at pp. 200-202.

109. A different Cambodian prosecutor is to be appointed for each Chamber, whereas only one foreign prosecutor will be named, with competence to appear in all three Extraordinary Chambers.

110. In early UN proposals, no international participation was envisaged at the crucial investigation stage, as it was assumed that the function would disappear, especially as the position is currently coming under fire from the domestic legal profession, increasingly composed of common law trained attorneys: see *Statement of Participants at a Workshop on the reform of Administration of Justice Relating to Police in Cambodia,* (Siem Riep, Cambodia, 22-24 January 2000), organised by the Cambodian Defenders Project/IHRLG.

judges, following the model of the Trial Chamber (Art. 20). However, in a complete turnaround compared with the Chambers themselves, a qualified majority of the Pre-Trial Chamber will be necessary in order to block the prosecution. The same procedure was later adopted for the co-investigating judges (Art. 23). In practise, however, it is to be feared that polarisation of prosecution teams will lead to disputes and time wasting, especially given the uncertainty concerning the exact state of Cambodian criminal procedure.

4.2   The unique rules relating to international participation

Under the terms of the draft MOU, international participation in the Extraordinary Chambers is governed by rules designed to guarantee respect for the international aspects of the trials, not only with respect to the Cambodian government but also to avoid the risk of any parallel bilateral intervention undercutting the Organisation's requirements. This led to the inclusion of specific rules relating to the selection of the international personnel participating in the Extraordinary Chambers as well as the financial and administrative organisation of the Chambers.

All the principle foreign personnel of the Extraordinary Chambers (judges, prosecutor and investigating judge) are to be appointed 'for the duration of the proceedings'.[111] This created no major problems as Cambodian law does not currently require such positions to be held by persons of Cambodian nationality. However, a procedural problem arose due to the fact that the 1993 Constitution requires the Cambodian Supreme Council of the Magistracy (SCM) to 'make proposals to the King on the appointment of judges and prosecutors to all courts'. (Art. 134). Accordingly, the Royal Government insisted that all personnel of the Extraordinary Chambers be appointed by the SCM, including the foreign staff. A compromise was finally found whereby the SCM is to appoint the foreign personnel 'upon nomination by the Secretary-General of the United Nations', from lists provided by the latter.[112] These lists must include at least two prosecutors, two investigating judges and 12 judges. If any of the appointees are absent, for any reason, they will be replaced by another person chosen from the UN lists, and not by a Cambodian, as required by the original governmental proposal.

However, the Tribunal Law provides that, in the event that those lists are exhausted, any vacancies are to be filled from other sources: first 'from candidates recommended by the governments of Member States of the United Nations or from among other foreign legal personalities'; failing that 'the Supreme Council of the Magistracy may choose replacement Cambodian judges, investigating judges or prosecutors'. This provision, which did not appear in the draft MOU, would only operate in the case of a UN pullout, to avoid rendering the Tribunal Law inoperable.

---

111. Tribunal Law, *supra* n. 6, Arts. 12, 21 and 26.
112. Ibid., Arts. 11, 18 and 26.

A special Office of Administration is to be set up, solely responsible for supervising the staff of the Extraordinary Chambers.[113] It is to have a Cambodian Director and a foreign Deputy Director. The Deputy will be responsible for recruiting the international administrative staff and managing any UN funding for the Chambers. Given the extreme importance of this position for the independence of the court, the UN insisted on choosing the Deputy directly. This led to slightly different wording in the Tribunal Law compared with the other posts, whereby he or she shall be 'appointed by the Secretary-General of the United Nations and assigned by the Royal Government of Cambodia' (Art. 31).[114]

The nature of funding for the Chambers has also evolved with fluctuations in the proposed international participation. In the finalised Tribunal Law, it is up to whoever provides personnel to cover the costs. This was included upon UN insistence, in response to Cambodian insistence on naming its own judges without any outside oversight. However, it leaves the Cambodian judges under the sole financial control of the government. As regards the international staff provided by the UN, the cost will not be appropriated from the ordinary budget of the Organisation (as is the case for the existing *ad hoc* Tribunals), but rather from a trust fund set up to receive voluntary donations from states (Art. 44).[115]

Despite the separate sources of funding for judges, the Tribunal Law responds to potential problems of corruption of underpaid local judges, or friction with highly paid foreign judges, by requiring that '[a]ll judges under this law shall enjoy equal status and conditions of service according to each level of the Extraordinary Chambers' (Art. 12). However, this is at the price of possible loss of independence *vis-à-vis* the CPP-controlled SCM of local judges seeking to be named to the highly paid posts within the Chambers. Moreover, nothing indicates how the Royal Government will finance the additional budgetary cost involved.

In a search for efficiency and cost effectiveness, the draft MOU proposes commencing the trials of those persons already in custody, without awaiting the end of investigations against the other suspects.[116]

4.3   A mixture of internal criminal procedure and international principles

In keeping with the tendency in other internationalised domestic tribunals, national criminal procedure is given pride of place in the Tribunal Law, in the hope that the practice of the temporary tribunal will leave a lasting legacy for the ordinary Cambodian courts. As Cambodia is not currently faced with a legal system in total fail-

---

113. Tribunal Law, *supra* n. 6, Chapter IX.

114. The 2003 Agreement further strengthens this wording; see *infra* part 6.

115. Despite resistance from the Secretary-General, the 2003 Agreement remains unchanged; see *infra* part 6.

116. According to one report, estimates of costs for such a tribunal are about US$ 60 million over three years, a relatively low cost operation compared with the *ad hoc* tribunals; see 'Cambodia: Road to Reconciliation? Cambodian and international efforts to address the legacy of the Khmer Rouge', *Oxford Analytica Asia Pacific Daily Brief* (2 October 2001); see also *infra* part 6.4.

ure, compared with other conflict-ridden countries, Article 33 of the Law simply specifies that the Extraordinary Chambers will conduct trials in accordance with existing Cambodian criminal procedure, yet with 'full respect for the rights of the accused and for the protection of victims and witnesses'. This apparent contradiction in terms, given the serious failings in Cambodian judicial practice,[117] is clarified by an additional provision to the effect that, '[i]f necessary, and if there are lacunae in these existing procedures, guidance may be sought in procedural rules established at the international level'.[118] Given the great uncertainty surrounding the exact content of Cambodian criminal procedure due to a multitude of overlapping laws,[119] the Chambers will have plenty of leeway to guarantee due process, especially as the wide terms of Article 33 may be interpreted as including UN soft law principles regarding human rights in the administration of justice as well as the Rules of Procedure and Evidence of other international tribunals.[120]

In reality, the Tribunal Law itself already contains a mixture of Cambodian procedure and international principles. Although the Cambodian government succeeded in imposing its own criminal justice system, especially concerning the investigation, the UN has insisted on incorporating some aspects of the procedural model currently taking shape within the purely international criminal courts. Moreover, Article 35 of the Law incorporates most of the minimum guarantees set out in Article 14(2) and (3) of the International Covenant on Civil and Political Rights (ICCPR).[121] Such interference is only justified, however, to the extent that this new model borrows the best elements from existing systems. Yet, especially as concerns the role of victims, the French-inspired Cambodian system offers more potential than is currently available in the international sphere.

4.3.1   *Difficulties in harmonising criminal procedure*

The concept of a 'Pre-trial Chamber' set up to resolve conflicts between the co-prosecutors and co-investigating judges is similar to the body of the same name within the International Criminal Court, which will supervise the investigation by the Prosecutor in the absence of any investigating judge. In Cambodia, however, the two systems overlap confusingly.

---

117. See e.g., Report of the UN Group of Experts, *supra* n. 3, paras. 123-130.

118. The draft MOU reiterates this provision and adds that the rights of the accused set out in Art. 14 ICCPR shall be repected throughout the trials (Art. 11); the 2003 Agreement expands and reinforces these provisions, see *infra* part 6.3.

119. In particular, two divergent texts adopted during the UN peacekeeping operation still appear to be on the books: Supreme National Council, Provisions Dated September 10, 1992 Relating to the Judiciary and Criminal Law and Procedure Applicable in Cambodia During the Transitional Period; and State of Cambodia, Kram [Law] dated 8 February 1993 on Criminal Procedure, both available at <http://www.bigpond.com.kh>.

120. Linton, loc. cit. n. 108, at p. 199.

121. UN Doc. GA Res. 2200 (1966), reprinted in 999 *UNTS* p. 171.

On another level, as before the *ad hoc* International Tribunals the UN insisted that *in absentia* trials not be allowed under the Tribunal Law, even though this procedure is generally available under the Cambodian Penal Code.[122]

Furthermore, the Cambodian Constitution formally prohibits the death penalty. As a result, the highest sentence provided for in Articles 38 and 39 of the Tribunal Law is life imprisonment. However, the Extraordinary Chambers will have jurisdiction over a certain number of serious domestic crimes, for which the death penalty was possible under the Cambodian penal code in force in 1975. In spite of the fact that the Minister confirmed, during parliamentary debate, that the general provision in Article 38 also applies to these domestic crimes, the Constitutional Council refused to approve the law before clarification of the point. This decision seems legally unfounded, given the general principle of criminal law according to which a later law, which is more favourable to the accused, takes precedence over the preceding provisions.[123] In any case, the Law was reintroduced into Parliament after the addition to Article 3 of the following sentence:

'The penalty under Articles 209, 500, 506 and 507 of the 1956 Penal Code shall be limited to a maximum of life imprisonment, in accordance with Article 32 of the Constitution of the Kingdom of Cambodia, and as further stipulated in Articles 38 and 39 of this Law.'

Accordingly, 'given that a Crime against humanity may carry the same sentence as genocide, deterrence and retribution would seem to be served equally by conviction for either offense'.[124] Clearly, however, conviction for genocide, the 'crime of crimes', carries a higher expressive impact for both the international community[125] and a Cambodian government which has systematically described the Khmer Rouge as a 'genocidal *clique*' for the last 20 years.

Also on the subject of the rights of the accused, the Tribunal Law confirms the right to be assisted by a court-appointed attorney (Arts. 24 and 35). However, the UN noted that the Law does not clearly lay down the accused's right to counsel of his choice,[126] as required by Article 14 ICCPR, nor the right to choose foreign counsel. When the question was raised before the National Assembly, the Minister

---

122. Pol Pot and Ieng Sary were tried in their absence in 1979, as was Prince Ranariddh in 1998 for collusion with the Khmer Rouge, under the 1994 Law Outlawing the movement. Although it is implicit in the general wording of the Tribunal Law that only those '[s]uspects who have been indicted and arrested shall be brought to the trial court ...' (*supra* n. 6, Art. 33), it is worth noting that the minimum guarantees set out in both Art. 35 of the Law and Art. 11 of the draft MOU omit the right 'to be tried in his presence' contained in Art. 14(4) ICCPR; it might thus be argued that the normal Cambodian *in absentia* procedure is not excluded: see State of Cambodia 1993 Law on Criminal Procedure, *supra* n. 119, Art. 111: 'If the accused, who is properly summoned, does not appear in court the judgment shall be proceeded by default.'

123. See e.g., Art. 15(1) ICCPR.

124. Amann, loc. cit. n. 12, at p. 117, speaking in the context of the ICTs.

125. Ibid., pp. 124-131.

126. However, the right to choose counsel does not necessarily imply the right to choose court-appointed counsel.

replied that the accused would have the right to choose any attorney admitted to the bar in Cambodia. Moreover, this right is clearly set out in Cambodian criminal law.[127] Sok An added that nothing prevented duly registered foreign attorneys from assisting such Cambodian counsel.[128]

4.3.2   *The victims*

In the Cambodian legal system, of French inspiration, the victims of a crime can become 'civil parties' to criminal proceedings.[129] Respect for this right in trials against the Khmer Rouge might strengthen the expressive effect of the trials while promoting national reconciliation. At the same time, action by the victims could provide an added guarantee that the facts are not misrepresented for political or ideological reasons. It is in recognition of this deficiency in common law systems that the Statute of the International Criminal Court provides an increased role for victims, although it is not comparable with full civil party rights. The Tribunal Law does not formally provide for intervention by victims, despite the fact that this right is guaranteed for lesser domestic crimes. Unsurprisingly, the Tribunal Law focuses solely on criminal trials. However, given that no reference is made to the question of civil party proceedings, it may be argued that the general reference to 'Cambodian procedure in force' covers civil party intervention, especially since Articles 36 and 37 of the Law confirm the right of victims to appeal against decisions at first instance and on appeal.[130]

Criticism by common law lawyers of such intervention, on the basis that it constitutes 'double jeopardy' forbidden by Article 14 ICCPR, undoubtedly stems from misconceptions concerning the civil party system, which is no more, in reality, than an alternate means of organising civil action in cases where the loss or damage results from a criminal act, thus avoiding the cost and inconvenience of conducting separate trials.

It is to be feared, however, given the extent of the crimes in question, that the Chambers would become bogged down with thousands of individual interventions. One solution would be the collective exercise of this right by victims associations, an approach which Cambodian criminal procedure does not currently recognise. Furthermore, any claim for damages would run afoul of Article 38 of the Law, which organises state confiscation of all ill-gotten property from anyone convicted by the Chambers. Such action may not, however, be the only solution for victims,

---

127. SNC, 1992 Provisions, op. cit. n. 119, Art. 10; and State of Cambodia, 1993 Law on Criminal Procedure, op. cit. n. 119, Arts. 75-78.

128. National Assembly of the Kingdom of Cambodia, debates on 2 January 2001 concerning Art. 24; unofficial English translation provided by the Documentation Center of Cambodia (copy on file with the author): this problem is resolved by express wording in the 2003 Agreement, see *infra* part 6.3.

129. For further reading see D. Boyle, *Ending the Impunity of the Khmer Rouge: A Possible Role for the Victims?* Available at <http://www.ridi.org/boyle/victims.htm.>

130. Indeed, it is difficult to see how those 'victims' having the right to appeal could be designated without some procedure akin to civil party intervention; this would also be in keeping with the ICT rules concerning civil proceedings before 'national courts', see *supra* n. 43, and accompanying text.

since parallel civil action is also possible under Cambodian criminal procedure, and time may not have run out since the Statute of Limitations would appear to be the same as the now extended limit for the underlying crimes.[131] This would be in keeping with the principles relating to victim compensation discussed above.[132]

Although the original proposals for a hybrid tribunal tabled by the parties in 1999 both corresponded to options that had already been considered and rejected by the UN Group of Experts in 1998, the structure finally adopted is a truly *sui generis* internationalised domestic tribunal. The Group of Experts had envisaged the establishment of a tribunal under UN administration and protection. The result was a court under Cambodian administration, albeit with international cooperation backed by significant financial clout.

4.4   Subject matter and personal jurisdiction

4.4.1   *An extensive subject matter jurisdiction*

The subject matter jurisdiction of the Extraordinary Chambers includes a reasonably faithful transposition of the conventional and customary prohibition of a wide range of international crimes, completed by limited jurisdiction over the most serious crimes under Cambodian law.

Beyond its function of establishing the Extraordinary Chambers, the Tribunal Law also effectuates a partial incorporation of 'international humanitarian law and custom, and international conventions recognized by Cambodia', into Cambodian criminal law.[133] Articles 4 to 6 of the Law, respectively, incriminate the three principle international crimes: genocide, crimes against humanity and war crimes. However, Articles 7 and 8 append the less well-known conventional infractions of 'destruction of cultural property during armed conflict',[134] and 'crimes against internationally protected persons'.[135]

Genocide, war crimes, destruction of cultural property and crimes against internationally protected persons are all defined by international conventions, even though the prohibition of some, if not all, of them has now become a customary rule of international law.[136] Although Cambodia had duly ratified all of these conventions before 1975, none of them had been incorporated into national law at that

---

131. See State of Cambodia, 1993 Law on Criminal Procedure, *supra* n. 119, Art. 16: 'The civil action may be filed together with the penal action at the same time and before the same judge. The civil action may also be filed separately. In the latter case, the exercise of the civil action shall be suspended as long as the penal action is not finally decided.'

132. See *supra* section 2.: The aims of international justice.

133. Partial, because this incorporation only applies to the Extraordinary Chambers and is thus limited by their personal and temporal jurisdiction.

134. Pursuant to the 1954 Hague Convention for Protection of Cultural Property in the Event of Armed Conflict, 249 *UNTS* 1954, 216.

135. Pursuant to the 1961 Vienna Convention on Diplomatic Relations, 500 *UNTS* 95.

136. As for genocide, see ICJ, Advisory Opinion on Reservations to the Genocide Convention, *ICJ Rep.* (1951); and ICTR, *Prosecutor* v. *Jean-Paul Akayesu,* Case No. IT-96-4-T, Judgement, 2 September 1998, para. 495.

time. Although such incorporation was thus essential, there were fears that Cambodia would take the opportunity of 'arranging' the definition of genocide so as to bring all of the crimes committed by the Khmer Rouge within this most odious of crimes. It should be noted in this respect that many authors agree that the treatment of national minorities was genocidal, but express doubt whether the crimes committed against the Khmer population in general amounted to more than crimes against humanity, to the extent that they arose out of the desire to eliminate social or political groups, which are not protected by the Genocide Convention.[137] Ratner argues that:

'Adoption of the alternative legal interpretation, though morally appealing, would, as a practical matter, enlarge the deliberately limited scope of the Convention's list of protected groups, insofar as almost any political, social, or economic elements of a population can be viewed as a part of a larger national group.'[138]

All attempts at 'hybrid' justice involve the risk of such political interference in the definition of crimes. Accordingly, the draft MOU insisted on the incrimination of genocide, war crimes and crimes against humanity, 'as defined in international instruments' (Art. 8). In the end, the Tribunal Law expressly linked the incriminations to their conventional definitions.[139] Furthermore, as suggested by the Group of Experts, the choice of the crimes included in the subject matter jurisdiction of the Extraordinary Chambers was dictated by the will to leave the Chambers free to characterise all of the Khmer Rouge crimes under international criminal law without having to denature each crime. This 'conventional' approach has resulted in wider jurisdiction being granted in Cambodia than exists before the *ad hoc* International Criminal Tribunals,[140] the subject matter jurisdiction of which is effec-

---

137. On this point, see e.g., the Report of the UN Group of Experts, *supra* n. 3, paras. 59-79; Boyle, loc. cit. n. 4, at pp. 783-789; S.P. Marks, 'Forgetting the Policies and Practices of the Past: Impunity in Cambodia', 18 *Fletcher Forum of World Affairs* (1994) pp. 17 at 25; W. Schabas and G. Stanton, 'Should Khmer Rouge Leaders be Prosecuted for Genocide or Crimes against Humanity?, debate in 22 and 23 *Searching For the Truth* (Phnom Penh, Documentation Center of Cambodia, October-November 2001); and Y. Jurovics, *Réflexions sur la spécificité du crime contre l'humanité* (Paris, LGDJ 2002) p. 169 fnn. 114-115, and pp. 312-313.

138. S. Ratner and J. Abrams, *Accountability for Human Rights Atrocities in International Law* (Oxford, Oxford University Press 2001) pp. 286-287; for an example of such extension, see e.g., H. Hannum, 'International Law and Cambodian Genocide: The Sounds of Silence', 11 *HRQ* (1998) p. 82.

139. For example, Art. 4 allows prosecution of persons having committed genocide, 'as defined in the Convention on the Prevention and Punishment of the Crime of Genocide of 1948'.

140. The only exception is the exclusion of violations of Art. 3 common to the 1949 Geneva Conventions, relating to non-international armed conflicts; however, this decision was not taken so much on the basis that there was no internal conflict in Cambodia at the time (a question for the judges to decide), but that such violations were not generally seen as being war crimes at the time: see Report of the UN Group of Experts, op. cit. n. 3, para. 75; contra see ICTY, *Prosecutor* v. *Zejnil Delalić et al.* *('Čelebići')*, Case No. IT-96-21-A, Appeal Judgement, 20 February 2001, paras. 163-168. In addition, it may have been difficult to prosecute simple perpetrators under common Art. 3, given that the exclusion of the defence of superior orders had undoubtedly not yet become a rule of customary international law at the time of the crimes: see ICTY, *Prosecutor* v. *Enver Hadzihasanović, Mehmed Alagić*

tively limited to 'rules of International Humanitarian Law which are beyond any doubt part of customary law'.[141]

The customary source of the prohibition of crimes against humanity[142] warrants special attention, as the definition of the crime could not be based on a single authoritative international text. Moreover, this crime was not prohibited by any international convention ratified by Cambodia at the time of the acts.[143] Article 5 of the Law incriminates certain inhuman acts 'committed as part of a widespread or systematic attack directed against any civilian population, on national, political, ethnical, racial or religious grounds'. In so doing, the Law simply reproduces Article 3 of the ICTR Statute. This text, dating from 1994, contains four noteworthy variations compared with the original Nuremberg definition: the absence of any link to an armed conflict; replaced by the formal requirement for a 'widespread or systematic attack'; the inclusion of supplementary inhuman acts (not only assassination, extermination, slavery, deportation and discriminatory persecutions, but also imprisonment, torture and rape); and the requirement (contrary to the ICTY and ICC Statutes) for a discriminatory intention, on 'national, political, ethnical, racial or religious grounds', in all cases.[144] The last point is important, as it might be difficult to fit all aspects of the Khmer Rouge treatment of the 'Khmer' group into the categories of national, political, ethnical, racial or religious discrimination.[145] This difficulty is resolved in the 2003 Agreement, which prefers the definition of crimes against humanity adopted in the ICC Statute.[146]

Finally, Article 29 of the Law globally respects contemporary rules of international criminal law concerning planning, instigation, ordering, attempt and other forms of indirect responsibility for these crimes.[147] The main exception is the apparent omission of 'direct and public incitement to commit genocide' from Article

---

and Amir Kubura ('Central Bosnia'), Case No. UN Doc. IT-01-47-PT, Response of Mehmed Alagić on the Challenge to Jurisdiction, 24 May 2002.

141. See the Secretary General's Report to the Security Council on establishment of the ICTY (UN Doc. S/25704, 3 May 1993), para. 34.

142. On the customary source of the incrimination, see IMT for Nuremberg, *United States* v. *Goering,* 1 October 1946, 13 *Annual Digest*, p. 203.

143. Cambodia never signed the 1968 Convention on the Non-Applicability of Statutory Limitations to War Crimes and Crimes Against Humanity; and only ratified the Rome Statue establishing the ICC, on 11 April 2002, after the passage of the Khmer Rouge Tribunal Law.

144. On the evolution of the definition of crimes against humanity, see D. Boyle, 'Génocide et crimes contre l'humanité - convergences et divergences', in E. Fronza and S. Manacorda, eds., *La justice pénale internationale dans les décisions des Tribunaux ad hoc. Etudes des Law Clinics en droit pénal international de Paris et Naples* (Milan, Giuffré 2003) pp. 124-140. These variations raise problems of retrospective criminal legislation which are considered *infra* part 4.4.4.

145. Khmer Rouge crimes against the clergy have been argued not to have involved religious discrimination because the members of all religions throughout the population were mistreated 'indiscriminately'; see Y. Jurovics, *Réflexions sur la spécificité du crime contre l'humanité* (Paris, LGDJ 2002) pp. 169-170. However, the treatment of religions could be seen as political discrimination or, extrapolating from recent *obiter dicta* of the ICTY, it might also be viewed as 'negative' religious discrimination against all those who did not share the atheist beliefs of the Khmer Rouge: ICTY, *Prosecutor* v. *Goran Jelisić*, Case No. IT-95-10-T Judgement, 14 December 1999, para. 71.

146. See *infra* part 6.

147. For details of ICT case law on this point, see J. Jones, *The Practice of the International Crim-*

4, which would thus have to be prosecuted as a form of complicity or 'instigation'. Command responsibility for the acts of subordinates is also provided for in terms akin to those in the ICC Statute. In return, the defence of superior orders is excluded.

It remains to be seen, however, whether these general rules are compatible with the rules applicable to the crimes drawn from the 1956 Penal Code.[148] In particular, following the orders of superiors holding 'legitimate authority' was a defence under Articles 99-100 of the 1956 Penal Code. Accordingly, applying the general rules in the Tribunal Law to the common crimes set out in Article 3 would seem to be contrary to the principle of legality. It may be, thus, that different standards will have to be applied to international and common crimes, a problem that will arise whenever mixed tribunals are granted jurisdiction over domestic infractions.[149] Moreover, as one author points out, in those cases where no specific provision is made concerning other defences, the logical conclusion is that the provisions of the 1956 Penal Code will also apply to international crimes, even if the defences available under international law at the time were more favourable.[150] Alternatively, the Extraordinary Chambers might deal with this apparent weakness in the Tribunal Law and 2003 Agreement[151] by following the case law of the ICTs, which have dealt with the absence of express enumeration of defences in their respective Statutes by reading in customary law rules and the 'general principles of international criminal law'.[152]

In reality, the quasi-totality of the inhuman acts perpetrated by the Khmer Rouge can also be seen as crimes under the 1956 Cambodian Penal Code in force when the Khmer Rouge took power. Article 3 of the Tribunal Law only allows prosecution for the most serious such crimes: murder, assassination, torture and religious persecution. However, in addition, the Penal Code incriminated certain acts of great relevance in this case: attacks on the King, his family and the free exercise of civil rights; profanation of religious sites; and inciting hatred between groups. It also prohibited arbitrary orders from government officials.[153]

---

inal Tribunals for the former Yugoslavia and Rwanda, 3rd edn. (Ardsley NY, Transnational Publishers 2003).

148. Royaume du Cambodge, 'Code pénal et Lois pénales', 7-8 *Recueil judiciaire* (1956) Arts. 89-104: insanity, youth, *force majeure*, superior orders and self-defence.

149. Major examples are the inclusion of the Indonesian crime of rape in the jurisdiction of the East Timor Serious Crimes Panel and the crime of sexual abuse of female minors in the jurisdiction of the Special Court for Sierra Leone, both of which are defined more restrictively than rape as a crime against humanity in international criminal law: see Linton, op. cit. n. 108, at pp. 211, 241.

150. Linton, ibid., at p. 197; however, given that most of the provisions of Cambodian law in this area provide for complete defences (the exception being obeying an *illegal* order, which is only a mitigating circumstance [1956 Code pénale, op. cit. n. 148]), it is unlikely that international law is more favourable.

151. See Amnesty International, *Kingdom of Cambodia: Amnesty International's position and concerns regarding the proposed 'Khmer Rouge' tribunal* (Report, AI Index ASA 23/005/2003) April 2002, available at <http://www.amnesty.org/>.

152. On this question, see Jones, op. cit. n. 147, at Part 6, Section 3: Defences.

153. 1956 Code pénale, *supra* n. 148, especially Arts. 203, 209, 211, 240 and 300 § d).

It must be said that it seems perfectly normal, in principle, for a domestic court such as the Extraordinary Chambers to try the Khmer Rouge for common crimes, even if the same acts may also be characterised as international crimes. In particular, it might seem appropriate in order to ensure the conviction of the physical perpetrators of the crimes, in the absence of evidence that they had the specific intent to commit crimes against humanity or genocide. However, such an approach, if applied to those who planned and implemented the criminal policy, would underestimate the full impact of their crimes. The point is particularly pertinent in the case of Cambodia, given the extremely limited personal jurisdiction of the Chambers, as few if any 'simple' perpetrators are likely to be prosecuted.

Consequently, the inclusion of common crimes may be seen as a fallback position aimed at ensuring convictions should the charges of international crimes be rejected. That being so, their inclusion also seeks to satisfy a desire to found the trials on solid grounds provided by incriminations already included in Cambodian law at the time the crimes were committed. However, in addition to doubts concerning the applicability of the 1956 Penal Code during the Democratic Kampuchea regime,[154] this search for legal legitimacy is weakened by a provision prolonging the statute of limitations for these common crimes.[155]

4.4.2   *An extremely limited personal jurisdiction*

Although there was global agreement on the need to limit prosecutions, the exact boundaries of the Chambers' personal jurisdiction was one of the most persistent sources of disagreement between Cambodia and the United Nations.

It was clear from the outset that the jurisdiction of the Khmer Rouge tribunal was going to be limited, well before the exact nature of the international participation had been determined. In the letter that set the whole process in motion in June 1997, the co-Prime Ministers requested 'the assistance of the United Nations and the international community in bringing to justice those persons responsible for the genocide and crimes against humanity during the rule of the Khmer Rouge from 1975 to 1979'.

In order to reach final agreement on the draft MOU, in July 2000 the UN accepted that the jurisdiction of the Extraordinary Chambers should cover only 'senior leaders of Democratic Kampuchea and those who were most responsible' for the crimes coming within its jurisdiction.[156] This form of words originated in the Report of the UN Group of Experts, which suggested the prosecution of persons who were '(...) most responsible for the most serious violations of human rights during the reign of Democratic Kampuchea (...)'. The Group of Experts admitted that inevitably these terms would not cover 'all persons at the senior levels of government of Democratic Kampuchea or even of the Communist Party of Kampuchea', but only the 'senior leaders with responsibility over the abuses as well as

---

154. It is open to argument that the Khmer Rouge operated a *tabula rasa* of all pre-existing 'reactionary' laws.

155. See *infra* part 4.4.4.

156. Arts. 1 and 2 of the Tribunal Law, *supra* n. 6.

those at lower levels who are directly implicated in the most serious atrocities'.[157] Sok An indicated during parliamentary debate that the aim of the added restriction was to limit prosecutions to a *very* small number of persons, so as to avoid alarming the thousands of former Khmers Rouge *cadre* who had joined forces with the Royal Government. Although arguably contrary to the general principles of criminal law, this sort of limitation is characteristic of the search for accountability in states where atrocities were committed in the past, regardless of whether the court is domestic or international.[158]

Thus, Article 2 of the Tribunal Law grants authority to

'bring to trial senior leaders of Democratic Kampuchea and those who were most responsible for the crimes and serious violations of Cambodian laws related to crimes, international humanitarian law and custom, and international conventions recognized by Cambodia, that were committed during the period from 17 April 1975 to 6 January 1979'.

Given the turbulent history of Cambodia since independence, a wider jurisdiction would have opened the way to prosecutions going well beyond the framework of Khmer Rouge crimes. However, neither the superpowers nor the countries of the region involved in the three Cambodian conflicts, nor even the current Cambodian government, had any interest in having their conduct before, during or after the Khmer Rouge period exposed to judicial scrutiny.

A further limitation is that only Cambodian leaders may be prosecuted, despite the possibility that Vietnamese forces may also have been responsible for war crimes during the period in question. This potential for discriminatory treatment led the UN Group of Experts to suggest excluding war crimes (a relatively minor aspect of Khmer Rouge crimes that is partly covered by the other international infractions) from the jurisdiction of the tribunal.[159] However, this advice was not followed.

The question also arose whether it was appropriate to formally include such a limitation in the law itself. Citing the examples of the *ad hoc* Tribunals for the Former Yugoslavia and Rwanda, the Group of Experts proposed that the Extraordinary Chambers be endowed with a wide personal jurisdiction covering 'any persons whose acts fall within its subject matter jurisdiction'. It would then be for the Prosecutor to decide which persons to indict, 'tak[ing] into account the twin goals of individual accountability and national reconciliation'.[160] In the end, the UN was forced to give in on this relatively theoretical point in July 2000, because Hun Sen made it a condition for his acceptance of guarantees concerning the independence of the international prosecutor and investigating judge. The recent practice of the

---

157. Report of the UN Group of Experts, *supra* n. 3, paras. 109-110.
158. 'Du droit international au droit national : l'exemple du génocide', in M. Delmas-Marty ed., *Les processus d'internationalisation,* Coll. Vers des principes directeurs internationaux de droit pénal, Vol. VII, (Paris, Editions de la Maison des Sciences de l'Homme 2001) pp. 171 at 216-218.
159. Report of the UN Group of Experts, *supra* n. 3, para. 151.
160. Ibid., paras. 110-111, 154 and 219(2).

ICTs relating to such questions[161] is clearly not transposable to the Extraordinary Chambers, because those cases not tried by the ICTs may still be heard by or transferred to the domestic courts of the countries concerned. In the Cambodian context, however, failure to try a person before the Extraordinary Chambers will automatically result in impunity, whether it be express, through time-barring of common crimes, or implied, as regards international crimes.[162]

Currently, the only persons to have been arrested are Ung Choeun, known as Ta Mok (the sole senior military commander who refused to surrender), and Kaing Khek Iev, known as 'Duch' (the former director of the Tuol Sleng interrogation facility in Phnom Penh). In order to avoid the obligation to release Ta Mok after expiration of the statutory period of pre-trial detention,[163] he has been successively charged with 'crimes against domestic security with the intention of serving the policies of the Democratic Kampuchea Group',[164] 'genocide' under Decree Law No. 1, 15 July 1979,[165] and finally 'crimes against humanity, in February 2002.[166] Other principle suspects, still living, include Nuon Chea, Ieng Sary and Khieu Samphan.[167]

4.4.3   *The effect of prior judicial decisions and immunities from jurisdiction*

Beyond these definitional problems, it was also necessary to take account of the possible effect of prior legal acts by the Cambodian authorities on the prosecution of certain persons who would otherwise come within the personal jurisdiction of the Extraordinary Chambers. Given that the trials will be held under Cambodian law, the problem of jurisdictional immunities, especially those of the Head of State of Democratic Kampuchea (successively, Norodom Sihanouk and Khieu Samphan), will undoubtedly be raised by the Defence. In addition, it is important to analyse the effects of both previous convictions by the Cambodian courts, by virtue of the principle *non bis in idem* (double jeopardy), and any royal pardons or amnesties granted to such persons.

The main *non bis in idem* problem derives from suggestions by Hun Sen that Ieng Sary (former Khmer Rouge number 2 and still a powerful player) should not be tried for genocide, as the Popular Republic of Kampuchea had already con-

---

161. See *supra* part 3.2.

162. This problem is limited somewhat by the fact that many subordinate members of the Khmer Rouge would be able to plead defences based on age, duress or mental health.

163. Six months for common crimes [SNC Provisions, *supra* n. 119, Art. 14(4)], extended to three years for international crimes by a law adopted *in extremis* on 11 August 1999.

164. Kingdom of Cambodia, Military Court, Phnom Penh, Order to Forward Case for Investigation, No. 019//99, 9 March 1999, based on the Law to Outlaw the Democratic Kampuchea Group, Law No. 064, 7 July 1994.

165. Kingdom of Cambodia, Military Court, Phnom Penh, Order to Forward Case for Investigation, No. 044/99, 6 September 1999; Duch was also charged with genocide in the same indictment.

166. 'Cambodia's Khmer Rouge "butcher" charged', CNN, 22 February 2002.

167. See S. Heder and B. Tittemore, 'Seven Candidates for Prosecution: Accountability for the Crimes of the Khmer Rouge', War Crimes Research Office, Washington College of Law, American University and Coalition for International Justice, June 2001, 129 pp.; available at <http://www.wcl.american.edu/pub/humright/wcrimes/khmerrouge.html>.

victed the 'Pol Pot-Ieng Sary clique' of this crime in 1979. In reality, this affirmation oversimplifies a complex legal problem. Firstly, the Tribunal Law makes no
specific reference to respect for the principle itself and domestic law is unclear on
the question. Although the principle is proclaimed by Article 14(7) ICCPR, Cambodia does not recognise the direct application of human rights treaties without
implementing legislation.[168] Secondly, even though the 1979 trial was considered
to be inconsistent with international principles of due process, the conviction may
still be considered binding within Cambodia's internal legal order. The point is not
conclusive, however, as this conviction followed a trial *in absentia*, and it may be
that Cambodian criminal law, based on the French system, allows for a new hearing after the arrest of the suspect, so as to respect his fundamental rights.[169]
Thirdly, the definition of the crime of 'genocide' in the 1979 Decree Law, concocted *ex post facto* to cover all of the Khmer Rouge Crimes,[170] varied so significantly from that of the 1948 Convention that it may be seen as a simple
incrimination under Cambodian law.[171] In fact, international law permits the prosecution of a person for international crime even though he or she has already been
convicted of a common crime based on the same acts.[172] In any case, the appropriate forum for deciding such complex legal problems is the competent court, not the
Cambodian Prime Minister.

Well aware of the historical links between the current government of Cambodia
and the Khmer Rouge,[173] the UN has repeatedly insisted on the clear exclusion of
any amnesty (before trial) or pardon (after conviction). Despite this, the Tribunal
Law only prohibits requests by the Royal Government of Cambodia for the amnesty or pardon of any persons who may be investigated for or convicted of crimes
coming within the jurisdiction of the Extraordinary Chambers (Art. 40). This incomplete provision was argued by Hun Sen to be the maximum possible without
revising the Constitution, which gives the King the unfettered right to grant pardons (Constitution, Art. 27) and provides for the adoption of amnesty laws by the
National Assembly (Constitution, Art. 90). As a result, no provision is made in the
Tribunal Law for persons having already received such a favour, such as Ieng Sary,

---

168. See *infra* part 5.1.

169. State of Cambodia, 1993 Law on Criminal Procedure, *supra* n. 119, Art. 115: '... if the notification [of conviction] is not made in person or if there is no writ of judgement enforcement to be
known to the accused, the decision may be opposed till the terms of limitation for punishment expires'.

170. The definition of genocide in PRK Decree-Law Nr. 1 may be consulted in UN Doc. A/C.3/34/
1, 30 July 1979; for further reading concerning the *ex-post facto* definition of genocide in the 1979
Decree-Law establishing a 'Revolutionary People's Tribunal' to try Pol Pot and Ieng Sary, see J.
Quigley, *Genocide in Cambodia: Documents from the Trial of Pol Pot and Ieng Sary* (Philadelphia,
University of Pennsylvania Press 2000); S. Heder, 'Pol Pot's First Trial: August 1979', paper presented at the *Legacies of Authoritarianism: Cultural Production, Collective Trauma, and Global Justice* Conference (University of Wisconsin, 3 April 1998); and Boyle, loc. cit. n. 4, at p. 803.

171. For an example of this reasoning concerning Australian War Crimes legislation, see High
Court of Australia, *Polyukhovic* v. *The Commonwealth*, (1991) 65 CLR 521, per Brennan J., p. 545,
available at <http://www.austlii.edu.au/au/cases/cth/high_ct/172clr501.html>.

172. See Art. 10(2) of the ICTY Statute, *supra* n. 43; and Art. 20 of the ICC Statute, *supra* n. 22.

173. Hun Sen is himself a former Khmer Rouge cadre.

who received a royal pardon granted by King Sihanouk when he surrendered in August 1996, with the formal approval of the Royal Government and Parliament. At the time, King Sihanouk made it known that this pardon was of purely internal application.

Furthermore, under a 1994 law outlawing Democratic Kampuchea, any Khmer Rouge soldier who surrendered within the ensuing six-month period could not be prosecuted for his crimes.[174] However, this law should have no effect on prosecutions before the Extraordinary Chambers, because Article 6 excludes Khmer Rouge leaders from the amnesty provisions.[175]

Finally, it should be noted that, even if a particular guarantee is not incorporated expressly in the Tribunal Law, the fact that the Constitutional Council has validated the law implies that it may be interpreted in such a way as to ensure compliance with constitutionally protected human rights standards. However, as mentioned above, it is not clear whether judicial review of a Chamber decision to allow prosecution of someone having already been amnestied is feasible.[176]

Be that as it may, in January 2001, the UN voiced its reservations concerning Article 40 of the Tribunal Law, pointing out that under Article 9 of the draft MOU, 'An amnesty granted to any person falling within the jurisdiction of the chambers shall not be a bar to prosecution.' The UN has even made respect for this principle a precondition for its participation, and further negotiations led to the inclusion of an amended provision in the 2003 Agreement.[177]

4.4.4   *Temporal and territorial jurisdiction*

At various stages in the negotiations, especially in January 1999, Hun Sen called for the widening of the trials to cover the period from 1970 to the present. This potentially opened the US to investigation for war crimes in relation to the B52 carpet bombings of Cambodia up until 1973, as well as Vietnam for crimes committed during the occupation of Cambodia from 1979 to 1989. It even raised the spectre of investigating the role of Western Nations and the UN itself in support for the Khmer Rouge against Vietnam.[178] Basically a negotiating ploy, this proposal was not retained and the temporal jurisdiction was limited to the exact period, down to the day, of Democratic Kampuchea, the Khmer Rouge regime: 17 April 1975 to 7 January 1979. This precision suggests that it is the regime that is being indirectly condemned through these criminal proceedings, as it excludes similar crimes committed by the Khmer Rouge before and after taking power.

---

174. Kingdom of Cambodia, Law to Outlaw the Democratic Kampuchea Group, Law No. 064, 7 July 1994, Art. 5.

175. A former Khmer Rouge General, Chhouk Rin, whose role in the death of three western backpackers was initially considered to have been covered by the amnesty provisions (see D. Boyle, 'Correspondents' Report – Cambodia', 3 *YIHL* (2000) pp. 437 at 439), was recently found guilty at a second trial, on this basis: 'Cambodia re-tries guerrilla commander', *BBC News*, 28 August 2002.

176. See *supra* part 4.1.

177. See *infra* part 6.

178. RGC, *Aide mémoire, supra* n. 67.

Apart from the obvious problem of retrospective criminal legislation raised by the Tribunal Law, there is also a problem of the statutory limitation on prosecuting certain common crimes. Given that the Khmer Rouge movement also committed crimes in neighbouring countries, the limited territorial jurisdiction of the Chambers also raises questions.

The principle, *nullum crimen sine lege*, as recognised in Cambodian law, prohibits all retrospective penal legislation. While it is true that the Khmer Rouge crimes were perpetrated after Cambodian ratification of the international conventions underlying the jurisdiction of the Extraordinary Chambers, all of the measures incorporating these international obligations into domestic law were adopted afterwards, including *a fortiori* the Tribunal Law adopted in 2001. There is some disagreement among jurists on the options open to Cambodia to satisfy its conventional obligation to prevent and punish Khmer Rouge crimes without infringing the *nullum crimen* principle.[179] However, the Cambodian government and the United Nations clearly consider that, as provided by Article 15 ICCPR,[180] it is licit to prosecute the Khmer Rouge for crimes that were prohibited by international law at the time they were committed, by virtue of later procedural legislation determining which tribunal has jurisdiction to try them. Accordingly, the Tribunal Law does not include crimes that have only been conventionally prohibited in international criminal law since 1979, such as torture and violations of the Additional Protocols to the Geneva Conventions.[181]

Crimes against humanity raise a particular problem in this respect. Although their inclusion is justified by the existence of a customary international prohibition of the crime before 1975, the exact contours of the infraction at the time of the facts are more difficult to define. Of the four variations in the Tribunal Law as compared with the Nuremberg Charter listed above, the absence of any link with a conflict and the inclusion of the material acts of imprisonment, torture and rape do not create any major problems as these variations have been incorporated into the customary definition since World War II.[182] However, the formal requirement of a widespread or systematic attack is the fruit of a more recent evolution in international criminal law, evidenced by the *ad hoc* International Tribunals and the ICC. Furthermore, the requirement for a discriminatory intention in all cases is specific to the ICTR Statute and is generally viewed as being more restrictive than the customary law concept. Although more restrictive retrospective legislation, thus

---

179. On the one hand, it is argued that the prosecution should only cover crimes that were defined by Cambodian national law before the acts were committed; on the other hand, it is argued that the courts can also prosecute crimes which were contrary to international law when committed, either by direct operation of international law or by subsequent legislative introduction into domestic law: see Boyle, loc. cit. n. 4, pp. 773-826.

180. *Supra* n. 121.: '1. No one shall be held guilty of any criminal offence on account of any act or omission which did not constitute a criminal offence, *under national or international law*, at the time when it was committed ...' [emphasis added].

181. Although torture was prohibited by the ICCPR prior to the torture convention, that treaty does not create international criminal offences; moreover, the negotiators clearly did not consider the argument that torture was prohibited under customary international law by 1975.

182. See in particular, Allied forces Control Council Law No. 10 for Germany, 20 December 1945.

more favourable to the accused, is not contrary to the principle of legality, these differences show that the case law of the ICTs must be handled with care when applied to the Cambodian situation. The same will apply to the replacement definition adopted in the 2003 Agreement, drawn directly from the ICC Statute.[183]

Apart from these minor question marks, the Tribunal Law seems to satisfy the criteria of valid penal legislation because it also provides for specific penalties. Prison terms range from five years to life and the confiscation of ill-gotten property is also allowed (chapter XI of the Law).

As requested by the UN, the Tribunal Law expressly excludes any statute of limitations for genocide and crimes against humanity. Despite the unfortunate absence of a similar provision for the other international crimes, including war crimes, it may be that the absence of any statute of limitations will be deduced *a contrario*, because the Tribunal Law only overrules existing statute of limitations provisions for common crimes under Cambodian law. Indeed, Article 3 of the Law prolongs by 20 years the limitation on prosecutions for the crimes set out in that Article. Added to the ten-year period already provided for in the 1956 Penal Code, these crimes will be time-barred between the years 2005 and 2009.

During parliamentary debate, Minister Sok An assured the MPs that such an extension, being of a purely procedural nature, does not violate the principle of non-retrospectivity. While this may be so for the extension of the limitation period for crimes which are not yet time-barred, one may wonder whether the specific facts of this case do not involve a violation of a fully acquired right not to be prosecuted, given that the initial period for prosecution had already expired more than ten years before the adoption of the Law. The UN Group of Experts, dominated by lawyers from common law systems where such limitations do not usually apply to crimes, considered that this was not a major problem.[184] However, the problem could have been avoided through a more subtle approach akin to those used in other civil law countries, for example, by suspending the commencement of the limitation period due to the absence of any effective legal system until at least the end of the UNTAC presence in 1993. Indeed, the UN Sub-Commission's report on the right to reparation for victims of gross violations of human rights specifies that

'Statutes of limitations shall not apply in respect of periods during which no effective remedies exist for violations of human rights and humanitarian law. Civil claims relating to reparations for gross violations of human rights and humanitarian law shall not be subject to statutes of limitations'.[185]

---

183. See *infra* part 6.3.

184. Report of the UN Group of Experts, *supra* n. 3, para. 90; however, the examples cited only concerned cases where the limitation was extended or declared not subject to a statute of limitations *before* becoming time-barred, and also only concerned international crimes and not common crimes.

185. *Supra* n. 45, para. 9.

However, Cambodia has not complied with these recommendations. This is but one example of the limits inherent in a hybrid system based as much on political considerations as legal principle.

In order to oppose the establishment of an international court, the Cambodian government insisted on its pre-emptive right to try the Khmer Rouge in the country where the crimes were committed, as provided by the Genocide Convention and the ICC Statute. However, some of these crimes were committed outside of Cambodian territory, especially the attacks on the population of Kampuchea *krom*, a Vietnamese-administered province claimed by the Khmer Rouge for historical reasons.

Although the Tribunal Law does not formally limit the Extraordinary Chambers' jurisdiction to the territory of Cambodia, it is open to argument whether active personal jurisdiction for acts committed abroad by state nationals is recognised in Cambodian law. The extensive territorial jurisdiction granted to the ICTR is an interesting, but not directly applicable, precedent for a wider approach. In addition, while the Law lists the obligations of Cambodian police and military authorities to find and arrest indicted suspects (Art. 31), no mention is made of judicial cooperation for the arrest of suspects that have left Cambodia. In such an eventuality, it will be necessary to rely on traditional extradition rules.[186]

While the jurisdiction granted to the Extraordinary Chambers in the Tribunal Law is globally in keeping with the principles of international criminal law, it does not fully satisfy Cambodia's international obligations. The Law clearly circumscribes not only the jurisdiction of the Chambers but also the extent of incorporation of international infractions into Cambodian domestic law. Of course, nothing prevents Cambodia from later extending this jurisdiction so as to prosecute lower level perpetrators of Khmer Rouge crimes in the future if the political will exists (or even crimes committed in other contexts), now that the legality of such prosecution has been established. The Royal Government is envisaging the inclusion of international crimes in the new penal code currently being drafted, but this could also be achieved through implementing legislation for the ICC Statute, at least as concerns future crimes.

In the meantime, one way of addressing many of the concerns raised by this hybrid system would be for the Extraordinary Chambers to adopt a set of Rules of Procedure and Evidence specific to the Chambers. The rules would be based on Cambodian procedure, but also incorporate the procedural aspects of the Tribunal Law and 2003 Agreement in a single document. The Rules could also contain provisions taken from the ICC Rules and other international documents, as required, in order to ensure fair trials. This would have the major advantage of providing the defence with greater procedural certainty and would avoid much time wasting recourse to the Pre-Trial Chamber to deal with problems as they arise.[187]

---

186. It should be remembered that *in absentia* proceedings seem to be excluded and that the Extraordinary Chambers were not established by the Security Council under Chapter VII of the Charter.

187. Even in East Timor, where the Courts were under direct UN Administration, UNTAET was eventually forced to adopt a transitional Criminal Procedure Code (UNTAET Reg. 2000/30, 25 September 2000), in order to clarify the interplay between existing legislation and UN Rules concerning

5.   THE LEGAL STATUS OF UN PARTICIPATION AND THE UN
       PULL-OUT

It was previously assumed that the draft MOU would be signed by the United
Nations and Cambodia once a law complying with its terms had been adopted.[188]
However, the reservations communicated to the government by the UN were not
incorporated into the final text of the Tribunal Law promulgated on 10 August
2001, thus putting its compliance in serious doubt.

UN Legal Counsel, Hans Corell, received official English and French translations of the Tribunal Law on 31 August 2001. At first, conciliatory comments were
made to the effect that the difficulties were not insurmountable, but that further
discussions would be necessary in order to bring the Tribunal Law into line with
the draft MOU.[189] The September terrorist attacks on the United States and air
strikes against Afghanistan reduced interest in the tribunal[190] and the parties began
blaming each other for failing to advance towards closure.[191]

Corell provided his comments on the Tribunal Law on 10 October, raising a
number of points and attaching a revised draft of the MOU. On 23 November, he
received a letter from Sok An indicating that a detailed response would follow.
However, the letter threw a new spanner into the works, categorically refusing any
modification of the Tribunal Law and reducing the MOU to the status of 'Articles
of Cooperation', determining 'the modalities of cooperation between the Royal
Government of Cambodia and the United Nations in implementing those provisions of the Law concerning foreign technical and financial support'.[192] On 22
January, Sok An finally replied to Hans Corell concerning all the points raised in
the latter's 10 October letter, but his answers clearly did not satisfy the UN.

On 8 February 2002, Kofi Annan took advantage of this new confrontation concerning the binding nature of its agreement with Cambodia to pull the UN out of
the process, indicating that the structure, as envisaged, did not allow the Organisation to guarantee respect for international standards of justice. The Secretary-General noted that the Royal Government wanted to reduce the Articles of Cooperation
'to the status of a technical and administrative document subordinate to the
Law'.[193] Sok An retaliated that this was not the case, proposing a conception of

---

the 'Serious Crimes Panels'; on this point, see S. Linton, 'Rising From the Ashes: The Creation of a
Viable Criminal Justice System in East Timor', 25 *Melbourne Univ. LR* (2001) p. 122 at 136.

    188. Draft MOU, *supra* n. 5, Art. 28.

    189. 'Cambodia: Invitation Sent U.N. For Negotiation On Khmer Rouge Trials', *United Nations
Foundation*, UNWire, 10 October 2001.

    190. M. Warren, 'Tribunals for Khmer Rouge "lost in the post" as rest of the world loses interest',
The Scotsman (26 October 2001).

    191. See e.g., F. Eckhard, Spokesman for the UN Secretary-General, 'UN Awaiting Comments by
Cambodia on Tribunal', New York, Excerpt from the noon briefing, 11 January 2002.

    192. Sok An, Letter to Hans Correll, 23 November 2001, available at <http://www.ocm.gov>:
'While the Articles of Cooperation may clarify certain nuances in the Law, and elaborate certain details, it is not possible for them to modify, let alone prevail over, a law that has just been promulgated.'

    193. F. Eckhard, Spokesman for the Secretary-General, Daily Press Briefing by the Office of the
Spokesman for the Secretary-General, 8 February 2002.

the MOU and the Law as being complementary documents of equal value, neither being superior to the other.[194]

This new element of disagreement concerned the exact legal status and corresponding effect of the MOU, once signed. Some rather tenuous legal reasoning on both sides has complicated this question. It is thus worth recalling a certain number of basic relevant principles. However, the argument concerning status also raises related questions regarding the nature of the UN action envisaged by the parties: participation, control, administration, supervision, verification or technical cooperation?

5.1   The exact legal status of the MOU

Although the draft MOU clearly states that the agreement will only *enter into force* after both parties have complied with the underlying legal requirements,[195] it leaves open the question whether formal *signature* was to come before or after adoption of the Tribunal Law.[196] The UN would have preferred that the Memorandum be signed before the legislation was passed, just as for any international agreement.[197] However, Hun Sen refused, insisting erroneously on full respect for the separation of democratic powers through the parliamentary process.[198] Accordingly, the draft MOU was never signed and never came into force. This puts paid to the UN claim that Cambodia's insistence on primacy of the Law over the MOU is in violation of the basic principle of international law, *pacta sunt servanda*, because Cambodia has not contracted any international obligations under the MOU. It has now been replaced by the largely identical 2003 Agreement.

The UN often refers to the fact that Cambodia requested its assistance in support of its criticism of the government's rejection of UN proposals. Yet it fails to mention that, by the time the Group of Experts arrived in Cambodia, the political situation had changed significantly and the new Prime Minister, Hun Sen, told them that he preferred an internal solution. It follows that the initial recommendations of the UN Group were not directly based on a Cambodian request for an *ad hoc* international tribunal, but on an independent determination that this was the most appropriate response to the situation in Cambodia, in accordance with the mandate granted by the UN General Assembly.

---

194. Sok An, Senior Minister in Charge of the Office of the Council of Ministers, Statement from the Royal Government of Cambodia in Response to the Announcement of UN Pullout from Negotiations on Khmer Rouge Trial, 12 February 2002, available at <http://www.ocm.gov>.

195. Draft MOU, *supra* n. 5, Art. 28. On the Cambodian side, the 'legal requirements' in question would include final promulgation of the Tribunal Law and, probably ratification of the MOU itself.

196. Art. 1 of the Draft MOU, ibid., contains two alternative formulations: '... the Law on the Establishment of Extraordinary Chambers, which has been adopted by the Cambodian Legislature under the Constitution of Cambodia / is subject to parliamentary approval, shall determine the jurisdiction of the court ...'.

197. H. Corell, Press Briefing by United Nations Legal Counsel, United Nations, 8 February 2000.

198. Parliamentary scrutiny of international agreements signed by the Executive is already assured, through the approval and ratification procedure set out in Arts. 26 and 99 of the 1993 Constitution (as amended), *supra* n. 56.

The response by the UN Secretariat to the Cambodian request for assistance does not fall squarely within its general grant of authority to provide technical assistance to Member States in judicial matters. The authority came from a specific grant by the UN General Assembly in December 1997.[199] It does not necessarily follow, however, that this change in nature of the UN participation changes its legal status. The parallels with technical assistance are evident, especially since no further intervention by the principle organs of the UN was required in order to validate the MOU.[200] The structure adopted does not involve the creation of a *sui generis* international court as in the case of Sierra Leone, clearly requiring a binding international agreement. The status of the agreement thus remained open for determination by mutual agreement between the parties.

In any event, the 'legislation first' approach places the establishment of the Extraordinary Chambers squarely within the authority of Cambodian national law,[201] as opposed to the 'Special Court' for Sierra Leone, which was 'established by an Agreement between the United Nations and the government of Sierra Leone and is therefore a treaty-based *sui generis* court of mixed jurisdiction and composition'.[202]

Nevertheless, in the absence of clear provisions in the MOU itself, hierarchical problems were bound to arise involving not only international rules but also Cambodian constitutional principles. Despite the Cambodian government's claim that there was no problem of hierarchy because the Law was 'parallel and complementary' to the MOU, which only covered the international aspects of the trials,[203] it seems quite clear from the terms of the draft MOU itself that there would be some overlap. Clarifying this point was the *raison d'être* for the renewed negotiations leading to adoption of the 2003 Agreement.

While the MOU was being finalised in July 2000, the UN was also setting up the Serious Crimes Panel for East Timor. In early 2002, the Organization also signed a treaty with Sierra Leone on the creation of the Special Court to try international crimes. In both cases, the administration of the courts remains firmly under UN control (either because the territory is under UN Administration, or under a binding treaty obligation), and the international judges and prosecutors named by the Secretary-General are in the majority. Although UN Legal Counsel made no

---

199. See *supra* n. 54.

200. It is to be noted that the General Assembly simply 'Welcome[d] the successful conclusion of the talks between the Government of Cambodia and the United Nations Secretariat on the question of the trial of the Khmer Rouge leaders ... and welcome[d] the efforts of the Secretariat and the international community in assisting the Government to this end': UN Doc. A/RES/55/95, 28 February 2001, para 18.

201. The Royal Government's systematic refusal to share UN drafts and comments with the legislator also demonstrates Hun Sen's desire to demonstrate the purely internal nature of the process leading to the establishment of the Extraordinary Chambers. The preamble to the Law does not mention any outside involvement.

202. Report of the Secretary-General on the Establishment of a Special Court for Sierra Leone, UN Doc. S/2000/915, 4 October 2000, para. 9, available at <http://www.specialcourt.org/documents/>.

203. Royal Government of Cambodia Task Force on the Khmer Rouge Trial, Statement on the Khmer Rouge Trial, 15 March 2002, available at <http://www.ocm.gov>.

reference to these achievements when announcing the Cambodia pullout, the Extraordinary Chambers system clearly suffers in comparison.

5.2   The nature of the UN participation

Regardless of its legal status, the MOU (and now the 2003 Agreement) clearly does not provide for UN 'control' over the Khmer Rouge trials. In fact the Organisation's role in filling out the structure of the Chambers is essentially a one-off contribution as compared with the ongoing Cambodian responsibility for providing premises, protecting participants, as well as identifying, arresting and detaining suspects and incarcerating those found guilty without later pardoning them.

In reality, control over funding of the international participation, through the deputy administrator, is the only real point of contact permitting the UN to have some ongoing influence over the proceedings. However, the main sanction for breach of the MOU would seem to be threatened withdrawal, and Hun Sen has proved to be an excellent poker player.

As regards the provision of international personnel to the Chambers from the lists drawn up by the UN Secretary-General,[204] it is difficult to see how the UN's role could even be classified as verification or supervision. Moreover, its administrative role is limited to the international staff and not the workings of the Chambers as such. The issue of what may happen in the event that the UN fails to provide sufficient candidates for nomination serves to underscore this point.

The draft MOU provided that any vacancy shall be filled by the SCM from the UN lists; thus guaranteeing continued international participation at the agreed levels.[205] In fact, the UN insistence on sole responsibility for providing potential nominees[206] was designed to preclude an unacceptable Cambodian provision in the January 2000 draft of the law, allowing the SCM to appoint foreign judges, 'at the request of the Secretary General of the United Nations, or of the governments of member States of the United Nations, or among other foreign legal personalities, after consultations with the Royal Government of Cambodia'.[207]

The Tribunal Law strikes a balance between these extreme positions. On the one hand, the SCM is initially to appoint foreign personnel only 'upon nomination by the Secretary-General of the United Nations', from the lists provided by him.[208] However, the reference to 'Governments of Member States of the United Nations or ... other foreign legal personalities' does not disappear. It resurfaces in Article 46, relating to any lack of UN-provided personnel, no longer as a concurrent

---

204. See *supra* part 4.2.

205. Draft MOU, *supra* n. 5, Arts. 2(8)-(10) [judges]; 4(4) and (5) [investigating judge]; and 5(5)-(7) [prosecutors].

206. Ibid., Art. 2(8): 'Appointment of international judges by the Supreme Council of the Magistracy shall be made *only* from the list submitted by the Secretary-General'.

207. An unofficial translation of this intermediate draft is currently available at <http://www.cambodian-parliament.org/Legislative_Act_/legislative_act_.html>; for a commentary on this draft, see 'Core Issues in Khmer Rouge tribunal law Unresolved', *Human Rights Watch* (Press release 2000/01, New York, 21 January 2000), available at: <http://www.hrw.org/press/2000/01/cambo0121.htm.>

208. Tribunal Law, *supra* n. 6, Arts. 11, 18 and 26.

source of personnel, but as a fall-back position allowing the nomination of supplementary candidates '[i]n the event those [UN] lists are exhausted'. As a last resort, if the required foreign staff are still not forthcoming after seeking foreign participation through bilateral arrangements, 'then the Supreme Council of the Magistracy may choose replacement Cambodian judges, investigating judges or prosecutors'. This is unlikely, however, given that the foreign judicial personnel is 'appointed for the duration of the proceedings',[209] ensuring that there should be little change.

Despite being a seemingly logical solution avoiding blockage of trials in the event of a UN pull-out, and despite the fact that the relevant provisions imply the right of the Secretary-General to place an unlimited number of names on each list,[210] the problem of exhaustion of the lists was one of the issues raised by UN Legal Counsel *after* passage of the Law.[211] This gives some idea of the extent of loss of UN confidence in Cambodian good faith, which Sok An was quick to reject in his detailed response on 22 January 2002, stating that '… in a spirit of cooperation … we have no intention of limiting the right and opportunity for the Secretary-General to send more names to supplement the lists during the course of the proceedings, should this become necessary'. He added '[t]his can be spelled out more precisely in the Articles of Cooperation.'[212] Stronger wording was indeed introduced into the 2003 Agreement on this point.[213]

However, the manner in which former Khmer Rouge commander, Ta Mok, was indicted for crimes against humanity, after passage of the Tribunal Law,[214] raises serious doubts as to the intention of the Cambodian authorities to respect its provisions relating to international cooperation. Indeed, the only Cambodian penal law relating to crimes against humanity being Article 5 of the Tribunal Law, the Extraordinary Chambers have exclusive jurisdiction.[215] Personnel appointed in accordance with the Tribunal Law should therefore have laid the charges, whereas it was the Prosecutor of the Phnom Penh Military Court who took action in this case. Even accepting that the fallback provisions in the law are open to a broad interpretation allowing Cambodian staff to act unilaterally while waiting for the international staff to be named, the Cambodian prosecutor and investigating judge should have been formally named to the Chambers before taking this decision. In reality, faced with the prospect of being forced to release Ta Mok on 6 March 2002 after the expiry of the maximum three-year period of pre-trial detention, the Cambodian

---

209. Draft MOU, *supra* n. 5, Arts. 12, 21 and 27.

210. Art. 11 refers to 'a list of *not less than* twelve candidates' and Arts. 18 and 26 refer to 'at least two candidates'.

211. H. Corell, Under Secretary-General for Legal Affairs, Letter dated 10 October 2001 [non-official document].

212. Sok An, Senior Minister in Charge of the Office of the Council of Ministers, *Cambodian response to the Eleven points raised in H.E. Hans Corell's letter of 10 October 2001* (Letter to H. Corell dated 22 January 2002, Annex).

213. See *infra* part 6.2.

214. 'Cambodia's Khmer Rouge "butcher" charged', CNN, 22 February 2002.

215. The 1979 and 1994 laws only referred to genocide.

government once more ran rough-shod over the finer points of the rights of the defence.[216]

6.   THE 2003 AGREEMENT

On 8 February 2002, after a global review of the concessions made by the UN, the Secretary-General, Kofi Annan, pulled the UN out of a process with which it had never been comfortable.[217] Widely supported by international and Cambodian civil society,[218] this decision was strongly contested by some of the most influential UN Member States.[219] In August 2002, Kofi Annan, 'made it clear that in order for him to engage in further negotiations, he need[ed] a clear mandate from either the General Assembly or the Security Council'.[220] This was forthcoming on 18 December 2002, when the General Assembly adopted a resolution requesting the Secretary-General to resume negotiations 'based on previous negotiations, to establish Extraordinary Chambers consistent with the provisions of the present resolution ...'.[221] The Secretary-General was given 90 days to report on implementation of the resolution and, on 17 March 2003, UN and Cambodian negotiators adopted a draft Agreement concerning the trials (the '2003 Agreement').[222] The text, as negotiated, was accepted by the Cambodian government on 28 March[223] and by the UN General Assembly on 13 May 2003.[224] The Agreement was officially signed by the parties in Phnom Penh on 6 June 2003 and will come into force once ratified by the Cambodian Parliament.[225] A discussion of the amendments follows.

6.1   Legal status of the 2003 Agreement

The legal status of the 2003 Agreement has been clarified. While it recognises the Cambodian position that the instrument only regulates international cooperation in

---

216. R. Charmichael and V. Sokheng, 'Aging Ta Mok on Ice for 3 more Years', *Phnom Penh Post*, Issue 11/05 (1-14 March 2002) available on subscription at <http://www.phnompenhpost.com/>.

217. F. Eckhard, Spokesman for the Secretary-General, Daily Press Briefing by the Office of the Spokesman for the Secretary-General, 8 February 2002.

218. For the reactions of the local NGO, Licadho, and Amnesty International, see 'Rights groups support UN stance on Khmer Rouge trial', Agence France-Presse (12 February 2002); see also Amnesty International, 'Cambodia: Flawed trials in no one's best interests' (Press release, AI Index ASA 23/001/2002) 11 February 2002, available at <http://www.amnesty.org/>.

219. 'US Ambassador and U.N. Secretary-General Discuss Cambodia', Associated Press (12 February 2002).

220. UN Press Release, Secretary-General replies to Cambodian Prime Minister's Letter on Trial of Khmer Rouge Leaders (UN Doc. SG/SM/8341, 20 August 2002), available at <http://www.un.org/News/>.

221. UN Doc. A/RES/57/228 (2002), 18 December 2002, para. 1.

222. *Supra* n. 7.

223. 'Cambodian cabinet approves Khmer Rouge trial law', Reuters (28 March 2003).

224. UN Doc. A/RES/57/228B, 13 May 2003, adopted without a vote.

225. Hua Jiang, Deputy Spokesman for the Secretary-General of the United Nations, 'UN and Cambodia Agree on Khmer Rouge Trial Structure', Highlights of the Noon Briefing, United Nations, UN Headquarters, New York, 6 June 2003.

the trials, it also specifies that it is the Agreement which provides the legal basis for such cooperation. In this respect, the Tribunal Law is thus relegated to the status of implementing legislation. Once ratified, the Agreement will be a binding international agreement between the United Nations and Cambodia, applying 'as law within Cambodia' (Arts. 1 and 2). Although the UN Secretary-General rightly sees this as a positive point, it also involves some drawbacks.

On the positive side, it means that the process is now under the auspices of the General Assembly, which was required to formally authorise the Secretary-General to sign it. This implies greater backing by the international community. Moreover, by virtue of the principle, *pacta sunt servanda*, the Agreement must be performed by the parties in good faith and Cambodia cannot invoke other provisions of its internal law as justification for failure to perform its engagements. The 2003 Agreement thus provides a legal guarantee that the Extraordinary Chambers will function and exercise their powers as envisaged in the Agreement, as well as providing an indisputable basis for determining breaches by Cambodia.

However, it is not clear that this formal change will place much additional pressure on Cambodia in practice to cooperate fully in the trials, over and above that already applied by NGOs, trading partners and international lending agencies. Of course, as envisaged in Article 28 of the 2003 Agreement, if the government were later to change the structure or cause the Chambers to function in a manner that did not conform to the agreement, the United Nations could threaten to put an end to its assistance. However, this convenient emergency exit for the UN would not help put an end to Khmer Rouge impunity.

Furthermore, the international status of the agreement creates potential for further time wasting by the Cambodian authorities. First, the Agreement must pass through the normal procedures of ratification including approbation by the National Assembly and Senate (Constitution, new Art. 26). Indeed, the earlier mutual understanding to that effect[226] has been formalised in the 2003 Agreement. Although this could undoubtedly be achieved rapidly by the Cambodian Parliament after the general elections in July 2003, the problems do not end there.

Unfortunately, there is no specific provision in the Cambodian Constitution establishing the status of validly ratified treaties in the domestic system. The government made it clear in its 1997 periodic report to the UN Committee on the Elimination of all Forms of Racial Discrimination ('CERD'), that it adheres to a dualist approach with respect to human rights conventions ratified by Cambodia. The latter 'may not be directly invoked before the courts or administrative authorities' and simply 'provide a basis for the development of national legislation ...'[227]

Accordingly, Cambodia would seem to require domestic law to be brought into conformity with the 2003 Agreement, especially the Tribunal Law. Indeed, although the Agreement provides that it will apply as law in Cambodia, implying that Cambodia does not need to adopt further legislation, this provision flies in the

---

226. See Statement on the Khmer Rouge Trial, *supra* n. 203, and UN Doc. SG/SM/7868, 27 June 2001.

227. CERD, Seventh periodic reports of States parties due in 1996: Cambodia (State Party Report, UN Doc. CERD/C/292/Add.2), 5 May 1997, para. 19.

face of Cambodia's dualist system. To the extent that the Agreement contains specific provisions in contradiction with the contents of the Tribunal Law, it is clearly preferable for the latter to be formally amended. Indeed, the failure to adopt legislation containing the new provisions might well be in breach Cambodia's international obligations towards the UN (eventually allowing the world body to withdraw from the process), but would not render the Tribunal Law as it stands invalid within the Cambodian legal system, or provide a basis for judicial review. However, amending the existing Tribunal Law would involve not only full parliamentary proceedings and constitutional review, but also further consultations with the UN as required by the Agreement itself (Art. 2(3)). Cambodia has previously drawn out such proceedings for as long as eight months.

6.2   Structure

The 2003 Agreement simplifies the structure of the Extraordinary Chambers by removing the intermediate appellate Chamber, leaving a two-tiered structure.[228] This new structure still provides the accused with appellate remedies similar to those enjoyed before the *ad hoc* International Criminal Tribunals, while significantly reducing the cost and length of trials. Accordingly, there will now be three out of five Cambodian judges at first instance; and four out of seven before the Supreme Court (Art. 3). Despite ongoing concerns regarding the independence of the Cambodian judiciary, the UN negotiating team was unable to convince the Cambodian authorities to accept a majority of foreign judges and a simple majority voting system.[229] As the 'super majority' system thus remains in place, the new voting formula is four out of five judges at first instance, and five out of seven before the Supreme Court (Art. 4).

An attempt by the UN Secretary-General to avoid potential blockage at the prosecution stage,[230] by providing for a single international prosecutor and investigating judge, or alternatively, by giving the international co-prosecutor and co-investigating judge the final say in case of disagreement (thereby rendering the Pre-Trial Chamber superfluous), was rejected outright by Cambodia.[231] The only Cambodian concession to worries about the nomination of foreign personnel in the 2003 Agreement was to accept formal confirmation that absent international investigating judges and prosecutors will also be replaced from the Secretary-General's list.[232] However, the Agreement still makes no provision for the case where the UN lists are 'exhausted'.

Article 26(3) of the Draft MOU subjected the UN role to outside factors: in the event that insufficient personnel is offered by states or insufficient funds are available in the United Nations Trust Fund, 'the United Nations shall be free from its

---

228. 2003 Agreement, *supra* n. 7, Art. 3.
229. See Report of the Secretary-General on Khmer Rouge trials, *supra* n. 7,*supra* n. 7.
230. See *supra* part 4.1.
231. Report of the Secretary-General on Khmer Rouge trials, *supra* n. 7, paras.16, 21 and 22.
232. *Supra* n. 7, Arts. 5(6) and 6(6).

obligations …' under the accord. However, in keeping with the binding treaty status of the 2003 Agreement, this provision has been removed.

As regards the extremely important position of the international Deputy Director of the administration, the 2003 Agreement strengthens the UN position with a specific provision to the effect that the assignment by the Cambodian government of the international Deputy Director appointed by the Secretary-General 'shall take place forthwith'(Art. 8(3)).

6.3   Jurisdiction and procedure

The 2003 Agreement introduces an important change to the subject-matter jurisdiction of the Extraordinary Chambers, because crimes against humanity are no longer defined in accordance with the ICTR definition, but that contained in the Statute of the International Criminal Court, ratified by Cambodia on 11 April 2002. While this avoids the problematical insistence of the ICTR Statute on a discriminatory motive for all crimes against humanity, it may cause new problems to the extent that the ICC definition incriminates acts which were not prohibited by customary international law at the time of the Khmer Rouge crimes. In particular, 'persecution' is widened to include acts 'against any identifiable group or collectivity on political, racial, national, ethnic, cultural, religious, gender.., or other grounds that are universally recognized as impermissible under international law …' (ICC Statute, Art. 7(h)).

The 2003 Agreement expands and reinforces the existing provisions concerning 'international standards of justice', notably by adding specific reference to Articles 15 ICCPR (Art. 12). Moreover, despite Cambodian assurances,[233] the UN insisted on including formal confirmation of the right to foreign or local counsel of one's own choice in the 2003 Agreement (Art. 13). While these additions are welcome, it has been pointed out that other pertinent principles of due process, such as the arrest provisions of ICCPR Article 9, are not included.[234] This problem is exacerbated by the fact that the Tribunal Law only requires the Chambers to 'seek guidance' in international rules, as compared with other internationalised courts, which only apply existing laws 'in so far as they do not conflict with' international standards.[235] Including these standards expressly in the 2003 Agreement would indeed resolve this weakness as it takes precedence over Cambodian law.

The 2003 Agreement also makes concessions to both sides concerning the legal status of prior amnesties and pardons. On the one hand, the Agreement bows to Cambodian constitutional concerns by replacing the broad MOU provision excluding all amnesties with the terms of the Tribunal Law prohibiting government requests for amnesties. On the other hand, the 2003 Agreement formally recognises that the question should be left to the Extraordinary Chambers to resolve (Art. 11 (2)). Despite this provision being described as 'disappointing' in comparison with

---

233. See *supra* part 4.3.1.

234. See Amnesty International's position and concerns regarding the proposed 'Khmer Rouge' tribunal, *supra* n. 151, p. 4.

235. See for East Timor, Linton, loc. cit. n. 187, p. 136.

the approach of other international tribunals, it is submitted that this is the only equitable solution to such complex issues raised by trials before domestic courts.[236]

6.4   **Funding**

The Secretary General has estimated the cost of international participation in the Extraordinary Chambers at more than 19 million US dollars over three years. In his 2003 report to the General Assembly, he argued that 'as a matter of constitutional principle', an operation of this nature, 'mandated by Member States', should constitute an expense of the Organization under Article 17 of the Charter of the United Nations and should be financed from assessed contributions, especially given 'the expressed wish of the General Assembly in resolution 57/228 that the Extraordinary Chambers be established as early as possible and that they begin to function promptly'. He added that 'A financial mechanism based on voluntary contributions would not provide the assured and continuous source of funding that would be needed', as 'the process of setting up the Extraordinary Chambers (...) could only be initiated once sufficient money was in place to fund the necessary personnel and the operations of the Chambers for a sustained period of time'. In support for his proposition, the Secretary-General pointed out that 'the Special Court for Sierra Leone has proved that ... it would probably be more than a year before sufficient contributions were received to make that possible'. In the case of Cambodia, 'the opportunity of bringing those responsible to justice might be lost' due to such delay.[237] This proposition was rejected by the Third Committee of the General Assembly, which confirmed that all costs would be met from voluntary contributions.[238]

On a related point, the Tribunal Law provides that Cambodia will ensure the security of all the personnel of the Chambers and persons appearing before them, with financial assistance from the UN. Despite clarification of this point in the 2003 Agreement, the recent murder of a Cambodian Judge, Sok Sethmony, who sentenced former Khmer Rouge commander Sam Bith to life in prison for the 1994 murders of 13 Cambodians and three Western backpackers,[239] shows that this remains a weak point in the entire concept of holding mixed international trials in the country itself.

---

236. See *supra* part 4.4.3.

237. Report of the Secretary-General on Khmer Rouge trials, *supra* n. 7, paras. 74-76.

238. Third Committee approves draft resolution on Khmer Rouge trials, UN Doc. GA/SHC/3734, 2 May 2003; the UN will also be responsible for the costs of fitting out and running the premises provided by Cambodia, the remuneration of defence counsel, witness travel and the cost of safety and security services provided by the Cambodian government. Detailed estimates of these costs were not yet available, but would also be met from voluntary contributions.

239. E. Unmacht, 'Senior Court Judge Murdered in Cambodia', Voice of America, 23 April 2003.

7.   CONCLUSION – NO NATIONAL RECONCILIATION WITHOUT
      FAIR TRIALS?

The Cambodian experience lends weight to the affirmation that 'a democratic society [cannot] be built on falsehood or disregard for a criminal past'.[240] Criminal
justice is clearly a necessary component of national reconciliation following the
crimes committed by the Khmer Rouge. The current process of harmonisation of
substantive law through the caselaw of the existing international tribunals and the
definition of infractions in new internationalised courts will accelerate with the
creation of the ICC. Nevertheless, due to the treaty-based structure of the ICC,
binding only on its State Parties, added to its prospective, complementary jurisdiction, the establishment of the ICC has not put an end to alternative mechanisms.

Within these parameters, a wide range of transitional justice options will remain
available, ranging from new *ad hoc* international tribunals to domestic prosecution.
The most appropriate form for any particular situation will depend on both legal
and extra-legal considerations. The good faith of the parties will probably be at
least as important as any technical guarantees of fair trials. It would seem that almost every possible solution, including a range of options for internationalised
domestic proceedings, have been envisaged for Cambodia at one time or another
in the last five years. Perhaps the only mechanism not having been the subject of a
formal proposal is the 'Special Court' system adopted for Sierra Leone. This is
partly because the concept evolved out of dissatisfaction with the solution adopted
for Cambodia in 2000, after Royal Government insistence on preservation of its
'sovereignty'.

If the Extraordinary Chambers ever do get off the ground, which now seems to
be a formality, their case law may provide interesting insights into the state of
international criminal law in the 1970s and the difficulties in rendering justice to
the victims of past crimes.

Such justice will miss its objective, however, unless the form chosen allows a
fair determination of individual responsibility for Khmer Rouge crimes. The appropriate mix should take account of the demands of Cambodians, including the
need to facilitate victim participation. Although the UN has not raised the question,
the Tribunal Law suffers seriously in comparison with the other internationalised
tribunals established since its structure was negotiated. The Cambodian solution
lies at the far end of the scale compared with the Sierra Leone Court. Detailed legal
analysis of the nature, structure and legal status of the Extraordinary Chambers
shows, however, that the interests of international justice support some, if not all,
of the UN concessions. The problem is that the Cambodian government seems
more interested in 'closure' than justice *per se*. In fact, clearer commitment to
justice for the victims of the Khmer Rouge will be needed from both parties if fair
trials are to be held in Cambodia. One way of limiting the chances of such devia-

---

240. R. Badinter, 'International Criminal Justice: From Darkness to Light', in A. Cassese et al.,
eds., *The Rome Statute of the International Criminal Court - A Commentary* (Oxford, Oxford University Press Oxford 2002) Vol. II, pp. 1931 at 1933.

tion would be for the Extraordinary Chambers to adopt rules of procedure incorporating all of the relevant provisions.

Kofi Annan's insistence on a new mandate before continuing with the negotiations showed that the structure as it then stood did not comply with his initial mandate, aimed at bringing about national reconciliation, strengthening democracy and addressing the issue of individual accountability in fair, impartial proceedings. It also showed that the UN is convinced that only sustained international support holds any hope of a successful outcome.

The decision to go ahead with UN participation will have repercussions going well beyond the domestic framework because, in the context of a body of international criminal law that is striving to lay down common principles, the Cambodian negotiations were followed closely. Despite early rhetoric, however, the UN clearly does not see the Cambodian compromise as a viable model. The mixture of temporal, political, cultural and even legal aspects unique to Cambodia would make it difficult to transpose to other situations even if the compromise were workable in Cambodia.

The South-African experience teaches us that veritable national reconciliation requires knowledge of the truth. However, every state faced with this problem must remain free to choose the means of discovering it. While it was not in the UN's interest that the negotiations fail simply for having insisted on a legal system foreign to Cambodian legal tradition, nothing is to be gained from trials that do not measure up to international standards.

The UN Member States chose to lead the Organisation back to the negotiating table, rather than by-passing the world body and entering into bilateral arrangements with Cambodia for the provision of international personnel, or wiping their hands of the entire affair. In principle, the fact that the Khmer Rouge trials are back on track is to be welcomed, given the damage done to the Cambodian social contract and the international moral order by their impunity. However, citing the current state of the Cambodian legal system, the Secretary General has warned that 'any deviation by the [Cambodian] government from the obligations undertaken could lead to the United Nations withdrawing its cooperation and assistance from the process.'[241] Since the General Assembly has approved the new compromise by consensus, it must now put the weight of the entire international community behind the process and the Cambodian people, to ensure that justice is done.

---

241. Report of the Secretary-General on Khmer Rouge trials, *supra* n. 7, summary.

INTERNATIONAL CRIMINAL PROCEDURE AND ITS PARTICIPANTS: AN EXAMINATION OF THE INTERACTION OF JUDGES, PROSECUTOR AND DEFENCE AT THE YUGOSLAV TRIBUNAL[1]

Christoph J.M. Safferling[2]

1. © C. Safferling, 2003.

2. Christoph Safferling, Dr. iur. (Munich), LL.M. (LSE) is Assistant Professor at the Institute for Criminal Law, Criminal Procedure and Criminology at the University of Erlangen-Nürnberg, Germany.

Yearbook of International Humanitarian Law
Volume 5 - 2002 - pp. 219-252

1.   INTRODUCTION

More than ten years have passed since the establishment of the International Criminal Tribunal for the Former Yugoslavia (ICTY) on 25 May 1993.[3] What was perceived then as being quite a scandalous step has come to seem somewhat normal both for international and criminal lawyers. The creation of the International Tribunal was a surprising move mainly for three reasons. First, from a public international law point of view, the UN Charter does not explicitly authorise anything like a 'judicial intervention'[4] as a possible means to react to an international conflict and establish peace and security.[5] Second, given that international criminal law at that time was hardly codified, the legality of prosecutions was questioned in view of the principle *nullum crimen sine lege.*[6] Third, the procedural system of an international criminal prosecution was unclear.[7]

The shock concerning the first problem was reduced by the establishment of the International Criminal Tribunal for Rwanda (ICTR) shortly thereafter,[8] and was later overcome by institutionalising 'judicial intervention' by Article 13(b) of the Statute of the International Criminal Court (ICC).[9] The second problem was solved by the first judgment of the Appeals Chamber of the ICTY itself.[10] The question of

---

3. The full name is International Criminal Tribunal for the Prosecution of Persons Responsible for Serious Violations of International Humanitarian Law Committed in the Territory of the Former Yugoslavia since 1991, founded by UN Security Council Resolution 827, 25 May 1993.

4. The term was coined by H. Roggemann, *Der International Strafgerichtshof* (Berlin, Spitz Verlag 1994) p. 8.

5. See J. Frowein and Ph. Kirsch, in B. Simma et al., eds., *The Charter of the United Nations - A Commentary* (Oxford, Oxford University Press 2002) 2nd edn. Introduction to Chapter VII, MN 33 and Art. 41 MN 6 and 19, 'atypical measures'.

6. This argument is still being brought forward by the defence, e.g., *Prosecutor* v. *Hadzihasanović et al.*, IT-01-47-PT, 12 November 2002, where the Trial Chamber II ruled that the concept of command responsibility was applicable to internal armed conflicts even before 1991.

7. *Ad hoc* institutions are frequently used in international law. In the field of international commercial relations, for example, *ad hoc* arbitration tribunals are an everyday phenomenon. Whereas arbitrators can be left with a relatively wide margin concerning the procedure they wish to adopt, a criminal trial requires strict adherence to quite a number of safeguards.

8. The full name is International Tribunal for the Prosecution of Persons Responsible for Genocide and Other Serious Violations of International Humanitarian Law Committed in the Territory of Rwanda and Rwandan citizens responsible for genocide and other such violations committed in the territory of neighbouring States between 1 January 1994 and 31 December 1994, founded by UN Security Council Resolution 955, 8 November 1994. As to the acceptance of this power of the SC see A. Paulus, 'Art. 29 MN 55-86', in Simma, op. cit. n. 5.

9. Rome Statute of the International Criminal Court, adopted on 17 July 1998, UN Doc. PCNICC/1999/INF/3 of 17 August 1999 (with corrections).

10. The problem was addressed and routinely solved by the Appeals Chamber of the ICTY in its first decision, *Prosecutor* v. *Tadić*, IT-94-1-AR72, 2 October 1995. See C. Greenwood, 'International Humanitarian Law and the Tadić Case', 7 *EJIL* (1996) p. 265; the very critical J.E. Alvarez, 'Nurem-

a fair procedure, however, prevails and will continue to be a core problem. The rights of the accused and efficiency depend heavily on the interaction between the participants. Furthermore, establishing the truth depends on the cooperation of the parties and the willingness to equip them with equal rights.[11]

This paper will first briefly introduce the participants and the procedural law in general (2), before exemplifying this interaction and addressing three procedural topics (3).

The first topic will be the treatment of witnesses and victims (3.1). From the viewpoint of the participants, there are three conflicting interest that need to be balanced: the interest to get as much evidence as possible (e.g., on the part of the Prosecutor, to corroborate the allegations contained in the indictment); the interest to discredit this evidence as much as possible (e.g., on the part of the defence, to counter the Prosecutor's case); and the interest to protect the witness (the role of the judges).

Secondly, the paper takes a look at evidence before the Tribunal (3.2). The communication and interaction between Prosecutor and defence can be demonstrated in particular in the field of pre-trial disclosure. The judges also have an interest to get the best evidence possible in order to find the truth.

Finally, the often-disputed subject of pre-trial detention at the ICTY is addressed (3.3). One can observe a rather typical struggle between liberty and efficiency in criminal prosecution. The defendant has a right to liberty, whereas the Prosecutor needs to ensure his presence at trial.

From these three examples it can be shown that the participants in the proceedings at the ICTY do show a great deal of respect for the rights of the accused. However, all three examples also bring to light flaws in the law or in the attitude of one or the other participants in interpreting and handling the existing law.

2.   PROSECUTION AT THE ICTY

Prosecution depends on institutions. In the case of international criminal law neither judge nor Prosecutor existed when the Security Council contemplated the establishment of the ICTY in 1993. In a rather roughly drafted Statute of a mere 34 articles, participating institutions had to be founded.

---

berg Revisited: The Tadić Case', 7 *EJIL* (1996) p. 245; H. von Heinegg, 'Die Errichtung des Jugosla-wien-Strafgerichtshofes durch Resolution 827 (1993)', in H. Fischer and S.R. Lüder, eds, *Völkerrech-tliche Verbrechen vor dem Jugoslawientribunal, nationalen Gerichten und dem Internationalen Strafgerichtshof* (Berlin, Spitz 1999) p. 63; polemic J. Bohnert, 'Kant in Jugoslawien', in G. Duttge, ed., *Gedächtnisschrift für E. Schlüchter* (Cologne, Heymanns 2002) p. 763.

11. The principle of 'equality of arms' is also contained in the human right to a fair trial, see e.g., ECourtHR *Bulut* v. *Austria*, Rep. 1996-II, para. 48; *Ankerl* v. *Switzerland*, Rep. 1996-V, para. 38; see also R. Esser, *Auf dem Weg zu einem europäischen Strafverfahrensrecht* (Berlin, De Gruyter 2002) pp. 407 et seq.

2.1   The participating institutions

The ICTY Statute has created three different organs under the same roof according to Article 11. The first is the institution of the judges (1). The second is the Office of the Prosecutor (2), and the third is the Registry (3). A fourth institution that participates in the proceedings before the ICTY but that is not included in the organisational structure of the Tribunal is the defence (4).

2.1.1   *The Chambers*

The Judges – or in the language of the Statute, the Chambers – constitute in a way the very heart of the Tribunal. They fulfil the duty which is the actual rationale of the entire institution: passing judgments. As is demanded by human rights law (Art. 14(5) ICCPR),[12] they are organised in a two-tier system. The Trial Chambers, of which there are now three,[13] constitute the first level. They hear the cases, evaluate the evidence, convict or acquit and lay down the sentences (Art. 23(1) ICTY Statute). The number of judges has been enlarged considerably by the introduction of so called *ad litem* judges (Arts. 13*ter* and 13*quater* ICTY Statute), resulting in the creation of sections within each Trial Chamber.[14] A rotation mechanism provides for a serious expedition of the trials. The Appeals Chamber, as the final arbiter of the law of the Tribunal between the parties,[15] controls the work of the Trial Chambers both in facts and in law (Art. 25 ICTY Statute).

The Statute foresees the election of a President of the Tribunal (Art. 14 ICTY Statute). The incumbent is vested with considerable powers, laid down in Rule 19, as he presides over all plenary meetings of the Tribunal and over the Appeals Chamber, coordinates the work of the Chamber, supervises the Registrar and issues Practice Directions, by which he regulates certain aspects of the proceedings in detail.[16] The President has, for example, regulated communication between the institutions by issuing a direction concerning the length of briefs and motions.[17] Furthermore, the President has issued a 'Practice Direction on the Procedure for the International Tribunal's Designation of the State in which a Convicted Person is to Serve his/her Sentence of Imprisonment'.[18] He has done so because it is the President who designates the place of imprisonment according

---

12. International Covenant on Civil and Political Rights, 999 *UNTS* 1966 p. 171; see C. Safferling, *Towards an International Criminal Procedure* (Oxford, Oxford University Press 2003) pp. 331, 334.

13. A third Trial Chamber was enacted by the amendment of Art. 11(a) Statute ICTY by Security Council Resolution 1166 of 13 May 1998.

14. Amendment of Article 13*ter* Statute ICTY by Security Council Resolution 1329 of 30 November 2000; see the 8th Annual Report of the ICTY, UN Doc. A/56/352 – S/2001/865, paras. 10-17.

15. See *Prosecutor* v. *Delalić et al.*, IT-96-21-A, 20 February 2001, App. Ch., para. 35.

16. The option to issue Practice Directions was introduced at the 13th Plenary Session on 25 July 1997. The various Presidents have since then made some use of this provision and drafted eight directions in this regard; to be found amongst other legal documents at: <http://www.un.org/icty/legaldoc/index.htm>.

17. Practice Direction on the Length of Briefs and Motions, IT/184/Rev.1, 5 March 2002.

18. IT/137, 9 July 1998 <http://www.un.org/icty/basic/detention/IT137.htm>.

to Rule 103.[19] It reads, however, more like an order to the Registry on how to prepare the President's decision formally. Should someone expect clarity on the criteria according to which the President decides the matter, he will be disappointed. Apart from a vague allusion to the proximity to the relations of the convicted, there is no normative standard which the President attempts to follow.[20] This shows that the President is a powerful and uncontrolled figure. The ICC has found a better solution by establishing a Presidency consisting of three persons (Art. 38 ICC Statute). This guarantees at least some control, e.g., as to the question where to enforce the sentence (Rule 199 ICC RPE).

2.1.2   *The Prosecutor*

The Prosecutor is a separate organisational entity (Art. 11(b) ICTY Statute).[21] Her duties are twofold (Art. 16 ICTY Statute):[22] first, the Prosecutor investigates the cases and decides whether or not to indict (investigative activity). Secondly, the Prosecutor tries the case before the bench (prosecution activity). In her work, the Prosecutor is to be seen as independent both from the other organs of the Tribunal and from any external source (Art. 16(2) ICTY Statute). She may therefore not receive instructions from a Chamber or from any government as concerns the conduct of an investigation. Closely connected to the question of independence is the question of 'objectivity'. In many continental systems the Prosecutor as a public figure is also called upon to investigate in favour of the suspect. The Statute and Rules do not entail any allusion to this continental approach.[23] Nevertheless, Trial Chamber II has held that

> 'the Prosecutor of the Tribunal is not, or not only, a Party to adversarial proceedings but is an organ of the Tribunal and an organ of international criminal justice whose object is not simply to secure a conviction but to present the case for the Prosecution, which

---

19. The enforcement system of the ICTY is shown in action by J. MacLean, 'The Enforcement of the Sentence in the Tadić Case', in H. Fischer, C. Kreß and S.R. Lüder, eds, *International and National Prosecution of Crimes Under International Law* (Berlin, Spitz 2001) p. 727; see also D. Tolbert, 'The International Criminal Tribunal for former Yugoslavia and the enforcement of sentences', 11 *Leiden JIL* (1998) p. 655.

20. I have tried to lay down some principles myself in Safferling, op. cit. n. 12, pp. 351-59; see for a detailed analysis of the law at the ICTY and the ICC, G. Sluiter and K. Kreß in A. Cassese, P. Gaeta and J.R.W.D. Jones, eds, *The Rome Statute of the International Criminal Court: A Commentary* (Oxford, Oxford University Press 2002) pp. 1757-1821; lately E. Lambert-Ardelgwad, 'Droit penal international – L'emprisonnement des personnes condamnées par les juridictions pénales internationales', *RSC* (2003) p. 162.

21. For a comparative analysis of international prosecutors, see M. Bergsmo, C. Cissé and C. Staker, 'The Prosecutor of International Tribunals: The Case of the Nuremberg and Tokyo Tribunals, the ICTY and ICTR, and the ICC Compared', in L. Arbour, A. Eser, K. Ambos and A. Sanders, eds, *The Prosecutor of a Permanent International Criminal Court* (Freiburg, Edition Iuscrim 2000).

22. See also 8th Annual Report ICTY, *supra* n. 14, paras. 186-194.

23. In detail, Safferling, op. cit. n. 12, pp. 64-79.

includes not only incriminating, but also exculpatory evidence, in order to assist the Chamber to discover the truth in a judicial setting'.[24]

The Chamber, consisting of Judges Cassese (Italy), May (UK) and Mumba (Zambia), prompted a considerable shift to the continental practice.

The ICC Statute has created an equally independent Office of the Prosecutor by Article 42 ICC Statute, but went one step further in explicitly obliging the Prosecutor to investigate against and in favour of the suspect (Art. 54(1)(a)) .

2.1.3   *The Registry*

The third organ is the Registry. The Office of the Registry is supposed to be the organisational centre of the entire institution with a 'myriad of tasks'.[25] It is supposed to serve both other organs, the Chambers and the Prosecutor (Arts. 11(c) and 17 ICTY Statute). It channels communication both within the different organs of the Tribunal (see Rule 33(A)) and to the public.[26] In some respects, the Registrar has considerable and growing power. He administers the legal aid system under which defence counsel are assigned to indigent accused. Moreover, he supervises the detention unit. The Victims and Witnesses Section within the Registry is responsible for the physical and psychological well-being of witnesses when they are in contact with the Tribunal. These activities all involve human rights issues. The Registry therefore is also an institution that can violate the human rights of accused persons who apply for legal aid or during their detention, or of witnesses when they come to The Hague to testify. It was thus necessary to establish judicial control of the Registrar's decisions. Trial Chamber II has derived its authority over the Registry from its duty to regulate in accordance with the statutory requirements for a fair and expeditious trial.[27]

The Registry has quite far-reaching powers over defence counsel. Where legal aid is warranted, not only does the Registry choose counsel, it also supervises and monitors the performance of defence counsel.[28] This influence is not without problems. A fair trial requires an independent and impartial tribunal (see Art. 14(1)(2) ICCPR or Art. 6(1)(1) ECHR[29]). In light of the principle of independence, it is of course preferable to have an institution designating counsel other than the judges themselves.[30] Nevertheless, what needs to be avoided is a selection of counsel

---

24. *Prosecutor* v. *Kupreskić et al.*, IT-95-16, 21 September 1998.

25. 5th Annual Report ICTY, UN Doc. A/53/219 – S/1998/737, para. 133.

26. Cf., 9th Annual Report ICTY, UN Doc. A/57/379 – S/2002/985, para. 238.

27. See concerning the decision on assignment of Counsel: *Prosecutor* v. *Blagojević*, IT-02-60-PT, 9 December 2002, T. Ch. II; more restrictively *Prosecutor* v. *Knezević*, IT-95-4-PT, IT-95-8/1-PT, 6 September 2002, T. Ch. III.

28. Cf., 9th Annual Report ICTY, *supra* n. 26, para. 299.

29. Convention for the Protection of Human Rights and Fundamental Freedoms, 213 *UNTS* (1950) p. 221; as amended by 11th protocol ETS No. 155.

30. In Germany it is the presiding judge that chooses the counsel; see para. 142 (1) German Code of Criminal Procedure.

based on their cooperativeness with the Registry rather than on what best suits defendants.

A further problem lies in the fact that there is only one Registry both for the Chambers and the Office of the Prosecutor (Rule 33(A)). Again, the principle of independence of the Tribunal is called into question.[31] The European Court of Human Rights (ECourtHR) has elaborated on the danger in this regard: '[T]he confidence which the court in a democratic society must inspire in the public and, above all, as far as criminal proceedings are concerned, in the accused' is the underlying rationale for the independence'.[32] This confidence on the side of the accused could be damaged as he could picture the Chambers and the Prosecutor as one body, which is institutionally mingled by the Registry.[33] The Chambers themselves have stressed the principle that justice must be seen to be done.[34] The problem is fuelled by the existence of the Coordination Council in Rule 23*bis*, which consists of the President, the Prosecutor and the Registrar. The visibility of the independence is further slanted by the Legal Support Section within the Registry. This section provides research and drafting assistance to the individual Chambers and to the Plenary, in particular with amendments to the RPE.[35] It is difficult to claim complete independence if legal support to the judges is provided by an institution that has to serve the Prosecutor at the same time.

The Office of the Registry of the ICC is organised in a similar manner. In Article 43(1) ICC Statute, however, the Registrar is cautioned to fulfil his duty without prejudice to the functions and powers of the Prosecutor.

2.1.4 *The defence*

The defence counsel is the link between the Tribunal and the accused. He is the only professional participant in the proceedings who is situated outside the formal tripartite organisational structure of the ICTY. According to Rule 42(A)(i), the defence counsel can be involved at the earliest stage, i.e., before interrogation of the accused by the Prosecutor.[36] The assignment of counsel is undertaken by the Registry if the accused lacks the means to remunerate such counsel (Rule 45).[37] If the accused chooses and pays for his own counsel, counsel shall file a power of attor-

---

31. As to the human right to an independent and impartial court or tribunal see Safferling, op. cit. n. 12, pp. 90-97.

32. *DeCubber* v. *Belgium*, 26 October 1984, Series A No. 86, para. 26.

33. The German system has frequently been suspected of producing a 'Schulterschlusseffekt' (to stand shoulder for shoulder) of the Prosecutor and the Judges; see B. Schünemann, 'Der Richter im Strafverfahren als manipulierter Dritter? Zur empirischen Bestätigung von Perseveranz- und Schulterschlusseffekt', 20 *Strafverteidiger* (2000) p. 159.

34. See *Prosecutor* v. *Hadzihasanović and Kubura*, IT-01-47, 26 March 2002, T. Ch. II; *Prosecutor* v. *Furundžija*, IT-95-17/1-A, 21 July 2000, App. Ch., Declaration Judge Shahabuddeen paras. 13, 14.

35. 6th Annual Report ICTY, UN Doc. A/54/187 – S/1999/846, para. 158.

36. This is a human rights requirement, cf., Safferling, op. cit. n. 12, pp. 106-107. At the ICC this requirement was incorporated in Art. 55 (2)(c) of the Statute.

37. Cf., as to the ICTR, M. Wladimiroff, 'The Assignment of Counsel before the International Criminal Tribunal for Rwanda', 12 *Leiden JIL* (1999) p. 957.

ney with the Registrar (Rule 44). The choice is not always easy for the Registry. The President has therefore issued a directive on assignment of counsel.[38] The Registrar retains a list of possible lawyers who have indicated their willingness to serve as counsel. Generally speaking, the prerequisite for being added to the list is that the counsel is admitted to the practice of law in a state and speaks one working language of the Tribunal.[39] The latter requirement can be overcome in cases where the interest of justice demand that counsel be assigned who does not speak either of the two working languages but speaks the native language of the accused (Rule 44(B)). Assignability further requires that the assignee is a member of the ICTY bar association, the Association of Defence Counsel – ICTY.[40] Although the fear of an independent advocacy makes this requirement understandable, the danger of producing closed shops and dependencies within the association is real.[41]

The Prosecutor complained about the assignment of a former ICTY Prosecutor as co-counsel to the accused *Kubura*.[42] As Article 13 of the Directive on Assignment of Counsel contains no explicit possibility for the Prosecutor to request a judicial review of the Registrar's decision, the Trial Chamber first had to rule on a jurisdictional matter. It allowed the request by virtue of Rules 54 and 73 and the overall responsibility of the Chamber to ensure the proper administration of justice. On the merits, the complaint was about conflict of interest and undue advantage on the side of the accused. To a continental lawyer, frankly this plea is astonishing. The Prosecutor on the continent, as an official and independent organ of the administration of justice,[43] cannot claim unfairness on his side. However, the Trial Chamber (the German Judge Schomburg presiding) ruled that it would be incompatible with representing the accused if the counsel was previously involved in the same case with the other party. This was not the case here. A general prior association with the Prosecutor may bring about certain advantages to the accused; in the eyes of the Chamber, however, this did not amount to unfairness of this trial.[44]

The performance of defence counsel is regulated in the Code of Conduct.[45] Dismissal of counsel is possible at the discretion of the Registrar if the accused (or co-counsel) so demand.[46] The conditions under which the Registrar could uphold an assignment despite a lack of trust between lawyer and client are not clear. Dismissal is mandatory if the Chamber refuses an audience to counsel or if counsel no

---

38. Directive No. 1/94, IT/73/REV. 9, as amended 12 July 2002.

39. In detail see Rules 44 and 45(B) and Art. 14 Directive of Assignment of Defence Counsel.

40. Information is accessible at <http://www.adcicty.com/home.htm>.

41. Membership with the ADC-ICTY has several levels; only full-members can exercise voting rights and be eligible themselves (see Art. 6 ADC-ICTY Constitution for the executive Committee; Art. 12 for the right to vote and Art. 14 for the Disciplinary Council).

42. *Prosecutor* v. *Hadzihasanović, Alagić and Kubura, supra* n. 32.

43. For the German system, cf., Safferling, op. cit. n. 12, at pp. 65 et seq.

44. *Prosecutor* v. *Hadzihasanović, Alagić and Kubura, supra* n. 32.

45. Code of Professional Conduct for Counsel Appearing before the International Tribunal (as amended on 12 July 2002) (IT/125 REV. 1).

46. Art. 19(A) Directive of Assignment of Defence Counsel. The decision is reviewable by the President, Art. 19(F) Directive of Assignment of Defence Counsel.

longer fulfils the qualification requirements or is held in contempt of court.[47] Contempt of court is regulated by Rule 77. The concept of contempt is foreign to civil law lawyers. It exists to uphold the integrity of the proceedings and can also serve to (indirectly) protect witnesses and victims. Defence counsel have been held in contempt at the ICTY because they have violated witness anonymity and prejudiced evidence.[48] Next to disciplinary measures ordered by the ICTY on the basis of the Code of Conduct[49] or ordered by a national association of the ADC-ICTY,[50] the ability to hold counsel in contempt of court is a powerful weapon to ensure their reliability.

2.2   The framework: the Statute and Rules of Procedure

The legal framework is set by the Statute and the RPE. What is interesting to note is the speed of their evolution: the Statute and RPE have been amended several times; the Rules 28 times at the time of writing.[51] They are developing at a pace that even the Office of the Prosecutor does not always seem to be able to keep up with.[52] Whilst the Statute rests on decisions of the Security Council of the United Nations, a body that is not known for celerity, the responsibility for the RPE lies with the judges (Art. 15 ICTY Statute). That judges draft their procedural law as they go along is, from a viewpoint of a separation of powers, a rather unfortunate solution.[53] It is however born out of the necessity to compromise and the impossibility of drawing up a static, concise system that is suitable for an evolving international institution like the ICTY. The legal framework also includes several other documents such as the Code of Conduct for Counsel,[54] the Rules for Detention[55] and a number of directives with external effects and enforcement agreements with separate states.

The procedural order consists of a mixed system; whereas the Statute was created with a clear inclination towards the adversarial system,[56] the Rules have incor-

---

47. Art. 19(C) Directive of Assignment of Defence Counsel.

48. *Prosecutor v. Tadić*, IT-94-1-A-R77, 'Judgement on Allegations of Contempt Against Prior Counsel, Milan Vujin', 31 January 2000; and *Prosecutor v. Tadić*, IT-94-1-A-R77, 'Appeal Judgement on Allegations of Contempt against Prior Counsel, Milan Vujin', 27 February 2001.

49. Arts. 37-50 of the Code of Professional Conduct For Counsel.

50. According to Art. 14 of the Constitution of the ADC-ICTY.

51. A short description of the development is provided by D. Mundis in 'From "Common Law" Towards "Civil Law": The Evolution of the ICTY Rules of Procedure and Evidence', 14 *Leiden JIL* (2001) pp. 367 at 370-374.

52. Cf., *Prosecutor v. Naletilić and Martinović*, IT-98-34-T, 27 February 2002, T. Ch. I., where the Prosecutor relied in her motion of January 2002 on a Rule that had been modified in December 2000.

53. S. De Gurmendi Fernandez and H. Friman seem to see this as rather normal in the international context. 'The Rules of Procedure and Evidence of the International Criminal Court', 3 *YIHL* (2000) pp. 157 at 158

54. IT/125 REV. 1.

55. Rules governing the Detention of Persons Awaiting Trial or Appeal Before the Tribunal or Otherwise Detained on the Authority of the Tribunal ('Rules of Detention') IT/38/REV.8, last amended 29 November 1999.

56. Gurmendi Fernandez and Friman, loc. cit. n. 53, pp. 157 at 164 et seq.

porated more and more inquisitorial elements.[57] The judges, as lawmakers, have introduced these changes principally out of the necessity to expedite proceedings.[58] The length of the proceedings is a cause for concern,[59] although it is understandable considering the complexity of the investigation and the relative immaturity of international criminal law. It should also be remembered that the ICTY does not have any alternative proceedings to a full-scale trial,[60] whereas domestic legal systems can avoid trial by the exercise of the discretionary powers of prosecutors. The application of inquisitorial elements to speed up the procedure at the ICTY might prove disappointing, however, as the continental system is often criticised for being too time consuming compared to the Anglo-American system.[61] The procedural difficulties the judges encounter are often related to the dichotomy between elements of the two different systems. The role of the judge in particular is considerably different than that of his Anglo-American counterpart.[62] Because the judge, as a professional jurist, is passing the judgement, and needs to give reasons for it,[63] he can or even must be equipped with inquisitorial elements.[64] This has consequences for several procedural problems. Some of these are discussed in the following part (3.).

At the ICC, the responsibility for the RPE lies with the Assembly of States Parties, and only in urgent cases can the judges issue provisional Rules (Art. 51 ICC Statute). From the viewpoint of the separation of powers, this solution is clearly preferable.

---

57. V. Tochilovsky, 'Rules of Procedure for the International Criminal Court: Problems to Address in Light of the Experience of the *ad hoc* Tribunals', in 46 *NILR* (1999) p. 343; Mundis, loc. cit. n. 51, pp. 367 at 368.

58. V. Tochilovsky, 'Legal Systems and Cultures in the International Criminal Court', in Fischer et al., eds., op. cit. n. 19, pp. 627 at 632; Mundis, loc. cit. n. 51, pp. 367 at 370 et seq.

59. The first criminal, Duško Tadić, was extradited 24 April 1995; the trial started 7 May 1996; the final conviction was on 26 January 2000. It is important to note that as regards the lengths of proceedings one must count from the charge to the end of the appeals proceedings; see Human Rights Committee General Comment 13 (Art. 14) para. 10. According to the ECourtHR even constitutional complaints are to be taken into account; see *Gast and Popp* v. *Germany*, Appl. No. 29357/95, 25 Feburary 2000, Rep. 2000-II, para. 64. Tochilovsky, loc. cit. n. 58, pp. 627 at 632 is misleading as he counts only the first instance trial.

60. Cf., S. Zappalà, *Human Rights in International Criminal Proceedings* (Oxford, Oxford University Press 2003) pp. 114-15.

61. Cf., D.J. Harris, M. O'Boyle and C. Warbrick, *Law of the European Convention on Human Rights* (London, Butterworths 1995) pp. 228 et seq, who demonstrate that most of the convictions by the ECourtHR concerning the 'reasonable time' requirement of Art. 6(1) ECHR originate in civil law jurisdiction.

62. Mundis, loc. cit. n. 51, pp. 367 at 369. A comparative study of the role of the judges in England and Germany is given by S. Schulte-Nover, *Strafrichter in Deutschland und England* (Frankfurt, Lang 2003).

63. In favour of a right to a reasoned judgment as a human right, Harris et al., op. cit. n. 61, pp. 215 et seq.

64. This is rightly stressed by Tochilovsky, loc. cit. n. 58, pp. 627 at 636.

3. PROCEDURAL DIFFICULTIES

3.1 Treatment of witnesses and victims

3.1.1 *The human rights framework*

The treatment of victims is not of central interest at the ICTY. In its Statute – which from a criminological point of view is rather conservative – the ICTY sees victims as possible witnesses without offering them the possibility of participation in the proceedings in their own right.[65] The ICC deals with this problem in a different, more modern, way. The Statute and Rules of Procedure provide for victims to be heard and to participate in the process (Art. 69(3) ICC Statute and Rules 89-93).[66] It seems, however, quite appropriate for the ICTY to concentrate on the main purpose of criminal proceedings, i.e., the prosecution of criminals.[67] This is primarily because of the inexperience[68] of international criminal law in dealing with victims,[69] and also because of the difficulties that national legal systems encounter in the proper treatment of victims of 'ordinary' domestic crimes in an ongoing prosecution.[70] The establishment of the ICTY did not present the right opportunity to experiment with victims. At the ICC, in contrast, a legal framework was established to develop a decent way to enable victims' participation.

Nevertheless, prosecution is hardly imaginable without victims.[71] The Prosecutor depends on their willingness to cooperate and testify against the offender. The role of the victim as a crucial witness puts him or her in a highly dangerous situa-

---

65. For an analysis of the position of the victim at the ICTY and the ICC, see C. Safferling, 'Das Opfer völkerrechtlicher Verbrechen', 115 *Zeitschrift für die gesamten Strafrechtswissenschaften* (2003), 352; see also De Gurmendi Fernandez and Friman, loc. cit. n. 53, pp. 157 at 181-192 and B. Timm, 'The Legal Position of Victims in the Rules of Procedure and Evidence', in Fischer et al., op. cit. n. 19, p. 289.

66. Cf., C. Jorda and J. de Hemptinne, 'The Status and the Role of the Victim', in Cassese et al., op. cit. n. 20, p. 1387; Timm, ibid., p. 289.

67. A rather bitter, disillusioned view of the work of the ICTY from a Croatian viewpoint is presented by Z.P. Separović, 'UN-Tribunal: Justice for the Victims?', in G.F. Kirchhoff and P.C. Friday, eds., *Victimology at the Transition From the 20th to the 21st Century* (Aachen, Shaker 2000) p. 325.

68. The predecessors of the ICTY, namely the Nuremberg and Tokyo Military Tribunals, have relied mostly on documents and have heard but a few witnesses. It has been suggested that the more high-ranking the accused the less need there is for witnesses; cf., Kreß, 'Witnesses in Proceedings Before the ICC', in Fischer et al., op. cit. n. 19, pp. 309 at 313, fn. 9. The trial of Slobodan Milošević, IT-02-54, does not seem to corroborate this assumption. In the first phase of the trial before Trial Chamber III concerning only Kosovo, the Prosecutor called some 124 witnesses to present his case; see <http://www.asil.org/insights/insigh90.htm>.

69. The victimological work in international criminal law has just started. The first attempt in this direction was the meeting of international experts at the International Workshop on 'War – Victimization – Security: The Case of the Former Yugoslavia'. For a report, see U. Ewald and C. von Oppeln, 'War – Victimization – Security: The Case of the Former Yugoslavia', 10 *Eur. J Crime, Crim. L & Crim. Jus.* (2002) p. 39.

70. For an analysis of the situation in Germany, see Th. Weigend, *Deliktsopfer und Strafverfahren* (Berlin, Duncker &Humblot 1989).

71. See e.g., *Prosecutor* v. *Tadić*, IT-94-1-T, 10 August 1995, T. Ch. II., para. 23.

tion for two reasons. First, the victim runs the risk of being persecuted by the offender or fellow criminals. Secondly, victims may suffer from what is often called secondary victimisation when they give testimony. Both risks may implicate human rights law. The risk of persecution by the offender can involve the right to life (Art. 6(1) ICCPR and Art. 2(1) ECHR). It is a sad truth that witnesses before international tribunals have not always testified without experiencing the most severe consequences. Two former witnesses at the Rwanda Tribunal were killed upon their return home.[72] The situation at the Yugoslav Tribunal is better due to the cooperation of states in offering their witness protection programmes.[73] It is however clear that the ICTY must do everything it can to guarantee the protection of the lives of witnesses. The victim is protected from secondary victimisation by virtue of the right to privacy (Art. 17 (1) ICCPR and Art. 8(1) ECHR).[74]

These human rights of the victim are in conflict with the right to a fair trial of the accused as found in Article 14 ICCPR and Article 6 ECHR and reiterated in Article 21 ICTY Statute. According to the right to a fair trial, the accused must be given the opportunity to confront[75] and question the witness against him (Art. 14 (3)(e) ICCPR, Art. 6(3)(d) ECHR and Art. 21(4)(e) ICTY Statute). In order to protect the victim as a witness, it can however sometimes be necessary not to disclose his or her identity to the accused or to prohibit direct questioning by the accused.

Another consideration is that the efficiency of prosecution requires that, first, the Judges can observe the demeanour of the victim when giving evidence and that, second, an atmosphere free of coercion, guaranteeing a true and reliable testimony.

3.1.2   *Procedural solutions*

On the basis of Article 22 of the ICTY Statute, the Rules of the ICTY foresee a witness protection scheme that has four main aspects:

1. According to Rule 34, the Victims and Witnesses Section established within the Registry is called upon to care for the physical security and for the psychological well being of witnesses. Although the possibilities of this unit were quite limited at first, the resources for victims and witness protection have since risen considerably.[76] The unit, which needs to provide services for 500 to 600 witnesses a year, can be regarded as an impressive and well-functioning organisation. This kind of witness support does not affect the trial procedure as such and

---

72. V. Morris and M. Scharf, *An Insider's Guide to the ICTY* (Irvington-on-Hudson NY, Transnational 1995) p. 536.

73. D. Donat-Cattin, 'Art. 68, no. 2', in O. Triffterer, ed., *A Commentary to the Rome Statute of the ICC* (Baden-Baden, Nomos 1999).

74. The ECourtHR has accepted this reading of Art. 8 ECHR in its decision, *Doorson* v. *The Netherlands*, 26 March 1996, Reports 1996-II, para. 70.

75. Cf., Kreß, loc. cit. n. 68, pp. 309 at 311.

76. The Victims and Witnesses Section is supported through donation of national states. It has been able to open a field office in Sarajevo to enhance the contact between the ICTY and the victims. In 2002 the Section consisted of 35 staff members; see 9th Annual Report of the ICTY, UN Doc A/57/379 – S/2002/85, 4 September 2002, paras. 267-270.

is therefore not in conflict with the rights of the accused.[77]

2. The possibilities of deposition of testimony or testimony by video-conference have been laid down in Rules 71 and 71*bis*. These two types of witness protection differ in the number of problems they raise with regard to the guarantee of a fair trial. The general rule is that a witness has to appear in person before the Tribunal and give oral testimony.[78] According to Rule 89(F), the written form of witness testimony is admissible only where the interests of justice so allow. A videolink is less problematic in this regard. Although the witness is physically outside the courtroom, he or she can still be seen, heard and addressed by the parties.[79]

The possibility of giving video testimony was not provided for in the original RPE. Notwithstanding, a Trial Chamber permitted hearing a defence witness by means of videolink from Banja Luka to The Hague, finding that it would infringe the rights of the accused to a lesser degree than a deposition, which was at that time foreseen in Rule 71.[80] Not long thereafter, the Rules were amended in this regard.[81] The introduction of video testimony was not, however, a revolutionary step. In national jurisdictions, in particular in the UK and Germany, videolink testimony at trial has been permitted for some time.[82] It is used mainly for child witnesses or other especially sensitive persons.[83] Videolinked interviews can therefore be seen as a generally accepted means to alleviate the situation of the witness,[84] and have thus been provided for in Articles 68(2) and 69 (2) ICC Statute and ICC Rule 87(3).

The presentation of evidence by deposition is more critical from the perspective of the rights of the accused, as the witness is neither present nor can he be questioned as if he were present. The accused therefore cannot confront the witness during the trial. Several problems with deposition will be discussed below (3.1.4).

3. Rules 69 and 75 give the judges the possibility to order witness anonymity. The witness's identity can be withheld from either the accused (Rule 69) or from the

---

77. A similar institution is foreseen at the ICC by virtue of Art. 43(6) ICC Statute.

78. Trial Chamber II has therefore summoned a journalist to give live evidence on one of his articles, see *Prosecutor* v. *Brdjanin and Talić*, IT-99-36-T, 7 June 2002, T. Ch. II.

79. The model practiced in Germany at the Regional Court (Landgericht) Mainz, 49 *Neue Juristische Wochenschrift* (1996) p. 208, critically reviewed by H. Dahs, 'Die gespaltener Hauptverhandlung', 49 *Neue Juristische Wochenschrift* (1996) p. 178, would probably be incompatible with the adversarial structure of the ICTY. The Judge interviewed the child witnesses in a different room. While this interrogation was transferred to the courtroom where Prosecutor, defence counsel and accused could watch, they were not in a position to take part in the questioning itself.

80. Cf., *Prosecutor* v. *Tadić*, IT-94-1-T, 25 June 1996, T. Ch. I.

81. First in Rule 90(A) and now in Rule 71*bis*, which is systematically the correct placement, next to the Depositions in Rule 71.

82. The different models are described by C. Keiser, *Das Kindeswohl im Strafverfahren* (Frankfurt, Lang 1998) pp. 352-367. Interrogations by video have also been discussed by the US Supreme Court in *Maryland* v. *Craig* 497 U.S. 836 (1990); a violation of the rights of the accused could not be found.

83. The practice deals mostly with child victims of sexual abuse.

84. Cf., F. Streng, 'Überfordern Sexualstraftaten das Strafrechtssystem?', in J. Schulz and Th. Vormbaum, eds., *Festschrift für Günter Bemmann* (Baden-Baden, Nomos 1997) pp. 443 at 448.

public (Rule 75). The difficulties as concerns the rights of the accused lie in the fact that the accused cannot question the witness properly if he does not know his identity. The identity of the witness is necessary data to develop a defence strategy. Requests for witness anonymity were put forward by the Prosecutor at the very beginning of the trial work at the ICTY.[85] The Trial Chamber struggled to find a just balance between the protection of the witness and the accused's right to fairness.[86] It has developed a number of criteria by which the necessity of withholding the identity will be evaluated (see below 3.3).

4. Lastly, Rule 96 establishes special protection for victims of rape or sexual violence when testifying at trial.[87] This special rule was warranted by the nature of the Yugoslav conflict and the allegations of systematic and mass rape of women.[88] The protection aims at reducing the effects of secondary victimisation.[89] Victims of sexual assault are particularly vulnerable, when they run the risk of being victimised a second time by testifying in court.[90] It is therefore prohibited to defend oneself against the allegation of sexual assault by presenting evidence of the prior sexual conduct of the victim (Rule 96(4)). Furthermore, consent is not admitted as a defence if the victim had been in a situation of duress. In any case, the offender has to convince the Judges *in camera* that his evidence for the victim's consent is relevant and credible (Rule 96(3)). In addition, no corroboration of the victim's testimony is needed (Rule 96(1)). As can be seen, the rule entails only regulations as regards the presentation of evidence. The protection of victims is an indirect one as it functions by limiting the right to cross-examination.[91] Consequently the victim can expect to be treated with more respect during examination in court.[92]

These four ways to protect witnesses can be ranked on a progressive scale: (1) is the normal protection scheme and produces not much difficulty with the rights of the accused. (2) causes difficulties with the right to a fair trial, in particular if the witness is not present and cannot be questioned and observed. (3) poses a great risk to the prospects of a defence. (4) is a special case, which makes the defence harder but not impossible. As (2) and (3) have the severest consequences on the fairness

---

85. The first was entered in the *Tadić* case on 18 May 1995.

86. *Prosecutor* v. *Tadić*, *supra* n. 71.

87. As to the functioning of Rule 96 see P.V. Sellers, 'Rule 89 (C) and (D): At Odds or Overlapping with Rule 96 and Rule 95?', in R. May et al., eds., *Essays on ICTY Procedure and Evidence in honour of Gabrielle Kirk McDonald* (The Hague, Kluwer Law International 2001) pp. 275 at 279-288.

88. Cf., *Prosecutor* v. *Delalić et al.*, IT-96-21-T, 5 June 1997, T. Ch. I. paras. 43-48.

89. R.W.D. Jones, *The Practice of the International Criminal Tribunal for the former Yugoslavia and for Rwanda* (Ardsley NY, Transnational 2000) 2nd edn., p. 429.

90. *Prosecutor* v. *Tadić*, *supra* n. 71, para. 46.

91. C.J.M. Safferling, 'Das Opfer völkerrechtlicher Verbrechen', 115 *Zeitschrift für die gesamten Strafrechtswissenschaften* (2003) pp. 352-384; see also A. Orie, 'Accusatorial v. Inquisitorial Approach in International Criminal Proceedings', in Cassese et al., op. cit. n. 20, pp. 1439 at 1472.

92. The comparable set of Rules at the ICC (Rules 63 (III), 70-72) is a little more restrictive than Rule 96 at the ICTY; D. K. Piragoff has tried to show, however, that they only differ in structure, in 'Procedural Justice Related to Crimes of Sexual Violence', in Fischer et al., op. cit. n. 19, pp. 385 at 389.

of the trial, a more detailed examination will be made of them in the following part.

3.1.3 *Protection of present witness*

3.1.3.1 Granting anonymity

The Office of the Prosecutor has made quite excessive use of the possibility to request anonymity for witnesses, which is laid down in Rule 69. According to Rule 69(A), the identity of a witness who may be in danger or at risk can be withheld in exceptional circumstances until he is brought under the protection of the Tribunal. After that, Rule 75 is applicable. The interplay between these two Rules is as follows: Rule 69 pertains to the pre-trial phase (phase one). It ends with the disclosure of the identity to the defence according to Rule 69(C). Disclosure, however, is limited by Rule 75 (phase two).

In Rule 75(B) the Chamber is given the power to exclude the public from trial,[93] i.e., to hold an *in camera* process.[94] If the identity of a witness should be withheld from the accused and the defence counsel, the Trial Chamber could order this by virtue of Rule 75(A), that is, if the need to ensure privacy and protection of the witness overrides the right of the accused.[95] This two-phase mechanism of the RPE is not always clear when reading the ICTY decisions.

The ICTY has developed the following criteria to evaluate the need to withhold the identity of the witness according to Rule 75(A):[96] (a) There must be real fear for the safety of the witness. The ruthless character of the crime would justify such fears; (b) the Prosecutor must establish the importance of the witness for her case; (c) the witness must be absolutely trustworthy and no evidence to the contrary should be available; (d) the ICTY's own protection scheme must be insufficient to protect the victim. As to the conduct of the trial – this could be seen as phase three – three further criteria are established: (e) the judge must know the identity of the

---

93. A possible infringement of the right to a public trial (Art. 14 (1)(2) ICCPR, Art. 6(1)(1) ECHR) is justified by explicit exceptions in the human rights treaties; cf., Safferling, op. cit. n. 12, at pp. 230-237.

94. The wording of Rule 75 (B) was modified at the 5th Plenary Session in January 1995. The term *ex parte* hearing was substituted by the term *in camera* in order to make clear that only the public is excluded from the trial. The accused and his defence counsel are certainly present; cf., Jones, op. cit. n. 89, at p. 384.

95. In the decision *Prosecutor* v. *Tadić, supra* n. 71, T. Ch. II, Judge Stephen delivered a separate opinion in which he ruled out the possibility that witness protection could necessitate anonymity during trial. The rights of the accused must prevail; see Kreß, loc. cit. n. 68, pp. 309 at 373-374. Trial Chamber I agreed with Judge Stephen in *Prosecutor* v. *Tihomir Blaškić*, Decision on the application of the prosecutor dated 17 October 1996 requesting protective measures for victims and witnesses, 5 November 1996, in principle, but then accepted the checking list put forward by the majority; see Jones, op. cit. n. 89, pp. 386 et seq.

96. *Prosecutor* v. *Tadić, supra* n. 71; these criteria have been accepted by *Prosecutor* v. *Blaškić*, ibid. Legal scholars have argued extensively about this issue, cf., M. Leigh, 'The Yugoslav Tribunal: Use of Unnamed Witnesses against Accused', 90 *AJIL* (1996) p. 216; C. Chinkin, 'Due Process and Witness Anonymity', 91 *AJIL* (1997) p. 74; M. Leigh, 'Witness Anonymity is Inconsistent with Due Process', 91 *AJIL* (1997) p. 80.

witness, (f) the judge must be able to observe the demeanour of the witness to assess his reliability, and (g) the defence must be in a position to question the witness on issues that are unlikely to reveal his identity.

The Prosecutor openly attempted to lower the threshold for witness anonymity. She has tried to argue, for example, that the volatile overall situation on the territory of the former Yugoslavia constituted *per se* 'exceptional circumstances' as required by Rule 69.[97] The Trial Chambers, however, have always been very cautious to emphasise the truly exceptional character of the measure, which requires a case-to-case evaluation of the situation.[98] The aim of the Prosecutor is clear: she wants to offer the best protection possible to fearful victims and witnesses. To establish an efficient and effective prosecution is undeniably one aim of the ICTY procedure. However, it is certainly not the only goal of international prosecution. Its main rationale is to establish a procedure in which the accused stands a fair chance to defend himself and is treated throughout the entire proceedings as a subject of the trial. Article 21 ICTY Statute incorporates two human rights provisions which are of relevance here: the defendant must be given sufficient time and facilities to prepare his defence (Art. 21(14)(b) ICTY Statute) and must have the right to scrutinise the testimony of the witness (Art. 2(4)(e) ICTY Statute). Both of these rights are endangered if the identity of the witness is withheld from the defence entirely or until shortly before the beginning of the trial.

There is another aspect to this, if one reads between the lines.[99] Trial Chamber II expressed concern that there was a tendency towards secrecy of the proceedings, which it intended to halt. The principle of a public trial (Art. 20(4) ICTY Statute), embodied as a human right in Article 14(1) ICCPR or Article 6(1) ECHR, is the issue here. The underlying reason for this democratic provision is twofold. First, it is formulated as a positive right for the accused so that the trial is supervised by the public. Secondly, it is meant to be an institutional guarantee for the public to be able to follow criminal proceedings and prevent arbitrary action on the part of the courts;[100] thirdly, the aims and purposes of any criminal law system can only be achieved if communication between the court and the public takes place.[101] The exact interpretation of the law at the ICTY lies in a just balance between those positions.[102]

---

97. See e.g., *Prosecutor* v. *Brdanin and Talić*, Decision on Motion by Prosecution for Protective Measures, IT-99-36-PT, 3 July 2000, T. Ch. II, para. 8.

98. Ibid., para. 11; *Prosecutor* v. *Furundžija*, IT-95-17/1, 11 June 1998, paras. 7, 8.

99. *Prosecutor* v. *Brdanin and Talić*, *supra* n. 95, T. Ch. II.

100. Cf., M. J. Bossuyt, *Guide to the* 'Travaux Préparatoires' *of the International Covenant on Civil and Political Rights* (Dordrecht, Nijhoff 1987) p. 284; J.E.S. Fawcett, *The Application of the European Convention on Human Rights* (Oxford, Oxford University Press 1987) 2nd edn., p. 161.

101. See for example, K. Ambos and H. Steiner, 'Vom Sinn des Strafens auf innerstaatlicher und supranationaler Ebene', *Juristische Schulung* (2001) p. 9; C. Safferling, 'The Justification of Punishment in International Criminal Law', 4 *Austrian Rev. Int. & Eur. L* (1999) p. 124; Ch. Möller, *Völkerstrafrecht und Internationaler Strafgerichtshof – kriminologische, straftheoretische und rechtspolitische Aspekte* (Münster, Lit 2003) pp. 416 et seq.

102. See ECourtHR, *Doorson* v. *The Netherlands*, *supra* n. 74; also *Visser* v. *The Netherlands*, Appl. No. 26668/95, 4 April 2002, paras. 48-52.

Witness anonymity according to Rule 69 is not too problematic; as long as the defence learns of the identity of the witness at a stage where there is still enough time to prepare for a proper defence, the rights of the accused are observed.[103] To withhold the identity from the public by virtue of Rule 75(B) is not detrimental to the right of the accused either, as long as the defence lawyers can properly investigate, which usually includes the help of third persons.[104] Granting anonymity during trial by virtue of Rule 75 (A), however, can only be the last resort. The Chamber may order non-disclosure only if it is convinced that no other method would protect the witness effectively. In weighing such evidence, the Chamber should insist on corroboration, or otherwise follow the maxim of *unus testis nullus testis.*[105]

The law of the ICC does not foresee a clear scheme for granting anonymity during trial. Rule 87(3) of its RPE accepts the use of pseudonyms, *in camera* proceedings and non-disclosure to third parties, but the wording (*'inter alia'*) indicates that the list is not exhaustive. Inevitably, the problem of anonymity during trial will sooner or later crop up at the ICC.[106]

3.1.3.2   Other means of protection

Other means of protection are far less contested. The possibility of a video-conference (Rule 75(B)(iii)) has been discussed above. One remarkable and apparently frequently used means is the interception of the questioning by the judges. The control power of the Chamber has been laid down in Rule 75(D). It is remarkable because common law judges do not like the idea of intervening in the examination by the parties.[107] In the continental system, on the other hand, the judge is in total control of the questioning.[108] Rule 75(D) is therefore one obvious sign that the ICTY procedure is moving towards a truly mixed system. The ICC has a similar provision in its Rule 140(2)(c).

3.1.4   *Non-present witness*

The reasons why a witness is not present can vary widely. A problem that is well known to all legal systems is that of a witness who dies before his testimony is required at trial but who has been interviewed by an investigator.[109] The general

---

103. There is no explicit time limit in the RPE; however, disclosure must take place before commencement of trial and not before the witness gives evidence, see *Prosecutor v. Brdjanin and Talić, supra* n. 78, para. 38, accepting 30 days as being sufficient for the proper preparation for the accused.

104. R.W.D. Jones, 'Protection of Victims and Witnesses', in Cassese et al., op. cit. n. 20, pp. 1355 at 1363.

105. See Zappalà, op. cit. n. 60, p. 132.

106. Jones, loc. cit. n. 104, pp. 1355 at 1366.

107. Cf., Kreß, loc. cit. n. 68, pp. 309 at 346-348.

108. See e.g., Art. 332 French CPP and § 238 German CPP.

109. In the first ICTY case in this regard, the dead witness was a defence witness who had been interviewed under oath by the Prosecutor, see *Prosecutor v. Blaškić,* IT-95-14-T, 29 April 1998, T. Ch. I.

rule of live in-court statements prevails.[110] However, ICTY law has been modified and amended several times to enable the introduction into evidence of written affidavits in certain circumstances. From December 1998 to December 2000, Rule 94*ter* foresaw the submission of affidavit evidence. Several safeguards were established: an affidavit was only permissible to corroborate evidence given by a present witness and only if it was laid down in strict accordance with the law of the state in which such document was signed. The opposing party could object to the use of the written statement and insist on a live, in-court examination. Obviously this regulation does not pertain to affidavits of deceased witnesses. The judges therefore had to rely on the general norm concerning admissible evidence in Rule 89. The test that needed to be applied was (1) whether the statement of the deceased had probative value (Rule 89(C)), and (2) whether it was not substantially outweighed by the need to ensure a fair trial (Rule 89(D)).[111] After difficulties arose and the Appeals Chamber had to intervene,[112] and driven also by the need to expedite the proceedings, the judges decided to generally revise the concept of written statements and created a catch all provision in Rule 92*bis*.[113] This provision – to be considered as *lex specialis* to Rule 89[114] – pertains to written statements, which go to proof of a matter other than the acts and conduct of the accused as charged in the indictment (Rule 92*bis*(A)). In subparagraphs (i) and (ii), the judges laid down circumstances that would either tend to favour or go against the admission of the evidence respectively. Usually it will be admissible if it serves as corroborative evidence or contains background information. Rule 92*bis*(B) establishes certain procedural requirements and demands a formal declaration of the person giving the written statement.[115] Rule 92*bis*(C) allows for a written statement, even if it is not in the form prescribed by paragraph (B). Such statement may be admissible if made by a person who has subsequently died, or by a person who can no longer with reasonable diligence be traced, or by a person who is by reason of bodily or mental condition unable to testify orally, if the Trial Chamber (i) is so satisfied on a balance of probabilities; and (ii) finds from the circumstances in which the statement was made and recorded that there are satisfactory indicia of its reliability. Rule 92*bis*(E) establishes the procedure: the submission of the written statement must be declared two weeks in advance and the opposing party has seven days to object. In that case, the Chamber will decide whether or not the witness is to be called for cross-examination. In contrast to the previous norm, the defence counsel cannot not demand a confrontation with the witness if the Trial Chamber decides otherwise.

---

110. Cf., e.g., *Prosecutor* v. *Naletilić and Martinović*, IT-98-34-T, 14 November 2001, T. Ch. I.
111. Cf., *Prosecutor* v. *Kordić and Cerkez*, IT-95-14/2-AR73.5, 21 July 2000, A. Ch.
112. Ibid., and *Prosecutor* v. *Naletilić and Martinović*, *supra* n. 52.
113. See 8th Annual Report of the ICTY, UN Doc. A/56/352 – S/2001/865 para. 51.
114. Cf., *Prosecutor* v. *Naletilić and Martinović*, *supra* n. 52.
115. The procedural requirements are further elaborated in the Practice Direction on Procedure for Implementation of Rule 92*bis*(B) of the Rules of Procedure and Evidence (the Presiding Officer), 20 July 2001, IT/192.

Trial Chamber I has given a rather narrow interpretation of Rule 92*bis*. Written statements of deceased witnesses can only be admitted as evidence if they go to prove matters other than the acts and conduct of the accused as charged in the indictment.[116] Paragraph (C) relieves only the formal declaration required by Paragraph (B).[117] But what are indicted acts and conduct of the accused? Trial Chamber I seemed to follow a rather formal approach. It asked whether the statement of the witness pertained to any count of the indictment. If it did, the statement should not be admitted.[118] Trial Chamber III elaborated further on this question. 'Acts and conduct' ought to be given its ordinary meaning.[119] Acts and conduct of other persons, like alleged co-perpetrators or subordinates, are not mentioned in the rule and therefore fall outside its scope of application.[120] The Appeals Chamber brought together the formal approach of Trial Chamber I and the requirements for individual responsibility of Article 7(1)-(3).[121] Trial Chamber III considered further that even if the requirements of Rule 92*bis* are formally fulfilled it still has discretion in deciding whether or not to admit the evidence.[122] This discretion is influenced by factors such as the cumulative nature of the evidence, which would favour its admissibility, or the importance of the issue between the parties,[123] which would require the attendance of the witness for cross-examination to fully test the Prosecutor's case. Likewise, concerns about the reliability of the evidence or any hearsay would speak for excluding the evidence.[124] The Appeals Chamber added another important case: it may well be that the written evidence pertains to a person other than the accused (and would therefore be permissible), but relates so closely to acts and conduct of the accused that it must be excluded. This could be the case, for example, when a charge of command responsibility (Art. 7(3) Statute ICTY) is at stake, where the conduct of subordinates could have prejudicial effect on the question whether the accused fulfils the subjective elements required by the norm.[125]

---

116. Cf., *Prosecutor* v. *Naletilić and Martinović, supra* n. 50; likewise *Prosecutor* v. *Galić*, IT-98-29-T, 2 August 2002, T. Ch. I. This reading of the norm was accepted by the Appeals Chamber in *Prosecutor* v. *Galić*, IT-98-29-AR73.2, 7 June 2002, App. Ch.; Zappalà, op. cit. n. 60, p. 138, welcomes this restriction.

117. *Prosecutor* v. *Galić*, ibid., paras. 24, 25.

118. *Prosecutor* v. *Naletilić and Martinović, supra* n. 52.

119. *Prosecutor* v. *Slobodan Milošević*, IT-02-54-T, 21 March 2002, T. Ch. III.

120. The Appeals Chamber follows this interpretation; *Prosecutor* v. *Galić, supra* n. 116.

121. The Appeals Chamber set up a list of acts and conduct accordingly, see *Prosecutor* v. *Galić*, ibid., paras. 9, 10.

122. *Prosecutor* v. *Slobodan Milošević, supra* n. 119.

123. *Prosecutor* v. *Galić, supra* n. 116, para. 15.

124. E.g., if the accused fears that the investigator who took the deposition influenced the witness, *Prosecutor* v. *Brdjanin and Talić*, IT-99-36-PT, 18 January 2002, T. Ch. 2.

125. *Prosecutor* v. *Galić, supra* n. 116, paras. 11-15, 19. The requirements of command responsibility have been discussed for the first time in international criminal law since the Nuremberg trials in *Prosecutor* v. *Delalić, Mucić, Delić, Landžo*, IT-96-21-T, 16 November 1998, T. Ch. II.; for a detailed analysis see K. Ambos, *Der Allgemeine Teil des Völkerstrafrechts* (Berlin, Duncker & Humblot 2002) pp. 284-292.

There is human rights case law on this point in the ECourtHR. The Court measures the proceedings as a whole against the human rights provisions of Article 6 ECHR. Written documents do not necessarily need to be excluded as a strict matter of principle. If the document only serves to present general background information or to corroborate other direct or indirect evidence, it could well be admitted.[126] Nevertheless, a verdict of guilt cannot be based on these written documents alone.[127] Because at the ICTY the verdict is handed down by professional judges and not by lay jurors, it can be expected that this sort of document will be accorded the value it deserves.[128] The wording of Rule 92*bis*(C) has its flaws when compared to the human rights provisions established by the ECourtHR. The reading of the Trial Chamber seems to conform to human rights requirements. If only evidence which goes to proof of a matter other than the acts and conduct of the accused is admissible, the admissibility concept of the ICTY is even more restrictive than that established by Article 6 ECHR. This development is to be welcomed and should be adopted in relation to Rule 68 ICC RPE and Article 69(2) ICC Statute.

3.2   Evidence before the Court

In contrast to national accusatorial systems, the ICTY has no strict rules of evidence. Moreover, the Chambers are not bound by any national rules of evidence (Rule 89(A)). Evidence rules are considered to be unnecessary at the ICTY because the trial operates without a jury.[129] The 'gatekeeper-function' of the judge is abandoned and the judicial input in a trial switches from admissibility to weight.[130] Therefore hearsay evidence, which is usually inadmissible, can be heard as the professional judges are in a position to give it the weight it deserves.[131] The matter of evidence is important for the interaction between Prosecutor and defence. Do the two parties have the same chance to produce evidence on their behalf and renounce evidence of the counterpart? Is the principle of equality of arms being observed? The following part addresses issues of disclosure (1.) and exculpatory

---

126. See for example, ECourtHR, *Isgrò* v. *Italy,* Series A 194-A para. 34, dealing with an earlier witness who had vanished.

127. See for example, ECourtHR, *Unterpertinger v. Austria,* Series A 110, para. 33; the Austrian Court based the conviction on a statement made to the police during investigation by the then-wife of the accused, who did not testify at trial; also *Saïdi* v. *France,* Series A 261-C para. 44, where a drug dealer was convicted only because he was identified by several persons whom he never had the chance of confronting during trial. More recently *Doorson* v. *The Netherlands, supra* n. 74, para. 76, also a drug dealer case. For a discussion of the Strasbourg case law from a German lawyer's perspective see Beulke, 'Konfrontation und Strafprozessreform', in E.-W. Hanack, H. Hilger, V. Mehle and G. Widmaier, eds., *Festschrift für Peter Riess* (Berlin, De Gruyter 2002) p. 3.

128. See for further discussion of this Safferling, op. cit. n. 12, pp. 283 et seq.

129. Orie, loc. cit. n. 91, pp. 1439 at 1485.

130. See I. Bryan and P. Rowe, 'The Role of Evidence in War Crimes Trials: The Common Law and the Yugoslav Tribunal', 2 *YIHL* (1999) p. 13; G. Boas, 'Admissibility of Evidence under the Rules of Procedure and Evidence of the ICTY: Development of the "Flexibility Principle"', in May et al., op. cit. n. 87, pp. 263 at 271.

131. Zappalà, op. cit. n. 60, pp. 133-135, with reference to the ICTY case-law concerning hearsay. See also A. Rodrigues and C. Tournaye, 'Hearsay Evidence', in May et al., op. cit. n. 87, p. 291.

evidence (2.). Finally, it takes a quick look at admission of evidence and human rights violations (3.).

3.2.1   *Disclosure of evidence*

The hassle about disclosure of evidence is something that a civil law jurist has difficulties understanding. In a civil law jurisdiction, the defence is granted access to the entire dossier of the investigation prior to trial.[132] The differences stem from the fact that in common law, the parties, that is, the Prosecutor and defence, are called to investigate. The court is only there to assist the parties in providing for coercive measures should that be necessary. Difficulties in balancing the rights of two equal parties are mirrored in the excessive energy that is needed in forming a just system of reciprocal disclosure to prohibit a trial by ambush.[133] Civil law criminal procedure is based on an official Prosecutor who investigates in an objective way collecting both incriminating and exonerating evidence.[134] The results of the investigation are collected in one 'dossier' which is made available to the defence. The defence need not disclose any additional material it wants to use for trial. The ICTY has adopted the disclosure system similar to the common law tradition. In Rule 66(A), the Prosecutor is obliged to make available to the defence copies of the material which supported the indictment and of prior statements of the accused.[135] Before the commencement of the trial, the Prosecutor also needs to hand over copies of statements of witnesses that the Prosecutor intends to call at trial. The exchange of further material according to Rule 66(B) is dependent on a request by the defence and triggers reciprocal disclosure of additional material by the defence by virtue of Rule 67(C).[136] The disclosure is in any case limited to evidence which is material to the preparation of the defence.

These Rules have produced a fair amount of case law. The term 'all prior statements' in Rule 66(A)(i) was interpreted with reference to Rule 16(a)(1)(A) of the US Federal Rules of Criminal Procedure, which served as a model for Rule 66.[137] The Trial Chamber at first broadened the scope of application as it held that all previous statements by the accused which appear in the Prosecutor's file must be disclosed irrespective of whether they were collected by the Prosecutor or by any other source. This wide interpretation, which was certainly positive for the rights of the accused, was later restricted when the Chamber decided that Rule 66(A) was subject to Rules 66(C) and 70(A).[138] The Prosecutor was thereby given a means to

---

132. Tochilovsky, loc. cit. n. 58, pp. 627 at 640.

133. Cf., Orie, loc. cit. n. 91, pp. 1439 at 1449.

134. At the ICC: Art. 54 (1)(a) Statute.

135. The provision was even more restrictive before and modified to enhance the rights of the accused at the 5th Plenary Session; 2nd Annual Report of the ICTY, UN Doc. A/50/365 – S/1955/728, para. 25.

136. Tochilvsky opines that this is the reason why the defence counsel is often reluctant to request disclosure according to Rule 66(B); see loc. cit. n. 58, pp. 627 at 641.

137. See *Prosecutor* v. *Blaškić*, IT-95-14, 27 January 1997, T. Ch. 1., paras. 35-38.

138. Rule 66 (C) was inserted at the 5th Plenary Session; 2nd Annual Report of the ICTY, UN Doc. A/50/365 – S/1955/728, para. 22; until November 1999 Rule 66 (B) referred to (C) expressly; see

reduce her obligation to disclose. The accused's own statements, which are the issue here, are highly important for the preparation of the defence. Indeed, the records of the accused are the very basis any defence must be built on. The restriction is therefore highly regrettable and unnecessary. How can security interests be affected if personal statements are handed out to the person who allegedly made them?

In another case, the defence tried to receive from the Prosecutor material pertaining to witnesses who testified against his client at a different trial by virtue of Rule 66(A)(ii).[139] The intention of the defence counsel was understandable. He wanted to observe the utterances of a witness after he testified against his client in order to get a better picture concerning the credibility and reliability of that witness.[140] The probative value of the evidence given by a witness who shows differences in his testimonies during different trials is of course reduced. The reason why the defence wanted the Prosecutor to hand over the material is a practical one: the defence cannot afford to follow all witness presentations at all trials. It would be much less of an organizational problem for the Prosecutor to do this, as representatives of her Office are present at every trial. Nevertheless, the Chamber held that those witnesses were no longer persons the Prosecutor 'intends to call' to testify within the meaning of Rule 66(A), and rejected the defendant's claim on this formal basis. This decision is quite unfriendly towards the defence. In particular with a view to the inequalities described above, it should be abandoned and the Prosecutor obliged to produce the trial transcripts.

Non-disclosure is further regulated in Rule 70. According to Rule 70(A), internal documents do not need to be disclosed.[141] Rule 70(B) deals with confidential information on the basis of which new evidence was found. The confidentiality stretches to the initial information only. Trial Chamber II has rightly stressed that the new evidence that could be collected on the ground of the confidential information itself must be handled in compliance with the obligations to disclose contained in Rules 66 and 67.[142] The norm, which was designed basically to grant to the Prosecutor the necessary means to shield confidential background information,[143] is under the overall control of the judges. By virtue of Rule 70(G), the Trial Chamber can still exclude any evidence if it sees the principle of a fair trial being tampered with (Rule 89(D)).

The complex system of disclosure seems to be counterproductive as concerns the need to expedite proceedings. But also because of the wide gap between the investigative means of the prosecution and those of the defence, it would be preferable if one would adopt a procedure wherein the Prosecutor presents the entire

---

Jones, op. cit. n. 89, at p. 336; As the rule reads now, systematically para. (C) operates as an exception to paras. (A) and (B).

139. See *Prosecutor* v. *Blaškić*, IT-95-14/2-AR73.6, 18 September 2000, App. Ch.

140. Trial Chamber II accepted in *Prosecutor* v. *Furundžija*, IT-95-17/1-T, T. Ch. II, 16 July 1998, the importance of evidence that affects the credibility of the witness for the defence under Rule 68; reported in *Prosecutor* v. *Furundžija*, IT-95-17/1-T, T. Ch. II, 10 December 1998, paras 18-22.

141. See *Prosecutor* v. *Blaškić*, IT-85-14-T, 27 January 1997, T. Ch. I.

142. See *Prosecutor* v. *Brdjanin and Talić*, IT-99-36-T, 23 May 2002, T. Ch. II.

143. Cf., Jones, op. cit. n. 89, p. 350.

package of evidence (dossier) to the defence team.[144] The ICC system, however, adheres to the disclosure system and has set up a whole set of rules to regulate it, in Rules 76-84 RPE ICC. The parties are well advised to adopt a practice that is not bureaucratic in order to achieve equality between the parties. However, in interpreting rules of disclosure one always has to keep in mind that structurally the defence is in a worse situation compared to the prosecution as concerns investigating powers and knowledge. This drawback needs to be equalised by information.[145]

3.2.2   Exculpatory evidence

The Prosecutor is obliged by virtue of Rule 68 to hand over exculpatory evidence to the defence team.[146] This provision is quite surprising to a common lawyer but absolutely standard for continental criminal prosecution.[147] The Prosecutor at the ICTY is supposed to be an objective organ of the Tribunal and her main objective is to assist the Chamber to discover the truth.[148] Rule 68 translates this to the relationship between the Prosecutor and the defence team. The duty to indicate the existence of exonerating evidence is not avoided by Rule 70(B) to (E).[149] The Prosecutor must disclose to the defence 'the existence of material known to the Prosecutor which in any way tends to suggest the innocence or mitigate the guilt of the accused or may affect the credibility of prosecution evidence'.[150] The question the Appeals Chamber had to deal with was whether Rule 68 is also applicable at the appeals stage.[151] If the defence counsel is viewed as the general contact person of the offender, the Prosecutor's obligation stretches even further until the end of the sentencing procedure. One might argue whether this obligation is rooted in Rule 68 or in the general principle of objectivity of the Office of the Prosecutor. However, as Rule 68 is without doubt an expression of this principle, the norm can and should be read in the widest sense possible as concerning the time question. On the basis of an extensive discussion, the Appeals Chamber came to the conclusion that the Prosecutor is 'under a continuing obligation under Rule 68 to disclose exculpatory evidence at the post-trial stage, including appeals'.[152]

---

144. See Mundis, loc. cit. n. 51, at pp. 378 at 380.

145. Similarly the jurisdiction of the German Bundesgerichtshof as concerns the principle of 'equality of arms', see e.g., 36 *BGHSt* p. 305.

146. Cf., Mundis, loc. cit. n. 51, p. 378; Mundis stresses that according to the existing law at the ICTY the Prosecutor is not obliged to point exculpatory evidence out to the Judges. However, the more the ICTY procedure moves towards civil law practice the more the Prosecutor must fulfil her role in a purely objective manner.

147. For a detailed comparison see Safferling, op. cit n. 12, pp. 64 et seq.

148. ICTY, Decision on Communication between the Parties and their Witnesses, *Prosecutor* v. *Kupreškić, Kupreškić, Kupreškić, Josipović, Papić and Šantić*, IT-95-16-T, T. Ch. I, 21 September 1998.

149. *Prosecutor* v. *Brdjanin and Talić*, IT-99-36-T, 23 May 2002, T. Ch. II.

150. See *Prosecutor* v. *Blaškić*, IT-95-14-T, 22 April 1999, T. Ch. I; relied on by Trial Chamber 2 in: *Prosecutor* v. *Brdjanin and Talić*, *supra* n. 140.

151. *Prosecutor* v. *Blaškić*, IT-95-14-A, 26 September 2000, App. Ch.

152. Ibid., para. 42.

Another question is how the exculpatory evidence must be presented by the Prosecutor. The Prosecutor tried to avoid handing over copies of the original documents or of parts of them and presented to the defence summaries instead. As a new attempt of the Prosecutor to make life for the defence counsel more complicated, the plea was rejected and it was found that the disclosure of the exculpatory material implies disclosure in the original form and not in the form of a summary.[153]

The duty of the Prosecutor to disclose exculpatory evidence is of immense importance to the defendant. The methods and means of the Office of the Prosecutor to investigate the case and to collect evidence are far-reaching and advanced compared to those available to defence counsel and his team. It is impossible to treat the Prosecutor, with her entire office, SFOR and cooperating police forces worldwide[154] and the accused as equal parties in the international context. The principle of equality of arms, which applies here,[155] warrants an adjustment, to compensate for the disadvantage that the defence team has in collecting evidence.

3.2.3   *Exclusionary rule*

Exclusion of evidence is regulated by Rule 89(C). This general rule gives to the Chambers the power to admit any evidence which it deems to have probative value. According to Rule 89(D), it may exclude evidence if there is danger that it will produce unfairness. Rule 92*bis*, which also pertains to the admissibility of evidence and establishes a special regulation, and therefore serves as *lex specialis* in this regard, has already been discussed.[156] On the basis of Rule 89(D), the question of admissibility is to be judged only by balancing the probative value and the fair trial principle. Questions as to the authenticity or reliability of the evidence are irrelevant at that stage.[157] These questions are significant for the final judgement, i. e., when deliberating whether the guilt of the accused has been proven beyond a reasonable doubt (Rule 87(A)(2)). Nevertheless, Trial Chamber II ruled that the submitting party could be called upon by the Chamber to provide a minimum of proof that would constitute *prima facie* indicia of reliability if the document so warrants.[158] The practice is generally in favour of admissibility as the rule.[159]

Apart from Rule 89(D), one finds another regulation governing the exclusion of evidence in Rule 95. It contains an exclusionary rule for evidence which was ob-

---

153. See *Prosecutor* v. *Brdjanin*, IT-99-36-T, 30 October 2002, para. 26.

154. States are obliged to cooperate according to Art. 29 ICTY Statute and the Chapter VII character of the Statute. In this regard, the ICTY is in a better situation than the ICC will be, where cooperation mostly depends on 'horizontal', inter-state relationships; see for a comprehensive analysis B. Swart, 'International Cooperation and Judicial Assistance', in Cassese et al., op. cit. n. 20, pp. 1589 at 1590-1598.

155. See *Prosecutor* v. *Brdjanin and Talić*, *supra* n. 149.

156. *Prosecutor* v. *Galic*, IT-98-29-AR73.2, 7 June 2002, App. Ch., para. 31.

157. See *Prosecutor* v. *Brdjanin and Talić*, IT-99-36-PT, 15 February 2002, T. Ch. II.

158. See *Prosecutor* v. *Brdjanin and Talić*, ibid., and *Prosecutor* v. *Stakić*, IT-97-24-PT, 25 February 2002, single judge (Schomburg), for the defence.

159. *Prosecutor* v. *Stakić*, ibid.

tained by methods which are contrary to international human rights standards,[160] although it does not say so explicitly. It refers only to methods of collecting evidence that cast substantial doubt on the reliability of the testimony or evidence whose admission would seriously damage the integrity of the proceedings. There is a certain gap between Rule 95 and the test of Rule 89(D) as discussed above. How would a Chamber know of the human rights violation if no information as to the reliability and authenticity needs to be presented when applying for admission? The Judges need to watch carefully and scrutinise the evidence presented intensely so that they can ask for more information if they have the slightest suspicion that human rights have been tampered with. It would be detrimental to the proper administration of justice if the general rule in favour of admission, which is the correct approach in principle, would be exercised automatically. The wording of Rule 95 is unclear and seems to leave room for discretion. Evidence achieved by improper means should be excluded, no matter how probative, according to the Tribunal's Second Annual Report.[161] This mean that the balancing test in Rule 89(D) is not applicable to Rule 95, which serves as *lex specialis* with regard to evidence obtained contrary to human rights. The Rule must be applied strictly. Human rights violations should never result in evidence at trial. The ICTY (as with the ICC[162]), as an institution that seeks to help to establish the rule of law, must itself adhere to the rule of law in the strictest sense.[163] Beyond the integrity of the proceedings, the dignity of human beings is put at risk if evidence obtained in violation of human rights is deemed admissible.[164] In the case of human rights infringements, the exclusionary rule in Rule 95 must therefore be interpreted as a mandatory one.[165]

3.3   Presence of accused: provisional release

One of the most contested issues of the procedural order at the ICTY is that of pre-trial detention. It is not surprising that in almost every case a motion has been filed requesting the provisional release of the accused. The granting of provisional release pending trial is crucial for the personal liberty of the accused. Likewise, the prosecution case depends on the presence of the alleged criminal. The jurisprudence of the Trial Chambers on this question cannot be considered to be uniform, as the judges do not seem to agree on the interpretation of the relevant norms. The following sub-section will take a closer look at the problem in general, after which the threshold requirements are addressed, in particular with regard to human rights. Finally, the guarantees given by third parties and the conditions the Chamber can impose on the provisionally released person are examined.

---

160. Rule 95 was amended several times; see Jones, op. cit. n. 89, pp. 427-428.

161. 2nd Annual Report of the ICTY, UN Doc. A/50/365 – S/1955/728, para. 26, fn. 9.

162. The exclusionary Rule is to be found in Art. 69(7) ICC Statute.

163. With regard to the ICC, see O. Lagodny, 'Legitimität und Bedeutung des Ständigen Internationalen Strafgerichtshofes', 113 *ZStW* (2001) pp. 800 at 823.

164. Safferling, op. cit n. 12, pp. 294-295.

165. See also M.C. Bassiouni and P. Manikas, *The Law of the International Criminal Tribunal for the Former Yugoslavia* (New York, Transnational 1996) p. 952.

3.3.1 *Provisional release: efficiency versus liberty*

The legal framework of pre-trial detention is given by Article 20(2) Statute and Rules 64 and 65. According to Rule 64, the accused is to be held on remand after his initial appearance at the Tribunal. Rule 65(A)-(C) states the conditions under which the accused may be released provisionally upon an order of the Trial Chamber.

The rationale of pre-trial detention is obvious: it is about safeguarding the functioning and effectiveness of the prosecution.[166] To this end, the presence of the accused at trial needs to be ensured and the reliability of evidence, both in the form of documents and in the form of witness testimony, must be upheld.[167] Finally, it must be guaranteed that the accused will not continue to break the law. In summary, pre-trial detention seeks to minimise three types of risks: the risk of escape, the danger of destruction of evidence and the risk of repetition of further offences. These efficiency criteria are countered by the right to liberty and security of the accused. This right is recognised by all major human rights treaties, including Article 9 ICCPR and Article 5 ECHR. One could paraphrase this position as the freedom from unlawful, arbitrary detention.[168]

These two positions need to be harmonised. Some guidance in achieving a proportionate balancing of these two conflicting objectives may be found in the human rights instruments. A precise rule is laid down in Article 9(3)(2) ICCPR, which provides that 'it shall not be the general rule that persons awaiting trial shall be detained in custody'. This rule-exception system[169] is clearly turned upside down by the wording of Rules 64 and 65. The Chambers justified this deviation by the spirit of the Statute (whatever this might be) and the gravity of the crimes.[170] The language modification of Rule 65 in 1999 has not changed the meaning of the norm. Before, provisional release was only allowed in 'exceptional circumstances',[171] to the effect that *in praxi* release was only granted for humanitarian purposes.[172] The amendment has led to a change of policy as release has been granted more frequently since then.[173]

---

166. Safferling, op. cit. n. 12, p. 137.

167. Cf., S. Zappalà, 'Rights of Persons during an Investigation', in Cassese et al., op. cit. n. 20, p. 1185

168. Cf., Art. 9(1)(2) ICCPR.

169. *Prosecutor* v. *Jokić*, IT-01-42-PT, 20 February 2002, para. 18 and *Prosecutor* v. *Ademi*, IT-01-42-PT, 20 February 2002, T. Ch. I, para. 19.

170. See *Prosecutor* v. *Blaškić*, IT-95-14-T, 20 December 1996, T. Ch. I.

171. Amendment of Rule 65 at the 21st Plenary Session of 15-17 November 1999, when the words 'exceptional circumstances' were deleted (IT/161); see also Zappalà, op. cit. n. 59, p. 95.

172. *Prosecutor* v. *Djukić*, IT-96-20-T, 24 April 1996, T. Ch. 1, General Djukić died before the trial commenced; cf., P. de Waart, 'From "Kidnapped" Witness to Released Accused "for Humanitarian Reasons": The Case of the Late General Djordje Djukić', 9 *Leiden JIL* (1996) p. 543; *Prosecutor* v. *Simić*, IT-95-9, 26 March 1998, T. Ch. I.

173. As to the case-law of the ICTY in this regard, see De Frank, 'ICTY Provisional Release: current Practice, a Dissenting Voice, and the Case for a Rule Change', 80 *Texas LR* (2002) pp. 1429 at 1451-1452.

The Trial Chambers have found differing answers to the question of rule-exception. Trial Chamber III (May, Robinson, Fassi Fihri) stated that provisional release continues to be the exception and not the rule.[174] Trial Chamber II (Schomburg, Mumba, Agius), in contrast, stated that detention should be the exception.[175] Maybe Trial Chamber I (Liu, Mahdi, Orie) intended to reach a compromise when it stated that the question of rule or exception could add nothing to the decision-reaching process.[176] Instead, the Chamber claimed that the relevant factors could only be found in a case-to-case evaluation. The language of Trial Chamber I is, however, misleading. Although it pretended not to decide on the rule-exception issue, it clearly treated Rule 65 as granting release only in exceptional circumstances and only if – and this seems to be the crucial point – the accused can prove that he meets the condition of Rule 65.[177] If one looks at the personal background of the judges, the discrepancy in interpretation can be traced back to the common law Judge May, presiding at Trial Chamber III and the German Judge Schomburg, presiding over Trial Chamber II. Although it is difficult to discern general tendencies, it seems that the focus in common law regarding bail is more on the exclusion of dangerous individuals,[178] whereas the German system puts the realisation of basic rights at the centre of pre-trial detention.[179] It could well be that these fundamental differences regarding such a central question arise from a generally differing approach to procedural law. The nature of international criminal law would for a common law jurist justify detention as the general rule.[180] Beyond cultural traditions, the dilemma of having to decide between efficiency of prosecution and liberty of persons can be found in any modern system of criminal prosecution.[181]

In order to answer the rule-exception question, one has to look at human rights jurisprudence in general. Human rights are often phrased as principles in the sense of the generally accepted discrimination of rights and principles as formulated by Dworkin.[182] As principles they do not entail clear orders; the legislator as the pre-

---

174. *Prosecutor* v. *Krajisnik et al.*, IT-00-39&40, 8 October 2001, T. Ch. III, para. 12. This was a 2:1 decision. Judge Robinson (Jamaica) vehemently dissented, voting in favour of a human rights based approach. An analysis of this dissent is given by De Frank, ibid., p. 1429.

175. *Prosecutor* v. *Hadzihasanović, Alagić, Kubura*, IT-01-47-PT, 19 December 2001, T. Ch. II, para. 7.

176. *Prosecutor* v. *Jokić*, para. 18 and *Prosecutor* v. *Ademi*, para. 19, both *supra* n. 169.

177. *Prosecutor* v. *Jokic*, ibid. and *Prosecutor* v. *Ademi*, ibid. The burden of proof is exactly the problematic consequence of the rule-exception mechanism; this is overlooked by T. Ch. I and De Frank, loc. cit. n. 175, pp. 1429 at 1450-1451.

178. L. Epstein and Th. G. Walker, *Constitutional Law for a Changing America: Rights, Liberties, and Justice* (Washington D.C., CQ Press 1992) pp. 412; N. Corre, *Bail in Criminal Proceedings* (London, Fourmat Publishing 1990) p. 4.

179. See e.g., L. Meyer-Goßner, *Strafprozessordnung* (Munich, C.H. Beck 2003) 46th edn., para. 112, Nos. 8-11.

180. I have tried to show that the special nature of international criminal law does not alter the legal arguments for or against pre-trial detention, Safferling, op. cit. n. 12, pp. 142-147.

181. A strong petitum for a renaissance of the principle of liberty in criminal policy has recently been issued by P.-A. Albrecht, *Die vergessene Freiheit* (Berlin, BWV 2003).

182. R. Dworkin, *Taking Rights Seriously* (London, Duckworth 1987).

constitutional addressee of human rights is called upon to incorporate the idea of the human right into his legal system. There are, however, cases in which the human rights norm does not leave room for legislative discretion. In some (rare) cases, a human right gives an unequivocal order. Article 9(3)(2) ICCPR is such a case; it contains a concrete and absolute instruction to the legislator not to foresee detention as the general rule. Albeit is difficult to find a proper dogmatic argument to establish a direct legal subordination of the ICTY to human rights treaties,[183] conformity with human rights is a corollary in cases where otherwise undue discrimination would be the effect. This is the case here, as it is often arbitrary whether a war criminal is tried by the ICTY or on the basis of the principle of universality by domestic courts.[184] Therefore, there might be a practical difference between the ICTY and domestic prosecution but not in theory.[185]

The ICTY Judges have certainly realised that Rules 64 and 65 are not in conformity with Article 9 ICCPR. Therefore, attempts have been made to water down the human rights prohibition of a mandatory pre-trial detention. To this end, Trial Chamber I has interpreted the Judgment *Ilijkov* v. *Bulgaria* of the ECourtHR[186] but has come to a different conclusion than Trial Chamber II in its interpretation of exactly this judgment. Trial Chamber I quoted the Court, which stated that '[a]ny system of mandatory detention on remand is *per se* incompatible with Article 5 (III)' ECHR[187] and 'the existence of the concrete facts outweighing the rule of respect for individual liberty must be … convincingly demonstrated',[188] but still drew the conclusion that the accused must show that he is to be provisionally released. Yet the next paragraph in the European Court's decision contains the following sentences suppressed by Trial Chamber I:

> '[m]oreover, the Court considers that it was incumbent on the authorities to establish those relevant facts. Shifting the burden of proof to the detained person in such matters is tantamount to overturning the rule of Article 5 of the Convention, a provision which

---

183. A conclusive argument has been brought forward by A. Reinisch, 'Das Jugoslawien Tribunal der Vereinten Nationen und die Verfahrensgarantien des II. VN-Menschenrechtspaktes', 47 *Austrian Journal of Public and International Law* (1995) pp. 173-213.

184. *Tadić* and *Erdemović* as rather small fish have been tried by the ICTY while *Djajić* (see C. Safferling, 'Public Prosecutor v. Djajić', 92 *AJIL* (1998) at p. 528) and *Jorgić* have been tried by German courts; the latter has been convicted for genocide: 45 *BGHSt* 64, 19 *Neue Zeitschrift für Strafrecht* (1999) p. 396; the decision was upheld by the Federal Constitutional Court, BVerfG *EuGRZ* 2001, 76; a critical analysis is given by C. Hoß and R.A. Miller, 'German Federal Constitutional Court and Bosnian War Crimes', 44 *GYIL* (2001) p. 576.

185. This against De Frank, loc. cit. n. 173, pp. 1429 at 1452-1453 and at 1460-1461. He opines that it would be 'grossly inappropriate' to equate domestic jurisdiction and the ICTY. The opposite is true. As concerns the applicability of the fair trial requirements there is no difference. An international prosecution cannot be a bit unfair just because it deals with war criminals.

186. ECourtHR *Ilijkov* v. *Bulgaria*, 26 July 2001, Appl. No. 33977/96.

187. Ibid. para. 84 with further references to the Courts case law; cf., also J. Meyer-Ladewig, *Hk-EMRK* (Baden-Baden, Nomos 2003), Art. 5, No. 36.

188. Ibid. para. 84.

makes detention an exceptional departure from the right to liberty and one that is only permissible in exhaustively enumerated and strictly defined cases.'[189]

This argument of Trial Chamber I raises several questions. First, it is unclear where the human rights standard that the Chamber applies comes from. There are no direct references to human rights norms when Rule 65 is being interpreted.[190] There is just one quote of the European Court, which is, as we have seen, incomplete. Secondly, why is the ECourtHR dealt as the sole authority in human rights law? The system of the Council of Europe is undoubtedly the best-working system of human rights protection, and indeed the ECHR and the case law of the Court may serve as an excellent tool for interpreting human rights.[191] However, the ICTY as a UN suborgan is not bound by the European system.[192] It has on the contrary to conform with the international and not purely regional human rights standard. Article 9(3) ICCPR therefore has a prominent position when Rule 65 is interpreted and cannot be simply left aside. Finally, it is astonishing that the Trial Chamber does not discuss the decisions of the other Chambers in substance, although it summarises their prior decisions.[193]

The decisions of the Trial Chambers remain highly controversial. The foregoing has tried to show that human rights law is unambiguous in holding that continued detention is always the exception and needs a special justification.[194] The circumstances under which pre-trial detention is justified are now discussed.

3.3.2   Conditions

3.3.2.1   General remarks

Rule 65(B) names two conditions that need to be met: the Trial Chamber needs to be satisfied that the accused will appear for trial and that he will not pose a danger to any victim, witness or other person if he is released. Before looking at these conditions separately, it must be stated that as a consequence of the rule-exception mechanism the burden of proof of the factual circumstances lies with the prosecution. This is not only derived from Article 9(3) ICCPR and Article 5(3) ECHR but also necessitated by the presumption of innocence in Article 14(2) ICCPR and

---

189. Ibid. para. 85.

190. *Prosecutor* v. *Ademi, supra* n. 169, paras. 18-22.

191. In this sense also Kreß, loc. cit. n. 68, pp. 309 at 369.

192. Cf., C. Safferling, 'Die EMRK und das Völkerstrafrecht', in J. Renzikowski, ed., *Die EMRK im Zivil-, Straf- und Öffentlichen Recht – Grundlagen einer Europäischen Rechtskultur* (Zürich, Schulthess 2003) forthcoming.

193. A deliberation of *Prosecutor* v. *Hadzihasanović, Alagić, Kubura, supra* n. 175, is missing, although both Chambers rely on the same decision of the ECourtHR.

194. As concerns burden of proof, De Frank seems to agree, loc. cit. n. 173, pp. 1429 at 1457-1458.

Article 6(2) ECHR.[195] This argument has been accepted by Trial Chamber II only.[196]

A second general remark on the application of Rule 65(B) is necessary. Trial Chamber I has opined that it still has discretion whether or not to grant provisional release even if the accused has been able to show that he meets the conditions spelled out in Rule 65(B).[197] The list contained in Rule 65 is not to be seen as exhaustive. Moreover the Trial Chamber 'may' deny the motion of the accused for provisional release, even if the Prosecutor does not object. Several misunderstanding can be observed here. First, human rights law clearly demands that a deprivation of liberty must adhere to both substantive and procedural law (Art. 9(1) ICCPR and Art. 5(1) ECHR). Consequently, legal requirements must be read as exhaustive, because otherwise the deprivation of liberty would not be based on grounds established by law.[198] Secondly, an implicit *d'accord* by the Prosecutor must lead to a release order by the Chamber. The party structure of the ICTY procedural system requires that the Tribunal restrict itself to the application of the facts brought before it by the parties. If the Prosecutor does not object to the evidence presented by the accused, the Chamber should not question it either.

Rule 65(B) incorporates two substantive criteria, which should be read as cumulative thresholds.[199] We now turn to look at them individually.

3.3.2.2   The presence of the accused

As previously mentioned, the rationale of pre-trial detention is to guarantee the presence of the accused at trial. If his presence can be ensured by other means, detention would not be necessary. The question is, how does the Chamber evaluate this issue? From a procedural point of view, there are two aspects. First, there is the accused himself. The Judges are confronted with a question of personal reliability and trustworthiness. Secondly, the state of residence of the indicted person is in a position to buttress the case for provisional release. The state can help to guarantee the presence of the accused by implementing several safeguards in the absence of a police force at the ICTY.[200] Procedurally, this means that these two sides must be heard.[201]

Substantially, the Chamber has to come to a prognosis as to the future behaviour of the accused. To base such a decision solely on the word of the accused,

---

195. ECHR *Ilijkov* v. *Bulgaria*, 26 July 2001, No. 33977/96, para. 84; *Letellier* v. *France*, 26 June 1991, Series A No. 207, paras. 35-53; *Clooth* v. *Belgium*, 12 December 1991, Series A No. 225, para. 44; *Muller* v. *France*, 17 March 1997, *Reports of Judgments and Decisions* 1997-II, paras. 35-45; *Jecius* v. *Lithuania*, 31 July 2000, No. 34578/97, paras. 93-94, ECHR 2000-IX.

196. *Prosecutor* v. *Hadzihasanović, Alagić, Kubura, supra* n. 175.

197. *Prosecutor* v. *Ademi, supra* n. 169, para. 22

198. Meyer-Ladewig, op. cit. n. 187.

199. This seems to be common ground. Cf., *Prosecutor* v. *Ademi, supra* n. 169, para. 21.

200. This is an important argument for the judges to interpret Rule 65 restrictively. See *Prosecutor* v. *Brdanin and Talić*, IT-99-36-PT, 25 July 2000, T. Ch. II, para. 18.

201. The necessity to question the accused before deciding has been established by the Appeals Chamber, see *Prosecutor* v. *Milutinović et al.*, IT-99-37-AR65, 30 October 2002, App. Ch.

who, after all, is an alleged war criminal, and on the statement of his state of residence does not suffice. The Chamber can expect that a person who asks to be released has already indicated his general acceptance of the competence of the Tribunal. Therefore, it is important for the Chamber's decision whether the accused has, upon a publicised indictment,[202] surrendered to The Hague voluntarily,[203] whether he cooperates substantially with the Prosecutor[204] and whether he can offer personal guarantees for his presence.[205] Having said this, it is necessary to emphasis that a lack of cooperation does not mean that release must be automatically denied. Trial Chamber I rightly pointed out[206] that such a mechanism could lead to an infringement of the right of the accused to remain silent as laid down in Article 14(3)(g) ICCPR and in Article 6 ECHR according to the ECourtHR.[207] It has also been reflected upon whether the severity of the crime and the expected long prison sentence create a presumption against the accused. But the likeliness of a lifelong prison sentence cannot as such establish the presumption that the indicted will not return for trial.[208] On this question, there is no difference to prosecution at a national level.

3.3.2.3   Influencing of evidence

The second requirement laid down in Rule 65(B) aims at securing evidence and protecting other persons who are involved in the case from the accused. As regards the latter goal, Rule 65(B) can be regarded as adequate. The mere possibility of influencing others, however, does not suffice; the Prosecutor must bring forward evidence of intimidation or specific hints of future ill behaviour.[209] The former aim of securing evidence in general is not phrased in a consistent manner. Trial Chamber I was right when it stressed that there are other ways of slanting evidence than by influencing victims and witnesses.[210] What has been forgotten is any reference to destruction of documentary evidence, effacement of traces of alleged crimes and potential conspiracy with co-accused who are at large. These dangers are real and can be reduced through pre-trial detention. Unfortunately, the law does not foresee such a condition. As the list in Rule 65(B) needs to be read as exhaustive, as was argued above, the destruction of written evidentiary material cannot be brought

---

202. On a sealed indictment the suspect can obviously not appear at the ICTY voluntarily; see *Prosecutor* v. *Brdanin and Talić, supra* n. 200; *Prosecutor* v. *Krajisnik and Plavsic*, IT-00-39&40-PT, 8 October 2001, T. Ch. III.

203. *Prosecutor* v. *Sainović and Ojdanić*, IT-99-37-PT, 26 June 2002, T. Ch. 3.

204. *Prosecutor* v. *Ademi, supra* n. 169, para. 27.

205. Ibid.

206. Ibid., para. 33.

207. See EcourtHR *Funke* v. *France*, Series A No. 256-A; *Saunders* v. *United Kingdom*, Rep. 1996-VI, 2064; *Murray* v. *United Kingdom*, 22 *EHRR* (1996) 29.

208. *Prosecutor* v. *Milutinović et al., supra* n. 201. This is also what the ECourtHR says in *Neumeister* v. *Austria* Series A No. 8, para. 10. p. 39, De Frank, loc. cit. n. 173, pp. 1429 at 1453 fn. 88 apparently misunderstood this judgment.

209. Cf., *Prosecutor* v. *Brdanin and Talić, supra* n. 200, para. 20.

210. *Prosecutor* v. *Ademi, supra* n. 169, para. 22.

forward against the motion for provisional release. The law is insufficient in this regard and should be amended.[211]

The Rome Statute of the ICC has found a better solution. According to Article 58(1)(b)(ii), detention can be ordered to ensure that the person does not obstruct or endanger the investigation of the court proceedings.[212] This wording is much more open and certainly more suitable for the rationale of pre-trial detention.

3.3.2.4   Guarantees by third parties

Safeguards offered by third parties can tip the scales for or against provisional release. As the ICTY is not equipped with a police force of its own or other coercive measures, it depends on the cooperation of entities that have these powers and can use them against the released person to ensure his presence. Such entity will usually be the state of residence of the accused. It is however not necessary that it is a state recognised by public international law. It suffices that such third party has effective control over the circumstances of the released person.[213] The safeguards offered by this third party must not be measured by an evaluation of the overall willingness of this entity to cooperate with the ICTY. There is no general assessment of the level of cooperation, but the Chamber needs to evaluate the individual case of the particular accused.[214] The assurances offered must pertain to a close monitoring of the accused in order to guarantee his presence for trial and likewise to prevent him from getting in contact with victims or witnesses.

3.3.2.5   Principle of proportionality

The checking of proportionality when scrutinising the legality of an official act is not unusual in public international law. In particular, humanitarian law requires that the applied methods and means of warfare need to be proportionate to the legitimate aim.[215] Likewise, the ECourtHR measures the legality of human rights infringements against the principle of proportionality. The principle has proven a workable means in balancing the individual's rights against possible infringements

---

211. This problem is found missing in the proposal made by De Frank, loc. cit. n. 173, pp. 1429 at 1456.

212. Cf., A. Schlunk, in O. Triffterer, eds., *Commentary on the Rome Statute* (Baden-Baden, Nomos 1999) Art. 58 No. 13.

213. *Prosecutor* v. *Blagojević and Obrenović et al.*, IT-02-60-AR65, 3 October 2002, App. Ch. The test could be found in the so-called *de facto regime* which is an accepted notion in public international law; see A. Verdross and B. Simma, *Universelles Völkerrecht* (Berlin, Duncker & Humblot 1984) 3rd edn., para. 961.

214. *Prosecutor* v. *Mrksić*, IT-95-13/1-AR65, 8 October 2002, App. Ch. In several cases, however, the Prosecutor intents to defeat the safeguards of the resident state by naming general lack of cooperation with the Office of the Prosecutor; cf., e.g., *Prosecutor* v. *Ademi*, *supra* n. 169, para. 35; *Prosecutor* v. *Brdanin and Talić*, *supra* n. 200, para. 15.

215. Cf., e.g., Art. 57(2) of the First Protocol to the Geneva Conventions; also D. Oeter, in D. Fleck, ed., *The Handbook of Humanitarian Law in Armed Conflicts* (Oxford, Oxford University Press 2000) para. 456 with further references as to the historic development and the customary law status of the principle of proportionality.

by official authorities. The principle of proportionality is a tool of constitutional law in Germany.[216] It has been explicitly applied to the question of pre-trial detention by the German Federal Constitutional Court.[217] Transferring this principle to the procedural law at the ICTY is therefore part of an international and European legal tradition. The question of pre-trial detention seems to be a suitable field of application of this principle.

Trial Chamber II, under the presidency of Judge Schomburg, has ruled that the principle of proportionality has to be observed when ruling on the question of pre-trial detention.[218] For the Chamber, the proportionality principle consists of three yardsticks: the denial of provisional release must be (1) suitable, (2) necessary and (3) its degree and scope must remain in a reasonable relationship to the envisaged target.

Other Chambers have also discussed certain issues that come within the ambit of the principle of proportionality without explicitly saying so. The question of the proximity of the trial is a good example.[219] Pre-trial detention has limits as concerns its duration. The further away the trial, the better the reasons must be for justifying the denial of provisional release.[220] The complexity of the case and the difficulties of the investigation are relevant criteria in this regard.[221]

4.   FURTHER DEVELOPMENTS

The picture of the procedural law at the ICTY which can be drawn from the examples discussed reveals a criminal court which functions in a manner that is quite comparable to national courts. At the same time, it operates as a genuine international institution with a truly mixed procedural system. The adherence of the original Statute and Rules to the Anglo-American system of criminal prosecution has not been abandoned entirely. Nevertheless, the shift towards a more inquisitorial practice is undeniable. This shift was necessary. First, the role of the judge is different from the English or American jury system. To adhere to evidence rules *à la* the US would neglect the fact that professional judges can weigh the evidence in a professional way and need not be protected from hearsay evidence, for example. Secondly, the protection of vulnerable witnesses and victims can demand a restriction on the side of the parties. A judge with inquisitorial powers can substitute for the parties' inabilities in this regard.[222] Thirdly, the role of the Prosecutor needed rethinking. The international element as well as the investigatory role require an independent and objective Prosecutor. Finally, the proceedings before the ICTY

---

216. Ibid.
217. Cf., Bundesverfasssungsgericht (German Federal Constitutional Court), 15 December 1965, in 19 *BVerfGE* (1966) pp. 342 at 348-351.
218. *Prosecutor* v. *Hadzihasanović, Alagić, Kubura, supra* n. 175, para. 7.
219. *Prosecutor* v. *Ademi, supra* n. 169, para. 22.
220. Cf., also Meyer-Ladewig, *supra* n. 187.
221. *Prosecutor* v. *Brdanin and Talić, supra* n. 200, para. 27.
222. Safferling, op. cit. n. 12, p. 75.

have turned out to be too time-consuming. The more the judge knows and the more the Prosecutor is aware of her service as an objective organ to discover the truth, the better a trial can be prepared and expedited.

Not all of these four aspects have been solved satisfactory in the practice of the ICTY. As to the general development of the law, one could ask whether it is wise for the Chambers to treat questions like provisional release as a competitive academic dispute. Is it in conformity with the rule of law when a Chamber 'feels it should set out … its view' of how to apply a norm?[223] In particular with regard to the necessity to expedite trials, it would suit the Tribunal better to aim at a concise, reliable and uniform interpretation of the Statute and Rules. The Prosecutor, it seems, has not entirely found her role in the proceedings. As was shown in particular as regards disclosure of evidence, the Prosecutor is too secretive towards the defence. Her role as an objective organ, which examines incriminating and exonerating evidence, likewise is not properly fulfilled when she tries to avoid communication and disclosure. The relationship between the defence and the Prosecutor must always be looked at with a view to the principle of equality of arms.[224] The defence is always behind the prosecution as regards knowledge and investigating powers. This disadvantage needs to be narrowed by the provision of information.

In general, however, the ICTY can be trusted in prosecuting criminals on a solid human rights basis. The strict adherence to the fairness of proceedings is necessary as the International Tribunal serves as a model for domestic courts. It is also indispensable because the international institution needs the help of national courts. The ICTY has come to accept the fact that it cannot and should not try any war criminal it can get hold of. It must restrict itself to the major figures and has thus modified its strategy (completion strategy).[225] The prosecution of lower-ranking subordinates should in the future be left to national courts.[226] The proceedings at the ICTY are also important because they serve as a model for the ICC. Most of the questions discussed here will sooner or later arise before the ICC. It would be best if that court where to take into account the different structural roles of the participants and aim at establishing true 'equality of arms' for the parties.

---

223. *Prosecutor* v. *Ademi*, *supra* n. 169, para. 11, concerning the interpretation of the amended Rule 65 (provisional release), see above 3.3.

224. Cf., Safferling 'Audiatur et altera pars – die prozessuale Waffengleichheit als Prozessprinzip?', 12 *Neue Zeitschrift für Strafrecht* (2003) (forthcoming).

225. Cf., B. Elberling, 'Rechtsprechung des Jugoslawien-Tribunals im Jahr 2002', 45 *GYIL* (2002) pp. 483 at 486-488.

226. See ICTY 9th Annual Report, UN Doc. A/57/379 – S/2002/985, para. 207.

CURRENT DEVELOPMENTS

THE YEAR IN REVIEW[1]

Avril McDonald[2]

---

1. © A. McDonald 2004.

2. Dr Avril McDonald is Head of the Section of International Humanitarian Law and International Criminal Law, TMC Asser Instituut for International Law, The Hague and Managing Editor of the *Yearbook of International Humanitarian Law*.

Yearbook of International Humanitarian Law
Volume 5 - 2002 - pp. 255-312

1.   INTRODUCTION

With the attacks of 11 September 2001 very much casting their shadow, 2002 was a year in which issues concerning both the *jus in bello* and the *jus ad bellum* occupied centre stage in international law and relations and dominated the news agenda, but often in a way that promoted confusion and misinformation rather than greater understanding of the law, and, as the year progressed, frustration and despair rather than optimism.

Transnational terrorism was cemented as the declared pre-eminent security concern of many states, and, as a consequence, full speed into the 'global war on terror' (hereinafter GWOT), the integrity of international humanitarian law, human rights law and international law in general, including the role of international organisations such as the United Nations, came under increasing challenge. Focal points of rancorous, polarised debate were the fact and the conditions of detention of persons, including minors,[3] at Guantánamo Bay, Cuba; the applicability and relevance of international humanitarian law in the context of the terrorist threat and the counter-terrorist response; the perceived conflict between human rights and national security; the coming into being of the International Criminal Court (ICC) and the US's almost obsessive opposition to it; and, as the year drew to a close, the spectre of the use of force against Iraq without Security Council authorisation by an increasingly belligerent United States and a handful of its allies.

As the scale and seriousness of the challenge to international peace and security posed by the phenomenon of transnational terrorism became increasingly obvious, so too did the vulnerability of what had been considered to be immutable, fundamental international rights. The willingness of some states to roll back or sacrifice human rights and humanitarian law standards in the face of the threat of terrorism called into question the sincerity of their avowed commitment to the rule of inter-

---

3. See 'Official: Youths Held at Guantánamo Bay', AP (23 April 2003); 'Teens held in Guantánamo', BBC News Online (23 April 2003). <http://news.bbc.co.uk/2/hi/south_asia/2970279.stm>.

national law and the underlying values it enshrines. Of great concern was the emergence of a view in some western states that human rights are not after all universal but can be denied wholesale to particular groups of persons. The most shocking manifestation of this attitude – an official policy not only of the United States but also other states – was the internment by the US at the ironically named Camp X-Ray,[4] Guantánamo Bay, of hundreds of persons detained in the context of the GWOT and the assertion that these persons are beyond both international and national law and, in particular, enjoy no rights of due process, either under human rights law or international humanitarian law.

Guantánamo detainees learned during 2002 that this government policy had judicial imprimatur, when several first instance courts in the United States found that they had no standing before US courts.[5] While some of these courts did not back the government view that these persons have no rights whatsoever – indicating that they have status and rights under international law, including international humanitarian law – since there is no court or judicial body available to them before which they can exercise these rights, the effect of these judgements was to leave the detainees in legal limbo, or, as the UK Court of Appeals put it, 'a legal black hole'.[6]

The legal fiction concocted to justify the denial of due process or any legal remedies to the Guantánamo detainees was the argument that as Guantánamo is not part of US sovereign territory, US courts have no jurisdiction over it, notwithstanding the fact that Guantánamo Bay and all persons found there are under the effective control of the US and the US, is the only state exercising control over the base. Striking was the cavalier attitude of the Bush government to the role and independence of the judiciary and the concept of the separation of powers under the US Constitution. In statements of interests filed in all of the cases brought on behalf of the Guantánamo detainees, the government opined that questions regarding both the procedural and substantive aspects of the detainees' status are beyond judicial review, being matters of executive privilege. According to the administration, the indefinite detention without trial of so-called unlawful combatants at Guantánamo represented an appropriate exercise of the President's war time powers.

Although the plight of the Guantánamo detainees earned most column inches, the US was by no means the only state tearing up the bill of rights for suspected terrorists or just persons of potential intelligence value. Its closest ally in the GWOT, the UK, also interned suspected terrorists with no intention of trying them pursuant to its Anti-Terrorism, Crime and Security Act 2001 at Belmarsh prison in London.[7] While such treatment of persons who have not been accused of any

---

4. Later renamed Camp Delta.

5. For details of these cases, see the USA report in Correspondents' Reports in this volume at pp. 626-636.

6. See the *Abbasi* case in the UK report in Correspondents' Reports in this volume at pp. 604-606.

7. See 'Suspected international terrorists detained in the United Kingdom: new visit by the Council of Europe's Anti-Torture Committee', Council of Europe, 24 March 2004. <http://www.cpt.coe.int/documents/gbr/2004-03-24-eng.htm>. See also <http://www.fairtrials.org.uk/.>

crime and who will probably never be indicted or tried for any offence is nothing new in some countries, it is the declared commitment of the USA and the UK, *inter alia*, to human rights and humanitarian law standards (to the extent that the latter actually applies in the context of the GWOT) that made the hasty abandonment of these norms in the face of the terrorist threat so remarkable.

Illustrative of the extent to which the commitment to humanitarian and human rights had been weakened in the face of the terrorist threat was the rehabilitation of a practice that before September 11 would have been considered unmentionable in civilised company. While few commentators could bring themselves to baldly utter the 'T' word, others had no such trepidation. The surreality of former human rights advocate and Harvard professor Alan Dershowitz appearing on prime time television and writing newspaper editorials advocating torture of suspected terrorists drove home how far the debate on appropriate responses to global terrorism had moved to the right.[8] The argument propounded by Professor Dershowitz, that in a so-called 'ticking time bomb' situation, torture could be resorted to in order to compel a detainee to reveal information, was greeted by many with horror but still found sympathetic ears. Professor Dershowitz advocated legalising torture in these cases and giving the responsibility for carrying it out to properly qualified and well-trained individuals. So-called 'torture warrants' could be issued either by the executive or the judiciary which would ensure that the practice was both legally sanctioned and transparent.[9] According to Dershowitz, since torture is inevitably going to be carried out in any event, it is better to ensure that those who are doing it know what they are doing and are upfront about it. For Professor Dershowitz, apparently it is better to be an honest torturer than a hypocrite.

It later transpired that torture had a seal of approval from even higher legal authorities than Professor Dershowitz.[10] In a secret memorandum prepared by the US Department of Justice's Office of Legal Counsel in 2002 at the request of the Central Intelligence Agency and addressed to the Counsel to the President, Alberto R. Gonzales, the Office of Legal Counsel offered the White House a range of possible defences that it said would negate any claim that certain interrogation methods violate Section 2340A of 18 U.S.C., which implements the 1984 Torture Convention in US law.[11]

---

8. See, *inter alia*, A.M. Dershowitz, *Why Terrorism Works – Understanding the Threat, Responding to the Challenge* (New Haven CO, Yale University Press 2002); A.M Dershowitz, 'Commentary', *LA Times* (8 November 2001); 'Dershowitz: Torture could be justified', CNN.com, 3 March 2003.

9. A.M. Dershowitz, 'Want to torture? Get a warrant', *Francisco Chronicle* (22 January 2002).

10. With the leaking in 2004 of several so-called 'torture memoranda' prepared for the Bush administration in 2002, namely, Memorandum by John C. Woo, US Justice Department, 9 January 2002; Memorandum from Alberto R. Gonzales to President Busy, 25 January 2002; Memorandum from Secretary of State Colin L. Powell to the White House, 26 January 2002; Memorandum from William H. Taft to Alberto R. Gonzales, 2 February 2002; Directive by Mr Bush on Treatment of Detainees, 7 February 2002; and, most notoriously, Memorandum for Alberto R. Gonzales, Counsel to the President, Re: Standards of Conduct for Interrogation under 18 U.S.C. 2340-2340A, U.S. Department of Justice Office of Legal Counsel, 1 August 2002. For commentary see A. Lewis, 'Making Torture Legal', 51 *The New York Review of Books* (15 July 2004) <http://www.nybooks.com/articles/17230>.

11. Memorandum for Alberto R. Gonzales, Counsel to the President, Re: Standards of Conduct for

Prepared by the Head of the Office of Legal Counsel, Jay S. Bybee,[12] what became known as the 'torture memorandum' advised that the Torture Convention 'prohibits only the most extreme acts by reserving criminal penalties solely for torture and declining to require such penalties for "cruel, inhuman, or degrading treatment or punishment"'. Noting that the question had arisen in the context of interrogations of detainees being held by the United States outside its territory,[13] Bybee advised that 'for an act to constitute torture as defined in Section 2340, it must inflict pain that is difficult to endure. Physical pain amounting to torture must be equivalent in intensity to the pain accompanying serious physical injury, such as organ failure, impairment of bodily function, or even death. For purely mental pain or suffering to amount to torture under Section 2340, it must result in significant psychological harm of significant duration, e.g., lasting for months or even years.'[14]

This view is not only morally repugnant and indefensible, it is legally incorrect. The difference between torture and cruel and inhumane treatment or punishment is not the nature or degree of the suffering inflicted (in both cases, the suffering is severe) but the purpose of inflicting the severe pain or suffering and the official status of the persons responsible for inflicting it.[15] There is no actual or legal hierarchy of suffering, with torture describing the most serious violations and cruel and inhuman treatment being a residual category encapsulating crimes which lack the severity of torture. This is clear from a reading of the element of the crimes of the ICC Statute. The elements of the war crime of torture and the war crime of inhuman acts are identical as regards the *actus reus* elements. In both cases, the elements are that 'the perpetrator inflicted severe physical or mental pain or suffering upon one or more persons'. The only difference between torture and cruel treatment as a war crime is that torture requires the purposive element that: 'The perpetrator inflicted the pain or suffering for such purpose as: obtaining information or a confession, punishment, intimidation or coercion or for any reason based on discrimination of any kind.'[16]

Interrogation under 18 U.S.C. 2340-2340A, US Dept. of Justice Office of Legal Counsel, 1 August 2002.

12. Who has since been appointed judge on the United States Court of Appeals for the Ninth Circuit.

13. *Supra* n. 11.

14. Ibid., at p. 1.

15. Art. 1 of the 1984 Convention Against Torture and Other Cruel, Inhuman or Degrading Treatment or Punishment states: '1. For the purposes of this Convention, the term 'torture' means any act by which severe pain or suffering, whether physical or mental, is intentionally inflicted on a person for such purposes as obtaining from him or a third person information or a confession, punishing him for an act he or a third person has committed or is suspected of having committed, or intimidating or coercing him or a third person, or for any reason based on discrimination of any kind, when such pain or suffering is inflicted by or at the instigation of or with the consent or acquiescence of a public official or other person acting in an official capacity. It does not include pain or suffering arising only from, inherent in or incidental to lawful sanctions.' But see on this point, *infra* at p. 285, The decision of the ICTY Appeals Chamber in *Kunarac*.

16. Elements of Crimes, Art. 8(2)(a)(II) – I, War Crime of Torture. Elements, para. 2. A. Cassese, P.

In any case, all acts of torture and cruel, inhuman and degrading treatment are equally prohibited under international human rights and humanitarian law. As long ago as 1948 the Universal Declaration of Human Rights prohibited in equally emphatic terms, without distinguishing between them, torture and cruel, inhuman or degrading treatment or punishment (Art. 5). Similarly, the 1975 Declaration on the Protection of All Persons from Being Subjected to Torture and Other Cruel, Inhuman or Degrading Treatment or Punishment equally prohibits torture as well as cruel, inhuman or degrading treatment and states that no state may permit or tolerate either. The Declaration makes it clear that 'torture constitutes an aggravated and deliberate form of cruel, inhuman or degrading treatment or punishment'.[17] It also states clearly that: 'Exceptional circumstances such as a state of war or a threat of war, internal political instability or any other public emergency may not be invoked as a justification of torture or other cruel, inhuman or degrading treatment of punishment.'[18] The International Covenant on Civil and Political Rights in Article 7 prohibits torture as well as cruel, inhuman or degrading treatment or punishment. Torture and cruel, inhuman and degrading treatment or punishment are also prohibited by both common Article 3 of the Geneva Conventions and as grave breaches of the Conventions and the First Additional Protocol. The ICTY Statute prohibits as a grave breach (b) 'torture or inhuman treatment, including biological experiments' and (c) 'wilfully causing great suffering or serious injury to body or health' (Art. 2). Article 5 of the Statute prohibits as a crime against humanity, (f) torture, and (i) other inhumane acts. Torture is also interdicted as a grave breach, a war crime and a crime against humanity in the ICC Statute.[19]

In several cases, Trial Chambers of the International Criminal Tribunal for the former Yugoslavia (ICTY) have been called upon to define the crimes of torture, wilfully causing great suffering or serious injury to body or health, cruel treatment and inhuman treatment. The *Čelebići* Judgement noted that the offence of wilfully causing great suffering or serious injury to body or health is prohibited as a grave breach in each of the four Geneva Conventions.[20] The *Čelebići* Judgement also noted that inhuman treatment is criminalised as a grave breach in each of the four

---

Gaeta and J.R.W.D. Jones, eds., *The Rome Statute of the International Criminal Court: A Commentary – Materials* (Oxford, Oxford University Press 2002) p. 159.

17. General Assembly Resolution 3452 (XXX), UN. Doc. A/10034 (1975), adopted by consensus on 9 December 1975, Art. 1(2).

18. Art. 3.

19. Art. 7(1) ICC Statute prohibits as a crime against humanity (f) torture and (k) other inhumane acts of a similar character intentionally causing great suffering, or serious injury to body or to mental or physical harm. Paragraph 2(e) explains that '"Torture" means the intentional infliction of severe pain or suffering, whether physical or mental, upon a person in the custody or under the control of the accused; except that torture shall not include pain or suffering arising only from, inherent in or incidental to, lawful sanctions.'

Art. 8 prohibits as a war crime in both an international or a non-international armed conflict torture or cruel and inhumane treatment including biological experiments (Art. 8(2)(a)(ii) and 8(2)(e)(i) and (ii)) and committing outrages upon personal dignity, in particular humiliating or degrading treatment (Art. 8(2)(b)(xxi)).

20. *Prosecutor* v. *Zejnil Delalić, Zdravko Mucić, Hazim Delić and Esad Landžo*, Case No. IT-96-21-T, Judgement, 16 November 1998, para. 498.

Geneva Conventions.[21] It stated that 'cruel treatment is treatment which causes serious mental or physical suffering or constitutes a serious attack upon human dignity, which is equivalent to the offence of inhuman treatment in the framework of the grave breaches provisions of the Geneva Conventions'.[22] Significantly, it found that 'the offence of torture under common Article 3 of the Geneva Conventions is also included within the concept of cruel treatment. Treatment that does not meet the purposive requirement of torture in common Article 3, constitutes cruel treatment.'[23]

But it was not only in relation to the treatment of suspected terrorists that the Bush administration binned the rule book. Many aspects of international humanitarian law and human rights law were called into question, including the definition of armed conflicts and the rules by which they are fought. Commentators wrote in 2002 that: 'A year after the terrorist attacks of September 11, it is evident that the United States' response represents a direct challenge to the laws of armed conflict as they have been understood for the past fifty years.'[24] The question of the adequacy of international humanitarian law in the face of the new realities invited impassioned debates amongst international legal scholars.[25] A spectrum of views was advanced, with some writers rejecting the idea that any change in the law is needed and others conceding that the goalposts have undeniably shifted and that international humanitarian law cannot remain unaffected by that fact.

Not surprisingly, the strongest proponent of the view that humanitarian law is adequate in a world in which new players, threats and types of conflicts have emerged was the ICRC. Its President, Jakob Kellenberger, rejected suggestions that Geneva law needs to be adjusted to deal with terrorism, stating that: 'After a thorough examination, I have not found any convincing argument to say the situation cannot be dealt with under existing rules.'[26] On the other side, one scholar (among many to hold such views) wrote that:

'... the Conventions and Protocols contain significant fault lines that impede effective functioning ... The problem is that terrorists have turned to tactics that can be answered effectively *only* through prolonged, often intense, military action. Yet, without a direct link to either an international or strictly internal armed conflict, humanitarian law does not apply (unless adopted by a State *as a matter of policy*). Thus, the first fault line

---

21. Ibid., para. 516.
22. Ibid., para. 551.
23. Ibid., para. 552.
24. A. Dworkin and D. Rieff, 'International law since September 11: Introduction', *Crimes of War online magazine*, <http://www.crimesofwar.org/sept-mag/sept-intro.html>.
25. See *inter alia*, S.R. Ratner, 'Jus ad bellum and jus in bello after September 11', 96 *AJIL* (2002) p. 905; A. Roberts, 'Counter-terrorism, Armed Force and the Laws of War', 44 *Survival* (2002) p. 7; H.-P. Gasser, 'Acts of terror, "terrorism" and international humanitarian law', *IRRC* No. 847 (2002) p. 547; B. MacPherson, 'Authority of the Security Council to Exempt Peacekeepers from International Criminal Court Proceedings', American Association of International Law (July 2002) <http://www.globalpolicy.org/intljustice/icc/crisis/200207asil.htm>. A comprehensive list and texts of documents on the issues are available at <http://www.globalpolicy.org/intljustice/icc/crisisindex.htm>.
26. 'ICRC rejects talk of Geneva Conventions review', Reuters (21 March 2004).

appears during high order military operations against transnational terrorists, either in direct response to a terrorist campaign or following the defeat of a State participating in it. Neither the Conventions nor the Protocols anticipated this form of hostilities and neither would seem malleable enough to fit comfortably.'[27]

Notwithstanding the stated ICRC position on the subject, it seemed clear that the much-needed serious debate on this subject was only beginning and would likely come to dominate scholarship in the field over the coming years.

The high watermark of 2002, and the greatest cause for hope, was the entry into force of the Statute establishing the world's first permanent International Criminal Court on 1 July. Still, the party was somewhat spoiled by the unwanted gift bequeathed it by a body that might have been expected to be more supportive of the Court. Resolution 1422, adopted by the United Nations Security Council on 12 July, was not only one of the most controversial and politicised of all UN SC resolutions in 2002, it set at odds two international organisations that might be expected to work in a complementary way.

Purportedly adopted pursuant to Article 16 of the ICC Statute,[28] the resolution sought to grant the personnel of non-States Parties complete immunity from the ICC for a renewable period of one year. It attracted a storm of criticism from states,[29] international organisations,[30] statesmen and even other UN organs,[31] not to mention international legal scholars. In particular, the resolution was slammed as being incompatible with Article 16 of the Statute and as a misuse of the SC's powers.

---

27. M. Schmitt, 'Rethinking the Geneva Conventions', *Crimes of War online magazine* (30 January 2003), <http://www.crimesofwar.org/expert/genevaConventions/gc-schmitt.html>.

28. Art. 16 provides that 'No investigation or prosecution may be commenced or proceeded with under this Statute for a period of 12 months after the Security Council, in a resolution adopted under Chapter VII of the Charter of the United Nations, has requested the Court to that effect; this request may be renewed by the Council under the same conditions.'

29. The range of opposition by states to the resolution is set out in M. El Zeidy, 'The United States Dropped the Atomic Bomb of Article 16 of the ICC Statute: Security Council Power of Deferrals and Resolution 1422', 35 *Vanderbilt JTL* (2002) pp. 1503 at 1518-1524. See <http://www.iccnow.org/documents/otherissues1422.html> for a comprehensive list and full texts of states' statements on resolution 1422, and <http://www.iccnow.org/documents/otherissues/1422/countrychart20020703.pdf> for a chart detailing the positions of governments.

30. On 25 September, the Parliamentary Assembly of the Council of Europe adopted resolution 1344 which called attention to the risk to the integrity of the ICC, *inter alia*, from the 'link made by some countries between the jurisdiction of the Court and the renewal of the United Nations Security Council mandates for peacekeeping operations [which] could put at risk the whole system of United Nations peacekeeping'. <http://assembly.coe.int/Main.asp?link=http://assembly.coe.int%2FDocuments%2FAdoptedText%2Fta02%2FERES1300.htm>. On 19 September, the European Parliament adopted a resolution which expressed its regret concerning the adoption of SC resolution 1422. <http://www.iccnow.org/documents/declarationsresolutions/intergovbodies/EP%20Resolution_19-Sept02.pdf>.

31. On 3 July, UN SG Kofi Annan wrote in a letter to US Secretary of State, Colin Powell that 'the method suggested in the proposal ... flies in the face of treaty law since it would force States that ratified the Rome Statute to accept a resolution that literally amends the treaty'. <http://www.iccnow.org/documents/otherissues/1422/SGlettertoSC3July2002.pdf>.

Resolution 1422 appeared to be at odds with the language and intention of Article 16, which seems to envisage a specific situation in which the SC has requested the Court for a temporary stay on investigation or prosecution for a renewable 12-month period, rather than the abstract and blanket immunisation of a specific group of persons from the Court's jurisdiction.

The resolution also seemed to be fundamentally in conflict with the underlying ethos and goals of the Statute, as expressed, *inter alia*, in the preamble. Another criticism is that the Security Council acted *ultra vires* in adopting resolution 1422, especially given the absence of an actual threat to international peace and security such as would have justified the adoption of a resolution under Chapter VII.[32] Indeed, the only genuine threat to peace and security came from the US threat to withdraw its forces from all overseas missions and not only from the UN mission in Bosnia (UNMIBH)![33]

One critic pointed out that resolution 1422 violated the fundamental principle of human rights that all persons enjoy equality before the law, and created a two-tiered system for international criminal justice.[34] Another noted that the resolution involved an unacceptable interference by the SC in the independence of the ICC Prosecutor.[35] Moreover, the resolution seemed unnecessary, given that the US has concluded bilateral agreements under Article 98 of the Rome Statute with a multiplicity of states,[36] and signs status of forces agreements with any state to which it actually sends troops, immunising its personnel from the jurisdiction of the territorial state.

As the year reached its conclusion, the Security Council became the locus of an even bigger fracas, with the USA and a few of its allies working flat out to win passage of a resolution which would either clear the way to war against Iraq or hopefully avoid it, depending on ones' interpretation of the wording of the resolution.

Unanimously adopted resolution 1441 set out an onerous series of steps that Iraq would have to take in order to avoid facing 'serious consequences', including allowing UN and International Atomic Energy Agency inspectors unprecedented access to all sites and making a declaration within 30 days of the adoption of the resolution detailing all and any Iraqi WMD programs or delivery systems.[37]

---

32. See F. Lattanzi, 'La Corte penale internazionale: una sfida per le guirisdizioni degli stati', III *Diritto Pubblico Comparato ed Europeo* (2002) pp. 1365 at 1372-1374;

33. Hanging over the SC debate on resolution 1422 was US veto on 30 June 2002 of the extension of the expiring mandate for the United Nation Mission in Bosnia and Herzegovina See <http://www. amicc.org/docs/peacekeeping.pdf>. See also Human Rights Watch, 'The ICC and the Security Council: Resolution 1422: *Legal and Policy Analysis*', <http://www.hrw.org/campaigns/icc/docs/1422legal. htm>.

34. See K. Ambos, 'International criminal law has lost its innocence', *German LJ* (1 October 2002) <http://www.germanlawjournal.com>.

35. See C. Stahn, 'The ambiguities of Security Council Resolution 1422', 1 *EJIL* (2003) pp. 85-104.

36. See in this volume, Correspondents' Reports, p. 622.

37. See *infra* at pp. 297-299.

Disagreement raged over the likely consequences of any failure to comply with resolution 1441 and even the ability of Iraq to meet the demands on it within the deadline. In supporting the resolution the US – with its troops amassed on the Kuwaiti border with Iraq ready to attack at the time of its adoption – reserved the right to resort to unilateral force without SC approval, if necessary, in this event. Other SC member states, however, took the view that another SC resolution would be needed, which would specifically order the use of force, and that any such use of force must have SC authorisation.[38]

2.   CONFLICTS, ARMED FORCES AND COMBATANTS

2.1   Types of conflicts

The Stockholm International Peace Research Institute (SIPRI) counted 21 major armed conflicts in 19 locations ongoing in 2002, four of which intensified substantially, namely, in Chechyna, Colombia, Israel-Palestine and Nepal, and four of which came close to resolution, namely, the Democratic Republic of the Congo, Sri Lanka, Somalia and Sudan. This represented a reduction on 2001, when SIPRI counted 24 major armed conflicts in 22 locations, and was the lowest number since 1998. The only active inter-state conflict was that between India and Pakistan. SIPRI stated that there was evidence that the effects of the terrorist attacks of 11 September 2001 had a direct impact on many of the conflicts. In particular, evidence that Al Qaeda might have links with fundamentalist Islamic organisations in Africa caused the USA to exert pressure on the warring parties in Somalia and Sudan, and move these conflicts towards resolution.[39]

3.   PROTECTED PERSONS

3.1   Civilians

On 26 November, the UN Secretary-General issued his third report to the Security Council on the protection of civilians in armed conflict.[40] The report was generally upbeat, reporting on progress achieved in several areas, including the resolution of a number of seemingly intractable conflicts. Several new challenges received particular attention in the report: sexual exploitation, commercial exploitation and terrorism.

---

38. See further *infra* at p. 297.

39. S. Wiharta and I. Anthony, 'Major armed conflicts', Chapter 2 of SIPRI Yearbook 2003 (Oxford, Oxford University Press 2003).

40. S/2002/1300, 26 November 2002. Issued pursuant to the request of the President of the Security Council dated 21 June 2001 (S/2001/614). For a discussion of the first and second reports of the Secretary-General, see 2 *YIHL* (1999) at pp. 214-216 and 4 *YIHL* (2001) at pp. 131-132.

In terms of strengthening the policy agenda, the report noted the development by the Office for the Coordination of Humanitarian Affairs of an aide-mémoire, which was adopted by the UN Security Council by Statement of its President dated 15 March 2002,[41] and which provides a basis for improved analysis and diagnosis of key civilian protection issues arising out of a conflict.[42] Furthermore, the Office for the Coordination of Humanitarian Affairs convened a series of regional workshops, with representatives of the UN, NGOs, governments and academia, at which participants were introduced to diagnostic tools, such as the aide-mémoire and had the opportunity to share their regional perspectives. The report also included as an annex a roadmap for the protection of civilians, designed to enhance the architecture of protection. The report noted that in the emerging context of the transition from conflict, practical action to protect civilians is required in three areas: secure humanitarian access; a clear separation of civilians and combatants; and the swift reestablishment of the rule of law, justice and reconciliation.[43]

Describing the problems arising from restrictions on humanitarian access, and the benefits that such access brings, including setting the stage for an end to conflict, the report noted that restrictions on access by non-state actors are a particular problem. '[V]ery few non-State actors recognize their responsibilities regarding humanitarian access as a component of international humanitarian law, and this leads to access being restricted, unpredictable or denied altogether.'[44] The report made some practical recommendations for how access to civilians during armed conflict could be improved.[45]

On the subject of separation of civilians and armed elements, the report noted two areas of particular concern: first, the intermingling of combatants and civilians in a range of situations, and second, the movement of combatants into refugee and internally displaced persons' camps. It noted that some of the methods adopted by governments to address these problems themselves violate international humanitarian law,[46] and listed the practical actions or requirements needed to deal effectively with the problem.[47]

Regarding re-establishing the rule of law in post-conflict societies and effecting reconciliation, the report noted the challenges to the culture of impunity in recent years, particularly the establishment of the International Criminal Court and other international criminal tribunals. It observed that: 'There are, however, no reconciliation templates. Each situation has unique requirements.'[48] It set out the practical requirements that address the needs of rule of law, justice and reconciliation in each case.[49]

---

41. S/PRST/2002/6.
42. Ibid., at para. 4.
43. Ibid., at para. 15.
44. Ibid., at para. 25.
45. Ibid., at para. 30.
46. Ibid., at paras. 33 and 34.
47. Ibid., at para. 40.
48. Ibid., at para. 51.
49. Ibid., at para. 53.

3.1.1   *Women*

On 16 October, the UN Secretary-General released a 12-page report on women, peace and security, which focused on 'the impact of armed conflict on women and girls, the role of women in peace-building and the gender dimensions of peace processes and conflict resolution',[50] and 'the challenges that must be addressed if progress is to be made in the achievement of the goal of gender equality in relation to peace and security'. The report included proposals for addressing situations affecting women and armed conflict and urged the UN Security Council to adopt them.[51]

The Secretary-General pointed to the many ways that armed conflicts affect women, beyond death and injury. These include exacerbating existing inequalities, sending women and children fleeing across borders, and subjecting them to sexual violence and torture. 'Women and children are disproportionately targeted in contemporary armed conflicts and constitute the majority of all victims. Women and children also constitute the majority of the world's refugees and internally displaced persons.'[52]

Concerning the legal dimensions of the problem, the report noted that humanitarian law and human rights protections apply on the basis of non-discrimination, and that some provisions are particularly relevant to women. He urged the Council to call on all parties involved in conflict to adhere to their obligations under applicable principles of international humanitarian law, human rights law and refugee law as they pertain to women and girls. He noted the strides taken in the past decade in addressing crimes against women in armed conflict, including the establishment of the ad hoc Tribunals for the Former Yugoslavia and Rwanda and the prosecution of gender crimes by these bodies, the ICC, the Special Court for Sierra Leone, *inter alia*, and the creation of other extra-legal mechanisms, such as Truth Commissions, which can provide redress. 'This comprehensive international legal framework has been increasingly responsive to the experiences of women and girls, particularly where sexual violence is concerned. ... The determination of individual command responsibility for many of the offences involving sexual violence against women and girls in armed conflict has been a major advance and has undermined the culture of impunity that previously pervaded discussion in this context.'[53] 'These advances must be maintained and further expanded.'[54] Efforts should be made to ensure that amnesty provisions included in conflict settlement agreements exclude impunity for all serious war crimes, including gender-based crimes.[55] Mr Annan also recommended that the Council explicitly integrate gender perspectives into the terms of reference of UN missions to countries and regions in conflict. He said that all UN-brokered peace accords should address the impact of

---

50. S/2002/1154 of 16 October 2002, para. 1.
51. S/2002/1154 of 16 October 2002.
52. Ibid., at para. 6.
53. Ibid., at para. 23.
54. Ibid., at para. 24.
55. Ibid., at para. 25, Action 4.

armed conflict on women and girls, their contributions to peace processes and their needs and priorities in the post-conflict context. Women should also be fully involved in peace negotiations.

The Secretary-General said the extent of human rights violations against women and girls must be factored into peace support operations, and recommended that contacts be set up with women's networks in order to gain more information on the issue. The report suggested that the Council ensure resources for setting up gender units in peacekeeping operations. Efforts aimed at reconstructing conflict-torn societies should incorporate activities focused on specific constraints facing women and girls. Urging recognition of the impact of armed conflict and displacement on family relations, the report called for developing programmes to prevent domestic violence.[56] Finally the Secretary-General stated that: 'We can no longer afford to minimize or ignore the contributions of women and girls to all stages of conflict resolution, peacemaking, peace-building, peacekeeping and the reconstruction processes. Sustainable peace will not be achieved without the full and equal participation of women and men.'[57]

3.1.2 *Children*

The 2000 Optional Protocol to the Convention on the Rights of the Child on the Involvement of Children in Armed Conflict entered into force on 12 February 2002, three months after the deposit of the tenth instrument of ratification or accession. The Optional Protocol prohibits both states and rebel groups from deploying children under the age of 18 in any form of armed conflict.[58] It was hoped that the new legal regime would impact on the problem of the more than 300,000 children estimated to be involved in armed conflict.

In other developments, from 8 to 10 May 2002, more than 7,000 people participated in the Special Session of the UN General Assembly on Children, convened to review progress since the World Summit for Children in 1990 and re-energise global commitment to children's rights.[59]

A report of the Secretary-General issued on 26 November 2002 on children and armed conflict followed up on the implementation of earlier SC resolutions on the subject.[60] As well as documenting the situation in a number of specific states, the report made some general observations, *inter alia*, on the needs of displaced children and particularly girls. It noted that the needs of the latter are specific, but they are often overlooked during post-conflict reconstruction.

---

56. Ibid., at para. 452.
57. Ibid., at para. 68.
58. See further the Year in Review in 4 *YIHL* (2001) at pp. 263-264.
59. <http://www.unicef.org/specialsession/>.
60. Report of the Secretary-General on children and armed conflict, S/2002/1299, 26 November 2002.

4.   METHODS, MEANS AND TYPES OF WARFARE

4.1   **Small arms**

On 20 September, the UN Secretary-General issued a short report on the subject of small arms.[61] Submitted pursuant to the statement of the President of the Council of 31 August 2001,[62] the report focused on identifying how the Council could contribute to dealing with the question of the illegal trade in small arms and light weapons. Twenty-two states, including the five permanent members and four non-permanent members of the Security Council, submitted their views on this issue to the Secretary-General. The report noted that there are an estimated '639 million small arms in the world today, nearly 60 per cent of which are legally held by civilians. These arms fuel, intensify and contribute to the prolongation of conflicts. As a conflict is prolonged, the need for more arms and ammunition grows, thus perpetuating a vicious cycle.'[63] The report said that small arms and light weapons pose a global threat to human security and human rights, and that at least 500,000 people die each year as a result of these weapons.[64] The widespread existence of these weapons in conflict zones also poses a threat to peacekeepers and hampers post-conflict reconstruction and development. The Report noted the various steps taken by the Council to deal with the problem, including the adoption of arms embargos to impede the flow of arms to conflict areas, and recently, the establishment of independent panels of experts and monitoring mechanisms to police compliance with these embargos. The Council has also addressed the issue of small arms as part of its conflict prevention initiatives, peacekeeping operations and peace-building activities. Part IV of the Report presented the observations and recommendations of the member states who had submitted them. They included that the Council must call upon member states to develop an international instrument to enable them to identify and trace illicit small arms and light weapons; member states should be called upon to enforce all Council resolutions on sanctions; member states should be called upon to enhance transparency in armaments; and the Council should continue its efforts to identify the link between the illegal trade in small arms and the illegal exploitation of natural resources, the drugs trade, and to develop innovative strategies to combat this phenomenon.

---

61. S/2002/1053.
62. S/PRST/2001/21.
63. Ibid., para. 3.
64. Ibid., para. 4.

5.   INTERNATIONAL CRIMINAL LAW

5.1   **The crimes**

5.1.1   *Terrorism*

Unsurprisingly, it was in the field of counter-terrorism that the most frenetic activity was witnessed.

On 10 April, the International Convention for the Suppression of the Financing of Terrorism[65] entered into force, having received more than the required 22 ratifications. The Convention was adopted by the United Nations General Assembly in New York on 9 December 1999, and was opened for signature on 10 January 2000. The Convention obliges States Parties to prosecute or extradite to affected states persons accused of funding terrorist activities, and requires banks to enact measures to identify suspicious transactions. It also request states to establish mechanisms to use such funds to compensate victims and/or their families.[66]

Efforts to draft a Comprehensive Convention against Terrorism as well as a Convention against Nuclear Terrorism continued within an ad hoc committee of the UN General Assembly and a working group, but stopped short of the adoption of the said draft treaties.[67]

On 6 August, the UN Secretary-General Kofi Annan sent to the Presidents of the Security Council and the General Assembly the report of the Policy Working Group on the United Nations and Terrorism (established in 2001), which set out to prioritise the Organisation's activities in the realm of counter-terrorism.[68] The report recommended that the UN focuses its counter-terrorism efforts on those areas where it enjoys a comparative advantage. 'In general terms, the United Nations should uphold, bolster and reassert the leading principles and purposes of the United Nations Charter, the core of which are undermined and threatened by terrorism. The Organization's activities should be part of a tripartite strategy supporting global efforts to: (a) dissuade disaffected groups from embracing terrorism; (b) deny groups or individuals the means to carry out terrorism and (c) sustain broad-based international cooperation in the struggle against terrorism.'[69]

The Security Council adopted a number of resolutions condemning terrorist attacks. Following the Bali bombing of 12 October, the Council adopted resolution 1438 on 14 October, condemning 'in the strongest possible terms the bomb attacks' as well as other such attacks, and stating that it regarded such attacks, like any terrorist acts, as a threat to international peace and security. It reaffirmed the

---

65. Adopted by the UN General Assembly, A/RES/54/109, 25 February 2000. <http://www.undcp.org/resolution_2000-02-25_1.html>.

66. For commentary on the law, see I. Bantekas, 'The International Law of Terrorist Financing', 97 *AJIL* (2003) p. 315.

67. See 'Completion of two further conventions against terrorism is urged in General Assembly's Legal Committee: delegates note ongoing efforts of bodies within mandated task', UN GA Press Release GA/L/3211, 4 October 2002. <http://www.un.org/News/Press/docs/2002/gal3211.doc.htm>.

68. A/57/273-S/2002/875, 6 August 2002.

69. See summary and para. 9.

need 'to combat by all means, in accordance with the Charter of the United Nations, threats to international peace and security caused by terrorist attacks', and its determination to do so, and urged all states to cooperate with the Indonesian authorities to bring the perpetrators of the Bali bombing to justice.

Following the taking hostage of Moscow theatre-goers by Chechen rebels on 23 October 2002, the Security Council adopted resolution 1440 on 24 October, which condemned in the strongest possible terms the act, and similar terrorist acts. It demanded the immediate and unconditional release of the hostages and urged all states to cooperate with the Russian authorities in bringing the perpetrators to justice.

Resolution 1450 of 13 December condemned the 28 November terrorist bomb attack at the Paradise Hotel in Kikambala, Kenya and the attempted missile strike on Arkia Israeli Airlines flight 582 departing Mombassa, Kenya and similar terrorist attacks elsewhere. It urged all states to cooperate in bringing to justice the perpetrators of these attacks, and reiterated the need to combat terrorism by all means within the Charter.

At the regional level, the locus of greatest activity was the Americas. There, the first international treaty dealing with terrorism adopted since the events of September 11, the Inter-American Convention Against Terrorism, was approved by the Permanent Council of the Organization of American States on 15 May 2002, and adopted at the second plenary session held on 3 June 2002.[70] The Convention, which will enter into force once six states have ratified it,[71] commits parties to improve regional cooperation in the fight against terrorism through information exchanges, technical cooperation, training programs and mutual legal assistance. Article 1 declares that the purposes of the Convention are 'to prevent, punish and eliminate terrorism. To that end, the states parties agree to adopt the necessary measures and to strengthen cooperation among them, in accordance with the terms of this Convention.' Other articles elaborate on the obligation to cooperate and assist other states. Under Article 2, acts considered as terrorist offences are those already criminalised in international terrorist conventions. Under Article 3, States Parties to the Inter-American Convention shall endeavour to become parties to these treaties, and to effectively implement them in their national law. Article 4 sets out the measures that states shall take to prevent, combat and eradicate the financing of terrorism. *Inter alia*, the Convention also commits parties to take the appropriate measures to ensure that asylum and refugee status is denied to persons suspected of having committed a terrorist offence (Arts. 12 and 13). By the end of 2002, all OAS states but Dominica had signed, and one (Canada) had ratified the Convention.

In 2002, the OAS's Inter-American Committee Against Terrorism (Comité Interamericano Contra el Terrorismo or CICTE), which was created in 1998, estab-

---

70. Inter-American Convention Against Terrorism. AG/Res. 1840 (XXXII-O/02). Adopted at the second plenary session held on 3 June 2002. <http://www.oas.org/xxxiiga/english/docs_items/AGres1840_02.htm>.

71. Art. 22.

lished a full-time secretariat, funded by voluntary donations from OAS member states.[72]

The Inter-American Commission on Human Rights issued an important report on terrorism and human rights on 22 October 2002, which focused in particular on the impact of terrorism and counter-terrorism on human rights and democracy.[73] The report made detailed reference to states' obligations under both human rights law and international humanitarian law in the context of the fight against terrorism. It noted that in undertaking several initiatives to counter terrorist violence, 'member states are equally obliged to remain in strict compliance with their other international obligations, including those under human rights law and international humanitarian law'.[74] It stressed that efforts to counter terrorism and to promote human rights and democracy are not antithetical but complementary.

Apropos the debate regarding the impact of new forms of transnational terrorism on traditional notions of warfare, the report stated that '… international law obliges member states [of the OAS] to take the measures necessary to prevent terrorism and other forms of violence and to guarantee the security of their populations. Indeed, it cannot be ruled out that these measures may include future developments in international law that will address recent manifestations of terrorism, as, for example, a new form of international warfare between private individuals or groups and states.'[75]

The report also made specific reference to the application of international humanitarian law by the Commission where situations of armed conflict are concerned: 'In interpreting and applying human rights protections in such circumstances, … it may be necessary for the Commission to refer to and consider pertinent provisions of international humanitarian law as the applicable *lex specialis*. This methodology is particularly significant where situations of international armed conflicts are concerned, as the four Geneva Conventions of 1949 and other applicable instruments prescribe extensive and specific rules and standards concerning the protection of victims of armed conflict and must be considered in order to properly interpret and apply international human rights protections during these armed conflicts.'[76]

Within Europe, on 13 June 2002 the Council of the European Union adopted a Framework Decision on Combating Terrorism.[77] The Framework Decision commits EU Member States to undertake to suppress certain terrorist offences.

---

72. <http://www.cicte.oas.org/history.htm>. See also US Dept. of State. 'Patterns of Global Terrorism 2002'. Released by the Office of the Coordinator for Counterterrorism, 30 April 2003. Western Hemisphere Overview. <http://www.state.gov/s/ct/rls/pgtrpt/2002/html/19987.htm>.

73. Report on Terrorism and Human Rights, Inter-American Commission on Human Rights. OEA/Ser.L/V/II.116, Doc. 5 rev. 1 corr., 22 October 2002. The report can be accessed online at <http://www.cidh.org/terrorism/eng/>.

74. Ibid., at para. 4.

75. Ibid., at para. 3.

76. Ibid., at para. 29.

77. 2002/475/JHA. The text of the Decision is available online at <http://europa.eu.int/eur-lex/pri/en/oj/dat/2002/l_164/l_16420020622en00030007.pdf> or <http://www.sisde.it/sito/Rivista24.nsf/ServNavig/20>.

5.1.2   *Torture*

On 18 December 2002, the UN General Assembly adopted the Optional Protocol to the UN Convention against Torture by an overwhelming majority of 127 in favour, four against (the USA, Nigeria, the Marshall Islands and Palau) and 42 abstentions. The Optional Protocol establishes a system for monitoring and inspections. 'The Protocol will allow independent international and national experts to conduct regular visits to places of detention within States Parties. The aim of these visits will be to assess the treatment of persons deprived of their liberty and their conditions of detention and make concrete recommendations for improvement. States Parties will be required to cooperate with the visiting mechanisms and to take steps to implement their recommendations ... It also establishes, for the first time in an international human rights instrument, a complementary inter-relationship between preventive efforts at the international and national level.'[78] The Optional Protocol opened for signature from 1 January 2003 and it enters into force upon the 20th ratification.

5.2   **Ad hoc International Criminal Tribunals**[79]

2002 was a pretty slow year for both Tribunals in terms of outcomes. Few judgements were rendered and fewer still of jurisprudential significance. The slow pace and the length of some trials is a concern given the stated need for the Tribunals to wind up their work by 2008, if the completion strategy is to be accomplished. The Prosecutor repeatedly said that the ICTY would not shut its doors while the two major accused, Ratko Mladić and Radovan Karadžić, remained at large. Whatever about the chances of the Yugoslav Tribunal being able to wind down by this date, and the regional courts of the former Yugoslavia being willing and able to prosecute the outstanding perpetrators and the others that are still being investigated by the ICTY Office of the Prosecutor (OTP), it was difficult to imagine how the 2008 deadline could be met in the case of Rwanda, where the national courts are already struggling to cope with a huge case-load, and the courts of other African states have no real incentive to take on Rwandan case.

Cooperation, or rather the lack of it, remained a problem for both Tribunals. On 23 October, ICTY President Jorda reported the Federal Republic of Yugoslavia to the UN Security Council for its failure to cooperate with the ICTY. It had failed to arrest accused persons on its territory, and had adopted a law on cooperation with the International Tribunal of 11 April 2002[80] which violates its commitments towards the Tribunal. The letter to the SC also noted that the ICTY's completion strategy (see below) could only be achieved if the major accused at large were arrested and transferred to the Tribunal for trial.[81]

---

78. See Amnesty International Press Release. 'UN: UN Adopts Protocol to Prevent Torture', AI Index: IOR 40/042/2002 (Public) News Service No: 237, 18 December 2002.

79. For internationalised tribunals, see under the relevant country in the Correspondents' Reports.

80. See further the FRY report in Correspondents' Reports in this volume at pp. 509-510.

81. 'Judge Claude Jorda, President of the International Criminal Tribunal for the Former Yugosla-

On 30 October, Chief Prosecutor Carla Del Ponte addressed the Security Council, and raised the issue of the lack of full cooperation by Rwanda, Croatia and the FRY, and mentioned that the completion strategy would not be achieved without 'timely arrests and timely access to the evidence'.[82]

On 19 December, the Security Council called for Yugoslavia and Rwanda to cooperate with the ICTY and ICTR, respectively.[83] The UN Security Council urged 'constructive dialogue between the Tribunals and the Governments concerned' but said that 'such dialogue or lack of dialogue must not be used by States as an excuse for failure to discharge their obligations to cooperate fully with the Tribunals.'

On 20 December, the Prosecutor held a press conference to protest the continued failure to cooperate of the FRY, as demonstrated by the refusal of the Yugoslav Foreign Minister to discuss the matter with her on 19 December.[84]

Another ongoing problem concerned the practice of fee splitting.[85] The Tribunals conducted investigations into the practice, according to which kickbacks are paid by Tribunal defence lawyers to their clients' families, but said that proving it was very difficult. On 13 March, the Registrars of both Tribunals issued a joint statement, pledging 'to make every effort possible to prevent abuses of the legal aid system of the two UN courts'.[86]

On 26 February, the UN Office of Internal Oversight Services (OIOS) released its report into fee splitting by defence lawyers,[87] following an earlier report in February 2001.[88] The report indicated that the legal systems of the Tribunals continue to be abused, with indigent detainees at the ICTR soliciting between $2,500 and $5,000 per month from their attorneys in order to continue retaining them as counsel. Steps taken by the ICTR to address the problem included the dismissal of one lead defence counsel on the grounds of financial dishonesty,[89] the imposition of limitations on gifts given to detainees by their lawyers and tighter screening of current and potential defence investigators. The ICTY prepared an amendment to the code of conduct that forbids fee splitting by defence counsel.

---

via, reports the continued non-cooperation by the Federal Republic of Yugoslavia to the Security Council', The Hague, 23 October 2002, JDH/P.I.S./706-e. <http://www.un.org/icty/pressreal/p706-e.htm>.

82. 'Address by the Prosecutor of the International Criminal Tribunals for the Former Yugoslavia and Rwanda, Mrs. Carla Del Ponte, to the United Nations Security Council', The Hague, 30 October 2002, JJJ/P.I.S./709-e. <http://www.un.org/icty/pressreal/p709-e.htm>.

83. 'Yugoslavia asked to work with UN war crimes court', AP (19 December 2002).

84. 'ICTY Prosecutor, Carla Del Ponte addresses once again "the unsatisfactory co-operation" of the Federal Republic of Yugoslavia with the Office of the Prosecutor', The Hague, 20 December 2002, FH/P.I.S./721-e. <http://www.un.org/icty/pressreal/p721-e.htm>.

85. M. Ilic and T. Walker, 'War criminals' families demand cash kickbacks', *The Sunday Times* (London) (14 April 2002).

86. See S. Chhatbar, 'ICTR and ICTY pledge to end fee splitting', *Internews* (13 March 2002).

87. <http://www.un.org/Depts/oios/reports/a56_836.pdf>.

88. <http://www.un.org/Depts/oios/reports/a55_759.pdf>.

89. In February, the ICTR announced that it had discharged one defence lawyer, Mr Andrew McCartan (UK), for financial irregularities. See 'Defence lawyer removed for financial dishonesty', ICTR/INFO-9-2-299.EN, Arusha, 6 February 2002. <http://www.ictr.org/ENGLISH/PRESSREL/2002/299.htm>.

The extraordinary extent to which Tribunal defendants can benefit from kickbacks from their counsel was revealed on 8 July, when the ICTY Registrar announced that the Tribunal would withdraw all legal aid from Zoran Zigić – who was sentenced in 2001 to 25 years' imprisonment – following the completion of a financial investigation by the Registry. Zigić, it turned out, had come into a lot of money, having received a total of 'at least 178,280 euros (approximately US $ 175,000) from members of his defence counsel team, according to a scheme organized by his former legal counsel, Mr. Simo Tosić, attorney-at-law from Banja Luka. The scheme included the assignment of two investigators who never actually worked for the defence.'[90] The withdrawal of legal aid from Zigić was without prejudice to any future attempt to recover the money from the accused.

5.2.1   *International Criminal Tribunal for the Former Yugoslavia*

5.2.1.1   The completion strategy

The Judges became increasingly focused on designing and putting into place the Tribunal's completion strategy, which would see it wrap up all investigations by the end of 2004 and all first instance cases by 2008. The strategy has two aspects: a focus only on the investigation and prosecution of high-ranking civilian and military personnel and the referral of cases of lesser importance to the national courts of the region.[91]

The President, Prosecutor and Registrar submitted a report to the Judges on the judicial status of the Tribunal and the prospects of referring some cases to the domestic courts of the former Yugoslavia, which the Judges discussed on 23 April at an Extraordinary Plenary session.[92] Among the recommended solutions were the establishment of a chamber at the envisaged state court of Bosnia and Herzegovina with specific jurisdiction to try war crimes suspects. The report also proposed that international judges or observers be appointed to serve at the state court and possibly provide training in international humanitarian law to the local judiciary and court personnel. The Judges agreed to the report's main proposals but said that Security Council authorisation would be required to implement some of them.[93]

From 17 to 21 June, Prosecutor Carla Del Ponte and President Claude Jorda visited Bosnia to discuss the deferral of cases to the Bosnian courts, and the establishment within the state court of a court with jurisdiction to try deferred cases.[94]

---

90. 'Legal aid to accused Zoran Zigic withdrawn following the completion of a financial investigation by the Registry', The Hague, 8 July 2002, CC/P.I.S./686-e. <http://www.un.org/icty/pressreal/p686-e.htm>.
91. See 'Address by his Excellency, Judge Claude Jorda', President of the International Criminal Tribunal for the Former Yugoslavia, to the United Nations General Assembly', The Hague, 29 October 2002, JdH/P.I.S./707-e. <http://www.un.org/icty/pressreal/p707-e.htm>.
92. 'Extraordinary plenary session of Tuesday 23 April 2002', The Hague, 24 April 2002, JdH/P.I.S./671e. <http://www.un.org/icty/pressreal/p671-e.htm>.
93. Ibid.
94. 'Visit of the President and Prosecutor of the International Criminal Tribunal for the Former

On 23 July, President Jorda presented the report on the completion strategy to the UN Security Council, and outlined the steps that had been taken to cooperate with the national authorities of Bosnia to prepare for the referral of cases back to its courts. He called on the SC to exert its influence on the recalcitrant states to cooperate and transfer accused persons to the Tribunal. 'This way – and this way alone – will we be able to fulfil our mandate in the time-limits envisaged.'[95] The same day, the President of the Security Council issued a Statement in which he indicated 'that the ICTY should concentrate its work on the prosecution and trial of the civilian, military and paramilitary leaders suspected of being responsible for serious violations of international humanitarian law committed in the territory of the former Yugoslavia since 1991, rather than on minor actors'.[96]

At their Extraordinary Plenary session held on 30 September, convened to implement the decisions stemming from the debate held at the Security Council, the judges discussed and adopted measures to facilitate implementing the referral of cases to national courts of the region. The Judges amended Rule 11 *bis* to permit judges to refer certain cases either to the courts of the territory of the state where the accused is arrested or the courts of the territory where the crimes were committed.[97]

The completion strategy was outlined to the General Assembly during President Jorda's Address to it on 29 October,[98] and again to the Security Council on 30 October.[99] On 13 December, President Jorda presented an oral report to the 27th Plenary of the Judges on the progress of the deferral strategy.[100]

5.2.1.2 An international bar for defence counsel and reform of the code of conduct

At their 23 April Extraordinary Plenary session, the Judges agreed on the principle of the establishment of an international bar association for defence counsel, whose *modus operandi* would be determined at the July plenary. As noted above, the

---

Yugoslavia to Bosnia and Herzegovina', The Hague, 24 April 2002, JdH/P.I.S./68-1e. <http://www.un.org/icty/pressreal/p681-e.htm>.

95. 'Address by His Excellency, Judge Claude Jorda, President of the International Criminal Tribunal for the Former Yugoslavia, to the United Nations Security Council', The Hague, 26 July 2002, JDH/P.I.S./690-ee. <http://www.un.org/icty/pressreal/p690-e.htm>.

96. S/PRST/2002/21 of 23 July 2002.

97. 'Extraordinary plenary session of 30 September 2002', The Hague, 1 October 2002, JdH/P.I.S./696e. <http://www.un.org/icty/pressreal/p696-e.htm>.

98. See 'Address by his Excellency, Judge Claude Jorda, President of the International Criminal Tribunal for the Former Yugoslavia, to the United Nations General Assembly', The Hague, 29 October 2002, JdH/P.I.S./707-e. <http://www.un.org/icty/pressreal/p707-e.htm>.

99. 'Address by his Excellency, Judge Claude Jorda', President of the International Criminal Tribunal for the Former Yugoslavia, to the United Nations Security Council', The Hague, 30 October 2002, JdH/P.I.S./708-e. <http://www.un.org/icty/pressreal/p708-e.htm>.

100. '27th Plenary of the ICTY Judges', The Hague, 13 December 2002, JdH/P.I.S./718e. <http://www.un.org/icty/pressreal/p718-e.htm>.

Judges also initiated a reform of the code of professional conduct relating in particular to the prohibition of fee-splitting.[101]

At their plenary session of 11 and 13 July, the Judges amended Rule 44 of the Rules of Procedure and Evidence relating to 'Appointment, Qualifications and Duties of Counsel', to provide that counsel who wish to practice before the ICTY must be a member of an association of counsels appearing at the ICTY. The plenary adopted a draft statute of a defence counsel association as a possible model for the proposed body. The Judges considered that the functions of such a body should include the provision of training for defence counsel, assistance with legal research and monitoring of professional conduct. The Judges also substantially amended the Code of Professional Conduct for Defence Counsel at the ICTY, extending it from 23 to 50 articles, including a provision explicitly prohibiting feesplitting.[102] On 19 December, the ICTY announced that it had formerly recognised the Association of Defence Counsel of the ICTY (ADC-ICTY)[103] as the body representing Defence Counsel appearing before it. The objectives of the Association are: to support the function and efficiency of defence counsel at the ICTY; to encourage defence counsel to participate in Tribunal activities; to advise the Tribunal regarding procedural changes; and to oversee the performance of defence counsel at the Tribunal.[104]

5.2.1.3   Arrests and new indictments

Following his voluntary surrender, on 31 January Dusan Fustar, a former shift commander at the Keraterm camp in Bosnia, was transferred to the ICTY detention unit. On 6 February, he made his initial appearance before the Tribunal. He is charged with both individual and command responsibility for crimes against humanity and war crimes.[105] On 1 April, SFOR detained Captain Momir Nikolić in Repovac, Bosnia and Herzegovina. He was transferred to the ICTY the following day. Nikolić, formerly the Assistant Commander (Chief) for Security and Intelligence of the Bratunac Brigade, which was involved in the massacre of Bosnian Muslim men at Srebrenica in July 1995, is accused of individual criminal responsibility for one count of genocide, four crimes against humanity and one violation of the laws or customs of war.[106] On 25 April, Dragoljub Ojdanić, the former Chief

---

101. 'Extraordinary plenary session of Tuesday 23 April 2002', The Hague, 24 April 2002, JdH/P. I.S./671e. <http://www.un.org/icty/pressreal/p671-e.htm>.

102. 'Judges' plenary session adopts reforms concerning defence counsel teams', The Hague, 19 July 2002, CC/P.I.S./688e. <http://www.un.org/icty/pressreal/ADV020205.htm>.

103. <http://www.adcicty.com>.

104. 'Association of Defence Counsel formally recognised by the ICTY', The Hague, 19 December 2002, JA/P.I.S./720e. <http://www.un.org/icty/pressreal/p720-e.htm>.

105. 'Voluntary surrender of Dusan Fustar to the International Criminal Tribunal for the Former Yugoslavia. The Hague, 31 July 2002, CVO/P.I.S./656e. <http://www.un.org/icty/pressreal/p656-e. htm>; 'Initial appearance of Dusan Fustar to take place on Wednesday 6 February 2002. The Hague, 5 February 2002, JL/P.I.S./PA042. <http://www.un.org/icty/pressreal/p688-e.htm>.

106. 'Arrest and transfer of Momir Nikolic', The Hague, 2 April 2002, RC/P.I.S./664. <http://www.un.org/icty/pressreal/p664-e.htm>.

of General Staff of the Yugoslav Army, was transferred from Serbia to the ICTY Detention Unit.[107] He is jointly charged with Milan Milutinović, Nikola Sainović and Vlajko Stojiljković, on the basis of individual and superior responsibility, with four counts of crimes against humanity and one count of violations of the laws or customs of war, allegedly committed during the execution of a campaign of terror and violence directed against Kosovar Albanian civilians.[108] On 2 May, Nikola Sainović and Momcilo Gruban were transferred to The Hague from Serbia. Sainović, the former Yugoslav Deputy Prime Minister, is charged with four crimes against humanity and one violation of the laws or customs of war. Gruban, a former shift commander at the Omarska camp, is charged with superior responsibility for crimes against humanity, grave breaches and violations of the laws or customs of war.[109]

On 15 May, Milan Martić and Mile Mrksić were transferred to The Hague. Martić, the former President of the self-proclaimed 'Republic of Serb Krajina' (RSK), is charged with individual and superior responsibility for one violation of the laws or customs of war, for ordering the military forces of the RSK to attack Zagreb on 2 and 3 May 1995, causing death and injury to a number of civilians. He was previously the subject of a Rule 61 proceeding. Mrskić, a former Colonel in the JNA and commander of the Guards Brigade, is charged with two others in the so-called Vukovar Three indictment. He is accused of individual and command responsibility for two crimes against humanity, two grave breaches and two violations of the laws or customs of war,[110] carried out against civilians removed from the Vukovar hospital in Croatia in 1991.[111]

On 19 May, Dusan Knežević was transferred to The Hague. He is charged with individual criminal responsibility for a total of 21 crimes against humanity, six grave breaches and 19 violations of the laws or customs of war, carried out at the Omarska and Keraterm camps in Bosnia. While Knežević did not have any position at the camp, he allegedly entered it as a visitor to carry out his crimes.[112]

On 14 June, SFOR arrested Darko Mrdja. He was transferred to The Hague the following day. The indictment, dated 16 April 2002 and unsealed on 14 June, charged Mrjda, the former commander of a Bosnian Serb police unit in Prejidor during 1992, with individual responsibility for two crimes against humanity and

---

107. 'Initial appearance of Dragoljub to take place on Friday 26 April 2002', The Hague, 25 April 2002, JL/P.I.S./PA049. <http://www.un.org/icty/pressreal/PA049e.htm>.

108. 'Transfer of Dragoljub Ojdanic to The Hague', The Hague, 31 July 2002, JL/P.I.S./672e. <http://www.un.org/icty/pressreal/p672-e.htm>.

109. 'Nikola Sainovic and Momcilo Gruban transferred to The Hague', The Hague, 2 May 2002, JL/P.I.S./673e. <http://www.un.org/icty/pressreal/p673-e.htm>.

110. 'Milan Martic and Mile Mrksic transferred to The Hague', The Hague, 15 May 2002, CC/P.I. S./675e. <http://www.un.org/icty/pressreal/675.htm>.

111. 'Initial appearance of Mile Mrksic to take place on Thursday 16 May 2002', The Hague, 15 May 2002, CC/P.I.S./PA052. <http://www.un.org/icty/pressreal/ADV020516.htm>.

112. 'Dusan Knezevic transferred to The Hague', The Hague, 19 May 2002, JL/P.I.S./676e. <http://www.un.org/icty/pressreal/676-e.htm>.

one violation of the laws or customs of war.[113] His initial appearance took place on 17 June.

Ranko Cesić was arrested by the Serb authorities on 25 May and was transferred to the ICTY on 17 June. A former camp guard at the Luka detention camp in Bosnia, Cesić was indicted alongside Goran Jelisić, and was charged with individual criminal responsibility for six crimes against humanity and six violations of the laws or customs of war.[114]

Miroslav Deronjić was arrested in Bosnia by SFOR on 7 July and transferred to the ICTY the following day. The former President of the Bratunac Crisis Staff in 1992, Deronjić is charged in an indictment issued on 3 July 2002 with individual criminal responsibility for two crimes against humanity and four violations of the laws or customs of war.[115] On 9 July, SFOR arrested Radovan Stanković in Foča and transferred him to the ICTY the next day. Stanković, a former member of an elite Bosnia Serb paramilitary group who was charged in the original Fŏca indictment, is accused of individual criminal responsibility for two crimes against humanity and two violations of the laws or customs of war.[116]

In addition to the two above-mentioned new indictments against Darko Mrdja and Miroslav Deronjić, on 6 September an indictment was confirmed against Ljubomir Borovcanin, the former Deputy Commander of the Bosnian Serb MUP[117] Special Police Brigade during the attack on July 1995 Srebrenica. He is charged with individual and command responsibility for complicity in genocide, four crimes against humanity and four violations of the laws or customs of war. The indictment remained sealed until 27 September.[118]

On 20 September, an indictment against General Janko Bobetko, the former Chief of Staff of the Croatian Army, was unsealed.[119] Warrants of arrest and orders were issued to Croatia on 17 and 20 September. On 29 November, the Appeals

---

113. 'Arrest and transfer of Darko Mrdja', The Hague, 14 June 2002, CVO/P.I.S./680e. <http://www.un.org/icty/pressreal/680-e.htm>.

114. 'Ranko Cesic transferred to The Hague', The Hague, 17 June 2002, CC/P.I.S./682e. <http://www.un.org/icty/pressreal/682-e.htm>.

115. 'Transfer of Miroslav Deronjic', The Hague, 8 June 2002, CC/P.I.S./685e. <http://www.un.org/icty/pressreal/685-e.htm>.

116. 'Transfer of Radovan Stankovic', The Hague, 10 July 2002, CC/P.I.S./687e. <http://www.un.org/icty/pressreal/687-e.htm>.

117. Internal Affairs Special Police.

118. 'Ljubomir Borovcanin: indictment unsealed for his alleged participation in crimes committed after the take-over of the Srebrenica enclave', The Hague, 30 September 2002, CC/P.I.S./695e. <http://www.un.org/icty/pressreal/695-e.htm>.

119. 'Indictment against General Janko Bobetko unsealed', The Hague, 20 September 2002, CVO/P.I.S./PA062. <http://www.un.org/icty/pressreal/ADV020920e.htm>.

Chamber rejected a challenge by Croatia[120] against Bobetko's indictment and a request for his arrest.[121]

5.2.1.4 Release and provisional release

Nenad Banović was released on 11 April from the ICTY detention unit following an order of the Trial Chamber withdrawing the indictment against him.[122] The decision followed the application by the Prosecutor on 27 March to withdraw the indictment, which stated that '... there is insufficient evidence to proceed to trial against Nenad Banović on the significant charges of the Indictment ...'.[123] On 26 July, another indictment was withdrawn at the request of the prosecution, this time against Milan Zec. According to the OTP, the evidence was insufficient to maintain it.[124] On 4 October, the indictment against an accused not in custody was withdrawn, again at the request of the prosecution. The justification was that Zoran Marinić was a low-level indictee, and as such, no longer corresponded to the criteria as set out in the completion strategy of the Prosecutor. The Prosecutor did not know the whereabouts of the accused.[125]

Several accused were granted provisional release pending their trials. On 20 February, Trial Chamber I granted Rahim Ademi and Miodrag Jokić's requests for provisional release, and set out its terms and conditions.[126] On 28 May, Dragan Jokić was granted provisional release by the Appeals Chamber, subject to a number of specific terms and conditions.[127] Momcilo Gruban was provisionally released on 20 July by Trial Chamber III subject to a number of conditions.[128] On 27 June, Trial Chamber II granted the applications for provisional release of

---

120. Croatia filed two applications with the Tribunal challenging Bobetko's indictment and the request for his arrest: Application of the Republic of Croatia to Submit an Interlocutory Appeal Against the Warrant of Arrest and Order of Surrender of 20 September 2002, filed on 30 September; and, Request from the Republic of Croatia for a Review of the Judge's Decision of 17 September Confirming the Indictment Against Janko Bobetko and the Order for his Arrest and Surrender of 20 September, filed on 4 October.

121. 'Appeals Chamber rejects applications made by Croatia in the *Prosecutor* v. *Janko Bobetko* case', The Hague, 29 November 2002, JL/P.I.S./714e. <http://www.un.org/icty/pressreal/p714-e.htm>.

122. 'Nenad Banovic released from ICTY custody following an order by Trial Chamber III withdrawing his indictment', The Hague, 11 April 2002, JL/P.I.S./667e. <http://www.un.org/icty/pressreal/667-e.htm>.

123. Ibid.

124. 'Indictment against Milan Zec withdrawn', The Hague, 29 July 2002, JL/P.I.S./691e. <http://www.un.org/icty/pressreal/p691-e.htm>.

125. 'Indictment against Zoran Marinic withdrawn', The Hague, 4 October 2002, JL/P.I.S./695e. <http://www.un.org/icty/pressreal/p695-e.htm>.

126. 'Provisional release granted to Rahim Ademi and Miodrag Jokic', The Hague, 20 February 2002, CVO/P.I.S./661-e. <http://www.un.org/icty/pressreal/p661-e.htm>.

127. 'Dragan Jokic granted provisional release', The Hague, 28 May 2002, JL/P.I.S./677-e. <http://www.un.org/icty/pressreal/p677-e.htm>.

128. 'Momcilo Gruban on provisional release', The Hague, 20 July 2002, CC/P.I.S./689-e. <http://www.un.org/icty/pressreal/p689-e.htm>.

Dragoljub Ojdanic and Nikola Sainovic, but stayed the decision, pending an appeal by the prosecution.[129]

On 30 July, President Jorda ordered the early release from ICTY detention of Milojica Kos. Kos was convicted on 2 November 2001 for persecution as a crime against humanity, and murder and torture as violations of the laws or customs of war, and sentenced to six years' imprisonment. Having already served three years, five months and five days in detention pending and during trial, he filed for early release on 5 June 2002. On 31 July, Kos was released, having served just over four years' for his crimes.[130]

On 20 September, Trial Chamber II granted the application of General Momir Talić for provisional release 'in light of his medical condition', subject to a number of terms and conditions.[131] Milorad Krnojelac was granted a five-day provisional release on 12 December for family reasons.[132]

5.2.1.5   Transfer of convicted persons

On 9 April, Drago Josipović was transferred to Spain to serve his 12-year sentence.[133] On 12 April, Vladimor Santić was transferred to Spain to serve out his 18-year sentence.[134] On 10 May, Dusko Sikirica and Damir Dosen were transferred to Austria to serve their sentences of imprisonment of 15 and five years, respectively. They were the first persons convicted by the ICTY to be sent to Austria.[135] On 28 November, Radomir Kovac and Zoran Vuković, two of the three persons convicted in the *Foča* case, were transferred to Norway to serve their sentences of 20 years and 12 years, respectively.[136] On 12 December, Dragoljub Kunarac, the remaining Foča accused, was transferred to Germany, pursuant to an ad hoc agreement, to serve his 28 year sentence.[137]

129. 'Dragoljub Ojdanic and Nikola Sainovic granted provisional release pending appeal by the prosecution', The Hague, 27 June 2002, JL/P.I.S./683e. <http://www.un.org/icty/pressreal/p683-e.htm>.

130. 'The President of the ICTY orders release of Milojica Kos', The Hague, 31 July 2002, RC/P.I.S./692e. <http://www.un.org/icty/pressreal/p692-e.htm>.

131. 'Momir Talic granted provisional release', The Hague, 20 September 2002, JL/P.I.S./694e. <http://www.un.org/icty/pressreal/p694-e.htm>.

132. 'Milorad Krnojelac granted a five-day provisional release for family reasons', The Hague, 13 December 2002, CC/P.I.S./717-e. <http://www.un.org/icty/pressreal/p717-e.htm>.

133. 'Drago Josipovic transferred to Spain to serve prison sentence', The Hague, 9 April 2002, JL/P.I.S./665e. <http://www.un.org/icty/pressreal/p665-e.htm>.

134. 'Vladimor Santic transferred to Spain his serve the remainder of his prison sentence', The Hague, 12 April 2002, JL/P.I.S./669e. <http://www.un.org/icty/pressreal/p669-e.htm>.

135. 'Dusko Sikirica and Damir Dosen transferred to Austria to serve prison sentence', The Hague, 10 May 2002, CVO/P.I.S./674e. <http://www.un.org/icty/pressreal/p674-e.htm>.

136. 'Radomir Kovac and Zoran Vukovic transferred to Norway to serve prison sentences', The Hague, 28 November 2002, CVO/P.I.S./712e. <http://www.un.org/icty/pressreal/p712-e.htm>.

137. 'Dragoljub Kunarac transferred to Germany to serve prison sentence', The Hague, 12 December 2002, JP/P.I.S./716e. <http://www.un.org/icty/pressreal/p716-e.htm>.

5.2.1.6   New trials

On 12 February, the long-awaited trial of former Yugoslav President Slobodan Milošević commenced before Trial Chamber III, before Judges Richard May (Presiding), Patrick Robinson and O-Gon Kwon, with the accused facing charges of genocide, crimes against humanity and war crimes.

On 1 February, the Appeals Chamber had upheld the prosecution's appeal on joinder of the three indictments against Milošević, concerning Croatia, Bosnia and Kosovo. It found that the Trial Chamber had misdirected itself in its application of Rule 49 as to whether there should be a joinder. Its error of law had 'invalidated the decision and vitiated the exercise by the Trial Chamber of its discretion'. Substituting its discretion for that of the Trial Chamber, it found that on the correct interpretation of Rule 49, the acts alleged in the three indictments did 'form the same transaction', and thus could be joined.[138]

On 12 April, the trial commenced of Dr Milomir Stakić, the President of the Municipality Crisis Staff in Prijedor, Bosnia, President of the Municipal Assembly and Head of the Prijedor Municipal Council for National Defence. He faced charges of individual and command responsibility for genocide or complicity in genocide, crimes against humanity and one violation of the laws or customs of war.[139]

5.2.1.7   Subpoenaing of war correspondents

In a decision issued in the *Brdjanin and Talić* case,[140] the Appeal Chamber ruled on the controversial question of whether it can subpoena war correspondents and compel them to testify at the Tribunal. The question had arisen when the Tribunal issued a subpoena against Mr Jonathan Randal, correspondent for the *Washington Post* newspaper, and he had appealed against it. The Appeals Chamber found the public interest in the work of a war correspondent must be balanced against the interests of justice in a particular case. In order to decide whether or not a particular war correspondent can be subpoenaed, a Trial Chamber must apply a two-pronged test: The petitioning party must demonstrate that: (1) that evidence sought is of direct and important value in determining a core issue in this case, and (2) it cannot reasonably be obtained elsewhere. In this case, it allowed the appeal and set aside the subpoena to Jonathan Randal.[141]

---

138. 'Milosevic case: the Appeals Chamber grants the prosecution's appeal for joinder', The Hague, 1 February 2002, XT/P.I.S./657-e. <http://www.un.org/icty/pressreal/p657-e.htm>.

139. 'Milomir Stakic trial to begin on Tuesday 16 April 2002', The Hague, 1 February 2002, JL/P.I.S./670e. <http://www.un.org/icty/pressreal/p670-e.htm>.

140. Case No. IT-99-36-PT.

141. '*The Prosecutor* v. *Radoslav Brdjanin & Momir Talic* "Randal Case" – Appeals Chamber defines a legal test for the issuance of subpoenas for war correspondents to testify at the Tribunal – Subpoena to Jonathan Randal set aside', The Hague, 11 December 2002, JL/P.I.S./715-e. <http://www.un.org/icty/pressreal/p715-e.htm>.

5.2.1.8   Guilty plea of Biljana Plavsić

On 2 October 2002, Biljana Plavsić, the former Bosnian Serb President, pleaded guilty to one count of persecution as a crime against humanity, following her earlier plea of not guilty to all counts on 11 January 2001.[142] Sentencing would follow.

5.2.1.9   Judgements

Prosecutor v. *Milorad Krnojelac*, Judgement, 15 March 2002

The accused was charged with individual and superior responsibility for six counts of crimes against humanity (persecution, torture, murder, inhumane acts, imprisonment and enslavement) and four counts of violations of the laws or customs of war (torture, cruel treatment, murder and slavery).

In its judgement of 15 March 2002, Trial Chamber II convicted Milorad Krnojelac, the warden of KP Dom prison in Foča, Bosnia from April 1992 until August 1993, of two crimes against humanity (persecution and inhumane acts) and two violations of the laws or customs of war (cruel treatment) committed at the prison against non-Serb detainees. Charges of grave breaches had been withdrawn by the Prosecutor before the trial began. During the pleading phase, and before the commencement of the trial, the prosecution admitted that it was unable to establish that the accused had personally participated in the crimes with which he was charged, but asserted that he was part of a joint criminal enterprise to commit them. The prosecution also alleged that the accused had aided and abetted those who had perpetrated the offences. These were the legal bases for holding him individually criminally responsible. Krnojelac was also responsible as a superior for failing to control the acts of his subordinates who carried out the crimes, said the Prosecutor. Krnojelac argued at trial that he had only limited authority as warden, and in particular had no authority over or responsibility for non-Serb detainees in the military unit of the prison.

In its judgement, the Trial Chamber rejected Krnojelac's defence and found that he exercised all the powers of the warden of KP Dom, including supervisory responsibility over all subordinate personnel and detainees.[143] It found that the accused was both individually responsible and responsible as a superior for the crime against humanity of persecution, responsible as a superior for the crime against humanity of inhumane acts, and both individually responsible and responsible as a superior for cruel treatment as violations of the laws or customs of war. Subsumed in those findings of individual responsibility for persecution, but not made the subject of cumulative convictions, were findings that the accused was individually responsible for imprisonment and inhumane acts as crimes against humanity.

---

142. See 'Top Serb changes plea to guilty', *The Guardian* (2 October 2002).
143. *Prosecutor* v. *Milorad Krnojelac*, Case No. 1T-97-25, Judgement, 15 March 2002, para. 107.

The Chamber found that the requirements of Articles 3 and 5 of the Statute had been met, and that Krnojelac's alleged acts were committed during an armed conflict between the Bosnian Serbs and the Bosnian Muslims and in the context of a widespread and systematic attack upon the Muslim population of Foča. It confirmed that 'there is no requirement under customary international law that the acts of the accused person (or of those persons for whose acts he is criminally responsible) be connected to a policy or plan. Such plan or policy may nevertheless be relevant to the requirement that the attack must be widespread or systematic and that the acts of the accused must be part of that attack.'[144] The accused must have the intention not only to commit the underlying act but must also know that there is an attack directed against the civilian population and that his acts are part of that attack, although knowledge of the details are not required.[145] These requirements were satisfied in this case.

The Trial Chamber departed from Trial Chamber I in *Prosecutor* v. *Krstić*[146] and *Prosecutor* v. *Kvocka*[147] in rejecting a rigid categorisation of accomplice liability for the purposes of sentencing and in the distinction drawn between a co-perpetrator and an accomplice.

> 'Categorising offenders may be of some assistance, but the particular category selected cannot affect the maximum sentence which may be imposed and it does not compel the length of sentences which will be appropriate in the particular case. This Trial Chamber, moreover, does not, with respect, accept the validity of the distinction which Trial Chamber I has sought to draw between a co-perpetrator and an accomplice.'[148] 'This Trial Chamber prefers to follow the opinion of the Appeals Chamber in *Tadić*, that the liability of the participant in a joint criminal enterprise who was not the principal offender is that of an accomplice.'[149]

Prosecutor v. *Dragoljub Kunarac, Radomir Kovac and Zoran Vuković*, Appeals Judgement, 12 June 2002

On 12 June, the Appeals Chamber rendered its verdict on the appeals against their convictions and sentences of Dragoljub Kunarac, Radomir Kovac and Zoran Vuković in the *Foča* case. The Chamber rejected all grounds of appeal and reaffirmed their sentences.

The judgement largely concurred with the findings of the Trial Chamber but offered some clarifications on a couple of point. Regarding the crime of torture, the Appeals Chamber further elucidated the nature of the definition of torture in

---

144. Ibid., at para. 58.
145. Ibid., at para. 59.
146. Case No. IT-98-33, Judgement, 2 August 2001.
147. Case No. IT-98-30/1, Judgement, 2 November 2001.
148. 'In *Prosecutor* v. *Krstic*, a distinction was drawn between an accomplice (as a secondary form of participation) and a co-perpetrator (as a direct and principal form of participation, but falling short of that of the principal offender).' At para. 76.
149. Ibid., at para. 77.

customary international law as it appears in the Torture Convention, in particular with regard to the participation of a public official or any other person acting in a non-private capacity, even though this point was not raised by the parties, 'in order that no controversy remains about this appeal or its consistency with the jurisprudence of the Tribunal'.[150] It emphasised that while the Trial Chamber in *Furundžija* was right to find that official capacity is an element of the crime of torture for the purposes of the Torture Convention, and that the definition of torture in the Torture Convention reflects customary international law as far as the obligation of States is concerned, this 'must be distinguished from an assertion that this definition wholly reflects customary international law regarding the meaning of the crime of torture generally'.[151]

'The Trial Chamber in the present case was therefore right in taking the position that the public official requirement is not a requirement under customary international law in relation to the criminal responsibility of an individual for torture outside of the framework of the Torture Convention.'[152]

The Appeals Chamber held that 'the assumption of the Appellants that suffering must be visible, even long after the commission of the torture, is erroneous. ... Sexual violence necessarily gives rise to severe pain or suffering, whether physical or mental, and in this way justifies its characterisation as an act of torture.'[153]

As regards the question whether the appellants had the intent to commit the crime of torture by means of rape, the Appeals Chamber stressed

> 'the important distinction between "intent" and "motivation". The Appeals Chamber holds that, even if the perpetrator's motivation is entirely sexual, it does not follow that the perpetrator does not have the intent to commit an act of torture or that his conduct does not cause severe pain or suffering, whether physical or mental, since such pain or suffering is a likely and logical consequence of his conduct. In view of the definition, it is important to establish whether a perpetrator intended to act in a way which, in the normal course of events, would cause severe pain or suffering, whether physical or mental, to his victims'.[154]

Prosecutor v. *Milan Simić*, Sentencing Judgement, 17 October 2002

More than four years following his initial not-guilty plea and after the commencement of his trial, Milan Simić, a member of the Bosnian Serb Crisis Staff and President of the Executive Board of the Municipal Assembly of Bosanski Samac at the time of his alleged crimes, entered a plea of guilty to two counts of the amended indictment against him (torture as crimes against humanity). Milan Simić

---

150. *Prosecutor* v. *Dragolub Kunarac, Radomir Kovac and Zoran Vuković* (Foča), Case Nos. IT-96-23 and IT-96-23/1, Appeals Judgement, 12 June 2002, para. 145.

151. Ibid., at para. 147.

152. Ibid., at para. 148.

153. Ibid., at para. 150. See also para. 151.

154. Ibid., at para. 153.

agreed that the crimes of torture to which he pleaded guilty were committed while he was acting in an official capacity.[155]

Upon the Trial Chamber's acceptance of this plea, the Prosecutor withdrew the remaining five counts against him (persecution as a crime against humanity, two counts of inhumane acts as crimes against humanity, and two counts of cruel treatment as violations of the laws or customs of war) and the Trial Chamber severed him from the case of *Prosecutor* v. *Blagoje Simić et al.*[156]

In its Sentencing Decision of 17 October, the Trial Chamber sentenced Milan Simić to five years' imprisonment for each count, to be served concurrently (as requested by the Prosecutor), from which would be subtracted the 835 days already served in pre-trial detention and during trial. In determining the sentence, the Trial Chamber weighed the usual aggravating and mitigating factors; regarding the former, his official position, the vulnerability of the victims, and his discriminatory intent, and regarding the former, his admission of guilt and expression of remorse, his voluntary surrender, lack of prior criminal record, and his comportment in the Detention Unit and attitude towards the proceedings, but seemed to be particularly influenced by the fact that Simić is a paraplegic. While saying on the one hand that his medical problems were not such as to justify a reduction of sentence, and should not be taken into account as a mitigating factor,[157] on the other hand the Chamber said that Simić's physical circumstances could not be ignored:

'The Trial Chamber notes that in the history of the Tribunal there has not been an accused in similar medical circumstances. Such a condition poses an exceptional circumstance that obliges this Trial Chamber, for reasons of humanity, to accept that Milan Simić's medical condition ought to be a consideration in sentencing, as a special circumstance. Accordingly a lesser sentence than Milan Simić would have otherwise received will be imposed. This is not to say that a long custodial sentence cannot be imposed on any accused in a similar state. Rather, each case must be treated according to its own circumstances.'[158]

Prosecutor v. *Mitar Vasiljević*, Judgement, 29 November 2002

On 29 November, Trial Chamber II convicted Mitar Vasiljević of persecution as a crime against humanity and murder as a violation of the laws or customs of war and acquitted him of eight counts. He was sentenced to 20 years' imprisonment.

Vasiljević worked as a waiter in the town of Visegrad during the war, and was said by the Prosecutor to have links to a paramilitary group run by Milan Lukić. However, the Chamber was 'not satisfied that the Accused was a member of Milan Lukic's paramilitary group, or that his association with that group was such that it is possible to draw an inference beyond reasonable doubt that the Accused shared the general homicidal intentions of that group. The Trial Chamber is satisfied that

---

155. *Prosecutor* v. *Milan Simić,* Sentencing Judgement, 17 October 2002, para. 12.
156. Ibid., at para. 116.
157. *Prosecutor* v. *Milan Simić,* Sentencing Judgement, 17 October 2002, para. 101.
158. Ibid., at para. 116.

he had some association with that group, in that he willingly acted as an informant to that group, and that this willingness arose from his close relationship with Milan Lukić.'[159]

On 7 June 1992, together with a number of other men, he was accused of having led seven Bosnian men to the bank of the Drina River, forced them to line up, and shot them from behind at close range. Two survivors escaped by pretending to be dead. On 14 June he was accused of involvement in a second incident, whereby about 70 Bosnian Muslim women, children and elderly men were directed to a house in Pionirska Street, which had been dosed with an inflammatory substance. Once inside it was set alight. Most died, although some escaped.

The Trial Chamber found that, in relation to the Drina River incident, the accused participated in a joint criminal enterprise that all seven men be killed. As only five died, he was found to be individually criminally responsible for the murder of those five, as a crime against humanity and as a violation of the laws or customs of war. In relation to the two men who escaped, Vasiljević was found to be individually criminally responsible for inhumane acts as a crime against humanity. The Chamber also found him guilty of persecution as a crime against humanity for the murder of the five men and inhumane acts in relation to the survivors. Given that the crime of persecution incorporates the ingredients of both murder and inhumane acts, and, according to the Chamber, is more specific than these crimes (although logically, it is in fact less specific than these other crimes, which are specific manifestations of the more general crime of persecution), the accused could not be cumulatively convicted of the three crimes against humanity for which he was found to be responsible but only that of persecution.

Concerning the Pionirska Street incident, the Chamber accepted the accused's alibi[160] and held that the prosecution had failed to prove any of the four crimes charged in relation to it (murder as a crime against humanity and a violation of the laws or customs of war and extermination and inhumane acts as crimes against humanity), and acquitted the accused of these charges. 'The Trial Chamber is not satisfied that the Prosecution has eliminated the reasonable possibility that the Accused was elsewhere at the time of the looting, transfer of the Kortinik group and setting on fire of the house.'[161]

In relation to the two counts of violence to life and person, one charged with respect to each incident, the Chamber was not satisfied that a violation to life and person as a violation of the laws or customs of war constitutes an offence under customary law giving rise to individual criminal responsibility, and acquitted the accused of these charges.

---

159. *Prosecutor v. Mitar Vasiljević*, Case No. IT-98-32-T, Judgement, 29 November 2002, at para. 95.
160. See at paras. 130, 143, 166.
161. Ibid., at para. 130.

'In the absence of any clear indication in the practice of states as to what the definition of the offence of "violence to life and person" identified in the Statute may be under customary law, the Trial Chamber is not satisfied that such an offence giving rise to individual criminal responsibility exists under that body of law.'[162]

5.2.2   *International Criminal Tribunal for Rwanda*

Following allegations of mistreatment of witnesses from Rwanda, on 4 March, in a letter sent by the Registrar to the Rwandan Minister of Justice and Institutional Relations, the Tribunal proposed establishing a Joint Committee with the government of Rwanda to verify the allegations.[163] However, after the Rwandan government responded to the offer by welcoming it, but asking that its terms of reference be expanded, the Tribunal withdrew the proposal.[164] 'The expanded terms of reference would assail the independence, impartiality and neutrality that must be the distinguishing feature of the Registry of the Tribunal.'[165]

On 29 July UN Secretary-General Kofi Annan requested the Security Council to remove Carla Del Ponte as Chief Prosecutor of the ICTR and appoint a dedicated prosecutor for the Kigali office.[166]

On 14 August, the UN Security Council adopted resolution 1431 (2002), amending the ICTR Statute (adding Articles 12 *ter* (election and appointment of ad litem judges) and *quater* (status of ad litem judges)) to provide for a pool of ad litem judges. The resolution requested the Secretary-General to expedite the election of a pool of 18 ad litem judges. At first sight, this may have appeared to provide a solution to the problem of how the ICTR can achieve its completion strategy. However, on closer examination, the resolution promised more than it actually offered. Only four ad litem judges can sit for their four year terms at any one time. The four sitting ad litem judges provided for in Article 11 was rather less than the nine that the ICTR President had recommended in order to expedite proceedings at the Tribunal and achieve completion by 2008.[167]

Under the now rather confusing Article 11 of the ICTR Statute, the Chambers are henceforth composed of 16 permanent judges (seven in the Appeals Chamber, five of whom sit in any one case, and nine in the three Trial Chambers). However,

---

162. *Prosecutor* v. *Mitar Vasiljević*, Case No. IT-98-32-T, Judgement, 29 November 2002, para. 203.

163. 'Tribunal proposes joint committee with government of Rwanda to verify allegations of mistreatment of witnesses from Rwanda', ICTR/INFO-9-3-08.EN, Arusha, 13 March 2002. <http://www.ictr/org/ENGLISH/PRESSREL/2002/9-3-08.htm>.

164. 'The Registrar decides to withdraw his proposal to establish a joint commission to investigate allegations of mistreatment of witnesses from Rwanda', ICTR/INFO-9-3-10.EN, Arusha, 17 April 2002. <http://www.ictr/org/ENGLISH/PRESSREL/2002/9-3-10.htm>.

165. 'Statement by the Registrar on the response of the government of Rwanda to the proposal to establish a Joint Commission to investigate the allegations of mistreatment of witnesses coming from Rwanda', ICTR/INFO-9-3-09.EN, Arusha, 28 March 2002. <http://www.ictr/org/ENGLISH/PRESS-REL/2002/9-3-09.htm>.

166. I. Arieff, 'Annan wants new Prosecutor for Rwanda Tribunal', Reuters, 29 July 2002.

167. 'ICTR President welcomes ad litem judges resolution', ICTR/INFO-9-2-312.EN, Arusha, 15 August 2002. <http://www.ictr/org/ENGLISH/PRESSREL/2002/312.htm>.

in an envisaged miracle of economy on a par with the loaves and the fishes, the Trial Chambers, with the addition of a mere four ad litem judges, may be divided into sections of three judges, each composed of both permanent and ad litem judges.

In October, in a passionate speech to the UN Security Council, ICTR President Judge Navanethem Pillay called on UN member states to help compensate the victims of the Rwandan genocide:

'Many Rwandans have questioned the ICTR's value and its role in promoting reconciliation if the issue of claims for compensation is not addressed. For every hour of every day over the past seven and a half years, we have lived with the voices of the survivors of genocide and so we strongly urge the United Nations to provide compensation for Rwandan victims.'[168]

5.2.2.1   Arrests

Quite a number of indictees appeared before the court for trial. Father Athanase Seromba, former Catholic priest at Nyange parish and one of two priests to be brought before the ICTR during the year, surrendered to the ICTR's jurisdiction and was transferred from Italy to Arusha on 6 February 2002.[169] He made his initial appearance before the court on 8 February when he pleaded not guilty to four counts of genocide, complicity in genocide, conspiracy to commit genocide and crimes against humanity.

March was the busiest month in terms of arrests and new arrivals at the detention unit. On 4 March, Vincent Rutaganira, former Councillor of Muguba, Gishyita Commune, was transferred from Tanzania to the ICTR detention centre in Arusha. He made his initial appearance on 26 March, when he pleaded not guilty to seven counts of genocide, conspiracy to commit genocide, crimes against humanity and war crimes.[170] On 18 March, two accused made their separate initial appearances before the ICTR. Aloys Simba, former Lieutenant Colonel in the Rwandan Armed Forces and a former Member of Parliament, pleaded not guilty to four counts of genocide, complicity in genocide and crimes against humanity. Simba was arrested in Senegal on 27 November 2001 and transferred to Arusha on 11 March 2002. Paul Bisengimana also entered a not guilty plea on 18 March to all 12 counts against him of genocide, complicity in genocide, incitement to genocide, crimes against humanity and war crimes. He was arrested in Mali on 4 December 2001 and transferred to the ICTR on 11 March. On 20 March 2002 Joseph Nzabirinda, a

---

168. 'ICTR President calls for compensation for victims', ICTR/INFO-9-2-326.EN, Arusha, 31 October 2002. <http://www.ictr/org/ENGLISH/PRESSREL/2002/326e.htm>.

169. 'Catholic priest surrenders to the Tribunal', ICTR/INFO-9-2-300.EN, Arusha, 7 February 2002. <http://www.ictr/org/ENGLISH/PRESSREL/2002/>.

'Father Seromba pleads not guilty', ICTR/INFO-9-2-301.EN, Arusha, 8 February 2002. <http://www.ictr/org/ENGLISH/PRESSREL/2002/>.

170. 'Vincent Rutaganira transferred to Arusha', ICTR/INFO-9-2-304.EN, Arusha, 4 March 2002. <http://www.ictr/org/ENGLISH/PRESSREL/2002/>; 'Vincent Rutaganira pleads not guilty', ICTR/INFO-9-2-309.EN, Arusha, 26 March 2002. <http://www.ictr/org/ENGLISH/PRESSREL/2002/>.

former youth organiser, was transferred to the Tribunal, following his arrest in Belgium on 21 December 2001. On 27 March, he pleaded not guilty to four counts of genocide, complicity in genocide and crimes against humanity. Amazingly, Nzabirinda previously worked as a defence investigator for the ICTR, as a member of the defence team in the case of Sylvain Nsabimana, one of the six accused in the *Butare* case.[171] Following his arrest in the Netherlands on 12 July 2001 and related legal proceedings there, on 27 March Simon Bikindi was transferred to the ICTR, where he made his initial appearance on 4 April. He pleaded not guilty to six counts of genocide, conspiracy to commit genocide, incitement to genocide, and crimes against humanity.[172] On 21 March, Father Hormisdas Nsengimana, the former Rector of Christ-Roi College in Butare Prefecture, was arrested in Cameroon.[173] He was transferred to the ICTR on 10 April, and made his initial appearance on 16 April, when he pleaded not guilty to four counts of genocide, conspiracy to commit genocide and crimes against humanity.[174]

On 15 May, Colonel Léonidas Rusatira, Former Colonel of the Rwandese' Armed Forces and Commandant of the École Supérieure Militaire, and former directeur de cabinet of the Ministry of Defence, was arrested in Belgium,[175] and he was subsequently transferred to the ICTR detention unit. However, on 15 August, the Tribunal dropped all charges against him, at the request of the Prosecutor, and ordered his immediate release.[176]

On 2 August General Augustin Bizimungu, Chief of Staff of the Rwandan Army from April to July 1994, was arrested in Angola. Following his transfer to the ICTR on 15 August,[177] he made his initial appearance on 21 August, when he pleaded not guilty to ten counts of genocide, conspiracy to commit genocide, crimes against humanity and war crimes.[178] He is jointly indicted with four other accused who are already in Tribunal custody, namely, General Augustin Ndindiliyimana, Major Francois-Xavier Nzuwonemeye, Captain Innocent Sagahutu and Major Protais Mpiranya.

---

171. 'Nzabirinda pleads not guilty to four counts', ICTR/INFO-9-2-310.EN, Arusha, 27 March 2002. <http://www.ictr/org/ENGLISH/PRESSREL/2002/>.
172. 'Bikindi the musician transferred to Arusha', ICTR/INFO-9-2-311.EN, Arusha, 28 March 2002. <http://www.ictr/org/ENGLISH/PRESSREL/2002/>;'Bikindi the musician pleads not guilty', ICTR/INFO-9-2-313.EN, Arusha, 4 April 2002. <http://www.ictr/org/ENGLISH/PRESSREL/2002/>
173. 'Former priest arrested in Cameroon; Nzabirinda alias "Biroto" transferred to Arusha'. ICTR/INFO-9-2-308.EN, Arusha, 21 March 2002. <http://www.ictr/org/ENGLISH/PRESSREL/2002/>.
174. 'Priest Nsengimana transferred to Arusha', ICTR/INFO-9-2-314.EN, Arusha, 10 August 2002. <http://www.ictr/org/ENGLISH/PRESSREL/2002/>.
'Father Nsengimana pleads not guilty', ICTR/INFO-9-2-315.EN, Arusha, 16 April 2002. <http://www.ictr/org/ENGLISH/PRESSREL/2002/>.
175. 'Colonel Leonidas Rusatira arrested in Belgium', ICTR/INFO-9-2-316.EN, Arusha, 15 May 2002. <http://www.ictr/org/ENGLISH/PRESSREL/2002/>.
176. M. Kimani, 'ICTR drops charges against genocide suspect Leonidas Rusatira,' *Internews*. <http://www.internews.org/activities/ictr_reports/ICTRnewsAug02.html>.
177. 'Augustin Bizimungu transferred to Arusha', ICTR/INFO-9-2-320.EN, Arusha, 15 August 2002. <http://www.ictr/org/ENGLISH/PRESSREL/2002/>.
178. 'Former army chief of staff pleads not guilty', ICTR/INFO-9-2-321.EN, Arusha, 21 August 2002. <http://www.ictr/org/ENGLISH/PRESSREL/2002/>.

On 11 September, Jean-Baptise Gatete, the former Mayor of Murambi Commune in Byumba, was arrested in the Republic of the Congo, and he was transferred to the ICTR on 13 September.[179] During his initial appearance on 20 September, he pleaded not guilty to the ten counts against him, including genocide, complicity in genocide, incitement to genocide, crimes against humanity and war crimes.[180]

Colonel Tharcisse Renzaho, former prefect of Kigaliville, was arrested on 29 September 2002 in the Democratic Republic of the Congo. He was transferred to the ICTR the following day. He made his initial appearance on 21 November, pleading not guilty to the three counts against him of genocide, or, in the alternative, complicity in genocide and crimes against humanity (murder).[181]

5.2.2.2 New trials

On 2 April, the so-called military trial began of Colonel Theoneste Bagosora, former Director of Cabinet in the Ministry of Defence; Lieutenant-Colonel Anatole Nsengiyumva, former Commander of Military Operations in Gisenyi sector; Major Aloys Ntabakuze, former Commander of Para Commando Battalion and Brigadier-General Gratien Kabiligi, former Chief of Military Operations.[182] They are charged with genocide, conspiracy to commit genocide, complicity in genocide, incitement to genocide and crimes against humanity.[183]

The trial of Eliezer Niyitegeka, former Minister of Information in the interim government in 1994, began on 17 June. The accused is charged with ten counts, including genocide, conspiracy to commit genocide, incitement to genocide and several crimes against humanity.[184]

5.2.2.3 Judgements

Prosecutor v. *Ignace Bagilishema*, Appeals Decision, 3 July 2002

In the shortest ever decision rendered by the Appeals Chamber, on 3 July it rendered a two-page judgement unanimously dismissing the appeal by the Prosecutor

---

179. 'Jean-Baptiste Gatete transferred to Arusha', ICTR/INFO-9-2-322.EN, Arusha, 16 September 2002. <http://www.ictr/org/ENGLISH/PRESSREL/2002/>.

180. 'Gatete pleads not guilty', ICTR/INFO-9-2-324.EN, Arusha, 20 September 2002. <http://www.ictr/org/ENGLISH/PRESSREL/2002/>.

181. 'First ICTR genocide suspect arrested in the Democratic Republic of Congo', ICTR/INFO-9-2-325.EN, Arusha, 30 September 2002. <http://www.ictr/org/ENGLISH/PRESSREL/2002/325e.htm>; 'Col. Renzaho pleads not guilty', ICTR/INFO/-9-2-328.EN. Arusha, 21 November 2002. <http://www.ictr/org/ENGLISH/PRESSREL/2002/328e.htm>.

182. For background on the trial and the accused see 'Military Trial – The Prosecutor vs Theoneste Bagasora, Anatole Nsengiyumva, Aloys Ntabakuze and Gratien Kabiligi', Arusha, 15 March 2002. <http://www.ictr.org/ENGLISH/PRESSREL/2002/bgmilitary.htm>.

183. 'Military trial opens', ICTR/INFO-9-2-312.EN, Arusha, 2 April 2002. <http://www.ictr.org/ENGLISH/PRESSREL/2002/312e.htm>

184. 'Trial of former Minister of Information starts', ICTR/INFO-9-2-317.EN, Arusha, 17 June 2002. <http://www.ictr.org/ENGLISH/PRESSREL/2002/317e.htm>.

against the acquittal by the Trial Chamber of Ignace Bagilishema.[185] The reasons would follow in due course.

5.3   International Criminal Court

On 1 July 2002, 60 days following the 60th ratification and just four years after its adoption, the Statute of the International Criminal Court entered into force. On 11 April, the four ratifications necessary to trigger its entry into force were exceeded when ten states lodged their instruments of ratification with the UN Secretary-General, bringing the number of States Parties at that time to 66.

The first meeting of the Assembly of States Parties took place from 3 to 10 September 2002 at UN headquarters in New York.

6.   IMPLEMENTATION OF IHL

6.1   International Committee of the Red Cross

On 25 September, the ICRC launched an Appeal on Biotechnology, Weapons and Humanity 'to promote consideration of the risks, rules and responsibilities related to advances in biotechnology which may lead to their hostile use to cause poisoning and deliberate disease'.[186]

6.2   Fact-finding, including the International Fact-Finding Commission

Three states recognised the competence of the International Fact-Finding Commission, namely, Cyprus on 14 October 2002, the Cook Islands on 7 November 2002 and the Democratic Republic of the Congo on 12 December 2002.[187]

7.   INTERNATIONAL ORGANISATIONS AND ACTIONS

7.1   United Nations Organization

7.1.1   The Security Council[188]

7.1.1.1   Afghanistan

Resolution 1390 of 28 January 2002, adopted by the SC under Chapter VII, reiterated the Council's condemnation of the attacks of 11 September 2001, noted the

---

185. See Year in Review, 4 *YIHL* (2001) pp. 298-299.

186. 'Use of nuclear, biological or chemical weapons: current international law and policy statements', Informal information note to Red Cross and Red Crescent National Societies about the ICRC position, <http://www.icrc.org/web/eng/siteeng0.nsf/iwpList512/0258785B15B3C484C1256CEE00>.

187. <http://www.ihffc.org/>.

failure of the Taliban to respond to its demands and condemned it for allowing Afghanistan to be used as a terrorist base and Al Qaeda and other terrorist groups for causing multiple civilian deaths. It stipulated a series of measures that states must take with respect to Osama Bin Laden, members of Al Qaeda and the Taliban and others associated with them: freezing of their assets, preventing weapons being supplied or sold directly or indirectly to them, and preventing their entry or transit through their territories.

Resolution 1401 of 28 March established a United Nations Assistance Mission in Afghanistan (UNAMA), for an initial period of 12 months, with a mandate and structure as laid out in the report of the Secretary-General of 18 March 2002 (S/2002/278). The resolution also reiterated the Council's support for the Bonn process and encouraged donor countries to make their contributions forthcoming.

Resolution 1413 of 23 May, adopted under Chapter VII, extended the authorisation for six months after 20 June 2002 of the International Security Assistance Force (ISAF), and authorised all member states participating in it to take 'all necessary measures to fulfill the mandate of the International Security Assistance Force'. It called upon member states to contribute personnel, equipment, and other resources to ISAF and to make contributions to the Trust Fund established pursuant to resolution 1386 (2001). It requested ISAF's leadership to provide monthly reports on the implementation of its mandate to the Secretary-General. The resolution also extended the Council's appreciation to the UK for taking the lead in organising and commanding ISAF, and welcomed Turkey's offer to assume the lead.

Security Council resolution 1419 of 26 June welcomed the election by the Emergency Loya Jira (held from 11 to 19 June) of Hamid Karzai as President of Afghanistan and the establishment of the Transitional Authority. It reiterated its strong support for the latter, in the full implementation of the Bonn Agreement, and called on all Afghan groups to cooperate in order to complete the peace process.

Resolution 1444 of 27 November extended ISAF's mandate for a further year beyond 20 December 2002, and authorised the participating member states to take all necessary measures to fulfill its mandate. It welcomed Turkey's assumption of ISAF's command, and called on all member states to contribute personnel and other resources to the Force and to contribute to the Trust Fund.

Resolution 1453 of 24 December welcomed the Kabul Declaration on Good-Neighbourly Relations signed by the Transitional Administration and the governments of China, Iran, Pakistan, Tajikistan, Turkmenistan and Uzbekistan on 22 December 2002 (S/2002/1416) and called on all states to respect it and support its implementation.

7.1.1.2   Angola

Resolution 1404 of 18 April, adopted under Chapter VII of the Charter, extended the mandate of the monitoring mechanism set up by the Council to monitor com-

---

188. The following does not mention every SC resolution but only those of particular interest to this readership, and merely highlights the most salient aspects of these resolutions.

pliance with the provisions of its earlier resolutions 864 (1993), 1127 (1997) and 1173 (1998) concerning the trade in conflict diamonds, and said that it would give full consideration to the expected report of the monitoring mechanism. It requested the monitoring mechanism to provide an additional report by 15 October 2002. It requested the Secretary-General to appoint four experts to serve on the monitoring mechanism and to make the necessary financial arrangements to support its work. All states should cooperate fully with the monitoring mechanism.

On 15 August, the Security Council adopted two resolutions concerning Angola, resolutions 1432 and 1433. Resolution 1432 suspended travel restrictions on UNITA members for 90 days in order to allow them to participate in the peace process. Resolution 1433 authorised the establishment of a United Nations Mission in Angola (UNMA) for a period of six months, until 15 February 2003. UNMA's mandate includes assisting the parties in concluding the Lusaka Protocol and assisting the Angolan government in a variety of tasks.

7.1.1.3   Bosnia and Herzegovina

Resolution 1423 of 12 July, adopted under Chapter VII considering that the situation in the region continued to constitute a threat to international peace and security, reaffirmed the Council's support for the General Framework Agreement for Peace in Bosnia and Herzegovina and the Dayton Peace Agreement and called upon all parties to strictly comply with their obligations under those Agreements. These included the duty to cooperate with all entities involved in the implementation of the peace settlement, including the International Tribunal for the Former Yugoslavia. It underlined that 'full cooperation by States and entities with the International Tribunal includes, *inter alia*, the surrender for trial of all persons indicted by the Tribunal and provision of information to assist in Tribunal investigations'. It authorised the Member States to continue SFOR (the multinational stabilisation force) for a further 12 months, authorised states to take all necessary measures to assist SFOR in carrying out its mission or in its defence, and recognised its right to take all necessary measures to defend itself from attack. The resolution also extended the mandate of the United Nations Mission in Bosnia and Herzegovina (UNMIBH), which includes the International Police Task Force (IPTF), until 31 December 2002.

7.1.1.4   Croatia

Resolution 1387 of 15 January authorised the United Nations Mission of Observers in Prevlaka (UNMOP) to continue monitoring the demilitarisation of the Prevlaka peninsula until 15 July 2002. It called on all parties to cease all violations of the demilitarised regime in the UN designated zones, to fully cooperate with the UN observers and to ensure their safety and free movement.

Resolution 1424 of 12 July further extended the military observers' mandate until 15 October. Resolution 1437 of 11 October authorised a final extension of UNMOP's mandate until 15 December 2002. It requested the Secretary-General to prepare for the termination of its mandate by gradually reducing the number of personnel, *inter alia*.

7.1.1.5   Cyprus

Resolution 1416 of 13 June extended the mandate of the United Nations Peace-keeping Force in Cyprus (UNFICYP) until 15 December 2001. Resolution 1442 of 25 November reaffirmed all of the Council's previous relevant resolutions on Cyprus and extended the mandate of UNFICYP until 15 June 2003. It urged the Turkish Cypriot side and Turkish forces to rescind restrictions imposed on UNFI-CYP operations and to restore the military status quo ante at Strovilia.

7.1.1.6   Democratic Republic of the Congo

The armed conflict in the Democratic Republic of Congo (DRC) remained a press-ing issue on the Council's active agenda. Resolution 1399 of 19 March condemned the fighting in Moliro in the DRC and the capture of Moliro by Rassemblement Congolais pour la Democratie-Goma (RCD-Goma). It stressed that no party to the Lusaka Ceasefire Agreement should be allowed to make military gains while a peace process is underway and while a peacekeeping operation is deployed. It de-manded an immediate withdrawal of all troops and the demilitarisation of such locations.

Resolution 1417 of 14 June extended the mandate of the United Nations Orga-nisation Mission in the Democratic Republic of Congo (MONOC) for one year until 30 June 2003 and called upon member states to support MONOC with per-sonnel to enable it to reach its authorised strength of 5,537 troops, including obser-vers. It expressed its intention to authorise a troop increase as soon as further progress had been achieved. The Council condemned ethnically- and nationally-based calls for violence and the killings of and attacks on civilians and soldiers in Kisangani, and reiterated that it held RCD-Goma, as the *de facto* authority, respon-sible to bring to an end all extrajudicial executions, human rights violations and harassment of civilians. It expressed its particular concern at the situation in the Ituri region and in South Kivu and called on all *de facto* authorities in the regions affected to ensure the protection of civilians and the rule of law. The resolution demanded the total and complete withdrawal of all foreign forces from DRC, and reiterated that all parties must submit their withdrawal plans to MONOC.

Following the signing on 30 July 2002 by the DRC and Rwanda of the Pretoria Agreement,[189] and on 6 September by the DRC and Uganda of the Luanda Agree-ment,[190] the Security Council adopted resolution 1445 on 4 December. It wel-comed the signing of these agreements and the decision made by all the foreign parties to fully withdraw from the DRC, and the progress made, including the verified withdrawal of 23,400 Rwandan troops on 24 October.

---

189. S/2002/914. <http://www.iss.co.za/AF/profiles/DRCongo/ptaagmt0702.htm>.
190. <http://www.usip.org/library/pa/drc_uganda/drc_uganda_09062002.html>.

The detailed resolution addressed many other aspects of the peace process, including disarmament, demobilisation, repatriation, reintegration and resettlement. It stressed that the main responsibility for ending the conflict lay with the parties themselves, who must demonstrate their will to fully respect their commitments and not provide support for any of the groups involved in the fighting, particularly in the Ituri area. Further efforts were necessary in order to achieve a comprehensive solution to the conflict. The Council called for a full cessation of hostilities involving regular forces and armed groups throughout the DRC, in particular in South Kivu and Ituri, and a cessation of all support to the armed groups. It called for the surrender to the ICTR of any indicted persons, and its concern at the humanitarian situation, particularly in Ituri. It expressed its deep concern 'over the intensification of ethnically targeted violence in the Ituri region', condemned 'all such violence or incitement to violence', requested 'all parties to take immediate action to defuse these tensions, ensure the protection of civilians and end violations of human rights', called on all parties to cooperate to set up the Ituri Pacification Commission, and requested the Secretary-General to authorise an increase in MONUC's presence in the area, 'if he determines that the security condition allows it'.

7.1.1.7   East Timor

Resolution 1392 of 31 January extended the mandate of the United Nations Transitional Administration in East Timor (UNTAET) until 20 May 2002, the date of independence.

On 17 May, the Council adopted resolution 1410, which established, as of 20 May and for an initial period of 12 months, a United Nations Mission of Support in East Timor (UNMISET) with the mandate: to provide assistance to East Timor's core administrative structures; to provide interim law enforcement and public security and to assist in the development of a new law enforcement agency, the East Timor Police Agency; and to contribute to the maintenance of the external and internal security of East Timor.

Headed by the Secretary-General's Special Representative, UNMISET had a civilian and a military component. The civilian component consisted of an Office of the Special Representative, with focal points for gender and HIV/AIDS; a Civilian Support Group, comprising up to 100 personnel; a Serious Crimes Unit and a Human Rights Unit. The military component had an initial strength of up to 5,000 troops, including 120 military observers. UNMISET was tasked to give effect to the following three Programmes of the Mandate Implementation Plan: Stability, Democracy and Justice; Public Security and Law Enforcement; and External Security and Border Control. Internationally accepted human rights principles should form an integral part of the training and capacity building carried out by UNMISET. Over a two year period, UNMISET had to fully devolve all operational responsibilities to the East Timorese authorities, without jeopardising stability. The resolution also referred to the need for cooperation between Indonesia and East Timor, *inter alia*, to ensure that those responsible for serious crimes committed in 1999 were brought to justice.

Resolution 1414 of 23 May admitted East Timor to the United Nations.

7.1.1.8 Ethiopia and Eritrea

Resolution 1398 of 15 March, which extended the mandate of the United Nations Mission in Ethiopia and Eritrea (UNMEE) until 15 September, reaffirmed the need for both parties to fulfill their obligations under international law, including international humanitarian law, human rights law and refugee law. It welcomed the anticipated final legal settlement of the border issues in accordance with the Algiers Agreements, and the parties' statement that they considered the border delimitation determination by the Boundary Commission[191] to be final and binding.

By resolution 1430 of 14 August, the Security Council adjusted UNMEE's mandate 'in order to assist the Boundary Commission in the expeditious and orderly implementation of its Delimitation Decision', to include demining and key area and administrative and logistical support for the Field Offices of the Boundary Commission. It called on both parties to cooperate with UNMEE in the implementation of its adjusted mandate, and reaffirmed 'the need for both parties to fulfill their obligations under international law, including international humanitarian law, human rights law and refugee law, and to ensure the safety of all personnel of the United Nations, the International Committee of the Red Cross (ICRC) and other humanitarian organisations. It again called on the parties to 'release and return without delay all remaining prisoners of war and civilian internees under the auspices of the International Committee of the Red Cross in accordance with the Geneva Conventions and the Algiers Agreements'.

Resolution 1434 of 6 September extended UNMEE's mandate until 15 March 2003. It welcomed 'the recent confirmations by both parties to implement fully their commitments under Article 2 of the Comprehensive Peace Agreement, in accordance with the Geneva Conventions, and in so doing', welcomed 'the recent release and repatriation by Eritrea of 279 prisoners of war (POWs)' and strongly encouraged 'Ethiopia to follow through on its pledge relating to the release and repatriation of its POWs and civilian internees', and called upon both parties 'to continue to clarify the cases of any remaining POWs and to resolve all other remaining issues in accordance with the Geneva Conventions, in cooperation with the International Committee of the Red Cross. It expressed its concern regarding reported incidents of cross border harassment and abductions of civilians on both sides and called on both parties to immediately put an end to such incidents and to fully cooperate with UNMEE investigations in this regard.

7.1.1.9 Georgia

Resolution 1393 of 31 January addressed the ongoing conflict in Abkhazia. Stressing that the continued lack of progress on key issues of a comprehensive settlement of the conflict in Abkhazia is unacceptable, it commended and supported the efforts of the Secretary-General and his Special Representative, the Russian Federation, the Group of Friends and the OSCE to stabilise the situation and achieve a

---

191. <http://www.un.org/NewLinks/eebcarbitration/EEBC-Decision.pdf>.

comprehensive political settlement, which must include a settlement of the political status of Abkhazia within the state of Georgia. Extending the mandate of the United Nations Observer Mission in Georgia (UNOMIG) until 31 July, the resolution called on the parties to take the necessary steps to identify those responsible for the shooting down of a UNOMIG helicopter on 8 October 2001 and to bring them to justice. It expressed its concern at the efforts of the parties to hinder the movement of UNOMIG and reminded Georgia to uphold its commitment to cease the activities of illegal armed groups crossing into Abkhazia from the Georgian-controlled side of the ceasefire line.

By July the situation had barely changed in Abkhazia and resolution 1427 of 29 July repeated many of the same sentiments as resolution 1393. It welcomed, however, the decrease of tensions in the Kodori Valley and the protocol signed by the two sides on 2 April and called on them to implement it fully. It once again stressed the need for progress on the issue of refugees and internally displaced people.

7.1.1.10 Iraq

On 14 May the Council, acting under Chapter VII of the Charter, adopted resolution 1409 adopting the revised Goods Review List[192] and the attached revised procedures concerning the humanitarian program in Iraq.

As the year progressed, controversy over Iraq's alleged weapons of mass destruction programs heated up, and the US gave increasingly strong signals of its willingness to go to war against Iraq, without SC authorisation if need be.

As noted in the introduction, on 8 November, the Council unanimously adopted resolution 1441, consisting of 14 operative paragraphs. It is clear from its preambular paragraphs that the resolution is based on the assumption that Iraq possessed weapons of mass destruction programs and such weapons themselves, as it recognised 'the threat Iraq's non-compliance with Council resolutions and proliferation of weapons of mass destruction and long-range missiles poses to international peace and security', and recalled 'that its resolution 678 (1990) authorized Member States to use all necessary means to uphold and implement its resolution 660 (1990) of 2 August 1990 and all relevant resolutions subsequent to resolution 660 (1990) and to restore international peace and security in the area'. It deplored Iraq's failure to provide an accurate, full, final and complete disclosure, as required by resolution 687 (1991), 'of all aspects of its programmes to develop weapons of mass destruction and ballistic missiles with a range greater than 150 km, and of all holdings of such weapons, their components and production facilities and locations, as well as all other nuclear programmes ...'

Operative paragraph 1 declared that 'Iraq has been and remains in material breach of its obligations under relevant resolutions, including resolution 687 (1991), in particular through Iraq's failure to cooperate with United Nations inspectors and the IAEA, and to complete the actions required under paragraphs 8 to

---

192. S/2002/515.

13 of resolution 687.' By paragraph 2 it extended to Iraq 'a final opportunity to comply with its disarmament obligations under relevant resolutions of the Council; and accordingly decides to set up an enhanced inspection regime with the aim of bringing to full and verified completion the disarmament process established by resolution 687 (1991) and subsequent resolutions of the Council'. The Council gave Iraq 30 days to provide to the United Nations Monitoring, Verification and Inspection Commission (UNMOVIC), the IAEA and itself, 'a currently accurate, full, and complete declaration of all aspects of its programmes to develop chemical, biological, and nuclear weapons, ballistic missiles, and other delivery systems … including any holdings and precise locations of such weapons, components, subcomponents, stocks of agents, and related material and equipment, the locations and work of its research, development and production facilities, as well as all other chemical, biological, and nuclear programmes, including any which it claims are for purposes not related to weapons production or material' (para. 3). Any false statement or omissions by Iraq in its declaration would constitute a further material breach of Iraq's obligations (para. 4).

Iraq was obliged to provide UNMOVIC and the IAEA with 'immediate, unconditional, and unrestricted access to any and all sites, including underground areas, facilities, buildings, equipment, records, and means of transport which they wish to inspect, as well as immediate, unimpeded, unrestricted, and private access to all officials and other persons whom UNMOVIC or the IAEA wish to interview in the mode or location of UNMOVIC's or the IAEA's choice pursuant to any aspect of their mandate' (para. 5). Iraq was given seven days to notify the Council of its intention to comply fully with the resolution, and had to immediately cooperate, unconditionally and actively, with UNMOVIC and the IAEA. All member states were requested to give full support to UNMOVIC and the IAEA in the discharge of their mandates. Any interference by Iraq with inspection activities or failure to comply with its disarmament obligations must be immediately reported by the Executive Chairman of UNMOVIC, Dr Hans Blix, and the Director-General of the IAEA, Dr Mohamed El Baredi, to the Council. Upon receipt of such a report, the Council would reconvene immediately. The resolution recalled that the SC had 'repeatedly warned Iraq that it will face serious consequences as a result of its continued violations of its obligations' (para. 13). In the meantime, it would remain seized of the matter. The resolution also deplored Iraq's failure to comply with its commitments under resolution 687 (1991) regarding terrorism, to end repression of its civilian population and to provide access for humanitarian workers to those in need, and to return or cooperate in accounting for Kuwaiti and third country nationals wrongfully detained by Iraq, or to return Kuwaiti property wrongfully seized by Iraq.

Resolution 1443 of 25 November, adopted under Chapter VII, extended the provisions of resolution 1409 (2002) until 4 December. Resolution 1447 of 4 December, adopted under Chapter VII, extended the Goods Review List for a new period of 180 days from 5 December. Resolution 1454 of 30 December approved for implementation beginning on 31 December of the adjustments to the Goods Review List and the revised procedure for implementation of the List specified in the annexes to the resolution, as the basis for the humanitarian programme in Iraq as referred to in resolution 986 (1995) and other relevant resolutions.

7.1.1.11 Israel/Occupied Territories

On 12 March, the Security Council passed resolution 1397 – introduced by the USA – endorsing the creation of a Palestinian state. The Council voted for it by 14 votes in favour, with one abstention (Syria). The resolution affirmed 'a vision of a region where two States, Israel and Palestinian, live side by side within secure and recognized borders', and stressed the need for all concerned to ensure the safety of civilians and respect the universally accepted norms of international humanitarian law. It demanded 'immediate cessation of all acts of violence, including all acts of terror, provocation, incitement and destruction' and urged Israel and the Palestinians to take steps towards resuming peace talks. The Palestinians praised the move, while Israel said it welcomed a 'balanced' resolution.[193] It was the first resolution on the conflict that the United States had introduced since fighting erupted in September 2000.[194]

On 30 March, the Council adopted resolution 1402 which expressed 'its grave concern at the further deterioration of the situation, including the recent suicide bombings in Israel and the military attack against the headquarters of the President of the Palestinian Authority'. It called upon both parties 'to move immediately to a meaningful ceasefire'; called for Israeli troops to withdraw from Palestinian cities, including Ramallah; and called upon the parties to fully cooperate with the peace process. It repeated its demand for an immediate cessation of all violence, including all acts of terror, provocation, incitement and destruction. Five days later the Council followed up with resolution 1403 of 4 April, which expressed its grave concern at the further deterioration of the situation and noted that resolution 1402 had not yet been implemented. It demanded its implementation without delay, and welcomed the mission of the US Secretary of State to the region, and efforts by others, particularly the Russian Federation, the EU and the UN Special Coordinator, to bring about a comprehensive, just and lasting peace in the Middle East.

On 24 September, the Council issued what was by its own standards a strongly worded resolution following Israeli reoccupation of Palestinian cities, including Ramallah, and Yassir Arafat's headquarters. Resolution 1435 expressed the Council's grave concern 'at the reoccupation of the headquarters of the President of the Palestinian Authority in the City of Ramallah that took place on 19 September 2002' and demanded 'its immediate end', and its alarm 'at the reoccupation of Palestinian cities as well as the severe restrictions imposed on the freedom on movement of persons and goods', and grave concern at the humanitarian crisis being faced by the Palestinian people. It reiterated 'its demand for the cessation of all acts of violence, including all acts of terror, provocation, incitement and destruction'; demanded that 'Israel immediately cease measures in and around Ra-

---

193. 'UN SC Resolution 1397: Constructive Contribution?', <http://www.nuerdetnok.dk/artikler/>.
194. UN backs Palestinian state', BBC Online News Report (13 March 2002).

mallah including the destruction of Palestinian civilian and security infrastructure', and demanded 'the expeditious withdrawal of the Israeli occupying forces from Palestinian cities towards the return of the position held prior to September 2000'. It also condemned all terrorist attacks against any civilians and called on 'the Palestinian Authority to meet its expressed commitment to ensure that those responsible for terrorist acts are brought to justice by it'. It expressed its full support for the efforts of the Quartet and called upon Israel, the PNA and all states in the region to cooperate with these efforts.

7.1.1.12 Lebanon

Resolution 1391 of 28 January 2002 extended the mandate of the United Nations Interim Force in Lebanon (UNIFIL) until 31 July 2002, and requested the Secretary-General to continue to take the necessary measures to implement the reconfiguration of UNIFIL. It called on the government of Lebanon to ensure the return of its effective authority in the south, including the deployment there of armed troops. It also condemned all acts of violence and expressed its great concern about the serious violations of the withdrawal line and urged them to cease these violations and respect the safety of UNIFIL personnel.

Resolution 1428 of 30 July extended UNIFIL's mandate for a further six months, until 31 January 2003, and otherwise addressed many of the same concerns as resolution 1391.

7.1.1.13 Liberia

Resolution 1408 of 6 May, adopted under Chapter VII, addressed, *inter alia*, the violations by Liberia of resolution 1343 (2001) concerning the trade in conflict diamonds, particularly through the acquisition of arms. The Council determined that 'the active support by the Government of Liberia to armed rebel groups in the region, in particular to former Revolutionary United Front (RUF) combatants who continue to destabilize the region, constitutes a threat to international peace and security in the region', and demanded that all states in the region cease military support for armed groups in neighbouring countries, take action to prevent armed individuals and groups from using their territories to prepare and commit attacks on neighbouring countries and refrain from any action that might contribute to further destabilisation of the situation on the borders between Guinea, Liberia and Sierra Leone. It called on the government of Liberia to fully cooperate with the Special Court for Sierra Leone; and reiterated its call upon Liberia to establish an effective Certificate of Origin regime for Liberian rough diamonds that is transparent and verifiable, taking into account the Kimberly process.[195] It called on the Secretary-General to establish a Panel of Experts to conduct a follow-up assessment mission to Liberia and neighbouring states in order to report on Liberia's compliance with SC demands, and requested all states and particularly arms ex-

---

195. See <http://www.kimberleyprocess.com:8080/>.

porting countries to exercise the highest degree of responsibility in transactions in small arms and light weapons to prevent their illegal diversion and re-export.

7.1.1.14 Sierra Leone

Resolution 1389 of 16 January authorised the United Nations Mission in Sierra Leone (UNAMSIL) to undertake certain election-related tasks in order to facilitate the smooth holding of elections. Resolution 1400 of 28 March 2002 extended the mandate of UNAMSIL for six months until 30 March 2002. It expressed the Council's serious concern at the violence, particularly sexual violence, suffered by women and children during the conflict in Sierra Leone and the importance of addressing these issues effectively. It expressed serious concern at the evidence of breaches of humanitarian law and human rights law uncovered by UNAMSIL, and at allegations that UN personnel may have been involved in sexual abuse of women and children in refugee and internally displaced persons' camps, and called on states to prosecute their nationals responsible for such crimes.

Resolution 1436 of 24 September was a detailed resolution concerning several aspects of the peace process in Sierra Leone. It extended UNAMSIL's mandate for a further six months from 30 September 2002 and welcomed the establishment of the Special Court for Sierra Leone and expressed its support for it. It encouraged donors to contribute to its Trust Fund, and urged UNAMSIL to rapidly negotiate a memorandum of understanding with the Court in order to provide all necessary administrative and related support, including on the identification and securing of crime scenes. It welcomed progress in establishing the Truth and Reconciliation Commission and urged donors to contribute to its budget. It demanded that the armed forces of Liberia and other states in the region refrain from illegal incursions into the territory of Sierra Leone, and called on all states to observe the arms embargo against Liberia. It encouraged the government of Sierra Leone to pay special attention to the needs of women and children affected by war, as outlined in the report of the Secretary-General.[196]

Resolution 1446 followed on 4 December 2002. It extended the measures restricting the export of illicit conflict diamonds for a period of six months from 5 December, given 'the role played by the illicit trade in diamonds in fuelling the recent conflict in Sierra Leone', and expressed 'its concern at the current large volume of illicit trade in diamonds and its potential negative impact on the fragile situation in Sierra Leone'. It welcomed GA resolution A/RES/65/263 of 13 March 2002 and ongoing efforts by states, the diamond industry and NGOs to break the link between the illicit trade in rough diamonds and armed conflict, particularly through the Kimberly process.

---

196. S/2002/987 of 5 September 2002.

7.1.1.15 Somalia

Resolution 1407, adopted on 3 May under Chapter VII, addressed the problem of the flow of weapons and ammunition to Somalia and its threat to peace and security. It requested the Secretary-General to establish within one month a team of experts consisting of two members, to prepare an action plan for an envisaged Panel of Experts detailing the resources and expertise that the Panel will require. The task of the Panel of Experts will be to generate independent information on violations of the arms embargo. The resolution called on all states to cooperate in the enforcement of the resolution.

By resolution 1425, adopted on 22 July, the Security Council, acting under Chapter VII, strengthened the arms embargo on Somalia. It decided that it 'prohibits the direct or indirect supply to Somalia of technical advice, financial and other assistance, and training related to military activities', and stressed that it 'prohibits financing of all acquisitions and deliveries of weapons and military equipment'. The resolution welcomed the Secretary-General's report and that of the expert team, and requested the Secretary-General to establish within one month a Panel of Experts consisting of three members to be based in Nairobi for six months, with the task of generating independent information on violations of the arms embargo as a step towards giving effect to and strengthening the embargo. It requested all states and the Transitional National Government and local authorities in Somalia to fully cooperate with the Panel of Experts.

7.1.1.16 Western Sahara

Security Council resolution 1394 of 27 February 2002 extended the mandate of the United Nations Mission for the Referendum in Western Sahara (MINURSO) until 30 April and requested the Secretary-General to provide a report on the situation before this date. On 30 April, MINURSO's mandate was further extended until 31 July, in order to consider further the report of the Secretary-General of 19 February.[197]

Resolution 1429 of 30 July addressed, *inter alia*, the plight of the prisoners of war held by both sides for many years.[198] 'Seeking to alleviate the consequences of conflict in Western Sahara, and accordingly to secure the immediate release of prisoners of war and other detainees, to establish the fate of persons unaccounted for, and to repatriate refugees, the resolution welcomed the release of 101 Moroccan prisoners of war,' and called upon the Polisario Front 'to release without further delay all remaining prisoners of war in compliance with international humanitarian law'. It called upon both Morocco and the Polisario Front 'to continue to cooperate with the efforts of the International Committee of the Red Cross to resolve the problem of the fate of all those unaccounted for since the beginning of the conflict'. The resolution further extended the mandate of MINURSO until 31 January 2003, and expressed its continued support for the efforts of the Secretary-

---

197. S/2002/178.
198. See the article by H.-P. Gasser in this volume at p 379.

General and his Personal Envoy to find a political solution to this long-standing dispute.

7.1.2 *The General Assembly*

In October, the Sixth (legal) Committee of the General Assembly discussed the status of ratifications of the four 1949 Geneva Conventions and their two Additional Protocols, following the GA's request in 2001 that the Secretary-General prepare a report on the status of the Protocols and measures taken to strengthen the existing body of international humanitarian law, based on information received from Member States and the International Committee of the Red Cross.

The Committee heard that compliance with international humanitarian law and widespread education about its rules and principles is of crucial importance, particularly these days when civilians are increasingly becoming direct targets rather than collateral victims of armed conflicts.[199]

Delegates welcomed recent positive developments, such as the formation of over 60 national committees to oversee implementation of international humanitarian law and to educate the public and armed forces about relevant rights and obligations, as well as the entry into force of the Statute of the International Criminal Court. The ICRC representative said the international community must regularly take stock of the law, clarify the rules where necessary and ensure that normative developments do not weaken the legal regime of protection. It is important for states not only to respect but also to ensure respect for humanitarian law in all circumstances.

7.1.3 *The International Court of Justice*[200]

On 28 May, the Democratic Republic of the Congo filed an application before the ICJ for provisional measures against Rwanda, which it alleged was committing 'massive, serious and flagrant violations of human rights and of international humanitarian law' resulting 'from acts of armed aggression perpetrated by Rwanda on the territory of the Democratic Republic of the Congo in flagrant violation of the sovereignty and territorial integrity of the Democratic Republic of the Congo, as guaranteed by the United Nations and OAU Charters'.

The application alleged that since August 1998, Rwanda's armed aggression had resulted in large-scale human slaughter, rape and sexual assault of women, assassinations and kidnapping of political figures and human rights activists, arrests, arbitrary detentions, inhuman and degrading treatment, systematic looting of public and private institutions, seizure of property belonging to civilians, human rights violations committed by the invading Rwandan troops and their rebel allies in the major towns in the East of the DRC, and destruction of the fauna and the flora of

---

199. 'Legal Committee is told observance of humanitarian law critical', UN General Assembly Press Release GA/L/3208, 2 October 2002.

200. For more detailed commentary see J. Crook, 'The 2002 Judicial Activity of the International Court of Justice', 97 *AJIL* (2003) p. 352.

the country. The application also alleged that Rwanda had shot down a Boeing 727 owned by Congo Airlines on 9 October 1998 in Kindu, causing the death of 40 civilians.

The DRC requested the Court to rule, *inter alia*, that Rwanda had breached its international obligations under Article 2(3) and (4) of the UN Charter and Articles 3 and 4 of the OAU Charter; the Universal Declaration of Human Rights and the main human rights treaties, including the Women's Convention, the Torture Convention, the Genocide Convention, the Constitutions of the WHO and UNESCO, the Convention on International Civil Aviation, the Hague Convention for the Suppression of Unlawful Seizure of Aircraft and the Montreal Convention for the Suppression of Unlawful Acts Against the Safety of Civil Aviation.

As a remedy, the DRC sought the withdrawal of all Rwandan armed forces from its territory; compensation for all acts of looting, destruction, slaughter, removal of property or persons and other acts of wrongdoing imputable to Rwanda. It reserved the right in the course of the proceedings to claim other damage suffered by it and its people.

At the time of filing its application, the DRC applied to the Court for provisional measures 'pending the Court's decision on the merits ... to prevent irreparable harm being caused to its lawful rights and to those of its population by reason of the occupation of part of its territory by Rwandan forces'.

On 7 November 2002, public hearings in the case concerning the *Application of the Convention on the Prevention and Punishment of the Crime of Genocide* (*Croatia* v. *Yugoslavia*) were concluded and the ICJ began its deliberations. On 4 November, Yugoslavia had requested the Court to dismiss the case. 'Yugoslavia was not a member of the United Nations, was not a state party to the statute of the court, and was not a state party to the genocide convention', said Yugoslav legal representative Tibor Varady.[201]

8.   REGIONAL ORGANISATIONS AND ACTIONS

8.1   North Atlantic Treaty Organisation

On 21 November at a summit meeting in Prague, NATO announced its intention to create a rapid reaction force to enable it to respond quickly to crisis situations. A declaration issued by the summit stated that NATO must be able to 'field forces that can move quickly to wherever they are needed ... including in an environment where they might be faced with nuclear, biological and chemical threats'.[202]

---

201. 'Yugoslavia fights genocide case', BBC World (4 November 2002).
202. 'Nato creates rapid response force', BBC Online News Report (21 November 2002).

8.2   European Union

In an extraordinary about-face, on 30 September 2002, EU foreign ministers reached a deal that would prevent them from surrendering to the ICC US agents, such as peacekeepers.[203] The agreement, known as the EU common position on the ICC, was all the more unexpected as for months prior to reaching it EU ministers had been vocal in their criticism of US efforts to exempt its nationals from the ICC,[204] whether through adoption of the American Servicemembers' Protection Act, its sponsorship of SC resolution 1422 or by trying to reach bilateral so-called Article 98 agreements with states.[205]

Earlier, a paper drafted by the EU legal service had advised that such an exemption had no legal basis under international law and was in violation of EU Member States' obligations under the ICC Statute,[206] being contrary to the purposes and principles of the Statue. However, the paper did not dispute the legality of EU Member States signing an Article 98 agreement with the US, so long as it concerned only US military personnel serving on mission and not all US nationals.[207] Under the EU agreement, there would be no exemption from prosecution for private citizens, such as mercenaries, suspected of committing ICC crimes.

8.3   European Court of Human Rights

On 23 March 2002, the European Court of Human Rights declared inadmissible an application by Slobodan Milošević concerning his detention and trial before the International Criminal Tribunal for the Former Yugoslavia.[208] The complainant alleged that his detention and trial by the ICTY was unlawful and violated Articles 5 (right to liberty and security of person), 6 (right to a fair trial), 10 (freedom of expression), 13 (right to an effective remedy) and 14 (prohibition of discrimination) of the European Convention on Human Rights. Milošević filed the application against the Netherlands on 20 December 2001, following the dismissal of his case before The Hague District Court on 31 August 2001.[209]

The ECHR struck out the application on the grounds of failure to exhaust domestic remedies. In particular, the applicant had not challenged the 31 August 2001 decision of the District Court of The Hague and had withdrawn an appeal against it before the Netherlands' Court of Appeals. In so doing he had also deprived himself of the possibility of a subsequent appeal on points of law to the Dutch Supreme Court.

---

203. See R. Wielaard, 'In nod to Bush administration, EU agrees to keep Americans out of war crimes court', AP (30 September 2002).

204. See for e.g., 'EU Slams U.S. Threat to World War Crimes Court', Reuters (18 June 2002).

205. See the USA report in Correspondents' Reports at pp. 622-624 of this volume.

206. See R. Wielaard, 'EU legal experts say nations have no right to exempt U.S. military from war crimes trials', AP (29 August 2002).

207. Ibid.

208. *Milosevic* v. *the Netherlands,* 22 March 2002. Reprinted in 41 *ILM* (2002) p. 801. See European Court of Human Rights 171, 27 March 2002. Press release issued by the Registrar.

209. See N. Keijzer, in Correspondents' Reports, 4 *YIHL* (2001) pp. 593-594.

8.4   **Inter-American Commission on Human Rights**

On 12 March, the Inter-American Commission on Human Rights, acting on a petition brought by the New York-based Center for Constitutional Rights, requested the US to 'take urgent measures necessary to have the legal status of the detainees at Guantánamo Bay determined by a competent tribunal'.[210] In its letter to the US, the Commission stated that:

'It is ... well known that doubts exists as to the legal status of the detainees. This includes the question of whether and to what extent the Third Geneva Convention and/or other provisions of international humanitarian law apply to some or all of the detainees and what implications this may have for their international human rights protections. According to official statements from the United States government, its Executive Branch has most recently declined to extend prisoner of war status under the Third Geneva Convention to the detainees, without submitting the issue for determination by a competent tribunal or otherwise ascertaining the rights and protections to which the detainees are entitled under US domestic or international law. To the contrary, the information available suggests that the detainees remain entirely at the unfettered discretion of the United States government. Absent clarification of the legal status of the detainees, the Commission considers that the rights and protections to which they may be entitled under international or domestic law cannot be said to be the subject of effective legal protection by the State.'

In its response of 11 April, the US argued that there was no legal or factual basis in fact or law for the Commission's request because: (a) international humanitarian law, not international human rights law, applied; (b) the IACHR had no jurisdiction to apply international humanitarian law; (c) the detainees, as a matter of public record, were unlawful combatants, not prisoners of war; and (d) the detainees were treated humanely. Therefore, the US asked the Commission to rescind its request for precautionary measures.[211]

On 15 July 2002, the US submitted an additional response to the Commission in which it maintained that the Commission had no jurisdiction to review its detention of enemy combatants or issue requests for precautionary measures to the US, much less binding ones.[212]

Rather than withdraw its request for precautionary measures as demanded by the US, the Commission, on 23 July 2002, again asked the US for information regarding how the US had complied with the request. The Commission stated that 'it has

---

210. Inter-American Commission on Human Rights (IACHR): *Decision on Request for Precautionary Measures (Detainees at Guantánamo Bay, Cuba)*. Reprinted in 41 *ILM* (2002) at p. 532. See also <http://www.humanrightsnow.org/oasconventiononguantanamodetainees.htm>.

211. See Response of US to Request for Precautionary Measures—*Detainees in Guantánamo Bay, Cuba*, IACHR 11 April 2002; American Society of International Law, *International Law in Brief* (4 June 2002).

212. Additional Response of US to Request for Precautionary Measures, *Detainees in Guantánamo Bay, Cuba*, IACHR 15 July 2002.

the competence and responsibility to monitor the human rights situation of the detainees and in so doing to look to and apply definitional standards and relevant rules of international humanitarian law in interpreting and applying the provisions of Inter-American human rights instruments in times of armed conflict'.[213]

On 23 August, the petitioners who had made the original request for precautionary measures requested a hearing before the Commission on the matter. That request was granted and an *in camera* meeting was held on 16 October.[214]

8.5   African Union

On 9 July 2002, the Protocol Relating to the Establishment of the Peace and Security Council of the African Union[215] was adopted by the 1st Ordinary Session of the Assembly of the African Union, held in Durban, South Africa.

The Protocol makes several references to international humanitarian law, and it is clear that ensuring respect for the law ranks amongst its key objectives. This is stated in Article 3 (objectives) which alludes to 'respect for the sanctity of human rights and international humanitarian law, as part of efforts for preventing conflicts' as being one of the African Union's objectives and states that 'respect for the rule of law, fundamental human rights and freedoms, the sanctity of human life and international humanitarian law' are amongst the principles that would guide the Union in its activities (Art. 4). Furthermore, while recognising as guiding principles the sovereignty and territorial integrity and the principle of non-interference in the internal affairs of member states, the Union equally recognises as a core guiding principle '[t]he right of the Union to intervene in a Member State pursuant to a decision of the Assembly in respect of grave circumstances, namely war crimes, genocide and crimes against humanity, in accordance with Article 4(h) of the Constitutive Act.'

The functions of the Peace and Security Council are, *inter alia*, to promote peace, security and stability in Africa, early warning and preventive diplomacy, peace-making, peace building and post-conflict reconstruction, humanitarian law and disaster action (Art. 6). Among the Peace and Security Council's powers are the power to 'anticipate and prevent disputes and conflicts, as well as policies that may lead to genocide and crimes against humanity' (Art. 7(a)) and to follow up progress made by states in respect for humanitarian law, *inter alia*, in the context of its conflict prevention activities (Art. 7(m)).

A particular innovation is the establishment of an African Standby Force, which shall be composed of standby multidisciplinary contingents with civilian and military components ready for rapid deployment (Art. 13(1)) Its functions shall include

---

213. IACHR Request to US, *Detainees in Guantánamo Bay, Cuba*, IACHR 23 July 2002.

214. For more details and a discussion see D. Weissbrodt, J. Fitzpatrick and F. Newman, eds., *International Human Rights – Law, Policy and Process*, 3rd edn. (Cincinnati OH, Anderson 2001). Supplement to Chapter 11: The Inter-American System and the Interpretation and Application of Human Rights Instruments (November 2003). <http://www1.umn.edu/humanrts/intlhr/chapter11.html>.

215. <http://www.africa-union.org/rule_prot/PROTOCOL-%20PEACE%20AND%20SECURITY %20COUNCIL%20OF%20THE%20AFRICAN%20UNION.pdf>.

observation and monitoring missions and other types of peace support operations; intervention in a state at its request in a grave situation; preventive deployment; peace-building, including post-conflict disarmament and demobilisation; and humanitarian assistance (Art. 13(3)). Significantly, training in both international humanitarian law and human rights law shall be an integral part of the training of both civilian and military contingents of standby forces.

9.   ARMS CONTROL AND DISARMAMENT

Considerable progress was made in the realm of arms control and disarmament, particularly concerning weapons of mass destruction (WMD), although here too there were notable disappointments. A common theme of the various efforts was a determination by participating states to prevent proliferation of weapons and in particular their acquisition by transnational terrorist groups.

9.1   Nuclear weapons

9.1.1   *Strategic Offensive Reductions Treaty*

On 24 May, the USA and the Russian Federation signed the Strategic Offensive Reductions Treaty (SORT), also known as, the Treaty of Moscow.[216] The bilateral treaty commits the signatories to reducing their stockpiles of strategic nuclear warheads to a maximum of 1,700 to 2,200 for each party by 31 December 2012 (Art. I). A Bilateral Implementation Commission will meet at least biannually to monitor implementation of the treaty (Art. III).

SORT continues where the five-Party Treaty on the Reduction and Limitation of Strategic Offensive Arms (START)[217] of 31 July 1991 left off. START remains in force. SORT will remain in force until 31 December 2012, unless the Parties decide to terminate it earlier, and may be extended by mutual agreement or replaced.[218]

In a Joint Declaration issued to coincide with the signing of SORT, the Parties elaborated on the types of cooperation envisaged under the new strategic relationship, including mutual political cooperation in resolving regional conflicts, economic cooperation and strategic cooperation, including in fighting transnational terrorism and preventing the proliferation of weapons of mass destruction.[219]

---

216. The text of the Treaty can be found at <http://fas.org/nuke/control/sort/sort.htm>.

217. The text of the START treaty can be found at <http://www.ceip.org/files/projects/npp/resources/start1text.htm>.

218. For an elaboration and detailed analysis of the terms of SORT see *Briefing Book on the Strategic Offensive Reductions Treaty or Treaty of Moscow* (Washington DC, Center for Arms Control and Non-Proliferation 2002).

219. The text of the Joint Declaration on the New Strategic Relationship is at <http://fas.org/nuke/control/sort/joint-decl.html>. See also 'President Bush, Russian President Putin sign nuclear arms treaty', Remarks by President Bush and President Putin at signing of Joint Declaration and press

9.1.2   *International Code of Conduct Against Ballistic Missile Proliferation*

On 25 November, the International Code of Conduct Against Ballistic Missile Proliferation (ICOC) was launched in The Hague.[220] Ninety-three states immediately signed up. The Netherlands was appointed as the Chair of the Code of Conduct for the first 12 months.[221]

The ICOC aims to fill some of the deficiencies of the 1987 Missile Technology Control Regime (MTCR)[222] – which it supplements but does not replace – by introducing demand-side controls on the acquisition of ballistic missile technology capable of delivering weapons of mass destruction.[223] The legally non-binding Code commits participating states to curb and prevent the proliferation of ballistic missiles capable of delivering weapons of mass destruction through regional and international efforts and to exercise maximum restraint in the development, testing and deployment of such weapons. The Code commits participating states to undertake various implementation and transparency measures. On the other hand, it was clear that these commitments only go so far. The US Under-Secretary for Arms Control and International Security, Mr John Bolton, stated that '… the United States – like other countries – understands this commitment as not limiting our right to take steps in these areas necessary to meet our national security requirements consistent with US national security strategy. This includes our ability to maintain our deterrent umbrella for our friends and allies, and the capabilities necessary to defeat aggression involving WMD attacks.'[224]

In a speech made following the launch of the Code of Conduct, UN Secretary-General Kofi Annan welcomed it, but at the same time stressed 'the need to continue international efforts to deal with the issue of missiles in its totality. There is no universally accepted norm or instrument specifically governing the development, testing, production, acquisition, transfer, deployment or use of missiles'.[225]

---

availability, The Kremlin, Moscow, Russia, 24 May 2002. <http://fas.org/nuke/control/sort/wh052402.html>.

220. The International Code of Conduct against Ballistic Missile Proliferation can be accessed online at the website of the Netherlands Ministry of Foreign Affairs. <http://www.minbuza.nl/default.asp?CMS_ITEM=MBZ460871>. See also International Code of Conduct Against Ballistic Missile Proliferation, Fact Sheet, Bureau of Nonproliferation, Washington, DC, 6 January 2004. <http://www.state.gov/t/np/rls/fs/27799.htm>.

221. See 'International Conference Against Ballistic Missile Proliferation in The Hague concludes', The Netherlands' Ministry of Foreign Affairs Press Release, 26 November 2002. <http://www.acronym.org.uk/docs/0211/doc13.htm>.

222. Missile Technology Control Regime (MTCR). Fact Sheet, Bureau of Nonproliferation, Washington DC, 23 December 2003. <http://www.state.gov/t/np/rls/fs/27514.htm>.

223. A. Harris, 'International Code of Conduct Against Ballistic Missile Proliferation', Basic Notes, 18 July 2002. <http://www.basicint.org/pubs/Notes/2002international_code.htm>.

224. See John. R. Bolton, Under Secretary for Arms Control and International Security, Remarks at the Launching Conference for the International Code of Conduct Against Ballistic Missile Proliferation, The Hague, the Netherlands, 25 November 2002. <http://www.state.gov/t/us/rm/15488.htm>.

225. 'Secretary-General welcomes launch of International Code of Conduct against Ballistic Missile Proliferation', UN Press Release SG/SM/8523, 25 November 2002. <http://www.un.org/News/Press/docs/2002/SGSM8523.doc.htm>.

9.1.3   *G-8 Global Partnership Against the Spread of Weapons and Materials of Mass Destruction*

In June 2002 at their meeting in Kananaskis, Canada, the leaders of the Group of Eight (G-8) formed a Global Partnership Against the Spread of Weapons and Materials of Mass Destruction, to provide material, technological and financial assistance to states (in the first instance, the Russian Federation) that lack the means to implement shared disarmament, non-proliferation and counter-terrorism objectives.[226] The focus of the Global Partnership will be non-proliferation, disarmament, counterterrorism and nuclear safety projects, and the project commits the G-8 nations to raise up to $20 billion over ten years to pay for these initiatives, half coming from the US.[227] As with SORT, a priority of the Global Partnership will be preventing WMD from falling into the hands of terrorists.

9.2   **Chemical weapons**

In early 2002 the Organisation for the Prohibition of Chemical Weapons (OPCW), seated in The Hague, was plunged into controversy when the US led a campaign to have its Director General, the Brazilian Jose Bustani, dismissed. It began in January when the US wrote to the Brazilian government asking it to recall Bustani, in contravention of the processes set out in the Chemical Weapons Convention. As justification, the US claimed that it did not like Bustani's management style, asserted that Bustani had ordered inspections in five countries for 'political reasons', and accused him of having a 'habit of refusing to consult' with member states, such as when he proposed anti-terrorism measures after the September 11 attacks without first approaching the United States. Brazil refused. In March, a smear campaign against Bustani duly commenced, in which Bustani was accused of 'financial mismanagement', 'demoralisation' of OPCW staff, 'bias' and 'ill-considered initiatives'. The US warned him that to avoid further damage to his reputation, he must resign. For his part, Bustani maintained that the campaign against him was politically motivated because he refused to treat the US as special but regarded it as on an equal footing with all other states, and stood firm. On 19 March the US proposed a vote of no confidence in Bustani, which it lost. At that point, the US, as the OPCW's biggest donor and threatening to withhold its dues unless the issue was resolved to its satisfaction, called a 'special session' of the member states to

---

226. See I. Anthony, 'Arms control in the new security environment', Chapter 14, *SIPRI Yearbook 2003* (Oxford, Oxford University Press 2003).

227. See 'The G8 global partnership against 'G-8 global partnership against the spread of weapons and materials of mass destruction', Kananaskis Summit 2002. <http://www.g8.fr/evian>. Alan. P. Larsen, Under Secretary for Economic, Business and Agricultural Affairs, Testimony before the House International Relations Committee, Washington DC, 25 July 2002. <http://www.state.gov/e/rls/rm/2002/12190.htm>.

oust him.[228] On 22 April, the OPCW voted 48-7 in favour of the US proposal dismissing Bustani. A further 43 nations abstained.[229]

Pundits and Bustani himself speculated that the real motivation behind the campaign was that the US wanted to discredit a person who might have removed any pretext for its planned war against Iraq,[230] although the US dismissed this as further evidence of Bustani's inflated ego and distorted sense of his responsibilities. It was known that Bustani had been trying to persuade Saddam Hussein to sign the Chemical Weapons Convention and open up Iraq to OPCW inspectors.[231]

9.3   Biological weapons

The final nail in the coffin of the hoped for optional verification protocol to the 1972 Biological Weapons Convention was hammered home at part two of the Fifth Review Conference of the States Parties to the Convention on the Prohibition of the Development, Production and Stockpiling of Bacteriological (Biological) and Toxin Weapons and on their Destruction, held in Geneva from 11-22 November 2002.[232] The meeting ended without the hoped for adoption of the verification protocol and the shelving of the entire project, probably indefinitely.[233]

At its eighth plenary meeting on 14 November 2002, the Conference decided on a number of steps for moving forward in other areas. In particular, it decided to hold three annual meetings of States Parties, commencing in 2003. The Sixth Review Conference would be convened no later than 2006. The goal of these interim meetings was to discuss and promote common understanding and effective action on: (i) the adoption of necessary national measures to implement the prohibitions set forth in the Convention, including the enactment of penal legislation; (ii) national mechanisms to establish and maintain the security and oversight of pathogenic micro-organisms and toxins; and (iii) enhancing international capabilities for responding to, investigation and mitigation of the effects of cases of alleged use of

---

228. 'U.S. confident of ousting chemical weapons chief', Reuters (29 March 2002).

229. 'Chemical weapons inspector sacked', CNN, 9 September 2002 <http://www.cnn.com/2002/WORLD/europe/04/22/chemical.weapons/index.html>; 'US Diplomatic Offensive Removes OPCW Director-General', *Disarmament Diplomacy*, Issue No. 64 (May-June 2002). Online at <http://www.acronym.org.uk/textonly/dd/dd64/64nr01.htm>; 'Anti-chemical chief sacked', Radio Netherlands, 23 April 2002. <http://www.rnw.nl/hotspots/html/opcw020423.html>; C. Lynch, 'Disarmament Agency Director Is Ousted: U.S. Assails Record on Chemical Arms', *Washington Post* (23 April 2002). <http://www.washingtonpost.com/ac2/wp-dyn?pagename=article&contentId=A31533-2002Apr22&-notFound=true>.

230. For the statement of Jose Bustani before being voted out of his job, see <http://www.opcw.org> (direct link to the statement is <http://www.opcw.org/SS1CSP/SS1CSP_DG_statement.html>.

231. G. Monbiot, 'The US wants to depose the diplomat who could take away its pretext for war with Iraq', *The Guardian* (16 April 2002).

232. The meeting had been reconvened after the meeting of the Fifth Review Conference held in Geneva from 19 November to 7 December ended without conclusion of a protocol and with the whole process heading for the rocks. See 4 *YIHL* (2001) p. 327.

233. For commentary, see O. Meier, 'The US Rejection of Bioweapons Verification, and Implications for Future Negotiations', International Network of Engineers and Scientists Against Proliferation, Bulletin No. 21, <http://www.inesap.org/bulletin21/bul21art26.htm>.

biological or toxin weapons or suspicious outbreaks of diseases; (iv) strengthening and broadening national and international institutional efforts and existing mechanisms for the surveillance, detection, diagnosis and combating of infectious diseases affecting humans, animals and plants; and (v) the content, promulgation and adoption of codes of conduct for scientists.[234]

10.   CONFLICT PREVENTION AND RESOLUTION

10.1   **Conflict prevention**

On 5 November, the Secretary-General issued a report titled 'Prevention of armed conflict: views of organs, organizations and bodies of the United Nations system',[235] which recorded the responses of all relevant UN organs, organisations and bodies to the recommendations made by the SG in his 2001 report on the prevention of armed conflict.[236] In the 2002 report, the SG noted that the 26 responses received reinforced the central findings of his 2001 report, in particular the emphasis on the importance of prevention of conflict to international peace and security as well as to sustainable development.[237] He stated further that the events of September 11 and the threat of transnational terrorism reinforced the urgency of prevention as well as the need for international cooperation in the move towards a culture of prevention.[238] 'The world cannot bear the moral, humanitarian and other costs of not preventing violent conflicts.'[239] *Inter alia*, the report urged the General Assembly to adopt a resolution on the issue of prevention.

234. For further details of the conclusions of the Fifth Review Conference see its Final Report. BWC/CONF.V/17, Geneva 2002.
235. A/57/588—S/2002/1269, 5 November 2002, prepared pursuant to GA resolution 55/281 of 1 August 2001.
236. A/55/985—S/2001/574 and Corr. 1. See 4 *YIHL* (2001) at pp. 310-311.
237. Ibid., at para. 5.
238. Ibid., at para. 6.
239. Ibid., at para. 8.

THE COMPLEMENTARY AND CONFLICTING RELATIONSHIP BETWEEN THE SPECIAL COURT FOR SIERRA LEONE AND THE TRUTH AND RECONCILIATION COMMISSION[1]

Abdul Tejan-Cole[2]

1. INTRODUCTION

Societies emerging from political turmoil and civil unrest associated with gross violations of human rights and humanitarian law face the crucial question of how to deal with these atrocities and put the past in its place.[3] Since the 1980s, this problem has been a major preoccupation of international law and scholarship. The traditional responses include outside intervention in such states pursuant to Chapter VII powers under the United Nations Charter, grants of conditional amnesty to perpetrators of war crimes and crimes against humanity, grants of some form of unconditional amnesty, and prosecution of perpetrators.

Nowhere is this question more pressing than in Sierra Leone, which recently emerged from a ten-year civil war characterized by systematic, serious and widespread violations of human rights and international humanitarian law.[4] The Gov-

---

1. © A. Tejan-Cole, 2004.

2. Law Lecturer, Fourah Bay College, University of Sierra Leone, Yale World Fellow 2002; Prosecutor Special Court for Sierra Leone. The views expressed herein are those of the author in his personal capacity and do not necessarily represent those of any organisation he works for or represents.

3. S.R. Ratner, 'New Democracies, Old Atrocities: An Inquiry in International Law', 87 *The Georgetown LJ* (1999) pp. 707-748. See also S.R. Ratner and J.S. Abrams, *Accountability For Human Rights Atrocities In International Law: Beyond The Nuremberg Legacy* (Oxford, Clarendon Press 1997) at pp. 140-141; J. Zalaquett, 'Confronting Human Rights Violations Committed by Former Governments: Principles Applicable and Political Constraints', in *State Crimes: Punishment or Pardon* (Denver CO, Aspen Inst. 1989) pp. 41-43; J. Sarkin, 'The Necessity and Challenges of Establishing a Truth and Reconciliation Commission in Rwanda', 21 *HRQ* (1999) at pp. 768-770, K. Henrard, 'The Viability Of National Amnesties in View of the Increasing Recognition Of Individual Criminal Responsibility At International Law', 8 *Journal of International Law MSU-DCL* (1999) pp. 595-649. See also L. Huyse, 'Transitional Justice', in P. Harris and B. Reilly, eds., *Democracy and Deep-Rooted Conflict: Options for Negotiators* (Stockholm, IDEA 1998) at pp. 273, 275; J. Malamud-Goti, 'Transitional Governments in the Breach: Why Punish State Criminals', in N.J. Kritz, ed., *Transitional Justice: How Emerging Democracies Reckon with Former Regimes* (Washington DC, US Inst. of Peace Press 1995) at pp. 189, 206; C.S. Nino, 'Response: The Duty to Punish Past Abuses of Human Rights put into Context: The Case of Argentina', in N.J. Kritz, ed., ibid., at pp. 417-419.

4. For a detailed account of the atrocities in Sierra Leone see A. Tejan-Cole, 'Human Right under the Armed Force Revolutionary Council - A catalogue of abuses', 10 *African JI & Comp. L* (1998) p. 481. See also <http://www.hrw.org.htm> and <http://www.amnesty.org>, in particular, the country and special reports on Sierra Leone from 1991 to date.

ernment of Sierra Leone had to make a choice between these four traditional strategies for dealing with these pervasive human rights violations. Many discussions on post-conflict accountability mechanisms focus on choosing between a truth commission, national or international criminal prosecutions, or some other form of establishing accountability. Sierra Leone is unique in trying almost all of these options in its attempt to address its post-conflict situation.

2.   HISTORY OF THE ESTABLISHMENT OF POST-CONFLICT MECHANISMS IN SIERRA LEONE

Atrocities were committed by rebel and government forces in the period after the conflict began in March 1991. Members of the Revolutionary United Front (RUF),[5] with the military and materiel support of the National Patriotic Front of Liberia (NPFL),[6] quickly gained control over a fifth of the territory of Sierra Leone and engaged in a campaign of violence whose only motivating factor seems to have been the control of Sierra Leone's abundant diamond wealth. In a counter offensive, the army hastily conscripted hundreds of recruits, as its number rose from 3,000 to 14,000 men in the first two years of the conflict. Most of the new government recruits were disaffected and the army was mismanaged and underpaid. In April 1992, a group of soldiers arrived in Freetown from the war front to demand better pay and conditions, but they soon overthrew President Momoh's government in a coup. Against a backdrop of rapidly deteriorating social conditions, labor and student unrest, and impending elections – which the opposition parties alleged the government was preparing to rig – the coup was extremely popular.

Over the next four years, the RUF continued to fight to overthrow the successive governments that followed. In 1996, Ahmad Tejan Kabbah was elected President of Sierra Leone but was overthrown in May 1997 in a military coup by the Armed Forces Revolutionary Council (AFRC).[7] The Sierra Leone Army supported the AFRC's leader, Major Johnny Paul Koroma, who in turn initiated an alliance with the RUF. During the RUF/AFRC rule, the rule of law and the economic situation of the country completely deteriorated. In February 1998, the Economic Community of West African States Monitoring Group (ECOMOG), which had been defending the Freetown airport, drove the RUF/AFRC out of Freetown and restored Kabbah to office. Sankoh was arrested in Nigeria, returned to Sierra Leone, tried, convicted and sentenced to death for treason. However, by the end of 1998, the rebels controlled over half the country, particularly in the areas of the major diamond mines.

---

5. The RUF is a loosely organized guerrilla group that started the war in 1991 seeking to topple the government of Sierra Leone and to retain control of the lucrative diamond-producing regions of the country. It was headed by a former Corporal in the Sierra Leone Army, Foday Sankoh.

6. Led by Charles Taylor, President of Liberia, it launched a civil war in neighbouring Liberia in 1989.

7. The Council formed by Johnny Paul Koroma after 25 May 1999

In January 1999, the AFRC/RUF entered Freetown and commenced 'Operation No Living Thing'. The subsequent human rights violations were among the worst of the conflict. ECOMOG, after several weeks, pushed the AFRC/RUF out of Freetown, but many children were abducted in the RUF retreat. The RUF continued to control many parts of the country. Many Sierra Leoneans were displaced as a result of the various occupations.

In May 1999, under the auspices of the Economic Community of West African States (ECOWAS), a ceasefire agreement was signed. In July, Sankoh was released from prison in order to attend negotiations with Kabbah in Lomé, Togo. On 7 July the Lomé Accord was signed.[8] To the dismay of many, Sankoh was appointed Chairman of the Board of the Commission for the Management of Strategic Resources, National Reconstruction and Development and with it control of the diamond mines, and was additionally appointed Vice-President of Sierra Leone, thereby making him answerable only to the President.

The Accord also provided a complete and unconditional blanket amnesty to all combatants since 1991. Although the UN witnessed the signing, it made it explicit that the amnesty and pardon provisions would not apply to violations of the international crimes of genocide, crimes against humanity, war crimes and other serious violations of international humanitarian law.[9] The Lomé Accord also provided for the creation of a Truth and Reconciliation Commission to aid in reconciling the various parties and provide a forum for victims and combatants to tell their stories, with the hope of beginning a healing process for all Sierra Leoneans.

In October 1999, the Security Council established the United Nation's Mission in Sierra Leone (UNAMSIL) to assist in carrying out the Lomé Accord. Although disarmament began and peacekeeping troops were present in Sierra Leone, the peace was tenuous. Hostilities did not cease and the atrocities continued.[10] In May 2000 the government of Sierra Leone and the United Nations reassessed their stance on the blanket amnesty after the rebels took United Nations peacekeepers as hostages[11] and Corporal Sankoh's security guards killed several people during a demonstration by civil society groups in front of his residence.[12]

---

8. Peace Agreement Between the Government of Sierra Leone and the Revolutionary United Front of Sierra Leone, 7 July 1999 [hereinafter Lomé Accord] <http://www.sierraleone.org/Loméaccord.html>.

9. Peace Agreement Between the Government of Sierra Leone and the Revolutionary United Front of Sierra Leone, 30 November 1996 [hereinafter Abidjan Accord] <http://www.sierra-leone.org/abidjanaccord.html>.

10. For a detailed account, see 'Sierra Leone: Getting Away With Murder, Mutilation, Rape-New testimony from Sierra Leone', Human Rights Watch, July 1999 <http://www.hrw.org/hrw/reports/1999/sierra/>, and A. Tejan-Cole, 'The Special Court for Sierra Leone: Conceptual Concerns and Alternatives', 1 *African Human Rights Law Journal* (2001) p. 107.

11. See <http://sierra-leone.org/slnews0500.html>, J. Rupert and D. Farah, 'Liberian Leader Urges Sierra Leone Rebels to Free Hostages', *Washington Post Foreign Service Saturday* (20 May 2000) p. A20.

12. N. Onishi, 'Gunmen Fire on Protesters in Sierra Leone', *New York Times* (9 May 2000). <http://sierra-leone.org/slnews0500-B.html> quoted MSF as saying that there were approximately 40 civilian casualties.

President Ahmed Tejan Kabbah wrote to the UN Secretary-General requesting the establishment of an independent Special Court for Sierra Leone to address the violations committed during the war. The Security Council passed a resolution mandating the Secretary-General to negotiate an agreement with the government of Sierra Leone to create an independent Special Court.[13] On 4 October 2000 the Secretary-General submitted his report to the Security Council, annexing the draft agreement between the UN and the government of Sierra Leone and the draft Statute for the establishment of the Court.[14] Several letters between the President of the Security Council and the Secretary-General from December 2000 to July 2001 made revisions to the Statute.[15]

In July 2001 the Security Council approved plans for a court that would prosecute 'persons who bear the greatest responsibility for serious violations of international humanitarian law and Sierra Leonean law committed in the territory of Sierra Leone since 30 November 1996'. In July 2001 the Security Council endorsed the establishment of a Special Court, and on 16 January 2002, Hans Correll[16] for the United Nations and Solomon Ekuma Berewa[17] for the government of Sierra Leone signed the Agreement establishing the Special Court for Sierra Leone.

Consequently, Sierra Leone will have both a national Truth and Reconciliation Commission and an international, UN-sanctioned Special Court. This situation is unique as it will be the first time a court and a truth commission with related jurisdiction have been established with the assistance of the United Nations. Both institutions will be operating at the same time with concurrent and somewhat overlapping jurisdiction.

3.   BASIS, COMPOSITION AND JURISDICTION OF THE TRUTH COMMISSION AND THE SPECIAL COURT

3.1   **Legal basis**

The Special Court for Sierra Leone will function under a unique mandate. Unlike the International Criminal Tribunal for Rwanda (ICTR) and the International Criminal Tribunal for the former Yugoslavia (ICTY), the Special Court for Sierra Leone was established by an agreement between the government of Sierra Leone and the UN under Security Council Resolution 1315 (2000), *not* pursuant to Chapter VII of the UN Charter. The Agreement determines, *inter alia*, the competence, jurisdic-

---

13. Res. 1315 (2000) of 14 August 2000. The Report of the Secretary-General on the Establishment of a Special Court for Sierra Leone, UN SCOR, UN Doc. S/2000/915 (2000).

14. See <http://www.sierra-leone.org/documents.html> and <http://daccess-ods.un.org/doc/UNDOC/GEN/N01/693/10/IMG/N0169310.pdf?OpenElement>.

15. Letters dated 22 December 2000, 12 January 2001 and 12 July 2001, respectively. <http://www.reliefweb.int>.

16. Deputy Under-Secretary for Legal Matters.

17. Then Attorney-General and Minister of Justice, now Vice President of Sierra Leone.

tion and organizational structure of the Special Court. No reference is made in either the Agreement or the Statute to Chapter VII of the United Nations Charter. Article 1 of the Agreement for the Special Court merely states: 'There is hereby established a Special Court for Sierra Leone ...' and the Statute of the Special Court traces its authority to an Agreement between the government of Sierra Leone and the UN 'pursuant to Security Council Resolution 1315 (2000)'.[18]

In a number of other resolutions on Sierra Leone the Security Council explicitly stated that it was acting pursuant to Chapter VII[19] but it failed to do so in Resolution 1315.[20] Although Resolution 1315 (2000)[21] used the same terminology found in Chapter VII of the Charter in reiterating 'that the situation in Sierra Leone continues to constitute a threat to international peace and security in the region', the Statute and Agreement do not explicitly state that the proposed court was established pursuant to this Chapter. Without such explicit reference, it seems clear that the Security Council was not exercising its powers under Chapter VII.

Despite its international component, the Truth and Reconciliation Commission is a national institution. The legal basis of the Truth and Reconciliation Commission is in Sierra Leonean law.[22] The Commission was first proposed under the Lomé Peace Accord. Unlike the Agreement with the Secretary-General establishing the Special Court, the Lomé Accord is not an international agreement but a compact between two national parties – the government and the Revolutionary United Front. The United Nations, Organisation of African Unity, the Economic Community of West African States and Jesse Jackson, US Presidential Special Envoy for the Promotion of Democracy in Africa, signed the agreement as witnesses and/or moral guarantors, not as parties.[23] Cementing the beginnings made through the signing of the Lomé Peace Accord, in 2000 the Parliament of Sierra Leone

---

18. <http://www.sierra-leone.org/specialcourtagreement.html>.

19. These Resolutions include 1343 (2001) (which imposed sanctions on Liberia for its support for the RUF and its involvement in the illicit arms-for-diamonds trade) <http://www.un.org/Docs/scres/2001/res1343e.pdf resolution>; resolutiion 1306 (2000) (prohibiting the direct or indirect import of all rough diamonds from Sierra Leone) <http://www.un.org/Docs/scres/2000/res1306e.pdf>; Resolution 1171 (1998) (terminating sanctions imposed on the military junta) <http://www.un.org/Docs/scres/1998/sres1171.htm> and resolution 1132 (1997) (demanding that the military junta take immediate steps to relinquish power in Sierra Leone and make way for the restoration of the democratically-elected government and a return to constitutional order) <http://www.un.org/Docs/scres/1997 / 9726713E.htm>.

20. There are numerous references in United Nations documents categorically stating that the Court was not established pursuant to Chapter VII. The Secretary-General of the UN in his Report on the establishment of the Special Court for Sierra Leone endorsed the view that the Court was not established pursuant to the Chapter VII of the Charter and noted that 'the Security Council may wish to consider endowing it with Chapter VII powers for the specific purpose of requesting the surrender of an accused from outside the jurisdiction of the Court.' The statements by UN officials constitute a part of the *travaux preparatoire* of the Special Court Agreement and will be used by the Courts when interpreting the Statute and the Agreement.

21. <http://daccessods.un.org/doc/UNDOC/GEN/N00/605/32/PDF/N0060532.pdf?OpenEle ment>.

22. See the Truth and Reconciliation Commission Act 2000, section 2(1), which states 'There is hereby established a body known as the Truth and Reconciliation Commission.'

23. <http://www.sierra-leone.org/lomeaccord.html>.

passed the Truth and Reconciliation Commission Act[24] specifying the scope, mandate and jurisdiction of the Commission.

3.2   Composition

The Special Court will be composed of one or more Trial Chambers, an Appeals Chamber, the Prosecutor's office and the Registry.[25] Three judges serve in the Trial Chambers – two appointed by the UN Secretary-General and one by the government of Sierra Leone.[26] Six months after the Court commences its functions, a second Trial Chamber may be set up if requested by the Secretary-General, the Prosecutor or the President of the Special Court.[27] In the Appeals Chambers, three judges were appointed by the Secretary-General and two by the government of Sierra Leone.[28]

The decision to require a mixed tribunal of national and international judges was due primarily to practical considerations and fears about the neutrality of national trials. The Sierra Leonean judicial system was largely decimated as a result of the war. It is only functional in Freetown and lacks the enormous human and financial resources required to undertake such trials.[29] Security Council Resolution 1315 noted '… the negative impact of the security situation on the administration of justice in Sierra Leone and the pressing need for international cooperation to assist in strengthening the judicial system of Sierra Leone'.[30]

The Truth and Reconciliation Commission is of mixed composition, as well. The Act provides for seven Commissioners: four citizens of Sierra Leone and three non-citizens.[31] The President of Sierra Leone appoints all the Commissioners as well as the Chairman and deputy Chairman of the Commission.[32] The decision to include international members was meant to ensure that the Commission creates an impartial historical record of the events in Sierra Leone.

---

24. <http://www.sierra-leone.org/trcact2000.html>.

25. Art. 11 of the Statute – Organisation of the Special Court. <http://www.sierra-leone.org/special-courtstatute.html>.

26. Art. 12(1) (a) of the Statute – Composition of the Chambers. <http://www.sierra-leone.org/specialcourtstatute.html>.

27. Art. 2(1) of the Statute (As amended by letter from the President of Security Council to the Secretary-General dated 22 December 2000.)

28. Art. 12(1)(b) of the Statute – Composition of the Chambers. <http://www.sierra-leone.org/specialcourtstatute.html>.

29. For the effect of the war on the Sierra Leone Judiciary see 'In Pursuit of Justice: A Report on the Judiciary in Sierra Leone', Report by the Commonwealth Human Rights Initiative. <http://www.humanrightsinitiative.org/publications/Sierra%20Leone%20Report.pdf>.

30. See n. 12 *supra*.

31. Section 3(1) of the Act.

32. Section 3(3) of the Act.

3.3   Subject-matter jurisdiction

The Sierra Leone Parliament passed the Truth and Reconciliation Commission Act in February 2000.[33] The broad functions of the Commission, as stated in Section 6 (1) are: (i) to create an impartial historical record of violations and abuses of human rights and international humanitarian law related to the armed conflict in Sierra Leone, from the beginning of the conflict in 1991 to the signing of the Lomé Peace Agreement in 1996; (ii) to address impunity; (iii) to respond to the needs of the victims; (iv) to promote healing and reconciliation and (v) to prevent a repetition of the violations and abuses suffered.

The Commission's mandate embraces investigating and reporting on the causes, nature and extent of the violations and abuses to the fullest degree possible – including their antecedents, their context, the role of both internal and external factors in the conflict, and whether the violations and abuses were the result of a deliberate policy or authorization by any government, group or individual.[34]

The Commission's task also includes helping to restore the human dignity of victims and promoting reconciliation by providing victims with the opportunity to give an account of the violations and abuses suffered and perpetrators the chance to relate their experiences. Its goal is to create a climate which fosters constructive interchange between victims and perpetrators, giving special attention to the subject of sexual abuse and to the experiences of children during the armed conflict.[35]

The Commission's subject-matter jurisdiction encompasses that of the Special Court but is much broader. Preconceived notions of the conflict will not limit the Commission's scope. Its task is to investigate and determine any and all violations and abuses of human rights and international humanitarian law related to the armed conflict in Sierra Leone.

In contrast, Resolution 1315 limits the subject matter jurisdiction of the Court to serious violations of international humanitarian law and crimes under Sierra Leonean law,[36] and prosecution, particularly with respect to crimes under international law, depends upon documented accounts of the war as well as predetermined ideas about the nature of the conflict and the acts committed during it. International humanitarian law prohibits crimes against humanity,[37] violations of Article 3 common to the Geneva Conventions and Additional Protocol II[38] and other serious

---

33. Act No. 6 of 2000.

34. Section 6(2) (a) of the Act.

35. Section 6(2)(b) of the Act.

36. <http://daccessods.un.org/doc/UNDOC/GEN/N00/605/32/PDF/N0060532.pdf?OpenElement>.

37. Art. 2 of the Statute of the Special Court for Sierra Leone gives the Court power to prosecute persons who committed murder, extermination, enslavement, deportation, imprisonment, torture, rape, sexual slavery, enforced prostitution, forced pregnancy and any other form of sexual violence, persecution on political, racial, ethnic and religious grounds and other inhumane acts as part of a widespread or systematic attack against a civilian population.

38. Art. 3 of the Statute of the Special Court for Sierra Leone gives the Court power to prosecute persons who committed or ordered the commission of serious violations of Art. 3 common to the Geneva Conventions of 12 August 1949 for the protection of War Victims and of Additional Protocol

violations of international humanitarian law – i.e., crimes considered to have had the status of customary international law at the time they were committed.[39] Crimes under Sierra Leonean law include offences relating to the abuse of girls under the Prevention of Cruelty to Children Act of 1960[40] and offences relating to the wanton destruction of property under the Malicious Damage Act of 1861.[41]

3.4   **Personal jurisdiction**

The Court has jurisdiction to try 'persons who bear the greatest responsibility' for serious violations of international humanitarian law and Sierra Leonean law committed in the territory of Sierra Leone since 30 November 1996.[42] The United Nations Secretary-General, in a letter dated 12 January 2001 and addressed to the President of the Security Council, cautioned that the term 'persons who bear greatest responsibility' does not limit personal jurisdiction to political and military leaders and is meant to provide a prosecutorial strategy, not form an element of the crime to be proven:[43]

> 'the determination of the meaning of the term 'persons who bear the greatest responsibility' in any given case falls initially to the Prosecutor and the Special Court itself. ... particular mention is made of those leaders who, in committing such crimes, have threatened the establishment and implementation of the peace process in Sierra Leone. It is my understanding that following from paragraph 2 above, the words "those leaders who ... threaten the establishment and implementation of the peace process" do not describe an element of the crime but rather provide guidance to the prosecutor in determining his or her prosecutorial strategy. Consequently, the commission of any of the statutory crimes without necessarily threatening the establishment and implementation of the

---

II thereto of 8 June 1977. These violations include violence to life, health and physical or mental well-being of persons, in particular murder as well as cruel treatment such as torture, mutilation or any other form of corporal punishment; collective punishments, taking of hostages; acts of terrorism; outrages upon personal dignity; pillage; the passing of sentences and the carrying out of executions without previous judgment pronounced by a regularly constituted court and threats to commit any of these acts.

39. Art. 4 of the Statute of the Special Court for Sierra Leone lists these as including intentionally directing attacks against the civilian population or against individual civilians not taking part in hostilities; intentionally directing attacks against personnel, installations, material, units or vehicles involved in a humanitarian assistance or peacekeeping mission in accordance with the Charter of the United Nations, as long as they are entitled to the protection given to civilians or civilian objects under the international law of armed conflict. In the letter from the President of Security Council to the Secretary-General dated 22 December 2000, the original Art. 4(c) was amended to read 'Conscripting or enlisting children under the age of 15 years into armed forces or groups or using them to participate actively in hostilities.'

40. Chapter 31 of the Laws of Sierra Leone. Art. 5(a) of the Statute of the Special Court for Sierra Leone.

41. Art. 5(b) of the Statute of the Special Court for Sierra Leone.

42. Art. 1 of the Statute of the Special Court for Sierra Leone as amended by letter from the President of the Security Council to the Secretary-General dated 22 December 2000.

43. UN Doc. S/2000/915, para. 1, sub-paras. 1-4.

peace process would not detract from the international criminal responsibility otherwise entailed for the accused.'

Whereas the Prosecutor in the Special Court will seek to try those who bear the greatest responsibility, the Commission has no such restriction and can investigate anybody and everybody. The government of Sierra Leone in its Briefing Paper noted that whereas 'the Special Court (is) for the few who meet the personal jurisdiction requirements, the Truth and Reconciliation Commission is for everybody else'.[44] Given the limited resources of the Special Court, it will only be able to prosecute a relatively limited number of persons despite the length of the conflict and the large number of fighting forces involved. The most optimistic estimates indicate that the Court may eventually try 24 persons,[45] whereas the Commission will almost certainly investigate in excess of this number.

Since the overlapping personal jurisdiction of the Special Court and the Truth and Reconciliation Commission is a potential source of conflict, the UN Expert Group suggested that the Prosecutor should define in his prosecutorial strategy 'those who bear the greatest responsibility'. Once defined, such defendants should be considered within the exclusive jurisdiction of the Court and outside that of the Commission.[46]

This solution to the personal jurisdiction conflict may not be entirely acceptable as there is nothing in the current law that restricts the Truth and Reconciliation Commission from taking evidence from or investigating the actors 'who bear the greatest responsibility'. Denying the Truth and Reconciliation Commission jurisdiction over such individuals would mean denying it access to the leaders of the conflict in Sierra Leone. The Commission would be unable to fulfill its mandate 'to create an impartial historical record of violations and abuses' without such access.

3.5   Temporal jurisdiction

The Special Court's jurisdiction covers events after 30 November 1996.[47] This date was meant to put the Sierra Leone conflict in perspective without unnecessarily extending the Special Court's temporal jurisdiction. The Special Court's jurisdiction is open-ended: it can prosecute offences for an indefinite period, and its life-

---

44. Briefing Paper on Relationship between the Special Court and the Truth and Reconciliation Commission - Legal Analysis and Policy Considerations of the Government of Sierra Leone for the Special Court Planning Mission <http://www.specialcourt.org/SLMission/PlanningMission/Briefing-Papers/SLGovTRC_SpCt_Relationship.doc>.

45. The United Nations, the Government or Court officials have not confirmed or denied this figure. However, in a statement quoted on Sierra Leone web on 13 October 2002, the Deputy Registrar of the Court, Robert Kirkwood, stated that the new court building will have 26 cells and that all of the accused will be held in individual cells built in accordance with international standards.

46. Communiqué issued by the 'Expert Meeting on the Relationship Between the Truth and Reconciliation Commission and the Special Court for Sierra Leone', United Nations, New York, 20-21 December 2001.

47. Art. 1 of the Statute of the Court.

span will be determined by a subsequent agreement between the government of Sierra Leone and the United Nations. This may happen when the judicial activities are completed, when local courts in Sierra Leone have acquired the capacity to assume prosecution of the remaining cases or when resources become unavailable.[48]

The commencement date for the Court's temporal jurisdiction is most unsatisfactory. The war in Sierra Leone began on 23 March 1991. The massive violations of human rights and humanitarian law that were committed by all the parties to the conflict between 23 March 1991 and 30 November 1996 will go unpunished.[49]

Before determining the temporal jurisdiction of the Court, the Secretary-General considered and eliminated several other starting dates. The date of commencement of the conflict was ruled out because it would have been too onerous a burden in terms of the time and cost of undertaking such investigations. The date of the AFRC coup, 25 May 1997, was rejected as having too many political overtones. Finally, 6 January 1999, the date of the rebel invasion of the capital, was rejected as giving the impression of favouring Freetown over the provinces.[50]

The Commission's jurisdiction begins much earlier, at the conflict's starting date of 23 March 1991, and concludes with the signing of the Lomé Peace Agreement on 7 July 1999. Therefore, the temporal jurisdiction of the two institutions overlaps between 30 November 1996 and 7 July 1999. However, the Commission will not be limited by the temporal jurisdiction in the course of establishing an impartial record, but must delve beyond the commencement date to determine the causes and reasons for the war.

4.   THE RELATIONSHIP BETWEEN THE TRUTH AND RECONCILIATION COMMISSION AND THE SPECIAL COURT

4.1   The need to determine the relationship

From the examination of the mandate and jurisdiction of both institutions, it is clear that their work overlaps. Both have related functions and the same common goals: ensuring accountability in Sierra Leone, bringing sustainable peace and building a culture of respect for human rights. There is a danger that without a clearly defined relationship, both institutions may duplicate the others' work and thereby waste limited financial and other resources.

Another problem is that because of the lack of a clear and well-defined relationship between the two institutions, the general populace in Sierra Leone is confused about their respective roles.[51] Clearly defining this relationship may also help reduce the tension and rivalry that usually exists between such institutions. Both

---

48. Para. 28 of the Report of the Secretary-General on the Establishment of a Special Court for Sierra Leone, UN SCOR, UN Doc. S/2000/1315 (2000).

49. For a critique of the temporal jurisdiction of the Court see Tejan-Cole, loc. cit. n. 10, p. 107.

50. <http://daccessods.un.org/doc/UNDOC/GEN/N00/661/77/PDF/N0066177.pdf?OpenEle ment>.

institutions will lose credibility if they are seen to be in conflict. It is of critical importance that this issue be resolved.

4.2   The Statutes

The Lomé Peace Accord Act[52] and the Truth and Reconciliation Commission Act,[53] which established the Truth and Reconciliation Commission, make no reference to the Special Court. At the time the Truth and Reconciliation Commission Act was enacted, four months before the President's requests to the UN, the Special Court was not contemplated. Similarly, the Agreement between the government of Sierra Leone and the Secretary-General of the United Nations establishing the Special Court makes no direct reference to the Truth and Reconciliation Commission.[54]

To all intents and purposes, their statutes treat the institutions as separate and distinct entities. Even the drafters of the Special Court Statute and Agreement, which came later and had an opportunity to address the issue, did not envision any relationship between the institutions or simply deemed it unnecessary to examine it.

4.3   The question of primacy

Although the Truth and Reconciliation Commission Act does not explicitly state its relationship with domestic courts or with the Special Court, reference is made to domestic courts. Section 8(2) provides that failure to respond to a summons or subpoena issue by the Commission, failure to truly and faithfully answer questions of the Commission after responding to a summons or subpoena, or intentionally providing misleading or false information to the Commission will be deemed contempt and the Commission can, at its discretion, refer the matter to the High Court of Sierra Leone for trial and punishment. Similarly, other offences created under the Act will be enforced by the High Court, a national court of Sierra Leone. Thus, under section 9(2) of the Act, if a person wilfully obstructs or interferes with the Commission or any of its members or officers in the discharge of their functions, he/she will be charged, tried and, if convicted, punished by the High Court of Sierra Leone.

Unlike the Special Court, despite having some international Commissioners, the Truth and Reconciliation Commission is a national institution and as such it does not have primacy over national courts. The Constitution of Sierra Leone provides

---

51. A recent story I heard confirmed this confusion. When a friend who ordered a taxi told the driver he was going to the Special Court, the driver took him to the TRC office.

52. <http://www.sierra-leone.org/lomeaccord.html>.

53. <http://www.sierra-leone.org/trcact2000.html>.

54. However, there is one indirect reference in the Statute of the Court. In Art. 15(5) under the rubric 'The Prosecutor', it provides as follows: 'In the prosecution of juvenile offenders, the prosecutor shall ensure that the child-rehabilitation program is not placed at risk and that, where appropriate, resort should be had to alternative truth and reconciliation mechanisms, to the extent of their availability.'

that the Supreme Court is the highest court and final court of appeal.[55] Section 125 of the Constitution provides that 'The Supreme Court shall have supervisory jurisdiction over all other Courts in Sierra Leone and over any adjudicating authority'.[56] Consequently, the Supreme Court will have supervisory jurisdiction over the Truth and Reconciliation Commission.[57]

None of the statutes gives the Truth and Reconciliation Commission primacy over the Special Court. The Statute of the Special Court gives it primacy over national courts. The Court may at any stage formally request a national court to defer to its competence in accordance with the Statute and the Rules of Procedure.[58] The Truth and Reconciliation Commission does not fall under the definition of national court and will be unaffected by this provision. It has functions akin to a court such as issuing subpoenas but it is certainly not a national court.

However, subsequent to the signing of the Statute, the government of Sierra Leone enacted the Special Court Agreement 2002 (Ratification) Act of 2002,[59] the enabling legislation providing 'for the ratification and implementation of the Agreement between the government of Sierra Leone and the United Nations signed on 16th January 2002, for the establishment of the Special Court for Sierra Leone'.[60] Section 21(2) of the Act requires that '[n]otwithstanding any other law, every natural person, corporation, or other body created by or under Sierra Leone law shall comply with any direction specified in an order of the Special Court.'[61]

In a letter to the Attorney-General[62] sent before the bill became law, Campaign for Good Governance, a national non-governmental organization,[63] noted that: 'It would seem from this bill that the consensus forged with regards to parity between the two institutions has not been officially recognized by any of the key decision-makers.' They requested that the government review the bill so as to ensure that 'the Act should in no way grant the Special Court primacy over the Truth and Reconciliation Commission, particularly with regards to demanding confidential information'. 'Such a move', they warned, 'would decimate any impression of Truth and Reconciliation Commission independence and demote it to a mere research arm of the Special Court'. [64] Its request fell on deaf ears.

Consequently, since both institutions came into existence the question of primacy in particular and the relationship between these institutions and the national

---

55. Section 122 of the Constitution. <http://www.sierra-leone.org/constitution-vii.html>.

56. <http://www.sierra-leone.org/constitution-vii.html>.

57. This supervisory power is not limited to the Supreme Court; all other courts forming part of the Superior Courts of Judicature that have supervisory powers also have such powers over the Truth and Reconciliation Commission.

58. Art. 8(2) of the Statute. <http://www.sierra-leone.org/specialcourtstatute.html>.

59. <http://www.specialcourt.org/documents/SpecialCourtAct.html>.

60. See the Memorandum of object and reasons of the Act. <http://www.specialcourt.org/documents/ImplLegn.html>.

61. <http://www.specialcourt.org/documents/ImplLegn.html>.

62. <http://www.slcgg.org/letterag.htm>.

63. A national Non-Governmental organisation in Sierra Leone. <http://www.slcgg.org>.

64. Similar views were expressed by a number of national and international NGOs including PRIDE, the National Forum for Human Rights and the International Centre for Transitional Justice.

courts in general has dominated the debate. It is clear that the Special Court will have primacy over persons who bear the greatest responsibility for the crimes listed in its Statute. What is uncertain is whether the Truth and Reconciliation Commission is obliged to comply with orders of the Special Court.

The Special Court's enabling legislation allows it to direct or order the Truth and Reconciliation Commission to do or omit to do a particular act. It may request and demand evidence from the Truth and Reconciliation Commission, whether the evidence is confidential or not. In stark contrast, Section 14(1) of the Truth and Reconciliation Commission Act makes the Commission an independent institution: 'in the performance of its functions under this Act, not ... subject to the direction or control of any person or authority'.[65]

Both institutions are steering clear of a confrontation. However, in the event this happens, the Courts of Sierra Leone may have to determine whether one institution has primacy over the other. The doctrine of subsequent legislation supports the Special Court's primacy over the Truth and Reconciliation Commission.[66] Under this doctrine, if provisions of an earlier bill are inconsistent with those of a later bill, they are impliedly repealed. Since the local enabling legislation giving the Truth and Reconciliation Commission its independence was enacted in February 2000, and the Special Court Agreement (Ratification) Act was passed in 2002, the latter will take precedence.

However, the Special Court Agreement (Ratification) Act aimed at giving effect to the signed Statute and Agreement. The Agreement and Statute do not expressly give the Special Court powers to direct the Truth and Reconciliation Commission. In its briefing paper, the government of Sierra Leone argued that

> ' ... it should also be remembered in this respect that the Agreement for the Special Court is a legally binding international agreement that cannot be circumvented by either pre-existing or subsequently enacted national law. Rather, should there be a conflict, domestic law has to be altered in order to comply with Sierra Leone's international obligations. Sierra Leone is therefore compelled to ensure that the necessary domestic legal conditions exist to enable it to fulfil this obligation as set out in the Agreement.'[67]

The government of Sierra Leone also noted that Article 17 of the Agreement governs obedience of national institutions to the Special Court and 'requires complete compliance'. Article 17 sets out Sierra Leone's obligation to cooperate with all the organs of the Court, including facilitating access to the Prosecutor to sites, persons and relevant documents required for the investigation. Article 17 is silent on the *scope* of this obligation, however. While the Agreement stresses cooperation, the enabling legislation emphasizes direction. The two characterizations of the rela-

---

65. <http://www.sierra-leone.org/trcact2000.html>.

66. Also known as the doctrine of implied repeal, *leges posteriores priores contrarias abrogant* states that an earlier Act cannot be used to amend or repeal a later Act. Instead, where any conflict arises between Acts of Parliament that cannot be smoothed by judicial interpretation, the later one always takes precedence.

67. 'Briefing Paper', *supra* n. 44.

tionship cannot be reconciled. The latter is obligatory, whilst the former is voluntary.

4.4   **Information sharing**

Whether or not to share information was one of the most imperative issues that dominated the initial debate about the relationship between two institutions.[68] The issue was raised not only as a matter of academic debate but was one of the most frequent questions asked at workshops in Freetown. At a preliminary sensitization session conducted by Post-Conflict Reintegration Initiative for Development and Empowerment (PRIDE) in Freetown in October 2001, ex-combatants made it clear that their willingness to participate in the Truth and Reconciliation Commission would depend in part on the relationship between the Commission and the Special Court.[69] The consensus was that perpetrators would be less willing to attend the Commission, or less inclined to tell the truth, if they believe their evidence would be used against them in the Special Court.

From the outset, the Commission was adamant that it would not share any confidential information with the Special Court. The Truth and Reconciliation Commission Act empowers the Commission to take evidence on a confidential basis. It further provides that the Commission will not be compelled to disclose any such information given to it in confidence.[70] Although the Commission is competent to disclose confidential information, it may not be compelled under the Act. It cannot be subpoenaed to give evidence about such confidential evidence.[71]

Special Court Prosecutor David Crane was quoted by Sierra Leone Web as saying that the Prosecutor's Office would not seek to use testimony taken by the Truth and Reconciliation Commission. Crane also said that the Court and the Truth and

---

68. The Government of Sierra Leone states in its Briefing Paper ibid. that the issue of information control has often been confused with the issue of primacy. However, 'Primacy refers solely to the question of which court has jurisdiction over a particular case or individual. As such, it only applies in respect of Sierra Leonean Courts and only in the limited situation where one body either is or could be seized of jurisdiction in a particular matter. Primacy is legally and conceptually different from the issue of information sharing or compliance with orders of the Court. Thus the fact that the Special Court has primacy over Sierra Leone courts is separate from the question of whether a national institution is required to comply with orders of the Special Court: this is governed solely by article 17 of the Agreement, which requires complete compliance.'

69. Report by the Post-Conflict Reintegration Initiative for Development and Empowerment, in partnership with the International Centre for Transitional Justice entitled 'Ex-Combatant views of the Truth and Reconciliation Commission and the Special Court in Sierra Leone', p. 19. <http://www.ictj. org/downloads/PRIDE%20report.pdf>. However, at the press conference launching the report, PRIDE Executive Secretary Joe Patrick Amara said that although the possibility of the Special Court using information from the Truth and Reconciliation Commission is a concern of some ex-combatants, 63% of those surveyed expressed a willingness to testify before the Truth and Reconciliation Commission, even if the information could be used by the Special Court.

70. The Act does not prohibit the sharing of information disclosed in public. Section 7(3) of the Act.

71. If the subsequent Special Court Agreement (Ratification) Act repeals this provision then the Special Court has the authority to demand any information from the Truth and Reconciliation Commission.

Reconciliation Commission would operate separately, but that both institutions would work to address 'the entrenched problem of impunity' and to ensure accountability.[72] As between the Office of the Prosecutor and the Truth and Reconciliation Commission, the matter seems to have been resolved. However, there is a likelihood that if the Commission is in possession of confidential exculpatory evidence, the defence may request access to such information.

This scenario may be less worrisome for the Commission. Perpetrators will not be afraid to make statements if they are aware that the only circumstance in which their statement will be used is to secure their acquittal or that of another perpetrator. Giving the defence limited access to confidential information from the Commission will address some fears and concerns and reduce the risk of the institutions undermining each other's work. A distinction must be drawn, however, between gaining access to confidential information and using such information as evidence in a court of law. This access must be very limited in order to ensure that the Commission is not seen as another chamber of the Court.

Since the defence must not be given free access to all information in the possession of the Commission, information should be given based on three preconditions: the information requested must be specific, essential to a fair determination of the innocence of the accused and it cannot reasonably be obtained from any other source.

This approach was also endorsed in the government's briefing paper. It suggests that the Truth and Reconciliation Commission should share with the Special Court 'confidential' material provided to it solely where the information can only be obtained from the Truth and Reconciliation Commission and the information is 'essential for the conviction or acquittal of the accused'.[73] This approach would preserve the confidentiality of most materials, yet allow the Special Court to trump that confidentiality to prevent a miscarriage of justice.

The question that then arises is who determines whether these preconditions have been met. It would certainly be undesirable for the institutions to use their enforcement powers against each other. As far as practicable, such matters may be resolved on a cooperative basis.

4.5   Sharing resources

The Truth and Reconciliation Commission and the Special Court have a common problem – lack of funding. Cooperating in three areas could make maximal use of these limited resources to improve accountability within Sierra Leone: investigation, disseminating public information, and witness protection.

The Special Court has sufficient resources for 18 months but the Secretary-General has warned that, as its funding is entirely voluntary, this will 'not provide the assured and continuous source of funding which would be required ...'[74] In 2001 a

---

72. <http://www.sierra-leone.org/slnews1202.html>.
73. See n. 65 *supra*.
74. Report of the United Nations Secretary-General on the Establishment of the Special Court for

revised budget was presented to Member States, putting the costs of the first three years of operation at US\$ 57 million, with US\$ 16.8 million reserved for the first year.[75] While the majority of funds for the first year were deposited into the Trust Fund and pledges for the following 24 months were made, there was still a significant gap between money actually pledged and the amounts contained in the budget.[76] It was uncertain whether these pledges would be honoured.

At the same time, the Truth and Reconciliation Commission is in dire straits. It has struggled to secure a fraction of its necessary operating budget. In an interview given to Sierra Leone Web, the interim Executive Secretary of the Commission stated that Commission was operating with a two person skeletal staff.[77] Commissioner William Schabas also drew attention to the Commission's critical funding situation. By September 2002 pledges amounted to US\$ 1,580,739, of which 1,107,825 had been received.[78] Although the government of Sierra Leone also donated the sum of US\$ 97,000 and contributed the premises of the Commission, the Commission was unable to get one-fifth of its estimated budget. With attention focusing on the war on terror, it seemed unlikely to receive any significant additional funding.

This shortage of funds means that the institutions must strive to work together, from necessity if nothing else. The government of Sierra Leone has endorsed this view and identified two main areas in which critical resources might be beneficially shared, viz., training of investigators, interviewers and other staff members, and public information and education.[79]

The government noted that it is crucial to the enterprise of both the Commission and the Court that investigators and interviewers be properly trained since they will frequently be the people who will be required to explain the mechanisms, answer questions and will often be the first people to whom witnesses tell their stories. Therefore, they should be 'properly trained both to facilitate the gathering of information as well as to make the process as beneficial as possible for the witness'.[80]

The underlying objectives of the public information campaigns for the Commission and the Special Court should be to: (i) dispel fear, confusion and misinformation because they are disruptive to the peace process; (ii) build confidence in the institutions through emphasizing their independence and credibility; and (iii) encourage the public's effective participation in and support of the Commission and

---

Sierra Leone issued on 4 October 2000. <http://daccessods.un.org/doc/UNDOC/GEN/N00/661/77/PDF/N0066177.pdf?OpenElement>.

75. Letter from the Secretariat, UN Doc. S/2001/693 (12 July 2001) <http://www.un.org/Docs/sc/letters/2001/693e.pdf> (referring to an amended budget and a letter of 14 June 2001 from the Secretariat to Member States regarding revised budget estimates). These numbers include contributions received up until 6 July 2001.

76. The shortfalls amount to approximately US\$ 1.8 million for the first year and US\$ 19.6 million for the second and third years combined.

77. <http://www.sierra-leone.org/slnews.html>.

78. Eighth weekly briefing of the truth and reconciliation commission chaired by Professor William Schabas, on 11 September 2002 <http://www.sierra-leone.org/trcbriefing091102.html>.

79. 'Briefing Paper', *supra* n. 44.

80. See n. 65 *supra*.

Court. The two institutions should commit themselves to a dual public information policy of 'do no harm' and together espouse the independence and distinctiveness of the Commission and the Special Court.

The collaborative aspects of the public information strategy of both institutions could include joint and shared training to ensure that those working on the information strategy are familiar with each other's role. The two bodies should also commit to sharing of public informational material for pre-release consideration by the other body. This will serve as a useful means of exchanging information and ensuring that the independence, credibility and efficiency of one body is not affected by a conflicting publication associated with the other.

A joint public information strategy for the Truth and Reconciliation Commission and the Court should emphasize that the Court will prosecute a limited number of perpetrators 'who bear the greatest responsibility' for atrocities, while the Truth and Reconciliation Commission will process all violations from 1991 until 1999. It should also indicate that proactive and full cooperation by a perpetrator with the Commission would be considered favourably by the Prosecutor in developing his short list of possible candidates for indictment, as well as during the sentencing phase.

The Commission and Special Court should also coordinate their methodologies on evidence gathering. For example, to the extent the Commission investigates a particular site or is provided with materials, it will be important to ensure that its investigators do not in any way disturb or taint evidence that the Court might need, or break a chain of custody that the Court might need to prove. If both the Commission and Court conduct the same investigations it will save resources, financial as well as human. There are very few qualified forensic experts within Freetown. Because bringing in two teams to do the same investigation would be very costly, experts brought from abroad will need to work together.

Another possible area for cooperation is the provision of protection services to victims and witnesses. This includes ensuring the safety and security of all witnesses brought before the relevant accountability mechanisms, which involves dealing with highly confidential information; linking national and local authorities; and ensuring safe transfer, accommodation and, if necessary, the relocation of witnesses. Protective measures are necessary not only for witnesses who actually appear before the Commission or the Special Court but also for potential witnesses. A perception that adequate protection may not be available will deter people from deciding to testify before either body in the first place.

The question facing Sierra Leone is not only what kind of protective measures should be adopted but also whether the Commission and the Special Court should adopt a joint structure within which to provide those measures. If there is *any* sharing of information between the Special Court and Truth and Reconciliation Commission, meetings between the two institutions will be needed to ensure that sharing of information does not inadvertently result in a person failing to be covered by witness protection.

However, their close cooperation could blur the distinction between the institutions and risk seriously damaging the independence of the institutions in the public eye. The perception that both institutions are the same when created may be difficult to erase. If the investigators of the Commission and the Court work too closely together, then people who would otherwise have cooperated with the Commission, but not the Court, will find excuses not to do even that. They may see the Commission as another chamber or an arm of the Court.

5.   CONCLUSION

The Special Court and the Truth and Reconciliation Commission have the capacity to contribute dramatically to the stability and longevity of peace, justice and democracy in Sierra Leone. However, if they are poorly designed or lose support civil society and the legal community, the impact could be minimal or even negative. They face a difficult dilemma: each must function and appear to the public as distinct, independent entities but simultaneously seek common goals: ensuring accountability for humanitarian law and human rights violations in Sierra Leone, bringing sustainable peace and building a culture of respect for human rights.

In order to be successful and avoid structural conflict, the relationship between the Commission and the Court should take account of the cultural, social and other contexts within which the institutions must operate. Enabling the people of Sierra Leone to have input into the establishment and operation of accountability mechanisms in their country would help ensure their cooperation.

The Special Court should set as a fundamental substantive and methodological priority to work together, cooperatively, with national institutions, including the Commission, and not to use its legal powers to impose its will. It should do everything it can to make national institutions effective in the short term and strong and self-sufficient in the longer term.

By developing a cooperative relationship that reduces or even removes the need for the Special Court to exercise its coercive powers, each institution will be better placed to serve the accountability process and contribute to a sustained peace in Sierra Leone. Furthermore, a proper explanation of these issues to the people of Sierra Leone can itself contribute to the accountability process and go a long way to reducing the confusion and distrust generated by misinformation that has already been widely disseminated regarding the respective roles and powers of the two institutions.

TRANSITIONAL JUSTICE: THE PROSECUTION OF WAR CRIMES IN BOSNIA AND HERZEGOVINA UNDER THE 'RULES OF THE ROAD'[1]

Janet Manuell and Aleksandar Kontić[2]

1.   THE JURISDICTION OF THE INTERNATIONAL CRIMINAL TRIBUNAL FOR THE FORMER YUGOSLAVIA

In May 1993, at the height of the wars in the former Yugoslavia, the United Nations' Security Council established the International Criminal Tribunal for the Former Yugoslavia (ICTY).[3] It did so in response to international outrage at evidence of war crimes being committed with impunity and on a scale unprecedented in Europe since World War II. The Statute empowered the ICTY to prosecute persons responsible for serious violations of international humanitarian law committed in the territory of the former Yugoslavia since 1 January 1991, in accordance with its provisions.

The ICTY was established by the Security Council rather than the General Assembly because it was thought that the situation in the former Yugoslavia was too serious to wait for a lengthy ratification process.[4] By characterising the war as a breach of the peace, the Security Council could act immediately under Chapter VII of the UN Charter.[5] Part of the international community's motivation in establishing the Tribunal was to prevent further war crimes being committed in the region, particularly against the people of Bosnia and Herzegovina and Croatia.[6]

The twin difficulties of the population's understandable preoccupation with the ongoing wars and the lack of political motivation in the former Yugoslav states to

---

1. © J. Manuell and A. Kontić, 2004.

2. Legal Officers, Rules of the Road Unit, Office of the Prosecutor, International Criminal Tribunal for the former Yugoslavia. The views expressed herein are those of the authors alone and do not necessarily reflect the views of the International Tribunal or the United Nations in general.

3. SC Res. 827 (S/Res/827 (1993)), 25 May 1993.

4. For a discussion of the relevant principles, see SC Res. 827, paras. 18-30.

5. Art. 39 of the UN Charter provides that: 'The Security Council shall determine the existence of any threat to the peace, breach of the peace, or act of aggression and shall make recommendations, or decide what measures shall be taken in accordance with Articles 41 and 42, to maintain or restore international peace and security.'

6. Commentators note, however, that this objective was not altogether successful. For instance, Antonio Cassese, a former ICTY President, in a newspaper interview given to *Slobodna Bosna* (a Bosnian and Herzegovinian weekly) and published on 12 May 2001 said: 'Something has happened that has surprised us all. Not only has the establishment of the Tribunal not persuaded warring factions, not only have future war crimes not been prevented, but in fact the worst crimes in Croatia and Bosnia and Herzegovina have taken place after the establishment of the Tribunal.'

Yearbook of International Humanitarian Law
Volume 5 - 2002 - pp. 331-343

prosecute their own high ranking suspects were addressed by situating the ICTY in The Hague. Once it was established, it was possible for war crimes' investigations and prosecutions to commence immediately. Since its inception, the ICTY has issued 50 public indictments (some incorporating multiple accused) and two contempt indictments. It has prosecuted more than 50 accused[7] in what are, frequently, extremely complex trials.[8]

The ICTY Statute envisaged a two-tiered mechanism for the prosecution of alleged war crimes: the first tier being the jurisdiction of the ICTY and the second tier being the national criminal jurisdiction of each of the states of the former Yugoslavia. The ICTY Statute provides that the jurisdictions are to be concurrent but that the Tribunal is to have primacy over the national courts.[9] Each state of the former Yugoslav republic therefore retains a residual war crimes' jurisdiction.

From the outset, it was clear that the ICTY was never going to be able to prosecute every suspect against whom there was sufficient *prima facie* evidence of the commission of war crimes. Instead, the aim of the ICTY was to prosecute only the key higher ranking individuals, namely, the military and civilian leaders and others who held senior command positions, while it was intended that the lower ranking suspects would be prosecuted in the national courts in the exercise of their state's residual jurisdiction.[10] However, in 1993, with various wars still underway, the reality of war crimes' prosecutions being conducted in the states of the former Yugoslavia was still a distant prospect. It is only with the development of peace in the region that national war crimes' prosecutions have become viable. The international community is now placing greater emphasis on national prosecutions in anticipation of the ultimate closure of the ICTY.

---

7. As of 21 October 2003.

8. The ICTY's Office of the Prosecutor (OTP) has grown from an initial staff of seven in 1993 to a staff of more than 800. In total, more than 1,500 staff are employed by the ICTY.

9. Art. 9 of the ICTY Statute provides that:

(1) The International tribunal and national courts shall have concurrent jurisdiction to prosecute persons for serious violations of international humanitarian law committed in the territory of the former Yugoslavia since 1991.

(2) The International tribunal shall have primacy over national courts. At any stage of the procedure, the International Tribunal may formally request national courts to defer to the competence of the International Tribunal in accordance with the present Statute and the Rules of Procedure and Evidence of the International Tribunal.

10. In his address to the General Assembly of the United Nations on 4 November 1997, Antonio Cassese, the then-President of the ICTY said:

'We are not capable of trying every war criminal at The Hague and it would help the tribunal in its task if there were more national prosecutions for the multiple crimes committed in the former Yugoslavia. The two approaches – international and national – should go hand-in-hand. The leaders of warring parties and other accused in command positions should be brought before The Hague Tribunal, whilst the other indictees should be tried by national courts.'

2.   BOSNIA AND HERZEGOVINA'S RESIDUAL JURISDICTION IN
         RESPECT OF WAR CRIMES' PROSECUTIONS

The war in Bosnia and Herzegovina (and Croatia) ended with the signing of the
Dayton Peace Agreement (Dayton) on 30 December 1995. A month later, General
Djordje Djukić and Colonel Aleksa Krsmanović, both of the Republika Srpska
Army, were driving near Sarajevo, the capital of Bosnia and Herzegovina. Extensive damage had been done to road signs in Bosnia and Herzegovina during the
war, and a damaged sign caused Djukić and Krsmanović to lose their way. They
were arrested at a Federation checkpoint and, by virtue only of their military positions, were immediately detained on suspicion of having committed war crimes.
They were indicted for war crimes a week later, on 6 February 1996, and it was
intended that they be prosecuted in Bosnian and Herzegovinian courts.

The ripple effect was immediate. In Bosnia and Herzegovina a series of arbitrary
retaliatory arrests and detentions were carried out by the formerly opposing forces
in the region. Local and national prisoner exchange programs were suspended indefinitely, and the emerging political cooperation between the former warring parties was swiftly eroded. The arbitrary arrests constituted a novel and dangerous
threat to peace and security in the country; not only was the right of free mobility
within the divided country in jeopardy but there was also the very real prospect of
many politically-motivated witch-hunt prosecutions and show trials taking place.
The death penalty was still, technically at least, an available sentencing option for
those convicted of war crimes.

This spate of reciprocal arrests caused serious concern among the Dayton signatories. Dayton had effectively divided Bosnia and Herzegovina into two territorial
entities (with separate governments, albeit under a single constitution), one of
which is predominantly Bosnian Muslim and Bosnian Croat (the Federation) and
the other, predominantly Bosnian Serb (Republika Srpska). Freedom of travel between the two entities was essential to ensure the viability of the divided country,
and any threat to freedom of travel was perceived to be a threat to Dayton itself.
Therefore, it was quickly apparent to the Dayton signatories that a mechanism was
needed to prevent retributive arrests, by ensuring that arrests of suspects on war
crimes' charges could be made only if the charges were founded on evidence that
satisfied international standards of fairness. As a result of their concern, the signatories gathered again, six weeks after Dayton and this time in Rome, to sign what
became known as the Rome Agreement.[11]

---

11. The discussions leading to the signing of the Rome Statement were sponsored by the international community and conducted primarily by the United States' Assistant Secretary of State, Richard
Holbrooke.

3.   THE ROME AGREEMENT

The Rome Agreement of 18 February 1996 consists of the Rome Statement on Sarajevo, with its numerous Annexes, and the Agreed Measures. The documents were signed on 18 February 1996. Different parties were signatories to the different documents. For instance, the Rome Statement was signed by President Izetbegović (Bosnia and Herzegovina), President Milošević (Federal Republic of Yugoslavia), Prime Minister Muratović (Federation), President Zubak (Federation) and Prime Minister Kasagić (Republika Srpska), while different Annexes were signed by various leaders according to their respective relevance to them, and the Agreed Measures were signed by Presidents Izetbegović, Milošević and Tudjman (Croatia).[12]

The Agreed Measures are expressed to apply to Bosnia and Herzegovina only; there is no similar mechanism in place in respect of Croatia, Serbia and Montenegro or any other state of the former Yugoslavia. The mischief of politically motivated arrests was addressed in Paragraph 5 of the Agreed Measures, which provides:

> Persons, other than those already indicted by the Tribunal, may be arrested and detained for serious violations of international humanitarian law only pursuant to a previously issued order, warrant or indictment that has been reviewed and deemed consistent with international legal standards by the International Tribunal. Procedures will be developed for expeditious decision by the Tribunal and will be effective immediately upon such action.[13]

The legal status of the Agreed Measures is uncertain. It is not, by itself, a treaty as defined by international law[14] and its umbrella, the Rome Agreement, is similarly not a treaty. The same signatories did not sign all of the documents comprising the Rome Agreement. The Agreed Measures have never been ratified or in any other way adopted by the signatories' states' legislatures, and there are no legislative sanctions for non-compliance with them.[15] Further, the obligation to comply with the Agreed Measures was imposed on only one country.

---

12. Although Presidents Milošević and Tudjman were presidents of neighbouring states, their agreement to the Agreed Measures (a mechanism applying solely to Bosnia and Herzegovina) was on the basis of their roles as the putative leaders of the Bosnian Serbs and Bosnian Croats, respectively.

13. The Agreed Measures and the other documents comprising the Rome Agreement can be found at <http://www.nato.int/ifor/general/d960218b.htm>.

14. The Vienna Convention on the Law of Treaties of 1969, Art. 2(1) defines a treaty as '… an international agreement concluded between states in written form and governed by international law …'

15. The only sanction for non-compliance with para. 5 of the Agreed Measures is procedural in nature. In the decision of *Bosnia and Herzegovina Federation* v. *Denis Behram*, Supreme Court of the Federation of Bosnia and Herzegovina, 28 May 1998, it was held that a prosecutor cannot indict a suspect unless the prosecutor first tenders to the court the ICTY Prosecutor's notification letter in which it is stated that a Standard Marking 'A' has been given in respect of charges against the suspect. The Bosnian and Herzegovinian courts have consistently applied this Supreme Court decision, and it has been discussed and adopted by the Human Rights' Chamber of Bosnia and Herzegovina.

After the Agreed Measures were signed, Richard Goldstone, the-then ICTY Prosecutor, agreed to assume responsibility for the administration of Paragraph 5. In recognition of the circumstances giving rise to Paragraph 5, the scheme established by the paragraph was colloquially referred to as the 'Rules of the Road'.

Procedures for the Tribunal's review of proposed Bosnian and Herzegovinian war crimes' prosecution files were subsequently developed by the ICTY. The ICTY Prosecutor determined that, to comply with Paragraph 5, the judicial authorities in Bosnia and Herzegovina were obliged to submit all of their proposed war crimes' prosecutions to the ICTY's Office of the Prosecutor (OTP) for legal review. Initially, the files were submitted to the ICTY and reviewed by OTP Legal Officers but then, as the number of files submitted increased, a Rules of the Road unit was established within the OTP. Currently, two Legal Officers (the writers) and four Language Assistants are employed in the Rules of the Road unit. The unit was initially funded by a grant from the American Bar Association,[16] and it has subsequently been funded independently of the ICTY. Because the Rome Agreement was negotiated separately from Dayton, the UN has taken the view that the review function exercise by the Rules of the Road unit is not part of the ICTY's formal mandate. Therefore, funding for the unit is not included in the ICTY's annual budget, and it has been raised directly from other sources through a trust fund.[17] The unit continues to function within the OTP today, although there are now plans to transfer its legal review function to Bosnia and Herzegovina in 2005.

Although Paragraph 5 of the Agreed Measures refers to the arrest and detention of suspects, in practice, the indictment of a person suspected of having committed war crimes is only permissible in Bosnia and Herzegovina if the ICTY's Prosecutor, on the recommendation of the Rules of the Road unit, has first approved the prosecution. Since its inception, more than 1,400 files containing allegations against more than 5,000 suspects have been submitted to the Rules of the Road unit for review. Files are submitted by those offices in Bosnia and Herzegovina that have the power of arrest. In broad terms, this means that files are submitted from the courts and the various Prosecutors' offices throughout the country, although the Federation's investigation agency, the Agency for Information and Documentation (AID), also submits files to the unit. The files consist of photocopies of the relevant evidence that has been gathered by the authorities, and upon which it is proposed to rely in the course of a prosecution. The Rules of the Road unit specifically requests that only photocopies of documents are sent to The Hague because of the potential for the chain of possession of original documents to be broken during the submission process. The files are delivered to The Hague by one of Bosnia and Herzegovina's three ICTY Liaison Officers (Muslim, Croat and Serb), or through one of the ICTY's Field Offices in Sarajevo and Banja Luka.

Unless a Bosnian/Croat/Serb-speaking Legal Officer is available, the proposed prosecution files are reviewed by the Rules of the Road unit in English. The review

---

16. Through its organ, the Central and Eastern European Legal Initiative (ABA-CEELI).

17. Funding countries have included the United States, the United Kingdom, Canada, Germany, Switzerland, Sweden, the Netherlands and Denmark.

is conducted solely on the papers submitted by the local prosecuting authorities; it does not take into account any evidence that may have been gathered independently by the ICTY or any evidence that may be contained in other, unrelated files. The sole purpose of the review is to determine whether there is sufficient *prima facie* evidence to establish a serious violation of international humanitarian law.[18] Other considerations, such as the past or present political positions of suspects or the ethnicity of witnesses or suspects, are irrelevant and are not considered.

When the unit receives a file, its particulars are entered into a database and its review is prioritised according to the request of the submitting authority. Some files, usually those where the suspect is amenable to immediate arrest, are reviewed as a matter of urgency and the result can be notified within a matter of days. Other files are reviewed according to criteria set by the unit's Legal Officers and Language Assistants. The Language Assistants translate each file into English and produce an English-language summary of it.[19] Some files relate to more than one suspect, usually because a joint criminal enterprise is alleged against the suspects. The summaries include everything on a file that is relevant to each suspect. There is often an overlap of witnesses' statements in various files, usually because Rules of the Road witnesses give evidence of criminal acts allegedly committed in a particular, confined area by a number of alleged perpetrators. In these circumstances, it is often more efficient to translate and summarise all files relating to a particular area at the same time.

A Rules of the Road Legal Officer reviews the file based on the summary and prepares a Recommendation. The Recommendation is reviewed by the other Rules of the Road Legal Officer, and it is then submitted to the ICTY Prosecutor or Deputy Prosecutor for approval and signature of the notification letter to the local prosecuting authorities. All notification letters are now delivered to the recently appointed State Prosecutor of Bosnia and Herzegovina, for distribution as required.

A system of Standard Markings has been developed in conjunction with the local prosecuting authorities to advise of the results of the legal review.[20] The use of this system leaves little room for misunderstanding. Every Recommendation

---

18. The Rules of the Road unit's legal reviews are conducted by applying international evidentiary standards. In practice, this means that the same evidentiary standards that are applied to ICTY prosecutions are applied to legal reviews done by the Rules of the Road unit.

19. The Language Assistants receive ongoing legal training from the OTP and are able to seek advice from the unit's Legal Officers as needed.

20. The protocols of the Rules of the Road scheme provide for the following Standard Markings on review:

Standard Marking 'A' The evidence is sufficient to establish the specified charge.

Standard Marking 'B' The evidence is insufficient to establish the charges. The deficiencies in the evidence are specified.

Standard Marking 'C' Further evidence is required, as specified.

Standard Marking 'D' The Prosecutor seeks a deferral of the prosecution to the ICTY.

Standard Marking 'E' The alleged crime is not within the jurisdiction of the Tribunal. An alternative crime, within the domestic jurisdiction of Bosnia and Herzegovina is specified.

Standard Marking 'F' The evidence is sufficient to establish a specified charge. The suspect is required as a witness by the ICTY and the local prosecuting authorities are requested to take action to protect the evidence.

gives Standard Markings in respect of the recommended charges against each suspect named on a file, and it is these Standard Markings that are notified to the local prosecuting authorities.

Historically, there has been patchy cooperation with the Rules of the Road unit. Part of the explanation is that war crimes' prosecutions were simply one of the many issues to be dealt with in the aftermath of the wars. Further, some prosecutors and investigative judges from certain Bosnian Herzegovinan regions were loath to submit any files because of a perceived loss of autonomy or because they resisted war crimes' prosecutions in their courts. On the other hand, some prosecutors and judges embraced Paragraph 5 from its first days. Prosecuting authorities throughout Bosnia and Herzegovina now comply with Paragraph 5 of the Agreed Measures although, for different reasons, the quality of the files is often lacking. This may reflect inadequate legal training of local prosecutors in respect of war crimes' prosecutions, inadequate investigative or judicial resources, or the reluctance of certain witnesses to testify. It is clear, however, that certain files are still being submitted to the Rules of the Road unit where the proposed prosecution is politically motivated and unsupported by the available evidence. The receipt of files such as these acts as a reminder of the continuing need for a review mechanism.

On occasion, the contents of the notification letters (advising of the result of the review) are made publicly available by the submitting authority, and given considerable local press coverage, usually with adverse comments about the perceived partiality of the ICTY. Often, however, public comment is made to indicate that the unit's integrity is in fact well regarded by local judicial officers and politicians.[21]

Notwithstanding the occasional criticisms, there are independent signs that the safeguard imposed by Paragraph 5 is working: there is freedom of movement and a greater degree of political stability within Bosnia and Herzegovina today than immediately after the arrests of General Djukić and Colonel Krsmanović, and there have not been widespread, sensationalised 'show' trials in respect of alleged war crimes.

Apart from facilitating freedom of movement in Bosnia and Herzegovina by implementing the mandate of Paragraph 5, the ICTY, through the Rules of the Road unit, has contributed to the developing legal system in Bosnia and Herzegovina in other ways. In October 2001, staff from the Rules of the Road unit held conferences in Sarajevo, the capital of Bosnia and Herzegovina, and in Banja Luka (the largest city and administrative centre of Republika Srpska) which were at-

---

Standard Marking 'G' The evidence for the charge specified by the local prosecuting authorities is insufficient, but it is sufficient for another crime, as specified by the ICTY.

21. For instance, commenting on a recent Rules of the Road funding shortage, the Prime Minister of Bosnia and Herzegovina, Adnan Terzić, was quoted as saying,

'This is worrying news for us and I intend to speak about it at the session of the Chamber for Peace Implementation in BH. We find that the Section for the Rules of the Road is absolutely necessary in ensuring the legality of the criminal proceedings.'

'A section of the Hague Tribunal under threat of shutting down', *Oslobodjenje* (a Bosnian Herzegovinan daily newspaper) (29 March 2003).

tended by more than 350 judges, lawyers and investigators.[22] Conference materials given to the participants included case studies, analyses of the applicable international law and suggestions on how a file should be prepared for review according to the Rules of the Road. Another aspect of the unit's contribution to the development of the national legal system is in the form of the notification letters sent by the ICTY's Prosecutor to the local prosecuting authorities (via the State Prosecutor) advising of the result of the legal review. If a prosecution is not approved, these notification letters specify the legal and evidentiary issues to be redressed, such as the need to properly identify alleged offences and the need to submit appropriate identification of suspects, relevant eyewitness evidence, medical evidence of injuries allegedly sustained and proof of death. The local prosecuting authority is invited to resubmit the file for further review after the additional evidence has been obtained. In this manner, the notification letters can perform an educative function.

One other important aspect of the Rules of the Road unit's work is its growing cooperation with the European Police Mission (EUPM) and the Organisation for Security and Cooperation in Europe (OSCE), both of which have missions in Bosnia and Herzegovina. Although the Rules of the Road unit has had a long history of cooperation with the Office of the High Representative (OHR) in Bosnia and Herzegovina,[23] it was only during the latter half of 2003 that open communication was established with EUPM and OSCE. EUPM has assumed the policing role in Bosnia and Herzegovina that was formerly carried out by the International Police

---

22. Branko Todorović, President of the Helsinki International Federation for Human Rights, Republika Srpska Branch, commented on the Rules of the Road unit's conferences in October 2001, saying:

'... the (Rules of the Road) conferences were tasked with giving a lasting contribution towards the completion of criminal procedures in Bosnia Herzegovina against persons suspected for violations of international humanitarian law. It is expected that the ICTY will process 200-300 main agents of the tragic violence in the area of former Yugoslavia. The remaining people, surely a large number, who are under suspicion for the commission of war crimes will be subject to domestic judiciary ...

Unfortunately, the courts still function as the longer arm of certain policies, rather than as the arm of justice. Some participants (of the Rules of the Road conferences) stressed the worrying fact that the politicians in Bosnia Herzegovina in various ways, and unfortunately successfully, exercise strong political control over the judiciary.

The essential question is: how could some of the local investigators, prosecutors and judges initiate proceedings aiming to establish criminal responsibility of those politicians who, during the war, participated in violations of international humanitarian law and who are, even today, in very high political positions or exercise public functions? ...'

The only thing we're left with is hope that the international community will very closely follow and support the activities in the Bosnia Herzegovinan judiciary, in order to punish all those who took part in the ethnic cleansing, violence and crimes. Without that, there is no future for this country.'

23. The Office of the High Representative (OHR) is the chief civilian peace implementation agency in Bosnia and Herzegovina. The High Representative is designated to oversee the implementation of the civilian aspects of Dayton in Bosnia and Herzegovina on behalf of the international community. The Steering Board of the PIC (international community) nominates the High Representative. The UN Security Council, which approved the Dayton Peace Agreement as well as the deployment of international troops in Bosnia and Herzegovina, is then required to endorse the nominee. The current High Representative of the international community in Bosnia and Herzegovina is Lord Paddy Ashdown (UK).

Taskforce (IPTF), and its mandate includes mentoring and monitoring war crimes' investigations in Bosnia and Herzegovina. The assistance that the Rules of the Road unit gives EUPM takes the form of advising it of investigations that may not have been properly or expeditiously conducted, and alerting it to any other investigative and arrest issues that require attention. To complete the prosecution process, OSCE has assumed the role of monitoring war crimes' trials and appeals conducted in Bosnia and Herzegovina to ensure that they are conducted with propriety. OSCE prepares reports of war crimes' prosecutions conducted in Bosnia and Herzegovina, and submits copies of those reports to the Rules of the Road unit. It is anticipated that the emerging cooperation between the Rules of the Road unit and EUPM and OSCE will develop throughout 2004 with a series of working group meetings, and that the cooperation will intensify as the time for the transfer of the ICTY Prosecutor's review function draws closer.

The evidence submitted to the Rules of the Road unit represents, in essence, a history of the war in Bosnia and Herzegovina because the submitting police, prosecutors, investigating judges and witnesses come from each side of the territorial divide. The Rules of the Road unit's database, therefore, uniquely, contains comprehensive data on every person who has ever been formally alleged to have committed a war crime in Bosnia and Herzegovina between 1992 and 1995. Clearly, this data will be valuable in assisting OHR, EUPM and OSCE in the exercise of their functions, and it will ultimately be valuable to government and police officials in Bosnia and Herzegovina.

4.   DIFFICULTIES ENCOUNTERED IN BOSNIAN AND
      HERZEGOVINIAN INDICTMENTS OF WAR CRIMES' SUSPECTS

The court system in Bosnia and Herzegovina has struggled to prosecute those suspects whose indictments have been approved by the ICTY's Prosecutor in accordance with Paragraph 5 of the Agreed Measures. From 1996 to the beginning of 2004, only about 50 war crimes' suspects were prosecuted in Bosnia and Herzegovina, which is less than 10 percent of those suspects who were given a Standard Marking 'A'. There are many reasons for this relatively low number of prosecutions: the country's court buildings, police stations and prisons were frequently damaged during the war and are only now being repaired; political and ethnic tensions still exist between certain investigating agencies and prosecutors; many victims and witnesses were displaced during the war and contact with them has since been lost; many victims and witnesses fear giving evidence in criminal proceedings in the absence of a witness protection scheme in the country; and many of the suspects live outside Bosnia and Herzegovina (or in the other entity within the country) and therefore have not been amenable to arrest.

A recurring obstacle to the indictment of alleged war criminals in Bosnia and Herzegovina has been the lack of cooperation between the police forces of Bosnia and Herzegovina's two entities. Each entity has a separate police force, and there has been little communication and cooperation between them since the Rome Agreement was signed. The practical effect of this, as far as national war crimes' prosecutions are concerned, is that suspects against whom indictments have been approved have rarely been amenable to arrest by the police force of the other territory. If, for instance, an indictment is approved for a Federation war crimes' prosecution against a Bosnian Serb suspect residing in Bosnian Serb territory, police from the Federation need the consent and cooperation of the Republika Srpska police to effect the arrest. Historically, there has been no such cooperation. Occasionally, a suspect has been arrested while travelling in the other entity to visit family or friends (or, as in one instance, to rob a bank[24]), but there has been no systematic procedure for the enforcement of arrest warrants across the entities. However, for the first time, in November 2003 the police forces of both the Federation and Republika Srpska cooperated in a joint operation to arrest a Serb suspect who was residing in Visegrád (in Republika Srpska) and wanted for prosecution in the Federation. This is an extremely encouraging development because it may herald a new era in war crimes' prosecutions in Bosnia and Herzegovina where the country's political boundaries no longer offer *de facto* immunity from arrest.

A fundamental problem is still posed by the absence of an effective witness protection scheme in Bosnia and Herzegovina, despite the enactment of the 'Law on the Protection of Witnesses under Threat and Vulnerable Witnesses' by the High Representative on 24 January 2003. Although some Rules of the Road suspects are alleged to have had a very high level of criminality in the planning of widespread joint criminal enterprises, the alleged crimes most frequently reviewed by the Rules of the Road unit range from a single rape to the murder of 100 people. Commonly, by virtue of the ICTY's exercise of its jurisdiction, the crimes alleged against Rules of the Road's are the 'grassroots' crimes. The witnesses whose statements are reviewed by the Rules of the Road unit are therefore, to use ICTY parlance, generally 'crime-base' witnesses. Because Bosnia and Herzegovina was so ethnically mixed prior to the war, to a much greater extent than say Serbia or Croatia, ethnic tensions were played out in towns, villages and hamlets in every municipality throughout the country. This means that, in many cases, Rules of the Road's suspects are alleged to have committed 'grass-roots' war crimes against their former neighbours and friends or acquaintances. Identification of suspects is therefore often easy for many of the alleged victims, but the concomitant of this is that the victims and witnesses - and their extended families and friends - are often well-known to suspects. Witness protection is therefore an extremely difficult, if not impossible, task because of the vulnerability of a victim's or witnesses' extended family circle. Although effective witness protection is an issue that is currently under the consideration of the judicial authorities and the international community in Bosnia and Herzegovina, this objective may be too difficult to ever achieve.

Another reason for the relatively low number of war crimes' prosecutions in Bosnia and Herzegovina is that political considerations still figure in the determination of who is to be prosecuted. The process of suspect identification by the local prosecuting authorities still appears, at times, to be politically motivated.[25] To date,

---

24. See 'The rapist Vitko "Vili" Jokić arrested', *Oslobodjenje* (12 March 2003).

prosecutions of alleged war criminals in Bosnia and Herzegovina have not been coordinated by a single authority, or even two single authorities (one for each entity); instead, each of the 15 Cantonal or District Prosecutors' Offices throughout the country has acted autonomously.[26] The legal system of Bosnia and Herzegovina has traditionally operated on the principle of territoriality of jurisdiction. If a suspect is alleged to have committed a war crime in one of Bosnia and Herzegovina's 154 municipalities, the Cantonal or District Prosecutors' Office with the territorial jurisdiction in respect of that municipality requests an investigative judge from its Cantonal or District Court to conduct an investigation. If the investigation reveals sufficient *prima facie* evidence, the prosecutor then seeks to lay an indictment against the suspect. The inevitably different levels of investigative and prosecutorial skills of lawyers throughout the country have resulted in vastly different approaches to the investigations and prosecutions that have taken place, although political motivation and pressure have also often played a role.

The principle of territoriality has been open to misuse. If, say, a Bosnian Muslim suspect were accused of committing a war crime against a Bosnian Serb in a municipality within the Federation, then it was unlikely the suspect would ever be prosecuted because a Federation court was the only court with the necessary jurisdiction. It has been a rare occurrence for a Bosnian Muslim or Bosnian Croat suspect to be indicted on war crimes' charges in a Federation court, and the same is true for a Bosnian Serb suspect in a Republika Srpska court. In the absence of a single prosecutor being responsible for the indictment of suspects and a single court being primarily responsible for war crimes' prosecutions in Bosnia and Herzegovina, the application of the territorial principle has left the legal system open to unevenness and political manipulation.

5.   THE ESTABLISHMENT OF A CHAMBER FOR WAR CRIMES WITHIN THE STATE COURT OF BOSNIA AND HERZEGOVINA AND THE APPOINTMENT OF A SPECIAL PROSECUTOR FOR WAR CRIMES

There is now a move to address the unfettered autonomy of the courts and the Cantonal or District prosecutors in Bosnia and Herzegovina, and to centralise the prosecution of alleged war crimes. Three initiatives have been adopted to dilute the principle of territoriality. The first, taken by the High Representative in November 2000,[27] was the establishment of a State Court. The second was the enactment of a

---

25. The ICTY Prosecutor's mandate given by para. 5 of the Agreed Measures is limited to a review of the *prima facie* evidence against a suspect, but only after the suspect has first been identified as a prosecution target. It is entirely a matter for the local prosecuting authorities as to which suspects are identified, and whose files are submitted for review. The Rules of the Road unit is not empowered to identify suspects and request local prosecuting authorities to submit particular files, and the ICTY Prosecutor does not have any other coercive powers in this respect.

26. There are ten Cantonal Courts in the Federation and five District Courts in Republika Srpska.

27. The High Representative was then Wolfgang Petrich.

new Criminal Code and Criminal Procedure Code in August 2003. This legislation gives the State Court of Bosnia and Herzegovina primary jurisdiction in respect of all war crimes' prosecutions conducted in the country. The third initiative was taken on 30 October 2003, when members of the international community met at a Donors' Conference in The Hague and agreed to establish a Chamber for War Crimes within the State Court of Bosnia and Herzegovina. Funding in the order of 15.7 million euros has been pledged for an initial two-year operation of the Chamber, an amount that includes building costs and the employment of local and international lawyers.[28] The work required to establish the Chamber started immediately.

The combined effect of these three initiatives is that the State Court's Chamber for War Crimes will have primary jurisdiction over all national war crimes' prosecutions in Bosnia and Herzegovina. The War Crimes' Chamber, staffed by national and international judges and assisted by the Special Prosecutor for War Crimes (overseen by the State Prosecutor), will provide a forum for those cases that the ICTY will not otherwise have the time to prosecute. In addition, the Special Prosecutor, who will not be bound by the territorial principle, may choose to prosecute those suspects whose prosecutions have already been approved by the ICTY's Prosecutor in accordance with Paragraph 5 of the Agreed Measures. The Special Prosecutor will be given the database maintained by the Rules of the Road unit, so that he or she will have all of the available data on all of those suspects who have already been identified. Currently, there are in excess of 600 suspects who have been given 'A' Standard Markings, which suggests that the immediate issue for the Chamber for War Crimes will be to determine its prosecutorial objectives. War crimes' prosecutions will continue to be conducted in the Cantonal and District courts by the relevant prosecutors, but only with the consent of the Special Prosecutor for War Crimes. It is anticipated that the Special Prosecutor will monitor those war crimes' prosecutions conducted in both the Cantonal and District courts.

Once the Chamber for War Crimes is established and a Special War Crimes' Prosecutor is appointed, the legal review function currently performed by the ICTY Prosecutor, through the Rules of the Road unit, will be transferred to Bosnia and Herzegovina. It is hoped that sufficient resources and staffing will be in place by 1 January 2005 to enable the review function to be transferred on that date. In pursuit of that goal, it is anticipated that Bosnia and Herzegovinian prosecutors from the Special War Crimes' Prosecutor's office will be seconded to the Rules of the Road unit in 2004, in order to develop a familiarity with the number, nature and quality of files reviewed by the unit. It is anticipated that these prosecutors will receive training from staff employed in the Rules of the Road unit, and from the ICTY more generally, as to the evidence required to establish a sufficient *prima facie* case according to international standards. After completing this training period, the prosecutors employed in the Special Prosecutor's office should then be able

---

28. Various Member States of the UN Security Council engaged in a public debate about the merits of establishing a War Crimes Chamber in Bosnia and Herzegovina, and expressed their 'in principle' approval of the Chamber, at the 4,837th and 4,838th Meetings of the UN Security Council on 8 and 9 October 2003.

to assume the review function exercised by the Rules of the Road unit, as well as pursue the prosecutions of suspects whose indictments have already been approved in accordance with Paragraph 5 of the Agreed Measures.

6.   CONCLUSION

By sponsoring the implementation of Paragraph 5 of the Agreed Measures to the Rome Statement, and now funding the establishment of a War Crimes' Chamber and the appointment of a Special Prosecutor for War Crimes, the international community hopes to ensure that a major function of transitional justice, namely the fair indictment of a large number of alleged war criminals, is implemented in Bosnia and Herzegovina. If this objective is successfully achieved, the people of Bosnia and Herzegovina will have a chance to see justice being done, and being done fairly, in their own national courts.[29]

---

29. Websites that may be of interest: <http://www.un.org>, <http://www.un.org/icty>, <http://www.ohr.int>, <http://;www.ictj.org>, <http://www.eupm.org> and <http://www.osce.org>.

THE LIABILITY OF CIVILIANS UNDER INTERNATIONAL HUMANITARIAN LAW'S WAR CRIMES PROVISIONS[1]

Roberta Arnold[2]

1.   INTRODUCTION

Contemporary international conflicts are witnessing an increasing involvement of civilians – such as, for example, suicide bombers[3] – in the conduct of hostilities. Unlike regular soldiers, however, whose job it is to fight, civilians are not allowed to participate in combat and may be tried under ordinary criminal law for such activity.[4] The question that this paper will attempt to answer is whether in the case where their engagement may lead to gross violations of humanitarian principles, they may be additionally subject to war crimes proceedings pursuant to international humanitarian law (IHL).

In order to assess the applicability of the war crimes' regime to civilians, this paper will be structured as follows. Part 2 will define who is a civilian. Part 3 will examine the position of international jurisprudence and doctrine on the question whether civilians may also be liable for war crimes and under what conditions. The fourth part will draw the conclusions.

2.   THE DEFINITION OF CIVILIANS

Pursuant to Article 4 of the Fourth Geneva Convention of 1949, persons that shall be protected as civilians are:

---

1. © R. Arnold, 2004.

2. Dr.iur. LL.M., Legal Advisor, Swiss Ministry of Defence. The author wishes to thank Prof. Walter Kälin (University of Bern), Col. Peter Hostettler (LOAC Section of the Swiss Dept. of Defence), Lt.Col. Bill Lietzau (Special Assistant to the General Counsel, U.S. Department of Defense) and Col. Charles Garraway (formerly, Directorate of Army Legal Services, UK) for their contributions to this discussion. The views expressed here are the author's solely, as well as the responsibility for any mistakes.

3. On this see E. Hale, 'Suicide bombers eager to enlist', *USA Today* (3 April 2003) <http://www.usatoday.com/news/world/2003-04-03-suicide-bombers-usat_x.htm>; T. Judah, 'Confusion reigns in Baghdad amid suicide bombers and hotel explosions', *Sunday Herald* (6 April 2003) <http://www.sundayherald.com/32892>.

4. K. Ipsen, 'Combatants', in D. Fleck, *The Handbook of Humanitarian Law in Armed Conflicts* (Oxford, Oxford University Press 1999) pp. 65-104, at 93, para. 317.

Yearbook of International Humanitarian Law
Volume 5 - 2002 - pp. 344-359

'... those who, at a given moment and in any manner whatsoever, find themselves, in case of a conflict or occupation, in the hands of a Party to the conflict or Occupying Power of which they are not nationals.

Nationals of a State which is not bound by the Convention are not protected by it. Nationals of a neutral State who find themselves in the territory of a belligerent State, and nationals of a co-belligerent State, shall not be regarded as protected persons while the State of which they are nationals has normal diplomatic representation in the State in whose hands they are.

The provisions of Part II are, however, wider in application, as defined in Article 13.

Persons protected by the Geneva Convention for the Amelioration of the Condition of the Wounded and Sick in Armed Forces in the Field of 12 August 1949, or by the Geneva Convention for the Amelioration of the Condition of Wounded, Sick and Shipwrecked Members of Armed Forces at Sea of 12 August 1949, or by the Geneva Convention relative to the Treatment of Prisoners of War of 12 August 1949, shall not be considered as protected persons within the meaning of the present Convention.'

Pursuant to this latter paragraph, civilians are defined in the negative. Namely, these shall be persons who do not qualify for better treatment under either the First, the Second or the Third Geneva Convention (GC) of 1949. The First and the Second GC protect the wounded and sick members of the armed forces, whereas the Third GC protects prisoners of war (POWs), i.e., either members of the regular armed forces of a state, or irregulars who belong to a Party to the conflict, are commanded by a person responsible, carry their arms openly, have a fixed distinctive sign and abide by the laws and customs of warfare.[5] This position is restated in Article 50 AP I:

'1. A civilian is any person who does not belong to one of the categories of persons referred to in Article 4 (A) (1), (2), (3) and (6) of the Third Convention and in Article 43 of this Protocol. In case of doubt whether a person is a civilian, that person shall be considered to be a civilian.

2. The civilian population comprises all persons who are civilians.

3. The presence within the civilian population of individuals who do not come within the definition of civilians does not deprive the population of its civilian character.'

---

5. See Art. 4 III GC. The definition of POW basically mirrors that of combatant. For details, see R. Arnold, 'Training with the opposition: the status of the "Free Iraqi Forces" in the US war against Saddam Hussein', 63 *Heidelberg JIL* (2003) (forthcoming).

Thus, no middle categories exist.[6] Someone is either a civilian or a combatant[7] with prisoner of war (POW) status in case of capture. Moreover, civilians retain their status even if they (unlawfully) engage in the hostilities:

> 'The (IV) GC does not state that civilians who engage in combat thereby lose their protection under the Convention. They lose their protection as civilians in the sense that they may become lawful targets for the duration of their participation in combat, but their status as civilians does not change according to the Convention.'[8]

Thus, individuals – like suicide bombers – who engage in hostilities without fulfilling the combatant status criteria set by Article 4 III GC and Articles 43-44 of the 1977 Additional Protocol I shall be considered civilians.[9]

3.   LIABILITY OF CIVILIANS FOR VIOLATIONS OF
      HUMANITARIAN LAW

Although, from a pragmatic point of view, we would all be inclined to subject these individuals to humanitarian law's war crimes provisions, as lawyers we must take into consideration the overall framework of humanitarian law and examine whether this regime was really intended to apply to civilians as well as combatants. As observed by the International Tribunal for Rwanda (ICTR) in the *Akayesu* Trial Judgement:

> 'The four Geneva Conventions – as well as the two Additional Protocols – as stated above, were adopted primarily to protect the victims as well as potential victims of armed conflicts. This implies thus that the legal instruments are primarily addressed to persons who by virtue of their authority, are responsible for the outbreak of, or are otherwise engaged in the conduct of hostilities. The category of persons to be held accountable in this respect then, would in most cases be limited to commanders, combatants and other members of the armed forces.'[10]

---

6. See J. Pictet, *Commentary to the IV Geneva Convention* (Geneva, ICRC 1958) at p. 50; Y. Sandoz, C. Swinarski and B. Zimmermann et al., eds., *Commentary on the Additional Protocols of 8 June 1977 to the Geneva Conventions of 12 August 1949* (Geneva, Nijhoff 1987), at paras. 1913 et seq.; O. Kimminich, *Schutz der Menschen in bewaffneten Konflikt* (Grünewald, Kaiser 1979) at p. 509, para. 1665.

7. Pictet, op. cit. n. 6, at p. 51; Sandoz et al., op. cit. n. 6, at para. 1678. For an analysis, including the exceptions such as the case of mercenaries and spies, see Arnold, loc. cit. n. 5, at fn. 91 et seq.

8. J. Elsea, 'Treatment of "Battlefield detainees" in the War on Terrorism', Congressional Research Service Report for Congress, 11 April 2002, at p. 11 (<http://www.fas.org/irp/crs/RL31367.pdf>); E. David, *Principes de droit des conflits armés*, 2nd edn. (Brussels, Bruylant 1999) at p. 245, para. 2.11.

9. On this see Arnold, loc. cit. n. 5, at pp. 12 et seq.

10. *Prosecutor v. Akayesu*, Judgement of 2 September 1998, Case No. ICTR-96-4, para. 630.

3.1 International jurisprudence

The most relevant recent decision on the *active* personal scope of application of international humanitarian law is the one taken by the ICTR in *Akayesu*.[11] After concluding that the members of regular armed forces are the primary addressees of war crimes provisions, the Trial Chamber held that:

> 'Due to the overall protective and humanitarian purpose of these international legal instruments, [...] the delimitation of this category of persons bound by the provisions in Common Article 3 and Additional Protocol II should not be too restricted. The duties and responsibilities of the Geneva Conventions and the Additional Protocols, hence, will normally apply only to individuals of all ranks belonging to the armed forces under the military command of either of the belligerent parties, or to individuals who were legitimately mandated and expected, as public officials or agents or persons otherwise holding public authority or de facto representing the Government, to support or fulfil the war efforts.'[12]

The issue was whether the accused, a civilian mayor, could be liable for war crimes for offences committed in relation to the conflict in Rwanda.[13] The Trial Chamber argued that the condition was the existence of a link between the accused and a Party to the conflict.[14] Reference was made to post-WWII judgements like the *Hadamar Trial*.[15] This case dealt with the liability of the civilian personnel of a civilian sanatorium for the killing of over 400 Polish and Soviet nationals by means of injection.[16] The US Military Commission in Wiesbaden (Germany) held that the accused, notwithstanding their civilian status, were guilty of 'violations of international law'. However, in that case there had been a clear link between the accused and a Party to the conflict, i.e., the Nazi regime.[17] Apparently the killings had been committed in compliance with a decree by Hitler authorising the killing of insane persons.[18]

Another relevant decision referred to was the one taken by the British Military Court in the *Essen Lynching* case.[19] The case dealt with the mistreatment and kill-

---

11. Ibid.
12. Ibid., at para. 631. This view was confirmed in *Prosecutor* v. *Musema*, Case No. ICTR-96-13-T, Judgement and Sentence, 27 January 2000, para. 274; *Prosecutor* v. *Rutaganda*, Case No. ICTR-96-3, Judgement of 6 December 1999, *Prosecutor* v. *Kayishema and Ruzindana*, Case No. ICTR-95-1, Judgement of 21 May 1999, para. 175.
13. Art. 4 ICTR Statute deals with violations of the laws of war (war crimes).
14. *Prosecutor* v. *Akayesu, supra* n. 10, para. 633.
15. *The Hadamar Trial*, Law Reports of Trials of War Criminals (LRTWC), The UN War Crimes Commission (UNWCC) Vol. I (London, HMSO 1947) pp. 47, at 53-54. (<http://www.ess.uwe.ac.uk/WCC/hadamar.htm>). The case was held between 8 and 15 October 1945.
16. *The Hadamar Trial, supra* n. 15.
17. Ibid., at p. 47.
18. Ibid., at p. 48.
19. *The Essen Lynching* case, LRTWC, UNWCC Vol. I, Case 8 (London, HMSO 1947) at p. 88 (<http://www.ess.uwe.ac.uk/WCC/essen.htm>). The case was held between 18-19 and 21-22 December 1945.

ing of allied POWs by civilians, with the compliance of the German military. Heyer, a Captain in the German Army, had given instructions that a party of three Allied prisoners of war was to be taken to a Luftwaffe unit for interrogation. He had ordered the escort not to interfere if civilians should molest the prisoners, while also saying that they ought to be shot, or would be shot. While marching through one of the main streets of Essen, a growing crowd of people started hitting them and throwing sticks at them. After reaching a bridge, the prisoners were thrown over the parapet. One of them was killed by the fall, whereas those who were not dead when they landed were killed by shots from the bridge and by members of the crowd, who beat and kicked them to death.[20] The Court held Captain Heyer and several civilians guilty of war crimes.[21] However, in this case there was also a clear link between the accused and a 'Party to the conflict', i.e., the German armed forces, who had clearly incited the commission of the crime. Moreover, interestingly, the Prosecution had pointed out that, with regard to the accused civilians:

'the charge alleged that the accused were concerned in the killing of the three British airmen. That was the wording of the charge, but, the Prosecutor added, for the purpose of this trial he would invite the Court to take the view that *this was a charge of murder and of nothing other than murder*. The allegation would be that all these seven Germans in the dock were guilty either as an accessory before the fact or as principals in the murder of the three British airmen.'[22]

This seems to suggest that, unlike the German military members of the escort, the civilians would have been tried under the ordinary English criminal legislation, even if this position was rejected by the Court.[23]

A third precedent, referred to by the ICTR in *Akayesu*[24] and in *Musema*,[25] is the *Zyklon B* case,[26] held in front of the British Military Court in Hamburg (Germany). The accused, owner of a firm dealing with the distribution of gases and gassing equipment for disinfecting public buildings, was charged with war crimes[27] for the supplying of the Zyklon B poison gas to the SS and the Wehrmacht for the extermination of allied nationals.[28] In this case there was also a clear link between the accused and a Party to the Conflict. On this basis, the ICTR in *Musema* concluded that:

---

20. Ibid., at p. 89.
21. Ibid., at p. 91.
22. Ibid., at p. 91.
23. Ibid., at pp. 91-92.
24. *Prosecutor* v. *Akayesu, supra* n. 10, para. 633.
25. *Prosecutor* v. *Musema, supra* n. 12, para. 270.
26. The *Zyklon B* case, Trial of Bruno Tesch and two others, LRTWC, UNWCC, Vol. I (London, HMSO 1947) at p. 94 (available at <http://www.ess.uwe.ac.uk/WCC/zyklonb.htm>).
27. Art. 46 of the Regulations annexed to the 1907 IV Hague Convention.
28. The *Zyklon B* case, *supra* n. 26, at p. 94.

'So it is well-established that the post-World War II Trials unequivocally support the imposition of individual criminal liability for war crimes on civilians where they have a link or connection with a Party to the conflict.'[29]

This view was reconfirmed by the ICTR in *Kayishema and Ruzindana*,[30] and by the ICTY in the *Kunarac Judgement*:

'It would appear to the Trial Chamber that common Art. 3 may also require some relationship to exist between a perpetrator and a party to the conflict. Since, in the present case, the three accused fought on behalf of one of the parties to the conflict, the Trial Chamber does not need to determine whether such a relationship is required, and if so, what the required relationship should be.'[31]

However, the ICTR changed its view in the *Akayesu* Appeal Judgement,[32] holding that:

'… common Article 3 requires a close nexus between violations and the armed conflict. This nexus … implies that, in most cases, the perpetrator of the crime will probably have a special relationship with one party to the conflict. However, such a special relationship is not a condition precedent to the application of common Article 3 and, hence of Article 4 of the Statute. Accordingly, the Appeals Chamber finds that the Trial Chamber erred on a point of law in restricting the application of common Article 3 to a certain category of persons, as defined by the Trial Chamber.'[33]

The Appeals Chamber argued that neither Article 4 of the ICTR Statute on war crimes nor common Article 3 of the 1949 Geneva Conventions set specific limitations on their active personal scope of application.[34] Thus, everyone could be liable of war crimes, as long as he or she had acted in furtherance of an armed conflict. The Chamber further observed that:

'the minimum protection provided for victims under common Article 3 implies necessarily effective punishment on persons who violate it. Now, such punishment must be applicable to everyone without discrimination, as required by the principles governing individual criminal responsibility as laid down by the Nuremberg Tribunal in particular. The Appeals Chamber is therefore of the opinion that international humanitarian law would be lessened and called into question if it were to be admitted that certain persons

---

29. *Prosecutor* v. *Musema, supra* n. 12 at para. 274. The Trial Chamber relied also on the findings of the Trial Chamber in *Prosecutor* v. *Akayesu, supra*, n. 10, paras. 640-644.

30. Prosecutor v. Kayishema, supra n. 12, para. 175.

31. *Prosecutor* v. *Kunarac, Kovac and Kunovic*'Foca', Case No. IT-96-23 and IT-96-23/1 Judgement, 22 February 2001, at para. 407.

32. *Prosecutor* v. *Akayesu*, Case ICTR-96-4, Judgement of 1 June 2001, paras. 444- 445.

33. Ibid., paras. 444-445.

34. Ibid., paras. 435-437.

be exonerated from individual criminal responsibility for a violation of common Article 3 under the pretext that they did not belong to a specific category.'[35]

Thus, the 'nexus criterion' requires only a link between the acts and the armed conflict, not between the perpetrator and a party to it.[36]

This view seems to be supported by several post WWII decisions – in particular the *Flick*,[37] *Krupp*[38] and Farben[39] judgements – in which only a nexus to the conflict was *explicitly* required. These dealt with the liability of the owners of three major German firms for the exploitation of slave labour provided by the Nazi regime.[40] In the *Farben* case, the US Military Tribunal held that:

'All of the defendants, acting through the instrumentality of Farben and otherwise, with divers other persons, during the period from 1 September 1939 to 8 May 1945, committed war crimes and crimes against humanity as defined by Article II of Control Council Law No. 10, in that they participated in the enslavement and deportation to slave labour on a gigantic scale of members of the civilian population of countries and territories under the belligerent occupation of, or otherwise controlled by, Germany; the enslavement of concentration camp inmates, including German nationals; the use of prisoners of war in war operations and work having a direct relation to war operations, including the manufacture and transportation of war material.'[41]

The court further observed that:

'The laws and customs of war are binding no less upon private individuals than upon government officials and military personnel. In case they are violated there may be a difference in the degree of guilt, depending upon the circumstances, but not in the fact of guilt.'[42]

---

35. Ibid., para. 443.

36. Ibid., paras. 439-444.

37. Trials of War Criminals before the Nuremberg Military Tribunals under Control Council Law No. 10, October 1946-April 1949, Military Tribunal IV, *US* v. *Friedrich Flick et al.*, Vol. VI, Case No. 5.

38. Trials of War Criminals before the Nuremberg Military Tribunals under Control Council Law No. 10, October 1946-April 1949, *US* v. *Alfred Krupp et al.*, Vol. 9, Case No. 10.

39. Trials of War Criminals before the Nuremberg Military Tribunals under Control Council Law No. 10, October 1946-April 1949, 'The I. G. Farben case', *US* v. *Carl Krauch et al.*, Vol. 7, Case No. 6 <http://www.mazal.org/archive/nmt/07/NMT07-C001.htm>.

40. Indictment of *Farben and others*, Trials of War Criminals before the Nuremberg Military Tribunals under Control Council Law No. 10, October 1946-April 1949, 'The I. G. Farben case', Ibid., at p. 50, para. 120. <http://www.mazal.org/archive/nmt/07/NMT07-T0050.htm>.

41. Ibid. With regard to Farben's role, see at p. 53, paras. 128 et seq. <http://www.mazal.org/archive/nmt/07/NMT07-T0053.htm>.

42. *US* v. *Alfred Krupp et al.*, *supra* n. 38 US Military Tribunal at Nuremberg, *US* v. *Alfred Krupp, et al.*, LRTWC, UNWCC, Vol. X, 1949, pp. 130-159, excerpt reported in A. Bouvier and M. Sassoli, *How does law protect in war?* (Geneva, ICRC 1999) at p. 671.

However, in this case there was, implicitly, a clear link between the defendant and a Party to the conflict, which may be the reason why the court did not deem it necessary to indicate it as an additional requirement.

A similar conclusion was reached in the *Flick* case, which also dealt with the exploitation of slave labour prevalently composed by Allied POWs.[43] The court held that:

> 'International law, as such, binds every citizen just as does ordinary municipal law. Acts adjudged criminal when done by an officer of the government are criminal also when done by a private individual. The guilt differs only in magnitude, not in quality. The offender in either case is charged with personal wrong and punishment falls on the offender in propria persona. The application of international law to individuals is no novelty.'[44]

This passage indicates that individuals, and not only states, can be subjects of international law and that they do not need to be *de jure* representatives of the state in order to be tried for war crimes. However, this conclusion does not detract from the fact that this may only hold true if the nexus with a party to the conflict is made.[45] In fact, in this case, the relationship between a Party to the conflict and the offender had been clearly established. The court had namely held that the accused had conducted his firm in strict relationship with the Nazi regime.[46]

This position may have been simplified under the ICC Statute. According to the *Elements of Crime* of Article 8 (which are not binding, however[47]), the condition

---

43. Trials of War Criminals before the Nuremberg Military Tribunals under Control Council Law No. 10, October 1946-April 1949, Military Tribunal IV, *US* v. *Friedrich Flick et al.*, Vol. VI, Case No. 5. Judgement <http://www.mazal.org/archive/nmt/06/NMT06-T1199.htm>.

44. Ibid., at p. 1192.

45. For example, in the *Israeli* case ADA 10/94, *Unnamed* v. *The Minister of Defence*, Appeal against the ruling of the District Court of Tel Aviv-Jaffa, 22 August 1994, at para. 4, Lebanese detainees claimed to be POWs subject to IHL provisions. The Court, however, rebutted this argument holding that since they did not meet the criteria of Art. 4 (A)(2) of the III GC, they amounted to mere terrorists, to be subject to common criminal proceedings. Similarly, it is arguable that also civilians who are not members of a terrorist group but who nevertheless fail to meet the criteria of this provision, and are not linked to any Party to the conflict, are not subject to IHL rules on warfare, including the war crimes provisions. They are common criminals who may nevertheless invoke the protection accorded to civilians by the IV GC, but who shall be prosecuted pursuant to ordinary criminal law or other headings like crimes against humanity. See also Elsea, loc. cit. n. 8, at p. 11.

46. Trials of War Criminals before the Nuremberg Military Tribunals under Control Council Law No. 10, October 1946-April 1949, *Flick et al.*, *supra* n. 37 paras. 18-19 of the indictment. <http://www.mazal.org/archive/nmt/06/NMT06-T0023.htm>. See also p. 43: Later in 1932, a basis was laid for permanent and systematic collaboration between Flick and the Nazi leaders. Hitler had asked his personal economic adviser, Keppler, to collect a small group of economic leaders 'who will be at our disposal when we come into power'. Keppler and Schacht approached Flick, Voegler, and others. The result was the formation of what was then called the 'Keppler Circle', which began to hold meetings to discuss the program of the Nazi Party in the economic field. <http://www.mazal.org/archive/nmt/06/NMT06-T0043.htm>. Flick was moreover a member of the Nazi party. See the Judgement, Volume VI, at 1222. <http://www.mazal.org/archive/nmt/06/NMT06-T1222.htm>.

47. Art. 9 ICC Statute states that the elements of crimes shall merely assist the Court in the interpretation and application of Arts. 6, 7 and 8. Thus, they are to be used merely as an interpretative aid.

for prosecution of war crimes is simply that 'the conduct took place in the context of and was associated with' an armed conflict.[48] There is no explicit requirement that the offender additionally has a link to a Party to the conflict. The question is whether the lack of any reference is to be interpreted as assertively excluding this requirement.

3.2   Doctrine and national precedents

It is generally agreed among scholars that civilians may be liable for war crimes.[49] The focus of the discussion, however, is on whether this liability is conditional upon a nexus to a Party to the conflict.[50]

The majority is opposed to this requirement, particularly for practical reasons related to the procedural hurdles of ordinary criminal law. One argument is that if individual liability for violations of IHL is made conditional on a nexus to a Party, it will only be possible to prosecute independent civilians who commit atrocities in war for ordinary offences like murder, which are not subject to universal jurisdiction. Such persons may find a safe haven in countries with neither personal nor territorial jurisdiction over the offence,[51] and which will not seek to extradite the offenders. Another argument is that if these civilians are not bound by IHL, their detention pursuant to ordinary criminal law may prove to be difficult, because of evidentiary problems. For example, in the case of the Al Qaeda members detained

---

See K. Dörmann, 'War Crimes in the Elements of Crimes', in H. Fischer et al., eds., *International and National Prosecution of Crimes Under International Law* (Berlin, Berlin Verlag 2001) pp. 95-139, at p. 95.

48. See the Elements of Crimes, UN Doc. PCNICC/2000/1/Add.2, at p. 18 (introduction to the Elements of Article 8).

49. According to L.C. Green: 'War crimes are violations of the laws and customs of the law of armed conflict and are punishable whether committed by combatants or civilians, including the nationals of neutral states'. Referred to in *Prosecutor* v. *Tadić*, Case IT-94-1-T, Decision on the Defence Motion on Jurisdiction, Judgement of 10 August 1995, at para. 61. Y. Dinstein, 'The distinction between war crimes and crimes against peace', in Y. Dinstein ed., *War Crimes in International Law*, 2nd edn. (The Hague, Martinus Nijhoff 1996) pp. 1-18, at p. 5. David, op. cit. n. 8, at p. 417, para. 2.243, and at p. 225, para 1.199 et seq. The term civilians used here is intended in the sense of Art. 50 AP I, i. e., both member of irregular forces who do not fulfill the combatant status criteria under III GC, thereby automatically constituting *de jure* civilians, and other 'pure' civilians in the sense of IV GC and Art. 43 AP I, who may however occasionally engage in the hostilities.

50. The dilemma is recalled by Bouvier and Sassoli, op. cit. n. 42, at p. 215: 'The most delicate case is that of individuals who cannot be considered as connected to one party, but nevertheless commit acts of violence contributing to the armed conflict for reasons connected with the conflict. If such individuals are not considered as addressees of IHL, most acts committed in anarchic conflicts would not be covered by IHL nor consequently punishable as violations of IHL.' However, these conclusions were drawn before the *Akayesu* Appeal Judgement of the ICTR in 2001.

51. This is in particular the view of Col. Charles Garraway, of the British Army legal branch, Col. Peter Hostettler, Head of the Law of Armed Conflict Section of the Swiss Ministry of Defence and Lt. Col. William Lietzau, Special Assistant to the General Counsel, U.S. Department of Defense, who said: 'I agree with the AC ... in the *Akayesu* case ... Of course civilians can commit war crimes. To conclude otherwise would, in large part, give immunity to unlawful combatants. While we might like to believe that domestic law could cover these violations, the fact is that, in most of the world, it does not.' (E-mail of 29 December 2002, on file with the author).

in the US naval base of Guantànamo Bay (Cuba), if the US authorities were to apply their domestic criminal provisions, they would have to bring the accused in front of a civil magistrate within 48 hours and establish probable cause for a specific criminal violation. In practice, this would mean that every alleged terrorist would have to be released as soon as captured and that an international criminal organisation with the capability to engage in war-like activities, would be able to secure immunity for its members.[52] The argument of the US authorities is that these persons are not combatants and do not fulfil the criteria of Article 4 III GC, but they have engaged in hostilities against the US and are therefore 'unlawful combatants', who may be retained until the end of the hostilities, with no specific charge.[53] However, as previously mentioned, there is no such category: someone is either a *de jure* combatant, with POW status in case of capture, or a civilian. If no link with the Afghan regime can be proven, Al Qaeda members should be tried for unlawful participation in combat pursuant to ordinary criminal law. For additional crimes, it is questionable whether they may be tried for war crimes. A much simpler solution would be prosecution under the heading of crimes against humanity, particularly in relation to the 11th September attacks, which did not occur within the framework of an already existing conflict.[54]

The fact that ordinary criminal legislation and international legal cooperation may not be adequate to prosecute these types of serious offenders is not a good reason to stretch IHL beyond its jurisdictional boundaries. If there is a gap, this should be filled otherwise than by extensive interpretation. Pursuant to the system of IHL, as well as the wording of common Article 2 to the Geneva Conventions, it seems that in international armed conflicts, only representatives of a High Contracting Party shall be subject to the war crimes provisions. All the others, like 'loose civilian combatants', who have no link with any Party, shall be prosecuted under ordinary criminal law not only for having engaged in hostilities without being authorised to, but also for other crimes committed in these circumstances.[55] Alternatively, they may be tried for crimes against humanity, which no longer require a nexus to an armed conflict.[56]

An objection may be that the point of holding civilians liable for engagement in combat under ordinary law is not that they cannot be charged with war crimes, too,

---

52. Opinion expressed by Lt. Col. William Lietzau, Special Assistant to the General Counsel, US Department of Defense, in an email of 7 April 2003 (on file with the author).

53. See A. McDonald, 'Defining the War on Terror and the Status of Detainees: Comments on the Presentation of Judge George Aldrich', 4 *Humanitäres Völkerrecht – Informationsschriften* (2002) pp. 202, 209.

54. Otherwise, it may have been possible to prosecute these type of acts pursuant to Art. 33 IV GC.

55. See G.H. Aldrich, 'The Taliban, al Qaida, and the Determination of Illegal Combatants', 4 *Humanitäres Völkerrecht* (2002) pp. 200, at p. 203: 'As persons [the Al Qaeda members ...] who have been combatants in hostilities and are not entitled to POW status, they are entitled [...] to humane treatment of the same nature as that prescribed by Art. 3 common to the four Geneva Conventions [...] but they may lawfully prosecuted and punished under national laws for taking part in the hostilities and for any other crimes, such as murder and assault, that they may have committed.' Ipsen, instead, confirms that participation in hostilities is an ordinary crime, without specifying the qualification of other crimes that may have been committed. Ipsen, loc. cit. n. 4, at p. 93, para. 317 et seq.

56. *Prosecutor* v. *Tadić*, Case No. IT-94-1, Judgement of 15 July 1999, at para. 623.

but that combatants have an immunity under domestic law for lawful acts of war. Therefore, a civilian who chooses to enter a conflict cannot claim the immunity of regular combatants. For example, in the case of Al Qaeda, the liability of its members would depend on their status. If proven that they belonged to a Party to the conflict – the Taleban regime – they would have immunity for lawful acts of war, but not for war crimes. Otherwise, they would amount to civilians with no immunity from domestic courts for *any* of their actions, *including* mere participation in combat. This, however, would *not* preclude the jurisdiction of other courts, including international tribunals.[57]

This conclusion, however, may give rise to confusion and unequal treatment. On the one hand, the question would be whether the jurisdictions – respectively for common offences and war crimes – would be concurrent or alternative. On the other hand, the severity of the proceedings may depend on which side the individual has been fighting. The following example will illustrate the problem. Let us assume that states A and B are at war. A citizen of A, X, decides to launch a terrorist attack against the civilian infrastructure of his own country (internal opposition), in order to support B's war effort. For the fact of having engaged in combat, X may be prosecuted under A's ordinary criminal laws. However, it is questionable whether he could be additionally prosecuted for breaches of IHL. In fact, since X did not belong to any party to the conflict, he would amount to an individual civilian engaged in internal sporadic acts of violence, which fall below the threshold of common Article 3 and AP II. Therefore, his attack would not constitute a breach of IHL (in particular Arts. 4 and 13 AP II). In order to be subject to IHL, the insurgency of X against state A should come within the framework of a parallel and more generalised internal conflict between A and opposition groups, organised and set up under a responsible command (this situation would constitute a mixed conflict).[58]

On the other hand, if X launched a terrorist attack against civilian installations of state B, since this action would come within the framework of an international conflict, X may be subject *both* to B's ordinary criminal laws for unlawful participation in combat *and* to war crimes proceedings for breach of Articles 33 IV GC and 51(2) AP I. Thus, depending on whether X engaged himself in hostilities

---

57. According to Col. Charles Garraway, Directorate of Army Legal Services, UK, in an opinion expressed in a mail to the author, on 31 August 2002 (on file with the author). See also G.I.A.D. Draper, 'The status of combatants and the question of guerrilla warfare', 45 *BYIL* (1971) pp. 183-218, at p. 193: 'Those participants in combat activities who fail to meet the requirements of Art. 4A(2) and (6) of the 1949 Convention not only stand under no benefit of prisoner-of-war status upon capture, but are exposed to allegations of war criminality for their participation in combat.' This, however, is not completely true, as the fact of having participated in combat would constitute an ordinary crime, not a war crime. On this see H.-P. Gasser, 'Protection of the civilian population', in Fleck, op. cit. n. 4, pp. 209-292, at p. 211, para. 501.

58. See Art. 1 AP II. This situation derives in part from the 'pairings theory'. On this aspect see R. Arnold, 'Human rights in times of war: the protection of POWs and the case of Ron Arad', 5 *HRLR* (2000) pp. 18, 20. <http://www.nottingham.ac.uk/law/hrlc/5.1.September.2000.pdf>. M. Hess, *Die Anwendbarkeit des humanitären Völkerrecht, insbesondere in gemischten Konflikten* (Zürich, Schulthess Polygraphischer Verlag 1985) p. 152.

against A or B, different consequences may apply. In the first case, he would be prosecuted only under ordinary criminal law, for unlawful participation in combat. In the second case, instead, he would be subject to double proceedings.

In order to avoid complications and inequalities, therefore, all *de facto* 'loose civilian combatants', including irregulars who do not fulfil the criteria of Articles 4(A)(2)(III) GC and 43-44 AP I, and civilians who occasionally engage in the hostilities, with no link to any party to the conflict,[59] should be subject to ordinary criminal law provisions.

It should be recalled that IHL was primarily drafted to regulate the conduct of *warfare*, an activity reserved to regular combatants. This view is confirmed by Article 3 of the Fourth Hague Convention of 1907, stating that: 'A belligerent Party which violates the provisions of the said Regulations shall, if the case demands, be liable for compensation. It shall be responsible for all acts committed by persons forming part of its armed forces.' The reference is limited to the Parties to the conflict, which do not encompass random and unorganised civilians, but groups claiming to represent their country, or part of it.[60] Similarly, Article 1 of the 1907 Hague Regulations states that:

'The laws, rights, and duties of war apply not only to armies, but also to militia and volunteer corps fulfilling the following conditions:
1. To be commanded by a person responsible for his subordinates;
2. To have a fixed distinctive emblem recognizable at a distance;
3. To carry arms openly; and
4. To conduct their operations in accordance with the laws and customs of war.
In countries where militia or volunteer corps constitute the army, or form part of it, they are included under the denomination "army".'

This provision clearly indicates that only members of a regular army, or of militias and volunteer corps commanded by a person responsible, etc. ... are subject to the rights and *duties* of war. Civilians *tout court*, with no *link* to any warring party, i.e., 'loose civilian combatants', cannot be active perpetrators of war crimes.

Another argument may be that since the grave breaches provisions of the 1949 GCs do not specify their active scope of application, everyone is bound by them. However, a systematic interpretation taking into consideration the aforementioned provisions permits rebuttal of this claim. The position that 'loose civilian combatants' are not encompassed is also supported by the fact that certain war crimes require *de facto* the involvement of public or public-related authorities. Examples are the compelling of a protected person to serve in the forces of a hostile Power or his/her deprivation of the right to a fair trial (Art. 147 IV GC).

---

59. The term refers to *de jure* civilians in the sense of Art. 50(1) AP I, who, by virtue of their engagement in the hostilities, are *de facto* combatants. However, since they have no link to any Party to the conflict, they are 'loose civilian combatants'.

60. L. Zegveld, *Accountability of Armed Opposition Groups in International Law* (Cambridge, Cambridge University Press 2002) at p. 15. J. Pictet, *Commentary on the First Geneva Convention of 1949* (Geneva ICRC 1952) at p. 37.

A further claim made in favour of the liability of civilians constituting 'loose combatants' under IHL is that since they can enjoy the *rights* of IHL, under the IV GC, they should also fulfil the *duties*. However, an analogy may be drawn with the so-called '*echte Sonderdelikte*' (genuine special offences) pursuant to central European criminal systems. These are offences that can only be committed by persons with specific professional affiliations (civil servants, specific professionals, etc.).[61] For instance, the principle of bank secrecy can only be breached by bank employees, even though every bank account holder in Switzerland is protected from it. The active and passive personal scope do not necessarily overlap. It should also be recalled that civilians' rights under IHL were only added at a later stage, to address the tendency towards greater victimisation among the civilian population. They reflect the duty of *combatants* to respect the rules of the 'game', if war can be defined as such. But they do not imply the inclusion of new duties for civilians. To claim that civilians can commit war crimes may also suggest that they have a right to participate in the hostilities. But the obligation of civilians to keep out of the 'game' is already imposed by the prosecution of their unlawful engagement under *ordinary* criminal law. With regard to additional serious offences like genocide, murder, rape, hostage-taking, these are already encompassed in most domestic criminal codes, with no need to resort to the war crimes provisions. For example, the war crime of pillaging is encompassed by the ordinary crime of theft. A possible objection is that this may also hold true for combatants. However, the reason why combatants should be prosecuted for war crimes rather than ordinary offences is that, because of their official position as representatives of a state, or of a non-state party alleging authority, they are expected to be disciplined and fight by lawful and *fair* methods of warfare. As observed by Roling: 'Criminal prosecution of war criminals is … one of the factors contributing to honourable behaviour in war.'[62] This is why the standards imposed on combatants should be more severe. Isolated crimes perpetrated by independent civilians should be prosecuted under domestic criminal law headings like murder, etc.[63] Should prosecution under ordinary offences prove to be insufficient in a particular case, given the gravity of the crime, it may be still possible to resort to prosecution for crimes against humanity, where the elements of that crime – namely, that they be part of a widespread or systematic attack – are otherwise met, since the aim of international law is to prosecute offences of a certain *gravity* rather than a certain type of person who violates those crimes.

Another argument is that civilians who engage in hostilities and who violate humanitarian law shall be subject to the same treatment as combatants undergoing

---

61. P. Noll and S. Trechsel, *Schweizerisches Strafrecht Allgemeiner Teil I – allgemeine Voraussetzungen der Strafbarkeit* (Zürich, Schulthess Polygraphischer Verlag 1998) at p. 76.

62. B.V.A. Röling, 'Criminal responsibility for violations of the laws of war', 12 *RBDI* (1976) pp. 8, 23.

63. See Pictet, op. cit. n. 6, at p. 601, with regard to the offence of appropriation: 'To constitute a grave breach, such destruction and appropriation must be extensive: an isolated incident would not be enough.' The fact that most war crimes imply widespread occurrence, implies the existence of an organised structure, suggesting that single individuals committing isolated acts are not encompassed. On this see also the heading of Art. 8 ICC Statute.

war crimes trials. However, unlike combatants, civilians cannot benefit from the judicial and substantive guarantees foreseen by POW status. Thus, a combatant and a civilian charged with the same offence would be treated unequally, if they were tried for the same war crime.

A further argument usually made in favour of the liability of civilians under IHL is the US decision *In Re Quirin*.[64] This preceded the coming into force of the 1949 GCs. Therefore, the only applicable provision was Article 29 of the 1907 Hague Regulations. The US Supreme Court stated that:

'... the law of war draws a distinction between the armed forces and the peaceful populations of belligerent nations and also between those who are lawful and unlawful combatants. Lawful combatants are subject to capture and detention as prisoners of war by opposing military forces. Unlawful combatants are likewise subject to capture and detention, but in addition they are subject to trial and punishment by military tribunals for acts which render their belligerency unlawful. The spy who secretly and without uniform passes the military lines of a belligerent in time of war, seeking to gather military information and communicate it to the enemy, or an enemy combatant who without uniform comes secretly through the lines for the purpose of waging war by destruction of life or property, are familiar examples of belligerents who are generally deemed not to be entitled to the status of prisoners of war, but to be offenders against the law of war subject to trial and punishment by military tribunals.'[65]

The accused were *de jure* civilians only because their engagement in spying activities had denied them the right to combatant and POW status.[66] However, there was a clear link between the accused and a Party to the conflict, i.e., Germany.[67] *De facto* the accused were combatants sent to the US in civilian clothing. Had they not engaged in espionage, they would have had the right to POW status, since this does not detract from the possibility of their being charged with the breach of the principle of distinction.[68]

---

64. US Supreme Court, Ex Parte Quirin, 317 US 1 (1942) <http://www.constitution.org/ussc/317-001a.htm#f>.

65. Ibid., at p. 31.

66. Ibid. The charges were: 1. Violation of the law of war. 2. Violation of Art. 81 of the Articles of War, defining the offence of relieving or attempting to relieve, or corresponding with or giving intelligence to, the enemy. 3. Violation of Art. 82, defining the offence of spying. 4. Conspiracy to commit the offences alleged in charges 1, 2 and 3.

67. Ibid., at p. 36: Specification 1 states that petitioners 'being enemies of the United States and acting for ... the German Reich, a belligerent enemy nation, secretly and covertly passed, in civilian dress, contrary to the law of war, through the military and naval lines and defenses of the United States ... and went behind such lines, contrary to the law of war, in civilian dress ... for the purpose of committing ... hostile acts, and, in particular, to destroy certain war industries, war utilities and war materials within the United States'.

68. In this respect, in fact, the decision is incorrect. There are authors suggesting that the criteria contained in Art. 4A(2) III GC apply also to regular members of the armed forces. This, however, is an interpretation that goes against the actual wording. For a critique see Aldrich, loc. cit. n. 55, at p. 204. He refers to Rosas and Mallison as supporters of this controversial view.

Another final argument against the liability of civilians constituting *de facto* 'loose combatants' under IHL is that there would be unequal treatment between perpetrators holding the nationality of a party engaged in the conflict, and nationals of neutral states or co-belligerent states holding normal diplomatic relations with the parties involved. In fact, there are three exceptional cases defined by Article 4 IV GC, in which civilians are not covered by IHL:

'— Nationals of a State which is not bound by the Convention;
— Nationals of a neutral State who find themselves in the territory of a belligerent State, and who has normal diplomatic representation in the State in whose hands they are;
— Nationals of a co-belligerent State, that has normal diplomatic representation in the State in whose hands they are.'[69]

The first situation is irrelevant, since the 1949 GCs have acquired customary law status. But with regard to the second case, it is possible to imagine the following scenario. For example (Y), a national of neutral state N, may decide to launch an attack against a civilian installation of state B (e.g., a TV station), in order to support state A, with which he sympathises. Due to Article 4 IV GC he would not be subject to the war crimes provisions. On the other hand if (Z), a national of state A, committed the same act, he may be charged with war crimes. This would be a discriminatory result. A similar problem may arise in relation to the third case. For example, Judge Aldrich observed that the US had normal diplomatic relations with the states of which many Al Qaeda members are nationals (UAE, Saudi Arabia, UK, etc.). Therefore, these members would fall under Article 4 IV GC and be excluded from IHL's scope of application.[70] This means that the Al Qaeda members responsible for terrorist attacks against the US should be prosecuted only under ordinary criminal law, unless it could be proven that they belonged to a 'Party to the conflict', i.e., the Afghani Taleban regime.[71] Only in this event could they be tried for war crimes. At the same time, though, 'loose' Afghan civilians who may have fought against the US may be tried for war crimes, should they be considered bound by IHL. But this, too, would be a discriminatory result.

4.   CONCLUSIONS

International humanitarian law's war crimes provisions were primarily designed to regulate the conduct of warfare by members of regular armed forces, or individuals somehow related to them. 'Loose civilian combatants' with no link to any official Party to a conflict who spontaneously decide to engage in the hostilities do not seem to have been envisaged by the drafters of the 1949 Geneva Conventions and

---

69. See Pictet, loc. cit. n. 6, at p. 48.
70. Aldrich, loc. cit. n. 55, at p. 203, fn. 4.
71. See McDonald, loc. cit. n. 52, at p. 207.

their Additional Protocols of 1977. However, recent conflicts have increasingly seen the involvement of these kinds of individuals, including suicide bombers, who have not been entrusted with the task to fight and who should keep out of the 'game'.

There are several practical reasons that would incline lawyers to hold civilians and irregulars short of combatant status liable under ordinary criminal law for a breach of the ban on the participation in combat, and under the war crimes provisions in case of serious violations. One in particular is that prosecution for war crimes would be subject to the principle of universal jurisdiction, thereby barring offenders from finding safe havens in states with no personal or territorial jurisdiction over the offence. Prosecution under ordinary criminal legislation is often faced with a lack of international cooperation. However, a systematic, teleological, historical and literal reading suggests that only regular combatants or other individuals, including civilians, who have a link to a Party to the conflict, may be subject to IHL's war crimes provisions for offences committed in international conflicts. This gap may be filled by prosecuting the others under ordinary criminal law or provisions on crimes against humanity. In addition, the ICC Statute may have opened the gates for a new development, by expressly requiring in the Elements of Article 8 on war crimes that the offences be simply related to the conflict, with no reference to a link between the offender and a Party to the conflict.

REGULATING EXPLOSIVE REMNANTS OF WAR[1]

Louis Maresca[2]

1. INTRODUCTION

There have been significant developments in recent years in the efforts to reduce the death, injury and suffering caused by anti-personnel landmines. These weapons are regarded as one of the major threats to civilians once an armed conflict has ended. Anti-personnel mines have killed and injured large numbers of men, women and children and slowed the rebuilding of war-affected countries. The long-term and indiscriminate effects of these weapons led to the adoption in 1997 of the Convention on the Prohibition of the Use, Stockpiling, Production and Transfer of Anti-personnel Mines and on their Destruction.

Anti-personnel mines, however, are one part of a broader problem. Modern armed conflict leaves behind a wide array of explosive ordnance which, like anti-personnel mines, causes large numbers of civilian casualties and has severe socio-economic consequences for years, and sometimes for decades, after the hostilities end. Until recently, international humanitarian law contained very few requirements to lessen the impact of these 'explosive remnants of war' (ERW).

This article will provide an overview of the problem of explosive remnants of war and the work being done to strengthen international humanitarian law in this area. In particular, it will focus on the work undertaken in the context of the 1980 Certain Conventional Weapons Convention (CCWC). In December 2002, States Parties agreed to negotiate a new international instrument in an effort to deal with the problem. While this article was commenced prior to the start of negotiations, its final section provides an overview of the contents of the protocol adopted by States Parties in November 2003.

---

1. © L. Maresca, 2003.

2. Legal Advisor, Mines-Arms Unit, Legal Division, International Committee of the Red Cross (ICRC). The views expressed in this article are those of the author and do not necessarily reflect those of the ICRC.

Yearbook of International Humanitarian Law
Volume 5 - 2002 - pp. 360-374

2.   EXPLOSIVE REMNANTS OF WAR: THE PREDICTABLE
        REMAINS OF MODERN ARMED CONFLICT[3]

The end of an armed conflict does not bring an end to the suffering of civilians
living in areas where fighting has taken place. There is often a wide range of dangers that threaten their lives and well-being. A significant threat is the presence of
unexploded ordnance. Modern armed conflicts leave behind enormous amounts of
ordnance that has failed to detonate as intended or has been left as part of stockpiles near battlefield positions. Ordnance commonly found includes artillery shells,
mortars, grenades, cluster bomb and other submunitions, air dropped bombs and
other similar explosives. These 'explosive remnants of war' continue to kill and
injure long after the fighting has ended.[4]

  Explosive remnants of war are not a new phenomenon. National authorities and
civilian populations in many regions of the world have had to deal with these
weapons throughout the Twentieth Century. It is estimated that 84 countries are
affected by explosive remnants of war.[5] Even today, countries across Europe continue to find and clear explosive munitions from the First and Second World Wars
and civilians still fall victim to these weapons.[6]

  While detailed information on the scale of the problem is scarce, information
from national authorities responsible for the clearance of explosive remnants of war
provides some insight. In Poland, for example, its Corps of Engineers have cleared
enormous amounts of explosive remnants of war left from World War II. Between
1944 and 2000 they removed and neutralized over 96 million pieces of ordnance.
While a large part of these were cleared between 1944 and 1956, nearly 700,000
were cleared in 2000.[7] The human costs are even more staggering. It is reported
that 4,094 civilians have been killed and another 8,774 injured by these weapons.[8]

---

3. This section draws heavily on the Report of the International Committee of the Red Cross to the
First Meeting of the Preparatory Committee for the 2001 Review Conference of the United Nations
Convention on Certain Conventional Weapons, UN Doc. CCW/CONF.II/PC.1/WP.1, 11 December
2000.

4. The phrase 'explosive remnants of war' has not been defined but it is generally understood to be
synonymous with 'unexploded ordnance'. Under the International Mine Action Standards (IMAS)
published by the United Nations Mine Action Service, unexploded ordnance is 'explosive ordnance
that has been primed, fused, armed or otherwise prepared for use or used. It may have been fired,
dropped, launched or projected yet remains unexploded either through malfunction or design or any
other reason'. IMAS, 04.10, 1st edn. 2001, at p. 26.

5. Landmine Action, 'Explosive Remnants of War: The Global Problem', Paper presented to the
Group of Governmental Experts to the Convention on Certain Conventional Weapons, December
2002.

6. 'Greek experts defuse bomb from Second World War at future Olympic site'. <http://ca.news.
yahoo.com/021129/6/qjiry.html>; 'British wartime bomb is defused as city holds its breath', <http://
archives.tcm.ie/irishexaminer/1999/09/23/fhead_268.htm>; 'Teen killed by World War I Bomb',
<http:www/news.com.au/common/story_page/0,4057,5395877%255E401,00.html>.

7. Engineering Forces of the Polish Armed Forces, 'Polish Experiences with Explosive Remnants
of War', Document distributed to the Group of Governmental Experts to the Convention on Certain
Conventional Weapons, December 2002.

8. B.A. Molaski and J. Pajak, 'Explosive Remnants of World War II in Poland', in A.H. Westing,
ed., *Explosive Remnants of War: Mitigating the Environmental Effects* (London, Taylor & Francis

Laos is another example of a country currently dealing with a long-existing explosive remnants of war problem. As a result of the conflicts in Southeast Asia during the 1960s and 1970s, it remains severely affected by explosive remnants of war. Information provided by the National UXO Programme in Laos shows that, since the end of the conflict in 1975, close to 12,000 people have been killed or injured by these weapons.[9] Particularly dangerous are cluster bomb submunitions, which were dropped in large numbers during the war. It is estimated that between nine and 27 million of these submunitions failed to explode as intended.[10] Unexploded mortars, projectiles, rockets, large bombs and landmines are also present throughout the country.[11]

More recent is the case of Kosovo. A study conducted by the International Committee of the Red Cross (ICRC) found that explosive remnants of war continued to kill and injure large numbers of civilians after the end of the conflict between NATO and the Federal Republic of Yugoslavia. In the year following the end of the fighting, 492 people were killed or injured by a variety of different explosive remnants of war.[12] These included anti-personnel mines, anti-vehicle mines, cluster bomb submunitions and other similar explosives. It is reported that through 2001, 54,808 pieces of ordnance were removed or destroyed in Kosovo by clearance agencies.[13]

In addition to the human casualties, explosive remnants of war produce a range of indirect, but nevertheless destructive, consequences. Like anti-personnel mines, these weapons can have a serious socio-economic impact. Their presence prevents people from returning to their homes and hampers the reconstruction of vital infrastructure after the conflict, such as housing, schools, water systems and roads.[14] This, in turn, can hinder development and the resumption of commercial activities. Particularly damaging is the effect on agriculture. Farmland or pastures contaminated by explosive remnants of war may be abandoned or cannot be farmed to capacity. Families and communities dependant on agriculture can be heavily affected.[15] Yet, in spite of the threat, economic necessity and other factors will often drive people to work their land or collect ordnance for scrap metal content. Such activities can increase the exposure to risk and result in even more casualties.

1985) p. 26. Statistics based on information of the Polish Ministry of National Defence, Warsaw, Army Combat Engineer annual reports (unpublished archives).

9. Lao National Unexploded Ordnance Programme, *Annual Report 2000* (Vientiane, UXO Lao 2001) p. 4.

10. Presentation of P. Bean, Programme Director Lao National UXO Programme, published in *Expert Meeting on Explosive Remnants of War: Summary Report* (Geneva, International Committee of the Red Cross 2000) p. 8.

11. UXO Lao <http://www.uxolao.org/clearance.htm>. See R. McGrath, *Cluster Bombs: The military effectiveness and impact on civilians of cluster munitions* (London, UK Working Group on Landmines 2002) p. 30.

12. International Committee of the Red Cross, *Explosive Remnants of War: Cluster bombs and Landmines in Kosovo* (Geneva, International Committee of the Red Cross 2000) p. 10.

13. International Campaign to Ban Landmines (ICBL), *Landmine Monitor Report 2002: Toward a Mine Free World* (Washington, Human Rights Watch 2002) p. 829.

14. Landmine Action, *Explosive Remnants of War: Unexploded ordnance and post-conflict communities* (London, Landmine Action 2002) pp. 23-25.

15. Ibid., pp. 33-35.

Laos, Kosovo and World War II Europe are just a few examples of countries and regions dealing with the problem of explosive remnants of war. Their experience is by no means unique. Similar scenarios are found in other parts of the world. It would seem safe to say that enormous amounts of explosive remnants of war, and, sadly, large numbers of unnecessary civilian casualties, are a predictable and persistent feature of modern warfare. As shown by the case of Kosovo, even conflicts of a short duration can produce a substantial problem that costs many lives. Unfortunately, with a growing capability of armed forces to rapidly deliver large amounts of ordnance over greater and greater distances, the scale of the problem may increase rather than diminish.

3.   THE REASONS WHY ORDNANCE FAILS TO EXPLODE AS INTENDED

The reasons why explosive remnants of war occur are varied. The presence of such weapons after the end of hostilities is generally due to their failure to detonate as intended once they are fired, dropped or otherwise delivered. Such failures are often the result of the design, production and use of the weapon as well as environmental factors that effect its operation.

Experts have identified the following as some of the reasons why explosive ordnance fails to function as intended:[16]

— *Poor design* – poorly designed fusing and poor inflight stabilization of air-delivered ordnance will often cause it to fail.

— *Production-related deficiencies* – such as poor manufacturing and the use of substandard materials and components in production.

— *Improper storage and handling* – the storage of ordnance in unfavourable conditions (i.e., too hot or too cold) can accelerate deterioration and adversely affect the functioning of mechanisms and explosive composition. Rough handling in storage and transport can also damage munitions and effect reliability.

— *Improper use of munitions* – common errors include the improper setting of fuses and incorrect launch profiles.[17]

— *Unfavourable target environment* – as many types of ordnance are designed to explode on impact, soft terrain, dense vegetation and heavy precipitation can prevent detonation.

— *Interaction with other exploding ordnance* – ordnance exploding nearby can cause damage to other munitions and prevent explosion.

---

16. Information collated from Geneva International Centre for Humanitarian Demining (GICHD), *Explosive Remnants of War: A Threat Analysis* (Geneva, Geneva International Centre for Humanitarian Demining 2002) p. 7; C. King, *Explosive Remnants of War: A study on submunitions and other unexploded ordnance* (Geneva, International Committee of the Red Cross 2000) pp. 38-39; McGrath, op. cit. n. 11, at pp. 25-27.

17. Examples of incorrect launch profiles would be the dropping of air-delivered weapons at too low an altitude, thus preventing them from arming properly.

It is difficult to accurately establish the extent to which ordnance may fail during a conflict. One indication of its reliability comes from data gathered during testing and in service trials prior to conflict. Militaries appear to accept a five percent failure rate during testing.[18] Conditions on the battlefield, however, often differ greatly from those found at testing sites and in testing procedures. As a result, failure rates during operations are known to be significantly higher.[19] In recent years, the data most widely available concerning the amount of explosive remnants of war found after a conflict has been that related to submunitions released from air-dropped cluster bombs or land-based delivery systems.

4.   THE PARTICULAR CONCERNS ABOUT SUBMUNITIONS

Submunitions have been cited as a particular problem within the broader category of explosive remnants of war.[20] In recent years, their consequences have been widely reported in the media.

Like other explosive ordnance, a certain percentage of submunitions will not explode as they are meant to. Yet submunitions are a special concern because of the very large numbers often used in conflict. During the war in Indochina, for example, perhaps as many as 90 million submunitions were dropped in Laos.[21] As stated above, it is believed that nine to 27 million failed to explode as intended; a 10-30 percent rate of failure.[22] Significant numbers of submunitions also failed to explode as a result of their use in Kosovo. NATO acknowledges dropping 1,392 cluster bombs, containing some 290,000 submunitions. While initial projections placed the number of unexploded submuntions at around 30,000, recent estimates have adjusted that figure to approximately 20,000.[23] Predictably, submunitions have caused large numbers of civilian casualties in situations where they have been used and pose serious challenges for organizations involved in the clearance of explosive remnants of war.[24]

---

18. King, op. cit. n. 16, at p. 9 indicates that US Army acceptance tests for munitions identify a failure rate of 2.5 percent - 5 percent as 'acceptable' for new ammunition. See also McGrath, op. cit. n. 11, at p. 27.

19. McGrath, op. cit. n. 11, at pp. 27-28.

20. Submunitions are often mislabelled as 'cluster bombs' in media reports. A submunition is any munition that, to perform its task, separates from a parent munition. This includes, for example, mines or munitions that form part of a cluster bomb, artillery shell or missile payload. A 'cluster bomb' is a bomb containing or dispensing submunitions. Cluster bombs are the dispensers, generally dropped from aircraft, which scatter submunitions over the area where an intended target is located. It is the submunitions that are the main focus of concern. GICHD, op. cit. n. 16, at p. 23.

21. McGrath, op. cit. n. 11, at p. 31.

22. Lao National Unexploded Ordnance Programme, *UXO Lao: Work Plan 2002* (Vientiane, UXO Lao 2002) p. 7; ICRC, op. cit. n. 10, at p. 8.

23. ICBL, op. cit. n. 13, at p. 824.

24. Submunitions have been cited as one of the principle causes of civilian casualties in conflicts in which they have been used. In Laos they are believed to have been responsible for a large part of the nearly 12,000 UXO related casualties. In Kosovo, submunitions were, along with anti-personnel mines, the leading cause of unexploded ordnance-related death and injury. Together, these weapons

An additional concern is the risks posed by submunitions during conflict when they are used against targets in or near populated areas. By design, submunitions are area weapons. Once released from the cluster bomb, rocket or other means of delivery, hundreds of them are dispersed over an area of up to several thousand square meters. In light of the wide area of dispersal, there is a substantial risk that significant numbers of civilians could be caught in a submunitions attack, particularly in situations where civilians and military targets are in close quarter. A report by Human Rights Watch has suggested that in such circumstances civilian casualties may be more extensive than those associated with traditional explosive ordnance.[25]

In addition, most submunitions cannot be precisely targeted once they are released and fall to the ground unguided. As such, their descent is often affected by environmental factors (wind, air density, etc.). Their small size, braking mechanisms (parachutes and ribbons) and other features mean that submunitions are prone to be affected by weather and land far from the intended target.

Based on these concerns, a number of non-governmental organizations called for a complete prohibition on the use of these weapons or a moratorium on use until the international regulations were strengthened.[26] At the Review Conference of States Parties to the Convention on Certain Conventional Weapons held in December 2001, several states, the ICRC and observer organizations participating in the conference called for a prohibition on the use of submunitions against any military target located in a concentration of civilians.[27]

5.   INTERNATIONAL HUMANITARIAN LAW

International humanitarian law contains a number of principles and rules which seek to limit the impact of weapons on civilians. Perhaps foremost is the principle that civilians enjoy a general protection against the dangers arising from military operations.[28] More detailed rules, such as the rules on distinction and the prohibition on indiscriminate attacks, give effect to this protection.[29]

---

accounted for 73 percent (approximately 36 percent each) of the 280 incidents individually recorded by the ICRC between 1 June 1999 and 31 May 2000. A variety of other ordnance accounted for the remaining 27 percent of the casualties. ICRC, op. cit. n. 12, at p. 9.

25. Human Rights Watch, *Fatally Flawed: Cluster Bombs and Their Use by the United States in Afghanistan* (Human Rights Watch, New York 2002) at p. 10.

26. These include Human Rights Watch, ICRC, Landmine Action and the Mennonite Central Committee. On 13 February 2003, the European Parliament adopted a resolution on the harmful effects of unexploded ordnance and depleted uranium ammunition which called on EU Member States to implement a moratorium on the further use of these weapons pending the conclusions of a comprehensive study of the requirements of international humanitarian law.

27. See *infra* Section 6.

28. Art. 51(1) Protocol Additional to the Geneva Conventions of 12 August 1949, and relating to the Protection of Victims of International Armed Conflicts (Protocol I), 8 June 1977 (hereinafter 1977 Additional Protocol I).

29. Art. 51(2) and 51(4) 1977 Additional Protocol I.

Specific rules to limit the consequences of certain forms of explosive remnants of war first found expression in the CCWC.[30] Protocol II annexed to the Convention requires that the parties to the conflict record the location of all mines, minefields and booby traps and take all necessary and appropriate measures to protect civilians from their effects once active hostilities have ended.[31] In 1996, States Parties adopted amendments to strengthen the Protocol in response to the widespread problems caused by anti-personnel mines.[32] In addition to further restricting the use of these weapons during conflict and improving the requirement to take all necessary and appropriate measures to protect civilians from their effects, the Protocol mandates the clearance of mines, booby traps and other devices without delay after the cessation of active hostilities.[33] The Protocol also establishes that parties to a conflict bear some responsibility for the mines, booby traps and other device employed by them.[34]

The Convention on the Prohibition of Anti-personnel Mines also requires that specific measures be taken to reduce the impact of anti-personnel mines.[35] Under its provisions, all areas containing anti-personnel mines must be cleared of these weapons. Until clearance is completed, the area must be marked, fenced and monitored for the effective exclusion of civilians.[36]

With the adoption of the amendments to Protocol II and the development of the Convention on the Prohibition of Anti-personnel Mines, the international community has begun to address the problems caused by explosive remnants of war through international humanitarian law. These instruments are important precedents and their provisions contain important elements to address the problem. Until now, however, most of the developments in the law have focussed on anti-personnel mines. Other explosive remnants of war, however, are not covered by the rules of amended Protocol II or the Convention on the Prohibition of Anti-personnel Mines. As has been indicated above, a wide range of other explosive remnants of war are nevertheless a significant part of the problem and cause large numbers of civilian casualties.

---

30. The full name is the Convention on Prohibitions or Restrictions on the Use of Certain Conventional Weapons Which May be Deemed to be Excessively Injurious or to Have Indiscriminate Effects (hereinafter CCWC). The Convention was adopted on 10 October 1980 and entered into force on 2 December 1983. As of 1 February 2003, there were 90 States Parties to the Convention.

31. Art. 7 Protocol on Prohibitions or Restrictions on the Use of Mines, Booby Traps and Other Devices.

32. Protocol on Prohibitions or Restrictions on the Use of Mines, Booby Traps and Other Devices as amended on 3 May 1996 (hereinafter amended Protocol II). The Protocol entered into force on 3 December 1997 and as of 1 February 2003 there were 68 States Parties.

33. Art. 10 Amended Protocol II. Under Art. 2(5), 'other devices' are defined as 'manually emplaced munitions and devices including improvised explosive devices designed to kill, injure or damage and which are actuated manually by remote control or automatically after a lapse of time'.

34. Art. 3(2) Amended Protocol II.

35. The full name is the Convention on the Prohibition of the Use, Stockpiling, Production, and Transfer of Anti-personnel Mines and on their Destruction. It was adopted on 18 September 1997 and entered into force on 1 March 1999. As of 1 February 2003 there were 131 States Parties.

36. Ibid., Art. 5.

It has been suggested that international humanitarian law rules governing the use of weapons during conflict may prohibit or restrict the deployment of weapons likely to become explosive remnants of war. This discussion has generally focussed on submunitions in light of the civilian casualties often associated with the large number that fail to explode as intended. One central issue is whether the use of submunitions, and presumably other explosive ordnance that may similarly fail to explode, would violate the prohibition on indiscriminate attacks found in Article 51 of the 1977 Additional Protocol I to the Geneva Conventions.

While there has not been extensive legal analysis published on this point, several commentators have suggested that the high numbers of submunitions that fail to explode, and the foreseeable civilian casualties likely to follow, may offend Article 51(4)(c). This is because submunitions will have effects that are indiscriminate and would violate key provisions of the Additional Protocol, such as the rule that a distinction between civilians and combatants must be made at all times.[37] Another argument is that the use of these weapons may offend the rule of proportionality under Article 51(5)(b).[38] The argument here is that the foreseeable civilian casualties caused by submunitions are likely to be excessive in relation to the military advantages gained.[39] This argument assumes that the long-term effects of explosive ordnance must be taken into account when making the determinations required by the principle of proportionality.

A more limited view of the role of the foreseeable effects of unexploded submunitions, and explosive remnants of war more generally, under Article 51(5)(b) has been taken by Professor Christopher Greenwood. In a paper submitted to the Group of Governmental Experts established by the States Parties to the CCWC, he suggested that the effects of explosive remnants of war do have a role to play in the determination of proportionality.[40] In his view, however, only the immediate risks, that is, the threats posed by explosive ordnance during an attack and the threat of explosive remnants of war in the hours following an attack, can be a factor. As the determination of proportionality must be based upon the information reasonably available at the time of an attack, he finds that the long-term risks of explosive remnants of war are too remote to be capable of assessment at that time.

---

37. Under Art. 51(4)(c) of Additional Protocol I, indiscriminate attack are 'those which employ a method or means of combat the effects of which cannot be limited as required by this Protocol'. Human Rights Watch, op. cit. n. 25, at p. 14; V. Wiebe, 'Footprints of Death: Cluster bombs as indiscriminate weapons under international humanitarian law', 22 *Michigan JIL* (2000) pp. 113-119.

38. Ibid.

39. Art. 51(5)(b) of 1977 Additional Protocol I considers an attack as indiscriminate if it 'may be expected to cause incidental loss of civilian life, injury to civilians, damage to civilian objects, or a combination thereof, which would be excessive in relation to the concrete and direct military advantage anticipated'.

40. C. Greenwood, 'Legal Issues Regarding Explosive Remnants of War.' Working Paper submitted to the Group of Governmental Experts of the States Parties to the Convention on Prohibitions or Restrictions on the Use of Certain Conventional Weapons Which May be Deemed to be Excessively Injurious or to Have Indiscriminate Effects, UN Doc. CCW/GGE/I/WP.10, 22 May 2002.

6.   THE WORK TO DEVELOP A NEW PROTOCOL TO THE
CONVENTION ON CERTAIN CONVENTIONAL WEAPONS

6.1   Background

The CCWC was widely viewed as the principal framework within which to discuss and develop new rules on explosive remnants of war. This instrument of international humanitarian law is intended to regulate conventional weapons that may cause excessive suffering to combatants or have indiscriminate effects on civilians.[41] The First Review Conference of the CCWC (1995-96) was the forum within which the international community first attempted to negotiate a complete prohibition on anti-personnel mines.[42]

The idea to address the problem of explosive remnants of war in the CCWC context was first made by the ICRC. With the Second Review Conference of States Parties to the CCWC scheduled to take place in December 2001, the ICRC convened a meeting of governmental and other experts in September 2000 to examine the problem and proposed that the issue be part of the Conference's agenda.[43]

Initial reactions to the ICRC's proposal were generally favourable. Many experts believed that a comprehensive approach to the problem of explosive remnants of war was necessary and logical and encouraged the ICRC to develop this issue further.[44] Other experts, however, felt that addressing this problem would be a long and complex process. Some experts felt that explosive remnants of war might be better placed on the agenda of a later review conference.[45]

As an organization with observer status in the preparations and work of the Second Review Conference, the ICRC submitted a report to the First Meeting of the Preparatory Committee.[46] In this document the ICRC called for the negotiation of a new protocol to the CCWC to reduce the death, injury and suffering caused by explosive remnants of war. The report proposed that this protocol cover all types of explosive remnants of war, except anti-personnel mines.[47] In the view of the ICRC, the main elements of a new protocol should include:

---

41. The rules regulating the weapons it covers are found in the five Protocols currently annexed to the Convention. Protocol I prohibits the use of weapons using fragments not detectable by X-ray. Protocol II, in both its original and amended versions, restricts the use of mines, booby traps and other devices. Protocol III restricts the use of incendiary weapons. Protocol IV prohibits the use and transfer of blinding laser weapons. Protocol V, as discussed *infra* Section 7, addresses ERW.

42. This effort was unsuccessful and led states supporting a prohibition on these weapons to pursue a ban in a separate process, the so-called Ottawa Process, which led to the adoption of the Convention on the Prohibition of Anti-personnel Mines in 1997.

43. International Committee of the Red Cross, Expert Meeting on Explosive Remnants of War, September 2000.

44. Ibid., pp. 14-15.

45. Ibid.

46. International Committee of the Red Cross, Report to the First Meeting of the Preparatory Committee For the 2001 Review Conference of the United Nations Convention on Certain Conventional Weapons, UN Doc. CCW/CONF.II/PC.1/WP.1, 11 December 2000.

47. The ICRC and many States Parties believed that anti-personnel mines were comprehensively dealt with by the Convention on the Prohibition of Anti-personnel Mines.

— The central principle that those who use munitions which remain after the end of active hostilities are responsible for clearing or providing the technical and material assistance needed to ensure the clearance of such ordnance. Explosive munitions and submunitions should self-destruct if they fail to detonate on impact and should be made detectable

— The principle that technical information to facilitate clearance should be provided to mine clearance organizations immediately after the end of active hostilities in an affected area.

— The principle that those who use munitions likely to have long-term effects should provide warnings to civilian populations on the dangers of such ordnance.

— For submunitions only (whether delivered by air or ground-based systems), a prohibition of use against military objects located in concentrations of civilians.[48]

The ICRC noted that obligations on clearance, the provision of information and warnings were already required for mines, booby traps and other devices under amended Protocol II of the CCWC and, thus, were already established in international humanitarian law. It also highlighted that the restriction on submunitions was similar to what was required for incendiary weapons under Protocol III of the CCWC.

Several States Parties also submitted proposals to address the problems caused by specific types of explosive remnants of war. Switzerland called for the adoption of new rules that would require all submunitions to have self-destruct and self-deactivation features to ensure that these weapons would be destroyed if the primary fuse failed to detonate as intended. The United States proposed new regulations to deal with the problems caused by anti-vehicle mines.[49] This proposal would require all such mines to be detectable and remotely-delivered anti-vehicle mines to possess self-destruct features in order to prevent the weapon from becoming a threat to civilians.

Discussion on these and other issues continued through the second and third meetings of the Preparatory Committee.[50] Presentations and papers submitted by States Parties, observer organizations and independent experts focussed on the nature of the explosive remnants of war problem; its impact on war-affected countries, and strategies for addressing the issue in the CCWC context. By the end of the third meeting of the Preparatory Committee, there was a growing consensus that explosive remnants of war was an issue which needed to be addressed by the inter-

---

48. ICRC, op. cit. n. 46, at pp. 11–12.

49. In the CCWC context, anti-vehicle mines are formally referred to as 'Mines Other than Anti-personnel Mines'. This proposal would later become a joint proposal of the United States and Denmark for a new protocol to the CCWC.

50. In addition to the proposals on explosive remnants of war, proposals were also submitted on extending the scope of application of the Convention and its Protocols to non-international armed conflicts (United States and the ICRC); wound ballistics regulations for small calibre weapons and ammunition (Switzerland), and a compliance mechanism for the Convention (United States, South Africa and the European Union).

national community and an issue which would be one of the primary areas of work for the 2001 Review Conference.

6.2   The 2001 Review Conference of the CCWC

The Second Review Conference of States Parties met from 11 to 21 December 2001 in Geneva, Switzerland. Despite some of the cautious statements made at the expert meeting convened by the ICRC in September 2000, no state spoke against work on explosive remnants of war or proposed that it be addressed at a later review conference. Instead, States Parties used the Conference to identify some of the issues they viewed as important elements of any further discussions or negotiations on this issue. These included the principles outlined in the proposal of the ICRC, the need to address explosive remnants of war from past conflicts and requirements for assistance and cooperation to prevent or address a future explosive remnants of war problem.

Many States Parties also expressed support for work on the proposals on submunitions and anti-vehicle mines made by Switzerland and the United States. By the start of the conference, the proposal for a new protocol on anti-vehicle mines had the co-sponsorship of 12 States Parties.[51] Yet in spite of this support, a number of crucial delegations were against further work on anti-vehicle mines. These States Parties cited legal and technical reasons as well as the financial burden of altering the design of anti-vehicle mines and modifying existing stocks with new technical features.[52]

In light of the range of proposals submitted to the Conference, States Parties decided to establish an expert group to examine the proposals on explosive remnants of war (including submunitions) and anti-vehicle mines. Along with the extension of the Convention's scope of application to non-international armed conflicts, the creation of the Group of Governmental Experts on Explosive Remnants of War and Anti-vehicle Mines was one of the principal results of the 2001 Review Conference.

6.3   The Group of Governmental Experts on Explosive Remnants of War and Anti-vehicle Mines

The Group of Governmental Experts met for a total of five weeks in 2002.[53] In accordance with the mandates adopted by the Review Conference, explosive remnants of war and anti-vehicle mines were discussed separately.[54]

---

51. Denmark, Finland, Germany, Guatemala, Hungary, Japan, the Republic of Korea, Poland, Romania, Slovakia, the United Kingdom and the United States.

52. China, India, Pakistan and Russia did not support work on anti-vehicle mines. For a good overview of the development of this issue see D. Kaye and S. Solomon, 'The Second Review Conference of the 1980 Convention on Certain Conventional Weapons', 96 *AJIL* (2002) pp. 931-933.

53. The Group's meetings were held from 21-24 May, 15-26 July and 2-10 December 2002 in Geneva, Switzerland.

54. Ambassador Chris Sanders of the Netherlands was appointed coordinator for the work on ex-

The work on explosive remnants of war was grouped into five main themes: 1) the factors and types of munitions that could cause humanitarian problems after a conflict; 2) technical improvements and other measures for munitions to reduce the risk of them becoming explosive remnants of war; 3) the adequacy of existing international humanitarian law in minimizing post-conflict risks of explosive remnants of war; 4) warnings to the civilian population, the clearance of explosive remnants of war, the provision of information to facilitate early and safe clearance, and associated issues and responsibilities; and 5) assistance and cooperation.[55]

The mandate for work on anti-vehicle mines was less specific.[56] However, the Group's discussions focussed on the humanitarian concerns posed by anti-vehicle mines; measures to facilitate rapid and safe clearance; the adequacy of existing law; technical measures to minimize the risk to civilians; as well as responses to sensitive fuses of anti-vehicle mines and anti-handling devices.

The Group of Governmental Experts included specialists from government and non-governmental circles. As the Group's work progressed, there was growing support for the development of generic, non-weapon specific, rules that could be applied after the end of hostilities to reduce the impact of explosive remnants of war. There was wide recognition that international humanitarian law did not adequately address the problem. The areas frequently mentioned as needing improvement were obligations on the clearance of explosive remnants of war, the sharing of information to facilitate clearance and risk education and the provision of warnings to civilian populations.

There was also support for considering generic measures that may be taken to prevent explosive ordnance from becoming remnants of war. These included measures related to quality control in the production of munitions and procedures for the handling and storage of munitions. Several experts spoke against developing specific regulations in these areas but there was a general recognition that the identification of 'best practices' may have a useful role to play.

There was less agreement on a technical, weapon-specific, approach to deal with the explosive remnants of war problem, specifically the proposal of Switzerland to require self-destruct and self-deactivation features on submunitions. The Swiss proposal was supported by experts from several European countries.[57] Yet, others voiced reservations about the costs of such requirements.[58] In their view, new technical features would entail significant costs both in terms of new technology and the alteration of existing stocks. Any requirements for technical improvements to

---

plosive remnants of war. Mr Peter Kolarov of Bulgaria was appointed coordinator for the work on Mines Other than Anti-personnel Mines.

55. Summary of the text adopted. For the full mandate see, Final Document, Second Review Conference of the States Parties to the Convention on Prohibitions or Restrictions on the Use of Certain Conventional Weapons Which May be Deemed to be Excessively Injurious or to Have Indiscriminate Effects, UN Doc. CCW/CONF.II/2, Geneva 2001, pp. 12-13.

56. Ibid., at p. 13. Under the mandate adopted by the Review Conference, the Group of Experts was to 'further explore the issue of mines other than anti-personnel mines'.

57. Experts from Switzerland, France, Germany and Ireland.

58. Experts from Brazil, China, Cuba, Pakistan and Russia, among others.

submunitions would need to be coupled with strong obligations for the provision of technology and assistance.

One proposal not widely supported in the Group of Governmental Experts was the call for a prohibition on the use of submunitions against any military object located in a concentration of civilians. This restriction was submitted by the ICRC and supported by several experts and non-governmental organizations as one element of the response to the problems posed by these weapons.[59] Among other experts, however, work in this area was not widely accepted. They believed that the existing rules of international humanitarian law were adequate and, in particular, there needed to be better implementation of Article 51 of 1977 Additional Protocol I. In this regard, several delegations gave presentations on how militaries implement international humanitarian law in targeting decisions.[60]

A range of views was presented during the discussions on anti-vehicle mines. Generally, there was wide support to strengthen the rules applicable to these weapons. There remained significant backing for the proposal for a new protocol on these weapons. Yet, a number of experts felt that the proposal did not go far enough in that its requirement for self-destruct features applied only to remotely delivered anti-vehicle mines and would not cover hand-emplaced mines which were seen as the more immediate problem. Several experts questioned the need for further regulation of anti-vehicle mines at this time. In their view, work should concentrate on promoting universal adherence and implementation of amended Protocol II to the CCWC, which also applies to these weapons, before the development of new instruments.

As a result of its discussions, the Group of Governmental Experts recommended to States Parties that the Group continue its work in 2003 with the following mandate:[61]

1. To negotiate an instrument on post-conflict remedial measures of a generic nature which would reduce the risks of explosive remnants of war, and to explore if these negotiations could include preventive generic measures for improving the reliability of explosive munitions, through voluntary best practices, on the manufacturing, quality control, handling and storage of munitions.
2. Separate from the negotiations, to continue to consider the implementation of existing principles of international humanitarian law and to further study preventive measures to improve the design of certain munitions, including submunitions, with a view to minimizing the risk of these munitions becoming explosive remnants of war.
3. To continue discussion on anti-vehicle mines and consider the most appropriate way to reduce the risks posed by their irresponsible use, including the possibi-

---

59. Experts from Norway, China, Mexico, Human Rights Watch and Landmine Action voiced support for the ICRC proposal.

60. International Humanitarian Law and Targeting: An Australian Approach, UN Doc. CCW/GGE/III/WP.6, 3 December 2002. See also Presentation of the United States, US Submunition Reliability Policy, December 2002.

61. Summarized from the Procedural Report of the Group of Governmental Experts, UN Doc. CCW/GGE/III/CRP.1/REV.1.

lity of concluding a negotiating mandate for a new instrument and other appropriate measures.

These recommendations were adopted by States Parties at a meeting of States Parties held on 12 and 13 December 2002.

7.   A NEW PROTOCOL ON EXPLOSIVE REMNANTS OF WAR

Negotiations on post-conflict remedial measures to reduce the risks of explosive remnants of war were held in Geneva from 10-14 March, 16-27 June and 17-24 November 2003. Basing their discussions on a series of papers prepared by the Coordinator of the negotiations, Ambassador Chris Sanders of the Netherlands, the Group made considerable progress. Agreement was reached in a number of important areas. The Protocol on Explosive Remnants of War was subsequently adopted by the Group and formally approved at a meeting of States Parties on 28 November 2003. It is the fifth protocol annexed to the CCWC.[62]

The Protocol is an important addition to international humanitarian law. It is the first multilateral international agreement to broadly deal with the problems caused by unexploded and abandoned ordnance. The Protocol's principal obligations require each party to an armed conflict to:

— Clear ERW in territory it controls after the end of active hostilities.
— Provide technical, material and financial assistance to facilitate the removal of unexploded or abandoned ordnance in areas it does not control resulting from its operations. This assistance can be provided directly to the party in control of the territory or through a third party, such as the UN, NGOs or other organizations.
— Record information on the explosive ordnance employed by its armed forces and to share that information with organizations engaged in ERW clearance or conducting programs to warn civilians of the dangers of these devices.
— Take all feasible precautions in its territory to protect civilians from the risks and effects of ERW. Such measures may include the marking, fencing and monitoring of ERW affected areas and the provision of warnings and risk education to civilians.

Although these obligations are only required 'where feasible' or 'where practicable', they nevertheless provide an outline of the measures required to address an ERW problem and a framework to support the activities of organizations conducting ERW clearance and risk education programs. The provisions on the recording and sharing of information will facilitate a rapid response to an ERW problem.

These rules also highlight that it is no longer acceptable for the parties to an armed conflict to do nothing when ERW are present. Regardless of whether the ERW are on their territory or resulting from munitions they have used, the parties will have an obligation to take specific action to reduce the danger. This is a further strengthening of international humanitarian law, which parallels developments to

---

62. It is reprinted in this volume of the Yearbook at p. 603.

remedy the problems caused by landmines. International humanitarian law now has a comprehensive approach towards addressing such problems.

The Protocol on Explosive Remnants of War will enter into force six months after 20 States have deposited their instruments of ratification with the depositary of the CCWC, the Secretary-General of the United Nations. Wide adherence to and faithful implementation of the Protocol will be necessary if its objectives are to be fulfilled. Like amended Protocol II of the CCWC, the Protocol on Explosive Remnants of War will apply to the problems arising from both international and non-international armed conflicts. As with Protocol II, one of the challenges will be ensuring compliance by non-state actors.

One of the ERW Protocol's limitations is that its substantive rules apply only to future conflicts. The obligations arising under it will not address the ERW currently found in many war-affected countries. For states already affected by ERW when they become a party, the Protocol gives them the right to seek assistance from other States Parties to help them address their ERW problems. In parallel, States Parties in a position to do so are obliged to provide assistance to help affected States Parties reduce the threats posed by these weapons.

As indicated above, proposals on anti-vehicle mines and measures on the use and design of submunitions were discussed separately from the ERW negotiations Several organizations and governments have proposed specific requirements in these areas. In order to consider these proposals, the mandate of the Group of Governmental Experts has been extended and these issues are on its agenda for 2004.

THE CONFLICT IN WESTERN SAHARA – AN UNRESOLVED ISSUE FROM THE DECOLONIZATION PERIOD[1]

Hans-Peter Gasser[2]

1.   INTRODUCTION

The territory of Western Sahara has an area of about 280,000 sq. km and approximately 250,000 inhabitants, known as Sahrawis. It is situated in the north-west of the African continent, where the Sahara Desert meets the Atlantic Ocean, and has a coastline of more than 1,000 km. In the north, Western Sahara has a common border of 443 km with Morocco, and in the south and west it is bordered by Mauritania (1,561 km). The territory also has a short common border of 42 km with Algeria. The climate is predominantly that of the desert: hot and dry in summer, cold in winter, with little or no rainfall. In the coastal regions vegetation may be abundant. While the Sahrawis were originally nomads, most of the population now lives in small towns and villages. The economy is based on agriculture and fishing, primarily destined for local consumption. Rich phosphate deposits are the main export commodity. There seem to be oil deposits off the Atlantic coast.

Following (and with the blessing of) the Berlin West Africa Conference of 1884, Spain established a protectorate in the same year over a territory called at that time Rio de Oro and now known as Western Sahara. However, the colonial power's effective control was confined to areas along the coast, where the main settlements were to be found. Little is known of the colonial period, except that resistance by some of the local population to the Spanish colonial power was already making itself felt at the beginning of the Twentieth Century. In the 1960s, the first claims to self-determination were voiced, and the first Sahrawi movements demanding independence for Western Sahara appeared on the scene. The Polisario Front, the main Sahrawi liberation movement, was formed in 1973 and started to wage a guerrilla war against the colonial power.

As early as 1956, Morocco, the neighbouring country to the north, had laid claim to part of Western Sahara. A few years later, Mauritania made known its interest in the southern part of the territory.

---

1. © H.-P. Gasser, 2003.

2. Former Senior Legal Adviser, International Committee of the Red Cross, Member of the Board of Editors, *Yearbook of International Humanitarian Law*.

Yearbook of International Humanitarian Law
Volume 5 - 2002 - pp. 375-380

In 1974 the United Nations expressed its concern about the situation.[3] In order to ascertain the Sahrawi population's wishes with regard to their future, the General Assembly decided that a referendum should be held and that, as a condition for a successful outcome of the voting procedure, a census of the Sahrawi population should be organized in order to compile a list of those entitled to take part in the referendum. The General Assembly also asked the International Court of Justice for an advisory opinion on legal issues related to the attribution of sovereignty over Western Sahara. Asked whether the territory of Western Sahara was *terra nullius* when the Spanish took control, the ICJ answered in the negative. The Court went on to say that neither Morocco nor Mauritania had any sovereign rights over (parts of) Western Sahara's territory.[4] This authoritative legal opinion clarifies the legal situation. However, it did not induce the various contending parties to adopt peaceful procedures to settle the issue of sovereignty over Western Sahara.

On 14 November 1975, Mauritania, Morocco and Spain signed a secret agreement, the Madrid Accords, according to which the territory of Western Sahara was to be divided into two: the northern part was to be annexed by Morocco and the southern part by Mauritania.[5]

On 26 February 1976, Spanish control over Western Sahara came to an end. The following day, the Sahrawi Arab Democratic Republic (*République arabe sahraouie démocratique – RASD*) was proclaimed by the Polisario Front. But the Sahrawi people did not gain their independence, and no sovereign state of Western Sahara was born. Instead, Spain's ill-prepared departure from that barren stretch of the Sahara Desert promptly sparked a conflict which, more than 25 years later, remains unresolved. While Morocco had already started to invade Western Sahara in November 1975 (the so-called 'Green March'), in the wake of the Madrid Agreement Moroccan military forces took control of the entire territory. A guerrilla war between the Moroccan Armed Forces and Polisario-led Sahrawi fighters ensued. In the early phase of the conflict, Algerian soldiers were also engaged in the fighting. In 1979 Mauritania gave up its claim and withdrew from the southern part of Western Sahara.

2.   THE CONFLICT

The past two decades have been characterized by frequent and sometimes severe clashes between the Moroccan armed forces and the Polisario Front. The latter adopted a hit-and-run strategy, which was fully adapted to the desert conditions. Hundreds were taken prisoner on both sides. In January 1976, a first group of civilian inhabitants fled Western Sahara and found refuge in neighbouring Algeria. Others followed in later years.

---

3. UNGA Res. 3292 (XXIX), 13 December 1974.

4. Western Sahara, Advisory Opinion of 16 October 1975, *ICJ Rep.* 1975.

5. Declaration of Principles on Western Sahara by Spain, Morocco and Mauritania, Madrid, 14 November 1975 ('Madrid Accords'), <http://www.wsahara.net/maccords.html>.

In view of the intractable situation, international bodies had to intervene and find a way out of the conflict. In 1980 the United Nations General Assembly reaffirmed the right of the Sahrawi people to self-determination and invited Morocco to participate in the search for a viable solution to the problem.[6] The following year, at the 18th Summit of the Organization of African Unity (OAU), the King of Morocco accepted the idea of a referendum in Western Sahara. In 1985 the UN Secretary-General, in cooperation with OAU, sent a first good offices mission to the region. On 20 June 1990 the Secretary-General submitted to the Security Council a report containing proposals for a settlement of the conflict[7] and, on 29 April 1991, the Council decided to establish the United Nations Mission for the Referendum in Western Sahara (MINURSO).[8] MINURSO's role was to assist the Special Representative of the UN Secretary-General in his task of organizing a referendum for the Sahrawis to decide on their future: independence or integration with Morocco. In particular, the UN body had to monitor respect for the ceasefire.

A ceasefire brokered by the UN Special Representative came into effect on 6 September 1991 and has generally been maintained until now, with a few exceptions. The referendum was scheduled to take place in January 1992, but never materialized. The main stumbling block has always been the question of who has the right to participate in the vote on self-determination. So, at the end of 2003, the situation was still basically the same as ten – or even 20 – years ago. MINURSO is still deployed in Western Sahara, the UN Special Representative is still trying to find an accommodation on the contentious issues and the Security Council keeps appealing to the parties concerned to accept a peaceful solution to the conflict.[9] The Security Council does not consider taking action under Chapter VII of the UN Charter in order to impose a settlement on the reluctant parties to the age-old conflict.

3.   HUMANITARIAN CONCERNS

The Western Sahara conflict has given rise to three major humanitarian concerns and continues to do so:
— the plight of the Sahrawi civilians living in refugee camps on Algerian territory;
— the situation of prisoners held by both parties to the conflict; and
— the whereabouts of missing persons.
In accordance with its mandate, the International Committee of the Red Cross (ICRC) offered its services to the two (originally three) parties to the armed con-

---

6. A/RES/35/19, 11 November 1980: Question of Western Sahara.

7. UN Doc. S/21360, 20 June 1990.

8. SC Res. 690 (1991). See the MINURSO website: <http://www.un.org/Depts/dpko/missions/minurso/index.html>.

9. The latest pertinent documents are: Report of the Secretary-General on the situation concerning Western Sahara, UN Doc. S/2003/565, 23 May 2003, and SC Res. 1495 (2003), 31 July 2003. See also the list of all Security Council resolutions at the MINURSO website, ibid., James A. Baker III, the former US Secretary of State, is the present Personal Envoy of the Secretary-General.

flict at the end of 1975. The ICRC expressed particular concern for the plight of the prisoners. But it also organized medical and food aid for the Sahrawi population in Western Sahara itself and in Algeria.

3.1   Civilians in refugee camps

To date, some 165,000 Sahrawi refugees are housed in camps on Algerian territory, close to the Saharan town of Tindouf.[10] Their living conditions are harsh, as the camps were set up in desert areas. The UN High Commissioner for Refugees and the World Food Programme are responsible for assistance to the refugees, with the help of a considerable number of non-governmental organizations, including the Sahrawi Red Crescent.[11]

3.2   Prisoners

The frequent clashes between the Moroccan Armed Forces and the Polisario fighters resulted in many prisoners on both sides. Captured Moroccan soldiers were taken to the Polisario Front's bases in western Algeria, whereas Morocco held captured Sahrawis in detention centres in Western Sahara. The Sahrawis were the first to consent to the ICRC's request to visit the prisoners, and towards the end of 1975 ICRC delegates for the first time visited Moroccan and Mauritanian prisoners in the hands of the Polisario Front. Morocco subsequently authorized the ICRC to see 99 Algerian prisoners captured by its Armed Forces. In April 1978 the ICRC received permission to see Polisario fighters held by Morocco, but it was not allowed to continue the visits on a regular basis. The ICRC, however, saw at regular intervals the Moroccan prisoners held by the Sahrawis.

In the years that followed, the ICRC attempted not only to get to see the prisoners in their camps but also to arrange for their repatriation. In 1987, under ICRC auspices, captured Algerian soldiers were released by Morocco and Moroccan soldiers were simultaneously sent home by the Polisario Front. For some of them, captivity had lasted more than 12 years. Subsequently, several repatriations of Moroccan prisoners took place. The most recent were on 7 July 2002, 26 February and 1 September 2003 when 101, 100 and 243 soldiers and civilians respectively were allowed to return home, some of them after more than 20 years in captivity. The difficulties encountered in negotiations for the prisoners' return to their respective countries bear witness to the extent to which political considerations can take precedence over the fate of human beings.

According to ICRC sources, 914 Moroccan soldiers were still held captive by the Polisario Front in September 2003; over half of them have been held for more than 20 years.[12] Morocco has declared that it has repatriated all Sahrawi prisoners. The Security Council has repeatedly appealed to both parties to the conflict, and

---

10. Figures according to estimates by the Algerian authorities (source: UNHCR).
11. The 'Sahrawi Red Crescent' does not fulfil the conditions for membership in the International Red Cross and Red Crescent Movement, as there is no sovereign state behind it.
12. ICRC Communication to the press 03/62, 1 September 2003.

later to the Polisario Front only, to release all persons taken prisoner during the conflict.[13]

3.3   Missing persons

The search for persons unaccounted for has been, and still is, one of the foremost concerns of the ICRC and the United Nations Envoy. Security Council Resolution 1429 (2002) again called upon Morocco and the Polisario Front to cooperate with the ICRC to resolve the fate of all persons missing since the beginning of the conflict. Nobody has a clear picture of the number of persons unaccounted for. The ICRC's activities in the unsettled Western Sahara conflict are now mainly concerned with the search for missing persons.

4.   LEGAL CONSIDERATIONS

In its Advisory Opinion of 1975, the ICJ did not examine the legal nature of the armed conflict being fought in Western Sahara, as it had not been asked to do so. Nor did the various Security Council Resolutions or the Reports of the UN Secretary-General. Yet there can be hardly any doubt that the Moroccan Armed Forces did indeed invade Western Sahara and that the territory has been under Moroccan control and administration ever 1976. This constitutes an occupation of foreign territory. International humanitarian law therefore applies, in particular the (Fourth) Geneva Convention relative to the Protection of Civilian Persons in Time of War, of 12 August 1949, with its chapter on occupied territories. These rules safeguard the rights of persons living in an occupied territory, and in particular the rights of persons detained for whatever reason by the occupying power.

Members of the Moroccan Armed Forces captured by the Polisario Front are under the protection of the Geneva Conventions, and so are Sahrawis, whether military or civilian, held by Morocco. Are captured members of the Armed Forces prisoners of war in the technical sense of the word? The answer depends on how the conflict between Morocco and the Polisario Front is categorized: is it an international or a non-international armed conflict? The Polisario Front claims to act in the name of the Sahrawi Arab Democratic Republic. Though a member of the Organization of African Unity, the said Republic has not been generally recognized as a sovereign state. It is not a member of the United Nations. Thus, it cannot be party to an international armed conflict, and the legal regime governing POWs does not apply to prisoners taken during the Western Sahara conflict. However, parties to such a conflict are not only free to apply the more favourable rules relating to international armed conflict, they are also strongly urged to do so.

---

13. SC Res. 1495 (2003), 31 July 2003, contains the most recent appeal.

5.   FINAL REMARKS

The Western Sahara conflict is one of those forgotten conflicts which tend to smoulder on interminably without any control. The Sahrawis are a forgotten people. Hardly any interest is aroused today by their struggle for self-determination and for decent living conditions of their own choice. Apart from the relevant international organizations, nobody seems to care any more about the victims of this conflict. It is high time to find a peaceful solution for a dispute whose parameters are well-defined.

TEACHING INTERNATIONAL HUMANITARIAN LAW IN UNIVERSITIES: THE CONTRIBUTION OF THE INTERNATIONAL COMMITTEE OF THE RED CROSS[1]

Antoine A. Bouvier and Katie E. Sams[2]

1.   INTRODUCTION

Although the promotion of international humanitarian law (IHL) in academic circles is a relatively new activity for the International Committee of the Red Cross (ICRC),[3] it has made rapid progress since the mid 1990s. Today, the organisation is following up on university-related activities in some 130 countries around the world. Overseen and harmonised by the ICRC headquarters in Geneva but implemented primarily by operational and regional delegations in the field, the ICRC's programmes targeting university professors and students are notable for their variety and diversity. Nevertheless, the organisation has made a concerted effort to ensure that all such programmes further the same broad objective and operate according to the same principles of action. In the second section of this paper, we examine the issues related to including IHL courses in the regular curricula of the universities and faculties concerned and present the *modus operandi* adopted by the ICRC on the basis of 'lessons learned'. In the third section, we highlight the ICRC's experience of promoting IHL in academic circles in the Russian Federation. Section 4 draws some conclusions.

2.   THE ICRC'S CONTRIBUTION TO THE PROMOTION OF IHL IN UNIVERSITIES

2.1   Background

The ICRC's approach to academic circles fits squarely within the more general framework of its dissemination programmes. Broadly, the organisation's dissemination efforts aim to spread knowledge of IHL and are premised on the belief that

---

1. © A.A. Bouvier and K.E. Sams, 2003.

2. Delegates to Academic Circles, International Committee of the Red Cross. The views expressed herein are those of the authors and do not necessarily reflect those of the International Committee of the Red Cross.

3. Academic circles have long been important contacts and partners for the ICRC. However, in the 1990s, the organisation began to intensify and systematise its activities targeting university professors and students.

Yearbook of International Humanitarian Law
Volume 5 - 2002 - pp. 381-393

this knowledge is an essential condition for the effective application of the law. In addition to university professors and students, the ICRC has specific programmes targeting armed police and security forces and other bearers of weapons,[4] young people[5] and communities affected by mines and explosive remnants of war (ERW).[6] In carrying out such activities, the ICRC supports States Parties to the Geneva Conventions and Additional Protocols in their obligation to 'disseminate' the texts of the treaties 'as widely as possible in their respective countries, and, in particular, to include the study thereof in their programmes of military and, if possible, civil instruction, so that the principles thereof may become known to the entire population …'[7]

It is important to bear in mind that the promotion of IHL *per se* is not the sole aim of the ICRC's contacts with the academic world. The organisation has long collaborated with scholars to analyse and develop the law. In the domain of communication, the ICRC and academic institutions have conducted courses for journalists and journalism students. The ICRC and university partners have also organised regular courses in the field of public health. Such relationships have enabled the ICRC to keep abreast of academic developments and have helped to position it as a reference institution for universities.

Over the past ten years, the ICRC has increasingly begun to approach academic circles with the specific aim of encouraging the teaching of IHL. The first formal programme in the field (in the former Soviet Union) was initiated in 1995, and the first position of Delegate to Academic Circles was created at headquarters in 1997. Programmes have since been launched in such diverse settings as Central Asia, Colombia, India, Indonesia, Jordan, Kenya, the Maghreb, Pakistan and South Africa. In an effort to harmonise and clarify the different goals of such programmes, the ICRC formulated internal guidelines in 2001.

2.2   Overall objective of ICRC programmes

ICRC programmes targeting academic circles aim to establish a sound teaching and research tradition in the field of IHL, with an eye towards students as the next generation of leaders. During their studies, university students must be made aware of the existence of IHL, understand its practical relevance and acquire a thorough knowledge of its basic principles. Logically, some of these students will maintain or even deepen their interest in the law after they enter the professional world.

---

4. These activities aim to ensure that all levels of armed forces and police and security forces know and apply IHL and human rights law and that other armed groups support humanitarian action.

5. The ICRC has launched two large-scale programmes for young people in educational settings since the mid 1990s: the secondary school programme for countries of the former Soviet Union and the Exploring Humanitarian Law programme. The objective of these programmes is to familiarise young people with the notion of human dignity and the rules and principles of IHL and humanitarian action.

6. The goal of this programme is to reduce the number of mine and ERW casualties by changing behaviour and promoting alternative, long-term solutions.

7. Art. 47, First Geneva Convention. See generally Arts. 47, 48, 49 and 144 of the 1949 Geneva Conventions, Art. 83 of the First Additional Protocol and Art. 19 of the Second Additional Protocol.

They will work to ensure that IHL is implemented and respected. They will influence the humanitarian debate and the development of existing law, and they will support the ICRC's activities.[8]

At this point it is worth clarifying an issue that often leads to confusion: whether these programmes are intended primarily to promote IHL or the ICRC. This question is basically flawed. The ICRC is one of the implementation mechanisms foreseen by the IHL treaties and is often the only one operating in practice. It is only logical, therefore, that the ICRC should be mentioned in disseminating IHL. On the other hand, IHL is an integral part of the ICRC's work, distinguishing it from that of many other humanitarian actors. It follows that teaching IHL (also) means promoting the ICRC. Nevertheless, the programmes will of course attract far wider support if emphasis is placed on promoting universally-accepted norms rather than on promoting the institution.

In furtherance of its goal of establishing a sound teaching and research tradition in IHL, the ICRC carries out a number of different activities. It promotes the inclusion and consolidation of IHL courses in the regular curricula of the world's leading universities. More concretely, the ICRC organises training courses and other events for professors and advanced students. It also sets up and maintains networks of academic experts to assist in the teaching, implementation and development of IHL. Finally, it provides professors with documentation and teaching aids that are specially designed to meet their needs.

2.3   Target population

Recognising that it would be impossible and indeed counter-productive to target all universities in a given country, the ICRC has adopted a selective approach. Priority is given to leading universities that train the next generation of decision-makers and opinion-makers.[9] Logically enough, the IHL training programmes are designed primarily for faculties of law, political science and international relations. Although IHL – by virtue of its content, principles of application and objectives – is relevant not only to jurists, some theoretical grounding (especially familiarity with certain general principles of public international law) is necessary for non-lawyers to understand and acquire expertise in the subject. Therefore, priority is given to a select and limited audience consisting of advanced students.

Clearly, however, certain aspects of IHL can (or even should) be covered by other faculties at a second stage. This applies in particular to faculties of medicine or even of theology, history, journalism and psychology. In this context, a resolutely interdisciplinary approach is the most appropriate. The aim is obviously not to turn out students who are experts in IHL but to encourage them to integrate

---

8. The 2001 guidelines provide in relevant part: 'In order to establish a sound teaching and research tradition in the field of IHL, students at universities and colleges that train future decision-makers and are targeted by the ICRC must be aware of the existence of IHL, understand its practical relevance and have a thorough knowledge of its basic principles. They must be familiar with the ICRC's activities and operating principles.'

9. In identifying such universities, an effort to avoid making 'political' choices must be made.

certain IHL principles in their respective fields of activity. Moreover, in some cases, the need to develop awareness of IHL among all students cannot be ruled out.

The distinctive characteristics of local academic systems must also be taken into account. To cite just one example, IHL seems to have become a staple ingredient of courses in faculties of 'conflictology', which are very common in a few countries of the former Soviet Union but virtually unknown in the rest of the world.

2.4   Principles of action

In furtherance of the overall objective of its university-related programmes, the ICRC pursues a variety of strategies. These strategies have been developed in light of the organisation's 'real life' experiences in different contexts around the world. Delegations are requested to apply these principles of action when launching new programmes.

2.4.1   *Capacity building*

Rather than advocating a do-it-yourself approach, IHL-teaching programmes (like programmes targeting different categories of combatants or secondary school students) call for vigorous application of a strategy to develop local capacities of self-reliance. The ICRC acts as a catalyst, identifying and providing training to local academic decision-makers and experts. The individuals who receive training, in turn, begin to teach IHL at the university-level. As soon as a new programme is launched, the ICRC should start to plan for its withdrawal and for local partners to take over its activities.

This strategy of developing local capacities of self-reliance is the only feasible, effective and appropriate approach. Even if it wanted to, the ICRC could never afford to take the place of university teaching staff. Moreover, it is essential to ensure that local actors will be able to run programmes themselves in the medium term; this is an infinitely preferable outcome to the 'flash in the pan' impact of programmes run entirely by short-stay delegates or ICRC-paid experts. This strategy is the best way of ensuring that IHL is fully 'appropriated' by the professors and students concerned and thus not perceived as an 'exotic' subject matter supported by foreign do-gooders. Participants in such programmes will be far more easily convinced of the relevance of IHL if it is their own teacher (or a representative of 'their' armed forces) who presents it to them as part of a regular course (even though the content of the course may not quite correspond to the ICRC's wishes or contain inaccuracies). Implicit in this approach is the recognition that the ICRC is not the sole authority on IHL; the capacity-building strategy is based on considerations of intercultural respect, responsiveness and empathy.

While the capacity-building approach allows the ICRC to withdraw from the programmes in the medium term, it requires a significant investment at the outset as well as a certain follow-up. Initially, the ICRC organises 'train the trainer' courses and ensures that professors are willing and able to begin teaching IHL. Even after IHL has been introduced into the curriculum, the organisation continues to conduct courses and advanced seminars for teaching staff. In conjunction with such activities, the ICRC maintains and replenishes a network of experts.

2.4.2   Adaptation

The success of IHL-teaching programmes generally depends on their adaptation to the procedures and systems particular to each context. The ICRC delegates in charge of these programmes should clearly identify the 'mandatory procedures' designated by a country's educational system. These procedures will depend, *inter alia*, on the amount of academic freedom enjoyed by individual universities and on the structure of the state or the type of university concerned (public, private or mixed system). Depending on the context, the inclusion of IHL in a faculty's regular curriculum, which is a prerequisite for the success of the programme, may be achieved simply through contacts with an interested member of the teaching staff, or may require far more complex action involving approaches (of varying degrees of formality) to the institutions responsible for designing the curriculum: Ministry of Education, Programming Committee, the Bar, University Senate, etc.

Convincing potential teachers about the necessity of introducing IHL in their regular curricula often proves difficult. Expertise and time are in short supply. In most countries the number of subjects already included in the curricula of universities makes it very difficult to add other topics. The fact that IHL is not considered 'economically profitable' often makes it particularly difficult to promote. In many universities, the financial resources required to introduce a new subject are also lacking.

ICRC delegates thus resort to a number of arguments 'justifying' the introduction of IHL in the regular curricula. They highlight the fact that IHL can be an effective tool for training legal reasoning. They also point out that knowledge of IHL will give students a better understanding of the reality of armed conflict and internal violence and stress that the law promotes impartiality and justice in an intrinsically unbalanced world. Finally, they emphasise that the subject could well be of professional value to many students who subsequently will pursue legal, diplomatic, judicial, political or military careers.[10]

In some contexts, teaching IHL as a separate subject is simply not a realistic option. In such situations, the ICRC advocates including certain aspects of the topic within existing survey courses and specialist seminars. Thus, for example, the origins and progressive development of the rules of IHL can be covered in a course on the history of international law, while the relationship between IHL and refugee law in situations of armed conflict can be highlighted in a refugee law course. At a minimum, the fundamental tenets of IHL should be presented in general public international law or human rights courses.

Adaptation should also be borne in mind when deciding on the content of the courses to be introduced. While there can be no question of modifying the content

---

10. For a more thorough analysis of the factors supporting the training of IHL, see M. Sassòli and A.A. Bouvier, *How does Law Protect in War?* (Geneva, ICRC 1999) pp. 1451-1453.

of the universal rules and principles of IHL in light of local contexts, a certain amount of flexibility is permissible with regard to the importance attached – within IHL courses – to certain related branches of study. A classic example is the question of human rights. In some countries where the notion of conflict is taboo, the only way to 'sell' an IHL course is to establish a close link with human rights. Conversely, the mere mention of links between IHL and human rights may, when dealing with certain authorities who find the latter's 'political' nature unacceptable, put an end to hopes of introducing a regular IHL course.

2.4.3   *Practice oriented teaching*

Wherever possible given local teaching traditions and educational facilities, IHL instruction should focus primarily on an examination of contemporary practice. It should serve to show the relevance of IHL, prove that it can be applied in contemporary conflicts and demonstrate that it can and must be respected, even in dire circumstances. Conversely, there seems to be little merit in seeking to impart the largest possible number of rules of conduct, since they are rapidly forgotten by students and the exercise thus remains purely academic.

Many teaching aids favour the practical approach: real or fictitious case studies; moot court competitions; role-playing; use of the Internet, etc. The ICRC strives to encourage this approach by providing the teaching staff concerned with suitable teaching materials and by adopting such methods itself whenever it directly participates in the training process. However, some modesty is naturally called for; the ICRC's task is not to radically call into question the teaching methods used in the countries where it is working.[11]

2.4.4   *Flexibility*

As amply demonstrated by experience, ICRC programmes targeting academic circles cannot and should not be identical everywhere. In each context, a number of parameters, including the structure of the academic community, the relative autonomy of academic institutions, the number of students, the financial resources available and the political and economic climate clearly depend on local factors. At the same time, these factors cannot be used to authorise any approach whatsoever or to 'justify' the abandonment of other basic principles of action.

---

11. For a more detailed analysis of teaching methodologies, see P.J. Martin, *Human Rights Education: Content and Methodologies in a Nutshell* (New York, Columbia University 2002). <http://www.owner-hr-education@rea.org>; M.T. Ladan, 'Issues in Curriculum Development of IHL', Paper Presented at Workshop on IHL Teaching and Research in Nigeria, Abuja, 2 December 2002; J.A. Georges and P.C. Richard, eds., *Human Rights Education for the 21st Century* (Philadelphia, University of Pennsylvania Press 1997) and Sassòli and Bouvier, ibid.

2.4.5   *Feasibility*

When considering launching university programmes, the ICRC must assess how realistic that goal is in light of the prevailing 'political' climate. Unfortunately, there are countries and systems where establishing a sound teaching and research tradition in the field of IHL in universities remains a long-term prospect. The ICRC should not force the issue if it determines that attempting to introduce the teaching of IHL appears unlikely, impossible to sustain or subject to inappropriate limitations or obstacles. In such situations, the ICRC should maintain contact with key actors within the Ministry of Education or university hierarchy and be prepared to expand its activities if and when the opportunity presents itself.

2.5   **Practical implementation by the ICRC**

Based on the experience it has gained over the past decade, the ICRC is now in a position to direct its efforts in a very precise manner. In line with the overall objective of its programmes targeting academic circles and its principles of action, the organisation has begun to concentrate on certain approaches while abandoning others that have proven fruitless. There are still a number of 'open questions' that must be addressed, as the ICRC seeks to fine tune its policies.

Before the first IHL course is taught in a given country, the ICRC may devote considerable time and energy to establishing the foundations for a solid, sustainable programme. In each context, it is imperative to systematically analyse curriculum design procedures. Although this process may prove frustrating, long, arduous or even disappointing, it is indispensable for ensuring the continuity of the ICRC's programmes. It is also essential for the ICRC to have systematic discussions and negotiations with all stakeholders, including relevant ministries, academic authorities and curriculum commissions.

Although the ICRC has long organised courses for academic circles, the institution has reoriented many of its training events to include practical elements in addition to covering the theory of IHL. To benefit fully from the train-the-trainer approach, the ICRC has begun to organise courses for and otherwise provide support to professors who are actually prepared to teach IHL but have not yet received the necessary training. Such courses, which have been held at the national, regional and international levels, include sessions on how to teach IHL. In parallel with these efforts, the ICRC conducts regional courses for advanced students and young professors, during which students, in small groups, work through a series of case studies.[12] An important by-product of such courses, whether organised for professors or students and at the national, regional or international levels, is the creation of networks of experts in IHL.

---

12. Such a course has been organised for over 20 years in Warsaw, Poland, for English-speaking students from Europe and North America. The same course has been held in French for more than 15 years. Similar courses are now offered on a regular basis in Africa, South Asia, Latin America and the Middle East.

In addition to more traditional academic courses, the ICRC supports the organisation of moot court competitions in IHL. Such competitions, which are highly motivating for students and professors alike, facilitate interaction between students from different universities and provide a good opportunity to assess the quality of the courses taught in the participants' universities. To this end, the ICRC regularly organises moot court competitions in the Central Africa, Central Asia, India and the Russian Federation, and supports independent competitions like the Jean-Pictet Competition in IHL.[13]

The ICRC seeks to ensure that professors have the requisite documentation and teaching aids at their disposal. The organisation regularly distributes standard IHL libraries to targeted universities.[14] The ICRC has also begun to study whether and how it can utilise 'e-learning' to communicate its message. When feasible, ICRC representatives encourage professors and students to use the ICRC website as a resource. The organisation plans to evaluate the possibility of developing an Internet-based, distance learning programme in IHL. Beyond that, a number of ICRC delegations furnish 'model courses' or computer presentations to interested professors.

The ICRC has recognised that it must continuously evaluate its programmes, in order to ensure that they further the priorities identified. In this regard, it is necessary to assess whether the universities supported by the ICRC are really those that train future leaders. Even if the universities targeted do play an important role in that regard, it is important to verify that their programmes of IHL instruction are appropriate. At times, it may be necessary for the ICRC to reorient its activities.

Largely as a result of such evaluations, the ICRC has abandoned certain approaches. For example, the ICRC does not favour the temporary insertion of foreign experts (from the ICRC or other sources) who are supposed to make up for local shortcomings by teaching courses themselves. Such initiatives prove untenable in the long-run and generally do nothing to encourage targeted universities to assume responsibility for mobilising the requisite financial and human resources themselves. While the ICRC makes teaching aids based on interactive educational methods available to interested professors, it does not advocate radically revising teaching methods. Moreover, the organisation generally declines to finance academic work, as this practice has sometimes led to rather questionable results and given rise to false expectations.

Finally, a number of issues must be gauged on a case-by-case basis. For example, should the ICRC encourage compulsory or optional courses? Which groups of students should be targeted? Should the ICRC encourage the translation of foreign books into local languages? Should ICRC-university relations be placed on a formal footing by concluding memoranda of understanding? What type of exit strategy should be contemplated? Although no final answers to such questions can be given at this stage, they must be addressed. Only detailed analysis and constructive

---

13. See <http://www.concourspictet.org>.

14. The Standard IHL Library contains over 80 titles, including relevant treaties and analytical texts.

discussion between local experts and ICRC delegates will permit the establishment of solid and sustainable programmes of IHL teaching in universities.

3.   CASE STUDY: THE RUSSIAN FEDERATION (1995-2004)

3.1   **Background**

The ICRC seized a window of opportunity in the mid 1990s and began to actively promote the teaching of IHL at the university level in the Russian Federation. Following the collapse of the Soviet Union, the Russian educational system began to undergo significant changes. Universities faced identity and financial crises, which forced them to become more competitive and to offer more popular specialisations. The educational authorities evidenced a certain amount of flexibility in terms of curriculum development and expansion, and new subjects were readily introduced.[15] In the Soviet era, international humanitarian law, if taught at all, was only included as a small component of the public international law course. Specialised studies in IHL were virtually nonexistent, as there was no tradition of teaching the subject and a lack of adequate documentation. In these circumstances, the ICRC delegation in Moscow launched its programme for promoting IHL among academic institutions in 1995. Although the bulk of the delegation's university-related activities cover the Russian Federation, a series of major events has been organised at the level of the Commonwealth of Independent States (CIS) countries,[16] in co-operation with the ICRC delegations located in those countries.

3.2   **Primary activities of the ICRC delegation in Moscow**

In line with the overall aims of the ICRC programmes targeting academic circles worldwide, the ICRC delegation in Moscow began to focus on the integration of IHL into the curricula of the country's leading universities from the outset. Following a series of meetings among the ICRC, the State Committee for Higher Education (now the Ministry of Education) and the Legal Department of the Presidential Administration, IHL was included into the draft State Standards for Higher Education at the 'specialist' degree level in 1996.[17] The ICRC also contacted target universities directly and facilitated the exchange of information between them. In mid 1997, for example, the ICRC, in cooperation with the Moscow State Institute of International Relations, organised a conference on the promotion of IHL at Kazan

---

15. Priority was generally given to 'economically profitable' subjects.

16. In addition to the Russian Federation, the CIS comprises all of the former Soviet republics except the three Baltic States: Armenia, Azerbaijan, Belarus, Georgia, Kazakhstan, Kyrgyzstan, Moldova, Tajikistan, Turkmenistan, Ukraine and Uzbekistan.

17. In the Russian Federation, students can obtain a university degree in one of two ways. The first option consists of two stages: the bachelor's level and the master's level. The second possibility is not divided into stages, and students obtain a specialist degree upon completion of their course of study. After obtaining a university degree, students can continue on to obtain a candidate of sciences degree, which is roughly equivalent to a Ph.D, or a doctor of sciences degree.

State University. Both civil servants and representatives of some 30 law faculties from around the region took part. The conference adopted a resolution highlighting the need to strengthen and coordinate measures aimed at integrating IHL into official humanities' curricula. In 1998, an academic working group convened at Moscow Lomonosov State University made conclusions concerning the possibilities of including IHL in the State Standards for Higher Education. In 1999, the ICRC, the Russian Red Cross and the Ministry of Education signed a cooperation agreement aimed at creating the conditions necessary for the study of IHL in institutions of higher education.

Largely as a result of such initiatives, IHL is now included in the State Standards for Higher Education, which were signed by the Ministry of Education in March 2000, and some 80 law faculties across the country have included IHL in their curricula. Specifically, for 'Jurisprudence' studies, IHL is a mandatory part of the compulsory international law course. Moreover, a compulsory course, entitled IHL and Mass Media, was included for 'Journalism' studies at the 'specialist' degree level. These State Standards for Higher Education make teaching the included subjects obligatory at all relevant faculties.

In addition to promoting the integration of IHL at the state level, the ICRC has lobbied for the inclusion of IHL in the Higher Education Standards for the CIS region. The ICRC made contact with the Commission on Education and Culture of the CIS Interparliamentary Assembly and promoted the adoption of recommendations on the inclusion of IHL into Higher Educational Standards in the CIS.[18] As no final decision has yet been taken, the ICRC will continue to follow up on this issue with the 'Council on Cooperation of the CIS States in the field of Education'.

In parallel with its efforts to promote the formal inclusion of IHL in the curricula, the ICRC provides comprehensive training to lecturers and supports academic research in the field of IHL. Since 1995, the ICRC has organised six regional training courses for law and international relations professors and three for journalism professors. Beyond the substance of IHL, these seminars include a practical component on how to teach IHL. More than 250 lecturers have attended such courses, and a large network of IHL experts has been established as a result. In addition to these more traditional training courses, the ICRC has created a forum for academics from the region to present their research and exchange their opinions on IHL-related issues. Since 2000, the ICRC and the law faculty of St. Petersburg State University have co-organised three regional 'Martens Readings' conferences, focusing on contemporary IHL issues. The ICRC is now making a special effort to use the professors who have received training as experts and trainers at the national and regional levels and to foster links between experts from the region and the rest of the world.

In order to facilitate teaching and research in the field of IHL, the ICRC supports the preparation and distribution of documentation and teaching aids. The organisa-

---

18. In addition to the Russian Federation, IHL is also included in the State Educational Standards for Higher Education in Belarus. At present, there are no State Educational Standards for Higher Education in other CIS countries.

tion has distributed extensive documentation to university libraries throughout the Russian Federation. It has translated certain texts[19] as well as supported the publication and distribution of a number of IHL manuals written by experts from the region.[20] In light of the lack of methodological tools for teaching, the ICRC has also commissioned the production of a teaching kit that will include IHL model courses, questionnaires and case studies.

The ICRC also works directly with students to deepen and improve their knowledge of IHL. ICRC representatives take part in a number of different academic events to raise awareness about IHL and the organisation's mandate. The ICRC delegation in Moscow works closely with students who are undertaking research projects on IHL issues, providing them with documentation as well as advice. Since 1997, the ICRC has regularly organised the Martens Competition – a regional, Russian-language moot court competition. In all, some 50 student teams from law and international relations faculties have taken part. In 2004, the ICRC plans to organise a ten-day IHL course targeting advanced students from the CIS countries, possibly in cooperation with the Russian Association of International Law (RAIL) and the Russian Red Cross. In recent years, the Moscow delegation has also initiated a number of national events. In May 2003, for example, the ICRC and the RAIL launched a national essay competition for law students from the Russian Federation with the aim of encouraging students to conduct independent research on key problems related to IHL.[21] The Moscow delegation planned to organise a moot court competition at the national level in 2004. The ICRC sponsors the participation of student teams at the Jean-Pictet Competition as well.

The ICRC is working to forge closer partnership with national organisations active and influential in the domain of international law in order to strengthen and support local capacities. In the mid- to long-term, these local partners will themselves host regular events on IHL at the national level, assuming many of the organisational responsibilities previously carried by the ICRC. It is hoped that this transfer of duties will carry with it a sense of 'IHL ownership' and will help change the perception that IHL is a western concept. In several countries in the region, national associations of international law are composed of influential persons at the academic and political levels. In June 2003, the ICRC and the RAIL signed a cooperation agreement covering the promotion of IHL and its implementation at the national level.[22]

---

19. In 2000, for example, the ICRC translated Professor Eric David's book, *Principes de Droit des conflits armés* (Brussels, Bruylant 1999) and distributed it widely.

20. For example, in 1997 the ICRC provided financial assistance to the Institute of State and Law of the Russian Academy of Sciences for the publication of Professor V.V. Pustogarov's book, *Fedor-Fedorovich Martens: Lawyer, Diplomat* [Russian title: *Fedor Fedorovich Martens: jurist, diplomat*] (Moscow, Meždunarodnyie Otnošenija 1999). More recently, the ICRC purchased copies of I.I. Kotlyarov's publication, *International Law in Armed Conflict* [Russian title: Mezhdunarodnoye Gumanitarnoye Pravo] (Moscow, Yurlitinform 2003), which is the most comprehensive IHL textbook published in Russian to date, for distribution to universities around the country.

21. The winners would be selected in December 2003, after a second round of competition, and the best works would subsequently be published.

22. Given the vast number of universities in the Russian Federation, collaborating with an umbrella

3.3   'Lessons learned' and future perspectives

In 2002, the Moscow delegation's university-related activities and its Advisory Service activities[23] were merged into a single IHL unit, in order to increase the synergies between academic circles and state officials and to create a larger pool of IHL experts. Although these two programmes initially had separate orientations, the need for a broader strategy became apparent in order to avoid duplicative efforts.[24] On the one hand, professors in the Russian Federation often serve as IHL experts for the authorities and parliamentarians. On the other hand, Russian government officials covering IHL-related files, such as the International Criminal Court or anti-personnel mines, are often requested to teach those themes in academic settings. Consequently, most of the events organised by the Moscow delegation since the end of 2002 have been attended by both target groups.

The wide range of activities undertaken to date has increased the visibility of IHL in academic circles throughout the Russian Federation, and many academic institutions have established impressive teaching and research traditions in the domain of IHL. Over the past eight years, the ICRC has made contact with a large number of universities and encouraged the teaching of IHL. Now that IHL has been included in the State Standards for Higher Education and is widely taught throughout the country, the ICRC has begun to adopt a more 'qualitative' approach, concentrating its support on those law, international relations and journalism faculties that train future decision- and opinion-makers. At the same time, however, the ICRC is examining ways of reaching out to new professors and students. The ICRC's Russian website, which was launched in 2003, will undoubtedly increase the organisation's visibility. With the support of ICRC headquarters, the Moscow delegation is also evaluating the possibility of developing its own distance-learning programme targeting academic circles.

---

association such as the RAIL should facilitate the task of maintaining regular and permanent contact with academic institutions. Moreover, by cooperating with an association, rather than a specific university, the ICRC will not be perceived as developing a privileged relationship with a particular academic institution.

23. The ICRC set up its Advisory Service on International Humanitarian Law in 1996 to step up its support to states committed to implementing IHL. Its three main priorities are: to encourage ratification of IHL treaties; to promote national implementation of the obligations arising from those treaties; and to collect and facilitate the exchange of information on national implementation measures. The Moscow delegation's Advisory Service programme was launched in 1996 and initially covered all of the countries of the former Soviet Union. In 2001, the Baltic States were attached to the ICRC delegation in Budapest, and in 2002, the Central Asian States were attached to the Tashkent delegation.

24. The holding of separate events was initially justified. Courses for state officials focused largely on specific issues of 'implementation', such as the repression of war crimes and the law on the protection of the red cross and red crescent emblems. The training courses for professors concentrated on general IHL issues.

4.   CONCLUDING REMARKS

Recent developments have generated an increased interest in IHL. Situations of armed conflict and internal violence are a daily reality for much of the world's population. The phenomenon of transnational terrorism and the international community's responses to it, have raised the profile of IHL considerably. The establishment of mechanisms to ensure more effective repression of violations of IHL, such as the *ad hoc* Tribunals and the International Criminal Court, has infused new life into IHL.

The ICRC has encountered an unprecedented receptiveness to teaching and studying IHL, and it has expanded its programmes targeting academic circles. The organisation's experience in the Russian Federation is but one example of this encouraging trend. An ever-increasing number of future decision- and opinion-makers around the world are acquiring a thorough knowledge of the basic principles of IHL during their university studies. Of course, knowledge of the rules does not, in and of itself, prevent violations of them. Yet without this knowledge, there is little chance that the rules will be followed. Therefore, the ICRC will continue to promote the inclusion of IHL in the curricula of the world's leading universities and to develop the capacities of local academic decision-makers and experts to teach IHL.

UNIVERSAL JURISDICTION: LESSONS FROM THE BELGIAN EXPERIENCE[1]

Luc Walleyn[2]

1.   INTRODUCTION

Belgium was variously praised, criticized and ridiculed for its 1993 law (as amended in 1999) giving it universal jurisdiction over war crimes, crimes against humanity and genocide.[3] The invocation of this law against Israeli and US defendants provoked an unprecedented conflict with Israel and serious tension with the United States of America in 2003. After months of diplomatic incidents, economic threats, provocative complaints and political debate, Belgium's controversial anti-atrocity law was repealed on 5 August 2003, ten years after entering into force. Even in the international legal community, real understanding of what happened in this legal laboratory is not common. This article is not a neutral study, but a contribution from an actor and a privileged witness.

2.   THE LONG HISTORY OF BELGIUM'S UNIVERSAL JURISDICTION LAW

Notwithstanding the development of international conventions relating to the laws of war (the Hague Conventions of 1907), and an attempt to launch an international trial against German Emperor Wilhelm after World War I, the history of international justice only truly began after World War II with the tribunals at Nuremberg and Tokyo. Those tribunals, although established by the war's victors, implemented the principles that we now consider as the basis of customary international criminal law. These principles have been further refined and confirmed in a number of international conventions, the most important of which are the Convention

---

1. © L. Walleyn, 2004.

2. The author was a member of the legal team in the *Sabra and Shatila* case and also represents victims of international crimes perpetrated in Guatemala and Rwanda.

3. Loi relative à la répression des infractions graves aux Conventions de Genève de 1949 et aux Protocoles I et II de 1977 additionnels à ces Conventions [Law of 16 June 1993 on the repression of grave breaches of the Geneva Conventions], *Moniteur belge* (MB), 5 August 1993, as amended by Loi du 10 février relative à la répression des violations graves du droit international humanitaire [Law of 10 February 1999 relating to the repression of serious violations of international humanitarian law], Published in MB, 23 March 1999. Both laws are reprinted in volume 2 of the *YIHL* (1999) at pp. 539 et seq.

on the Prevention and Punishment of the Crime of Genocide of 1948, the four Geneva Conventions of 1949 (with the Additional Protocols of 1977), and the Torture Convention of 1984, as well as different regional conventions.

2.1 Universal jurisdiction for war crimes

Clearly, the four Geneva Conventions provide for universal jurisdiction over war crimes. According to Article 49 of the First Geneva Convention[4]:

> 'Each High Contracting Party shall be under the obligation to search for persons alleged to have committed, or to have ordered to be committed, such grave breaches, and shall bring such persons, regardless of their nationality, before its own courts. It may also, if it prefers, and in accordance with the provisions of its own legislation, hand such persons over for trial to another High Contracting Party concerned, provided such High Contracting Party has made out a prima facie case.'

As early as 1952, the Belgian Ministry of Foreign Affairs created a commission to draft the legal framework that would enable Belgium to implement the obligation to repress war crimes as provided for in the Geneva Conventions. Initially, the draft was intended to be an international model, and was submitted as such to an expert committee formed in Geneva by the International Committee of the Red Cross (ICRC) in 1956.[5] The expert committee concluded, however, that a uniform penal law, proposed as an annex to the Geneva Conventions, would not be realistic given the considerable differences in the various states' legal systems. So the bill was redrafted merely as a national law for Belgium. In 1963 an initial draft of the law was to be submitted to the Belgian parliament, but work on this draft was suspended when the Diplomatic Conference on the Development of Humanitarian Law was launched, eventuating in the adoption of the two Additional Protocols to the Geneva Conventions of 1977. After many years of consultation in the framework of NATO, Belgium finally ratified these protocols in 1986.

With the end of the Cold War in the late 1980s and early 1990s, the pace of progressive legal developments in Belgium quickened. On 5 July 1989, the government decided on a draft bill implementing the provisions of the Geneva Conventions, providing for universal jurisdiction in Belgium's courts based on the principle *aut dedere aut judicare*.[6] In April 1991, upon receiving the advice of the *Conseil d'Etat*,[7] this proposal was submitted to Belgium's parliament. The debates in the parliament clearly demonstrated that representatives and senators had in mind the types of grave violations of humanitarian law witnessed in recent and ongoing conflicts: Iraq-Kuwait, the former Yugoslavia and Somalia. On the initiative of the Senate, violations of Protocol II were also incorporated, although this

---

4. The three other conventions contain a similar rule in Arts. 50, 129 and 149.
5. 6 *Revue de Droit Pénal et de Criminologie* (1955-1956) pp. 594-633.
6. 'Extradite or prosecute', a rule initially used in the law concerning extradition.
7. The 'Council of State' is the highest administrative court, which also gives non-binding advice on proposed legal bills.

protocol does not prescribe universal jurisdiction. By introducing universal juris-diction for grave breaches of the Geneva Conventions, Belgium followed the ex-ample of countries like Switzerland and Germany.[8]

The law of 16 June 1993 was passed unanimously by both chambers of the parliament just as the world witnessed a major development in international jus-tice: the creation of the International Criminal Tribunal for the Former Yugoslavia by the UN Security Council on 22 February 1993.

Some months after the law entered in force, the Belgian public was shocked by the genocide in Rwanda and the killing of Belgian peacekeepers. Complaints were lodged by victims against perpetrators of the genocide who had found refuge on Belgian soil but also against those responsible for the organization of the genocide and the killing of the blue helmets. Complaints were even lodged against two for-mer Belgian ministers on the grounds that they had withdrawn Belgian peace-keepers and thereby had contributed to a paralysis of UNAMIR (United Nations Assistance Mission in Rwanda). A Belgian officer appeared before a court martial for negligent behavior in Rwanda but was acquitted.

At this point, Belgium became very politically active. It supported the creation of a second *ad hoc* tribunal in Arusha (the International Criminal Tribunal for Rwanda), sponsored the rebuilding of the Rwandan judiciary and assisted in orga-nizing the defense in the Rwandan genocide cases. International humanitarian law soon emerged as a major political issue when, under the presidency of Prime Min-ister Guy Verhofstadt, the Senate established a commission to investigate the in-volvement of Belgium in the Rwanda events. On 16 October 1997, a new legal proposal was submitted by a group of senators providing for the possibility of ex-ercising universal jurisdiction over the crime of genocide.[9]

2.2   Genocide and crimes against humanity incriminated

Universal jurisdiction to pursue and punish the crime of genocide stems primarily from *jus cogens*,[10] and notably from the 1948 Genocide Convention. Although Article VI of the Genocide Convention expressly mentions prosecution before the courts of the state directly concerned with the events and an international criminal court, these jurisdictions are not exclusive. In its 11 July 1996 decision in the *Bos-nia and Herzegovina* v. *Yugoslavia* case, the International Court of Justice declared about the 1948 Convention:

---

8. The Military Code of the United States of America also contains provisions for an enlarged jurisdiction over war crimes: 'The jurisdiction of the United States military tribunals in connection with war crimes (...) extends also to all offences of this nature committed against nationals of allies and of co-belligerents and stateless persons'. US Army Field Manual 27-10, §507(a).

9. The 1948 Convention for the Repression of Genocide does not assert universal jurisdiction for this crime, though many have argued that *jus cogens* already provides the basis for universal jurisdic-tion over genocide.

10. That part of international law that is always binding for every nation, even without agreement upon any convention.

'... the rights and obligations enshrined by the Convention are rights and obligations erga omnes. The Court notes that the obligation each State thus has to prevent and to punish the crime of genocide is not territorially limited by the Convention.'[11]

The ICTY Appeals Chamber declared in the *Blaškić* case that the obligation for each national jurisdiction 'to judge or to extradite the persons presumed responsible for grave violations of international humanitarian law' was customary in character.[12]

The Belgian senators who proposed the 1997 bill wanted to adopt a procedural law relative to universal jurisdiction for the crime of genocide, and to make it immediately and retroactively applicable. The Belgian legislature had clearly applied the same principle in the same domain with the 22 March 1996 law relative to the recognition of the International Tribunals for the former Yugoslavia and Rwanda.[13] This recognition rests, in effect, on a formal competence in positive Belgian law in relation to deeds committed after 1991, well before the law of 22 March 1996.

On 17 July 1998, the diplomatic conference in Rome adopted the Statute for a permanent International Criminal Court, and in October of that same year, Augusto Pinochet, former president of Chile, was arrested in London in execution of an international arrest warrant issued by a Spanish judge. At the request of Chilean victims, a Belgian judge also accepted his jurisdiction when the British government envisaged the release of Pinochet.[14] This decision and a subsequent warrant of arrest were welcomed by the Belgian government and by public opinion at large. Investigating Judge Damien Vandermeersch could not base his decision on the 1993 law, however, so he justified it by reference to international customary law, which considers that torture and forced disappearances, as crimes against humanity, are incriminated by *jus cogens*.

Similar reasoning can be found in a number of decisions pronounced in other countries, such as, for example, in the *Demjanjuk* decision, in which a United States federal court decided:

'The universality principle is based on the assumption that some crimes are so universally condemned that the perpetrators are the enemies of all people. Therefore, any na-

---

11. ICJ, 11 July 1996. *Case concerning application of the Convention on the Prevention and Punishment of the Crime of Genocide* (*Bosnia and Herzegovina* v. *Yugoslavia*), par. 31. <http://www.icj-cij.org/icjwww/idocket/ibhy/ibhyjudgment/ibhy_ijudgment_19960711_frame.htm>

12. *Prosecutor* v. *Tihomir Blaškić*, Case IT-95-14-AR, 29 October 1997, <http://www.un.org/icty/blaskic/appeal/decision-e/71029JT3.html>. Para. 29: '(...) The International Tribunal does not have the mission of replacing the jurisdiction of any State. By virtue of Article 9 of the Statute, the International Tribunal and the national jurisdictions are concurrently competent. The national jurisdictions of the States of Ex-Yugoslavia, as those of all States, are required by customary law to judge or to extradite those persons presumed responsible for grave violations of international humanitarian law. The primacy of the Tribunal foreseen in Article 9 (2) is applicable to all national jurisdictions or, if these jurisdictions lack this customary obligation, it can intervene and judge.'

13. Loi relative à la reconnaissance du Tribunal international pour l'ex-Yougoslavie et du Tribunal international pour le Rwanda, et à la coopération avec ces Tribunaux. MB, 27 April 1996.

14. Brussels Investigation and hearing judge, 6 November 1998, *Journal des Tribunaux* (1999) p. 308.

tion which has custody of the perpetrators may punish them according to its law applicable to such offences ... Israel or any other nation ... may undertake to vindicate the interest of all nations by seeking to punish the perpetrators of such crimes.'[15]

During the discussion on the genocide bill, the government proposed to include provisions on genocide and on crimes against humanity in the 1993 law, making it a general law applicable to serious breaches of humanitarian law.[16] The government also proposed a provision inspired by the *Pinochet* ruling of the British House of Lords, one that – as all were soon to discover – proved to be quite revolutionary: the principle that no immunity should be able to bar prosecution based on the law.[17] The genocide bill was merged with the existing war crimes statute and became a general 'law on grave breaches of international humanitarian law' *(loi relative aux violations graves du droit international humanitaire)* of 10 February 1999.[18]

The spring of 2001 witnessed the final test of the Belgian universal jurisdiction law when a Brussels court tried four Rwandan genocide perpetrators. During the six weeks of the trial, all of Belgium was transfixed by the proceedings, which demonstrated the depth of public support for combating impunity and for the necessity of universal jurisdiction in that effort.

For a good understanding of the Belgian laws on universal jurisdiction, it should be stressed that these laws were definitely seen as an implementation of international obligations. Hosting Europe's capital, Belgium has a tradition of open-mindedness towards international law. The Belgian Supreme Court has considered since the 1970s that a rule stemming from an international convention is superior to a national statute.[19] Where social and economic law are in large part determined by the European Union's regulations, and penal and family law substantially influenced by the European Convention on Human Rights and the jurisprudence of the Strasbourg Court, implementing international law is a natural process.

3.   A VICTIM FRIENDLY PROCEDURE

Belgium is certainly not the only country that translated international humanitarian law into universal jurisdiction for international crimes. It is not even the only country to practice universal jurisdiction *in absentia*.[20] It is, however, a country of civil law tradition, highlighting the institution of the *'partie civile'* (private prosecutor).

---

15. *Petrovsky* v. *Demjanjuk*, US Appeals Court, 6th Circuit, 31 October 1985. 776 F.2d 571 (6th Cir. 1985).

16. The Belgian government and legislature expressly confirmed international customary law as a basis for jurisdiction and noted the procedural character of the law of 10 February 1999. As such, and particularly with regard to universal jurisdiction, it is thus for immediate application, irrespective of the date of the violation.

17. Art. 5, Law of 16 July 1993.

18. MB, 23 March 1999.

19. Cour de Cassation, 27 May 1971, arrêt Franco-Suisse/Le Ski.

20. Other countries include Germany, Australia, New Zealand, South-Africa, Bolivia and Canada.

As in France and some other civil law countries, the victim is not only an active party in the criminal procedure but can even instigate a criminal investigation without the consent of the public prosecutor. The investigation is then conducted by an independent judge, investigating *à charge et à décharge*.[21] The sole condition necessary to lodge a complaint and to instigate an investigation is to claim damages that bear a reasonable relationship to the alleged crime, and to pay an amount determined by the judge to cover court fees if the claim turns out to be less than well founded.

A recent reform of the criminal procedural law, introduced in the aftermath of the *Dutroux* case,[22] granted even more rights to victims. Plaintiffs in Belgium could now more directly influence the work of the investigating judge, request access to file records, suggest certain acts of investigation (search, arrest warrant) and lodge an appeal to the Court of Appeal if the judge refuses to accept such requests.

The universal jurisdiction and immunity provisions of the 1993 and 1999 laws, the success of the 2001 Rwandan trial,[23] as well as the possibilities of Belgium's civil law procedure, attracted victims from all over the world to Brussels in the hope of lodging complaints against alleged perpetrators of war crimes and crimes against humanity, including such prominent political leaders as Saddam Hussein, Laurent-Désiré Kabila, Paul Kagame and Ariel Sharon.[24]

4.   FROM PINOCHET TO SHARON

The Belgian arrest warrant against Augusto Pinochet elicited the support of the government, but a year later the same judge issued a warrant against Yerodia Ndombasi, the Congolese Minister of Foreign Affairs, for publicly encouraging and calling for an assassination campaign against Rwandan Tutsis in Kinshasa. Some diplomatic problems arose as a result, but the Congo opted for a purely legal approach to the problem and brought its grievances against Belgium before the International Court of Justice (ICJ).[25] The pending procedure in The Hague did not damage the relationship between the two countries. Yerodia himself welcomed a Belgian minister on a visit to the Congo when the former was already the subject of an international search warrant confirmed by the Belgian government.

Despite its status as the former colonial power, Belgium was not confronted with an anti-Belgian movement in the Congo, nor did it witness any negative press

---

21. Against and in favor of the suspect.

22. A famous paedophile who abducted, abused and killed young girls. The trial is planned to start March 2004.

23. Cour d'Assises Bruxelles, 8 June 2001. Full information on the trial, including the trial can be found on <http://www.asf.be/AssisesRwanda2/fr/frStart.htm>.

24. More than 40 complaints were filed, but only a few of these cases originated a real investigation.

25. ICJ, 14 February 2002. R.D.C./Belgium. Case of the arrest warrant of 11 April 2000. 121/2002. For commentary, see J. Wouters and L. De Smet, 'The ICJ's judgement in the case concerning the arrest warrant of 11 April 2000: some critical notes', 4 *YIHL* (2003) p. 373.

campaigns or threats against Belgians living in the Congo. Congo's case at the ICJ even dropped an initial challenge against Belgium's practice of universal jurisdiction and focused instead on the immunity of the Minster of Foreign Affairs. Eventually, on 14 February 2002, the ICJ found that the Belgium law violated the internationally accepted principle of immunity of the head of a country's diplomatic service. The issue of universal jurisdiction, however, was pointedly left open, notwithstanding the pressure of Court President Gilbert Guillaume, who opposed universal jurisdiction in his separate opinion.[26]

Unlike the complaint against Congolese President Laurent-Désiré Kabila and the warrant against his Minister of Foreign Affairs, the complaint against Ariel Sharon, the first ruler of a country of the 'North' accused under the principle of universal jurisdiction in Belgium, provoked an immediate and vituperative storm of political reactions. Israel did not seize the ICJ but combined diplomacy and lobbying with a strong legal defense in the Belgian courts. The Brussels Court of Appeal declared on 16 April 2002 in the *Yerodia* case that investigation was not admissible as long as one of the suspects could not be found on Belgian territory.[27] Similar decisions were taken on 26 June 2002 in the *Sabra and Shatila* case[28] and in the case against the president of the Ivory Coast.[29]

Many observers expected that this would be the end of the Belgian law on universal jurisdiction. As a result of a strong lobbying campaign initiated by victims' groups and human rights NGOs, however, a proposal for an 'interpretative law' to clarify and reconfirm the intent and meaning of the 1993 and 1999 laws was submitted by a group of senators,[30] and more importantly, was supported by the Belgian government, especially the prime minister, who decided to back this initiative and link it to a second, more general proposal.[31]

The first bill was intended to confirm the interpretation of the law which the members of parliament themselves had in mind at the time, contrary to the above-mentioned decisions of the Brussels Appeal Court, which were wrongly based on the presumed will of the legislator. The purpose of the second bill was to take into account two key developments in international law: the *Yerodia* ruling of the ICJ and the Rome Statute of the International Criminal Court. But this bill also included some serious restrictions on the rights of plaintiffs to instigate an investigation, providing for a more consistent role for the Federal Prosecutor in cases lacking any nexus with Belgium. Both bills were negotiated with the representa-

---

26. Different individual opinions within the ICJ suggest a split on this issue within the Court. Clearly the majority of the judges did not want to close the future development of universal jurisdiction.

27. Cour d'Appel Bruxelles, Chambre des Mises en Accusation, *Kabila et Cs*. 16 February 2002, unpublished.

28. Cour d'Appel Bruxelles, o.c., *Sharon et Cs*. 26 June 2002, unpublished.

29. Ibid.

30. Belgian Senat. Proposal 1255-02. All quoted proposals and the record of the discussions in both chambers of the parliament can be found on the site of the Belgian senate <http://www.senate.be>.

31. Belgian Senat. Proposal 1256-02.

tives of human rights NGOs, who were concerned that the bills might jeopardize pending cases.

On 29 January 2003, the Senate adopted the two proposals, notwithstanding considerable pressure from Israel and the USA and not to mention pressure from the Federation of Belgian Enterprises, a group that was keenly aware of the consequences that prosecution of war crimes could have for Belgian exports to some countries. These businessmen were especially alarmed since complaints had already been lodged against multinational companies for their support of some regimes in Asia and Africa.

Immediately after the justice commission of the Senate adopted the bill, the General Prosecutor of the *Cour de Cassation* (Belgium's Supreme Court) set a date for a hearing in the *Sabra and Shatila* case. Although he rejected the reasoning of the Brussels Appeals Court, he still advised to confirm the decision for other reasons. He argued in a brief[32] that universal jurisdiction *in absentia* was not based on international customary law, and stipulated that the Belgian legislator had not made clear any intention to go beyond the international obligation of *aut dedere aut judicare*. Additionally, the General Prosecutor elaborated on the statute's objective. In his opinion, an *in absentia* trial would be an imperfect tool that would eventuate in a virtual rather than a real judicial process. With no defendant present, a trial would take place in a vacuum. The General Prosecutor concluded that such a trial would not further the effective prosecution of these crimes, but would instead do more harm than good to the law's objective. Furthermore, the General Prosecutor argued that an *in absentia* trial would raise questions as to its legality, as it might be a violation of the defendant's right to a fair trial.[33]

5.   THE 12 FEBRUARY RULING OF THE COUR DE CASSATION IN THE *SHARON* CASE

In its ruling of 12 February 2003, the *Cour de Cassation*, hearing the *Sharon* case, clearly rejected the reasoning of the General Prosecutor, and stressed that prosecution based on the law of 16 June 1993, as amended in 1999, for acts of genocide, crimes against humanity and grave breaches of the Geneva Conventions is not limited by the restrictions provided for by the Code of Procedure, and does not require the presence of the accused on Belgian soil. The Court observed, however, that defendant Ariel Sharon was sitting prime minister of Israel at the time the complaint was lodged, and that he was still the incumbent of that position. Recalling the customary principle that grants ruling heads of states and governments immunity from prosecution, the Court stated that no international convention pro-

---

32. The General Prosecutor's brief and the judgment of 12 February 2003 can be found on the site of the Cour de Cassation at <http://www.juridat.be/juris/jucf.htm>. An unofficial translation of the decision on <http://www.indictsharon.net>.

33. It is true that Belgian law permits not only investigation but also trial *in absentia*. For serious crimes, however, such trials are not usual and generally the prosecution seeks the arrest and extradition of the accused before starting the trial, in order to avoid a second procedure after the arrest occurs.

vides for an exception to that principle in case of prosecution for international crimes.

The Court recalled that Article IV of the 1948 Genocide Convention does exclude immunity but also takes into consideration that Article VI of the same convention only provides for prosecution before national courts of the state on whose territory the crimes were committed, and before an international criminal court, and does not provide for prosecution before national courts judging on the basis of universal jurisdiction. The exception to the customary law principle of immunity thus cannot be extended to national courts applying the principle of universal jurisdiction. The Court argued that the provision of Article 5 of the law of 16 June 1993, stating that no immunity can bar prosecution based on this law, should be limited to what is permitted under international customary law, and be seen as prohibiting impunity based on official status; at the same time it does not provide an exception to the principle of international immunity for heads of states and governments.

The *Cour de Cassation* concluded that the ruling of the Brussels Appeals Court was acceptable when it declared prosecution against Ariel Sharon inadmissible, but for the reason mentioned cancelled the same ruling as it considered that prosecution against Amos Yaron and others involved in the Sabra and Shatila massacre required their presence on Belgian territory.

On 10 June 2003, the Brussels Appeals Court decided to also reject the other arguments advanced by the defense, and the investigating judge announced he would reopen the investigation.

6.   THE IRAQ WAR AND ITS COLLATERAL DAMAGE FOR UNIVERSAL JURISDICTION

The decision of the Supreme Court provoked a huge reaction from Israel, which recalled its ambassador in Brussels for more than three months. It was also followed by a new wave of complaints, some of them purely provocative and even a few that were lodged with the express intention of challenging the law itself, such as a genocide complaint brought against the Belgian Minister of Foreign Affairs based on his approval of an arms contract with Nepal. On the very eve of the US invasion of Iraq, a group of Iraqi citizens, survivors of a US bombing of a bomb shelter in Baghdad during the first Gulf War, lodged a complaint against George W. Bush, Sr. Immediately thereafter, the US joined the Israeli campaign against the Belgian universal jurisdiction law

Just before the close of the parliamentary session, the government split over the reform of the 1993 law. On the last day before the dissolution of the Chambers, the quite moderate proposal that had already been adopted by the Senate passed in the Chamber of Representatives but an important amendment was added, with the support of the opposition, in order to neutralize the majority which was in favor of universal jurisdiction.[34] This amendment provided for a procedure making it possi-

---

34. Art. 7(4) of the law of 23 April 2003.

ble to withdraw a case from the Belgian courts, and to send it to another country if that country indicts for genocide, crimes against humanity and war crimes and can furthermore grant a fair trial to all parties concerned. The provision was heavily criticized by the Council of State in its advice as a violation of the separation of the judiciary and the government.[35] It was still not enough, however, to calm American anger and suspicion.

At this time, a second Iraqi complaint was lodged to test the new law, this time against US Commander General Tommy Franks and other high-ranking American officers. While the State Department carefully expressed satisfaction about the Belgian decision to change the law, albeit stressing 'the need to be diligent in taking steps to prevent abuse of the legal system for political ends',[36] Democratic Congressman Gary Ackerman presented his 'Universal Jurisdiction Rejection Act',[37] explicitly referring to Belgium. This acts provides that US authorities will refuse judicial cooperation in cases based on universal jurisdiction. Although an investigation could no longer be initiated on the initiative of the Federal Prosecutor, and notwithstanding the fact that the old government was supposed to handle only 'current affairs',[38] the government didn't wait for the prosecutor's decision upon the opening of an inquiry, and decided immediately to refer the case to the US judiciary. A string of other mostly frivolous complaints followed, which received the same treatment. The situation became more and more ridiculous in the eyes of public opinion.

Visiting Brussels in June 2003, US Secretary of Defense Donald Rumsfeld claimed in a press conference that without the withdrawal of the universal jurisdiction law, Brussels could no longer be the seat of NATO headquarters, since, in his view, representatives of NATO Member States would be at risk of arrest and prosecution every time they visited Belgium.[39] On 12 July 2003, the Belgian political parties involved in negotiations on a new coalition government program reached an agreement to withdraw the 'Law on the Prosecution of Serious Breaches of Humanitarian Law', with integration of the different material provisions of the law into the Penal Code but abandonment of the universal jurisdiction principle.[40] This agreement would lead to the statute of 5 August 2003.[41]

---

35. Doc. Senat. 1999-2003. 2-1256/13. <http://www.senate.be>.

36. Statement of State Department spokesmen Boucher. <http://www.Expatica.com>, 9 May 2003.

37. House of Representatives. Bill No. 2050, 9 May 2003. The bill contains: a prohibition on any kind of American cooperation with an investigation or prosecution under a universal jurisdiction act; a requirement that the President ensure US classified material is not used for such investigations or prosecutions; an authorization for the President to use all necessary means to assist any American or ally imprisoned due to enforcement of a universal jurisdiction act.

38. Between election date and the date a new government is installed, the dismissed government has only a limited power.

39. See statement of Human Rights Watch, 12 June 2003. <http://www.hrw.org/press/2003/06/belgium061303.htm>.

40. Press release of the Belgian government, 14 July 2003. <http://www.diplomatie.be/en/press/homedetails.asp?TEXTID=8273>.

41. Loi relative aux violations graves du droit international humanitaire (law on grave breaches of international humanitarian law) of 5 August 2003. MB, 8 August 2003. The law entered in force on the day of its publication.

7.   CURRENT BELGIAN LAW ON GRAVE BREACHES OF INTERNATIONAL HUMANITARIAN LAW

The new provisions regarding jurisdiction for international crimes abolished the principle of universal jurisdiction for all cases lacking a nexus with Belgium. Jurisdiction based on the principle of active and passive personality is enforced. Thus, Belgium will retain jurisdiction over its own nationals involved in international crimes committed abroad, without any condition of double prohibition.[42] The most important form of jurisdiction based on the active personality principle is the possibility of prosecution of residents involved in crimes against humanity and war crimes committed abroad, or of non-nationals for extraterritorial crimes if they are resident in Belgium (this was the scenario in the case of the four Rwandans accused in the 2001 trial). Victims of such perpetrators will still have the possibility to instigate a judicial inquiry acting as private prosecutor.

Even *in absentia* the Belgian courts will also retain jurisdiction over international crimes committed against Belgian citizens or residents, but the initiative for prosecution rests with the federal prosecutor. The prosecutor's decision is no longer open to appeal. He or she can still initiate prosecution when required by an international convention and/or by customary law. Victims of torture will be able to use this provision, as the 1984 Convention against Torture provides for jurisdiction over perpetrators present on the territory of a State Party.

A decision of the Supreme Court is now required in order to close investigations pending in cases not covered by these new criteria. In fact, on 24 September 2003, the Supreme Court ended the two most controversial cases: the investigation into the massacre in Sabra and Shatila involving the Prime Minister of Israel, Ariel Sharon, and the complaint against former US president George Bush, Sr. A transitory rule states that cases in which at least one of the initial plaintiffs is a Belgian citizen can still be investigated and judged.[43]

8.   THE END OF UNIVERSAL JURISDICTION?

Notwithstanding the maintenance of an enlarged jurisdiction based on the passive and active personality principles, the new Belgian legislation is now more restrictive than that of either Spain or Germany. Human rights organizations and victims' groups were very disappointed about the devolution of the Belgian anti-atrocity law. For years, Belgium was considered a country standing at the forefront of the struggle against impunity. Given the negative Belgian experience, some other countries could be more reluctant than before in prosecuting war crimes.

Nevertheless, Belgium's decision to retreat will probably not put an end to attempts in other countries to pass legislation according with the general obligation

---

42. The new Art. 10*bis* of the Belgian code of criminal procedure.
43. This provision concerns mainly the investigation against the former president of Chad, Hissene Habré.

to prosecute perpetrators of war crimes and crimes against humanity. Countries pursuing this course of action can learn from Belgium's experience and avoid the mistakes made by the Belgian authorities.

One of the most important lessons is that the prosecution of crimes against humanity and war crimes should be coordinated at an international level. Since Belgium was – incorrectly – known as the only country where victims could find redress, it attracted cases from over the world. Some were very serious matters that could not find any other forum; others were frivolous or politically motivated actions, but all of them together created a heavy burden for the judiciary of such a small country.

A serious approach to the prosecution of war crimes requires harmonizing legislation and coordinating actions in different states. Harmonization of legislation would also limit the pressure from countries fearing the prosecution of their own nationals abroad. Some initiatives have already been taken at the level of the European Union.

On 13 June 2002, the European Council created a 'European network of contact points in respect of persons responsible for genocide, crimes against humanity and war crimes'.[44] On 8 May 2003, the European Council of Ministers issued a framework decision on the prosecution of genocide, crimes against humanity and war crimes, that aims to increase cooperation among national units in member states in that field.[45] The establishment of the ICC and the necessity of adapting national legislation implementing the principle of complementarity (subsidiarity) embedded in the preamble of the Rome Statute should make mandatory some form of universal jurisdiction and encourage international cooperation, at least at the European level.

A second lesson is that actions against impunity cannot be sustained if they are not supported by public opinion in the country where the prosecution is taking place. The prosecution against four perpetrators of the Rwandan genocide, including two nuns, faced opposition from the Catholic Church and conservative parties. This opposition could be overcome, however, thanks to significant public support for the victims. The plaintiffs, Belgian-Rwandan families and genocide survivors living in Belgium who encountered their torturers in Brussels streets, could also build on the guilty conscience about the Rwanda tragedy. The fact that Belgian soldiers were killed in Rwanda and the presence of a Rwandan community in Belgium were additional elements creating support. The Palestinian victims from Sabra and Shatila initially received widespread support, but this support evaporated in the face of external political pressure. When victims as well as perpetrators are living abroad, cases can easily appear to be politicized, even if the legal case itself is strong and solid.

Creating support based on international solidarity and ethical principles is more difficult than creating solidarity with people living in the same country. Similarly,

---

44. Council Decision 2002/494/JHA, 13 June 2002, (*OJ* L 167, 26/06/2002 P-0002).
45. Council Decision 2003/335/JHA, May 2003 on the investigation and prosecution of genocide, crimes against humanity and war crimes. (*OJ* L 118, 15/05/2003, P 0012 – 0014).

it is easier to spark outrage about the fact that a well-known criminal has found asylum in the country than to instill concerns about a war criminal thousands of miles away. Although the requirement of a nexus with the country is not based on international law, it facilitates public understanding of and support for the necessity of extraterritorial jurisdiction.

A third lesson is that the adoption of legislation incorporating universal jurisdiction should not be seen as a political move or an ethical statement from the legislator, but rather should be undertaken with the sincere intent to combat the most serious forms of crime in a framework of international cooperation. Prosecuting crimes against humanity is as necessary as combating terrorism, international drug trafficking or the trafficking of human beings.

Attractive laws are insufficient. Undertaking prosecutions also necessitates that additional means be made available to the judiciary. A law that creates a new scope of activity for the judiciary must be accompanied by measures to manage the additional tasks that arise in its wake. Neglecting this will hurt prosecutors and judges, and only provoke a negative attitude towards the new legislation, when this group should be one of the key constituencies within the population who are aware of the importance of this kind of prosecution.

The combination of universal jurisdiction with an unlimited access for victims to the courts placed enormous pressure on Belgium. The remedy that has been chosen is to limit the scope of universal jurisdiction, even though the problems were not provoked by the existence of a legal framework for universal jurisdiction as such. The option taken by the law of 23 April 2003 to discourage victims without any link with the country from lodging cases was probably a better compromise between principles and realism.

Giving more responsibility to national prosecutors while enhancing international cooperation between prosecutors should make it possible to eliminate frivolous and purely political complaints while refocusing judicial attention on the most serious crimes as well as on those crimes that cannot be prosecuted in the country of the perpetrator or where the crimes were committed. Universal jurisdiction should definitely remain an option for the victims, but only as the last resort for those cases in which only an international approach can assure them redress.

THE FIRST OPCW REVIEW CONFERENCE OF THE CHEMICAL WEAPONS CONVENTION[1]

Ralf Trapp[2] and Lisa Tabassi[3]

'... the exercise we are about to tackle goes beyond a normal review of the operations of a disarmament agreement. From our common deliberations, a renewed sense of commitment must emerge. In the past few months, preparatory work has shown that there is indeed a vast area of convergence among Member States, but that, at the same time, there remain issues that require further efforts to forge a common understanding and a shared vision.'

Rogelio Pfirter, Director-General of the OPCW, 28 April 2003[4]

1.   INTRODUCTION AND BACKGROUND

The First Special Session of the Conference of the States Parties to Review the Operation of the Chemical Weapons Convention (the First Review Conference) was convened by the Organisation for the Prohibition of Chemical Weapons (OPCW) from 28 April to 9 May 2003 in The Hague, the Netherlands. This article examines the mandate of the Review Conference, as stipulated by the Chemical Weapons Convention (Convention or CWC),[5] the preparations undertaken by the

---

1. © R. Trapp and L. Tabassi, 2003.

2. Senior Planning Officer (formerly Secretary to the OPCW Executive Council's Working Group on Preparations for the Review Conference and the OPCW Technical Secretariat's Review Conference Steering Group) in the Office of the Deputy Director-General of the Technical Secretariat of the OPCW. The views expressed are the author's own and do not necessarily reflect those of the Secretariat.

3. Legal Officer in the Office of the Legal Adviser of the Technical Secretariat of the OPCW. The views expressed are the author's own and do not necessarily reflect those of the Secretariat.

4. Para. 2 of the Opening Statement by the Director-General to the First Special Session of the Conference of the States Parties to Review the Operation of the Chemical Weapons Convention, OPCW Doc. RC-1/DG.3, 28 April 2003, <http://www.opcw.org>.

5. Convention on the Prohibition of the Development, Production, Stockpiling and Use of Chemical Weapons and on Their Destruction, *UNTS* (1974) No. 33757, p. 45. Corrected and changed [amended] text available at <http://www.opcw.org>; L. Tabassi, ed., *OPCW: The Legal Texts* (The Hague, OPCW/TMC Asser Press 1999) pp. 3-115; or from the OPCW Technical Secretariat, Johan de Wittlaan 32, 2517 JR The Hague, the Netherlands.

The corrected text of the Convention consists of the Appendix to Conference on Disarmament Doc. CD/1170, dated 26 August 1992, corrected by Depositary Notifications C.N.246.1994.TREATIES-5 of 31 August 1994 (procès-verbal of rectification of the original of the Convention: Arabic, Chinese, English, French, Russian and Spanish texts); C.N.359.1994.TREATIES-8 of 27 January 1995 (procès-verbal of rectification of the original of the Convention: Spanish text); C.N.454.1995.TREATIES-12

OPCW and its Member States, the issues that could have been raised, and those that were addressed in the Political Declaration and the Report adopted by the First Review Conference.

The OPCW was established as an intergovernmental organisation in The Hague on 29 April 1997, the date of the entry into force of the CWC. As the implementing body for the treaty, the OPCW's mandate is 'to achieve the object and purpose of [the] Convention, to ensure the implementation of its provisions, including those for international verification of compliance with it, and to provide a forum for consultation and cooperation among States Parties'.[6] The OPCW has three organs: the Conference of the States Parties (Conference), the Executive Council (Council) and the Technical Secretariat (Secretariat), the latter which is composed of approximately 500 staff members, approximately half of who are inspection team members. Six years after entry into force of the CWC, the OPCW is fully operational, the verification regime is being implemented, all declared stockpiles of chemical weapons have been inspected and are being destroyed or prepared for destruction, and the programmes for implementation support, international cooperation for the peaceful use of chemistry, and protection and assistance against the use or threat of use of chemical weapons are being developed and carried out.

At the time of the First Review Conference there were 151 States Parties to the Convention,[7] of which 113 participated in the Review Conference. Two signatory states, Haiti and Israel, and two other states, Angola and the Libyan Arab Jamahiriya, participated as observers in accordance with the Rules of Procedure of the Conference. Five international organisations and bodies, 22 non-governmental organisations (NGOs) and six chemical industry associations also participated as observers in accordance with the Rules of Procedure.

2.   THE PURPOSE OF THE REVIEW CONFERENCE

Article VIII, paragraph 22, of the Convention and Part IX, paragraph 26, of the Verification Annex to the Convention respectively provide:

'22. The Conference shall not later than one year after the expiry of the fifth and the tenth year after the entry into force of this Convention, and at such other times within that time period as may be decided upon, convene in special sessions to undertake reviews of the operation of this Convention. Such reviews shall take into account any

---

of 2 February 1996 (procès-verbal of rectification of the original of the Convention: Arabic and Russian texts); C.N.916.1999.TREATIES-7 of 8 October 1999 (acceptance of amendment for a change to Section B of Part VI of the Annex on Implementation and Verification ('Verification Annex'), effective 31 October 1999); and C.N.157.2000.TREATIES-1 of 13 March 2000 (acceptance of corrections to the amendments, effective 9 March 2000).

6. Art. VIII(1) of the Convention.

7. See Status of Participation in the Chemical Weapons Convention. <http://www.opcw.org> under documents, S series. As of 20 October 2003, the number of States Parties had increased to 157 to include Afghanistan, Andorra, Sao Tome and Principe, Timor-Leste and Tonga.

relevant scientific and technological developments. At intervals of five years thereafter, unless otherwise decided upon, further sessions of the Conference shall be convened with the same objective.'

'26. At the first special session of the Conference convened pursuant to Article VIII, paragraph 22, the provisions of [the regime for other, unscheduled discrete organic chemical production facilities][8] shall be re examined in the light of a comprehensive review of the overall verification regime for the chemical industry (Art. VI, Parts VII to IX of this Annex) on the basis of the experience gained. The Conference shall then make recommendations so as to improve the effectiveness of the verification regime.'

Article VIII of the CWC established the Conference to, *inter alia,* oversee the implementation of the Convention and review compliance with it, and the Conference meets annually in regular sessions to do so. Article VIII also mandates the Executive Council to, *inter alia,* promote the effective implementation of and compliance with the Convention, and it meets at least four times per year to do so. The Technical Secretariat is mandated to, *inter alia*, carry out the verification measures under the Convention and report on these to the Conference and Council. Because, in the case of the CWC, there is already an ongoing daily, quarterly and annual review of implementation and compliance, the purpose, function and organisation of CWC review conferences is consequently distinct from the review conferences of treaties which lack an implementing body.

The CWC stipulates that its review conferences shall examine the operation of the Convention, taking into account any relevant scientific and technological developments and a comprehensive overview of the verification regime for the chemical industry. The scope of the mandates of the OPCW organs implies that review conferences step back and view the Convention from a broader perspective, and link the review to specific purposes, i.e., the progress made towards universal adherence to the Convention, the progress of the destruction of chemical weapons and their production facilities, and any possible security concerns of States Parties. These issues are especially crucial for the first 10-15 years after the entry into force of the Convention, which is the time frame stipulated by the Convention for com-

---

8. The Verification Annex Part IX provisions on 'other chemical production facilities' are deliberately evolutionary. The negotiators of the Convention failed to agree on a regime for 'capable' facilities. Capable facilities are those in which the technological processes or nature of activities are such that they can quickly be converted to produce chemical weapons, if so desired. All modern chemical industries have certain facilities that are 'capable' but agreement could never be reached on the development of another schedule listing, for example, technological processes or equipment. Instead it was decided to create a category for unscheduled discrete organic production facilities in which thousands of plants would be declared (with some differentiation based on chemistry – the so-called PSF facilities producing discrete organic chemicals containing one or more of the elements of phosphorus, sulphur or fluorine), while at the same time OPCW capacity for inspecting them would be finite. Random selection of sites for inspection, use of information available to the Secretariat, and involvement of Member States in the selection process was envisaged by the Convention to target inspections. The First Review Conference was to review this entire verification concept for other chemical production facilities producing discrete organic chemicals, in the light of experience gained, and as part of an overall review of industry verification.

pletion of destruction of all declared chemical weapons.[9] The First Review Conference was also to review the regime for verification of the chemical industry, and particularly the verification of what the Convention calls 'other chemical production facilities' producing non-treaty-regulated organic chemicals.

As would ordinarily happen in any review conference, it was to be expected that the first CWC Review Conference would reaffirm commitment to the CWC and the OPCW, make recommendations to strengthen the implementation process, and give guidance on future directions for CWC implementation (reaffirmation, common understandings, recommendations and priorities).

3.   THE PREPARATORY PROCESS

Article VIII, paragraph 32(c) mandates the Council to make the arrangements for the sessions of the Conference, including the preparation of the agenda. To this end, and pursuant to a recommendation of the Conference,[10] the Council established an open-ended Working Group on the Preparations for the Review Conference (Working Group) on 28 September 2001 which was to, with the assistance and cooperation of the Secretariat, review relevant background documentation prepared by the Secretariat as well as national papers submitted by a number of States Parties, and make recommendations to the Council on the substantive and organisational aspects of the Review Conference.[11]

Between November 2001 and March 2003, the Working Group, chaired by Argentina, met 30 times. It addressed procedural matters related to the First Review Conference and received and reviewed 18 background papers prepared by the Secretariat, an interim report prepared by the OPCW Scientific Advisory Board on relevant scientific and technological developments, 33 national papers and 12 written submissions by NGOs.

The Chairman of the Working Group considered that it would be difficult to develop the final document(s) of the Review Conference during its two-week time span unless a considerable portion was already prepared in draft form before commencement of the Review Conference. He therefore proposed to use the means of a Chairman's paper to issue initial draft(s) under his own responsibility and without prejudice to the work of the Review Conference. In the last few months before the Review Conference was due to begin, and following the structure of the draft provisional agenda of the Review Conference, the Chairman began issuing elements of his eventual paper to the Working Group. These were later revised by him, with the help of the Secretariat, taking into account the comments and national papers received from delegations, into a consolidated Chairman's Paper con-

---

9. W. Krutzsch and R. Trapp, *A Commentary on the Chemical Weapons Convention* (Dordrecht, Martinus Nijhoff 1994) pp. 143-145.

10. Report of the Sixth Session of the Conference of the States Parties, subparas. 21.2 of OPCW Doc. C-VI/6, dated 19 May 2001, <http://www.opcw.org>.

11. Decision on the Establishment of the Open-Ended Working Group on Preparations for the Review Conference, OPCW Doc. EC-XXV/DEC.4, dated 28 September 2001, <http://www.opcw.org>.

taining an initial draft political declaration and the substantive section of the Review Conference Report (Agenda item 7: review of the operation of the CWC), which formed the initial basis for discussion and negotiation during the Review Conference itself. Although the Chairman's Paper was submitted with the caveat that it would not prejudice the work of the Review Conference, in practical terms it reflected to a considerable degree the desired outcome of the Review Conference since it already represented a certain measure of consensus achieved among States Parties, or at least those participating in the preparatory process.

The work of the Working Group reached its successful conclusion largely due to the concerted efforts made in 2003 in the months just preceding the Review Conference. A number of other matters besides the Review Conference competed for the attention of delegations throughout the existence of the Working Group. At the Group's inception in late 2001 and throughout much of 2002 the main focus of attention in the OPCW centred on other matters: the OPCW's contribution to counter-terrorism in the wake of 11 September 2001; the OPCW budgetary crisis of 2001-2002; the removal of the Director-General and the appointment of his replacement in 2002; and, finally, the decision on implementation of the tenure policy for OPCW staff. Consensus on the last matter was reached only in late March 2003 and the Council requested a Special Session of the Conference to decide the matter before 1 May. Accordingly, the Review Conference had to interrupt its work for one afternoon in order for the Conference to convene in special session to decide upon implementation of the tenure policy.[12]

In short, despite the short time frame and the other competing, complex matters to be addressed, the efforts of the Working Group and its Chairman, the Secretariat, States Parties, the Scientific Advisory Board and NGOs resulted in 28 documents for review at the opening of the Review Conference: the Chairman's texts, a Note by the Director-General, seven background papers by the Secretariat, a report by the Scientific Advisory Board, and 19 national papers. All of these were issued just days before the Review Conference convened. A further ten national papers were issued after the Review Conference opened.

The issuance of the documents so late in the process meant that there was little time for prior reflection on them in the capitals of participating states. There was some speculation during the preparatory process that the Review Conference would not reach consensus on the political declaration and, in particular, the substantive portions of its report. However, the concerted effort by the Working Group in its last stages and the issuance of the Chairman's texts created a momentum which enabled the Review Conference to successfully complete its work. There was a pervasive sense of commitment by delegations to finding consensus and this was, of course, the key factor in ensuring the Review Conference's success.

---

12. Decision: Tenure Policy of the OPCW, OPCW Doc. C-SS-2/DEC.1, 30 April 2003, <http://www.opcw.org>.

4.   THE REVIEW CONFERENCE

4.1   **Potentially contentious issues**

The first morning was taken up with decisions on procedural matters. The following three and a half days were devoted to general debate and another half-day was set aside for the special session of the Conference to decide on the tenure policy. During the remainder of the two weeks, the Review Conference met only briefly and sporadically in plenary session as the substantive work was conducted in two arenas: (1) meetings conducted by a group of friends of the chair (of the Committee of the Whole), in which delegations devoted their time to revising the Chairman's text of the draft political declaration for submission to the Committee of the Whole (the main committee of the Conference of the States Parties[13]); and (2) the Committee of the Whole, which devoted its time to revising the Chairman's text on Agenda Item 7 and considering and adopting its Report to the Review Conference.[14]

Two potentially contentious matters arose at the opening of the Review Conference which could have led to divisive political debate: (a) the legality of the employment of incapacitating chemical agents in 'non-lethal weapons' and the use of toxic chemicals other than riot control agents for law enforcement purposes, an issue raised by the International Committee of the Red Cross (ICRC)[15] among others;[16] and (b) the statement by the United States during the general debate that two States Parties, the Islamic Republic of Iran and Sudan, were actively pursuing chemical weapons programmes.[17] Furthermore, early in the Review Conference preparations, there was speculation that article-by-article scrutiny of the Convention at the Review Conference would raise the likelihood of deadlock over certain issues. These included the maintenance of export control policies outside of the CWC regime by a small group of CWC States Parties participating in the informal, pre-CWC 'Australia Group', who were refusing to export CWC scheduled chemi-

---

13. Rule 45 of the Rules of Procedure of the Conference of the States Parties, OPCW Doc. C-I/3, 12 May 1997. <http://www.opcw.org>.

14. Committee of the Whole: Report to the First Special Session of the Conference of the States Parties to Review the Operation of the Chemical Weapons Convention, OPCW Doc. RC-1/CoW.1, 9 May 2003. <http://www.opcw.org>.

15. D. Ruppe, 'Red Cross Says it was Muzzled over Stand on Incapacitating Weapons', *Global Security Newswire* (30 April 2003); I. Daoust, R. Coupland and R. Ishoey, 'New Wars, New Weapons? The Obligation of States to Assess the Legality of Means and Methods of Warfare', 84 *IRRC* (2002) pp. 345-363. <http://www.icrc.org>.

16. See for example, M. Dando, 'The Danger to the Chemical Weapons Convention from Incapacitating Chemicals', First CWC Review Conference Paper No. 4, University of Bradford Department of Peace Studies, March 2003, <http://www.brad.ac.uk/acad/scwc/cwcrcp/cwcrcps.htm>; and M. Wheelis, '"Non-Lethal" Chemical Weapons – A Faustian Bargain', *Issues in Science and Technology* (Spring 2003) pp. 74-78; and a later report, '"Non-Lethal" Weapons, the CWC and the BWC', 61 *The CBW Conventions Bulletin* (September 2003) p. 102, <http://www.sussex.ac.uk/spru/hsp/>/pdfbulletin. html>.

17. D. de Luce and O. Burkeman, 'US Accuses Iran of Stockpiling Chemical Arms', *The Guardian* (16 May 2003).

cals to some other CWC States Parties.[18] There were also concerns that the Review Conference might turn into an amendment exercise, something most States Parties were clearly not prepared to entertain.

Perhaps underscoring the pervasive commitment by States Parties to pragmatically achieving consensus and results at the Review Conference, the potentially contentious issues remained topics for the margins of the Conference. Although the ICRC was not allowed to address the Review Conference directly, its Statement and documentation were made available to delegations. The Islamic Republic of Iran, exercising the right of reply, denied the statement of the United States that it had a chemical weapons program and affirmed its compliance with and commitment to the CWC. The statement by the United States was not discussed again in the plenary of the Review Conference and any action further to that statement remains to be seen. Agreed language implicitly referring to the issue of the Australia Group export control policy was eventually reflected in both the Political Declaration and Report of the Review Conference. Conflict was avoided by adopting language that could be interpreted by some States Parties to mean that export control regulations of dual use chemicals needed to be reviewed and, if necessary, adjusted to become consistent with the Convention. At the same time, it could be interpreted by others as meaning that they have the right to continue with the export control measures under the Australia Group.[19]

It was not clear until the end of the second week whether consensus would be achieved on the substantive portions of the Report or whether only a political declaration would be agreed upon. Nevertheless, the primary outcomes of the Review Conference were its Political Declaration[20] and its Report,[21] both of which will be discussed further below.

4.2   The Political Declaration

The Political Declaration was intended primarily for the outside world. It is a reflection of States Parties' views on the role of the CWC in the present security

---

18. See for example, A. Kelle, 'The First CWC Review Conference: Taking Stock and Paving the Way Ahead', in UNIDIR, 4 *Disarmament Forum* (2002) pp. 3 at 6.

19. See for example, paras. 17 and 21 of the Political Declaration of the First Review Conference OPCW Doc. RC-1/3, 9 May 2003: '17. The States Parties reaffirm that national implementation measures must reflect all relevant provisions of the Convention and the comprehensive nature of its prohibitions, to ensure that they apply to all toxic chemicals and precursors except where intended for purposes not prohibited under the Convention, as long as their types and quantities are consistent with such purposes.' and '21. The States Parties ... reaffirm their undertaking not to maintain among themselves any restrictions that are incompatible with the obligations undertaken under the Convention, which would restrict or impede trade and the development and promotion of scientific and technological knowledge in the field of chemistry for peaceful purposes.'

20. Political Declaration of the First Special Session of the Conference of the States Parties to Review the Operation of the Chemical Weapons Convention (First Review Conference), OPCW Doc. RC-1/3, 9 May 2003, <http://www.opcw.org>.

21. Report of the First Special Session of the Conference of the States Parties to Review the Operation of the Chemical Weapons Convention (First Review Conference), OPCW Doc. RC-1/5, 9 May 2003, <http://www.opcw.org>.

environment and reflects their commitment to chemical weapons disarmament, full treaty implementation and to the OPCW. It also calls for universal adherence to the CWC. Concrete action called for in the Political Declaration includes: intensifying States Parties' bilateral and multilateral efforts towards universality of the Convention; the adoption of national implementing legislation; continued efforts to destroy chemical weapons global stockpiles in accordance with the requirements of the CWC; further optimisation of the verification system; efforts to curb CW proliferation; enhancement where possible of the assistance measures States Parties have elected to provide for protection against chemical weapons; enhancement of the OPCW's international cooperation programmes; and development of partnerships with other relevant international and regional organisations.

4.3   The Report of the First Review Conference

From the outset of the preparatory process, the working group did not seek to undertake a systematic article-by-article review but instead structured its work into thematic clusters. Thus, the Report reflects the review of treaty operations, 'taking note' of the impact of science and technology,[22] and gives general guidance and direction to States Parties, the Council and the Secretariat, following the thematic clusters conceived during the preparatory process.

4.3.1   *General issues (the role of the CWC and universality)*

The roles of the CWC and the OPCW remain important to States Parties. While the need for full compliance was emphasised, it was linked to the ability to fully implement the CWC. In the new post-11 September security environment, the contribution of the CWC is considered to be significant for counter-terrorism. The Review Conference noted with concern that, along with the continued threat of the possible use of chemical weapons by states, the international community faces a growing danger of such use by terrorists as well. The importance of universal adherence was stressed and both the quantitative and qualitative aspects of universality were considered. Unspoken but understood was the positive effort needed to encourage adherence by states not party to the CWC in the Middle East and by the Democratic People's Republic of Korea. The Review Conference recommended that the Council and the Secretariat develop an action plan to further encourage, in a systematic and coordinated matter, adherence to the Convention and to assist states ready to join the Convention in their national preparations to implement it. This recommendation became one of the main foci of attention by delegations in the months following the conclusion of the Review Conference.

---

22. The Review Conference left it to the Executive Council to study the recommendations and observations made by the OPCW Scientific Advisory Board in its Report on Developments in Science and Technology (OPCW Doc. RC-1/DG.3, dated 28 April 2003, with a view to preparing recommendations to the Conference on them, <http://www.opcw.org> .

4.3.2   *General obligations and declarations related thereto (Arts. I – III of the CWC)*

The prohibitions under Article I were reaffirmed, together with the definition of 'chemical weapons' and 'chemical weapons production facility', which were found to be adequate to cover developments in science and technology. The Council was requested to consider additional chemicals that may be relevant to the Convention and assess whether these compounds should be considered in the context of the Schedules of Chemicals. All States Parties were called upon to submit the required declarations when due, and the Secretariat was tasked with offering assistance and keeping the Council informed. The Council was called upon to reach agreement on the declaration criteria for former chemical weapons' development facilities, which are necessary to promote confidence among States Parties.

4.3.3   *Verification in general*

The CWC verification system, unique in arms control and disarmament, was reaffirmed as one of the most important provisions of the Convention. Although it was noted with satisfaction that the OPCW had established a verification system that meets the requirements of the Convention, it was felt that efficiency should be increased, i.e., the use of resources should be optimised. The recommendations of the OPCW Scientific Advisory Board were to be taken up by the Council. In respect of declarations, States Parties were called upon to work with the Secretariat to clarify any ambiguities contained in their declarations. The Secretariat was encouraged to apply information technology more effectively in the implementation of the verification regime, including the electronic submission of declarations. In respect of inspections, implementation by all States Parties of the standing arrangements required by the Convention was stressed as being important to the proper conduct of inspections. The Council and Secretariat were requested to intensify the study of how to further optimise the OPCW verification system. In respect of reporting, the Council and Secretariat were encouraged to further improve the form and content of the Verification Implementation Report. Other proposals, such as expert meetings by governments, were dropped at the end.

4.3.4   *Chemical weapons issues*

In this cluster, the language of the report did not go as far as some states would have wanted. The commitments to destruction of chemical weapons and chemical weapons production facilities were reaffirmed, and States Parties that are in a position to do so were called upon to assist possessor States Parties with destruction. The Review Conference stressed to possessor States Parties the importance of securing their storage facilities and preventing any movement of the weapons except for removal for destruction. The timely reimbursement of Articles IV and V verification costs was brought to the attention of States Parties. The Secretariat's intention after 29 April 2003 to inspect all chemical weapons production facilities that are subject to conversion was noted. Progress on the destruction of old chemical weapons was also noted and, in respect of destruction of abandoned chemical weapons, the positive effect of cooperation between the territorial and abandoning States Parties was emphasised.

4.3.5   *Article VI issues (activities not prohibited under the CWC)*

The right of States Parties, subject to the provisions of the Convention, to develop, produce, otherwise acquire, retain, transfer and use toxic chemicals and their precursors for purposes not prohibited under the Convention was reaffirmed and linked to the obligation of States Parties to adopt the necessary measures to ensure that they are only intended for purposes not prohibited in any place under their jurisdiction or control. The Secretariat was encouraged to continue providing technical assistance to States Parties to identify declarable facilities and submit declarations, receive inspections and address other technical questions. Regarding Schedule 1 chemicals, the study of a proposed *de minimis* rule for notification was tasked to the Council. In respect of inspection of Part IX 'other chemical production facilities', it was agreed that there is a need to concur on the selection process and to increase the number of this type of inspection as appropriate. The Council and Secretariat were tasked to resolve outstanding chemical industry cluster issues, improve the submission and handling of industry declarations, refine inspection conduct, improve the Secretariat's reporting and study the need for a recommendation about the future treatment of the salts of Schedule 1 chemicals not specifically mentioned in Schedule 1. The impact on universality of the full and effective implementation of the Schedules 2 and 3 transfer regulations was noted, and the Council was requested to produce a recommendation on whether additional measures are necessary for transfers of Schedule 3 chemicals to states not party to the CWC.

The First Review Conference did not attempt to further develop the verification regime for Verification Annex Part IX 'other chemical production facilities' and further work will remain for the run-up to the Second Review Conference.

4.3.6   *National implementation measures*

The single most important request by the Review Conference, and the one that received most attention by delegations in its aftermath, was its request to the Council to recommend to the Conference at its October 2003 session an Action Plan regarding the implementation of Article VII obligations. The Review Conference noted the status of implementation and agreed that urgent attention is needed to ensure that all States Parties establish a National Authority, enact national implementing legislation and adopt administrative implementation measures. It encouraged States Parties to assist each other with that task which, in view of the fact that the majority of States Parties do not have legislation covering all areas essential to adequately enforce the Convention obligations, would be necessary since it is beyond the resources of the Secretariat to address all the assistance needs in the short term. States Parties were called upon to report before October 2003 on the status of adoption of national implementing legislation, any problems encountered and any assistance needed. The momentum created by the Review Conference carried over into the development of this plan and, indeed, a plan was adopted at the Annual Session of the Conference in October 2003. The Review Conference also interpreted Article VII, paragraph 5, to mean that States Parties are required to submit the actual text of their implementing legislation to the OPCW.

4.3.7 *Article IX issues, including challenge inspections*

States Parties were encouraged to make full use of bilateral consultations to clarify and resolve any doubts about compliance with the Convention. It noted that the Council had received no clarification requests under Article IX and that the challenge inspection provisions of the Convention remain untested. The Review Conference expressed its confidence that States Parties would not abuse the challenge inspection process and requested the Secretariat to continue to maintain a high standard of readiness to conduct such inspections.

4.3.8 *Assistance and protection against chemical weapons*

The Review Conference noted the additional relevance that Article X has in today's security context. It also noted concerns related to the possibility that chemical facilities may become the object of attack, including by terrorists, which could lead to deliberate releases or theft of toxic chemicals. States Parties were called upon to meet their obligation to submit information on their national programmes related to protective purposes and the Council was requested to develop and submit for adoption the procedures for submission of this information. The Secretariat was requested to continue working on the OPCW data bank on protection and States Parties were invited to contribute to it. States Parties which had not met their obligation to elect the measure of assistance they will provide through the OPCW in case of use of chemical weapons were requested to do so. The Review Conference stressed that the OPCW must have the capacity and be ready at all times to investigate allegations of chemical weapons use and to determine the need for follow-up action by the OPCW and by individual Member States, and to facilitate the delivery of assistance. It noted that the Secretariat had established and tested the Assistance Coordination and Assessment Team (ACAT) and declared that defining the overall function of ACAT is an important and urgent matter. It stressed that the OPCW must coordinate its activities in an assistance operation with other international agencies involved in emergency response in order to avoid duplication of efforts.

4.3.9 *International cooperation*

The Review Conference's extensive reaffirmation of the provisions of Article XI disguises the fact that there is deep disagreement over the interpretation of those provisions. Concretely, the Review Conference encouraged the OPCW to establish relations and partnerships with relevant regional and international organisations, including chemical industry associations and civil society, in order to build on existing competencies, develop synergies and avoid duplication of efforts. The Council was tasked with elaborating guiding principles on international cooperation programmes. The Secretariat was charged with taking those guiding principles into account when developing proposals and the Council was requested to apply them when evaluating the Secretariat's reports on international cooperation programmes and proposals for new ones.

4.3.10   Protection of confidential information

The importance attached to the OPCW's protection of confidential information was reiterated. The Review Conference underlined the need for adequate training of staff. It urged States Parties to meet the requirement to provide details on their handling of confidential information provided to them. It also took cognisance of the fact that 85 percent of the information submitted to the Secretariat had been classified as confidential by the originating State Party. It encouraged the Secretariat and States Parties to review their respective practices in assigning levels of classification and to reduce the levels in order to increase work efficiency and ensure the smooth functioning of the confidentiality system. It requested the Secretariat to evaluate which resources would be required to adopt the ISO-17799 information security standard.[23] It noted the need to ensure that confidential information is protected when the OPCW proceeds to electronic submission of declarations.

4.3.11   The functioning of the OPCW

States Parties were called upon to fully participate in the activities of the OPCW's policy-making organs. The Council was urged to increase momentum and strive to conclude the unresolved issues. The importance of the Chairperson and Vice-Chairpersons being engaged with the work of the facilitation groups was noted. The Confidentiality Commission was tasked with being fully operational at all times and the Secretariat was requested to support it. The Review Conference, recognising the important contributions made by the Scientific Advisory Board, recommended that the interaction between the Scientific Advisory Board and delegations should be further enhanced in the context of the Council's facilitation process. The valuable contributions of the Advisory Body for Administrative and Financial Matters were recognised. The Review Conference underlined the importance of putting in place a more effective budgetary process. The dedication of Secretariat staff was noted with satisfaction. The Conference decision on the start date of the tenure policy was welcomed.[24] The Council was counselled to resolve

---

23. ISO-17799 is an internationally recognised generic information security standard with a comprehensive set of rules for best practices in information security. It comprises a code of practice and a specification for an information security management system and is intended to serve as a single reference point for identifying a range of controls needed for most situations where information systems are used in industry and commerce. For more information see <http://www.iso17799software. com>.

without delay the issues of the OPCW's Staff Rules, amendments to Staff Regulation 3.3,[25] and classification of posts. The Review Conference noted the evolving relationship between the OPCW and other international, regional, and sub-regional organisations, and in particular stressed the importance of its relationship with the United Nations.

5.   THE OPEN FORUM

The Open Forum convened by the OPCW on 1 May 2003 at the Peace Palace in The Hague was open to the public and advertised on the OPCW website and in mailings to relevant institutions and interested individuals listed in the OPCW database. It was opened by the OPCW Director-General, Mr Rogelio Pfirter. The keynote speaker, His Excellency, Dr Adolf von Wagner of Germany, former Chairman of the Ad Hoc Committee on Chemical Weapons during the concluding period of CWC negotiations in the Conference on Disarmament in Geneva, delivered a paper on the development, stockpiling and use of toxic chemicals for law enforcement purposes, including domestic riot control purposes under the CWC. Papers were delivered under the rubric 'Implementation of the Chemical Weapons Ban' on the following topics: chemical weapons destruction, status of implementing legislation, Article VI issues and industry verification, and advances in science and technology. Papers were also delivered under the rubric 'the Chemical Weapons Ban and the Use of Incapacitants in Warfare and Law Enforcement' on the following topics: the general purpose criterion, law enforcement, riot control agents, incapacitants, and implications for international humanitarian law. Participating panellists were respectively affiliated with the Bradford University Department of Peace Studies, the Federation of American Scientists, Global Green/USA, Green Cross Russia, the Harvard Sussex Program on CBW Armament and Arms Limitation (HSP), the International Committee of the Red Cross (ICRC), the International Council of Chemical Associations (ICCA), the International Union of Pure and Applied Chemistry (IUPAC), the London School of Economics, and the Mountbatten Centre for International Studies. At the time of writing, arrangements were underway for the papers to appear on the HSP website.[26]

---

24. The authors note that this decision was taken despite the impact that it will undoubtedly have in terms of loss of institutional memory, reduction of operational capacity of the OPCW to implement its mandate, and cost.

25. The version of Staff Regulation 3.3 adopted in July 1999 stipulates that, on reimbursement of national income taxes paid by Secretariat staff on OPCW net salaries and emoluments, the OPCW shall refund to staff the amounts of those taxes paid, but only to the extent that the OPCW is reimbursed the amounts by the State Party concerned (a qualifier that is not consistent with the regulations and practice of other international organisations).

26. <www.sussex.ac.uk/spru/hsp/publications.html>.

6.   CONCLUSIONS AND LESSONS LEARNED

Structurally, the establishment of the working group to prepare for the First Review Conference proved valuable and should be repeated again for the Second Review Conference. To support that working group, a temporary task force should be established in the Secretariat to coordinate the internal review of experience gained by the Secretariat, as well as the preparation of all background materials, the support of the preparatory negotiations of States Parties, and to coordinate the preparation of the Note by the Director-General to the Second Review Conference. Improvements must be made to ensure the timely issuance of the background documents required by the working group. The preparation and editing of such documents needs to be streamlined. Six months should be set aside for the substantive discussions of the working group, and the timing should be such that the work on the draft documents can be completed in good time for the opening of the Review Conference.

Substantively, 37 recommendations were made by the First Review Conference to States Parties, 37 to the Council and 43 to the Secretariat. Many of the recommendations were not new but only reinforced existing trends or tasks. No radical new directions or drastic changes or amendments were suggested. The incremental progress achieved by the OPCW was recognised, past achievements were consolidated and current trends and directions were confirmed. In the current environment of disarmament and arms control, especially in light of some of the events in other fora where earlier advances are even being backtracked, together with the evidence of the decline of political interest in achieving progress in disarmament, the outcome of the First Review Conference for the CWC can be considered to be quite positive on balance. Specific guidance was given and a number of pragmatic recommendations were made. There was no dismantling of the CWC regime; on the contrary, the momentum of the Review Conference has since been maintained and the resulting political commitment and pressure should contribute greatly to improved national implementation of the Chemical Weapons Convention. The deep integration of States Parties into assistance activities through the Action Plan for universality and the one for Article VII implementation, both recently adopted, should ensure the degree of success that will be achieved as follow-up to the First Review Conference.

Did civil society have a voice in the process? During the preparatory phase, the interaction of the Working Group and non-governmental actors was limited to the submission of written material, on invitation by the Working Group's Chairman. During the Review Conference itself, under the Rules of Procedure of the Conference, of the observers, only signatory states are explicitly entitled to make statements and submit their views in writing to the Conference. This is no different from other Review Conferences, although normally NGOs are allowed to make statements in a session specifically set aside for that purpose. This is usually not a formal part of the conference programme but is conducted nevertheless with the Conference president presiding over the proceedings. This did not happen at the First CWC Review Conference. Rather, on 1 May, an 'Open Forum' was convened by the OPCW in which members of civil society participated.

The extent of involvement of NGOs in the preparatory process as well as in the Review Conference itself was thus not as intensive as that enjoyed by NGOs in some other disarmament fora. However, the relationship between the OPCW and NGOs is slowly evolving. This question should be approached more systematically and well before the next Review Conference, and private discussions may be needed with key delegations to gain support for more effective involvement of the NGO community.

What tasks remain for the Second Review Conference? A number are already apparent: the further development of the Verification Annex Part IX regime for 'other chemical production facilities' and the consideration of whether new chemical agents will need to be added to the Schedules annexed to the CWC. Developments in chemical and life science research and chemical manufacturing will continue at a fast pace, posing new challenges to the verification regime of the CWC in the chemical industry. The so called 'General Purpose Criterion' of the CWC will continue to bring any new agents within the scope of CWC prohibitions but enforcement issues will continue to be a challenge. In this context, one should assume that the quality of national implementation will again be an important issue for the review. There are also structural changes within the industry that need to be taken into account: a focus on core business, adaptation to market requirements and production on demand, and the emergence of 'world plants' on the one hand and increased reliance on contractual manufacturing on the other. All tend to increase the complexity of chemical industry operations and need to be assessed in respect of their impact on verification. Regulation, declaration and verification of activities relevant to the CWC will increasingly become a challenge to effective implementation.

The next Review Conference is expected to take place in 2008. This is one year after the ten-year destruction period for chemical weapons, and (only) four years before the maximum possible extension date of the period of CW destruction (10 +5). There is, of course, no use in speculating today about what the situation will be like in five years, but it is clear that this will be a crucial moment for the OPCW to review the progress achieved in the elimination of CW stockpiles, to make realistic projections about what still needs to be achieved, and to consider whether there will then be a need to take certain decisions in respect of the implementation of the destruction provisions of the Convention.

CORRESPONDENTS' REPORTS

CORRESPONDENTS' REPORTS[1]
A Guide to State Practice
Concerning International Humanitarian Law

---

1. Correspondents' Reports is compiled and edited by Avril McDonald and Maria Nybondas, primarily from information provided to the *YIHL* by its correspondents but also drawing on other sources. Dr Avril Mc Donald is Head of the Section of International Humanitarian Law and International Criminal Law, TMC Asser Institute for International Law and Managing Editor of the *Yearbook of International Humanitarian Law*. Maria Nybondas is Assistant Managing Editor of the *Yearbook of International Humanitarian Law*, a researcher at the TMC Asser Institute for International Law and a Ph.D. candidate in international law at the University of Utrecht.

The section does not purport to be a fully inclusive compilation of all international humanitarian law-related developments in every state, reporting in this volume mainly developments since the beginning of 2002 until the end of 2002 that have come to the Yearbook's attention. Developments from early 2003 that are part of a sequence of events starting in 2002 or earlier are noted in brief. Legal developments in early 2002 that were noted in volume 4 of the *YIHL* are not repeated here. Readers are thus advised to consult this section in conjunction with Correspondents' Reports in volume 4. We apologise for this inconvenience. Further, some 2001 humanitarian law-related developments came to our attention after volume 4 went to press and could not be noted there. For the sake of completeness we have included them here. Reference is also included to a number of legal developments which are not strictly-speaking related to IHL but which are nonetheless interesting and relevant for our readers, in particular, relating to justice issues, jurisdictional questions, *jus ad bellum*, state security, human rights, refugee law and terrorism. Presentation of subject matter roughly follows the sequence in the Classification of Documents at pp. 649, with the exception that all cases are grouped together at the end of each report, followed by news of pending developments. Where citations, dates or other details have not been provided, they were not available or obtainable. Where not otherwise specified, comments are prepared by Avril McDonald and Maria Nybondas, mainly based on reports of NGOs and IGOs and news media, *inter alia*. The *YIHL* is actively seeking new correspondents, particularly in Africa, Asia and Latin America. Interested persons and anyone who is willing to contribute information should contact the Managing Editor at A.McDonald@asser.nl.

Editor's Note: The Yearbook has decided not to include information concerning signings or ratifications of treaties. This information, constantly updated and referring to over 100 IHL treaties, is provided by the ICRC at its IHL database: <http://www.icrc.org/ihl>. Current information regarding ratifications, as well as full texts of reservations and declarations, is also available from the UN Treaty Website at <http://untreaty.un.org/>.

ALBANIA

International Criminal Court
☛ Decision of 23 September 2002 of the Constitutional Court on the ICC

'On 23 September 2002, the Constitutional Court concluded that the 1998 Rome Statute of the ICC was compatible with the Albanian Constitution. In particular, the Court examined questions relating to the transfer of jurisdiction to international bodies, to immunity from criminal prosecution provided for by Albanian law for persons serving in several official capacities, and to the principle of *non bis in idem*. The Court concluded that the ICC Statute guaranteed the fundamental human rights and freedoms proclaimed in the Albanian Constitution, including the presumption of innocence, the principle of *nullum crimen sine lege, nullum poena sine lege*, the non-retroactivity of criminal law, the right to be assisted by a lawyer, the independence of judges, presentation to a court before being remanded in custody, and the right to appeal against the verdict. Furthermore, the nonapplicability of the statute of limitations to the crimes within the jurisdiction of the ICC is also in conformity with Albanian legislation. The Court consequently ruled that there were no constitutional obstacles to ratification of the ICC Statute by Albania.'[2]

ANGOLA

Peace Process
☛ Luena Memorandum of Understanding [Memorandum de Entendimento Complementar ao Protocolo de Lusaka Para a Cessação das Hostilidades e Resolução das Demais Questões Militares Pendentes nos Termos do Protocolo de Lusaka], UN Doc. S/2002/ 483 (2002), 4 April 2002

This agreement established an immediate ceasefire and called for UNITA's return to the peace process as laid down in the 1994 Lusaka Protocol.[3]

ARGENTINA

Geneva Law
☛ Statement of the Argentine Republic to the Swiss Confederation rejecting the claim of Britain to extend the application of the indicated Protocols to the Falkland Islands, South Georgia and the South Sandwich Islands, and to accept the competence of the International Fact Finding Commission in accordance with Protocol I in relation to these territories, 9 December 2002[4]

The Argentine Republic on 9 December 2002 rejected the British claim to extend the application of Protocols I and II of the 1949 Geneva Conventions to the Falkland Islands, South

---

2. Source: ICRC Advisory Service, National Implementation of International Humanitarian Law – Biannual update on national legislation and case-law, July-December 2002. <http://www.icrc.org/ Web/eng/siteeng0.nsf/htmlall/5LVLHV/$File/irrc_849_National_Implem.pdf>.
3. For an extended analysis of the Luena Memorandum and the Angolan peace process generally, see further the article by J. Doria in this volume at pp. 25 et seq.
4. The British claim and the Argentine response are reprinted in this volume at pp. 602 et seq.

Georgia and the South Sandwich Islands, and to accept the competence of the International Fact Finding Commission in relation to these territories (see also the British report, *infra*).[5]

Children
- Law No. 25.616, approving Facultative Protocol on the Convention on Children's Rights, concerning the participation of children in armed conflicts. Approved by the Congress on 17 July 2002, promulgated on 9 August 2002, published in *Boletín Oficial* of 12 August 2002, without any reservation or interpretative declaration

Implementation
- The Commission for the Application of International Humanitarian Law (CADIH) agreed to a request of the Ministry of Foreign Affairs that the Legal Council of the Ministry assume the functions of the National Information Office required by Geneva Convention III, Articles 122-124 and Geneva Convention IV, Articles 136-141. The Office was due to be created in 2003 by a Ministerial Resolution.

Cultural Property
- Law No. 25.478 on the Second Protocol of The Hague Convention of 1954 for the Protection of Cultural Property in Case of Armed Conflict. Adopted in The Hague on 26 March 1999, approved by the Congress on 24 October 2001, promulgated on 19 November 1999, published in *Boletín Oficial* of 26 November 2001
- CADIH has presented a request for technical and financial assistance to the government, in order to obtain help with the exploration and identification of cultural property that should be protected in case of armed conflict in Argentine territory. Furthermore, CADIH has asked for help and experience from states that offer cooperation in this field.

Education and Training on International Humanitarian Law
- On 7 October 2002, the ICRC and the Deputy and Senate Chamber organised a seminar for the strengthening of national IHL application measures. The seminar was supported by Parliamentarians for Global Action, the Inter-Parliamentarian Union and CADIH. Two hundred and forty persons attended the seminar: senators, deputies, civil and military authorities, academics and the public. The publication of the seminar proceedings was declared to be of parliamentary interest.

Pending
- Argentina's legislation to implement the ICC Statute

In early February 2002, the Inter-Ministerial Commission created by the government in August 2000 to formulate draft implementing legislation for the Rome Statute made public its first draft and submitted the final version of the draft implementing legislation to the President. On 9 October 2002, the final version of Argentina's implementing legislation was submitted by the President to Congress. It must be approved by both chambers before becoming law. The Argentine project includes all the Statute norms about crimes against humanity, war crimes and genocide. It includes not only all the acts incriminated in Article

---

5. The text is reproduced in the Documentation section of this volume at pp. 602 et seq.

8 of the Statute but also the major breaches of the four Geneva Conventions and Protocol I that were not included in the Rome Statute, for example, starvation of the civilian population in an internal conflict or attacks against installations containing dangerous forces, etc. The project also includes cooperation with the ICC.

☛ The Commission of Study to analyse and evaluate the adaptation of Argentine legislation to the ICC Statute[6] finished its work on 12 February 2002 and its report was presented to the Senate's Foreign Affairs Commission in October 2002.

☛ Project of law on the emblem of the Red Cross proposed by the CADIH to the Argentine Parliament to replace existing Law 2976.[7] This Project of law was rejected. A new proposal will be made in March 2003.

☛ On October 2002, the Deputy Chamber prepared a project of declaration, asking the Executive Power to authorise that the membership of CADIH could be increased by one member of the Deputy Chamber and one of the Senate Chamber.

☛ A project for the modification of the Code of Military Justice, including the specific acts that constitute major breaches of IHL, has been under the examination of the Defense Commission of the Deputy Chamber since August 2002.

José Consigli and Gabriel Valladares

ARMENIA

The Emblem

☛ Law of the Republic of Armenia on the Use and Protection of the Emblems of the Red Cross and Red Crescent. Adopted 5 February 2002, promulgated 2 March 2002, entered into force 2 March 2002

The law regulates the emblem's use as a protective device (by the medical and religious personnel of the armed forces, troops of the Ministry of the Interior, border guards, other military formations and public authorities responsible for action in emergencies, civilian medical units, and the medical personnel of the Armenian Red Cross Society and other National Red Cross and Red Crescent Societies) and as an indicative device (by bodies belonging to the International Red Cross and Red Crescent Movement and, in peacement, by authorised ambulances and aid stations providing free treatment to the injured and sick).[8]

---

6. See 3 *YIHL* (2000) p. 413.
7. Ibid., p. 414.
8. Source: ICRC Advisory Service, National Implementation of International Humanitarian Law – Biannual update on national legislation and case-law, January-June 2002. <http://www.icrc.org/Web/eng/siteeng0.nsf/html/5FLE9G?OpenDocument>.

AUSTRALIA[9]

Armed Forces/Child Soldiers

☛ Minister for Foreign Affairs, Alexander Downer and the Minister Assisting the Minister for Defence, Danna Vale, Joint Media Release: 'Australia Signs Protocol on Child Soldiers', 22 October 2002 <http://www.foreignminister.gov.au/releases/2002/fa151c_02.html>

☛ Defence Instructions (General) PERS 33-4 *Recruitment and Employment of Members Under 18 Years in the Australian Defence Force*, 28 June 2002

On 21 October 2002, Australia signed the 2000 Optional Protocol to the Convention on the Rights of the Child on the Involvement of Children in Armed Conflict. The Optional Protocol raises the age for participation in hostilities from 15 to 18 years and the minimum age for voluntary recruitment to 16 years.

Prior to signature by the Australian Government, the Secretary of the Australian Department of Defence and the Chief of the Australian Defence Force (ADF) issued Defence Instructions (General) PERS 33-4 on 28 June 2002. The purpose of the Instructions was to incorporate the provisions of the Optional Protocol into the ADF's recruitment and deployment procedures. In line with, and exceeding the minimum requirements of, the Optional Protocol, the minimum voluntary recruitment age for the ADF is now 17 years. The Instructions specify that all feasible measures should be taken to ensure that persons under the age of 18 are not deployed to an area of hostilities, in accordance with Australia's international responsibilities.

As at 31 December 2002, Australia had not yet ratified the Optional Protocol. The Optional Protocol must be considered by a parliamentary committee (the Joint Standing Committee on Treaties) which reports to the Parliament of Australia before the Australian government deposits its instrument of ratification. It was anticipated that Australian ratification would occur sometime during 2003.

International Criminal Court

☛ 'The Statute of the International Criminal Court', Report No. 45 of the Joint Parliamentary Standing Committee on Treaties, 14 May 2002 <http://www.aph.gov.au/house/committee/jsct/icc/report/fullreport.pdf>

☛ The Minister for Foreign Affairs Alexander Downer and the Attorney-General Daryl Williams QC, Joint Media Release: 'Australia Ratifies International Criminal Court', 2 July 2002 <http://www.foreignminister.gov.au/releases/2002/fa095b_02.html>

☛ Australian Declaration upon ratification of the ICC Statute, 29 July 2002 <http://un-treaty.un.org/ENGLISH/bible/englishinternetbible/partI/chapterXVIII/treaty10.asp>

The failure of the Australian government to lodge its instrument of ratification of the Rome Statute by 31 December 2001 was explained in the Correspondents' Report for Australia in Vol. 4 of the *YIHL*.[10] Following the federal election in November 2002, the Joint Parliamentary Standing Committee on Treaties (JSCOT) was reconstituted with a new chair, Julie

---

9. Information and commentaries by Tim McCormack, Australian Red Cross Professor of International Humanitarian Law, University of Melbourne and Foundation Director of the Asia-Pacific Centre for Military Law, member of the Board of Editors, *Yearbook of International Humanitarian Law*.

10. See 4 *YIHL* (2001) pp. 443-447.

Bishop. Under Ms Bishop's leadership, the Committee conducted a second public enquiry, this time into the draft implementing legislation for the Rome Statute.[11] Written submissions were received by the Committee and several recommendations for amendment of the draft legislation were included in the Committee's Report. In particular, the submission of the Australian Red Cross was relied upon extensively by the Committee and was cited multiple times in the Report.

JSCOT tabled its Report in May 2002 unanimously recommending Australian ratification of the Rome Statute. Five members of JSCOT appended a joint statement to the Committee Report expressing concern about the potential for the International Criminal Court to act inconsistently with Australia's national interests.[12] The five signatories to the statement all indicated that their qualified support for ratification was conditional on the implementation of all the Committee's recommendations and particularly a declaration of Australia's primary national jurisdiction; reaffirmation that Australia defines the crimes in Articles 6-8 of the Statute in accordance with the definitions assigned to those crimes in the national implementing legislation; and that the Australian government monitor the work of the International Criminal Court and report to Parliament annually.

Entry into force of the Rome Statute had already been triggered following the deposit of the 60th instrument of ratification in New York in April 2002 at the time of the tabling of the JSCOT Report. JSCOT was clearly cognisant of the need for Australia to ratify by 1 July 2002 to be among the original States Parties to the Statute. Following the tabling of JSCOT's Report an intense public debate ensued, with a number of government backbenchers indicating their opposition to Australian support for the Rome Statute, often on ill-informed grounds. The Prime Minister announced on 20 June 2002 that the government had decided to ratify the Rome Statute and that he would proceed with the introduction of draft implementing legislation into Parliament.[13] With uncommon speed and efficiency the draft legislation passed through the requisite stages of parliamentary consideration, entering into law with the Royal Assent of the Governor-General on 27 June 2002.[14] The instrument of ratification was personally carried to New York on 29 June 2002 by the Foreign Ministry's Senior Legal Adviser and deposited in the UN Treaties Office on 1 July 2002.

In an attempt to placate the opponents of the Australian ratification of the Rome Statute, the government drafted a 'Declaration' to accompany the deposit of the instrument of ratification. The Declaration reaffirms the primacy of Australia's national jurisdiction and explains the requirement of the issuance of a certificate by the Attorney-General for the surrender of any person to the International Criminal Court. Most controversially, the Declaration states the Australian understanding 'that the offences in Articles 6, 7 and 8 [of the Statute] will be interpreted and applied in a way that accords with the way they are implemented in Australian domestic law'. The intention behind this particular wording originates from concerns expressed by the five joint signatories of the statement appended to the JSCOT Report – concerns about an alleged lack of precision in the definitions of crimes within the subject matter jurisdiction of the International Criminal Court, opening the possibility for the International Criminal Court to wander from trials of the most serious inter-

---

11. Ibid., pp. 445-446.

12. See the Joint Statement at <http://www.aph.gov.au/house/committee/jsct/icc/report/appendixa.pdf>.

13. See <http://www.pm.gov.au/news/media_releases/2002/media_release1708.htm>.

14. See media release by the Foreign Minister at <http://www.foreignminister.gov.au/releases/2002/fa095a_02.html>.

national crimes in pursuit of politically motivated prosecutions in contempt of the primacy of national jurisdiction.[15] Unfortunately, the choice of wording in the Declaration smacks of national arrogance – a State Party purporting to instruct the Court to follow its implementing legislation rather than the Statute itself. When the text of the Declaration was lodged with the instrument of ratification in New York, it was necessary for the Australian government to add the explicit rider that the Declaration 'is not a reservation' to avoid other States Parties objecting to the words of the Declaration on the grounds that it constituted a reservation inconsistent with Article 120 of the Statute. Australian ratification of the Statute was no sure thing and the opponents of it ran a highly effective and very nearly successful campaign. However, many of the arguments against Australian participation were spurious and misinformed. It is a reasonable expectation that as the International Criminal Court commences its work and establishes its jurisprudential and political credibility many of the arguments that are voiced against it in Australia will evaporate.

- ☛ International Criminal Court Act (No. 41, 2002). Enacted 27 June 2002, entered into force on the date of entry into force of the Rome Statute for Australia, namely 26 September 2002 <http://scaleplus.law.gov.au/html/pasteact/3/3500/rtf/0412002.rtf>
- ☛ International Criminal Court (Consequential Amendments) Act (No. 42, 2002). Enacted 27 June 2002, entered into force on the date of entry into force of the Rome Statute for Australia, namely 1 July 2002 <http://scaleplus.law.gov.au/html/pasteact/3/3501/rtf/0422002.rtf>

The final version of Australia's implementing legislation does not differ extensively either in general approach, structure or content from the original draft legislation described in Vol. 4 of the *YIHL*.[16] Although some amendments were made to the legislation following the tabling of the JSCOT Report, as well as by the Attorney-General's Department and by the Office of Parliamentary Counsel following the normal inter-governmental department review of the draft legislation, overall the final legislation closely resembles the originally tabled drafts.

Of particular interest to international humanitarian lawyers is that Schedule 3 of the International Criminal Court (Consequential Amendments) Act repeals Part II of the Geneva Conventions Act 1957 – the part of the legislation rendering grave breaches of the four Geneva Conventions and of Additional Protocol I crimes under Australian domestic law. Those particular crimes are now all covered under the new legislation and it would be superfluous to deal with them pursuant to two separate pieces of legislation. The Australian Red Cross was keen to ensure that the Geneva Conventions Act continued to operate in respect of alleged grave breaches occurring between 1957 when the legislation became operative and 2002 when the implementing legislation for the Rome Statute took effect. Article 8(b) of the Australian Acts Interpretation Act 1901 covers this particular situation to the effect that the 1957 legislation continues to operate for the period up to the date of its repeal. However, JSCOT did recommend, on the basis of the submission of the Australian

---

15. See Appendix A to the JSCOT Report at <http://www.aph.gov.au/house/committee/jsct/icc/report/appendixa.pdf>.

16. See 4 *YIHL* (2001) at pp. 443-447. For a more detailed discussion of the legislation see T.L.H. McCormack, 'Australia's Legislation for the Implementation of the *Rome Statute*', in M. Neuner, ed., *National Legislation Incorporating International Crimes: Approaches of Civil and Common Law Countries* (Berlin, Berliner Wissenschafts-Verlag 2003) pp. 65-82.

Red Cross, that the government state explicitly that the Geneva Conventions Act 1957 continues to operate for alleged acts committed between 1957 and 2002.[17]

It has become apparent that the relative speed of Parliamentary enactment of the legislation to facilitate ratification of the Rome Statute by the date of its entry into force has come at some cost. For example, the decision to incorporate Australia's new substantive war crimes, crimes against humanity and genocide as a new schedule of crimes into the existing Criminal Code Act 1995 renders those crimes subject to the general criminal law principles of the Code, including issues such as *mens rea* requirements. The Criminal Code Act 1995 deals primarily with domestic crimes and a number of Australian criminal lawyers have begun to query whether or not it is desirable to spell out the elements of international crimes in the detailed way followed in the implementing legislation but then to subject those international crimes and their elements to general principles usually only applicable to domestic crimes. The extent to which the legislation is ever relied upon remains to be seen. The Geneva Conventions Act, for example, has been operative for 46 years and not a single prosecution has been initiated in that time – despite the fact that the legislation allows Australian courts to exercise universal jurisdiction in respect of alleged grave breaches. It seems hardly likely, given that paucity of utilisation, that the International Criminal Court (Consequential Amendments) Act is about to open the floodgates of Australian trials of alleged perpetrators of international crimes.

Establishment of the Asia-Pacific Centre for Military Law
☛ Minister for Defence Senator the Hon. Robert Hill, Media Release: Launch of NewMilitary Law Centre, 8 August 2002 <http://www.minister.defence.gov.au/Hilltpl.cfm?CurrentId=1770> [Centre Website at: <http://www.apcml.org>]

On 8 August 2002 the Minister for Defence, Senator Robert Hill, publicly launched the Asia-Pacific Centre for Military Law at HMAS Penguin in Sydney. The Centre is a new collaborative initiative of the University of Melbourne Law School and the Australian Defence Force Legal Service with the aim of facilitating cooperation amongst military forces of the Asia-Pacific Region in the research, training and implementation of the laws governing military operations.

The Centre has a University node operating at the Law School in Melbourne and a military node temporarily based at Randwick Army Barracks in Sydney. The Centre conducts a number of activities including annual training courses in Operations Law for Commanders and Planning Staff, Operations Law for Legal Advisers, Civil and Military Cooperation (CIMIC) in Military Operations and the Law of Peace Operations. Courses commenced in 2002 involving officers from militaries in South East and East Asia and the South Pacific participating alongside Australian Defence Force officers. In the case of the CIMIC Course in particular, participants also include representatives of both the inter-governmental community, the humanitarian non-government community and the International Committee of the Red Cross. The Centre is the Australian partner in the international 'Challenges of Peacekeeping Project' coordinated by the Swedish Folke Bernadotte Academy. The Rt. Hon. Sir Ninian Stephen is the Foundation Patron of the Centre.

---

17. See Recommendation 9 of the JSCOT Report on p. 105 at <http://www.aph.gov.au/house/committee/jsct/icc/report/fullreport.pdf.

Cases (Application of Article 1(F) of the Refugee Convention)
- *SRJJJ* v. *Minister for Immigration & Multicultural & Indigenous Affairs*, [2002] *AATA* 264 (17 April 2002) <http://www.austlii.edu.au/cgi-bin/disp.pl/au/cases/cth/aat/2002/264.html>

Applicant 'SRJJJ' (real name not disclosed) was born in Kosovo and claimed to have worked as a police officer from 1972 to 1990. He further claimed that he was 'thrown out of the police force' when the Serbian authorities extended their control over Kosovo in 1990. SRJJJ then managed a shop until the Serbian Army occupied the town in which he lived in 1999. He fled to Macedonia with his family and stayed in a refugee camp for about two months until Australia granted him and his family a temporary protection visa. SRJJJ applied for a permanent protection visa in 2000.

In his protection visa application, SRJJJ indicated that he feared for his safety and that of his family if he returned to Kosovo. During his time as a police officer SRJJJ claimed that he was 'ordered to fulfil [his] duties which were: arresting, intimidating, imprisonment and sometimes [he] was forced to shoot'. The administrative decision-maker apparently relied upon this statement to exclude SRJJJ from the protection of the Refugee Convention in accordance with Article 1(F)(a).

Before the Tribunal, SRJJJ conceded that he arrested people suspected of committing crimes but denied ever saying that he had used force in order to extract confessions and information. He claimed to only have used a baton in self-defence. He denied having said that he shot people, and denied any knowledge of police using 'torture techniques'. This gave rise to a series of apparent inconsistencies in his evidence, which SRJJJ claimed arose from interpretation errors; SRJJJ is not literate in English, and at the initial interview, the interpreter was Albanian, whereas SRJJJ speaks Croatian. In further support of his position that he was not a violent person and had not committed crimes against humanity, SRJJJ tendered character evidence which depicted him as a friendly, honest and hardworking person who contributed to his community.

The Minister for Immigration submitted that there were serious reasons for considering that in his employment as a police officer, SRJJJ regularly engaged in cruel and brutal treatment of suspected criminals, in breach of human rights. The Minister contended that SRJJJ was deliberately misleading the Tribunal and that the inconsistencies in his evidence should be construed against him.

Tribunal Member Handley determined that the claimed 'mistranslation' from the initial interview was too extensive to be plausible. However, in light of the considerable character evidence and the applicant's demeanour before him, he also determined that SRJJJ's claims in the protection visa application were exaggerated in order to give support to his fear of return to Kosovo. The Tribunal was not convinced of sufficiently strong evidence of SRJJJ's participation in crimes against humanity in Kosovo to exclude him from the protection of the Refugee Convention.

- *SAH* v. *Minister for Immigration & Multicultural & Indigenous Affairs*, [2002] *AATA* 263 (18 April 2002) <http://www.austlii.edu.au/au/cases/cth/aat/2002/263.html>

Applicant 'SAH' (real name not disclosed) applied to the Australian Administrative Appeals Tribunal ('the Tribunal') for review of an administrative decision denying his application for refugee status in Australia. His application had been rejected on the basis that there were serious reasons for considering that SAH had committed a war crime or a crime against humanity within the meaning of Article 1(F)(a) of the Refugee Convention, excluding SAH from its protection.

SAH was an Iraqi national and a Shi'a Moslem. He arrived in Australia by boat at the end of 2000 accompanied by his second wife and children. SAH was involuntarily conscripted to the Iraqi national army after graduating from university in 1985. He was discharged from the army in 1990 at the end of the Anfal Campaign against the Kurds. He was recalled to the army six months later as a result of the war against Kuwait. When his unit was given orders to mobilise, he deserted the army and returned to his family. He remained in hiding until the uprising by the Kurds and Shi'a Moslems in March 1991, in which he participated by encouraging people to join the uprising and by distributing supplies. It appeared that a death sentence had been passed on SAH *in absentia* for deserting the army and for his part in the uprising. SAH fled to Iran when the Iraqi army came to crush the uprising, where he stayed until coming to Australia. He left Iran to alleviate the Iraqi government's security measures against his first wife, who had undergone arrest and torture and deprivation of rations.

The Tribunal's Deputy President Forgie provided information on the atrocities committed as part of the Anfal Campaign and the Iraqi invasion of Kuwait. SAH was adamant that despite being in active service during the campaigns, he had only ever been an administrative officer and had never been involved in battle. He claimed that he had been involved in the distribution of food and clothes to the regiment. As a Shi'a Moslem, he was not trusted with the distribution of munitions. He did, however, admit to knowing about the atrocities committed but claims that his function precluded him from participation in their commission.

Discussion of the law applicable to the interpretation of Article 1(F)(a) now follows a standard format in Tribunal reasoning. Most notably, in determining the definition of crimes against humanity and war crimes as set out in Article 1(F)(a), Tribunal members commonly draw on the Nuremberg Charter, common Article 3 of the Geneva Conventions, the Statutes of the *ad hoc* International Criminal Tribunals for the former Yugoslavia and Rwanda and the Rome Statute of the International Criminal Court.

Similarly, there is a standard recitation of the prerequisites for serious reasons for considering that an applicant may be liable as an accessory to war crimes or crimes against humanity. Reference is made to Articles 25(3)(b) and (c) of the Rome Statute and Article 6 of the Nuremberg Charter to the effect that accessorial liability will be found where the accused knowingly contributes to a common criminal objective or purpose: see *W97/164*, [1988] *AATA* 618 (10 June 1988) <http://www.austlii.edu.au/au/cases/cth/aat/1988/618.html>.

Deputy President Forgie found that the Iraqi army committed war crimes and crimes against humanity during both the Anfal Campaign and the invasion of Kuwait. He also held that SAH was a member of the Iraqi army when these atrocities were committed. It is clear from the preceding discussion of the applicable law that the direct commission of an act is not the only way that criminal responsibility can be engaged. Where a person aids, abets or otherwise assists in the commission of a crime, or is complicit in its commission, that person may be held responsible as an accessory. Deputy President Forgie held that:

'[m]erely supplying clothes and food and paying salaries as an administrative officer to Army personnel without any evidence of any closer involvement in the activities amounting to war crimes and crimes against humanity does not make him part of any common purpose in carrying out those activities. That is so even though he may, as part of his service activities, have supplied clothes and food to, and paid the salaries of, those soldiers engaged in the activities.'

As a result, Deputy President Forgie was not satisfied of sufficiently strong evidence of SAH's participation in war crimes or crimes against humanity to exclude the protection of the Refugee Convention and he set aside the administrative decision.

☛ *AXOIB* v. *Minister for Immigration & Multicultural Affairs*, [2002] *AATA* 365 (17 May 2002) <http://www.austlii.edu.au/au/cases/cth/aat/2002/365.html>

Applicant 'AXOIB' was a Sri Lankan national. His family had strong political associations with the United National Party (UNP), which governed Sri Lanka for 17 years, ending in 1994. As noted by the Australian Administrative Appeals Tribunal Deputy President Wright, during the reign of the UNP there were many arbitrary arrests, extra-judicial murders and widespread use of torture against opponents of the UNP, most notably against members of the LTTE (Tamil Tigers).

AXOIB was a member of the UNP for 14 years, commencing in 1982. Throughout that time he was employed by the UNP, including as Assistant Secretary, with responsibility for over 100 branches of the UNP. In his protection visa application, AXOIB claimed that in 1988 he wrote a report exposing and naming certain subversive elements who were subsequently arrested and 'punished' by the Sri Lankan security forces. He repudiated this claim before the Tribunal. He did agree, however, that as Assistant Secretary he was required to obtain information about terrorist activities and their methods of operation so that law enforcement authorities could deal with them.

The inconsistencies and contradictions in the evidence given by AXOIB were viewed unfavourably by Deputy President Wright, who stated that: 'I regard the applicant as a patently unreliable witness … his obvious evasions were unconvincing and exposed him as a deliberate liar.' The Tribunal concluded that there was little doubt that AXOIB was well aware that in reporting people to the UNP they could be tortured and detained or killed by the army or security forces. The Minister to whom AXOIB directly reported is documented as having headed a group of thugs who engaged in activities leading to murder, illegal detention and disappearances. Deputy President Wright was 'convinced that the applicant was aware of these activities … although he denied such knowledge.' It is apparent that the adverse character findings were extremely relevant in a case turning largely on circumstantial evidence.

Whilst the Tribunal did not find sufficient evidence implicating AXOIB in the commission of war crimes or crimes against humanity as a principal actor, it did find that the applicant was involved as an accomplice. The Tribunal noted that Article 7 of the Rome Statute includes torture in its definition of crimes against humanity and that both murder and ill treatment of persons can constitute war crimes. Whilst there was no direct admission from the applicant that he knew that the people he reported were, in fact, tortured or killed, he was deemed to have been aware that this was the likely consequence of his reporting them. According to Deputy President Wright, 'his clear awareness of the terror campaign being waged by both the government and anti-government forces [meant] that he knew full well that they would be assaulted by the security forces'.

Deputy President Wright concluded that there were serious reasons for considering that AXOIB aided and abetted the commission of war crimes or crimes against humanity by reporting individuals to the security forces 'if he knew the outcome of his impugned conduct was likely to be torture or murder of those individuals'. The intent to achieve such a result, 'could and should be inferred' in this case. Furthermore, there was no suggestion of coercion or duress to exculpate the applicant's conduct. The applicant was therefore excluded from the protection of the Refugee Convention.

☞ *WAV* v. *Minister for Immigration & Multicultural Affairs*, [2002] *AATA* 463 (14 June 2002) <http://www.austlii.edu.au/au/cases/cth/aat/2002/463.html>

Applicant 'WAV' was an Afghani national of Tajik ethnicity. During the Communist reign in Afghanistan, he worked as a prison officer in Kabul. His role mostly involved liaising with family members of people held within the prison. Once the Taliban took control, however, he became fearful for his life and moved around within the country. He came to Australia with the assistance of people smugglers in 2001, accompanied by his wife and children, who were granted protection visas. His application was refused on the ground that there were serious reasons for considering that he had committed war crimes or crimes against humanity during his time as a prison officer.

The claim that there were serious reasons for considering that WAV had committed war crimes or crimes against humanity was based on the fact that the State Intelligence Service – KHAD – had a compound within the prison at which WAV worked. WAV maintained that the KHAD operated in secret and that he had no direct contact with KHAD nor did he participate in its activities. The ordinary prison officers had no access to the KHAD compound within the prison. The only contact that WAV ever had with KHAD was if a KHAD prisoner was executed or transferred to the regular prison, in which case the applicant would sometimes advise the prisoner's family. WAV maintained that the passing on of information does not constitute participation in a crime against humanity.

Deputy President Wright concurred with this argument. Despite general evidence being tendered about the civilian police force in Kabul providing KHAD with assistance, including the arrest and torture of suspects, this evidence was held to be insufficiently detailed to found a claim for accessorial liability on the part of WAV. The applicant's testimony had been inconsistent in places, giving rise to 'suspicion' about his innocence, but 'mere suspicion is not enough'. The evidence in this case did not demonstrate serious reasons for considering that WAV was involved in an organisation with a 'limited brutal purpose' or that he was personally engaged in activities within the police force which afforded him knowledge of torture or unlawful killings and implicated him in an accessorial role. The applicant was not excluded from the protection of the Refugee Convention.

☞ *SAL* v. *Minister for Immigration & Multicultural & Indigenous Affairs*, [2002] *AATA* 1164 (12 November 2002) <http://www.austlii.edu.au/au/cases/cth/aat/2002/1164.html>

Applicant 'SAL' was an Uzbek of the Muslim Sunni religion born in Afghanistan. He fled Afghanistan for Australia in 2001 and applied for refugee status on the grounds that his life was endangered by the Taliban because of his ethnicity and by the Uzbek militia because he had refused to fight with the militia against the Taliban.

Between 1984 and 1992, SAL was employed by the State Intelligence Services – KHAD – and was based in the Samangan province, not far from Kabul. Had he not joined KHAD, he would have had to join the army, which he did not want to do. Throughout his career he was promoted many times, eventually holding the rank of Major. From 1988, he was based at the main security compound in Samangan. The compound did not have a prison or detention facilities.

SAL described his role as involving the interviewing of mullahs throughout the province and reporting back to his superiors on the results of the interviews. He was not armed and generally did not wear a uniform. It was not his job to arrest or detain people or even to give orders to others to do so; that was the domain of other units. Furthermore, he did not have access to any interrogation rooms. His boss did have access to such a room, but SAL claimed he did not know what happened there as it was 'seriously secret'.

The main question to be determined by the Tribunal was whether SAL had any part to play – directly or indirectly – in any acts of atrocity. Expert evidence on the nature of KHAD and its activities was relied upon by the Minister for Immigration. According to that evidence, only people very loyal to the government were selected to work for KHAD. Promotions within KHAD depended upon proving loyalty by conducting arrests, interrogations, torture and even executions. According to the expert testimony, anyone employed with KHAD would have to have been personally involved in such activity. The expert gave evidence that he did not find it plausible that SAL would not know what his colleagues were doing.

Deputy President Forgie quoted the conclusion of Deputy President Wright in *AXOIB* (discussed above) that there were 'serious reasons for considering that he aided and abetted either war crimes or crimes against humanity by reporting individuals ... if he knew the outcome of his impugned conduct was likely to be torture or murder of those individuals'.

Deputy President Forgie held that SAL was an officer of KHAD at a time when the organisation committed war crimes and crimes against humanity. He also held that there was strong evidence that SAL would have been aware of the activities KHAD engaged in, even if he was not directly involved. He concluded that SAL was aware that his reporting of information had consequences for those whom he reported. Whilst SAL 'distanced himself from these consequences', as they were carried out by others, the Tribunal held that there was strong evidence that he made his reports in the knowledge that KHAD was likely to engage in activities amounting to crimes against humanity. This was considered to constitute strong evidence that SAL had participated in war crimes and/or crimes against humanity and so he was excluded from the protection of the Refugee Convention pursuant to Article 1(F)(a).

☞ *VAG* v. *Minister for Immigration & Multicultural & Indigenous Affairs*, [2002] *AATA* 1332 (23 December 2002) <http://www.austlii.edu.au/au/cases/cth/aat/2002/1332.html>

Applicant 'VAG' was an Iraqi Kurd, of the Sunni Moslem faith. In the early 1960s, he was involved in Kurdish political organisations. He surrendered himself to Iraqi authorities in 1974 and signed a declaration acknowledging that he would be executed if he became involved in such organisations again. Despite having signed the declaration, in 1976 he joined the Patriotic Union of Kurdistan (PUK) and worked secretly for it in his town. VAG claimed that in 1986 the Iraqi authorities became aware of his involvement in the PUK and issued a warrant for his arrest but he managed to avoid arrest. He participated in the Kurdish revolt against the Iraqi regime in 1991 as a political worker, distributing propaganda and protecting public buildings and documents.

After the uprising, parts of Iraq were under Kurdish control and, in 1991 VAG became a political leader of the PUK in a province of about 25,000 people. However, he conceded that his role in the PUK was not a very senior one. In 1993 members of the PUK fought the

Islamic Revolutionary Party near to VAG's town and 150 prisoners were captured and brought to the town to be detained. VAG organised for injured prisoners to be treated and for relatives to be informed of their whereabouts. Most of the prisoners were collected the next day and removed to another location. VAG had been informed that all were subsequently released, except for two prisoners who were killed. VAG did not know anything about the circumstances surrounding their deaths, but he was concerned that the relatives of those who had died would blame him for the deaths.

In 1994 VAG was suspended from the PUK due to his criticism of the way it was operating. He rejoined the party but did not continue in a political role. In 1995 the PUK appointed him as Head of Authorities for Soran Province – a civil administrative role ensuring that there was adequate food, housing and safety for the people in the province. After holding this role, VAG became the head of the Martyr's Department, which is not affiliated with any political party and helps Kurdish families who have lost family members in the Kurdish struggle. He retired from that position in 2001 and since retiring 'no longer enjoy[s] the protection of the PUK'. He understands that his name is on a death list held by the Islamic Revolutionary Party.

There was no evidence that VAG was directly involved in the commission of war crimes or crimes against humanity, so potential accessorial liability was the Tribunal's focus. The submission of the Minister for Immigration that there were serious reasons for considering that VAG was an accomplice to the commission of war crimes or crimes against humanity rested on two main points. The first was that the Kurdish Democratic Party (KDP) and PUK had been involved in countless human rights violations over the years, including torture, executions and arbitrary arrest. The second was that due to the level of VAG's duties and knowledge of the PUK's activities, he was a knowing participant in the crimes committed by members of the PUK. VAG's evidence suggested that whilst he had been politically active with the PUK for a long time, he was not involved in fighting, nor did he have any control over those who were; he was only ever engaged in purely political activities. His general association with the PUK was not a sufficient basis to give rise to strong grounds for considering that he was an accomplice to war crimes or crimes against humanity as he was not in a position 'where he could influence the course of events ... [and] there is no evidence that he participated in acts of atrocity, was present at any as a bystander or instigated or directed any'.

However, the killings of the two prisoners who had been in his care and were subsequently transferred and then executed raised different questions. The killings appear to be extra-judicial in nature and could therefore constitute a war crime or crime against humanity. Members of the PUK carried out the two killings, but there was no evidence suggesting that VAG knew that this would occur once the prisoners left his control. Deputy President Forgie dealt with this issue in the following way:

> 'VAG was at arm's length from the killings that ultimately occurred and there is no evidence to suggest that he was able to prevent their occurring. Unlike an informer who may be able to choose whether or not he passes on information, this was not a case in which VAG could choose not to send the prisoners as he had been directed to do without consequence to himself ... I do not consider that he can be said to have been part of any common purpose in carrying out the killings.'

As a result, VAG was not excluded from the protection of the Refugee Convention.

TIM McCORMACK

AUSTRIA[18]

Law of Armed Conflict

☛ Federal Law amending *inter alia* the Penal Code [Bundesgesetz, mit dem das Strafgesetzbuch, die Strafprozessordnung 1975, das Strafvollzugsgesetz, das Suchtmittelgesetz, das Gerichtsorganisationsgesetz, das Waffengesetz 1996, das Fremdengesetz 1997 und das Telekommunikationsgesetz geändert werden (Strafrechtsänderungsgesetz 2002)]. Adopted by Parliament on 25 July 2002, entered into force on 1 October 2002, published in the Austrian Federal Law Gazette, *BGBl* [*Bundesgesetzblatt*][19] I Nr. 134/2002. For the Explanatory Memorandum see *RV* [*Regierungsvorlage*] 1166 *BlgNR* [*Beilagen zu den Stenographischen Protokollen des Nationalrates*][20] 21, *GP* [*Gesetzgebungsperiode*]

This law amends the provision in paragraph 320 of the Penal Code concerning the unlawful support of parties to armed conflicts. Subparagraph 2 of this provision stipulates that the prohibition on support to parties of an armed conflict does not apply to situations where any of the following decisions are implemented: a decision of the Security Council of the United Nations, a decision on the basis of title V of the Treaty on the European Union, a decision within the framework of the OSCE, or any other peace operation in the framework of an international organisation in conformity with the principles of the Charter of the United Nations, such as measures to avert a humanitarian catastrophe or to stop severe and systematic human rights violations.

Prisoners of War

☛ Federal Law amending the Federal Law on the Compensation of Prisoners of War [Bundesgesetz, mit dem das Kriegsgefangenenentschädigungsgesetz geändert wird]. Entered into force on 1 January 2002, adopted by Parliament on 21 February 2002, published in *BGBl* I Nr. 40/2002. For the Explanatory Memorandum see *RV 944 BlgNR* 21, *GP*

With this law the right to claim compensation according to the Federal Law on the Compensation of Prisoners of War was extended to persons who were taken as prisoners of war by the Western Allies, as well as to civilian internees having been detained outside Austrian territory, and to persons residing outside Austria.

Children

☛ Optional Protocol to the Convention on the Rights of the Child on the involvement of children in armed conflict [Fakultativprotokoll zum Übereinkommen über die Rechte des Kindes betreffend die Beteiligung von Kindern an bewaffneten Konflikten]. According to its Article 10(1), this Agreement entered into force on 12 February 2002, published in *BGBl* III Nr. 92/2002. For the Explanatory Memorandum see *RV 766 BlgNR* 21, *GP*

---

18. Information and commentaries by Dr Thomas Desch, Federal Ministry of Defence, Vienna, and Mag. Peter Kustor, Federal Chancellery, Vienna.
19. The Federal Law Gazette is also available at <http://www.ris.bka.gv.at>.
20. Parliamentary documents are also available at <http://www.parlament.gv.at>.

On the occasion of the ratification of this Optional Protocol on 1 February 2002, Austria made the following Declaration according to Article 3(2) of the Optional Protocol:

'Under Austrian law the minimum age for the voluntary recruitment of Austrian citizens into the Austrian army (Bundesheer) is 17 years.'

According to § 15, in conjunction with § 65c of the Austrian National Defence Act 1990 (Wehrgesetz 1990), the explicit consent of parents or other legal guardians is required for the voluntary recruitment of a person between 17 and 18 years.

The provisions of the Austrian National Defence Act 1990, together with the subjective legal remedies guaranteed by the Austrian Federal Constitution, ensure that legal protection in the context of such a decision is afforded to volunteers under the age of 18. A further guarantee derives from the strict application of the principles of the rule of law, good governance and effective legal protection.

Cultural Property
- Regulation of the Federal Minister for Education, Science and Culture in the field of the Federal Law concerning restrictions on the possession of objects of historical, artistic or cultural value [Verordnung der Bundesministerin für Bildung, Wissenschaft und Kultur über Regelungen auf dem Gebiet des Denkmalschutzgesetzes (Denkmalschutzverordnung – DMSVO)]. Entered into force 1 March 2002, published in *BGBl* II Nr. 97/2002

This Regulation provides *inter alia* for details for the selection, classification, registration and identification of cultural property under the Hague Convention on the Protection of Cultural Property in the Event of Armed Conflict of 1954, thus implementing Paragraph 13 of the Federal Law concerning restrictions on the possession of objects of historical, artistic or cultural value.[21]

Chemical Weapons
- Agreement between the Republic of Austria and the Organisation for the Prohibition of Chemical Weapons on the Privileges and Immunities of the OPCW [Abkommen zwischen der Republik Österreich und der Organisation für das Verbot chemischer Waffen über die Privilegien und Immunitäten der OPCW]. According to its Article 12(1), this Agreement entered into force on 1 September 2002, published in *BGBl* III Nr. 200/2002. For the Explanatory Memorandum see *RV 964 BlgNR* 21, *GP*

Whereas the 1997 Convention on the Prohibition of the Development, Production, Stockpiling and Use of Chemical Weapons and on Their Destruction only contains certain provisions concerning privileges and immunities of the Director-General and the staff of the Technical Secretariat of the OPCW during the conduct of verification activities, this Agreement extends the privileges and immunities to the Organisation as a whole and its personnel in order to facilitate the performing of its functions in Austria.

---

21. Cf., 3 *YIHL* (2000) p. 421.

Nuclear Weapons

☛ Statement by H.E. Dr Benita Ferrero-Waldner, Federal Minister for Foreign Affairs of Austria, on the occasion of the Fifth Anniversary of the CTBTO Preparatory Commission, Vienna, 18 March 2002 <http://www.un.int/austria/Statements/docs/2002/ctbto.html>[22]

At the time when the Foreign Minister delivered the Statement, five years had elapsed since the Executive Secretary and a small team of experts of the Provisional Technical Secretariat of the Comprehensive Test Ban Treaty Organisation (CTBTO) Preparatory Commission had taken up their work at the Vienna International Centre. The Secretariat had evolved into a full-fledged international organisation with some 280 staff members and an annual budget of almost $84 million. The Foreign Minister called upon all States Signatories to continue to provide the CTBTO Preparatory Commission and the Provisional Technical Secretariat with sufficient support for the timely establishment of the International Monitoring System. This would include the creation of a global verification network of 321 monitoring stations and 16 radionuclide laboratories. The first of the planned laboratories was the radionuclide laboratory at Seibersdorf, Austria, formally certified by the Provisional Technical Secretariat in Autumn of 2001 and formally opened in December 2001. Proficiency tests had demonstrated that this laboratory would be capable of detecting extremely tiny concentrations of 'suspicious' radionuclides stemming from nuclear tests.

International Criminal Tribunals

☛ Memorandum of Understanding between the Federal Government of Austria and the United Nations on the Extension and Amendment of the Memorandum of Understanding between the Federal Government of Austria and the United Nations for the Loan of Prison Staff to the International Criminal Tribunal for the former Yugoslavia[23] [Vereinbarung zwischen der Österreichischen Bundesregierung und den Vereinten Nationen über die Verlängerung und Abänderung der Vereinbarung zwischen der Österreichischen Bundesregierung und den Vereinten Nationen zur leihweisen Beistellung von Gefängnispersonal an den Internationalen Strafgerichtshof für das ehemalige Jugoslawien]. Entered into force on 1 June 2002. The Agreement is laid up for insight at the Federal Ministry for Foreign Affairs (cf., Austrian Federal Law Gazette, *BGBl* III Nr. 143/2002)

On 10 May 2002 the ICTY delivered for the first time for imprisonment in Austria two persons from Bosnia and Herzegovina sentenced for crimes against humanity. This delivery is based on the Agreement between the United Nations and the Federal Government of Austria on the Enforcement of Sentences of the International Criminal Tribunal for the former Yugoslavia of 1999.[24]

---

22. For Austrian Statements in the framework of the UN in general, see <http://www.un.int/austria/Statements/>.

23. For the original version of the agreement cf., 3 *YIHL* (2000) p. 422.

24. Ibid., p. 423.

International Criminal Court

☞ Rome Statute of the International Criminal Court [Römisches Statut des Internationalen Strafgerichtshofs samt Erklärung der Republik Österreich]. According to its Article 126 (1), the Agreement entered into force on 1 July 2002. Published in *BGBl* III Nr. 180/ 2002

As Articles 27(1) and 89(3) of the Rome Statute, when incorporated in the Austrian legal order, would modify or complement Austrian constitutional law, they had to be approved by the Austrian Parliament with a qualified majority. When depositing its instrument of ratification on 28 December 2000, the Republic of Austria made the following Declaration:

'Pursuant to Article 87 para. 2 of the Rome Statute the Republic of Austria declares that requests for cooperation and any documents supporting the request shall either be in or be accompanied by a translation into the German language.'

☞ Federal Law on the Cooperation with the International Criminal Court [Bundesgesetz über die Zusammenarbeit mit dem Internationalen Strafgerichtshof], entered into force on 1 October 2002. Published in *BGBl* I Nr. 135/2002. For the draft text and the Explanatory Memorandum see *RV 1168 BlgNR* 21. *GP*

The Austrian Parliament (on 10 July 2002 the Austrian National Council and on 25 July 2002 the Federal Council) adopted this Federal Law, which specifies Austria's obligation to cooperate with the International Criminal Court. It obliges all organs of the Federation, in particular the courts, the public prosecutors, the relevant authorities for the execution of sentences and the security authorities, to comprehensively cooperate with the International Criminal Court, including its Chambers and the Presidency, the Prosecutor and the Registrar. It entails provisions concerning the granting of access to information and documents on suspected crimes falling within the competence of the Court, the provision of judicial assistance to the Court, the deliverance of arrested persons to the Court, the acceptance of sentenced persons for imprisonment and the execution of fines.

Terrorism

☞ International Convention for the Suppression of the Financing of Terrorism [Internationales Übereinkommen zur Bekämpfung der Finanzierung des Terrorismus], ratified by Austria on 15 April 2002. According to its Article 26(2), it entered into force for Austria on 15 May 2002. Published in *BGBl* III Nr. 102/2002, and the internationally corrected version in *BGBl* III Nr. 103/2002. For the text, draft translation into German and Explanatory Memorandum see *RV 902 BlgNR* 21. *GP*

This Convention applies, *inter alia*, to the financing of any act intended to cause death or serious bodily injury to a civilian or any other person not taking an active part in the hostilities in a situation of armed conflict, when the purpose of such act, by its nature or context, is to intimidate a population, or to compel a government or an international organisation to do or to abstain from doing any act (cf., Art. 2(1)(b)).

☞ Federal Law amending, *inter alia*, the Penal Code [Bundesgesetz, mit dem das Strafgesetzbuch, die Strafprozessordnung 1975, das Strafvollzugsgesetz, das Suchtmittelgesetz, das Gerichtsorganisationsgesetz, das Waffengesetz 1996, das Fremdengesetz 1997 und das Telekommunikationsgesetz geändert werden (Strafrechtsänderungsgesetz 2002)]. Entered into force on 1 October 2002, published in *BGBl* I Nr. 134/2002. For the Explanatory Memorandum see *RV* 1166 *BlgNR* 21. *GP*

This law introduces into the Penal Code a new provision concerning the financing of terrorism (para. 278(d)), thereby implementing the 1999 International Convention for the Suppression of the Financing of Terrorism into Austrian law.

THOMAS DESCH and PETER KUSTOR

AZERBAIJAN

The Emblem

☞ Law of the Republic of Azerbaijan 'on the changes and additions to the criminal code of the Republic of Azerbaijan and the code of administrative offences of the Republic of Azerbaijan' in keeping with the law 'on the use and protection of the red cross and red crescent emblems'. Adopted and promulgated on 16 April 2002, entered into force on 23 June 2002, published in *Azerbaijan (Official Gazette)*, No. 141 (3153) of 23 June 2002

'Essentially, it amends the Criminal Code in order to add penalties for misuse in wartime of the distinctive signals and the names "Red Cross" and "Red Crescent" and of signs that constitute an imitation of the red cross or red crescent emblems. It also adds penalties to the Code of Administrative Offences for such misuse in time of peace.'[25]

BELGIUM[26]

Cases

☞ *Case concerning the Arrest Warrant of 11 April 2000 (The Democratic Republic of the Congo* v. *Belgium)*, International Court of Justice, Judgement of 14 February 2002[27]

☞ Proceedings against *Abdulaye Yerodia Ndombasi and L.-D. Kabila*, Chamber of indictments of the Brussels Court of Appeals, Decision of 16 April 2002, *JLMB* [*Jurisprudence de Liège, Mons et Bruxelles*] (2002), liv. 21, p. 918 <www.ulb.ac.be/droit/cdi/fichiers/CMA-Yerodia-0402.rev.pdf>

☞ *Cour de cassation*, Judgement of 22 November 2002 (not yet published) <www.ulb.ac.be/droit/cdi/fichiers/arret-cass-Yerodia.pdf>

On 14 February 2002, the ICJ decided, against Belgium and in favour of the Democratic Republic of the Congo (DRC), that the Court had jurisdiction to entertain the DRC application, that the application was admissible and that the case was not moot.[28] As to the merits,

---

25. Source: ICRC Advisory Service, National Implementation of International Humanitarian Law – Biannual update on national legislation and case-law, January-June 2002. <http://www.icrc.org/Web/eng/siteeng0.nsf/html/5FLE9G?OpenDocument>.

26. Information and commentaries by Eric David, Professeur ordinaire, Brussels Free University.

27. For commentary on the case, see J. Wouters and L. De Smet, 'The ICJ's Judgement in the Case concerning the Arrest Warrant of 11 April 2000: Some Critical Observations', 4 *YIHL* (2001) p. 373.

28. For background on the proceedings before the Belgian courts, see 3 *YIHL* (2000) pp. 430-431 and 4 *YIHL* (2001) pp. 457-458.

the ICJ ruled that the issuance by Belgium of the arrest warrant of 11 April 2000 against Abdulaye Yerodia Ndombasi, and its international circulation, constituted violations of a legal obligation of Belgium towards the DRC, in that they failed to respect the immunity from criminal jurisdiction and the inviolability which the incumbent Minister for Foreign Affairs of the DRC enjoyed under international law.[29]

The Judgement, which gave rise to a lot of comments, negative and positive,[30] will not be discussed here.

A day after the ICJ rendered the Judgement mentioned above, a Belgian investigating judge withdrew the arrest warrant issued against Yerodia. However, the case remained *sub judice* and was brought before the Chamber of Indictments (*chambre des mises en accusation*) of the Brussels Court of Appeals in order to decide whether the Belgian judge had jurisdiction in this case. The question before the Brussels Court of Appeals did not concern Yerodia's immunity since, at the time, Yerodia did not carry out any official function in the Congolese government. Therefore, there was no longer an immunity problem. However, another question arose regarding the power of the Belgian judge to exercise jurisdiction *in absentia* according to the Belgian law.

As a reminder, Article 7 of the Law of 16 June 1993 (as modified on 10 February 1999; hereinafter: 'the 1993 law' or 'the 1993/1999 law') on the punishment of grave breaches of international humanitarian law[31] stated that 'the Belgian courts have jurisdiction over offences provided for in this law, irrespective of the place where they have been committed'.[32] On the other hand, Article 12 of the Preliminary Title of the Code of Criminal Proceedings provided for the jurisdiction of the Belgian judge with regard to extraterritorial offences only if the presumed author of the offence was found on Belgian soil. However, this provision only concerns offences that are enumerated in the Preliminary Title, and not

---

29. See <http://www.icj-cij.org>. For a discussion of the case, see the article by J. Wouters and L. De Smet in volume 4 of the *YIHL* (2001) at p. 373.

30. E.g., M. Sassòli, 'L'arrêt Yerodia: quelques remarques sur une affaire au point de collision entre les deux couches du droit international', 106 *RGDIP* (2002) pp. 791-818; M. Henzelin, 'La compétence universelle: une question non résolue par l'arrêt Yerodia', 106 *RGDIP* (2002) pp. 819-854; A. Cassese, 'When May Senior State Officials Be Tried for International Crimes? Some Comments on the *Congo v. Belgium* Case', 13 *EJIL* (2002) pp. 853-876; S. Wirth, 'Immunity for Core Crimes? The ICJ's Judgement in the *Congo v. Belgium* Case', 13 *EJIL* (2002) pp. 877-894; M. Spinedi, 'State Responsibility v. Individual Responsibility for International Crimes: *Tertium non Datur?*', 13 *EJIL* (2002) pp. 895-900; J. Salmon, 'Libres propos sur l'arrêt de la CIJ du 14 février 2002 dans l'affaire relative au *mandat d'arrêt du 11 avril 2000*', 35 *RBDI* (2002) pp. 512-517; M. Kamto, 'Une troublante "immunité totale" du ministre des Affaires étrangères (sur un aspect de l'arrêt du 14 février 2002 dans l'affaire relative au *mandat d'arrêt du 11 avril 2000*)', 35 *RBDI* (2002) pp. 518-530; J. Verhoeven, 'Quelques réflexions sur l'affaire relative au *mandat d'arrêt du 11 avril 2000*', 35 *RBDI* (2002) pp. 531-536; P. Sands, 'What is the ICJ for?', 35 *RBDI* (2002) pp. 537-545; J.-P. Cot, 'Eloge de l'indécision de la Cour et la compétence universelle', 35 *RBDI* (2002) pp. 546-553; M.N. Shaw, 'The *Yerodia* case: Remedies and judicial functions', 35 *RBDI* (2002) pp. 554-559; J.-P. Queneudec, 'Un arrêt de principe: L'arrêt de la C.I.J. du 14 février 2002', <http://www.ridi.org/adi/articles/2002/>.

31. Reprinted in 2 *YIHL* (1999) pp. 120 et seq. L. De Smet and F. Naert, 'Making or breaking international law? An international law analysis of Belgium's act concerning the punishment of grave breaches of international humanitarian law', 35 *RBDI* (2002) pp. 471-511.

32. Correspondent's translation. Original text: 'Les juridictions belges sont compétentes pour connaître des infractions prévues dans la présente loi, indépendamment du lieu où celles-ci ont été commises.'

the crimes embodied in other laws, such as the 1993/1999 law which constituted the basis of the complaints.

In its judgement of 16 April 2002, the Chamber of Indictments ruled that Article 12 of the Preliminary Title of the Code of Criminal Proceedings was a general provision which applied to all crimes committed outside Belgium, including, consequently, the crimes embodied in the 1993/1999 law. As the accused had never been on Belgian soil, the prosecution against them was inadmissible. It is noticeable that the court did not invoke the extinguishment of the case concerning L.-D. Kabila on account of his death (he had been killed on 17 January 2001) since the Court considered, in the upstream of this event, that the case was not admissible from the outset.

This judgement was cancelled by the *Cour de cassation* on 22 November 2002, not on the merits but only for procedural reasons.

☛ Proceedings against *A. Sharon, A. Yaron et al.*, Chamber of Indictments of the Brussels Court of Appeals, Decision of 26 June 2002
☛ *Cour de cassation*, Decision of 12 February 2003, *JLMB* (2003) pp. 368 et seq.; *Journal des Procès*, 21 February 2003, p. 22 <http://www.cass.be/juris/jucf.htm>

As in the *Yerodia* case, the issue of the admissibility of the prosecution of serious violations of international humanitarian law *in absentia* was raised in respect of the complaints lodged by Palestinian victims of the Sabra and Shatila massacres (Beirut, 16-18 September 1982) against the Israeli Prime Minister Ariel Sharon (who was Minister of Defence in 1982), the former division commander General Amos Yaron (who exercised military control over the Sabra and Shatila camps), and others. The complaint was brought, once again, on the basis of the 1993/1999 law.

On 26 June 2002, another Chamber of Indictments of the Brussels Court of Appeals ruled, as in the *Yerodia* case but on different grounds, that the prosecution was not admissible because of the fact that the accused had not been found in Belgium.[33] The Chamber founded its conclusions mainly on a mistake which appeared in the *travaux préparatoires* of the draft law of 1993. At the time, it was stated that the 1993 law had to be applied even if the accused was not found in Belgium, but this should not have been expressly specified in the law, since Article 12 of the Preliminary Title of the Code of Criminal Proceedings would be repealed very soon. In other words, the legislator erroneously suggested that Article 12 could cover the 1993 Law.

This judgement was reversed by the *Cour de cassation* on 12 February 2003.[34] In its judgement, the Court, rightly, considered that the letter of Article 12 confined its scope to the extraterritorial offences provided for in the Preliminary Title of the Code of Criminal Proceedings and did not extend to crimes provided for in the 1993/1999 law.

---

33. The judgement, initially foreseen on 6 March 2002 (see Belgian Report of 2001), was eventually passed on 26 June 2002, *JT* (2002) pp. 539-543. <http://www.ulb.ac.be/droit/cdi/>.

34. Commentaire J. Kirkpatrick, 21 March 2003, pp. 16-23; *JT* (2003), obs. P. d'Argent, pp. 243 et seq.

☛ Ongoing Proceedings against *Hissène Habré*

In connection with a complaint brought on 30 November 2000[35] before an investigating judge against the former Chadian president Hissène Habré, the investigating judge, Daniel Fransen, accompanied by the public prosecutor and officials of the Belgian judicial police, visited Chad from 26 February until 2 March 2002, in the framework of an international rogatory commission, in order to question victims and witnesses of atrocities attributed to Habré.[36] Apart from the investigations carried out in Africa into the Rwandan genocide, it was the first time that an investigating judge in Belgium carried out an overseas mission in connection with the application of the 1993/1999 law.

Pending
☛ Draft law interpreting the 1993/1999 Law on the Punishment of Grave Breaches of International Humanitarian Law, 12 December 2002, *Doc. parl.*, Sénat, 2001-2002, 2-1255/2, 23 December 2002

The *Yerodia* and *Sharon* judgements (above), passed by the Chambers of Indictments, raised much concern and disappointment among the NGOs and the members of Parliament who support the fight against impunity. Therefore, on 18 July 2002, several members of the Senate introduced a draft interpretative law clearly specifying that Article 7(1) of the 1993 law 'must be interpreted as applicable irrespective of the place where the presumed author of the crime can be found'.[37]

As this draft was proposed at the time of judicial proceedings and could interfere in these proceedings, a stream of public opinion feared that the draft law could strike a blow to the non-retroactivity principle.[38] Therefore, on 19 September 2002, the President of the Senate decided to request the opinion of the Council of State (legislation section) about the draft law.

On 12 December 2002, the Council of State admitted that it was possible to adopt an interpretative law but that great care should be taken not to undermine the non-retroactivity principle and the requirement that the law ought to be foreseeable.

As to the merits, the Council of State considered that the question had to be examined in light of a new Article 12*bis* introduced by the law of 18 July 2001 in the Preliminary Title of the Code of Criminal Proceedings.[39] Article 12*bis* provided for an automatic extension of the jurisdiction of the Belgian courts each time a treaty binding Belgium obliged Belgian judicial authorities to exercise a criminal competence which did not yet exist in Belgian law. The main object of the provision was to enable a Belgian court to judge the presumed

---

35. See 4 *YIHL* (2001) p. 454.
36. <http://www.fidh.org/communiq/2002/td2602f.htm>.
37. Original text: 'L'art. 7, al. 1er, de la loi du 16 juin 1993 [...] doit être interprété comme s'appliquant sans considération du lieu où l'auteur présumé du crime peut être trouvé'. *Doc. parl.*, Sénat, 2001-2002,   2-1255/1.   <http://www.senate.be/www/webdriver?MIval=index_senate&M=3&-LANG=fr>. Correspondent's translation.
38. See the debate in the Belgian newspapers against the interpretative law; against the interpretative law: G. Haarscher, P. Mertens and F. Ringelheim, 'La compétence universelle et l'esprit des lois', *Le Soir* (6 September 2002); in favour of the interpretative law: E. David, S. Parmentier and J. Wouters, *Le Soir* (14 and 15 November 2002).
39. *Moniteur belge* (1 September 2001) 1st edn.

author of an international crime committed abroad when the said person was found in Belgium, when there was no link between the crime and Belgium and when Belgium did not extradite him or her.

According to the Council of State, this provision necessarily affected Article 7 of the 1993/1999 law since, during the *travaux préparatoires* of draft Article 12*bis*, the Minister of Justice mentioned the 1948 Genocide Convention, the 1949 Geneva Conventions and the 1977 Additional Protocol I among the instruments aimed at by Article 12*bis*. In other words, inasmuch as genocide and war crimes committed in an international armed conflict were concerned, this new provision limited the prosecution of their presumed authors, on the basis of Article 7, to the case of authors found in Belgium. Prosecution *in absentia* remained possible only for other crimes provided for in the 1993/1999 law, i.e., crimes against humanity and war crimes committed in a non-international armed conflict. The interpretative law could only concern those crimes. Anyway, the Council of State remained reluctant about the adoption of this law considering the abovementioned principles of non-retroactivity and the requirement that the law ought to be foreseeable.

The opinion of the Council of State was far from being convincing. Firstly, it was strange to contend that Article 12*bis* modified Article 7 of the 1993/1999 law while one does not find in the *travaux préparatoires* of Article 12*bis* the slightest allusion to any link of this provision with the 1993/1999 law in general, and with its Article 7 in particular. Secondly, the concern regarding the retroactivity of an interpretative law does not make much sense since the interpretation of the law is supposed to be an inherent and integral part of the law as it is from the date of its adoption; thirdly, even if there were any kind of retroactivity in the law to be passed – *quod non* –, this would not be a violation of the principle of the legality of crimes and penalties given that the law did not create any new crime or any new penalty which did not exist earlier: the law only concerned procedural and jurisdictional matters, not substantive ones. This explains why the Senate did not follow the Council of State's opinion, voted the law *ne varietur* and transmitted it to the Chamber on 30-31 January 2003.[40]

For the final fate of the law, see the 2003 report.

☞ Draft law modifying the 1993/1999 Law on the Punishment of Grave Breaches of International Humanitarian Law

At the same time as the draft interpretative law was introduced, members of the Senate brought in a draft law with a view to modifying the 1993/1999 Law.[41] The draft had a triple purpose:
1. Adapting the list of war crimes embodied in current Article 1(3) of the 1993 law to the list of war crimes enumerated in Article 8 of the Rome Statute and in Article 15 of the Second Protocol of 16 March 1999 Additional to the Hague Convention of 1954, relating to the protection of cultural objects. The new Article 1*ter* would include all the war crimes mentioned in these instruments and would apply in the same contexts (international or non-international armed conflicts) as the ones defined by these instruments;

---

40. *Doc. parl.*, Sénat, 2001-2002, 2-1255-4 and 5; *Ann. Parl.*, Sénat, 2002-2003, 30 January 2003, 2-265.

41. *Doc. parl.*, Sénat, 2001-2002, 2-1256/1, 18 July 2002. <http://www.senate.be/www/webdriver? MIval=index_senate&M=3&LANG=fr>.

2. Adapting the current Article 5(3) to the judgement of the ICJ in the *Yerodia* case (see above). Interestingly, the new paragraph 3 does not completely abrogate the actual provision, which excludes any procedural immunity that would be an obstacle to the prosecution.[42] Taking into account the limitations of criminal immunity recognised by the ICJ Judgement itself, and more particularly, by the common separate opinion of Judges Higgins, Kooijmans and Buergenthal, the new paragraph 3 continues to exclude immunity, but to the limits established by international law.[43] For example, if a current foreign minister was prosecuted before the ICC and if he was found in Belgium, he could be arrested in order to be surrendered to the ICC in spite of any immunity he would claim;[44]

3. Modifying current Article 7 which, combined with the legal possibility for the victims of a crime to lodge a complaint before an investigating judge (Code of Criminal Proceedings, Article 63 et seq.), allows the victims to submit an international humanitarian law crime to a Belgian judge whatever the place of the crime, the nationality of the presumed author, the nationality of the victim, and even in the absence of the presumed author in Belgium (universal jurisdiction *in absentia*). This liberal system in 2000 and 2001 provoked a flood of about 30 complaints in Belgium, not only by Belgian victims but also by many foreign victims. Some of these complaints (more especially, the *Yerodia* and the *Sharon* cases) put Belgium in diplomatic difficulties *vis-à-vis* the DRC and Israel. Furthermore, the Belgian government felt that a number of complaints were politically motivated and the result of a forum shopping strategy; these reasons were not as clearly stated in the draft Article 7, but everyone knew that they were behind the suggested modifications. The modifications included the following:

   a. It was expressly stated that the Belgian courts have jurisdiction over crimes mentioned in the law, wherever they were committed and even if their presumed author was not found in Belgium;

   b. If the crime was committed outside Belgium, its presumed author was not Belgian and was not found in Belgium, and if the victim was not Belgian or had not been residing in Belgium for one year, the prosecution could only proceed upon the request of the federal prosecutor. This provision was designed to filter complaints and to get rid of complaints which seemed fanciful or not reliable. This provision, however, did not apply to complaints submitted before 1 July 2002 (the date of the entry into force of the Rome Statute). In other words, most complaints already brought before the Belgian justice could continue to be dealt with;[45]

   c. If the crime was committed abroad, the Belgian Minister of Justice was entitled to refer it to the ICC on the basis of Article 14 of the Rome Statute. If the ICC decided

---

42. Current Art. 5(3) reads as follows: 'The immunity linked to the official capacity of a person does not prevent the application of the present act' (correspondent's translation, French text: 'L'immunité attachée à la qualité officielle d'une personne n'empêche pas l'application de la présente loi').

43. Draft Art. 5(3) reads as follows: 'The international immunity linked to the official capacity of a person prevents the application of the present act only in the limits established by international law' (correspondent's translation, French text: 'L'immunité internationale attachée à la qualité officielle d'une personne n'empêche l'application de la présente loi que dans les limites établies par le droit international').

44. See Rome Statute, Art. 27(2), and *Yerodia* Judgement, *ICJ Rep.* (2002) para. 61.

45. See 4 *YIHL* (2001) pp. 454-455.

not to indict the presumed author, the case could be submitted again to the Belgian courts;

d. Instead of referring the case to the ICC, the Belgian Minister of Justice was also entitled to refer it to the state *loci delicti commissi*, or to the state of the nationality of the presumed author, or to the state where the presumed author happened to be. If one of these states decided to exercise its jurisdiction, and if this state respected the rules of fair trial, the Belgian *Cour de cassation* would remove the case from the Belgian courts.

On 18 September 2002, the President of the Senate requested the opinion of the Council of State regarding the above draft modifications. On 16 December 2002, the Council of State gave a detailed opinion,[46] which was rather critical of the draft modifications. The Council of State observed not only that universal jurisdiction *in absentia* is legally questionable, but also, and rather surprisingly, that universal jurisdiction, as such, would be disputable with regard to 'the superior norms of international law'! Obviously, the members of the Council of State needed some retraining in public international law … Be that as it may, there was one observation in the opinion of the Council of State which deserved consideration, namely, the removal of a case from a Belgian court to the ICC by the Minister of Justice. Such a removal would be a clear interference by the executive in judicial matters and a violation of the separation of powers. The Senate was to amend the draft on this point and some other minor details. As this and other important events were to occur in 2003, the reader is invited to consult volume 6 of the Yearbook for subsequent developments.

ERIC DAVID

BOLIVIA

The Emblem
- Law No. 2390 on the Use and Protection of the Red Cross Emblem [Ley No. 2390 El uso y la protección del emblema de la Cruz Roja]. Adopted on 14 May 2002, promulgated on 23 May 2002, entered into force on 19 June 2002, published in *Gaceta Oficial de Bolivia*, 19 June 2002

'It sets out in particular the different authorised uses of the emblem (use as a protective device by the medical and religious services of the armed forces, civilian hospitals, medical units and religious personnel attached thereto, and by the Bolivian Red Cross; use as an indicative device by this Society and by other National Red Cross or Red Crescent Societies; and use by the International Red Cross organisations) and provides for the punishment of misuse, including perfidious use in time of war, in accordance with the Criminal Code and/or the Military Criminal Code. The illegal marking with the emblem of various documents (letters, leaflets, etc.) or goods or their packaging, and the selling or putting on the market of items so marked, are subject to a specific sanction. The red crescent emblem, the names "Red Cross" and "Red Crescent" and the distinctive signals for the identification of medical units or transports are also covered by this law.'[47]

---

46. *Doc. parl.*, Sénat, 2001-2002, 2-1256/3, 6 January 2003; <http://www.senate.be/www/webdri ver?MIval=index_senate&M=3&LANG=fr>.
47. Source: ICRC Advisory Service, National Implementation of International Humanitarian Law

International Criminal Court
- On 24 May 2002, the Ombudsman's Office reported that Bolivia had ratified the legislation incorporating the Rome Statute into national law. Following its ratification of the ICC Statute on 27 June 2002, in September the Minister of Justice began the process of drafting implementing legislation.[48]

BOSNIA AND HERZEGOVINA

The Emblem
- Law on the Use and Protection of the Red Cross Emblem and the Title of the Red Cross Society of Bosnia and Herzegovina. Adopted on 29 April 2002, entered into force on 8 June 2002, published in the *Official Gazette of Bosnia and Herzegovina*, Year VI, No. 11, 30 May 2002, pp. 274-276

'The Law on the use and protection of the red cross emblem and the title of the Red Cross Society of Bosnia and Herzegovina ... sets out rules on the use of the red cross and red crescent emblems and names, of the distinctive signals for the identification of medical units and transports, and of the title of the Red Cross Society of Bosnia and Herzegovina. It distinguishes between protective and indicative use and, in connection with the latter, between time of war and time of peace. It lists in detail the establishments, units, means of transport and persons entitled to use the names and emblems for different purposes, and lays down the conditions governing such use. The International Red Cross organisations are expressly permitted to use the emblems at any time for all their activities. The law also provides for the dissemination of the text of the Geneva Conventions among members of the armed forces, health workers, university students and the population in general. Misuse of the emblems and, for certain medical or religious personnel, failure to wear the armlet or carry an identity card when performing relevant duties, or failure to return such items after losing the corresponding status, are punishable by a fine. Perfidious use of an emblem or distinctive signal is considered a war crime which is to be punished in accordance with the provisions of the Criminal Code.'[49]

Genocide
- Report of the Republika Srpska on the massacre at Srebrenica, 3 September 2002

The report denied that a genocide or a massacre of up to 8,000 Muslim men and boys had taken place at Srebrenica in July 1995. Instead it claimed that between 1,800 and 1,900 Muslim soldiers died in combat or of their wounds. About 100 more were killed by Serbs angry over alleged Muslim atrocities. The report also sought to portray the Serbs as victims.[50]

– Biannual update on national legislation and case-law, January-June 2002. <http://www.icrc.org/Web/eng/siteeng0.nsf/html/5FLE9G?OpenDocument>.

48. Source: CICC/The Americas: Bolivia. <http://www.iccnow.org/countryinfo/theamericas/bolivia.html>.

49. Source: ICRC Advisory Service, National Implementation of International Humanitarian Law – Biannual update on national legislation and case-law, January-June 2002. <http://www.icrc.org/Web/eng/siteeng0.nsf/html/5FLE9G?OpenDocument>.

However, as critics of the report noted, not even General Krstić, who was convicted by a Trial Chamber of the ICTY for genocide with respect to Srebrenica, nor former President Milošević, have denied that a massacre took place there. They have simply disclaimed personal or command responsibility for it.[51]

International Criminal Court
☞ Law to ratify the Rome Statute. Adopted by Parliament on 5 February 2002, published in the *Official Gazette of Bosnia and Herzegovina* on 6 March 2002, ratification entered into force at the domestic level on 14 March 2002[52]

Criminal Law Reform – Rule of Law
☞ Endorsement of a reinvigorated strategy for judicial reform to strengthen the rule of law efforts in Bosnia and Herzegovina in 2002/2003 by the Steering Board of the Peace Implementation Council, 28 February 2002
☞ Communiqué of the Steering Board of the Peace Implementation Council issued at Sarajevo on 7 May 2002

The Communiqué stated that the establishment of a single High Judicial and Prosecutorial Council would 'lay the foundations for further reform of the judiciary, such as the restructuring of the court and prosecutorial system'.

☞ Communiqué of the Steering Board of the Peace Implementation Council issued at Sarajevo on 31 July 2002

The Communiqué stated that the Board welcomed the establishment within the Court of Bosnia and Herzegovina of a Special Chambers and endorsed the proposal of the High Representative for Bosnia and Herzegovina to include national and international judges in a Special Panel/Department for Organised Crime, Economic Crime and Corruption in the Court of Bosnia and Herzegovina and the Prosecutor's Office of Bosnia and Herzegovina.

☞ Decision No. 13/02 of the High Representative of Bosnia and Herzegovina enacting the Law on Amendments to the Law on Court of Bosnia and Herzegovina.[53] Adopted on 6 August 2002, entered into force eight days after its publication in the *Official Gazette of Bosnia and Herzegovina*, in accordance with its Article 11,[54] published in the *Official*

---

50. 'New Srebrenica report condemned', *Southeast Europe Times* (2 September 2002.) <http://www.balkantimes.com/html_text_only2/english/020904-SVETLA-001.htm>.

51. See Radio Free Europe/Radio Liberty Balkan Report of 6 September 2002, Vol. 6, No. 33. <http://www.rferl.org/balkan-report/>; 'Bosnian Serbs deny Srebrenica massacre', Radio Netherlands, 4 September 2002. <http://www.rnw.nl/hotspots/html/sre020904.html>.

52. Source: CICC/Europe/CIS:Bosnia and Herzegovina. <http://www.iccnow.org/countryinfo/europecis/bosniaherzegovina.html>.

53. The Law on Court of Bosnia and Herzegovina of 12 November 2000 was published in the Official Gazette of Bosnia and Herzegovina of 29/00. It was subsequently adopted by the Bosnia and Herzegovina Parliamentary Assembly and published in the *Official Gazette of Bosnia and Herzegovina* of 16/02. The Law provided for the establishment of a Court of Bosnia and Herzegovina, in order to ensure the effective exercise of the competencies of the State of Bosnia and Herzegovina and the respect of human rights and the rule of law in the territory of the state (Art. 1).

54. The High Representative's Decision stipulated that '[t]he said Law shall enter into force as a

Gazette of Bosnia and Herzegovina, 24/02; *Official Gazette of the Federation of Bosnia and Herzegovina*, 43/02; and *Official Gazette of the Republika Srpska*, 55/02

This decision of the High Representative of Bosnia and Herzegovina enacting the Law on Amendments to the Law on Court of Bosnia and Herzegovina, to which was attached the mentioned Law, was designed to address the problems of organised and economic crime and criminal offences committed by public officials in the course of their duties. *Inter alia*, the Law provided for the establishment of special panels within the Criminal Division of the Court of Bosnia and Herzegovina to deal with organised crime, economic crime and corruption (Art. 6) and a Special Appellate Panel for Organised Crime, Economic Crime and Corruption within the Appellate Division. It also gave the Court jurisdiction over crimes defined in the Laws of the Federation of Bosnia and Herzegovina, the Republika Srpska and the Brčko District which occurred prior to the entry into force of the Criminal Code of Bosnia and Herzegovina, when those crimes include elements of international or inter-Entity crime as defined in the Criminal Code of Bosnia and Herzegovina (Art. 9).

☞ Decision No. 14/02 of the High Representative of Bosnia and Herzegovina enacting the Law on the Prosecutor's Office of Bosnia and Herzegovina. Adopted on 6 August 2002, entered into force eight days following its publication in the *Official Gazette of Bosnia and Herzegovina*[55] <http://www.ohr.int/ohr-dept/rule-of-law-pillar/doc/HRs-Decision-Enacting-The-Law-on-Prosecutor%27s-Office.doc>

By this law, a Prosecutor's Office of Bosnia and Herzegovina, whose seat is in Sarajevo, was established in order to ensure the effective exercise of the competence of the state of Bosnia and Herzegovina and the respect of human rights and the rule of law in the territory of Bosnia and Herzegovina (Art. 1). Article 2 provided that the Prosecutor's Office is an independent organ of the state. The Office consists of a Chief Prosecutor of Bosnia and Herzegovina, assisted by three Deputy Chief Prosecutors and a number of Prosecutors, who shall be selected and appointed by the High Judicial and Prosecutorial Council of Bosnia and Herzegovina from the Prosecutors of the Prosecutor's Office (Art. 3(1) and (2)). Within the Prosecutor's Office, a Special Department for Organised Crime, Economic Crime and Corruption was established (Art. 3(3)).

Regarding the criminal jurisdiction of the Prosecutor's Office, it was established by Article 12 that it should be 'the authority competent to investigate the offences for which the Court of Bosnia and Herzegovina is competent, and to prosecute offenders before the Court of Bosnia and Herzegovina, in accordance with the Criminal Procedure Code of Bosnia and Herzegovina and other applicable laws (Art. 12(1)). Further, the Prosecutor's Office is the competent authority to 'receive requests for international assistance in criminal matters as stipulated by law, multilateral and bilateral treaties and conventions, including requests for extradition or surrender of persons sought, from Courts or authorities within the territory of Bosnia and Herzegovina and from other states or International Courts or Tribunals. Where a

---

law of Bosnia and Herzegovina as provided for in Article 11 thereof on an interim basis, until such time as the Parliamentary Assembly of Bosnia and Herzegovina adopts this Law in due force, without amendment and with no conditions attached.'

55. The Law entered into force on an interim basis as provided for in Art. 21 until such time as the Parliamentary Assembly of Bosnia and Herzegovina adopts it in due force, without amendment and with no conditions attached.

court decision is necessary to carry out the request, the Prosecutor's Office shall be competent to make an application for such a decision (Art. 12(2)). Article 12(3) provided that the 'Special Department shall, *inter alia*, undertake measures defined by law with a view to investigating and prosecuting the perpetrators of Organised Crime, Economic Crime and Corruption offences as provided by State Law, when provision is made in the said laws that the Court of Bosnia and Herzegovina has such jurisdiction'.

The law further provided for the various aspects of the powers and functioning, including funding, of the Office and the Special Department.

☛ Decision No. 32/02 of the High Representative of Bosnia and Herzegovina enacting the Law on the Federation Prosecutor's Office of the Federation of Bosnia and Herzegovina. Adopted 21 August 2002, entered into force eight days following its publication in the *Official Gazette of the Federation of Bosnia and Herzegovina*[56]

The law established a Federation Prosecutor's Office as an autonomous state body, empowered to undertake certain measures concerning the investigation and prosecution of persons who may have committed criminal offences and economic violations, and the conduct of other activities as defined by Federation law (Arts. 1 and 16). The Federation Prosecutor's Office was to consist of a Chief Federation Prosecutor, two Deputy Chief Federation Prosecutors and a number of Federation Prosecutors (Art. 5), who should be appointed by the High Judicial and High Prosecutorial Council.

According to Article 16(2) of the law, the Federation Prosecutor's Office 'shall have first instance jurisdiction to investigate and prosecute persons who may have committed the criminal acts of terrorism, inter-cantonal crime, illicit drug trafficking and organised crime, which the Law on the Supreme Court of the Federation of Bosnia and Herzegovina … defines as the competencies of that Court'. The Chief Federation Prosecutor was also empowered under the law, where he determines that due to a violation of a Federation law or an International Treaty there are well-founded reasons for him/her to pursue a legal remedy against an executive Court decision or a decision issued in administrative or other proceedings, to demand that the enforcement of such a decision be postponed or cancelled, if its enforcement may cause detrimental consequences (Art. 18(1)).

The law also provided for, *inter alia*, the organisation, work and funding of the Federation Prosecutor's Office.

☛ Decision No. 33/02 of the High Representative of Bosnia and Herzegovina enacting the Law on the Prosecutor's Office of the Republika Srpska. Adopted on 21 August 2002, entered into force eight days following its publication in the *Official Gazette of the Republika Srpska*[57] <http://www.ohr.int/ohr-dept/rule-of-law-pillar/doc/HRs-Decision-RS-Prosecutor%27s-Office.doc>

---

56. The Law entered into force on an interim basis as provided for in Art. 40 until such time as the Parliament of the Federation of Bosnia and Herzegovina adopts it in due force, without amendment and with no conditions attached.

57. The Law entered into force on an interim basis as provided for in Art. 53 until such time as the Republika Srpska National Assembly adopts it in due force, without amendment and with no conditions attached.

The law established Prosecutors' Offices of the Republika Srpska as autonomous state bodies empowered to undertake, within the rights and duties of the Republika Srpska, certain measures concerning the investigation and prosecution of persons that may have committed criminal offences (Arts. 1 and 16) and provided for their general responsibilities and powers, organisation and work and funding.

War Crimes Prosecutions
- ☛ Establishment of a three-member team of experts tasked to handle the handover of the processing of war crimes cases from the ICTY to the Bosnian war crimes court, 26 February 2002
- ☛ 'Non Paper' of Carla Del Ponte to establish a single Bosnia and Herzegovina court to prosecute war crimes

According to Amnesty International, during 2002, '[d]espite thousands of investigations relating to war crimes, few suspects were brought to justice in domestic courts, largely as a result of the lack of cooperation between the criminal justice systems of the two entities. According to unofficial estimates, some 10,000 potential suspects were listed in local investigation files, of which 2,500 had been reviewed by the [Yugoslav] Tribunal Prosecutor who approves domestic prosecutions in individual cases [under the so-called "Rules of the Road"].'[58]

The secret 'Non Paper' delivered by ICTY Chief Prosecutor Carla Del Ponte to the Chairman of Bosnia's Council of Ministers proposed establishing a single war crimes court, to deal with war crimes cases at the 'lower and medium levels'. The court would have branches in the major cities of Bosnia and Herzegovina. It would employ both international and domestic legal experts from both entities, and would be supervised by the ICTY, the Office of the High Representative and domestic authorities.[59]

According to Amnesty International, 'the proposal had not been officially adopted at the end of 2002, apparently because of insufficient funds'.[60]

- ☛ Joint statement of High Representative Paddy Ashdown and Chief Prosecutor of the International Criminal Tribunal for the former Yugoslavia Carla Del Ponte, 19 November 2002 <http://www.ohr.int/ohr-dept/presso/pressr/default.asp?content_id=28527>

The joint statement said that: 'The Chief Prosecutor of the ICTY and the High Representative have agreed that the issue of building the capacity of the BiH authorities to prosecute war crimes is essential. This capacity will complement the ICTY in bringing those indicted for war crimes to justice. BiH cannot be a fully functioning state without that capacity, which is a key part of bringing future closure to the war. The Chief Prosecutor and the High Representative both expressed their determination to build this capacity …'

---

58. Amnesty International, 'Bosnia-Herzegovina' (Covering events from January-December 2002). <http://www.amnesty.org/web/wb/nsf/print/bih-summary-eng>. For more on the Rules of the Road, domestic prosecutions in Bosnia and Herzegovina and the handover of cases from the ICTY to the Bosnian courts, see the article in this volume by J. Manuell and A. Kontić in this volume at p. 331.

59. J. Pavkovic, 'A Mini-Hague in Sarajevo', *Vecernji List*, <http://www.ohr.int/ohr-dept/presso/bh-media-rep/round-ups/default.asp?content_id=5804>.

60. Amnesty International, 'Bosnia-Herzegovina' (Covering events from January-December 2002). <http://www.amnesty.org/web/wb/nsf/print/bih-summary-eng>.

Cases

☛ Arrest of five former Bosnian Serb police officers in May on suspicion of involvement in the disppearance of the Matanović family in 1995

'In the RS, five former Bosnian Serb police officers were arrested in May on suspicion of involvement in the disppearance of the Matanović family in 1995. The police investigation into the case, which had been ordered by the Human Rights Chamber in 1995, only progessed after intense pressure from the UN Mission in Bosnia and Herzegovina (UNMIBH) and the International Police Task Force (IPTF). Evidence implicating a further 18 former and serving police officers in Prijedor, was revealed in May. In November, the Tribunal approved the opening of judicial investigations relating to these additional subjects, after judicial proceedings were delayed for several months by counter-complaints from the suspects.'[61]

☛ Arrest of *Ivan Banković*, 22 June 2002

On 22 June, the authorities arrested Ivan Banković, 30, suspected of killing nine Muslim civilians in the village of Mokronoge during the war.[62]

☛ Decision of the Human Rights Chamber on the handover of four Algerian terrorist suspects to US authorities in January 2002, 11 October 2002

On 11 October 2002, the Human Rights Chamber ruled that the government had violated the rights of four Algerian terrorist suspects, including those relating to expulsion, illegal detention and prohibition of the death penalty, when they handed them over to the United States in January 2002.[63] The Human Rights Chamber ruled that the Federation and state authorities had violated multiple human rights, and ordered the authorities to pay $5,000 in compensation to the four men and to retain lawyers to represent them in any forthcoming trial proceedings in the USA, and to do everything possible to ensure that they are not subjected to the death penalty.[64]

The men were among six Algerians holding Bosnian citizenship, Bensayah Belkacem, Mustafa Adir, Saber Lamar, Muhamed Nehle, Lakhdar Bumedien and Boudellah Hadz, who had been handed over to US custody by the Bosnian government in January, without obtaining guarantees that they would not be subjected to the death penalty, torture or ill-treatment, or unfair trial. 'The transfer ignored a decision of the Human Rights Chamber which stated that four of them should not be forcibly removed from Bosnian territory, pending a full examination of their case. The six men were reportedly taken to the US-run detention facility in Guantanamo Bay, Cuba. They had been arrested by the Federation police in October 2001 on suspicion of "international terrorism" in connection with an alleged plan to attack foreign embassies in Sarajevo. On 17 January [2002] the Federation Supreme

---

61. Amnesty International, 'Bosnia-Herzegovina' (Covering events from January-December 2002). <http://www.amnesty.org/web/wb/nsf/print/bih-summary-eng>. See also OHR BiH Media Round-up, 10 May 2002.
62. 'Bosnian police arrested two men, one suspected of committing war crimes', AP, 22 June 2002.
63. 'Bosnia violated rights of terror suspects: court', AFP, 11 October 2002.
64. K. Kratovac, 'Bosnia's top human rights court rules handover of Algerians illegal', AP, 11 October 2002.

Court ordered their release from custody but instead the men were immediately redetained by Federation special police forces and hours later handed over to US officials.'[65] The handover was widely condemned, including by the Office of the UN High Commissioner for Human Rights. A statement issued by the latter said that: 'Our concern is that the rule of law was clearly circumvented in this process. There was no legal basis upon which the Interior Ministry could have taken these individuals from the prison, consequently it would appear that this is an arbitrary arrest and detention.'[66]

Pending
☞ Compensation claims against the Netherlands, 15 November 2002
☞ Compensation claims against the United Nations, 19 December 2002

In December 2002, the families of those killed in the Srebrenica massacre (about 8,000 people) filed a request for compensation with the UN Secretary-General, claiming that the UN had failed to protect the inhabitants of the enclave. In November, Srebrenica survivors demanded compensation from the Dutch government for the failure of Dutchbat to protect the people of Srebrenica. The amount sought was not specified.

'Failure of the Netherlands and the UN to protect the civilian population of Srebrenica is unlawful under the laws of war and human rights law,' a statement from the lawyers said. 'The plaintiffs hold the Netherlands and UN liable for all losses suffered as a result of this,' it added.[67]

AVRIL McDONALD

BRAZIL

International Criminal Court
☞ Legislative Decree No. 112 of 6 June 2002
☞ Legislative Decree No. 4388 of 25 September 2002

At the end of 2001, the Minister of Justice appointed a working group of legal experts whose task was to study the possible means by which Brazil could comply with the provisions contained in the Rome Statute, which was approved by Decreto Legislativo No. 112 of 6 June 2002 and enacted by Decreto Legislativo No. 4388 of 25 September 2002.

On 24-25 October 2002 the working group delivered its considerations with regard to the national implementation of the ICC Statute and thereby submitted a draft bill which provided for the required amendments to Brazilian legislation.

The bill provides Brazil with the possibility of exercising primary jurisdiction and enables the necessary cooperation with the International Criminal Court.

The bill is divided into seven chapters. Chapter I deals with the general principles applicable to the crime of genocide, crimes against humanity and war crimes. In particular, Article 3 specifies that these crimes are imprescriptible and not subject to bail, nor to amnesty,

---

65. Amnesty International, 'Bosnia-Herzegovina' (Covering events from January-December 2002). <http://www.amnesty.org/web/wb/nsf/print/bih-summary-eng>.
66. 'UN human rights agency condemns Algerian terror suspect handover', Deutsche Press-Agentur, 22 January 2002.
67. E. Onstad, 'Srebrenica survivors seek Dutch, UN compensation', Reuters, 15 November 2002.

clemency, or pardon. Article 4 sets forth the principle of territorial (universal) jurisdiction, satisfied even when the offender is a foreigner or stateless but 'enters territory under Brazilian jurisdiction'.

Chapter II provides the elements of the crime of genocide, while Chapters III and IV set forth respectively the definition of crimes against humanity and war crimes. In particular, in Chapter III Section II the number of the specific offences constituting crimes against humanity has been increased. For instance, Article 7.1(g) of the ICC Statute has been translated into the separate offences of sexual violence and sexual aggression, followed by the crimes of presence at sexual violence, aggression, sexual slavery, forced prostitution, forced pregnancy and forced sterilisation. Moreover, the offence of deprivation of rights is also seen as a crime against humanity when the victim has been deprived of his or her basic rights, 'for belonging to a political, racial, ethnic, religious, cultural, or gender-based group'. The crime against humanity of inhuman acts concludes Chapter III.

Chapter IV provides for those offences 'carried out during periods of armed conflict or, after hostilities have ceased, so long as the victim is under the domination of a belligerent party'. Three sections of Chapter IV respectively refer to general provisions applicable (Arts. 41 to 49), war crimes committed in the context of an international armed conflict (Arts. 50 to 86) and war crimes of a non-international character (Art. 87). The distinction between the two categories of war crimes relies entirely on Article 87, which establishes that the offences included in Section II of Chapter IV are also punishable under the headings of Chapter IV when committed during non-international armed conflict with the sole exception of those included in Article 55 (coercion to render military service to an enemy force), Article 65 (displacement of the civilian population by the Occupying Power) and Article 86 (failing to repatriate).

Chapter V deals with crimes against the administration of justice by the ICC. Article 88 affirms the principle of complementarity and therefore the 'responsibility' of Brazil to prosecute the above-mentioned crimes when not tried by the ICC. Section II introduces the specific crimes, such as the prohibition to use false testimony (Art. 90), and active and passive corruption (respectively, Arts. 91 and 97).

Chapters VI and VII set forth terms and conditions for the cooperation with the ICC and some procedural rules.

Generally speaking, the draft bill tries to respect as much as possible the principles and rules peculiar to the Brazilian justice system while, at the same time, it puts forward some innovations, such as the narrower discipline regarding the cause of extinction of accountability. Moreover, Chapter II harmonises the previous regime of the crime of genocide under Brazilian law, which provided for different penalties depending on the civil or military nature of the crime. In particular, the death penalty provided for in the wartime military code has been abrogated. New offences have been introduced in Chapter III, such as those regarding sexual crimes and those dealing with forced disappearance of people and racial segregation. Chapter IV gives emphasis to a more stringent protection of people and goods.

The final chapter of the draft bill confirms the applicability of the ordinary rules of procedure and fixes a maximum term of two years for the conclusion of the investigation, where the accused is subjected to pre-trial detention.

ANNA DANIELI

BULGARIA

Pending
☛ Legislation to implement the Statute of the International Criminal Court

On 15 March 2002, Parliament ratified the Rome Statute. Following Bulgaria's ratification of the ICC Statute on 14 April 2002, in September draft implementing legislation was sent to the Council of Ministers for its approval. This legislation must thereafter be sent to the General Assembly for adoption.

Bulgaria has amended its Criminal Code and Criminal Procedural Code in order to achieve full compatibility with the ICC regime.[68]

BURUNDI

Peace Process
☛ Ceasefire agreement (S/2002/1329) between the Transitional Government of Burundi and the Conseil national pour la défense de la démocratie-Forces pour la défense de la démocratie (CNDD-FDD), 2 December 2002

On 2 December 2002, a ceasefire agreement (S/2002/1329) between the Transitional Government of Burundi and the Conseil national pour la défense de la démocratie-Forces pour la défense de la démocratie (CNDD-FDD) was signed.[69] The agreement was to enter into force on 30 December 2002. The period between the signature and the coming into force of the agreement was meant to allow for the armed forces to attain knowledge about the agreement.[70] The agreement followed on several important developments earlier in the year. The Implementation Monitoring Committee (IMC), under the Chairmanship of the United Nations, which had been relocated from Arusha, Tanzania to Bujumbura in Burundi in 2001, held several ordinary sessions in 2002. This body had been given the responsibility to ensure that the provisions of the Arusha Agreement,[71] signed in 2000, were fully and speedily implemented. Accordingly, the IMC in 2002 engaged in various tasks, such as work for the adoption of a number of laws, including a law on 'provisional immunity for political leaders returning from exile' and a 'law against genocide, war crimes and crimes against humanity'. IMC further worked on publicising the Arusha Agreement. This was to ensure information about the peace process at the grassroots level. The inauguration of the Transitional National Assembly and the Transitional Senate on 10 January and 6 February 2002, respectively, followed on the establishment of the Transitional Government in 2001. The different political views within these bodies led to some difficulties in their decision-making and even to the arrest of one member of the UPRONA[72] party, and the house arrest of a

---

68. Source: <http://www.iccnow.org/countryinfo/europecis/bulgaria.html>. See also <http://legal.coe.int/icc/Default.asp?fd=docs&fn=Docs.htm>.
69. See <http://www.un.org/Depts/dpa/prev_dip/africa/burundi/fr_burundi_background_3.htm>. See also the Statement of the Secretary-General of the United Nations, Press Release SG/SM/8539. <http://www.un.org/News/Press/docs/2002/sgsm8539.doc.htm>.
70. See Press Release from the United Nations Security Council, UN Doc. SC/7586 (4 December 2002). <http://www.un.org/News/Press/docs/2002/sc7586.doc.htm>.
71. See Arusha Peace and Reconciliation Agreement for Burundi. <http://www.usip.org/library/pa/burundi/pa_burundi_08282000.html>. See also reference to draft Peace Agreement in Correspondents' Report on Burundi in 3 *YIHL* (1999) at p. 436.

member of the PARENA[73] party.[74] These difficulties, however, did not stop the signing of the ceasefire agreement.

Pending
☛ Establishment of a Truth and Reconciliation Commission

The Secretary-General of the United Nations, in his report to the Security Council on the situation in Burundi, stated that a 15-member Truth and Reconciliation Commission had been established by the Transitional Government of Burundi.[75] However, Human Rights Watch reported a failure to actually ratify legislation on the establishment of a truth and reconciliation commission.[76] In August 2002, the Burundian cabinet considered a bill to establish a Truth and Reconciliation Commission.

Education and Training
☛ The ICRC set up a pilot project called Exploring Humanitarian Law, which aimed at providing basic knowledge of international humanitarian law to teenagers in Burundi. Four secondary schools took part in the programme in the 2001-2002 school year. The aim of the programme was to broaden it so as to cover more secondary schools in the following school year and to ultimately have it included in the curriculum of Burundian secondary schools.[77]

MARIA NYBONDAS

CAMBODIA[78]

The Emblem
☛ Royal Decree on the Use and Protection of the Red Cross or Red Crescent Emblem. Adopted on 6 May 2002 and immediately entered into force

'It regulates the different authorised uses of the emblems (as a protective device by the medical and religious services of the armed forces, by civilian hospitals and medical personnel, transports and units, and by religious personnel attached to such units, and by the Cambodian Red Cross; use as an indicative device by the Cambodian Red Cross and other National Red Cross or Red Crescent Societies; and use by the international components of the Movement). It provides for punishment of misuse, including perfidious use in time of war, which qualifies as a war crime under the applicable law.'[79]

---

72. UPRONA – Union for National Progress Party.

73. PARENA – Party for National Recovery.

74. See Report of the Secretary-General to the Security Council on the situation in Burundi, UN Doc. S/2002/1259 (18 November 2002). <http://www.hri.ca/fortherecord2002/documentation/security/s-2002-1259.htm>.

75. Ibid., para. 13.

76. See Human Rights Watch, World Report 2003, covering the period between November 2001 and November 2002. <http://www.hrw.org/wr2k3/africa2.html>.

77. See *ICRC Annual Report 2002*, Burundi: October 2002. <http://www.icrc.org>.

78. Information and commentaries by David Boyle, Solicitor admitted to the Bar of the New South Wales Supreme Court, Australia; instructor at the Paris Law Clinic in international criminal law, University of Paris I; Doctorate candidate, University of Paris II.

79. Source: ICRC Advisory Service, National Implementation of International Humanitarian Law

Khmer Rouge Trials
- Law on the Establishment of the Extraordinary Chambers in the Courts of Cambodia for the Prosecution of Crimes Committed during the Period of Democratic Kampuchea [*Kram* NS/RKM/0801/12]. Adopted on 10 August 2001 [Official translation available at <http://www.ocm.gov.kh/> Khmers rouges Law as promulgated; unofficial copy also available at <http://www.ridi.org/boyle/kr_law_10-08-02.htm>

Negotiations for the implementation of the Law, which was finally promulgated in July 2001, continued throughout 2002 without any sign of success.[80]

International Criminal Court
- Cambodia's National Assembly unanimously endorsed the ICC ratification bill on 26 November 2001 and the Senate subsequently approved the bill on 20 December 2001.

After the King's signature, Cambodia ratified the treaty on 11 April 2002, participating in the simultaneous deposit at the special UN treaty ceremony to mark the 60 ratifications necessary for entry into force, thus becoming the first country in the ASEAN and South Asia to ratify the Rome treaty.

However, by the end of 2002 there had been no progress towards adoption of implementation legislation, either as a separate bill or as part of the still pending Code of Criminal Law and Procedure.

Cases
- *Nuon Paet*, Cambodian Supreme Court, Phnom Penh, 4 September 2002, unreported
- *Chhouk Rin*, Cambodian Court of Appeal, Phnom Penh, 6 September 2002, unreported
- *Sam Bith*, Phnom Penh Municipal Court, 23 December 2002, unreported

In the first of a series of developments in cases involving the kidnapping and murder of three Western backpackers by the Khmer Rouge in July 1994, the Cambodian Supreme Court decided on 4 September 2002 to uphold the sentence of life imprisonment against General Nuon Paet for a range of charges, including terrorism. The former Khmer Rouge officer has now exhausted all legal options for appeal.

On 6 September 2002, another rebel officer, Colonel Chhouk Rin, had his acquittal by the Phnom Penh Municipal Court on similar charges overturned *in absentia* by the Cambodian Court of Appeal. The acquittal, based on an amnesty law passed three weeks before the attack, had led to heavy pressure for a retrial from donor countries.

Finally, on 23 December 2002, Sam Bith, the officer in command of the area in southwestern Cambodia where the train was ambushed, was also sentenced to life imprisonment for his part in the killing of the backpackers.

– Biannual update on national legislation and case-law, January-June 2002. <http://www.icrc.org/Web/eng/siteeng0.nsf/html/5FLE9G?OpenDocument>.

80. For a detailed analysis of the law and the work to establish Extraordinary Chambers for Cambodia, see the article by D. Boyle in this volume at p. 167.

☞ *Cambodian Freedom Fighters*, Phnom Penh Municipal Court, 28 February 2002, unreported

The Cambodian Freedom Fighters (CFF) emerged in November 1998 in the wake of political violence that brought the Cambodian People's Party to power. The US-based group, which has an avowed aim of overthrowing the government, claimed responsibility for an armed attack in late November 2000 on several government installations, killing at least eight persons and wounding more than a dozen civilians.

Cambodian courts in February and March 2002 prosecuted a total of 38 CFF members suspected of staging the attack. The courts convicted 19 members, including one US citizen, of terrorism and/or membership in an armed group and sentenced them to terms of five years to life imprisonment. These convictions followed two earlier trials in June and November 2001, involving a total of 56 convictions.

Various criticisms have been made concerning these mass trials, including uncertainty concerning the applicable criminal law, arrest without a warrant, exceeding the six month limit on pre-trial detention, failure to allow counsel sufficient access to the accused and failure to present key prosecution witnesses in court. Given the inclusion of prominent opposition politicians in lists of suspected members of the CFF, there have also been claims of political manipulation of the courts.

DAVID BOYLE

CANADA[81]

Armed Forces

☞ Annual Report of the Judge Advocate General to the Minister of National Defence on the Administration of Military Justice in the Canadian Forces: A review from 1 April 2001 to 31 March 2002 <http://www.forces.gc.ca/jag/office/publications/annual_reports/2002annualreport_e.pdf>

This was the third annual report by the Judge Advocate General (JAG) on the administration of justice in the Canadian Armed Forces, with the aim of increasing the public accountability and transparency of military justice. The report describes the function of the JAG and its links with other institutions, and explains the Canadian military justice measures that have been taken to improve its administration. It also reviews summary charges, proceedings and court martial decisions from April 2001 to March 2002. According to the report, no charges were made during that period for violations of humanitarian law of armed conflict.

Landmines

☞ Donation to Canadian Landmine Fund

Marking the fifth anniversary of the signing of the Ottawa Convention banning antipersonnel mines, the Minister of Foreign Affairs announced on 29 November 2002 that Canada

---

81. Information and commentaries by René Provost, Associate Professor and Associate Dean, Faculty of Law and Institute of Comparative Law, McGill University, Montreal. This report was prepared with the assistance of Ms Caroline Deschênes.

would provide an additional $72 million for the Canadian Landmine Fund over a five-year period beginning in April 2003. The new funding was to be used to promote adherence to the Ottawa Convention but also to support global mine action activities, such as mine risk education, destruction of stockpiled mines and mine-clearing projects. This $72 million was in addition to the $120,000 announced by the Minister in July 2002 for the Mine Action Resource Centre located in Colombo, Sri Lanka. The Canadian Landmine Fund was created in 1997 to provide direct assistance to mine-affected communities around the world, and since then it has disbursed approximately $72 million toward mine action activities in more than 25 developing countries.[82]

War Crimes
☛ Canada's War Crimes Program, 5th Annual Report 2001-2002, published on 11 October 2002 at <http://www.cic.gc.ca/english/pub/war2002/index.html>

Based on the premise that 'Canada will not become a safe haven for those individuals who have committed war crimes, crimes against humanity or any other reprehensible acts during armed conflict', Canada's War Crimes Program provides a financial and operational framework to ensure that appropriate enforcement action is taken against suspected war criminals. The Program works through a special partnership between the Department of Justice Canada, the Department of Citizenship and Immigration and the RCMP (Royal Canadian Mounted Police), who, in 1998, were allocated $46.8 million over three years to investigate and litigate new cases, expand capacity for interdiction abroad, improve case processing in Canada and provide enhanced infrastructure for the War Crimes Program.

This fifth annual report, covering the fiscal year 2001-2002, details the government's progress in bringing to justice those involved in war crimes during World War II and more recent wars, and provides information concerning Canada's war crimes strategy, international cooperation, partnerships and the resources set aside to achieve the government's objectives. The report reveals that 445 people were prevented from entering Canada in 2001-2002 (bringing the total to 2,011 for the last five years) and that 46 people were removed from Canada for war crimes-related allegations, which represents an increase of ten percent over 2000-2001 (bringing the total to 233 since the inception of the Program). There are approximately 79 active World War II files and 205 immigration cases under study by the Department of Citizenship and Immigration, dealing with modern war crimes-related allegations.

The fifth report also contains the conclusions of the final report on the formal evaluation of Canada's War Crimes Program. The purpose of this evaluation was to assess the effectiveness of the Program and to review its internal and external outcomes by answering specific evaluation questions relating to its relevance, design, delivery and program success levels. It concluded that since the inception of the War Crimes Program, Canada has the mechanisms in place to deal effectively with war criminals and persons who have com-

---

82. <http://www.dfait-maeci.gc.ca/minpub/Publication.asp?FileSpec=/Min_Pub_Docs/105746. htm&bPrint=False&Year=&ID=&Language=E>; <http://www.dfait-maeci.gc.ca/minpub/Publication. asp?FileSpec=/Min_Pub_Docs/105740.htm&bPrint=False&Year=&ID=&Language=E>; <httphttp:// www.dfait-maeci.gc.ca/minpub/Publication.asp?FileSpec=/Min_Pub_Docs/105375.htm&bPrint= False&Year=&ID=&Language=E>.

mitted crimes against humanity and that it will continue to apply and improve these mechanisms in order to achieve greater compliance with international norms.

Cases
☛ *Vujović* case, Decision of the Convention Refugee Determination Division, 4 April 2002

The 5th Annual Report of Canada's War Crimes Program, covering the fiscal year 2001-2002, contains illustrations of expulsion of refugee claimants for their participation in contemporary war crimes. The following case is a good example of the legal processes followed to remove such individuals from Canada.

In March 1997 Zoran Vujović, a Yugoslav citizen, was admitted as a visitor at Vancouver International Airport with a fraudulent British passport. The following month, he applied for refugee status, alleging that he was a trained employee of the Yugoslav State Security administration and a member of the secret police. On 28 June 1998, the Minister of Citizenship and Immigration filed an intervention and evidence was introduced to demonstrate that Vujović was complicit in crimes against humanity for his delivery of weapons to Serbian combatants in Albania, Bosnia and Herzegovina and Croatia during the war. The Convention Refugee Determination Division (CRDD) emphasized that prior to making these arms deliveries, which assisted the Serbian military and paramilitary groups in committing crimes against humanity, such as the execution of Croatian prisoners, Vujović knew of the atrocities perpetrated against Croatian civilians in Vukovar. However, Vujović left Yugoslavia immediately prior to an inquiry into alleged war crimes committed by his associates. On the basis of these facts, the CRDD excluded Vujović from refugee determination on 4 April 2000. He applied to the Federal Court for judicial review, but was refused leave to appeal. On 20 February 2002, Vujović was removed to the Federal Republic of Yugoslavia under escort.

☛ *Aleksić* v. *Canada (Attorney General)*, Ontario Superior Court of Justice, 8 July 2002. Reported at (2002) 215 DLR (4th) 720; (2002) 13 C.C.L.T. (3rd) 139

In January 2001, an Ontario Superior Court of Justice Judge held that a group of 50 Canadians of Serbian origin and seven Serb nationals could sue the Canadian government for its participation in the NATO missile and aerial bombardments of parts of the Federal Republic of Yugoslavia in 1999. The group alleged that Canada thereby contravened international law and infringed the Canadian Charter of Rights and Freedom,[83] and demanded $76 million in compensation for deaths, injuries and property damage suffered by their relatives in Serbia. The judge gave them 60 days to update their statement of claim to establish exactly how each of them was directly affected by the bombing. The Canadian government appealed the decision, contending that the statement of claim should be struck down on the basis that the claims were not justiciable and did not disclose a reasonable cause of action.

In July 2002, a majority of the Ontario Superior Court of Justice allowed the appeal, mainly on the grounds that Canada should be immune from tort liability in matters of pure policy, as was the case with respect to its decision to participate in NATO bombing, and that

---

83. Constitution Act, 1982 (79). Enacted as Schedule B to the *Canada Act 1982* (UK) 1982, c. 11, which came into force on 17 April 1982.

the Crown and its agents were under no duty of care to avoid causing injury or damage to private individuals during the course of military hostilities. An application for leave to appeal to the Ontario Court of Appeal was filed on 16 September 2002, but no decision had been rendered by the end of the year.

☛ Citizenship revocation and extradition proceedings against Michael Seifert

In November 2000, an Italian Military Tribunal found Michael Seifert, a naturalized Canadian citizen, guilty of war crimes, including murder and torture, committed while he was a guard at a German police transit camp in Northern Italy in 1944-1945. The Military Court of Appeal of Verona dismissed his appeal of the conviction on 18 October 2001.[84] As a result, the Canadian Minister of Citizenship and Immigration served a Notice of Intent to revoke Seifert's Canadian citizenship. Seifert then requested, pursuant to Section 18(2) of the 1998 Citizenship Act, that the matter be referred to the Federal Court to determine whether he was admitted to Canada on the basis of false representation, fraud or by knowingly concealing material circumstances. On 13 November 2001, a statement of claim was issued in Vancouver. Seifert was arrested in Vancouver, on 1 May 2002, pursuant to an arrest warrant that had been issued following an extradition request from Italy,[85] but was subsequently released while the citizenship revocation proceeding and the extradition request were still pending before the courts.

Ongoing Cases
☛ *Ribich* case

In 2002, Nicholas Ribich, a Canadian of Serb descent who joined the Bosnian Serb Army as a volunteer, faced four charges of hostage-taking under Canadian law for his alleged involvement in the abduction of four military observers who were used as human shields in order to prevent air strikes by NATO on Bosnian Serb positions during the NATO bombing of Bosnia in May 1995. The Canadian Criminal Code was amended in 1989 to allow for prosecutions of hostage-taking committed abroad, but this was believed to be the first time a Canadian was being prosecuted under this new provision, which provided for a maximum sentence of life in prison. Ribich was arrested in Germany in February 1999 and was subsequently extradited to Canada in May 1999. The trial began on 7 October 2002, but the judge of the Ontario Superior Court declared a mistrial on 20 January 2003, after the lawyers of the defendant argued that their defence rested on national security issues, some of which were currently before the Federal Court of Canada Appeals Division. A new trial date was to be fixed in March 2003.[86]

RENÉ PROVOST

---

84. See 4 *YIHL* (2001) pp. 566-568.
85. See further the Italian Report, *infra* in this volume p. 555.
86. See S. Thorne, 'Judge declares mistrial in case of Canadian who fought for Serb Army', Canadian Press, 23 January 2003. <http://cnews.canoe.ca/CNEWS/Canada/2003/01/20/13377-cp.html>.

CHILE[87]

Cases

☛ Opinion of the Constitutional Court regarding the Rome Statute of the International Criminal Court, 8 April 2002 <http://www.tribunalconstitucional.cl>

Within the context of the procedure of approval of the Rome Statute (the Statute) by the Chilean Parliament, on 4 March 2002 the Deputies Chamber submitted the correspondent bill to the Constitutional Court (the Court), asking it to render an opinion on the compatibility of the Statute with the Chilean Constitution (the Constitution). As with France, Portugal, Luxembourg and Ireland before Chile, the Court established the need for constitutional amendment prior to the approval by the Parliament and later ratification by the Chilean government of the Statute, on the following grounds:

— The juridical nature of the jurisdiction of the International Criminal Court (the ICC) is in fact not complementary to national criminal jurisdictions, as stated in the Statute, but corrective and even substitutive or supplementary, in certain cases, to that of national jurisdictions. This means that the Statute is deferring to a new jurisdiction, not contemplated in the Constitution, the right to begin procedures for crimes committed in Chile, which amounts to a transfer of sovereignty not authorised by Chilean constitutional law.

— Unlike other international courts established in international treaties ratified by Chile, such as the American Convention on Human Rights and the Statute of the International Court of Justice, that can neither correct nor substitute national courts' resolutions, the ICC is a supranational tribunal that is enabled to examine the intentions and motivations of Chilean national tribunals, a right not given in the Chilean constitutional order to any other state power besides the judiciary.

— According to the Statute, the ICC could disregard pardons and amnesties previously granted by competent national authorities. This in fact limits the power of the President of the Republic to issue individual pardons and also deprives the legislature of its power to issue general pardons and amnesties, in relation to the crimes mentioned in Article 5 of the Statute.

— The parliamentary exemption and privileges and immunities established in the Constitution for judges of the judiciary generally, judges of the Court, judicial prosecutors, the National Prosecutor, regional prosecutors and adjunct prosecutors would no longer apply where the Statute considers their direct processing before the ICC.

— The Statute creates certain powers of the ICC Prosecutor – among which are those to investigate in the territory of the parties to the treaty, gather and examine evidence, subpoena and interrogate those persons investigated and the victims and witnesses – that infringe the constitutional norm that entrusts the direction of the investigation of the facts that constitute crimes exclusively to the State Attorney's General Office.

Following this decision of the Constitutional Court, the government sent a draft of a constitutional amendment to the Parliament that was still pending in the legislative organ by the end of 2002.

---

87. Information and commentaries by Hernán Salinas Burgos, Professor of Public International Law, Catholic University of Chile and Sebastián Lopéz Escarcena, Assistant Professor of Public International Law, Catholic University of Chile.

☛ Decision of the Supreme Court regarding the definitive dismissal of the criminal process against *General Augusto Pinochet Ugarte*, 1 July 2002

Based on the judicially established incurable nature of the mental illness affecting General Pinochet, the Supreme Court declared the definitive dismissal of the process initiated against the former Chilean ruler for the crimes perpetrated by the military party led by General Sergio Arellano Stark in the month of October 1973. With this sentence, the Supreme Court annulled the temporal dismissal dictated by the Court of Appeals of Santiago in 9 July 2001 which allowed for the reopening of the process in case General Pinochet recovered from his already established mental illness.[88]

The Court's conclusion on General Pinochet's mental health followed from medical experts' reports, according to which it was acquired after the perpetration of the crimes investigated. The incurable nature of the mental illness of the former ruler would make him unable to be part of a criminal procedural relationship every time his legal capacity to act in a criminal procedure is affected by what is technically called 'moderate insanity' in Chilean legislation.

The decision of the Supreme Court was founded in the application of certain provisions of the Criminal Procedure Code established in favour of those accused in this type of procedure, such as Article 349 of the mentioned Code, compelling judges to submit any accused person older than 70 years to a mental examination, notwithstanding the penalty for the correspondent crime, and Article 686 of the same Code, providing that if an incurable mental illness is established in the process, the respective criminal procedure must be definitively dismissed.

HERNÁN SALINAS BURGOS and SEBASTIÁN LOPÉZ ESCARCENA

COLOMBIA[89]

Landmines

☛ Law No. 759 of 25 July 2002 implementing the Ottawa Convention [Ley 759 de 2002 (25 de julio) por medio de la cual se dictan normas para dar cumplimiento a la Convención sobre la Prohibición del Empleo, Almacenamiento, Producción y Transferencia de minas antipersonal y sobre su destrucción y se fijan disposiciones con el fin de erradicar en Colombia el uso de las minas antipersonal]. Adopted by the Senate on 20 July 2002, promulgated on 25 July 2002, entered into force on 30 July 2002, the date of its publication, published in *Diario Oficial (D.O.)* No. 44883, 30 July 2002, p. 2

By adding a new article (Art. 367A) to the chapter on International Humanitarian Law in the Colombian Penal Code, Law 759 criminalised the use, production, sale and stockpiling of antipersonnel mines, and specified penalties from ten to 15 years imprisonment, a fine of 500 to 1,000 times the minimum legal monthly salary in force and interdiction from exercising rights and public functions for between ten and 15 years.[90] Abetting or induction is also penalised (Art. 367B).[91]

---

88. See 4 *YIHL* (2001) at pp. 477-478.

89. Information and commentaries by Professor Rafael A. Prieto Sanjuán (Paris II), Consultant and Professor of Public International Law and International Relations at Externado University of Colombia, Bogotá, D.C.

Chemical Weapons

☛ Decree No. 1419 establishing the National Authority for the Prohibition of the Development, Production, Stockpiling and Use of Chemical Weapons and for their Destruction. Signed on 10 July 2002, entered into force on 13 July 2002

The National Authority is an inter-sectoral commission, established in accordance with Article VII(4) of the 1993 Convention on Chemical Weapons, 'which comprises the Ministers (or their representatives) of Foreign Affairs, National Defence, Agriculture and Rural Development, Trade, Environment and Health. The mandate of the Authority is: to facilitate implementation of the Convention; to coordinate the activities of the governmental and industrial sector to that effect; to serve as a liaison office between the government and the Organisation for the Prohibition of Chemical Weapons (OPCW); to defend national interests within the framework of the OPCW and in relations with other States Parties; to draft the rules for implementation of the Convention; to assist the government in programmes, to undertake planning, projects and recommendations to implement the Convention; and to undertake any other appropriate activity.[92]

International Criminal Court

☛ Law No. 742 of 5 July 2002 by which is approved the Rome Statute of the International Criminal Court, done in Rome on 17 July 1998 [Ley 742 del 5 de junio de 2002 'Por medio de la cual se aprueba el Estatuto de Roma de la Corte Penal Internacional, hecho en Roma el día diecisiete (17) de julio de mil novecientos noventa y ocho (1998)']. Published in *D.O.* No. 44826, 7 June 2002, p. 1

☛ Constitutional Judgement C-578 of 30 July 2002 in the revision process of Law 742/2002 (dossier LAT-223) [Sentencia de Constitucionalidad C-578 del 30 de julio de 2002 en el proceso de revisión de la Ley 742/2002 (expediente LAT-223)] <http://juriscol.banrep.gov.co:8080>

☛ Ratification with Interpretative Declarations of the ICC Statute, Ministry of Foreign Affairs, 2 August 2002 (instrument deposited 5 August 2002) [Ratificación con declaraciones interpretativas del Estatuto de la Corte Penal Internacional (instrumento depositado el 5 de agosto de 2002)] <http://untreaty.un.org/ENGLISH/bible/englishinternetbible/partI/chapterXVIII/treaty10.asp#Declarations>

---

90. Colombian Penal Code, Art. 367A. '*Empleo, producción, comercialización y almacenamiento de minas antipersonal.* El que emplee, produzca, comercialice, ceda y almacene, directa o indirectamente, minas antipersonal o vectores específicamente concebidos como medios de lanzamiento o dispersión de minas antipersonal, incurrirá en prisión de diez (10) a quince (15) años, en multa de quinientos (500) a mil (1.000) salarios mínimos mensuales legales vigentes, y en inhabilitación para el ejercicio de derechos y funciones públicas de cinco (5) a diez (10) años.'

91. Ibid., Art. 367B. '*Ayuda e inducción al empleo, producción y transferencia de minas antipersonal.* El que promueva, ayude, facilite, estimule o induzca a otra persona a participar en cualquiera de las actividades contempladas en el artículo 367A del Código Penal, incurrirá en prisión de seis (6) a diez (10) años y en multa de doscientos (200) a quinientos (500) salarios mínimos mensuales legales vigentes.'

92. Source: ICRC Advisory Service, National Implementation of International Humanitarian Law – Biannual update on national legislation and case-law, January-June 2002. <http://www.icrc.org/Web/eng/siteeng0.nsf/html/5FLE9G?OpenDocument>.

Despite its active support for the ICC during the Rome Conference and during the subsequent Preparatory Commissions drafting the Elements of Crimes and the Rules of Procedure and Evidence, by the end of 2001 the Colombian government had yet to present a bill or project in the Congress for the implementation of the Rome Statute into Colombian law.[93] What was the reason for this failure and what solution was adopted in order to rectify the Executive's omission?

The most obvious explanation for the government's reticence was the negotiation process pursued by the former government, which placed its hopes on the possibility of achieving peace or the reinsertion into civilian life of the armed opposition, and which feared that the possibility of the negotiators of the armed insurgence being indicted by the ICC would impede this goal. Another explanation may be the so-called American Servicemembers' Protection Act of 2002,[94] an Act which provides, *inter alia*, that those states – with some exceptions – that ratify the Rome Statute will be sanctioned by the withholding of US military assistance. As is well known, Colombia at the relevant time was the second greatest beneficiary of this help in the world, and had very little interest in losing US support, particularly as the option of a negotiated solution to the conflict seemed to fade.

The answer to the Executive's inefficiency came from the Republic's Congress. Via a reform project (or so-called Legislative Act) of the Constitution, the first step was research into the question of incorporation of the ICC Statute from a constitutional point of view. Even though it is not easy to reform the Constitution in Colombia, this procedure had the advantage of ignoring the faculties of the President in relation to international relations and evading constitutional review by the court, which is competent only to examine the formal conditions of the legislative act but not its substantive conditions.[95] This is mainly due to the fact that the people represented by the parliament are sovereign in these matters. The only uncertainty concerned the form of the deposit of the ratification instrument that would bind Colombia, and whether the government would oppose the Congress, in which case the development of the mechanisms for cooperation with the ICC would be an arduous task.

Finally, the Congress and the government came to an agreement: the former would reform the Constitution, reserving the application of the Rome Statute only in matters competent to it. This means that it would not modify or apply in its internal order. For its part, the government would be authorised (and tacitly compromised) to expedite the corresponding norms that would enable the ratification and implementation of the Statute.[96] In this way, once the legislative act that reformed Article 93 (adding a second paragraph) of the Constitution had been approved,[97] the government deposited the ICC Statute incorporation bill

---

93. See Correspondents' Reports in 3 *YIHL* (2000) p. 454.

94. US Public Law (PL) 107-206: 2 August 2002 (signature of President George W. Bush). For the text, analysis and chronology of this law, see the site of the Washington Working Group on the International Criminal Court <http://www.wfa.org/issues/wicc/aspafinal/aspahome.html>. Reprinted in this volume at p. 619. See also the US report *infra* in this volume at p. 621.

95. Art. 188, §§ 2 and 6; Arts. 241 and 379 of the Colombian Constitution.

96. Documents on the implementation process may be consulted on the website of the Coalition for the ICC. See in particular <http://www.iccnow.org/espanol/colombia/col_2vuelta.pdf>.

97. Art. 93. — 'Los tratados y convenios internacionales ratificados por el Congreso, que reconocen los derechos humanos y que prohíben su limitación en los estados de excepción, prevalecen en el orden interno. Los derechos y deberes consagrados en esta Carta, se interpretarán de conformidad con los tratados internacionales sobre derechos humanos ratificados por Colombia.

Adicionado. A.L. 02/2001, art. 1º. El Estado colombiano puede reconocer la jurisdicción de la Corte Penal Internacional en los términos previstos en el Estatuto de Roma adoptado el 17 de julio de 1998

before the Congress, which approved it without major inconveniences. It was then sent for presidential sanction and revision by the Constitutional Court, which subjected it to a fast and formal procedure. Finally, after this, the former government of President Andrés Pastrana, which was due to leave office on 7 August 2002, deposited, two days before this date, the ratification instrument that binds it as a party to the ICC Statute.

To the apparent surprise of Congress, *inter alia*, the ratification Act made use of the safeguard (opting-out) clause contained in Article 124 of the Statute.[98] An 'authorisation to assassinate and massacre' for some, this clause was considered by the outgoing government, and endorsed by the new one of President Alvaro Uribe, as a 'window for peace', in order to leave open the possibility of a negotiated resolution of the armed conflict. Notwith-

---

por la Conferencia de plenipotenciarios de la Naciones Unidas y, consecuentemente, ratificar este tratado de conformidad con el procedimiento establecido en esta Constitución.

La admisión de un tratamiento diferente en materias sustanciales por parte del Estatuto de Roma con respecto a las garantías contenidas en la Constitución tendrá efectos exclusivamente dentro del ámbito de la materia regulada en él.'

98. In total, Colombia included six declarations with the deposit of the ratification instrument of the ICC Statute:

1. None of the provisions of the Rome Statute concerning the exercise of jurisdiction by the International Criminal Court prevent the Colombian State from granting amnesties, reprieves or judicial pardons for political crimes, provided that they are granted in conformity with the Constitution and with the principles and norms of international law accepted by Colombia.

Colombia declares that the provisions of the Statute must be applied and interpreted in a manner consistent with the provisions of international humanitarian law and, consequently, that nothing in the Statute affects the rights and obligations embodied in the norms of international humanitarian law, especially those set forth in article 3 common to the four Geneva Conventions and in Protocols I and II Additional thereto.

Likewise, in the event that a Colombian national has to be investigated and prosecuted by the International Criminal Court, the Rome Statute must be interpreted and applied, where appropriate, in accordance with the principles and norms of international humanitarian law and international human rights law.

2. With respect to articles 61(2)(b) and 67(1)(d), Colombia declares that it will always be in the interests of justice that Colombian nationals be fully guaranteed the right of defence, especially the right to be assisted by counsel during the phases of investigation and prosecution by the International Criminal Court.

3. Concerning article 17(3), Colombia declares that the use of the word "otherwise" with respect to the determination of the State's ability to investigate or prosecute a case refers to the obvious absence of objective conditions necessary to conduct the trial.

4. Bearing in mind that the scope of the Rome Statute is limited exclusively to the exercise of complementary jurisdiction by the International Criminal Court and to the cooperation of national authorities with it, Colombia declares that none of the provisions of the Rome Statute alters the domestic law applied by the Colombian judicial authorities in exercise of their domestic jurisdiction within the territory of the Republic of Colombia.

5. Availing itself of the option provided in article 124 of the Statute and subject to the conditions established therein, the government of Colombia declares that it does not accept the jurisdiction of the Court with respect to the category of crimes referred to in article 8 when a crime is alleged to have been committed by Colombian nationals or on Colombian territory.

6. In accordance with article 87(1)(a) and the first paragraph of article 87(2), the government of Colombia declares that requests for cooperation or assistance shall be transmitted through the diplomatic channel and shall either be in or be accompanied by a translation into the Spanish language.'
<http://untreaty.un.org/ENGLISH/bible/englishinternetbible/partI/chapterXVIII/treaty10.asp#Declarations>.

standing, peace talks broke down in Spring 2002, although the guerrilla groups seemed to prefer to stage acts of a terrorist nature rather than engage in direct military confrontation.[99]

Apart from the internal situation, other difficulties persisted in the international order which contributed to Colombia's reticence to join the ICC Statute. The United States insisted that Colombia sign a bilateral (Art. 98) agreement excluding US nationals from the ICC's jurisdiction, similar to those it has negotiated with other countries. In the face of strong public opinion, Bogotá responded by stating that a cooperation accord previously signed with the US in 1962 gives full guarantees of immunity from international criminal jurisdiction to American soldiers. Nonetheless, Washington insisted on getting a new and clear agreement that expressly excludes military and civil personnel from the ICC's jurisdiction. The situation presently seems to be in a *status quo* as both countries are interdependent in their fight against drug trafficking and terrorism.

Finally, attacks against the civilian population that could constitute crimes against humanity, even genocide, are under the jurisdiction of the ICC if national jurisdictions are not able or willing to prosecute individuals charged with these crimes. Amnesties granted as a condition for political agreements with unlawful armed groups could indicate such inability or unwillingness. Colombia's ratification of the ICC Statute will thus constitute a special limit on its freedom of manoeuvre in dealing with armed opposition groups: peace cannot be founded on impunity for the gravest crimes without the establishment of responsibility, both state (entity) and individual (public or private).

RAFAEL A. PRIETO SANJUÁN

Disciplinary Code
☛ Law No. 734 introducing a new disciplinary code. Adopted on 5 February 2002, published on 13 February 2002, entered into force on 5 May 2002

'It contains disciplinary rules that must be observed by public officials. Article 34 provides in particular that every public official must "accomplish and ensure accomplishment of duties contained in international humanitarian law treaties", and Article 48 states that "committing serious violations of international humanitarian law" and "failure to obey orders and instructions contained in Presidential Orders intended to promote human rights or implement international humanitarian law" are considered to be very serious offences.'[100]

(DEMOCRATIC REPUBLIC OF THE) CONGO

The Peace Process
☛ Pretoria Peace Accord. Signed by President Joseph Kabila of the Democratic Republic of the Congo and the Republic of Rwanda President Paul Kagame on 30 July 2002 in Pretoria, South Africa

---

99. See the database of the Presidential Program on Human Rights: <http://www.derechoshuma nos.gov.co/observatorio>.

100. Source: ICRC Advisory Service, National Implementation of International Humanitarian Law – Biannual update on national legislation and case-law, January-June 2002. <http://www.icrc.org/Web/eng/siteeng0.nsf/html/5FLE9G?OpenDocument>.

The President of the Democratic Republic of the Congo (DRC) Joseph Kabila and Rwandan President Paul Kagame signed the peace agreement in Pretoria in the presence of representatives of the African Union and the United Nations. The agreement represented the end of the conflict between the DRC and the Republic of Rwanda. The conflict in the unstable Great Lakes region intensified in 1998 and up until the agreement had claimed a huge number of victims. The peace agreement was supported by the Security Council of the United Nations and the government of South Africa.[101] Incorporated in the peace accord were measures that were to be taken by both the DRC and Rwanda. The government of the DRC committed itself to, among other things, disarm the Interahamwe and ex-FAR (former Rwandan Army) within the territory of the DRC under its control and repatriate Rwandan ex-combatants to Rwanda. Rwanda was to withdraw its troop from the DRC when the security concerns in the DRC had been adequately addressed. Both the DRC and Rwanda agreed on a 90-day programme for the implementation of the peace agreement.[102]

Pending
☛ Legislation to implement the Statute of the International Criminal Court

Following its ratification of the Rome Statute on 11 April 2002, the government of the DRC drafted implementing legislation. 'The draft legislation includes provisions on cooperation and the incorporation of crimes under the Rome Statute. The draft also raises the age of criminal responsibility from 16 to 18, and calls for supplementary measures to ensure objective assessments of the age of the accused. Furthermore, the legislation reasserts the universal jurisdiction of the Congolese courts (provided under Article 3 of the Criminal Code). The draft was presented and defended before a range of stakeholders (the Law Reform Commission, Judiciary Section of the Supreme Court, Presidency and various Ministries) in October 2002.'[103]

(REPUBLIC OF THE) CONGO-BRAZZAVILLE

Constitution
☛ New Constitution, 20 January 2002

'On 20 January 2002 the new Constitution was approved by referendum. Article 10 of the new Constitution states that no one is bound to obey an order which would obviously constitute a violation of human rights or of any public freedom. Likewise, such violations cannot be justified by citing superior orders. Article 11 states that war crimes, crimes

---

101. 'Accord signed towards ending Congolese conflict', UN Chronicle, Vol. XXXIV, Issue 3, United Nations 2002. Online Edition: <http://www.un.org/Pubs/chronicle/2002/issue3/081902_rwanda_congo_accord.html>.
102. DRC-RWANDA: Text of the Pretoria Memorandum of Understanding, IRINnews.org, Integrated Regional Information Networks (IRIN), 31 July 2002, <http://www.irinnews.org/report.asp?ReportID=29111&SelectRegion=Great_Lakes&SelectCountry=DRC-RWANDA> and DRC-RWANDA: Kabila, Kagame sign peace pact, IRINnews.org, Integrated Regional Information Networks (IRIN), 30 July 2002, <http://www.irinnews.org/report.asp?ReportID=29092&SelectRegion=Great_Lakes&SelectCountry=DRC-RWANDA>.
103. Source: CICC/Africa: Congo, Democratic Republic. <http://www.iccnow.org/countryinfo/africa/congodemrep.html>.

against humanity and the crime of genocide will be punished in accordance with the law and that such crimes are not subject to statutory limitations.'[104]

International Court of Justice
☛ Petition against France filed before the International Court of Justice, 10 December 2002

On 10 December 2002, the Republic of the Congo filed a petition with the ICJ seeking to block France from putting the Congolese Minister of the Interior, Pierre Oba, on trial for crimes against humanity and torture. In its petition, Congo said that the effort by France to prosecute Mr Oba for crimes allegedly committed 'in connection with the exercise of his powers for the maintenance of public order in his country' amounted to a breach of the principle that one country cannot exercise its authority on the territory of another. The court document also stated that in issuing a warrant instructing police officers to examine President Denis Sassou Nguesso as a witness in the case, France violated 'the criminal immunity of a foreign Head of State, an international customary rule recognised by the jurisprudence of the Court', and asked the Court to annul all investigation and prosecution efforts.[105]

France's agreement to the Court's jurisdiction in this case was required for the Court to exercise jurisdiction. The petition and a request for preliminary measures were transmitted to Paris, but no action had been taken by the end of the year.

COOK ISLANDS

Geneva Law
☛ Geneva Conventions and Additional Protocols Act 2002 (An Act to consolidate and amend the Geneva Conventions Act 1958). Adopted and entered into force on 11 February 2002

'It provides for the punishment of grave breaches of the 1949 Geneva Conventions and of the 1977 Additional Protocol I on a universal jurisdiction basis. It also makes it an offence to use, without the consent of the Ministry of Foreign Affairs or if not otherwise authorised under Section 12 of the *Cook Island Red Cross Society Act 2002*, the red cross, red crescent and red lion and sun emblems; the designations linked to each of these emblems; the heraldic emblem of the Swiss Confederation; the distinctive sign of civil defence; the distinctive signals of Annex I to Additional Protocol I; the special sign for works and installations containing dangerous forces; and any emblem, designation or signal too closely resembling these. It regulates certain aspects of legal proceedings instituted against prisoners of war or other protected internees. The texts of the Conventions and Protocols are not annexed, but the Act provides for the distribution of copies to those concerned or interested.'[106]

---

104. Source: ICRC Advisory Service, National Implementation of International Humanitarian Law – Biannual update on national legislation and case-law, January-June 2002. <http://www.icrc.org/Web/eng/siteeng0.nsf/html/5FLE9G?OpenDocument>.
105. 'Congo petitions world court to block trial of government petition in France', UN News Centre Report, 10 December 2002. <http://www.un.org/news>.
106. Source: ICRC Advisory Service, National Implementation of International Humanitarian Law

The Emblem
- Cook Islands Red Cross Society Act 2002. The Act to Establish, Recognise and Regulate the Cook Islands Red Cross Society. Adopted and entered into force on 11 February 2002

COSTA RICA

Landmines
- Law No. 8231 on the prohibition of anti-personnel mines [Ley No 8231: prohibición de minas antipersonales]. Adopted on 18 March 2002, promulgated on 2 April 2002, published in *La Gaceta: Diario Oficial*, No. 73, 17 April 2002 and entered into force on the same day

'This law was adopted in order to implement the 1997 Ottawa Convention on Landmines. In particular, it makes it illegal to use and to encourage the use of mines, to develop, produce, acquire, stockpile, retain, import, export, possess, transfer, trade or move about, directly or indirectly, mines, anti-handling devices, constituent parts or raw material for the manufacture thereof. It provides for the destruction of all mines and other prohibited objects in accordance with Article 4 of the Ottawa Convention and for the creation of a special unit to this end. Any violation of this law is punishable by three to six years imprisonment regardless of any penal or civil action that may arise in connection with the death of or injury to a person, or damage to private or public property.'[107]

War Crimes and Crimes Against Humanity
- Law No. 8272 on penal repression to sanction war crimes and crimes against humanity [Ley No 8272: represión penal como castigo por los crímenes de guerra y de lesa humanidad]. Adopted on 25 April 2002, promulgated on 2 May 2002, published in *La Gaceta: Diario Oficial*, No. 97, 22 May 2002 and entered into force the same day

'It amends Article 7 of the Penal Code to include acts committed in contravention of international humanitarian law in the list of acts punishable under national law irrespective of the law applicable at the place where they were committed and irrespective of the nationality of the perpetrator, and adds two new articles (Arts. 378 and 379) that define and fix penalties for war crimes (serious violations of or war crimes under an international humanitarian law treaty) and crimes against humanity (crimes against humanity under a human rights treaty or under the Rome Statute of the International Criminal Court).'[108]

CROATIA

Cases
- Conviction of three former Croatian military policemen for crimes committed in the 1991 war, Bjelovar County Court, 25 January 2002

– Biannual update on national legislation and case-law, January-June 2002. <http://www.icrc.org/Web/eng/siteeng0.nsf/html/5FLE9G?OpenDocument>.
107. Ibid.
108. Ibid.

Three Croatian former military policemen received minimum one-year sentences for illegal arrests and torture leading to the deaths of an unknown number of Croatian Serb civilians. The judge explained the low sentences saying, 'they were Homeland defenders who committed crimes during war circumstances'. The judge also said that there was not enough evidence to convict the three on murder charges since the bodies of the Serbs had not been found.[109]

☛ Conviction of *Nikola Alaica, Mile Bekić, Drago Karagaca, Petar Manula, Milan Prusac* and *Sreto Jovandić*, Osijek District Court, 5 April 2002

The Osijek District Court on 5 April 2002 convicted six ethnic Serbs for war crimes committed against Croatian civilians during the 1991 war in Croatia and sentenced them to prison terms of between two and six years. Nikola Alaica, Mile Bekić, Drago Karagaca, Petar Manula, Milan Prusac and Sreto Jovandić were found guilty of illegally abducting Croat civilians from their homes in eastern Croatia during the minority Serb rebellion against the country's secession from Yugoslavia. The court found that the victims were held in makeshift prisons for several months and some were subjected to physical abuse.[110]

☛ Conviction of *Fikret Abdić*, Karlovac County Court, 31 July 2002

On 31 July 2002, Fikret Abdić, the former warlord who ruled the small breakaway fiefdom of Bihac in northwestern Bosnia during the 1992-1995 Bosnian war, was sentenced to 20 years' imprisonment for war crimes by the Karlovac County Court.[111] The judgement was pronounced a few months before the elections in October 2002 of the three-party Presidency of Bosnia. Abdić had been one of the candidates for the Presidency.[112]

☛ Arrest of *Nikola Ivankovia* and *Enes Viteškia*, 14 September 2002

Two persons suspected of participating in war crimes against 19 civilians in Paulin Dvor, near Osijek, on 11 December 1991, were arrested and taken to the Osijek County Court investigating centre on 14 September 2002.[113] The suspects were said to be a 43-year-old member of the military and a 33-year old civilian, from the Osijek area.[114]

☛ Acquittal of *Tonci Vrkić, Miljenko Bajić, Josip Bikić, Davor Banić, Emil Bungur, Ante Gudica, Andjelko Botić* and *Tomo Dujić* on charges of killing and torturing Serb civilians, Split County Court, 22 November 2002

---

109. 'Former Croat military police sentenced for war crimes', Deutsche Presse-Agentur, 25 January 2002.

110. 'District court convicts six Serbs of war crimes against Croats', AP, 5 April 2002.

111. <http://www.diplomatiejudiciaire.com/Abdic.htm>; 'Bosnia: Croatian Court Convicts Warlord Abdic', 1 August 2002. <http://www.rferl.org/features/2002/08/01082002145759.asp>.

112. For background on the case, see 4 *YIHL* (2001) at pp. 486-487.

113. 'Croatia: Two war crimes suspects arrested in eastern town', BBC Worldwide Monitoring, 14 September 2002.

114. 'Croatia holds two in war-crimes probe', AFP, 14 September 2002.

A court in Split on 22 November 2002 acquitted eight former military police on charges of killing and torturing Serb prisoners in 1992, ending the longest war crimes trial to that date. The local state prosecutor said that he would appeal to the Supreme Court against the acquittal.

The eight were indicted in March 2000 for allegedly killing and beating civilians at the Lora military prison outside Split in 1992. They were also charged with killing two detainees and seriously injuring another two. The 23-page indictment against them said that they had violated the Geneva Conventions on the treatment of prisoners of war.[115] The trial began on 10 June 2001.[116] One of the eight has been on the run since 2001 and was tried *in absentia*. The court released the remaining seven from custody in July. The Supreme Court later ordered their rearrest, but two had meanwhile gone into hiding.[117]

☛ Decision of Constitutional Court on the indictment against General Janko Bobetko, 12 November 2002

On 12 November, the Constitutional Court ruled that it had no authority to rule on the merits of an ICTY war crimes indictment against General Janko Bobetko, charging him with commanding a 1993 operation in which at least 30 Serbs were killed. The ruling said: 'Proving a criminal act and establishing responsibility for such an act can only be done before the relevant court that has raised the indictment.' Croatia was awaiting a ruling from the ICTY Appeals Chamber on its formal complaint against the indictment.[118]

On 23 September 2002, Prime Minister Ivica Racan had said that his cabinet had concluded that 'we cannot act upon the arrest warrant', which had been delivered to the government earlier that day. 'We will not budge from this position and we will pursue all means at our disposal – legal, political and diplomatic' to oppose the indictment.[119]

On 14 November, Prime Minister Ivica Racan said that the government had decided to forward the entire file in the *Bobetko* case, including the medical records, to the competent county court for further procedures.[120]

☛ Decision on the health of General Janko Bobetko, Zagreb County Court, 29 November 2002

The Zagreb County Court ruled on 29 November that General Janko Bobetko, indicted by the ICTY for war crimes, could not be surrendered as he is medically unfit to stand trial.

---

115. 'Trial opens against 8 military policemen charged with wartime killings of Serbs', AP, 10 June 2002.

116. G. Vezić, 'Lora Trial Prosecutors Seek Relocation', Institute for War and Peace Reporting. Tribunal Report No. 272, June 24-30, 2002. <http://www.iwpr.net/index.pl?archive/tri/tri_272_8_eng.txt>.

117. 'Croat court acquits ex-policemen of war crimes', Reuters, 22 November 2002.

118. 'Croatia court says cannot rule on war crimes cases', Reuters, 12 November 2002; 'Constitution Watch, Volume 11/12 Number 4/1, Winter 2002/Spring 2003. <http://www.law.nyu.edu/eecr/vol11_12num4_1/constitutionwatch/croatia.html>.

119. 'Prime minister: Croatia will not extradite wartime army chief to the U.N. court', AP, 23 September 2002.

120. 'PM says government to forward Bobetko file to county court', Hina, 14 November 2002.

The court found that any mental and physical stress put upon the 83-year-old general, could have fatal consequences, given his history of heart problems and diabetes.[121]

Ongoing Cases
☛ The *Gospić five* case

The trial of General Mirko Norac and four others (Tihomir Oresković, Stjepan Grandić, Ivica Rozić and Milan Canić) opened on 28 January 2002, and was continuing as the year closed. Tihomir Oresković, Ivica Rozić, Stjepan Grandić, Milan Canić and Mirko Norac were indicted on charges of war crimes against the civilian population, relating to the killing of at least 40 Serbian civilians in the Gospić area at the end of 1991. If convicted, they could face up to 20 years in prison. At the proceedings, all the defendants except Oresković pleaded not guilty.[122]

☛ Civil suit by Croatian former detainees of Serb-run camps, 7 September 2002

A group of Croatian former detainees of Serb-run detention camps during the conflict in Croatia filed a class action suit against more than 300 Serbs suspected of war crimes with Prosecutor Mladen Bajić.[123]

AVRIL McDONALD

CYPRUS

International Criminal Court
☛ Law to ratify the Rome Statute, 28 February 2002

'On 28 February 2002, the Parliament passed the bill of ratification, which was then signed by the President before deposit at the UN. Previously, the translation of the ICC Statute was completed and the draft ratification legislation was approved by the Council of Ministers and the House of Representatives. There were no major obstacles for ratification, and no need to amend the Constitution.'[124]

Death Penalty
☛ Amendment of the Military Criminal Code to remove the death penalty, 19 April 2002

On 19 April 2002 the Military Criminal Code of Cyprus was amended to remove the provisions that provided for the death penalty for the military offences of treason and piracy. While the death penalty had been abolished for all crimes committed in times of peace in

---

121. 'Croatian suspect "unfit for trial"', BBC World/Europe, 29 November 2002.
122. Balkan Reconstruction Report. L. Kozole, 'Test for the government', 5 February 2002. <http://www.tol.cz/look/BRR/article.tpl?IdLanguage=1&IdPublication=9&NrIssue=1&NrSection=1&NrArticle=3221>; 'Croatian war crimes trial opens', UPI, 28 January 2002. <http://www.upi.com/print.cfm?StoryID=28012002-113048-3145r>.
123. 'Croat camp detainees to ask Belgrade for 300 million euros in compensation for torture', AFP, 7 September 2002.
124. Source: CICC/Europe/CIS: Cyprus. <http://www.iccnow.org/countryinfo/Europe/Cyprus.html>.

1999, the maximum sentence for committing these two offences in wartime had up until the amendment been the death penalty. The last execution in Cyprus took place in 1962.[125] Cyprus announced that it would sign the Protocol to the European Convention on Human Rights concerning the abolition of the death penalty in all circumstances. The signature took place on 3 May 2002 during the 110th session of the Committee of Ministers of the Council of Europe.[126]

Small Arms
☞ Agreement between the government of Cyprus and UNFICYP to destroy small arms, 10 July 2002

The government of Cyprus on 10 January 2002 agreed with UNFICYP, the United Nations Peacekeeping Force in Cyprus, on the destruction of weapons that had been held under UN custody at Nicosia Airport since 1972. The small arms had been imported to Cyprus by the government of Archbishop Makarios as a measure to face the paramilitary groups that were felt to form a threat to it. However, the presence of these weapons was opposed by both the Turkish and the Greek Cypriots. After intensive negotiations, it was agreed that the UN would take control of the weapons.

The decision to destroy the weapons followed on a unilateral initiative from the government. This initiative was taken in order to improve the possibilities to continue peace negotiations between the Greek Cypriot and the Turkish Cypriot leaders, Mr Clerides and Mr Denktash. UNFICYP had proposed several other options instead of destruction of the weapons. However, the government did not approve of any of these proposals, for example returning the weapons to their official owners or to the Cyprus police or the UN. According to reports, a document containing the proposal for the destruction of the small arms was submitted to the UN.[127]

Pending
☞ Bill to ratify the Landmines Convention

On 24 January 2002 the government of Cyprus announced that it had decided to push for ratification of the 1997 Convention on the Prohibition of the Use, Stockpiling, Production and Transfer of Anti-Personnel Mines and on their Destruction.[128] It had introduced a bill to the House of Representatives on 17 January, in which it pleaded 'for the early approval and ratification of the Convention and its subsequent implementation'. The government was also committed to take steps to remove landmines from the ceasefire line. This decision

125. Amnesty International, Death Penalty News, AI Index: ACT 53/004/2002, 1 September 2002. <http://www.amnesty.org/library/engindex>.

126. Cyprus News Agency: News in English, 26 February 2002. <http://www.hri.org/news/cyprus/cna/2002/02-02-26.cna.html#06>.

127. J. Christou, 'Government agrees to destroy arms cache held at airport since 1972', *Cyprus Mail*, 26 January 2002. <http://www.cyprus-mail.com/2002/January/26/news1.htm>. See also 'Cyprus ready to destroy weapons under UN custody since 1972', Cyprus News Agency: News in English, 25 January 2002. <http://www.hri.org/news/cyprus/cna/2002/02-01-25.cna.html#05>.

128. 18 September 1997, 2056 UNTS 211.

was not believed to create any problems for the defence capability of the country.[129] On 29 January, the Cyprus delegation to the Mine Ban Treaty Standing Committee meeting made a statement on the progress towards ratification of the treaty and on the clearance of the minefields. It stated that the government was willing to carry out the clearing operation on a unilateral basis, in cooperation with UNFICYP, but hoped that the Turkish Cypriot side would respond positively to the project. On 29 March, the Turkish Cypriot side stated that it considered that the issue should be dealt with only after a political settlement had been reached. The Turkish Cypriots were not prepared to join in the project at this stage. Consequently, UNFICYP decided to focus on giving assistance to the government of Cyprus in clearing the minefields in question. A team from the UN Mine Action Service visited Cyprus in June in order to assess the situation and make recommendations regarding the clearance of the minefields on the Greek Cypriot side.[130]

MARIA NYBONDAS

CZECH REPUBLIC[131]

Dissemination
☛ Framework Agreement on Cooperation [Rámcová dohoda o spolupráci], April 2002

In April 2002, the Ministry of Defence of the Czech Republic and the Czech Red Cross concluded a seven-Article Framework Agreement on Cooperation. Article 3 of that Agreement, on the Cooperation in the field of dissemination of international humanitarian law, provides for a possibility of disseminating information on international humanitarian law for members of the Czech armed forces as well as their civilian personnel by experts and professionals of the Czech Red Cross. This Article stipulates *expressis verbis* that the main aim of the cooperation in the field of dissemination of international humanitarian law is to ensure that members of the Czech Armed Forces and their civilian personnel and, in particular, those preparing for participation in humanitarian operations, will know the basic rules of international humanitarian law, particularly the Geneva Conventions, and be able to make use of them in practice.

JAN HLADÍK

Pending
☛ Ratification of the ICC Statute

'In December 2002, a working group of deputies and senators, established by the Czech government, began preparing a new bill amending the Constitution. The government has expressed its commitment to submit a request for ratification [of the ICC Statute] as soon as Parliament passes the constitutional amendment. According to the Ministry of Foreign

---

129. 'Cyprus government engaged in moves to remove landmines', Cyprus News Agency: News in English, 24 January 2002. <http://www.hri.org/news/cyprus/cna/2002/02-01-24.cna.html#05>.
130. Land Monitor Report 2002. <http://www.icbl.org/lm>.
131. Information and commentaries provided by Jan Hladík, Programme Specialist, International Standards Section, Division of Cultural Heritage, UNESCO.

Affairs, a new proposal for ratification is also being prepared. This ratification bill will first be submitted to the government and then to Parliament.'[132]

DENMARK[133]

International Crimes

☛ Establishment of a Special International Crimes Office. The official mission of the office is outlined in Article 3 of Administrative Regulation No. 1146 of 13 December 2002. Published in *Lovtidende* A (2002) pp. 8197-8198 <http://www.retsinfo.dk>

On 1 June 2002 the Special International Crimes Office was established. The Director of the Special International Crimes Office is responsible for investigating and prosecuting international crimes, including, in particular, genocide, crimes against humanity, war crimes, acts of terrorism and other serious crimes committed outside Denmark, provided such investigation and prosecution requires special knowledge and insight into circumstances abroad as well as cooperation with authorities abroad, international institutions, organisations, etc.

Mrs Birgitte Vestberg, a highly experienced prosecutor who has for a number of years served as the District Attorney for Funen, was appointed as the first Director. Her office is based in Copenhagen.

The establishment of a special office for international crimes is seen as a consequence of the continued international focus on combating impunity. On ordering the setting up of the office, the Minister of Justice, Mrs Lene Espersen, said: 'War criminals and similar perpetrators of violations of international humanitarian law should not be allowed to find a safe haven in Denmark but must be investigated and punished if such punishment is warranted.'[134]

Counter-terrorism

☛ Legislation in connection with the implementation of United Nations' initiatives related to combating terrorism. Law No. 378 of 6 June 2002. Published in *Lovtidende* A (2002) pp. 2416-2420 <http://www.retsinfo.dk>

The terrorist attacks against the USA on 11 September 2001 forced a number of nations to reconsider national legislation as well as amending such legislation as a consequence of Security Council Resolution No. 1373 (2001). Already before 'September 11', Denmark had ratified and implemented a number of UN Conventions relating to terrorism, with the exception of the International Convention for the Suppression of the Financing of Terrorism adopted by the General Assembly of the United Nations on 9 December 1999. However, this Convention was signed on 25 September 2001, and legislation to implement the Convention as well as further enhancing investigation and prosecution of terrorist activities in general was passed in June 2002 as Law No. 378 of 6 June 2002. The law amends the Penal

---

132. Source: CICC/Europe/CIS: Czech Republic. <http://www.iccnow.org/countryinfo/europecis/czechrepublic.html>.

133. Information provided by Peter Otken, LL.M., Special Assistant to the Judge Advocate General, Copenhagen.

134. As quoted in *Politiken*, 16 April 2002.

Code, the Administration of Justice Act, the Weapons and Explosives Act, the Extradition Act and other legislation. This note, however, will only mention the introduction into Danish law of a specific definition of terrorism since the other amendments are considered to be mainly of domestic interest.

Article 114 of the Penal Code providing for sentences up to and including life imprisonment for terrorism is new. Elements of the crime include the intent to seriously scare any population or to force Danish or foreign authorities or international organisations to take or refrain from taking action, or to destabilise or destroy a country's or an organisation's fundamental political, constitutional, economic or institutional structures. The *actus reus* of the crime can be either murder, serious violence, detention, and other serious crimes already described in the Penal Code. Transportation of weapons or explosives as well as threats to commit acts mentioned in Article 114 with the above-mentioned intent also fall under the provision.

Jurisdiction over International Crimes
☞ Government Commission on Jurisdiction. The Terms of Reference of the Commission were published on the Internet at <http://www.jm.dk/nyheder/11.07.2002> Justitsministeren nedsætter et jurisdiktionsudvalg

The Minister of Justice, Mrs Lene Espersen, in July 2002 decided to set up a commission with the purpose of going over the provisions in the Danish penal code related to jurisdiction over offences committed abroad. The reason behind this decision is the increased frequency of international travel, which raises the question whether the existing Danish provisions are satisfactory.

One of the issues to be investigated by the commission is the principle of double criminality. This principle implies that Danish courts can only adjudicate an act that is criminal according to the Danish Penal Code and committed abroad, provided that such an act is also punishable according to the penal legislation of the country where the act was committed. It has been debated whether this principle should still apply in cases where people living in Denmark leave the country in order to perform female circumcision or to have sex with children ('sex tourism') in countries where such acts are not punishable.

Furthermore, the commission is to look into the provision relating to particular serious crimes such as war crimes and torture. The commission is tasked to consider how rules on jurisdiction can be most conveniently drafted in order to ensure prosecution of persons committing such particularly serious crimes.

In relation to war crimes and other international crimes, it should be remembered that since 1986 Danish courts have jurisdiction over criminal acts committed outside Denmark irrespective of the nationality of the perpetrator, where the act is covered by an international convention in pursuance of which Denmark is under an obligation to start legal proceedings (Article 8(5) of the Penal Code). In 1995 the Supreme Court used this provision to hold a Bosnian responsible for war crimes committed in Bosnia-Herzegovina against fellow Bosnians.[135]

---

135. 1 *YIHL* (1998) p. 431.

Ongoing Cases
☛ Continuing investigation of possible war crimes committed in 1988 by a former senior Iraqi general officer

As mentioned in the 2001 report, a person described in the press as a former senior Iraqi army officer was in late 2001 made the object of a criminal investigation by Danish authorities.[136]

During 2002 more information was made public. The General was *Nizar Al-Khazraji*, who according to press reports was commander of the Iraqi 1st Army in 1984-1988 and later became Chief of the Iraqi Army. The press also reported that the Danish authorities were investigating allegations that he carried out orders or failed to prevent personnel and material being provided for actions carried out with the intention of making possible the total or partial destruction of the Kurdish population in Northern Iraq. It was also alleged that *Nizar Al-Khazraji* failed to take any measures to ensure that those participating in the above-mentioned actions were prosecuted.

During the autumn of 2002 the investigation was taken over by the new Special International Crimes Office. In November the Office moved to ensure that the General did not travel out of Denmark. The Court of First Instance in Soroe on 19 November ruled that the General could not travel out of Denmark and that he should continue to be under police supervision, including by depositing all his travel documents with the Special International Crimes Office.

By the end of the year, no decision as to the formal indictment of the General had been made public.

PETER OTKEN

EAST TIMOR

International Criminal Court
☛ Resolution of the National Parliament on the 'Rome Statute for the International Criminal Court'. Signed for publication on 24 August 2002

Court of Appeals
☛ Executive Order 2002/4, 1 April 2002 concerning the appointment of temporary international judges

In April 2002, the Transitional Administrator recommended the temporary appointment of two international judges to fill the places left on the Court of Appeals by the departure of Judges Frederick Egonde-Entende and Claudio Ximenes de Jesus. By Executive Order 2002/04 of 1 April 2002, two international judges who were at that time serving as judges on the Special Panels for Serious Crimes, the Honorable Antero Luis and the Honorable Benfeito Mosso Ramos, were appointed to serve as judges on the Court of Appeals. These appointments were to expire on 20 May 2002. The Court disposed of one appeal during the time of this configuration.

Prior to the appointment of the temporary judges, the Court had not been functional since October 2001, when Judge Frederick Egonde-Entende completed his term. Lacking the

---

136. 4 *YIHL* (2001) p. 491.

required number of international judges, the Court could not be constituted. Aside from the brief period of appointment of the temporary judges, there was no functioning appeals court from October 2002 to the end of 2002.

In the absence of a functioning Court of Appeals, during 2002 it was not possible to exercise the right of appeal in East Timor on either interlocutory matters or final decisions. However, 38 appeals were filed in 2001 and 19 in 2002.[137]

Special Panels for Serious Crimes

As of December 2002, 240 people had been accused in 45 indictments of the Special Crimes Investigation Unit of the Dili District Court. Thirty-one people had been tried and convicted, with sentences ranging from 11 months to 33 years.[138]

Commission for Reception, Truth and Reconciliation in East Timor (CAVR)[139]
☛ Swearing in of National Commissioners, 21 January 2002

The Commission for Reception, Truth and Reconciliation in East Timor (Commissão de Acolhimento, Verdade e Reconciliação de Timor Leste (CAVR)) started its work on 21 January 2002, when the National Commissioners were sworn in. 'Since then CAVR has focussed its efforts not only on hearing the truth and facilitating reconciliation but also in the reception of returnees from West Timor.'[140] The CAVR is a predominantly Timorese institution; its 240 member staff are mainly from East Timor, assisted by a few foreign experts.

By February 2003, the Commission had heard more than 2,500 statements,[141] including more than 200 from perpetrators.[142]

Pending
☛ Draft law on Amnesty <http://www.jsmp.minihub.org/Legislation/Draf_%20Law_Amnesty_eng.pdf>

In May 2002, a draft Law on amnesty and pardons, consisting of just eight articles, was prepared by President Kay Rala Xanana Gusmão. It was introduced to the Constitutent Assembly in the hope that it would be passed in time for independence on 20 May 2002.

---

137. Judicial System Monitoring Programme, 'The Right to Appeal in East Timor', JSMP Thematic Report 2, Dili, East Timor, October 2002, p. 3.

138. Human Rights Watch, 'Justice Denied for East Timor: Indonesia's Sham Prosecutions, the Need to Strengthen the Trial Process in East Timor, and the Imperative of U.N. Action', New York, 20 December 2000. <http://www.jsmp.minihub.org/Reports/Copy%20of%20Justice%20Denied%20for%20East%20Timor%20NB13_1_02.pdf>.

139. For background on the TRC see C. Stahn, 'Accomodating Individual Criminal Responsibility and National Reconciliation: The UN Truth Commission for East Timor', 95 *AJIL* (2001) p. 46.

140. Address by His Excellency President Kay Rala Xanana Gusmão at the inauguration of the newly rehabilitated former Balide Prison as the National Office of the CAVR and the opening of the National Public Hearing on Political Imprisonment, Dili, 17 February 2003. <http://www.jsmp.minihub.org/Reports/XGcavrjr18feb03.htm>.

141. Ibid.

142. Commissão de Acolhimento, Verdade e Reconciliação de Timor Leste (CAVR), Update December 2002-January 2003.

However, the Assembly declined to discuss the draft and referred it for redrafting. After some minor amendments, the bill was reintroduced to the National Parliament.

The Law, which is drafted using vague language, would offer immunity from criminal prosecution for a broad swathe of past crimes committed in connection with the struggle for independence, and reduced prison sentences for such crimes. Article 1 states that all crimes against property committed before 19 May 2002 that do not involve violence or threats are granted amnesty. Article 2 grants amnesty for all non-violent crimes and non-bloody crimes committed on or before 30 September 1999 by East Timorese who were forced to join the militias. Article 3 grants amnesty for all acts committed by the Resistance but specifically exempts from amnesty war crimes, crimes against humanity and genocide. Article 4 provides for substantial reduction in prison terms for crimes committed prior to 20 May 2002 but not covered by the amnesty provisions. Article 5 is also concerned with sentencing. Article 6 provides that no amnesty is provided against civil actions arising from crimes committed. Article 7 states that any doubts or omissions arising from the implementation of the Law are to be resolved by the Court of Appeal. Finally, Article 8 states when the Law (had it been passed) would have come into operation, i.e., 20 May 2002.[143]

Human Rights Watch criticised it as undermining due process and equal protection of the law and because it would allow those responsible for some of the most serious abuses to go unpunished.[144]

AVRIL MCDONALD

ECUADOR

Pending

☞ Draft implementation legislation regarding crimes under the jurisdiction of the International Criminal Court [Proyecto de ley sobre delitos contra la humanidad]

Draft implementing legislation was submitted to Congress on 18 December 2002. The draft legislation was thereafter to be studied by the Specialized Permanent Commission on Civil and Penal Issues.

The draft implementation law recognises that Ecuadorian law does not define or criminalise international crimes. It thereafter states the applicability of the new legislation and provides a definition of genocide, crimes against humanity and war crimes. The draft law also includes provisions on the relationship between the state of Ecuador and the International Criminal Court.[145]

---

143. For a detailed report on the Law, see 'The Draft Law on Amnesty and Pardon', Judicial System Monitoring Programme, November 2002. <http://www.jsmp.minihub.org/Reports/Final%20Amnesty%20English%20050203.pdf>.

144. 'East Timor Amnesty Bill Flawed: Perpetrators of War Crimes May Excape Prosecution', Human Rights Watch Press Release, New York, 18 July 2002. <http://www.hrw.org/press/2002/07/etimor0718.htm>.

145. ICC Update, 32nd edn., January 2003, <http://www.iccnow.org/publications/update/iccupdate32Eng.pdf>.

ERITREA

Border Dispute

☛ Decision of the Permanent Court of Arbitration on the border dispute between Ethiopia and Eritrea, 13 April 2002   <http://www.reliefweb.int/w/rwb.nsf/vID/221AAF25202 CEEA6C1256B9C0041F66B?OpenDocument>

ESTONIA[146]

Penal Code

☛ Entry into force on 1 September 2002 of Penal Code adopted on 6 June 2001

'Chapter 8, entitled "Offences against humanity and international security", provides for prison sentences for offences against humanity (§§ 89 and 90), including crimes against humanity and genocide; offences against peace (§§ 91-93); war crimes (§§ 94-109), including "acts of war against the civilian population", "illegal use of means of warfare against civilians", "attacks against civilians", "unlawful treatment of prisoners of war or interned civilians", "attacks against prisoners of war or interned civilians", "refusal to provide assistance to sick, wounded or shipwrecked persons", "attacks against persons *hors de combat*", "attacks against protected persons", "use of prohibited weapons", "environmental damage as a method of warfare", "exploitative abuse of emblems and marks of international protection", "attacks against nonmilitary objects", "attacks against cultural property", "destruction or illegal appropriation of property in a war zone or occupied territory" and "marauding" and offences against international security (§§ 110-112). It stipulates that the perpetrator of the offence shall be punished, as well as the State representative or the military commander who issued the order to commit the offence, or who consented to, or failed to prevent, the commission of the offence, if prevention was in his or her power. The defence of superior orders shall not preclude the punishment of the principal offender. The Penal Code also provides that there shall be no statute of limitations for "offences against humanity" and "war crimes" (§ 5(4)). It further states that "regardless of the law of the place of commission of an act, the penal law of Estonia shall apply to an act committed outside the territory of Estonia if the punishability of the act arises from an international agreement binding on Estonia" (§ 8).'[147]

ETHIOPIA

Border Dispute

☛ Decision of the Permanent Court of Arbitration on the Border Dispute between Ethiopia and Eritrea, 13 April 2002 <http://www.reliefweb.int/w/rwb.nsf/vID/221AAF25202 CEEA6C1256B9C0041F66B?OpenDocument>

---

146. Source ICRC Advisory Service, National Implementation of International Humanitarian Law – Biannual update on national legislation and case-law, January-June 2002. <http://www.icrc.org/ Web/eng/siteeng0.nsf/html/5FLE9G?OpenDocument>. See also CICC/Europe/CIS:Estonia. <http:// www.iccnow.org/countryinfo/europecis/estonia.html>.

147. Source ICRC Advisory Service, National Implementation of International Humanitarian Law – Biannual update on national legislation and case-law, January-June 2002. <http://www.icrc.org/ Web/eng/siteeng0.nsf/html/5FLE9G?OpenDocument>. See also CICC/Europe/CIS:Estonia. <http:// www.iccnow.org/countryinfo/europecis/estonia.html>

FEDERAL REPUBLIC OF YUGOSLAVIA[148]

A. MONTENEGRO

Cases
☛ *Nebojša Ranisavljević* case, Judgement of the High Court of Bijelo Polje, Montenegro, 9 September 2002

On 9 September 2002, the High Court in Bijelo Polje found Nebojša Ranisavljević guilty of a war crime against the civilian population under Article 142(1) of the Federal Republic of Yugoslavia Criminal Code, and sentenced him to 15 years in prison.

According to the indictment: 'On 27 February 1993 in Višegrad, Bosnia-Herzegovina, and as a member of an armed formation – a group of some 25 armed men under the command of Milan Lukić of Višegrad – during the armed conflict in Bosnia-Herzegovina, [Ranisavljević] took part in taking and carrying out a decision to, in contravention of international law, attack a Yugoslav Railways passenger train, abduct from it civilian passengers, and to rob and murder them.'

Explaining the decision, Judge Golubović said the Court had borne in mind that Ranisavljević's direct involvement in the planning and commission of the crime had not been proved, but that his membership of the armed group who had abducted the passengers and murdered them was established beyond a doubt.

The Humanitarian Law Centre in Belgrade noted that 'the trial was unduly prolonged ... primarily because of the refusal of the Republika Srpska authorities in Bosnia to cooperate with the High Court in the early stages of the proceedings. As a result, Ranisavljević was held in pre-trial custody for six years, from 22 October 1996. Under international standards, persons charged with a criminal offense have the right to a trial within a reasonable period. In the *Ranisavljević* case, the indictment was filed on 14 March 1997 and his trial opened on 4 May 1998.'[149]

On 7 May, a document submitted to the Court by the Belgrade Rail Company (ZTP) revealed that top military, police and civilian officials of Serbia and Yugoslavia knew of the plan to abduct Bosniac passengers from the Belgrade to Bar train in 1993 and took no steps to prevent it.[150]

B. SERBIA

Truth and Reconciliation Commission
☛ Inauguration of the Truth and Reconciliation Commission, 22 February 2002

On 22 February 2002, Yugoslav President Vojislav Kostunica inaugurated the country's Truth and Reconciliation Commission to investigate war crimes committed in Slovenia, Croatia, Bosnia and Kosovo over the previous decade. The Commission members are: Sve-

---

148. Information and commentaries by Miodrag Starčević, Professor of International Humanitarian Law at the Military High Schools Centre, Belgrade, Avril McDonald, Managing Editor of the *YIHL* and Michael E. Hartmann, International Prosecutor, Kosovo. The latter can be reached at Intprosecutor @yahoo.com.
149. <http://www.hlc.org.yu/english/War_Crimes_Trials_Before_National_Courts/Serbia/index. php?file=67.html>.
150. Ibid.

tozar Stojanović, Mirjana Vasović, Rodovan Bigović, Svetlana Velmar Janković, Mihajlo Vojvodić, Djordjije Vuković, Ljubodrag Dimić, Slavoljub Djukić, Aleksandar Lojpur, Bosko Mijatović, Radmila Nakarada, Predrag Palavestra, Zoran Stanković, Darko Tanasković and Sulejman Hrnjica. The Commission was established in March 2001, with a three-year mandate.[151]

AVRIL McDONALD

International Criminal Tribunals
☛ Law on Cooperation of the Federal Republic of Yugoslavia with the International Criminal Tribunal for the Prosecution of Persons Responsible for Serious Violations of International Humanitarian Law Committed in the Territory of the Former Yugoslavia since 1991. Adopted and published on 11 April 2002 in *Official Gazette of the Federal Republic of Yugoslavia*, No. 18, 11 April 2002 and entered into force the following day

'The law sets out rules for the provision of legal assistance to the International Tribunal, for the operation of its officers on the territory of the Federal Republic of Yugoslavia, for the transmittal of criminal proceedings or the transfer of indictees to the International Tribunal, and for the execution of its sentences by the Yugoslav authorities.'[152]

One of the most difficult problems which Serbia and Montenegro faced during 2002 was cooperation with the Hague Tribunal. Despite the coming to power of a new government and the surrender in 2001 of former President Milošević to the ICTY, there were continuing disputes between officials of the FRY and the Hague Tribunal, particularly the Prosecutor.

According to official governmental statements, there is no doubt that there was good will for cooperation and for surrender of accused persons who are the responsibility of or in the power of the FRY. The main evidence for that, according to their statements, is Milošević's surrender by the government as well as that of several other high level military and political officials of the previous regime.

From the Hague side, there were oft-repeated requests to imprison and extradite the remaining accused persons at large from Bosnia and Herzegovina (particularly, Mr Karadžić and General Mladić), in spite of the repeated statements of Belgrade's officials that neither of them was under the control of FRY. Despite this, the Prosecutor of the Hague Tribunal continued to assert that they were in Serbia, enjoying – particularly in the case of General Mladić – the protection of the FRY Army, notwithstanding the absence of evidence produced to support this claim. In addition, the Prosecutor, from time to time declared her intention to bring new accusations against Yugolav citizens.

This long-lasting disagreement seriously undermined the efforts of the government of Serbia and Montenegro to take a step forward in international cooperation, as many international organisations, including the United Nations and its Security Council, made cooperation with the Hague Tribunal one of the most essential conditions for the acceptance of the FRY in some international organisations. At the same time, the public in the FRY increasingly felt the state to be under a kind of never-ending pressure. Some politicians and even some experts accused the Prosecutor, and the Hague Tribunal in general, of bias by

---

151. AFP, 4 August 2001; BBC Monitoring Europe – Political, 22 February 2002.
152. Source: ICRC Advisory Service, National Implementation of International Humanitarian Law – Biannual update on national legislation and case-law, January-June 2002. <http://www.icrc.org/Web/eng/siteeng0.nsf/html/5FLE9G?OpenDocument>.

virtue of the fact that there were no more accusations of people from other parts of the former Yugoslavia and from Kosovo and Metohija particularly. Some extremists even saw such attitude of the Hague Tribunal as proof that it was created against the Serbian people in general.

MIODRAG STARČEVIĆ

Cases

➤ *Ivan Nikolić* case, District Court of Prokuplje, 8 July 2002

Nikolić was indicted on 19 April 2002 by the district court in Prokuplje for the killing of two Kosovo Albanian civilians in May 1999. Nikolić had previously been charged with murder, but the prosecutor in Prokuplje amended the indictment to include war crimes charges. The trial opened on 11 June 2002. On July 8, the court found Nikolić guilty and sentenced him to eight years in prison.[153]

➤ *Zlatan Mančić, Rade Radivojević, Danilo Tešić* and *Mišel Seregij* case, Military Court of Niš, 11 October 2002

In an indictment of 19 July 2002, the military prosecutor charged Lt. Col. Zlatan Mančić and Captain Rade Radivojević with incitement to murder (Art. 47(2) Serbian Criminal Code, in conjunction with Article 23 Federal Criminal Code); and Privates Danilo Tešić and Mišel Seregij as accomplices (Art. 47(2) Serbian Criminal Code, in conjunction with Article 22 Federal Criminal Code). Mančić was in addition charged with abuse of official position (Art. 174(1) Federal Criminal Code).

At the instruction of the Supreme Military Prosecutor, the military prosecutor of Niš, on 16 September 2002 amended the indictment and charged the two officers with a war crime against the civilian population (Art. 142(1) Federal Criminal Code), and the two former privates as accomplices. The count of abuse of official position in respect to Mančić was retained in the amended indictment. At the last session of the trial on 11 October, and before imposition of the sentence, the prosecutor again amended the indictment against Mančić and, instead of a violation of common Article 3 of the 1949 Geneva Conventions, charged him with violating Article 33(3) in conjunction with Article 5 of the Federal Criminal Code on the protection of civilians in international armed conflicts.[154]

On 11 October 2002, the Military Court of Niš found the four defendants guilty of war crimes against civilians in Kosovo, the first war crimes conviction of Yugoslav soldiers with respect to the Kosovo conflict. The court sentenced Lt. Col. Zlatan Mančić to seven years' imprisonment and Captain Rade Radivojević to five years' imprisonment on charges of ordering two soldiers to kill two unidentified Albanians in April 1999. The law specifies jail terms of five to 40 years for those convicted of war crimes. Mančić was also found guilty of extorting money from Albanian civilians in a refugee convoy. Radenko Miladino-vić, presiding over the trial chamber, said that Mančić and Radivojević, as security officers, had been obliged to ensure that civilians were protected but had instead ordered their mur-

---

153. 'Human Rights Concerns in the Federal Republic of Yugoslavia'. Human Rights Watch Briefing Paper. <http://www.hrw.org/backgrounder/eca/yugo-bck0711.htm>.

154. <http://www.hlc.org.yu/english/War_Crimes_Trials_Before_National_Courts/Serbia/index. php?file=67.html>.

ders. Both officers denied the charges. The two former soldiers who actually carried out the murders, Danilo Tešić and Mišel Seregij, both 34 years of age, were sentenced to three years' imprisonment. They admitted murdering the two Albanians and burning their bodies. The court gave those soldiers less than the minimum sentences in view of extenuating circumstances. Judge Miladinović explained that they had committed the murders in the belief that they themselves would be killed if they refused to carry out the order. Nevertheless, he found that all four men had violated the Geneva Convention on the protection of civilians. They were released pending appeals within the next 15 days.[155]

According to the Humanitarian Law Centre: 'This trial was important in both political and legal terms since it was the first before a military tribunal in Serbia for war crimes. The Humanitarian Law Center, however, has some serious reservations with regard to how the Court applied the Geneva Conventions and determined the facts of the case.'[156]

Ongoing Cases
☛ Trial of *Sasa Cvjetan and Dejan Demirović*, Members of the 'Scorpians', Prokuplje District Court

Two members of a special anti-terrorist police unit known as the 'Scorpians' are being tried before the Prokuplje District Court for war crimes against the civilian population in Kosovo. They are accused in connection with the killing of several Albanian civilians in the Kosovo town of Podujevo on 28 March 1999.[157]

AVRIL MCDONALD

C. Kosovo[158]

Cases
☛ *Juvenile V.* case[159]

In late 2001 UNMIK transferred juvenile V. to Serbian authorities to serve his 'one to five years in custody', in a locked educational facility. This was lauded by some since Kosovo has no such facilities appropriate for a Serbian minor in custody which could provide both educational and psychological/counseling services.

---

155. Source: <http://www.preventgenocide.org/punish/domestic/index.htm>.
156. Ibid.
157. Ibid.
158. Information and commentaries by Michael E. Hartmann, written while Senior Fellow, United States Institute of Peace, Washington, DC, January-September 2003; currently International Prosecutor 2000-2004, Office of the Public Prosecutor of Kosovo (before the Supreme Court), Unmik, at email intprosecutor@yahoo.com. This report concerns only that small minority of war crimes cases that reached a court trial. Many more cases were under investigation by the Complex Criminal Investigative Unit of the Unmik Police, with guidance from international prosecutors, and other cases were selected by international prosecutors and judges at the judicial investigation stage and resulted in no indictment being filed.
159. For background, see 4 *YIHL* (2001) at pp. 506-507.

☛ *Radovan Apostolić* case, District Court of Mitrovica/Mitrovicë, Decision of 28 January 2002

On 28 January 2002, Radovan Apostolić, who was originally indicted on 8 September 2000 by a local prosecutor for war crimes, but which charges were over the course of several months reduced by an international public prosecutor first to arson, and then to theft, was acquitted on all counts. In summing up to the court at the end of the ten-month case, the international public prosecutor had taken the unusual step of arguing that the main witness, also the injured party and the owner of the looted property, had lied to the court numerous times, so that at most the court should believe that the accused took only candles and tea, not the hundreds of thousands of Deutsche Marks claimed by the victims.[160]

☛ *Sava Matić* case, District Court of Prizren, Decision of 27 March 2002

Sava Matić was tried in 2001 for war crimes under Article 142 of the applicable Federal Republic of Yugoslavia Criminal Code (FRYCC).[161] He was alleged to have obeyed orders to take part in the murders of 42 civilians from one village. On 29 January 2001, the majority international judge Regulation '64' Panel found him guilty only of light bodily injury in connection with an incident that was not mentioned in the indictment. Both the prosecutor and the defense appealed.[162]

The Supreme Court, composed of an international majority panel, reversed the conviction on 13 June 2001, as it was for a crime different from that alleged in the indictment. The retrial began on 22 November 2001, again with a local prosecutor. Matić again maintained his defence of alibi, and on 27 March 2002 an all-international panel found him not guilty.

☛ *Dragan Nikolić* case, District Court of Gjilan/Gnjilane, Decision of 2 April 2002

The original conviction by a Kosovan majority panel of the accused for murder within the context of an armed conflict was overturned by an international majority Supreme Court on 9 April 2001, upon defence appeal, and sent back for retrial on the basis of (1) incorrect and insufficient findings of fact and (2) the refusal of the trial court to hear proposed Serb and Croat defence witnesses.[163] The retrial began on 12 September 2001 before a majority international panel, with an international prosecutor. The defence again presented an alibi. The trial panel found the inculpatory witnesses unconvincing, and found Nikolić not guilty on 18 April 2002. The international public prosecutor for Gjilan/Gnjilane filed an appeal, and it was pending before the Supreme Court at the end of 2002.

---

160. Ibid., at p. 514.
161. UNMIK Regulation 1999/24, as amended by 2000/59, prescribes the 1989 Kosovo and FRY law as applicable, as modified by Regulations, and international human rights standards. For background, see 4 *YIHL* (2001) at pp. 500-506.
162. For background, see 4 *YIHL* (2001) at pp. 511-512.
163. Ibid., at p. 508.

☞   *Milos Jokić* case, District Court of Gjilan/Gnjilane, Decision of 3 May 2002

The Kosovan trial panel had originally found Jokić guilty of war crimes (ordering and committing murder) under Article 142 of the FRYCC. This decision was reversed on appeal by an international majority (under Regulation 2000/64) Supreme Court panel on 26 April 2001, due to insufficient facts in the record and a failure to hear witnesses proposed by the defense.[164]

An international public prosecutor and a '64' Panel of international judges retried the case. The accused maintained his alibi defence during the retrial, and on 3 May 2002 Jokić was found not guilty on all counts.

☞   *Miroslav Vucković* case, Detention Decision Analysing ECHR Jurisprudence, Supreme Court, 16 July 2002

Meriting notice is a well-reasoned decision by the Kosovo Supreme Court, by the most senior international judge Presiding over a three-judge '64' Panel, the first Supreme Court or District Court decision to address the claims of accused war criminals – some of whom had been held since July and August 1999 – under Article 5(3) of the European Convention on Human Rights (ECHR) and consider the post-conflict environment and circumstances as affecting the justice system. The judge was presiding over a '64' panel deciding on whether to extend the detention of *Vucković*, which analysed the lengthy pretrial and post-trial detentions of the accused, which also applied to other Kosovan-Serbians accused of war crimes.

The 16 July 2002 decision held that the UNMIK judiciary was forced by the circumstances of post-war reconstruction to reflect upon its own capacity to try war crimes within a reasonable time given its situation of insufficient judicial personnel, limited logistics and civil unrest on the ground.

While the Supreme Court ordered the continuation of the 3.5 year detention of the accused, it implicitly warned that it was time to cut the matter short.[165]

---

164. Ibid., at pp. 508-509.

165. 'The complexity of the case must be considered as a factor which might justify the lengthiness, as discussed *supra*. ... The scope and complexity of this case are thus of greater magnitude than in most cases heard by Kosovo courts, and therefore the length of the proceedings cannot properly be compared to such other cases.

The most questionable time period of this proceeding which concerns the court in light of ECHR Art. 5(3) is that approximately seven months between the filing of the first indictment and the commencement of the main trial. We are aware that during this time, the local judiciary was in the process of being organised, that there was a boycott by appointed ethnic Serbian judges who refused to participate in what was a homogenous ethnic Albanian judiciary, a hunger strike by Serb prisoners charged with genocide and war crimes, violent demonstrations and clashes in Mitrovica, and the closure of the Mitrovica District Court on numerous occasions due to violence and threats to security. The UNMIK administration during this time acted diligently through both existing legal procedures, and by establishing through Regulations 2000/6 and 2000/34, to enact a special section [now division] of International Judicial Support in the Department of Judicial Affairs, to support the appointment and work of international judges and prosecutors. The first international judge sat upon the panel of the first trial in this case, and we understand that one of the reasons for the delay was the desire to have Judge Christer Karphammar to participate on that panel. [footnote omitted] Later, UNMIK increased the participation of international judiciary with the enactment of Regulation 2000/64 which is being used to re-try this case now.

☛ *Sasa Grković* case, District Court of Prizren, Decision of 4 September 2002

On 19 February 2002, the accused was indicted by the international public prosecutor of Prizren for war crimes under Article 142 FRYCC, allegedly committed in late March 1999. The accused was charged with participating in three massacres of Kosovar Albanian civilians, as well as destruction of real and personal property, while he was a member of an armed and uniformed Serb militia. The trial started on 29 July 2002 with an international public prosecutor before an international majority '64' panel, and on 4 September 2002 the accused was acquitted of all charges by the court, due to insufficient evidence that he committed the acts with which he was charged.

☛ *Miroslav Vucković* case, District Court of Mitrovica/Mitrovicë, Decision of 25 October 2002

Miroslav Vucković had his Kosovan majority five-judge trial panel genocide conviction reversed by an international majority Supreme Court panel in 2001,[166] and the retrial began on 4 January 2002. The international public prosecutor for Mitrovica/Mitrovicë filed an amended indictment charging Vucković with war crimes under Article 142 of the FRYCC, including murder. The Regulation 2002/64 Trial Panel of one Kosovan judge and two internationals (one presiding) retried the case from 4 January through 24 October 2002.[167] On 25 October 2002, in one of the best reasoned and most comprehensive Kosovo war crimes verdicts, the Court found that Vucković:

We note that normally a shortage of judicial personnel is not accepted by ECHR jurisprudence as an excuse for overly long detention. However, the circumstances stated above are not normal nor taken into account by most ECHR decisions on the length of detention, since those decisions are set in states with established judicial systems unlike Kosovo. These circumstances related in Kosovo do show that the applicable state authorities, the Mitrovica District Court, UNMIK and the then Department of Judicial Affairs, took all possible efforts to expedite this case. To cite the Council of Europe Commentary on ECHR [Art.] 5(3), "in such cases [of delay] it can be particularly significant that a special unit has been created to deal with the case or that additional resources have been provided for existing ones expected to handle a case of an exceptional character...". [footnote omitted]

Accordingly, overall, the length of delay in light of all circumstances is not so manifest as to require the Supreme Court, with our limited knowledge of the facts specific to this trial, and without any specific arguments of the parties to this effect, to order immediate release of the accused. However, we are quite concerned about the lengthiness, and must require the trial court panel to seriously consider the offered bail in light of the delay. This very long detention of the accused should properly be considered as an additional and critical factor in deciding bail, especially if there are additional elements of family situation, and of other guarantees, as well as whether the bail offered will be properly secured to allow the effective threat of levying upon any property so encumbered.'

166. For background, see 4 *YIHL* (2001) at pp. 510-511.

167. The applicable Kosovo procedure, unlike US and other common law procedures where juries are involved, allows trials to be conducted on non-consecutive days, and thus there were in this case one to 12 trial days per month; given the schedules of the international judges and prosecutors and commitments to appear in other cases, this was not unusual for UNMIK.

'As part of an armed group of civilians, some of whom were Yugoslav Army reservists; and being closely associated with them and other Yugoslav Army members acting on behalf of the Yugoslav armed forces, especially during the period 14 April to 22 April 1999 when the worst village attacks occurred; at times (between September 1998 and 9 May 1999) where, in the territory of Kosovo, a state of internal armed conflict existed between the [Kosovo Liberation Army (KLA)] and the armed forces of the Federal Republic of Yugoslavia, both armed forces being under a responsible command, and exercising control over parts of the territory of Kosovo that enabled them to carry out sustained and concerted military operations and whilst an international armed conflict co-existed alongside the internal armed conflict during the period 24 March 1999 to 9 May 1999, and a nexus existed between the acts committed and the armed conflict; committed the following acts the victims of which were members of the civilian population:

1. Illegal and self-willed destruction of property, as per Article 142 in conjunction with Article 22 of the CCY [Criminal Code of the Socialist Federal Republic of Yugoslavia] and encompassed by Article 147 of the Fourth Geneva Convention of 1949 (Grave Breach);

2. Stealing on a large scale of property, as per Article 142 of the CCY in conjunction with Article 22 of the CCY and as encompassed by Article 4, paragraph 2(g) of Additional Protocol II (1977) to the Geneva Conventions of 1949; and

3. Application of measures of intimidation and terror and endangering the safety of other persons, as per Article 142 of the CCY in conjunction with Article 22 of the CCY and as encompassed by paragraph 1(a) of Common Article 3 to the Geneva Conventions of 1949, Article 4, paragraph 2(a) of Additional Protocol II (1977) to the Geneva Conventions of 1949.'

The Court also found that 'between September 1998 and 24 March 1999 the accused's acts were committed during an internal armed conflict and that between 24 March 1999 and 9 May 1999 they were committed during an internal armed conflict co-existing alongside with an international armed conflict'. The Court based its findings upon UN official documents; OSCE official documents; and the testimony of Col. Richard Heaslip, Member of the Irish Defence Forces, Head of the Activation Team of the OSCE Kosovo Verification Mission in December 1998 and then Chief of Liaison Branch of Kosovo.

As to the liability of the accused for war crimes, the Court found 'that the accused in spite of his civilian activity as a hospital driver, was acting in concert and on behalf of the Yugoslav armed forces'. The Court was also specific as to its finding a nexus between the acts committed and the armed conflict:

'The court already explained that the accused acted in concert and on behalf of the armed forces and that their common purpose was the evacuation of the Albanian population from the region and that looting properties and setting them on fire were clearly aimed at preventing the return of the population in question. Therefore the court considered that the actions of the accused were not only facilitated by the existence of an armed conflict but were closely linked with its existence and extent.'

During the trial and retrial, there was testimony that the accused's war crimes included acts of murder and attempted murder; however, the Court did not find that Vucković committed any such acts.

The defence appealed the verdict, and as of the end of 2002 it had not been decided.

☛ *Lulzim Ademi* case, Supreme Court, Decision of 8 December 2002

This phase of the *Ademi* case concerned the legality of an *in absentia* war crimes conviction under Article 142 of the FRYCC by a Kosovan majority five-judge panel, with one international judge and a presiding Kosovan judge.[168] After the conviction but before the appeal, UNMIK Regulation 2001/1 was promulgated, which forbids *in absentia* trials. The Regulation states that it 'entered into force on 12 January 2001 and shall apply also to criminal proceedings pending as of that date'. The question presented was whether it applied to the *Ademi* verdict and pending appeal.

The Supreme Court on 9 December 2002 cancelled (reversed) the verdict and sent it back for retrial 'with the participation of the accused'. The Supreme Court approved the International Public Prosecutor of Kosovo's proposed interpretation of UNMIK Regulation 2001/1, which had proposed that any *in absentia* war crimes case not yet final (under the applicable law a case is not final until all possible appeals have been decided) was proscribed by Regulation 2001/1.[169] The Supreme Court also found that the charges of possession of a large amount of weapons under Article 199(3) of the Kosovo Criminal Code (KCC), for which there was a conviction, and Complicity (Art. 22 FRYCC) in Murder under Article 30 of the KCC for which there was an acquittal, 'were intrinsically linked to war crimes charges'. Hence, the proscription under Regulation 2001/1 also applies to the entire factual *gravaman* under appeal. The determination of the allegation and facts pleaded in the indictment must therefore be postponed until such time as the accused is captured or voluntarily appears before the trial court in connection with the indictment.

☛ *Andjelko Kolasinac* case, District Court of Prizren and Supreme Court, Decision of 31 January 2003 of the District Court of Prizren

On 2 November 2001, a majority international panel of the Supreme Court reversed Andjelko Kolasinac's conviction for ordering the destruction of evidence of forced deportation.[170] The retrial[171] of the case against Kolasinac, the President of the Municipal Assembly in Rahovec and the Head of the local Civil Defence Unit and the highest-ranking

---

168. For background, see 4 *YIHL* (2001) at pp. 507-508.

169. The Supreme Court stated: 'This panel of the Supreme Court has closely observed and is satisfied with the interpretation of this Regulation done in the second Opinion of the Public Prosecutor's Office of Kosovo. The [International Public Prosecutor's] Opinion states: "There is no question that our procedure here was 'pending' on this date. That an appeal rather than trial or investigation was pending is significant, since the Regulation's use of the phrase 'criminal proceedings' rather than 'trials' must be given meaning, which is obviously to broaden the scope of the regulation's proscription; otherwise Section 4 would have had only the entry into force date. The fact that the drafters added the phrase, 'and shall apply also to criminal proceedings pending' as of 12 January 2001, can only mean that the definition of 'criminal proceedings' includes both appeals and investigations, which are not trials, but are therefore also 'included'. Once this Regulation is applied to an appeal the only reasonable interpretation of the protection is that the Courts cannot allow a trial verdict of guilt done in absentia to be affirmed and stand, if it has jurisdiction over such a verdict while it is on appeal and thus not final. There is no other reasonable interpretation of the Section 4 requirement that it 'shall apply also to criminal proceedings pending'." It should be noted that the first Opinion, by the Kosovan Public Prosecutor of Kosovo, recommended that the Court affirm the trial verdict.

170. For background, see 4 *YIHL* (2001) at p. 513.

171. The first verdict of the District Court in Prizren dated 14 June 2001, as a result of the appeals from both parties was overturned by the decision of the Supreme Court of 2 November 2001

Serb government employee ever indicted by a court in Kosovo, took place before a '64' Panel composed of two internationals and one local judge during the last quarter of 2002. The initial indictment, characterised by sweeping statements, which *inter alia* had caused the reversal of the first verdict due to its disparity with the charge, was developed by the international public prosecutor in a set of amendments. The verdict in the trial was announced on 31 January 2003.[172]

The court found Kolasinac guilty of the following: that during April/May 1999, he acted in complicity with other Serb officials in organising the registration of the population for use in connection with the forced displacement and deportation of Kosovar Albanians in Rahovec; that in complicity with other Serb officials he participated in organising an estimated 100 Kosovar Albanians from the Rahovec municipality to be utilised as forced labour in connection with the cleaning of the roads in Malishevë/Mališhevo and the pruning of the vineyards in the Rahovec area; last, that during the cleaning of the roads in Malishevë/Mališhevo, the accused, as Commander of the Headquarters of the Civil Defense, failed to prevent the looting, pillaging and destruction of the forcefully abandoned property of the thousands of Kosovar Albanians that had been forcefully displaced and deported by the military. These acts were qualified as a War Crime Against the Civilian Population pursuant to Article 142 of the FRYCC in relation to: (a) the displacement or forced repatriation through registration, (e) forced labour, (g) the pillaging and looting of the property of the population, including (h) the illegal and wilful destruction and taking possession of property on a large scale, under the doctrine of command responsibility. The District Court acquitted Andjelko Kolasinac regarding allegations of concealing the traces of crimes, partly because it found such charges absorbed by the acts for which it had already pronounced the accused guilty, and partly because it found the allegations unsupported by evidence.

This verdict attributed criminal responsibility to Kolasinac more broadly than did the first verdict, where he had been found guilty only for the non-IHL crime under the Kosovo Criminal Code of concealing traces of a crime, albeit a war crime. Accordingly, the sentence was increased from five to eight years' imprisonment. The defense again appealed to the Supreme Court, and the Kosovo Supreme Court '64' Panel was expected to hear the parties and issue its decision in 2004.

The history of these proceedings to date proves the awkwardness of the old Yugoslav definition of a war crime, under which it is not allowed to atomise specific acts constituting a war crime for separate adjudication, whereupon a reversal of a judgement creates an opportunity for proving and arguing all issues involved until the verdict becomes final as a whole.

☞ *Alexander Mlladenović* case, District Court of Pristina/Prishtinë, Decision of 23 November 2001

This case was not reported in 2001 due to the original indictment being for robbery, albeit in the context of the armed conflict (the crimes were alleged to have occurred on 4 and 22 April 1999 and to have been committed by a Kosovar Serb against Kosovar Albanians), and for setting fire to several houses (alleged to have occurred on 4 April and 4 June

---

172. The retrial started on 1 October 2002 and lasted through January 2003, with the last month devoted mainly to hearing the closing speeches. The verdict was handed down on 31 January 2003.

1999). However, after the trial began on 14 June 2001, the international public prosecutor filed an amended indictment on 5 July 2001, charging property damage, arson and robbery as war crimes under Article 142 FRYCC.

On 23 November 2001, the international majority '64' Panel acquitted the accused due to insufficient evidence, and on 9 November 2002 it issued a comprehensive and lengthy written verdict analysing in great depth the facts and the law.

The verdict implied that the court had expected the international prosecutor to take much greater efforts than he did to attempt to prove some of the essential elements of a war crime, especially since the prosecutor had amended the indictment to include war crimes charges.[173] The verdict properly put prosecutors on notice that amending 'up' to war crimes

---

173. The Court specified:

'16. The Prosecution during the case appeared to take for granted the existence of critical elements of a war crime, contrary to the need to prove such elements. Upon reading SFRY CC Article 142, the applicable Legal Commentary, and reviewing pertinent international humanitarian law agreements and law, it is obvious that the elements of an Article 142 war crime which must be proven are:

An act or omission, *actus reus*, of the perpetrator, as listed in Article 142, with the accompanying *mens rea* of the perpetrator; Status of the perpetrator, that is, who orders or commits; Status of the victim; Armed conflict, in particular its existence, parties and character [internal or international]; Nexus of the perpetrator's acts to the Armed Conflict; That this criminal conduct must also be a violation of international law. The Prosecution did not even argue or attempt to prove most of these elements.

17. *Actus Reas, Mens Rea*, and Status of the Perpetrator: These separate requirements seem to be merged by the Prosecution, which requests the Court to find the accused criminally liable for all crimes done by 'Serb Forces' in the area, even if the accused himself did not personally do those acts. Yet Article 142 requires the accused to either order or commit. It is also true, however, that criminal liability may also be found against the accused even if he has not ordered or personally committed the proscribed acts, through the principles of complicity, Art. 22 SFRY CC; Incitement, Art. 23 SFRY CC; or Aiding, Art. 24 SFRY CC. Yet these bases of liability must also be proven based on facts. The Prosecution does not prove the accused's liability under any of these theories.

18. Rather, the Prosecution simply assumes the accused's liability based on assumptions which were built upon other assumptions. The Prosecution first made the unproven assumption that the 3 groups of the military, police, and vaguely-defined paramilitary forces are all part of one group with apparently one overall plan of intimidation and goal of expulsion, also referred to as the "State's plan," which is then classified without more evidence as "Serb forces." Neither this plan of intimidation or goal/State plan of expulsion is proven.

19. Second, the Prosecution then assumes that the accused is part of the "Serb forces" group, without clearly identifying to which subgroup he belongs, since he is seen in uniforms, paramilitary black, and civilian clothing, these witnesses thus giving contradictory testimony. Indeed, the accused is also seen with and without a firearm.

20. Third, the Prosecution then assumes that the accused had the *mens rea* of intimidation of the Albanian population, apparently with the objective to expel the population from Lipjan, and thus was part of the "Serb forces" and accordingly liable for all acts of the group based on accomplice liability, although the Prosecution does not attempt to prove the *mens rea* and *actus reas* requirements of Art. 22, such as joint participation.

21. In sum, the Prosecution simply assumes that a Serb who is in proximity of the police or military or paramilitaries is automatically one of that group with the aims and *mens rea* of that group, whatever they may be. However, during this time, when the Serbian government called up and armed many of its civilians with past military experience, and declared war against NATO, it cannot be assumed that the mere presence near or around others in such groups, even if armed, can be in itself equated to physically and mentally joining them for purposes of criminal liability. No attempt was made to prove more than mere proximity to such "group," which was in itself consisting of different groups and individuals, which were not necessarily homogeneous in purpose or action.

22. Armed Conflict. The Prosecution does not even discuss the issues involved with the need to prove the existence, parties to and character of an Armed Conflict. That there was a declaration of war by Yugoslavian authorities against NATO does not automatically cause this to be an Armed Conflict as between the Kosovar-Albanians and Serb authorities, and the issue of Nexus also requires proof of an Armed Conflict involving the Kosovar-Albanian victims, at least as relating to the war effort to the advantage of the Serbs. Thus the parties to the conflict must be articulated in the proof. Yet the Prosecution did not even articulate any of the parties. Even if the Prosecution had claimed that the Kosovar-Albanian "party" is acting on behalf of or in concert with NATO, that must be proven. Otherwise, the character of the conflict concerning the Albanian-Kosovar and Serb forces may be only internal.

23. As to the existence of an armed conflict, it must be proven that it is not a situation of internal disturbances and tensions, such as riots, isolated and sporadic acts of violence and other acts of a similar nature, as defined in Additional Protocol II, Art. 1(2). Once there is proven a conflict exists, the issue is at what level. Art. 3 common to [the] four Geneva Conventions directly applies to non-international armed conflicts, but the level of hostilities required to "qualify" under

charges must be supported by additional elements and proven, in contrast to this case where even the lesser charges were found to be insufficiently proven. However, the acquittal resulted from the findings of the court that there was insufficient evidence that the accused had participated in the events; thus, even if the prosecutor could have proven the predicate elements for war crimes and the acts themselves, the identity of the perpetrators could not be sufficiently proven. The verdict became final in 2003.

☛ *Igor Simić et al.* case

After the international public prosecutor of Mitrovica/Mitrovicë dismissed this genocide case during the trial for insufficient evidence on 1 April 2001,[174] the attorney for some injured parties attempted to resume the prosecution as an injured party prosecution, as allowed under the applicable Law of Criminal Procedure Articles 61 et seq. However, the absence of the accused Simić and UNMIK Regulation 2001/1 prohibition against *in absentia* war crimes trials prevented any further proceedings.

Ongoing Cases
☛ *Momcilo Trajković* case, District Court of Gjilan/Gnjilane and Supreme Court

The retrial of this case[175] – the seminal case on command responsibility in Kosovo – had begun before the District Court of Gjilan/Gnjilane but not yet finished by the end of the year.[176]

Article 3 is lower than that defined in the Additional Protocol II, Art. 1, which is harder to prove, but accordingly provides a higher level of protection for civilians.

24. Nexus. There must be a nexus between the alleged crime and the relevant armed conflict. Where the Prosecution has not yet attempted to prove whether it was an international or internal conflict, it could then hardly have proven this nexus requirement.

25. This is also a requirement under international law. See ICTY *Tadić* Appeals Chamber jurisdiction decision (1995), para. 70 ('closely related to the hostilities'); ICTY *Kunarać* Trial Court Judgement, paras. 402 and 407 ('a close nexus'), ICTY *Delalić* Trial Court judgement, 16 Nov. 1998, para. 193 ('an obvious link'), and ibid., para. 197 ('a clear nexus'). The existence of an armed conflict must, at a minimum, have played a substantial part in the perpetrator's ability to commit it, his decision to commit it, the manner in which it was committed or the purpose for which it was committed. Hence, if it can be established '… that the perpetrator acted in furtherance of or under the guise of the armed conflict, it would be sufficient to conclude that his acts were closely related to the armed conflict'. ICTY *Kunarać* Appeals Chamber judgement, para. 58.

26. In determining whether or not the act in question is sufficiently related to the armed conflict, the following *factors*, amongst others, may be relevant: the fact that the perpetrator is a combatant (or a member of the armed forces or an armed group); the fact that the victim is a civilian or a non-combatant; the fact that the victim is a member of the opposing party; the fact that the act may be said to serve the ultimate goal of a military campaign; and the fact that the crime is committed as part of or in the context of the perpetrator's official duties. See ICTY *Kunarać* AC judgement, para. 59.

27. This is the applicable law, but unfortunately the Prosecution did not even argue or attempt to prove the factual circumstances that would support an argument on this Nexus requirement.

28. Violation of International Law. Each act committed by the accused must be proven to be a violation of international law. For example, the scope of international law relating to non-international armed conflicts is more limited than the law relating to international armed conflicts. If the Serbian/Kosovar-Albanian conflict is characterized as an internal conflict, not all of the conduct otherwise listed in Art. 142 is prohibited by international law. If conduct referred to in Art. 142 is not prohibited in Art. 3 common to [the] four Geneva Conventions, or Additional Protocol II, it cannot be a war crime in an internal armed conflict pursuant to Art. 142.'

Cf., this comprehensive *Mlladenović* verdict with the equally detailed *Vucković* case verdict cited above; in *Vucković* the verdict painstakingly analysed the elements and factors discussed in this *Mlladenović* verdict, and the *Vucković* verdict explained how they were sufficiently proven.

174. For background, see 4 *YIHL* (2001) at p. 509.

175. Ibid., at pp. 512-513.

☛ *Veselin Besović* case, District Court of Peć/Pejë

The accused was indicted by an international prosecutor on 11 November 2001 for war crimes under Article 142 FRYCC on the charges that in late May through December 1998, and in late March through May 1999, the accused was a member of armed and uniformed Serbian forces which committed murder and torture, and other acts of terror, with the motivation of persecuting Kosovar Albanians and causing them to flee Kosovo. The trial began on 20 May 2002.

Unfortunately, the trial was not completed because an international judge left UNMIK to return to his country.[177] The trial was adjourned due to it not having completed at least one evidentiary session within 30 days – with a new panel not being constituted during that time as required by the local procedure[178] – resulting in the accused being released from custody on 13 December 2002, after signing a pledge to reappear before the court. A new panel was constituted with a new presiding judge and trial was rescheduled for 28 January 2003 before the Peć/Pejë District Court, with the necessity of all witnesses being required to testify anew.

---

176. On 30 May 2003, the '64' Panel international-majority trial court announced the verdict of the retrial, which was not guilty on all eleven counts of war crimes. The accused was found guilty of postwar attempted murder (shooting at a Kosovar Albanian hoisting an Albanian flag at the Department of Internal Affairs in Kaminica, the accused's office). The retrial court's 2003 verdict had been foreshadowed by the International Public Prosecutor of Kosovo's lengthy Opinion on the first verdict, which called for reversal on several grounds, including a detailed analysis of the lack of evidence supporting the finding of command responsibility liability for the acts of police officers which were the basis of the war crimes counts.

177. That first trial panel stated: 'A major reason for failure of the panel to complete the trial of the accused prior to the departure of the panel member resulted from the complexity of the case alleged against him. The amended indictment charges the accused with 26 counts, 23 of which are charged as war crimes. The factual allegations underpinning those counts are highly complex and to date the panel has heard thirty-nine witnesses, six of whom were defense witnesses, which required the panel to organize to travel to Belgrade in order to receive their evidence. Delays in being able to complete the trial prior to the departure of one of the panel members resulted from difficulties associated with collecting evidence alleged to be relevant to the defense of the accused, including documents from the Zastava factory, medical records from the Belgrade hospital, and information regarding the mobilization or otherwise of the accused from the Ministry of the Interior. To date the panel still has not received any of the requested materials and the causes of the delay are currently being investigated by the Department of Justice.'

178. Art. 305 of the 1986 Yugoslav Law of Criminal Procedure provides:

'(1) A main trial which is adjourned shall recommence from the beginning if the membership of the panel has changed, but after the parties have been examined, the panel may decide that in such a case the witnesses and expert witnesses shall not be examined again, and that a new on-the-spot inquest will not be performed again, but that the testimony of witnesses and expert witnesses given in the previous main trial shall be read or the record of the on-the-spot inquest will be read.

(2) If a main trial which was adjourned is held before the same panel, it shall be resumed, and the presiding judge shall briefly summarize the course of the previous main trial, but even in that case the panel may order that the trial recommence from the beginning.

(3) If the adjournment has lasted longer than one month, or if the trial is being held before another presiding judge, the main trial must recommence from the beginning, and all evidence must again be presented.'

☛ *Latif Gashi, Rrustem Mustafa aka 'Commander Remi', Naim Kadriu* and *Nasif Mehme-ti* case, District Court of Pristina/Prishtinë

On 28 January 2002, the first war crimes case against Kosovar Albanians began with the arrests of Latif Gashi, who was allegedly the Director of the Intelligence Service of Kosovo (KSHiK) and a KLA/UCK officer, and of former UCK/KLA[179] soldiers Naim Kadriu and Nasif Mehmeti. On 11 August 2002, the international investigating judge expanded her investigation to include Rrustem Mustafa, aka UCK/KLA 'Commander Remi'. The criminal investigation generated controversy and some demonstrations among the Kosovar Albanian community, due to the support enjoyed by the accused based on their ex-UCK/KLA status. The investigation was continued through November 2002, occasioning demonstrations, media attacks against the investigation and against some of the injured parties and witness intimidation. It resulted in an indictment on 19 November 2002 that was subsequently amended in 2003. The November 2002 indictment charged illegal arrests and detention by the UCK/KLA of Kosovar Albanian civilians, which allegedly resulted in inhumane treatment through detentions in inhumane conditions, beatings, torture and murder.[180] The trial was due to begin in 2003 before the District Court of Pristina/Prishtinë.

MICHAEL E. HARTMANN

FINLAND

International Criminal Court

☛ Entry into force on 1 July 2002 of Act No. 1284/2000 on the implementation of the ICC Statute[181]

Adopted on 28 December 2000, 'this Act clarifies and supplements the Act on International Legal Assistance in Criminal Matters with respect to cooperation between Finland and the ICC, in particular in the following matters: arrest and surrender to the Court of a person found in Finland's territory (Section 3); judicial assistance for investigation and prosecution (Section 4); summoning of witnesses (Sections 5 and 6); enforcement of a sentence of imprisonment (Section 7); and forfeiture of proceeds, property and assets derived from the crime (Sections 7 and 8). ... It notably introduces punishment for "offences against the administration of justice by the ICC" (Chapter 15, Section 12a), "offences against the ICC", such as violent resistance to, or bribery of, a person who is in the service of the ICC (Chapter 16, Sections 19a and 20) and offences by an official of the ICC, such as acceptance of a bribe (Chapter 40, Section 9).'

Pending

☛ Government Bill (188/2002 vp) of 18 October 2002 to the Parliament, on the amendment of some provisions of the Penal Code – Terrorist Crimes, Biological Weapons
☛ Act No. 17/2003 to amend the Penal Code – Terrorist Crimes, Biological Weapons. Approved by Parliament on 24 January 2003, entered into force on 1 February 2003

---

179. 'UCK' is the Albanian-language acronym for 'KLA' or Kosovo Liberation Army.
180. While there was one Serbian Forest Ranger as an injured party, all of the other victims were Kosovar Albanians. This was a case which relied upon the testimony of Kosovar Albanians.
181. See 3 *YIHL* (2000) pp. 498-499.

The goal of the Government Bill was to carry out changes in the law that would enable Finland to live up to the requirements of the Framework Decision (2002/475/RIF) of the European Union on combating terrorism and those of other international instruments. The Bill suggested that a new chapter on terrorist crimes should be included in the Penal Code. This chapter was to contain provisions on, among other things, crimes intended to spread terror, preparation of terrorist acts, participation in the activities of a terrorist group and financing of terrorism. Definitions of terrorism-related terms were also part of the new chapter. These definitions were based on the European Union Framework Decision. The purpose of the law according to the Finnish government was to secure the criminality of the acts mentioned in the Framework Decision.

In the same Bill, the government proposed criminalising biological weapons. Finland has ratified the 1972 Convention on the Prohibition of the Development, Production and Stockpiling of Bacteriological (Biological) and Toxin Weapons and on Their Destruction, but no criminalisation of biological weapons has been incorporated in the Penal Code. The Convention did not oblige a criminalisation of biological weapons, and thus incorporating the provision into the Penal Code was considered as one possible means to comply with the treaty obligation to prohibit and prevent biological weapons from being developed or used. The government considered a more limited prohibition of biological weapons, namely, the prohibition of biological weapons for terrorist activities as mentioned in the European Framework Decision on combating terrorism, as not satisfactory. It was considered that criminality related to the use of biological weapons could in general be considered serious, not only in the case of terrorist activities. The intention of this prohibition was to further eliminate possible gaps in the law concerning criminal behaviour in relation to dangerous weapons. The Government Bill noted that the provisions on biological weapons did not concern their use in armed conflict. Accordingly, the Bill stated that the biological weapons provision was only to be applicable regarding use of these weapons in another way than use in accordance with the provisions included in Chapter 11, paragraphs 1-3 of the Penal Code on war crimes and crimes against humanity. Use of biological weapons in armed conflict was to be punished as a crime against the laws of war. After approval by the Parliament, the Act amending the Penal Code entered into force on 1 February 2003.

Maria Nybondas

FRANCE[182]

Prisoners of War

☛ National Advisory Commission on Human Rights. Opinion on the situation of detainees captured during the international armed conflict in Afghanistan [Commission nationale consultative des droits de l'homme (CNCDH): Avis concernant la situation des personnes détenues après avoir été arrêtées dans le cadre du conflit armé international en Afghanistan]. Adopted 7 March 2002 <http://www.commission-droits-homme.fr/bin Travaux/AffichageAvis.cfm?IDAVIS=663&iClasse=1>

---

182. Information and commentaries provided by Professor Paul Tavernier, Professor Paris-Sud University, Director, Centre de Recherches et d'Etudes sur les droits de l'Homme et le droit humanitaire (CREDHO), with the assistance of Alexandre Balguy-Gallois, CREDHO and Catholic Law Faculty, Paris.

The National Advisory Commission on Human Rights, in its opinion of 7 March 2002, expressed its concern about the prisoners taken during the conflict in Afghanistan and kept at Guantánamo Bay, a military base of the United States of America in Cuba. Condemning acts of terrorism, and in particular the attacks of 11 September 2001, the Commission at the same time noted the lack of official information about those who had been arrested in relation to these terrorist acts. The Commission especially pointed out the lack of clarification of the legal status of the detainees. Moreover, the Commission laid down the international rules and principles that should be applied to the detainees. Finally, it requested the French government to take these principles into account when determining its position on the issue and to continue its work for the respect of the Geneva Conventions and its diplomatic efforts in order to facilitate the mission of the International Committee of the Red Cross.

☛ Decision of the Tribunal de Grande Instance of Paris of 31 October 2002 concerning two French nationals detained at Guantánamo Bay

'On 18 October 2002, the families of two French nationals detained in Guatánamo Bay had petitioned the *Tribunal de Grande Instance* of Paris with a view to clarifying their situation under the Third Geneva Convention of 1949, including the question of their prisoner-of-war status. On 31 October 2002, the Tribunal stated that it did not consider itself competent to examine the case. Following this decision, the lawyers of the two detainees filed a charge in Lyon, against persons unknown, for "arbitrary detention" and "kidnapping and restraint".'[183]

Children
☛ Law No. 2002-271 of 26 February 2002 authorising the ratification of the Optional Protocol to the Convention on the Rights of the Child and Concerning the Involvement of Children in Armed Conflict [Loi No 2002-271 du 26 février 2002 autorisant la ratification du Protocole facultatif à la Convention relative aux droits de l'enfant concernant l'implication d'enfants dans les conflits armés]. Published in the *Official Gazette of the French Republic/Journal Officiel de la République française* No. 49, 27 February 2002

Conventional Weapons
☛ Decree No. 2002-23 of 3 January 2002 modifying Decree No. 95-589 of 6 May 1995 relating to the application of the Decree of 18 April 1939 establishing the regime for weapons of war, arms and munitions [Décret, 2002-23 du 3 janvier 2002 modifiant le décret No 95-589 du 6 mai 1995 relatif à l'application du décret du 18 avril 1939 fixant le régime des matériels de guerre, armes et munitions]. Published in the *Official Gazette of the French Republic/Journal Officiel de la République française* No. 5, 6 January 2002, p. 409
☛ Decree No. 2002-123 of 25 January 2002 of the President of the Republic not discussed in the Council of Ministers concerning publication of the Additional Protocol to the Convention on Prohibitions or Restrictions on the Use of Certain Conventional Weapons which May Be Deemed to Be Excessively Injurious or to Have Indiscriminate Ef-

---

183. Source: ICRC Advisory Service, National Implementation of International Humanitarian Law – Biannual update on national legislation and case-law, July-December 2002. <http://www.icrc.org/Web/eng/siteeng0.nsf/htmlall/5LVLHV/$File/irrc_849_National_Implem.pdf>.

fects. Adopted at Vienna (Austria) on 13 October 1995 (Protocol on Blinding Laser Weapons, Protocol IV) [Décret du Président de la République non délibéré en Conseil des Ministres No 2002-123 du 25 janvier 2002 portant publication du protocole additionnel à la Convention sur l'interdiction ou la limitation de l'emploi de certaines armes classiques qui peuvent être considérées comme produisant des effets traumatiques excessifs ou comme frappant sans discrimination, adopté à Vienne le 13 octobre 1995 (Protocole relatif aux armes à laser aveuglantes, Protocole IV)]. Published in the *Official Gazette of the French Republic/Journal Officiel de la République française* No. 27, 1 February 2002, p. 2151

☞ Decree No. 2002-1019 of 24 July 2002 abrogating Decree No. 92-489 of 5 June 1992 concerning the application of the regime of materials of war, arms, munitions and comparable materials to Security Council resolution 757 concerning the Federal Republic of Yugoslavia. [Décret simple 2002-1019 du 24 juillet 2002 abrogeant le décret N° 92-489 du 5 juin 1992 relatif à l'application au régime des matériels de guerre, armes, munitions et matériels assimilés de la résolution 757 du Conseil de sécurité des Nations unies concernant la République fédérale de Yougoslavie]. Published in the *Official Gazette of the French Republic/Journal Officiel de la République française* No. 173, 26 July 2002, p. 12799

☞ Decree No. 2002-1364 of 14 November 2002 publishing the Protocol on the Prohibition or Restriction on the Use of Incendiary Weapons (Protocol III), adopted at Geneva, 10 October 1980 [Décret No 2002-1364 du 14 novembre 2002 portant publication du protocole sur l'interdiction ou la limitation de l'emploi des armes incendiaires (Protocole III), adopté à Genève le 10 octobre 1980]. Published in the Official Gazette of the French Republic/*Journal Officiel de la République française* No. 271, 21 November 2002, p. 19240

Regarding the latter document, the text of Protocol III is published together with two declarations of the French government on Article 2(2) and (3) concerning launching of incendiary weapons from an aircraft and distinction between military objectives and concentration of civilians.

Specific Situations

OCCUPIED PALESTINIAN TERRITORIES

☞ Israel-Palestine: 'The urgency of international engagement', Parliamentary proceedings: Information report, 20 April 2002, Middle East [Israël-Palestine: 'L'urgence d'un engagement international'], Doc. Senate, No. 285. Published in *Travaux parlementaires*: *Rapport d'information*, 20 April 2002, Middle/East Moyen-Orient, <http://www.senat. fr/rap/r01-285/r01-285.html>

From 17 to 31 March 2002, a delegation of the Ministries of Foreign Affairs and Defence and the Armed Forces visited Israel and the Occupied Palestinian Territories. The delegation, presided over by Mr Xavier de Villepin, was composed of Mr Michel Pelchat, Mrs Danielle Bidard-Reydet, Mr Daniel Goulet, Mrs Monique Cerisier-Ben Guiga and Mr Jean-Guy Branger. The purpose of the visit was information gathering for further parliamentary discussion and to inform public opinion.

CHECHNYA
☛ National Advisory Commission on Human Rights (CNCDH), Opinion on the humanitarian situation and human right in Chechnya [Commission nationale consultative des droits de l'homme (CNCDH), *Avis sur la situation humanitaire et des droits de l'homme en Tchétchénie*]. Adopted 7 March 2002 <http://www.commission-droits-homme.fr/binTravaux/AffichageAvis.cfm?IDAVIS=664&iClasse=1>
☛ National Advisory Commission on Human Rights (CNCDH), Opinion on the humanitarian situation in Chechnya and Ingushetia [Commission nationale consultative des droits de l'homme (CNCDH), *Avis sur la situation en Tchétchénie et en Ingouchie*]. Adopted 19 December 2002 <http://www.commission-droits-homme.fr/binTravaux/AffichageAvis.cfm?IDAVIS=675&iClasse=1>

INDIA-PAKISTAN
☛ Senate, Information Report for the Ministries of Foreign Affairs, Defence and the Armed Forces following a mission to India and Pakistan [Sénat, Rapport d'information de la commission des affaires étrangères, de la Défense et des Forces armées à la suite d'une mission effectuée en Inde et au Pakistan], Doc. Sénate, No. 336 of 24 June 2002 <http://www.senat.fr/rap/r01-336/r01-336.html>

IRAQ
☛ Senate 2002, Iraq at the crossroads. Acts of the Colloquium of 27 June 2002 [Sénat 2002 – L'Iraq à la croisée des chemins. Actes du colloque du 27 juin 2002]. Under the high patronage of Christian Poncelet, President of the Senate, Jean-Daniel Gardère, Director-General of the French Centre of Foreign Commerce, and under the guidance of the Inter-Parliamentary group France-Iraq <http://www.senat.fr/international/colloqiraq/colloqiraq.html>
☛ Report, Iraq in Danger, Mission to Iraq by a delegation of a friendly senatorial group from 18 to 23 June 2001 [Rapport, *L'Irak en danger*, mission effectuée en Irak par une délégation du groupe sénatorial d'amitié France-Irak du 18 au 23 juin 2001] Report No. 38, 19 March 2002 <http://www.senat.fr/rapga.html>

Crimes Against Humanity
☛ Private bill No. 223 aiming to exclude sentences for crimes or complicity in crimes against humanity from applicability of Law No. 2002-303, adopted 4 March 2002 and regarding the rights of sick persons and the quality of the healthcare system [Proposition de loi N° 223 tendant à exclure du champ d'application de la loi no. 2002-303 du 4 mars 2002 relative aux droits des malades et à la qualité du système de santé les condamnations pour crime ou complicité de crime contre l'humanité]. This private bill was registered by the Presidency of the National Assembly on 24 September 2002; Doc. National Assembly, 24 September 2002 <http://www.assemblee-nationale.fr/12/propositions/pion0223.asp>

Genocide
☛ Revisionism and genocide denial. Private bill aiming at the strengthening of the fight against revisionism and to authorise prosecution of persons who deny genocide acknowledged by France or by an international organisation of which France is a member. National Assembly document No. 300, 15 October 2002, Registered with the Presidency of the Assembly on 15 October 2002 [Révisionnisme, négateurs des génocides.

Assemblée nationale No 300, douzième legislature. Enregistré à la Présidence de l'Assemblée nationale le 15 octobre 2002. Proposition de loi tendant à renforcer la lutte contre le révisionnisme et à permettre les poursuites à l'encontre des négateurs des génocides reconnus par la France ou une organisation internationale dont la France est membre] <http://www.assemblee-nationale.fr/12/propositions/pion0300.asp>

Terrorism
➤ Colloquium on 'Terrorism and International Criminal Responsibility', Tuesday 5 February 2002 at the National Assembly [Colloque 'Terrorisme et responsabilité pénale internationale', le mardi 5 février 2002 à l'Assemblée nationale]
   [Program and some documents are available at: <http://www.assemblee-nationale.fr/dossiers/attentats-2.asp> <http://www.sos-attentats.org/juridique/etudes_articles/34.pdf> <http://www.sos-attentats.org/index2.htm>]

International Criminal Tribunals
➤ Law No. 2002-287 of 28 February 2002 authorising the approval of the agreement between the government of the French Republic and the United Nations Organisation concerning the execution of penalties pronounced by the International Criminal Tribunal for the former Yugoslavia [Loi No 2002-287 du 28 février 2002 autorisant l'approbation de l'accord entre le Gouvernement de la république française et l'Organisation des Nations-Unies concernant l'exécution des peines prononcées par le Tribunal pénal international pour l'ex-Yougoslavie], published in the *Official Gazette of the French Republic/Journal Officiel de la République française* No. 51, 1 March 2002, p. 3905

International Criminal Court
➤ Law No. 2002-268 of 26 February 2002 concerning cooperation with the International Criminal Court [Loi No 2002-268 du 26 février 2002 relative à la cooperation avec la Cour pénale internationale]. Published in the *Official Gazette of the French Republic/Journal Officiel de la République française* No. 47, 27 February 2002, p. 3684

The purpose of this law is to adapt the French Criminal Procedure Code to the obligations accepted by the French government under the Rome Statute as regards cooperation with the ICC. New clauses are added in the Criminal Procedure Code concerning judicial cooperation (judicial assistance, arrest and surrender) and enforcement of sentences (penalties imposed by the Court). Another law is needed to amend the Criminal Code to introduce in French legislation clauses concerning crimes provided for in the Rome Statute, especially Articles 6 (Genocide) and 7 (Crimes Against Humanity).

➤ Decree No. 2002-925 of 6 June 2002 publishing the Convention establishing the Statute of the ICC, adopted in Rome 17 July 1998, including declarations by the French Republic [Décret No 2002-925 du 6 juin 2002 portant publication de la Convention portant Statut de la Cour pénale internationale, adoptée à Rome le 17 juillet 1998, avec les déclarations de la République Française]. Published in the *Official Gazette of the French Republic/Journal Officiel de la République française* No. 134, 11 June 2002, p. 10327

In France, publication of treaties and conventions in the Official Gazette is a prerequisite for their application by the French courts. Generally, publication occurs after the entry into force of the agreement. Therefore it is noticeable that in this case publication occurred before the entry into force of the ICC Statute on 1 July 2002. Following the text of the Statute are attached three declarations made by France when it ratified it. The first one is an interpretative declaration concerning self-defence as provided in Article 51 of the UN Charter and some key points about Article 8 (use of nuclear weapons, military objectives, etc.). The second declaration is made under Article 8 of the Statute: documents concerning cooperation will be written in the French language. The third declaration is made under Article 124 of the Statute (opt-out clause): France does not accept the Court's jurisdiction as regards war crimes perpetrated on its territory or by nationals/citizens for a seven-year period.

☞ National Advisory Commission on Human Rights (CNCDH), Opinion on implementation of the International Criminal Court Statute [Commission nationale consultative des droits de l'homme (CNCDH), *Avis sur la mise en oeuvre du Statut de la Cour pénale internationale*]. Adopted 19 December 2002 <http://www.commission-droits-homme.fr/binTravaux/AffichageAvis.cfm?IDAVIS=673&iClasse=1>

In the Advisory Opinion, the National Advisory Commission approved the government's position on the integrity of the Rome Statute, especially concerning the French Declaration made before the extradition treaty signed in Paris on 23 April 1996 between the United States and France entered into force on 1 February 2002. In this declaration, the French government stated that the French Republic ratified the Rome Statute establishing the ICC and that the French authorities are therefore obliged to carry out requests for cooperation issued by the ICC.[184]

In the second part of the opinion, the Commission was very critical of the procedure followed for presentation of a French candidate for an ICC judge and deplored the lack of transparency. In the third part, it recalled its previous opinion, adopted on 23 November 2001, on French legislation implementing the ICC Statute.

Compensation

☞ Retirement pensions and invalidity grants for war veterans who are natives of overseas territories. State Council Decision No. 216172 of 6 February 2002. *Minister of Defence and Minister of Economy, Finance and Industry* v. *Mrs Doukouré*, published in the Lebon Record [Pensions de retraite et d'invalidité des anciens combattants l'outremer. Décision du conseil d'état du 6 février 2002. *Ministre de la Défense et Ministre de l'Économie, des Finances et de l'Industrie* c. *Mme Doukouré*. Publié aux Tables du Recueil Lebon]

☞ Private Bill, presented by M. Gilbert Gantier, aiming to specify conditions for implementation of Article L.273, military and war victims grants code, 15 October 2002, Doc. National Assembly No. 277 [Proposition de loi de M. Gilbert Gantier visant à préciser les conditions d'application de l'article L. 273 du code des pensions militaires

---

184. Decree No. 2002-117 of 29 January 2002, publishing the extradition treaty between France and the United States of America (with an agreement's statement on representation), signed in Paris, 23 April 1996) [Décret No 2002-117 du 29 janvier 2002 portant publication du traité d'extradition entre la France et les Etats-Unis d'Amérique (ensemble un procès-verbal d'accord sur la représentation), signé à Paris le 23 avril 1996]. Published in the *Official Gazette of the French Republic/Journal Officiel de la République française* No. 25, 30 January 2002, p. 2002.

d'invalidité et des victimes de guerre, déposée le 15 octobre 2002, No. 277 (renvoyée à la commission des affaires culturelles)] <http://www.assemblee-nationale.fr/12/documents/index-propositions_2003.asp>

☛ Sénate, Question No. 675 of Mr Sauvadet François concerning veterans and victims of war [Sénat, Question No. 675 de M. Sauvadet François se rapportant aux anciens combattants et victimes de guerre]

☛ National Assembly No. 164, 12th legislature. Registered with the Presidency of the National Assembly on 1 August 2002 [Assemblée nationale, No 164, douzième législature, Enregistré à la Présidence de l'Assemblée nationale le 1er août 2002. Proposition de loi visant à instaurer des mesures de réparation aux orphelins de déportés, à ceux des fusillés et massacrés pour fait de résistance et à ceux des patriotes résistant à l'Occupation. Pars MM Lucien Guichon, Michel Voisin, Gérard Voisin, Bernard Schreiner and Patrick Beaudouin, deputies] <http://www.legifrance.gouv.fr/> <http://www.assemblee-nationale.fr/12/propositions/pion0164.asp>

PAUL TAVERNIER

GEORGIA

☛ Statement by the Parliament of Georgia on the 23 August 2002 bombing by the Russian Federation,[185] 24 August 2002

The statement expresses the Georgian Parliament's indignation and protest regarding the violation of Georgian airspace and bombing of Georgian territory by the Russian Federation on 23 August 2002, which resulted in civilian casualties. Georgian officials said that a woman and child were killed when four military aircraft presumed to be Russian bombed the Pankisi Gorge on 23 August. Seven other people were injured. A Russian Defense Ministry spokesman denied that Russian aircraft flew any such bombing raid.[186] Characterising 'this barbaric act as the military aggression against the sovereignty of Georgia', the Parliament said that it threatened the development of civilized relations between Georgia and Russia and posed a threat to stability in the entire region. The US White House also issued a statement condemning the bombing.[187]

GERMANY[188]

Protection of Civilians and Humanitarian Workers

☛ Speech of the Federal Minister for Foreign Affairs at the 58th Session of the United Nations Commission on Human Rights, Federal Foreign Office, Press Release of 20 March 2002 <http://www.unhchr.ch/huricane/huricane.nsf/NewsRoom?OpenFrameSet>

---

185. Reprinted in the Documentation section of this volume at p. 819.

186. Russia denies bombing Pankisi, while Georgia claims two killed', RFE/RL Newsline, 23 August 2002. <http://w ww.h ri.o rg/news/balkans/rferl/2002/02-08-23.rferl.Html#20>.

187. 'White House Deplores Russian Bombing of Georgian Villages, August 23, 2002', 24 August 2002. <http://www.usembassy.it/file2002_08/alia/a2082401.htm>.

188. Information and commentaries provided by Sascha Rolf Lüder, Research Fellow at the Chair for Criminal Law, Criminal Procedure and Legal History, Fern Universität Hagen, and Gregor Schotten, Desk Officer in the Political Department of the Federal Foreign Office, Berlin. the views expressed in these commentaries are those of the authors alone.

☞ Question of the Violation of Human Rights and Fundamental Freedoms in any Part of the World, Situation of Human Rights in the Sudan, United Nations Commission on Human Rights Draft Resolution, UN Doc. E/CN.4/2002/L.27, 12 April 2002

☞ Question of the Violation of Human Rights and Fundamental Freedoms in any Part of the World, Situation of Human Rights in the Democratic Republic of the Congo, United Nations Commission on Human Rights Draft Resolution, UN Doc. E/CN.4/2002/L.25/Rev.1, 17 April 2002

In his speech before the 58th Session of the United Nations Commission on Human Rights, the German Minister for Foreign Affairs, Joschka Fischer, said that Russia had a '... legitimate right to maintain its territorial integrity' but that, at the same time, the use of military force against the civilian population was '... unacceptable and not compatible with European and international norms'. With regard to the situation in the Middle East, the German Minister for Foreign Affairs emphasised that '... measures against medical and humanitarian institutions and their staff were totally unacceptable. The functioning of these institutions had to be guaranteed'.

Germany co-sponsored a draft resolution in the United Nations Commission on Human Rights on the 'Situation of Human Rights in the Sudan'. In this resolution, the Commission on Human Rights expressed its deep concern at '... the widespread and indiscriminate aerial bombardments and attacks by the government of the Sudan, particularly bombings of schools and hospitals, churches, food distribution areas and marketplaces ...'. The resolution urged '... parties to the conflict, ... to protect civilians and civilian facilities from military attacks and in particular the government of the Sudan to cease immediately all indiscriminate aerial bombardments and attacks against the civilian population and civilian installations ...'.

The draft resolution also urged all parties to the conflict in the Sudan '... to grant full, safe and unhindered access to all international agencies and humanitarian organisations in order to facilitate by all possible means the delivery of humanitarian assistance, in conformity with international humanitarian law, to all civilians in need of protection and assistance ...'.

In another draft resolution also co-sponsored by Germany on the 'Situation of Human Rights in the Democratic Republic of Congo', the Commission on Human Rights expressed its concern regarding '... the indiscriminate attacks on civilian populations, including hospitals, in areas held by rebel and by foreign forces'. The draft resolution also condemned 'the killings of six ICRC humanitarian workers on 26 April 2001 in Ituri Province, the perpetrators of which must be brought to justice'.

Prisoners of War

☞ Release of 101 Moroccan POWs Held Captive over 20 Years, Federal Foreign Office, Press Release of 7 July 2002 <http://www.germany-info.org/relaunch/politics/new/pol_morocco_pow.htm>

☞ Question of the Violation of Human Rights and Fundamental Freedoms in any Part of the World, Situation of Human Rights in Iraq, United Nations Commission on Human Rights Draft Resolution, UN Doc. E/CN.4/2002/L.26, 11 April 2002

After more than 20 years in captivity, 101 Moroccan prisoners of war were released on 7 July 2002.[189] The Polisario Front had announced beforehand that 100 Moroccan prisoners of war were going to be released in response to a humanitarian initiative by the German government. The Federal government also supported the calls made by the ICRC and the United Nations for the immediate release of the remaining prisoners without political pre-conditions.

In April 2002, Germany co-sponsored a draft resolution on the 'Situation of Human Rights in Iraq' in the United Nations Commission on Human Rights. The resolution calls upon the government of Iraq '... to release immediately all Kuwaitis and nationals of other States who may still be held in detention and inform families about the whereabouts of arrested persons, to provide information about death sentences imposed on prisoners of war and civilian detainees and to issue death certificates for deceased prisoners of war and civilian detainees'.

International Criminal Court

☛ Act of Implementation of the Rome Statute of the International Criminal Court [*Gesetz zur Ausführung des Römischen Statutes des Internationalen Strafgerichtshofes*]. Adopted on 21 June 2002, published in *Bundesgesetzblatt* (2002) II on 28 June 2002, pp. 2144 et seq., entered into force on 1 July 2002

☛ International Criminal Code of 26 June 2002 [*Gesetz zur Einführung des Völkerstrafge-setzbuches vom 26. Juni 2002*]. Published in *Bundesgesetzblatt* (2002) II on 29 June 2002, pp. 2254 et seq., entered into force the same day

In parallel to the ratification of the Rome Statute of the International Criminal Court (the Court), work began on the bill of a German law implementing the Rome Statute, which shall govern the details of cooperation between the German courts and authorities and the Court, as well as on a draft International Criminal Code that transposes the crimes defined in the Rome Statute into German criminal law. Both bills passed through the German Parliament in Spring of 2002 with an overwhelming majority.

Already before the Court commenced operation, the International Criminal Code entered into force on 30 June 2002.[190] So far, the International Criminal Code has been translated into Arabic, Chinese, English, French, Greek, Russian and Spanish.[191] On 1 July 2002 the Act of Implementation of the Rome Statute of the International Criminal Court[192] entered into force.

---

189. See further the article by H.-P. Gasser in this volume at p. 375.

190. See H. Kreicker, 'Die völkerstrafrechtliche Unverjährbarkeit und die Regelung im Völker-strafgesetzbuch', 56 *Neue Justiz* (2002) pp. 281 et seq.; S.R. Lüder and T. Vormbaum, eds., *Materialien zum Völkerstrafgesetzbuch: Dokumentation des Gesetzgebungsverfahrens* (Münster, Lit 2002); H. Satzger, 'German Criminal Law and the Rome Statute: A Critical Analysis of the New German Code of Crimes against International Law', 2 *International Criminal Law Review* (2002) pp. 261 et seq.; G. Werle and F. Jeßberger, 'Das Völkerstrafgesetzbuch', 19 *Juristenzeitung* (2002) pp. 725 et seq.

191. See Max Planck Institute for Foreign and International Criminal Law [*Max Planck-Institut für ausländisches und internationales Strafrecht*]. <http://www.iuscrim.de/info/profile.html>.

192. See J. MacLean, 'Gesetzentwurf über die Zusammenarbeit mit dem Internationalen Strafge-richtshof', 35 *Zeitschrift für Rechtspolitik* (2002) pp. 260 et seq.; J. Meißner, *Die Zusammenarbeit mit dem Internationalen Strafgerichtshof nach dem Römischen Statut* (Munich, C.H. Beck 2003); P.

The German government pledged to continue to do its utmost to ensure that the Court was established in The Hague as quickly as possible.

Cases

☛ *Fredrich Engel* case, Hamburg State Court, 5 July 2001

Fredrich Engel was convicted by the Hamburg State Court on 5 July 2001 on 59 counts of murder and sentenced to seven years in prison for the reprisal killings of 59 Italian prisoners of war at a Turchino mountain pass outside Genoa, Italy, in 1944.

'The trial revealed that Engel headed the intelligence unit with tracking enemies of the Nazis. Engel admitted he had approved the list of prisoners from Genoa's Marassi jail to be shot and was present during the killings, but did not order the massacre or shoot anyone. One witness, however, told the Court that Engel "clearly had the job of supervising the killings" and at one point ordered a lieutenant to shoot a captive who was not yet dead. Judge Seedorf ... said to Engel: "You were the highest-ranking person at that site, so one must conclude that events unfolded the way you had imagined, and, I might add, to your satisfaction". ... Despite the prosecutor's request for a life sentence, the Court took into account the "exceptional circumstances" created by the long interval since the crimes, and a spotty witness testimony and issued a lesser sentence of seven years. The Court said that Fredrich Engel was too old to serve his seven-year sentence.'[193]

☛ *Viel* case, Ravensburg District Court, Judgement of 3 April 2001 [*Landgericht Ravens-burg, Urteil vom 3. April 2001*]

On 3 April 2001, Julius Viel, a former SS commander, was sentenced to 12 years in prison for the murder of seven Jewish prisoners at the Theresienstadt concentration camp in 1945. Eighty-three year-old Julius Viel was convicted of murdering the victims in Nazi-occupied Czechoslovakia.[194] They were digging anti-tank trenches at Leitmeritz, near the camp, when they were killed. The judge in the Ravensburg District Court said he had acted 'out of lust for murder and base motives', and not on orders.

Viel had been investigated for the murders in the 1960s, but the case was closed for a lack of evidence. The case was reopened when a former Nazi trainee, Hungarian-born Adalbert Lallier, decided to break half a century of silence to reveal that he had witnessed the killings. Lallier, an economics professor in Canada, told the court in Ravensburg that Viel had shot the victims in cold blood. He was the only person to give evidence, but the German judge said he had believed his account. 'Lallier certainly did not imagine what happened', said Judge Hermann Winkler. He said Viel had escaped a life sentence because of the time that had elapsed since the crime.

A number of other investigations into Nazi killings have been continuing, but most defendants are now considered too old or too ill to stand trial.

SACHA ROLF LÜDER and GREGOR SCHOTTEN

Wilkitzki, 'The German Law on Co-operation with the ICC', 2 *International Criminal Law Review* (2002) pp. 195 et seq.

193. Source: <http://www.preventgenocide.org/punish/domestic/index.htm>.
194. 'German Nazi jailed at 83', BBC News, 3 April 2001.

GREECE

International Criminal Court
☛ Law to ratify the Rome Statute, 27 March 2002

'A draft law of ratification, completed by an ad-hoc inter-ministerial committee, was submitted to the Parliament on 13 January 2002. The ratification bill was approved by Parliament on 27 March 2002, and was then signed by the President and published in the official gazette.'[195]

GUATEMALA

International Criminal Court
☛ Advisory Opinion of the Constitutional Court on the compatibility of the Rome Statute with the Guatemalan Constitution, 26 March 2002

'In January 2002, the President of Guatemala, Alfonso Portillo, asked for the opinion of the Constitutional Court with regard to the Rome Statute. Previously, sources from the Ministry of Foreign Affairs indicated that the Statute was examined in order to identify possible constitutional issues. Extradition and life imprisonment were identified as two issues that might raise the need for a constitutional amendment. On 26 March 2002, the Constitutional Court rendered its advisory opinion, and concluded that there is no incompatibility between the Guatemalan Constitution and the Rome Statute. There is reportedly strong resistance to ratification from conservative members of the government alliance.'[196]

Cases
☛ *Juan Valencia Osorio, Edgar Augusto Godoy Gaytán* and *Guillermo Oliva Carrera* case, Fourth Appeals Court, 4 October 2002

Army Colonel Juan Valencia Osorio was sentenced to 30 years' imprisonment for having ordered the 1990 killing of anthropologist Myrna Mack. General Edgar Augusto Godoy Gaytán and Colonel Guillermo Oliva Carrera were acquitted of the same charge. According to Amnesty International, it was the first time that a high-ranking military official had been convicted for a crime committed during Guatemala's 36-year civil war, and only the second time that an officer had been convicted of a political crime.[197]

☛ *Byron Lima Estrada, Byron Lima Oliva, Obdulio Villanueva*, and *Mario Orantes* case (Bishop Juan José Gerardi case), Appeals Court of Guatemala City, 8 October 2002

On 8 October 2002, an Appeals Court in Guatemala annulled the landmark convictions of three military men and a priest in the 1998 murder of prominent bishop and human rights

---

195. CICC/Europe/CIS: Greece. <http://www.iccnow.org/countryinfo/europecis/greece.html>.
196. CICC/The Americas: Guatemala. <http://www.iccnow.org/countryinfo/the americas/guatemala.html>.
197. See Guatemala Human Rights Update, Vol. 15, No. 5, 1 March 2003. <http://www.ghrc-usa.org/updates/vol15no5.pdf>; News Release Issued by the International Secretariat of Amnesty International, AMR 34/062/2002, 4 October 2002.

defender Juan José Gerardi. The three-judge panel ordered a retrial and said it annulled the convictions because of irregulaties in the testimony of a witness who claimed he saw the accused on the night of the murder.

Retired Col. Byron Lima Estrada, his son Capt. Byron Lima Oliva, former Presidential bodyguard Obdulio Villanueva, and a Roman Catholic Priest Mario Orantes had been convicted in June 2001 of Gerardi's murder. The Appeals Court said: 'The court is convinced that the sentencing court did not weigh up the proof. The sentence is annulled ... We order a new trial.'[198]

GUINEA

International Criminal Court
- ☛ Law to ratify the Rome Statute, approved by the National Assembly on 13 November 2002[199]

HONDURAS

International Criminal Court
- ☛ Law to ratify the Rome Statute, 29 May 2002

'During its session in January 2002, the Plenary [Meeting] of the Supreme Court of Justice rendered a favourable opinion on the ratification of the Rome Statute. This opinion was sent to the Secretary of Foreign Affairs, Guillermo Perez Cadalso, former Supreme Court Justice who presided over the commission that wrote the favourable opinion. On 29 May 2002, the Minister of Foreign Affairs and the President signed the Executive Agreement to submit the Statute to the National Congress. The following day, the Rome Statute was considered by the National Congress, and was unanimously approved. The legislation was then sent to the Honduran President for his sanction and promulgation, and published in the official journal, La Gaceta, in order to be incorporated into domestic law. In November 2002, the Executive branch expressed an interest in discussing draft implementing legislation for the Rome Statute. The Ministries of Justice and Foreign Affairs may consider a new amendment to the Penal Code, an addendum to the already drafted amendment or a new and autonomous act on crimes under international law.'[200]

HUNGARY[201]

Conventional Weapons
- ☛ Parliamentary Resolution 81/2002 (XI.13) on the Ratification of the Protocol Modifying the Convention on Prohibitions or Restrictions on the Use of Certain Conventional Weapons Which May Be Deemed to Be Excessively Injurious or to Have Indiscrimi-

---

198. G. Brosnan, 'Guatemala court annuls rights convictions', Reuters, 8 October 2002; 'New trial in killing of Guatemala cleric', AP, 8 October 2002.

199. CICC/Africa: Guinea. <http://www.iccnow.org/countryinfo/africa/guinea.html>.

200. CICC/The Americas: Honduras. <http://www.iccnow.org/countryinfo/the americas/honduras.html>.

201. Information and commentaries by Péter Kovács, Professor of International Law, Péter Pázmany Catholic University of Budapest and Miskolc University.

nate Effects [Resolution 81/2002(XI.13) OGY határozat a mértéktelen sérülést okozónak vagy megkülönböztetés nélkül hatónak tekinthetõ egyes hagyományos fegyverek alkalmazásának betiltásáról, illetõleg korlátozásáról szóló Egyezmény módosításának megerõsítésérõl]. Adopted on 12 November 2002. See the short text in the *Official Journal* (*Magyar Közlöny*), No. XI.13 <http://www.complex.hu/kzldat/o02h0081.htm/o02h0081.htm#lbj1>

With its Resolution 81/2002(XI.13), the Parliament ratified the Convention on Prohibitions or Restrictions on the Use of Certain Conventional Weapons Which May Be Deemed to be Excessively Injurious or to Have Indiscriminate Effects.

Counter-terrorism

☛ Act XXV/2002 on the promulgation of the International Convention for the Suppression of Terrorist Bombings, adopted on 15 December 1997 in New York by the United Nations General Assembly at its 52th Session [2002. évi XXV. törvény a robbantásos terrorizmus visszaszorításáról, New Yorkban, az Egyesült Nemzetek Közgyûlésének 52. ülésszakán, 1997. december 15-én elfogadott nemzetközi egyezmény kihirdetésérõl]. Adopted on 10 September 2002. The promulgation occurred on the date of its publication in the *Official Journal* (*Magyar Közlöny*) <http://www.complex.hu/kzldat/t0200025.htm/t0200025.htm>

☛ Act LIX/2002 on the promulgation of the International Convention for the Suppression of the Financing of Terrorism adopted on 9 December 1999 in New York by the United Nations General Assembly at its 54th session [2002. évi LIX. törvény a terrorizmus finanszírozásának visszaszorításáról, New Yorkban, az Egyesült Nemzetek Közgyûlésének 54. ülésszakán, 1999. december 9-én elfogadott nemzetközi Egyezmény kihirdetésérõl]. Adopted on 17 December 2002. The promulgation occurred on the date of its publication in the Official Journal (*Magyar Közlöny*) <http://www.complex.hu/kzldat/t0200059.htm/mun_2.htm#kagy1>

The two recent and important UN conventions against international terrorism were promulgated (according to the dualistic approach), namely, the International Convention for the Suppression of Terrorist Bombings (New York, 1997) with Act XXV/2002 and the International Convention for the Suppression of the Financing of Terrorism (New York, 1999) with Act LIX/2002.

Medical Assistance

☛ Parliamentary Resolution 111/2002 (XII.18) on the participation of a Hungarian medical military unit in the International Security Assistance Force in Afghanistan [Resolution 111/2002 (XII.18) OGY határozat az afganisztáni Nemzetközi Biztonsági Közremûködõ Erõk mûveleteiben magyar katonai egészségügyi kontingens részvételérõl], adopted on 17 December 2002. Entered into force on the date of its adoption. See the short text in the *Official Journal* (*Magyar Közlöny*), No. XII.18 <http://www.complex.hu/kzldat/o02h0111.htm/o02h0111.htm>

With its resolution 111/2002 (XII.18), the Parliament authorised the government to send a small military medical unit to Afghanistan in order to work in the International Security Assistance Force (ISAF).

Cases
- Arrest of *Rade Varga*, 30 January 2002

On 30 January 2002 Hungarian police, acting on an international arrest warrant issued at Croatia's request, arrested Rade Varga, a 39-year old ethnic Serb from Croatia wanted in Croatia for war crimes allegedly committed against Croatian POWs during the war. Reports said that Croatia would request his extradition within 40 days.[202]

Pending
- Following the ratification of the Statute of the International Criminal Court in 2001, Hungary continued the preparatory works in her national legislation necessary for the promulgation of the Statute. The promulgation was scheduled for 2003.

PÉTER KOVÁCS

INDIA[203]

Counter-terrorism
- The Prevention of Terrorism Act, Act No. 15 of 2002. Assented to by the President on 28 March 2002, published in the *Gazette of India*, Extraordinary of 29 March 2002

The Prevention of Terrorism Bill, having been passed by the Indian Parliament, received the assent of the President on 28 March 2002. It entered the Statute Books as The Prevention of Terrorism Act, 2002.

Peacekeeping
- In 2002, more than 5,885 personnel were deployed as part of peacekeeping contingents in UNMIK (Kosovo), UNMEE (Ethiopia-Eritrea), MONUC (Democratic Republic of Congo) and UNGCI (Iraq). Two liaison officers deputed to serve in UNMA (Angola) during the year remained there as part of the force.
- A national seminar on emerging trends in peacekeeping operations, organised by the Ministry of External Affairs, was held at the United Service Institution of India, New Delhi on 30 and 31 July 2001. Its special focus was on peace enforcement operations.

Education and Training
- The ICRC was involved in conducting six seminars for the officers of the Indian Armed Forces. A total of 390 Indian Army/Air Force officers attended the seminar. The ICRC supported the Indian Army by sponsoring two officers on courses at the Institute of San Remo in Italy.
- The National Academy of Legal Studies and Research (NALSAR) University of Law, Hyderabad, introduced a web-based Diploma Programme in International Humanitarian Law. This is the first such course in South Asia conducted through distance education.[204]

---

202. 'Hungarian police confirm arrest of alleged war criminal', Deutsche Presse-Agentur, 30 January 2002.

203. Information and commentaries by Major General Nilenadra Kumar, Judge Advocate General of the Indian Army.

204. The programme is presented on the website <http://www.nalsarpro.org>.

☛ A two-day seminar was organised by North Bengal University on 23 and 24 February 2002 as part of a judicial officers' training programme. A paper on 'Efficacy of Executive Provision in the Army towards the Cause of Environment and Military Law' was presented by the Judge Advocate General of the Army.[205]

Cases (interrogation of security suspects)

☛ *Ms Anguri* v. *Commissioner of Police, Delhi and Others*, Delhi High Court, Judgement of 25 May 2001. Published in *Criminal Law Journal* (Delhi) (2001) p. 3697

In this case, the judiciary commented upon the process of interrogation for security suspects. Several persons were implicated in some cases of military intelligence leakage. The husband of the petitioner, a Havildar (equivalent to Sergeant), was amongst them. He was interrogated at the Military Intelligence Interrogation Centre, where he was subjected to severe beating and other forms of torture, which led to his death. The petitioner approached the Delhi High Court seeking payment of compensation.

The Court held that there could be no gainsaying that freedom of an individual must yield to the security of the state.

'The right of preventive detention of individuals in the interest of security of the State in various situations prescribed under different statutes has been upheld by the Courts. The right to interrogate the detenus, culprits or arrestees in the interest of the nation, must take precedence over an individual's right to personal liberty.

The welfare of an individual must yield to that of the community. The action of the State, however, must be right, just and fair. Using any form of torture for extracting any kind of information would neither be right nor just nor fair and therefore would be impermissible, being offensive to Article 21. Such a crime suspect must be interrogated – indeed subjected to sustained and scientific interrogation determined in accordance with the provisions of law. He cannot however be tortured or subjected to third degree methods or eliminated with a view to elicit information, extract confession or divulge knowledge about his accomplices, weapons etc. His constitutional right cannot be abridged except in the manner permitted by law, though in the very nature of things there would be qualitative difference in the method of interrogation of such person as compared to an ordinary criminal. The challenge of terrorism must be met with innovative ideas and approach. State terrorism is no answer to combat terrorism. State terrorism would only provide legitimacy to terrorism. That would be bad for the State, the community and above all for the rule of law. The State must, therefore, ensure that the various agencies deployed by it for combating terrorism act within the bounds of law and not become a law onto themselves. There is a need therefore to develop scientific methods of investigation and to train the investigators properly to interrogate to meet the challenge.'

Cases (compensation)

☛ *Mrs. Damyanti Barua* v. *Union of India*, Gauhati High Court Writ Petition No. 59 of 1999, Judgement of 21 June 2002

---

205. N. Kumar, *Courts Martial Under Scrutiny* (New Delhi, Universal Law Publishing Company 2002).

☛ *Hiren Chandra Ray* v. *Union of India*, Gauhati High Court Writ Petition No. 2730 of 2002, Judgement of 21 June 2002

These two landmark judgements given by the Gauhati High Court gave practical relief to the victims of armed violence by award of compensation.

The first case was of *Damyanti Barua* v. *Union of India*. The husband of the petitioner was picked up by army troops from the petitioner's house. Later his whereabouts could not be ascertained. He was not brought before the Magistrate or handed over to the police. The army authorities denied having arrested the individual. Dealing with a *habeas corpus* petition filed before it, the Gauhati High Court directed the District and Session Judges to conduct an enquiry, in which army personnel participated. The report of the enquiry upheld the course of events as described by the petitioner. The High Court then dealt with the matter for grant of compensation.

In its judgement dated 21 June 2002, the High Court held that as the state had failed to protect the life of a citizen, the petitioner was entitled to compensation. Considering the age of the missing person and his economic condition etc., a sum of Rs.1,00,000 (Rupees one lakh)[206] was ordered. The High Court stated that 'The petitioner will be at liberty to seek other remedies by way of damages in any civil/other competent court as available and grant of such compensation will be in addition to this.'

In the second case, *Hiren Chandra Ray* v. *Union of India*, the son of the petitioner was picked up by army personnel at night, on 10 November 2000, from a civilian area and was taken to an army camp. During interrogation he was alleged to have revealed his involvement in ULFA (United Liberation Front of Assam), a banned militant outfit. A rifle was said to have been recovered based on the information extracted from him. Later, while returning to the army camp, the party was ambushed and came under indiscriminate fire. The son was reported to have been killed in the crossfire. The petitioner father prayed for appropriate compensation.

Gauhati High Court recorded that uncontroverted facts had revealed that the deceased was picked up by the army and died while in army custody. The army failed to protect the life of the deceased. The High Court stated:

'This is not a case where the deceased had contributed to his own death either attempting to flee or doing something that prompted his killing. Hence, the petitioner being the father of the deceased is entitled to compensation in public litigation. Considering the age of the deceased and the other relevant factors, compensation is determined at Rs.1,00,000 (Rupees one lakh).[207] This is not a cause where the Union of India is entitled to charge [an] individual officer and collect the amount of compensation from him. Moreover in addition to the compensation awarded in this case, the petitioner will be at liberty to seek relief before the competent forum for other claim and compensation in accordance with any other law.'[208]

☛ *Tekarongsen Sir & Others* v. *Union of India*, Gauhati (Kohima) High Court, Civil Rule No. 115(K) of 1997, Judgement of 5 September 2002

---

206. Equivalent to US $2,225.
207. Equivalent to US $2,225.
208. Order dated 21 June 2002.

Damage due to indiscriminate firing was the subject matter of the case of *Tekarongsen Sir & Others* v. *Union of India*. Certain innocent civilians were killed and maimed by the Army personnel of 12 MADRAS Regiment in an alleged 'encounter' with the underground. The Kohima bench of Gauhati High Court directed a judicial enquiry to be held and also payment of adequate compensation to the deceased and two other injured persons. On perusal of the enquiry report, the High Court did not accept the same and ordered a fresh enquiry. The probe was held again and its findings were placed before the High Court. The report did not show that the injuries had been caused during a crossfire when the security forces were operating against the underground. The evidence presented by the Central Government was found to be inconsistent and contradictory. The High Court concluded that the Army personnel had indulged in indiscriminate firing.

The Court held such action on the part of the respondents to be a clear violation of the right to life and personal liberty guaranteed under Article 21 of the Constitution of India:[209]

'Nobody is authorised under the mandate of the Constitution to take away the right to life and liberty of a person except according to procedure established by law. Respect for the rights of individuals is the bedrock of true democracy. A person is born free to his basic human rights. Hence it is the bounden duty of the State to repair the damages done by its officers to the individual's rights. In order to prevent the violation of such right reasonably and also to secure the due compliance of Article 21, it is needed to mulch its violators in the payment of monetary compensation. Accordingly the victims of such firing are entitled to get adequate compensations.'

The respondents were directed to pay compensation of Rs. 2,00,000/- (Rupees two lakhs)[210] to the next of kin of the person killed and a sum of Rs. 1,00,000 (Rupees one lakh) each to the two victims who were injured.[211]

NILENADRA KUMAR

INDONESIA

Cases

Following the issuance in April 2001 of a Presidential Decree establishing an ad hoc Human Rights Court at the Central Jakarta District Court with the competence to hear cases of crimes committed by Indonesian and other officials in East Timor,[212] in August 2001, the Ad Hoc Court for East Timor was established. In January 2002, President Megawati Sukarnoputri appointed 18 non-career judges to sit on the Court. According to Human Rights Watch: 'The judges for the Ad Hoc Court were chosen during the course of secret hearings by a closed session of Indonesia's Supreme Court. It is unclear what the criteria were for the selection. Most have no training in, or experience with, international law or human rights

---

209. Art. 21 – Protection of life and personal liberty – provides: 'No person shall be deprived of his life or personal liberty except according to procedure established by law.'
210. Equivalent to approximately US $4,450.
211. Order dated 5 September 2002.
212. Pursuant to Law 26 of 2000 on Human Rights Courts. Reprinted in 3 *YIHL* (2000) at p. 717. See also 4 *YIHL* (2001) pp. 536-537.

law.'[213] Twenty-four prosecutors were inducted in February. The same month, the first indictments were issued against seven individuals, including Abilio Soares, the former Governor of East Timor, and General Timbul Silaen, the former Police Chief. Trials against these seven persons began in March 2002.

The outcomes of these and other cases tried in 2002 revealed serious problems with the Ad Hoc Special Court.[214] Human Rights Watch criticised the 'seeming lack of will to indict high- and mid-level military officers'. Further, '[w]hen charges have been filed, it appears that the prosecution has not been eager to succeed. Indictments have been factually inaccurate. Observer reports from the trials have suggested that prosecutors are actively seeking acquittals. Prosecutors have made little or no attempt to portray the military as an active participant in the violence.'[215] The court was also lambasted for failing to provide adequate witness protection or logistical support to witnesses: 'No provisions were made for the first witnesses to be met at the airport. In addition, they had to walk, in public, to the courthouse, due to roadblocks. No safe space was arranged for them at the courthouse, and no safe passage to travel between the courtroom and other parts of the building. On one occasion, a defendant was let in to see protected witnesses.'[216]

As of mid-January 2003, ten military and police officers had been acquitted, one military officer had been convicted and sentenced to five years, pending appeal, and two civilians had been convicted.

Appeals in these cases against convictions would be heard by the High Court, and then go to the Supreme Court, while appeals against acquittals would go straight to the Supreme Court. 'The appeals process will be discharged by a mixed panel of career and non-career judges with little or no experience of international law or crimes of this complexity.'[217]

☞ *Adam Damiri* case, Decision of the Ad Hoc Court for East Timor, 5 August 2002 <http://socrates.berkeley.edu/~warcrime/East_Timor_and_Indonesia/Indictments_and_ judgements/Indonesia_Damiri_Judgement.htm>

Major General Adam R. Damiri, as Military Commander IX/Udayana, was indicted by the Ad Hoc Court on Human Rights on 1 July 2002 on two charges of crimes against humanity: (1) Murder as a crime against humanity in violation of Article 9(a) of Indonesia's Law 26 of 2000 on Human Rights Courts pursuant to Article 42(1) of the same law concerning military command responsibility; and (2) Assault as a crime against humanity in violation of Article 9(h) pursuant to Article 42(1) concerning military command responsibility.[218]

Damiri as a military commander was alleged to be responsible for the involvement of his subordinates in relation to: the attack on the Liquisa Church and Pastor Rafael Dos Santos' residence on 6 April 1999; the attack on Isaac Leandro's house and Manuel Carrascalao's

---

213. Human Rights Watch, 'Justice Denied for East Timor: Indonesia's Sham Prosecutions, the Need to Strengthen the Trial Process in East Timor, and the Imperative of U.N. Action', New York, 20 December 2002. <http://www.hrw.org/backgrounder/asia/timor/etimor1202bg.htm>.

214. See 'Indonesia: Implications of the Timor Trials', International Crisis Group, 8 May 2002. <http://www.crisisweb.org/library/documents/report_archive/A400643_08052002.pdf>.

215. Human Rights Watch, *supra* n. 213.

216. Ibid.

217. Ibid.

218. <http://socrates.berkeley.edu/~warcrime/East_Timor_and_Indonesia/Indictments_and_judge ments/Indonesia_Damiri_Indictment.htm>.

house in Dili on 17 April 1999; the attack on Dili Diocese on 5 September 1999; the attack on Bishop Belo's residence on 6 September 1999; and the Suai Ave Maria Church massacre on 6 September 1999.

On 5 August 2002, the Human Rights Court in Jakarta convicted Major General Damiri of two counts of crimes against humanity and sentenced him to three years' imprisonment. He was at liberty pending his appeal.

☛ *Abilio Soares* case, Decision of the Ad Hoc Court for East Timor, 14 August 2002 <http://socrates.berkeley.edu/~warcrime/East_Timor_and_Indonesia/Indictments_and_judgements/Indonesia_Soares_Judgement.htm>

Soares, the former Governor of East Timor, was indicted on 20 February 2002 on two cumulative charges of crimes against humanity: (1) murder as a crime against humanity under Article 9(a) of Indonesia's Law 26 of 2000 on Human Rights Courts, and (2) assault/persecution as a crime against humanity under Article 9(h) of the said law. He was accused of command responsibility for the failings and actions of his subordinates as well as the actions of organisations and groupings, such as Pamswakarsa (a private militia), with respect to the attack on the Liquisa church on 6 April 1999; the attack on Manuel Carrascalao's house in Dili on 17 April 1999; the attack on Bishop Belo's house in Dili on 6 September 1999; and the Suai Ave Maria Church massacre on 6 September 1999.[219]

The trial began on 14 March 2002, and concluded on 17 April. A total of 12 prosecution witnesses were called, including some other persons accused by the Ad Hoc Human Rights Court. 'The court rejected challenges by the defence to the jurisdiction of the court and the indictment. The court ruled that retroactive use of criminal legislation was not necessarily inconsistent with international law, citing the practice that has developed since Nuremburg and Tokyo, as illustrated by the practice at the ICTY and ICTR, and cited cases from Israel and France. But it held that it was up to an Indonesian constitutional court to decide whether the law relied upon in the indictment against Soares violates the Constitution of the Republic of Indonesia. As no such court currently exists, the court rejected the defence arguments and ordered that the hearing continue.'[220]

On 14 August 2002, the Human Rights Court convicted Soares on both counts. 'We hereby declare the defendant Abilio Osorio Soares has been proven legally guilty of the first and second charges of gross rights violations', presiding judge Emmy Marni Mustafa told the court.[221] He was sentenced to three years' imprisonment, well below the minimum sentence of ten-years stipulated under Indonesian law, or the ten-and-a-half year sentence requested by the Prosecutor. Soares appealed his conviction and the verdict, saying that he was being made a scapegoat.[222] He remained at liberty pending the outcome of the appeal.

---

219. <http://socrates.berkeley.edu/~warcrime/East_Timor_and_Indonesia/Indictments_and_judgements/Indonesia_Soares_Indictment.htm>.

220. 'Wiranto testifies in Jakarta', Judicial System Monitoring Program, 4 April 2002. <http://www.jsmp.minihub.org/News/4_4.htm>.

221. 'Former East Timor governor jailed', *The Age*, 15 August 2002.

222. 'East Timor governor jailed over violence', BBC News, 14 August 2002. <http://news.bbc.co.uk/2/hi/asia-pacific/2192033.stm>.

☛ *Timbul Silaen* case, Decision of the Ad Hoc Court for East Timor, 15 August 2002
<http://socrates.berkeley.edu/~warcrime/East_Timor_and_Indonesia/Indictments_and_
judgements/Indonesia_Silaen_Judgement.htm>

Brigadier General Timbul Silaen, East Timor's former Chief of Police, was indicted on 20
February 2002 on two cumulative charges of crimes against humanity: (1) murder as a
crime against humanity under Article 9(a) of Indonesia's Law 26 of 2000 on Human Rights
Courts, and (2) assault/persecution as a crime against humanity under Article 9(h) of the
said Law.[223] The defendant was accused of being involved in the Suai massacre on 6 September 1999. He was charged with command responsibility for the actions of his subordinates with respect to the attack on the Liquisa church on 6 April 1999; the attack on Manuel
Carrascalao's house in Dili on 17 April 1999; the attack on the UNAMET office in Liquisa
on 4 September 1999; and the attack on Bishop Belo's house in Dili on 6 September 1999.

The trial began on 4 April and ran through 30 May. A total of 12 witnesses were called
by the prosecution, including several other persons accused by the Human Rights Court.

On 15 August 2002, the Ad Hoc Court for East Timor acquitted Silaen due to lack of
evidence.

☛ *Herman Sedyono*, *Lili Kusardiyanto*, *Ahmad* Syamsudin Sugito and *Gatot Subiaktoro*
(Suai Church massacre) case, Decision of the Ad Hoc Court for East Timor, 15 August
2002 <http://socrates.berkeley.edu/~warcrime/East_Timor_and_Indonesia/Indictments
_and_judgements/Indonesia_Sedyono_Judgement.htm>

This case also concerned the massacre at the Ave Maria Church in Suai on 6 September
1999. Lieutenant Colonel Herman Sedyono, the former Bupati (district administrator) of
Covalima district in East Timor; Lieutenant Colonel Lili Kusardiyanto, the former Commander of Suai District Military Command; Captain Ahmad Syamsudin, the former Chief-
of-Staff of Suai District Military Command; Lieutenant Sugito, the former Commander of
Suai Military Sector Commandl and Lieutenant Colonel Gatot Subiaktoro, the former Police Chief of Suai district, were jointly indicted on 20 February 2002 on charges of crimes
against humanity. The primary charges against all accused was murder as a crime against
humanity, under Article 9(a) of Law 26 of 2000 on Human Rights Courts, and pursuant to
Article 42(1) concerning military command responsibility. The subsidiary charge against all
five accused was murder as a crime against humanity under Article 9(a), and pursuant to
Article 41, attempting, plotting or assisting in the perpetration of crimes within the jurisdiction. In addition, Sedyono was subsidiarily charged under Article 9(a) of the Law on Human Rights Court pursuant to Article 42(2) concerning civilian command responsibility;
Kushadiyanto was subsidiarily charged under Article 9(a) pursuant to Article 42(1) with
military command responsibility; Subiaktoro was subsidiarily charged under Article 9(a)
pursuant to Article 42(1) concerning military command responsibility; Syamsudin was subsidiarily charged under Article 9(a) pursuant to Article 42(1), and Sugito was subsidiarily
charged under Article 9(a) pursuant to Article 42(1).[224]

---

223. <http://socrates.berkeley.edu/~warcrime/East_Timor_and_Indonesia/Indictments_and_judge
ments/Indonesia_Silaen_Indictment.htm>.

224. <http://socrates.berkeley.edu/~warcrime/East_Timor_and_Indonesia/Indictments_and_judge
ments/Indonesia_Sedyono_Indictment.htm>.

The accused were alleged to be criminally responsible for the acts of those subordinates under their effective control, because they did not exercise the correct and lawful control over their subordinates; to have known or deliberately ignored information that clearly indicated that their subordinates were committing or had just committed crimes against humanity as part of a widespread and systematic attack against the civilian population of East Timor; and to have failed to take any or the necessary steps to prevent or stop the attack, or to surrender the perpetrators to the authorities for investigation, prosecution and punishment.

The trial began on 19 March and concluded on 28 May. The prosecutor called 11 witnesses.[225]

On 15 August 2002, all five accused were acquitted. The Court, while finding evidence that a crime against humanity had been committed by the Laksaur and Mahidi militias, held that there was no command relationship between the five accused and these groups. Thus, the accused could not be held responsible for the crimes perpetrated under Article 42(1). As regards the lesser charge of attempting, plotting or assisting in the perpetration of a crime against humanity, the Court held, first, that as the offence had been committed and completed, there was no need to deal with the question of whether there had been any attempt; second, that it was not satisfied that any of the accused had conspired in the commission of the offence; and third, that it had not been proven that the accused deliberately aided in the commission of the offence.

☛ *Eurico Guterres* case, Decision of the Ad Hoc Court for East Timor, 27 November 2002 <http://socrates.berkeley.edu/~warcrime/East_Timor_and_Indonesia/Indictments_and_ judgements/Indonesia_Guterres_Judgement.htm>

Former pro-Jakarta militia leader Eurico Guterres, as a superior or Deputy Commander of Prointegration Forces or superior or commander of the group Aitarak, was indicted on 18 February 2002 on two charges of murder as a crime against humanity in violation of Article 9(a) of the Law 26 of 2000 on Human Rights Courts and assault as a crime against humanity under Article 9(h) of the Law, pursuant to Article 42(2) concerning civilian or police command responsibility, in connection with an attack on the house of Manuel Viegas Carrascalao on 17 April 1999.[226] According to the indictment, Guterres did not control his subordinates in a correct and proper manner. He knew or deliberately ignored information that clearly showed that his subordinates were committing or had just committed gross violations of human rights amounting to murder as part of a widespread or systematic attack directly aimed at the civilian population. He did not take the appropriate and necessary steps within his competence to stop these actions of his subordinates or to surrender the perpetrators to the suitable authorities for investigation and prosecution. Despite the existence of a videotape in which Guterres was shown ordering his men to capture and kill independence supporters, Guterres was not charged with individual criminal responsibility but only with failure to control his subordinates, and the Court could not therefore find him guilty of having ordered, incited or participated in the attacks.

---

225. Judicial Systems Monitoring Program. Case Status. Suai Church Massacre. <http://www. jsmp.minihub.org/Indonesia/caseupdates/UpdSuai.pdf>.

226. <http://socrates.berkeley.edu/~warcrime/East_Timor_and_Indonesia/Indictments_and_judge ments/Indonesia_Guterres_Indictment.htm>.

Guterres was convicted of command responsibility and sentenced to the minimum ten years' imprisonment. 'We find him guilty of having allowed his followers to murder and torture people in the house of Manuel Viegas Carrascalao on April 17, 1999, in Dili, where 12 people were killed and three others injured,' said presiding judge Herman Heller Hutapea.

Earlier, in 2001, Eurico Guterres was charged in relation to an incident in Atambua, West Timor. He was accused of incitement for resisting efforts by the authorities to disarm the militias and sentenced to six months in prision by the North Jakarta District Court. However, he served only 23 days before being released.[227]

☞ *Asep Kuswani, Adios Salova, Leoneto Martins* and *Endar Priyanto* (Liquisa Church massacre) case, Human Rights Court, Decision of the Ad Hoc Court for East Timor, 29 November 2002 <http://socrates.berkeley.edu/~warcrime/East_Timor_and_Indonesia/Indictments_and_judgements/Indonesia_Kuswani_Judgement.htm>

The three accused, Asep Kuswani, Adios Salova and Leoneto Martins, were jointly indicted on 31 May 2002 with command responsibility for two counts of crimes against humanity, allegedly perpetrated during the massacre at Liquisa Church on 6 April 1999. Lt.Col. Kuswani, the former Liquisa Military Commander; Lt.Col. Salova, the former Police Chief of Liquisa; and Martins, the former Bupati (district administrator) of Liquisa, were primarily charged with murder as a crime against humanity under Article 9(a) of the Law on Human Rights Courts. Subsidiarily, Kuswani was charged under Article 9(a) pursuant to Article 42 (1) with military command responsibility; while Salova and Martins were charged under Article 9(a) pursuant to Article 42(2) with civilian/police command responsibility.

On 29 November 2002, Presiding Judge Cicut Sutiarso acquitted the three accused of the charge of failing to prevent pro-Indonesian militias from attacking Liquisa Church and killing at least 22 people. The fourth defendant, Lt.Col. Endar Priyanto, the Army Chief of East Timor's capital Dili when militiamen attacked the house of a prominent independence leader, killing 12 civilians, was acquitted of the charge of failing to stop the massacre.

☞ *Soedjarwo* case, Decision of the Ad Hoc Court for East Timor, 27 December 2002 <http://socrates.berkeley.edu/~warcrime/East_Timor_and_Indonesia/Indictments_and_judgements/Indonesia_Soedjawro_Judgement.htm>

Lieutenant Colonel Soedjarwo, the former Dili Military Commander, was indicted on 31 May 2002 in connection with the attacks on the Diocese of Dili and the residence of Bishop Belo. The indictment was publicly read on 25 June 2002. He was primarily charged with murder as a crime against humanity in violation of Article 9(a) of the Law 26 of 2000 on Human Rights Courts, pursuant to Article 42(1) concerning military command responsibility, and secondarily with assault as a crime against humanity under Article 9(h), pursuant to Article 42(1).[228]

With regard to the primary charge, the indictment charged that the accused, as a military commander, should have controlled TNI (Indonesian Army) troops who took part in gross

---

227. Human Rights Watch, *supra* n. 213. See also 4 *YIHL* (2001) p. 543.

228. <http://socrates.berkeley.edu/~warcrime/East_Timor_and_Indonesia/Indictments_and_judgements/Indonesia_Soedjawro_Indictment.htm>.

violations of human rights but failed to do so. After the incidents, the accused should have surrendered the persons who took part in the violations, but he failed to do so. With regard to the secondary charge, according to the indictment, the accused did not take the necessary steps to direct his force to restore the situation at the Diocese of Dili, with the result that several people died and others were seriously injured.

Soedjarwo was convicted on 27 December 2002, and sentenced to five years' imprisonment. He remained free pending the outcome of his appeal.

☛ *M. Yayat Sudrajat* case, Decision of the Ad Hoc Court for East Timor, 30 December 2002 <http://socrates.berkeley.edu/~warcrime/East_Timor_and_Indonesia/Indictments_and_judgements/Indonesia_Sudrajat_Judgement.htm>

Colonel M. Yayat Sudrajat, the former military chief of the Tribuna VIII military intelligence unit, was indicted on 4 July 2002 on two primary charges of military command responsibility for murder (Art. 9(a)) and assault (Art. 9(h)) as crimes against humanity under Law 26 of 2000, and two subsidiary charges of attempting, plotting or aiding the commission of murder and assault as crimes against humanity under Law 26. Sudrajat was alleged to be responsible as a military commander, pursuant to Article 42(1) of Law 26, for the involvement of three members of his unit in the attack on the Liquisa church which resulted in the death of 22 people and injury to 21 others. The subsidiary charges alleged that Sudrajat aided the commission of the attack on the Liquisa church by deliberately providing the opportunity for it to occur. He was alleged to have done this by not fulfilling his duties as he was obliged to. In particular he was alleged to have failed to fulfill his duty to create an atmosphere which was conducive to reconciliation between pro-independence and pro-integration groups.

On 30 December 2002, the Jakarta Human Rights Court acquitted Sudrajat of all charges.

The Court's decision means that ten Indonesian security officials who had been tried thus far for crimes against humanity in the former Indonesian territory had been acquitted.[229]

Ongoing Cases
☛ *M. Noer Muis* case

Brigadier General M. Noer Muis was indicted on 4 July 2002 on two cumulative charges of murder (under Art. 9(a) Indonesia's Law 26 of 2000 on Human Rights Courts) and assault/persecution as crimes against humanity (under Art. 9(h)) of the same law).

The first charge related to the attacks on the Dili Diocese, Bishop Belo's house and the Suai Ave Maria Church. The accused's potential liability for the attacks arose under Article 42(1)(a)(b) (military command responsibility).

It was alleged that the attacks were carried out by pro-integration militia, TNI forces and members of the police. It was further alleged that the accused knew or ought to have known that those under his command were committing or had just committed crimes against humanity and did not take all necessary steps available to him, as the military commander of East Timor at the time of the alleged attacks, to prevent or stop them. Likewise, it was

---

229. Ibid.

alleged that the accused did not hand over the perpetrators of the attacks to be questioned and charged.

The second charge was brought on the same basis except that it was limited to the attacks on the Diocese of Dili and Bishop Belo's house.

AVRIL McDONALD

IRELAND[230]

Emergency Law
☛ Report of the Committee to Review the Offences Against the State Acts 1939-1998 and Related Matters. Dublin, May 2002[231]

On 10 April 1998 the participants in the multiparty negotiations in Belfast concluded the so-called 'Belfast Agreement'.[232] In the section of the Agreement dealing with security issues, the Irish government undertook to 'initiate a wide-ranging review of the Offences Against the State Acts 1939-1985 with a view to both reform and dispensing with those elements no longer required as circumstances permit'.[233] Later, the Offences Against the State (Amendment) Act 1998 was passed following an especially serious bombing in Omagh by a dissident republican group, and this legislation was subsequently included in the review. The Committee was established in May 1999, and it was requested to examine all aspects of the Offences Against the State Acts 1939-1998, taking into account:

(1) The view of the participants to the multi-party negotiations that the development of a peaceful environment on the basis of the Agreement they reached on 10 April 1998 can and should mean normalisation of security arrangement and practices;

(2) The threat posed by international terrorism and organised crime;

(3) Ireland's obligations under international law.

The Report contains a detailed consideration of the legislative enactments that were originally intended to deal with the perceived threat to the institutions of the state from paramilitary groups arising from the conflict taking place in Northern Ireland. The Report contains widely divergent views on the necessity for and use of the Acts under review.

The first Offences Against the State Act was passed in 1939, after the outbreak of World War II, and various amendments were passed since then, usually as a result of increased tension and violence associated with the conflict in Northern Ireland. However, as the Committee pointed out, the central core of the legislation came before the enactment of various international human rights covenants, and the law had not undergone a thorough review in this context.

Essentially, the Report contained two views. The majority view favoured retaining but amending the legislation, and thus keeping its key elements in place, while the minority view was to the effect that much of the legislation should be repealed, as it did not belong in a modern democratic society. However, even within these two groups, there was not a

---

230. Information and commentaries by Ray Murphy, Irish Centre for Human Rights, School of Law, National University of Ireland, Galway.

231. Can be purchased directly from Government Publications Sales Office, Sun Alliance House, Molesworth Street, Dublin 2.

232. British-Irish Agreement done at Belfast on 10 April 1998. <http://www.gov.ie/iveagh/angloir ish/goodfriday/default.htm>.

233. Ibid., Chapter on Security, para. 5.

consensus of opinion on every issue. The legislation under review referred, *inter alia*, to the continued existence of the non-jury Special Criminal Court, its use for non-terrorist 'ordinary' crimes, the statutory provision providing for internment without trial, the right of a suspect to have a solicitor present during questioning, and whether inferences should be drawn from a suspect exercising his or her right to silence.

Speaking at the launch of the Report, the Minister for Justice stressed the need to study all the issues it raised carefully, and to have a full public debate before rushing to conclusions about this body of legislation that has been a central feature of the criminal justice system since 1939.[234] In conclusion, this is a comprehensive report that contains much useful information and commentary on a wide range of emergency and related provisions in Irish law, and the recommendations reflect the complexity of the issues and principles at stake.

Pending
☛ European Convention on Human Rights Bill

This is probably the most important piece of legislation currently before the Irish legislature. However, the passage of the bill has been delayed indefinitely, and it is not clear when it will return to the Dail (Parliament) for consideration. It is now some five years since the Belfast Agreement, where Ireland agreed to begin the process of incorporation. Ireland is the only state of the 44-state Council of Europe not to have implemented the European Convention on Human Rights.[235]

☛ Criminal Justice Terrorist Offences Bill, 2002, No. 46/2002 <http://www.irlgov.ie/ag>

This proposed piece of legislation was introduced to the Irish Dail (Parliament) on 17 December 2002. It was considered that this date was not accidental, and that the bill was introduced at a time close to the Christmas holiday break when debate and reaction would be muted. The purpose of the bill was to implement into Irish law the European Union's Framework Decision on Combating Terrorism adopted by the Council of the European Union on 13 June 2002, as well as a number of UN anti-terrorism agreements.[236] The UN aspects of the bill are not significant, and deal for the most part with mechanisms for international cooperation. They include commitments arising from UN Security Council Resolution 1373 adopted in response to the events of 11 September 2001. The bill is also intended to amend Irish law more generally to enhance the capacity of the state to address the problem of international terrorism.

The European provisions have proved contentious in Ireland. Article 34 of the Treaty on European Union[237] provides that the European Council may adopt framework decisions for the purpose of approximation of the laws and regulations of the member states. It also provides that framework decisions will be binding on the member states as to the result to

---

234. The *Irish Times*, 30 May and 2 August 2002.
235. For further details see the report on Ireland in 4 *YIHL* (2001) pp. 545-547.
236. The Conventions concerned are the International Convention for the Suppression of the Financing of Terrorism, the International Convention for the Suppression of Terrorist Bombings, the International Convention for the Prevention and Punishment of Crimes Against Internationally Protected Persons and the International Convention Against the Taking of Hostages.
237. <http://europa.eu.int/en/record/mt/top.html>.

be achieved, but will leave to the national authorities the choice of form and methods. The Framework Decision on Combating Terrorism is directed to the approximation of the laws of member states in relation to a common definition of terrorist offences, including offences relating to terrorist groups.

This is a long and complex piece of legislation that was intended to become part of Irish law during 2003. Commenting on the bill, the Minister for Justice, Equality and Law Reform, Mr Michael McDowell, said the 'enactment of this legislation will significantly strengthen our law for the purpose of dealing with the threat posed by international terrorism in the light of the events of 11 September 2001 and since and will also enable Ireland to meet a number of commitments it has made as part of the international community's response to such events'.[238]

Key features of the bill include provisions providing that specified offences will become terrorist offences when committed with the requisite intent; that terrorist groups who commit terrorist offences in or outside the state will be unlawful organisations for the purposes of the Offences Against the State Acts 1939-1998 and the relevant provisions of those Acts; concerning the exercise of jurisdiction in relation to terrorist offences and offences relating to terrorist groups when committed outside the state in certain circumstances; relating to the creation of new offences consistent with certain international UN Conventions; and provisions to enable funds which are being used, or which may be intended to be used, for the purposes of committing terrorist offences, including financing terrorism, to be frozen.

The main difficulty with the Framework Decision, which is replicated in the bill, is that it attempts to define terrorism by providing in Section 4 that a wide range of offences if committed with the intent of 'unduly compelling a government or an international organisation to perform or abstain from performing an act' are to be deemed terrorist activities. The problem with such a definition is that it covers a broad range of offences from the most serious to the relatively minor. While murder and assault come within its remit, so too do summary or minor offences such as damage to property or vehicles. In this way, damage to property committed as part of an anti-war or similar protest, if those on the protest are seeking to unduly compel a change in or overturn government policy, could potentially be terroristic under the bill. Not surprisingly, the introduction of the bill was criticised by civil liberty groups such as the Irish Council for Civil Liberties.[239]

RAY MURPHY

ISRAEL[240]

Armed Forces

☛ Amendment No. 3 to the Implementation of the Agreement on the Gaza Strip and the Jericho Area (Restrictions on Activities) Law 1994 [Hok Letikun (Mispar 3) Hok Yesum Heskem Habeinaim Bidvar Hafada Hama'aravit VeRetzuat Azza (Hagbalat Pe'ilut), 755, 1995]. Adopted on 6 May 2002, entered into force on 19 May 2002, published in

---

238. Department of Justice, Equality and Law Reform Press Release, 18 December 2002.

239. <http://www.iccl.ie>.

240. Information and commentaries by Dr Yuval Shany, School of Law, Academic College of Management, Israel. The reporter would like to thank the Research Foundation of the Law School of the Academic College of Management for their financial support of this research. Additional thanks are due to Ms Matat Gutterman, who assisted in the research for this report. For the report on the Occupied Palestinian Territories, see *infra* pp. 580 et seq.

Official Gazette vol. 1842, p. 398 <http://www.knesset.gov.il/ laws/heb/FileD.asp? Type=1&SubNum=2&LawNum=1842> [in Hebrew]

Article 7A to the amended Law provides that any person who recruits an Israeli citizen to service in the armed forces of the Palestinian Council, or to another foreign armed force operating in the territories subject to the jurisdiction of the Council, could be sentenced to a period of up to seven years of imprisonment. An Israeli citizen who serves in such armed forces, belongs to such forces, or acts on behalf of such forces, could be sentenced to up to five years of imprisonment.

The amendment was mainly designed to address the recruiting of Palestinian residents of Jerusalem who hold Israeli citizenship to Palestinian militias operating in the Occupied Territories and in Palestinian Controlled Territories. Such a phenomenon is considered to create significant political and security problems for Israel, as it is thought to weaken Israel's political hold in East Jerusalem and, at the same time, enable Palestinian terror groups to use Israeli identification cards as a means to increase their ability to move freely in and out and within Israel and to carry out terror attacks.

Security Provisions
- Security Provision (Amendment No. 84) (Judea and Samaria) (No. 1510) Order 2002. Adopted on 1 August 2002, entered into force on the date of its adoption
- Security Provision (Amendment No. 87) (Gaza Strip) (No. 1155) Order 2002. Adopted on 1 August 2002,[241] entered into force on the date of its adoption

According to Security Provision (Judea and Samaria) (No. 378) Order 1970, the Israel Defence Force (IDF) West Bank Military Commander can subject individuals living in the territory to special supervision measures, if justified by imperative military needs. These supervisory measures are to be periodically reviewed (every six months) by an appellate committee. In light of the deteriorating security situation in the West Bank and Gaza Strip, in 2002 two new decrees were issued: Amendments No. 84 and No. 87, which expanded the application of Order 378 to the Gaza Strip, and specifically permitted the West Bank military commander to order that West Bank residents, subject to special supervision, would be assigned to reside in the Gaza Strip.

Detention
- The Incarceration of Unlawful Combatants Law 2002 [Hok Kliatam Shel Lohamim Bilti Hukiyim, 762, 2002]. Adopted on 4 March 2002, entered into force on 14 March 2002, published in 1834 *Official Gazette* (2002) p. 192 <http://www.knesset.gov.il/ laws/heb/FileD.asp?Type=1&SubNum=2&LawNum=1834> [in Hebrew][242]

The law authorises the Israel Defence Force (IDF) Chief of Staff to order the incarceration of 'unlawful combatants' involved in armed hostilities against the state of Israel, who are

---

241. Security Provision (Amendment No. 84) (Judea and Samaria) (No. 1510) Order 2002, adopted on 1 August 2002 (copy with author); Security Provision (Amendment no. 87) (Gaza Strip) (No. 1155) Order 2002, adopted on 1 August 2002 (copy with author).

242. An unofficial translation of the full text of the Law is provided in the Documentation section of this volume at pp. 669 et seq.

not entitled to prisoner of war status under the Geneva Conventions. According to Article 3 of the law, the Chief of Staff can issue an order only if he believes that the imprisoned person compromises national security. Imprisoned persons must be released at the end of hostilities, or sooner if they no longer constitute a security threat. As in cases of administrative detentions, incarceration orders under the law are subject to periodical review by the Israeli District Court, whose decisions can be appealed before the Supreme Court.

The law is mainly designed to enable Israel to continue to detain senior Hezbollah leaders whom it captured during its occupation of southern Lebanon. After the Supreme Court in 2000[243] held that the Emergency Powers (Detention) Law 1979 did not permit the holding of Lebanese nationals as 'bargaining chips' for future negotiations concerning the fate of IDF soldiers missing in action, the Knesset moved to introduce new legislation on the matter. It created a special status for unlawful combatants, analogous to that of prisoners of war. In particular, the law was intended to provide that unlawful combatants could be detained for the entire duration of the hostilities in which their organisations might have been involved, and, thus, could be prevented from rejoining such forces while the armed conflict continued. However, it should be noted that the final version of the law was modelled after the provisions of the Fourth Geneva Convention governing administrative detention (Arts. 43 and 78). It adopted a 'personal risk' approach and introduced periodic judicial safeguards by District Court judges (over which the Supreme Court exercises appellate jurisdiction). The two main innovations of the law can be found in Articles 7-8. Article 7 creates a refutable presumption that a person belonging to a hostile organisation, or who participated in hostile acts perpetrated by such an organisation (including indirect participation), represents a threat to national security for the duration of the hostilities. Article 8 invests authority in the Minister of Defense to issue determinations regarding the involvement of organisations in hostilities against the state and concerning the continuation of hostilities. These determinations constitute *prima facie* methods of proving the facts that underlie the legality of incarceration orders under the law. It should be also noted that incarcerated unlawful combatants can be released before the end of hostilities if they no longer pose a security threat, or if release is warranted for special reasons.

☛ The Incarceration of Unlawful Combatants Regulations 2002 [Takanot Kliatam Shel Lohamim Bilti Hukiyim, 762, 2002]. Adopted on 11 April 2002, entered into force the same day, published in *Regulations Series (Kovetz Hatakanot)* Vol. 6161, p. 588[244]

The Regulations, adopted with a view to guaranteeing the basic needs of incarcerated unlawful combatants, provide that persons imprisoned under the Unlawful Combatants Law are entitled, subject as a rule to security considerations, to conditions which resemble the conditions afforded to prisoners of war. In particular, they are entitled to clothing, food and medical services; to be held in hygienically proper conditions; to have two hours of daily exercise; to work at will; to keep personal belongings, literature and religious items; to smoke; to receive visitors (including representatives of the International Committee of the Red Cross); to meet with an attorney; and to send and receive letters. The Regulations also introduce guidelines for disciplinary and penal proceedings.

---

243. *Anonymous v. Minister of Defence*, Crim. F.H. 7048/97, 54(1) *Piskey Din* [*P.D.*] 721.

244. An unofficial translation of the full text of the Regulations is provided in the Documentation section of this volume at pp. 672 et seq.

☛ Detention in Time of Combat (Temporary Provision) (Judea and Samaria) (No. 1500) Order 2002. Adopted on 5 April 2002, entered into force on the day of its adoption, published in 198 *Judea and Samaria Proclamations, Orders and Appointments (Minsharim, Tzavim VeMinuyim)* (2002) p. 3133

☛ Detention in Time of Combat (Temporary Provision) (Amendment) (Judea and Samaria) (No. 1502) Order 2002. Adopted on 1 May 2002, entered into force on the day of its adoption, published in 198 *Judea and Samaria Proclamations, Orders and Appointments (Minsharim, Tzavim VeMinuyim)* (2002) p. 3136

☛ Detention in Time of Combat (Temporary Provision) (Amendment no. 2) (Judea and Samaria) (No. 1505) Order 2002. Adopted on 4 June 2002, entered into force on the day of its adoption, published in 199 *Judea and Samaria Proclamations, Orders and Appointments (Minsharim, Tzavim VeMinuyim)* (2002) p. 3150

☛ Detention in Time of Combat (Temporary Provision) (Amendment no. 3) (Judea and Samaria) (No. 1512) Order 2002. Adopted on 4 September 2002, entered into force on the day of its adoption

Military Order 1500, which was issued during Operation 'Defensive Shield', in which the IDF recaptured most West Bank cities, was designed to accommodate the mass arrests that Israel had carried out at the time (some 7,000 Palestinians were detained in the first week of the operation). Given the inability of military authorities to process and interrogate the detainees within the ordinary timeframe provided by military law applicable in the West Bank and Gaza Strip,[245] a new temporary Order was issued. Order 1500 relaxed the normal conditions of judicial supervision over the detention of Palestinian suspects arrested during the combat activities, which were initiated on 29 March 2002, so as to enable the Israeli authorities to 'filter' the detainees while in custody.

The Order, originally designed to be in force for two months, provided that Palestinians suspected of constituting a security threat could be detained for a period of up to 18 days, on the written order of IDF officers. During that initial period of detention, the detained persons were not entitled to meet with their attorneys.[246] Detained persons were entitled to challenge their arrest before the detaining authority within the first eight days of detention; they could not, however, initiate proceedings before military judicial authorities concerning the legality of detention within the first 18-day period.[247] However, any extension of the initial 18-day period of detention had to be approved by a military judge. Finally, detained persons were entitled to meet with their attorneys at the end of the initial period of detention (subject to the ordinary law in force in the West Bank and Gaza Strip relating to postponement of attorney-client meetings for security reasons).[248]

---

245. Security Provisions (Judea and Samaria) (No. 378) Order, 1971. The preexisting legislation required that detainees in security-related offences would be brought before a judge within eight days following their arrest.

246. See *infra* at p. 531 of this report the case of *Center for the Defense of the Individual* v. *IDF West Bank Military Commander*, which challenged the legality of the Order.

247. It is unclear whether detained persons were allowed to petition the Supreme Court in the initial 18-day period. Under Israeli administrative law such restriction could never be presumed. However, the Court often insists upon exhaustion of alternative remedies as a prerequisite for seizing its jurisdiction.

248. Art. 78C(c)(2) of Order 378 authorizes the Israeli authorities to postpone attorney-client meetings for an additional period of up to 15 days, for imperative security reasons.

A number of subsequent Orders, extending and modifying the terms of Order 1500, were issued throughout 2002. On 1 May 2002, the IDF West Bank military commander issued Order 1502, which enabled military authorities to complete the processing of all detainees who had not been brought before a military judge within 18 days, as required by Order 1500, by 10 May 2002. Order 1505 extended the application of Order 1500 by three more months, and introduced two important changes: 1) the initial period of detention was shortened from 18 to 12 days; and 2) the period in which attorney-client meetings were barred was shortened from 18 to four days. Order 1505 was extended by Order 1512 for four more months. At the end of 2002, a claim challenging the legality of the detention orders was still pending before the Israeli Supreme Court.

Emergency Law
☛ The Extension of Validity of Emergency Regulations (Judea, Samaria and the Gaza Strip – Criminal Jurisdiction and Legal Cooperation) Law 2002 [Hok LeHa'arachat Tokpan Shel Takanot-Sh'at-Herum, 762, 2002]. Adopted on 26 June 2002, entered into force on 27 June 2002, published in *Official Gazette* Vol. 1853, p. 458 <http://www.knesset.gov.il/laws/heb/FileD.asp?Type=1&SubNum=2&LawNum=1853> [in Hebrew]

The Law extended the application of the Emergency Regulations (Judea, Samaria and the Gaza Strip – Criminal Jurisdiction and Legal Cooperation) 1967 for a period of five more years. In pursuance of these Regulations, Israeli courts and military courts have concurrent jurisdiction to try persons who have committed crimes in the West Bank and Gaza Strip (provided that they are proscribed by both Israeli law and the law applicable in the West Bank and Gaza Strip). The Regulations also introduce provisions on legal cooperation between Israeli civil and military courts relating to offences perpetrated in the West Bank and Gaza Strip, and authorise the Israeli police to exercise their powers of investigation in respect of violations of Israeli law in the West Bank and Gaza Strip.

Compensation
☛ Amendment No. 4 to the Civil Torts (State Responsibility) Law, 1952 [Hok Letikun (Mispar 4) Hok Hanezikim HaEzrahiyim (Ahrayut Hamedina), 712, 1952]. Adopted on 24 July 2002, entered into force on 1 August 2002, published in *Official Gazette* Vol. 1862, p. 514 <http://www.knesset.gov.il/laws/heb/FileD.asp?Type=1&SubNum=2&LawNum=1862> [in Hebrew]

In light of the increase in the number of *intifadah*-related civil claims (arising from both the first (1987-1992) and the second (2000-present) *intifadas* brought by Palestinian individuals against the state of Israel before the Israeli courts (totalling millions of NIS (New Israeli Sheqel) in sought damages), and given the numerous practical difficulties the state encounters in defending such claims (especially, when claims are presented long after the alleged events), the government initiated legislation designed to improve the state's position in such litigation. The Amendment adds to Article 5 of the Law – which absolves the state of Israel from incurring civil responsibility for injurious acts of war committed by the Israel

Defence Force[249] – a new Article 5A.[250] This specifically addresses tort claims filed against the state of Israel for damages inflicted by Israeli security forces in the Occupied Territories. Article 5A subjects such tort claims to four restrictions: (1) prompt notification of damage by the claimant to the competent authorities (normally, within 60 days from the day of injury); (2) short period of limitations (normally, two years); (3) inapplicability of evidentiary presumptions reversing the burden of proof upon the alleged tortfeasor (*res ipsa loquitur* and control over dangerous objects); (4) lack of determination that the state's right to fair trial had been deprived from it as a result of a breach of the existing legal cooperation agreements in force between Israel and the Palestinian Authority. Most restrictions do not apply retroactively with regard to pending claims, but they do apply with regard to certain, at the relevant time, unclaimed injuries.[251]

Cases

A. DETENTION

☛ *Bassam Natshe* v. *IDF West Bank Military Commander*, H.C.J. 2307/02, Supreme Court of Israel, Judgement of 26 February 2002. Not yet published

The Court rejected a challenge to the detention law which was in force in the West Bank prior to the promulgation of Military Order 1500 (see above). The preexisting Order provided that suspects of security-related offences could be arrested and detained for up to eight days without judicial supervision; that a military judge could extend pre-trial detentions by periods of 30 days, up to 90 days altogether; and that a military appeals court could extend pre-trial detention by 90 more days. The Court held that under the prevailing security conditions there was no basis for nullifying the Order.

☛ *The Center for the Defense of the Individual* v. *IDF West Bank Military Commander*, H.C. 2901/02, Supreme Court of Israel, Judgement of 7 April 2002. Published in 56(3) *P.D.*[252] 19

The case was brought before the Court by four Israeli human rights NGOs which challenged the lawfulness of Article 3 of Military Order 1500,[253] which provided that all persons detained under it would be barred from meeting with attorneys in the first 18 days of their detention. The applicants argued that postponement of attorney-client meetings must be decided on a case-by-case basis. The Court rejected the petition and held that while the right of detained individuals to meet with their attorneys is a fundamental right, it could be postponed in certain circumstances for security reasons. In the circumstances of the case, the Court accepted the state's position that the temporal proximity between the mass arrests under Order 1500 and active combat (Operation 'Defensive Shield') precluded the immedi-

---

249. However, the Supreme Court recently held the article to be inapplicable in many *intifadah*-related claims. See *Benni Udah* v. *State of Israel*, C.A. 6051/92, 56(4) *P.D.* 1. The case is discussed below.

250. An unofficial translation of the text of Art. 5A is provided in the Documentation section of this volume at p 799.

251. See the OTP report in this volume at p. 585

252. Law Reports or Judicial Decisions.

253. See *supra* p. 529 of this report.

ate weighing of the individual circumstance of each and every detainee and the assessing whether a meeting with an attorney might represent a security threat. Once conditions in the area were stabilised, the military authorities would be obligated to reconsider their decision with regard to each individual detainee separately. The Court also dismissed allegations of torture and maltreatment of detainees as ill-founded.

☞ *Arad* v. *Dirani*, H.C.R. 7060/0, Supreme Court of Israel, Decision of 22 April 2002. Published in 2002(2) *Takdin* 340

A request by family members of Ron Arad – a navigator with the Israeli Air Force, who was captured on 16 October 1986 by members of the Lebanese AMAL Militia, after parachuting out of his Phantom jet – for reexamination of the decision by the Supreme Court in *Sheikh Abed al-Karim Obeid and Mustafa al-Dirani* v. *Minister of Defense* (H.C. 794/98, Supreme Court of Israel, Judgement of 23 August 2001) was rejected on 23 April 2002. The reviewing judge held that no legal ground for a reexamination hearing had been established, as the challenged judgement constituted a mere application of the well-known administrative law doctrine of reasonableness to the concrete facts of the case and did not purport to establish an innovative legal precedent.

☞ *Anonymous* v. *Minister of Defense*, Crim. F.H. 2645/02, Supreme Court of Israel, Judgement of 8 May 2002. Published in 56(4) *P.D.* 231

According to data published by B'Tselem, an Israeli NGO, by the end of 2002 some 1,000 Palestinians were held by Israel in administrative detention.[254] In this case, the lawfulness of administrative detention orders was confirmed.

☞ *Doctors for Human Rights* v. *Commander of the 'Ofer' Camp*, H.C. 5553/02, Supreme Court of Israel, Decision of 8 August 2002. Not yet published

The Supreme Court held that an NGO does not have the right to inspect the medical conditions in a detainment camp in the West Bank, since there is no legal basis for the request. This was especially relevant in light of the fact that the camp was regularly visited by representatives of the International Committee of the Red Cross.

☞ *Nadal Abed al Fatah Abdallah Nazal* v. *IDF West Bank Military Commander*, H.C.J. 8834/02, Supreme Court of Israel, Judgement of 11 November 2002. Published in 2002 (3) *Takdin* 104

In the *Nazal* case it was noted that failure on the part of the detaining authority to append its name and rank to the signature of the administrative detention order would not invalidate it. Still, it would be proper to require explicit inclusion of these details in future cases.

☞ *Sheikh Abed al-Karim Obeid and Mustafa al-Dirani* v. *Minister of Defense*, H.C.J. 2055/02, Supreme Court of Israel, Judgement of 12 December 2002. Published in 2002 (2) *Pador* 228

---

254. <http://www.btselem.org/English/Administrative_Detention/Statistics.asp>.

A challenge against the constitutionality of the 2002 Incarceration of Unlawful Combatants Law brought by two Lebanese detainees before a court in Israel, and based on the same law, was rejected by the Supreme Court. The Court held that the detainees had failed to exhaust alternative procedural remedies before seizing the Supreme Court and that the proper forum to challenge the law was the District Court, which periodically monitored incarceration orders issued under the Incarceration of Unlawful Combatants Law.

☞ *The Center for the Defense of the Individual v. IDF West Bank Military Commander*, H. C. 3278/02, Supreme Court of Israel, Judgement of 18 December 2002. Published in 57 (1) *Pador* 385 [an English version of the Judgement is available at <http://62.90.71.124/ Files_ENG/02/780/032/a06/02032780.a06.HTM>]

The case dealt with a petition submitted to the Supreme Court by seven Israeli and Palestinian human rights NGOs challenging the conditions of detention of hundreds of Palestinian detainees arrested during and after Operation 'Defensive Shield' and held in temporary internment facilities located in various military headquarters and in the permanent 'Ofer' detention camp near Ramallah. In its unanimous decision, the Court held that all detainees were entitled to receive humane treatment and to be held in humane conditions, as established by Israeli administrative law and by international instruments such as the Fourth Geneva Convention (citing Arts. 27, 85, 89-92, 94, 97, 100), Article 10 of the International Covenant on Civil and Political Rights (which the Court accepted as reflective of customary international law) and the UN Standard Minimum Rules for the Treatment of Prisoners[255] (citing Rules 10, 19, 21, 26). While the Court acknowledged that the provisions of the Geneva Convention were formally meant to apply only with regard to 'interned' persons – i.e., persons held in administrative detention – it held that these standards should also influence the treatment of persons detained for other purposes, such as interrogation.

In the circumstances of the case, the Court held that international standards had been violated by the IDF, especially in the first days of detention when detainees were held in makeshift facilities. Some detainees had been subjected to excessively strict handcuffing; some had been deprived of shelter and regular use of toilet facilities in the first hours following their arrest (up to 48 hours in some cases); and property belonging to some of the detainees was confiscated without proper record being taken thereof. The first days of the operation of the 'Ofer' camp were also characterised by breaches of humanitarian standards, especially in terms of exposure of detainees to severe weather conditions due to lack of proper shelter and shortage in supply of blankets, and intolerable overcrowding of the detainees. The Court specifically held that there were no military needs that could justify these breaches of the law.

However, the Court held that conditions in the 'Ofer' camp had markedly improved since, and that present conditions in the camp met and, sometimes exceeded, international minimum standards for detainment. Still the Court pointed out two deficiencies: 1) it found the refusal of the military authorities to provide the detainees with dining tables, relying upon security reasons, as unreasonable; 2) it ordered the IDF to facilitate the provision of or to provide the detainees with books, newspapers and recreational games. It also recom-

---

255. Standard Minimum Rules for the Treatment of Prisoners, 30 August 1955, UN Doc. A/ CONF/611, annex I, E.S.C. Res. 663C, 24 UN ESCOR Supp. (No. 1) at 11, UN Doc. E/3048 (1957), amended E.S.C. Res. 2076, 62 UN ESCOR Supp. (No. 1) at 35, UN Doc. E/5988 (1977).

mended the creation of new procedures of review over conditions of detention (a permanent advisory oversight committee to review detention facilities and new legislation providing for first-instance judicial review over detainees' complaints before a court or commission other than the Supreme Court).

☛ *Hala Yassin* v. *Yoni Ben David – Commander of the Ketziot Military Base – Detention Facility Ketziot*, H.C. 5591/02, Supreme Court of Israel, Judgement of 18 December 2002. Published in 57(1) *P.D.* 403 [an English version of the judgement is available at <http://62.90.71.124/Files_ENG/02/910/055/a03/02055910.a03.HTM>]

The petitioners, Palestinians held in administrative detention in the Ketziot detention facility and a group of Israeli and Palestinian NGOs, brought a challenge against the conditions of detention in the camp. The Court held that although initial conditions at the camp fell below international and Israeli standards, there have been significant improvements since. Still, the Court noted four issues of concern. The Court requested the IDF to reconsider its decision to accommodate the detainees in tents (and not in permanent structures). It further recommended that arrangements should be provided so that the detainees' beds were elevated from the ground; hygienic conditions in the toilets needed to be reexamined; and the issue of dining tables needed to be resolved. The Court also recommended that appropriate review procedures be introduced by the military and that the Israeli Prisons Authority take over the running of the camp.

☛ *Islam Muhammad Rushdi Jerar* v. *IDF West Bank Military Commander*, H.C. 9332/02, Supreme Court of Israel, Decision of 20 December 2002. Published in 2002(4) *Takdin* 737

The Court held that the military authorities were under an obligation to provide immediate information regarding the detainment of individuals to inquiring family members, since such information is a fundamental due process guarantee, which also protects important humanitarian interests. In the *habeas corpus* case at hand, details regarding the detention of a Palestinian individual were provided to the detainee's family during the pendency of proceedings before the Court. Consequently, the petition was withdrawn by the applicants, but the Court ruled that the state should incur the costs of the proceedings. A similar outcome was reached in several other cases decided in 2002.[256]

B. COMPENSATION

☛ *Jamal Kassem Benni Udah* v. *State of Israel*, C.A. 5964/92, Supreme Court of Israel, Judgement of 20 March 2002. Published in 56(4) *P.D.* 1

This case dealt with the application of Article 5 of the Civil Torts (State Responsibility) Law 1952 to the hundreds of *intifadah*-related cases pending before Israeli courts (see above under Compensation). Article 5 exempts the state from incurring liability in tort for 'acts of war committed by the Israel Defence Force'. The question before the Supreme

---

256. See e.g., *Habiba* v. *The IDF West Bank Military Commander,* H.C.J. 8352/02, 2002(4) *Takdin* 235; *Nabtiti* v. *The IDF West Bank Military Commander,* H.C.J. 8488/02, 2002(4) *Takdin* 216; *Elbuchari* v. *The IDF West Bank Military Commander*, H.C.J. 5829/02, 2002(3) *Takdin* 1106.

Court was whether the use of force by the IDF in order to quell mass uprisings could be regarded as an act of war. In light of the failure of the Knesset to regulate *intifadah* claims by way of legislation until the date of the judgement, the case was based upon ordinary Israeli tort law.[257]

The Court, sitting in an expanded nine-judge chamber, held unanimously that only acts of actual warfare or acts of an operational-military nature, generating special risks to combatants and potential victims, could be viewed as acts of war that justify the inapplicability of ordinary tort law. While acts such as military raids, exchange of fire, bombings etc., were clearly acts of war, ordinary law enforcement operations in an occupied territory were clearly not. In the circumstances of the case, one of the claimants died and another was injured during an attempt by the IDF to arrest suspects. The Court held that the dominant features of the incident were that of a 'police operation', and no special risk justifying exemption from liability had come into being. Thus, the ruling of the District Court awarding the claimants damages by reason of the negligent conduct of the state was upheld.

☞ *Ahmed Abu-Samra* v. *State of Israel*, C.A. 6051/99, Supreme Court of Israel, Judgement of 20 March 2002. Published in 56(6) *P.D.* 185

The Court rejected an appeal by residents of the Dir-Al-Balah area in the Gaza Strip whose property was damaged by acts of violence perpetrated by settlers in 1992, in revenge for the murder of a settler. The Court accepted the claim that the army is under a duty to protect the lives and property of Palestinians residing in areas subject to belligerent occupation, even in situations where the threat is created by non-state entities. However, it held that this duty is of a relative nature, and that it was not established in the circumstances of the case that the precautionary acts taken by the army to prevent disorder were unreasonable. Still, the Court recommended that the state consider making an *ex gratia* payment to those appellants who had suffered proven damages.

C. ASSIGNED RESIDENCE/DEPORTATION – APPLICATION OF THE FOURTH GENEVA CONVENTION

☞ *Kipah Mahmad Ahmed Ajuri* v. *IDF West Bank Military Commander*, H.C.J. 7015/02, Supreme Court of Israel, Judgement of 3 September 2002. Published in 56(6) *P.D.* 352 [an English version of the Judgement is available at <http://62.90.71.124/files_eng/02/150/070/a15/02070150.a15.HTM>]

The case dealt with a challenge to the legality of assigned residence orders issued by the IDF West Bank Military Commander against three Palestinians whose brothers had been involved in terrorist activities. The first issue addressed by the Court was whether the case should be reviewed in accordance with the standards of international humanitarian law. President Barak, who wrote the judgement for the Court, held that:

'*first*, all the parties before us assumed that in the circumstances currently prevailing in the territory under the control of the IDF, the laws of international law concerning belli-

---

257. On 24 July 2002, Amendment No. 4 to the Civil Torts (State Responsibility) Law 1952 was adopted, introducing some limitations upon the bringing and conducting of *intifadah*-related claims. See *supra* at p. 530 of this report.

gerent occupation apply...; *second*, the rules of international law that apply in the territory are the customary laws (such as the appendix to the (Fourth) Hague Convention respecting the Laws and Customs of War on Land of 1907, which is commonly regarded as customary law...). With regard to the Fourth Geneva Convention, counsel for the Respondent reargued before us the position of the State of Israel that this convention – which in his opinion does not reflect customary law – does not apply to Judea and Samaria. Notwithstanding, Mr Nitzan told us – in accordance with the long-established practice of the government of Israel ... that the government of Israel decided to act in accordance with the humanitarian parts of the Fourth Geneva Convention. In view of this declaration, we do not need to examine the legal arguments concerning this matter, which are not simple... It follows that for the purpose of the petitions before us we are assuming that humanitarian international law – as reflected in the Fourth Geneva Convention (including article 78) and certainly the Fourth Hague Convention – applies in our case.'

This brief assertion is of great importance as it deviates from the traditional position of the Court on the status of the Fourth Geneva Convention in cases involving the West Bank and Gaza Strip. First, it evaded the dispute surrounding the formal application of the Convention in the Occupied Territories,[258] by holding that the unilateral declaration to abide by the humanitarian provisions of the Convention, adopted by Israel in the early 1970s, could lead to the direct application of the Convention in specific cases. This could have clear implications for the applicability of the Convention in future cases. Second, without any discussion the Court rejected a proposition adopted in its earlier case-law that significantly constrained the application of the Convention, according to which persons who represented a security threat could not rely upon the humanitarian provisions of the Convention.[259] Instead, the Court applied the protections of the Convention to the applicants, notwithstanding their alleged 'lack of clean hands'. Finally, the Court moved farther away from the traditional rules governing the incorporation of international law in the Israeli legal system, which provided that treaty law was not part of the law of the land without a legislative act of transformation, and relied directly upon a unilateral undertaking to respect the terms of a treaty in order to examine the validity of an administrative measure (an order by the military commander). While Israeli law did recognise that declarative treaties are automatically part of the law of the land, it is remarkable that the Court in *Ajuri* reached the conclusion that the relevant provisions of the Fourth Geneva Convention were directly applicable without discussing their customary status (in fact, its earlier case-law specifically provided that the Fourth Geneva Convention did not represent customary law).[260] This has considerable implications for the status of international treaty law in general, and international humanitarian law in particular, under the Israeli legal system. It seemed, however, that this last holding should be limited in its effect to cases involving a challenge to the legality of secondary legislation. According to an interpretative presumption applied in recent case-

---

258. As is well known, Israel has long held that the conditions for application of the Fourth Geneva Convention to occupied territories, specified in Art. 2 of the Convention, have not been met, since the Occupied Territories did not rightfully belong prior to 1967 to any party to the Geneva Conventions. For a recent critique of this position, see D. Kretzmer, *The Occupation of Justice* (Albany NY, Suny Press 2002).

259. *Afo* v. *IDF West Bank Military Commander*, H.C.J. 785/87, 42(2) *P.D.* 4.

260. *Kawasme* v. *Minister of Defense*, H.C.J. 320/80, 35(3) *P.D.* 113.

law,[261] Israeli law should be construed so as to conform to the state's international obligations. On this legal basis, secondary legislation which is inconsistent with such obligations could be deemed unlawful. Hence, it is perhaps correct to assume that the automatic incorporation of treaty law (or of unilateral declarations) would not be possible in cases where no domestic norm, which needed interpretation, could be relied upon.

After asserting the applicability of both Geneva and Hague law, President Barak proceeded to inspect the specific legal framework governing the challenged act – the removal of persons from the West Bank to the Gaza Strip. He accepted the position of the state that the assigned residence orders constituted, in principle, application of the powers of the occupying authority under Article 78 of the Fourth Geneva Convention, and that they should not have been viewed as deportation orders, generally prohibited under Article 49. This is perhaps the most controversial part of the decision. At the time of the issuing of the order, government spokespersons widely referred to them as *deportation* orders,[262] probably revealing the true intent of the policy makers. Further, the orders, as executed, did not seem to meet the central rationale of Article 78 – supervision over persons who threaten security by way of movement restrictions. It was hardly reasonable to view an outcome which leads to the removal of suspected individuals from the West Bank, an area in which the IDF had effective control and could exercise powers of supervision, to Gaza City, where Israel had no effective control, as a measure of supervision. It is also arguable, given this last observation, that the order resulted in removal of persons from territory subject to Israel's effective control to an area situated outside it, i.e., a prohibited act of deportation. While President Barak maintained that 'the two areas [West Bank and Gaza Strip] were conceived by all concerned as one territorial unit' (relying, *inter alia*, on Articles 11 and 31 of the Interim Agreement between Israel and the PLO),[263] his position was not totally convincing, especially in light of the fact that Israel had maintained in a number of international fora that it did not have effective control over areas subject to the rule of the Palestinian Authority (during the second half of 2002, this proposition could probably only have applied with regard to some parts of the Gaza Strip).[264]

The final part of the decision addressed the question whether the individual circumstances of the three applicants justified the issuing of orders relating to them, namely, if they could be viewed as constituting a security threat. The Court was clear on the point that the orders would have been deemed unlawful if no personal risk to the security of the region could be established, notwithstanding their importance as an effective deterrent against would-be terrorists (still, considerations of deterrence could be weighed when all other conditions had been met). In the case of two of the three applicants, the Court found that the burden had been met: the Ajuris – the brother and the sister of a suspected terrorist – knew of their next of kin's terrorist activities and provided him with material assistance (the sister sewed explosive belts and the brother served as a look out while his brother was

261. See e.g., *Anonymous* v. *Minister of Defense*, Crim. F.H. 7048/97, 54(1) *P.D.* 721.

262. See e.g., N. Gilbert, 'Gov't to expel family of Emmanuel terrorist', *Jerusalem Post*, 1 August 2002; 'Hearings in the High Court of petitions of candidates for deportations have ended with no results', *Ma'ariv*, 26 August 2002 (in Hebrew) [Hadiyun BeBagatz BeAtirrot HaMeumadim Legerush Histayem BeLo Hachra'a].

263. Interim Agreement on the West Bank and Gaza Strip (Israel-PLO), 28 September 1995, 36 *ILM* (1997) p. 551.

264. See e.g., Second Periodic Report of the State of Israel under the International Covenant on Civil and Political Rights, para. 8, UN Doc. CCPR/C/ISR/2001/2 (2001).

removing explosives from a hideout place). In the case of the third applicant, the Court found that his mere awareness of the criminal acts of his brother could not justify a harsh measure such as assigned residence and invalidated the order pertaining to him.

D. House Demolitions

☛ *Yihye Al-Matib* v. *The IDF Gaza Strip Military Commander*, H.C.J. 2264/02, Supreme Court of Israel, Judgement of 19 March 2002. Published in 2002(1) *Takdin* 698

The petitioners requested the Court to instruct the army to refrain from demolishing their houses during military operations in the Gaza Strip. The parties reached a settlement, according to which the IDF would notify each house owner if and when it intended to demolish his or her house, and would give them sufficient time to challenge the decision before the military authorities and, subsequently, to the Supreme Court prior to actual demolition.

☛ *Adalah – The Legal Center for Arab Minority Rights in Israel* v. *The IDF West Bank Military Commander*, H.C.J. 2977/02, Supreme Court of Israel, Judgement of 9 April 2002. Published in 56(3) *P.D.* 6

The petitioner, an Israeli NGO, asked the Court to order the IDF to refrain from demolishing houses during its operations in the Jenin refugee camp without affording residents the right to a fair hearing. It was alleged that no sufficient prior warning was given to residents before house demolitions and that this practice resulted in civilian casualties. In response, the IDF stated that demolitions of houses in the camp is justified by operational needs – the need to reduce risks to Israeli soldiers during combat in residential areas in which houses are often used as booby-traps and hideouts for armed militants. Further, it was alleged that according to standard operational guidelines, residents of areas in which demolishing equipment operates are given notice of 1-1.5 hours before actual demolition begins.

The Court rejected the proposition that the right to fair hearing could apply in combat situations such as the one ongoing in Jenin. Still it noted that it presumes that the IDF had instructed its service members to do everything they can to prevent unnecessary infliction of damage upon innocent civilians.

☛ *Yosef Muhammad Gosin* v. *The IDF Gaza Strip Military Commander*, H.C.J. 4219/02, Supreme Court of Israel, Judgement of 30 May 2002. Published in 56(3) *P.D.* 608

The petition challenged an order issued by the IDF, pursuant to Article 23(g) of the 1907 Hague Regulations, to destroy a gas-producing factory owned by the petitioner, situated in proximity to a major road in the Gaza Strip. The army justified the order by reference to numerous incidents where shooting took place from within the factory compound aimed in the direction of the road, which resulted in a number of Israeli casualties. The Court rejected the state's position that the justiciability of the petition was questionable and stated that the Court was invested with authority to examine the lawfulness of the acts undertaken by military commanders, as opposed to the wisdom underlying the acts: 'the military commander must act within the confines of the law, and the Court's task is to provide an authoritative interpretation of the law'.

As for the merits of the case, the Court accepted the position that the challenged order was justified by military necessity. Further, it accepted that the IDF was entitled to resort to urgent military measures and to demolish one of the structures comprising the factory while litigation was still pending, in response to a new shooting incident and to intelligence reports that indicated that the structure might be used for additional terrorist attacks. The Court also rejected the assertion by the petitioner that the purpose of protecting the road, which was used by Israeli settlers, was unlawful in light of the illegality of Israeli settlements. According to the Court, the final status of the settlements would be decided in political negotiations, and until then the military commander was responsible for protecting all civilians – Israelis and Palestinians – in the area subject to his control.

☞ *Nahil Adal Sa'ado Amar* v. *The IDF West Bank Military Commander*, H.C.J. 6696/02, Supreme Court of Israel, Judgement of 6 August 2002. Published in 56(3) *P.D.* 110

The petitioners, family members of persons accused by Israel of terrorist acts, requested the Court to order the IDF to refrain from demolishing their houses before providing them with the right to fair hearing. The Court rejected the petition for being of an overly general nature. However, it stated that while normally the IDF was not allowed to use its legal authority to demolish houses without offering the owners a fair hearing, there could be circumstances in which operational considerations pertaining to the need to minimize risk to the lives of the soldiers involved in demolition operations would justify derogation from the right to fair hearing (e.g., to prevent ambushes against IDF soldiers). A subsequent request presented to Court to conduct a further hearing in the matter was rejected.[265]

☞ *Mahmud Iada Adi Salah-A-Din* v. *The IDF West Bank Military Commander*, H.C.J. 6868/02, Supreme Court of Israel, Judgement of 8 August 2002. Published in 2002(3) *Takdin* 258

In a case similar to the *Amar* case, the petitioners and the IDF reached a settlement, according to which family members who feared that their house might be targeted for demolition without prior notice would be able to present all information militating against such a measure to the IDF authorities, and the latter would consider that information before deciding on any pre-planned house demolition operation.

☞ *Yosef Hamid Mustafah Za'arub* v. *The IDF Gaza Strip Military Commander*, H.C.J. 6996/02, Supreme Court of Israel, Judgement of 20 August 2002. Published in 56(3) *P. D.* 407
☞ *Muhammad Id Baher* v. *The IDF West Bank Military Commander*, H.C.J. 7473/02, Supreme Court of Israel, Judgement of 17 September 2002. Published in 56(3) *P.D.* 488

Both cases dealt with demolition of houses of terrorists, pursuant to the authority of military commanders under Regulation 119 of the Defence (Emergency) Regulations 1945. In the *Za'arub* case, the Court reaffirmed the position that personal involvement on the part of the remaining house dwellers in terrorist activity is not a *sine qua non* for the lawfulness of house demolition measures.[266] In the specific case, it accepted the IDF's position that the sensitive location of the Mawasi neighbourhood in which the house was situated (its unhin-

---

265. *Garadat* v. *The IDF West Bank Military Commander*, H.C.F.H. 7206/02, 2002 *Pador* 362.
266. *Nazal* v. *The IDF Military Commander in Judea and Samaria*, H.C.J. 6026/94, 48(5) *P.D.* 338.

dered proximity to Israeli settlements in the Gaza Strip) required special deterrence, in light of the deteriorating security conditions in that area. Hence, in circumstances in which a terrorist went directly from his house to a Jewish settlement in order to commit a terror attack with a weapon stashed near his house, the IDF's decision to demolish that house is not unreasonable.

In the *Baher* case, the petitioners, family members of two suicide bombers, appealed against the decision of the IDF West Bank Military Commander to demolish their houses. The Court refused to address arguments concerning the futility of house demolition operations, and held that the effectiveness of this measure is an issue within the proper discretion of the military authorities. As for the arguments that the sanction of demolition would be unjust given the petitioners' lack of involvement in the terrorist activities of their next of kin, the Court reaffirmed the ruling that proof of such involvement is not always necessary. In any event, the Court noted that the petitioners cannot rely upon considerations of justice in the circumstances of the case: the evidence shows that they were aware of their next of kin's potential to engage in terrorism; one of the houses served as the meeting place of the two terrorists; the mother of one of the terrorists praised the terror attack in a newspaper interview; and none of the petitioners have denounced it.

It is notable that the approach of the Supreme Court with regard to house demolition cases is markedly different than the approach taken in the assigned residence cases. While in the first category of cases, there was no requirement that persons affected by the measure be personally involved in hostile activities, a more stringent standard of personal threat to the security of the occupying power was adopted in the *Ajuri* case.

E. TARGETED KILLINGS

☛ *Member of Knesset, Muhammad Barrake* v. *Prime Minister, Ariel Sharon*, H.C.J. 5872/ 01, Supreme Court of Israel, Judgement of 29 January 2002. Published in 56(3) *P.D.* 1

The petitioner, an Israeli Member of the Knesset, challenged the lawfulness of the IDF's policy of targeted killings aimed against Palestinian militants. The Court rejected the petition as non-justiciable, since the Court should not determine which fighting methods the army should resort to in its attempts to prevent terror attacks, and since the petition was of a too general nature.

☛ *The Public Committee Against Torture in Israel* v. *Government of the State of Israel*, H. C.J. 769/02, Supreme Court of Israel, Decision of 18 April 2002. Published in 2002(2) *Takdin* 239

The petitioners, Israeli and Palestinian NGOs, filed a new petition challenging the legality of targeted killings. The Court decided to accept detailed briefs on the matter from the parties, including on the preliminary objections to jurisdiction. The case was still pending by the end of the year.

F. APPROPRIATION OF PRIVATE PROPERTY

☛ *Omar Dari* v. *Minister of Defense*, H.C.J. 5577/02, Supreme Court of Israel, Judgement of 18 July 2002, published in 2002(2) *Takdin* 823

The Court approved the seizure of Palestinian agricultural land located in the West Bank by the military for transportation purposes after the army undertook to shorten the period of seizure from two years to one year. At the expiration of the initial period of seizure, the necessity of extending it will be considered. The question of compensation was not addressed by the Court.

G. PROTECTION OF CIVILIANS AND OTHERS FROM MILITARY OPERATIONS

☞ *Canon (Law) – The Palestinian Society for the Protection of Human Rights and the Environment* v. *General Yitzhak Eitan, the IDF West Bank Military Commander*, H.C.J. 3022/02, Supreme Court of Israel, Judgement of 10 April 2002. Published in 56(3) *P.D.* 9

The Petitioners, Israeli and Palestinian NGOs, filed a petition during the course of Operation 'Defensive Shield' in which the Court was requested to order the IDF to stop its practice of attacking civilian targets in Jenin during combat operations in the city. The Court held that the petition is non-justiciable as it asks the Court to intervene in specific methods applied during military operations. Still, the Court noted a statement by the IDF that during the operation in Jenin it undertook every effort to minimise damage to civilians (the Court noted, in this regard, the army's decision to refrain from using all of its firepower in the combat operation in Jenin and to resort instead to door-to-door fighting – a tactic which cost the lives of at least 14 IDF soldiers). The Court also stated that the Palestinian civilian population in Jenin is in fact being held hostage by Palestinian militants.

☞ *Adalah – The Legal Center for Arab Minority Rights in Israel* v. *The IDF West Bank Military Commander*, H.C.J. 3799/02, Supreme Court of Israel, Decisions of 23 May 2002 and 18 August 2002. Published in 2002(2) *Takdin* 1298; 2002(2) *Takdin* 3811

The petitioner, an Israeli NGO, requested the Court to issue an interim injunction ordering the IDF to refrain from using Palestinian civilians as human shields or hostages. It was filed in response to numerous reports that army units apply in their operations in Palestinian residential areas a 'neighbour procedure', according to which local residents are asked to inspect suspected houses situated in their neighbourhood or to try and convince militants hiding or operating from within local houses to surrender to the Israeli authorities. In response, the IDF undertook, notwithstanding its reservations concerning the veracity of the allegations, to refrain from seeking assistance from Palestinian civilians in circumstances which could endanger them. The army also stated that detailed procedures for cooperation with local residents would be prepared in the near future and that any specific allegations concerning the use of the 'neighbour procedure' will be investigated. In light of these statements, the Court held that no interim measures were necessary.

In light of subsequent NGO reports alleging the continued use of the 'neighbour procedure',[267] the Court reversed its initial position and issued a short-term interim measure banning the use of such procedure. The measure was extended since then by the Court on several occasions, and is still in force. In the meantime, following an event in which a Palestinian was killed while allegedly participating in a 'neighbour procedure', the petitioners requested the Court to declare the state in contempt of court.

---

267. See e.g., B'Tselem, *Human Shield: Use of Palestinian Civilians as Human Shields in Violation of the High Court of Justice Order* (Jerusalem, 2002), also at <http://www.btselem.org/Download/2002_Human_Shield_Eng.doc>.

H. Exclusion of Civilians from Military Zones

☞ *Member of Knesset, Muhammad Barrake* v. *Minister of Defense, Benjamin Ben-Eliezer*, H.C.J. 9293/01, Supreme Court of Israel, Judgement of 10 January 2002. Published in 56(2) *P.D.* 509

☞ *Doctors for Human Rights* v. *IDF West Bank Military Commander – Chief of Southern Command*, H.C.J. 727/02, Supreme Court of Israel, Judgement of 2 May 2002. Published in 56(3) *P.D.* 39

The Court held that the IDF may prevent for security reasons the entrance of Israeli citizens, including members of the Knesset and NGO activists, to areas designated as 'closed military areas', in which active fighting take place.

I. Siege of Bethlehem

☞ *Custodia Internazionale di Terra Santa* v. *Government of Israel*, H.C.J. 3436/02, Supreme Court of Israel, Judgement of 24 April 2002, published in 56(3) *P.D.* 22

☞ *Muhammad Almadani* v. *Minister of Defense*, H.C.J. 3451/02, Supreme Court of Israel, Judgement of 2 May 2002. Published in 56(3) *P.D.* 30 [an English version of the Judgement is available at <http://62.90.71.124/files_eng/02/510/034/a06/02034510.a06. HTM>]

The two cases pertained to the siege of the Church of the Nativity in Bethlehem between 14 April to 10 May 2002.[268] The Church was surrounded by the IDF after some 200 Palestinian militants took refuge within the Church compound. Almost 50 clergymen were in the Church at the beginning of the siege and it is unclear whether or not they were held by the militants against their will (the IDF officially maintained that the clergymen were held as hostages in the compound).

In the first petition, the *Custodia*, who owns the Church compound, requested the Court to order the IDF to allow in food, water, drugs and other necessary supplies to the clergymen; to reconnect water and electricity; to permit doctors to enter the compound to examine the sick and wounded; and to allow for the removal of two dead bodies present in the Church. The Court refused to intervene in the situation, citing the fact that negotiations to end the siege were still underway and that the petition pertained to the course of an ongoing military operation. Still, the Court noted that the IDF had allowed all clergymen who wished to leave the Church to do so, it had brought in food, water and drugs for use by the clergymen, and it agreed to permit the entry of additional food supplies on demand. It also noted that there was some water and electricity (produced by generators) in the compound, despite the fact that the army disconnected the Church from outside utilities in order to pressurise the militants into surrendering.

The second petition was brought by the Palestinian governor of the City of Bethlehem, who was inside the Church compound, and by two Israeli Members of the Knesset. The petitioners asked the Court to instruct the army to permit the entry of medical teams and

---

268. The siege ended as a result of an agreement brokered by the EU and the US. The agreement provided for the exile of 13 top militants to European destinations, for the transfer of 26 other militants to the Gaza Strip and for the release of the other 86 activists after being identified and searched by the IDF. American security personnel undertook to sweep the church compound for booby-traps and other weaponry.

representatives of the International Committee of the Red Cross into the compound in order to treat the wounded and collect the dead, and to permit the supply of food and drugs to the people inside the Church. The Court reaffirmed the obligation of the state of Israel to comply with international humanitarian law in its struggle against terror. President Barak noted that this commitment stems not only from pragmatic considerations but also from deeper democratic values: 'the State fights in the name of the law, for upholding the law. The terrorists fight against the law and in breach of the law. The war against terror is also the fight of the law against those who challenge it.' Indeed, the Court noted that the taking over of the Church compound by Palestinian militants is a serious breach of international humanitarian law. The Court held that the problems pertaining to medical treatment and removal of the dead had already been resolved by the parties. As for the refusal of the IDF to permit food supplies, citing concern that food earmarked for use by civilians would be seized by the militants, the Court held that the position adopted by the IDF – to supply food to the clergymen, on demand, and to enable all civilians in the compound who do not take part in hostilities to leave and reenter the compound in order to get food and water – was compatible with the terms of Article 23(a) of the Fourth Geneva Convention. This is particularly in light of the fact that some stored food was still available within the compound.

J. Responsibility for Human Remains on the Battlefield
☞ *Member of Knesset, Muhammad Barrake* v. *The Minister of Defense, Benjamin Ben-Eliezer*, H.C.J. 3114/02, Supreme Court of Israel, Judgement of 14 April 2002. Published in 56(3) *P.D.* 11 [an English version of the Judgement is available at <http://62.90.71.124/files_eng/02/170/021/l06/02021170.l06.htm>]

The petitioners, two Members of the Israeli Knesset and two NGOs (an Israeli NGO and a Palestinian NGO), filed a petition asking the Court to instruct the IDF to refrain from examining, removing and burying the bodies of Palestinians who died during combat in the Jenin refugee camp, and to assign this task to local medical teams, accompanied by representatives of the International Committee of the Red Cross and family members of the victims. The Court held that the IDF bears the ultimate responsibility for handling bodies left behind on the battlefield. However, it noted that the petitioners and the respondents have been able to reach an agreement, which would enable local Palestinians and Red Cross and Red Crescent employees to participate, subject to the prevailing military conditions, in the process of locating and identifying the bodies, and that the IDF was also willing to enable the Palestinian side to bury its dead, provided that it moved to do so immediately.

In *obiter dicta,* the Court addressed allegations made by the petitioners that a massacre had been committed in Jenin:

'A fight took place in Jenin – a fight in which many of our soldiers died. The army fought house to house and not by way of air bombardment in order to prevent, as much as possible, civilian casualties… The petitioners failed to meet their burden. A massacre is one thing. A difficult fight is another thing.'

K. Criminal Law
☞ *State of Israel* v. *Marwan Bin Khatib Barghouti*, Crim. Case (T.A.) 92134/02, Tel Aviv District Court, Decision of 12 December 2002. Not yet published <http://www.mfa.gov.il/mfa/go.asp?MFAH0mz80>

The defendant, leader of the Tanzim militant organisation, Member of the Palestinian Council and the former Secretary-General of the Fatah movement in the West Bank, was arrested in Ramallah and brought to trial in Israel, under ordinary Israeli criminal law, for his involvement in the murder and attempted murder of hundreds of Israeli citizens. He raised five principal preliminary objections to the jurisdiction of the Israeli Court: 1) that the Oslo accords barred criminal proceedings against Palestinians for acts committed in areas transferred to the Palestinian Authority; 2) that he was entitled to a prisoner of war status, by virtue of being a freedom fighter; 3) that his arrest in Ramallah was an illegal act of kidnapping; 4) that his status as a Parliament member conferred upon him personal immunity; and 5) that his indictment was a political and not a legal act.

The Court rejected all of these objections, ruling that 1) the Oslo accords did not bar prosecution of Palestinians for offences against Israel, and that in any event the accords could not be relied upon as they were not part of the Israeli legal system and because they had been materially breached by the Palestinian side; 2) the defendant did not meet the conditions set out in the Third Geneva Convention for prisoner of war status – his organisation did not fight with a distinctive sign, members of his organisation did not carry their arms openly, and most significantly, the Tanzim systematically targeted civilians in violation of the laws of war. As a result, the defendant was an unlawful combatant and was criminally responsible for all acts of violence in which he was involved (including those acts which constitute war crimes); 3) the arrest of an unlawful combatant during conflict is permissible, and, in any event, the manner in which the defendant was brought into Israel had no bearing upon the jurisdiction of the Court. The Court also rejected the argument that the removal of the defendant from the West Bank and Gaza Strip constituted an unlawful deportation, prohibited by Article 49 of the Fourth Geneva Convention. According to the Court, this provision only barred mass transfers of population and was not customary law (and thus, not part of the Israeli legal system). Furthermore, the defendant was estopped from relying upon the protections of the Convention, as his involvement in attacks on civilians demonstrated a repudiation on his part of the Convention's basic principles; 4) membership of Parliament did not confer immunity before the courts of another country; and 5) the offences attributed to the defendant clearly pertained to criminal action.

Pending

☞ Civil Torts (State Responsibility) (Amendment No. 5) (Submission of Claims against the State of Israel by an Enemy State National or by a Conflict Area Resident) Draft Law, 2002 [Hatza'at Hok Hanezikim HaEzrahiyim (Ahrayut Hamedina) (Tikun Mispar 5) (Hagashat T'viot Neged Hamedina Al-Yedei Natin Medinat Oyev O Toshav Ezor Imut), 762, 2002]. Published in the *Official Gazette* for draft legislation on 15 July 2002 <http://www.knesset.gov.il/Laws/Data/BillAllOld/3173/3173_All.html> [in Hebrew]

The purpose of the proposed bill, submitted to the Knesset by the government of the state of Israel, is to further limit tort claims against the state relating to the second Palestinian *intifadah* (2000-present). This purpose is supposedly justified by the asymmetry created by the inability of Israeli victims of terrorism and other forms of armed hostilities to bring claims against the Palestinian Authority,[269] and by the practical difficulties the state encoun-

---

269. It should be noted that several tort claims against the Palestinian Authority are currently pend-

ters in defending such claims (inaccessibility to evidence and witnesses; high number of incidents). According to the government, the ability of victims belonging to an enemy entity to bring civil claims in Israeli national courts has no parallel in states such as the US, the UK, France and Germany.

The legislation would exempt the state from civil liability in claims brought by enemy nationals or by members of terrorist organisations, and those acting on their behalf, except if the injurious act was committed while he or she was in Israeli custody. Similarly, residents of an area situated outside the territory of the state of Israel, and designated by the Minister of Defense as a 'conflict area', would not be able to bring claims against the state for conflict-related torts or any other claim against the security forces of the state of Israel (except if the act in question was committed while he or she were in Israeli custody if the injury was inflicted by Israeli civil administration in the West Bank and Gaza Strip and was unrelated to the conflict or if the claim involved a traffic accident, unrelated to the conflict). The Minister of Defense was authorised to appoint a commission to propose *ex gratia* payments to conflict area residents with regard to exempted claims.

YUVAL SHANY

ITALY[270]

Children

👉 Law No. 46 of 11 March 2002 ratifying the Optional Protocols to the United Nations Convention on the Rights of the Child, done in New York on 6 September 2000 [Legge 11 marzo 2002, n. 46 'Ratifica ed esecuzione dei protocolli opzionali alla Convenzione dei diritti del fanciullo, concernenti rispettivamente la vendita dei bambini, la prostituzione dei bambini e la pornografia rappresentante bambini ed il coinvolgimento dei bambini nei conflitti armati, fatti a New York il 6 settembre 2000']. Entered into force on 12 March 2002, published in the *Italian Official Journal* [*Gazzetta Ufficiale della Repubblica italiana*], Ordinary Supplement No. 77, 2 April 2002 <http://www.parla mento.it/parlam/leggi/020461.htm>

By Law No. 46 of 11 March 2002, the Italian Parliament authorised the ratification of the Optional Protocols to the United Nations Convention on the Rights of the Child of 1989, namely, on the sale of children, child prostitution and child pornography (Optional Protocol I), and on the involvement of children in armed conflict (Optional Protocol II).[271] Their ratification was discussed on 26 September 2001 at the Senate, which approved it on 28 November 2001. On 10 December 2001, the matter came before the Chamber of Deputies, which approved it on 20 February 2002.[272]

---

ing before Israeli courts. The District Court of Jerusalem has recently asked the Minister of Foreign Affairs for an official certificate determining whether the Palestinian Authority enjoys sovereign immunity. *Noriz* v. *The Palestinian Authority*, C.A. (Jer.) 2538/00, 2003(1) *Takdin* 4968.

270. Information and commentaries provided by Clara Bosco, Rosa Dinuzzi, Valeria Eboli, Valentina Della Fina, Giovanni Carlo Bruno and Ornella Ferrajolo of the Institute for International Legal Studies, National Research Council (CNR), Rome.

271. The two Optional Protocols, which were adopted by the United Nations General Assembly on 25 May 2000, entered into force on 18 January 2002 and on 12 February 2002, respectively, three months after the deposit of the tenth instrument of ratification or accession.

272. By that time, the Italian legislation had already regulated the issues dealing with the Conven-

In compliance with Article 3 of the Second Optional Protocol on the Involvement of Children in Armed Conflict, the government declared that Italian legislation on voluntary recruitment requires a minimum age of 17 years with respect to requests for early recruitment for compulsory military service or voluntary recruitment (military duty on a short-term and yearly basis). It also declared that the legislation in force guarantees the application, at the time of voluntary recruitment, of the provisions of Article 3(3) of the Protocol, *inter alia*, as regards the requirement of the consent of the parent or guardian of the recruit.

CLARA BOSCO[273]

International Criminal Tribunals
- Law No. 181 of 2 August 2002, Provisions concerning cooperation with the International Tribunal having jurisdiction over serious violations of international humanitarian law committed in the territory of Rwanda and neighbouring States [Legge 2 agosto 2002, No. 181, Disposizioni in materia di cooperazione con il Tribunale internazionale competente per gravi violazioni del diritto umanitario commesse nel territorio del Ruanda e Stati vicini]. Published in the *Italian Official Journal* [*Gazzetta Ufficiale della Repubblica italiana*] No. 190, 14 August 2002, entered into force on 15 August 2002 <http://www.parlamento.it/parlam/leggi/>

Law No. 181, providing for cooperation between Italy and the International Criminal Tribunal for Rwanda (ICTR), is based on the similar Law No. 120 of 14 February 1994 on the cooperation with the International Criminal Tribunal for the former Yugoslavia.[274]

According to Article 3 of Law No. 181, cooperation with the ICTR implies the Italian judge's duty, at any stage of a procedure against a person accused of crimes within the ICTR's jurisdiction, to defer to the Tribunal's competence should the latter decide to apply the 'primacy clause' under Article 8 of the Statute, and where the following two conditions are met.

First, Article 3 of the Law states that the Italian judge, declaring the existence of the Tribunal's primary jurisdiction, must refer only to the Tribunal's territorial and temporal jurisdiction. Here the legislator aimed at restricting the national judge's evaluation only to objective and verifiable data, such as *locus* and *tempus commissi delicti*, excluding any evaluation of the jurisdiction *ratione materiae* of the ICTR. The legislator, in fact, considered that the International Tribunal, in comparison with the Italian judge, possesses different and more suitable data to frame a specific event in one of the cases covered by its competence and regulated by Articles 2 and 5 of its Statute.

The second condition for the transfer of the proceeding requires that the ICTR and the national court both proceed for the 'same act'. The jurisdiction over the transfer of the proceeding – dealing with a jurisdiction withdrawal case – belongs to the judge of the pending case. If the proceeding is at the pre-trial stage, the preliminary hearing judge is the person competent to decide on it, according to the general rules.

---

tion on the Rights of the Child and related Protocols through the dispositions contained in the Laws No. 166, 27 May 1991; No. 269, 3 August 1998; No. 148, 25 May 2000; and No. 2, 8 January 2001.

273. Clara Bosco is a consultant at the Institute for International Legal Studies, National Research Council (Cnr), Rome.

274. 1 *YIHL* (1998) p. 468.

Law No. 181 also provides for the reopening of the national proceeding in front of the Italian judicial authority if, according to Articles 17 and 18 of the Statute, the Tribunal decides not to formulate the charge or not to confirm the indictment or to dismiss the indictment for lack of jurisdiction.[275] Therefore, the reopening of the proceeding in Italy is allowed unless the Tribunal has already decided on the merits of the charge formulated pursuant to its norms and rules of procedure.

Should one of the above-mentioned hypotheses occur, a grounded decree for the reopening of the investigation shall be issued by the judge for the preliminary hearing on the Public Prosecutor's request and, in this case, the pre-trial investigation terms start to run again. If the criminal action has already commenced, the preliminary hearing judge or the President of the Tribunal should order the renewal of the introductory act.

The law also indicates the duty of the Italian judicial authority to give timely notice of pending cases over which the International Tribunal might have priority jurisdiction in order to promptly grant a request of the proceeding transfer, thereby avoiding that the request be transmitted when the national proceeding is at an advanced stage.[276]

Article 7 of the law provides for the procedures concerning the recognition of the ICTR judgement, which, pursuant to paragraph 2 of the same article, cannot be given if the judgement has not become final, according to the Statute and the other provisions governing the International Tribunal; if the judgement is contrary to the fundamental rules of the legal order of the state; if the act for which the judgement has been pronounced is not considered as a crime by Italian law; or if a final judgement on the same person for the same act has already been pronounced.

Law No. 181, in implementation of Article 28 of the Statute governing cooperation and judicial assistance with the International Tribunal, states the duty of the Minister of Justice to transmit the acts requested by the Tribunal to the Court of Appeal of Rome, which will implement them by decree (Art. 10). If the request of the Tribunal concerns the surrender of the accused, the Court of Appeal may state that the conditions for the surrender do not exist only in the following circumstances: if the Tribunal has not adopted any measure restraining the personal liberty of the accused; if there is no physical similarity between the person requested and the person surrendered; if the fact for which the surrender is requested does not fall under the temporal and territorial jurisdiction of the International Tribunal; if the fact under question is not considered as a crime by Italian law; or if a final judgement on the same person for the same act has already been pronounced.

One can observe that the legislator has precisely regulated the case of the surrender of the accused, considering the great importance of the topic under discussion, which involves the fundamental rights guaranteed at constitutional level, and in particular, the right to personal liberty. In this context, the legislator's specific attention towards the regulation of the application of preventive measures has to be underlined. This attention is motivated by the fact that Article 28(2)(d) of the Statute states that the Tribunal can also request the arrest or the detention of the person with respect to whom an application for preventive measures has been demanded. In particular, Law No. 181 states that preventive detention can be replaced by an alternative measure in case of serious medical grounds.[277] Moreover, pursuant to Articles 12(5) and 13(3), preventive measures can be revoked if the competent judicial

---

275. Art. 4(1) of the Law.
276. Art. 6(1) of the Law.
277. Art. 12(4) of the law.

authorities did not pronounce on the surrender request of the defendant within the terms of the law or if the defendant has not been transferred to the International Tribunal within the terms stated.

In conclusion, in accordance with Article 17(1) of the ICTR Statute, the legislator states that national and international non-governmental organisations that are authorised to collect and transmit relevant information to the Tribunal shall receive the full cooperation of the Italian state.

ROSA DINUZZI[278]

The National Society

☛ Decree of the President of the Council of Ministers No. 208 of 5 July 2002 concerning the approval of New Statute of the Italian Red Cross Association [Decreto del Presidente del Consiglio dei Ministri n. 208 del 5 luglio 2002 'Approvazione del nuovo statuto dell'Associazione italiana della Croce rossa']. Entered into force on 9 October 2002, published in the *Italian Official Journal* [*Gazzetta Ufficiale della Repubblica italiana*] No. 224 of 24 September 2002 <http://www.cri.it/bibliocri/docscri.htm>

On 5 July 2002, the Italian Premier, acting in concert with the Ministers of Defence and Health, approved a new Statute for the Italian Red Cross Association, the Italian national society.[279]

Article 2 of the approved Statute concerns the duties of the Association and directly mentions international humanitarian law. It states that the Italian Red Cross fulfils all of the duties provided for in the Geneva Conventions of 12 August 1949 and their Additional Protocols, which form the basis for the Association, under Article 1 of the Statute.[280]

In conformity with Article 4 of the Statute, the Association, a national society, is recognised by the Italian government as the only 'voluntary aid society, auxiliary to the public authorities in the humanitarian field' acting on the national territory.

---

278. Rosa Dinuzzi is a consultant at the Institute for International Legal Studies, National Research Council (Cnr), Rome.

279. The Italian Red Cross Association was founded on 15 June 1864 and recognised by Royal Decree No. 1243, 7 February 1884, when the first Statute was approved. A further Statute was approved by Royal Decree No. 111 of 21 January 1929, followed by various Acts containing special rules on specific aspects of the Association up to the Decree No. 613 of the President of the Republic of 31 July 1980, on the 'Reorganization of the Italian Red Cross'. In the Italian legal system, the Red Cross Association is established as a public body, because a number of the duties it performs have a public character. Decree No. 613/1980 used to qualify the association as a private body of public relevance (*ente privato di interesse pubblico*), granting the body a private nature. This qualification could better lay emphasis on the volunteer component marking the social tissue, as remarked by P. Benvenuti, 'Croce rossa internazionale', in *Enciclopedia giuridica Treccani* (Rome, Istituto della Enciclopedia italiana 1988). The importance awarded to the volunteer component is stressed, at the present time, by the dualistic structure of the Association, made up of both an institutional part and a volunteer part, *ex* Art. 16(2) of the new Statute. See also P. De Cesare-Sanino, 'Il riordinamento della Croce rossa italiana', in *Il Foro amministrativo* (Milan, Giuffrè 1981) pt. 1, pp. 194-199; P. Balocchi, 'Osservazioni sulla disciplina giuridica della Croce rossa italiana', in *Diritto e società* (1986) pp. 31-64; P. Gargiulo, 'Croce rossa internazionale', in *Digesto Discipline pubblicistiche*, IV (1989) pp. 488-493, 492.

280. The Geneva Conventions have been executed in Italy by Law No. 1739 of 27 October 1951.

The Italian Association Statute recalls the conditions for admission provided for under the International Red Cross Movement Statute, and adhesion to them has been established, as provided for by Article 2(i) of the new Statute.[281]

The duties of the Association include the following field activities: the treatment of the wounded and sick, and all the victims of an armed conflict; the fulfilment of all duties of a sanitary character related to civil defence activities; the search for and provision of aid to prisoners of war, interned and missing people and refugees. As provided for by the Statute, the Association is founded on the seven fundamental principles of humanity of the International Red Cross. Additionally, the Association is charged with the promotion and diffusion of these principles (Art. 2(h)).

A remark is required about the extension of the wartime activities of the Red Cross to all kinds of armed conflicts. This enlarged notion embraces all situations involving the use of armed force. It is also important to note that the Italian Red Cross has important duties even during peacetime, when, in addition to the continued preparation for its wartime and armed conflict duties, it works on tasks including social and sanitary activities, civil welfare and, generally, aid in situations of public disaster.

The Italian Red Cross is a Member of the League of the Red Cross National Societies and the International Red Cross and Red Crescent Movement (or International Red Cross), having been recognised by the International Red Cross Committee, in accordance with Article 5(2)(b) of the Statute of the Movement.

VALERIA EBOLI[282]

Peace Enforcement – Participation in Military Operations Abroad

☞ Law No. 6 of 31 January 2002, 'Conversion in law, with modifications, of the Decree-law No. 421 of 1 December 2001, concerning urgent dispositions for the participation of military staff to the multifunctional operation called "Enduring Freedom". Amendments to the Military Penal Code of War, approved by Royal Decree No. 303 of 20 February 1941' [Legge 31 gennaio 2002, n. 6 'Conversione in legge, con modificazioni, del decreto-legge 1° dicembre 2001, n. 421, recante disposizioni urgenti per la partecipazione di personale militare all'operazione multinazionale denominata *"Enduring Freedom"*. Modifiche al codice penale militare di guerra, approvato con regio decreto 20 febbraio 1941, n. 303']. Adopted on 31 January 2002, entered into force on 3 February 2002, published in the Italian *Official Journal [Gazzetta Ufficiale della Repubblica italiana]* No. 28, 2 February 2002

'This law ... transformed the Decree-Law No. 421 on the multinational operation "Enduring Freedom" into a law and amended the Military Criminal Code of War. ... It extends the applicability of the Military Criminal Code of War to military personnel on mission for armed operations outside Italian territory, such as the troops taking part in the "Enduring Freedom" operation. The Law also emphasizes that the provisions of Book II, Title 4, of the Code ("Acts against the laws and customs of war") applies to all armed conflicts, irrespec-

---

281. It was already stated in the former Statute of 1997. For instance, the use of the emblem as a distinctive sign remains the same as required of the Italian Society Statute in Art. 4(5) of the International Movement Statute.

282. Valeria Eboli is a Ph.D. Candidate in International Law at the University 'La Sapienza' of Rome.

tive of whether or not there was a declaration of war. It adds new Articles 184*bis* and 185*bis* which impose prison sentences for the taking of hostages; for the threat to wound or kill a person who is unarmed, is not acting in a hostile manner or is captured in connection with the conflict, with the aim to force the hand-over of persons or objects; and for torture or other inhuman treatments, illegal transfers or any other act prohibited under international conventions, including biological experiments or medical treatments which are not required by the state of health of prisoners of war, civilians or other persons protected by the said conventions.'[283]

☛ Report of the Military Attorney-General of the Republic at the Military Appeal Court for the opening of judicial year 2002 (General Assembly of the Military Appeal Court, Rome, 22 January 2002)

The Report contains some critical evaluations related both to Decree Law No. 421 of 1 December 2001 – which establishes some urgent dispositions for the participation of Italian military personnel in the multifunctional operation called 'Enduring Freedom', against international terrorism in Afghanistan – and to the bill brought before the Senate on 14 December 2001 (Senate Act No. 915) for the review of the Military Penal Code of War of 1941.[284]

The Attorney-General, Mr Vindicio Bonagura, defined as 'not necessary' the government decision to introduce in Decree Law No. 421 a specific norm according to which the Military Penal Code of War applies to contingents participating in Operation 'Enduring Freedom'. In fact, Article 9 of the Military Penal Code of War already states that it is also to be applied in peacetime to contingents engaged in military operations abroad.

The Attorney-General's considerations also relate to the substance of the question. It has been stressed that by the adoption of an *ad hoc* measure, the government has demonstrated its intention to distinguish the mission in Afghanistan from other missions abroad, as in this case Italian contingents are engaged in a real armed conflict. However, there remains a legislative gap concerning the punishment of crimes committed by Italian soldiers during missions abroad. In the Attorney-General's opinion, it would have been more appropriate to adopt a wider law with the aim of determining a common discipline for all Italian missions abroad, which have become more and more frequent.

As far as the review of the Military Penal Code of War is concerned, the Attorney-General shared the idea that a comprehensive reformulation is needed, in the light of deep changes that have occurred since the time of its elaboration. Notwithstanding the reform, Mr Bonagura predicted that the Military Penal Code of Peace will continue to be applied to

---

283. ICRC Advisory Service, National Implementation of International Humanitarian Law – Biannual update on national legislation and case-law, January-June 2002. <http://www.icrc.org/Web/eng/siteeng0.nsf/html/5FLE9G?OpenDocument>. See also CICC/Europe/CIS:Estonia. <http://www.iccnow.org/countryinfo/europecis/estonia.html>.

284. As regards the Law converting Decree-Law No. 421 of 2001, including also the amendments to the Military Penal Code of War, *Law No. 6 of 31 January 2002, 'Conversion in law, with modifications, of the Decree-law No. 421 of 1 December 2001, concerning urgent dispositions for the participation of military staff to the multifunctional operation called 'Enduring Freedom'. Amendments to the Military Penal Code of War, approved by Royal Decree No. 303 of 20 February 1941*, in 4 *YIHL* (2001) pp. 563-565.

traditional peacekeeping operations, which now constitute an ordinary activity for the Italian armed forces, derogating from Article 9 of the Military Penal Code of War.

The Attorney-General made two different proposals in order to solve the problem of the normative gap concerning the discipline to be applied to Italian contingents taking part in missions abroad. The first one concerns the elaboration of an *ad hoc* law; the second one would provide for the amendment of the Military Penal Code of Peace in order to make it more suitable for the new exigencies.

In the first case, we would have specific rules able to satisfy the particular requirements of missions abroad which go beyond the traditional dichotomy 'code of peace – code of war', which is anachronistic in the Attorney-General's view. The second option has the advantage of simply modifying and integrating a text which already includes the great part of the discipline now applied to the contingents participating in peacekeeping operations.

The Report also deals with an important issue which has not yet been solved, namely, the structure of the military judicial system, which has not been treated in the new discipline introduced by Law No. 6 of 31 January 2002.

VALENTINA DELLA FINA[285]

Cases

☛ Proceedings against *Goran Jelisić*, Court of Appeal of Rome, Judgement No. 8 of 31 January 2002

This decision recognises the judgement delivered on 5 July 2001 by the Appeals Chamber of the International Criminal Tribunal for the former Yugoslavia (ICTY) against Goran Jelisić,[286] the Serbian officer found guilty of genocide, violations of the laws or customs of war and crimes against humanity, committed in May 1992 in the municipality of Brčko in the north-eastern part of Bosnia-Herzegovina and sentenced to 40 years of imprisonment.

On 23 October 2001, the Ministry of Justice addressed the request of the Rome Court of Appeal's Attorney-General that the Court promote the recognition proceeding of the aforesaid judgement, in order to obtain the enforcement of the sentence in Italy, according to Law No. 120 of 14 February 1994[287] and to Law No. 207 of 7 June 1999, the latter ratifying the agreement between the United Nations and Italy 'on the enforcement of judgments of the International Criminal Tribunal for the Former Yugoslavia', done on 6 February 1997 in The Hague. The Italian state, following its accession to this Agreement, indicated its willingness to enforce the sentences imposed by the ICTY. The latter submitted to the Italian government a request for the enforcement of the judgement delivered against Jelisić, providing the supporting documentation requested by Article 2 of the 1997 Agreement.

In the decision under examination, the Court of Appeal of Rome confirmed the existence of all the conditions requested by the law and the aforesaid 1997 Agreement for the recognition of the ICTY's judgements. In this regard, the Court specified that the judgement against Jelisić was delivered by the ICTY and that it had become final according to the Statute and the other rules governing the Tribunal's activities. Moreover, the acts for which

---

285. Valentina Della Fina is a researcher at the Institute for International Legal Studies, National Research Council (CNR), Rome.

286. *The Prosecutor* v. *Goran Jelisić*, Case No. IT-95-10-A, Appeal Judgment, 5 July 2001. For a summary of the decision, see 4 *YIHL* (2001) pp. 280-283.

287. 1 *YIHL* (1998) p. 468.

the sentence had been imposed constitute criminal offences according to the law of the state of enforcement,[288] and, according to the Court's ascertainments, no final judgement had already been delivered by the Italian state against the same person for the same act.

As far as the sentence to be served by the convicted in Italy is concerned, the Court stated that, according to Article 3 of the 1997 Agreement, the competent national authorities of the state designated for the sentence enforcement are bound by the length of the sentence imposed by the judgement (in this case 40 years). For this reason, the last provision of Article 7(4) of Law No. 120 of 1994, which states that the length of the sentence must not exceed 30 years' imprisonment, must be considered repealed by the first paragraph of Article 3 of the 1997 Agreement, in compliance with the principle of *lex specialis derogat generali*.

According to the Court, the fact that the rules under examination must be interpreted in the aforesaid manner is easily understandable considering the specific nature and the profound meaning of the 1997 Agreement, whose provisions prevail over Italian law, pursuant to Article 696 of the Italian Criminal Procedure Code.

In this respect, the Court of Appeal also specified that the above-mentioned agreement is a framework agreement: in other words, it does not refer to the enforcement of a specific sentence, given that the practical definition of the judgements to be enforced in Italy shall be taken care of, on a case-by-case basis, following the procedure referred to in Article 2 of the 1997 Agreement. The latter is founded on three fundamental pillars which derive from the provisons of the ICTY's Statute, especially from Articles 24 and 27: pursuant to them, the penalty imposed by the International Tribunal must be respected by the applicable law of the state concerned; the minimum conditions of detention must respect the widely accepted international standards governing the treatment of prisoners; and finally, the enforcement of a sentence of imprisonment must be subject to the supervision of the International Tribunal.

In this context, the Court reaffirmed that Italy, following its accession to this 1997 Agreement, agreed, along with the other signatory states, to implement a set of substantial rules directed at the punishment of serious violations of international humanitarian law, even if these rules should provide for different penalties than those imposed by Italian legislation. The reason behind this lies in the fact that, unlike the process for the recognition of foreign criminal judgements provided for by the European Convention on the Transfer of Sentenced Persons of 21 March 1983 – that is, judgements with regard to which the Italian authority was not the 'author' of the substantial rule governing the specific case and the subsequent penalty – the International Tribunal's judgements enforce substantial common law, established and agreed upon at an international level by the contracting parties, and for this reason the Italian state must be considered, from the legal point of view, the author of this substantial common law as well.

In the end, the Court underlined that the compulsory nature of United Nations law for Italy stems from its hierarchically superior position to the state's internal laws. This superior position, according to Chapter VII of the UN Charter, is characteristic of Security Council resolutions and of the International Tribunal's Statute, as it had been adopted by SC Resolution 827 of 1993.

Therefore, following its accession to the 1997 agreement, Italy renounced its jurisdiction, recognising, on the one hand, the international and intangible nature of the penalty imposed by the ICTY – which implies that the length of penalty must not be altered by the internal

---

288. Italian Law No. 962 of 9 October 1967.

laws of the enforcing state – and on the other hand, the supervisory power of the ICTY in the sentence enforcement phase. In this regard, the President of the Tribunal may decide to transfer the sentenced person back to the International Tribunal should he realise that the prisoner was not granted a pardon or a commutation of the sentence which he should have been entitled to according to the national law of the state designated for the sentence enforcement.

In the light of the principles stated by the Court, Goran Jelisić shall serve in Italy the overall penalty of 40 years of imprisonment imposed by the ICTY, and therefore, in consideration of the supporting documentation attesting the convicted's arrest on 22 January 1998, Jelisić shall be imprisoned until 22 January 2038.

ROSA DINUZZI

☛ *Marcović and Others* v. *Presidency of the Council of Ministers*, Court of Cassation (Joint Sections), Order No. 8157 of 5 June 2002

The Order under review basically addresses questions of jurisdiction with regard to state responsibility for damages allegedly incurred due to acts of war, and in particular for the conduct of aerial warfare. The United Sections of the Court of Cassation decided that the Italian courts lacked jurisdiction to rule on a case concerning possible Italian responsibility, as a state, for violations of international humanitarian law deriving from the bombing of one of the Radio Televizije Srbije (RTS) buildings on 23 April 1999, during the air strikes (Operation Allied Forces) carried out by NATO against the Federal Republic of Yugoslavia. In the reasoning of the Court, the non-self-executing nature of the First Additional Protocol of 1977 to the Geneva Conventions of 1949 (Arts. 35(2), 48, 49, 51, 52, 57) as well as the European Convention on Human Rights (Arts. 2 and 15) was reaffirmed.

The case originated from an application for damages filed against the Presidency of the Council of Ministers, the Italian Ministry of Defence and the Command of Allied Forces in Southern Europe (AFSOUTH) before the Tribunal of Rome. The applicants were relatives of Yugoslav nationals killed in the bombing of RTS on 23 April 1999. In their opinion, the bombing of the RTS building constituted a methods and means of war prohibited by the First Additional Protocol of 1977, mainly because the building had to be considered as a non-military objective and because the act was intentionally directed against civilians. In addition, they argued that the same act violated Article 174 of the Italian Military Criminal Code applicable in time of war, which provides for the punishment of the commanding officer authorising or ordering, *inter alia*, the use of methods or means of war contrary to law and international treaties. According to the petitioners, the responsibility arising from the above-mentioned acts had to be attributed to Italy, since as a NATO Member State it concurred in determining the conduct of war and because the war action was initiated on Italian territory.

In the applicants' opinion, the London Agreement of 19 June 1951 between NATO Member States regarding the status of their armed forces, which was executed in Italy by Law No. 1335 of 30 November 1955, was also applicable to the case. In particular, the claim was said to have arisen

'out of acts or omissions of members of a force or civilian component done in the performance of official duty, or out of any other act, omission or occurrence for which a force or civilian component is legally responsible, and causing damage in the territory of the receiving State to third parties, other than any of the Contracting Parties' (Art. VIII (5) of the Agreement).

The respondents invoked the lack of jurisdiction on different grounds and asked the Court of Cassation for a preliminary ruling on that question. In order to avoid a judgement on the merits, the State Attorneys put forward a rather abstract reasoning, maintaining that the acts ascribed to the state organs in the case under examination had to be considered as an expression of a 'sovereign subject' in the international community. Claims deriving from activities performed as a sovereign subject in the domain of international relations might be judged only by those international courts or tribunals whose jurisdiction had been specifically accepted by the state.

Moreover, the Ministry of Defence considered that the 1951 London Agreement was not applicable to the case because casualties had not been caused on the territory of a 'receiving State' – which, according to the Agreement, is 'the Contracting Party in the territory of which the force or civilian component is located, whether it be stationed there or passing in transit' (Art. I(1)(e)).

As a reaction to the state's argument, the applicants maintained, *inter alia*, that limits on the modalities of waging an act of war can be derived from international treaties on humanitarian law. Beyond the said limits any state could be responsible for damages caused by its activities even toward individual victims, who may claim for damages before a national tribunal.

On the second question introduced by the Ministry of Defence, they responded that whether certain facts happened or not on the Italian territory was not a question of jurisdiction, but an issue of responsibility.

The Attorney-General expressed the opinion, in his written conclusions, that the Italian jurisdiction should be affirmed, but challenged the existence of 'rules or principles' affirming the state's responsibility in such cases.

In its Order, the Court of Cassation reaffirmed, first of all, its competence to decide questions of jurisdiction. This competence stems from Article 382(2) of the Italian Civil Procedure Code and well-established case-law. As for the case in hand, it ruled in favour of the request of the Presidency of the Council of Ministers and the Ministry of Defence, and decided that the Italian courts lacked jurisdiction.

According to the Court, the reasons for its decision have to be found in the peculiarity of the act under examination. The *Marcović and others* case concerns an issue of state responsibility deduced from an act of war, in particular from aerial war, considered among modalities of war conduct. According to the Court, the choice of the modalities of waging war has to be included among governmental acts. The said acts constitute an expression of a political function, attributable to an organ – the government – by the Constitution. In the accomplishment of the political function a 'situation of protected interest', which aims to give or to deny a specific content to acts, cannot be provided for. And, with respect to the said acts, no judge can have the power of challenging the way in which the political function is carried out.

As for international humanitarian law, and in particular the First Additional Protocol of the Geneva Conventions (Arts. 35(2), 48, 49, 51, 52, 57) and the European Convention on Human Rights (Arts. 2 and 15), the Court of Cassation emphasised that, although the above-mentioned provisions concerning the conduct of hostilities are aimed at protecting civilians in case of attacks, they are not self-executing and only govern relations among states.

Internal laws executing the international treaties in question do not provide for, either expressly or implicitly, any rule allowing alleged victims to claim damages directly deriving from a violation of international law by a contracting state before the latter state's tribunals.

The rationale of this contention is that it would not in any case be possible to recognise the judicial protection of individual interests against activities performed in connection with a state's political function.

GIOVANNI CARLO BRUNO[289]

☛ Extradition request for *Michael Seifert*

After the life imprisonment sentence handed down by the Military Court of Appeal of Verona on 18 October 2001 in proceedings *in absentia* against Michael Seifert,[290] the Italian government formally requested the extradition from Canada of the convicted war criminal. Since 1951 Seifert had been living in Vancouver where, on 1 May 2002, he had been arrested following the issuance of a warrant of arrest by the British Columbia Supreme Court. That same court, on 3 May 2002, denied Seifert bail on the grounds that releasing him would 'undermine the public's confidence in the administration of justice', given the serious nature of the crimes he was accused of in Italy. But on 24 May 2002, after a bail review in the British Columbia Court of Appeal, Seifert was released from custody until his extradition hearing, which began on 15 October 2002 and had yet to be completed by the end of the year.

ROSA DINUZZI

Pending

☛ International Criminal Court: draft-bills concerning the implementation of the Rome Statute in the Italian legal system (Chamber of Deputies, No. 2724; Senate, No. 1638)

Italy ratified the Statute establishing the International Criminal Court on 26 July 1999 pursuant to Law No. 232 of 12 July 1999, by which the Italian Parliament authorised the Statute's ratification. The Law also contains an implementing order (so-called 'ordine d'esecuzione': 'Full and entire execution shall be given to the Statute ...') that became effective when the Statute of the ICC entered into force on 1 July 2002. The implementing order places the Statute in the Italian legal system, because the Act by which the Parliament authorised the ratification and the implementation of a treaty implies that the treaty, once in force, becomes part of Italian law.

However, Law No. 232/1999 does not contain provisions to implement non-self-executing norms of the Statute in the Italian legal system. In fact, the original bill authorising the ratification also delegated authority to the government to adapt Italian criminal legislation, but this authorisation was removed from the final text, in order to speed up the bill's approval.[291] Law No. 232/1999 consequently seems to be insufficient to fully implement the Statute of the ICC in the Italian legal system.

---

289. Giovanni Carlo Bruno is a researcher at the Institute for International Legal Studies, National Research Council (CNR), Rome.

290. 4 *YIHL* (2001) pp. 566-568.

In 2002 two draft-bills containing provisions for further implementation were introduced in the Parliament, both on the initiative of parliamentary members. The first was presented in the Chamber of Deputies on 9 May (draft-bill No. 2724) and submitted for first consideration to the Justice Committee, acting in a reporting capacity, on 17 June. The second was introduced in the Senate on 24 July 2002, and submitted to the Justice Committee on 4 December (draft-bill No. 1638).[292]

The texts of the two bills are almost identical. Taking into account the complementary character of the Court's jurisdiction, it intends: 1) to introduce into domestic legislation, when necessary, the crimes within the competence of the Court, so that Italian tribunals can exercise their primary jurisdiction; and 2) to make the national legal system consistent with Italy's obligation to cooperate fully with the Court, whenever it exercises its own jurisdiction. The text is thus conceived as a comprehensive 'international criminal code', addressing a number of substantive and procedural issues. This raises, of course, some problems of coordination with the existing Italian criminal law.

As for crimes within the competence of the Court – genocide, crimes against humanity and war crimes – the draft-bills restate their definitions by reference to Articles 5-8 of the Rome Statute and to the 'Elements of Crimes' approved by the Assembly of States Parties in September 2002.[293] This approach is certainly correct from the point of view of the relationship between international law and national legislation. Moreover, as regards some crimes the draft-bill would, once approved, fill some gaps in domestic legislation, such as the long-lasting lack of specific provisions on the crime of torture.[294] The same is true for some 'new' crimes against humanity mentioned in Article 7 of the Rome Statute, including sexual slavery, forced pregnancy, enforced sterilisation and other form of sexual violence, or the enforced disappearance of persons. It is generally recognised that these provisions of the Statute do not reflect customary international rules, and could not be considered, by consequence, as part of Italian law under Article 10 of the Constitution.[295] Rather, it can be said that these crimes have been made subject to Italian legislation by virtue of Law No. 232/199 implementing the Statute in the Italian legal system. However, relevant sanctions are lacking.

As for other crimes already subject to existing Italian laws (i.e., war crimes and crimes against humanity as defined by relevant treaties to which Italy is a party), it should be recalled that their legal definitions, deriving from other international treaties, may differ

---

291. V. Della Fina, 'Law No. 232 of 12 July 1999 Concerning the Statute Establishing the International Criminal Court', 3 *YIHL* (2000) pp. 535 et seq.

292. This procedure is admissible in the Italian legal system; it is a task of the Presidency Offices of the Chamber of Deputies and the Senate to provide coordination at later stages, in order to avoid duplication.

293. Assembly of States Parties to the Rome Statute of the International Criminal Court, First Session, New York, 3-10 September 2002, *Official Records*, UN Doc. ICC-ASP/1/3, Part II, pp. 108 et seq.

294. It has to be said, however, that various draft-bills were presented in the Parliament in 2002, in order to introduce the crime of torture into the Italian Penal Code: see *infra*, V. Della Fina, 'Bill concerning the introduction of the crime of torture (Senate, No. 1608, presented on 16 July 2002)'.

295. This is why we cannot completely share the view that 'the subject-matter jurisdiction of the ICC is already part of Italian Law, because Art. 10 of the Italian Constitution provides for automatic implementation of customary international law into domestic law' (fact-sheet on the Statute's implementation by Italy available on the website of the International Criminal Court: <http://www.icc-cpi. int/statesparties>).

from those found in the Statute. In this context, both draft-bills concerning the Statute's implementation establish that their own provisions on war crimes and on crimes against humanity have to be considered as a *lex specialis*, prevailing over any other applicable rules. That is in compliance with the practice generally followed by the Italian judicial organs when applying rules aimed at implementing a treaty in the domestic legal system. It may be asked, however, if this criterion would be sufficient to solve all the problems that might arise, for example, from the existence of different legal definitions of a given crime, or from possible conflicts of competence between judicial organs.[296]

Some coordination with norms already in force is also needed for the implementation of Part 9 of the Rome Statute, concerning international cooperation and judicial assistance to the Court. On this point, the provisions of the draft-bills are conceived as a set of complementary rules in respect of the existing legislation on criminal proceedings, and take into account that a complete reform of the Procedural Penal Code is currently under consideration by the Italian government. This is why many members of Parliament seem to be favourable to the postponement of the adoption of the Statute's implementing legislation until the said reform is approved.

Another critical point concerns the compatibility of Article 27 of the Statute, which affirms the irrelevance of official capacity, with the constitutional immunities guaranteed to ministers, members of Parliament and judges of the Constitutional Court. No problems should arise regarding the extradition of nationals, as this is allowed in Italy when requested under international agreements (Art. 26 of the Constitution), and specifically for the crime of genocide (Constitutional Act No. 1/1967).

Finally, the two draft-bills also aim to establish a national procedure for the nomination of candidates for election as judges to the International Criminal Court, in accordance with Article 36 of the Statute. Lack of such provisions, however, did not impede Italy from nominating Mr Mauro Politi as a candidate in the first election; he was actually elected in the first resumed session of the Assembly of States Parties held in February 2003.[297]

ORNELLA FERRAJOLO[298]

☞ Bill No. 1608, presented on 16 July 2002 in the Senate: introduction of the crime of torture into Italian law

The Italian Constitution contains some relevant provisions concerning the prohibition of torture. In particular, Article 13(4) provides for the punishment of any physical and moral violence against persons deprived of their liberty; Article 27(3) establishes that penalties cannot be contrary to the principles of humanity and must aim at the reeducation of the

---

296. According to the draft-bills, judicial competence in respect of war crimes, which generally rests with military tribunals, would be attributed in the case of war crimes envisaged in the ICC Statute to the ordinary jurisdiction ('Corte d'assise').

297. The composition of the Court is as follows: P. Kirsch (President, Canada); A. Kuenyehia (First Vice President, Ghana); E. Odio Benito (Second Vice President, Costa Rica); R. Blattmann (Bolivia); M.H. Clark (Ireland); F.D. Diarra (Mali); A. Fulford (United Kingdom); K.T. Hudson-Phillips (Trinidad and Tobago); C. Jorda (France); H.P. Kaul (Germany); E. Kourula (Finland); G.M. Pikis (Cyprus); N. Pillay (South Africa); M. Politi (Italy); T.N. Slade (Samoa); S. Song (Republic of Korea); S. de Figueiredo Steiner (Brazil); A. Usacka (Latvia).

298. Ornella Ferrajolo is a senior researcher at the Institute for International Legal Studies, National Research Council (CNR), Rome.

convict; and finally, Article 28 concerns the penal, civil and administrative liability of public officials who violate individual constitutional rights.

Notwithstanding these provisions, unlike in other European countries, the Italian Penal Code does not contain the crime of torture. It only provides for the imprisonment for 30 months of a public officer who subjects to 'severe measures not allowed by the law' a person under arrest or under his custody (Art. 608) and for the offences of strokes and wounds (Art. 582).

Nevertheless, Italy has ratified the Convention against Torture and Other Cruel, Inhuman or Degrading Treatment or Punishment, adopted by the General Assembly of the United Nations on 10 December 1984,[299] which contains a definition of torture (Art. 1) and requests each State Party to ensure that all acts of torture are offences under its criminal law (Art. 4).

Italy has also ratified the International Covenant on Civil and Political Rights, which contains a provision on the prohibition of torture (Art. 7),[300] and the Statute of the International Criminal Court, which includes torture among the grave breaches and crimes against humanity and gives a definition of the term (Art. 7(2)(e)).[301] At the regional level, Italy is a party to the European Convention on Human Rights, which provides for an absolute prohibition of torture (Arts. 3 and 15), and of the European Convention for the Prevention of Torture and Inhuman or Degrading Treatment or Punishment of 1987.[302]

In order to implement its international obligations,[303] seven bills on the introduction of the crime of torture in the Penal Code were presented before the Italian Parliament.[304] In particular, bill No. 1608, presented before the Senate on 16 July 2002, enlarges the definition of torture contained in the UN Convention by including among the authors of this crime private citizens (Art. 1). In compliance with Articles 3 and 10 of the UN Torture Convention, the bill prohibits the expulsion, return or extradition of a person to a state where there are substantial grounds for believing that he would be subjected to torture (Art. 2) and envisages special training on human rights for public officers and other persons who may be involved in the custody, interrogation or treatment of any individual subjected to any form of arrest, detention or imprisonment (Art. 3). Besides, the bill establishes that any statement made as a result of torture shall not be invoked as evidence in any proceeding, except against a person accused of torture (Art. 4); it also excludes diplomatic immunities for foreigners subjected to a criminal proceeding or condemned for the crime of torture in another country or by an international tribunal (Art. 5).

---

299. Italy ratified the Convention with Law No. 498 of 3 November 1988.

300. Italy ratified the Covenant with Law No. 881 of 25 October 1977. It is noteworthy that Art. 5 of the 1948 Universal Declaration of Human Rights also prohibits torture.

301. Italy ratified the Statute of the Court with Law No. 232, of 12 July 1999. According to Art. 7 (2)(e), 'Torture means the intentional infliction of severe pain or suffering, whether physical or mental, upon a person in the custody or under the control of the accused; except that torture shall not include pain or suffering arising only from, inherent in or incidental to, lawful sanctions.'

302. Italy ratified both the Conventions respectively with Laws No. 848 of 4 August 1955 and No. 7 of 2 January 1989.

303. The UN Committee against torture has made some critical observations on the Italian criminal law during the examination of the first and second Italian Reports, requesting to introduce the crime of torture in the Penal Code, see CAT/C/9/Add. 9; CAT/C/SR. 109 and 110/Add.; CAT/C/25/Add. 4 and CAT/C/SR. 214 at Add. 1.

304. Six bills were presented during this legislature (XIV). For the texts see <http://www.senato.it/ app./ricerca/sddl.asp>.

Finally, it should be noted that the bill, in compliance with the international obligations, recognises the right to fair and adequate compensation for the victims of torture and establishes a Committee for the rehabilitation of the victims with the task of managing a special Fund (Art. 6).

VALENTINA DELLA FINA

JAPAN[305]

Peacekeeping
☛ Sending of forces to UNTAET, March 2002

Pursuant to the International Peace Cooperation Law (Law No. 79 of 19 June 1992), in March 2002 the government dispatched 680 persons from engineering units of the Self-Defense Force (SDF) to the United Nations Transitional Administration in East Timor (UNTAET). Their mission was to provide rear support such as road and bridge repair work. In addition, ten SDF personnel were sent as the staff of UNTAET's military component headquarters. The mission of contingent and headquarters staff continued after the replacement of UNTAET with the United Nations Mission of Support in East Timor (UNMISET) on 20 May, and was extended to 20 August 2003.

Counter-terrorism
☛ Anti-Terrorism Specific Measures Law, Law No. 113 of 2 November 2001

Based on the Anti-Terrorism Specific Measures Law (Law No. 113 of 2 November 2001), on 19 November the Cabinet approved the extension of rear-area logistic support of the SDF for the US-led military campaign in Afghanistan until 19 May 2003. Three destroyers, two supply ships and a transport ship can be dispatched to the Indian Ocean. On 16 December, a destroyer equipped with the advanced Aegis missile-system was sent to provide security for the SDF's refueling of US and British ships in the Arabian Sea. The Aegis ship also serves as a flagship among SDF vessels.

Emergency Law
☛ Bill Concerning Measures to Ensure National Independence and Security in a Situation of Armed Attack

The subject of this draft emergency legislation, which outlines how to respond to a military attack against Japan, was a longtime taboo under the Constitution. Believing that the legislation was indispensable and should be prepared in time of peace, the government first submitted a set of emergency response bills, including the Law Concerning Measures to Ensure National Independence and Security in a Situation of Armed Attack, to the 154th ordinary session of the Diet in April 2002.

During Diet discussions on the bills, the definitions of 'military attack situation', 'when such a situation is feared', and 'when such a situation is predicted' as stated in the bills

---

305. Information and commentaries provided by Professor Hideyuki Kasutani, Professor of International Law, Setsunan University, Japan, and Professor Seigo Iwamoto, Professor of International Law, Suzuka International University, Japan.

proved too vague. Moreover, the bills failed to address the new type of threats, such as terrorist attacks and spy ship incidents, and lacked provisions for civil defense to protect the people. The bills were severely critised, and finally did not pass.

Cases

☞ The victims of Japanese germ warfare case, Tokyo District Court, Decision of 26 August 2002

A Tokyo court acknowledged for the first time that Japan had engaged in biological warfare during World War II, killing thousands of Chinese victims. 'Koji Iwata, the Presiding Judge, said that the Imperial Army had contravened the Geneva and Hague Conventions by spreading plague, typhoid and other diseases in Ouzhou, Ningbo and Changde between 1940 and 1942. "The evidence shows that Japanese troops, including Unit 731 [the secret experimental unit] and others, used bacteriological weapons on the orders of the imperial army's headquarters and that many local residents died."' 'But the court rejected the claims of 180 mostly Chinese plaintiffs for about $16,355 each in compensation on the ground that all reparation issues had been settled inter-governmentally by international peace treaties.'[306]

Unit 731, a special division of the Japanese Army, located in Manchuria, in Japanese-occupied northern China, was the largest and most notorious of the Japanese experimental facilities. Chinese, Korean and Russian POWs and civilians were experimented on, including by vivisection, and exposed to bubonic plague, cholera, typhus, dysentery and anthrax, *inter alia*. The persons involved in Unit 731's operation have never been brought to trial, because at the end of the war the Japanese officers involved were given immunity from prosecution in return for the US receiving the experimental data. The information is locked away in US military archives.

With neither Japan nor the US admitting to the cover up, in June 1996 the Association to Reveal the Historical Fact of Germ Warfare by the Japanese Armed Forces was established by an alliance of Japanese and Chinese human rights activists, doctors and lawyers. In 1997, a civil suit was filed by 108 survivors and family members in Tokyo against the Japanese government, for 10 million yen (£53,000 per victim).[307]

Ongoing Cases

☞ The *former Allied POWs* case, Tokyo High Court, Judgement of 27 March 2002[308]

On 11 March 2002, the Tokyo High Court rejected an appeal by seven former Allied POWs, who sought $22,000 each in compensation from the Japanese government for abuses they suffered in former Japanese Imperial Army camps. The plaintiffs claimed compensation on the ground that some members of the Japanese military forced plaintiffs to perform slave labour and abused them in the camps during World War II in breach of Arti-

---

306. J. Watts, 'Japan guilty of germ warfare against thousands of Chinese: Tokyo judges rule that second world war atrocities did take place but reject claims for compensation', *The Guardian*, 27 August 2002.

307. A. McNaught, '"Sorry is not enough", relatives of more than 300,000 Chinese killed in secret germ warfare are taking the Japanese government to court', *The Times* (London), 1 February 2002.

308. As to the Judgement of 26 November 1998 by the Tokyo District Court, see 2 *YIHL* (1999) pp. 389-390. See also *The Dutch former POWs* case, 4 *YIHL* (2001) p. 571.

cle 3 of the 1907 Hague Convention respecting the Laws and Customs of War on Land and international customary law.

The plaintiffs had appealed a November 1998 ruling by the Tokyo District Court, in which they had demanded $22,000 (16.2 million yen) each in damages on the basis of the Hague Convention, which stipulates that a national government has a responsibility to compensate for its inhumane actions during a war.

However, the Tokyo High Court, Justice Kengo Ishii presiding, dismissed their claim by upholding a lower court ruling that damages for war victims should be provided collectively for their respective countries through peace treaty negotiations.

'The Hague Convention does not stipulate on individual rights to make claims against an aggressor nation. You cannot demand the Japanese government pay damages even if you had been forced to do hard labor and physically abused by the Japanese army'.

In October 2002, the Tokyo High Court also rejected an identical compensation suit filed by eight Dutch former POWs seeking compensation for the mistreatment they suffered.

HIDEYUKI KASUTANI AND SEIGO IWAMOTO

Pending
☞ Bills to improve Japan's ability to respond to a military attack

Three pending bills aim to improve Japan's ability to respond to a military attack. One bill stipulates the creation of a government task force with authority over government ministries and local bodies in the event of an attack on Japan. It would also provide for more cooperation with the 35,000 US military personnel stationed in Japan and sets out punishments for those who fail to comply with instructions to provide supplies such as food and fuel to the military in the event of an attack.[309]

JORDAN

Military Penal Code
☞ Military Penal Code, adopted 28 May 2002. Entered into force 17 July 2002, published in the *Official Journal* No. 4568, 16 June 2002

On 17 July 2002 the government of Jordan enacted a new Military Penal Code, which was adopted on 28 May 2002. One chapter of the Military Penal Code deals with war crimes and their criminalisation. The basis for the definition of these crimes is the 1949 Geneva Conventions and the 1977 Additional Protocols.[310]

International Criminal Court
☞ Law of 16 April 2002 establishing Jordan's compliance with the Rome Statute

---

309. 'Japan looks to boost military power', CNN Online News Report, 17 April 2002.

310. UN Press Release, GA/L/3208, 2 October 2002, at <http://www.un.org/News/Press/docs/2002/gal3208.doc.htm>, and ICRC Advisory Service, National Implementation of International Humanitarian Law – Biannual update on national legislation and case-law, July-December 2002. <http://www.icrc.org/Web/eng/siteeng0.nsf/htmlall/5LVLHV/$File/irrc_849_National_Implem.pdf>.

'The law contains three articles: Art. 1 incorporates the full text of the Rome Statute; Art. 2 sets the date of entry into force; and Art. 3 provides the need for the Statute's implementation into national law.'[311]

Implementation
☛ Temporary Law No. 63 for the year 2002, The Law on the National Committee for the Implementation of International Humanitarian Law. Endorsed by the government of Jordan on 20 August 2002 entered into force on 16 October 2002, published in *The Official Gazette of the Hashemite Kingdom of Jordan*, No. 4568, 16 October 2002

'It provides a legal basis for the pre-existing national committee. The Chairman of the Committee is to be appointed by the King and the Jordan Red Crescent is in charge of the secretariat. The members of the Committee are representatives of the following parties: Prime Minister; Ministry of Justice; Ministry of Foreign Affairs; Ministry of the Interior; Ministry of Education; Ministry of Health; Directorate of Military Courts; Public Security Directorate; Directorate of Civil Defence; Jordan University; and the National Assembly. In addition three persons with experience and expertise are to be appointed by the Chairman of the Committee, and the Jordan Red Crescent is represented by its President (as Vice-Chairman of the Committee). The Committee is mandated, *inter alia*: to devise and implement the general policy, strategy, plans and programmes for raising awareness of the principles of international humanitarian law at the national level; to promote, together with the ICRC and the parties concerned, efforts to disseminate the principles of international humanitarian law; to exchange information and experiences with national, Arab, regional and international organisations and commissions concerned with international humanitarian law and strengthen ties with them; to carry out research and studies for the parties concerned, present proposals to them and give them advice; to issue publications on international humanitarian law and the means by which it may be implemented; to adopt, together with the parties concerned, recommendations and reports related to the principles of humanitarian law and its development; and to help improve legislation related to international humanitarian law. An Executive Committee is to be formed to follow up the affairs of the National Committee.' [312]

Education and Training
☛ Round Table on IHL for Judges and Prosecutors, 24-25 September 2002

The ICRC together with the Judicial Institute of Jordan held a round table for judges and prosecutors on 24 and 25 September. The initiator of the meeting was the Jordanian National Commission for the Implementation of International Humanitarian Law.[313] The aim of the round table was to find out whether international humanitarian law could be included in the training of Jordanian judges. The outcome of the round table was a recommendation to include IHL in the training programme for judges and to create a documentation centre for IHL materials.

---

311. Source: CICC Website: North Africa/Middle East/Jordan. <http://www.iccnow.org/country info/northafricamiddleeast/jordan.html>.
312. Source: ICRC Advisory Service, National Implementation of International Humanitarian Law – Biannual update on national legislation and case-law, July-December 2002. <http://www.icrc.org/Web/eng/siteeng0.nsf/htmlall/5LVLHV/$File/irrc_849_National_Implem.pdf>.
313. *ICRC Annual Report 2002*, Jordan. <http://www.icrc.org>.

KAZAKHSTAN[314]

The Emblem

☛ Law No. 268-II of the Republic of Kazakhstan of 14 December 2001, Concerning the Emblem and Distinguishing Sign of Medical Services of the Armed Forces of the Republic of Kazakhstan [Закон Республики Казахстан от 14 декабря 2001 года N 268-II Об эмблеме и отличительном знаке медицинской службы Вооруженных Сил Республики Казахстан] <http://base.zakon.kz/result.asp?uid=FD2F2FA6-6690-43C4-911E-7D6B965DEA13&language=rus&vid=null&reqsrch=0&type=-1&source=1&class=-1&start_date=&end_date=&number=268-II+&mj_start_date=&mj_end_date=&mj_number=&name=&name_concat=1&text=&text_concat=1&status=all&sort=power>

The Law states that the Republic of Kazakhstan shall use the blazon of a red crescent on a white background as an emblem and distinguishing sign of the medical services of the Armed Forces of the Republic of Kazakhstan (Art. 1).

Implementation

☛ Resolution No. 1794 of the Government of the Republic of Kazakhstan of 1 December 2000 Concerning the Creation of the Inter-Departmental Commission on International Humanitarian Law (with amendments introduced by the Republic of Kazakhstan Government's Resolution No. 645 of 14 June 2002) <http://base.zakon.kz/doc/?uid=449CA0B4-200C-4C37-97A2-9B47F0C58C13&language=rus&doc_id=1020812&language=rus&forprint>[315]

The Inter-Departmental Commission on International Humanitarian Law consists of representatives of the Ministries of Justice, Foreign Affairs, Economics, Education, Interior, Culture, Environment, Defence, Civil Defence and Public Health as well as from the Public Prosecutor's Office, Supreme Court, the Commission on the Family and Women and academic circles. The objectives of the Committee are to promote, review and evaluate the compliance of national legislation with provisions of humanitarian law treaties, to draw up proposals for national implementation of international humanitarian law, and to coordinate activities of the bodies involved in the implementation, *inter alia*.

Education and Training

☛ Introduction of IHL into the state curriculum

In 2002 Kazakhstan included IHL in its state standards for study of international law.[316]

DANA ZHANDAYEVA

---

314. Information and commentaries by Dana Zhandayeva, LL.M., independent researcher, Almaty, Kazakhstan.

315. The contact information of the Commission is: Ministry of Justice, 45 Prospect Pobedy St., 473000, Astana, Kazakhstan, Tel.: 7-3172-39-12-13.

316. For more information on the ICRC's activities in Central Asia, including Kazakhstan, including the promotion of the teaching of IHL, see <http://www.icrc.org/Web/Eng/siteeng0.nsf/htmlall/E38FE767BB309C16C1256D43002CD9BE/$File/icrc_ar_02_tashkent.pdf?OpenElement> and <http://www.icrc.org/web/eng/siteeng0.nsf/iwpList182/2E7CAD8419C44B8AC1256B74005C49AD>.

(REPUBLIC OF) KOREA
Truth and Reconciliation
☛ Establishment of Presidential Truth Commission on Suspicious Deaths, 17 October 2000 [The website of the Commission is at <http://truthfinder.go.kr/eng/index.htm>]

On 17 October 2000, President Kim Dae-Jung inaugurated the Presidential Truth Commission on Suspicious Deaths[317] to investigate the deaths of citizens opposed to past authoritarian regimes in South Korea. Earlier that year, on 15 January, the enactment of the Special Act to Find the Truth on Suspicious Deaths created the commission and established its mandate to investigate deaths upon the request of petitioners, to report its findings and recommendations to the president, and to identify human rights perpetrators for prosecution. The commission received 80 petitions by the deadline of 2 January 2001 and had until 20 April 2002 to complete its work.

The commission was composed of nine members, led by law professor Yang Seung-Kyu, Kim Hyoung-Tae, Mun Deok-Hyoung, Lee Suk-Young, Ahn Byung-Ook, Pak Un-Jong, Lee Yoon-Seong, Lee Won-Young and Baik Seung-Hun.

Implementation and Dissemination
☛ Presidential Decree No. 15602 establishing the 'Korean National Committee for International Humanitarian Law'
☛ Decision No. 42 of the Ministry of Foreign Affairs and Trade, 17 October 2002

'The Ministry of Foreign Affairs and Trade is in charge of the Chairmanship and Secretariat of the Committee. The functioning of the Committee is defined in Decision No. 42 of the Ministry of Foreign Affairs and Trade of 17 October 2002. Members of the Committee are representatives of the Ministries of: Foreign Affairs, Education and Human Resources, Justice and National Defence, the Cultural Properties Administration, the Korean Red Cross Society and academic circles. The Commission's mandate includes the following tasks: to monitor and coordinate the dissemination and implementation of international humanitarian law; to advise on matters relating to ratification of humanitarian law treaties; to review national legislation and propose measures to implement the rules of international humanitarian law; to promote international humanitarian law in educational institutions, armed forces and among the general public; and to cooperate and exchange information with national committees of other countries, the ICRC and international organisations.' [318]

LITHUANIA[319]
Cases[320]
☛ *Pranas Preikšaitis and others* case, Judgement of Vilnius Regional Court, 4 June 2002

---

317. Presidential Truth Commission on Suspicious Deaths. <http://truthfinder.go.kr/eng/index.htm>.
318. ICRC Advisory Service, National Implementation of International Humanitarian Law – Biannual update on national legislation and case-law, July-December 2002. <http://www.icrc.org/Web/eng/siteeng0.nsf/htmlall/5LVLHV/$File/irrc_849_National_Implem.pdf>.
319. Information and commentaries by Rytis Satkauskas, Universidad de Madrid, Spain.
320. According to the information provided by the Prosecutor's General Office, more than 130

Charges for the genocide of the Lithuanian population pursuant to the provisions of the Law on the Responsibility for the Genocide of the Population of Lithuania of 9 April 1992[321] and Article 71 of the Lithuanian Penal Code of 1998, as amended in 2000, were brought against three former members of the security forces – Pranas Preikšaitis, 72, Ignas Tamošiūnas, 73, and Algirdas Lapinskas, 78 – for the killing of members of the Lithuanian resistance, the so-called 'forest brothers', in the post-war period.

Amendment of Article 71 of the Lithuanian Penal Code of 1998 broadened the definition of genocide provided for in the 1948 Genocide Convention by introducing the category of 'social and political group'.[322] A similar definition of genocide remained in the New Penal Code, adopted in 2000.[323]

The accused Preikšaitis moved to dismiss on the ground that his participation in the security forces was a necessity because he refused to become a member of the guerilla fighters in 1948 and he knew another person who was killed after such a refusal. Besides, he agreed with the policy of the Ministry of Social Security because the 'forest brothers' were killing innocent people. All the accused were found not guilty, as their participation in alleged executions was not proven.

☛ *Bronius Viater and Kazys Kregždė* case, Judgement of Vilnius Regional Court, 4 June 2002[324]

The proceedings were instituted against two former guerilla fighters, who, after being arrested by the State Security of the Lithuanian Soviet Socialist Republic in 1951, agreed to collaborate. Working undercover for the State Security, they continued fighting as part of the resistance, and during this period participated in the execution of several resistance fighters.

The Court stressed that the objective of the activities of the Ministry of State Security was the elimination of a defined political group – those resisting the occupational regime. Therefore, the activities of the accused qualified as genocide of this political group on the basis of Article 71 of the 1998 Penal Code. The charges were based, *inter alia*, on the reports of the accused and the correspondence of the State Security. However, the case was discontinued by the decision of 4 June 2002 due to the poor health of both accused.

---

criminal proceedings relating to genocide and/or war crimes have been instituted by the public prosecutors in Lithuania since the restoration of independence in 1990. However, only 13 cases have reached the courts: five persons were sentenced, four were acquitted, while the remaining cases were discontinued because of the death or illness of the accused or due to a lack of evidence. By the end of 2002, preliminary questioning was being conducted in approximately 20 war crimes and/or genocide cases. The Prosecutor General's Office also issued on 18 September 2001 a list of 76 entries of persons whose rehabilitation for the crimes of genocide and the killings of defenseless people was cancelled by the Supreme Court.

321. Text in Lithuanian on <http://www3.lrs.lt/cgi-bin/getfmt?C1=w&C2=2006>.

322. Text of Art. 71 'Genocide' of the former Penal Code of the Republic of Lithuania, as amended on 1998, is available in the Report of Lithuania under International Convention on the Elimination of all Forms of Racial Discrimination, UN Doc. CERD/C/369/Add.2 (13 February 2001). <http://www.hri.ca/fortherecord2002/documentation/tbodies/cerd-c-369-add2.htm>.

323. 4 *YIHL* (2001) pp. 578-579. An English translation of Art. 99 'Genocide' and Art. 100 'Crimes Against Humanity' is available at <http://www.preventgenocide.org/lt/LRBK99.htm>.

324. *Lietuvos Rytas*, 5 June 2002.

Despite the lack of precise definition by the legislator, participation in the oppressive unit alone was not considered as participation in the genocide of the population.

☛ *Vincas Misiunas* case, Judgement of Vilnius Regional Court, 30 December 2002[325]

Charges for the deportation of a Lithuanian 'kulak' family in 1951 were brought in this case against a former officer of the Ministry of State Security of the puppet government of the Lithuanian SSR.

The court found that by executing orders the accused had participated in the deportation of a Lithuanian countryman into Siberia and therefore committed a war crime – 'Deportation of the civilian population of the occupied country' – as described in Article 334 of the 1998 Penal Code. The court dismissed the argument that the accused was forced to execute the orders. A penalty of five years' imprisonment was imposed as well as confiscation of property.

RYTIS SATKAUSKAS

MALTA

International Criminal Court
☛ Act to implement the Rome Statute. Passed by Parliament in November 2002

In January 2002, the Ministry of Justice announced its commitment to ratify the Rome Statute. In order to implement the Rome Statute, Parliament passed an ICC Act in November 2002. Malta ratified on 29 November 2002, becoming the 85th State Party. The Minister for Justice, in exercising his powers granted in the ICC Act, must now issue legislation to bring the Act into force. The Office of the Attorney-General had previously concluded a study on the implications of ratification.[326]

MEXICO[327]
Children
☛ Ratification of the Optional Protocol to the Convention on the Rights of the Child on the involvement of children in armed conflicts, 15 March 2002. Published in the *Official Gazette of the Federation*, 3 May 2002, Vol. DLXXXIV, No. 2, Section 1, pp. 8-12

Truth and Reconciliation
☛ Appointment of a Special Prosecutor to investigate the crimes of the past, 4 January 2002

On 4 January 2002, pursuant to recommendation 26/2001 issued on 27 November 2001 by the National Commission for Human Rights (NCHR), the Attorney-General (AG) desig-

---

325. *Atgimimas*, 24-30 January 2003.
326. CICC Website: Europe/CIS: Malta. <http://www.iccnow.org/countryinfo/europecis/malta.html>.
327. Information and commentaries by José A. Guevara, Researcher at the Human Rights Programme of the Iberoamericana University and Lecturer in International Human Rights Law at the Law Faculty of the Iberoamericana University.

nated Ignacio Carrillo Prieto as Special Prosecutor for the Attention of Actions that Might Constitute Federal Crimes Committed Either Directly or Indirectly by Public Servants Against Persons Related to Social or Political Movements of the Past (SPO). The SPO was created in lieu of and with the intention of addressing the demands for a 'Truth Commission' for Mexico, and to consolidate the existing 'democratic institutions' created for the protection of human rights, like the NCHR, and for the investigation of crimes, like the AG (Ministerio Público).

Following the Presidential Accord ordering the creation of the SPO, the Mexican transitional policy to address the crimes of the past seeks to reflect the three traditional elements: justice, truth and reparations. The justice requirement was addressed through the establishment and granting of powers to the SPO to investigate. The need to establish the truth about past crimes was addressed through the creation of a committee composed of five members of civil society named by the AG, who will support the investigations of the SPO with historical, sociological, political and legal elements. The official information that this committee will need to perform its duties will be concentrated in the General Archive of the Nation (AGN). The Presidential Accord establishes the duty of all organs of the executive branch to surrender all existing files created before 1985 to the AGN, and obliges the agencies of government that might have been involved in the crimes of the past or that possess relevant information related thereto to allow all citizens and authorities involved in the investigation of such crimes, i.e., NCHR and the SPO, to freely access the files created after 1985. Finally, the Presidential Accord ordered the Minister of the Interior to create an interdisciplinary committee to determine the procedure by means of which the victims of the crimes of the past will be allowed to receive 'just administrative reparation'. This committee should be composed of public servants of the Executive Branch and by experts in reparations, serving as advisors. Up to 31 December 2002 the SPO did not present charges against any accused before the judiciary, and there was no existing or available public information relating to the reparations interdisciplinary committee.

War Crimes and Crimes Against Humanity
☞ Ratification of the Convention on the Non-Applicability of Statutory Limitations to War Crimes and Crimes Against Humanity and interpretative declaration. Published in *Official Gazette of the Federation*, 22 April 2002, Vol. DLXXXIII, Section 1, pp. 10-13

On 15 March 2002, Mexico deposited its instrument of ratification of the Convention on the Non-Applicability of Statutory Limitations to War Crimes and Crimes Against Humanity before the Secretary-General of the United Nations. Mexico signed the Convention on 3 July 1969. The Convention was published in the *Official Gazette of the Federation* on 22 April 2002, which included an interpretative declaration for Article 1, which provides:

'In conformity with Article 14 of the United Mexican States' Political Constitution, the Mexican government at the moment of ratifying the Convention on the Non-Applicability of Statutory Limitations to War Crimes and Crimes Against Humanity approved by the General Assembly of the United Nations on November 26, 1968, understands that Mexico will not apply statutory limitations to the crimes recognised in the Convention exclusively when committed after the entry in force of the Convention to Mexico.'

It would appear, however, that this interpretative declaration is null and void due to the fact that it infringes the object and purpose of the Convention by limiting the application of its

Article I, which provides: 'No statutory limitation shall apply to the following crimes, irrespective of the date of their commission.'

Enforced Disappearances
☞ Ratification of the Inter-American Convention on Forced Disappearance of Persons and interpretative declaration and reservation, 4 May 2001. Published in the *Official Gazette of the Federation*, 18 January 2002, Vol. DLXXX, No. 14, p. 4

Mexico's ratification instrument was deposited before the Secretary-General of the Organisation of American States on 9 April 2002 with an interpretative declaration and a reservation. The former provides as follows:

'In conformity with Article 14 of the United Mexican States' Political Constitution, the Mexican government at the moment of ratifying the Inter-American Convention on Forced Disappearance of Persons, adopted in the City of Belem, Brazil on June 9, 1994, understands that the norms of such Convention will be applied to facts that constitute forced disappearance of persons, when ordered, executed or committed after the entry in force of the Convention to Mexico.'

The reservation presented by Mexico provided as follows:

'The government of the United Mexican States in ratifying the Inter-American Convention on Forced Disappearance of Persons, adopted in the City of Belem, Brazil on June 9, 1994, applies an express reservation to article IX thereto, in conformity with the Political Constitution that recognises the war privilege (fuero de guerra), when the military official commits a crime during its service. The fuero de guerra is not considered as a special jurisdiction in the sense of the Convention and in conformity with article 14 of the Mexican Constitution no person could be deprived from life, liberty or property, possessions or rights but through a trial followed before a previously established tribunal, in which the due process of law is guaranteed and applicable law was previously adopted to the perpetration of the acts that might constitute a crime.'

On 19 April 2002, the government of the Federal District of Mexico City (GDF) initiated a constitutional proceeding before the Supreme Court of Justice of the Nation against the Executive and the Senate in order to nullify the interpretative declaration presented by Mexico to the Inter-American Convention. For the GDF, the declaration affects preexisting norms of the Criminal Code for the Federal District that recognises the non-applicability of statutory limitations for the crime of forced disappearance of persons. Up till 31 December 2002, no decision had been rendered by the Supreme Court.

International Criminal Court
☞ Constitutional Amendment to enable ratification of the Rome Statute of the ICC

On 6 December 2001, the Executive requested that the Senate amend Article 21 of the Constitution in order to enable the ratification of the Rome Statute.

During the first period of the 2002 parliamentary sessions (which began on 15 March and ended on 30 April), the Senate did not discuss the Executive's request. As a reprisal, the Executive sent the Rome Statute to the Senate on 28 August, just before the second ordinary period of sessions started, and on 15 December 2002 the Senate discussed and approved an amendment to Article 21 of the Constitution, which was intended to emulate the French constitutional amendment. Notwithstanding, the Senate approved the following formulation: 'The Executive Branch might recognise the jurisdiction of the International Criminal Court, with the authorisation of the Senate, on a case-by-case basis.' The Senate based its amendment on an Analysis (Dictamen) prepared by the Senate's Committees of Constitutional Affairs; Foreign Relations; International Organisations; Justice; Human Rights; and Legislative Studies, which recognised that various countries amended their constitutions to enable the ratification of the Rome Statute. The Dictamen mentioned France, Colombia, Germany and Brazil. It is important to point out that Brazil did not amend its Constitution.

It remains for the Mexican Constitutional amendment to be approved by the Chamber of Deputies, and following that, to obtain the approval of the majority of the legislature of the federated states. Up till 31 December 2002, the Chamber of Deputies had not included the matter in its agenda. If the constitutional amendment is approved and the Rome Statute ratified, Mexico could still be in violation of various international obligations. First, if a request for cooperation is denied by the Mexican state for reasons other than those allowed by Chapter IX of the Rome Statute but based exclusively on the joint decision of the Senate and the Executive, the duty to cooperate fully with the ICC as stipulated in the Rome Statute might be breached. Secondly, following the Vienna Convention on the Law of Treaties, Mexico could not deny cooperation with the ICC by alleging the insufficiency of its national law. In particular, the Executive and the Senate will not be able to refuse to surrender a person to the ICC unless such refusal is in conformity with the Rome Statute. On the other hand, such a joint decision of the Executive and the Senate might result in impunity if it impedes Mexico from complying with its duty to investigate, prosecute and punish genocide, crimes against humanity and war crimes. Furthermore, other international human rights and humanitarian law treaties might be breached if the Mexican judiciary does not investigate and seriously punish those responsible for international crimes, i.e., violations of the International Covenant on Civil and Political Rights, the Inter-American Convention on Human Rights, the 1948 Genocide Convention, the UN Torture Convention, the Inter-American Convention on Forced Disappearance of Persons, the four Geneva Conventions of 1949 and their Protocol I, among others.

Mexican NGOs and individuals have criticised the Constitutional Amendment of Article 21 approved by the Senate alleging, *inter alia*, that the Senate will be performing judicial functions when analysing whether national prosecutions are taken with the intention of shielding an individual from his or her criminal responsibility or whether there is an 'unjustified delay in the proceedings' or such proceedings 'were not or are not being conducted independently or impartially' or 'were or are being conducted in a manner which, in the circumstances, is inconsistent with an intent to bring the person concerned to justice'.

International Committee of the Red Cross
☛ Host Country Agreements for the Establishment of a Regional Delegation of the International Committee of the Red Cross [Acuerdo entre los Estados Unidos Mexicanos y el Comité Internacional de la Cruz Roja relativo al establecimiento en México de una Delegación Regional del Comité], 3 April 2002, published in the *Official Gazette of the Federation*, 24 May 2002 <http://tratados.sre.gob.mx/>

On 3 April 2002, the Mexican Senate approved the Host Country Agreement for the Establishment of a Regional Delegation of the International Committee of the Red Cross.

Education and Training
☛ A Human Rights Manual for Mexican Navy Personnel, published as Accord 036 of the Minister of the Navy, Marco Antonio Peyrot González, in the *Official Gazette of the Federation*, 6 May 2002, Vol. DLXXXIV, No. 3, Section 1, pp. 7-22

The Accord recognises that the Navy is in constant contact with the civilian population as part of its duty to prevent and repress crimes within its maritime jurisdiction. The Manual will guarantee that all officials from the Navy will understand and apply human rights and international humanitarian law norms in their missions and everyday operations.

Cases
☛ Spanish application for the extradition of Ricardo Miguel Cavallo

On 2 February 2001, the Mexican Ministry of Foreign Affairs (MFA) issued an Accord authorising the extradition of Ricardo Cavallo to Spain, to face charges there of genocide, terrorism and torture. Spanish magistrate Baltasar Garzón Real indicted Cavallo on 1 September 2000 for genocide, torture and terrorism, for crimes allegedly committed during Argentina's 'dirty war' of the 1970s and 1980s.

Following this Accord, Cavallo requested the protection of the *amparo* before the Judiciary. Judge Juan García Orozco (Judge García), from the Amparo Tribunal 1st B specialised in Criminal Matters in Mexico City was responsible for the case. Cavallo argued that the Accord breached 42 constitutional rights, among others that the crimes of genocide, terrorism and torture could not be judged as they were subject to the applicability of statutes of limitations. Cavallo also alleged that the Spanish universal jurisdiction norms were invalid under Mexican and the applicable international laws.

After an analysis of the arguments of the MFA, the Attorney-General and Cavallo, Judge García, on 25 March 2002, determined that the statutes of limitations, as recognised by the Mexican and Spanish applicable laws during the period when the crimes were committed (1976-1983), covered neither genocide nor terrorism. However, Judge García found that the crime of torture benefited from such statutory limitations under the Mexican and Spanish laws applicable during such period of time, and therefore the new extradition accord that should be issued by the MFA should not authorise Spanish tribunals to investigate or prosecute the tortures attributed to Cavallo. On the other hand, Judge García ruled that the Spanish universal jurisdiction norms are valid under Mexican and international law. For him, the extraterritoriality principle applies to certain crimes like genocide due to the fact that such crimes affect the international community as a whole, and it is in the interest of such community that such crimes are investigated and those responsible are punished by any state. For Judge García, a state that investigates, prosecutes and punishes is acting on behalf of the international community as a whole. Further, Spain and Mexico and even Argentina are obliged to amend their internal legislation to enable their courts either to extradite or to prosecute the accused for genocide, terrorism and torture.

Following this ruling, the MFA, the AG and Cavallo asked for a review proceeding before the higher Federal Tribunals, on 12, 15 and 16 April 2002, respectively. Both the MFA and the AG alleged that the crime of torture was not subject to statutory limitations in conformity with the applicable Mexican law. Cavallo argued that his constitutional rights were violated on 22 separate grounds with the issuance of the extradition Accord. Among them, Cavallo included arguments that the crimes of genocide and terrorism were prescribed and that the applicable international treaties had not entered into Mexican law in conformity with the Constitution, because they were not signed personally by the Executive.

The review proceeding will be treated by a Tribunal Colegiado de Circuito and by the Mexican Supreme Court (the latter on the question of the constitutionality of the treaties). Neither Tribunal had issued its ruling by the end of 2002.

José A. Guevara

MOROCCO[328]

'Status Quo' Agreement

☛ In July 2002, after intense negotiations, Morocco and Spain came to an agreement about the island Perejil, 200 m off the Moroccan coast, which earlier that month had been the object of an international dispute between the two countries. The agreement led to the acceptance of the demilitarised status of the island, which it enjoyed prior to the dispute. However, disagreement remained regarding the question whether the island belongs to Spain or Morocco.[329]

Dissemination

☛ General Assembly forming the Moroccan Network of International Humanitarian Law

On 18 March 2002, the constitutive General Assembly of the Moroccan Network of International Humanitarian Law was held in Marrakesh. The first meeting to create the Network had been held on 28 May 2001. The main objectives of the Network are to promote training and education, dissemination, research and implementation of IHL in Morocco; to encourage the introduction of IHL to the non-academic public (the Armed Forces, Ministries, the Red Crescent and civil society); to contribute to a focus on IHL research; to assist the ministries concerned with implementation of IHL; and to facilitate exchanges between the members of the network and networks of the same nature in other countries.

Khadija Elmadmad and Abderrahim Kounda

NAMIBIA

International Criminal Court

☛ Law on ratification of the Rome Statute. Tabled by the Minister of Justice in the National Assembly on 20 June 2002, where it was unanimously adopted[330]

---

328. Information and commentary by Dr Khadija Elmadmad, Professor of Public International Law and English at the University of Casablanca and holder of the Unesco Chair on Migration and Humanitarian Laws at the University of Casablanca and by Dr Abderrahim Kounda, a specialist in International Humanitarian Law at the University of Casablanca.

329. See news reports: 'Spain sends in the gunboats', 13 July 2002, and 'Stand-off tinged with farce on Parsley Island', 14 July 2002. <http://www.telegraph.co.uk>, and 'Morocco-Spain row over island flares anew', 24 September 2002. <http://www.aljazeerah.info>.

330. CICC/Africa: Namibia. <http://www.iccnow.org/countryinfo/africa/namibia.html>.

International Criminal Court

☛ The ICC Implementation Act [Uitvoeringswet Internationaal Strafhof], Act of 20 June
2002. Entered into force on 1 July 2002, published in *Staatsblad* (Bulletin of Acts and
Orders) (2002) p. 314[332]

The Act contains rules concerning the cooperation between the International Criminal
Court (ICC) and the Netherlands. It does not make punishable any crimes; an International
Crimes Bill to that effect was approved by the Lower House in the last days of December
2002 but had still to be discussed by the Senate as the year closed.

The Act consists of a general part and three specific chapters. The three chapters relate to
the transfer to the ICC of requested persons, cooperation regarding investigation and prosecution and the execution of sentences. Some final paragraphs relate to assistance to the ICC
by the Netherlands as the Host State.

Article 7 of the Act expresses the general rule – in conformity with Article 97 of the ICC
Statute – that, in the case of an existing impediment to compliance with a request from the
ICC, compliance will not be refused without the ICC having been consulted about possible
ways of resolving the matter.

TRANSFERAL OF A REQUESTED PERSON

Transferal on request of a person to the ICC is considered to be a different concept than
extradition; the 1967 Extradition Act is not applicable.

Article 12 of the Act expresses the specialty rule: the transfer of a requested person will
always be subject to the general condition that without the explicit permission of the Minister of Justice of the Netherlands this person will not be prosecuted by the ICC for any other
crime than that for which the request for transfer has been granted, and that in relation to
such a crime he will not be transferred to a third state without the explicit permission of the
Minister of Justice.

Decisions on a request by the ICC for transferal are normally taken in two steps. First,
the District Court of The Hague decides on the permissibility of the transfer. Only if the
Court has deemed the transfer permissible may the Minister of Justice grant the request. If
the requested person has in front of an examining magistrate agreed with the requested
transferal, however, the Public Prosecutor may order the transfer to be directly executed
without the involvement of the District Court, provided that the Minister of Justice is kept
informed. In the latter case, the specialty rule is not applicable.

The Act provides for the possibility of the preliminary arrest and detention of a person, in
anticipation of a formal request from the ICC for his transferal. The preliminary detention
can be ordered by a public prosecutor for a period of not more than three days. Subsequent
detention can only be ordered by an examining magistrate. After the formal request from
the ICC has been received, further detention can be ordered by the District Court of The
Hague.

---

331. Information and commentaries by Professor Emeritus Nico Keijzer, Professor of Criminal
Law, University of Tilburg; Advocate-General at the Supreme Court of the Netherlands.
332. The Act applies to the whole Kingdom, including the Netherlands Antilles and Aruba.

The Hague District Court has to decide whether the requested transfer is allowable. At the Court's hearing, which normally is in public (unless the requested person prefers a hearing *in camera*), the requested person may give his views. If he has no lawyer, the Court will appoint one for his assistance. If the person brought before the Court appears not to be the person referred to in the request of the ICC, the Court will, if consultation with the ICC does not solve the matter, declare the transfer not allowable. Otherwise, the transfer will be declared allowable. Circumstances that traditionally would inhibit extradition, such as the lack of double incrimination, the political character of the crime or statutory limitation, do not preclude the Court from deciding that the requested transfer is allowable. The District Court's decision is not subject to appeal.

If the District Court has deemed the requested transfer allowable and the Minister of Justice has decided that the request shall be granted, the requested person will be transferred to the ICC. If at that moment the requested person is being prosecuted before a Dutch court for the same facts, this prosecution will be discontinued. If he is serving a sentence imposed by a Dutch court, the Minister of Justice can decide that the requested person will nevertheless be transferred right away and that the period of his being at the disposal of the ICC will be deducted from his time to be served.

OTHER FORMS OF COOPERATION

The Act prescribes that requests for assistance in relation to investigations or prosecutions, as meant in Article 93 of the ICC Statute, shall as much as possible be complied with, including requests for 'any other type of assistance which is not prohibited by the law of the requested State' (Art. 93(1)(l) of the Statute).

Although the Dutch Code of Criminal Procedure does not provide for examination of witnesses or experts by means of videoconference link, the Act enables evidence to be given to the ICC by such means.

Requested application of coercive measures, such as interrogation of persons against their will or seizure of documents, will be executed under the supervision of an examining magistrate; in such cases, the requested person has the right to be assisted by a lawyer. In other cases, requests are complied with under the supervision of a public prosecutor. Seizure of documents or other pieces of evidence can be contested before the District Court by interested persons.

EXECUTION OF PENALTIES

On request of the ICC, its sentences can be executed in the Netherlands.

Penalties of imprisonment, imposed by the ICC in relation to core crimes as mentioned in Article 5 of its Statute, cannot be pardoned; requests for remission will be forwarded to the ICC. Penalties imposed in relation to obstruction, as mentioned in Article 70(1) of the Statute, can be pardoned after consultation with the ICC.

In relation to the core crimes, the articles of the Dutch criminal code that provide for early release after two-third of the sentence has been served, are not applicable.

Article 71 of the Act provides for confidential communication between a person serving a sentence imposed by the ICC and the ICC.

The Act also contains provisions for the execution of fines and confiscation orders.

ASSISTANCE BY THE NETHERLANDS AS THE HOST STATE

Persons requested by the ICC will be transferred through the territory of the Netherlands by the Dutch authorities.

Until 15 days after their release by the ICC, such persons cannot be arrested or prosecuted in the Netherlands for offences committed before their arrival in the Netherlands.

Dutch law does not apply to deprivations of liberty of persons on the premises which have been made available to the ICC by the Netherlands.

Peacekeeping
☛ The Srebrenica report of the Netherlands Institute for War Documentation: *Srebrenica, a 'safe' area – Reconstruction, background, consequences and analyses of the fall of a safe area* [Srebrenica, een 'veilig' gebied – Reconstructie, achtergronden, gevolgen en analyses van de val van een Safe Area], 10 April 2002 [the Dutch and English versions of the report are available on <http://www.Srebrenica.nl>]

In September 1996, the Minister for Foreign Affairs and the Minister of Defence instructed the Netherlands Institute for War Documentation to investigate events before, during and after the fall of Srebrenica in Bosnia and Herzegovina during July 1995.

On 10 April 2002, this Institute presented its report: 'Srebrenica, a "safe" area – Reconstruction, background, consequences and analyses of the fall of a safe area' ('Srebrenica, een "veilig" gebied – Reconstructie, achtergronden, gevolgen en analyses van de val van een Safe Area').

The report is over 3,000 pages long. The following is an abbreviated summary of its main conclusions.

The promise made by UN General Morillon in 1993 to the people of Srebrenica that they were under the protection of the UN and would not be abandoned produced a *fait accompli*, which the Security Council turned into the decision to label Srebrenica as a 'safe area', a new and undefined concept. Nothing was clear about it except that it ruled out a mandate for a genuine military defence of the area or its population. The presence of UN troops was intended rather to be a warning by the international community not to attack ('to deter by presence'). The proclamation of the zone as a safe area created an illusion of security for the population.

Humanitarian motivation, coupled with the ambition to improve Dutch credibility and prestige in the world, led the Netherlands to offer to dispatch its Air Brigade for this role. In practice, 'Dutchbat' was dispatched:
— on a mission with a very unclear mandate;
— to a zone described as a 'safe area' although there was no clear definition of what that meant;
— to keep the peace where there was no peace;
— without obtaining in-depth information from their Canadian predecessors in the enclave;
— without adequate training for this specific task in those specific circumstances;
— virtually without military and political intelligence work to gauge the political and military intentions of the warring parties;
— with misplaced confidence in the readiness to deploy air strikes if problems arose; and
— without any clear strategy for leaving.
The supposed demilitarisation in the Srebrenica enclave was virtually a dead letter. The Bosnian Army (ABiH) followed a deliberate strategy of using limited military actions to tie

up a relatively large part of the manpower of the Bosnian Serbian army (VRS), to prevent it from heading in full force for the main area around Sarajevo. This was also done from the Srebrenica enclave. ABiH troops had no qualms about breaking all the rules in skirmishes with the VRS. They provoked fire by the Bosnian Serbs and then sought cover with a Dutchbat unit, which then ran the risk of being caught between two fires. On the other hand, the VRS blockade policy was a significant contributor to a frustrating and demotivating situation. As a result, the strength of Dutchbat had been depleted by one third by the beginning of July 1995 and there was a serious shortage of supplies, from food to diesel oil for the vehicles. The last two battalions in particular became mentally and physically exhausted in the course of their mission.

From a military perspective, Dutchbat had few grounds for mounting a counterattack on its own initiative, because:

— active defence of the enclave by military means was not in accordance with the mandate, the UN policy (the maintenance of impartiality) or the rules of engagement;
— the instruction ('to deter by presence') was for military reaction to be above all reticent;
— the military balance of power was such that, without outside support, Dutchbat would have been defenceless in a serious confrontation;
— as a result of the 'stranglehold strategy' (the blockade policy of the VRS), Dutchbat was no longer a fully operational battalion in terms of manpower, supplies or morale;
— military means could only be deployed if the safety of the battalion was in danger and if it was the target of direct fire – the 'smoking gun' requirement – which the VRS deliberately avoided;
— the circumstances, such as the failure of air support to materialise and the death of a Dutchbat member through an action by a Bosnian Muslim, hardly encouraged the mood for a counterattack on its own initiative.

The expectation on the part of Dutchbat and the Sector North East in Tuzla that help would come from outside on the morning of 11 July 1995 in the form of massive air strikes was misguided. The UNPROFOR command had completely ruled out air strikes but was also extremely reticent about lighter support from the air in the form of close air support. It thereby crushed the Dutchbat illusion, and the enclave became an easy target for the VRS. On the Dutch side, the potential for the deployment of air support was overestimated.

The tragic nadir of the fall of Srebrenica was the mass killing of thousands of Muslim men by Bosnian Serbian units. A large number of the men were members of the ABiH who had attempted to break out of the enclave to Tuzla with some of the male population during the night of 11 July. The decision to break out and thus to give up further resistance was taken entirely outside the UN and UNPROFOR. The flight to Tuzla and the mass executions which followed took place entirely out of view of Dutchbat. Suggestions that the Muslims were killed 'under the eyes of Dutchbat' are unfounded in relation to this mass slaughter.

It was precisely in the treatment of the many prisoners that the Bosnian Serbs lost control of themselves. In some places the Muslims were slaughtered like beasts. They included men who had been separated from the women outside the Dutch compound in Potočari during the transfer of the population to Tuzla. That mass murder was the intention is also clear from the fact that, after the prisoners had been taken, no measures were taken to see whether there were 'war criminals' among them, no prisoner-of-war facilities were found, no food or drink were organised, identity cards were destroyed, and no distinction was made between combatants and non-combatants.

A number of Muslim men had already been killed by the Bosnian Serbs in Potočari in a local act of revenge. The battalion command received limited information about this, but what was reported was alarming enough: two sightings of nine or ten corpses and indications that assaults were taking place during interrogations in a house near the compound. Much more happened in Potočari than what the members of Dutchbat saw. But not all of what they saw was reported in those days. Communication was a complete failure at the time. One reason for this is the great stress to which the members of Dutchbat were exposed, their narrowing of focus, and their shutting themselves off from the world around them. In some cases too, concern about their own survival meant more to them than the fate of the Muslim men who had made things so difficult for Dutchbat.

One week after the presentation of this report, and seven years after the fall of the Srebrenica enclave, the Dutch cabinet decided to collectively resign from office in response. After the general elections which followed, a parliamentary inquiry was held in order to shed more light on who – on the Dutch side – had been politically responsible for the disaster. At the end of 2002, the parliamentary commission had not yet finished its report of this inquiry.

Cases
☛ *Milošević* v. *ICTY and The State of the Netherlands*, The Hague District Court, 26 February 2002 [Milošević tegen (1) Joegoslaviëtribunaal en (2) de Staat, Rechtbank Den Haag (Voorzieningenrechter) 26 februari 2002, LJN-nummer: AD9602 Zaaknummer KG 02/105]

The plaintiff Slobodan Milošević, former president of the FRY, detained in the detention centre made available by the Netherlands to the ICTY, brought interim injunction proceedings (*kort geding*) against the ICTY and the State of the Netherlands before the President of the District Court (*arrondissementsrechtbank*) of The Hague. He sought an order directed against the ICTY and against the State of the Netherlands, to enter into consultation with each other, in order to end the violation by the Tribunal of the plaintiff's right to correspond and consult out of hearing of other persons with the lawyers representing him in a complaint lodged with the European Court of Human Rights.

In support of his claim, the plaintiff argued that by preventing him from confidentially communicating with his lawyers, the Tribunal was in violation of Article 6, Sections 3(b) and 3(c) of the European Convention for the Protection of Human Rights and Fundamental Freedoms (ECHR) and Article 14 of the International Covenant on Civil and Political Rights, and in violation of Article 21(4) of the Tribunal's own Statute. Under Articles 1 and 13 ECHR and Article VI of the Headquarters Agreement between the Netherlands and the United Nations of 29 July 1994, the Netherlands is obliged, in the plaintiff's view, to counteract any violations of human rights on its territory, including those by the Tribunal.

The Registrar of the Tribunal, in a letter to the Court, invoked the Tribunal's immunity. The Court recognised that immunity on the basis of Articles 105(1) of the UN Charter, 30 (1) of the ICTY Statute, IV and VIII of the Headquarters Agreement, and II of the Convention on the Privileges and Immunities of the United Nations of 13 February 1946.

The Court held that, the Kingdom of the Netherlands having lawfully transferred its jurisdiction over ICTY detainees to the ICTY, Dutch law is not applicable. Support for this holding was found in Articles VI and XX of the Headquarters Agreement, 17 of the Act implementing the Statute of the ICTY into Dutch law,[333] and 9(2) and 29(1) of the Statute itself. From Article 103 of the UN Charter it follows that regulations given by the Security Council prevail over any other regulations. Accordingly, the state of the Netherlands has nothing to do with deprivation of liberty by the Tribunal; the same goes for the Dutch courts.

Moreover, the Court took into account that Rules 84-88 of the Rules governing the detention of persons awaiting trial or appeal before the Tribunal or otherwise detained on the authority of the Tribunal include a complaint handling procedure. The plaintiff had not submitted a complaint under this procedure against the alleged violations by the Tribunal of his right of free communication with his lawyer. He still had a possibility to do so. Besides, it had been brought forward by the state that, according to the Registrar, the plaintiff's lawyer will have access to the plaintiff and will be able to communicate with him confidentially.

As a consequence of all this, the Court ruled that it had no jurisdiction in the matter.

NICO KEIJZER

NEW ZEALAND[334]

Nuclear Materials

☞ New Zealand Nuclear Free Zone Extension Bill 2000, No. 32-1 <http://www.knowl edge-basket.co.nz/tkbgp/welcome.html>

The Bill, awaiting its Second Reading in Parliament at the time of the 2001 report,[335] was defeated on 29 May 2002.[336] Had it become law, it would have extended the existing New Zealand Nuclear Free Zone to include New Zealand's exclusive economic zone and would have prohibited the passage within that area of nuclear-propelled ships or ships carrying radioactive waste or reprocessed nuclear fuel.

Opposition to the Bill was based on the view that it would lead New Zealand to breach its international law obligations, in particular, the right of innocent passage as provided for in the 1982 Law of the Sea Convention. In response, the Green Party (which introduced the Bill and was the only Party to vote for its passage) argued that the right of navigation in the Law of the Sea Convention was a qualified right which gives states the right to qualify the freedom for navigational purposes. Other members were not persuaded, however, and the Bill was defeated by 108 votes to seven.

Pending

☞ Counter-Terrorism Bill 2002, No. 27-1 <http://www.knowledge-basket.co.nz/tkbgp/ welcome.html>

The aim of the Bill is to amend and supplement the Suppression of Terrorism Act 2002 which in turn aims at implementing New Zealand's obligations under the International Con-

---

333. Act of 21 April 1994. See 1 *YIHL* (1998) p. 482.
334. Information and commentaries by Treasa Dunworth, Lecturer in Law, Faculty of Law, University of Auckland.
335. See 4 *YIHL* (2001) p. 599.
336. 601 *Parliamentary Debates* (29 May 2002) pp.16683-16700

vention on the Suppression of Terrorist Bombings, the International Convention on the Suppression of the Financing of Terrorism and Security Council Resolution 1373 of 28 September 2001.

The 2002 Bill, which provides for new terrorism-related offences and penalties and a range of investigative measures designed to combat terrorism, was subjected to intense public criticism both as to its substantive terms and the process by which it was enacted. Clause 12 creates a number of new offences, two of which are of interest in the present context. The first offence relates to the importation, acquisition, possession or control of radioactive material. If the Bill is enacted, this will become section 13D of the Act. The second offence is unlawful dealings with 'nuclear material' (as defined in Art. 1(a) of the 1980 Convention on the Physical Protection of Nuclear Material), which would become section 13C. The Bill also provides for extraterritorial jurisdiction over these offences by virtue of its Clauses 13 and 14.

The Bill was introduced in Parliament on 17 December 2002 and was to have its first reading in 2003.

TREASA DUNWORTH

NICARAGUA

The Emblem

☛ Law No. 418 on the protection and use of the name and emblem of the Red Cross [Ley No 418 de Protección y Uso del Nombre y del Emblema de la Cruz Roja], adopted on 26 February 2002, promulgated on 15 March 2002, published in *La Gaceta: Diario Oficial*, No. 57, 22 March 2002, pp. 1995-1998, entered into force on the day of its publication

'It sets out in particular the different authorised uses of the red cross emblem (use as a protective device by the medical and religious services of the armed forces, civilian hospitals, medical units and religious personnel attached to them, and the Nicaraguan Red Cross; use as an indicative device by this Society and by other National Red Cross or Red Crescent Societies; and use by the International Red Cross organisations) and provides for the punishment of misuse, including perfidious use in time of war, according to the applicable law. The red crescent emblem, the distinctive signals for the identification of medical units or transports, and all other emblems or signs that may be adopted in future international treaties and used for purposes similar to the red cross or red crescent are also covered by this law.'[337]

NORWAY

Universal Criminal Jurisdiction

☛ Complaint against Russian President Vladimir Putin

---

337. ICRC Advisory Service, National Implementation of International Humanitarian Law – Biannual update on national legislation and case-law, January-June 2002. <http://www.icrc.org/Web/eng/siteeng0.nsf/html/5FLE9G?OpenDocument>.

The Norwegian Penal Code recognises the right to bring charges in Norway for serious crimes committed by foreigners abroad. In October 2002 seven people of Chechen origin living in Norway reported Russian President Putin to the police for having violated the Geneva Conventions of 1949 and the 1984 Torture Convention. The crimes allegedly committed were the use of heavy weaponry against the civilian population, torture and rape of women and men, among others. The complaint asserted that Norway has an obligation to prosecute serious crimes like torture regardless of the nationality of the accused or of the place where the crime was committed. The complaint included a request to the Public Prosecutor to exercise universal jurisdiction and prosecute Mr Putin on the basis of paragraph 12(4) of the Penal Code, including the provisions of the law concerning serious bodily harm.[338]

Pending
☛ Inclusion of torture in the new Penal Code

At the early 'høring' stage (where affected bodies and organisations have an opportunity to comment on draft legislation before it becomes a proposition) of the legislation process which will lead to a new Norwegian Penal Code, the Ministry of Justice gave its analysis of the need to include torture as a separate crime. The present Penal code does not include a specific clause on torture. Crimes constituting torture have been prosecuted under other penal provisions, such as those criminalizing bodily harm, use of force or threat or misuse of official capacity.

Norway has been criticised by the UN Torture Committee for not having acted in accordance with Article 4(1) of the Torture Convention, which states that 'Each State Party shall ensure that all acts of torture are offences under criminal law. The same shall apply to an attempt to commit torture and to an act by any person which constitutes complicity or participation in torture.' The Norwegian view has been that other provisions of the Penal Code cover the crime of torture without a specific mention of the crime, and that this is still an acceptable interpretation of the duty as laid down in the Torture Convention. According to the Ministry, it would be difficult to foresee any acts of torture that would not already be punishable under existing provisions. Moreover, the same approach to the crime of torture has been applied in the other Nordic countries. Nevertheless, as the starting point is that the use of torture is unacceptable and as there has been international criticism of the present situation, the Norwegian Ministry of Justice decided to submit its analysis, including a proposed definition based on the Torture Convention, for further reflection by the 'høringsinstansene' (the organisations submitting comments).[339]

MARIA NYBONDAS

☛ Inclusion of the ICC crimes in the Penal Code

'In April 2002, the Permanent Commission for Penal Law submitted its reports and a proposal to include the crimes in the Rome Statute into the Norwegian Penal Code. … The

---

338. 'Politianmeldelse av folkerettsbrudd begått av russisk militært personell i Tsjetsjenia', Oslo, 31 October 2002. <http://www.tsjetsjenia.no/anmeldelse.htm>.

339. See Høring – ny straffelov, Norwegian Ministry of Justice. <http://www.odin.dep.no/jd/norsk/aktuelt/hoeringssaker/paa_hoering/012101-080026/index-dok000-b-n-a.html>.

need for legislative enactments or amendments was described in the ratification bill in order to ensure compliance with the obligations envisaged under the Statute, as well as to enable Norwegian authorities to provide voluntary assistance to the Court. Thus, implementation legislation was deemed necessary in the field of international cooperation and judicial assistance, and with regard to enforcement of sentences of imprisonment. Under consideration are legislative enactments similar to those pertaining to cooperation with the international criminal tribunals for the former Yugoslavia and Rwanda. (…) Irrespective of the need for legislative enactments referred to above, the Rome Statute will also be considered closely in the context of future reviews of Norwegian criminal legislation, i.e., particular relevance to crimes and general principles of criminal law in the Statute.'[340]

OCCUPIED PALESTINIAN TERRITORIES[341]

The Peace Process

☛ Development of a Performance-Based Roadmap to a Permanent Two-State Solution to the Israeli-Palestinian Conflict, 30 April 2003[342] <http://www.state.gov/r/pa/prs/ps/2003/20062pf.htm>

In 2002 close to no Israeli-Palestinian contacts were witnessed on both the diplomatic and operational levels. The year also witnessed the worst record of human rights atrocities in the Occupied Palestinian Territories (OPTs) since the Israeli-Palestinian negotiation process was inaugurated in 1991 and the Palestinian National Authority (PNA) was established in 1993.

With the failure of the Israeli and Palestinian authorities to reach agreement on any of the issues at the core of the Israeli-Palestinian conflict, namely the status of Jerusalem; the right of Palestinian refugees to return; borders; statehood; and the Israeli colonies in the OPTs, including Jerusalem, – together referred to as 'final status negotiations' issues' – the level of violence in the OPTs rose to unprecedented levels. The Israeli Army's invasion and occupation of all West Bank Palestinian towns, villages and refugee camps since the beginning of 2002 had, by the end of the year, turned into effective reoccupation and control by the Israeli occupation army of the entire West Bank and much of the Gaza Strip, including areas hitherto under the authority of the PNA. This occupation brought with it an increase in the death toll amongst Palestinian civilians. Israelis, including civilians, were also targets of increased violence by Palestinians, both inside and outside of the OPTs.

During 2002 a quartet, composed of representatives of the UN and the governments of the US, UK and Russia, developed a 'Road Map for Peace in the Middle East' as part of their efforts to revive the Israeli-Palestinian negotiation process. The contents of the Road Map, which is not a treaty of any sort but simply a performance-based list of sequential steps the Israeli and Palestinian authorities could take, with the backing of the 'quartet'

---

340. CICC/Europe/CIS: Norway: <http://www.iccnow.org/countryinfo/europecis/norway.html>.

341. Information and commentaries by Dr Mustafa Mari, Professor of Laws, Institute of Law, Bir Zeit University, Bir Zeit, Palestine. For the report on Israel, see *supra* pp. 526 et seq.

342. Released by the Office of the Spokesman of the US State Department on 30 April 2003, Press Statement # 2003/451. The document was developed in 2002, but its release by the US was conditioned on the creation of the position of a Prime Minister for the PNA, and the swearing in of the first Palestinian Prime Minister.

members, was, however, not officially released during 2002 although it circulated widely on an informal basis.

The Road Map was largely based on a speech the President of the US delivered on 24 June 2002, in which he conditioned any support for the resumption of Israeli-Palestinian negotiations on Palestinian reform, including a change in the leadership of the PNA. Although the Palestinian people elected their president in 1996, the selection of a Prime Minister was made, under Israeli and US pressure, without any recourse to the voters.[343]

There was no explicit reference to any provisions of international law in the Road Map, and its implementation and monitoring were not to be entrusted to any international organisation or state, including the UN. The Road Map was based on the premise that the parties should reach a negotiated settlement but it did not stipulate that the outcome should be in conformity with international law dictates.[344]

Principles of Distinction and Prohibition of Indiscriminate Attacks and Disproportionate Force
☛ UNSC Resolution No. 1405, dated 19 April 2002, respecting the establishment of a fact-finding commission to investigate events which took place in the Jenin Refugee Camp, in the northern part of the West Bank <http://www.un.org/Docs/scres/2002/sc2002.htm>

Starting in February 2002, the Israeli Army invaded and reoccupied all major towns in the West Bank and entered and carried out attacks in much of the Gaza Strip. Among the bloodiest incursions by the Israeli Army were those in the Jenin Refugee Camp and Nablus, which occurred in early 2002.

On 3 April 2002, the Israeli Army started an offensive in the Jenin Refugee Camp, which lasted until 18 April. Media and other eyewitnesses reported heavy, disproportionate and indiscriminate fire by the army during the onslaught, which resulted in the killing of several dozen Palestinians. More than half of them were civilians, including people with disabilities, women, elderly persons and medical personnel. The incursion also involved the total or partial destruction of whole neighbourhoods of the camp: the army used bulldozers to level entire camp blocks, thus leaving almost a third of the camp's refugees homeless.

International personalities and human rights groups who visited the camp following the withdrawal of Israeli troops on 18 April supported the claims of Palestinian officials that the army had committed war crimes in the camp. Amongst the first to visit the camp was the United Nations Special Coordinator for the Middle East Peace Process, Mr Terje Roed-Larsen, who stated that the camp 'is totally destroyed; it is like an earthquake; we have

---

343. The US and Israel explicitly demanded that the PNA replace its elected President, Mr Yasser Arafat. When the PNA refused, the US accepted an alternative plan, by which much of Mr Arafat's powers have been transferred to an appointed Prime Minister, a position which did not exist in the Palestinian political-constitutional system until the Palestinian Legislative Council adopted relevant amendments to the Basic Law on 18 March 2003.

344. See 'Roadmap Fails Rights Test', Human Rights Watch, 8 May 2003, and 'The "Roadmap": Repeating Oslo's Human Rights Mistakes', Human Rights Watch, 8 May 2003. On the role of international law, and principle generally, in the Palestinian – Israeli negotiation processes, see 'The Negotiation Process: The lack of a human rights component', 10 *Palestine-Israel Journal of Politics, Economics and Culture* (2003) pp. 5-16.

expert people here who have been in war zones and earthquakes and they say they have never seen anything like it'.[345]

On 19 April 2002, the UN Security Council unanimously adopted Resolution 1405 (2002), in which it welcomed the initiative the Secretary-General of the UN had taken to develop accurate information regarding the events in the Jenin Refugee Camp. The establishment of a UN Fact-Finding Commission was followed by the appointment of Mr Martti Ahtisaari, former President of Finland, as its head. [346]

Israel expressed numerous reservations respecting the composition and proposed role of the Commission. However, according to William L. Nash, a retired US Army Major General and one of the advisors appointed to the Commission: 'Israel's need for clarification turned to obstruction and then to backlog.' Although Mr Ahtisaari tried to answer Israeli queries and concerns, Israel was not willing to cooperate with the Commission, and as Nash concluded, 'it soon became clear that the Israelis were fundamentally hostile to the very concept of finding out what had happened in Jenin'.[347]

On 1 May 2002, the UN Secretary-General wrote to the President of the UN Security Council notifying him of his intention to disband the Fact-Finding Commission, due to the lack of Israeli government commitment to cooperate with it.[348] On 3 May the UN Secretary-General announced, in a letter he sent to the President of the Security Council, his decision to disband the team.[349]

The UN Security Council failed to ensure that its resolution would be respected by the government of Israel, when the Secretary-General informed the Council he would not be able to overcome Israel's objections to the Fact-Finding Commission's composition and assignment. This was both disappointing and sent the wrong message to perpetrators of war crimes.In addition to the above-mentioned indiscriminate attacks, Israeli, Palestinian and international human rights groups, including Amnesty International, Human Rights Watch, B'Tselem, Al-Haq, the Palestinian Center for Human Rights, LAW, and the Palestinian Independent Commission for Citizens' Rights (PICCR), all documented violations by the Israeli Defence Forces of the rights of Palestinian civilians, in some cases possibly amounting to war crimes.[350]

---

345. See *Report of the High Commissioner for Human Rights submitted pursuant to decision 2002/ 103*, UN Doc. E/CN.4/2002/184 (24 April 2002) para. 48.

346. In addition to Mr Ahtisaari, the team included former United Nations High Commissioner for Refugees, Ms Sadako Ogata, and former President of the ICRC, Mr Cornelio Sommaruga. The team was supported by technical experts from various fields. See *Fact-Finding Team: Letter from the Secretary-General to the President of the Security Council*, UN Doc. S/2002/475 (23 April 2002). See also *Jenin Refugee Camp Fact-finding Team: Letter from the Secretary-General to the President of the Security Council*, UN Doc. S/2002/504 (1 May 2002).

347. W.L. Nash, 'My team should have investigated Jenin', *Washington Post*, 12 May 2002, p. B04.

348. *Jenin Refugee Camp Fact-finding Team: Letter from the Secretary-General to the President of the Security Council*, UN Doc. S/2002/504 (1 May 2002).

349. *Letter from the Secretary-General to the President of the Security Council*, UN Doc. S/2002/ 511 (3 May 2002). Following his failure to ensure Israeli compliance with the dictates of the international community, as they are laid down in Security Council Resolution 1405 (2002), the Secretary-General submitted to the UN General Assembly a report, based on General Assembly Resolution ES-10/10 (7 May 2002), which was based on publicly-available information, as opposed to a visit to the area where the event took place, as Resolution 1405 demands. *Report of the Secretary-General prepared pursuant to General Assembly resolution ES-10/10*, UN Doc. A/ES-10/186 (30 July 2002).

350. On this generally see *Israeli Violations of Palestinian Citizen's Rights During 2002* (Palesti-

Palestinian individuals, including those belonging to organisations committed to violent resistance of the Israeli occupation of Palestinian territory, carried out operations targeting Israeli occupation troops in the OPTs. On many occasions such operations were carried out in circumstances suggesting that either civilians were purposefully targeted or due care was not taken to ensure that civilians were not harmed, in violation of international humanitarian law.[351]

The Israeli military's use of lethal, disproportionate force against Palestinian civilians during 2002 resulted in the death of more than 1,000 Palestinians, among them 178 children and 48 women. Additionally, Israel stepped up its wilful killing of Palestinians, by assassinating 82 Palestinians within the Palestinian territories, in clear violation of international humanitarian law rules.[352]

Israeli troops continued the use of Palestinian civilians as human shields during raids in Palestinian towns, villages and UN-administered refugee camps in the West Bank and the Gaza Strip, thus endangering the lives of these civilians.[353]

2002 also witnessed the imposition of ever more severe limitations on the freedom of emergency crews, including ambulance and other medical crews operating in the OPTs, which persisted even after the Israeli major offensive, which began in March 2002, ended.[354] Individuals killed included a British UNRWA employee killed by Israeli troops in the Jenin Refugee Camp, and several Palestinian and foreign medical personnel and journalists.[355]

Israel deported a large number of Palestinians. In May 2002, 13 Palestinians were deported to Cyprus, where they stayed until a number of European countries agreed to receive them. The position of the ICRC with respect to this act by the occupying power was that:

---

nian Independent Commission for Citizens' Rights 2003). <http://www.piccr.org>; *Report of the Secretary-General prepared pursuant to General Assembly resolution ES-10/10*, UN Doc. A/ES-10/186 (30 July 2002); *Human Rights Watch World Report 2003*, pp 459-472; Amnesty International Annual Report Summaries, AI Index: POL 10/008/2003 (Public), News Service No: 114, 28 April 2003; *The heavy price of Israeli incursions*, Amnesty International, AI Index MDE 15/042/2002, April 2002; *Jenin: IDF Military Operations*, Human Rights Watch, May 2003. For more on this visit, see <http://www.lawsociety.org>; <http://www.alhaq.org>; <http://www.piccr.org>; <http://www.hrw.org>; <http://www.amnesty.org>; and <http://www.btselem.org>.

351. On this see *Erased in a Moment: Suicide Bombing Attacks Against Israeli Civilians*, Human Rights Watch, October 2002.

352. *Summary of Annual Report 2003*, Amnesty International. <http://www.amnesty.org>, and *PICCR's Annual Report 2003*. <http://www.piccr.org>. PICCR, however, puts the number at 1,071 Palestinians, and provides a complete list of Palestinians killed and assassinated during the year. See above PICCR report for details.

353. See *Summary of Annual Report 2003*, Amnesty International, available at <http://www.amnesty.org; *Human Rights Watch Annual Report 2003*, p. 461, and *In a Dark Hour: The Use of Civilians During IDF Arrest Operations*, Human Rights Watch, April 2002.

354. For details see, e.g., *Multiple Violations of International Humanitarian Law by the Israeli Defense Forces in the Palestinian Occupied Territories and Measures Taken against International Humanitarian Workers,* Médecins du Monde, 12 April 2002. <http://www.reliefweb.int/w/Rwb.nsf/s/D8EEDA7EEB8F2EEDC1256B9C002E544E>; *PICCR's Annual Report 2003*, and *Human Rights Watch Annual Report 2003.*

355. See *PICCR's Annual Report 2003.*

'Transfers outside occupied territory are illegal and that covers the 13 men.'[356] Curfews were imposed on almost all parts of the OPTs for long periods during the year.[357]

Human rights organisations also documented an unprecedented surge in the number of Palestinians placed under administrative detention by the Israeli army during the re-occupation. By the end of 2002, B'Tselem reported that more than 1,000 Palestinian civilians had been placed in administrative detention.[358] Administrative detention is carried out with total disregard for fair trial guarantees, including the duty to give reasons for such action and provide an opportunity to challenge it before an independent court.

The treatment by the Israeli military occupation authorities of the thousands of Palestinians it detained was a continuing source of concern. Violence and torture during interrogations by Israeli authorities remained common, according to testimonies received by human rights groups from current and ex-detainees and prisoners.[359] Most detainees and prisoners were held outside the OPTs, making communication between them and their families and lawyers almost impossible. The detention of residents of occupied territory elsewhere is not permitted under international humanitarian law.[360]

The destruction of homes and other Palestinian property by the Israeli military authorities intensified during the year. At least 2,000 homes were destroyed by the Israeli occupation authorities in the West Bank and the Gaza Strip during 2002, compared to about 300 during the first 12 months following the beginning of the Intifada in September 2000.[361]

Compensation

☛ Civil Wrongs Law (State Responsibility) (Amendment Number 4), 24 July 2002[362] <http://www.knesset.gov.il/laws/heb/FileD.asp?Type=1&SubNum=2&LawNum= 1862> [in Hebrew]

On 24 July 2002, the Israeli parliament passed an Amendment of the Civil Wrongs Law (State Responsibility), exempting the state of Israel from claims by Palestinian civilians,

---

356. R. Fisk, 'Red Cross attacks exile of Palestinians', *The Independent*, 23 May 2002. <http://news.independent.co.uk/world/middle_east/story.jsp?story=297948>.

357. The UN Committee Against Torture on 23 November 2001 expressed its concern that a 1999 Israeli Supreme Court decision banning certain practices employed by Israeli authorities during the interrogation of Palestinians did not definitely prohibit torture, and that Israel's policies of closure and house demolitions might, in some cases, constitute cruel, inhuman or degrading treatment or punishment. See 'UN: Israel torture ban has loopholes', AP, 23 November 2001. See also *Human Rights Watch Annual Report 2003*, p. 462.

358. According to B'Tselem, Israeli authorities currently hold 1,007 Palestinians under administrative detention, the largest number at any given date since 1991. See *For the First Time Since 1991 – Over 1000 Administrative Detainees*, press statement by B'Tselem, 1 January 2003. <http://www.btselem.org/English/Press_Releases/2003/030102.asp>. For administrative detention updates, check <http://www.btselem.org/English/Administrative_Detention/Statistics.asp>.

359. *Human Rights Watch Annual Report 2003*, p. 464.

360. See *PICCR's Annual Report 2003*.

361. Ibid. See also *Human Rights Watch Annual Report 2003*, p. 462. For 2001 estimates see *Human Rights Watch World Report 2002*, p. 443. For a graphic description of the massive destruction of homes in the Jenin Refugee Camp, see T. Yeheskeli, 'I made them a stadium in the middle of the camp', *Yediot Aharonot*, 31 May 2002.

362. Copy of the approved amendment, in Hebrew, is available online at <http://www.knesset.gov.il/provatelaw/data/2645_3_1.rtf>. Unofficial translation of an earlier draft is available online at <http://www.btselem.org>.

even in cases where it was proven before Israeli courts that occupation army troops, or other Israeli security forces, had acted illegally. The Amendment renders the Israeli army immune from almost all civil suits.[363] Although the Amendment is generally not retroactive, its provisions setting time limits on reporting Israeli occupation force actions and submitting claims for compensation apply, under certain conditions, to events that took place earlier. For example, the provision respecting the bringing of a claim against the Israeli authorities for compensation within two years of the date of the action also applies to actions which took place prior to the Amendment's entry into force, although the two year period starts from the date the law entered into force.

The Amendment used two means to reach this result:

1. It widens the definition of 'military operation' to include acts undertaken in the context of fighting or preventing terrorism, hostile activity and popular uprising or civil unrest.[364] The law as it existed prior to the Amendment already exempted the Israeli authorities from paying compensation for damages resulting from wartime action. This Amendment widens the scope of the exemption by broadening the definition of wartime action to include actions that were not necessarily part thereof, such as stone throwing, flag-raising or other actions which take place when confronting demonstrations or operating patrols in the OPTs.[365]

2. It authorises Israeli courts to reject almost all claims for compensation brought against the Israeli Army, or other Israeli security forces, for the actions of their troops in the West Bank and the Gaza Strip, unless the actions were reported to the proper Israeli authorities within a specified period of time. The law introduces a reduced time limit of 60 days, during which actions which give rise to compensation claims have to be reported to the proper Israeli authorities, and mandates that claims respecting reported incidents should be submitted within a period of two years, down from seven years under the provisions which still apply to similar incidents taking place outside of the OPTs.[366] Short time limits are thus specific to actions taking place in the OPTs. The discriminatory imposition of the shortened time limits causes concern, as it makes clear the intention of the drafters of the law: preventing Palestinian victims from obtaining compensation for damages caused by Israeli army actions in the OPTs.[367]

Education and Training
☛ Memorandum of Understanding Between the Palestinian Ministry of Education and Higher Education and the ICRC, 16 April 2003

---

363. See the press statement four leading Israeli human rights organizations issued following the adoption of this law, entitled *Human Rights Organizations Call Law a Black Stain on Israel's Statutes*, 24 July 2002. <http://www.btselem.org/english/special/020724_compensation.asp>. See also *Human Rights Watch Annual Report 2003*, p. 462. For an analysis of an earlier draft of the law see also M. Mari and M. Pujara, *In Light of the Israeli Draft Law on Denying Compensation to Palestinians: Accountability of the Israeli Occupier for Violations of Palestinian Rights* (Ramallah, Al-Haq 1998).

364. Civil Wrongs (State Responsibility) Law (Amendment number 4), 24 July 2002, Art. 2.

365. For more on this see *Position of Human Rights Organizations on the Proposed Law to Deny Compensation to Persons Injured by Israeli Security Forces in the Occupied Territories*, 26 June 2002. <http://www.btselem.org/English/Special/Compensation_Law/Position_Paper.asp>.

366. Civil Wrongs (State Liability) Law (Amendment number 4), 24 July 2002, Art. 3.

367. For an Israeli perspective on the law, see *supra* at p. 530.

The purpose of the memorandum is to pave the way for the formal introduction of the teaching of international humanitarian law in Palestinian school curricula. With assistance from and cooperation with the ICRC and the Palestinian Red Crescent Society, the Palestinian Authority is organising training opportunities for teachers at selected pilot schools.[368]

Cases

☛ *Jamal Bani Odeh et al.* v. *State of Israel*, SC 5964/92, and *State of Israel* v. *Jamal Bani Odeh*, SC 6051/92, Decision of the High Court, 20 March 2002 Decisions available at <http://www.courts.gov.il> [in Hebrew]

The decision of the Israeli High Court in two appeals relating to compensation sought by Palestinians arising from injury or death caused by the Israeli Army and other security forces actions in the OPTs was rendered almost a decade after the case was submitted to it in order to clarify the position of the judiciary as to the matters the Civil Torts (State Responsibility) (Submission of Claims against the State of Israel by an Enemy State National or by a Conflict Area Resident) Draft Law was designed to address.

The Court distinguished between 'belligerent acts' by the army, in which the state of Israel enjoys immunity from compensation suits, and policing acts, for which no such immunity exists.[369] This finding is contrary to the argument presented by attorneys for the state of Israel, who argued that all actions by the Israeli army in response to the Palestinian Intifada were acts of war, thus denying compensation to victims of such acts.

Mustafa Mari

PANAMA

International Criminal Court

☛ Law to ratify the Rome Statute. Passed by the Legislative Assembly on 7 March 2002[370]

PARAGUAY

International Criminal Court

☛ Presidential Decree No. 19.685 of 10 December 2002

This decree 'created a committee on implementation of the Rome Statute. This committee will consist of three members from the Ministries of Foreign Affairs, Justice and Defence. The committee is required to complete its work by 10 March 2003.'[371]

---

368. *Exploring Humanitarian Law to be introduced in Palestinian Schools*, Palestinian Red Crescent Society, Press Release dated 16 April 2003. <http://www.palestinercs.org/pressreleases/PR160403WBRR.htm>.

369. See 'Court: not all IDF actions in territories are war', *Haaretz*, 21 March 2002.

370. CICC/The Americas: Panama. <http://www.iccnow.org/countryinfo/theamericas/panama.html>.

371. CICC/The Americas: Paraguay. <http://www.iccnow.org/countryinfo/theamericas/paraguay.html>.

PERU

Education and Training

☛ Law No. 27741 setting up education policy in the field of human rights and a national plan for their dissemination and teaching [Ley No 27741 que establece la política educativa en materia de Derechos Humanos y crea un plan nacional para su difusión y enseñanza]. Adopted on 9 May 2002, promulgated on 28 May 2002, entered into force two days later for most of its provisions, published in *El Peruano: Diario Oficial*, 29 May 2002, p. 223774

'It provides for the compulsory teaching of the country's Constitution, human rights and international humanitarian law at all levels of the education system, civilian or military. It asks the executive power to adopt a national plan for the implementation of this provision within 120 days following publication of the law.'[372]

☛ Law on the Ministry of Defence. Adopted on 11 November 2002, promulgated on November 2002

'Article 7(e) stipulates that the duties and responsibilities of the Ministry of Defence include determining the objectives of the armed forces with regard to the defence and promotion of human rights and international humanitarian law.'[373]

Cases

☛ Arrest of *Santiago Martin Rivas*, 19 November 2002

'In a dramatic arrest that could shed light on former president Alberto Fujimori's possible involvement in human rights crimes, Peru captured the head of an army death squad that killed 25 people in two of Peru's most notorious massacres in the early 1990s. Maj. Santiago Martin Rivas was leader of the Grupo Colina death squad. ... He was one of 10 officers sentenced to up to 20 years in prison for the La Cantuta killing ... He was released after Fujimori decreed an amnesty in 1995. But he became a fugitive after Peru's top military tribunal ruled [in 2001] that the sentences should be upheld, and a warrant was issued for his arrest. His detention brings to seven the number of Grupo Colina members behind bars; 14 are still at large.'[374]

Pending

☛ Review of the Penal Code to ensure harmonisation with the ICC Statute and other international treaties

'In mid-September 2002, the government enacted a law, establishing a committee to amend the Penal Code and other penal norms so as to harmonize them' with the Rome Statute and other treaties ratified by Peru. The Committee was composed of representatives of the gov-

---

372. ICRC Advisory Service, National Implementation of International Humanitarian Law – Biannual update on national legislation and case-law, January-June 2002. <http://www.icrc.org/Web/eng/siteeng0.nsf/html/5FLE9G?OpenDocument>.

373. Ibid.

374. <http://www.preventgenocide.org/punish/domestic/index.htm>.

ernment and civil society. In March 2002, the National Committee on International Humanitarian Law started working on cooperation legislation. Proposed legislation was expected to be submitted to the Congress within one year.'[375]

Commission of Inquiry
☞ Report by the Institute for National Remembrance 'Around Jedwabne', 2 November 2002

The 1,500 page report documents the massacres of Jews in and around Jedwabne, Poland, in 1941. As many as 1,600 Jews were killed in Jedwabne. The report revealed that at least 30 organised massacres were carried out by local people rather than by the occupying Nazis. The report said that the Jedwabne pogram was not an isolated incident, and that hundreds of Jews were murdered in similar attacks by Poles in more than 20 towns in the same region.[377]

Cases
☞ *Henryk Mania* case, Konin Regional Court, 8 July 2001
☞ *Henryk Mania* case, Poznan Appeals Court, 5 February 2002

A Polish national, Henryk Mania, 78, of Szczevin in northwestern Poland, was arrested in November 2000 on charges of having assisted in the killing of Jews in a World War II extermination camp. 'It was the first case brought by the government's Institute of National Remembrance',[378] which in June 2000 began investigating archives and documents relating to Communist- and Nazi-era crimes.

He was convicted in July 2001 by the Konin Regional Court and sentenced under Poland's 1944 decree on prosecuting Nazi-era criminals to eight years in prison for participating in acts of genocide at the Chelmno death camp from 8 December 1941 to 7 April 1943. Up to 300,000 persons are believed to have been killed at Chelmno. During the trial, Mania testified that he had been forced to work in the camp and threatened with death if he tried to escape.

Mania appealed the decision, again arguing that he could not be prosecuted for genocide, as he had been forced to work at the camp by the Nazis and was threatened with death if he tried to escape.

On 5 February 2002, the Poznan Court of Appeals rejected his appeal against his conviction and sentence. It upheld the District Court's ruling that Mania could have escaped. 'It also cited evidence that he had shown eagerness to beat victims and take their belongings. "The camp in Chelmno was a hell for people prepared by other people and it was not as a victim that the defendant took part in it," Judge Marian Pogorzelski said.'[379] Judge Pogor-

---

375. CICC/The Americas: Peru. <http://www.iccnow.org/countryinfo/theamericas/peru.html>.
376. <http://www.preventgenocide.org/punish/domestic/index.htm>.
377. Ibid.
378. <http://www.ipn.gov.pl/index_eng.html>.
379. 'Polish court rejects appeal of elderly death camp killer', AP, 5 February 2002.

zelski said the defendant and other Poles who worked at the camp had 'lived on friendly terms with German commanders'.[380]

International Criminal Court
☛ Law No. 111/2002 (ratification Act). Adopted by the Romanian Chamber of Deputies on 26 February 2002, signed by the President on 12 March 2002, published in the *Official Gazette* on 28 March 2002

Following the adoption of the ratification Act, a working group on implementation of the Rome Statute, composed of representatives of the government and civil society, was created to study the definition of crimes. It was due to begin work in Autumn 2002.[381]

Conflict in Chechnya
☛ Report of the Parliamentary Assembly of the Council of Europe/Russian State Duma Joint Working Group on the Conflict in the Chechen Republic, Document 9559, 22 September 2002

This joint report called for greater speed and efficiency by the law enforcement authorities in reviewing and pursuing all complaints about unlawful killing and about missing, maltreated and tortured persons in Chechnya.

'In April, a joint Council of Europe-Russian Duma working group compiled a list of 358 criminal investigations into alleged abuses against civilians. But only about 20 percent of the cases were under active investigation; more than half had been suspended. In "disappearance" cases as many of 79 percent of the investigations had been suspended. The criminal investigations did not include a single case of torture or ill treatment. Very few abuse cases had progressed to the courts. Courts issued guilty verdicts against servicemen in eleven cases, five of which resulted in prison sentences.'[382]

Cases
☛ *Budanov* case, North Caucasian District Military Court, Rostov-on-Don, 31 December 2002

The trial of Colonel Yuri Budanov, a senior Russian officer charged with the murder of the 18 year-old Chechen girl Kheda 'Elza' Kungaeva, and the only high-ranking military official to face trial for abuses in Chechyna, ended on 31 December 2002.

On the night of 26-27 March 2000, Kungaeva was forcibly taken from her parents' house on the orders of Russian military commander Colonel Yuri Budanov, the commander of

---

380. <http://www.preventgenocide.org/punish/domestic/index.htm>.
381. CICC/Europe/CIS: Romania. <http://www.iccnow.org/countryinfo/europecis/romania.html>.
382. *Human Rights Watch World Report 2002*. Russian Federation. <http://www.hrw.org/wr2k2/europe16.html>.

division 13206. She was subsequently interrogated, beaten and raped before finally being strangled.

Following his arrest on 29 March 2000, Budanov admitted strangling Kungaeva, alleging that she had been a Chechen sniper, but said that he did so during a moment of temporary insanity.[383] The case was unusual insofar as the highest echelons of the Russian military publicly acknowledged and condemned Budanov's actions, and initiated an investigation into them. It was the first time since the commencement of military operations in Chechnya by the Russian military that criminal proceedings had been initiated against a Russian serviceman for alleged crimes in the course of duty.[384]

Following the initial investigation into the case by the Russian military, which confirmed that no members of Kungaeva's family were involved in the Chechen conflict, nor was she a sniper, the rape charges were dropped, despite forensic evidence that she had had been subjected to both forced vaginal and anal penetration. Budanov was charged with kidnapping resulting in death (Art. 126 of the Russian Criminal Code), abuse of office accompanied by violence with serious consequences (Art. 286), and murder of an abductee (Art. 105). No charges were brought for the beating and torture. Three of Budanov's subordinates, Sergeant Li-En-Shou, Sergeant Grigoriev and Private Yegorev, were charged with concealing a serious crime, although these were subsequently dropped under the 26 May 2002 amnesty law.[385]

After four psychiatric examinations, Budanov was found to have been temporarily insane. He was acquitted by the Court on 31 December and sent for compulsory psychiatric treatment, on the recommendation of the psychiatric panel.[386]

The appeal by the Chief State Prosecutor Aleksandr Savenko was lodged on 9 January 2003, and on 10 January Kungaeva's parents also filed an appeal.

AVRIL MCDONALD

Pending
☛ Criminal Law Reform

'In June, the State Duma passed a criminal procedure code in its second reading, the last step before adoption. If adopted and signed into law, the code would introduce some long-awaited changes, such as a transfer from the procuracy to the judiciary of the authority to approve arrest and search warrants. However, the draft omitted steps that would help com-

---

383. See 3 *YIHL* (2000) pp. 568-569.

384. 'Russian servicement, killed 18-year-old Chechen girl, stands trial', *Pravda*, 28 February 2001. <http://newsfromrussia.com/chechnya/2001/02/28/2767.html>.

385. Source: 'Accountability for violations of human rights and humanitarian law in Chechnya: the trial of Colonel Yuri Budanov', BOFAX No. 231E, 9 January 2003, Institute for International Law of Peace and Humanitarian Law of the Ruhr-University Bochum. See also *Backgrounder on the case of Kheda Kungaeva, Trial of Yuri Budanov Set for February 28*. Human Rights Watch, <http://www.hrw.org/backgrounder/eca/chech-bck0226.htm>; A. Yurkovsky, 'Mirror of a war', *World Press Review*, 30 January 2002.

386. See Y. Tumanov, 'Chechen murder case colonel acquitted', Caucasus Reporting Service No. 11, 9 January 2003. Institute of War and Peace Reporting. <http://www.iwpr.net/index.pl?archive/cau/cau_200301_161_1_eng.txt; 'Accountability for violations of human rights and humanitarian law in Chechnya: the trial of Colonel Yuri Budanov', BOFAX No. 231E, 9 January 2003; A. Badkhen, 'Russian absolved in Chechen death; insanity verdict worries rights activists', *San Francisco Chronicle*, 1 January 2003.

bat torture. … The State Duma also adopted amendments to several laws on the judiciary to introduce jury trials throughout Russia and to combat corruption among judges. Under the amendments, jury trials would be adopted in all [eighty]-nine regions of Russia by 2003. Draft amendments would also facilitate the [prosecution] of corrupt judges.'[387]

SIERRA LEONE

Special Court for Sierra Leone
☛ The Special Court (Agreement, 2002), (Ratification) Act 2002.[388] Published in the *Sierra Leone Gazette*, Vol. CXXX, No. II, Supplement, 7 March 2002 <http://www.special court.org/documents/SpecialCourtAct.html>
☛ Appointment of key Special Court personnel and prosecutorial policy

On 19 April, US military lawyer David Crane was appointed by UN Secretary-General Kofi Annan as the Prosecutor of the Special Court for Sierra Leone and Robin Vincent of the UK was named Registrar.[389]

During the year, Mr Crane made it a point to travel widely around Sierra Leone, conducting town meetings to interface with what he called his 'clients'. He also visited many schools and community groups.

In September, the Prosecutor's investigators cordoned off their first crime scene, in the village of Tombodu in the Kono district, and exhumations followed.[390]

On 2 October, Chief Prosecutor David Crane said that he would investigate, indict and prosecute all those who bear the greatest responsibility for atrocities committed during the conflict in Sierra Leone, regardless of which side they belonged to.[391]

On 2 November, during a visit to a secondary school in Karbala, Crane said that he would not indict children, even though he had the power to indict anyone over the age of 15 years under the Statute. 'The children of Sierra Leone have suffered enough both as victims [and] as perpetrators. I am not interested in prosecuting children. I want to prosecute the people who forced thousands of children to commit unspeakable crimes.' He added that he intended to establish 'crimes against children', such as forced recruitment and abduction, as war crimes.[392]

In an interview given on 21 November 2002, Crane said that 'Gender crimes will be emphasized as a core crime and will be pursued from the onset. It will not be an afterthought. We are making gender crimes a top priority of our investigation and prosecution because rape and sexual assault used as a tool of war needs to be prosecuted.' Crane also

---

387. *Human Rights Watch World Report 2002*. Russian Federation. <http://www.hrw.org/wr2k2/europe16.html>.

388. Reprinted in this volume at p. 800.

389. 'Pentagon lawyer named prosecutor in Sierra Leone', Reuters, 19 April 2002.

390. 'Special Court investigators cordon off their first crime scene', Special Court for Sierra Leone, Press and Public Affairs Office, Press Release, Sierra Leone, 2 November 2002. <http://www.sc-sl.org/pressrelease-092702b.html>.

391. During a visit to Koidu Community Center. See 'For Special Court, no one is above the law', I. Barrie, *Standard Times*, 2 October 2002.

392. 'Special Court Prosecutor says he will not prosecute children', Special Court for Sierra Leone, Press and Public Affairs Office, Press Release, Sierra Leone, 2 November 2002. <http://www.sc-sl.org/pressrelease-110202.html>.

said that the Special Court has 'international jurisdiction' and '[w]e fully expect to utilize that jurisdiction.'[393]

By the beginning of November, the Prosecutor's Office was almost fully staffed and was fully operational, according to Crane, and included more Sierra Leoneans than any other nationality.[394]

On 10 December, in a speech given to mark International Human Rights Day, Mr Crane expounded on how his office would interrelate with the Truth and Reconciliation Commission. 'I will not demand any information from the Truth and Reconciliation Commission! Victims, perpetrators, and witnesses who testify before the TRC should do so without fear of having their statements subpoenaed by my office.' Crane added that the work of both the Special Court and the Truth and Reconciliation Commission must succeed and referred to them as 'two key pillars to stabilize the peace in Sierra Leone …'[395]

Meanwhile, on 2 December 2002, the eight judges of the Special Court were sworn in.[396] Two of the three trial judges were appointed by the UN and the others by Sierra Leone. Of the five appeals judges, three were appointed by the UN and two by the government of Sierra Leone.[397]

The judges are Emmanuel O. Ayoola of Nigeria; Geoffrey Robertson from the UK; George Gelaga King of Sierra Leone; Hassan B. Jallow of The Gambia; Renate Winter from Austria (Appeals Chamber); Pierre Boutet of Canada; Benjamin M. Itoe of Cameroon; and Rosolu John Bankole Thompson of Sierra Leone (Trial Chamber).

On 5 December 2002, the eight judges of the Court elected as President Judge Geoffrey Robertson, who also became presiding judge of the Appeals Chamber. The presiding judge of the Trial Chamber is Judge Bankole Thompson.[398]

Work on the permanent court building was expected to be completed by mid 2003.[399]

Truth Commission
☞ Establishment and funding of the Truth and Reconciliation Commission

393. C. Cobb Jr., 'Sierra Leone's Special Court: will it hinder or help?', Interview, allAfrica.com, 21 November 2002.

394. 'More Sierra Leoneans in Prosecutor's office than any other nationality', Special Court for Sierra Leone, Press and Public Affairs Office, Press Release, Sierra Leone, 6 November 2002. <http://www.sc-sl.org/pressrelease-110602.html>. ·

395. 'Remarks by Prosecutor David M. Crane for International Human Rights Day, Victoria Park, Freetown', Special Court for Sierra Leone, Press and Public Affairs Office, Press Release, Sierra Leone, 2 November 2002. <http://www.sc-sl.org/pressrelease-121002.html>.

396. 'Special Court Judges sworn-in', IRIN, 2 December 2002.

397. 'International judges arrive in Sierra Leone for swearing-in', Special Court for Sierra Leone, Press and Public Affairs Office, Press Release, Sierra Leone, 28 November 2002. <http://www.sc-sl.org/pressrelease-112802.html>; 'Special Court judges sworn-in', Special Court for Sierra Leone, Press and Public Affairs Office, Press Release, Sierra Leone, 2 November 2002. <http://www.sc-sl.org/pressrelease-120202.html>.

398. 'Judges elect Geoffrey Robertson QC as President', Special Court for Sierra Leone, Press and Public Affairs Office, Press Release, Sierra Leone, 2 November 2002. <http://www.sc-sl.org/pressrelease-120302.html>.

399. Special Court for Sierra Leone, Press and Public Affairs Office, Press Release, Sierra Leone, 11 October 20002. <http://www.sc-sl.org/pressrelease-101103.html>.

Sierra Leone's Truth and Reconciliation Commission, a "'home-grown" initiative',[400] whose legal basis is the 1999 Lomé Peace Agreement[401] and the Truth and Reconciliation Act 2000,[402] started out with next-to-no resources. The Interim Secretariat was set up in late March 2002 with only one staff member. By July, it had grown to 14, including international advisers and national consultants. During the interim preparatory phase, lasting from July to 4 October, the Commission was expected to: hire staff; procure office space; design and undertake a public education campaign; prepare a budget and secure funds; and undertake a sensitisation program and preliminary background research. Some research activities were performed on behalf of the Commission by the Office of the High Commissioner for Human Rights.[403]

In its weekly briefing of 11 September, the Commission called attention to the 'critical funding situation. To date, pledges amount to US $1,580,739, of which $1,107,825 has been received, not taking into account the sum of US $97,000 donated by the government of Sierra Leone and its contribution of the premises of the Commission.' The Commission also noted its concern that some members of the public were still misconstruing the purpose of the TRC and its relationship with the Special Court.[404]

According to a report of the International Crisis Group: 'On 4 December 2002, the TRC deployed statement takers, who are to collect the stories from all citizens who wish to come forward, regardless of war-time affiliation. These stories will be the basis for public hearings in early 2003 and for the creation of an official historical record of the war. However, the TRC commissioners are still a largely dysfunctional body that has not yet developed a comprehensive operational plan.'[405]

Ongoing Cases
- Trial of Foday Sankoh for the deaths of 22 peace protesters by shooting outside his home on 8 May 2000, High Court of Sierra Leone

On 11 March 2002, Foday Sankoh, the former Head of the Revolutionary United Front (RUF), appeared in court to answer charges of murder brought on 4 March. Days before, President Ahmed Tejan Kabbah lifted a four-year state of emergency, which had enabled the government to detain Sankoh indefinitely without charge.[406]

---

400. 'Peace with Justice? The Special Court and the Truth and Reconciliation Commission (TRC)', in M. Malan, P. Rakate and A. McIntyre, Peacekeeping in Sierra Leone, UNAMSIL
Hits the Home Straight, Chapter 11, Monograph No. 68 (Cape Town, Institute for Social Studies). <http://www.iss.co.za/Pubs/Monographs/No68/Chap11.html>.
401. <http://www.sierra-leone.org/lomeaccord.html>.
402. <http://www.sierra-leone.org/trcact2000.html>. See 4 *YIHL* (2001) pp. 613-614.
403. 'Statement by Rt. Rev. Dr. Joseph Humper, Chairman of the Truth and Reconciliation Commission on the Occasion of its First Weekly Briefing, on Wednesday 24th July 2002'. <http://www.sierra-leone.org/trcbriefing072402.html>.
404. 'Eighth Weekly Briefing of the Truth and Reconciliation Commission Chaired by Professor William Schabas, on Wednesday 11th September 2002'. <http://www.sierra-leone.org/trcbriefings091102.html>.
405. 'Sierra Leone's Truth and Reconciliation Commission: A Fresh Start?', International Crisis Group, 20 December 2002.
406. T. McKinley, 'Sankoh murder trial begins', BBC Online News Report, 11 March 2002. See also M. Doyle, 'Sierra Leone rebels face murder charge', BBC Online News Report, 4 March 2002.

On 5 June, the trial of Sankoh and 49 other RUF members opened before the High Court of Sierra Leone. Sankoh faced 70 counts, including murder, conspiracy to murder and shooting with intent to kill. If he was found guilty, he faced the death penalty.[407] The trial was adjourned the next day until 10 July to allow Sankoh's Nigerian-born lawyer to obtain permission to practice at the Sierra Leone bar and to allow the prosecution time to prepare its case and to issue indictments.

Sankoh was also expected to be indicted by the Special Court for Sierra Leone.

AVRIL McDONALD

SLOVAKIA

International Criminal Court
☛ Act to ratify the International Criminal Court, approved by Parliament in the first week of April 2002, signed by the President on 8 April 2002[408]

National Committee
☛ Committee on International Law, established by a Decision of the Ministry of Foreign Affairs on 20 September 2001, entered into force on 1 January 2002

'Chaired by the Ministry of Foreign Affairs and with the Slovak Red Cross providing the secretariat, it includes representatives of the Ministries of Foreign Affairs, Defence, Justice, Interior, Health, Education and Culture, the Office of the Ombudsman, the armed forces and the Slovak Red Cross itself. The Commission's mandate is to analyse the degree of implementation of international humanitarian law in national law and its application by national courts and administrative authorities, to propose to the authorities the adoption of measures to ensure effective implementation of this body of law, to propose Slovakia's participation in other humanitarian law treaties, to help spread knowledge of this body of law in schools, the armed forces and the police, and to cooperate with national committees of other countries and with international organisations.'[409]

SLOVENIA

International Criminal Court
☛ Act on Cooperation with the International Criminal Court, adopted by the Slovenian National Assembly on 25 October 2002, entered into force after promulgation by the President and publication in the *Official Gazette*[410]

'It establishes the jurisdiction of Slovenian courts over the crimes defined in the 1998 Rome Statute of the ICC (Chapter IV) and contains provisions dealing, *inter alia*, with the arrest of persons and their surrender to the ICC (Chapter VI), the protection of Slovenia's national

---

407. T. Pitman, 'Once mighty ex-leader of Sierra Leone rebels hovers on verge of madness', AP, 5 June 2002.

408. CICC/Europe/CIS: Slovakia. <http://www.iccnow.org/countryinfo/europecis/slovakia.html>.

409. ICRC Advisory Service, National Implementation of International Humanitarian Law – Biannual update on national legislation and case-law, January-June 2002. <http://www.icrc.org/Web/eng/siteeng0.nsf/html/5FLE9G?OpenDocument>.

410. CICC/Europe/CIS: Slovenia. <http://www.iccnow.org/countryinfo/europecis/slovenia.html>.

security interests (Chapter VIII), the privileges and immunities of the ICC (Chapter IX) and the enforcement in Slovenia of reparation orders made and fines imposed by the ICC (Chapter XI).'[411]

SOUTH AFRICA[412]

International Criminal Court

☞ The International Criminal Court Act 27 of 2002 (Act to provide for a framework to ensure the effective implementation of the Rome Statute of the International Criminal Court in South Africa; to ensure that South Africa conforms with its obligations set out in the Statute; to provide for the crime of genocide, crimes against humanity and war crimes; to provide for the prosecution in South African courts of persons accused of having committed the said crimes in South Africa and beyond the borders of South Africa in certain circumstances; to provide for the arrest of persons accused of having committed the said crimes and their surrender to the said Court in certain circumstances; to provide for cooperation by South Africa with the said Court; and to provide for matters connected therewith), assented to on 12 July 2002, entered into force 16 August 2002, published in the *Government Gazette* No. 236421, 18 July 2002, pp. 1-160 <http://www.parliament.gov.za/bills/2001/b42-01.pdf>

The new law is modeled along the lines of the 1999 SADC ICC Enabling Act.[413] The law seeks to assist SADC countries in fulfilling their obligations to investigate and prosecute nationally and to provide for mechanisms necessary in order to cooperate with international enforcement regimes.

The purpose and objective of the Act is to implement substantive international humanitarian law into South African municipal law in order to enable national courts to prosecute ICC crimes. The new law further seeks to enable national courts and relevant authorities to cooperate and assist, if necessary, the ICC in conducting its investigations and prosecuting persons alleged to have committed crimes within the jurisdiction of the Court in South Africa[414] – specifically:

'(i) to enable the Court to make requests for assistance;
(ii) to provide mechanisms for the surrender to the Court of persons accused of having committed crimes referred to in Article 5 of the Statute [war crimes, crimes against humanity and genocide];
(iii) to enable the Court to sit in the Republic;
(iv) to enforce any sentence imposed or order made by the Court.'[415]

---

411. ICRC Advisory Service, National Implementation of International Humanitarian Law – Biannual update on national legislation and case-law, January-June 2002. <http://www.icrc.org/Web/eng/siteeng0.nsf/html/5FLE9G?OpenDocument>.

412. Information and commentaries by Phenyo Keiseng Rakate, B.Juris, LL.B (UNW), LL.M (Stell), LL.D. Candidate (UNISA), Deputy-Director, Directorate: Research and Analysis, Department of Defence, Pretoria, Republic of South Africa.

413. <http://www.sirente.com/catalogue/rsdlo_i/lex/sadc/sadc_1.html>.

414. Section 3(c).

415. Ibid.

Consequently, it follows that incorporating the Rome Statute into South African domestic law necessitated the amendment of the 1977 Criminal Procedure Act to include crimes of genocide, crimes against humanity and war crimes in the list of punishable offences in South African criminal law.[416] Similarly, the amendment of the Correctional Services Act was needed in order to empower the Minister of Correctional Services to enforce the imprisonment sentence of a person sentenced by the Court.[417] Also, the Military Discipline Supplementary Measures Act of 1999 was also amended to grant military courts jurisdiction to prosecute any of its members responsible for crimes under the jurisdiction of the ICC.[418] Although military courts have always enjoyed extraterritorial jurisdiction, their powers and status are now elevated significantly. However, given the seriousness of ICC crimes, military courts require the consent of the National Director of Public Prosecutions before they can institute proceedings against the alleged person.[419]

The ICC can now exercise jurisdiction over any person who is a South African citizen, resident in the Republic or fugitive from justice, irrespective of whether such crimes where committed inside or outside South Africa.[420]

The new law seeks to ensure cooperation with the ICC and national jurisdictions. The fact that a domestic court or the Director of Public Prosecutions would decline to prosecute would not preclude the ICC from conducting investigations or prosecuting the alleged person.[421] Further provisions are made for the arrest and surrender of persons to the Court and cooperation and judicial assistance to the Court, such as the transfer of prisoners to give evidence or assist in investigations, requests for assistance in obtaining evidence and search and seizure of documents.[422]

☛ The UN Mission in the Democratic Republic of the Congo

In 2002 preparations were made for the deployment of South African National Defence Force (SANDF) members to the eastern part of the Democratic Republic of the Congo as part of the third phase of the United Nations peacekeeping mission in the Democratic Republic of the Congo (MONUC III). The SANDF was to form part of the United Nations disarmament, demobilisation, reintegration, repatriation and resettlement programme. South Africa previously deployed 150 technical staff for MONUC Phase II mission in the DRC. For MONUC phase III, South Africa was to deploy 1,268 SANDF members. The President, as required in the Constitution, had to inform parliament of the reasons, place, period and number of people expected to be deployed.[423] The National Office for the Coordination of Peace Missions, located in the Department of Foreign Affairs, was responsible for coordinating all peace missions, including MONUC phase III.

Pending
☛ The Defence Bill, 2001

---

416. Act 51 of 1977, Section 18(g).
417. Act 111 of 1998, Section 31 of the Act; Cf., Art. 103 of the ICC.
418. Section 3(4) of the Act.
419. Section 4(3) of the Act.
420. Section 4(2) of the Act.
421. Section 4(6) of the Act.
422. See generally Parts 2, 3 and 4 of the Act.
423. Section 228(4)(a) of the 1993 Constitution read with Section 201(3) of the 1996 Constitution.

The Defence Bill, 2001 was approved by Cabinet and was to be tabled in Parliament during the 2003 parliamentary session. The Bill repeals the 1957 Defence Act[424] to give effect to the values enshrined in the 1996 Constitution[425] in respect of security services. There are at least two features which demonstrate South Africa's commitment to comply with the four Geneva Conventions of 12 August 1949. First, in line with the 1998 White Paper on Defence, membership of the force is voluntary. However, persons eligible for mobilisation may not be less than 18 years of age.[426] Secondly, persons contracted for services will be obliged to remain in the service during times of war, a state of national defence or a state of emergency.[427] In the case of a state of national defence, the president, acting in accordance with the Constitution,[428] may declare a state of national defence if the sovereignty of the country is (i) threatened by war, including biological or chemical warfare, or invasion, armed attack or armed conflict; (ii) being or has been invaded or is under armed or cyber attack or subject to a state of armed conflict.[429]

PHENYO KEISENG RAKATE

SPAIN[430]

Landmines

☛ Order of the Ministry of Defence 610/2002 of 8 March 2002. Published in *Boletín Oficial del Estado* (*B.O.E.*), 21 March 2002, No. 69, p. 11479

Since the entry into force in Spain in 1998 of Amended Protocol II annexed to the Convention on Certain Conventional Weapons, and the ratification in 1999 of the Ottawa Treaty, which deals with the use, storage, production and transfer of anti-personnel landmines, the government has decided to institutionally develop the Directive of National Defence 1/2000. This establishes the active participation of the Spanish state in initiatives of armament control and disarmament, by means of the Order of the Ministry of Defence 610/2002 of 8 March 2002, which establishes the International Demining Centre. The Centre was created to respond to the new needs that have arisen as a result of Spain's increasing participation in peace operations and humanitarian aid. It has been established as the national reference organisation on matters of humanitarian demining and, in conjunction with the Ministry of Foreign Affairs, its mission is to boost Spain's role in international demining.

Children

☛ Ratification Instrument to the Facultative Protocol of the Convention of Children's Rights, about the Participation of Children in Armed Conflicts, of 25 May 2000. Issued by the King of Spain on 1 March 2002. Entered into force for Spain on 8 April 2002, in conformity with the provisions of Article 10, published in *B.O.E.*, 17 April 2002, No. 92, p. 14494

---

424. Act 44 of 1957.
425. Act 108 of 1996.
426. Section 91(2)(a) of the Bill.
427. Section 58 of the Bill.
428. Section 203 of the Constitution.
429. Section 89 of the Bill.
430. Information and commentaries by Santiago Castellá, Professor of Criminal Law, and Antoni Pigrau, Professor of International Law, at the Rovira I Virgili University, Tarragona.

Annexed to the Ratification Instrument is the following Declaration by the government of Spain: 'In accordance with the provisions of article 3 of the Protocol, Spain states that the minimum age for voluntary enlistment in her armed forces is eighteen years old.'

SANTIAGO CASTELLÁ AND ANTONI PIGRAU

SWEDEN[431]

International Criminal Court
☛ Act on Co-operation with the International Criminal Court [Lag (2002:329) om samarbete med Internationella brottmålsdomstolen]. Adopted 8 May 2002, entered into force 1 July 2002, published in *Svensk Författningssamling* (*SFS*) 2002:329

The ratification of the ICC required Sweden to make amendments to existing law concerning cooperation with the Court. A law[432] already existed in Sweden concerning the cooperation with the International Criminal Tribunals for the former Yugoslavia and Rwanda.[433] Due to the unique character of the International Criminal Court, it was, however, found to be appropriate to enact a law that deals specifically with the ICC. The provisions of the new law are to apply in case of an ICC request that Sweden take measures based on the Statute of the Court. The law deals with investigation and prosecution in relation to the crimes of genocide, crimes against humanity and war crimes. It also applies to investigation and prosecution of crimes directed against the ICC. Finally, it contains provisions concerning enforcement of the Court's sentences and transfer of arrested persons through Sweden.

International Crimes
☛ International Crimes and Swedish Jurisdiction. Report of the Commission on International Criminal Law, Swedish Governmental Official Report. Published in *Statens Offentliga Utredningar* (*SOU*) 2002:98[434]

The purpose of the Commission was to review Swedish legislation on criminal responsibility for international crimes and jurisdiction over such crimes. The assignment of the Commission was extended to include a review of Swedish legislation on criminal jurisdiction in general.

With the provisions of the Rome Statute as its primary model, the Commission proposed a new Swedish Act on International Crimes. The Act would make it possible to hold individuals responsible for genocide, crimes against humanity and war crimes. The scope of the proposed Act was, however, somewhat wider than the Rome Statute, *inter alia* as regards responsibility for war crimes committed during non-international armed conflicts.

The provisions on general conditions for criminal responsibility and various forms of defences, found under the heading of 'General Principles of Law' in the Rome Statute, are largely compatible with Swedish law. There are, however, exceptions and the Commission proposed new legislation in accordance with the provisions of the Rome Statute. It pro-

---

431. Information and commentaries by Ola Engdahl, Doctoral Candidate in International Law at Stockholm University and the Swedish National Defence College.

432. *SFS* 1994:569.

433. 1 *YIHL* (1998) p. 507.

434. The following text is largely based on the English summary of the Report.

posed that special provisions on military and other commanders' responsibility be introduced. Furthermore, it proposed that genocide, crimes against humanity and war crimes be exempt from the normal statutes of limitation.

Swedish legislation in general provides for a very wide jurisdiction over crimes committed abroad. In some aspects, at least formally, it extends beyond the limits of international law. This was one of the reasons for the principal rule, requiring the leave of the government or the Prosecutor-General to prosecute crimes committed abroad.[435] In addition, the courts were obliged to observe the rules on jurisdiction that follow from international law.

In the Commission's proposal, the provisions regarding the competence of Swedish courts were based on the traditional principles of international law allowing for state jurisdiction. The formal limits of competence were narrowed and made more precise. The system requiring leave to prosecute crimes committed abroad was to be retained. The competence to grant leave was to be moved from the government to the Prosecutor-General. In individual cases, however, the Prosecutor-General could hand over the case to the government.

On Swedish legislation on jurisdiction over international crimes, the Commission proposed that Swedish courts would have universal jurisdiction over genocide, crimes against humanity and war crimes, i.e., be competent to try charges on such crimes regardless of where or by whom they have been committed. The proposal in this part also encompassed acts of torture under the 1984 UN Convention against Torture and Other Cruel, Inhuman or Degrading Treatment or Punishment. Furthermore, a special provision was proposed regarding crimes under international treaties that are binding on Sweden. If a treaty obliges Sweden to prosecute in a case where the alleged offender is not extradited, Swedish courts are competent to try the crime in question.

Implementation
- ☛ Press release from the Ministry for Foreign Affairs, 27 June 2002, regarding governmental appointment of International Humanitarian Law Delegation <http://www.reger ingen.se/galactica/service=irnews/owner=sys/action=obj_show?c_obj_id=45872>

---

435. In June 2002, the youth organisation of the Swedish Social Democratic Party submitted an indictment of several highly placed commanders of the Israeli Defence Forces for alleged war crimes in the West Bank and the Gaza Strip. The facts were largely based on reports from several human rights organisations. According to the prosecutor, the request of leave of government did not in itself hinder the prosecutor from undertaking a preliminary investigation. Such a preliminary investigation did not normally commence without a prior informal contact with the government or its representative. Only when the preliminary investigation had reached the point where there were enough reasons to start a prosecution, a formal decision in the matter of appointment for prosecution would be taken (such decision did not include any assessment of the strength or the character of the evidence presented). The prosecutor decided not to undertake a preliminary investigation of the case. The decision was based primarily on the fact that an investigation would in practice be impossible to conclude (the necessary legal assistance to conduct such investigation would in fact need the authorisation of the Israeli government) and passing of sentences would be even less likely (requiring extradition of Israeli officers). The indictment and the decision by the prosecutor appear in English on the web page of the youth organisation at <http://www.ssu.se>. See also <http://www.agera.ssu.se/dokument/anm_Sharon _eng.pdf> and <http://www.agera.ssu.se/dokument/beslutet_engelska.pdf>.

The government decided to establish an International Humanitarian Law Delegation, whose task it is to identify, follow-up and propose priorities in international humanitarian law that are of importance for Swedish foreign policy. The delegation is to, *inter alia*, monitor and analyse developments in international humanitarian law, and its interplay with other related fields of international law, including disarmament and human rights.

The Swedish tradition of commitment in the field of humanitarian law, reflected in its advisory group, goes back 30 years. What distinguishes the new International Humanitarian Law Delegation from previous groups is that it will have somewhat different working forms and other powers, in order to be able to meet new needs and challenges as efficiently as possible. Working groups are to be appointed, for example, to make analyses and to act as think tanks.

The State Secretary for Foreign Affairs at the Ministry for Foreign Affairs is to be appointed as Chairman of the Delegation and the State Secretary at the Ministry of Defence is to become Vice-Chairman.

Cases
☛ Case against *Fredrik Sandberg*, Gotland District Court, 4 January 2002

On 4 January 2002, Fredrik Sandberg, age 25, was convicted for 'Hets mot folkgrupp' (agitation against an ethnic group) in violation of Sweden's hate speech law and sentenced to six months' imprisonment by the Gotland District Court. In 2000, Sandberg's neo-Nazi organisation, the Nationalsocialistisk Front (National Socialist Front), published a new, 60-page edition of the 1936 Nazi booklet *Die Judenfrage* (The Jewish Question), and sold it on its website.[436]

Pending Legislation
☛ Decision to ratify the Optional Protocol to the Convention on the Rights of the Child on the Involvement of Children in Armed Conflicts

The Swedish Parliament approved Government Bill 2001/02:178 proposing to ratify the Optional Protocol to the Convention on the Rights of the Child on the involvement of children in armed conflicts.[437] Article 2 of the Optional Protocol requires States Parties to deposit a binding declaration upon ratification on the minimum age at which it will permit voluntary recruitment into its national armed forces. All services within the Swedish Armed Forces require a minimum age of 18 years. A declaration of a minimum age of 18 years for voluntary recruitment would therefore not lead to any change in Swedish legislation.

The fact that youths under the age of 18 may learn how to handle firearms dressed in uniform, within, for example, the National Home Guard has, however, been criticised by the Swedish Red Cross. It argued that, although these youths are not *serving* in the Armed Forces, there is a risk that they could be used in battle if Sweden were to participate in an armed conflict. According to the Swedish Red Cross, a minimum age of 18 years should be implemented in all relevant legislation.

---

436. <http://www.preventgenocide.org/punish/domestic/index.htm>.

437. The decision to ratify the Optional Protocol was thereafter taken by the government in December but instruments of ratification were not deposited during 2002.

There is no specific Act to prevent recruitment of persons under the age of 18 years to armed groups – as distinct from the national armed forces – to take part in hostilities outside Sweden. Such recruitment is, however, largely penalised in Swedish legislation through the provisions in the Penal Code on kidnapping, unlawful deprivation of liberty, placing a person in a distressful situation, arbitrary conduct concerning a child and unlawful recruitment. However, recruitment of individual children in the age range of 15-18 years not involving any deprivation of liberty, coercion, or deceit will probably not be covered by any of the aforementioned provisions. To fully comply with Article 4 of the Optional Protocol, adoption of new legal measures therefore seems necessary, and it is also the intention of the government to propose new legislation on this matter at a later stage.

OLA ENGDAHL

SWITZERLAND[438]

International Criminal Court
☞ The Federal Law on Cooperation with the International Criminal Court of 22 June 2001. Entered into force on 1 July 2002[439]

Military Penal Code
☞ Revision of Article 17 of the Swiss Military Penal Code [rechtfertigender Notstand] dealing with self-defence

Article 17 of the Swiss Military Penal Code dealing with self-defence was revised following the suggestion of the Swiss Judge Advocate [Oberauditor]. It now incorporates a new paragraph 2, establishing that:

'he who, during wartime, commits an act which is normally subject to a criminal sanction, acts lawfully if the act is perpetrated in the interest of the national defence and if the author, with this act, warrants higher interests.' (unofficial translation)
['War dem Täter nicht zuzumuten, das gefährdete Gut preiszugeben, so handelt er nicht schuldhaft'][440]

ROBERTA ARNOLD and PETER HOSTETTLER

TAJIKISTAN

The Emblem
☞ Resolution No. 28 on the implementation of the law of the Republic of Tajikistan 'on the usage and protection of the red cross and red crescent emblems and appellations in the Republic of Tajikistan'. Published on 4 February 2002

---

438. Information and commentary by Dr Roberta Arnold, Legal Advisor, Swiss Department of Defence, Staff Caf-Loac Section, and Peter Hostettler, Head of Section Law of Armed Conflict, Swiss Department of Defence.
439. See 4 *YIHL* (2001) p. 622.
440. The original states as follows: 'Wer während Kriegszeiten eine mit Strafe bedrohte Tat begeht, handelt rechtmässig, wenn die Tat im Interesse der Landesverteidigung geboten ist und der Täter dadurch höherwertige Interessen wahrt.'

'The purpose of the decree is to assign responsibilities to the various ministries for the following activities: marking medical establishments, health-care units and transports of medical equipment with the red crescent emblem in accordance with the law; providing medical personnel with identification material; producing armlets, identification cards and the equipment necessary for the sending of distinctive signals; preventing misuse of the red cross and red crescent emblems and names; designing a distinctive sign with which to mark medical and pharmaceutical establishments providing paid services; designing new road signs to mark first-aid posts and hospitals; and working out a draft law for Tajikistan "on the Red Crescent Society of Tajikistan".'[441]

TANZANIA

International Criminal Court
☛ Protocol on the Rome Statute, ratified on 2 August 2002

Following Tanzania's ratification of the ICC Statute, an implementation network was formed in October 2002 consisting of representatives of civil society. It is studying Tanzanian law to see what steps need to be taken to implement the Statute into national law.[442]

UNITED ARAB EMIRATES

The Emblem
☛ Law on the Red Crescent in the United Arab Emirates. State Law No. 9 of 2002 on the Red Crescent in the United Arab Emirates. Issued and entered into force on 28 July 2002, published in the *Official Journal*, No. 384, 28 July 2002

'Its Chapters IV and V (Arts. 22 to 27) deal only with the protection of the red crescent emblem in time of peace. They provide for a prison sentence or a minimum fine of 5,000 Dirham for any unauthorised use of the emblem.'[443]

UNITED KINGDOM[444]

Geneva Conventions 1949 and Additional Protocols 1977
☛ The Geneva Conventions (Amendment) Act (Overseas Territories) Order 2002, Statutory Instruments, 2002 No. 1076, made on 17 April 2002, entered into force on 1 May 2002 [United Kingdom primary and subordinate legislation (Acts of Parliament and

---

441. ICRC Advisory Service, National Implementation of International Humanitarian Law – Biannual Update on national legislation and case-law, January-June 2002. <http://www.icrc.org/web/eng/siteeng0.nsf/html/5FLE9g?o pendocument>.

442. CICC/Africa: Tanzania. <http://www.iccnow.org/countryinfo/africa/tanzania.html>.

443. ICRC Advisory Service, National Implementation of International Humanitarian Law – Biannual update on national legislation and case-law, January-June 2002. <http://www.icrc.org/Web/eng/siteeng0.nsf/html/5FLE9G?OpenDocument>.

444. Information and commentaries provided by A.P.V. Rogers, Fellow of the Lauterpacht Research Centre for International Law, University of Cambridge. Thanks to Ms Helen Upton, Assistant Legal Adviser, Mr Nick McDuff, United Nations Department, Foreign and Commonwealth Office, London, and Major Joanne Bowen, Army Legal Services.

statutory instruments) are published by The Stationery Office Limited and can be found on <http://www.legislation.hmso.gov.uk>]

This Act extended the Geneva Conventions (Amendment) Act 1995, the national implementing legislation for the Additional Protocols of 1997, with exceptions and modifications, to Anguilla, Bermuda, the British Antarctic Territory, the British Indian Ocean Territory, the Cayman Islands, the Falkland Islands, Montserrat, Pitcairn, Henderson, Ducie and Oeno Islands, St Helena and Dependencies, South Georgian and the South Sandwich Islands, the Sovereign Base Areas of Akrotiri and Dhekelia, Turks and Caicos Islands and the Virgin Islands.

☛ Diplomatic Note No. 49 dated 1 July 2002 from the British Embassy, Berne, to the government of the Swiss Confederation.

This note makes a declaration to the depositary of the Geneva Conventions and Additional Protocols to extend the United Kingdom's ratification of the Additional Protocols of 1977 to the territories listed above. This extension is made on the basis of the same statements made on ratification of the 1977 Additional Protocols by the United Kingdom. In addition, the declaration extends the United Kingdom's acceptance of the competence of the International Fact-Finding Commission under Article 90 of Additional Protocol I to those territories.[445]

☛ Note 339/2002 of 9 July 2002 from the United Kingdom Mission to the United Nations to the Secretary-General of the United Nations on measures regarding the status of the Additional Protocols of 1977 and the dissemination and implementation of international humanitarian law

The Secretary-General had requested the government to submit any relevant information for inclusion in the report of the Secretary-General on the Additional Protocols, as referred to in General Assembly Resolution 55/148 of 12 December 2000. The government submitted this note with information on the implementation of the Additional Protocols in United Kingdom law and recent developments in the field. The information has been published in volumes 3 and 4, as well as the current volume, of this yearbook.

Explosive Remnants of War
☛ In 2002 the United Kingdom actively participated in United Nations discussions on explosive remnants of war (ERW), through the Group of Governmental Experts of the States Parties to the United Nations Convention on Certain Conventional Weapons (CCW) established to address that issue. The United Kingdom government supported the development of a legally binding instrument on ERW within the CCW framework, to address issues such as post-conflict clearance of unexploded ordnance and warnings to civilians. At the December 2002 meeting of States Parties, a mandate was secured to begin negotiations in 2003 and the UK participated in the first meeting of the Group of Governmental Experts in March 2003.

---

445. 3 *YIHL* (2000) p. 598.

International Criminal Tribunals
☛ UK involvement in establishment of the Special Court for Sierra Leone

The United Kingdom was significantly involved in the formulation of the Agreement, signed on 16 January 2002, between the United Nations and the government of Sierra Leone establishing the Special Court for Sierra Leone. Officials from the United Kingdom participated in the planning mission for the Special Court to prepare the groundwork for its operations, including premises, prosecution and investigation. The Special Court was to have, *inter alia*, the power to prosecute persons who bear the greatest responsibility for serious violations of international humanitarian law committed in Sierra Leone since 30 November 1996.

Dissemination
☛ The United Kingdom interdepartmental committee on international humanitarian law[446] held its fourth meeting on 9 October 2002. Two of its members, Helen Upton of the Foreign and Commonwealth Office and Michael Meyer of the British Red Cross, attended the International Committee of the Red Cross conference for national committees in March 2002, which addressed issues relevant to the work of national IHL committees and facilitated networks between them.

Education and Training
☛ The Foreign and Commonwealth Office, in conjunction with the UK interdepartmental committee and the British Red Cross Society, organised two training events on international humanitarian law for civil servants on 5 May 2002 and 11 March 2003 (for lawyers and non-lawyers, respectively). The aim of this training was to increase general awareness of international humanitarian law in government departments, in furtherance of the UK's common obligation in the Geneva Conventions and their Additional Protocols to disseminate the Conventions as widely as possible.

Cases
☛ *R. (Abbasi and another)* v. *Secretary of State for Foreign and Commonwealth Affairs and another*, Court of Appeal (Civil Division) in London, Judgement of 6 November 2002, [2002] EWCA Civ159[447]

Feroz Ali Abbasi, a British national, was captured by United States forces in Afghanistan. In January 2002 he was transported to Guantánamo Bay in Cuba, a naval base on territory held by the United States on a long lease pursuant to a treaty with Cuba. By the time of the hearing before the Court of Appeal, he had been held captive for eight months without access to a court or any other form of tribunal or even to a lawyer. The proceedings were brought on his behalf by his mother. It was sought, by judicial review, to compel the Foreign Office to make representations on his behalf to the United States government or to take other appropriate action or to give an explanation as to why this had not been done.

---

446. Ibid.
447. Reprinted in the Documentation section of this volume at p. 726. A summary of the Judgement can be found on <http://www.lawreports.co.uk>.

It was understood by the Court of Appeal that Mr Abbasi was being held by the United States as an enemy combatant, pursuant to a Military Order issued by the President of the United States. There was no indication whether he was going to be tried, and courts in the United States had ruled that, as the military base at Guantánamo Bay was outside the sovereign territory of the United States, those courts had no jurisdiction to entertain petitions for writs of *habeas corpus* from aliens detained there.[448] Those decisions were, however, subject to appeal. The Court of Appeal expressed surprise that the writ of the United States courts did not run in respect of individuals held by the government on territory that the United States held as a lessee under a long-term treaty.

Evidence on behalf of the United Kingdom government was to the effect that there had been close and regular contact between the UK government and the government of the United States about the situation of the British nationals detained at Guantánamo Bay and their treatment. The UK government had raised with the US government on a number of occasions questions regarding their welfare and proper treatment and there had been periodic visits to the detainees. They had also been the subject of direct discussions at Secretary of State level as well as at official level.

On behalf of Mr Abbasi it was submitted that he was being arbitrarily detained in violation of his fundamental human rights, and that the Foreign Secretary owed him a duty under English public law to take positive steps to redress the position, or at least to give a reasoned response to his request for assistance.

For the Secretary of State it was argued that the authorities clearly established two principles that barred the relief sought: that the English court would not (1) examine the legitimacy of action taken by a foreign sovereign state nor (2) adjudicate upon actions taken by the executive in the conduct of foreign relations.

The Court of Appeal considered, on the first point, that, while recognising the need for due caution in the case of allegations that a foreign state was in breach of its international obligations, the Court was free to express a view about what it conceived to be a clear breach of international law, particularly in the context of human rights. It went on to express the view that it was objectionable that Mr Abbasi should be subject to indefinite detention in territory over which the United States had exclusive control with no opportunity to challenge the legitimacy of his detention before any court or tribunal. It was clear that there could be no direct remedy in the Court of Appeal, as the US government was not before the Court and no order of the Court would be binding on it.

As for the second point, the Court of Appeal considered that, although the Secretary of State must be free to give full weight to foreign policy considerations, which are not justiciable, that did not mean that the whole process was necessarily immune from judicial scrutiny. The Court of Appeal found that while the Foreign Office had discretion to protect British citizens, including, where appropriate, to make representations to other states on their behalf, there was no enforceable duty to do so. However, there was no reason why the Foreign Office's decision or inaction should not be reviewable if it could be shown that the same were irrational or contrary to legitimate expectations; but the court could not enter forbidden areas such as decisions affecting foreign policy. Foreign Office policy statements indicated that where certain criteria were satisfied, the government would 'consider' making representations. The citizen's legitimate expectation was that such a request would be considered and that, in the process, all relevant factors (including foreign policy considera-

---

448. For a discussion of these cases, see *infra*, the US report at pp. 626 et seq.

tions and the nature and extent of the injustice claimed to have been suffered) would be taken into account.

In this case the Court of Appeal rejected the claim to relief on a number of grounds, including the fact that it was quite clear from the evidence that the Foreign Office had considered Mr Abbasi's request for assistance and that the steps taken by the Foreign Office in Mr Abbasi's case were those that could reasonably have been expected in the circumstances.

A.P.V. ROGERS

☛ *A. and others* v. *Secretary of State for the Home Department*, Appeal No. SC/ 1-7/2002, Special Immigration Appeals Commission of 30 July 2002

This decision of Justice Collins found that parts of Britain's Anti-Terrorism, Crime and Security Act 2001[449] were in violation of Article 14 of the European Convention on Human Rights prohibiting discrimination on grounds of national origin. The decision is interesting for the Commission's observations on the extent to which international terrorism constitutes a state of emergency, and the margin of appreciation that states enjoy with respect to derogation from the right to liberty during emergencies.

The Commission, the body competent under the Anti-Terrorism, Crime and Security Act to hear challenges to it, was concerned in particular with the compatibility of Part 4 of the Act (Sections 21 to 25), titled 'Immigration and Asylum', which enables the certification and detention of persons suspected of being threats to national security or international terrorists, with a view to removing them from the UK. Such a person could be detained despite the fact that their removal from the UK was either temporarily or permanently prevented. A particular feature of the Act is that only non-UK citizens can be detained, because only they can be removed from the country.

Justice Collins found that such detention violated Article 5 of the European Convention on Human Rights (right to liberty and security of persons), which became part of UK law under the Human Rights Act 1998. The only relevant ground for detention would be Article 5(1)(f), 'but, since removal is impossible, detention would be unlawful. ... Since no removal can (or so it is believed) be effected, it is apparent that no action is being taken with a view to deportation.'[450]

The Judgement noted that the UK Secretary of State had made a derogation order from Article 5 of the Convention on 11 November 2001.[451] The public emergency justifying derogation was the 'terrorist threat to the United Kingdom from persons suspected of involvement in international terrorism'. Some foreign nationals present in the UK were suspected of involvement in the commission, preparation or instigation of terrorist acts, or of having linked with international terrorist organisations, and constituted a threat to the UK's national security.

---

449. 4 *YIHL* (2001) pp. 631-632.
450. At para. 6 of the Judgement.
451. Human Rights Act 1998 (Designated Derogation) Order 2001 (2001 No. 3644), 11 November 2001. Came into force on 13 November 2001. Art. 2 reads: 'The proposed derogation by the United Kingdom from Article 5(1) of the Convention, set out in the Schedule to this Order, is hereby designated for the purposes of the 1998 Act in anticipation of the making by the United Kingdom of the proposed derogation.'

A key question for the Commission was whether there actually existed a state of emergency justifying derogation under Article 15 of the ECHR. The Commission distinguished between the imminence of a terrorist threat and the imminence or actuality of the emergency:

> 'It would be absurd to require the authorities to wait until they were aware of an imminent attack before taking the necessary steps to avoid such an attack. ... What is required is a real risk that an attack will take place unless the necessary measures are taken to prevent it. ... An emergency can exist and can certainly be imminent if there is an intention and a capacity to carry out serious terrorist violence even if nothing has yet been done and plans have not yet reached the stage when an attack is actually about to happen.'[452]

The Commission concluded that there was in fact a public emergency which threatened the life of the nation within the terms of Article 15. Appreciation of the risks of international terrorism had increased post-11 September 2001. The UK was a prime target, second only to the US. If an attack occurred, the results would be devastating. It was not unreasonable for the UK to derogate from Article 15 of the ECHR, where other Council of Europe states had not, given the particular risk to the UK posed by international terrorists.

It then dealt with the question whether the measures taken by the government in Part 4 of the 2001 Act were 'strictly required' by the exigencies of the emergency. It found that the existence of possible alternative measures did not of itself mean that the measures taken were not strictly necessary. As to the appellants' argument that there was no rational connection between the measures taken and the objectives sought to be achieved (a proportionality argument), the Commission found, first, that the provisions were not 'over-inclusive' as applied or as they lawfully could be applied; and second, the fact that under the Act persons certified as international terrorists could leave the UK if they could find a country to accept them was not irrational. It accepted the Attorney-General's argument that there was an advantage to the UK in the removal of a potential terrorist from circulation within the state, as he cannot operate effectively if he is neither in the country nor at liberty, and his removal disrupts the organisation of terrorist activities.

The Commission also considered the question of notification of derogation under both the ECHR and the ICCPR and concluded that a failure of proper notification does not invalid a derogation, and that 'the requirements of Article 15(3) of the ECHR and Article 4(3) of the ICCPR are directory, not mandatory'.[453]

In examining the UK's Designated Derogation Order, the Commission found, however, that it purported to derogate only from Article 5(1) of the ECHR, with the result that under national law at least, all the other human rights recognised in the Human Rights Act would continue to exist, and if the appellants could show a breach of any right other than those recognised in Article 5(1), they could succeed under Section 7 of the Human Rights Act even if they could not succeed in an international forum. Appellants argued that the measures in Sections 21 to 25 of the Act breached their rights under Articles 3 (torture), 6 (fair trial) and 14 (discrimination) of the Act, as well as under Article 5.

---

452. At para. 24 of the Judgement.
453. At para. 62 of the Judgement.

The Commission rejected the argument that there was any breach of Article 3. The conditions of the detention, the mere fact of the detention, and the fact that no fixed term for it had been set were not derogation issues and therefore not issues for it to decide. The Commission also denied that there was a breach of Article 6. The appellants had not been charged with a crime; their certification as suspected international terrorists was a statement of suspicion. The whole nature of the procedure is that there is no charge.

As to the argument that the detention breached Article 14, the Commission noted that discriminatory measures could only be justified if the threat which the measures are intended to address emanates exclusively from the group that is the subject of the discrimination. It noted that the state has a right to control immigration, which is not restricted to the point of entry, and that differences between nationals and non-nationals could be made under the ECHR for this purpose, but found that an alien who cannot be deported must be allowed to remain:

> 'A person who is irremovable cannot be detained or kept in detention simply because he lacks British nationality. In order to detain him there must be some other justification, such as that he is suspected of having committed a criminal offence. If there is to be an effective derogation from the right to liberty enshrined in Article 5 in respect of suspected international terrorists, – and we can see powerful arguments in favour of such a derogation – the derogation ought rationally to extend to all irremovable suspected international terrorists. It would only be confined to the alien section of the population only if, as the Attorney-General contends, the threat stems exclusively or almost exclusively from that alien section. But the evidence … demonstrates that the threat is not so confined. There are many British nationals already identified – mostly in detention abroad – who fall within the definition of "suspected international terrorists", and it was clear from the submissions made to us that in the opinion of the respondent there are others at liberty in the United Kingdom who could be similarly defined. In those circumstances we fail to see how the derogation can be regarded as other than discriminatory on grounds of national origin.'

AVRIL MCDONALD

UNITED STATES OF AMERICA[454]

Armed Forces and Combatant Status

- ☛ Fact Sheet. Status of Detainees at Guantánamo. White House Press Release of 2 February 2002[455]
- ☛ United States response, submitted to the Inter-American Commission on Human Rights on 15 April 2002, to a petition on behalf of the Guantánamo prisoners, 41 *ILM* (2002) p. 1023
- ☛ Department of Defense News Release Number 497-02, 2 October 2002. 'DOD Responds to ABA Enemy Combatant Report'[456] <http://www.freerepublic.com/focus/news/765425/posts>

---

454. Information and commentaries by Burrus M. Carnahan, Professorial Lecturer in Law, the George Washington University, Washington, D.C., and Dr Avril Mcdonald.

455. Reprinted in the Documentation section of this volume at pp. 662 et seq.

456. Reprinted in the Documentation section of this volume at p. 665.

One of the most controversial United States' policies adopted following the Al Qaeda attacks of 11 September 2001 has been the decision to detain some persons as 'unlawful combatants', without recognising them as prisoners of war under the Third Geneva Convention. The first and third documents expand upon the scope and implications of this policy, as applied to the 2002 armed conflict in Afghanistan.

The first document, a White House press release of 2 February 2002, summarizes the US President's determinations in regard to the legal status of Al Qaeda and Taliban personnel captured during the armed conflict in Afghanistan. Briefly, the President, exercising his powers as Commander-in-Chief of the US Armed Forces, determined that fighting in Afghanistan between the forces under his command and the forces of the unrecognised Taliban government was an armed conflict between two States Parties to the Third Geneva Convention. In accordance with Article 2 of the Convention, it therefore applied to the conflict in principle. However, the Al Qaeda forces fighting in alliance with the Taliban, and the Taliban forces themselves, were both determined by the President not to meet the requirements of Article 4 of the Convention, and were therefore not directly protected by its terms. Nevertheless, the President ordered that, 'to the extent appropriate and consistent with military necessity', both the Al Qaeda and Taliban captives be treated 'in a manner consistent with the principles of the Third Geneva Convention of 1949'.

United States Department of Defense News Release Number 497-02, issued on 2 October 2002, summarizes the official response of the Department's General Counsel to a report critical of the policies adopted earlier in 2002 (and described in the first document). It was prepared by a committee of the American Bar Association (ABA), and focused on the situation of two American citizens being held as Al Qaeda combatants. The ABA, a nongovernmental organization, is the largest professional organisation of lawyers in the United States. Much of the discussion in the response deals with wartime authority under the US Constitution, but it also addresses issues of international legal significance.

Among the more important of these are the General Counsel's conclusions that 'the United States is currently in a state of war with al Qaeda', and governments have 'wartime authority to detain enemy combatants in order to prevent them from furthering enemy attacks ... in the future'. This authority is asserted to exist regardless of whether the detainees are prisoners of war or unlawful combatants. Finally, the General Counsel declared that detained enemy combatants have no right under international law to legal advice to contest their detention under the law of the detaining power.

These positions were also reflected, with somewhat different details, in another document published in 2002. This was the United States' response submitted to the Inter-American Commission on Human Rights on 15 April 2002, to a petition on behalf of the Guantánamo prisoners.[457]

Taken together, these documents reflect the continuing importance for the United States of custom as a primary source of international humanitarian law. On its face, the Third Geneva Convention of 1949 may appear to create a comprehensive legal regime for the treatment of captured enemy combatants in international armed conflict. Yet by applying the customary concept of the unlawful combatant or unprivileged belligerent, every enemy combatant captured by US forces in Afghanistan has been excluded from direct protection by the Convention.

---

457. 'US Response to the Inter-American Commission on Human Rights, 15 April 2002', 41 *ILM* (2002) at p. 1023.

The doctrine that unlawful combatants are completely excluded from the category of prisoners of war, and therefore from conventions protecting prisoners of war, is by no means a recent creation arising from the events of 11 September 2001. The doctrine has a venerable history in American law of war practice, going back at least as far as the US Civil War of 1861-1865. United States Army General Order number 100, issued on 24 April 1863 by order of President Lincoln (the Lieber Code), defined the nature and consequences of unlawful combatancy as follows:

> 'Article 82. Men, or squads of men, who commit hostilities, whether by fighting, or inroads for destruction or plunder, or by raids of any kind, without commission, without being part and portion of the organised hostile army, and without sharing continuously in the war, but who do so with intermitting returns to their homes and avocations, or with the occasional assumption of the semblance of peaceful pursuits, divesting themselves of the character or appearance of soldiers – such men, or squads of men, are not public enemies, and, therefore, if captured, are not entitled to the privileges of prisoners of war, but shall be treated summarily as highway robbers or pirates.'[458]

Under this Article, one could become an unlawful combatant either by fighting without a significant link, express or tacit, to a party to the conflict ('without commission, [or] without being part and portion of the organised hostile army'), or by engaging in hostilities in a clandestine manner ('with the occasional assumption of the semblance of peaceful pursuits, divesting themselves of the character or appearance of soldiers').

The adoption of the 1949 Geneva Conventions altered, but did not eliminate, this old doctrine. For example, according to Professor Howard Levie, one of the foremost American authorities on the Third Geneva Convention:

> '... even individuals who fall within the categories specifically enumerated in Article 4 [of the Third Convention] are not entitled to prisoner-of-war status if, at the time of capture by the enemy they were dressed in civilian clothes and were engaged in an espionage or sabotage mission behind enemy lines'.[459]

The continuing vitality of these ancient distinctions is well illustrated by the President's differing decisions on Al Qaeda and Taliban personnel. While the President found the conflict in Afghanistan to be an international armed conflict, the Al Qaeda fighters were found to have no adequate connection to any party to that armed conflict; they were not members of the organised armed forces of any *de facto* or *de jure* government of Afghanistan. As fighters, their loyalty was to a non-state, supranational political movement, not a legitimate party to the conflict under Article 2 of the Third Geneva Convention. For similar reasons, they would not be considered part of a *levee en masse* under Article 4A(6) of the Convention because they were not 'inhabitants' of an invaded territory 'who on the approach of the enemy spontaneously take up arms to resist the invading forces, without having had time to form themselves into regular armed units'. Al Qaeda had organised themselves into regular

---

458. <http://www.au.af.mil/au/awc/awcgate/law/liebercode.htm>.
459. H. Levie, *Prisoners of War in International Armed Conflict*, International Law Studies, Vol. 59 (Newport RI, US Naval War College 1978) p. 82.

armed bands long before the arrival of US and allied forces, and had already taken up arms for purposes unrelated to the spontaneous defense of any nation's territory.

The United States could have sought to achieve the same result within the text of the Third Convention, but elected not to. The alternative approach would have accorded Al Qaeda personnel preliminary protection under the Convention either as members of a *levee en masse* or a volunteer corps or partisan group, and then litigated their status on a case-by-case basis before a tribunal convened under Article 5 of the Convention (see below). That a comprehensive determination of status by the US commander-in-chief was adopted instead reinforces the importance, for the United States, of custom, usage and other sources of international law outside the text of the Geneva Conventions themselves.

After noting the United States' position that Al Qaeda fighters cannot be prisoners of war because Al Qaeda is a non-state entity, it is somewhat arresting to find that both the General Counsel of the US Defense Department and the ABA also believe that 'the United States is currently in a state of war' with Al Qaeda (third document). Some commentators, most notably the distinguished British military historian Michael Howard, have criticized the United States for using the terminology of 'war' to describe its current armed conflict with Al Qaeda and other terrorist groups. In this view, for a national government to say that it is at war with such groups accords them too much dignity and respectability. This criticism neglects the unique significance that the term 'war' has attained in United States' constitutional law.

For almost 200 years it has been accepted that if the US government is involved in a 'war', the President, as commander-in-chief of the armed forces, is invested with all the powers necessary to wage and win that war. American lawyers are generally comfortable with the idea that a war, in this sense, can occur between the federal government and a non-state entity. Historically, international law has been consulted to determine what powers the President will legitimately need to wage any war, whether international or internal. When the President announced a 'war on terrorism' after 11 September 2001 he was therefore claiming the right to use historically defined powers under the US Constitution, rather than conceding any international recognition to Al Qaeda.

The President took a somewhat different approach in his decision on the status of the Taliban forces. These could be considered as members of the regular forces of an unrecognised government of a party to the conflict under Article 4A(3) of the Third Convention. The decision to deny prisoner of war status to the Taliban purports to be based not on the customary doctrine of unlawful combatancy but rather on the the terms of the [Third] Geneva Convention itself. Specifically, it appears that the US government applied the four criteria for militia, volunteer corps and resistance movements in Article 4A(2) to the Taliban,[460] and found that the latter failed to meet the requirements to distinguish themselves from the civilian population and to conduct their operations in accordance with the laws of war.[461]

Article 5 of the Third Geneva Convention provides that '[s]hould any doubt arise as to whether persons, having committed a belligerent act and having fallen into the hands of the enemy, belong to any of the categories enumerated in Article 4, such persons shall enjoy the protection of the present Convention until such time as their status has been determined by

---

460. Cf., ibid., pp. 36-37.
461. 'US Response to the Inter-American Commission on Human Rights', *supra* n. 457, at p. 1023.

a competent tribunal.' In regard to both the Al Qaeda and Taliban detainees, the United States has asserted that there was no doubt as to their correct status, and that there was therefore no need to resort to tribunal proceedings under Article 5.[462]

Afghanistan and the United States are not parties to Protocol I Additional to the Geneva Conventions. Article 45 of the Protocol supplements the provisions of Article 5 of the Third Convention. It is not clear, however, whether Article 45, had it been applicable, would have precluded the United States from adopting a blanket determination of unlawful combatancy for all Al Qaeda and Taliban detainees. Article 45 of Protocol I provides, in pertinent part, as follows:

> '1. A person who takes part in hostilities and falls into the power of an adverse Party shall be presumed to be a prisoner of war, and therefore shall be protected by the Third Convention, if he claims the status of prisoner of war, or if he appears to be entitled to such status, or if the Party on which he depends claims such status on his behalf by notification to the detaining Power or to the Protecting Power.'

A presumption of prisoner of war status would appear to preclude a detaining power from making the kind of comprehensive determinations that the United States made in the case of the Al Qaeda and Taliban detainees. The presumption does not arise, however, unless prisoner of war status is claimed, either by the detainee or his power of origin. With the fall of the Taliban government, Afghanistan would be unlikely to claim prisoner of war status for detainees whom the current government may regard as traitors. Since the United States has decided that there was no 'doubt' that the Al Qaeda and Taliban detainees were not entitled to prisoner of war status, it is even more unlikely that it would determine that any detainee 'appears to be entitled to such status'. By all reports, the detainees are a relatively unsophisticated group, unlikely to understand the significance of claiming prisoner of war status themselves. As a practical matter, application of Article 45 of Protocol I may have not affected the decision of the US authorities to treat the Al Qaeda and Taliban detainees as unlawful combatants. Again as a practical matter, it is indeed possible that application of Article 45 might have adversely affected the situation of the detainees. At present, the US government is allowing the International Committee of the Red Cross to have regular access to the detainees. Such access might have been severely curtailed if US authorities became concerned that it might induce the individual detainees to claim the Article 45 presumption of prisoner of war status.

Some of the Al Qaeda and Taliban detainees may face future judicial proceedings as a result of their belligerent activities, either in Afghanistan or elsewhere. It is not clear how the President's 2002 determination of the detainees' status will affect their individual ability to claim prisoner of war status in any future proceedings. Depending on the offences charged and the nature of the prosecution evidence, such proceedings might be tried either before regular federal civilian courts in the United States or before military commissions sitting at Guantánamo, Cuba. Even if a US civilian court entertained a motion to regard an accused as a prisoner of war under the Third Convention, precedent suggests that the court would accord great weight to the President's formal determination that they are not lawful combatants.

---

462. Ibid.

Military commissions are established under the President's powers as commander-in-chief of the armed forces. Such tribunals might rationally conclude that, since they are established by the authority of the President, they have no jurisdiction to review the legality of Presidential determinations. On the other hand, the Department of Defense Instructions for the conduct of military commission trials, issued in 2003 (which shall be discussed in Vol. 6 of the *YIHL*) indicate that accused detainees would be allowed to argue and present evidence that specific acts charged against them were covered by the 'combatant privilege', i.e., that they were lawful actions under the laws of war. For such a defense to prevail, the accused must be allowed to establish that he was a lawful combatant at the time of the hostile act charged. The standard of proof required for conviction before these tribunals is the Anglo-American common law standard of proof of guilt beyond a reasonable doubt. If the defense is able to raise a reasonable doubt as to the accused's status as a lawful combatant, a US military commission should acquit.

While denying that the Al Qaeda and Taliban fighters in its custody are entitled to prisoner of war status, the United States claims that, as a matter of 'policy' (i.e., not a matter of legal obligation), it is treating the detainees, 'to the extent appropriate and consistent with military necessity, in a manner consistent with the principles of the Third Geneva Convention of 1949' (document 1). The scope and content of 'general principles of the Geneva Conventions' or 'general principles of humanitarian law' have been controversial for some time. In 1986, a majority of the judges of The International Court of Justice was unwilling to go beyond Common Articles 1 and 3 in determining the 'minimum yardstick' for behavior in armed conflict.[463]

The United States has adopted a considerably wider definition of 'general principles of the Third Convention' in its treatment of the Al Qaeda and Taliban detainees. In particular, an effort has been made to respect the Third Convention's provisions on shelter, clothing, diet and cultural and spiritual needs. Only where inconsistent with 'military necessity' or when considered not 'appropriate' have the Convention's standards been deliberately disregarded. While not mentioned in these documents, 'military necessity' will undoubtedly be invoked to deny Al Qaeda and Taliban detainees the right, under Articles 85 and 102 of the Third Convention, to be tried by the same courts using the same procedures as in cases involving military personnel of the detaining power. Members of the US military would be tried by courts martial established by statutory authority, not military commissions. The proceedings of courts martial are open to the public, thus severely limiting the prosecution's ability to use secret evidence, while military commission proceedings could involve such evidence. So far, provisions of the Third Convention not considered 'appropriate' for the Al Qaeda and Taliban detainees have been limited to tangential and obsolete privileges, such as advance pay, canteen facilities and the right to receive scientific equipment, musical instruments or sports outfits.

The right of detainees to eventual release and repatriation has been the subject of considerable discussion. The United States has insisted that, under customary law, it has the right to hold unlawful combatants for at least as long as it would have the right to hold prisoners of war under Article 118 of the Third Convention, that is until the end of active hostilities. In principle, this might be a valid interpretation of customary law. However, given the open-ended nature of a 'war on terrorism', where the enemy is one or more non-state actors

---

463. Military and Paramilitary Activities in Nicaragua (Merits) (*US* v. *Nicaragua*), paras. 218-220 (1986).

which are notoriously subject to shifting identities and locations, the 'end of active hostilities' standard has not satisfied critics. As an example of the limited utility of this standard, they could point to the ongoing conflict between Morocco and the non-state Polisario Liberation Front, where some Moroccans have been held as prisoners of war for over 15 years.[464]

In document 3, the Defense Department General Counsel offers some indication as to when usage and custom, as reflected in the principle of military necessity, might require release of a detainee short of the end of hostilities. The government has no interest in detaining enemy combatants any longer than necessary, and is reviewing the requirement for their continued detention on a case-by-case basis. But as long as hostilities continue and the detainees retain intelligence value or present a threat, no law requires that the detainees be released, and it would be imprudent to do so.

This formulation suggests that a detainee might reasonably expect release, and could even have a right to release, when he is no longer of intelligence value to the detaining power, and where the military situation has changed to the point that he is no longer a threat to the detaining power. The latter contingency might arise when the detainee's own government has changed, and no longer supports terrorist activities, or when the terrorist organisation with which he was affiliated has been broken up. Physical or severe mental disability of the detainee might also meet this test.

Burrus M. Carnahan

- ☞ President's Order of 9 June 2002 designating José Padilla as an enemy combatant
- ☞ Statement of Deputy Secretary of Defense Paul Wolfowitz on the arrest of Abdullah al Mujahir, also known as José Padilla, 10 June 2002[465] <http://www.defenselink.mil/news/Jun2002/t06102002_t0610dsd.html>
- ☞ News Briefing, Department of Defense, 12 June 2002

In a 9 June 2002 Order addressed to the US Secretary of Defense, the President set forth his findings in relation to Jose Padilla, also known as Abdullah al Mujahir, who became known in the media as 'the dirty bomber'.

The seven-paragraph Order concluded that Padilla is an enemy combatant, and provides, in summary, the basis for that conclusion, namely, that Padilla is 'closely associated with al Qaida'; is engaged in 'hostile and war-like acts', including 'preparation for acts of international terrorism' directed at the US; 'possesses information that would be helpful in preventing al Qaida attacks'; and 'represents a continuing, present and grave danger to the national security of the United States'.[466] Paragraph 6 of the Order directed Secretary Rumsfeld to detain Padilla.

In his statement of 10 June, Deputy Secretary of Defense, Paul Wolfowitz, presented the administration's position on the legal status of Padilla. He said that Padilla had been arrested in the United States and turned over to the US Department of Defense, which held him at the Naval Consolidated Brig in Charleston, South Carolina. The authorities claimed that he was an agent of Al Qaeda and had been planning to plant a 'dirty bomb', that is, an

---

464. See H.-P. Gasser, 'The Conflict in Western Sahara – An Unresolved Issue from the Decolonization Period', in this volume at p. 375.

465. Reprinted in the Documentation section of this volume at p. 664.

466. 9 June Order, paras. 2-5.

ordinary bomb capable of dispersing radioactive material, on US territory. Notwithstanding the fact that Al Mujahir is a US citizen, Wolfowitz stated that he was being held under the laws of war as an enemy combatant. The legal basis for his detention was the 9 June 2002 Order of the President, pursuant to the Military Order of 13 November 2002,[467] and the legal authority for his designation as an unlawful combatant was said to be the 1942 Supreme Court case *ex parte Quirin* and the 1946 Supreme Court case in *re Territo*.

In *Quirin*,[468] a US citizen was captured after having been covertly put ashore in the US by a German U-boat during World War II for the purpose of engaging in acts of sabotage on behalf of Germany. He was tried and convicted by the Armed Forces. The Court stated: 'Unlawful combatants are … subject to capture and detention, but in addition they are subject to trial and punishment by military tribunals for acts which render their belligerency unlawful.' In *Territo*,[469] a US citizen fighting in the Italian Army against the US during World War II was captured by the Americans and held prisoner of war. Territo sought a writ of *habeas corpus*, claiming that his incarceration as a prisoner of war was unlawful. The court found that 'all persons who are active in opposing an army in war may be captured and except for spies and other non-uniformed plotters and actors for the enemy are prisoners of war'. US citizenship was no bar to being treated as an enemy combatant. The court held that 'Territo upon capture was properly held as a prisoner of war'.

In a Press Briefing of 12 June 2002, during a trip to Doha, Qatar, Secretary of Defense, Donald Rumsfeld said that Padilla was 'an individual who unquestionably was involved in terrorist activities against the United States'. He said that Padilla would be held 'by the United States government through the Department of Defense and be questioned'. Secretary Rumseld made it clear that Padilla was being held not so much as to prevent him from carrying out a terrorist act but to gather information:

> 'Here is an individual who has intelligence information, and … our interest in his case is not law enforcement, it is not punishment because he was a terrorist or working with the terrorists. Our interest at the moment is to try and find out everything he knows so that hopefully we can stop other terrorist acts.'

In December 2002, the United States District Court for the Southern District of New York decided, *inter alia*, that Padilla's designation as an enemy combatant by the President was lawful.[470]

AVRIL MCDONALD

Methods and Means of Warfare
- ☛ Status of Investigations during Operation Enduring Freedom, CENTCOM News Release, 29 March 2002[471]
- ☛ United States Department of Defense News Release, Statement on Hazar Qadam raid, 21 February 2002[472]

---

467. See *infra* at p. 626 of this report.
468. 317 *US* 1 (1942); 317 *US* 1; 87 *L Ed.* 7.
469. 156 *F 2d* 142, 145 (9th Cir. 1946).
470. See *infra* at pp. 662 at 664-665 of this report.
471. Reprinted in the Documentation section of this volume at p. 658.
472. Reprinted in the Documentation section of this volume at p. 657.

☛ Investigation of Civilian Casualties, Oruzgan Province, Operation Full Throttle, 30 June 2002[473]

It is well settled that military commanders have an obligation to investigate possible violations of humanitarian law involving their own forces and, if appropriate, to initiate legal process to punish such offences. The obligation to investigate and punish war crimes committed by a commander's own troops was implicit in national directives such as the following from US Army General Order number 100, 24 April 1863 (the Lieber Code):

> 'Art. 44. All wanton violence committed against persons in the invaded country, all destruction of property not commanded by the authorised officer, all robbery, all pillage or sacking, even after taking place by main force, all rape, wounding, maiming, or killing of such inhabitants, are prohibited under the penalty of death, or such other severe punishment as may seem adequate for the gravity of the offense.
>
> …
>
> Art. 46. Neither officers nor soldiers are allowed to make use of their position or power in the hostile country for private gain, not even for commercial transactions otherwise legitimate. Offences to the contrary committed by commissioned officers will be punished with cashiering or such other punishment as the nature of the offense may require; if by soldiers, they shall be punished according to the nature of the offense.
>
> Art. 47. Crimes punishable by all penal codes, such as arson, murder, maiming, assaults, highway robbery, theft, burglary, fraud, forgery, and rape, if committed by an American soldier in a hostile country against its inhabitants, are not only punishable as at home, but in all cases in which death is not inflicted, the severer punishment shall be preferred.'

In occupied territory, the obligation to investigate and punish became more definite with the adoption of Article 43 of the Hague Regulations on Land Warfare of 1899 and 1907, which required the occupying power to 'take all the measures in his power to restore, and ensure, as far as possible, public order and safety'. Following World War II, the 1945 trial of General Yamashita by a US Military Commission, for failure to investigate and punish atrocities committed by his soldiers in the Philippines, established that failure to investigate could result in personal penal liability for a military commander.

The exact scope and nature of this liability remained the subject of debate for two decades. By 1977, both expert and diplomatic consensus had finally settled on the proper formula to state the legal obligations of commanders to deal with war crimes by members of their command. This consensus was reflected in Article 87 of Additional Protocol I as follows:

> '1. The High Contracting Parties and the Parties to the conflict shall require military commanders, with respect to members of the armed forces under their command and other persons under their control, to prevent and, where necessary, to suppress and to report to competent authorities breaches of the Conventions and of this Protocol.
>
> …
>
> 3. The High Contracting Parties and Parties to the conflict shall require any commander who is aware that subordinates or other persons under his control are going to commit or

---

473. Reprinted in the Documentation section of this volume at p. 660.

have committed a breach of the Conventions or of this Protocol, to initiate such steps as are necessary to prevent such violations of the Conventions or this Protocol, and, where appropriate, to initiate disciplinary or penal action against violators thereof.'

These provisions are widely regarded as reflecting customary international law, binding on states, such as the United States, that are not party to Additional Protocol I to the Geneva Conventions.

The above documents, all issued in 2002, are public summaries of US military investigations of incidents involving civilian casualties and damage during the fighting in Afghanistan in 2001 and 2002. They illustrate how commanders in the United States military view their obligation to initiate necessary steps to suppress possible violations of international humanitarian law.

The investigation in each case was ordered by the Commander-in-Chief of Central Command who had operational command over US forces engaged in Afghanistan. The most serious incidents arose out of attacks on Hazar Qadam on 23 January 2002 and Operation Full Throttle on 20 June 2002. Both incidents involved attacks on villages believed to be Taliban strongholds which resulted in significant civilian deaths and injuries.

The Central Command investigation of Operation Full Throttle focused on legally significant issues, including whether the buildings attacked were legitimate targets, whether the persons killed or injured were directly engaged in hostilities, and the ability of US forces to distinguish enemy combatants from non-combatants. The investigation's conclusion relied in part on the legal principle that parties to a conflict deliberately using civilians to shield military actions are legally responsible for collateral civilian casualties, rather than the attacking forces. This legal position has been repeatedly asserted by the United States since the 1970s.

The Central Command investigation of the raid on Hazar Qadam was forwarded to the US Department of Defense, the superior authority immediately above Central Command. The Department determined that no legal liability attached to the US participants in the Hazar Qadam raid.

BURRUS M. CARNAHAN

Nuclear Weapons
- ☞ National Security Presidential Directive 17, 14 September 2002 <http://www.fas.org/irp/offdocs/nspd/nspd-17.html>
- ☞ National Strategy to Combat Weapons of Mass Destruction, 11 December 2002 <http://www.whitehouse.gov/news/releases/2002/12/WMDStrategy.pdf>
- ☞ White House, The National Security Strategy of the United States of America, 13 September 2002 <http://www.whitehouse.gov/nsc/nss.pdf>

The first document specifically allows for the use of nuclear weapons in self-defense to a biological or chemical weapons attack. The National Security Presidential Directive 17 states: 'The United States will continue to make clear that it reserves the right to respond with overwhelming force – including potentially nuclear weapons – to the use of [weapons of mass destruction] against the United States, our forces abroad, and friends and allies.'

The second document released on 11 December, a public version of the Presidential Directive 17, closely parallels the first one, although the text departs from the phrase 'including potentially nuclear weapons' to say 'including through resort to all of our options … .', [474]

The National Security Strategy (see also below) linked the US policy of preemption generally to the threat of nuclear and other weapons of mass destruction, particularly in the hands of terrorists who would not be deterred by the usual modes of deterrence and containment.

Biological Weapons
- The Bioterrorism Act of 2002, enacted by Congress on 23 January 2002, signed into law by President Bush on 12 June 2002 <http://www.fda.gov/oc/bioterrorism/PL107-188.pdf>

This law, otherwise known as the 'Public Health Security and Bioterrorism Preparedness and Response Act of 2002', regulates various aspects of the threat posed by bioterrorism. Its various parts deal with: national preparedness for bioterrorism and other public health emergencies; enhancing controls on dangerous biological agents and toxins; protecting safety and security of food and drug supplies; drinking water security; and safety, *inter alia*.

Military Commissions
- Military Commission Order No. 1 of 21 March 2002 establishing Rules of Procedure for operating the Military Commissions <http://www.defenselink.mil/news/Mar2002/d20020321ord.pdf>

Military Commission Order No. 1 of 21 March 2002 (the Order) establishing Rules of Procedure for operating the Military Commissions was intended to elaborate on the legal regime for non-US citizens detained by the US who may face trial before US military commissions established in Presidential Military Order of 13 November 2001, relating to Detention, Treatment, and Trial of Certain Non-Citizens in the War on Terrorism. [475]

The Order 'implements policy, assigns responsibilities, and prescribes procedures … for trials before military commissions of individuals subject to the President's Military Order'. The commissions shall have jurisdiction over persons suspected of violations of the laws of war and all other offences triable by military commission.

The Secretary of Defense or a designee appointed, shall appoint three to seven members to the commission, and one to two alternate members. Members must be commissioned officers of the US Armed Forces. The Presiding Officer's role is similar to that of a judge. He or she must be a military officer who is a Judge Advocate of any branch of the US Armed Forces. The Chief Prosecutor must be a Judge Advocate. Generally, they will be military officers, although they must include special prosecutors from the Department of Justice. The Chief Defense Counsel must be a Judge Advocate. He or she supervises the overall defense efforts and will have a staff of military defense counsel. The accused may choose to hire a civilian counsel. That person must be a US citizen licensed to practice law in the US, and must be able to obtain at least a secret clearance.

---

474. R. Tomkins, 'U.S. threatens Nuke response to WMD attack', UPI, 11 December 2002; N. Kralev, 'Bush signs paper allowing nuclear response', *Washington Times*, 31 January 2003.
475. 4 *YIHL* (2001) pp. 633-635.

A guilty verdict must be pronounced by at least two-thirds of the members (the same as US courts martial). However, a death sentence can only be imposed by a unanimous seven member panel.

Significantly, the Order provides in Section 1(f) that 'Given the danger to the safety of the United States and the nature of international terrorism, and to the extent provided by and under this order, I find consistent with section 836 of title 10, United States Code, that it is not practicable to apply in military commissions under this order the principles of law and the rules of evidence generally recognised in the trial of criminal cases in the United States district courts.'

The Order points out that the terrorist threat amounts to 'an extraordinary emergency ... for national defense purposes, that this emergency constitutes an urgent and compelling government interest, and that issuance of this order is necessary to meet the emergency' (Section 1(g)).[476]

International Criminal Court

☛ Letter from John R. Bolton, US Under Secretary of State for Arms Control and International Security, to Kofi Annan, UN Secretary-General, announcing America's decision to 'unsign' the ICC Statute, 6 May 2002 <http://www.state.gov/r/pa/prs/ps/2002/9968.htm>

☛ Secretary Rumsfeld's Statement on the ICC Treaty, Department of Defense, No. 233-02, 6 May 2002 <http://www.defenselink.mil/news/May2002/b05062002_bt233-02.html>

☛ Issues Update: US Has No Legal Obligation to the International Criminal Court, Pierre-Richard Prosper, US Ambassador for War Crimes Issues, Foreign Press Center Briefing – Washington DC, 6 May 2002 <http://www.wfa.org/issues/wicc/unsigning/prosperunsigning.html>

☛ Letter from 45 members of the US House of Representatives to President George W. Bush, 22 May 2002 <http://www.wfa.org/issues/wicc/unsigning/crowleyopletter.html>

On 6 May 2002, in an internationally unprecedented step, by letter sent from John R. Bolton, Under Secretary of State for Arms Control and International Security, to UN Secretary-General Kofi Annan, the United States 'unsigned' the Rome Statute of the International Criminal Court.[477]

The short text of the letter read:

'This is to inform you, in connection with the Rome Statute of the International Criminal Court adopted on July 17, 1998, that the United States does not intend to become a party to the treaty. Accordingly, the United States has no legal obligations arising from its signature on December 31, 2000. The United States requests that its intention not to become a party, as expressed in this letter, be reflected in the depositary's status lists relating to this treaty.'

---

476. A national emergency was proclaimed on 14 September 2001 by Proclamation 7463, Declaration of National Emergency by Reason of Certain Terrorist Attacks.

477. J. Garamone, 'U.S. withdraws from International Criminal Court Treaty', American Forces Press Service, 7 May 2002. <http://www.defenselink.mil/news/May2002/n05072002_200205071.html>; J. Lobe, 'Bush "unsigns" war crimes treaty', Alternet, 6 May 2002. <http://www.alternet.org/story.html?StoryID=13055>.

The Statute had been signed by President Clinton on 31 December 2001, just hours before the final deadline for signing.[478]

US Secretary of Defense Donald Rumsfeld said in a separate written statement issued on 6 May:

> 'The United States will regard as illegitimate any attempt by the court or states parties to the treaty to assert the ICC's jurisdiction over American citizens. ... We have an obligation to protect our men and women in uniform from this court and to preserve America's ability to remain engaged in the world. And we intend to do so.'

Rumsfeld outlined the administration's main points of opposition to the Court, including:

> 'the lack of adequate checks and balances on powers of the ICC prosecutors and judges; the dilution of the U.N. Security Council's authority over international criminal prosecutions; and the lack of an effective mechanism to prevent politicized prosecutions of American servicemembers and officials. These flaws would be of concern at any time, but they are particularly troubling in the midst of a difficult, dangerous war on terrorism. There is a risk that the ICC could attempt to assert jurisdiction over U.S. service members, as well as civilians, involved in counterterrorist and other military operations – something we cannot allow.'[479]

In a separate statement issued on 6 May, Pierre-Richard Prosper, the State Department's Ambassador for War Crimes, said:

> 'The president has also made clear and is making clear that he is committed to combating war crimes, committed for the United States to play a leadership role in the world to address these abuses as they occur. We took this rare but not unprecedented action today in order to give us the flexibility to protect our interests and the flexibility to pursue alternative approaches. ... In support of this alternative mechanism, the United States will be prepared to support politically, financially, technically and logistically any state – post conflict state – that seeks to credibly pursue accountability for violations of humanitarian law ... We will be asking Congress to help us in finding the necessary resources in order to combat these problems. We will seek to mobilize the private sector, to see if the private sector can play a role in this regard, either through funding or other contributions. We will seek to create a pool of experienced judges, lawyers and prosecutors, who will be willing to work on short notice, in order to help ingrain the rule of law in these societies. And we will take steps within the United States to fill any gaps that we may have in our laws, to ensure that the United States does not become a safe haven for war criminals and indicted persons. ...'

In a press conference given following the issuance of the statement, Mr Prosper said that the ICC 'should not expect any support for cooperation from the United States government'. In response to a different question he stated that the US would not 'take aggressive action or wage war, if you will, against the ICC or the supporters of the ICC. Again, he

---

478. <http://www.npwj.org/pressmon/un_wireicc_usasign.htm>.
479. See Garamone, *supra* n. 477.

respects the decisions of states to be part of this treaty consensually, but in turn, he also wants states to respect our decision not to be part of it'. However, this statement is difficult to reconcile with the provisions of the American Servicemembers' Protection Act (see *infra*) or the US's aggressive campaign to persuade states to sign so-called 'Article 98 agreements' with it (see *infra*).

On 13 May, the European Union, in a Declaration supported by the Central and Eastern European countries associated with the EU and Norway, Cyprus and Malta, expressed its disappointment and regret about the decision to unsign, stating, *inter alia*, that: 'While respecting the sovereign rights of the United States, the European Union notes that this unilateral action may have undesirable consequences on multilateral Treaty-making and generally on the rule of law in international relations.' The statement further noted that US fears about the Court were unfounded and regretted that it had not waited until it had had the benefit of the Court's actual experience. It expressed the Union's concern about the potentially negative effect the US action would have on the development and reinforcement of recent trends towards individual accountability for the most serious international crimes, and its determination to encourage the widest possible support for the ICC.[480]

On 22 May, 45 members of the US House of Representatives sent a signed letter to President Bush, which conveyed their opposition to his withdrawal from the Statute. '"Unsigning" the treaty in this manner will provide no substantive benefit but has created a harmful precedent that will undermine efforts by the United States to compel other countries to adhere to their obligations under international law.'

☞ American Servicemembers' Protection Act of 2002 (Adopted as part of the 2000 Supplemental Appropriations Act for further recovery from and response to terrorist attacks on the United States for the fiscal year ending 30 September 2002, and for other purposes). Public Law. 107-206, signed by President George W. Bush on 2 August 2002 <http://www.usaforicc.org/ASPA.htm>

This Act, which was introduced by Senator Jesse Helms on 10 May 2000,[481] was finally signed into law by President Bush on 2 August 2002.

The main purposes of the Act are to prevent any US Court, or any agency or entity of any state or local government, from cooperating with or supporting the International Criminal Court (Section 2004); to restrict US participation in certain United Nations peacekeeping operations (Section 2005); to prohibit direct or indirect transfer of classified national security information and law enforcement information to the ICC (Section 2006); to prohibit US military assistance to parties to the ICC (except NATO Member States; major non-NATO allies, including Australia, Egypt, Israel, Japan, Jordan, Argentina, the Republic of Korea and New Zealand, and Taiwan) (Section 2007); to authorise the freeing of members of the US Armed Forces and certain other persons who have been detained or imprisoned by the ICC (Section 2008). The authority to rescue persons detained or imprisoned by the ICC extends not only to US personnel but allied persons.

According to Section 2005, it is US policy to seek permanent exemption from the ICC for US troops in every UN peacekeeping authorization, and the President should use the

---

480. Declaration by the EU on the Position of the US Towards the International Criminal Court, 13 May 2002. <http://www.wfa.org/issues/wicc/unsigning/euonunsigning.html>.

481. 3 *YIHL* (2000) p. 615.

voice and veto of the United States in the UN SC to ensure that each resolution of the SC authorizing any peacekeeping operation under Charter VI of the Charter or peace enforcement operation under Chapter VII permanently exempts, at a minimum, members of the US Armed Forces participating in such operation from criminal prosecution or other assertation of jurisdiction by the ICC for actions undertaken in connection with the operation.

Section 2003 grants to the President authority to waive Sections 2005 (prohibition on US participation in UN peacekeeping) and 2007 (prohibition on assistance to States Parties) for a single period of one year if he notifies congressional committees and reports that the International Criminal Court has entered into a binding agreement with the US not to exercise jurisdiction over US and allied personnel. Under Section 2007, US military assistance to States Parties to the Rome Statute will cease one year after the date of its entry into force pursuant to Article 126.

The motivation for the Act is explained in Section 2002, where Congress set out its findings on the matter. It found, *inter alia*, that any American prosecuted by the Court would be denied procedural safeguards to which all Americans are entitled under the Bill of Rights, including the right to trial by jury; that members of the US Armed Forces should be free from the risk of prosecution by the Court, especially where they are stationed or deployed around the world to protect the vital national interests of the US: 'The United States government has an obligation to protect the members of its Armed Forces, to the maximum extent possible, against criminal prosecutions carried out by the International Criminal Court.' It also expressed concern that not only servicemembers but also the President and other senior elected and appointed officials of the US government might be prosecuted by the ICC. 'No less than members of the Armed Forces of the United States, senior officials of the United States government should be free from the risk of prosecution by the International Criminal Court, especially with respect to official actions taken by them to protect the national interests of the United States.' Moreover, 'Any agreement within the Preparatory Commission on a definition of the Crime of Aggression that usurps the prerogative of the United Nations Security Council under Article 39 of the Charter of the United Nations to "determine the existence of any ... act of aggression" would contravene the charter of the United Nations and undermine deterrence.' Finally, the US pointed to the legal principle that a treaty is only binding on its parties and does not create obligations for non-parties to be bound without their consent. 'The United States is not a party to the Rome Statute and will not be bound by any of its terms. The United States will not recognize the jurisdiction of the International Criminal Court over United States nationals.'

➡ Article 98 Agreements

Following its unsigning of the Treaty, the United States actively pursued bilateral so-called Article 98 agreements with States Parties to the ICC Statute. The effect of such agreements is to immunise either or both forces and the nationals of the co-signatory from the criminal jurisdiction of the ICC.[482]

Various international NGOs monitoring the work of the Court expressed their concern at the worldwide campaign to enter into what Amnesty International and Human Right Watch,

---

482. 'US Bilateral Immunity or So-called "Article 98" Agreements', Coalition for an International Criminal Court. <http://www.globalpolicy.org/intljustice/icc/2003/0606usbilaterals.htm>.

inter alia, called 'impunity agreements'.[483] Amnesty expressed its view that these agreements were limited to existing Status of Forces Agreements (SOFAs) and did not apply to SOFAs that are entered into after a state becomes a party to the ICC. Further, 'even if the International Criminal Court were to hold that this provision also applies to renewed or new SOFAs, those SOFAs would, of course, have to be consistent with the Rome Statute and other international law. In addition, … a state entering into a US impunity agreement that had previously signed the Rome Statute would be acting in a manner that would defeat the object and purpose of the Statute and, therefore, would be in violation of its obligations under customary international law governing treaties.' Human Rights Watch stated that Article 98 agreements 'violate the Rome Statute' and that any state that has ratified the Statute may not lawfully sign an agreement with a state that has repudiated or not signed the Statute, as to do so would violate and undermine it.[484]

In an article published in the *Wall Street Journal*, David Scheffer, the Ambassador for War Crimes under the Clinton administration and the chief US negotiator at the ICC Prepcoms and the Rome conference, expressed his view that the agreements sought by the US were permitted under Article 98, although they had limitations. But significantly, he said that they immunised only state officials and not private individuals. He recalled that:

'the original intent of Article 98 agreements was to ensure that Status of Forces Agreements … between the United States and scores of countries would not be compromised and that Americans on official duty could be specially covered by agreements that fit Article 98's terms. I first put that requirement on the table in early 1995 in Madrid. … Throughout five years of treaty negotiations, the Article 98 safeguard was a major U.S. objective and it was successfully achieved … Significantly, Article 98 does not prevent the new court from investigating or even indicting an American official. But if there is an Article 98 agreement with another country, that country would not be able to surrender an indicted official covered by that agreement to the court without Washington's consent. … However, the Bush administration overreaches, if it attempts, with Article 98 agreements, to immunize any U.S. national living abroad or travelling for any reason from surrender to the court and to blanket the entire world with such agreements. The negotiating objective never was to protect American mercenaries or any other citizen engaged in unofficial activities. (We would have used "state of nationality" rather than "sending state" if that had been our intent.) As I often said as a negotiator, rogue citizens act at their own risk.'[485]

On 25 September 2002, the Parliamentary Assembly of the Council of Europe adopted a resolution on the subject of Article 98 agreements, in which it expressed, *inter alia*, the Assembly's view that these '"exemption agreements" are not admissible under the international law governing treaties, in particular the Vienna Convention on the Law of Treaties,

---

483. Amnesty International, 'International Criminal Court: US Efforts to Obtain Impunity for Genocide, Crimes against Humanity and War Crime' [sic], AI Index: IOR 40/025/2002, August 2002. <http://www.amnesty.org/library/Index/engIOR400252002?OpenDocument&of=THEM>; Human Rights Watch, 'United States Efforts to Undermine the International Criminal Court: Impunity Agreements', 4 September 2002. <http://www.hrw.org/campaigns/icc/docs/art98analysis.htm>.

484. Ibid.

485. D.J. Scheffer, 'Original intent at the global criminal court', *Wall Street Journal Europe*, 20 September 2002.

according to which States must refrain from any action which would not be consistent with the object and the purpose of a treaty'.[486] It further called on all Council of Europe Member States and observer States to, *inter alia*, not enter into bilateral 'exemption agreements' which would compromise or limit in any manner their cooperation with the Court in the investigation and prosecution of crimes within the jurisdiction of the Court.

In the final analysis, the legality of Article 98 agreements entered into by the US, either in their entirety or in part, will remain an open question until and unless the ICC itself is called upon to make a determination on the matter.

The US also succeeded in pushing through a resolution at the UN which would shield peacekeepers from non-States Parties from the jurisdiction of the Court for a period of one year.[487]

Jus Ad Bellum
- ☛ USA: Joint Resolution of Congress to authorise the use of United States Armed Forces against Iraq, 10 October 2002[488] <http://www.freerepublic.com/focus/news/761620/posts>

The joint resolution of the US Congress (Senate and House of Representatives) authorizing the US invasion of Iraq makes it clear that, so far as Congress was concerned at least and to the extent that it considered the question, the principal international legal basis for the US resort to force against Iraq was self-defense. US reliance on Iraq's material breach of SC resolutions for use of force was not a question of it volunteering for the role of international policeman or self-appointed vigilante acting in lieu of the SC and on behalf of the international community. Iraq's material breaches of earlier SC resolutions were only relevant as a legal basis insofar as they involved its involvement in activities which threatened the security and interests of the US, or the Persian Gulf region, whose peace and security was also declared to be in the national security interests of the United States.

In fact, the resolution was Congress's imprimatur for a test drive of the doctrine of anticipatory self-defense (see below). However, the threat posed by Iraq, as outlined in the resolution, was so vague and remote as to exemplify the problems with the doctrine of pre-emption, at least as understood in this case, and its adoption as a matter of policy rather than military necessity. Whether or not the resolution was grounded in firm intelligence, given that it was a licence for the use of preemptive force, it is striking that it characterised the apparent threat to the security interests of the US posed by Iraq in such imprecise language.

The resolution stated that Iraq, in material breach of UN Security Council resolutions, had thwarted the efforts of UN weapons inspectors to destroy its weapons stockpiles and had continued to develop weapons of mass destruction (WMD). The resolution referred to Iraq's demonstrated capability and willingness to use WMD, its support for terrorist organisations, including Al Qaeda – members of which were apparently known to be in Iraq – and its manifest hostility towards the United States, and

---

486. Resolution 1300 (2002) (1) on the 'Risks for the integrity of the Statute of the International Criminal Court' from Article 98 agreements. <http://www.pgaction.org/uploadedfiles/CoERes BIAs25June03Eng.pdf>.
487. See the Year in Review in this volume at p. 269.
488. Reprinted in the Documentation section of this volume at p. 819.

'the risk that the current Iraqi regime will either employ those weapons to launch a surprise attack against the United States or its Armed Forces or provide them to international terrorists who would do so, and the extreme magnitude of harm that would result to the United States and its citizens from such an attack, combine to justify action by the United States to defend itself'.

It referred to UN SC Resolution 678 (1990) which authorised the use of 'all necessary means' to enforce Resolution 660 (1990), and to subsequent SC Resolutions, particularly 687 (1991) and 949 (1994), as well as to earlier congressional authorizaton for the use of the US Armed Forces in order to enforce the relevant SC resolutions, and stated:

'… the United States is determined to prosecute the war on terrorism and Iraq's ongoing support for international terrorist groups combined with its development of weapons of mass destruction in direct violation of its obligations under the 1991 cease-fire and other United Nations Security Council resolutions make clear that it is in the national security interest of the United States and in furtherance of the war on terrorism that all relevant United States Security Council resolutions be enforced, including through the use of force if necessary'.

Preemptive Self-defence
☛ President George W. Bush, State of the Union Address, 29 January 2002 <http://www.whitehouse.gov/news/releases/2002/01/20020129-11.html>
☛ President George W. Bush, Remarks by the President at 2002 Graduation Exercise of the United States Military Academy at West Point, 1 June 2002 <http://www.whitehouse.gov/news/releases/2002/06/20020601-3.html>
☛ White House, The National Security Strategy of the United States of America, 13 September 2002 <http://www.whitehouse.gov/nsc/nss.pdf>

In several documents released in the course of 2002, the Bush administration set out its doctrine of preemptive or anticipatory self-defense, or what has become known as the 'Bush doctrine'.

The doctrine was unveiled during President Bush's State of the Union Address on 29 January 2002, in which he first referred to the so-called 'Axis of evil', consisting of North Korea, Iran and Iraq. The President warned:

'I will not wait on events, while dangers gather. I will not stand by, as peril draws closer and closer. The United States of America will not permit the world's most dangerous regimes to threaten us with the world's most destructive weapons.'

The policy was elaborated during President Bush's address to the graduating class at West Point Military Academy. In particular, he explained the rationale behind preemption: new threats, such as terrorism, which cannot be contained in the old ways:

'For much of the last century, America's defense relied on the Cold War doctrines of deterrence and containment. In some cases, those strategies still apply. But new threats also require new thinking. Deterrence – the promise of massive retaliation against nations – means nothing against shadowy terrorist networks with no nation or citizens to defend. Containment is not possible when unbalanced dictators with weapons of mass destruction can deliver those weapons on missiles or secretly provide them to terrorist allies.

We cannot defend America and our friends by hoping for the best. We cannot put our faith in the word of tyrants, who solemnly sign non-proliferation treaties, and then systemically break them. If we wait for threats to fully materialize, we will have waited too long.

Homeland defense and missile defense are part of stronger security, and they're essential priorities for America. Yet the war on terror will not be won on the defensive. We must take the battle to the enemy, disrupt his plans, and confront the worst threats before they emerge. In the world we have entered, the only path to safety is the path of action. And this nation will act.'

Further refinement of the policy came in September 2002, when the Bush administration released a policy paper known as the National Security Strategy that fleshed out the doctrine of preemption. America would

'not hesitate to act alone, if necessary, to exercise our right of self-defense by acting preemptively against such terrorists, to prevent them from doing harm against our people and our country ... We must be able to stop rogue states and their terrorist clients before they are able to threaten or use weapons of mass destruction against the United States and our allies and friends. ...

The United States has long maintained the option of preemptive actions to counter a sufficient threat to our national security. The greater the threat, the greater is the risk of inaction – and the more compelling the case for taking anticipatory action to defend ourselves, even if uncertainty remains as to the time and place of the enemy's attack. To forestall or prevent such hostile acts by our adversaries, the United States will, if necessary, act preemptively. The United States will not use force in all cases to preempt emerging threats, nor should nations use preemption as a pretext for aggression. Yet in an age where the enemies of civilization openly and actively seek the world's most destructive technologies, the United States cannot remain idle while dangers gather.'[489]

The National Security Strategy also makes clear that the US will make 'no distinction between terrorists and those who knowingly harbor or provide aid to them'.

Cases (status of detainees)
- ☞ *Coalition of Clergy, et al.* v. *George Walker Bush, et al.*, United States District Court for the Central District of California, Case No. CV 02-570 AHM, Order dismissing petition for writ of *habeas corpus* and first amended petition for writ of *habeas corpus*, 19 February 2002[490] <http://www.politechbot.com/docs/guantanamo.decision.022202. pdf>
- ☞ *Shafiq Rasul, Skina Bibi, as Next Friend of Shafiq Rasul, et al.* v. *George Walker Bush, et al.; Fawzi Khalid Abdullah Fahad Al Odah, et al.*, Plaintiffs, v. *United States of America, et al.*, Defendants, United States District Court for the District of Colombia,

---

489. See M.J. Glennon, 'Why the Security Council Failed', *Foreign Affairs* (May/June 2003) pp. 16 at 20.

490. Reprinted in this volume at pp. 626 et seq.

30 July 2002[491] <http://news.findlaw.com/hdocs/docs/terrorism/rasulvbush073102dsm.
pdf>

☛ *Padilla* v. *Bush*, United States District Court for the Southern District of New York, No.
02 CIV. 445 (MBM) 2002 WL 31718308 (S.D.N.Y. 4 December 2002) <http://faculty.
maxwell.syr.edu/tmkeck/Cases/PadillavBush2002.htm>

☛ *Hamdi* v. *Rumsfeld*, US Court of Appeals for the Fourth Circuit, 316 *F.3d* 450, 8 January 2003[492] <http://www.runet.edu/~mfranck/images/490%20seminar/Hamdi%20v%
20Rumsfeld.pdf>

The question of the legality of the detention of persons being held at Guantánamo Bay was
brought before a number of US courts in 2002.

The first and second cases involved similar legal questions, chiefly, the right of non-
citizens detained outside the sovereign territory of the US to apply for *habeas corpus* in US
court. The third and fourth cases concerned the legal status of US citizens who are considered to be unlawful combatants. These cases indicated that the lower courts at least paid the
utmost deference to executive powers in matters concerning determination of conflict, designation of unlawful combatant status, and detention of unlawful combatants. The canny
decision of the executive to detain persons captured both in Afghanistan and in connection
with the wider war on terrorism in Guantánamo Bay in Cuba, an area not subject to US
sovereignty if within US jurisdiction, was vindicated as the courts found the question of
sovereignty to be dispositive.

In the first case, *Coalition of Clergy, et al.* v. *George Walker Bush, et al.*, the United
States District Court for the Central District of California dismissed an order of petition for
habeas corpus by the applicants, a group of interested persons acting on behalf of persons
detained in Guantánamo Bay. The petition alleged that detainees at Guantánamo Bay were
being held in violation of the US Constitution or the laws and treaties of the US, in that they
(1) have been deprived of their liberty without due process of law; (2) have not been informed of the nature and cause of the accusations against them; and (3) have not been
afforded the assistance of counsel. The petition also claimed that the detainees had rights
under the Geneva Convention which had been breached, such as relating to the prohibition
against the transfer of prisoners from their country of capture.

The Court found that (1) the petitioners did not have standing to assert a claim on behalf
of the detainees; (2) Even if the petitioners did have standing, the Court lacked jurisdiction
to entertain the claims; (3) Since no federal court would have jurisdiction over the petitioners' claims, there was no basis to transfer the case to another federal district court.

Assuming that the detainees lacked access to the courts themselves, the Court nevertheless held that the applicants lacked *locus standi* to appear on their behalf as they lacked a
'significant relationship with the detainees – indeed, any relationship' and there was no
evidence that they had sought authorization to do so.

As regards the jurisdictional question, the Court justified its finding that it lacked jurisdiction to hear the case on the ground that no custodian responsible for the custody of the
detainees was within its territorial jurisdiction. Some of the custodians named by the petitioners were within the territorial jurisdiction of the District Court for the District of Colombia, and if a federal court within that district could exercise jurisdiction, federal law

---

491. Reprinted in this volume at p. 456.
492. Reprinted in this volume at p. 482.

mandated a transfer of the case to that court rather than its dismissal. However, such a transfer was not possible in this case since neither the courts within that district nor indeed any US court had jurisdiction to hear the case given that the detainees were outside the sovereign territory of the United States.

Applying *Johnson* v. *Eisentrager*,[493] the Court found that the detainees were at no relevant time within any territory over which the US had sovereignty:

'In all key respects, the Guantanamo detainees are like the petitioners in *Johnson*: They are aliens; they were enemy combatants; they were captured in combat; they were abroad when captured; they are abroad now; since their capture, they have been under the control of only the military; they have not stepped foot on American soil; and there are no legal or judicial precedents entitling them to pursue a writ of habeas corpus in an American civilian court. Moreover, there are sound practical reasons, such as legitimate security concerns, that make it unwise for this or any court to take the unprecedented step of conferring such a right on these detainees.'

Distinguishing territorial jurisdiction from sovereignty, the Court noted that the latter concept is the dispositive issue: 'The Court finds that Guantanamo Bay is *not* within the sovereign territory of the United States and therefore rejects petitioners' argument.' The Court found that the legal status of Guantánamo Bay was governed by the 1903 lease agreement between the United States and Cuba, which was extended in 1934,[494] and which recognised Cuba's ultimate sovereignty over Guantánamo at the same time that it recognised US jurisdiction and control over it.

In concluding, the Court noted *obiter* that it had not been presented with the question of whether the Guantánamo detainees had no rights at all. Citing *Johnson*, it said that:

'this Court is "not holding that these prisoners have no right which the military authorities are bound to respect. The United States, by the [1949] Geneva Convention ... concluded an agreement upon the treatment to be accorded captives. These prisoners claim to be and are entitled to its protection. It is, however, the obvious scheme of the Agreement that responsibility for observance and enforcement of these rights is upon political and military authorities. Rights of alien enemies are vindicated under it only through protests and intervention of protecting powers as the rights of our citizens against foreign governments are vindicated only by Presidential intervention."'[495]

The *Rasul* action, filed on 19 February 2002,[496] was brought on behalf of two British citizens (Rasul and Iqbal) and an Australian (Hicks) detained in Guantánamo Bay. It requested

---

493. 339 *U.S.* 763; 70 *S.Ct.* 936 (1950).

494. Lease to the United States of Lands in Cuba for Coaling and Naval Stations, February 16-23, 1903, U.S.-Cuba, T.S. N. 418; Treaty Between the United States of America and Cuba Defining Their Relations, May 29, 1934, Art. III, 48 Stat. 1682, 1683. Under Art. III of the 1903 Agreement: 'While on the one hand the United States recognizes the continuance of the ultimate sovereignty of the Republic of Cuba over the above described areas of land and water, on the other hand, the Republic of Cuba consents that during the period of occupation by the United States of said areas under the terms of this agreement the United States shall exercise complete jurisdiction and control over and within said areas.'

495. In part VI of the judgement, quoting *Johnson* v. *Eisentrager*, 339 U.S., at p. 789.

that they be released and permitted to meet with their counsel. The *Odah* case was brought on behalf of 12 Kuwaitis,[497] and requested a preliminary and permanent injunction allowing the detainees to meet with their family members and counsel, and to be informed of the charges against them. The US government filed motions to dismiss. Like the earlier case of *Coalition of Clergy*, the question for the Court was whether aliens held outside the sovereign territory of the United States can use the US courts to pursue claims under the US Constitution. Oral argument was held on 26 June 2002.

In late July 2002, the US District Court, Judge Colleen Kollar-Kotelly presiding, found that the Court lacked jurisdiction to hear the claims and dismissed both cases.

As to claims brought by the plaintiffs under the Alien Tort Claims Act (ATCA), the Judge dismissed them, holding that no ATCA relief was available to the *Rasul* or *Odah* plaintiffs as *habeas corpus* was the only potential remedy for wrongful detention. The court held in the alternative that in order to be sued under the ATCA, the government must waive its immunity and it had not done so here.[498]

As to the jurisdictional question, in viewing the cases as *habeas corpus* petitions, the Court found that '*Eisentrager* is applicable to the aliens in this case, who are held at Guantanamo Bay, even in the absence of a determination by a military commission that they are "enemies". ... *Eisentrager* broadly applies to prevent aliens detained outside the sovereign territory of the United States from invoking a petition for a writ of *habeas corpus*.' The *situs* of a petitioner for *habeas corpus* was only relevant if he was an alien (if he was held outside the sovereign territory, he had no right of *habeas corpus*); for a citizen, the only question was one of status. The Court found that the petitioners Rasul, Iqbal and Hicks were captured in an area where the US was engaged in active military hostilities.[499]

The Court addressed the question of whether Guantánamo Bay is part of US sovereign territory and stated: 'It is undisputed, even by the parties, that Guantanamo Bay is not part of the sovereign territory of the United States.' The only remaining question was whether this fact alone is an absolute bar to suit or whether aliens on a US military base situated in a foreign country could be considered to be within the territorial jurisdiction of the US under a *de facto* theory of sovereignty, as petitioners argued. The Court found that the relevant case-law, including cases specifically concerned with the question of *de facto* sovereignty in relation to Guantánamo,[500] either did not support their claim or rejected it.

---

496. *Rasul* v. *Bush*, Civil Action No. 02-299 (CKK) (D.D.C. filed 19 February 2002).

497. *Odah* v. *United States*, Civil Action No. 02-828 (D.D.C. filed 1 May 2002).

498. See J. Green and P. Hoffman, 'Litigation Update: Summary of Recent Developments in U.S. Cases Brought under the Alien Tort Claims Act and Torture Victim Protection Act', in American Civil Liberties Union, *ACLU International Civil Liberties Report 2002*. <http://www.civilrightslawla.com/ICLR/ICLR_2002/ICLR2002.html>.

499. The petitioners claimed that they were in Afghanistan to offer humanitarian assistance. They claimed that at no time did they join a terrorist force or engage in belligerency against the US or support the Taliban, and if they ever took up arms it was only in the form of a *levee en masse*. The petititioners in *Odah* claimed to have been volunteers providing humanitarian assistance in Afghanistan.

500. *Bird* v. *United States*, 923 F. Supp. 338 (D. Conn. 1996); *Cuban American Bar Ass'n, Inc.* v. *Christopher*, 43 F.3d 1412 (11th Cir. 1995), *cert. denied*, 515 *U.S.* 1142 (1995).

Finally, the Court stated that 'just as the *Eisentrager* Court did not hold "that these prisoners have no right which the military authorities are found to respect,"[501] this opinion, too, should not be read as stating that these aliens do not have some form of rights under international law.' It had earlier noted in passing that the notion that these detainees could be held incommunicado from the rest of the world was inaccurate. '[T]he government recognizes that these aliens fall within the protections of certain provisions of international law and diplomatic channels remain an ongoing and viable means to address the claims raised by these aliens.'

The 4 December 2002 decision of the District Court for the Southern District of New York in the case of *Padilla* v. *Bush* was the most detailed of all those rendered thus far by US courts dealing with the status of detainees. As noted above,[502] Padilla was arrested in Chicago on 8 May 2002 on a material witness warrant issued by the Court pursuant to 18 U.S.C. § 3144 to enforce a subpoena to secure his testimony before a grand jury in the District. On 9 June 2002, he was designated an enemy combatant. Since giving his testimony to the grand jury, Padilla had been detained without charge or any prospect of release at the Consolidated Naval Brig in Charleston, South Carolina. Through his attorney, he petitioned for *habeas corpus*, challenged the lawfulness of his detention and sought an order directing that he be permitted to consult with his counsel. The respondent moved to dismiss, arguing that his counsel lacked *locus standi* and that the court lacked personal jurisdiction. Alternatively, it moved to have the case transferred to the District of South Carolina, where Padilla was being held.

The President's Order of 9 June 2002 designing Padilla as an enemy combatant,[503] along with a redacted declaration[504] of Defense Department employee Michael H. Mobbs (the Mobbs Declaration)[505] setting forth the relevant facts, had been submitted to the Court, and the government argued that the Mobbs Declaration was a sufficient basis for its designation of Padilla as an enemy combatant. The Mobbs Declaration stated that Padilla was born in New York, and had criminal convictions for murder and weapons offences. After his release from prison, he changed his name to al Muhajir and travelled to Egypt and also to Saudi Arabia and Afghanistan. In 2001, while in Afghanistan, he is alleged to have approached a senior lieutenant of Osama bin Laden and proposed stealing radioactive material within the US in order to build and detonate a 'radiological dispersal device', otherwise known as a 'dirty bomb'. Padilla was alleged to have researched the project at an Al Qaeda safehouse in Pakistan. While Padilla was not necessarily a member of Al Qaeda, he had 'extended contacts with senior Al Qaida members and operatives' and acted under the direction of Al Qaeda operatives, received training from them and was sent to the US to conduct reconnaissance and/or conduct other attacks on their behalf.

The Court held (1) that Padilla's attorney, as next friend, could pursue the petition and the government's motion to dismiss for lack of standing was denied; (2) that Secretary Rumsfeld is the proper respondent in this case, and the Court had jurisdiction over him; thus the motion to dismiss for lack of jurisdiction or to transfer the case to South Carolina

---

501. *Johnson* v. *Eisentrager, supra* n. 493, at p. 789, fn. 14.

502. See *supra* at p. 614 of this report.

503. Ibid.

504. An unredacted version of the Declaration (the 'Sealed Mobbs Declaration') had been provided to the Court, but the government maintained that it must remain confidential.

505. The unredacted Mobbs Declaration was the basis for the conclusions expressed in the 9 June Order.

was denied; (3) the President is authorized under the Constitution and by law to direct the military to detain enemy combatants in the circumstances present here, such that Padilla's detention is not *per se* unlawful; (4) Padilla may consult with his counsel in aid of pursuing this petition, under conditions that minimize the likelihood that he can use his lawyers as unwilling intermediaries for the transmission of information to others, and may, if he chooses, submit facts and arguments to the Court in aid of his petition; and (5) in deciding whether or not Padilla was lawfully detained, the Court needed only to examine whether the President had some evidence to support his finding that Padilla was an enemy combatant and whether that evidence had become moot due to events subsequent to his detention.

The most relevant part of the judgement concerned the lawfulness of Padilla's detention. The issue broke down into the following subsidiary questions: (1) Did the President have the authority to designate as an enemy combatant an American citizen detained on American soil, and, through the Secretary of Defense, to detain him for the duration of armed conflict with Al Qaeda?; (2) If so, could the President exercise that authority without violating 18 U.S.C. § 4001(a), which bars the detention of American citizens except pursuant to an Act of Congress;[506] (3) If so, by whatever standard the Court must apply – itself a separate issue – is the evidence adduced by the government sufficient to justify Padilla's detention?

The Court found that the answer to the first two questions was yes; the answer to the third awaited a further submission by Padilla, should he choose to make one.

Regarding the President's authority to order the seizure and detention of enemy combatants in a time of war, the Court found that neither Padilla nor any of the *amici* had sought to deny the President's authority in this respect but had merely sought to distinguish this case from cases in which the President may make such an order on the grounds that this is not a time of war, and that therefore the President may not use his powers as Commander-in-Chief or apply the laws of war to Padilla, and that Padilla in any event must be treated differently because he is an American citizen captured on American soil where the courts are functioning. Specifically, petitioners argued that because Congress did not declare war on Afghanistan, the only nation state against which the US has taken direct action, the measures sanctioned in war are not available here. Second, because the current conflict is with Al Qaeda, which is essentially a criminal organization that lacks clear corporal definition, the conflict can have no clear end and then the detention of enemy combatant is potentially indefinite and therefore unconstitutional. The Court found both of these arguments to be unconvincing.

As regards the first argument, the Court noted that it was essentially besides the point, as the real issue concerned what powers the President may exercise in the present circumstances. '[A] formal declaration of war is not necessary in order for the executive to exercise its constitutional authority to prosecute an armed conflict – particularly when, as on September 11, the United States is attacked'. It was for the President, even without specific congressional authorization, and not the courts, to decide when force to repel aggressive acts by third parties is required, and courts may not review the level of force selected.[507] Even if congressional authorization were deemed necessary, the Joint Resolution[508] passed

---

506. 18 U.S.C. § 4001(a) (2000).

507. Quoting with approval *The Prize Cases*, 67 *U.S.* (2 Black) 635 (1862).

508. According to the judgement, Authorization for the Use of Military Force, § 2(a) 'authorises the President to use necessary and appropriate force in order, among other things, "to prevent any

by both Houses of Congress provides it. The Court noted that the laws of war, which the President had invoked as to Padilla, apply regardless of whether or not a war has been declared.

The Court found it unnecessary to address the question as to when the conflict with Al Qaeda may end:

> 'So long as American troops remain on the ground in Afghanistan and Pakistan in combat with and pursuit of al Qaida fighters, there is no basis for contradicting the President's repeated assertion that the conflict has not ended. At some point in the future, when operations against al Qaida fighters end, or the operational capacity of al Qaida is effectively destroyed, there may be occasion to debate the legality of continuing to hold prisoners based on their connection to al Qaida, assuming such prisoners continue to be held at that time.'

The Court found Padilla's argument that because the period of his detention is at this moment indefinite, it is therefore perpetual, and therefore illegal, to be 'illogical', and his assumption that indefinite confinement of a person not accused of a crime is unconstitutional to be 'simply wrong'.

The Court distinguished between lawful and unlawful combatants, noting that the former could not be tried for lawful acts of combatancy and could claim POW status, whereas the latter could be tried for such acts but could not claim POW status. But punishment is discretionary, and there is no basis to impose a requirement that unlawful combatants be punished. Still, both lawful and unlawful combatants could be detained for the duration of hostilities. The detention of the latter 'is supportable – again, logically and legally – on the same ground that the detention of prisoners of war is supportable: to prevent them from rejoining the enemy'.

Coming to the central issue of the case – whether the President has the legal authority to designate an American citizen captured on American soil as an enemy combatant and detain him without trial – the Court, relying heavily on *Quirin*,[509] first found that detention of unlawful combatants was permitted:

> 'If, as seems obvious, the Court [in *Quirin*] in fact regarded detention alone as a lesser consequence than the one it was considering – trial by military tribunal – and it approved even that greater consequence, then our case is *a fortiori* from *Quirin* as regards the lawfulness of detention under the law of war.'

The legal basis for the President's authority to order the detention of an unlawful combatant arose both from the terms of the Joint Resolution of Congress to authorize the use of United States Armed Forces against Iraq, and from his constitutional authority as Commander-in-Chief, as set forth in the *Prize* cases,[510] *inter alia*. No principle of the Third Geneva Convention impeded the exercise of that authority. Neither was Padilla's detention barred by

---

future acts of international terrorism against the United States," and thereby engages the President's full powers as Commander in Chief'.

509. *Ex Parte Quirin*, 317 U.S. 1 (1942).

510. *Supra* n. 507.

Statute, specifically, 18 U.S.C. § 4001(a) or the USA Patriot Act.[511] '... § 4001(a), which by its terms applies to Padilla, bars confinement only in the absence of congressional authorisation, and there had been congressional authorisation here; the Patriot Act simply does not bear on this case'.

The Court noted the considerable deference which the judiciary owes to the executive in matters relating to foreign policy, national security and military affairs, which had not been disputed by Padilla. While Padilla in essence argued that he was entitled to a trial on the issue of whether he is an enemy combatant or not, that issue was not a question for the Court as

'The President ... has both constitutional and statutory authority to exercise the powers of commander in chief, including the power to detain unlawful combatants, and it matters not that Padilla is a United States citizen captured on United States soil. ... In the decision to detain Padilla as an unlawful combatant, ... the President is operating at maximum authority, under both the Constitution and the Joint Resolution.'

The Court noted the paucity of jurisprudence on these matters:

'*Quirin* offers no guidance regarding the standard to be applied in making the threshold determination that a *habeas corpus* petitioner is an unlawful combatant. ... However, if the case-law seems sparse and some of the cases abstruse, that is not because courts have not recognized and do not continue to recognize the President's authority to act when it comes to defending this country.'

The *Hamdi* case also concerned an American citizen whom the US had designated an enemy combatant. Hamdi was born in the US and raised in Saudi Arabia. He was captured in Afghanistan, where the government claimed he was fighting with the Taliban, and initially detained there before being sent to Guantánamo Bay. He was subsequently transferred to the Norfolk Naval Station Brig in Norfolk, Virginia on 15 April 2002, when US officials confirmed that he was a US citizen.

The petitioners argued that 'as an American citizen ... Hamdi enjoys the full protections of the Constitution', and that the government's current detention of him in this country without charges, access to a judicial tribunal, or the right to counsel, 'violate[s] the Fifth and Fourteenth Amendments to the United States Constitution'. Specifically, Hamdi and his *amici* relied on two legal grounds: 18 U.S.C. § 4001, which regulates the detention of US citizens, and Article 5 of the Third Geneva Convention. According to the US government, Hamdi is an 'enemy combatant' in spite of being a US citizen. As such, he has no right to a lawyer. Enemy combatants have none of the rights of ordinary criminal defendants, or even foreigners who might face military tribunals.

The sole question that had been certified for the Court was '[w]hether the Mobbs Declaration,[512] standing alone, was sufficient as a matter of law to allow a meaningful judicial

---

511. Pub. L. No. 107-56, 115 Stat. 272 (2001). See 4 *YIHL* (2001) pp. 636-637.

512. The Mobbs Declaration refers to an affidavit from Michael Mobbs, Special Adviser to the Under Secretary of Defence for Policy, which confirmed the material factual allegations in Hamdi's petition, namely, the circumstances in which Hamdi had been captured, his designation as an 'enemy combatant' by the executive, and his transfer to the Norfolk Naval Brig.

review of Yaser Esam Hamdi's classification as an enemy combatant', although the Court noted that it was not limited in its findings to this single question.

In its decision of 8 January 2003, the US Court of Appeals for the Fourth Circuit noted that Hamdi's due status as an American citizen and as an enemy combatant raised 'important questions about the role of the courts in times of war'. The Court acknowledged the importance of judicial deference to the executive and limitations on judicial activities in times of war, which may be inferred from the allocation of powers under the US Constitution. 'These powers include the authority to detain those captured in armed struggle. These powers likewise extend to the executive's decision to deport or detain alien enemies during the duration of hostilities, and to confiscate or destroy enemy property.' In its conclusion, the Court wrote that 'separation of powers takes on a special significance when the nation itself comes under attack. Hamdi's status as a citizen, as important as that is, cannot displace our constitutional order or the places of courts within the Framer's scheme. Judicial review does not disappear during wartime, but the review of battlefield captures in overseas conflicts is a highly deferential one.'

It is interesting to note that the Court found that Hamdi had been captured in the context of the global war on terror rather than the international armed conflict in Afghanistan. It noted that the interests that the separation of powers seeks to protect, including the security, liberty and self-determination of the people, carry no less weight

> 'because the conflict in which Hamdi was captured is waged less against nation-states than against scattered and unpatriated forces. … Nor does the nature of the present conflict render respect for the judgements of the political branches any less appropriate. We have noted that the "political branches are best positioned to comprehend this global war in its full context,"[513] and neither the absence of set-piece battles nor the intervals of calm between terrorist assaults suffice to nullify the warmaking authority entrusted to the executive and legislative branches.'

Again noting the executive's power to exercise jurisdiction over members of the armed forces, including enemy belligerents, and recognizing that the government has no more profound responsibility than the protection of American citizens from further terrorist attacks, the Court found that detention of enemy combatants serves at least two vital purposes:

> 'First, detention prevents enemy combatants from rejoining the enemy and continuing to fight against America and its allies. … In this respect, "captivity is neither a punishment nor an act of vengeance", but rather "a simple war measure".[514] And the precautionary measure of disarming hostile forces for the duration of a conflict is routinely accomplished through detention rather than the initiation of criminal charges. To require otherwise would impose a singular burden upon our nation's conduct of war. Second, detention in lieu of prosecution may relieve the burden on military commanders of ligitating the circumstances of a capture halfway around the globe. This burden would not be inconsiderable and would run the risk of "saddling military decision-making with the

---

513. Quoting the judgement in *Hamdi II*, 296 *F.3d* at p. 283.
514. Quoting W. Winthrop, *Military Law and Precedents*, 2nd edn. (1920) p. 788.

panoply of encumbrances associated with civil litigation" during a period of armed conflict.'[515]

The Court observed that '[a]s the nature of threats to America evolves, along with the means of carrying those threats out, the nature of enemy combatants may change also. In the face of such change, separation of powers doctrine does not deny the executive branch the essential tool of adaptability.'

The Court rejected Hamdi's argument that his detention was contrary to 18 U.S.C. § 4001(a), insofar as it lacked congressional authorization. It found that even if congressional authorization for his detention was required, Congress had authorized the President to 'use all necessary and appropriate force against those nations, organisations or persons he determines planned, authorized, committed, or aided the terrorist attacks' or 'harboured such organisations or persons'.[516]

'... the "necessary and appropriate force" referenced in the congressional resolution necessarily includes the capture and detention of any and all hostile forces arrayed against our troops. Furthermore, [referring to Congressional authorization of funds for persons similar to prisoners of war[517]] [i]t is difficult if not impossible to understand how Congress could make appropriations for the detention of persons "similar to prisoners of war" without also authorizing their detention in the first place. ... If Congress had intended to override [the] well-established precedent and provide American belligerents some immunity from capture and detention, it surely would have made its intentions explicit.'

There was no indication that § 4001(a) was intended to overrule the longstanding rule that an armed and hostile American citizen captured on the battlefield during wartime may be treated like the enemy combatant that he is.

Regarding Hamdi's claim that Article 5 of the Third Geneva Convention applied, which requires a formal determination of his status by a competent tribunal, the Court found that:

'[t]his argument falters also because the Geneva Convention is not self-executing.' The Geneva Convention evinced no intent to be self-executing, and '[c]ertainly there is no explicit provision for enforcement by any form of private action. And what discussion there is of enforcement focuses entirely on the vindication by diplomatic means of treaty rights inhering in sovereign nations. ... Hamdi provides no reason to conclude that 28 U.S.C. § 2241 makes these diplomatically-focused rights enforceable by a private right of petition.'

Moreover, regardless of any determination of status under Article 5, and the outcome of that determination, the detaining power would be entitled to detain unlawful belligerents in the same way that it can detain prisoners of war, although it also had the option of trying

---

515. Quoting *Hamdi II, supra* n. 513, at pp. 283-284.

516. Authorization for Use of Military Force, Pub. L. No. 107-40, 115 Stat. 224 (18 September 2001).

517. 10 U.S.C. § 956(5) (2002).

unlawful belligerents for the acts that rendered their belligerency unlawful. 'For all these reasons, we hold that there is no purely legal barrier to Hamdi's detention.'

The Court found that while Hamdi as an American citizen did have rights under the Bill of Rights, and would be entitled to due process if he was charged with a crime, he had not been charged with a crime, but was being held as an enemy combatant pursuant to the laws and customs of war. 'Hamdi's citizenship rightfully entitles him to file this petition to challenge his detention, but the fact that he is a citizen does not affect the legality of his detention as an enemy combatant.' Furthermore, 'the fact that Hamdi is presently being detained in the United States – as opposed to somewhere overseas – does not affect the legal implications of his status as an enemy combatant'.

That much determined, the Court had to examine whether the Mobbs Declaration of itself provided a sufficient legal basis for the detention. The Court found that it did, and overturned the 16 August request for production of supporting materials by the District Court. 'Asking the executive to provide more detailed factual assertions would be to wade further into the conduct of war than we consider appropriate and is unnecessary to a meaningful judicial review of the case.'

In conclusion, the Court addressed Hamdi's contention that even if his detention as an unlawful combatant had been lawful, it no longer was as the relevant hostilities had ended. It said: 'Whether the timing of a cessation of hostilities is justiciable is far from clear. ... The executive branch is also in the best position to appraise the status of a conflict, and the cessation of hostilities would seem no less a matter of political competence than the initiation of them.' Still, the Court did not have to look further into the matter since, '[b]ecause under the most circumscribed definition of conflict hostilities have not yet reached their end, this argument is without merit.'

Cases (aiding the Taliban)
☞ *United States of America* v. *John Phillip Walker Lindh*, United States District Court for the Eastern District of Virginia, Alexandria Division, Criminal No. 02-37-A. Plea Agreement, 15 July 2002. 212 *F. Supp.2d* 541, 552 et seq. (E.D. Va. 2002)[518]
☞ *United States of America* v. *John Phillip Walker Lindh*, United States District Court for the Eastern District of Virginia, Alexandria Division, Criminal No. 03-37-A. Sentencing Memorandum, 4 October 2002

In the case of *United States* v. *Walker Lindh*, the defendant, the so-called 'American Taliban', pleaded guilty on 15 July 2002 to count nine of the Indictment against him,[519] of supplying services to the Taliban, in violation of Title 50, United States Code, Section 1705(b), Title 18, United States Code, Section 2, and Title 31, Code of Federal Regulations, Sections 545.204 and 545.206(a), and to a Criminal Information charging him carrying an explosive during the commission of a felony. In doing so, he avoided possible multiple life sentences. In exchange, prosecutors dropped eight other charges against him, including conspiracy to murder US citizens.[520] The plea agreement, in which Walker Lindh also

---

518. For the complete docket in the *Walker Lindh* case, see <http://notablecases.vaed.uscourts.gov/ 1:02-cr-00037/DocketSheet.html>.

519. For a copy of the indictment, see <http://www.usdoj.gov/ag/2ndindictment.htm>.

520. '"I plead guilty," Taliban American says', CNN.com, 17 July 2002. <http://www.cnn.com/ 2002/LAW/07/15/walker.lindh.hearing>.

agreed to fully cooperate with law enforcement and intelligence officials in their investigations into the Taliban and Al Qaeda; to testify fully and truthfully at any grand juries, trials or other proceedings, including military tribunals; and to withdraw claims that he was mistreated while in US military custody, had the full approval of the White House.[521] Walker Lindh also agreed that neither he nor any members of his family could accept any money for selling his story. The agreement stated: 'The defendant hereby assigns to the United States any profits or proceeds which he may be entitled to receive in connection with any publication or dissemination of information relating to illegal conduct alleged in the indictment.' A 20-year sentence was recommended.

Walker Lindh, a 21-year-old US citizen, converted to Islam as a teenager, and after studying Arabic in Saudi Arabia and Pakistan,[522] had travelled to fight on the side of the Taliban against the Northern Alliance. He was captured and taken into custody along with other Taliban fighters in Afghanistan in December 2001, and was then identified as a US citizen.[523]

On 4 October 2002, he was sentenced to 20 years in federal prison. During his sentencing hearing, he made an emotional plea of remorse for his actions, saying that he had made a mistake by joining the Taliban.[524] The Court in its Sentencing Memorandum said that 'the claims that the 20-year custody sentence is either too lenient or too severe are all unpersuasive. Indeed, that sentence appears in all respects to be just and reasonable and to serve in appropriate measure the various goals of the criminal justice system, namely, deterrence, rehabilitation, retribution, and incapacitation.'

Cases (Alien Tort Claims Act[525])

☛ *Mehinović* v. *Vucković*, US District Court for the Northern District of Georgia, 198 *F. Supp.2d* 1322 (N.D. Ga. 2002), 29 April 2002 <http://www.cacd.uscourts.gov/CACD/RecentPubOp.nsf/bb61c530eab0911c882567cf005ac6f9/c604172936988c5688256c29007f770b?OpenDocument>

'On 29 April 2002, in a civil action against a Bosnian Serb, the District Court of the Northern District of Georgia found that the accused had committed and was liable to prosecution for torture, cruel, inhuman or degrading treatment, arbitrary detention, war crimes, crimes against humanity, assault and battery, false imprisonment, intentional infliction of emotional distress and civil conspiracy. More specifically regarding war crimes, the court found that the man had committed torture and other abuses against civilians in the context of an armed conflict and that he had therefore violated Article 3 common to the four Geneva Conventions of 1949 and the customary international humanitarian standards enshrined in it, and at the same time committed a grave breach of those Conventions in that he had

---

521. 'Bush gave nod to plea agreement, officials say', CNN.com, 15 July 2002. <http://www.cnn.com/2002/LAW/07/15/bush.plea.deal/index.html>.

522. 'John Walker Lindh sentenced to 20 years: American Taliban fighter apologizes at sentencing', *Washington Post*, 5 October 2002, p. A.1.

523. '"American Taleban" jailed for 20 years', BBC News, 4 October 2002. <http://news/bbc.co.uk/2/hi/americas/2298433.stm>.

524. S. Candiotti, 'Walker Lindh sentenced to 20 years', CNN.com. <http://www.cnn.com/2002/LAW/10/04/lindh.statement/index.html>.

525. This is not an exhaustive survey of all ATCA and TVPA cases, but a summary only of those cases concerned with IHL violations or of related interest.

wilfully caused great suffering or serious injury and unlawful confinement. The Court's jurisdiction regarding these matters was based on the Alien Tort Claims Act and the Torture Victim Protection Act. The Court ordered the defendant to pay damages to each of the four victims who brought the lawsuit.'[526] The plaintiffs were each awarded $35 million in punitive and compensatory damages.[527]

☞ *William Ford et al.* v. *José Guillermo García et al.*, No. 01-10357, D.C. Docket No. 99-08359-CV-DTKH, US Court of Appeals for the 11th Circuit, 30 April 2002 <http://www.cja.org/cases/Romagoza_Docs/RomagozaChurchAppeal.htm>

The eleventh circuit upheld the jury verdict of 3 November 2000 in favour of the defendant Salvadoran generals,[528] in this case brought by relatives of four American churchwomen killed in El Salvador in December 1980. Generals José Guillermo García and Carlos Vides Casanova served as Ministers of Defense at different times during the relevant period.

The main legal issue presented in the appeal was the allocation of the burden of proof in a civil action involving the command responsibility doctrine brought under the Torture Victims' Protection Act (TVPA).[529] The case was one of the first brought under the TVPA to deal at length with the question of command responsibility. The Appellants contended that the jury instructions at trial contained errors of law, which placed on them the burden of establishing elements that they are not required to prove under either the TVPA or the international law which the TVPA has adopted. The instructions required Appellants to prove by a preponderance of the evidence, first, that the perpetrators of the crimes were under the Appellees' 'effective command', defined as the legal authority and the practical ability of the Generals to control the guilty troops, and second, that the Generals failed to take all reasonable steps to prevent or repress the murders of the churchwomen. Appellants argued that both of these showings are properly affirmative defenses that the Appellees had the burden of proving at trial. Finally, Appellants contended that the district court's instructions erroneously included proximate cause as a required element before liability could be established under the TVPA and command responsibility doctrine.

The Court, Judge Daniel T.K. Hurley presiding, applying the standard of responsibility followed by the *ad hoc* International Criminal Tribunals for the former Yugoslavia and Rwanda, found that the 'essential elements of liability under the command responsibility doctrine are: (1) the existence of a superior-subordinate relationship between the commander and the perpetrator of the crime, (2) that the commander knew or should have known, owing to the circumstances at the time, that his subordinates had committed, were committing, or planned to commit acts violative of the law of war, and (3) that the commander failed to prevent the commission of the crimes, or failed to punish the subordinates after the commission of the crimes. Although the TVPA does not explicitly provide for liability

---

526. ICRC Advisory Service, National Implementation of International Humanitarian Law – Biannual update on national legislation and case-law, January-June 2002. <http://www.icrc.org/Web/eng/siteeng0.nsf/html/5FLE9G?OpenDocument>. See also <http://www.cja.org/cases/Mehinovic_-Docs/Mehinovic_Judgement_Summary.html>; <http://www.civilrightslawla.com/ICLR/ICLR_2002/9_sondheimer.pdf>.

527. American Civil Liberties Union, *ACLU International Civil Liberties Report 2002*, Chapter 9, pp. 57 at 57-58. <http://www.aclu.org/International/International.cfm?ID=11742&c=36>.

528. 3 *YIHL* (2000) pp. 613-614.

529. For details of a second case against the same defendants, see *infra* p. 639.

of commanders for human rights violations of their troops, legislative history makes clear that Congress intended to adopt the doctrine of command responsibility from international law as part of the Act.'

The appellants acknowledged that they had to prove the three elements identified, but argued that once having done so, the burden shifts to the defence to prove that they did not have the practical ability to control their troops or that they took all necessary and reasonable measures to control the troops, either one of which would serve to exonerate them from liability. The Court disagreed. 'Despite Appellants' assertions that the district court's definition of "effective command" misplaced the burden of persuasion, we find no plain error.' The Court noted that international jurisprudence dealing with the doctrine of command responsibility since *In re Yamashita*, including that of the ICTY and ICTR, has consistently required the effective control by a commander over his troops before imposing liability under the doctrine of command responsibility:

'A reading of the cases suggests that a showing of the defendant's actual ability to control the guilty troops is required as part of the plaintiff's burden under the superior-subordinate prong of command responsibility, whether the plaintiff attempts to assert liability under a theory of *de facto* or *de jure* authority.... Even were we to read these cases in the light most favorable to Appellants, however, the decisions at least suggest that the burden of persuasion on this matter is not altogether certain. We therefore hold that there was no plain error here because the district court's instruction included an element which properly must be proved in command responsibility cases, and no case-law exists clearly assigning the burden of persuasion away from the plaintiff on this matter.'

☛ *Juan Romagoza Arce, Neris Gonzalez and Carlos Mauricio* v. *José Guillermo García and Carlos Eugenio Vides Casanova*, Federal District Court of Florida, Case No. 99-8364 Civ-Hurley, Verdict 23 July, Final Judgement 31 July 2002

In this case, which followed on the above case brought against the same defendants under the TVPA by victims of torture, killings and crimes against humanity committed in El Salvador in the 1980s,[530] the plaintiffs claimed that Generals José Guillermo García and Carlos Eugenio Vides Casanova were responsible for the crimes committed by persons acting under their command and control.

In the earlier case, the complaint against García and Casanova was rejected by the jury, acting on the judge's instructions. The judge told the jury that they should only find the respondents responsible if they were found to have exercised effective command over the troops who committed the crimes, meaning that 'the commander has the legal authority and the practical ability to exert control over his troops'.

In the extant case, Judge Hurley departed from his earlier instructions to the jury. He stated that the generals could be held liable even if the plaintiffs had been tortured by non-soldiers, so long as the generals had the same authority over those civilian 'volunteers' as they would have had over their own troops. Regular military commanders could be held accountable for crimes committed by death squad members or paramilitaries.

---

530. 3 *YIHL* (2001) pp. 613-614.

The trial, which began on 24 June, ended with the jury's verdict of 23 July. The jury found both generals liable on all counts and ordered them to pay the three plaintiffs $14.6 million in compensatory damages and $40 million in punitive damages. Final judgement was entered on 31 July 2002.[531]

☛ *Alexis Holyweek Sarei, et al.* v. *Rio Tinto plc and Rio Tinto Limited*, Case No. CV 00-11695 MMM (AIJx), U.S. District Court, Central District of California, 9 July 2002, 221 *F. Supp.2d* 1116 (C.D. Cal. 2002) <http://www.cacd.uscourts.gov/CACD/Recent PubOp.nsf/bb61c530eab0911c882567cf005ac6f9/c604172936988c5688256c29007 f770b?OpenDocument>

In this case, the plaintiffs sued Rio Tinto and a subsidiary, which are part of an international mining group, under the Alien Tort Claims Act (ATCA) for violations of international norms prohibiting crimes against humanity, war crimes, racial discrimination, torture, cruel, inhuman and degrading treatment, and violations of environmental rights. They alleged that the companies acted in complicity with the governments of Papua New Guinea (PNG) and Australia in forcibly evicting the plaintiffs from their land and destroying the rain forest through their copper mining.

The District Court requested the State Department's opinion on whether the outcome of *Rio Tinto* could have a potential political impact on US foreign interests.

After reviewing the State Department's Statement of Interest, the court granted the defendants' motion to dismiss and denied the plaintiffs' motion to amend their complaint. It concluded that 'all claims must be dismissed on the basis of the political question doctrine':[532]

> 'Ruling on the merits of these allegations will inevitably require passing judgement on the pre-war and wartime conduct of the PNG government. It is this type of judgement that the Statement of Interest indicates may have serious implications for the future of the peace agreement that has been reached, and thus for the foreign policy objectives the executive branch has set. It is also the type of judgement that risks placing the court in the position of announcing a view that is contrary to a coordinate branch of government, with all the attendant embarrassment that would ensue. The situation is thus quintessentially one that calls for the invocation of the political question as to each of plaintiffs' causes of action.'[533]

☛ *John Doe I et al.* v. *Unocal Corp. et al.*, U.S. 9th Circuit Court of Appeals, 18 September 2002 <http://www.ca9.uscourts.gov/ca9/newopinions.nsf/3D534390583B882 F88256C380004FE18/$file/0056603.pdf?openelement>

---

531. For news reports of the case, see R. Collier, 'Florida jury convicted two Salvadorean generals of atrocities $54.6 million awarded to three torture victims', *San Francisco Chronicle*, 24 July 2002, p. A12; D. Gonzalez, 'Torture victims in El Salvador are awarded $54 million', *The New York Times*, 24 July 2002; M. Roig-Franzia, 'Torture victims win lawsuit against Salvadoran general', *Washington Post*, 24 July 2002, p. A01; 'El Salvadoran generals guilty of torture', BBC News, 23 July 2002.

532. At p. 133 of the Judgement.

533. At pp. 117-118 of the Judgement.

In a landmark decision, on 18 September 2002, the US 9th Circuit Court of Appeals in Pasadena, California ruled that multinational corporations can be held liable in US courts for aiding and abetting human rights violations committed by others abroad.

In the case brought by a group of Burmese villagers against oil giant Unocal Corp., the multinational was accused of turning a blind eye to alleged human rights abuses in Burma committed by the Burmese military against persons working on a $1.2 billion oil pipeline being constructed for Unocal. These included torture, murder, rape, forced labor and beatings.

The case was originally filed in September 1996 in US federal court by four Burmese villagers, who demanded that Unocal pay tens of millions of dollars in compensation for alleged abuses by Burmese soldiers against Burmese indentured labourers. They alleged that even if Unocal's involvement did not rise to the level of active criminal participation, the corporation benefited from the abuses.

The federal judge found that the evidence suggested that 'Unocal knew that forced labor was being utilized and that the joint venturers benefited from the practice'. But he threw out the case on the grounds that the company's conduct did not rise to the level of active participation (the standard of liability used in the Nuremberg cases involving the role of German industrialists in the Nazi forced-labor program).

The villagers then refiled their case in a superior court in Los Angeles, bringing many of the same claims but this time under state law. That court sent the case back to the lower federal court. It is the latter process which resulted in the finding of 18 September.

A key legal issue in the case before the 9th Circuit Court of Appeals was the liability standard. Although the judges agreed that Unocal should be held liable, it disagreed over the applicable standard of liability. The majority, consisting of Judges Harry Pregerson and Stephen Reinhardt, said that Unocal should be held to the international law standard developed in the jurisprudence of the ICTY and ICTR: 'Given the sufficient evidence in the present case that Unocal gave assistance and encouragement to the Myanmar Military ... we may impose aiding and abetting liability for knowing practical assistance or encouragement, which has a substantial effect on perpetuation of the crime.'

Commentators on the case noted that while there was nothing unusual about holding US corporations liable under tort law for aiding and abetting criminal behaviour, the legal significance of the ruling lay in the fact that in this case, a transnational corporation could be held liable under this standard.[534]

☛ *Wiwa* v. *Royal Dutch Petroleum Co.*, 226 *F.3d* 88 (2d Cir. (N.Y.) 2000); Slip Copy 2002 WL 319887 (S.D.N.Y., Decided 22 February; filed on 28 February 2002) <http://www.earthrights.org/shell/mtd02.shtml>

In this action, Nigerian émigrés sued two foreign holding companies, Royal Dutch Petroleum and Shell Transport and Trading Company, based in the Netherlands and the US, respectively, under the Alien Tort Claims Act and other laws. They alleged that the corpora-

---

534. See J. Green and P. Hoffman, 'Litigation Update: Summary of Recent Developments in U.S. Cases Brought under the Alien Tort Claims Act and Torture Victim Protection Act', in American Civil Liberties Union, *International Civil Liberties Report 2002*. <http://www.civilrightslawla.com/ICLR/ICLR_2002/ICLR2002.html>.

tions participated in human rights violations against them in retaliation for their political opposition to the companies' oil exploration activities in Nigeria.

On 22 February, a New York District Court ruled that 'a civil lawsuit charging multinational oil giant Shell with complicity in human rights violations will go forward'. The ruling by Judge Kimba Wood held that Shell Transport and Trading Company and Royal Dutch Petroleum Company can be held liable in the US for cooperating in the persecution and execution of environmental activists in Nigeria. The ruling includes an analysis of forced exile as a form of cruel, inhuman or degrading treatment.[535]

Pending
☛ *Presbyterian Church* v. *Talisman Energy Co. Inc.*, 01 CV 9882 (AGS) (S.D.N.Y), 8
   November 2001; amended complaint filed on 25 February 2002

The Presbyterian Church of Sudan and one of its pastors filed a class action on behalf of non-Muslims in Sudan, alleging that Talisman, a Canadian oil production company, supported the ethnic cleansing campaign of the Islamic government in Khartoum. The plaintiffs alleged that Talisman was complicit in the actions of the government against Christians who lived near oil fields or transportation systems, including kidnapping, rape, murder and land confiscation. The February 2002 amended complaint added the Sudanese government as a co-defendant.[536]

☛ *Doe* v. *ExxonMobil*, D.D.C. 2002, 20 June 2001 <http://www.indonesia-house.org/
   focus/aceh/Exxon-Lawsuit01.htm>

On 20 June 2001, a claim was filed in the Federal District Court for the District of Columbia under the Alien Tort Claims Act against ExxonMobil. The plaintiffs, 11 villagers from Aceh province in Indonesia, alleged that they were victims of human rights abuses committed by security forces employed by the oil company. They claimed that it knowingly employed brutal tactics to protect its operations, and aided and abetted human rights violations through financial and other material support to the security forces. In addition, the plaintiffs claimed that the security forces were either employees or agents of ExxonMobil, and thus the oil company was liable for their actions.[537]

In May 2002, the Court asked the US State Department whether proceeding with the case would jeopardize US-Indonesia relations.

The State Department on 29 July 2002, in a letter to Presiding Judge Louis F. Oberdorfer by the Legal Advisor, William H. Taft IV, recommended that the lawsuit be dropped, claiming that it would 'risk a seriously adverse impact on significant interests of the United States, including interests related directly to the ongoing struggle against international terrorism'.[538]

---

535. Ibid.
536. Ibid.
537. P. Ravindran, 'Alien tort legislation in the US – why it should not be tampered with', *The Hindu Business Line*, 13 August 2003.
538. The letter of interest is available online at <http://www.hrw.org/press/2002/08/exxon072902.pdf>.

☞ *Ntsebeza* v. *Citigroup*, 02 Civ. 4712 (RCC), June 2002

In June 2002, a class action on behalf of over 5,000 victims of Apartheid in South Africa was filed against dozens of multinational corporations. They are accused of propping up the regime in the mid 1980s, when it faced financial collapse because of international sanctions.[539]

☞ *Reyes et al.* v. *Juan Evangelista López Grijalba*, U.S. District Court for the Southern District of Florida, No. 02-22046-Civ-Lenard, 15 July 2002 <http://www.cja.org/cases/ Grijalba_Docs/Grijalba_Complaint.html>

On 15 July 2002, the Centre for Justice and Accountability filed a civil suit against Juan Evangelista López Grijalba in Miami in the US District Court for the Southern District of Florida, on behalf of six Hondurans, alleging his involvement in and command responsibility for torture, disappearance and extrajudicial killings committed by Battalion 3-16 of the Honduran Army. Grijalba was a colonel in the Honduran Army and served as the Head of the National Investigations Directorate in 1981 and head of the Department of Intelligence for the Armed Forces General Staff in 1982, and it was in those positions that he was in command of the members of Battalion 3-16. According to the complaint, members of Battalion 3-16 and others acting in coordination with the battalion kidnapped and brutally tortured plaintiffs Oscar and Gloria Reyes in 1982; abducted, tortured and disappeared Manfredo Velásquez (the brother of plaintiff Zenaida Velásquez and father of plaintiff Hector Ricardo Velásquez) in 1981; and disappeared the brothers of plaintiffs Jane Doe I and II.[540]

In April 2002, Grijalba was taken into detention in Florida by the Immigration and Naturalisation Service for immigration violations.[541]

☞ *Burnett, St.* v. *Al Baraka Investment and Development, et al.*, No. 02-CV-1616 (JR) (D. D.C. 14 August 2002)

This suit was brought by more than 3,000 survivors and relatives of those killed in the 11 September 2001 attacks on the World Trade Center in New York against defendants which include seven international banks, eight Islamic foundations and their subsidiaries, and several individuals alleged to be terrorist financiers, including Osama bin Laden and members of the Saudi royal family. It relies on the Foreign Sovereign Immunities Act, the Torture Victims' Protection Act, the Alien Tort Claims Act, RICO (Racketeer Influenced and Corrupt Organizations) and tort claims, including wrongful death and conspiracy. The plaintiffs seek $1 trillion in compensation and punitive damages.[542]

---

539. See J. Green and P. Hoffman, 'Litigation Update: Summary of Recent Developments in U.S. Cases Brought under the Alien Tort Claims Act and Torture Victim Protection Act', in American Civil Liberties Union, *International Civil Liberties Report 2002*. <http://www.civilrightslawla.com/ICLR/ ICLR_2002/ICLR2002.html>.

540. American Civil Liberties Union, *ACLU International Civil Liberties Report 2002*, ibid., Chapter 9, pp. 57 at 57-58. <http://www.aclu.org/International/International.cfm?ID=11742&c=36>.

541. G. Epstein Nieves, 'Honduran linked to killings: Miami lawyers says charges are false', *Miami Herald*, 22 July 2002.

542. See J. Green and P. Hoffman, 'Litigation Update: Summary of Recent Developments in U.S.

☛ *Ashton et al.* v. *Al Qaeda Islamic Army et al.*, No. 02 CV-6977

☛ *Beyer et al.* v. *Al Qaeda Islamic Army et al.*, No. 02 CV-6978 (S.D.N.Y. filed 4 September 2002)

1,400 victims and survivors of the 11 September 2001 attacks by Al Qaeda on the World Trade Center in New York filed a massive class action on 4 September 2002, under the Anti-Terrorism Act, the Torture Victims' Protection Act and the Anti-Terrorism and Effective Death Penalty Act. It charges Al Qaeda; Osama Bin Laden; 37 Al Qaeda associates; the estates of the 19 hijackers who died in the attacks; Zacharias Moussaoui; the Taliban and its leader, Mohammad Omar; Iraq; Saddam Hussein and his two sons; the Iraqi intelligence agency; 13 individual Iraqi officials; and 64 co-conspirators, including banks, charities, corporations and individuals that are alleged to have provided funds to support acts of terror against the US, with involvement in the attacks of 11 September.[543]

☛ *Kiobel, et al.*, v. *Royal Dutch Petroleum*, S.D.N.Y. 02 Civ. 7618 (KMW), 20 September 2002

On 20 September 2002, 14 persons filed a class action under the ATCA charging Shell with complicity in human rights violations committed between 1990 and 1999 in Nigeria. These included the purchasing of ammunition and providing logistical support for the repression of anti-Shell protesters. As part of their motion to dismiss the case, the defendants filed a US Department of Justice *amicus* brief that challenged the ACTA itself, which was filed in the Ninth Circuit in the *Unocal* case.[544]

☛ *Khulumani et al.* v. *Barclays et al.*, New York Eastern District Court, 12 November 2002

On 12 November 2002, a lawsuit was filed in the New York Eastern District Court on behalf of the Khulumani Support Group (which counsels more than 32,000 South Africans affected by Apartheid), which demands reparations from the 22 named respondent corporations. It alleges that these multinationals, which invested in South Africa during the Apartheid era, aided and abetted a crime against humanity. *Inter alia*, the suit charges IBM and Fujitsu ICL with supplying technology for the Apartheid government to create so-called 'passbooks' for the black majority population which were used to limit their movement and employment and opportunities. The case, brought under the Alien Tort Claims Act, also charges financial institutions such as Citicorp with lending funds used to bolster police and the armed forces, and claims that arms manufacturers and oil companies violated international arms embargoes on sales to South Africa.[545]

AVRIL MCDONALD

Cases Brought under the Alien Tort Claims Act and Torture Victim Protection Act', in American Civil Liberties Union, *International Civil Liberties Report 2002*. <http://www.civilrightslawla.com/ICLR/ICLR_2002/ICLR2002.html>.

543. Ibid.

544. Ibid.

545. A. Raphael, 'Apartheid victims sue global corporations', OneWorld US, 13 November 2002. See further <http://www.cmht.com/casewatch/cases/cwapartheid4.html>.

URUGUAY

International Criminal Court
☞ Decision of the Supreme Court regarding the International Criminal Court

'On 2 May 2002, the Executive branch submitted the ratification bill to Parliament. The Supreme Court then declared that a constitutional amendment would not be necessary as interpretation of the treaty can resolve concerns regarding immunities and amnesties.'[546]

THE VATICAN

Genocide
☞ Release of World War II-era documents announced, 15 February 2002

On 15 February 2002, the Vatican announced that it would release documents from World War II to counter accusations that the then-Pontiff did little to denounce the Holocaust. It said that it wished to end the 'unjust and ungrateful speculation' that Pope Pius XII had not raised concerns during the war that European Jews were being massacred. The first batch of 640 documents, to be released in 2003, cover relations between the Vatican and Germany from 1922 to 1939, and deal with the pontificate of Pope Pius' predecessor, while a second batch, dating from 1939 to 1945, deals with wartime prisoners. The Vatican statement said that the documents 'show great works of charity and assistance undertaken by Pius XII with respect to the numerous prisoners and other victims of the war, of any nation, religion and race'.[547]

VENEZUELA

Pending
☞ Review of the Penal Code

In June 2002, the Penal Code was taken up for review, in order to include in it the crimes of genocide and crimes against humanity.[548]

---

546. Source: CICC/The Americas: Uruguay. <http://www.iccnow.org/countryinfo/theamericas/uruguay.html>.
547. 'Vatican to release war archives', BBC Online News Report, 15 February 2002.
548. Source: CICC/The Americas: Venezuela. <http://www.iccnow.org/countryinfo/theamericas/venezuela.html>.

DOCUMENTATION[1]

---

1. The Documentation section has been prepared by Avril McDonald, Managing Editor of the *YIHL*, from materials provided to the *YIHL* by its correspondents, *inter alia*. Restricted space forces us to be selective in the documents included. The *YIHL's* general policy is to prefer documents to which access might otherwise be difficult, in particular regarding state practice, or which are particularly topical and relevant to the readership. In general, we will tend not to publish documents that are easily and widely available, although we may make exceptions, particularly where the material supports an article in the yearbook. The documents are reproduced as we have received them, although some may be in a slightly condensed form. All spelling, grammatical and layout irregularities are therefore in the original. The source of the document and translation, where applicable, is indicated alongside each document. The titles of documents listed in the table of contents *infra* at p. XXX are not the exact titles. The latter appear alongside the particular documents. Regarding footnotes, the number placed in square brackets is the number of the footnote in the original document.

CLASSIFICATION OF DOCUMENTS

0.	**Zero:**	**INTERNATIONAL HUMANITARIAN LAW IN GENERAL**

1.	**One:**	**SOURCES AND GENERAL PRINCIPLES**
1.1	I	SOURCES
1.11		A. Pre-Hague
1.12		B. Hague Law
1.13		C. Geneva Law
1.14		D. Post-1977 Developments
1.15		E. Customary Law
1.2	II	GENERAL PRINCIPLES
1.21		A. Martens Clause
1.22		B. Superfluous Injury and Unnecessary Suffering
1.23		C. Principle of Distinction
1.24		D. Principle of Proportionality
1.25		E. Military Necessity

2.	**Two:**	**CONFLICTS, ARMED FORCES AND COMBATANTS**
2.1	I	TYPES OF CONFLICTS
2.11		A. International
2.12		B. Non-international
2.13		C. Other
2.2	II	TYPES OF ACTOR(S)
2.21		A. Armed Forces and Combatant Status
2.22		B. Non-State Actors
2.23		C. Specific Groups
2.231		1. Mercenaries
2.232		2. Spies
2.233		3. Other

3.	**Three:**	**PROTECTED PERSONS**
3.1	I	TYPES OF PROTECTED PERSONS
3.11		A. Wounded, Sick and Shipwrecked
3.12		B. Prisoners of War
3.13		C. Civilian Population
3.131		1. Civilians Generally
3.132		2. Women and Children
3.133		3. Medical and Religious Personnel
3.134		4. Journalists
3.135		5. Other
3.2	II	SPECIFIC SITUATIONS AND PROHIBITIONS
3.21		A. Internment
3.22		B. Occupation
3.23		C. Prohibition of Collective Punishment
3.24		D. Prohibition of Deportation and Transfer
3.25		E. Reprisals

NOTE: Many international and national documents related to international humanitarian law are available on the Internet through an on-line access to the ICRC IHL database (ICRC website: http://www.icrc.org). This database now contains almost 100 treaties and texts on the conduct of hostilities and the protection of victims of war (dating from 1856 to the present); the commentaries on the four Geneva Conventions and their Additional Protocols; an up-to-date list of signatures, ratifications, accessions or successions to IHL treaties; and, the full text of reservations. Constantly updated, this data is also regularly replicated on a D-ROM that can be obtained from the ICRC (Public Information Division, 19, av. de la Paix, CH-1202 GENEVA; e-mail: webmaster.gva@icrc.org; Fax: ++ 41 22 733 20 57; CHF 49.- or USD 39,-). National implementing legislation (Geneva Conventions Acts, extracts from Penal Codes, laws related to the protection of the emblem, laws on cooperation with the international Tribunals, etc.) and jurisprudence are also available for an increasing number of countries.

DOCUMENTS

1.13   GENEVA LAW

☞ UK: The Geneva Conventions (Amendment) Act (Overseas Territories) Order 2002 No. 1076, 17 April 2002

[…]

At the Court at Windsor Castle, the 17th day of April 2002

Present,

The Queen's Most Excellent Majesty in Council

Her Majesty, in exercise of the powers conferred on Her by section 8(2) of the Geneva Conventions Act 1957,[2] as applied to the Geneva Conventions (Amendment) Act 1995[3] by section 7(4) of that Act, or otherwise in Her Majesty vested, is pleased, by and with the advice of Her Privy Council, to order, and it is hereby ordered, as follows:

1. This Order may be cited as the Geneva Conventions (Amendment) Act (Overseas Territories) Order 2002. It shall come into force on 1st May 2002.

2. The provisions of the Geneva Conventions (Amendment) Act 1995 shall extend to the Territories specified in Schedule 1 hereto, subject to the exceptions and modifications specified in Schedule 2 hereto.

A. K. Galloway
Clerk of the Privy Council

Schedule 1
Article 2

---

2. [1] 5 & 6 Eliz. 2. c.52.
3. [2] 1995 c.27.

Territories to which the Geneva Conventions (Amendment) Act 1995 extends

Anguilla
Bermuda
British Antarctic Territory
British Indian Ocean Territory
Cayman Islands
Falkland Islands
Montserrat
Pitcairn, Henderson, Ducie and Oeno Islands
St Helena and Dependencies
South Georgia and the South Sandwich Islands
Sovereign Base Areas of Akrotiri and Dhekelia
Turks and Caicos Islands
Virgin Islands

Schedule 2
Article 2

Exceptions and modifications to be made in the extension of the Geneva Conventions (Amendment) Act 1995 to the Territories specified in Schedule 1

1. For the words "the Geneva Conventions Act 1957" in subsection (1) of section 1 there shall be substituted the words "the Geneva Conventions Act 1957 as extended to the Territory by the Geneva Conventions Act (Colonial Territories) Order in Council 1959".[4]

2. Subsection (4) of section 1 shall be omitted.

3.   (1) In subsection (2) of section 2, paragraph (a) shall be omitted.

(2) In subsection (3) of section 2, paragraph (a) shall be omitted.

(3) In subsection (4) of section 2, for paragraph (a) there shall be substituted the following paragraph: –
    "(a) for the words "fifty pounds" there shall be substituted the words "five thousand pounds or its equivalent";"

(4) In subsection (5) of section 2, for the words "the passing of this Act" there shall be substituted the words "the coming into operation of this Act in the Territory"; and for the words "the passing of the Geneva Conventions (Amendment) Act 1995" there shall be substituted the words "the coming into operation of the Geneva Conventions (Amendment) Act 1995 in the Territory".

(5) In subsection (6) of section 2, for paragraph (b) there shall be substituted the following paragraph: –

---

4. S.I. 1959/1301.

" (b) for the words "ship or aircraft" there shall be substituted the words "ship, aircraft or hovercraft"."

(6) In subsection (7) of section 2, paragraph (b) shall be omitted.

4. In section 3, for the words "the Secretary of State" wherever they occur there shall be substituted the words "the Governor"; and the words from "(3)" to "Parliament" shall be omitted.

5. For subsection (7) of section 4 there shall be substituted the following subsection: –
   "(7) After subsection (2) there shall be inserted the following subsection: –
   "(2A) The first protocol and the second protocol shall for the purposes of this Act be construed subject to and in accordance with: –
   (a) any reservation or declaration certified by Her Majesty by Order in Council[5] to have been made by the United Kingdom on ratification of the protocols, and which has not been so certified as having been withdrawn;

   (b) any amendment to the Fifth Schedule to this Act made by Her Majesty by Order in Council so as to ensure that the Schedule sets out the text of the first protocol as in force in relation to the United Kingdom.""

6. In section 5, paragraph (b) shall be omitted.

7. In section 7, subsections (2), (3) and (4) shall be omitted.

Explanatory Note *(This note is not part of the Order)*

This Order extends to the Territories specified in Schedule 1 the Geneva Conventions (Amendment) Act 1995, subject to the exceptions and modifications specified in Schedule 2.

☛ **Argentina: Statement of the Argentine Republic to the Swiss Confederation rejecting the claim of Britain to extend the application of the Additional Protocols to the Falkland Islands, South Georgia and the South Sandwich Islands, and to accept the competence of the International Fact Finding Commission in accordance with Protocol I in relation to these territories, 9 December 2002**

The Embassy of the Argentine Republic to the Swiss Confederation is honored to address the Federal Council, in its capacity as depository of the Protocols Additional to the Geneva Conventions of 12 August 1949, adopted at Geneva on 8 June 1977, in relation to the communication sent by the Permanent Mission of Switzerland to the United Nations in Geneva dated 5 November 2002, in regards to a petition made by the United Kingdom on 2 July 2002 to extend the application of said Protocols to the Falkland Islands, South Georgia and the South Sandwich Islands, and to accept the competence of the international Fact-Finding Commission in accordance with Protocol I in relation to these territories.

---

5. [4] See S.I. 1998/1754.

The Argentine Republic rejects the British claim to extend the application of the indicated Protocols to the Falkland Islands, South Georgia and the South Sandwich Islands, and to accept the competence of the International Fact Finding Commission in accordance with Protocol I in relation to these territories.

The Protocols Additional to the Geneva Conventions of 12 August 1949, adopted at Geneva on 8 June 1977 apply to the Falkland Islands, South Georgia and the South Sandwich Islands as being an integral part of the territory of the Argentine Republic, by virtue of the ratification of said Protocols by the Argentine government on 26 November 1996 and the acceptance of the competence of the International Fact-Finding Commission announced on 91 October 1996.

In relation to the question of the Falkland Islands, the United Nations General Assembly adopted resolutions 2065 (XX), 3160 (XXVIII), 31/49, 37/9, 38/12, 39/6, 40/21, 41/40, 42/19 and 43/25, in which there is a dispute over sovereignty, and asked that the Argentine Republic and the United Kingdom re-initiate negotiations with a view to find a peaceful and definite solution to the dispute, with the mediation of the United Nations Secretary-General, who will inform the General Assembly about any progress.

The Argentine Republic reaffirms its right of sovereignty over the Falkland Islands, South Georgia and the South Sandwich Islands, and the surrounding maritime spaces.

The Argentine Republic kindly requests that the Federal Council advise the High Contracting Parties to the Additional Protocols of this communication.

The Embassy of the Argentine Republic wishes to convey to the Swiss Confederation the assurance of its highest regard.

Berne, 9 December 2002

1.23   PRINCIPLE OF DISTINCTION

☛ USA: United States Department of Defense News Release No. 083-02. Statement on Hazar Qadam Raid, 21 February 2002

Today, the Secretary of Defense provided information during a Pentagon press briefing about the initial results of a commander in chief, U.S. Central Command-directed investigation into the circumstances surrounding the Jan. 23 raid of two compounds near Hazar Qadam. In order to ensure the record accurately reflects the findings of the investigation, the following clarification is provided.

The total number of Afghans who were killed during the raid is 16, with 14 killed at one compound and two killed in the other compound. The number of Afghans taken into custody by U.S. forces was 27. Those 27 were taken to a U.S. forward operating base at Qandahar airport for questioning. On Feb. 6, after being questioned about their identities and actions, they were released to the custody of Afghan officials in Oruzgan Province.

The 16 Afghans were killed after they fired on U.S. forces conducting a raid at two compounds believed to contain elements of Taliban or al Qaeda leadership. While we regret the loss of life, we are confident that the U.S. forces did their jobs to the best of their abilities, using the best information available to them in a very difficult situation.

☛ USA: Centcom News Release – Status of Investigations during Operation Enduring Freedom, 29 March 2002

[…]

Release Number 02-03-09

[…]

MacDill AFB, FL – For the past six months, Coalition forces have engaged in extensive combat activities as a part of Operation Enduring Freedom. Coalition forces have flown 36,564 sorties and dropped 21,737 weapons. During the course of those operations, the Commander in Chief of U.S. Central Command (USCINCCENT) determined there have been ten incidents that warranted review. The following is the most current information available on these ten investigations, listed in chronological order:

October 2001

International Committee of the Red Cross (ICRC) – The ICRC maintained certain facilities in Kabul, Afghanistan within a compound known as Kabul Army Storage Depot North. This compound had a long and continuous association with Afghan military activities. Additionally, facilities within the compound were used by the Taliban. The ICRC, in advance of our military action in Afghanistan, was asked to provide the coordinates for all of their facilities in Afghanistan. Coordinates for the ICRC facilities in this Depot were not included in the information provided by the ICRC. On October 16, the compound was attacked by Coalition air forces. Following that attack, USCENTCOM was made aware that ICRC facilities were located within this compound. The compound was struck again on October 26. A preliminary inquiry conducted by USCENTCOM was passed to the Chief of Staff of the Air Force on 30 November 2001 for follow-on action as he deemed appropriate. (See Oct. 26, 2001, CENTCOM release # 01-10-06).

November 2001

United Nations Convoy – USCENTCOM became aware through press reporting that on November 11 a United Nations convoy had suffered damage from aerial bombardment while traveling to Bamian, Afghanistan. A Preliminary Inquiry was conducted by USCENTCOM. The inquiry determined that the convoy was not the target of a strike. Rather, high altitude bombers were striking steep cliffs alongside a road in order to block the route to enemy forces. Additionally, the inquiry disclosed that the UN Convoy was not traveling on the days for which it had requested and received clearance. The coalition had no reason to suspect the presence of the UN convoy nor was the convoy visible to the bombers. The convoy was struck by flying debris. No one was killed or injured. This incident is closed.

[…]

January 2002

Hazar Qadam Direct Action Mission – On January 23, Coalition forces conducted a direct action mission against two suspected al Qaida/Taliban compounds located near the town of Hazar Qadam. Fourteen personnel at one compound and two at the other were killed. One U.S. person was injured. Twenty-seven people were detained and transported to Qandahar for interrogation. The interrogation determined that the personnel might have been friendly Afghans. USCINCCENT directed the U.S. Army Forces Central Command (ARCENT) Commander to conduct an investigation. That investigation did not substantiate that the compounds at Hazar Qadam were, at the time of the direct action mission, being used by Al Qaida/Taliban. Nevertheless, the investigation concluded that there were no systemic errors in the targeting process, mission planning or mission execution. This incident is closed. (See DoD release # 083-02)

Allegations by Hazar Qadam Detainees of Abuse at Qandahar – Several detainees taken from Hazar Qadam alleged that they had been physically mistreated while in U.S. custody at Qandahar. USCINCCENT directed ARCENT to conduct an investigation into the allegation. The investigation found no evidence of mistreatment. All the detainees underwent normal in-processing at the facility upon arrival. They were photographed and subjected to a medical review. Those requiring medical attention were promptly treated. There was no evidence that any of them suffered any additional injury while there. The injuries noted upon their arrival were not serious or life-threatening and were consistent with what might be expected from the application of force reasonably necessary to secure them during the direct action mission at Hazar Qadam. This incident is closed.

February 2002

Allegation that a Detainee was Mistreated While at Qandahar – One of the detainees moved from Qandahar to the U.S. base at Guantanamo Bay, Cuba, on or about February 12, claimed U.S. guards at Qandahar had beaten him. The detainee had signs of physical injury that were not documented in the file that accompanied him from Qandahar. The allegation was reported to USCENTCOM, and USCINCCENT directed ARCENT to conduct an investigation. The investigation found that the detainee, while at Qandahar, struggled and fought with his guards, and was injured during efforts to gain control of him. The detainee was seen immediately by medical personnel at Qandahar and a report of the incident prepared. That report, however, was inadvertently omitted from the file that was forwarded to Guantanamo Bay, Cuba. Corrective measures to ensure proper forwarding of documentation were instituted. This incident is closed.

March 2002

[…]

Suspected Leadership Target Engaged Near Shikin, Afghanistan – On March 6, Coalition forces attacked a suspected Al Qa'ida leader traveling in a vehicle near Shikin, Afghanistan. The attack resulted in 14 fatalities and one wounded. Among the killed were eight adult males, three adult females and three children. To more fully understand the entire incident, USCINCCENT directed the Task Force Commander to conduct an investigation, which is ongoing. Once the investigation is complete, it will be forwarded to USCENT-COM for review. (See Mar. 12, 2002, CENTCOM release # 02-03-04)

In addition to these investigations, there have been several aircraft mishaps during Operation ENDURING FREEDOM. Investigations of these incidents are within the exclusive purview of the Service that operated the aircraft. Since aircraft investigations are not under the control or authority of USCENTCOM, they are not included in this investigation update.

☛ USA: Centcom News Release – Investigation of Civilian Casualties, Oruzgan Province, Operation Full Throttle, 30 June 2002

[...]

The Deh Rawod area of Afghanistan is considered the "home" of the Taliban and remains an area where the Taliban enjoy popular support. The extended families of both Mullah Mohammed Omar, the former "Supreme Leader" of the Taliban, and Mullah Berader, the former "Senior Military Commander" of the Taliban, reside in the area.

Coalition aircraft have regularly been the target of hostile fire from the Deh Rawod area. While ineffective, the fire was clearly intentional and directed toward coalition forces. Two weeks prior to Operation Full Throttle (OFT), covert reconnaissance of the area was conducted. Gunfire from various caliber weapons was observed throughout the day and at night, including mortars and AAA[6] fire. The Deh Rawod area appeared to support enemy military training.

OFT was intended to deny Deh Rawod as an enemy sanctuary. Afghan forces were involved [in] the execution of the mission.

Two days before the incident, additional reconnaissance teams were inserted into positions where they could observe the specific objectives and the approaches that coalition ground and airborne forces would take to execute their missions. Hostile fire was directed at coalition helicopters conducting these insertions, forcing at least one to land at an alternate site. During this period of increased and focused reconnaissance, every time a coalition aircraft appeared overhead or could be heard at night, ground fire was directed at it. These fires were traced back to their source locations on the ground. From the nature and characteristics of the fires, it was clear that these were AAA and not small arms.

Several compounds in the Deh Rawod area were positively identified as sources of this AAA fire. AAA fire had emanated from these compounds on repeated occasions over the previous two days and the source of the fires did not change. In all cases, the locations of these compounds were such that they could range and threaten coalition ground and airborne forces that were to execute OFT. On-call close air support assets were assigned to

---

6. [1] AAA = Anti-Aircraft Artillery [editor's note].

OFT to counter these threats should AAA in those compounds become active in the moments immediately preceding the introduction of coalition forces into the area.

As coalition ground and airborne forces approached the area, fire erupted from some of the compounds. By firing, these AAA batteries established that they were manned, armed and operational. Their proximity to the objectives, landing zones and blocking positions made them a threat to inbound coalition forces. Consequently, these sites were valid targets and AC-130 aircraft[7] were directed toward them.

Significant efforts were expended to ensure only the compounds that were the sources of fire were targeted. At the first targeted compound, the apparent location of most of the deaths and injuries, AAA fire was directed at the AC-130 as it approached. At one location, however, the AC-130 arrived at a target and found it to be "cold" and elected not to strike it.

The AC-130 was not able to observe the AAA weapon itself. Rather, the ground location of the source of the fire was identified and fires were directed to that area. Just as the weapon itself is not seen, it is also not possible to determine if the fires from the AC-130 have damaged or destroyed the weapon. Consequently, personnel at the weapon's location were the primary targets. Unfortunately, it is also not possible to distinguish men from women or adults from children.

The dead and wounded later observed by coalition forces were mostly women and children. Coalition medical personnel treated the wounded. Four wounded children were medically evacuated by helicopter. A search of the first targeted compound, about two to four hours after the AC-130 had departed, revealed bloodstains and evidence of the AC-130 weapons impacts. There were no weapons or spent cartridges of any type readily observed within the compound. Further, the local Afghans maintained that most of the dead had already been buried – although no fresh gravesites were observed.

Near the second compound that had been targeted, coalition forces established a checkpoint. The checkpoint identified approximately 20 injured personnel being transported to local medical facilities. Of the 20, 2 were adult males.

Villagers had initially claimed 250 dead and 600 injured, but a village elder later admitted that the real numbers were only about 25% of those figures. The Afghan government presented a report listing 48 dead and 117 wounded. Coalition forces could only confirm 34 dead and approximately 50 wounded. An exact number will never be able to be confirmed.

Although the AC-130 struck 6 AAA sites, the local Afghans claimed that all of the dead and injured were located at only the first two compounds. Both of these targets were east of the Helmand River, while the other 4 targets were on the west side. Due to difficult terrain, safety and other limitations, neither coalition forces immediately following OFT, CJTF-180

---

7. [2] The AC-130 is a medium-sized cargo plane, commonly known as a "Hercules," converted to combat use by placing several machine guns and/or rapid-firing cannon to fire out of windows on one side of the aircraft. The AC-130 attacks a target on the ground by circling the target with its "armed" pointed towards the target. [editor's note]

representatives during the fact-finding mission on 3-4 July, nor Investigation Board members during the Investigation Board's visit to the area on 24 July were able to visit any of the sites on the west side of the river. The visits to the two compounds did not reveal the presence of any antiaircraft weapons or even a significant presence of shell casings from any weapon. The fact-finding team found two small piles of RPK rounds (about 12 total shells), but also noted that the two compounds showed no signs of having been occupied and had recently been raked. By the time the Investigation Board visited on 24 July, they were only able to confirm the existence of battle damage at the two compounds consistent with fires from an AC-130. Local Afghans continued to maintain that all the deaths and injuries were confined to these two compounds and did not facilitate visits to the other compounds.

In the period immediately following the incident, village elders admitted to Coalition forces that people within the village regularly had fired at aircraft using AK-47s, RPK's (squad machine gun) and DShK's (heavy machine gun), but not with a weapon larger than 23 mm. In fact, village elders acknowledged holding a local Shura (town meeting) the day prior to the incident to discuss firing weapons into the air during weddings and firing at aircraft. Also, two freshly completed drawings on the walls of the local pharmacy/hospital depicted people firing at helicopters and fixed wing aircraft.

There were people within this area of Oruzgan Province that regularly aimed and fired of variety of weapons at coalition aircraft. These weapons represented a real threat to coalition forces. As OFT commenced, AAA weapons were fired and, as a result, an AC-130 aircraft, acting properly and in accordance with the rules, engaged the locations of those weapons. Great care was taken to strike only those sites that were actively firing that night. While the coalition regrets the loss of innocent lives, the responsibility for that loss rests with those that knowingly directed hostile fire at coalition forces. The operators of those weapons elected to place them in civilian communities and elected to fire them at coalition forces at a time when they knew there were a significant number of civilians present.

2.21   ARMED FORCES AND COMBATANT STATUS

☛ **USA: Fact Sheet. Status of Detainees at Guantanamo. White House Press Release of 7 February 2002**

United States Policy.
The United States is treating and will continue to treat all of the individuals detained at Guantanamo humanely and, to the extent appropriate and consistent with military necessity, in a manner consistent with the principles of the Third Geneva Convention of 1949.

The President has determined that the Geneva Convention applies to the Taliban detainees, but not to the al-Qaida detainees.

Al-Qaida is not a state party to the Geneva Convention; it is a foreign terrorist group. As such, its members are not entitled to POW status.

Although we never recognized the Taliban as the legitimate Afghan government, Afghanistan is a party to the Convention, and the President has determined that the Taliban are covered by the Convention. Under the terms of the Geneva Convention, however, the Taliban detainees do not qualify as POWs.

Therefore, neither the Taliban nor al-Qaida detainees are entitled to POW status.

Even though the detainees are not entitled to POW privileges, they will be provided many POW privileges as a matter of policy.

All detainees at Guantanamo are being provided:

— three meals a day that meet Muslim dietary laws
— water
— medical care
— clothing and shoes
— shelter
— showers
— soap and toilet articles
— foam sleeping pads and blankets
— towels and washcloths
— the opportunity to worship
— correspondence materials, and the means to send mail
— the ability to receive packages of food and clothing, subject to security screening

The detainees will not be subjected to physical or mental abuse or cruel treatment. The International Committee of the Red Cross has visited and will continue to be able to visit the detainees privately. The detainees will be permitted to raise concerns about their conditions and we will attempt to address those concerns consistent with security.

Housing. We are building facilities in Guantanamo more appropriate for housing the detainees on a long-term basis. The detainees now at Guantanamo are being housed in temporary open-air shelters until these more long-term facilities can be arranged. Their current shelters are reasonable in light of the serious security risk posed by these detainees and the mild climate of Cuba.

POW Privileges the Detainees will not receive. The detainees will receive much of the treatment normally afforded to POWs by the Third Geneva Convention. However, the detainees will not receive some of the specific privileges afforded to POWs, including:

— access to a canteen to purchase food, soap, and tobacco
— a monthly advance of pay
— the ability to have and consult personal financial accounts
— the ability to receive scientific equipment, musical instruments, or sports outfits

Many detainees at Guantanamo pose a severe security risk to those responsible for guarding them and to each other. Some of these individuals demonstrated how dangerous they are in uprisings at Mazar-e-Sharif and in Pakistan. The United States must take into account the need for security in establishing the conditions for detention at Guantanamo.

Background on Geneva Conventions. The Third Geneva Convention of 1949 is an international treaty designed to protect prisoners of war from inhumane treatment at the hands of their captors in conflicts covered by the Convention. It is among four treaties concluded in the wake of WWII to reduce the human suffering caused by war. These four treaties provide protections for four different classes of people: the military wounded and sick in land conflicts; the military wounded, sick and shipwrecked in conflicts at sea; military persons and civilians accompanying the armed forces in the field who are captured and qualify as prisoners of war; and civilian non-combatants who are interned or otherwise found in the hands of a party (e.g. in a military occupation) during an armed conflict.

☞ USA: United States Department of Defense, Deputy Secretary of Defense Wolfowitz at a Special Department of Justice Press Conference, Monday, 10 June 2002

(Special Department of Justice press conference on the arrest of Abdullah al Mujahir, also known as Jose Padilla. Hosted by Larry Thompson, deputy attorney general. Also participating was Robert Mueller, director, Federal Bureau of Investigation.)

Thompson: Good morning. I'm pleased to be here with Deputy Secretary of Defense Paul Wolfowitz and FBI Director Bob Mueller.

By now all of you have heard the attorney general's statement regarding the arrest of Abdullah al Mujahir and his transfer to military control. Secretary Wolfowitz has a few brief remarks, and then all three of us will be available for a few questions regarding the attorney general's announcement. I'll turn it over to Deputy Secretary Wolfowitz.

Wolfowitz: Thanks, Larry. Yesterday, at the direction of the president, the Department of Justice transferred control of Jose Padilla, who is a U.S. citizen, to the Department of Defense. As of today, he will be held at the Naval Consolidated Brig in Charleston, South Carolina.

Based on information available to our government, Padilla met with senior al Qaeda members to discuss plans for exploding a radioactive device, a radioactive dispersal device, or what is commonly called a "dirty bomb," in the United States. He researched nuclear weapons and received training in wiring explosives while in Pakistan, and he was instructed to return to the United States to conduct reconnaissance operations for al Qaeda.

Under the laws of war, Padilla's activities and his association with al Qaeda make him an enemy combatant. For this reason, Jose Padilla has been turned over to the Department of Defense.

Our number one priority is to defend the American people from future attacks. To do that, we must root out those who are planning such attacks. We must find them, and we must stop them. And when we have them in our control, we must be able to question them about plans for future attacks.

The FBI's initial detention of Padilla is one important step in this process. It demonstrates the successful sharing of information and close cooperation among U.S. government agencies that will be key to winning the war against terrorism. I would like to commend all of those who worked to bring about this result that makes the American people safer.

Q: Mr. Thompson or Secretary Wolfowitz, what is his status then? I thought the administration's rules on military tribunals said they would be only for non-American citizens. Is the whole point of holding him as a military combatant to be able to question him without using the conventional criminal process?

Thompson: His status, as the attorney general said in his statement, is as an enemy combatant. He is being attained under the laws of war as an enemy combatant. There's clear Supreme Court and circuit court authority for such a detention.

Q: What is the Supreme Court precedent?

Thompson: It's a 1942 case ex parte Quirin. And there's a 9th Circuit case, and I forgot the name of it – it's in re Territo; it's a 1946 case. Beverly?

Q: Does he have legal representation at the moment?

Thompson: He was being held under the authority of a federal judge, and he had legal representation in connection with that. Yes?

Q: Does he now? Does he now?

Q: Larry, how far did they get? How far did they get? Did they have – had they assembled any parts of the weapon in the United States? Or try to acquire any parts of the weapon?

Thompson: I'll defer to the director on that question.

Mueller: Let me just start off by saying that we have worked closely with the CIA for many months now. And the detention of this individual was a result of the close cooperative work of FBI agents and CIA agents, not only overseas, but also here in the United States. And I would like to thank our counterparts at the CIA for their work on this particular case. As we've emphasized – and by we, I mean, I think, the intelligence agencies, as well as Department of Defense – our principal priority is preventing future terrorist attacks. And this instance is an example of prevention. Now, with regard to the specific question as to the extent of the planning, as it states, I think, in the attorney general's statement, there were discussions about this possible plan, and it was in the discussion stage. And it had not gone, as far as we know, much past the discussion stage, but there were substantial discussions undertaken.

Q: Director Mueller, how long has the government been tracking this guy? And can you tell us what the origin of that was? Was it based on information from Zubaidah or prior to that?

Mueller: Well, let me just say, I cannot get into much of the background of the case because there are sources and methods that would be – that would be disclosed if we got into much detail at this particular point in time.

Q: (Off mike) – confirm that the attack was planned against the Washington, D.C., area? And also, what's happened to him if he's been arrested? He was detained March 8th. What happened to him in all that time?

Thompson: I'll defer to where he might be by Secretary Wolfowitz – where he –

Q: If that were –

Wolfowitz: We don't know. I mean, as Director Mueller said, this was still in the initial planning stages. It certainly wasn't at the point of having a specific target. He had indicated some knowledge of the Washington, D.C., area, but I want to emphasize again, there was not an actual plan. We stopped this man in the initial planing [sic] stages. But it does underscore, I think, the continuing importance of focusing particularly on those people who may be pursuing chemical or biological or radiological or nuclear weapons. This is but one such individual.

☛ **USA: United States Department of Defense News Release No. 497-02: DoD Responds to ABA Enemy Combatant Report, 2 October 2002**

Department of Defense General Counsel William J. Haynes II last week asserted the President's authority to detain enemy combatants in response to an American Bar Association report critical of the policy.

In a letter to ABA President Alfred P. Carlton regarding conclusions in the recently released "Preliminary Report of the ABA Task Force on Treatment of Enemy Combatants," Haynes said, "Mr. Hirshon was kind enough to send me the August 8, 2002 Preliminary Report ('Report') of the ABA Task Force on Treatment of Enemy Combatants ('Task Force'). The Task Force asks the Administration to explain the basis and scope of its authority to detain U.S. citizens as enemy combatants (pp. 20-21). We have explained our position in various filings and arguments before federal courts, and elsewhere. Nevertheless, I am happy to respond now, especially since the Report contains legal errors that I am sure the Task Force will want to correct before the ABA considers whether to endorse the Report.

"There are many areas in which the Task Force's Report concurs with the government's analysis of its authority to detain enemy combatants. First, the Report acknowledges that the United States is currently in a state of war with al Qaeda, one that triggers Executive Branch authority to prevent further attacks. Second, the Report recognizes that the United States government possesses wartime authority to detain enemy combatants in order to prevent them from furthering enemy attacks on the United States in the future. Finally, the Report concludes that a state of war necessarily confers upon the government additional authority that it does not possess in time of peace.

"My comments address the two central issues in the Report: (1) The President's authority to detain enemy combatants during wartime; and (2) Judicial review of the President's determination of enemy combatant status.

"Without question, the President can detain enemy combatants, including those who are U.S. citizens, during wartime. See Ex parte Quirin, 317 U.S. 1, 31, 37 (1942); Colepaugh v. Looney, 235 F. 2d 429, 432 (10th Cir. 1956); In re Territo, 156 F. 2d 142, 145 (9th Cir. 1946). The Fourth Circuit recently reaffirmed this proposition. See Hamdi v. Rumsfeld, 296 F.3d 278, 281, 283 (4th Cir. 2002). The purposes of detaining enemy combatants during wartime are, among other things, to gather intelligence and to ensure that detainees do not return to assist the enemy. Presidents have detained enemy combatants in every major conflict in the Nation's history, including recent conflicts such as the Gulf, Vietnam, and Korean wars. During World War II, the United States detained hundreds of thousands of prisoners of war in the United States (some of whom were U.S. citizens) without trial or counsel. Then, as now, the purpose of detention was not to punish, but to protect.

"Article II of the Constitution is the primary basis for the President's authority to detain enemy combatants. Article II vests the 'executive Power' in the President and provides that he 'shall be Commander in Chief of the Army and Navy of the United States.' U.S. Const. art. II, § 1, cl. 1; id., § 2, cl. 1. These provisions invest 'the President alone . . . with the entire charge of hostile operations' during wartime. Hamilton v. Dillin, 88 U.S. (21 Wall.) 73, 87 (1874); see also Johnson v. Eisentrager, 339 U.S. 763, 788 (1950). The determination that an individual should be detained as an enemy combatant has traditionally been one of the President's most fundamental military judgments.

"While Article II is a sufficient basis for the President's authority to detain enemy combatants, in the current conflict the President also enjoys the support of Congress. In its Joint
Resolution of September 18, 2001, Congress authorized 'the President . . . to use all necessary and appropriate force against those nations, organizations, or persons he determines
planned, authorized, committed, or aided the terrorist attacks that occurred on September
11, 2001, or harbored such organizations or persons, in order to prevent any future acts of
international terrorism against the United States by such nations, organizations or persons.'
Pub. L. No. 107-40, § 2(a), 115 Stat. 224 (2001) (emphasis added); see also 10 U.S.C.§
956. Congress thus specifically authorized the President not only to use deadly force, but
also any lesser force needed to capture and detain enemy combatants to prevent them from
engaging in continued hostilities against the United States. The President's constitutional
power is at its apex when he enjoys such support from Congress, especially in the field of
foreign affairs. See Dames & Moore v. Regan, 453 U.S. 654, 674 (1981); Youngstown
Sheet and Tube Co. v. Sawyer, 343 U.S. 579, 635-37 & n. 2 (1952) (Jackson, J., concurring).

"The Report incorrectly suggests (p. 9) that the absence of a 'formal Congressional 'Declaration of War' somehow affects the President's power to detain enemy combatants. As
explained above, Article II alone gives the President the power to detain enemies during
wartime, regardless of congressional action. In any event, Congress's September 18, 2001
Joint Resolution provides ample congressional sanction. It has long been settled that congressional approval of presidential military action need not take the form of a declaration,
see, e.g., Talbot v. Seeman, 5 U.S. (1 Cranch) 1 (1801); Bas v. Tingy, 4 U.S. (4 Dall.) 37
(1800). Indeed, the vast majority of U.S. military actions have not been preceded by a congressional declaration of war. The President has exercised the power to detain enemy combatants in many wars that lacked a formal declaration from Congress, including, most
recently, the Gulf, Vietnam, and Korean wars. And the Fourth Circuit recently confirmed
that the government currently possesses the authority to detain enemy combatants even
though Congress has not declared war against al Qaida. See Hamdi, 296 F.3d at 283.

"The Report also errs in suggesting (p. 9) that the President may detain only enemy combatants who wear uniforms. This position was implicitly rejected in Quirin, a case involving
enemy saboteurs captured wearing civilian clothes. See Quirin, 317 U.S. at 31 ('Lawful
combatants are subject to capture and detention as prisoners of war by opposing military
forces. Unlawful combatants are likewise subject to capture and detention . . .'). Any other
rule would reward enemy combatants for violating the traditional law of war requirement to
wear uniforms or a distinctive insignia as a condition of lawful combat.

"Finally, the President's authority to detain enemy combatants is not affected by 18 U.S.C.
§ 4001. Section 4001 requires that '[n]o citizen shall be imprisoned or otherwise detained
by the United States except pursuant to an act of Congress.' The text and legislative history
of Section 4001, as well as its placement in Title 18 of the U.S. Code, demonstrate that
Congress intended Section 4001(a) to govern only the administration of federal civilian
prisons, and not to restrict the President's constitutional authority as Commander in Chief
to detain enemy combatants. Moreover, as explained above, there is an act of Congress that
supports the detentions – the September 18, 2001 Joint Resolution. If Section 4001 nonetheless purported to apply to enemy combatant detentions, it would impinge on the President's constitutional powers under Article II. Section 4001 should be read to avoid this

constitutional difficulty. See, e.g., Franklin v. Massachusetts, 505 U.S. 788, 800-01 (1992) (citations omitted).

"The Report suggests that the government's position in the Hamdi and Padilla habeas litigation is that 'with no meaningful judicial review, an American citizen alleged to be an enemy combatant could be detained indefinitely without charges or counsel on the Government's say-so.' That statement warrants three comments.

"First, the government welcomes meaningful judicial review of its detention in the United States of 'enemy combatants.' As part of its Returns in Hamdi and Padilla, the government submitted ample factual evidence supporting its determinations that Hamdi and Padilla are enemy combatants. These executive branch submissions to the judiciary are literally unprecedented in our nation's long history of wartime detentions of enemy combatants, and demonstrate our commitment to judicial review in this context. The Fourth Circuit reaffirmed that the judiciary owes the executive branch 'considerable' deference in the context of foreign relations and national security, especially when the President acts with congressional support, and that this considerable deference 'extends to military designations of individuals as enemy combatants in times of active hostilities, as well as to their detention after capture on the field of battle.' Hamdi, 296 F.3d at 281.

"Second, I am puzzled about the basis for the Report's recommendation (pp. 23-24) that a detainee should be given counsel for purposes of seeking habeas relief. The Report correctly acknowledges (p. 23) that 'the 6th Amendment right to counsel does not technically attach to uncharged enemy combatants,' and that giving detainees access to counsel may sometimes be 'unwise, impractical, or dangerous.' But the Report goes on to argue for a right to counsel on the basis of a vague and unexplained reference (p. 24) to 'full Due Process rights.' There is no due process or any other legal basis, under either domestic or international law, that entitles enemy combatants to legal counsel. And providing such counsel as a matter of discretion at this time would threaten national security in at least two respects: It would interfere with ongoing efforts to gather and evaluate intelligence about the enemy. And it might enable detained enemy combatants to pass concealed messages to the enemy. Al Qaida training manuals emphasize the 'importance,' when detained, of 'mastering the art of hiding messages,' and teach that al Qaida detainees should '[t]ake advantage of visits to communicate with brothers outside prison and exchange information that may be helpful to them in their work outside prison . . .' See Birmingham UK Al Qaida Manual, page 16, para. 6, available at <http://www.usdoj.gov/ag/manualpart1_4.pdf; cf. United States v. Ahmed Abdel Sattar, et al., Indictment 02 Crim. 395, 7, 16, 30 (Grand Jury Indictment, S.D.N.Y., April 9, 2002) (attorney for member of terrorist group related to al Qaida indicted for passing messages to and from convicted terrorist Sheik Omar Abdel-Rahman).

"Third, the Report misleadingly asserts that Hamdi and Padilla are being detained 'indefinitely.' The suggestion appears to be that Hamdi and Padilla are being detained lawlessly and without limit. That is not true. As I just explained, the constitutional power to detain during wartime is well settled. In addition, international law – including the Third Geneva Convention – unambiguously permits a government to detain enemy combatants at least until hostilities cease. I appreciate that there may be uncertainty about when hostilities cease in the novel conflict with al Qaida. But I believe that disquiet about indefinite detention is misplaced for two reasons. First, the concern is premature. In prior wars combatants (including U.S. prisoners of war) have been legally detained for years. We have not yet approached that point in the current conflict. And second, the government has no interest in detaining enemy combatants any longer than necessary, and is reviewing the requirement for their continued detention on a case-by-case basis. But as long as hostilities continue and the detainees retain intelligence value or present a threat, no law requires that the detainees be released, and it would be imprudent to do so.

"Much of the foregoing analysis responds to your query about the basis of presidential power to detain enemy combatants during wartime. But there is more at work here than the exercise of prerogatives. The Constitution confers extraordinary power on the President to enable him to carry out his ultimate responsibility of ensuring that the American people are safe and secure. To fail to exercise this power would be to fail to discharge this most basic of all presidential responsibilities.

"I agree with the Report (p. 4) that '[h]ow we deal with citizens suspected of terroristic activity will say much about us as a society committed to the rule of law.' This is one of the many reasons why the government has paid such careful attention to the legal basis for its actions. In our view, the detention of enemy combatants is authorized by the Constitution, by Congress, by long historical practice, by the laws and customs of war, by Supreme Court precedent, and by lower court precedent. In this light, the Report's ubiquitous suggestion that the detention of Hamdi and Padilla is inconsistent with the rule of law is misplaced. I hope that an examination of the precedents and arguments above will lead the Task Force to rethink its analysis and conclusions.

3.21   INTERNMENT

☛ Israel: The Incarceration of Unlawful Combatants Law 2002 and Appendix, 4 March 2002

1) Purpose

This Law is designed to regulate the incarceration of unlawful combatants, who are not entitled to prisoner of war status, in a way which conforms to the State of Israel's obligations under the rules of international humanitarian law

2) Definitions

In this Law –
"The Chief of Staff" – The Chief of General Staff of the Israel Defense Force;
"Unlawful combatant" – a person who has taken a part in hostilities against the State of Israel, directly or indirectly, or is a member of a force engaged in hostilities against the State of Israel who does not meet the conditions which confer a prisoner of war status under international humanitarian law, as enumerated in article 4 of the Third Geneva Convention Relative to the Treatment of Prisoners of War of 12 August 1949;

"Imprisoned person" – any person who is detained by force of an order issued by the Chief of Staff in accordance with the provisions of this Law.

3) Incarceration of unlawful combatant

(a) In the event that the Chief of Staff has reasonable grounds to believe that a person held by State authorities is an unlawful combatant, and that his release will compromise national security, he may issue an hand signed warrant, ordering his incarceration in a designated location (hereinafter – "incarceration order"); an incarceration order shall contain the reasons for incarceration, without compromising the requirements of national security.

(b) An incarceration order may be issued without the presence of the person held by State authorities.

(c) An incarceration order will be notified to the imprisoned person at the earliest possible date, and he will be afforded the opportunity to present his arguments concerning the order before an army colonel or a higher ranked officer, who is appointed by the Chief of Staff; the arguments of the imprisoned person will be recorded by the officer and brought before the Chief of Staff; if the Chief of Staff concludes, after reviewing the imprisoned person's arguments, that the conditions provided in section (a) have not been met, he will annul the incarceration order.

4) Annulment of incarceration order

If the Chief of Staff believes, at any time after the issuance of the incarceration order, that the conditions provided in article 3(a) are not met, or that there are special reason justifying the release of the imprisoned person, he will order the annulment of the incarceration order.

5) Judicial review

(a) An imprisoned person shall be brought before a District Court judge no later than 14 days following the day in which the incarceration order was issued; if a District Court judge found that the conditions provided in article 3(a) have not been met he will annul the incarceration order.

(b) In the event that the imprisoned person was not brought before the District Court and proceedings did not begin before the court within 14 days following the day in which the incarceration order was issued, the imprisoned person shall be released, unless there exists another ground for his detention under any law.

(c) Once every 6 months from the day in which the incarceration order was issued under article 3(a), the imprisoned person shall be brought before a District Court judge; if the court finds that his release would not compromise national security or that there exist special reasons justifying his release, it will annul the incarceration order.

(d) The District Court's decision under this article may be appealed within 30 days to the Supreme Court, which will hear it in a single-judge chamber; the Supreme Court shall have all of the powers granted to the District Court under this Law.

(e) In proceedings under this Law, rules of evidence may be derogated from, for noted reasons; the court may admit a piece of evidence, even if the imprisoned person or his attorney are not present or without disclosing it to them if, after reviewing the evidence or hearing arguments, even if the imprisoned person or his attorney are not present, it became convinced that disclosure of the evidence to the imprisoned person or his attorney might compromise national security or public safety; this provision does not derogate from any right not to disclose evidence provided in Chapter C of the Evidence Ordinance (New Version) 1971.

(f) Proceedings under this Law will be held *in camera* unless the court provided otherwise.

6) Right of imprisoned person to meet a lawyer

(a) The imprisoned person may meet a lawyer at the earliest date in which the meeting could be arranged without compromising the requirements of national security, but no more than 7 days before he is to be brought before a District Court judge, in pursuance with the provisions of article 5(a).

(b) The Minister of Justice may, by way of an Order, limit the right of representation in proceedings under this Law to persons who have been granted unrestricted authorization to serve as defense counsel before military courts under the provisions of article 318(C) of the Military Judging Law 1955.

7) Presumption

For the purpose of this Law, a person who was a member of a force conducting hostilities against the State of Israel, or who has participated in hostilities undertaken by such a force, directly or indirectly, will be regarded as a person whose release will compromise national security for as long as hostilities undertaken by that force against the State of Israel had not ended, unless it was proven otherwise.

8) Determination concerning hostilities

A determination by the Minister of Defense, in a hand signed certificate, that a certain force engages in hostilities against the State of Israel or that hostilities undertaken by such a force against the State of Israel have ended or have not ended, shall serve proof in any legal proceedings, unless proven otherwise.

9) Criminal proceedings

(a) Criminal proceedings may be initiated against an unlawful combatant pursuant to any law.

(b) The Chief of Staff may issue an order of incarceration of an unlawful combatant in accordance with article 3, even if criminal proceedings under any law are pending against him.

10) Conditions of incarceration

(a) An imprisoned person shall be held in proper conditions which shall not compromise his health and dignity.

(b) The conditions of incarceration of imprisoned persons shall be determined by the Minster of Defense in Regulations

11) Delegation of authorities

The Chief of Staff may delegate his authorities under this Law to an army General appointed by him.

12) Transitional provisions

(a) The provisions of this Law shall also apply to an unlawful combatant held by State authorities at the date of its entry into force.

(b) Until the Regulations under article 10(b) have been introduced, conditions of incarceration of imprisoned persons will be governed by the Emergency Powers (Detention) (Conditions of Administrative Detention) Regulations 1981.

13) Implementation and Regulations

(a) The Minister of Defense is responsible for the implementation of this Law.

(b) The Minister of Justice may introduce Regulations governing procedure in proceedings under this Law.

Appendix III
Detention of Unlawful Combatants (Conditions of Detention) Regulations-2002[8]

1) Definitions

In these regulations –
"Place of Detention" – the prison, where the detainee is detained, as defined in the Prisons Ordinance [New Version]-1971, or a military detention facility (hereinafter – military facility), where the detainee is detained, determined as a the place of detention in an Order under Section 3(a) of the Law;
"The Commandant" – the director of the place of detention.

2) Separate Detention

The detainee shall be held in the place of detention separate from sentenced detainees and from detainees awaiting their trial.

3) Solitary Confinement

(a) The Commandant may order that a detainee be held in solitary confinement, if he

----

8. Footnotes omitted. Translation provided with the courtesy of the Legal Department, International Committee of the Red Cross, Tel Aviv.

is convinced that such is necessary for State security, for maintaining discipline at the place of detention, or for protection of the well-being or health of the detainee or of other detainees.

(b) The Commandant may also, at his discretion, order that a detainee be held in solitary confinement, if the detainee so requests.

(c) The Commandant, having ordered that a detainee be held in solitary confinement, shall reconsider his order at least once every two months, or at an earlier date, if the detainee so requested and the Commandant saw reason to do so.

(d) A detainee held in solitary confinement for a period exceeding three months may appeal to the Chief of Staff against the Commandant's last decision under which he is being held in solitary confinement; in considering the appeal, the Chief of Staff may, at his discretion, order continuation of solitary confinement or its cancellation.

(e) The Commandant shall not order that a detainee be held in solitary confinement for a period exceeding six months before he receives authorisation to do so from the Chief of staff.

4) Clothing

(a) A detainee shall wear no symbols or decorations, save for symbols serving religious purposes being of a reasonable and acceptable material and size.

(b) A detainee shall not wear uniform.

(c) A detainee shall wear such clothes, undergarments and shoes issued to him by the Commandant.

(d) The provision of sub-Regulation (c) notwithstanding, a detainee shall be entitled to wear his private clothes where wearing them does not interfere with health or proper order.

5) Receiving Food and Food Products

(a) A detainee in a place of detention shall receive the food ration supplied to the wardens at that place of detention, with consideration for, to the extent possible, his religious beliefs.

(b) In places of detention with a canteen, the Commandant may permit the detainee to purchase products therein.

(c) Food shall not be supplied to the detainee in the place of detention in a manner not set forth in this Regulation, except with permission of the Commandant.

6) Medical Examination and Care

(a) As soon as possible after his arrival to the place of detention, the detainee shall be examined by a physician appointed by the Commandant; the detainee shall likewise be examined by a physician once a month and at any time necessary.

(b) A detainee is entitled to receive medical care and medical equipment as required by his health condition.

(c) A physician, having determined that the detainee's health or life is in danger, and the detainee refuses to accept the care prescribed by the physician, it is permissible to use, in the physician's presence, such degree of force necessary for carrying out the physician's instructions.

7)   Hygienic Conditions

The Commandant will ensure that the detainee is detained in appropriate hygienic conditions and is granted appropriate sleep arrangements, which do not endanger the detainee's health or impairs his dignity.

8)   Walk

(a) A detainee shall have a walk under the sky for at least two hours daily; the Commandant may, as per the detainee's request and if he saw reasonable ground for so doing, exempt the detainee from the obligation to have a walk.
(b) The Commandant may order that a detainee would not go out for a walk, during a period not exceeding three consecutive days each time, if he is convinced that this is necessary for State security or for preserving the well-being or health of the detainee.
(c) The arrangements of the walk shall be determined by the Commandant.

9)   Labour

(a) As per the detainee's request, and subject to the existence of suitable arrangements enabling this at the place of detention, the Commandant may, in his discretion, permit the detainee to engage, within the bounds of the place of detention, in labour to be specified in the permission; in consideration for the said permitted labour, the detainee shall be paid wages according to the Prisons Regulations 1978; likewise, the Commandant may permit the detainee to engage in other labour for himself.
(b) A detainee is obliged to make his bed, to clean and keep in order the cell where he is staying; except for this obligation, the detainee shall be exempt from labour.

10) Right to Receive Personal Items and Practice Religious Worship

(a) A detainee may receive from the Commandant his own personal items which were deposited upon his entry to detention, if he needs them for his own use in the place of detention; he may also receive necessary wash and cleaning products necessary for his use, all this on condition that the items are not items the possession of which are prohibited at the place of detention.
(b) A detainee may have in his possession a Bible, Koran or the New Testament and items of worship required for prayer according to his religion.
(c) A detainee not held in solitary confinement under sub-Regulation 3(a), may practice joint prayer with other detainees, unless the Commandant considers that, for reasons of State security, security or discipline in the place of detention, or for reasons of health, this has to be prevented.
(d) A detainee may receive for reading such newspapers and books as ordered by the Commandant.

11) Receiving Cigarettes

A detainee who has proven to the Commandant that it is his habit to smoke, shall be provided with the cigarette ration standard for prisoners in the place of detention.

12) Visit to Detainees

    (a) A detainee may receive, in a location to be determined by the Commandant, such visitors as set forth below:

        (1) Delegates of the International Red Cross Organisation;

        (2) Any other visitor, including a family member, to whom regulation 13 does not applies – [only] with special permission which the Chief of Staff may grant in his discretion.

    (b) Sub-regulation (a)(1) notwithstanding, the Minister of Defence may prohibit a detainee from receiving a visit of Delegates of the International Red Cross Organisation, for a period not exceeding three months, if he is convinced that this will endanger State security; the prohibition shall be communicated to the detainee.

    (c) The Minister of Defence, having ordered a prohibition of visits under sub-Regulation (b), shall reconsider his order at least once a month or, if the detainee or the aforementioned visitor requested that the order is reconsidered at an earlier date and the Minister of Defence saw reason to do so.

    (d) The number of visitors in a visit shall not exceed three, except under special permission which the Commandant may grant in his discretion.

    (e) The provisions of this Regulation shall not derogate from the provisions of Regulation 13.

13) Visit by Attorney to Detainees

    (a) Where a detainee requested to meet an attorney in order to deal with a legal matter pertaining to the detainee himself, the Commandant shall permit such a meeting, at the earliest date at which it can take place without impairing the requirements of State security, but no later than seven days prior to his being brought before a Court under Section 5 of the law; the meeting will take place at a location to be determined by the Commandant

    (b) Where the right to representation has been restricted by an order issued under Section 6(b) of the Law, the Commandant shall not authorize a meeting under sub-Regulation (a), unless the attorney presented to him the unqualified permit granted to him, as required by said order.

    (c) The provisions of Regulation 14 shall not apply to Attorney visits under this Regulation.

14) Presence During a Visit to A Detainee

    (a) During a visit to a detainee under the provisions of Regulation 12(a)(2), a person authorized by the Commandant for this purpose shall be present, if the Commandant is convinced that his presence is required for State security, public security, or the security of the place of detention.

(b) A person so authorized may terminate the conversation of the visitor with the detainee, if he is convinced that terminating the conversation is necessary for maintaining State security, public security, or the security of the place of detention. He may also take any other reasonable measure which is necessary for preventing harm to the abovementioned.

(c) The detainee may appeal the termination of the conversation to the Commandant, and the Commandant may, in his discretion, decide to have the conversation continued or terminated.

15) Letters

(a) In this Regulation, "letter" – any matter written, in print, in drawing, in illustration, or any other means of transmitting words, digits or forms.

(b) A detainee shall not send or receive a letter, save for through the Commandant.

(c) A detainee may send a person located outside of the place of detention four letters and four postcards per month; the Commandant may, at his discretion, permit the detainee a larger number.

(d) Letters of the detainee to the authorities of the State or to his attorney shall not be counted as the letters mentioned in sub-Regulation (c).

(e) Sub-regulation (a) notwithstanding, a detainee may not send outside the place of detention books or newspapers received by him, unless permitted by the Commandant, at his discretion.

(f) A detainee may receive letters sent to him from outside the place of detention.

(g) The Commandant may open and examine any letter and any other document of a detainee or addressed to a detainee for reasons enumerated in sub-Regulation (h).

(h) The Commandant may prohibit the sending of a detainee's letter, in whole or in part, or the transmission of a letter to a detainee, in whole or in part, if convinced that it is necessary for reasons of State security, public security, security or discipline of the place of detention or fear of impairment of interrogation or legal proceedings.

(i) The Commandant, having decided to prevent transmission of a letter to its destination, shall give the grounds for his decision in writing, and shall instruct the archiving of that letter in a specially designated place.

(j) The prevention of transmission of a letter to its destination, in whole or in part, shall be notified to the detainee; the Commandant may fail to notify the detainee of the prevention of transmission of the letter to its destination, in whole or in part, if convinced that it is necessary for reasons enumerated in sub-Regulation (h), with the exception of a letter sent to a relative or from him; for the purpose of this Regulation, "relative" – parent, the parent of a parent, spouse, descendant, brother or sister.

(k) The provisions of sub-Regulation (g), (h), (i) and (j) shall not apply to Court documents intended for the Court, or to letters to an attorney representing the detainee in accordance with regulation 13(a).

16) Receipt of Money or Payments

A detainee shall not receive money or pay money to another person, unless permitted by the Commandant in his discretion.

17) Place of Detention Offences

A detainee who committed or attempted to commit any of the following, or who assisted another detainee to so commit, has committed a place of detention offence:
(1) An act interfering with the discipline and proper order in the place of detention;
(2) Violation of a legal order or a warden or another person acting on behalf of the Commandant;
(3) Communicating in writing, orally or by other means with an outside person in violation of these Regulations.
(4) Inciting another to disrupt the proper order of the prison.

18) Penalties for Place of Detention Offences

(a) The Commandant may impose on a detainee who committed a place of detention offence all or some of these penalties:
  (1) Revoking the right to buy goods at the canteen;
  (2) Revoking the right to have a walk or limitation thereof in another manner;
  (3) Revoking the right to receive books and newspapers;
  (4) Revoking the right to receive cigarettes;
  (5) Revoking the right to receive or send letters;
  (6) Revoking the right to receive money;
  (7) Isolation;
Derogation of a right under paragraphs (1) to (7) shall be for a period not exceeding fourteen days.
(b) An Officer or Warden authorized by the Commandant for this purpose in writing, may impose on a detainee who committed a place of detention offence the penalties specified in sub-Regulations (a)(1)-(7), for a period not exceeding seven days.
(c) A detainee will not serve cumulative isolation penalties for a period exceeding 14 days, except with the written permission of the Commandant.

19) Rules for Imposing Penalties

(a) Penalties shall not be imposed on a detainee who committed a place of detention offence, unless the charges against him were read to him and he was given an opportunity to be heard.
(b) Penalties may be imposed on a detainee for each and every one of the offences for which was found guilty, as long as he is not punished more than once for the same act.
(c) A penalty imposed under these Regulations shall not exempt a detainee from punishment under any law.
(d) A penalty imposed on a detainee under these Regulations shall be recorded in his personal file.

20) Escape from Legal Detention

The Commandant may impose on a detainee who escaped, conspired to escape, committed an attempted escape, or abetted another to escape, the penalty of isolation not exceeding 21 days; this Regulation is without prejudice to the provision of any other law.

21) Consulting

(a) These Regulation shall be notified to a detainee as soon as possible after he is brought to the place of detention.
(b) A detainee may, at any reasonable time, consult these Regulations if he so requests, as well as copy them.
(c) Notifying the detainee of the Regulations and the right to consult them shall be carried out in a language that the detainee understands.

☞ **USA:** *Coalition of Clergy, et al.* **v.** *George Walker Bush, et al.*, **19 February 2002**

United States District Court Central District of California

Coalition of Clergy, et al., Petitioners
v.
George Walker Bush, et al., Respondents

Case No. CV 02-570 AHM

Order dismissing petition for writ of habeas corpus and first amended petition for writ of habeas corpus

I. Procedural Background and Summary of Ruling

This case results from the sudden attacks on the United States on September 11, 2001, resulting in the deaths of thousands of innocent civilians. Within a few days, the President, with the approval of Congress (Pub. L. No. 107-40 (September 8, 2001)), commanded the Armed Forces of the United States to use all necessary and appropriate force against the persons responsible for those attacks, who soon came to be known as the "Al Qaeda terrorist network." The President dispatched American forces to Afghanistan, where that group was believed to be functioning with the active support of the "Taliban" government then in power in that country. In the course of combat operations, American forces, as well as other nations allied with the United States, captured or secured the surrender of thousands of persons. Beginning in early January 2002, the Armed Forces transferred scores of these captives to the United States Naval Base at Guantanamo Bay, Cuba ("Guantanamo"). Their confinement in Guantanamo led to this action.

Petitioners are a group referring to themselves as the "Coalition of Clergy, Lawyers, and Professors." They include at least two journalists; ten lawyers; three rabbis; and a Christian pastor. Some of these individuals are prominent professors at distinguished law schools or schools of journalism. One is a former Attorney-General of the United States. On January

20, 2002 they filed a Verified Petition for Writ of Habeas Corpus on behalf of "Persons Held Involuntarily at Guantanamo Naval Air Base, Cuba." In substance, the petition alleges that the captives held at Guantanamo (the "detainees") are in custody in violation of the Constitution or the laws or treaties of the United States, in that they: (1) have been deprived of their liberty without due process of law, (2) have not been informed of the nature and cause of the accusations against them and (3) have not been afforded the assistance of counsel. The petition also suggests, somewhat elliptically, that the detainees have rights under the Geneva Convention that have been violated, such as "prohibition of [*sic*] transferring persons taken prisoner in [*sic*] war from the country of their capture." (Pet. Memo. 7:16-17) Petitioners allege that "[b]ecause the persons for whom relief is sought appear to be held incommunicado and have been denied access to legal counsel, application properly is made by petitioners acting on their behalf. 28 U.S.C. § 2242. . . ." (*Id.* 7:20-23)

The relief that petitioners seek is a writ or order to show cause (1) directing the respondents to "identify by full name and country of domicile and all other identifying information in their possession each person held by them within three days;" (2) directing respondents "to show the true cause(s) of the detention of each person;" and (3) directing respondents to produce the detainees at a hearing in this court. (*Id.* 8:14-23; 9:1-3)

The persons named as respondents are President George W. Bush; Secretary of Defense Donald H. Rumsfeld; Richard B. Myers, the Chairman of the Joint Chiefs of Staff; Gordon R. England, the Secretary of Navy; and five other named individuals and "1000 Unknown Named United States Military Personnel," all of whom are alleged to be military officers responsible for the operations at the Guantanamo Naval Base.

On January 22, 2002, two days after the petition was filed, the Court presided over a brief hearing at which it expressed strong doubts that it has jurisdiction to entertain the petition. The Court ordered the parties to address that threshold question in written briefs. They have done so and appeared at a second hearing today.[9]

Having reviewed and considered all the arguments and conducted additional research on its own, the Court rules as follows:
1. Petitioners do not have standing to assert claims on behalf of the detainees.
2. Even if petitioners did have standing, this court lacks jurisdiction to entertain those claims.
3. No federal court would have jurisdiction over petitioners' claims, so there is no basis to transfer this matter to another federal district court.
4. The petition must be dismissed.

---

9. [1] On February 11, 2002, after the parties had filed their respective briefs on the threshold jurisdictional issues, petitioners filed a "First Amended" petition purporting to add a claim under what they refer to as the "cruel and unusual clause" of the Eighth Amendment. Counsel for petitioners had acknowledged at the hearing "I'm going to have to proceed on the petition as it is right now. And if a decision is reached to add an Eighth Amendment claim, then I'm going to have to ask for permission to do that." He neither sought nor received permission. Moreover, the court instructed the parties that "if there is jurisdiction the petition could be amended at a later time." (Tr., p.10-11) The Amended Petition does not affect, much less cure, the jurisdictional defects described below, and this Order applies to both petitions.

II. The Writ of Habeas Corpus

Given the importance of the issues that petitioners proclaim are at stake in this case, a decidedly abbreviated description of the writ of habeas corpus is appropriate.

The writ of habeas corpus, providing a means by which the legal authority under which a person is detained can be challenged, is of immemorial antiquity . . . The precise origin of the writ . . . is not certain, but as early as 1220 A.D. the words "*habeas corpora*" are to be found in an order directing an English sheriff to produce parties to a trespass action before the Court of Common pleas. . . . Today it is regarded as "perhaps the most important writ known to the constitutional law of England . . . ."

Its significance in the United States has been no less great. Article I, 9 of the Constitution gives assurance that the privilege of the writ of habeas corpus shall not be suspended, unless when in cases of rebellion or invasion the public safety may require it, and its use by the federal courts was authorized [as long ago as in] . . . the Judiciary Act of 1789. Wright, Miller and Cooper, Federal Practice and Procedure: Jurisdiction 2d § 4261 and n. 3 (citations omitted).

The statutory authorization for a federal judge to issue a writ of habeas corpus currently is set forth in 28 U.S.C. § 2241, *et. seq.* In essence, when a judge issues such a writ, the authorities responsible for the petitioner's custody are required to demonstrate that he is being detained lawfully. As Mr. Justice Black put it, the "grand purpose" of the writ of habeas corpus is "the protection of individuals against erosion of their right to be free from wrongful restraints upon their liberty." *Jones v. Cunningham*, 371 U.S. 236, 243, 83 S.Ct. 373, 377 (1963).[10] Although the writ of habeas corpus plays a central role in American jurisprudence, there are many limitations on a court's authority to issue such a writ. Here, in urging the court to dismiss the petition – i.e., effectively refuse to issue a writ – respondents invoke three such limitations. They contend: (1) petitioners lack "standing" to come to this court – i.e., they are not entitled to ask the court on the detainees' behalf to order respondents to justify the detention of the detainees; (2) this particular federal court lacks jurisdiction to entertain the petition; and (3) no federal district court anywhere has jurisdiction. Respondents are correct as to all three contentions.

III. Petitioners Do Not Have Standing

Respondents argue that petitioners lack standing to assert claims on behalf of the detainees. Whether a plaintiff (or, in the case of a habeas proceeding, a petitioner) has standing "is the threshold question in every federal case, determining the power of the court to entertain the suit . . . . The Art. III judicial power exists only to redress or otherwise to protect against injury to the complaining party, even though the court's judgment may benefit others collaterally. . . ." *Warth v. Seldin*, 422 U.S. 490, 498-499, 95 S. Ct. 2197, 2205 (1975). 28 U.S. C. § 2242 provides that "[a]pplication for a writ of habeas corpus shall be in writing signed

---

10. [2] The foregoing discussion involves only the writ of habeas corpus "ad subjiciendum," which compels an inquiry into the cause of restraint. There are other writs of habeas corpus, but they are irrelevant here.

and verified by the person for whose relief it is intended *or by someone acting in his behalf.*" (Emphasis added). Courts use the term "next friend" to describe the person who acts on behalf of another person (the "real party in interest") for whom the relief is sought. The "next friend" has the burden "clearly to establish the propriety of his status and thereby justify the jurisdiction of the court." *Whitmore v. Arkansas*, 495 U.S. 149, 110 S. Ct. 1717, 1727 (1990).

A number of courts have allowed habeas petitions to be filed by "next friends," although in circumstances different from those here. *See, e.g., U.S. ex rel. Toth v. Quarles*, 350 U.S. 11, 76 S. Ct. 1 (1955) (sister, on behalf of ex-serviceman civilian who was arrested by military authorities and taken to Korea to stand trial before a court-martial); *Vargas v. Lambert*, 159 F.3d 1161 (9th Cir.1998) (mother of state court prisoner slated to be executed for murder, where mother made showing sufficient to establish her son's lack of mental competence to waive his right of appeal); *Nash v. MacArthur*, 184 F.2d 606 (D.C. Cir. 1950) (attorney, on behalf of seven Japanese nationals convicted of war crimes by military commissions).

In seeking dismissal of this petition on the basis that petitioners lack "next friend" standing, respondents rely primarily on *Whitmore v. Arkansas, supra.* In *Whitmore*, the named petitioner was a death row inmate. He sought to intervene in an Arkansas state court criminal proceeding in order to prosecute an appeal on behalf of one Simmons, who had been convicted of multiple murders and had waived his right to direct appeal. Whitmore tried to get permission to appeal on behalf of Simmons on the basis that the heinous facts in Simmons's cases would become included in a database that Arkansas uses for purposes of comparative reviews of capital sentences. Whitmore contended that inclusion of the information about Simmons would make him – Whitmore – appear less deserving of execution. Whitmore also purported to proceed as "next friend" of Simmons, hoping to overturn the latter's death sentence on appeal. Although Whitmore was not seeking a writ of habeas corpus on behalf of Simmons, the Supreme Court analogized his effort to that of a "next friend" in a habeas case, and defined the prerequisites for "next friend" standing.

> First, a "next friend" must provide an adequate explanation – such as inaccessibility, mental incompetence, or other disability – why the real party in interest cannot appear on his own behalf to prosecute the action .... [Citation]. Second, the "next friend" must be truly dedicated to the best interests of the person on whose behalf he seeks to litigate . ... [Citation]. [It also] has been further suggested that a "next friend" must have some significant relationship with the real party in interest. *Id.* at 162-64 (citations omitted).

The Court then held that Whitmore lacked standing because "there was no meaningful evidence that [Simmons] was suffering from a mental disease, disorder or defect that substantially affected his capacity to make an intelligent decision." *Id.* at 166.

The Ninth Circuit has stated that under the *Whitmore* test, "[i]n order to establish next friend standing, the putative next friend must show (1) that the petitioner is unable to litigate his own cause due to mental incapacity, lack of access to court, or other similar disability; and (2) the next friend has some significant relationship with, and is truly dedicated to the best interests of, petitioner." *Massie ex. rel. Kroll v. Woodford*, 244 F.3d 1192, 1194 (9th Cir. 2001). The court will now address this two-prong test.

A. Lack of Access to the Court.

Whitmore and the other cases on which respondents rely are all factually distinguishable because the real party in interest clearly *did* have access to the court, could have filed a petition in his own behalf and chose not to do so. Thus, in *Brewer v. Lewis*, 989 F.2d 1021 (9th Cir. 1993), the person denied standing to seek a writ of habeas corpus was a condemned prisoner's mother. Her son had explicitly sought to abandon all further judicial proceedings, and the mother was unable to establish that he was incompetent. *Id.* at 1025-1026. Similarly, in *Massie* a death row inmate filed a federal habeas corpus petition but then moved to dismiss it. A journalist who had dealt with the inmate for fifteen years thereupon filed a "next friend" petition on behalf of the inmate. Like the mother in *Brewer* and the "next friend" in *Whitmore*, the journalist failed to present "meaningful evidence" of the inmate's alleged incompetency to dismiss his own habeas corpus petition. Moreover, at oral argument before the Ninth Circuit, the inmate explicitly opposed the journalist's petition. *Id.* at 1195. Not surprisingly, the Court found that the journalist lacked standing. *Id.* at 1199.[11]

Here, although the hastily-prepared petition is far from a model of precision or clarity, it does at least allege that the Guantanamo detainees "appear to be held incommunicado and have been denied access to legal counsel. . . ." Pet. Memo. 7:20-23. This is tantamount to alleging lack of access to the court. But standing alone, conclusory allegations such as these are not sufficient to establish standing. *Brewer,* 989 F.2d at 1026; *Massie,* 244 F.3d at 1197 ("meaningful evidence" required; "conclusory opinions" are insufficient). In this case, petitioners' assertions that the detainees are totally incommunicado are not supported by the news articles they attached to the petition. Indeed, as respondents point out, the news articles actually contradict the assertions. Some of the articles reflect that the detainees were given the opportunity to write to friends or relatives (Pet. Mem. p.10); others state that some detainees had already been in contact with diplomats from their home countries (Pet. Mem. pp.16:20-21); yet other articles state that a team from the International Red Cross met with the detainees (Pet. Mem. p.15). In their brief filed a week after respondents' brief, petitioners did not explain these inconsistencies, much less provide a basis for the court to disregard them.[12] Moreover, the Court has been informed that on February 19, 2002, the parents of three specified Guantanamo detainees did file suit on behalf of their respective sons. *Shafiq Rasul, et al. v. Bush,* No. 02-CV 00299 (D., D.C.) *See,* "Suit Says U.S. Violates Prisoners Rights in Cuba," Wall Street Journal, February 20, 2002, at A10. Respondents are correct that as to the first prong of the *Whitmore-Massie* test, the immediate question before this court is the adequacy of the allegations in the petition concerning lack of access to court. They are also correct that the allegations fail to satisfy that prong. But in court today, counsel for respondents displayed commendable candor in acknowledging that from a practical point of view the detainees cannot be said to have unimpeded or free access

---

11. [3] Compare *Groseclose* v. *Dutton*, 594 F. Supp. 949 (M.D. Tenn. 1984), where next friends, including a death row inmate, minister and two anti-death penalty organizations, were permitted to proceed. There, the real party in interest did not oppose their efforts and the petitioners demonstrated that his previous waiver of the right to file a habeas petition was involuntary. *Groseclose*, 594 F. Supp. at 951, 961-62.

12. [4] The Court may take judicial notice of the information in the articles attached to the petition. Fed. R. Evid. 201(b). Indeed, both sides cite these articles for different purposes.

to court. Despite the recent filing of a second lawsuit, it would be naive for this court to find that they do enjoy such access. Thus, although it makes no actual finding on the issue, the court will proceed to analyze the second prong under the supposition that the detainees lack access to court.

B. Significant Relationship With The Detainees or "Uninvited Meddlers."

The second prong of the *Whitmore-Massie* "next friend" test requires the petitioners to demonstrate that they have a "significant relationship" with the detainees. Respondents argue that petitioners cannot demonstrate that they are dedicated to the best interests of the Guantanamo detainees because they have not demonstrated such a relationship. On the question of what constitutes a significant relationship, respondents cite *Davis v. Austin*, 492 F. Supp. 273 (N.D. Ga. 1980), in which a distant relative and a minister were not permitted to proceed on behalf of a death row inmate. But in *Davis* the real party in interest explicitly made a competent decision to forego further proceedings. It was because the "next friends" were proceeding *contrary* to the inmate's wishes that the court found they lacked standing – not because their ties were too remote. *Id.* at 275-276.

Respondents also cite *Lenhard v. Wolff*, 443 U.S. 1306, 100 S. Ct. 3 (1979), in arguing that petitioners fail to demonstrate a significant relationship with the detainees. In *Lenhard*, then-Justice Rehnquist granted a stay of a prisoner's execution on an application filed by two deputy public defenders who had been appointed by the trial court. In *dicta*, Justice Rehnquist noted that "however worthy and high minded the motives of 'next friends' may be, they inevitably run the risk of making the actual defendant a pawn to be manipulated on a chessboard larger than his own case." *Id.* at 1312. However, in *Lenhard*, the lawyers' right to petition on behalf of the inmate was not in question. Indeed, Justice Rehnquist lauded them for their "commendable fidelity to their assignment . . . ." *Id.* at 1308. More-over, he stated,

> [I]t strikes me that from a purely technical standpoint a public defender may appear as "next friend" with as much justification as the mother of [the real party in interest] . . . . *Id.* at 1310.

Although *Davis* and *Lenhard* are weak authority for respondents, *Whitmore, supra*, does buttress their contention that petitioners lack standing, particularly this language:

> [L]imitations on the "next friend" doctrine are driven by the recognition that it was not intended that the writ of habeas corpus should be availed of, as a matter of course, by intruders or uninvited meddlers, styling themselves next friends . . . . Indeed, if there were no restriction on "next friend" standing in federal courts, the litigant asserting only a generalized interest in constitutional governance could circumvent the jurisdictional limits of Art. III simply by assuming the mantle of "next friend." *Whitmore,* 495 U.S. at 163.

The court recognizes that the named petitioners have filed this petition because they perceive there are rights that need to be vindicated. But that consideration, standing alone, does not necessarily make them "uninvited meddlers" within the meaning of *Whitmore*.[13] *See Warren v. Cardwell*, 621 F.2d 319, 321 n.1 (9th Cir. 1980) (California lawyer who filed a petition in his own name on behalf of an Arizona inmate not accessible because of a prison lockdown "was not an uninvited meddler"). There is a difference between being "uninvited because you are meant to be excluded" and being "uninvited but welcome." The next friend/would-be petitioners in the cases upon which respondents rely fall into the former category, because their efforts were at odds with the desires of the real parties on whose behalf they were attempting to proceed. That is not the case here, because there is no evidence that the Guantanamo detainees affirmatively object to the petitioners' efforts, and common sense suggests that they would not.[14] But neither is there evidence that they are welcome, so petitioners cannot demonstrate that they fall into the latter category.

More than four weeks have elapsed since petitioners filed the original petition. In that period, petitioners' counsel has filed a brief on jurisdiction, an amended petition and numerous other memoranda and declarations on other issues. During that same period, the names of at least some of the detainees have been published by the national press and, as indicated above, parents of three specified detainees have filed suit. Yet there is nothing in the record even suggesting that *any* of the Guantanamo detainees supports this petition. Not one friend, relative, diplomatic or religious representative, fellow countryman or anyone with a direct tie to a particular detainee has authorized this petition. Common sense suggests that something is seriously awry in petitioners' claims to be the appropriate representatives of the detainees. This conclusion is reinforced by yet another telling factor: nowhere have petitioners alleged, much less filed a declaration, that they *attempted* to communicate with the detainees and were prevented from doing so. Although petitioners may regard such efforts as futile and thus unnecessary, to bolster their claimed standing as "next friends" it would have been helpful if they had tried anyway.[15]

To summarize, the court finds that the cases on which respondents rely to establish that petitioners lack a sufficient relationship with the detainees or that petitioners can be dismissed as "uninvited meddlers" are all factually distinguishable. Yet these cases state the

---

13. [5] In using the term "uninvited meddlers" in *Whitmore*, Chief Justice Rehnquist cited to *United States ex rel. Bryant v. Houston*, 273 F. 915, 916 (2d Cir. 1921). There, the named petitioner failed to disclose anywhere in her petition who she was, what relationship, if any, she had with the real party in interest or whether the real party was unable to file the petition himself. Chief Justice Rehnquist also cited to *Rosenberg v. United States*, 346 U.S. 273, 291-292, 75 S. Ct. 1152, 1161-1162 (1953). There, the real parties in interest already had several attorneys but their habeas petition was prepared by another lawyer who sought to intervene. Justice Frankfurter noted that the legitimate counsel of record "simply had been elbowed out of the control of their case" by the lawyer who filed the habeas petition. *Idem.*

14. [6] As Justice Frankfurter stated in a different context, "Nor does law lag behind common sense." *Ludecke v. Watkins*, 335 U.S. 160, 167, 68 S. Ct. 1429, 1432 (1948).

15. [7] The court is not suggesting that the mere failure of a "next friend" to establish direct communication with the prisoner and obtain explicit authorization from him is enough to preclude "next friend" petitioners. If it were, then there would be an incentive for the government to keep all captives, even United States citizens, incommunicado. Although respondents are not advocating that unacceptable and illegal result, a too-expansive interpretation of "uninvited meddlers" could lead to it.

governing legal principles of standing, and this district court is required to apply them. Petitioners may not be "uninvited meddlers" in the same sense as the petitioners in those cases, but they do lack a "significant relationship" with the detainees – indeed, any relationship. To permit petitioners to seek a writ of habeas corpus on a record devoid of any evidence that they have sought authorization to do so, much less obtained implied authority to do so, would violate the second prong of the *Whitmore-Massie* test. And it would invite well-meaning proponents of numerous assorted "causes" to bring lawsuits on behalf of unwitting strangers. For these reasons, then, the court finds that petitioners lack standing to file this petition on behalf of detainees.[16]

Under standard principles governing leave to amend pleadings, if petitioners sought to amend their petition in order to supplement their claims of standing, this court would be expected to grant such leave. That is not the case, however, if the amended petition, or any amended petition, would be a legal "futility" because it could not satisfy the other jurisdictional requirements. For that reason, the court must proceed to discuss those requirements, for if they preclude this court from exercising jurisdiction then the petition should be dismissed without leave to amend.

IV. This Court Lacks Jurisdiction to Issue the Writ Because No Custodian is Within the Territorial Jurisdiction of the Court

Respondents argue that even if petitioners have standing this court lacks jurisdiction to entertain this petition because no custodian responsible for the custody of the detainees is present in the territorial jurisdiction of this district. Respondents are correct.

The federal statute governing habeas petitions provides that "writs of habeas corpus may be granted by the Supreme Court, any justice thereof, the district courts and any circuit judge *within their respective jurisdictions*." 28 U.S.C. § 2241(a) (emphasis added). As the Supreme Court has explained, "the phrase 'within their respective jurisdictions' acts as an obvious limitation upon the action of individual judges" because it reflects the conclusion of Congress that it would be "inconvenient, potentially embarrassing, certainly expensive and on the whole quite unnecessary to provide every judge anywhere with the authority to issue the Great Writ on behalf of applicants far distantly removed from the courts whereon they sat." *Carbo v. United States*, 364 U.S. 611, 617, 81 S. Ct. 338, 342 (1961).[17] In *Schlanger v. Seamans*, 401 U.S. 487, 91 S. Ct. 995 (1971), the Supreme Court held that the Arizona District Court lacked jurisdiction over a habeas petition because the only custodian

---

16. [8] At the hearing today, Prof. Erwin Chemerinsky, one of the named petitioners (but not the author of petitioners' court papers), argued that the requirement that "next friends" demonstrate a "significant relationship" with the real parties in interest should be relaxed where the real parties lack access to court. He urged that general principles of standing under the constitutional requirements of Art. III favor such an approach. The court chooses to apply the standards enunciated in the *Whitmore-Massie* line of cases and notes that in *Whitmore* the Supreme Court noted that the limitations on standing that it was applying were in fact consonant with Article III, and were not based merely on "prudential" limitations. 492 U.S. at 156 n. 1.

17. [9] In *Braden v. 30th Judicial Circuit Court*, 410 U.S. 484, 93 S. Ct. 1123 (1973), the Supreme Court noted that a writ of habeas corpus is issued to the person who has allegedly detained the prisoner unlawfully and held that a federal court with jurisdiction over the custodian can exercise jurisdiction even if the prisoner is outside that court's jurisdiction.

of the petitioner was outside that district. *Id.* at 490-91. It stated, "the District Court in Arizona has no custodian within its reach against whom its writ can run. . . . [T]he absence of [petitioner's] custodian is fatal to the jurisdiction of the Arizona District Court." *Id.* at 491. The Ninth Circuit has applied this rule several times, and the rule is so well-settled that it is unnecessary to cite these cases. Moreover, the Ninth Circuit has expressly held that 28 U.S.C. § 1391(e), which provides for nationwide service of process on officers of the United States, does not extend habeas corpus jurisdiction to persons outside the territorial limits of the district court. *Dunne v. Henman*, 875 F. 2d 244, 248 (9th Cir. 1989); *accord, Schlanger,* 401 U.S. at 490 n.4.[18]

It is clear, then, that because there is no showing or allegation that any named respondent is within the territorial jurisdiction of the Central District of California, this court lacks jurisdiction to issue the writ requested by petitioners. It is also true, however, that in cases where the petitioner's direct custodian is outside the territorial jurisdiction of the court where the petition is filed, jurisdiction does lie in a district court where anyone in the "chain of command" with control over the petitioner is present. *Ex Parte Hayes*, 414 U.S. 1327, 1328, 94 S. Ct. 23, 24 (1973); *cf. Kinnell v. Warner*, 356 F. Supp. 779, 782 (D. Hawaii 1973) ("Anyone in the 'chain of command' with control over petitioner's whereabouts is that petitioner's proper custodian for habeas purposes."). Here, petitioners have named as respondents several individuals who are custodians of the detainees, either because they are directly responsible for their detention or are within the "chain of command" of those directly responsible. At least some of those respondents are present within the territorial jurisdiction of the District Court for the District of Columbia. If the federal court in that district can exercise jurisdiction over this petition, federal law, at least in this circuit, mandates not dismissal, but transfer to that court. Whenever a civil action is filed in a court . . . and that court finds that there is a want of jurisdiction, the court shall, if it is in the interest of justice, transfer such action . . . to any other such court in which the action or appeal could have been brought at the time it was filed or noticed . . . 28 U.S.C. § 1631. In *Miller v. Hambrick*, 905 F. 2d 259 (9th Cir. 1990), the Court of Appeals stated,

> Normally, transfer will be in the interest of justice because normally dismissal of an action that could be brought elsewhere is "time-consuming and justice defeating."… [This approach] was adapted to habeas corpus in applying 28 U.S.C. § 2241(d), the provision to habeas corpus in a State which contains two or more judicial districts… Now under 28 U.S.C.§ 1631 the same approach can be taken generally in habeas corpus proceedings… *Id.* at 262 (citations omitted).

In *Cruz-Aguilera v. INS*, 245 F.3d 1070, 1073-74 (9th Cir. 2001), the Court of Appeals cited the above language from *Miller* and added that "[b]ecause the statute's language is mandatory, federal courts should consider transfer without motion by the parties."

Transfer to the United States District Court for the District of Columbia is appropriate if three conditions are met: (1) the transferring court lacks jurisdiction; (2) the transferee court could have exercised jurisdiction at the time the action was filed; and (3) the transfer is in

---

18. [10] Despite the clear holding of these cases, petitioners' counsel argued in his brief that section 1391 permits this court to subject the respondents to jurisdiction on this basis.

the interest of justice. *Id*. As to condition (1), this Court has already found that it lacks jurisdiction. As to condition (3), a court is required to construe a habeas petition in the light most favorable to the petitioners. That requires this court to assume, without actually finding, that the allegations in this petition that the detainees' rights have been violated are true. Construing the petition that way, transfer would be in the interests of justice, for it would avoid a "time-consuming" and "justice-defeating" dismissal. *Miller*, 905 F.2d at 262 (quoting *Goldlawr, Inc. v. Heiman*, 369 U.S. 463, 467, 82 S. Ct. 913 (1962)).

What remains for determination, therefore, is whether even though respondents are within the jurisdiction of another court – the District of Columbia – that court (or *any* federal court) has the authority to exercise jurisdiction over the parties and claims asserted in this petition. It is to that question that the Court will now turn.

V. No District Court has Jurisdiction Over This Petition

A. *Johnson* v. *Eisentrager* Compels Dismissal If the Detainees Are Outside the Sovereign Territory of the United States.

As this Court suggested in its previous order, the key case is *Johnson v. Eisentrager*, 339 U. S. 763, 70 S. Ct. 936 (1950). Because the Supreme Court's holding in *Johnson* is controlling here, the decision warrants careful review. In *Johnson*, Mr. Justice Jackson described "the ultimate question" as "one of jurisdiction of civil courts of the United States vis-a-vis military authorities in dealing with enemy aliens overseas." *Id*. at 765. The case arose out of World War II. The habeas petitioners were twenty-one German nationals who claimed to have been working in Japan for "civilian agencies of the German government" before Germany surrendered on May 8, 1945. They were taken into custody by the United States Army and convicted by a United States Military Commission of violating laws of war by engaging in continued military activity in Japan after Germany's surrender, but before Japan surrendered.[19] The Military Commission sat in China with the consent of the Chinese government. After trial and conviction there, the prisoners were repatriated to Germany to serve their sentences in a prison whose custodian was an American Army officer. While in Germany, the petitioners filed a writ of habeas corpus claiming that their right under the Fifth Amendment to due process, other unspecified rights under the Constitution and laws of the United States and provisions of the Geneva Convention governing prisoners of war all had been violated. *Id*. at 765-767. They sought the same relief as petitioners here: that they be produced before the federal district court to have their custody justified and then be released. They named as respondents the prison commandant, the Secretary of Defense and others in the civilian and military chain of command.

Reversing the Court of Appeals, the Supreme Court in *Johnson* upheld the district court's dismissal of the petition on the ground that petitioners had no basis for invoking federal judicial power in any district. *Id*. at 790-91. In reaching that conclusion, the Supreme Court stated the following:

---

19. [11] The Supreme Court has "characterized as 'well-established' the power of the military to exercise jurisdiction over . . . enemy belligerents, prisoners of war or others charged with violating the laws of war." *Johnson*, 339 U.S. at 286 (citations deleted).

— "[T]he privilege of litigation has been extended to aliens, whether friendly or enemy, only because permitting their presence in the country implied protection. No such basis can be invoked here, for these prisoners at no relevant time were within any territory over which the United States is *sovereign* and the circumstances of their offense [and] their capture . . . were all beyond the territorial jurisdiction of any court of the United States." *Id.* at 777-78 (emphasis added).[20]

— "We are cited to no instance where a court, in this or any other country where the writ is known, has issued it on behalf of an alien enemy who, at no relevant time and in no stage of his captivity, has been within its territorial jurisdiction. Nothing in the text of the Constitution extends such a right, nor does anything in our statutes." *Id.* at 767.

— "A basic consideration in habeas corpus practice is that the prisoner will be produced before the court. . . To grant the writ to these prisoners might mean that our army must transport them across the seas for hearing . . . The writ, since it is . . . [argued] to be a matter of right, would be equally available to enemies during active hostilities. . . . Such trials would hamper the war effort . . . It would be difficult to devise more effective fettering of a field commander than to allow the very enemies he is ordered to reduce to submission to call him to account in his own civil courts and divert his efforts and attention from the military offensive abroad to the legal defensive at home . . ." *Id.* at 778-79.

Although there has been no decision since *Johnson* that involves facts comparable to those in this case, other courts have either followed *Johnson* or acknowledged its precedential authority. *See, e.g., Zadvydas v. Davis*, 533 U.S. 678, 121 S. Ct. 2491, 2500 (2001) ("It is well established that certain constitutional protections available to persons inside the United States are unavailable to aliens outside of our geographic borders. *See, United States v. Verdugo-Urquidez*, 494 U.S. 259, 269, 273-275, 110 S. Ct 1056 (1990) (Fifth Amendment's protections do *not* extend to aliens outside the territorial boundaries); *Johnson v. Eisentrager*, 339 U.S. 763, 784 (same).") In *Verdugo-Urquidez, supra*, the Supreme Court also cited *Johnson* (494 U.S. at 273) and added, "If there are to be restrictions on searches and seizures of aliens outside of the United States which occur incident to . . . American action [abroad], they must be imposed by the political branches through diplomatic understanding, treaty or legislation." *Verdugo-Urquidez, supra*, 494 U.S. at 275.

In all key respects, the Guantanamo detainees are like the petitioners in *Johnson*: They are aliens; they were enemy combatants; they were captured in combat; they were abroad when captured; they are abroad now; since their capture, they have been under the control of only the military; they have not stepped foot on American soil; and there are no legal or judicial precedents entitling them to pursue a writ of habeas corpus in an American civilian court. Moreover, there are sound practical reasons, such as legitimate security concerns, that make it unwise for this or any court to take the unprecedented step of conferring such a right on these detainees. Petitioners nevertheless argue that *Johnson* "is both factually and legally

---

20. [12] In emphasizing the importance of sovereignty, the Court distinguished its earlier decision in *In re Yamashita*, 327 U.S. 1, 66 S. Ct. 340 (1946). There, a Japanese general convicted by an American Military Commission in the Philippines, challenged the authority of the Commission to try him. The Supreme Court denied his habeas petition on the merits. The *Johnson* court noted that, unlike the status of Guantanamo (*see infra*), the United States had "sovereignty" over the Philippines at the time, which is why Yamashita was entitled to access to the courts. *Id.* at 781.

inapposite for numerous reasons." Petitioners' first supposed distinction is that in *Johnson* the petitioners already had been given access to American courts. Not so; the tribunal in *Johnson* was a Military Commission functioning in China; the petitioners there, as here, were seeking to get *into* a federal court.[21] Next, petitioners argue that there are issues of fact that underlie jurisdiction which must be resolved before dismissal. Petitioners do not state what those supposed issues are and in any event the question before this court *is* a purely legal one, as in *Johnson*. Finally, as petitioners put it, "[m]ost importantly the detainees are 'present' in the United States of America, because Guantanamo Naval Base is, as a matter of both fact and law, the United States of America." (Response, p.15). Petitioners' last argument requires the Court to assess the legal and juridical status of the Guantanamo Bay Naval Base.

B. Detainees were seized and at all times have been held outside the sovereign territory of the United States.

Johnson establishes that whether the Guantanamo detainees can establish jurisdiction in any district court depends not on the nature of their claims but on whether the Naval Base at Guantanamo Bay is under the sovereignty of the United States. Petitioners argue that the detainees are now within the territorial jurisdiction of the United States and thus are entitled to a writ of habeas corpus. But there is a difference between territorial jurisdiction and sovereignty, and it is the latter concept that is key. *See United States v. Spelar*, 338 U.S. 217, 70 S. Ct. 10, 11 (1949), in which the Supreme Court observed, "We know of no more accurate phrase in common English usage than 'foreign country' to denote territory subject to the sovereignty of another nation." The Court finds that Guantanamo Bay is *not* within the sovereign territory of the United States and therefore rejects petitioners' argument.

The legal status of Guantanamo Bay is governed by a lease agreement entered into by the United States and Cuba in 1903 and extended by those countries in 1934. *See* Lease to the United States of Lands in Cuba for Coaling and Naval Stations, Feb. 16-23, 1903, U.S.-Cuba, T.S. No. 418 ("Lease Agreement"); Treaty Between the United States of America and Cuba Defining Their Relations, May 29, 1934, art. III, 48 Stat. 1682, 1683. The 1903 agreement provides that the United States shall lease Guantanamo Bay from the Republic of Cuba for use as a coaling or naval station. Lease Agreement, art. I. Article III of the 1934 Treaty provides that the 1903 lease shall "continue in effect" until the parties agree to modify or abrogate it.

As to the legal status of Guantanamo Bay so long as it is leased to the U.S., the 1903 agreement states:

---

21. [13] It appears that the Guantanamo detainees will also be subjected to trial before military commission. On November 13, 2001, the President issued an Executive Order entitling members of Al Qaeda and other individuals associated with international terrorism who are under the control of the Secretary of Defense to be tried before "one or more military commissions" that will be governed by "rules for the conduct of the proceedings . . .[and] which shall at a minimum provide for . . . a full and fair trial, with the military commission sitting as the triers of both fact and law ..." *See* Detention, Treatment and Trial of Certain Non-Citizens in the War Against Terrorism, 66 Fed. Register 57,833 (November 13, 2001). Thus, it appears that the detainees are similar to the petitioners in *Johnson* in this respect, too.

While on the one hand the United States recognizes the continuance of the ultimate sovereignty of the Republic of Cuba over the above described areas of land and water, on the other hand the Republic of Cuba consents that during the period of occupation by the United States of said areas under the terms of this agreement the United States shall exercise complete jurisdiction and control over and within said areas. Lease Agreement, art. III.

It is telling that in their brief petitioners do not even mention the first clause of the 1903 agreement, which provides that Cuba explicitly retained sovereignty. The omission suggests that they realize that sovereignty is the dispositive issue. Relying instead only on the second clause, petitioners argue that because the Lease Agreement provides that Guantanamo Bay is under the "complete jurisdiction and control" of the United States, the detainees effectively are being held within United States territory and thus are entitled to the writ of habeas corpus.

One need only read the lease to realize that petitioners' argument that "jurisdiction and control" is equivalent to "sovereignty" is wrong. The agreement explicitly distinguishes between the two in providing that Cuba retains "sovereignty" whereas "jurisdiction and control" are exercised by the United States. Cuba and the United States defined the legal status of Guantanamo Bay, and this court has no basis, much less authority, to ignore their determination. *Vermilya-Brown Co. v. Connell*, 335 U.S. 377, 380, 69 S. Ct. 140 (1948). ("[T]he determination of sovereignty over an area is for the legislative and executive departments.").

In addition to the express terms of the Lease Agreement, the only federal courts that have addressed the issue have held that Guantanamo Bay is not within the sovereign territory of the United States and is not the functional equivalent of United States sovereign territory. In *Cuban American Bar Assoc. v. Christopher*, 43 F. 3d 1412, 1425 (11th Cir. 1995), *cert. denied*, 515 U.S. 1142, 115 S. Ct. 2578 and 516 U.S. 913, 116 S. Ct. 299 (1995), the Eleventh Circuit had to determine whether Cuban and Haitian migrants temporarily detained at the Guantanamo Bay Naval Base could assert rights under various United States statutes and the United States Constitution. *Cuban American Bar Assoc.*, 43 F. 3d at 1421. Citing the language of the Lease Agreement quoted above, the Court of Appeals stated "the district court erred in concluding that Guantanamo Bay was a 'United States territory.' We disagree that control and jurisdiction is equivalent to sovereignty." *Id*. at 1425. The Court of Appeals then went on to reject the argument that United States military bases which are leased abroad and remain under the sovereignty of foreign nations are "'functionally equivalent' to being . . . within the United States." *Id. See also Bird v. United States*, 923 F. Supp. 338, 342-43 (D. Conn. 1996) (holding that sovereignty over Guantanamo Bay rested with Cuba and therefore plaintiff's tort claim was barred under the "foreign country" exception of the Federal Tort Claims Act). The court finds the analyses and conclusions of these courts persuasive.[22]

---

22. [14] The cases on which petitioners mainly rely to avoid this result do not support their arguments. *United States* v. *Corey*, 232 F.3d 1166 (9th Cir. 2000), not a habeas case, merely reached the unexceptional conclusion that federal courts have jurisdiction over a criminal case charging a *United*

For the foregoing reasons, the court finds that sovereignty over Guantanamo Bay remains with Cuba. The court therefore holds that petitioners' claim that the Guantanamo detainees are entitled to a writ of habeas corpus is foreclosed by the Supreme Court's holding in *Johnson*.

VI. Conclusion

The Court understands that many concerned citizens, here and abroad, believe this case presents the question of whether the Guantanamo detainees have *any* rights at all that the United States is bound, or willing, to recognize. That question is *not* before this Court and nothing in this ruling suggests that the captives are entitled to no legal protection whatsoever. For this Court is not holding that these prisoners have no right which the military authorities are bound to respect. The United States, by the [1949] Geneva Convention . . . concluded an agreement upon the treatment to be accorded captives. These prisoners claim to be and are entitled to its protection. It is, however, the obvious scheme of the Agreement that responsibility for observance and enforcement of these rights is upon political and military authorities. Rights of alien enemies are vindicated under it only through protests and intervention of protecting powers as the rights of our citizens against foreign governments are vindicated only by Presidential intervention. *Johnson*, 339 U.S. at 789.[23]

For the foregoing reasons, the Verified Petition For Writ of Habeas Corpus and the Verified First Amended Petition are both dismissed with prejudice.

It is so ordered.

Dated: February 19, 2002

☛ **USA: *Shafiq Rasul, Skina Bibi, as Next Friend of Shafiq Rasul, et al.*, Plaintiffs, v. *George Walker Bush, et al.*, Respondents, 31 July 2002**
☛ ***Fawzi Khalid Abdullah Fahad Al Odah, et al.*, Plaintiffs, v. *United States of America, et al.*, Defendants, 31 July 2002**

United States District Court for the District of Columbia
Civil Action No. 02-299 (CKK)
Civil Action No. 02-828 (CKK)

States citizen with offenses committed at United States installations abroad. *Cobb* v. *United States*, 191 F.2d 604 (9th Cir. 1951) does not hold – indeed, rejected the view – that America's exclusive control over the Guantanamo Naval Base constitutes *de jure* sovereignty; Okinawa, not Guantanamo Bay, was at issue in *Cobb* and the court found that *de jure* sovereignty over Okinawa had *not* passed to the United States, so Okinawa was still a "foreign country" within the meaning of the Federal Tort Claims Act. *Idem* at 608. Finally, the judgment in *Haitian Centers Council, Inc.* v. *McNary*, 969 F.2d 1326 (2d Cir. 1992) was vacated by the Supreme Court in *Sale* v. *Haitian Centers Council, Inc.*, 509 U.S. 918, 113 S. Ct. 3028 (1993).

23. [15] The President recently declared that the United States will apply the rules of the Geneva Convention to at least some of the detainees. See "*U.S. Will Apply Geneva Rules to Taliban Fighters*," Los Angeles Times, February 8, 2002 at A1.

Memorandum Opinion
(July 31, 2002)

I. Introduction

Presently before the Court are two cases involving the federal government's detention of certain individuals at the United States Naval Base at Guantanamo Bay, Cuba. The question presented to the Court by these two cases is whether aliens held outside the sovereign territory of the United States can use the courts of the United States to pursue claims brought under the United States Constitution. The Court answers that question in the negative and finds that it is without jurisdiction to consider the merits of these two cases. Additionally, as the Court finds that no court would have jurisdiction to hear these actions, the Court shall dismiss both suits with prejudice. Throughout their pleadings and at oral argument, Petitioners and Plaintiffs contend that unless the Court assumes jurisdiction over their suits, they will be left without any rights and thereby be held *incommunicado*. In response to this admittedly serious concern, the government at oral argument, conceded that "there's a body of international law that governs the rights of people who are seized during the course of combative activities." Transcript of Motion Hearing, June 26, 2002 ("Tr.") at 92. It is the government's position that "the scope of those rights are for the miliary and political branches to determine–and certainly that reflects the idea that other countries would play a role in that process." *Id.* at 91. Therefore, the government recognizes that these aliens fall within the protections of certain provisions of international law and that diplomatic channels remain an ongoing and viable means to address the claims raised by these aliens.[24] While these two cases provide no opportunity for the Court to address these issues, the Court would point out that the notion that these aliens could be held *incommunicado* from the rest of the world would appear to be inaccurate. After reviewing the extensive briefings in these cases, considering the oral arguments of the parties and their oral responses to the Court's questions, and reflecting on the relevant case law, the Court shall grant the government's motion to dismiss in both cases on the ground that the Court is without jurisdiction to entertain these claims.[25]

---

24. [1] The Court notes that, at least for Petitioner David Hicks in the *Rasul* case, diplomatic efforts by the Australian government have already commenced. First Am. Pet. for Writ of Habeas Corpus ("Am. Pet."), Ex. C., "Affidavit of Stephen James Kenny," Attach. 2 (Letter from Robert Cornall, Australian Attorney-General's Office to Stephen Kenny, counsel for Petitioner Terry Hicks) ("Australia has indicated to the United States that it is appropriate that Mr Hicks remain in US military custody with other detainees while Australia works through complex legal issues and conducts further investigations . . . Australian authorities have been granted access to Mr Hicks and will be granted further access if required.").

25. [2] In reaching its decision in the *Rasul* case, the Court considered the First Amended Petition for Writ of Habeas Corpus, the Exhibits to the Amended Petition for Writ of Habeas Corpus, the Memorandum in Support of the Amended Petition for Writ of Habeas Corpus, Respondents' Motion to Dismiss Petitioners' First Amended Petition for Writ of Habeas Corpus, Petitioners' Memorandum in Opposition to Respondents' Motion to Dismiss, and Respondents' Reply in Support of Their Motion to Dismiss Petitioners' First Amended Petition for Writ of Habeas Corpus. In reaching its decision in the *Odah* case, the Court considered the Amended Complaint, Plaintiffs' Motion for a Preliminary Injunction, Plaintiffs' Request for Expeditious Hearing on Plaintiffs' Motion for a Preliminary Injunction and Supporting Statement of the Facts that Make Expedition Essential, Defendants' Motion to Dismiss Plaintiffs' Complaint and Motion for a Preliminary Injunction, Plaintiffs' Opposition to Defendants' Motion to Dismiss Plaintiffs' Complaint and Motion for a Preliminary Injunction, Defen-

II. Procedural History

Petitioners in *Rasul v. Bush*, Civil Action No. 02-299, filed their case on February 19, 2002, and have styled their action as a petition for writ of habeas corpus. Petitioner Shafiq Rasul and Asif Iqbal are citizens of the United Kingdom and are presently held in Respondents' custody at the United States Naval Base at Guantanamo Bay, Cuba. Am. Pet. ¶¶ 10, 14. Petitioner David Hicks is an Australian citizen who is also detained by Respondents at the military base at Guantanamo Bay. *Id.* ¶ 5. Also included in the Petition are Skina Bibi, mother of Shafiq Rasul, Mohammed Iqbal, father of Asif Iqbal, and Terry Hicks, father of David Hicks. Petitioners request, *inter alia*, that this Court "[o]rder the detained petitioners released from respondents' unlawful custody," "[o]rder respondents to allow counsel to meet and confer with the detained petitioners, in private and unmonitored attorney client conversations," and "[o]rder respondents to cease all interrogations of the detained petitioners, direct or indirect, while this litigation is pending." Am. Pet., Prayer for Relief, ¶¶ 4-6. Plaintiffs in *Odah v. United States*, Civil Action No. 02-828, filed their action on May 1, 2002. The *Odah* case involves the detention of twelve Kuwaiti nationals who are currently being held in the custody of the United States at the United States Naval Base at Guantanamo Bay, Cuba. Am. Compl. at 4. The action is concurrently brought by twelve of their family members who join the suit and speak on behalf of the individuals in United States custody. *Id.* Unlike Petitioners in *Rasul*, the *Odah* Plaintiffs disclaim that their suit seeks release from confinement. Rather, Plaintiffs in *Odah* ask this Court to enter a preliminary and permanent injunction prohibiting the government from refusing to allow the Kuwaiti nationals to "meet with their families," "be informed of the charges, if any, against them," "designate and consult with counsel of their choice," and "have access to the courts or some other impartial tribunal." *Id.* ¶ 40.[26] Plaintiffs' Amended

---

dants' Reply in Support of Motion to Dismiss, Plaintiffs' Opposition to Defendants' Motion for Leave to Late File Their Reply In Support of Defendants' Motion to Dismiss and Response to Plaintiffs' Request for Expeditious Hearing, Plaintiffs' Consent Motion for Leave to File Post-Argument Brief Correcting Erroneous Statements by Defense Counsel at Oral Argument, Defendants' Response to Plaintiffs' Post-Argument Brief, and Plaintiffs' Reply to Defendants' Response to Plaintiffs' Post-Argument Brief.

26. [3] After full briefing and oral argument on Defendants' Motion to Dismiss in the *Odah* case, Plaintiffs filed an Amended Complaint, which they filed as of right pursuant to Rule 15 of the Federal Rules of Civil Procedure. In a conference call with the Court, Plaintiffs represented that there were three specific differences between the Amended Complaint and the original Complaint. First, the Amended Complaint added two new plaintiffs to the action, a Kuwaiti national held at the military base at Guantanamo Bay and a member of his family who brings the suit on his behalf. Originally, there had only been twenty-two Plaintiffs. *Compare* Compl. 3, 4, *with* Am. Compl. 3, 4. Second, Plaintiffs abandoned their request that the Court order Defendants to turn Plaintiffs, held at the military base at Guantanamo Bay, over to the Kuwaiti government. Compl. 44. Third, Plaintiffs made an effort to clarify the four specific requests for relief that they seek in this case. *Compare* Compl. 42, *with* Am. Compl. 40. Ordinarily, when the Court receives an amended complaint after a defendant files a motion to dismiss, it denies the motion to dismiss without prejudice and requests that the defendant re-file the motion based on the allegations presented in the amended complaint. In this case, based on the Court's review of the Amended Complaint, it appears that such a procedure would be a useless exercise since the legal theories underlying Defendants' present motion to dismiss will not be affected by the filing of the Amended Complaint. Defendants agree with the Court and contend that the amendments will not impact upon the Court's ruling on the motion to dismiss. Accordingly, the Court will apply Defendants' motion to dismiss to Plaintiffs' Amended Complaint. *See Nix v. Hoke*, 62 F. Supp. 2d 110, 115 (D.D.C. 1999) (citing cases); *see also* 6 Charles Alan Wright & Arthur R. Miller, *Federal Practice and Procedure* § 1476 (2d ed. 1990) ("[D]efendants should not be required to

Complaint contains three counts. First, Plaintiffs contend that Defendants' conduct denies the twelve Kuwaiti nationals due process in violation of the Fifth Amendment to the Constitution. *Id.* ¶ 37. Second, Plaintiffs argue that Defendants' actions violate the Alien Tort Claims Act, 28 U.S.C. § 1350. *Id.* ¶ 38. Lastly, Plaintiffs allege that Defendants' conduct constitutes arbitrary, unlawful, and unconstitutional behavior in violation of the Administrative Procedure Act, 5 U.S.C. §§ 555, 702, 706. *Id.* ¶ 39.

In the *Rasul* case, Respondents moved to dismiss the First Amended Petition for Writ of Habeas Corpus on March 18, 2002. This motion was fully briefed on April 29, 2002. On May 1, 2002, the *Odah* case was filed and Plaintiffs designated it as related to the *Rasul* matter. Thus, *Odah* was assigned to this Court. Plaintiffs in *Odah* moved for a preliminary injunction at the time they filed their suit. Instead of filing a memorandum in opposition to the motion for preliminary injunction, Defendants in the *Odah* case moved to dismiss the action. That motion was fully briefed on June 14, 2002.[27]

At the time the Court received the motion to dismiss in the *Odah* matter, it became obvious to the Court that the government was moving to dismiss both cases primarily on jurisdictional grounds. Accordingly, the Court found it appropriate to make a threshold ruling on the jurisdictional question in both cases before conducting any further proceedings. Mindful of the importance of these suits, which raise concerns about the actions of the Executive Branch, the Court heard oral argument on the government's motion to dismiss in both cases on June 26, 2002.

III. Factual Background[28]

A. *Rasul v. Bush*

Little is known about Petitioner David Hicks except that he was allegedly living in Afghanistan at the time of his seizure by the United States Government. Am. Pet. ¶ 22. As for Peti-

---

file a new motion to dismiss simply because an amended pleading was introduced while their motion was pending. If some of the defects raised in the original motion remain in the new pleading, the court simply may consider the motion as being addressed to the amended pleading. To hold otherwise would be to exalt form over substance.").

27. [4] The Court's initial briefing schedule in the *Odah* case did not contemplate that Defendants would be moving to dismiss the entire action. Rather the Court's briefing schedule set forth a date for Defendants to respond to Plaintiffs' motion for preliminary injunction. *Odah v. United States*, Civ. No. 02-828 (D.D.C. May 14, 2002) (order setting forth briefing schedule). Instead of filing an opposition to the motion for a preliminary injunction, on the date that their opposition to the preliminary injunction was due, Defendants moved to dismiss the entire case (and, by inference, the motion for preliminary injunction). Plaintiffs filed a timely opposition to Defendant's motion. Defendants then filed a reply, which Plaintiffs argued was inappropriate since the Court's initial briefing schedule did not set a date for Defendants to file a reply. However, when the Court set the initial briefing schedule, it was only concerned with receiving a response to the motion for preliminary injunction. Defendants were clearly within their right to move for dismissal of the entire action, which would permit them the opportunity to file a reply to their motion to dismiss. Although Defendants filed their reply late, the Court shall grant them leave to file the reply. To the extent that Plaintiffs' opposition to Defendants' filing of a reply brief responds to new issues first raised in Defendants' reply, the Court shall consider Plaintiffs' response as a surreply to Defendants' motion to dismiss.

28. [5] For purposes of the instant motions to dismiss, the allegations of the Amended Petition/Amended Complaint are taken as true. The facts in this section are presented accordingly, and do not constitute factual findings by this Court.

tioner Rasul, in the summer of 2001, he allegedly took a hiatus from studying for his computer engineering degree to travel. *Id.* ¶ 24. Allegedly, Petitioner Rasul's brother convinced him to move to Pakistan "to visit relatives and explore his culture." *Id.* Petitioner Rasul left the United Kingdom after September 11, 2001, and allegedly traveled to Pakistan solely to attempt to continue his education at less expense than it would cost to take similar courses in the United Kingdom. *Id.* Petitioner Rasul allegedly stayed with an Aunt in Lahore, Pakistan before engaging in further travel within that country. *Id.* Allegedly, forces fighting against the United States captured and kidnapped Petitioner Rasul after he left Lahore. *Id.* As for Petitioner Iqbal, it is alleged that in July of 2001, his family arranged for him to marry a woman living in the same village in Pakistan as Petitioner Iqbal's father. *Id.* ¶ 23. After September 11, 2001, Petitioner Iqbal left the United Kingdom and allegedly traveled to Pakistan solely for the purpose of getting married. *Id.* In early October of 2001, shortly before the marriage, Petitioner Iqbal's father allegedly allowed Petitioner Iqbal to leave the village briefly. *Id.* After leaving the village, forces working in opposition to the United States allegedly captured Petitioner Iqbal. *Id.* Petitioners Rasul, Iqbal, and Hicks were picked up in a region of the world where the United States is actively engaged in military hostilities authorized by a Joint Resolution of the United States Congress, passed on September 18, 2001, in the wake of the September 11, 2001, terrorist attacks. The Joint Resolution authorizes the President to: use all necessary and appropriate force against those nations, organizations, or persons he determines planned, authorized, committed, or aided the terrorist attacks that occurred on September 11, 2001, or harbored such organizations or persons, in order to prevent any future acts of international terrorism against the United States by such nations, organizations or persons. Authorization for Use of Military Force, Pub. L. No. 107-40, § 2, 115 Stat. 224 (2001) (cited in Am. Pet. ¶ 25). In the course of the military campaign authorized by the Joint Resolution, the United States attacked the Taliban, the ruling government of Afghanistan. Am. Pet. ¶ 25. While seeking to overthrow the Taliban, the United States provided military assistance to the Northern Alliance, "a loosely knit coalition of Afghani and other military groups opposed to the Taliban Government." *Id.* ¶ 26.

The Northern Alliance captured Petitioner David Hicks in Afghanistan and transferred custody of him to the United States on December 17, 2001. *Id.* ¶ 27. The precise circumstances surrounding Petitioner Rasul's and Petitioner Iqbal's capture are unknown. However, they appear to have been transferred to United States control in early December of 2001. *Id.* ¶ 28. It is alleged in the Amended Petition that at no time did any of the Petitioners in United States custody voluntarily join any terrorist force. *Id.* ¶ 30.[29] Additionally, if any of the Petitioners in United States custody "ever took up arms in the Afghani struggle, it was only on the approach of the enemy, when they spontaneously took up arms to resist the invading forces, without having had time to form themselves into regular armed units, and carrying their arms openly and respecting all laws and customs of war." *Id.* Additionally, it is alleged

---

29. [6] While denying a role in any terrorist activity, Petitioners in their Amended Petition for Writ of Habeas Corpus conspicuously neglect to deny that they took up arms for the Taliban. In fact, in an exhibit attached to the Amended Petition, Petitioner Terry Hicks, who has brought this suit on behalf of his son, indicates that his son had joined the Taliban forces. Am. Pet., Ex. C., "Affidavit of Stephen James Kenny," Attach. 8 (Letter from Stephen Kenny, counsel for Petitioner Terry Hicks to Respondent Bush) ("It is our client's understanding that his son subsequently joined the Taliban forces and on 8 December 2001 was captured by members of the Northern Alliance."). Interestingly, this fact has been omitted from the text of the Amended Petition, but can be found only by a careful reading of an exhibit attached to the Amended Petition. *Id.*

in the Amended Petition that if Petitioners Rasul, Iqbal, and David Hicks were in Afghanistan prior to being captured, "it was in order to facilitate humanitarian assistance to the Afghani people." *Id.* ¶ 31. Furthermore, these Petitioners allegedly "have taken no step that was not fully protected as their free exercise of their religious and personal beliefs." *Id.*

B. *Odah v. United States*

The twelve Kuwaiti nationals in the *Odah* case, who are in United States custody at the military base at Guantanamo Bay, were in Afghanistan and Pakistan, some before and some after, September 11, 2001. Am. Compl. ¶ 14. These individuals were allegedly in those countries as volunteers for charitable purposes to provide humanitarian aid to the people of those countries. *Id.* The government of Kuwait allegedly supports such volunteer service by continuing to pay the salaries of its Kuwaiti employees while they engage in this type of volunteer service abroad. *Id.*

According to the Amended Complaint, none of those held in United States custody are, or have ever been, a combatant or belligerent against the United States, or a supporter of the Taliban or any terrorist organization. *Id.* ¶ 15. Villagers seeking bounties or other promised financial rewards allegedly seized the twelve Kuwaiti Plaintiffs against their will in Afghanistan or Pakistan. *Id.* ¶ 16. Subsequently these twelve Plaintiffs were transferred into the custody of the United States. *Id.* At various points in time, beginning in January of 2002, these twelve Plaintiffs were transferred to Guantanamo Bay. *Id.* ¶¶ 19-21.[30]

IV. Legal Standard District Courts Use in Evaluating Motions to Dismiss Under Federal Rule of Civil Procedure 12(b)(1)

In both matters before the Court, the government has moved to dismiss on jurisdictional grounds. Before a federal court can hear a case, it must ascertain that it has jurisdiction over the underlying subject matter of the action. *Bender v. Williamsport Area School Dist.*, 475 U.S. 534, 541 (1986) ("Federal courts are not courts of general jurisdiction; they have only the power that is authorized by Article III of the Constitution and the statutes enacted by Congress pursuant thereto.").

Motions to dismiss for lack of jurisdiction over the subject matter of the action are proper under Federal Rule of Civil Procedure 12(b)(1). In the Rule 12(b)(1) context, the plaintiff bears the burden of proving jurisdiction. *McNutt v. General Motors Acceptance Corp.*, 298 U. S. 178, 182-83 (1936). In both matters, the government challenges the actual complaint (and/or petition) itself, without relying on matters outside the pleadings. *See generally Hohri v. United States*, 782 F.2d 227, 241 (D.C. Cir. 1986), *vacated on other grounds*, 482 U.S. 64 (1987) (explaining that materials *aliunde* pleadings can be considered on a Rule 12(b)(1) motion). One commentator has referred to this type of motion as a "facial challenge" to a complaint, because a district court is not asked to review documents outside the pleadings. 2 James Wm. Moore et al., *Moore's Federal Practice*, § 12.30[4], at 39 (3rd ed. 2002) ("A facial attack questions the sufficiency of the pleading."). As both motions to dismiss before the Court present such "facial challenges," the Court must accept all of the Amended Petition's/Amended Complaint's well-pleaded factual allegations as true and draw all reasonable inferences from

---

30. [7] It has not been confirmed that Plaintiff Mohammed Funaitel Al Dihani is currently in custody at Guantanamo Bay. Am. Compl. ¶ 21.

those allegations in Petitioners'/Plaintiffs' favor. *United Transp. Union v. Gateway Western R. R.*, 78 F.3d 1208, 1210 (7th Cir. 1996) (*citing Rueth v. EPA*, 13 F.3d 227, 229 (7th Cir. 1993)).[31]

V. Discussion

A. Alien Tort Statute and Administrative Procedure Act Claims

1. *Rasul v. Bush*

The Amended Petition for a Writ of Habeas Corpus in the *Rasul* action states that "Petitioners bring this action under 28 U.S.C. §§ 2241 and 2242, and invoke this Court's jurisdiction under 28 U.S.C. §§ 1331, 1350, 1651, 2201, and 2202, 5 U.S.C. § 702; as well as the Fifth, Sixth, Eighth, and Fourteenth Amendments to the United States Constitution, the International Covenant on Civil and Political Rights ("ICCPR"), the American Declaration on the Rights and Duties of Man ("ADRDM"), and Customary International Law." Am. Pet. ¶ 2. While Petitioners seek to invoke this Court's jurisdiction under a host of separate provisions, the suit is *brought* explicitly as a petition for writs of habeas corpus pursuant to 28 U.S.C. §§ 2241 and 2242.

It has long been held that challenges to an individual's custody can only be brought under the habeas provisions. *See Chatman-Bey v. Thornburgh*, 864 F.2d 804, 807 (D.C. Cir. 1988) (*en banc*) ("Habeas is . . . 'a fundamental safeguard against unlawful custody.'") (quoting Justice Harlan's dissent in *Fay v. Noia*, 372 U.S. 391, 449 (1963)); *Monk v. Secretary of the Navy*, 793 F.2d 364, 366 (D.C. Cir. 1986) ("In adopting the federal habeas corpus statute, Congress determined that habeas corpus is the appropriate federal remedy for a prisoner who claims that he is 'in custody in violation of the Constitution . . . of the United States.'") (quoting 28 U.S.C. § 2241(c)(3)). As Petitioners seek to be "released from respondents' unlawful custody," the Court can consider this case only as a petition for writs of habeas corpus and not as an action brought pursuant to the Alien Tort Statute, 28 U.S.C. § 1350, or any of the other jurisdictional bases suggested in the Amended Petition. The exclusive means for securing the relief Petitioners seek is through a writ of habeas corpus.

2. *Odah v. United States*

Seeking to avoid having the Court consider their case as a petition for writ of habeas corpus, Plaintiffs in *Odah* disclaim any desire to be released from confinement. Am. Compl. at 4. In fact, Plaintiffs have filed an Amended Complaint that eliminates an earlier request that this Court consider transferring the twelve Kuwaiti detainees to Kuwait. By eliminating this request, Plaintiffs endeavor to distance themselves from anything that might be construed as an effort to seek their release from United States custody. Instead, Plaintiffs in *Odah* ask this Court to enter a preliminary and permanent injunction prohibiting the government from refusing to allow the Kuwaiti nationals to "meet with their families," "be informed of the charges, if any, against them," "designate and consult with counsel of their choice," and "have access to the courts or some other impartial tribunal." Am. Compl. ¶ 40. While purport-

---

31. [8] Notably, there are a few attachments to the Amended Petition for Writ of Habeas Corpus which the Court cites in this Memorandum Opinion. The Court does not consider these matters to be outside the pleadings because they were attached as exhibits to the Amended Petition.

ing not to seek release from confinement, Plaintiffs in their Amended Complaint plainly challenge the lawfulness of their custody. The Supreme Court has held that "the essence of habeas corpus is an attack by a person in custody upon the legality of that custody." *Preiser v. Rodriguez*, 411 U.S. 475, 484 (1973). As the United States Court of Appeals for the District of Columbia Circuit stated in *Chatman-Bey*, "[a]s previously suggested, the modern habeas cases teach, broadly, that habeas is designed to test the lawfulness of the government's asserted right to *detain* an individual." *Chatman-Bey*, 864 F.2d at 809 (emphasis in original); *see also Razzoli v. Federal Bureau of Prisons*, 230 F.3d 371, 373 (D.C. Cir. 2000) ("[W]e adhere to *Chatman-Bey*: for a federal prisoner, habeas is indeed exclusive even when a non-habeas claim would have a merely probabilistic impact on the duration of custody."). In the present case, Plaintiffs' fourth request for relief squarely challenges the validity of Plaintiffs' detention. Plaintiffs seek to have "access to the courts or some other impartial tribunal." Am. Compl. ¶ 40. Elaborating on this request, Plaintiffs have told the Court that they seek access to an impartial tribunal in order to "expeditiously establish their innocence and be able to return to Kuwait and their families." Pls.' Mem. of P. & A. in Supp. of Mot. for a Prelim. Inj. ("Pls.' Mem.") at 2. Without question, this prayer for relief is nothing more than a frontal assault on their confinement. While Plaintiffs in this case state that they do not seek immediate release, neither did the plaintiffs in *Chatman-Bey* or *Monk*. Nevertheless, the District of Columbia Circuit in both of those cases found that the federal habeas statute was the only lawful way for the petitioners to challenge their confinement. *Chatman-Bey*, 864 F.2d at 809; *Monk*, 793 F.2d at 366. In the *Odah* case, Plaintiffs seek to be presented immediately before a court to exonerate themselves "expeditiously." This type of claim is within the exclusive province of the writ of habeas corpus.[32] The other provisions of Plaintiffs' request for relief, namely that they be permitted to "meet with their families," "be informed of the charges, if any, against them," and "designate and consult with counsel of their choice," Am. Compl. ¶ 40, are directly related to their request to be brought before a court which would determine the extent of their entitlement to rights. Plaintiffs cannot escape having the Court convert their action into writs for habeas corpus by adding these three additional requests for relief.

Plaintiffs argue that they merely seek to challenge the *conditions* of their confinement relying principally on *Gerstein v. Pugh*, 420 U.S. 103 (1975). Pls.' Opp'n to Defs.' Mot. to Dismiss Pls.' Compl. and Mot. for a Prelim. Inj. ("Pls.' Opp'n") at 19-20. The Supreme Court in *Gerstein* found that, pursuant to 42 U.S.C. § 1983, a declaratory judgment action against state officials was a permissible means to address whether a person arrested and held for trial under a prosecutor's information was constitutionally entitled to a probable cause hearing before a judge. *Gerstein*, 420 U.S. at 107 n.5. Thus, the Supreme Court concluded that such an action did not need to be filed as a habeas petition. *Id.* n.6 ("Respondents did not ask for release from state custody, even as an alternative remedy. They asked only that the state authorities be ordered to give them a probable cause determination.").

There are clear differences between the claims presented in *Odah* and those addressed by the Court in *Gerstein*. As the Third Circuit has noted, "[I]n *Gerstein v. Pugh*, the constitutional validity of a method of pretrial procedure, *rather than its application to any particular case,*

---

32. [9] Plaintiffs cite to the habeas statutes as a basis for the Court's jurisdiction over their claims. Am. Compl. 1. Even though Plaintiffs have disavowed that their action is one sounding in habeas, the *Amended* Complaint continues to rely on the habeas statutes to provide this Court with jurisdiction.

was the focus of the challenge." Tedford v. Hepting, 990 F.2d 745, 749 (3d Cir. 1993) (emphasis added). The *Gerstein* Court recognized that the pretrial custody of the named plaintiffs had long since expired. *Gerstein*, 420 U.S. at 110 n.11. Accordingly, the claims the *Gerstein* Court addressed were focused on the constitutional adequacy of a pretrial procedure as it existed in the abstract. Plaintiffs in *Odah*, on the other hand, each seek a hearing on the merits of their individualized detentions. In addition, Plaintiffs have not brought a declaratory judgment action seeking to invalidate some procedure that would not impact the duration of their confinement. The issue in *Odah* is Plaintiffs' desire to have a hearing before a neutral tribunal. For such a claim, a petition for writ of a habeas corpus is the exclusive avenue for relief.[33] Thus, as it does in *Rasul*, the Court shall review the jurisdictional basis of the *Odah* case as if it were styled as a petition for writ of habeas corpus.[34]

---

33. [10] Plaintiffs' citation to *Brown v. Plaut* is similarly unavailing. Pls.' Opp'n at 20 (citing *Brown v. Plaut*, 131 F.3d 163 (D.C. Cir. 1997)). The *Brown* case involved a prisoner's challenge to a decision to place him in administrative segregation. The Court of Appeals held that such action did not have to be brought as a petition for writ of habeas corpus. *Id.* at 167. In that case, the appellate panel observed that the Supreme Court "has never deviated from *Preiser*'s clear line between challenges to the fact or length of custody and challenges to the conditions of confinement." *Id.* at 168. Plaintiffs' broad request to be produced before a tribunal is obviously a challenge "to the fact . . . of custody." *Id.* Accordingly, *Brown* does not apply to this case.

34. [11] Alternatively, the Court notes that in order for the government to be sued under the Alien Tort Statute, the government must waive its sovereign immunity. *FDIC v. Meyer*, 510 U.S. 471, 475 (1994) ("Absent a waiver, sovereign immunity shields the Federal Government and its agencies from suit."). Plaintiffs argue that Section 702 of the Administrative Procedure Act provides such a waiver. Pls.' Opp'n at 24 (citing *Sanchez-Espinoza v. Reagan*, 770 F.2d 202, 207 (D.C. Cir. 1985) (Scalia,J.) (stating that while the Alien Tort Statute does not provide a waiver of sovereign immunity, "[w]ith respect to claims against federal [officials] for *nonmonetary* relief . . . the waiver of the Administrative Procedure Act . . . is arguably available") (emphasis in original)). Assuming that Section 702 of the Administrative Procedure Act provides a waiver, the Court finds that the actions of the government in this case would be exempt by 5 U.S.C. § 701(b)(1)(G) (providing an exemption for, "military authority exercised in the field in time of war or in occupied territory"). Cases that have analyzed Section 701(b)(1)(G) have had occasion to address it only in the context of "judicial interference with the relationship between soldiers and their military superiors." *Doe v. Sullivan*, 938 F.2d 1370, 1380 (D. C. Cir. 1991). Despite the absence of pertinent case law, the language of Section 701(b)(1)(G) supports the view that this Court is unable to review the claim Plaintiffs make under the Administrative Procedure Act. There is no dispute that Plaintiffs were captured in areas where the United States was (and is) engaged in military hostilities pursuant to the Joint Resolution of Congress. Am. Compl. 16 ("the Kuwaiti Detainees were seized against their will in Afghanistan or Pakistan"). This situation plainly falls within Section 701(b)(1)(G). The Court was unable to find any material in the legislative history that addressed Section 701(b)(1)(G) of the Administrative Procedure Act, *see, e.g.*, S. Rep. No. 89-1350, at 32-33 (1966); H.R. Rep. No. 89-901, at 16 (1965), and the parties have not provided any legislative history, that would change the Court's view of this provision. Furthermore, granting Plaintiffs relief under the Administrative Procedure Act would produce a bizarre anomaly: United States soldiers would be unable to use the courts of the United States to sue about events arising on the battlefield, while aliens, with no connection to the United States, could sue their United States military captors while hostilities continued. Such an outcome defies common sense. Accordingly, even if the Court did not treat the *Odah* case as a petition for writs of habeas ccorpus, Count III, brought pursuant to the Administrative Procedure Act, fails because the actions complained of by Plaintiffs are exempt pursuant to 5 U.S.C. § 701(b)(1)(G). Additionally, as Plaintiffs have not set forth another basis for the government's waiver of its sovereign immunity outside the Administrative Procedure Act, Count II brought pursuant to the Alien Tort Statute would be subject to dismissal.

B. The Ability of Courts to Entertain Petitions for Writs of Habeas Corpus Made By Aliens Held Outside the Sovereign Territory of the United States

The Court, therefore, considers both cases as petitions for writs of habeas corpus on behalf of aliens detained by the United States at the military base at Guantanamo Bay, Cuba. In viewing both cases from this perspective, the Court concludes that the Supreme Court's ruling in *Johnson v. Eisentrager*, 339 U.S. 763 (1950), and its progeny, are controlling and bars the Court's consideration of the merits of these two cases. The Court shall briefly provide an overview of the *Eisentrager* decision, discuss the distinction in *Eisentrager* between the rights of citizens and aliens, analyze whether *Eisentrager* applies only to enemy aliens, and lastly, discuss the meaning of the concept of "sovereign territory" as presented in *Eisentrager*.

1. *Johnson* v. *Eisentrager*

The *Eisentrager* case involved a petition for writs of habeas corpus filed by twenty-one German nationals in the United States District Court for the District of Columbia. *Eisentrager*, 339 U.S. at 765. The prisoners in *Eisentrager* had been captured in China for engaging in espionage against the United States following the surrender of Germany, but before the surrender of Japan, at the end of World War II. *Id*. at 766. Since the United States was at peace with Germany, the actions of the *Eisentrager* petitioners violated the laws of war. *Id*. Following a trial and conviction by a United States military commission sitting in China, with the express permission of the Chinese government, the prisoners were repatriated to Germany to serve their sentences at Landsberg Prison. *Id*. Their immediate custodian at Landsberg Prison was a United States Army officer under the Commanding General, Third United States Army, and the Commanding General, European Command. *Id*. The district court dismissed the petition for want of jurisdiction. *Id*. at 767. An appellate panel reversed the decision of the district court and remanded the case for further proceedings. *See Eisentrager v. Forrestal*, 174 F.2d 961 (D.C. Cir. 1949). In an opinion by Judge E. Barrett Prettyman, the Court of Appeals for the District of Columbia Circuit held that "any person who is deprived of his liberty by officials of the United States, acting under purported authority of that Government, and who can show that his confinement is in violation of a prohibition of the Constitution, has a right to the writ." *Id*. at 963. A divided panel of the Supreme Court reversed the decision of the District of Columbia Circuit and affirmed the judgment of the district court. *Eisentrager*, 339 U.S. at 791. In finding that *no* court had jurisdiction to entertain the claims of the German nationals, the Supreme Court, in an opinion by Justice Robert Jackson, found that a court was unable to extend the writ of habeas corpus to aliens held outside the sovereign territory of the United States. *Id*. at 778.

2. The Critical Distinction Between Citizens and Aliens

Justice Jackson began his opinion by noting the legal differences between citizens and aliens, and between friendly aliens and enemy aliens. *Id*. at 769. Noting that citizenship provides its own basis for jurisdiction, Justice Jackson observed that "[c]itizenship as a head of jurisdiction and a ground of protection was old when Paul invoked it in his appeal to Caesar." *Id*. Such protections, Justice Jackson noted, also apply to an individual seeking a fair hearing on his or her claim to citizenship. *Id*. 769-70 (citing *Chin Yow v. United States*, 208 U.S. 8 (1908)). In the case of the alien, Justice Jackson wrote that "[t]he alien, to whom the United

States has been traditionally hospitable, has been accorded a generous and ascending scale of rights as he increases his identity with our society." *Id*. at 770. For example, presence within the country provides an alien with certain rights that expand and become more secure as he or she declares an intent to become a citizen, culminating in the full panoply of rights afforded to the citizen upon the alien's naturalization. *Id*. In extending constitutional protections beyond the citizenry, Justice Jackson noted that the Supreme Court "has been at pains to point out that it was the alien's presence within its territorial jurisdiction that gave the Judiciary power to act." *Id*. at 771. Justice Jackson's sentiment is borne out by the case law. Courts of the United States have exercised jurisdiction in cases involving individuals seeking to prove their citizenship, *Chin Yow*, 208 U.S. at 13 (1908) (habeas action permitted for one seeking admission to the country to assure a hearing on his claims to citizenship), or in situations where aliens held in a port of the United States sought entry into the country, *Nishimura Ekiu v. United States*, 142 U.S. 651, 660 (1892) ("An alien immigrant, prevented from landing by any such officer claiming authority to do so under an act of congress, and thereby restrained of his liberty, is doubtless entitled to a writ of *habeas corpus* to ascertain whether the restraint is lawful."). In the cases at bar it is undisputed that the individuals held at Guantanamo Bay do not seek to become citizens. Nor have Petitioners or Plaintiffs suggested that they have ever been to the United States or have any desire to enter the country. Petitioners and Plaintiffs do not fall into any of the categories of cases where the courts have entertained the claims of individuals seeking access to the country.

3. Does the *Eisentrager* Opinion Apply Only to "Enemy" Aliens?

Justice Jackson continued his analysis in *Eisentrager* by noting that enemy aliens captured incident to war do not have even a qualified access to the courts of the United States as compared to an alien who has lawful residence within the United States. *Eisentrager*, 339 U.S. at 776 ("[T]he nonresident enemy alien, especially one who has remained in the service of the enemy, does not have . . . this qualified access to our courts, for he neither has comparable claims upon our institutions nor could his use of them fail to be helpful to the enemy."); *id*. (quoting *Clarke v. Morey*, 10 Johns. 69, 72 (N.Y. Sup. Ct. 1813) ("A lawful residence implies protection, and a capacity to sue and be sued. A contrary doctrine would be repugnant to sound policy, no less than to justice and humanity.")). Petitioners in *Rasul* and Plaintiffs in *Odah* argue that the determination by the military commission in China that the petitioners in *Eisentrager* were enemy aliens is fatal to the government's reliance on *Eisentrager*. Pet'rs Mem. in Opp'n to Resp'ts Mot. to Dismiss ("Pet'rs Opp'n") at 12; Pls.' Opp'n at 6-7. Insisting that no determination has been made about the aliens presently held by the government at Guantanamo Bay, Plaintiffs and Petitioners argue that the holding in *Eisentrager* is inapplicable to the instant cases.

   To the contrary, the Supreme Court's conclusion in *Eisentrager*, that the district court was without jurisdiction to consider the petition for writs of habeas corpus on behalf of the twenty one German nationals, did not hinge on the fact that the petitioners were enemy aliens, but on the fact that they were aliens outside territory over which the United States was sovereign. The Supreme Court held:

   We have pointed out that the privilege of litigation has been extended to aliens, whether friendly or enemy, only because permitting their presence in the country implied protection. No such basis can be invoked here, for these prisoners at no relevant time were within any territory over which the United States is sovereign, and the sences of their offense, their capture, their trial and their punishment were all beyond the territorial jurisdiction of any court of the United States.

Id. at 777-78. In fact, the Supreme Court has consistently taken the position that *Eisentrager* does not apply only to those aliens deemed to be "enemies" by a competent tribunal. *See Zadvydas v. Davis*, 533 U.S. 678, 693 (2001) (Breyer, J.); *United States v. Verdugo-Urquidez*, 494 U.S. 259, 270 (1990) (Rehnquist, C.J.). These later Supreme Court cases reinforce the conclusion that there is no meaningful distinction between the cases at bar and the *Eisentrager* decision on the mere basis that the petitioners in *Eisentrager* had been found by a military commission to be "enemy" aliens.[35]

In *Zadvydas*, the Court cited *Eisentrager* for the proposition that "[i]t is well established that certain constitutional protections available to persons inside the United States are unavailable to aliens outside of our geographic borders." *Zadvydas*, 533 U.S. at 693 (discussing also that "once an alien enters the country, the legal circumstance changes, for the Due Process Clause applies to all 'persons' within the United States, including aliens, whether their presence here is lawful, unlawful, temporary, or permanent"). In *Verdugo-Urquidez*, the Court quoted a passage from *Eisentrager* for the proposition that the Supreme Court has emphatically rejected "extraterritorial application of the Fifth Amendment." *Verdugo-Urquidez*, 494 U.S. at 269. The Court of Appeals for the District of Columbia Circuit has taken a similarly broad view of *Eisentrager*. *Harbury v. Deutch*, 233 F.3d 596, 605 (D.C. Cir. 2000), *rev'd on other grounds sub nom. Christopher v. Harbury*, 122 S. Ct. 2179 (2002) (observing that the Supreme Court's citation to *Eisentrager* in *Verdugo-Urquidez* was binding, and expressing its view that extraterritorial application of the Fifth Amendment was not available for aliens).

If there exists any doubt as to the sweeping nature of the holding in *Eisentrager*, the dissent in that opinion clearly crystalizes the extent of the decision. Justice Douglas, writing for himself and two other Justices, stated:

> If the [majority's] opinion thus means, and it apparently does, that these petitioners are deprived of the privilege of habeas corpus solely because they were convicted and imprisoned overseas, the Court is adopting a broad and dangerous principle. . . . [T]he Court's opinion inescapably denies courts power to afford the least bit of protection for any alien who is subject to our occupation government abroad, even if he is neither enemy nor belligerent and even after peace is officially declared.

---

35. [12] The government has encouraged this Court to take "judicial notice" that these individuals are "enemy combatants." Tr. 9-10. In reviewing this case, the Court has taken the allegations in the Amended Petition and Amended Complaint as true as required by Rule 12(b)(1). Petitioners and Plaintiffs allege that the individuals held at Guantanamo Bay were initially taken into custody and detained in Afghanistan and Pakistan where military hostilities were in progress. Am. Pet. 22-24; Am. Compl. 16. David Hicks, who had joined the Taliban, *see supra* note 6, arguably may be appropriately considered an "enemy combatant." The paucity, ambiguity, and contradictory information provided by the Amended Petition and the Amended Complaint about Petitioners Rasul and Iqbal and the twelve Kuwaiti Plaintiffs held at the military base at Guantanamo Bay prevents the Court from likewise concluding that these individuals were engaged in hostilities against the United States, or were instead participating in the benign activities suggested in the pleadings. While another court with apparently the same factual record has labeled, without explanation, the individuals held at Guantanamo Bay "enemy combatants," *Coalition of Clergy v. Bush*, 189 F. Supp. 2d, 1036, 1048 (C.D. Cal. 2002), this Court on the record before it, declines to take that step because taking judicial notice of a fact requires that the fact be "not subject to reasonable dispute." Fed. R. Evid. 201.

Eisentrager, 339 U.S. at 795-96 (Douglas, J., dissenting). Thus, even Justice Douglas noted that according to the majority's opinion in *Eisentrager*, the Great Writ had no extraterritorial application to aliens.

Accordingly, the Court finds that *Eisentrager* is applicable to the aliens in these cases, who are held at Guantanamo Bay, even in the absence of a determination by a military commission that they are "enemies."[36] While it is true that the petitioners in *Eisentrager* had already been convicted by a military commission, *id.* at 766, the *Eisentrager* Court did not base its decision on that distinction. Rather, *Eisentrager* broadly applies to prevent aliens detained outside the sovereign territory of the United States from invoking a petition for a writ of habeas corpus.

In sum, the *Eisentrager* decision establishes a two-dimensional paradigm for determining the rights of an individual under the habeas laws. If an individual is a citizen or falls within a narrow class of individuals who are akin to citizens, i.e. those persons seeking to prove their citizenship and those aliens detained at the nation's ports, courts have focused on status and have not been as concerned with the situs of the individual. However, if the individual is an alien without any connection to the United States, courts have generally focused on the location of the alien seeking to invoke the jurisdiction of the courts of the United States. If an alien is outside the country's sovereign territory, then courts have generally concluded that the alien is not permitted access to the courts of the United States to enforce the Constitution. Given that *Eisentrager* applies to the aliens presently detained at the military base at Guantanamo Bay, the only question remaining for the Court's resolution is whether Guantanamo Bay, Cuba is part of the sovereign territory of the United States.

4. Is Guantanamo Bay Part of the Sovereign Territory of the United States?

The Court in *Eisentrager* discusses the territory of the United States in terms of sovereignty. *Id.* at 778 ("for these prisoners at no relevant time were within any territory over which the United States is sovereign"). It is undisputed, even by the parties, that Guantanamo Bay is not part of the sovereign territory of the United States.[37] Thus, the only question remaining for resolution is whether this fact alone is an absolute bar to these suits, or

---

36. [13] The United States confronts an untraditional war that presents unique challenges in identifying a nebulous enemy. In earlier times when the United States was at war, discerning "the enemy" was far easier than today. "[I]n war 'every individual of the one nation must acknowledge every individual of the other nation as his own enemy.'" *Eisentrager* 339 U.S. at 772 (quoting *The Rapid*, 8 Cranch 155, 161 (1814)). The two cases at bar contain nationals from three friendly countries at peace with the United States, demonstrating the difficulty in determining who is the "enemy."

37. [14] The United States occupies Guantanamo Bay under a lease entered into with the Cuban government in 1903. Agreement Between the United States and Cuba for the Lease of Lands for Coaling and Naval Stations, Feb. 16-23, 1903, U.S.-Cuba, art. III, T.S. 418. The lease provides: While on the one hand the United States recognizes the continuance of the ultimate sovereignty of the Republic of Cuba over [the military base at Guantanamo Bay], on the other hand the Republic of Cuba consents that during the period of occupation by the United States of said areas under the terms of this agreement the United States shall exercise complete jurisdiction and control over and within said areas with the right to acquire . . . for the public purposes of the United States any land or other property therein by purchase or by exercise of eminent domain with full compensation to the owners thereof. *Id.* As is clear from this agreement, the United States does not have sovereignty over the military base at Guantanamo Bay.

whether aliens on a United States military base situated in a foreign country are considered to be within the territorial jurisdiction of the United States, under a *de facto* theory of sovereignty. Petitioners and Plaintiffs assert that the United States has *de facto* sovereignty over the military base at Guantanamo Bay, and that this provides the Court with the basis needed to assert jurisdiction. Pet'rs Opp'n at 21; Pls.' Opp'n at 11. In other words, Petitioners and Plaintiffs argue that even if the United States does not have *de jure* sovereignty over the military facility at Guantanamo Bay, it maintains *de facto* sovereignty due to the unique nature of the control and jurisdiction the United States exercises over this military base. According to Petitioners and Plaintiffs, if the United States has *de facto* sovereignty over the military facility at Guantanamo Bay, then *Eisentrager* is inapplicable to their cases and the Court is able to assume jurisdiction over their claims. However, the cases relied on by Petitioners and Plaintiffs to support their thesis are belied not only by *Eisentrager*, which never qualified its definition of sovereignty in such a manner, but also by the very case law relied on by Petitioners and Plaintiffs. At oral argument, when asked for a case that supported the view that *de facto* sovereignty would suffice to provide the Court with jurisdiction, both Petitioners and Plaintiffs directed the Court to *Ralpho v. Bell*, 569 F.2d 607 (D.C. Cir. 1977). Tr. at 33, 62-63. The *Ralpho* case involves a claim brought under the Micronesian Claims Act of 1971, which was enacted by the United States Congress to establish a fund to compensate Micronesians for losses incurred during the hostilities of World War II. *Ralpho*, 569 F.2d at 611. The plaintiff in that case, a citizen of Micronesia, argued that the Micronesian Claims Commission, established by the Act to adjudicate settlement claims, violated his due process rights by relying on secret evidence in deciding his claim. *Id.* at 615. While the United States did not have sovereignty over Micronesia, the District of Columbia Circuit found that the plaintiff was entitled to the protections of the due process clause. *Id.* at 618-19. Petitioners and Plaintiffs have seized upon this case as an example of a court granting an alien due process rights in a geographic area where the United States was not sovereign. Petitioners and Plaintiffs contend that if the plaintiff in *Ralpho* was able to secure constitutional rights in an area where the United States was not sovereign, constitutional rights are arguably available to aliens located in places where the United States is the *de facto* sovereign. The problem for Petitioners and Plaintiffs is that *Ralpho* does not stand for the proposition that a court can grant constitutional rights over a geographical area where *de facto* sovereignty is present. Rather, *Ralpho* stands for a limited extension of the uncontested proposition that aliens residing in the sovereign territories of the United States are entitled to certain basic constitutional rights. As the Court of Appeals explained in *Ralpho*, "[t]hat the United States is answerable to the United Nations for its treatment of the Micronesians does not give Congress greater leeway to disregard the fundamental rights and liberties of a people as much American subjects as those in other American territories." *Id.* After this observation, the *Ralpho* Court quoted the remarks of the United States Representative to the United Nations Security Council Meeting that considered whether to award trusteeship to the United States: "My government feels that it has a duty toward the peoples of the Trust Territory to govern them with no less consideration than it would govern any part of its sovereign territory." *Id.* n.72 (internal citation omitted). Additionally, when the United States was appointed by the United Nations to administer Micronesia as a trust territory, no other nation had sovereignty over Micronesia, and the United States had "full powers of administration, legislation, and jurisdiction over the territory subject to the provisions of [the trust] agreement." Trusteeship Agreement for the Former Japanese Mandated Islands Approved at the One Hundred and Twenty-Fourth Meeting of the Security Council, July 18, 1947, 61 Stat. 3301, T.I.A.S. No. 1665, art. 3; *id.*, preamble (noting that "Japan, as a result of the Second World War, has ceased to exercise any authority in these islands"). As clearly set forth in the case, the *Ralpho* Court treated Micronesia as the equivalent of a United States territory, such as Puerto Rico or Guam. In fact, *Ralpho* relies solely on the cases establishing constitutional rights for persons living in the territories of the United States as support for the view that the plaintiff located in Micronesia was deserving of certain due process rights. *Ralpho,* 569 F.2d at 619 n.70 (citing, *inter alia, Balzac v. Porto Rico,* 258 U.S. 298, 313 (1922)). The *Balzac* case, which predates *Eisentrager,* stands for the proposition that the limits of due process apply to the sovereign territories of the United States. *Balzac,* 258 U.S. at 313; *id* at 312 ("The Constitution, however, contains grants of power, and limitations which in the nature of things are not always and everywhere applicable and the real issue in the Insular Cases was not whether the Constitution extended to the Philippines or [Puerto] Rico when we went there, but which ones of its provisions were applicable by way of limitation upon the exercise of executive and legislative power in dealing with new conditions and requirements.").[38] Thus, the Court in *Ralpho* analogized the situation before it to those cases granting constitutional rights to the peoples of United States territories, even though the trust agreement with the United Nations did not provide for sovereignty over Micronesia. *Ralpho,* 569 F.2d at 619 n.71. The cases involving the territories of the United States, relied on by the *Ralpho* Court, are fundamentally different from the two cases presently before the Court. The military base at Guantanamo Bay, Cuba, is nothing remotely akin to a territory of the United States, where the United States provides certain rights to the inhabitants. Rather, the United States merely leases an area of land for use as a naval base. Accordingly, the Court is hard-pressed to adopt Petitioners' and Plaintiffs' view that the holding in *Ralpho* favors their claims. In fact, another district court considering whether a *de facto* sovereignty test should be used to analyze claims occurring at the military base at Guantanamo Bay flatly rejected the idea. *Bird v. United States,* 923 F. Supp. 338 (D. Conn. 1996). In *Bird,* a plaintiff alleged a misdiagnosis of a brain tumor at the United States Medical Facility at Guantanamo Bay. *Id.* at 339. Seeking to sue under the Federal Tort Claims Act ("FTCA"), the plaintiff sought to distinguish prior case law which held that injuries occurring on leased military bases were exempt from the FTCA under the "foreign country" exemption. In order to circumvent this case law, the plaintiff in *Bird* argued that the unique territorial status of the military base at Guantanamo Bay brought

---

38. [15] In *Harbury,* the Court of Appeals referred to *Balzac* as a situation where foreign nationals were under "de facto U.S. political control." *Harbury,* 233 F. 3d at 603. This phrase does not imply that in situations where *"de facto* sovereignty" might arguably be present, constitutional rights are available to aliens. In making this statement, the Court of Appeals cited to two cases involving Puerto Rico, *Examining Bd. of Eng'rs., Architects & Surveyors v. Otero,* 426 U.S. 572, 599 n.30 (1976) and *Balzac,* 258 U.S. at 312-13, and another case involving a special court of the United States that was held in Berlin, *United States v. Tiede,* 86 F.R.D. 227, 242-44 (U.S. Ct. Berlin 1979). In the two cases involving Puerto Rico, it is undisputed that the United States had sovereignty over the territory.

In the case involving the special court convened in Berlin, the court was a United States court convened in an occupation zone controlled by the United States. *Tiede,* 86 F.R.D. at 244-45 ("The sole but novel question before the Court is whether friendly aliens, charged with civil offenses in a United States court in Berlin, under the unique circumstances of the continuing United States occupation of Berlin, have a right to a jury trial."). Accordingly, the fact that the panel in *Harbury* used the phrase "de facto U.S. political control" to describe a category of cases where constitutional rights were provided to non-citizens does not aid Petitioners and Plaintiffs. The cases relied upon by the Court of Appeals in *Harbury* for this statement do not support the view that where the United States has *de facto* sovereignty, courts of the United States have jurisdiction to entertain the claims of aliens.

injuries occurring on its soil within the FTCA. *Id*. at 340. Rejecting the plaintiff's argument that the United States had *de facto* sovereignty over the military base at Guantanamo Bay, the court wrote, "[b]ecause the 1903 Lease of Lands Agreement clearly establishes Cuba as the *de jure* sovereign over Guantanamo Bay, this Court need not speculate whether the United States is the *de facto* sovereign over the area." *Id*. at 343. While *Bird* dealt with the foreign country exemption to the FTCA, it expressly disavowed a *de facto* sovereignty test, when it was clear that Cuba was the *de jure* sovereign over Guantanamo Bay. The *Bird* case is not the only court to reject a *de facto* sovereignty test for claims involving aliens located at the military base at Guantanamo Bay. *Cuban American Bar Ass'n, Inc. v. Christopher*, 43 F.3d 1412 (11th Cir. 1995), *cert. denied*, 515 U.S. 1142 (1995). The *Cuban American Bar Association* case involved Cuban and Haitian migrants held in "safe haven" at Guantanamo Bay after they left their respective countries and were intercepted in international waters by the United States Coast Guard. *Id*. at 1417, 1419. The Eleventh Circuit specifically addressed the question of whether migrants "outside the physical borders of the United States have any cognizable statutory or constitutional rights." *Id*. at 1421. In *Cuban American Bar Association*, the Eleventh Circuit held: The district court here erred in concluding that Guantanamo Bay was a "United States territory." We disagree that "control and jurisdiction" [as set forth in the lease between the United States and Cuba] is equivalent to sovereignty. . . . [W]e again reject the argument that our leased military bases abroad which continue under the sovereignty of foreign nations, hostile or friendly, are "functional[ly] equivalent" to being land borders or ports of entry of the United States or otherwise within the United States. *Id*. at 1425 (internal citations omitted). Thus, *Cuban American Bar Association* stands for the proposition that the military base at Guantanamo Bay is not within the territorial jurisdiction of the United States simply because the United States exercises jurisdiction and control over that facility. Plaintiffs seek to distinguish *Cuban American Bar Assoication* by citing a Second Circuit opinion that has been vacated as moot by the Supreme Court. Pls.' Opp'n at 12-13 (citing *Haitian Centers Council, Inc. v. McNary*, 969 F.2d 1326 (2d Cir. 1992), *vacated as moot sub nom. Sale v. Haitian Centers Council, Inc.*, 509 U.S. 918 (1993) [hereinafter "*HCC*"]). Ordinarily the Court would give short shrift to a case that has been vacated by the Supreme Court and not issued by the District of Columbia Circuit. However, since Plaintiffs in their papers, emphasize the importance of the reasoning in this vacated decision, the Court considers it necessary to briefly address the case. The Court determines that *HCC* is distinguishable on its facts. In *HCC*, migrants were housed at the military base on Guantanamo Bay and determinations were made by Immigration and Naturalization Service ("INS") officers regarding their status. *Id*. at 1332-33. Those migrants that an INS officer deemed to have a credible fear of political persecution were "screened in" and were to be brought to the United States to pursue asylum claims. Those who did not fit within this class were repatriated to Haiti. *Id*. The crucial distinction in their rights as aliens is that the aliens in *HCC* had been given some form of process by the government of the United States. Once the United States made determinations that the migrants had a credible fear of political persecution and could claim asylum in the United States, these migrants became vested with a liberty interest that the government was unable to simply deny without due process of law. The situation in *HCC* is fundamentally different from the cases presently before the Court. The individuals held at Guantanamo Bay have no desire to enter the United States and no final decision as to their status has been made. At this stage of their detention, those held at Guantanamo Bay more closely approximate the migrants in *Cuban American Bar Association* than the migrants "screened in" for admission to the United States in *HCC*.[39]

VI. Conclusion

The Court concludes that the military base at Guantanamo Bay, Cuba is outside the sovereign territory of the United States. Given that under *Eisentrager*, writs of habeas corpus are not available to aliens held outside the sovereign territory of the United States, this Court does not have jurisdiction to entertain the claims made by Petitioners in *Rasul* or Plaintiffs in *Odah*. Of course, just as the *Eisentrager* Court did not hold "that these prisoners have no right which the military authorities are bound to respect," *Eisentrager*, 339 U.S. at 789 n.14, this opinion, too, should not be read as stating that these aliens do not have some form of rights under international law. Rather, the Court's decision solely involves whether it has jurisdiction to consider the constitutional claims that are presented to the Court for resolution. Petitioners and Plaintiffs argue that as long as the United States has *de facto* sovereignty over Guantanamo Bay, Fifth Amendment protections should apply. For this proposition, Petitioners and Plaintiffs rely on *Ralpho*, a case that involves land so similar to United States territory that the District of Columbia Circuit extended constitutional protections to its inhabitants. Clearly, Guantanamo Bay does not fall into that category. The Court, therefore, rejects the holding in *Ralpho* as a basis for this Court to exercise jurisdiction over the claims made by Petitioners and Plaintiffs. Accordingly, both cases shall be dismissed for want of jurisdiction.

Colleen Kollar-Kotelly
United States District Judge

➤ **USA: *Hamdi* v. *Rumsfeld*, 8 January 2003**

U.S. 4th Circuit Court of Appeals

[...]

No. 02-7338

Yaser Esam Hamdi; Esam Fouad Hamdi, as next friend of Yaser Esam Hamdi, Petitioners – Appellees,

versus

Donald Rumsfeld; W.R. Paulette, Commander,
Respondents – Appellants.

---

39. [16] While there is dicta in the *HCC* opinion which indicates a broader holding with regard to the constitutional rights of individuals detained at the military base on Guantanamo Bay, such dicta in *HCC* is not persuasive and not binding. *HCC*, 969 F.2d at 1343. The Supreme Court in *Eisentrager*, *Verdugo-Urquidez*, and *Zadvydas*, and the District of Columbia Circuit in *Harbury*, have all held that here is no extraterritorial application of the Fifth Amendment to aliens.

[…]

Appeal from the United States District Court for the Eastern District of Virginia, at Norfolk. Robert G. Doumar, Senior District Judge. (CA-02-439-2)

Argued: October 28, 2002 Decided: January 8, 2003

Before Wilkinson, Chief Judge, and Wilkin and Traxler, Circuit Judges.

Reversed and remanded with directions to dismiss by published opinion. Opinion by Wilkinson, Chief Judge, and Wilkin and Traxler, Circuit Judges, in which all three concur.

[…]

Yaser Esam Hamdi filed a petition under 28 U.S.C. § 2241 challenging the lawfulness of his confinement in the Norfolk Naval Brig.[40] On this third and latest appeal, the United States challenges the district courts order requiring the production of various materials regarding Hamdi's status as an alleged enemy combatant. The district court certified for appeal the question of whether a declaration by a Special Advisor to the Under Secretary of Defense for Policy setting forth what the government contends were the circumstances of Hamdi's capture was sufficient by itself to justify his detention. Because it is undisputed that Hamdi was captured in a zone of active combat in a foreign theater of conflict, we hold that the submitted declaration is a sufficient basis upon which to conclude that the Commander in Chief has constitutionally detained Hamdi pursuant to the war powers entrusted to him by the United States Constitution. No further factual inquiry is necessary or proper, and we remand the case with directions to dismiss the petition.

I.

As recounted in earlier appeals regarding Hamdi's detention, *Hamdi v. Rumsfeld*, 294 F.3d 598 (4th Cir. 2002) ("*Hamdi I*"), and *Hamdi v. Rumsfeld*, 296 F.3d 278 (4th Cir. 2002) ("*Hamdi II*"), the al Qaida terrorist network, utilizing commercial airliners, launched massive attacks on the United States on September 11, 2001, successfully striking the World Trade Center in New York City, and the Pentagon, the military headquarters of our country, near Washington, D.C. A third unsuccessful attack upon at least one additional target, most likely within Washington, D.C., was foiled by the efforts of the passengers and crew on the highjacked airliner when it crashed in Somerset County, Pennsylvania, southeast of Pittsburgh. In total, over 3,000 people were killed on American soil that day.

In the wake of this atrocity, Congress authorized the President "to use all necessary and appropriate force against those nations, organizations, or persons he determines planned, authorized, committed, or aided the terrorist attacks" or "harbored such organizations or persons." Authorization for Use of Military Force, Pub. L. No. 107-40, 115 Stat. 224 (Sept.

---

40. [1] The court expresses its appreciation to the Public Defender's Office for the Eastern District of Virginia, the United States Attorney's Office for the Eastern District of Virginia, and the Solicitor General's Office for the professionalism of their efforts throughout these expedited appeals.

18, 2001). The President responded by ordering United States armed forces to Afghanistan to subdue al Qaida and the governing Taliban regime supporting it. During this ongoing military operation, thousands of alleged enemy combatants, including Hamdi, have been captured by American and allied forces.

The present case arises out of Hamdi's detention by the United States military in Norfolk, Virginia. Hamdi apparently was born in Louisiana but left for Saudi Arabia when he was a small child. Although initially detained in Afghanistan and then Guantanamo Bay, Hamdi was transferred to the Norfolk Naval Station Brig after it was discovered that he may not have renounced his American citizenship. He has remained in Norfolk since April 2002.

In June 2002, Hamdi's father, Esam Fouad Hamdi, filed a petition for writ of habeas corpus, naming as petitioners both Hamdi and himself as next friend.[41] The petition alleged that Hamdi is a citizen of the United States who was residing in Afghanistan when he was seized by the United States government. According to the petition, "[i]n the course of the military campaign, and as part of their effort to overthrow the Taliban, the United States provided military assistance to the Northern Alliance, a loosely-knit coalition of military groups opposed to the Taliban Government," and thereby "obtained access to individuals held by various factions of the Northern Alliance." The petition further alleges that "Hamdi was captured or transferred into the custody of the United States in the Fall of 2001" in Afghanistan, transported from Afghanistan to Camp X-Ray at the United States Naval Base in Guantanamo Bay, Cuba, in January 2002, and ultimately transferred to the Norfolk Naval Station Brig in Norfolk, Virginia, in April 2002.

Although acknowledging that Hamdi was seized in Afghanistan during a time of active military hostilities, the petition alleges that "as an American citizen, . . . Hamdi enjoys the full protections of the Constitution," and that the government's current detention of him in this country without charges, access to a judicial tribunal, or the right to counsel, "violate[s] the Fifth and Fourteenth Amendments to the United States Constitution." By way of relief, the petition asks, inter alia, that the district court: (1) "Order Respondents to cease all interrogations of Yaser Esam Hamdi, direct or indirect, while this litigation is pending"; (2) "Order and declare that Yaser Esam Hamdi is being held in violation of the Fifth and Fourteenth Amendments to the United States Constitution"; (3) "To the extent Respondents contest any material factual allegations in th[e] Petition, schedule an evidentiary hearing, at which Petitioners may adduce proof in support of their allegations"; and (4) "Order that Petitioner Yaser Esam Hamdi be released from Respondents' unlawful custody."

On June 11, before the government had time to respond to the petition, the district court appointed Public Defender Frank Dunham as counsel for the detainee and ordered the government to allow the Defender unmonitored access to Hamdi. On July 12, we reversed the district court's order granting counsel immediate access to Hamdi. *Hamdi II*, 296 F.3d at

---

41. [2] This court has previously determined that Esam Fouad Hamdi is a proper next friend. *Hamdi I*, 294 F.3d at 600 n.1. Two earlier petitions filed by the Federal Public Defender for the Eastern District of Virginia Frank Dunham and Christian Peregrim, a private citizen from New Jersey, were dismissed. Neither Dunham nor Peregrim had a significant relationship with the detainee, and Hamdi's father plainly did. Id. at 606.

279. We cautioned that Hamdi's petition involved complex and serious national security issues and found that the district court had not shown proper deference to the government's legitimate security and intelligence interests. We did not order the petition dismissed outright, however, noting our reluctance to "embrac[e] [the] sweeping proposition . . . that, with no meaningful judicial review, any American citizen alleged to be an enemy combatant could be detained indefinitely without charges or counsel on the government's say-so." *Id.* at 283. Rather, we sanctioned a limited and deferential inquiry into Hamdi's status, noting "that if Hamdi is indeed an 'enemy combatant' who was captured during hostilities in Afghanistan, the government's present detention of him is a lawful one." *Id.* (citing *Ex parte Quirin*, 317 U.S. 1, 31, 37 (1942)). We also instructed that, in conducting the inquiry, "the district court must consider the most cautious procedures first, conscious of the prospect that the least drastic procedures may promptly resolve Hamdi's case and make more intrusive measures unnecessary." *Id.* at 284.

Following this remand, the district court held a hearing on July 18. During this hearing, the court expressed its concern over possible violations of Hamdi's rights as an American citizen. The court also questioned the government's most basic contentions regarding the ongoing hostilities, asking "with whom is the war I should suggest that we're fighting?" and "will the war never be over as long as there is any member [or] any person who might feel that they want to attack the United States of America or the citizens of the United States of America?" The court directed that "[a]ll of these [answers should] be provided in the answer that the government is to file to the petition" and directed the United States to file such a response to Hamdi's petition by July 25.

On July 25, the government filed a response to, and motion to dismiss, the petition for a writ of habeas corpus. Attached to its response was an affidavit from the Special Advisor to the Under Secretary of Defense for Policy, Michael Mobbs, which confirms the material factual allegations in Hamdi's petition – specifically, that Hamdi was seized in Afghanistan by allied military forces during the course of the sanctioned military campaign, designated an "enemy combatant" by our Government, and ultimately transferred to the Norfolk Naval Brig for detention. Thus, it is undisputed that Hamdi was captured in Afghanistan during a time of armed hostilities there. It is further undisputed that the executive branch has classified him as an enemy combatant.

In addition to stating that Hamdi has been classified as an enemy combatant, the Mobbs declaration went on further to describe what the government contends were the circumstances surrounding Hamdi's seizure, his transfer to United States custody, and his placement in the Norfolk Naval Brig. According to Mobbs, the military determined that Hamdi "traveled to Afghanistan in approximately July or August of 2001" and proceeded to "affiliate[] with a Taliban military unit and receive[] weapons training." While serving with the Taliban in the wake of September 11, he was captured when his Taliban unit surrendered to Northern Alliance forces with which it had been engaged in battle. He was in possession of an AK-47 rifle at the time of surrender. Hamdi was then transported with his unit from Konduz, Afghanistan to the Northern Alliance prison in Mazar-e-Sharif, Afghanistan and, after a prison uprising there, to a prison at Sheberghan, Afghanistan. Hamdi was next transported to the U.S. short term detention facility in Kandahar, and then transferred again to Guantanamo Bay and eventually to the Norfolk Naval Brig. According to Mobbs, interviews with Hamdi confirmed the details of his capture and his status as an enemy combatant.

In keeping with our earlier instruction that the district court should proceed cautiously in reviewing military decisions reached during sanctioned military operations, we directed the district court to first "consider the sufficiency of the Mobbs declaration as an independent matter before proceeding further." Following this order, the district court held a hearing on August 13 to review the sufficiency of the Mobbs declaration.

During this hearing, the district court recognized that "the government is entitled to considerable deference in detention decisions during hostilities." The court also noted that it did not "have any doubts [Hamdi] had a firearm [or] any doubts he went to Afghanistan to be with the Taliban." Despite these observations, however, the court asserted that it was "challenging everything in the Mobbs' declaration" and that it intended to "pick it apart" "piece by piece." The court repeatedly referred to information it felt was missing from the declaration, asking "Is there anything in here that said Hamdi ever fired a weapon?" The court questioned whether Mr. Mobbs was even a government employee and intimated that the government was possibly hiding disadvantageous information from the court.

The district court filed an opinion on August 16, finding that the Mobbs declaration "falls far short" of supporting Hamdi's detention. The court ordered the government to turn over, among other things, copies of Hamdi's statements and the notes taken from any interviews with him; the names and addresses of all interrogators who have questioned Hamdi; statements by members of the Northern Alliance regarding the circumstances of Hamdi's surrender; and a list of the date of Hamdi's capture and all of the dates and locations of his subsequent detention.

Upon the Government's motion to certify the August 16 production order for immediate appeal, the district court certified the following question: "Whether the Mobbs Declaration, standing alone, is sufficient as a matter of law to allow a meaningful judicial review of Yaser Esam Hamdi's classification as an enemy combatant?" We then granted the Government's petition for interlocutory review pursuant to 28 U.S.C.A. § 1292(b). In so doing, we noted that "this court 'may address any issue fairly included within the certified order because it is the order that is appealable, and not the controlling question identified by the district court'." *Hamdi v. Rumsfeld*, No. 02-7338 (4th Cir. Sept. 12, 2002) (order granting petition for interlocutory review) (quoting *Yamaha Motor Corp. v. Calhoun*, 516 U.S. 199, 205 (1996)).

II.

Yaser Esam Hamdi is apparently an American citizen. He was also captured by allied forces in Afghanistan, a zone of active military operations. This dual status – that of American citizen and that of alleged enemy combatant – raises important questions about the role of the courts in times of war.

A.

The importance of limitations on judicial activities during wartime may be inferred from the allocation of powers under our constitutional scheme. "Congress and the President, like the courts, possess no power not derived from the Constitution." *Ex parte Quirin*, 317 U.S. 1, 25 (1942). Article I, section 8 grants Congress the power to "provide for the common Defence and general Welfare of the United States . . . To declare War, grant Letters of Marque and Reprisal, and make Rules concerning Captures on Land and Water; To raise and support armies . . . [and] To provide and maintain a navy." Article II, section 2 declares that "[t] he President shall be Commander in Chief of the Army and Navy of the United States, and of the Militia of the several States, when called into the actual Service of the United States."

The war powers thus invest "the President, as Commander in Chief, with the power to wage war which Congress has declared, and to carry into effect all laws passed by Congress for the conduct of war and for the government and regulation of the Armed Forces, and all laws defining and punishing offences against the law of nations, including those which pertain to the conduct of war." *Quirin*, 317 U.S. at 26. These powers include the authority to detain those captured in armed struggle. *Hamdi II*, 296 F.3d at 281-82.[42] These powers likewise extend to the executive's decision to deport or detain alien enemies during the duration of hostilities, *see Ludecke v. Watkins*, 335 U.S. 160, 173 (1948), and to confiscate or destroy enemy property, *see Juragua Iron Co. v. United States*, 212 U.S. 297, 306 (1909).

Article III contains nothing analogous to the specific powers of war so carefully enumerated in Articles I and II. "In accordance with this constitutional text, the Supreme Court has shown great deference to the political branches when called upon to decide cases implicating sensitive matters of foreign policy, national security, or military affairs." *Hamdi II*, 296 F.3d at 281.

The reasons for this deference are not difficult to discern. Through their departments and committees, the executive and legislative branches are organized to supervise the conduct of overseas conflict in a way that the judiciary simply is not. The Constitution's allocation of the warmaking powers reflects not only the expertise and experience lodged within the executive, but also the more fundamental truth that those branches most accountable to the people should be the ones to undertake the ultimate protection and to ask the ultimate sacrifice from them. Thus the Supreme Court has lauded "[t]he operation of a healthy deference to legislative and executive judgments in the area of military affairs." *Rostker v. Goldberg*, 453 U.S. 57, 66 (1981).

The deference that flows from the explicit enumeration of powers protects liberty as much as the explicit enumeration of rights. The Supreme Court has underscored this founding principle: "The ultimate purpose of this separation of powers is to protect the liberty and security of the governed." *Metro. Wash. Airports Auth. v. Citizens for the Abatement of Air-*

---

42. [3] Persons captured during wartime are often referred to as "enemy combatants." While the designation of Hamdi as an "enemy combatant" has aroused controversy, the term is one that has been used by the Supreme Court many times. *See, e.g., Madsen v. Kinsella*, 343 U.S. 341, 355(1952); *In re Yamashita*, 327 U.S. 1, 7 (1946); *Quirin*, 317 U.S. at 31.

craft Noise, Inc., 501 U.S. 252, 272 (1991). Thus, the textual allocation of responsibilities and the textual enumeration of rights are not dichotomous, because the textual separation of powers promotes a more profound understanding of our rights. For the judicial branch to trespass upon the exercise of the warmaking powers would be an infringement of the right to self-determination and self-governance at a time when the care of the common defense is most critical. This right of the people is no less a right because it is possessed collectively.

These interests do not carry less weight because the conflict in which Hamdi was captured is waged less against nation-states than against scattered and unpatriated forces. We have emphasized that the "unconventional aspects of the present struggle do not make its stakes any less grave." *Hamdi II*, 296 F.3d at 283. Nor does the nature of the present conflict render respect for the judgments of the political branches any less appropriate. We have noted that the "political branches are best positioned to comprehend this global war in its full context," *id.*, and neither the absence of set-piece battles nor the intervals of calm between terrorist assaults suffice to nullify the warmaking authority entrusted to the executive and legislative branches.

B.

Despite the clear allocation of war powers to the political branches, judicial deference to executive decisions made in the name of war is not unlimited. The Bill of Rights which Hamdi invokes in his petition is as much an instrument of mutual respect and tolerance as the Fourteenth Amendment is. It applies to American citizens regardless of race, color, or creed. And as we become a more diverse nation, the Bill of Rights may become even more a lens through which we recognize ourselves. To deprive any American citizen of its protections is not a step that any court would casually take.

Drawing on the Bill of Rights' historic guarantees, the judiciary plays its distinctive role in our constitutional structure when it reviews the detention of American citizens by their own government. Indeed, if due process means anything, it means that the courts must defend the "fundamental principles of liberty and justice which lie at the base of all our civil and political institutions." *Powell v. Alabama*, 287 U.S. 45, 67 (1932) (internal quotation marks omitted). The Constitution is suffused with concern about how the state will wield its awesome power of forcible restraint. And this preoccupation was not accidental. Our forebears recognized that the power to detain could easily become destructive "if exerted without check or control" by an unrestrained executive free to "imprison, dispatch, or exile any man that was obnoxious to the government, by an instant declaration that such is their will and pleasure." 4 W. Blackstone, *Commentaries on the Laws of England* 349-50 (Cooley ed. 1899) (quoted in *Duncan v. Louisiana*, 391 U.S. 145, 151 (1968)).

The duty of the judicial branch to protect our individual freedoms does not simply cease whenever our military forces are committed by the political branches to armed conflict. The Founders "foresaw that troublous times would arise, when rulers and people would . . . seek by sharp and decisive measures to accomplish ends deemed just and proper; and that the principles of constitutional liberty would be in peril, unless established by irrepealable law." *Ex Parte Milligan*, 71 U.S. (4 Wall.) 2, 120 (1866). While that recognition does not dispose of this case, it does indicate one thing: The detention of United States citizens must be subject to judicial review. *See Hamdi II*, 296 F.3d at 283.

It is significant, moreover, that the form of relief sought by Hamdi is a writ of habeas corpus. In war as in peace, habeas corpus provides one of the firmest bulwarks against unconstitutional detentions. As early as 1789, Congress reaffirmed the courts' common law authority to review detentions of federal prisoners, giving its explicit blessing to the judiciary's power to "grant writs of habeas corpus for the purpose of an inquiry into the cause of commitmen" for federal detainees. Act of Sept. 24, 1789, ch. 20, § 14, 1 Stat. 81-82. While the scope of habeas review has expanded and contracted over the succeeding centuries, its essential function of assuring that restraint accords with the rule of law, not the whim of authority, remains unchanged. Hamdi's petition falls squarely within the Great Writ's purview, since he is an American citizen challenging his summary detention for reasons of state necessity.

C.

As the foregoing discussion reveals, the tensions within this case are significant. Such circumstances should counsel caution on the part of any court. Given the concerns discussed in the preceding sections, any broad or categorical holdings on enemy combatant designations would be especially inappropriate. We have no occasion, for example, to address the designation as an enemy combatant of an American citizen captured on American soil or the role that counsel might play in such a proceeding. *See, e.g., Padilla v. Bush*, No. 02 Civ. 445 (MBM), 2002 WL 31718308 (S.D.N.Y. Dec. 4, 2002). We shall, in fact, go no further in this case than the specific context before us – that of the undisputed detention of a citizen during a combat operation undertaken in a foreign country and a determination by the executive that the citizen was allied with enemy forces.

The safeguards that all Americans have come to expect in criminal prosecutions do not translate neatly to the arena of armed conflict. In fact, if deference to the executive is not exercised with respect to military judgments in the field, it is difficult to see where deference would ever obtain. For there is a "well-established power of the military to exercise jurisdiction over members of the armed forces, those directly connected with such forces, [and] enemy belligerents, prisoners of war, [and] others charged with violating the laws of war." *Duncan v. Kahanamoku*, 327 U.S. 304, 313-14 (1946) (footnotes omitted). As we emphasized in our prior decision, any judicial inquiry into Hamdi's status as an alleged enemy combatant in Afghanistan must reflect this deference as well as "a recognition that government has no more profound responsibility" than the protection of American citizens from further terrorist attacks. *Hamdi II*, 296 F.3d at 283.

In this regard, it is relevant that the detention of enemy combatants serves at least two vital purposes. First, detention prevents enemy combatants from rejoining the enemy and continuing to fight against America and its allies. "The object of capture is to prevent the captured individual from serving the enemy. He is disarmed and from then on he must be removed as completely as practicable from the front . . . " *In re Territo*, 156 F.2d 142, 145 (9th Cir. 1946). In this respect, "captivity is neither a punishment nor an act of vengeance," but rather "a simple war measure." W. Winthrop, *Military Law and Precedents* 788 (2d ed. 1920). And the precautionary measure of disarming hostile forces for the duration of a conflict is routinely accomplished through detention rather than the initiation of criminal charges. To require otherwise would impose a singular burden upon our nation's conduct of war.

Second, detention in lieu of prosecution may relieve the burden on military commanders of litigating the circumstances of a capture halfway around the globe. This burden would not be inconsiderable and would run the risk of "saddling military decision-making with the panoply of encumbrances associated with civil litigation" during a period of armed conflict. *Hamdi II*, 296 F.3d at 283-84. As the Supreme Court has recognized, "[i]t would be difficult to devise more effective fettering of a field commander than to allow the very enemies he is ordered to reduce to submission to call him to account in his own civil courts and divert his efforts and attention from the military offensive abroad to the legal defensive at home." *Johnson v. Eisentrager*, 339 U.S. 763, 779 (1950).[43]

The judiciary is not at liberty to eviscerate detention interests directly derived from the war powers of Articles I and II. As the nature of threats to America evolves, along with the means of carrying those threats out, the nature of enemy combatants may change also. In the face of such change, separation of powers doctrine does not deny the executive branch the essential tool of adaptability. To the contrary, the Supreme Court has said that "[i]n adopting this flexible understanding of separation of powers, we simply have recognized Madison's teaching that the greatest security against tyranny . . . lies not in a hermetic division among the Branches, but in a carefully crafted system of checked and balanced power within each Branch." *Mistretta v. United States*, 488 U.S. 361, 381 (1989). If anything, separation of powers bears renewed relevance to a struggle whose unforeseeable dangers may demand significant actions to protect untold thousands of American lives.

The designation of Hamdi as an enemy combatant thus bears the closest imaginable connection to the President's constitutional responsibilities during the actual conduct of hostilities. We therefore approach this case with sensitivity to both the fundamental liberty interest asserted by Hamdi and the extraordinary breadth of warmaking authority conferred by the Constitution and invoked by Congress and the executive branch.

III.

After the district court issued its August 16 production order, it granted respondent's motion for an interlocutory appeal of that order. The following question was certified for our review:

> Whether the Mobbs Declaration, standing alone, is sufficient as a matter of law to allow a meaningful judicial review of Yaser Esam Hamdi's classification as an enemy combatant?

As the Supreme Court has made clear, we are not limited to this single question. Rather, an appellate court may address any issue fairly included within the certified order, because 'it

---

43. [4] The government has contended that appointment of counsel for enemy combatants in the absence of charges would interfere with a third detention interest, that of gathering intelligence, by establishing an adversary relationship with the captor from the outset. *See Hamdi II*, 296 F.3d at 282 (expressing concern that the June 11 order of the district court "does not consider what effect petitioner's unmonitored access to counsel might have upon the government's ongoing gathering of intelligence"). That issue, however, is not presented in this appeal.

is the *order* that is appealable, and not the controlling question identified by the district court.' *Yamaha Motor Corp., U.S.A. v. Calhoun*, 516 U.S. 199, 205 (1996) (internal quotation marks omitted).

On this appeal, it is argued that Hamdi's detention is invalid even if the government's assertions were entirely accurate. If that were clearly the case, there would be no need for further discovery such as that detailed in the August 16 production order, because Hamdi's detention would be invalid for reasons beyond the scope of any factual dispute. Indeed, any inquiry into the August 16 production order or any discussion of the certified question would be unnecessary, because neither could suffice to justify a detention that, as a threshold matter, was otherwise unlawful. Moreover, the burden of the August 16 order would necessarily outweigh any benefits if, quite independent of the disputed factual issues, Hamdi were already entitled to relief. *See* Fed. R. Civ. Proc. 26(b)(1)-(2). For that reason, any purely legal challenges to Hamdi's detention are fairly includable within the scope of the certified order. *See Juzwin v. Asbestos Corp.*, 900 F.2d 686, 692 (3d Cir. 1990) (stating that, on § 1292(b) review of an order denying a dispositive motion, an appellate court is "free to consider all grounds advanced in support of the grant of [the motion] and all grounds suggested for sustaining its denial" (internal quotation marks omitted)).

In this vein, Hamdi and amici have in fact pressed two purely legal grounds for relief: 18 U.S.C. § 4001(a) and Article 5 of the Geneva Convention. We now address them both.[44]

A.

18 U.S.C. § 4001 regulates the detentions of United States citizens. It states in full:

(a) No citizen shall be imprisoned or otherwise detained by the United States except pursuant to an Act of Congress.

(b)(1) The control and management of Federal penal and correctional institutions, except military or naval institutions, shall be vested in the Attorney General, who shall promulgate rules for the government thereof, and appoint all necessary officers and employees in accordance with the civil-service laws, the Classification Act, as amended[,] and the applicable regulations.

(2) The Attorney General may establish and conduct industries, farms, and other activities and classify the inmates; and provide for their proper government, discipline, treatment, care, rehabilitation, and reformation.

18 U.S.C. § 4001 (2002). Hamdi argues that there is no congressional sanction for his incarceration and that § 4001(a) therefore prohibits his continued detention. We find this contention unpersuasive.

---

44. [5] We reject at the outset one other claim that Hamdi has advanced in abbreviated form. He asserts that our approval of his continued detention means that the writ of habeas corpus has been unconstitutionally suspended. *See* U.S. Const. art. I, § 9. We find this unconvincing; the fact that we have not ordered the relief Hamdi requests is hardly equivalent to a suspension of the writ.

Even if Hamdi were right that § 4001(a) requires Congressional authorization of his detention, Congress has, in the wake of the September 11 terrorist attacks, authorized the President to "use *all necessary and appropriate force* against those nations, organizations, or persons he determines planned, authorized, committed, or aided the terrorist attacks" or "harbored such organizations or persons." Authorization for Use of Military Force, Pub. L. No. 107-40, 115 Stat. 224 (Sept. 18, 2001) (emphasis added). As noted above, capturing and detaining enemy combatants is an inherent part of warfare; the "necessary and appropriate force" referenced in the congressional resolution necessarily includes the capture and detention of any and all hostile forces arrayed against our troops. Furthermore, Congress has specifically authorized the expenditure of funds for "the maintenance, pay, and allowances of prisoners of war [and] other persons in the custody of the [military] whose status is determined . . . to be similar to prisoners of war." 10 U.S.C. § 956(5) (2002). It is difficult if not impossible to understand how Congress could make appropriations for the detention of persons "similar to prisoners of war" without also authorizing their detention in the first instance.

Any alternative construction of these enactments would be fraught with difficulty. As noted above, the detention of enemy combatants serves critical functions. Moreover, it has been clear since at least 1942 that "[c]itizenship in the United States of an enemy belligerent does not relieve him from the consequences of [his] belligerency." *Quirin*, 317 U.S. at 37. If Congress had intended to override this well-established precedent and provide American belligerents some immunity from capture and detention, it surely would have made its intentions explicit.

It is likewise significant that § 4001(a) functioned principally to repeal the Emergency Detention Act. That statute had provided for the preventive "apprehension and detention" of individuals inside the United States "deemed likely to engage in espionage or sabotage" during "internal security emergencies." H.R. Rep. 92-116, at 2 (Apr. 6, 1971). Proponents of the repeal were concerned that the Emergency Detention Act might, inter alia, "permit[] a recurrence of the round ups which resulted in the detention of Americans of Japanese ancestry in 1941 and subsequently during World War II." *Id.* There is no indication that § 4001(a) was intended to overrule the longstanding rule that an armed and hostile American citizen captured on the battlefield during wartime may be treated like the enemy combatant that he is. We therefore reject Hamdi's contention that § 4001(a) bars his detention.

B.

Hamdi and amici also contend that Article 5 of the Geneva Convention applies to Hamdi's case and requires an initial formal determination of his status as an enemy belligerent "by a competent tribunal." Geneva Convention Relative to the Treatment of Prisoners of War, Aug. 12, 1949, art. 5, 6 U.S.T. 3316, 75 U.N.T.S. 135.

This argument falters also because the Geneva Convention is not self-executing. "Courts will only find a treaty to be self-executing if the document, as a whole, evidences an intent to provide a private right of action." *Goldstar (Panama) v. United States*, 967 F.2d 965, 968 (4th Cir. 1992). The Geneva Convention evinces no such intent. Certainly there is no explicit provision for enforcement by any form of private petition. And what discussion there is of enforcement focuses entirely on the vindication by diplomatic means of treaty rights inhering in sovereign nations. If two warring parties disagree about what the Convention requires of them, Article 11 instructs them to arrange a "meeting of their representatives" with the aid of diplomats from other countries, "with a view to settling the disagreement." Geneva Convention, at art. 11. Similarly, Article 132 states that "any alleged violation of the Convention" is to be resolved by a joint transnational effort "in a manner to be decided between the interested Parties." *Id.* at art. 132; *cf. id.* at arts. 129-30 (instructing signatories to enact legislation providing for criminal sanction of "persons committing . . . grave breaches of the present Convention"). We therefore agree with other courts of appeals that the language in the Geneva Convention is not "self-executing" and does not "create private rights of action in the domestic courts of the signatory countries." *Huynh Thi Anh v. Levi,* 586 F.2d 625, 629 (6th Cir. 1978) (applying identical enforcement provisions from the Geneva Convention Relative to the Protection of Civilian Persons in Time of War, Feb. 2, 1956, 6 U.S.T. 3516, 75 U.N.T.S. 287); *see also Holmes v. Laird,* 459 F.2d 1211, 1222 (D. C. Cir. 1972) (noting that "corrective machinery specified in the treaty itself is nonjudicial").

Hamdi provides no reason to conclude that 28 U.S.C. § 2241 makes these diplomatically-focused rights enforceable by a private right of petition. Indeed, it would make little practical sense for § 2241 to have done so, since we would have thereby imposed on the United States a mechanism of enforceability that might not find an analogue in any other nation. This is not to say, of course, that the Geneva Convention is meaningless. Rather, its values are vindicated by diplomatic means and reciprocity, as specifically contemplated by Article 132. There is a powerful and self- regulating national interest in observing the strictures of the Convention, because prisoners are taken by both sides of any conflict. This is the very essence of reciprocity and, as the drafters of the Convention apparently decided, the most appropriate basis for ensuring compliance. As the Court in *Eisentrager* observed about the predecessor to the current Geneva Convention, "the obvious scheme of the Agreement [is] that responsibility for observance and enforcement of these rights is upon political and military authorities." 339 U.S. at 789 n.14.

Even if Article 5 were somehow self-executing, there are questions about how it would apply to Hamdi's case. In particular, it is anything but clear that the "competent tribunal" which would determine Hamdi's status would be an Article III court. Every country has different tribunals, and there is no indication that the Geneva Convention was intended to impose a single adjudicatory paradigm upon its signatories. Moreover, Hamdi's argument begs the question of what kind of status determination is necessary under Article 5 and how extensive it should be. Hamdi and the amici make much of the distinction between lawful and unlawful combatants, noting correctly that lawful combatants are not subject to punishment for their participation in a conflict. But for the purposes of this case, it is a distinction without a difference, since the option to detain until the cessation of hostilities belongs to the executive in either case. It is true that unlawful combatants are entitled to a proceeding before a military tribunal before they may be punished for the acts which render their belligerency unlawful. *Quirin,* 317 U.S. at 31. But they are also subject to mere detention in precisely the same way that lawful prisoners of war are. *Id.* The fact that Hamdi might be an unlawful combatant in no way means that the executive is required to inflict every consequence of that status on him. The Geneva Convention certainly does not require such treatment.

For all these reasons, we hold that there is no purely legal barrier to Hamdi's detention. We now turn our attention to the question of whether the August 16 order was proper on its own terms.

IV.

As we will discuss below, we conclude that Hamdi's petition fails as a matter of law. It follows that the government should not be compelled to produce the materials described in the district court's August 16 order.

We also note that the order, if enforced, would present formidable practical difficulties. The district court indicated that its production request might well be only an initial step in testing the factual basis of Hamdi's enemy combatant status. The court plainly did not preclude making further production demands upon the government, even suggesting that it might "bring Hamdi before [the court] to inquire about [his] statements."

Although the district court did not have "any doubts [that Hamdi] had a firearm" or that "he went to Afghanistan to be with the Taliban," the court ordered the government to submit to the court for in camera, ex parte review: (1) "[c]opies of all Hamdi's statements, and the notes taken from any interviews with Hamdi, that relate to his reasons for going to Afghanistan, his activities while in Afghanistan, or his participation in the military forces of the Taliban or any other organization in that country"; (2) "[a] list of all the interrogators who have questioned Hamdi, including their names and addresses, and the dates of the interviews"; (3) "[c]opies of any statements by members of the Northern Alliance" regarding Hamdi's surrender; (4) "[a] list that includes the date of Hamdi's capture, and that gives all the dates and locations of his subsequent detention"; (5) "[t]he name and title of the individual within the United States Government who made the determination that Hamdi was an illegal enemy combatant"; (6) "[t]he name and title of the individual within the United States Government who made the decision to move Hamdi from Guantanamo Bay, Cuba to the Norfolk Naval Station"; and (7) "the screening criteria utilized to determine the status of Hamdi." The court's order allows the government to redact "intelligence matters" from its responses, but only to the extent that those intelligence matters are outside the scope of inquiry into Hamdi's legal status.

Hamdi argues vigorously that this order should be affirmed. Because of the alleged "breadth with which Respondents construe their authority to imprison American citizens whom they consider to be enemy combatants," Br. of the Petitioners/Appellees at 27, Hamdi argues we must allow the district court to subject the government's classification of him to a searching review. While the ordinary § 2241 proceeding naturally contemplates the prospect of factual development, *see* 28 U.S.C. §§ 2243, 2246, such an observation only begs the basic question in this case – whether further factual exploration would bring an Article III court into conflict with the warmaking powers of Article I and II. Here, the specific interests asserted by the government flow directly from the warmaking powers and are intimately connected to them. Whatever the general force of these interests (which we discussed extensively above), they are most directly implicated by captures in a zone of active combat operations.

A review of the court's August 16 order reveals the risk of "stand[ing] the warmaking powers of Articles I and II on their heads," *Hamdi II*, 296 F.3d at 284. The district court, for example, ordered the government to produce all Hamdi's statements and notes from interviews. Yet it is precisely such statements, relating to a detainee's activities in Afghanistan, that may contain the most sensitive and the most valuable information for our forces in the field. The risk created by this order is that judicial involvement would proceed, increment by increment, into an area where the political branches have been assigned by law a preeminent role.

The district court further ordered the government to produce a list of all interrogators who have questioned Hamdi, including their names and addresses and the dates of the interviews, copies of any statements by members of the Northern Alliance regarding Hamdi's surrender, and a list that includes the date of Hamdi's capture and all the dates and locations of his subsequent detention. Once again, however, litigation cannot be the driving force in effectuating and recording wartime detentions. The military has been charged by Congress and the executive with winning a war, not prevailing in a possible court case. Complicating the matter even further is the fact that Hamdi was originally captured by Northern Alliance forces, with whom American forces were generally allied. The district court's insistence that statements by Northern Alliance members be produced cannot help but place a strain on multilateral efforts during wartime. The court also expressed concern in its order that the Northern Alliance did not "identify the unit [to which Hamdi was affiliated]," "where or by whom [Hamdi] received weapons training or the nature and extent thereof," or "who commanded the unit or the type of garb or uniform Hamdi may have worn . . . " In demanding such detail, the district court would have the United States military instruct not only its own personnel, but also its allies, on precise observations they must make and record during a battlefield capture.

Viewed in their totality, the implications of the district court's August 16 production order could not be more serious. The factual inquiry upon which Hamdi would lead us, if it did not entail disclosure of sensitive intelligence, might require an excavation of facts buried under the rubble of war. The cost of such an inquiry in terms of the efficiency and morale of American forces cannot be disregarded. Some of those with knowledge of Hamdi's detention may have been slain or injured in battle. Others might have to be diverted from active and ongoing military duties of their own. The logistical effort to acquire evidence from far away battle zones might be substantial. And these efforts would profoundly unsettle the constitutional balance.

For the foregoing reasons, the court's August 16 production request cannot stand.

V.

The question remains, however, whether Hamdi's petition must be remanded for further proceedings or dismissed.

Hamdi's American citizenship has entitled him to file a petition for a writ of habeas corpus in a civilian court to challenge his detention, including the military's determination that he is an "enemy combatant" subject to detention during the ongoing hostilities. Thus, as with all habeas actions, we begin by examining the precise allegations presented to us by the respective parties. In this case, there are two allegations that are crucial to our analysis. First, Hamdi's petition alleges that he was a resident of and seized in Afghanistan, a country in which hostilities were authorized and ongoing at the time of the seizure, but that his continued detention in this country without the full panoply of constitutional protections is unlawful. Second, the Government's response asserts that Hamdi is being detained pursuant to the Commander-in-Chief's Article II war powers and that the circumstances underlying Hamdi's detention, as reflected primarily in the Mobbs declaration, establish that Hamdi's detention is lawful.

Generally speaking, in order to fulfill our responsibilities under Article III to review a petitioner's allegation that he is being detained by American authorities in violation of the rights afforded him under the United States Constitution, we must first determine the source of the authority for the executive to detain the individual. Once the source of the authority is identified, we then look at the justification given to determine whether it constitutes a legitimate exercise of that authority.

A.

Here the government has identified the source of the authority to detain Hamdi as originating in Article II, Section 2 of the Constitution, wherein the President is given the war power. We have already emphasized that the standard of review of enemy combatant detentions must be a deferential one when the detainee was captured abroad in a zone of combat operations. The President "is best prepared to exercise the military judgment attending the capture of alleged combatants." *Hamdi II*, 296 F.3d at 283. Thus, in *Quirin*, the Supreme Court stated in no uncertain terms that detentions "ordered by the President in the declared exercise of his powers as Commander in Chief of the Army in time of war and of grave public danger" should not "be set aside by the courts without the clear conviction that they are in conflict with the Constitution or laws of Congress constitutionally enacted." *Quirin*, 317 U.S. at 25.

This deferential posture, however, only comes into play after we ascertain that the challenged decision is one legitimately made pursuant to the war powers. It does not preclude us from determining in the first instance whether the factual assertions set forth by the government would, if accurate, provide a legally valid basis for Hamdi's detention under that power. Otherwise, we would be deferring to a decision made without any inquiry into whether such deference is due. For these reasons, it is appropriate, upon a citizen's presentation of a habeas petition alleging that he is being unlawfully detained by his own government, to ask that the government provide the legal authority upon which it relies for that detention and the basic facts relied upon to support a legitimate exercise of that authority. Indeed, in this case, the government has voluntarily submitted – and urged us to review – an affidavit from Michael Mobbs, Special Advisor to the Under Secretary of Defense for Policy, describing what the government contends were the circumstances leading to Hamdi's designation as an enemy combatant under Article II's war power.

The Mobbs affidavit consists of two pages and nine paragraphs in which Mobbs states that he was "substantially involved with matters related to the detention of enemy combatants in the current war against the al Qaeda terrorists and those who support and harbor them." In the affidavit, Mobbs avers that Hamdi entered Afghanistan in July or August of 2001 and affiliated with a Taliban military unit. Hamdi received weapons training from the Taliban and remained with his military unit until his surrender to Northern Alliance forces in late 2001. At the time of his capture, Hamdi was in possession of an AK-47 rifle. After his capture, Hamdi was transferred first from Konduz, Afghanistan to the prison in Mazar-e-Sharif, and then to a prison in Sheberghan, Afghanistan where he was questioned by a United States interrogation team. This interrogation team determined that Hamdi met "the criteria for enemy combatants over whom the United States was taking control." Hamdi was then transported to the U.S. short term detention facility in Kandahar, and then transferred again to Guantanamo Bay and eventually to the Norfolk Naval Brig. According to Mobbs, a subsequent interview with Hamdi confirmed the details of his capture and his status as an enemy combatant.

The district court approached the Mobbs declaration by examining it line by line, faulting it for not providing information about whether Hamdi had ever fired a weapon, the formal title of the Taliban military unit Hamdi was with when he surrendered, the exact composition of the U.S. interrogation team that interviewed Hamdi in Sheberghan, and even the distinguishing characteristics between a Northern Alliance miliary unit and a Taliban military unit. Concluding that the factual allegations were insufficient to support the government's assertion of the power to detain Hamdi under the war power, the court then ordered the production of the numerous additional materials outlined previously. We think this inquiry went far beyond the acceptable scope of review.

To be sure, a capable attorney could challenge the hearsay nature of the Mobbs declaration and probe each and every paragraph for incompleteness or inconsistency, as the district court attempted to do. The court's approach, however, had a signal flaw. We are not here dealing with a defendant who has been indicted on criminal charges in the exercise of the executive's law enforcement powers. We are dealing with the executive's assertion of its power to detain under the war powers of Article II. *See Eisentrager*, 339 U.S. at 793 (Black, J., dissenting) ("[I]t is no 'crime' to be a soldier."); *cf. In re Winship*, 397 U.S. 358, 363 (1970) (explaining that elevated burden of proof applies in criminal cases because of consequences of conviction, including social stigma). To transfer the instinctive skepticism, so laudable in the defense of criminal charges, to the review of executive branch decisions premised on military determinations made in the field carries the inordinate risk of a constitutionally problematic intrusion into the most basic responsibilities of a coordinate branch.

The murkiness and chaos that attend armed conflict mean military actions are hardly immune to mistake. Yet these characteristics of warfare have been with us through the centuries and have never been thought sufficient to justify active judicial supervision of combat operations overseas. To inquire, for example, whether Hamdi actually fired his weapon is to demand a clarity from battle that often is not there. The district court, after reviewing the Mobbs affidavit, did not "have any doubts [Hamdi] had a firearm [or] any doubts he went to Afghanistan to be with the Taliban." To delve further into Hamdi's status and capture would require us to step so far out of our role as judges that we would abandon the distinctive deference that animates this area of law.

For these reasons, and because Hamdi was indisputably seized in an active combat zone abroad, we will not require the government to fill what the district court regarded as gaps in the Mobbs affidavit. The factual averments in the affidavit, if accurate, are sufficient to confirm that Hamdi's detention conforms with a legitimate exercise of the war powers given the executive by Article II, Section 2 of the Constitution and, as discussed elsewhere, that it is consistent with the Constitution and laws of Congress. *See Quirin*, 317 U.S. at 25. Asking the executive to provide more detailed factual assertions would be to wade further into the conduct of war than we consider appropriate and is unnecessary to a meaningful judicial review of this question.

B.

We turn then to the question of whether, because he is an American citizen currently detained on American soil by the military, Hamdi can be heard in an Article III court to rebut the factual assertions that were submitted to support the "enemy combatant" designation. We hold that no evidentiary hearing or factual inquiry on our part is necessary or proper, because it is undisputed that Hamdi was captured in a zone of active combat operations in a foreign country and because any inquiry must be circumscribed to avoid encroachment into the military affairs entrusted to the executive branch.

In support of its contention that no further factual inquiry is appropriate, the government has argued that a "some evidence" standard should govern the adjudication of claims brought by habeas petitioners in areas where the executive has primary responsibility. That standard has indeed been employed in contexts less constitutionally sensitive than the present one, albeit in a procedural posture that renders those cases distinguishable. *See, e.g., INS v. St. Cyr*, 533 U.S. 289, 306 (2001) (describing historical practice under which, so long as "there was some evidence to support" a deportation order, habeas courts would not "review factual determinations made by the Executive"); *Eagles v. Samuels*, 329 U.S. 304, 312 (1946); *Fernandez v. Phillips*, 268 U.S. 311, 312 (1925). In each of these cases, the Court indicated that the role of the writ is not to correct "mere error" in the executive's exercise of a discretionary power, but rather to check the executive branch if it asserts a "power to act beyond the authority granted." *Eagles*, 329 U.S. at 311-12. Thus, the government asserts, the role of a habeas court is not to reconsider the executive's decision, but rather only to confirm that "there was *some* basis for the challenged executive determination." Br. for Respondents-Appellants at 29. Once that determination is made, the government further asserts, the detainee may not offer any rebuttal evidence and no further factual inquiry is allowed.

It is not necessary for us to decide whether the "some evidence" standard is the correct one to be applied in this case because we are persuaded for other reasons that a factual inquiry into the circumstances of Hamdi's capture would be inappropriate.

1.

As we have emphasized throughout these appeals, we cannot set aside executive decisions to detain enemy combatants "without the clear conviction that they are in conflict with the Constitution or laws of Congress constitutionally enacted." *Quirin*, 317 U.S. at 25. We cannot stress too often the constitutional implications presented on the face of Hamdi's petition. The constitutional allocation of war powers affords the President extraordinarily broad authority as Commander in Chief and compels courts to assume a deferential posture in reviewing exercises of this authority. And, while the Constitution assigns courts the duty generally to review executive detentions that are alleged to be illegal, the Constitution does not specifically contemplate any role for courts in the conduct of war, or in foreign policy generally.

Indeed, Article III courts are ill-positioned to police the military's distinction between those in the arena of combat who should be detained and those who should not. Any evaluation of the accuracy of the executive branch's determination that a person is an enemy combatant, for example, would require courts to consider, first, what activities the detainee was engaged in during the period leading up to his seizure and, second, whether those activities rendered him a combatant or not. The first question is factual and, were we called upon to delve into it, would likely entail substantial efforts to acquire evidence from distant battle zones. *See Eisentrager*, 339 U.S. at 779. The second question may require fine judgments about whether a particular activity is linked to the war efforts of a hostile power – judgments the executive branch is most competent to make.

Hamdi's petition places him squarely within the zone of active combat and assures that he is indeed being held in accordance with the Constitution and Congressional authorization for use of military force in the wake of al Qaida's attack. *Quirin*, 317 U.S. at 25. Any effort to ascertain the facts concerning the petitioner's conduct while amongst the nation's enemies would entail an unacceptable risk of obstructing war efforts authorized by Congress and undertaken by the executive branch.

2.

Hamdi contends that, although international law and the laws of this country might generally allow for the detention of an individual captured on the battlefield, these laws must vary in his case because he is an American citizen now detained on American soil. As an American citizen, Hamdi would be entitled to the due process protections normally found in the criminal justice system, including the right to meet with counsel, if he had been charged with a crime. But as we have previously pointed out, Hamdi has not been charged with any crime. He is being held as an enemy combatant pursuant to the well-established laws and customs of war. Hamdi's citizenship rightfully entitles him to file this petition to challenge his detention, but the fact that he is a citizen does not affect the legality of his detention as an enemy combatant.

Indeed, this same issue arose in *Quirin*. In that case, petitioners were German agents who, after the declaration of war between the United States and the German Reich, were trained at a German sabotage school where they "were instructed in the use of explosives and in methods of secret writing." *Quirin*, 317 U.S. at 21. The petitioners then journeyed by submarine to the beaches of New York and Florida, carrying large quantities of explosives and other sabotage devices. All of them were apprehended by FBI agents, who subsequently learned of their mission to destroy war industries and facilities in the United States. All of the petitioners were born in Germany but had lived in the United States at some point. One petitioner claimed American citizenship by virtue of the naturalization of his parents during his youth. The Court, however, did not need to determine his citizenship because it held that the due process guarantees of the Fifth and Sixth Amendments were inapplicable in any event. It noted that "[c]itizenship in the United States of an enemy belligerent does not relieve him from the consequences of a belligerency which is unlawful." *Id.* at 37. The petitioner who alleged American citizenship was treated identically to the other German saboteurs.

The *Quirin* principle applies here. One who takes up arms against the United States in a foreign theater of war, regardless of his citizenship, may properly be designated an enemy combatant and treated as such. The privilege of citizenship entitles Hamdi to a limited judicial inquiry into his detention, but only to determine its legality under the war powers of the political branches. At least where it is undisputed that he was present in a zone of active combat operations, we are satisfied that the Constitution does not entitle him to a searching review of the factual determinations underlying his seizure there.

3.

Similarly, we reject Hamdi's argument that even if his initial detention in Afghanistan was lawful, his continuing detention on American soil is not. Specifically, Hamdi contends that his petition does not implicate military concerns because "the underlying claims in this case are designed to test the legality of Hamdi's imprisonment in a naval brig in Norfolk, Virginia, not a military determination made overseas on the basis of caution rather than accuracy." Br. of the Petitioners/Appellees at 44. But the fact that Hamdi is presently being detained in the United States – as opposed to somewhere overseas – does not affect the legal implications of his status as an enemy combatant. For the same reason that courts are ill-positioned to review the military's distinction between those who should or should not be detained in an arena of combat, courts are not in the position to overturn the military's decision to detain those persons in one location or another. It is not clear why the United States should be precluded from exercising its discretion to move a detainee to a site within this country, nor do we see what purpose would be served by second guessing the military's decision with respect to the locus of detention.

4.

To conclude, we hold that, despite his status as an American citizen currently detained on American soil, Hamdi is not entitled to challenge the facts presented in the Mobbs declaration. Where, as here, a habeas petitioner has been designated an enemy combatant and it is undisputed that he was captured in an zone of active combat operations abroad, further judicial inquiry is unwarranted when the government has responded to the petition by setting forth factual assertions which would establish a legally valid basis for the petitioner's detention. Because these circumstances are present here, Hamdi is not entitled to habeas relief on this basis.

C.

Finally, we address Hamdi's contention that even if his detention was at one time lawful, it is no longer so because the relevant hostilities have reached an end. In his brief, Hamdi alleges that the government "confuses the international armed conflict that allegedly authorized Hamdi's detention in the first place with an on-going fight against individuals whom Respondents refuse to recognize as 'belligerents' under international law." Id. at 53-54. Whether the timing of a cessation of hostilities is justiciable is far from clear. See Ludecke, 335 U.S. at 169 ("Whether and when it would be open to this Court to find that a war though merely formally kept alive had in fact ended, is a question too fraught with gravity even to be adequately formulated when not compelled."). The executive branch is also in the best position to appraise the status of a conflict, and the cessation of hostilities would seem no less a matter of political competence than the initiation of them. *See United States v. The Three Friends*, 166 U.S. 1, 63(1897) ("[I]t belongs to the political department to determine when belligerency shall be recognized, and its action must be accepted according to the terms and intention expressed."). In any case, we need not reach this issue here. The government notes that American troops are still on the ground in Afghanistan, dismantling the terrorist infrastructure in the very country where Hamdi was captured and engaging in reconstruction efforts which may prove dangerous in their own right. Because under the most circumscribed definition of conflict hostilities have not yet reached their end, this argument is without merit.

VI.

It is important to emphasize that we are not placing our imprimatur upon a new day of executive detentions. We earlier rejected the summary embrace of "a sweeping proposition – namely that, with no meaningful judicial review, any American citizen alleged to be an enemy combatant could be detained indefinitely without charges or counsel on the government's say-so." Hamdi II, 296 F.3d at 283. But, Hamdi is not "any American citizen alleged to be an enemy combatant" by the government; he is an American citizen captured and detained by American allied forces in a foreign theater of war during active hostilities and determined by the United States military to have been indeed allied with enemy forces.

Cases such as Hamdi's raise serious questions which the courts will continue to treat as such. The nation has fought since its founding for liberty without which security rings hollow and for security without which liberty cannot thrive. The judiciary was meant to respect the delicacy of the balance, and we have endeavored to do so.

The events of September 11 have left their indelible mark. It is not wrong even in the dry annals of judicial opinion to mourn those who lost their lives that terrible day. Yet we speak in the end not from sorrow or anger, but from the conviction that separation of powers takes on special significance when the nation itself comes under attack. Hamdi's status as a citizen, as important as that is, cannot displace our constitutional order or the place of the courts within the Framer's scheme. Judicial review does not disappear during wartime, but the review of battlefield captures in overseas conflicts is a highly deferential one. That is why, for reasons stated, the judgment must be reversed and the petition dismissed. It is so ordered.

☛ **UK:** *Abbasi & Another* v. *Secretary of State for Foreign and Commonwealth Affairs, et al.*, **6 November 2002**

Neutral Citation Number: [2002] EWCA Civ 1598
Case No: C/2002/0617A; 0617B
6th November, 2002

In the Supreme Court of Judicature Court of Appeal (Civil Division) on Appeal from High Court of Justice Queen's Bench Division Administrative and Divisional Court, The Hon. Mr Justice Richards

Before:

The Queen on the Application of Abbasi & Anor. Claimants

And

Secretary of State for Foreign and Commonwealth Affairs & Secretary of State for the Home Department, Defendants

Mr N Blake QC; Mr Philippe Sands and Mr Ben Cooper (instructed by Messrs Christian Fisher Khan for the Claimants)
Professor C Greenwood QC; Mr Philip Sales (instructed by The Treasury Solicitor for the Defendants)
Hearing Dates: 10, 11 and 12 September 2002

Lord Phillips:
This is the judgment of the Court to which all members have contributed.

Introduction

1. Feroz Ali Abbasi, the first claimant, is a British national. He was captured by United States forces in Afghanistan. In January 2002 he was transported to Guantanamo Bay in Cuba, a naval base on territory held by the United States on long lease pursuant to a treaty with Cuba. By the time of the hearing before us he had been held captive for eight months without access to a court or any other form of tribunal or even to a lawyer. These proceedings, brought on his behalf by his mother, the second claimant, are founded on the contention that one of his fundamental human rights, the right not to be arbitrarily detained, is being infringed. They seek, by judicial review, to compel the Foreign Office to make representations on his behalf to the United States Government or to take other appropriate action or at least to give an explanation as to why this has not been done.

2. On 15 March 2002 Richards J. refused the application for permission to seek judicial review. However, on 1 July 2002 this court granted that permission, retained the matter for itself, and directed that the substantive hearing commence on 10 September 2002. It did so because the unusual facts of this case raise important issues. To what extent, if at all, can the English court examine whether a foreign state is in breach of treaty obligations or public international law where fundamental human rights are engaged? To what extent, if at all, is a decision of the executive in the field of foreign relations justiciable in the English court? More particularly, are there any circumstances in which the court can properly seek to influence the conduct of the executive in a situation where this may impact on foreign relations? Finally, in the light of the answers to these questions, is any form of relief open to Mr Abbasi and his mother against the Secretary of State for Foreign and Commonwealth Affairs?

Mr Abbasi's predicament

3. Mr Abbasi was one of a number of British citizens captured by American forces in Afghanistan. He was, with others, transferred to Guantanamo Bay. Those currently detained there include seven British citizens. As soon as she learned what had happened to her son, Mrs Abbasi made contact with the Foreign Office. Through lawyers, she pressed the Foreign Office to assist in ensuring that the conditions in which her son was detained were humane. She has also pressed the Foreign Office to procure from the United States authorities clarification of her son's status and of what is to be done with him in the future.

4. Evidence of action taken by the United Kingdom Government in relation to Mr Abbasi and the other British detainees in Guantanamo Bay has been provided in a witness statement by Mr Fry, a Deputy Under-Secretary of State for Foreign and Commonwealth Affairs. He speaks of close contact between the United Kingdom Government and the United States Government about the situation of the detainees and their treatment and of the consistent endeavour of the government to secure their welfare and ensure their proper treatment. To that end, we are told, the circumstances of the British detainees have been the subject of regular representations by the British Embassy in Washington to the United States Government. They have also been the subject of direct discussions between the Foreign Secretary and the United States Secretary of State as well as 'numerous communications at official level'.

5. The government was able to obtain permission from the United States Government to visit detainees at Guantanamo Bay on three occasions, between 19 and 20 January, between 26 February and 1 March and between 27 and 31 May. These visits were conducted by officials of the Foreign and Commonwealth Office and members of the security services. The former were able to assure themselves that the British prisoners, including Mr Abbasi, were being well treated and appeared in good physical health. By the time of the third visit, facilities had been purpose built to house detainees. Each was held in an individual cell with air ventilation, a washbasin and a toilet. It is not suggested by the claimants that Mr Abbasi is not being treated humanely.

6. The members of the security services took advantage of these visits to question Mr Abbasi with a view to obtaining information about possible threats to the safety of the United Kingdom. Initially this was the subject of independent complaint by the claimants, but before us the argument has focussed on the allegation that the Foreign and Commonwealth Office is not reacting appropriately to the fact that Mr Abbasi is being arbitrarily detained in violation of his fundamental human rights.

7. The position of the Foreign and Commonwealth Office is summarised by Mr Fry in the following terms:

    "In cases that come to us with a request for assistance, Foreign and Commonwealth Ministers and Her Majesty's diplomatic and consular officers have to make an informed and considered judgement about the most appropriate way in which the interests of the British national may be protected, including the nature, manner and timing of any diplomatic representations to the country concerned. Assessments of when and how to press another State require very fine judgements to be made, based on experience and detailed information gathered in the course of diplomatic business.

In cases where a person is detained in connection with international terrorism, these judgements become particularly complex. As regards the issue of the detainees now at Guantanamo Bay, as well as satisfying the clear need to safeguard the welfare of British nationals, the conduct of United Kingdom international relations has had to take account of a range of factors, including the duty of the Government to gather information relevant to United Kingdom national security and which might be important in averting a possible attack against the United Kingdom or British nationals or our allies; and the objectives of handling the detainees securely and of bringing any terrorist suspects to justice."

8. In or about February 2002 the claimants initiated habeas corpus proceedings in the District Court of Columbia. As we shall explain, rulings in proceedings brought by other detainees in a similar position demonstrate that Mr Abbasi's proceedings have, at present, no prospect of success.

The position according to the United States Government and the United States Courts

9. On 2 July 2002 the First Secretary at the American Embassy in London wrote to solicitors acting for the claimants in the following terms:

"The United States Government believes that individuals detained at Guantanamo are enemy combatants, captured in connection with an on-going armed conflict. They are held in that capacity under the control of U.S. military authorities. Enemy combatants pose a serious threat to the United States and its coalition partners.

Detainees are being held in accordance with the laws and customs of war, which permit the United States to hold enemy combatants at least for the duration of hostilities. I can assure you that the United States is treating these individuals humanely and in a manner consistent with the principles of the Third Geneva Convention 1949. Representatives of the International Committee of the Red Cross are at Guantanamo Bay and meet with detainees individually and privately.

Under international humanitarian law, captured enemy combatants have no right of access to counsel or the courts to challenge their detention. If and when a detainee is charged with a crime, he would have the right to counsel and fundamental procedural safeguards."

10. The Third Geneva Convention 1949 relates to Prisoners of War. The United States has not, however, accepted that prisoners held at Guantanamo have the status of prisoners of war. The position of the United States is made plain in the following passage of a statement made by the United States Press Secretary on 2 February 2002:

"Taliban detainees are not entitled to POW status ... they have not conducted their operations in accordance with the laws and customs of war ... al Qaeda is an international terrorist group and cannot be considered a state party to the Geneva Convention. Its members, therefore, are not covered by the Geneva Convention, and are not entitled to POW status under the treaty."

The distinction between lawful and unlawful combatants is drawn in a passage in a Supreme Court decision *ex parte Quirin* (1942) 317 U.S. 1 30-31 (quoted at p.7 of A-G's response in proceedings in the United States District Court for the Eastern District of Virginia, Norfolk Division *Hamdi v Rumsfeld* of Bundle 2 to which we shall return):

"By universal agreement and practice, the law of war draws a distinction between the armed forces and the peaceful populations of belligerent nations and also between those who are lawful combatants and unlawful combatants. Lawful combatants are subject to capture and detention as prisoners of war by opposing military forces. Unlawful combatants are likewise subject to capture and detention, but in addition they are subject to trial and punishment by military tribunals for acts which render their belligerency unlawful."

11. Mr Abbasi is, as we understand the position, detained pursuant to the executive authority entrusted to the President as Commander in Chief of the US Military. It is not clear whether he is detained pursuant to a Military Order issued by the United States President on 13 November 2001 relating to "Detention, treatment, and trial of certain non-citizens in the war against terrorism". We can summarise the effect of that Order as follows. The Order stipulates that it applies to any individual who is not a citizen of the United States with respect to whom the President has determined in writing that there is reason to believe (1) that such individual is a member of al-Qaeda or (2) that he was engaged in international terrorism, or (3) that it is in the interests of the United States that he should be subject to the order. The order provides that any such individual will be detained at an appropriate location and treated humanely. It provides that any individual "when tried" will be tried by a military tribunal, and contains extensive provisions relating to such trial. It further provides:

"With respect to any individual subject to this order … the individual shall not be privileged to seek any remedy or maintain any proceeding, directly or indirectly, or to have any such remedy or proceeding sought on the individual's behalf, in (i) any court of the United States, or any State thereof, (ii) any court of any foreign nation, or (iii) any international tribunal."

There is no indication whether Mr Abbasi is going to be tried and thus whether the Order applies to him.

12. On 19 February 2002 three prisoners detained at Guantanamo Bay, two British and one Australian, commenced a civil action in the District Court of Columbia – *Rasul et al. v George Walker Bush et al.* in which they petitioned for a writ of habeas corpus. The government moved to dismiss the action for want of jurisdiction. A similar motion was brought to dismiss an action brought by relatives of ten Korean citizens, who were also detained at Guantanamo Bay – *Odah et al. v United States of America et al.* The petitioners sought an order that the detainees be informed of the charges, if any, against them, be permitted to consult with counsel and have access to a court or other impartial tribunal. The Court treated this as an application for habeas corpus. After hearing argument the Court ruled that the military base at Guantanamo Bay was outside the sovereign territory of the United States and that, in consequence of this fact and the fact that the claimants were aliens, the Court had no jurisdiction to entertain their claims. The position would have been different had they been American subjects.

13. In so holding, the District Court purported to follow a majority decision of the Supreme Court in *Eisentrager v Forrestal* (1949) 174 F.2d 961. That case concerned German citizens who had been convicted of espionage by a United States military commission after the surrender of Germany at the end of the Second World War and repatriated to Landsberg Prison in Germany to serve their sentences. The prison was under the control of the United States army. The prisoners petitioned for writs of habeas corpus. Giving the decision of the majority, Justice Robert Jackson held that a court was unable to extend the writ of habeas corpus to aliens held outside the territory of the United States. He distinguished between aliens and citizens, observing that "citi-

zenship as a head of jurisdiction and a ground of protection was old when Paul invoked it in his appeal to Caesar".

14. The District Court distinguished the position of aliens held at a port of entry into the United States and seeking immigration. They are entitled to a writ of habeas corpus to ascertain whether the restraint is lawful – *Nishimura Ekiu v. United States* (1892) 142 U.S. 651, 660.

15. We are informed that the decision in *Rasul* is subject to appeal. We are further informed that regardless of the outcome of the appeal, a petition for certiorari is almost certain to be filed with the Supreme Court. In these circumstances we cannot proceed on the basis that the last word has been spoken by the United States courts on their jurisdiction to entertain a claim for habeas corpus on behalf of detainees at Guantanamo. On the face of it we find surprising the proposition that the writ of the United States courts does not run in respect of individuals held by the government on territory that the United States holds as lessee under a long term treaty.

16. Mr Fry has placed before the court a pleading in a case, *Hamdi v Donald Rumsfeld*, concerning a national of Saudi Arabia, born in Louisiana and claiming to be an American citizen. He was captured in Afghanistan, held initially in Guantanamo Bay but then transferred to custody in Norfolk, Virginia. His father has petitioned on his behalf for habeas corpus in the District Court for the Eastern District of Virginia, Norfolk Division. No point has been taken on jurisdiction, no doubt because Mr Hamdi is detained on United States territory and claims American citizenship. The pleading in question is the response of the Attorney-General in what appears to be the final stages of the hearing at first instance. The material parts of this response can be summarised as follows:

   i. Hamdi's detention is lawful since he has been seized by the military and is detained as an enemy combatant;

   ii. there is no obligation under the law and customs of war for captors to charge combatants with an offence;

   iii. prisoners of war have no right to counsel;

   iv. the military has properly determined that Hamdi was an enemy combatant, "the executives' determination that someone is an enemy combatant and should be detained as such [being] one of the most fundamental military judgments of all",

   v. the sworn declaration explaining the military's determination readily satisfies any constitutionally appropriate standard of judicial review.

   Thus, in essence, the submission is that the war on terrorism is at least the equivalent to a conventional war, the military's judgment as to who is an enemy combatant should be upheld, and the rights available to citizens in relation to ordinary criminal prosecutions, e.g. the right to counsel, and the right to be brought before a court and charged within a reasonable time, are inapplicable.

17. The Attorney-General's response indicates that his submissions accord with observations of the Court of Appeals of the Fourth Circuit in interlocutory hearings in the same proceedings. Once again it seems likely that these proceedings will, whatever their outcome, be subject to appeal and thus will not represent the last word on the extent to which the status of a person held as an enemy combatant is open to review by the courts.

Expressions of concern

18. There have been widespread expressions of concern, both within and outside the United States, in respect of the stand taken by the United States government in cases such as *Hamdi*. On 16 January 2002 the United Nations High Commissioner for Human Rights issued a statement which included the following assertions

> "All persons detained in this context are entitled to the protection of international human rights law and humanitarian law, in particular the relevant provisions of the International Covenant on Civil and Political Rights (ICCPR) and the Geneva Conventions of 1949.
>
> The legal status of the detainees, and their entitlement to prisoner-of-war (POW) status, if disputed, must be determined by a competent tribunal, in accordance with the provisions of Article 5 of the Third Geneva Convention."

19. Submissions made in *Hamdi* seem, however, to entail that the decision of the military as to who is an enemy combatant is almost unchallengeable. Furthermore, whereas in a conventional war prisoners of war have to be released at the end of hostilities, there is the possibility that, by denying the detainees captured during the war against terrorism the status of prisoners of war, their detention may be indefinite. The position of the United States Administration was described in an article about two Australian detainees in the Sydney Morning Herald for 17 May 2002, entitled 'At the President's Pleasure', in this way:

> "What received less attention until recently was the Administration's plan to detain the men for as long as it deemed they posed a threat to American security. The White House is upfront about its intention to change the established rules of war. "What the Administration is trying to do is create a new legal regime," the Deputy Assistant Attorney-General, John Yoo, said in a speech earlier this year.
>
> The old legal regime is the Geneva Convention, designed to protect legitimate prisoners of war captured during conflicts. Under the convention, it is not a crime to be a member of an enemy's army, and POWs are free to go home after the end of hostilities unless they are charged with a war crime or a crime against humanity."

20. In her 8th Witness statement Miss Christian suggests that countries other than the United Kingdom are also concerned about their citizens being held without due process. One matter of particular concern relates to the length of detention. As Miss Christian points out, a citizen of the United States has the right to go before a court to challenge the legality of his detention. That right at the very least compels the US military to say whether the particular individual is being held as an enemy combatant. In practice, it enables that individual to argue the points of concern and challenge the response of the US government exemplified by the A-G's response in *Hamdi*. Thus Miss Christian submits that there is serious discrimination between US citizens and non-US citizens held as enemy combatants.

21. The Inter-American Commission on Human Rights is an organ of the Organisation of American States, of which the United States is a member. By letter dated 12 March 2001 the Commission requested that the United States:

> "take the urgent measures necessary to have the legal status of the detainees at Guantanamo Bay determined by a competent Tribunal."

The United States response was delivered under cover of a letter dated 11 April, the letter stating:

"The United States wishes to inform the Commission that the legal status of the detainees is clear, that the Commission does not have jurisdictional competence to apply international humanitarian law, that the precautionary measures are neither necessary nor appropriate in this case, and that the Commission lacks authority to request precautionary measures of the United States."

The Commission made observations on 13 May 2002, and the US further responded on 15 July. Following this the Commission reasserted its authority requesting precautionary measures by letter dated 23 July 2002. Two paragraphs of that decision are worth quoting:

"In this connection, the Commission must emphasize the importance of ensuring the availability of effective and fair mechanisms for determining the status of individuals falling under the authority and control of a state, as it is upon the determination of this status that the rights and protections under domestic and international law to which those persons may be entitled depend. This fundamental prerequisite is reflected in the provisions of numerous international instruments, including Article 5 of the Third Geneva Convention and Article XVIII of the American Declaration, which must be interpreted and applied so as to be given practical effect. Partly for this reason, human rights supervisory bodies such as this Commission may raise doubts concerning the status of persons detained in the course of an armed conflict, as it has in the present matter, and require that such status be clarified to the extent that such clarification is essential to determine whether their human rights are being respected. In light of the principle of efficacy, it is not sufficient for a detaining power to simply assert its view as to the status of a detainee to the exclusion of any proper or effectual procedure for verifying that status.

Notwithstanding this basic precept which underlies the Commission's present request for precautionary measures, the United States has not provided the Commission with any information concerning steps that have been taken to clarify the legal status of each of the detainees at Guantanamo Bay. Rather, it has reiterated the view asserted by the United States prior to the adoption of the Commission's measures, namely that the legal status of the detainees is clear because the Executive Branch of the US government considers that neither the Taliban nor the al Qaeda detainees meet the criteria applicable to lawful combatants under the Third Geneva Convention. The Commission has already determined, however, that doubts continue to exist concerning the legal status of the detainees, and that it remains entirely unclear from their treatment by the United States what minimum rights under international human rights and humanitarian law the detainees are entitled to. The United States has only said that it "is treating and will continue to treat all of the individual detained at Guantanamo Bay humanely and, to the extent appropriate and consistent with military necessity, in a manner consistent with the principles of the [Geneva Convention]." While the Commission is encouraged that the United States intends to treat the detainees humanely, this statement appears to confirm the Commission's previous finding that, in the State's view, the nature and extent of rights afforded to the detainees remain entirely at the discretion of the US government. And as indicated by the Commission in its initial request, this is not sufficient to comply with the United States' international obligations."

The claimants' complaint

22. The submissions of Mr Blake QC, on behalf of the claimants, echo the points made by the Commission. Those submissions can be summarised as follows: The status of Mr Abbasi is unclear; it is unclear precisely how long the US authorities intend to hold him; it is unclear whether they intend to bring charges against him before a military tribunal or a court. Of critical significance, he has no access to a court to clarify the legitimacy of his continued detention, even to the extent of clarifying that the President continues to rule that he is an individual to whom the Presidential decree applies. Even less does he have any opportunity to challenge the validity of that decree. The United States has chosen to place non-US citizens in a different position from US citizens. It is an open question whether US citizens' challenges will ultimately be successful, but they have had, and do have, access to the courts in the United States. Non-US citizens are detained in a place over which the United States has de facto control, but from which the detainee has no ability to test the legality of his detention. Indeed the Presidential decree purports to deprive the detainee of the right to go to any court. He is in (as it was described during the hearing) 'a legal black hole'.

The relief sought

23. By the re-amended claim form the claimants request the court to declare:
    Against the First Respondent [Defendant]:
    (i) That the government of the United Kingdom has the right to protect the interests of its nationals, within the limits permitted by international law;
    (ii) That acts or omissions with respect to the said right are exercises of jurisdiction and/or acts of sovereignty over the said nationals;
    (iii) That in the exercise of such sovereignty or jurisdiction, the United Kingdom government should act compatibly with the Convention rights of such nationals;
    (iv) That the Second Claimant [this and other references to the Second Claimant in Section 7 should be references to the First Claimant] as a British national temporarily present detained abroad without access to a local court or tribunal for determination of the legality, purpose and intended duration of the detention, is held arbitrarily contrary to international standards in the ECHR, the ICCPR or the ADHR respectively;
    (v) That the Second Claimant accordingly is in need of the exercise of the said jurisdiction and powers enjoyed by the Defendants;
    (vi) That accordingly, the Respondents [Defendants] are under a duty to take all reasonable steps within their jurisdiction to cause, seek or require the government of the United States to: –
        a. release the Second Claimant from detention or;
        b. return him to the custody or control of the Respondents [Defendants] in the United Kingdom; or
        c. bring the Second Claimant before a competent court or tribunal to determine whether the Claimant is being held in accordance with law, and applicable international standards;
        d. permit access by the Second Claimant to a lawyer of his choice for the purpose of c. above, and/or advising of his rights with respect to any criminal law investigation to which he may be subject.

(vii) That in the discharge of the said duty, the Respondents [Defendants] should make diplomatic representations to the United States authorities at whichever level and in whatever terms is considered most appropriate to achieve the ends stated in vi. above.

24. Relief was also claimed against the Second Defendant, but the Claimants have not pursued a separate claim against the Second Defendant before us, and we shall say no more of this.

25. Although the formulation of this relief was the result of a process of amendment and re-amendment, it was almost comprehensively abandoned by Mr Blake in the course of oral submissions. He had, so it seemed to us, great difficulty in advancing his claim to relief in a form which could readily be transposed into an order of the court. The essence of his submissions was that Mr Abbasi was subject to a violation by the United States of one of his fundamental human rights and that, in these circumstances, the Foreign Secretary owed him a duty under English public law to take positive steps to redress the position, or at least to give a reasoned response to his request for assistance. Mr Blake accepted that no legal precedent established such a duty, but submitted that the increased regard paid to human rights in both international and domestic law required that such a duty should be recognised.

The issues

26. For the Secretary of State, Mr Greenwood QC submitted that the authorities clearly established two principles that posed insuperable barriers to the relief claimed in these proceedings: (1) the English court will not examine the legitimacy of action taken by a foreign sovereign state; (2) the English court will not adjudicate upon actions taken by the executive in the conduct of foreign relations. Most of the debate focussed on the question of whether these principles do, indeed, bar the claimants' claim to relief.

The submissions

27. We propose to outline the submissions made in respect of each of the principles relied upon by Mr Greenwood.

Is the legitimacy of action taken by a foreign sovereign state justiciable?

28. A lengthy section of Mr Blake's argument was devoted to demonstrating that the United States was in breach of a fundamental right, or 'ius cogens', in subjecting Mr Abbasi to arbitrary detention. Mr Blake did not suggest that there might not be good grounds for detaining Mr Abbasi. He accepted that the application of the principles of the rules of war, and the provisions of the Geneva Convention, raised difficult questions in the context of the events of September 11th and the military campaign in Afghanistan which followed. The status of Mr Abbasi was in doubt. The violation of international law consisted in his denial of access to any tribunal before which that doubt could be resolved. He was, in truth, subject to arbitrary detention.

29. In support of this submission, Mr Blake referred us to a number of instruments which, so he submitted, established that the prohibition of arbitrary detention had reached the status of a norm of customary international law: Article 9 of the United Nations Declaration of Human Rights; Article 9 of the International Covenant on Civil and Politi-

cal Rights; Article 5 of the European Convention for the Protection of Human Rights and Fundamental Freedoms; Article 7 of the American Convention of Human Rights.

30. Mr Blake also relied on the 3rd Geneva Convention. Article 5 provides that where there is doubt as to whether persons who have committed belligerent acts are prisoners of war, they are to be accorded the protection of the Convention until their status has been determined 'by a competent tribunal'. It was contrary to the Convention and to international law to deny Guantanamo prisoners both the protection of the Convention and the right to have their status determined by a competent tribunal. Principles of humanitarian law and human rights alike would not permit the denial of access to a review by a court of whether detention was lawful.

31. Mr Greenwood did not challenge the proposition that arbitrary detention violated a fundamental human right. He emphasised that the United States government denied that the detention of prisoners at Guantanamo was unlawful and submitted that the legality of that detention was not justiciable in an English court.

32. In support of the proposition that the English court has no jurisdiction to determine whether a foreign State is in breach of its treaty obligations, Mr Greenwood referred us to the observations of Lord Diplock in *British Airways v. Laker Airways* [1985] AC 58 at 85-6. He further submitted that it is well established that the English court will not adjudicate upon the legality of a foreign State's transactions in the sphere of international relations in the exercise of sovereign authority, citing *Buttes Gas and Oil v Hammer* [1982] AC 888 at 932 (per Lord Wilberforce); *Westland Helicopters Ltd v AOI* [1995] QB 282. To do so would involve a serious breach of comity: see *Buck v AG* [1965] 1 Ch 745 at 770-771 (per Lord Diplock) and *R v Secretary of State*, ex parte *British Council of Turkish Cypriot Associations* 112 ILR 735 at 740 (per Sedley J). He observed that the relief sought by the claimants was founded on the assertion that the United States government was acting unlawfully. For the court to rule on that assertion would be contrary to comity and to the principle of State immunity.

33. The cases cited by Mr Greenwood unquestionably support the general proposition for which they were cited. It is not, however, a proposition that affords of no exception. Mr Greenwood accepted that there were exceptions to the rule. He submitted, however, that the exceptions applied only in exceptional circumstances and had no application to the facts of the present case. Examples of cases where the rule was not applied are *Oppenheim v Cattermole* [1976] AC 249, *R v Secretary of State for the Home Department, ex parte Adan* [2001] 2 AC 477 and *Kuwait Airways Corp v Iraqi Airways Co (Nos 4 and 5)* [2002] 2 WLR 1352. We shall revert to these decisions when we come to review the merits of the rival contentions.

34. Mr Blake for his part did not challenge the general proposition that the English court will not adjudicate on the legality of the executive actions of a foreign State. He held, however, that this principle of comity, founded in public international law, has no application to the facts of this case. The United States are not impleaded in the present proceedings. The rights and liabilities of the United States are not in issue. What is here sought is domestic relief against the Secretary of State.

35. Mr Blake laid emphasis on the fact that international law recognises that municipal law may afford the individual a right to diplomatic protection against breaches of international law by another State. He referred us to the following passage from the *Barcelona Traction Company* case – 1970 ICJ Reports at page 44:

"The Court would here observe that, within the limits prescribed by international law, a State may exercise diplomatic protection by whatever means and to whatever extent it thinks fit, for it is its own right that the State is asserting. Should the natural or legal person on whose behalf it is acting consider that their rights are not adequately protected, they have no remedy in international law. All they can do is resort to national law, if means are available, with a view to furthering their cause or obtaining redress. The municipal legislator may lay upon the State an obligation to protect its citizens abroad, and may also confer upon the national a right to demand the performance of that obligation, and clothe the right with corresponding sanctions. However, all these questions remain within the province of municipal law and do not affect the position internationally." (1970 ICJ reports, p. 3, para. 78).

He submitted that this passage demonstrates that no breach of comity is involved where a court adjudicates on a claim for a domestic law remedy that is founded on an alleged breach of international law by another State.

36. This argument overlapped with the submissions made by Mr Blake in relation to the next issue – can the English court adjudicate upon the conduct of the executive in the field of international relations? In support of the submission that it was desirable that the court should assert such jurisdiction, Mr Blake referred us to the views of Professor Dugard, Special Rapporteur to the Fifty Second Session of the International Law Commission. Professor Dugard advocated municipal law rights to diplomatic protection and observed that in some States such rights were already recognised. It was implicit that the exercise of such rights did not infringe any principle of international law.

Is executive action in the conduct of foreign affairs justiciable?

37. Mr Greenwood referred to a formidable line of authority in support of his submission that the decisions taken by the executive in its dealings with foreign states regarding the protection of British citizens abroad are non-justiciable, starting with *Council of Civil Service Unions v Minister for the Civil Service* [1985] 1 AC 374 (the *GCHQ* case). Mr Greenwood drew particular attention to the observations of Lord Diplock at p.411. He submitted that the courts have repeatedly held that the decisions taken by the executive in its dealings with foreign states regarding the protection of British nationals abroad are non-justiciable. He cited the following passages from recent decisions in support of this proposition:

(1) *R. v. Secretary of State for Foreign and Commonwealth Affairs, ex parte Pirbhai* (107 ILR 462 (1985)):

"… in the context of a situation with serious implications for the conduct of international relations, the courts should act with a high degree of circumspection in the interests of all concerned. It can rarely, if ever, be for judges to intervene where diplomats fear to tread." (p.479, per Sir John Donaldson MR)

(2) *R. v. Secretary of State for Foreign and Commonwealth Affairs, ex parte Ferhut Butt* (116 ILR 607 (1999)):

"The general rule is well established that the courts should not interfere in the conduct of foreign relations by the Executive, most particularly where such interference is likely to have foreign policy repercussions (see *R. v. Secretary of State for Foreign and Commonwealth Affairs*, ex parte *Everett* [1989] 1 QB 811 at 820).

This extends to decisions whether or not to seek to persuade a foreign government of any international obligation (e.g. to respect human rights) which it has assumed. What if any approach should be made to the Yemeni authorities in regard to the conduct of the trial of these terrorist charges must be a matter for delicate diplomacy and the considered and informed judgement of the FCO. In such matters the courts have no supervisory role." (p.615, per Lightman J).

"Whether and when to seek to interfere or to put pressure on in relation to the legal process, if ever it is a sensible and a right thing to do, must be a matter for the Executive and no one else, with their access to information and to local knowledge. It is clearly not a matter for the courts. It is clearly a high policy decision of a government in relation to its foreign relations and is not justiciable by way of judicial review." (p.622, per Henry LJ).

(3) *R. (Suresh and Manickavasagam) v. Secretary of State for the Home Department* [2001] EWHC Admin 1028 (unreported, 16 November 2001):

"... there is, in my judgement, no duty upon the Secretary of State to ensure that other nations comply with their human rights obligations. There may be cases where the United Kingdom Government has, for example by diplomatic means, chosen to seek to persuade another State to take a certain course in its treatment of British nationals; but there is no *duty* to do so." (paragraph 19, per Sir Richard Tucker).

38. To the above he added a citation from the judgment of Laws LJ in the matter of *Foday Saybana Sankoh* (119 ILR (2000) 389 at 396) where he described as a hopeless proposition that "the court should dictate to the executive government steps that it should take in the course of executing government foreign policy."

39. Mr Blake embarked with fervour on the task of persuading us that there were good reasons why the court should extend the boundaries of judicial review to embrace decisions as to the exercise of diplomacy where fundamental rights of British subjects were threatened in a foreign country. Public international law governed relations between states. It could not be expected to be in the van in imposing duties on individual States to protect their own subjects against violation of their human rights. There was, however, a growing recognition that international law could and should give rise to individual rights. This country should take the lead in recognising that the government owed a duty to British citizens to take appropriate steps to protect them against violation of their fundamental human rights by other countries.

40. Mr Blake started with the position under international law. The conventional view is that where a state intervenes by diplomatic action in aid of a subject who has been treated by another state in a manner which infringes international law, the injury that has been done is to the state and the right asserted is that of the state. Mr Blake drew our attention to recent developments of international law under which it has been recognised that the right infringed in such a case is that of the subject and the intervention of the state is in support of the right of its subject. It is only a short further step for the municipal law of a state to recognise a duty owed to the subject to intervene to protect the subject against the violation of the rights that he enjoys under international law.

41. Mr Blake referred us to the *First Report on Diplomatic Protection* by Professor Dugard, to which we have already referred. The Dugard Report proposed that a State should have legal duty (under general international law) "to exercise diplomatic protec-

tion on behalf of the injured [national] upon request, if the injury results from a grave breach of a jus cogens norm attributable to another State" (draft Article 4(1)). It suggested that such a duty (and the corresponding right of the national) should exist where the national was unable to bring a claim before a competent international court or tribunal. Mr Blake recognised that this proposal had not yet been accepted by all states parties (including the US and the UK). Indeed Professor Dugard himself had accepted that his proposal would not in fact go forward. He later said:

> "The Special Rapporteur recognised that he had introduced Article 4 *de lege ferenda*. As already indicated, the proposal enjoyed the support of certain writers, as well as some members of the Sixth Committee and of the International Law Association; it even formed part of some Constitutions. It was thus an exercise in the progressive development of international law. But the general view was that the issue was not yet ripe for the attention of the Commission and that there was a need for more state practice and, particularly, more *opinio juris* before it could be considered." (ILC Report, 2000, para. 456).

42. Mr Blake referred us, in addition, to an article by Professor Warbrick on Diplomatic Representations and Diplomatic Protection in (2002) 1 Ch 723. That article recognised, at p.724, the present position in English municipal law:

> "The government adheres to the orthodoxy of the 'Vattelian' fiction that diplomatic protection is the right of the State, that it is a right to claim for breaches of international law ... which affects its nationals. Whether or not to bring the claim, on what terms it is settled and the destination of the proceeds of any settlement are for the State alone to decide. This international perspective is replicated in domestic law, where the presentation of claims is an exercise of the foreign affairs prerogative, which, despite the advances in accountability for the exercise of prerogative powers in recent years, has remained outside the scope of judicial review."

43. Professor Warbrick went on, however, at p.733, to observe that German constitutional case law suggested that the state had a duty to protect German nationals and that South African writers had argued for a constitutional right to diplomatic protection. He then contemplated the possibility of such a right under English domestic law, at least in a situation where urgent intervention was required to prevent torture or similar gross ill-treatment.

> "What would be required of the English court is to identify a minimum obligation on the government to give an account of what steps it has taken by way of intervention and why, given the circumstances, it has not done more."

This was the minimum obligation that Mr Blake urged the court should recognise in the present case.

44. In this context Mr Blake drew attention to the 1963 Convention on Consular Relations, to which both this country and the United States are party. In the *La Grand case (Germany v United States)* 27 June 2001 the International Court of Justice held that Article 36 of this Convention created individual rights of detained persons to have consular access. Initially the applicants had sought to enforce such a right in these proceedings, but this remedy was not pursued before us. Mr Blake did, however, submit that this was a pertinent example of international law creating individual rights, to which effect should be given under domestic law.

45. Mr Blake also submitted that, as a matter of international law, the European Conven-

tion on Human Rights was capable of creating rights to seek diplomatic intervention on the part of a person in the position of Mr Abbasi. These submissions overlapped with submissions that the Human Rights Act should be so interpreted as to give rise to such rights under domestic law, and we shall consider them in that context, to which we now turn.

46. In answer to the case advanced by Mr Greenwood, Mr Blake submitted that the mere fact that the decision sought to be reviewed related to the exercise of prerogative power by the Foreign Office did not place a complete embargo on relief being obtained from the court. He referred to *ex parte Everett* [1989] 1 QB 811 relating to the issue of passports, and to *Lewis v A-G of Jamaica* [2001] 2 AC 50 a case concerned with the prerogative of mercy, where a procedural irregularity was held to be the subject of review. He, in his turn, relied on the *GCHQ* case where he pointed out that the court held that executive action was not immune from judicial review merely because it was carried out in pursuance of a power derived from a common law or prerogative, rather than a statutory source. This is an authority to which we will return.

47. Mr Blake then proceeded to develop his case as to why, on the facts of this case, the exercise of prerogative should be subject to judicial review. In essence his submissions were as follows: (i) a continuing and serious wrong was being done to Mr Abbasi, a British national, abroad; (ii) it was within the power of the Foreign and Commonwealth Office to make representations to the United States; (iii) those representations might bring the wrong to an end; (iv) the Foreign and Commonwealth Office had taken no relevant action, nor given any explanation for their failure; (v) in these circumstances judicial review should lie.

48. Mr Blake sought to derive assistance from the Human Rights Convention and the Human Rights Act, although once again he accepted that this required an extension of the existing jurisprudence. Article 1 of the Convention provides:

> "The High Contracting Parties shall secure to everyone *within their jurisdiction* the rights and freedoms defined in Section 1."

49. Section 6(1) of the Human Rights Act provides that it is unlawful for a public authority to act in a way which is incompatible with a Convention right. Mr Blake accepted that the applicants had to establish that Mr Abbasi was *within the jurisdiction* of the United Kingdom in order to invoke the Act and the Convention. He submitted however that this requirement was satisfied because, as Mr Abbasi was a British national, the United Kingdom government had *jurisdiction* to take measures in relation to him.

50. In support of this submission, Mr Blake relied on the reasoning of Stanley Burnton J. in *R (Carson) v Secretary of State for Employment and Pensions* (23rd May 2002), a case concerned with the pension rights of a British subject resident abroad. Mr Blake accepted that there was no Convention right to diplomatic protection, but argued that if there was a causal link between the failure to accord Mr Abbasi diplomatic protection and his continued arbitrary detention, then the Foreign and Commonwealth Office was acting in a way which was incompatible with Mr Abbasi's Convention right to liberty under Article 5 and was thus in breach of Section 6 of the Human Rights Act.

Discussion

Is the legitimacy of executive action taken by a foreign State justiciable?

51. A passage in the judgment of Lord Nicholls in *Kuwait Airways Corporation v Iraqi Airways Co (nos 4 and 5)* [2002] 2 WLR 1353 at p.1362 identifies the relevant principles and the limits to those principles:

> "24. On behalf of IAC Mr Donaldson submitted that the public policy exception to the recognition of provisions of foreign law is limited to infringements of human rights. The allegation in the present action is breach of international law by Iraq. But breach of international law by a state is not, and should not be, a ground for refusing to recognise a foreign decree. An English court will not sit in judgment on the sovereign acts of a foreign government or state. It will not adjudicate upon the legality, validity or acceptability of such acts, either under domestic law or international law. For a court to do so would offend against the principle that the courts will not adjudicate upon the transactions of foreign sovereign states. This principle is not discretionary. It is inherent in the very nature of the judicial process: see *Buttes Gas and Oil Co v Hammer (No 3)* [1982] AC 888, 932. KAC's argument, this submission by IAC continued, invites the court to determine whether the invasion of Kuwait by Iraq, followed by the removal of the ten aircraft from Kuwait to Iraq and their transfer to IAC, was unlawful under international law. The courts below were wrong to accede to this invitation.
>
> 25. My Lords, this submission seeks to press the non-justiciability principle too far. Undoubtedly there may be cases, of which the *Buttes* case is an illustration, where the issues are such that the court has, in the words of Lord Wilberforce, at p.938, "no judicial or manageable standards by which to judge [the] issues":
>
> > "the court would be asked to review transactions in which four sovereign states were involved, which they had brought to a precarious settlement, after diplomacy and the use of force, and to say that at least part of these were 'unlawful' under international law."
>
> This was Lord Wilberforce's conclusion regarding the important inter-state and other issues arising in that case: see his summary, at p.937.
>
> 26. This is not to say an English court is disabled from ever taking cognisance of international law or from ever considering whether a violation of international law has occurred. In appropriate circumstances it is legitimate for an English court to have regard to the content of international law in deciding whether to recognise a foreign law. Lord Wilberforce himself accepted this in the *Buttes* case, at p 931D. Nor does the "non-justiciable" principle mean that the judiciary must shut their eyes to a breach of an established principle of international law committed by one state against another when the breach is plain and, indeed, acknowledged. In such a case the adjudication problems confronting the English court in the *Buttes* litigation do not arise. The standard being applied by the court is clear and manageable, and the outcome not in doubt. That is the present case."

52. It is of interest to see to what Mr Donaldson was referring when he sought to limit the policy exception to the rule to the infringement of human rights. In *Oppenheim v Cattermole* [1976] AC 249 one issue that arose was whether a decree passed in Germany in 1941 depriving Jews who had emigrated from Germany of their citizenship should be recognised by the English court. Lord Cross of Chelsea at 277G said this:

"... if the decree had simply provided that all Germans who had left Germany since Hitler's advent to power with the intention of making their homes elsewhere should cease to be German nationals it may be that our courts would have had to recognise it even though many of those concerned were not in truth voluntary emigrants but had been driven from their native land. But the 1941 decree did not deprive all "émigrés: of their status as German nationals. It only deprived Jewish émigrés of their citizenship. Further, as the later paragraphs of the decree show, this discriminatory withdrawal of their rights of citizenship was used as a peg upon which to hang a discriminatory confiscation of their property. A judge should, of course, be very slow to refuse to give effect to the legislation of a foreign state in any sphere in which, according to accepted principles of international law, the foreign state has jurisdiction. He may well have an inadequate understanding of the circumstances in which the legislation was passed and his refusal to recognise it may be embarrassing to the branch of the executive which is concerned to maintain friendly relations between this country and the foreign country in question. But I think – as Upjohn J thought (see *In re Claim by Herbert Wagg & Co Ltd* [1956] Ch. 323, 334) – that it is part of the public policy of this country that our courts should give effect to clearly established rules of international law. Of course on some points it may be by no means clear what the rule of international law is. Whether, for example, legislation of a particular type is contrary to international law because it is "confiscatory" is a question upon which there may well be wide differences of opinion between communist and capitalist countries. But what we are concerned with here is legislation which takes away without compensation from a section of the citizen body singled out on racial grounds all their property on which the state passing the legislation can lay its hands and, in addition, deprives them of their citizenship. To my mind a law of this sort constitutes so grave an infringement of human rights that the courts of this country ought to refuse to recognise it as a law at all."

53. This passage lends support to Mr Blake's thesis that, where fundamental human rights are in play, the courts of this country will not abstain from reviewing the legitimacy of the actions of a foreign sovereign state. A more topical support for this proposition can be can be derived from the exercise that the court has to undertake in asylum cases, where the issue is often whether the applicant for asylum has a well-founded fear of persecution if removed to a third country. In such circumstances consideration of the claim for asylum frequently involves ruling on allegations that a foreign state is acting in breach of international law or human rights.

54. In *R v Home Secretary, ex parte Adan* [2001] 2 WLR 143 the issue was raised of whether the courts of this country should entertain a contention that the courts of France and Germany were mis-applying the Refugee Convention. That case was concerned with certificates issued pursuant to s.2 of the Asylum and Immigration Act 1996.

55. The United Kingdom took the view that under Article 1A(2) of the Refugee Convention protection extended to asylum seekers who feared persecution by persons other than the state if for any reason the state could not protect them against such persecution. France and Germany were known to interpret that Article more narrowly. The United Kingdom accepted that two asylum seekers, Adan and Aitsegeur should not be returned to Somalia having regard to the United Kingdom's interpretation, but the Se-

cretary of State had been prepared to certify in relation to their return to Germany and France respectively under s.2(3) of the Act, that those countries would not send them to another country "other than in accordance with the Convention". The House of Lords held first that there was one autonomous meaning of the Convention which was that adopted by the United Kingdom, and that the Secretary of State was not entitled to certify as he did on the basis that there were other legitimate interpretations in relation to which Germany and France should be left to take their own view. One point taken by Mr Pannick QC, for the Secretary of State in that case, was that:

> "having regard to the principle of comity under which the courts of one country are very slow to adjudicate upon the actions or decisions of another country or its courts acting within the territory of that country, Parliament could not have intended that the Secretary of State or the courts of this country might, in effect, have to make a decision that an action by the German or French governments or a ruling of a German or French court was wrong in law."

56. This comity point was dealt with by Lord Slynn at p.147; Lord Steyn at pp.155/6, Lord Hutton at p.163 and Lord Hobhouse at pp.167/8. They rejected the submission. In essence their reasoning was that what the court was concerned with was the United Kingdom's obligation under the Convention as interpreted by the United Kingdom, and the Secretary of State's obligation under the Statute. Lord Steyn put it this way:

> "Fifthly, counsel for the Secretary of State raised a matter which did cause me concern at one stage, namely whether the view I have adopted contains an implicit criticism of the judicial departments of Germany and France. I certainly intend no criticism of the interpretations adopted in good faith in Germany and France. Unanimity on all perplexing problems created by multilateral treaties is unachievable. National courts can only do their best to minimise the disagreements. But ultimately they have no choice but to apply what they consider to be the autonomous meaning. Here the difference is fundamental and cannot be overcome by a form of words. The House is bound to take into account the obligations of the United Kingdom Government and to apply the terms of section 2(2)(c) of the 1996 Act."

57. Although the statutory context in which *Adan* was decided was highly material, the passage from Lord Cross' speech in *Cattermole* supports the view that, albeit that caution must be exercised by this court when faced with an allegation that a foreign state is in breach of its international obligations, this court does not need the statutory context in order to be free to express a view in relation to what it conceives to be a clear breach of international law, particularly in the context of human rights.

Our view of Mr Abbasi's predicament

58. Mr Blake has founded his case upon Mr Abbasi's predicament as it currently appears. If the decision of the District Court of Columbia accurately represents the law of the United States, then the United States executive is detaining Mr Abbasi on territory over which it has total control in circumstances where Mr Abbasi can make no challenge to his detention before any court or tribunal. How long this state of affairs continues is within the sole control of the United States executive. Mr Blake contends that this constitutes arbitrary detention contrary to the fundamental norms of international law. It is not the fact that Mr Abbasi is detained on which Mr Blake relies – it is the fact that

Mr Abbasi has no means of challenging the legality of his detention. It is this predicament which, so Mr Blake contends, gives rise to a duty on the part of the Foreign Secretary to come to Mr Abbasi's assistance. That assistance is claimed as a matter of last resort. We do not consider that we can deal satisfactorily with this appeal without addressing those submissions and we consider, in the light of the jurisprudence discussed above, that it is open to us to do so.

59. The United Kingdom and the United States share a great legal tradition, founded in the English common law. One of the cornerstones of that tradition is the ancient writ of habeas corpus, recognised at least by the time of Edward I, and developed by the 17th Century into "the most efficient protection yet developed for the liberty of the subject" (per Lord Evershed MR, *Ex p Mwenya* [1960] 1 QB 241, 292, citing Holdsworth's History of English Law, vol 9 pp.108-125). The court's jurisdiction was recognised from early times as extending to any part of the Crown's dominions:

> "for the King is at all times entitled to have an account why the liberty of any of his subjects is restrained wherever that restraint is inflicted"

(Blackstone, Commentaries (1768) vol 3 p.131, cited by Lord Evershed MR, *ibid*, p.292; see also the recent review of the authorities by Laws LJ, *R (Bancoult) v Foreign Secretary* [2001] 2 WLR 1219, 1236).

60. The underlying principle, fundamental in English law, is that every imprisonment is prima facie unlawful, and that:

> "... no member of the executive can interfere with the liberty ... of a British subject except on the condition that he can support the legality of his action before a court of justice" (*R v Home Secretary ex p Khawaja* [1984] 1 AC 74, 110, per Lord Scarman; citing the classic dissenting judgment of Lord Atkin in *Liversidge v Anderson* [1942] AC 206, 245 and Eshugbayi Eleko v Government of Nigeria [1931] AC 662, 670).

This principle applies to every person, British citizen or not, who finds himself within the jurisdiction of the court: "He who is subject to English law is entitled to its protection." (per Lord Scarman, *ibid* p.111). It applies in war as in peace; in Lord Atkin's words (written in one of the darkest periods of the last war):

> "In this country, amid the clash of arms, the laws are not silent. They may be changed, but they speak the same language in war as in peace." (*Liversidge v Anderson* [1942] AC 206, 245 at p.244)

61. As one would expect, endorsement of this common tradition is no less strong in the United States. In *Fay v Noia* (1963) 372 US 391, 400, Justice Brennan referred to:

> "the 'extraordinary prestige' of the Great Writ, *habeas corpus ad subjiciendum*, in Anglo-American jurisprudence ... It is 'a writ antecedent to statute, and throwing its root deep into the genius of our common law ... It is perhaps the most important writ known to the constitutional law of England, affording as it does a swift remedy in all cases of illegal restraint or confinement ...'" (adopting the words of Lord Birkenhead LC, in *Secretary of State v O'Brien* [1923] AC 603, 609).

62. Like Lord Atkin, he emphasised its importance in times of national emergency:

> "It is no accident that habeas corpus has time and again played a central role in national crises, wherein the claims of order and liberty clash most acutely, not only in England in the 17th Century, but also in America from our very beginnings and today." (*ibid* p.401)

63. The recognition of this basic protection in both English and American law long pre-

dates the adoption of the same principle as a fundamental part of international human rights law. Of the many source documents to which we have been referred, it is enough to cite the International Covenant of Civil and Political Rights, to which the United Kingdom and the United States are parties. Article 9, which affirms "the right to liberty and security of person" provides:

"4. Anyone who is deprived of his liberty by arrest or detention shall be entitled to take proceedings before a court, in order that a court may decide without delay on the lawfulness of his detention and order his release if the detention is not lawful."

By Article 2, each state party undertakes to

"ensure to all individuals within its territory and subject to its jurisdiction" the rights recognised by the Covenant "without distinction of any kind, such as ... national origin ..."

64. For these reasons we do not find it possible to approach this claim for judicial review other than on the basis that, in apparent contravention of fundamental principles recognised by both jurisdictions and by international law, Mr Abbasi is at present arbitrarily detained in a 'legal black-hole'.

65. That is not to say that his detention as an alleged "enemy combatant" may not be justified. This court has very recently had occasion to consider the legitimacy of legislation that empowers the Secretary of State to detain within this jurisdiction aliens who are suspected of being international terrorists – *A, X and Y and Others v Secretary of State for the Home Department [2002] EWCA Civ 1502*. We would endorse the summary of the position under international law of Brooke LJ at paragraph 130:

"What emerges from the efforts of the international community to introduce orderly arrangements for controlling the power of detention of non-nationals is a distinct movement away from the doctrine of the inherent power of the state to control the treatment of non-nationals within its borders as it will towards a regime, founded on modern international human rights norms, which is infused by the principle that any measures that are restrictive of liberty, whether they relate to nationals or non-nationals, must be such as are prescribed by law and necessary in a democratic society. The state's power to detain must be related to a recognised object and purpose, and there must be a reasonable relationship of proportionality between the end and the means. On the other hand, both customary international law and the international treaties by which this country is bound expressly reserve the power of a state in time of war or similar public emergency to detain aliens on grounds of national security when it would not necessarily detain its own nationals on those grounds."

These comments can be applied with equal force to those suspected of having taken part in military operations involving terrorist organisations.

66. What appears to us to be objectionable is that Mr Abbasi should be subject to indefinite detention in territory over which the United States has exclusive control with no opportunity to challenge the legitimacy of his detention before any court or tribunal. It is important to record that the position may change when the appellate courts in the United States consider the matter. The question for us is what attitude should the courts in England take pending review by the appellate courts in the United States, to a detention of a British Citizen the legality of which rests (so the decisions of the United States Courts so far suggest) solely on the dictate of the United States Government, and, unlike that of United States' citizens, is said to be immune from review in any court or

independent forum.

67. It is clear that there can be no direct remedy in this court. The United States Government is not before the court, and no order of this court would be binding upon it. Conversely, the United Kingdom Government, which, through the Secretaries of State is the respondent to these proceedings, has no direct responsibility for the detention. Nor is it suggested that it has any enforceable right, or even standing, before any domestic or international tribunal to represent the rights of the applicant, or compel access to a court.

Is the conduct of the Secretary of State justiciable?

68. Mr Blake submitted that we should find that the Foreign Secretary owed Mr Abbasi a duty to respond positively to his, and his mother's, request for diplomatic assistance. He founded this submission on (i) the assertion that international law is moving towards the recognition of such a duty and that customary international law forms part of our common law; (ii) the alleged recognition of such a duty under the constitutions of Germany and, possibly, other states; (iii) the assertion that such a duty arises under the Human Rights Convention together with the Human Rights Act. It is convenient to deal with this last point first.

69. It is clear that international law has not yet recognised that a State is under a duty to intervene by diplomatic or other means to protect a citizen who is suffering or threatened with injury in a foreign State. This emerges clearly from the passage from the *Barcelona Traction case* which we have cited at paragraph 35 above, and from the concession made by Professor Dugard to which we have referred at paragraph 41. Mr Blake accepted this to be the case, but suggested that our municipal law should lead so that international law may follow. In these circumstances it does not seem to us that Mr Blake can derive any assistance from established principles of international law.

70. We turn to Mr Blake's reliance on the European Convention on Human Rights and the Human Rights Act. Section 2 of the Act requires us to take into account any relevant decisions of the Strasbourg Court. There are two recent decisions which are particularly in point. In *Al-Adsani v United Kingdom* (2002) 34 EHRR 11 the applicant, who had joint British and Kuwaiti citizenship, wished to pursue proceedings in England against the Government of Kuwait in respect of torture, to which he alleged he had been subjected in Kuwait. He was unable to do so by reasons of the provisions of the State Immunity Act 1978. He alleged before the Strasbourg court that this immunity violated Article 3 of the Convention, when read in conjunction with Articles 1 and 13. In dealing with the question of whether the torture had been committed within the jurisdiction of the United Kingdom the Court said:

> "In the above-mentioned *Soering* case the Court recognised that Article 3 has some, limited, extraterritorial application, to the extent that the decision by a Contracting State to expel an individual might engage the responsibility of that State under the Convention, where substantial grounds had been shown for believing that the person concerned, if expelled, faced a real risk of being subjected to torture or to inhuman or degrading treatment or punishment in the receiving country. In the judgment it was emphasised, however, that insofar as any liability under the Convention might be incurred in such circumstances, it would be incurred by the

expelling Contracting State by reason of its having taken action which had as a direct consequence the exposure of an individual to proscribed ill-treatment.

The applicant does not contend that the alleged torture took place within the jurisdiction of the United Kingdom or that the United Kingdom authorities had any causal connection with its occurrence. In these circumstances, it cannot be said that the High Contracting Party was under a duty to provide a civil remedy to the applicant in respect of torture allegedly carried out by the Kuwaiti authorities."

71. This passage demonstrates (i) that the concept of *jurisdiction* under Article 1 of the Convention is essentially territorial, but (ii) that acts within the territory of the United Kingdom that cause an individual to suffer violation of his human rights outside the territory may infringe the Convention. It is a considerable extension of that principle to postulate that the Convention requires a state to take positive action to prevent, or mitigate the effects of, violations of human rights that take place outside the jurisdiction and for which the state has no responsibility.

72. In *Bankovic and Others v Belgium and Others* (App. No. 52207/99) [11 BHRC 435] citizens of the Federal Republic of Yugoslavia ('FRY') sought to complain to the Strasbourg Court that deaths and injuries caused by air strikes carried out by members of Nato in the course of the conflict in Kosovo violated, among others, Article 2 of the Convention. The respondent governments contended that the applicants and their deceased relatives were not at the material time within their jurisdictions, within the meaning of Article 1. The applicants argued that the very act of carrying out the air strikes was an assertion of effective control, which brought the applicants within the jurisdiction of those carrying out the strikes. They further argued that the decision to carry out the air-strikes had been taken within the territories of the respondent governments, so that the principle in *Soering v UK* [1989] ECHR 14038/88 was applicable.

73. As to the latter point the Court noted at paragraph 68 that:

"...liability is incurred in such cases by an action of the respondent state concerning a person while he or she is on its territory, clearly within its jurisdiction, and that such cases do not concern the actual exercise of a state's competence or jurisdiction abroad."

As to the former point, the Court held that the argument was inconsistent with the terms of Article 1 of the Convention.

74. The conclusions of the Court were encapsulated in this sentence from paragraph 61 of the judgment:

"The court is of the view, therefore, that article 1 of the convention must be considered to reflect this ordinary and essentially territorial notion of jurisdiction, other bases of jurisdiction being exceptional and requiring special justification in the particular circumstances of each case."

75. In paragraphs 71 and 73 the Court had this to say about the circumstances in which the exercise of an extra-territorial jurisdiction would bring an act within the ambit of the Convention:

"In sum, the case law of the court demonstrates that its recognition of the exercise of extra-territorial jurisdiction by a contracting state is exceptional: it has done so when the respondent state, through the effective control of the relevant territory and its inhabitants abroad as a consequence of military occupation or through the consent, invitation or acquiescence of the government of that territory, exercises all or some of the public powers normally to be exercised by that government.

...

Additionally, the court notes that other recognised instances of the extra-territorial exercise of jurisdiction by a state include cases involving the activities of its diplomatic or consular agents abroad and on board craft and vessels registered in, or flying the flag of, that state. In these specific situations, customary international law and treaty provisions have recognised the extra-territorial exercise of jurisdiction by the relevant state."

76. We derive the following principles from the decisions considered above:

i. The jurisdiction referred to in Article 1 of the Convention will normally be territorial jurisdiction.

ii. Where a State enjoys effective control of foreign territory, that territory will fall within its jurisdiction for the purposes of Article 1.

iii. Where, under principles of international law, a state enjoys extra-territorial jurisdiction over an individual and acts in the exercise of that jurisdiction, that individual will be deemed to be within the jurisdiction of the state for the purposes of Article 1, insofar as the action in question is concerned.

77. These principles come nowhere near rendering Mr Abbasi within the jurisdiction of the United Kingdom for the purposes of Article 1 on the simple ground that every state enjoys a degree of authority over its own nationals. Mr Blake has not identified any relevant control or authority exercised by the United Kingdom over Mr Abbasi in his present predicament. Nor has he identified any act of the United Kingdom government of which complaint can be made that it violates Mr Abbasi's human rights.

78. Finally in this context we should refer to the decision of the Commission in *Bertrand Russell Peace Foundation v United Kingdom* (2 May 1978). The applicant, which was unquestionably within the jurisdiction of the United Kingdom, complained of the failure by the British postal authorities to make representations to the Soviet authorities in respect of the interception and destruction of mail sent by the applicant to Russia. The applicant alleged that this failure violated Articles 8 and 10 of the Convention. The Commission held that the application was not admissible. The following passages from its judgment are material:

"In this respect the Commission observes that no right to diplomatic protection or other such measures by a High Contracting Party on behalf of persons within its jurisdiction is as such guaranteed by the Convention. The question nevertheless remains whether any right to diplomatic or other intervention vis-à-vis a third state, which by action within its own territory has interfered with the Convention rights of a person "within the jurisdiction" of a Contracting State, can be inferred from the obligation imposed on the Contracting State by Article 1 of the Convention to "secure" that person's rights.

Having considered the parties' submissions the Commission has come to the conclusion that no such right can be inferred from Article 1 of the Convention, in conjunction in particular with articles 8 and 10 of the Convention which are invoked in the present case, reaching this conclusion it has particularly taken into account the general arguments put forward by the respondent Government as to the implications of accepting such an interpretation of the Convention. In Particular it does not consider that Article 1 of the Convention can, consistently with the generally recognised principle set forth in Article 34 of the Vienna Convention on the Law of Treaties, be interpreted so as to give rise to any obligation on the Contracting Parties to secure that non-contracting states, acting within their own juris-diction, respect the rights and freedoms guaranteed by the Convention, even though, as in the present case, their failure to do so may have adverse effects on persons within the jurisdiction of the Contracting State. It has therefore concluded that, as the respondent Government have submitted, the act or omission forming the substantive basis of the alleged violation of the Convention must be one falling within the jurisdiction of the Contracting State, at least in the sense that it consti-tutes an exercise of "jurisdiction" by that state or a failure to exercise lawful jur-isdiction in the sense of sovereign power. It is not sufficient that the "victim" alone is within that state's jurisdiction. Accordingly, even though, as the applicant points out, Article 10 of the Convention guarantees the right to receive and impart infor-mation "regardless of frontiers", this does not imply any right to intervention in respect of the acts of a non-contracting state for which the Contracting State is in no way responsible. It implies merely that the Contracting State must, in the ex-ercise of its jurisdiction, itself respect this right."

While this is a decision of relative antiquity, we are not aware of any more recent Strasbourg jurisprudence that throws doubt on it. The principles that it enunciates are fatal to this limb of the applicants' argument.

79. For these reasons we do not consider that the European Convention on Human Rights and the Human Rights Act afford any support to the contention that the Foreign Secre-tary owes Mr Abbasi a duty to exercise diplomacy on his behalf.

80. If Mr Blake is unable to demonstrate that, either through the incorporation of interna-tional law or under the Human Rights Act, Mr Abbasi enjoys a right to diplomatic assistance under our domestic law, do the authorities relied upon by Mr Greenwood close the door to any possibility of establishing such a right by way, as Mr Blake would contend, of a beneficial development of our public law? The authorities relied upon by Mr Greenwood, of which we have cited relevant passages at paragraphs 37 and 38 above, are powerful indeed. There are, however, three considerations which have led us to reject the proposition that there is no scope for judicial review of a refusal to render diplomatic assistance to a British subject who is suffering violation of a funda-mental human right as the result of the conduct of the authorities of a foreign state.

81. The first consideration is the development of the law of judicial review in relation (i) to the doctrine of legitimate expectation and (ii) to the invasion of areas previously im-mune from review, such as the exercise of the prerogative.

82. As to the first, under the modern law of judicial review, the doctrine of "legitimate expectation" provides a well-established and flexible means for giving legal effect to a settled policy or practice for the exercise of an administrative discretion. The expecta-tion may arise from an express promise or "from the existence of a regular practice which the claimant can reasonably expect to continue", per Lord Fraser, *Council of Civil Service Unions v Minister for Civil Service* [1985] AC 374, 401; and see de Smith, Judicial Review 5th Ed p. 419 ff. The expectation is not that the policy or prac-tice will necessarily remain unchanged, or, if unchanged, that it will not be overridden by other policy considerations. However, so long as it remains unchanged, the subject is entitled to have it properly taken into account in considering his individual case; see de Smith pp. 574-5, citing *Re Findlay* [1985] AC 318, 388, per Lord Scarman.

83. For the second development, it is necessary to refer to the landmark decision in *Coun-cil of Civil Service Unions -v- Minister for the Civil Service* [1985] AC 374 (the

'*GCHQ*' case), which established that the mere fact that a power derived from the Royal Prerogative did not necessarily exclude it from the scope of judicial review. The House of Lords did, however, accept that there were certain areas which remain outside the area of justiciability. Thus, at p.398, Lord Fraser referred to:

> "many of the most important prerogative powers concerned with control of the armed forces and with foreign policy and with other matters which are unsuitable for discussion or review in the Law Courts"

84. Lord Scarman said, at p.407, that the controlling factor in considering whether a particular exercise of prerogative power was subject to review was "not its source but its subject matter." Lord Diplock, at p.411, expanded on the categories of prerogative decision which remained unsuitable for judicial review:

> "Such decisions will generally involve the application of Government policy. The reasons for the decision-maker taking one course rather than another do not normally involve questions to which, if disputed, the judicial process is adapted to provide the right answer, by which I mean that the kind of evidence that is admissible under judicial procedures and the way in which it has to be adduced tend to exclude from the attention of the court competing policy considerations which, if the Executive discretion is to be wisely exercised, need to weighed against one another – a balancing exercise which judges by their upbringing and experience are ill-qualified to perform."

85. Those extracts indicate that the issue of justiciability depends, not on general principle, but on subject matter and suitability in the particular case. That is illustrated by the subsequent case of *R -v- Foreign Secretary ex p. Everett* [1989] 1QB 811. This court held, following the *GCHQ* case, that a decision taken under the prerogative whether or not to issue a passport was subject to judicial review, although relief was refused on the facts of that particular case. Lord Justice Taylor, at p.820, summarised the effect of the *GCHQ* case as making clear that the powers of the court "cannot be ousted merely by invoking the word 'prerogative'":

> "The majority of their Lordships indicated that whether judicial review of the exercise of a prerogative power is open depends upon the subject matter and in particular whether it is justiciable. At the top of the scale of executive functions under the Prerogative are matters of high policy, of which examples were given by their Lordships; making treaties, making war, dissolving parliament, mobilising the armed forces. Clearly those matters and no doubt a number of others are not justiciable but the grant or refusal of a passport is in a quite different category. It is a matter of administrative decision affecting the right of individuals and their freedom of travel. It raises issues which are just as justiciable as, for example, the issues arising in immigration cases."

86. The interaction of these two developments in the law of judicial review can be seen in *R -v- Home Secretary ex p. Ahmed and Patel* [1998] INLR 570. The applicants were illegal immigrants who had married persons with indefinite leave to remain in the UK and had children in the UK. In support of their applications for leave to remain on the basis of their marriages, they relied on legitimate expectations created by the UK's ratification of two international conventions relating to the rights of the child and of the family. Lord Woolf MR accepted that in principle a legitimate expectation could be created by the State's act in entering into a treaty. He relied, at p.584, on the approach of the High Court of Australia in *Minister for Immigration -v- Teoh* [1995] 183 CLR 273:

"...Ratification of a convention is a positive statement by the Executive Government of this country to the world and the Australian people that the Executive Government and its agencies will act in accordance with convention that positive statement is an adequate foundation for a legitimate expectation, *absent statutory or executive indications to the contrary*, that administrators will act in conformity with the Convention..." (p.291, per Mason CJ and Deane J – Lord Woolf's emphasis).

At p.592 Hobhouse LJ also accepted the approach of the Australian case, but emphasised that where the Secretary of State had adopted a specific policy, as he had in the instant case, it was not possible to derive any expectation from the treaty going beyond the scope of the policy.

87. The second consideration is that, to a degree, the Foreign and Commonwealth Office have promulgated a policy which, so it seems to us, is capable of giving rise to a legitimate expectation.

88. The practice of the United Kingdom Government in respect of diplomatic protection was explained in 1999, in comments presented to the United Nations General Assembly, as part of the discussion of a report of the International Law Commission (reproduced in British Yearbook of International Law 1999 at p.526). Under the heading "Diplomatic protection: United Kingdom Practice", the paper notes that this is a matter "falling within the prerogative of the Crown" and that "there is no general legislation or case law governing this area in domestic law". It distinguishes between "formal claims" and "informal representations".

89. In relation to formal claims, "a considered statement of the Government's policy" is contained in "rules" issued by the Foreign Office, based on "general principles of customary international law". It is said, citing *Mutasa v Attorney General* [1980] 1 QB 114 (see below), that the rules are "a statement of general policy and have no direct effect in domestic law". We have been shown the current version of the rules (reproduced in (1988) 37 ICLQ p.1006). It is not suggested that any are directly relevant to this case, but we note rule VIII, which provides:

> "If, in exhausting any municipal remedies, the claimant has met with prejudice or obstruction, which are a denial of justice, HMG may intervene on his behalf in order to secure justice."

90. In relation to informal representations, the 1999 British Year Book of International Law records two further Ministerial statements of policy. The first refers to a "review of our policy" on making such representations about convictions and sentencing of British prisoners abroad:

> "At present we consider making representations if, when all legal remedies have been exhausted, the British national and their lawyer have evidence of a miscarriage or denial of justice. We are extending this to cases where fundamental violations of the British national's human rights had demonstrably altered the course of justice. In such cases, we would consider supporting their request for an appeal to any official human rights body in the country concerned, and subsequently giving advice on how to take their cases to relevant international human rights mechanisms."

91. This review was further explained in a Parliamentary Answer on 16th December 1999 by Baroness Scotland. Having referred to the revised policy, she said:

"We are very conscious of the other government's obligations to ensure the respect of the rights of British citizens within their jurisdiction. This includes the right to a fair trial. In cases where a British citizen may have suffered a miscarriage of justice we believe that the most appropriate course of action is for the defendant's lawyers to take action through the local courts. If concerns remain, their lawyers can take the case to the United Nations Human Rights Committee, where the State in question has accepted the right of individual petition under the ICCPR. *The UK Government would also consider making direct representations to third governments on behalf of British citizens where we believe that they were in breach of their international obligations.*" (emphasis added)

92. Taken together, these statements indicate a clear acceptance by the government of a role in relation to protecting the rights of British citizens abroad, where there is evidence of miscarriage or denial of justice. In the present case none of the avenues suggested in the last quotation is available. The words emphasised contain no more than a commitment "to consider" making representations, which will be triggered by the "belief" that there is a breach of the international obligations. This seems to imply that such consideration will at least start from a formulated view as to whether there is such a breach, and as to the gravity of the resulting denial of rights.

93. The traditional view, repeated in the comments to the General Assembly, is that the practice reflected in these statements has no effect or relevance in domestic law, but we are not persuaded that this is correct. In this context it is relevant to give further consideration to *Butt,* a decision upon which, as we observed at paragraph 37, Mr Greenwood relied. In that case the applicant sought an order that the Foreign and Commonwealth Office should make representations to the President of the Yemen that a flawed criminal trial in progress in the Yemen should be halted and a retrial ordered before the verdict was given. In the leading judgment in the Court of Appeal Henry LJ recorded the following concession by the Secretary of State:

"Much has been done for those who are on trial. This is because, as is accepted by the Secretary of State before us, there lies on the respondent a common law duty to protect its citizens abroad. The extent and the limits of that duty are set out in a leaflet that is available for those who travel abroad."

94. The leaflet referred to was one of two, which set out the assistance to be expected by British subjects abroad from a British consul. These expressly excluded intervention in a criminal trial, which was fatal to the application. But it seems to us that, in the light of the concession made by the Secretary of State it would have been difficult, in that case at least, for him to have denied that there was a legitimate expectation that such assistance as was proffered in the leaflets would be provided.

95. The published government policy in relation to consular assistance has no direct relevance to Mr Abbasi's case. We shall revert to the extent of any legitimate expectation in a case such as his after we have referred to the third consideration which weighs in favour of the possibility of judicial review.

96. In *Al Adsani v United Kingdom* the Government contended, as recorded at paragraph 50, that:

"There were other, traditional means of redress for wrongs of this kind available to the applicant, namely diplomatic representations or an inter-State claim."

97. In *Rasul* the United States District Court expressed the "serious concern" that the court's decision would leave the prisoners without any rights, and recorded the gov-

ernment's recognition that:

> "these aliens fall within the protections of certain provisions of international law and that diplomatic channels remain an ongoing and viable means to address the claims raised by these aliens." (p.2)

98. These statements reflect the fact that, to use the words of *Everett,* it must be a 'normal expectation of every citizen' that, if subjected abroad to a violation of a fundamental right, the British Government will not simply wash their hands of the matter and abandon him to his fate.

99. What then is the nature of the expectation that a British subject in the position of Mr Abbasi can legitimately hold in relation to the response of the government to a request for assistance? The policy statements that we have cited underline the very limited nature of the expectation. They indicate that where certain criteria are satisfied, the government will "consider" making representations. Whether to make any representations in a particular case, and if so in what form, is left entirely to the discretion of the Secretary of State. That gives free play to the "balance" to which Lord Diplock referred in *GCHQ.* The Secretary of State must be free to give full weight to foreign policy considerations, which are not justiciable. However, that does not mean the whole process is immune from judicial scrutiny. The citizen's legitimate expectation is that his request will be "considered", and that in that consideration all relevant factors will be thrown into the balance.

100. One vital factor, as the policy recognises, is the nature and extent of the injustice, which he claims to have suffered. Even where there has been a gross miscarriage of justice, there may perhaps be overriding reasons of foreign policy which may lead the Secretary of State to decline to intervene. However, unless and until he has formed some judgment as to the gravity of the miscarriage, it is impossible for that balance to be properly conducted.

101. Although Mr Blake did not rest his case on "legitimate expectation", the position as it emerges from the authorities to which we have referred seems very close to what he was ultimately contending should be the content of the "duty" which he asserts. As he said in his reply: –

> "The claimants are not seeking relief against the US Government and nor are they seeking to dictate to the Executive how it should conduct foreign policy and by what means; they are merely stating their case why the Government should intervene with another foreign sovereign state".

Orally he made clear what he wanted was the case considered by the Foreign and Commonwealth Office.

102. The width of discretion enjoyed by the executive in this field is exemplified by the decision of the German Federal Constitutional Court in the case of *Rudolph Hess* (Case number 2 BVR4 19/80), 90 ILR 386, on which Mr Blake relied as supporting a "duty" of diplomatic protection. That concerned an application by Rudolph Hess for the Federal Republic to take diplomatic steps to secure his release on compassionate grounds, some twenty years after his imprisonment by the International Military Tribunal following the War. The court accepted that the Federal Republic were under a constitutional duty to provide diplomatic protection to German nationals, but said that the government enjoyed "wide discretion in deciding whether and in what manner to grant such protection in each case". It had to be left to the government to assess the foreign policy considerations, from the standpoint of both the interests of the Federal

Republic and those of Hess, and decide on that basis how far further steps were appropriate or necessary.

103. The court rejected the application in that case, because it could not be said that the government had in any way abused its wide discretion. It is noteworthy that the court rejected the suggestion that the government should have done more to object to the detention on legal grounds, accepting that it was open to the Federal Government to consider that "the political significance of the decisions at issue was essentially more important than the effect of legal arguments on the position of the occupying powers" (pp.396-397). However, it was not suggested that the legal arguments could be ignored altogether.

104. The extreme case where judicial review would lie in relation to diplomatic protection would be if the Foreign and Commonwealth Office were, contrary to its stated practice, to refuse even to consider whether to make diplomatic representations on behalf of a subject whose fundamental rights were being violated. In such, unlikely, circumstances we consider that it would be appropriate for the court to make a mandatory order to the Foreign Secretary to give due consideration to the applicant's case.

105. Beyond this we do not believe it is possible to make general propositions. In some cases it might be reasonable to expect the Secretary of State to state the result of considering a request for assistance, in others it might not. In some cases he might be expected to give reasons for his decision, in others he might not. In some cases such reasons might be open to attack, in others they would not.

106. We would summarise our views as to what the authorities establish as follows:

i. It is not an answer to a claim for judicial review to say that the source of the power of the Foreign Office is the prerogative. It is the subject matter that is determinative.

ii. Despite extensive citation of authority there is nothing which supports the imposition of an enforceable duty to protect the citizen. The European Convention on Human Rights does not impose any such duty. Its incorporation into the municipal law cannot therefore found a sound basis on which to reconsider the authorities binding on this court.

iii. However the Foreign Office has discretion whether to exercise the right, which it undoubtedly has, to protect British citizens. It has indicated in the ways explained what a British citizen may expect of it. The expectations are limited and the discretion is a very wide one but there is no reason why its decision or inaction should not be reviewable if it can be shown that the same were irrational or contrary to legitimate expectation; but the court cannot enter the forbidden areas, including decisions affecting foreign policy.

iv. It is highly likely that any decision of the Foreign and Commonwealth Office, as to whether to make representations on a diplomatic level, will be intimately connected with decisions relating to this country's foreign policy, but an obligation to consider the position of a particular British citizen and consider the extent to which some action might be taken on his behalf, would seem unlikely itself to impinge on any forbidden area.

v. The extent to which it may be possible to require more than that the Foreign Secretary give due consideration to a request for assistance will depend on the facts of the particular case.

Are the applicants entitled to relief in the present case?

107. We have made clear our deep concern that, in apparent contravention of fundamental principles of law, Mr Abbasi may be subject to indefinite detention in territory over which the United States has exclusive control with no opportunity to challenge the legitimacy of his detention before any court or tribunal. However, there are a number of reasons why we consider that the applicants' claim to relief must be rejected:

> i. It is quite clear from Mr Fry's evidence that the Foreign and Commonwealth Office have considered Mr Abbasi's request for assistance. He has also disclosed that the British detainees are the subject of discussions between this country and the United States both at Secretary of State and lower official levels. We do not consider that Mr Abbasi could reasonably expect more than this. In particular, if the Foreign and Commonwealth Office were to make any statement as to its view of the legality of the detention of the British prisoners, or any statement as to the nature of discussions held with United States officials, this might well undermine those discussions.

> ii. On no view would it be appropriate to order the Secretary of State to make any specific representations to the United States, even in the face of what appears to be a clear breach of a fundamental human right, as it is obvious that this would have an impact on the conduct of foreign policy, and an impact on such policy at a particularly delicate time.

> iii. The position of detainees at Guantanamo Bay is to be considered further by the appellate courts in the United States. It may be that the anxiety that we have expressed will be drawn to their attention. We wish to make it clear that we are only expressing an anxiety that we believe was felt by the court in *Rasul*. As is clear from our judgment, we believe that the United States courts have the same respect for human rights as our own.

> iv. The Inter-American Commission on Human Rights has taken up the case of the detainees. It is as yet unclear what the result of the Commission's intervention will be. It is not clear that any activity on the part of the Foreign and Commonwealth Office would assist in taking the matter further while it is in the hands of that international body.

108. For all these reasons the application before us must be dismissed.

4.1   METHODS AND MEANS OF WARFARE

☞ **USA: DoD News Briefing – Secretary Rumsfeld, Secretary of Defense and General Myers, Chairman of the Joint Chiefs of Staff, 12 February 2002**

Rumsfeld: Greetings. Good morning. I have a brief comment, and then General Myers has some remarks. As a country, we've lost thousands of innocent civilians on September 11th, and certainly our country and the people of our country understand what it means to lose fathers and mothers, and sons and daughters, and brothers and sisters. I think it's useful to remind ourselves that the Taliban and the al Qaeda made a practice of doing harm and repressing the Afghan people. The Afghan people were starved in some measure because the Taliban and al Qaeda stole humanitarian food aid and kept it from them. There was a refugee crisis in the country with internally dislocated people, as well as large camps external to the country. They purposefully used women and children in residential areas to shield their military activities. They deliberately positioned military equipment next to schools and mosques. Even before September 11th, the United States had been the larger donor of food aid to Afghan people, providing something in excess of 170 million dollars' worth prior to September 11th. In the first days of the war, DOD alone dropped more than a half a million rations of meals into Afghanistan to feed the starving. President Bush has pledged $320 million more, in addition to the military program. And every single day since the war begin, in the midst of the conflict, coalition forces, including American service people, have risked their lives to deliver humanitarian assistance to alleviate the suffering of the Afghan people. Today, U.S. and coalition forces are on the ground, digging wells, building schools, supporting other civilian missions to help the Afghan people recover from years of Taliban oppression, and they're doing a fine job at it. And those who perpetrated these crimes against their own people are no longer in power. Hundreds are in detention, and they will have to answer for their crimes. General Myers?

Myers: Thank you, Mr. Secretary. And good morning again. I'd like to follow up with the status on the Zhawar Kili strike from last week. The material we found around the site is being sent back to the United States for analysis. The search team was able to locate what we think was the exact impact point of the missile. And then the team cleared snow around that site out to 200 yards. There was anywhere from a foot to three to four feet of snow that had to be cleared. And I think yesterday Admiral Stufflebeem gave you a list of the type of material that they took from that site, and as I said before, that's currently being sent back to the United States for analysis.

Our team has left that site, but we'll continue to surveil (sic) that particular site and the region for some time to come. The Hazar Qadam investigation is progressing. At this point in the investigation, I don't believe that any of the detainees – this was the 27 that were detained – were subject to beatings or rough treatment after they were taken into custody. All 27 detainees were medically screened upon arrival in Kandahar, and there were no issues of beatings or kickings or anything of that sort. As we've told you before, we continue the full investigation there, and General Franks will make that available once it is complete. As an addendum here, the total number of detainees now in U.S. control is 474; 220 in Afghanistan, and 254 detainees in Guantanamo Bay, Cuba. And with that, we'll take your questions.

Rumsfeld: Questions. Charlie?

Q: Mr. Secretary, speaking of Admiral Stufflebeem, he lamented yesterday that this war has turned into what he called a "shadow war" and that you're chasing al Qaeda and Taliban and it's difficult to find them. You're very reluctant to discuss now the secret things that are going on, especially while they're going on – Special Forces troops, what they're doing. It seems the things that you are announcing, for instance, the attack at Zhawar Kili and the attack north of Kandahar, later to turn out to be mistakes. Are you worried that this is turning into some kind of public relations disaster where the headlines in the newspapers, the preponderance of them, are on mistakes rather than accomplishments?

Rumsfeld: Well, I mean, the first thing one has to say is that any time there is a suggestion that U.S. forces have, as you characterized it, made a mistake, it is something that we take very seriously as a country, and certainly the armed forces and the Pentagon do. When that occurs, we ask the appropriate people to undertake an investigation and to look into the charges or the allegations that have been made. We do that because we care that things be done as well as it's humanly possible to do them. You say that everything we do is being called a mistake. I don't know that that's the case. Maybe I didn't quote you quite right. But it seems to me there's a great deal we're doing in the country. We're in the process of assisting them to develop their own national military force. We're providing humanitarian assistance. We're assisting the government with a host of specific things. The forces everywhere they are located are helping the people in those communities. So there's a great deal of good being done. And the harm that the Taliban was doing is no longer being done. The al Qaeda that had taken – pretty much taken over the country, in a major sense, are on the run. And the Taliban have been thrown out. So the repression that existed – the circumstance of the Afghan people today is vastly better. Now, does that mean that when there's an operation and someone suggests that it was in one way or another inappropriate that we shouldn't investigate it? No. We do investigate it. And we care about it. And we'll in good time find out actually what took place.

Q: I didn't mean to suggest everything you do was a mistake. You're very reluctant to discuss the positive things that you say you're doing. For instance, details on what attacks you might have foiled, what evidence –

Rumsfeld: I see your point.

Q: – and perhaps the weight is going in the other direction on bad publicity.

Rumsfeld: Well, you're right. I mean, to some extent, when a – the forces in the country are doing a variety of things. And among them are some things that are not public; that is to say, they are observing things that are taking place, and trying to make judgments about where people might be located or who might be moving things around in a country in a way that's inappropriate. So we don't announce those things. They're out doing that on a covert basis. There are other things they do which are not announced until they happen. And those are direct action against a compound, for example, that is believed to be harboring al Qaeda or Taliban, senior Taliban people. The other thing that's taking place is there's a good deal of discussion going on, and people are, in fact, being discovered, being taken into custody. A lot of intelligence information's being gathered, and that intelligence information has been helpful in preventing other terrorist attacks. So no one ever likes to see an event where someone charges that it was improper, as we saw with respect to the operation that General Myers commented about. But it happens, and all you can do is go at it, find out what took place, and tell the world what actually happened.

Q: Are you concerned over these two high-profile events and what they might be doing to the campaign, in the eyes of the world?

Rumsfeld: I'm always concerned when there is an allegation made that suggests that some innocent person was – that an attack was inappropriate or that some innocent person was killed or injured. Obviously, anyone would be concerned about that.

Myers: Can I add a little something – just something to that?

Rumsfeld: Sure.

Myers: You know, I think the secretary and I would – we are anxious to share some of these successes with you. The problem is that once you do that, then the tactics and the techniques and the procedures that are being used in this very difficult mission of locating leadership and other pockets of al Qaeda or Taliban, once we tell you how successful we've been, then we reveal those tactics, techniques and procedures, and sometimes they're easy to thwart. So that's why we have to be very careful. This is an ongoing operation, if you will, and we've just got to be very, very careful. The second thing I'd say, that no matter how these investigations turn out, as some of you know because you've been in the field with our forces, they are the most professional and disciplined forces there are. They make life and death decisions when they come upon this group – these two compounds, where we had the 27 detainees and the 15 that were killed. Some of those detainees could have easily been killed. They were armed. The rules of engagement permit you to shoot back. And the fact that they were detained and not killed I think is an indication of just how professional and disciplined and dedicated our folks are. Now, if there were mistakes made, we're going to find that out when General Franks finishes his investigation. But I think the American people need to know that we have the best forces in the world, the best-trained forces, who are making these decisions and 99.9 percent of the time make them exactly right.

Rumsfeld: Let me – let me elaborate, Charlie, on your question, because when you ask the question, "Are you concerned?", there's always a risk, if one says they're not concerned, that the headline will be that the Pentagon is not concerned. And it happened to me when I was asked in a lengthy interview by BBC about the detainees and how they were being treated. And I described how they were being treated; they were being treated very, very well, and properly, and humanely, and consistent with the Geneva Convention. And we went through all this and I described it. And then he said something to the effect, "Well, are you concerned about how they're being treated?" And I said something to the effect – no – meaning, as I said in the context, because I know how they're being treated and they've been treated very, very properly and humanely. And that has roared around Europe that the Secretary is not concerned about how they're being treated, when the context was that I was not concerned because I know how they're being treated, and they're being treated and handled very, very well. Now, when you say, "Are you concerned about these?" and if I say, no, I am not concerned about what – as you cast the question, which is, are you concerned that they are going to be negative and take support away from the campaign of the war against terrorism, if I had answered and said no, I'm not, because I have confidence in the American people and in the people of the world recognizing how much better off the people in Afghanistan are today than they were, and yet I do have a concern when someone makes an allegation, because obviously we don't want people to be improperly handled, and we do not want operations against targets that are not appropriate targets. So I'm concerned about the specifics. But I did not want to simply answer it in a way that the headline would become inflammatory. I've become very cautious. Yes.

Q: Mr. Secretary, several people now from this podium have said that this target at Zhawar Kili is believed to have been legitimate and appropriate, yet stories persist out of the region that the missile may have killed three innocent civilians who were out collecting scrap metal. Can you provide for us today any additional information besides what this Predator may have seen that led U.S. forces to attack that site? And second of all, what is –

Rumsfeld: You mean the three individuals?

Q: The three. At Zhawar Kili.

Rumsfeld: Okay. Let's do that one.

Q: Okay.

Rumsfeld: I don't know that I can add anything to it. It's my understanding that the people who operate the Predator were watching a large number of people – 15 or – 10, 15, 20 people – over a period of time. And out of this group came three people. And they moved in and among various outcroppings of rocks and trees. And the people who have the responsibility for making those judgments made the judgments that, in fact, they were al Qaeda and that they were a proper target. And they make those judgments based on behavior, based on various types of equipment in information that they have developed over a sustained period now of weeks and weeks and weeks. A decision was made to fire the Hellfire missile. It was fired. It apparently hit three people – one or more people. There is an investigation underway. Special Forces could not get up there because of the weather. They went up there. They cleared away a large diameter area of snow, anywhere from a foot to two feet of snow, and picked up a great deal of material from the site, and they are in the process of checking into that, and they're also interviewing people in the region. Now, someone has said that these people were not what the people managing the Predator believed them to be. We'll just have to find out. There's not much more anyone could add, except there's that one version and there's the other version.

Q: Was there any additional intelligence that led to this site to begin with that may have contributed to the perception that these were al Qaeda?

Rumsfeld: These are people who have been doing this now for a good many weeks. And they monitor sites, and they go back to sites where they know al Qaeda have been. And they check things out. And they are honorable, fine people doing the best that's possible to be done. I was not in the control booth. I have not reviewed the – I have not compared the elements that went into their decisions. I am sure people will do that. Yes, Ron.

Q: What is your personal confidence that this, in fact, was an appropriate, legitimate target?

Rumsfeld: It's not for me to say. I have great confidence in the people doing it. They're honorable people. They're talented people. They're skillful. They've been doing it for weeks and weeks and weeks now, and they've got a darned good record and I've got a lot of respect for them. Yes.

Q: Mr. Secretary, you said earlier there's a great deal of good being done in Afghanistan, and you were nodding in particular at the humanitarian effort that's being made daily. But in the hunt for al Qaeda and Taliban leaders on the military front, what has gone right lately? We've heard nothing but problems lately. What's gone right?

Rumsfeld: Well, we have gathered some intelligence from them that has been beneficial to the United States and other countries and to our deployed forces – and not just a little, but more than a little. Second, we continue to gather in additional people, senior people, in the Taliban and al Qaeda. It's a fairly steady flow; it's not large numbers at any given time, but we are continuing to bring them in and to interrogate them at Bagram or at Kandahar, and ultimately in Guantanamo Bay. So I feel quite good about the progress.

Q: Senior people – can you – how senior? Any names or –

Rumsfeld: As you know, we've got what they say their names are, and we have what we think them to be, and some of their aliases. And we've decided that it's not useful to announce their names because then, for one thing, it could be wrong because they don't always tell the truth, and for a second thing, it can tell everyone else in those organizations who we have and what types of information we conceivably will be hearing from them, in which case it makes it much easier for others to get away. Yes?

Q: I want to pick up on that point a second. About three weeks ago, from the podium, you said you would think about releasing a list of who was killed in the al Qaeda leadership. About two weeks ago, President Bush told the Washington Post that he keeps a scorecard like a baseball game, and 16 of 22 al Qaeda leaders remain at large. This is about a couple of weeks ago. Can you shed any light on that? Is that roughly the number at large – six maybe killed and another 16 at large?

Rumsfeld: It changes every day. And there is such a list, and it does indicate whether or not they have been killed for sure, or presumed dead, or in captivity, or at large. And where people fit on that, an individual's status may change from week to week, depending as more information becomes available. And in many cases they're qualified, that is to say it says "presumed" as opposed to certainty. And we have thought about it, and we've decided not to release it.

Q: Was it six – is that roughly, though, six, roughly, have been killed?

Rumsfeld: I can't say. I haven't – I have to go back and – I'm sure when he said it, it was correct. My guess is the numbers have changed since.

Q: General Myers, I have a quick one on the Predator. There's been a lot of attention on this one strike. Roughly how many of these Predator Hellfires have been fired in the campaign by the CIA? Are we talking in the 40 or 50 range, and one or two have been controversial?

Myers: I don't have – I don't have that at my fingertips. And probably if I did, we wouldn't talk about how many. But let me just add a little comment to the earlier question on success here. You know, we said early on that one of the ideas – and the president has said this, and others, that we wanted to disrupt these operations, and part of disruption is getting them to move. And, you know, I think, at least I have said, if they leave Afghanistan, that's not all bad because they're going to be in their second-favorite place, and they're going to be in a place where they're less comfortable, where they have to spend more resources to buy their security, and so forth. It has turned out that that is – that's been true. Some of the folks we've gotten our hands on have been actually through other countries, and we've been fairly successful there. And when the time comes, that will all be released. So it's having the kind of effect, I think, that we want to have. Yes?

Q: Two questions about the Predator attack. First of all, yesterday it was described as an appropriate target. Is it still the feeling in this building that it was an appropriate target?

Rumsfeld: As I said, it is from the people I've talked to. The building? I can't speak for the building. But there is no change in opinion on the part of the people who were involved in the process, except for the fact that because people have raised a question about it, that there is an investigation going on, and people, as I say, have gone up there to take a look at it.

Q: Second question. There was a little confusion yesterday. Admiral Stufflebeem said that there was no real-time interaction between the CIA and CENTCOM when this attack was going down, when the CIA was pulling the trigger. And then we saw comments that seemed to contradict that on the wires a little later. Can you bring some clarification to that? How much interaction was there between the DOD and the CIA about this target at the time it was going down?

Rumsfeld: I can't speak to that, except to say that there tends to be a high degree of interaction between CENTCOM and CIA on a whole host of things, and certainly on these matters.

Q: Okay, explain the contradictions we got yesterday –

Myers: I don't know why you got the contradictions because there was close coordination, like there always is. And I don't know why you got the contradiction. I can't explain that.

Q: So General Stufflebeem was incorrect when he said there was no real-time coordination?

Myers: I didn't hear what he said, so I don't know – I can't say that. And I don't know what he was thinking or the context he said it in. I would just reiterate –

Rumsfeld: He's getting careful too. I like that! (laughter) Way to go, General!

Myers: (laughs) Thank you, sir!

Q: Well, explain what were the facts, if you could.

Myers: Well, again, without divulging too much of how this all works, there is close coordination between what the CIA is doing and what Central Command is doing.

And it just – it's virtually continuous. And so I don't know what Admiral Stufflebeem said or told you, but – and that was the case here. I don't know what else there is to say.

Rumsfeld: Yes.

Q: Mr. Secretary, General Myers, both of you talked last week before Congress about developing a joint task force headquarters that would deploy in the event of something like that. If we had had that in place, how could this have helped this operation now? Could the joint task headquarters that the Joint Forces Command is developing right –

Myers: I'll take a stab at it, if I can. Central Command's a little different situation because, in a sense, they are already a joint task force headquarters. So it's a little different for them. A better one to take would be Pacific Command, in doing something in their region, where the unified commander might designate a joint task force. But let's assume it's Central Command. What we're envisioning there is not only the habitual relationships which CEN-TCOM does have with all its components – its Army and its Navy and its Marine and its air components; they have that relationship that we're trying to establish in other unified commands, and maybe more than one. In Central Command, they essentially have this one big joint task force. And one of the issues is what is the suite of equipment that you equip them with when they go in to conduct an operation, whether it's humanitarian or whether it's combat or whatever? And that's the part we need to focus on. Then you take a suite of equipment that plugs everybody in so they all have the relevant pictures of what's happening and so forth. So I think it'd be very relevant in terms of the equipment.

Rumsfeld: Yes.

Q: Can you adapt this to the other –

Myers: Yes. Oh, absolutely. Yes. Have to be adaptable.

Q: This is apparently the most specific information in the last five months about another terrorist attack today. Without divulging anything you don't want to, can you say anything about whether and how DOD's reacting?

Rumsfeld: Well, first let me say that the – as I understand it, the information that the Department of Justice used to come to the conclusion it came to, that an announcement was appropriate, was information that has been gained in large measure from the interrogations that have been taking place and the other information that has been a result of the efforts of the multi- departmental groups that do the interrogation. The Department of Defense was pretty much at a level of alert that it didn't require many additional things, although I understand some elements have taken some additional steps which I'd prefer not to discuss.

Q: Can you say anything generally about what you mean by that?

Rumsfeld: About what?

Q: The last thing you said. Can you generally – what are you referring to?

Rumsfeld: No, because it's –

Q: (off mike) – at Guantanamo Bay, by the way, or in Afghanistan?

Rumsfeld: I don't know. It could – we interrogate at Bagram, Kandahar and Guantanamo. So – and where that particular information came from, I think it was Guantanamo, but I don't know.

Myers: Yes, I think that's right.

Rumsfeld: Yes?

Q: Getting back to the Taliban leadership, about three weeks ago, prior to the Special Forces raid north of Kandahar, Afghan officials said that they were in negotiations with three top Taliban officials, including Omar's secretary, to try to bring them in from the cold, and then the attack happened and they lost contact with these three folks. Were you aware of those negotiations? And if so, do you know what the status is of those today?

Rumsfeld: I can't run a thread back to that particular comment. I do know that at any given time, including this moment, there are discussions taking place about Taliban, and particularly Taliban more than al Qaeda, people who are trying to understand what's going to happen to them if they turn themselves in, or if they decide to give us assistance in finding other people, and that type of thing. So it's a continuous process.

Q: And you're in contact with the Afghan officials, parties to the negotiations with these folks?

Rumsfeld: See, I don't know what you mean by "these folks." But certainly the –

Q: Well, the three top Taliban officials.

Rumsfeld: I can't speak to that. As I said, I know that at any given moment of the day or night, there are discussions going on, and we are certainly in touch with Afghan people who are involved in those kinds of discussions. Yes?

Q: Mr. Secretary, you said recently, or just actually a couple of moments ago, that the folks firing Predators have a good record. What did you mean when you said that?

Rumsfeld: I mean that they're serious people. They've been doing this now since – some months, and that I have observed how they handle themselves, and they develop patterns of behavior which give them information. They use human intelligence from the ground. They observe a variety of things from the ground and the air and they connect those things, and then they make judgments. And they have, on a number of occasions, been successful in doing exactly that which they intended to do.

Q: But "record" implies a scorecard. Do you have some sort of scorecard in mind you can share with us?

Rumsfeld: I – no. It is a series of events that I have observed, and that others have observed, rather than keeping score on it.

Q: Secretary Rumsfeld, on the Predator strike question again, in late November, when people were asking you about the relationship between CIA operations and CENTCOM – and then it was more about ground operations – but you said very specifically that General Franks was the man at the steering wheel coordinating or in control of all military operations. Now, with the Predator strikes, you're talking more about an exchange of information, coordination. So I was wondering if you could clarify the situation of how CIA-military operations are coordinated or in control by CENTCOM.

Rumsfeld: Yeah. That's a good question, and it's hard to answer. The overwhelming bulk of all activity in Afghanistan since the first U.S. forces went in have been basically under the control of the Central Command. And that's particularly true after the first month. The one exception has been the armed Predators – I shouldn't say "the one exception." An exception has been the armed Predators, which are CIA-operated.

Q: Why is that – why is that an exception?

Rumsfeld: It is just a fact. They were operating them before the United States military was involved, and – the armed Predators – and doing a good job. And so rather than changing that, we just left it.

Q: Why not plug them into the command and control at CENTCOM? You have three operators at a Predator.

Rumsfeld: It's just a historical fact that they were operating these things over recent years, and they were in Afghanistan prior to the involvement of CENTCOM. And they continued during this period. That's just the way it is. Yes.

Q: Could I just get the two of you maybe to free associate a little bit more on that subject? We're seeing a –

Rumsfeld: To do what? (laughter)

Q: Free associate. (laughs) It's a sort of touchy-feely '70s term. (laughter)

Myers: I don't believe I can –

Rumsfeld: You got the – you got the wrong guys! (laughter)

Myers: I don't think I can do that with you. It's illegal. I – (laughter)

Q: The general subject matter is there is this growing sort of military role for the CIA, and we have you guys up here every day and can ask questions. But the CIA is obviously – operates in a lot more shadowy way. People are thinking back and remembering some of the excesses of that agency in Latin America 20, 30 years ago, and I think there's – there tends to be a growing sense of, hmm, what are getting into here? Could you all talk more philosophically about the dealings between the Pentagon and the CIA, and what the parameters are that you're developing or thinking about for how to manage this new world where the CIA now has its own real military capabilities that are not necessarily under the control of the U.S. military, which has transparency with the American public?

Rumsfeld: I can give you a couple of paragraphs on the subject.

Q: All right. That would be the free association.

Rumsfeld: Is that right? The relationship between the Defense Department and the CIA today is as good as I've ever seen it: that is to say, in the relationships and the interaction and the connectivity. We have people involved with things they're doing, and in – for example, in counterterrorism or in intelligence cells, where we're trying to bring all kinds of intelligence information into one place. They have people involved in things that we're doing in a sense of connecting their capabilities and their assets to what we do. The concern you're expressing, from a decade or two or three ago, I think is not apt simply because people are sensitive to those things and there's all kinds of congressional consultation, there's all kinds of procedures within the executive branch so that things that the agency is planning to do are well vetted in the appropriate ways before they do them. I think the general relationship on the ground tends to be that if we're not there, the CIA, obviously, has the reporting relationship straight up through the CIA and we're not involved. To the extent they are there, and we then get involved, there's an early period where they're both there and they're doing somewhat different things, needless to say. And then, at a certain point, the defense element is large enough that it becomes – things tend to chop over to it and the chain of command goes up through the combatant commander, except for, obviously, things that don't fit within our statutory responsibilities.

Q: Secretary Rumsfeld, a number of administration officials have spoke (sic) recently about the need for a regime change in Iraq – probably the highest-profile being Secretary of State Colin Powell. Do you favor such a regime change sooner rather than later? And how concerned should Saddam Hussein be that the U.S. military may be the force of that regime change?

Rumsfeld: Well, I think that the Congress passed legislation relating to regime change. I've forgotten the name of the statute. (to General Myers) Do you know?

Myers: I don't remember either.

Rumsfeld: But I –

Q: Aid to the opposition.

Rumsfeld: Well, that was part of it. But I think it was also broader. And I think that's – I don't know many people who have developed a great deal of admiration for that regime and the way it treats its people and the way it treats its neighbor, and the fact that it's engaging in the development of weapons of mass destruction. The timing, and whether or not anything is done with respect to any country is something that is for the president and the country to make those judgments. And it's not for me to express views on that. So I don't.

Q: Has something new come to the attention of the United States with regard to Iraq that has kicked us into an apparently higher gear for planning and the contemplation of dealing with Iraq? Or is this a continuum that –

Rumsfeld: I think the United States since Desert Storm has always had a various planning with respect to Iraq and what it might do to its neighbors. It's threatened – it's invaded Kuwait. It's threatened the Shi'a in the south and harmed them. It's harmed the Kurds in the north. It has expressed its view that the regimes of its neighboring countries are illegitimate and ought not to be there. This is – it is a country that threw out the inspectors, that has an active weapons of mass destruction program. I don't know if anything's changed.

Q: Maybe it is a misperception here. Previous administrations have adopted the policy of trying to contain Saddam Hussein. And it appears from what the president has said and what Colin Powell has said that containment no longer works in the view of this administration, that the threat has somehow changed, increased, that the dynamics are different, and therefore regime change has become a more substantial goal for this administration than previous ones. Is that a – is that true?

Rumsfeld: Well, if you think about what the president and Secretary Powell have said, what they have said, it seems to me, is pretty much self-evident, that every year that goes by and the inspectors are not there, the development of their weapons of mass destruction proceed apace, bringing them closer to a time when they will have those weapons developed in a form that is more threatening than it had been the year before or the year before that. The second thing that's occurred is the technologies have advanced. And to the extent that the sanctions – which historically is the case: sanctions tend to weaken over time, they're relaxed in one way or another. And as those sanctions are relaxed and as dual use capabilities flow into that country, their capability is restored in terms of their ability to impose harm on their neighbors or threaten others. Third, the September 11th attack, if you think of the president's words and Secretary Powell's position, it reminded the world and the United States that terrorist networks exist, that, in fact, they – we now know from the intelligence we've gathered that they've had a very active effort underway to get chemical, biological and radiation capabilities – terrorist networks. And we know that Iraq has those and does not wish much of – many of its neighbors well, if any. I don't think it has a neighbor that it wishes well – maybe. So it's that combination of things that I would suspect led to the president's comments and to the secretary's comments.

Q: But would it be accurate to say that this building, that the Pentagon is now spending more time considering Iraq than it had previously, in terms of your planning process?

Rumsfeld: This building has always been attentive, for at least more than a decade now, 10, 12 years, to Iraq. We've had Northern no-fly zones and Southern no-fly zones; been flying flights there attempting to contain that country and prevent them from jumping on one of their neighbors. Yes?

Q: Could I follow up, Mr. Secretary, on what you just said, please? In regard to Iraq weapons of mass destruction and terrorists, is there any evidence to indicate that Iraq has attempted to or is willing to supply terrorists with weapons of mass destruction? Because there are reports that there is no evidence of a direct link between Baghdad and some of these terrorist organizations.

Rumsfeld: Reports that say that something hasn't happened are always interesting to me, because as we know, there are known knowns; there are things we know we know. We also know there are known unknowns; that is to say we know there are some things we do not know. But there are also unknown unknowns – the ones we don't know we don't know. And if one looks throughout the history of our country and other free countries, it is the latter category that tend to be the difficult ones. And so people who have the omniscience that they can say with high certainty that something has not happened or is not being tried, have capabilities that are – what was the word you used, Pam, earlier?

Q: Free associate? (laughs)

Rumsfeld: Yeah. They can – (chuckles) – they can do things I can't do. (laughter)

Q: Excuse me. But is this an unknown unknown?

Rumsfeld: I'm not –

Q: Because you said several unknowns, and I'm just wondering if this is an unknown unknown.

Rumsfeld: I'm not going to say which it is.

Q: Mr. Secretary, if you believe something –

Rumsfeld: Right here. Right here. Right here.

Q: Mr. Secretary, point of clarification –

Rumsfeld: No, this is a promise.

Q: – I think under Wright's rules, that a point of clarification – (laughter)

Q: I just wanted to ask a real bottom line question. And many apologies for taking you back to Zhawar Kili one last time. But you mentioned here a couple of times that that incident is now under investigation and cited that the team went up there for that reason.

Rumsfeld: This is to the three individuals. Correct.

Q: That's right. But, of course, the team went up there when people from this podium were saying it was definitely what you believed to be senior al Qaeda and you were simply going there to find out which al Qaeda you killed. Not that there – at that time there were, of course, no at least public allegations that perhaps these people were innocent. So this investigation clearly that you were referring to perhaps has emerged since the team went up there. So what is – are you –

Rumsfeld: I don't know that.

Q: Are you investigating it? Is the CIA investigating it? Or – you mentioned –

Rumsfeld: No, I'm not. This – no. This is something that CENTCOM has decided and done, and properly so.

Q: So what is it that CENTCOM is now investigating in regard to the Zhawar Kili attack?

Rumsfeld: I don't know what the right word is. I know that when a – I know – you're correct. There was an interest in getting some positive identification, if that were possible. And second, every time an allegation comes up that seems to have some – that raises questions that ought to be addressed, then CENTCOM on its own decides that they're going to have people go look at that. And whatever that word is – some call it, an investigation, others call it something else. But that's what's taking place, is they are going up there doing that.

Q: But that's – they're – so CENTCOM – just to make sure I really understand. CENTCOM is investigating these potential allegations that perhaps these were innocent people. Is that what – and why is CENTCOM investigating that and not the CIA, since it was their missile and their targeting?

Rumsfeld: Well, I don't know that I said that CIA wasn't.

Q: Could you explain that a little more, and –

Rumsfeld: No. I just don't know what they're doing.

Q: But you do know that CENTCOM's looking into it.

Rumsfeld: I do.

Q: And could you just one more time explain something to me? Does the CIA have the ability, the approval to pull the trigger without coming to the military? Does the CIA have that bottom line authority to pull the trigger without coming to the military?

Rumsfeld: I don't know that I am going to start responding to questions for the Central Intelligence Agency.

Q: Well, have you given – let me try it the reverse way, then. Has the U.S. military – I don't know what the right verb is – given the CIA the approval, the authority, the whatever to pull the trigger without coming to Central Command first?

Rumsfeld: I don't know that it's for us to give that authority. If they have capabilities, they do them, what they wish to do.

Q: So they have the legal – the legal authority to do things without coming to you?

Rumsfeld: I'm not going to answer what the CIA does. But it's not – it is not the Pentagon that gives other agencies of government authority. We're going to make the last – the last question here.

Q: I just want to – because you so cleverly buried Jim Miklaszewski's question by characterizing it as something that was unknowable. But he didn't ask you something that was unknowable. He asked you if you knew of evidence that Iraq was supplying – or willing to supply weapons of mass destruction to terrorists –

Rumsfeld: He cited reports where people said that was not the case.

Q: Right. He's done that and –

Rumsfeld: And was my response was to that, and I thought it was good response.

Q: But if we are to believe things –

Rumsfeld: I could have said that the absence of evidence is not evidence of absence, or vice versa.

Q: But we just want to know, are you aware of any evidence? Because that would increase our level of belief from faith to something that would be based on evidence.

Rumsfeld: Yeah, I am aware of a lot of evidence involving Iraq on a lot of subjects. And it is not for me to make public judgments about my assessment or others' assessment of that evidence. I'm going to make that the last question.

Q: I wanted to go back to the terrorist attack. Can you provide any information that – and would this be also another one of the successes that you might cite about the interrogation in Cuba? Did you learn that the man might have al Qaeda connections? Is there anything you can elaborate on the terrorist attack?

Rumsfeld: Other than to say what I said; that interrogations have produced information and, indeed, in this instance, produced some of the evidence that led to the decision by the Department of Justice.

Q: General Myers?

Myers: No, I sticking with the secretary. (laughter).

Q: Thank you.

Myers: Nice try!

5.5   MILITARY COMMISSIONS AND TRIBUNALS

☛ USA: United States Department of Defense, Military Commission Order No. 1, 21 March 2002

Subject: Procedures for Trials by Military Commissions of Certain Non-United States Citizens in the War Against Terrorism

References:

(a) United States Constitution, Article II, section 2

(b) Military Order of November 13, 2001, "Detention, Treatment, and Trial of Certain Non-Citizens in the War Against Terrorism," 66 F.R. 57833 (Nov. 16, 2001) ("President's Military Order")

(c) DoD 5200.2-R, "Personnel Security Program," current edition

(d) Executive Order 12958, "Classified National Security Information" (April 17, 1995, as amended, or any successor Executive Order)

(e) Section 603 of title 10, United States Code

(f) DoD Directive 5025.1, "DoD Directives System," current edition March 21, 2002

1. Purpose

This Order implements policy, assigns responsibilities, and prescribes procedures under references (a) and (b) for trials before military commissions of individuals subject to the President's Military Order. These procedures shall be implemented and construed so as to ensure that any such individual receives a full and fair trial before a military commission, as required by the President's Military Order. Unless otherwise directed by the Secretary of Defense, and except for supplemental procedures established pursuant to the President's Military Order or this Order, the procedures prescribed herein and no others shall govern such trials.

2. Establishment of Military Commission

In accordance with the President's Military Order, the Secretary of Defense or a designee ("Appointing Authority") may issue orders from time to time appointing one or more military commissions to try individuals subject to the President's Military Order and appointing any other personnel necessary to facilitate such trials.

3. Jurisdiction

A. Over Persons

A military commission appointed under this Order ("Commission") shall have jurisdiction over only an individual or individuals ("the Accused") (1) subject to the President's Military Order and (2) alleged to have committed an offense in a charge that has been referred to the Commission by the Appointing Authority.

B. Over Offenses

Commissions established hereunder shall have jurisdiction over violations of the laws of war and all other offenses triable by military commission.

C. Maintaining Integrity of Commission Proceedings

The Commission may exercise jurisdiction over participants in its proceedings as necessary to preserve the integrity and order of the proceedings.

4. Commission Personnel

A. Members

(1) Appointment
The Appointing Authority shall appoint the members and the alternate member or members of each Commission. The alternate member or members shall attend all sessions of the Commission, but the absence of an alternate member shall not preclude the Commission from conducting proceedings. In case of incapacity, resignation, or removal of any member, an alternate member shall take the place of that member. Any vacancy among the members or alternate members occurring after a trial has begun may be filled by the Appointing Authority, but the substance of all prior proceedings and evidence taken in that case shall be made known to that new member or alternate member before the trial proceeds.

(2) Number of Members
Each Commission shall consist of at least three but no more than seven members, the number being determined by the Appointing Authority. For each such Commission, there shall also be one or two alternate members, the number being determined by the Appointing Authority.

(3) Qualifications
Each member and alternate member shall be a commissioned officer of the United States armed forces ("Military Officer"), including without limitation reserve personnel on active duty, National Guard personnel on active duty in Federal service, and retired personnel recalled to active duty. The Appointing Authority shall appoint members and alternate members determined to be competent to perform the duties involved. The Appointing Authority may remove members and alternate members for good cause.

(4) Presiding Officer
From among the members of each Commission, the Appointing Authority shall designate a Presiding Officer to preside over the proceedings of that Commission. The Presiding Officer shall be a Military Officer who is a judge advocate of any United States armed force.

(5) Duties of the Presiding Officer
(a) The Presiding Officer shall admit or exclude evidence at trial in accordance with Section 6(D). The Presiding Officer shall have authority to close proceedings or portions of proceedings in accordance with Section 6(B)(3) and for any other reason necessary for the conduct of a full and fair trial.
(b) The Presiding Officer shall ensure that the discipline, dignity, and decorum of the proceedings are maintained, shall exercise control over the proceedings to ensure proper implementation of the President's Military Order and this Order, and shall have authority to act upon any contempt or breach of Commission rules and procedures. Any attorney authorized to appear before a Commission who is thereafter found not to satisfy the requirements for eligibility or who fails to comply with laws, rules, regulations, or other orders applicable to the Commission proceedings or any other individual who violates such laws, rules, regulations, or orders may be disciplined as the Presiding Officer deems appropriate, including but not limited to revocation of eligibility to appear before that Commission. The

Appointing Authority may further revoke that attorney's or any other person's eligibility to appear before any other Commission convened under this Order.

(c) The Presiding Officer shall ensure the expeditious conduct of the trial. In no circumstance shall accommodation of counsel be allowed to delay proceedings unreasonably.

(d) The Presiding Officer shall certify all interlocutory questions, the disposition of which would effect a termination of proceedings with respect to a charge, for decision by the Appointing Authority. The Presiding Officer may certify other interlocutory questions to the Appointing Authority as the Presiding Officer deems appropriate.

B. Prosecution

(1) Office of the Chief Prosecutor
The Chief Prosecutor shall be a judge advocate of any United States armed force, shall supervise the overall prosecution efforts under the President's Military Order, and shall ensure proper management of personnel and resources.

(2) Prosecutors and Assistant Prosecutors
Consistent with any supplementary regulations or instructions issued under Section 7(A), the Chief Prosecutor shall detail a Prosecutor and, as appropriate, one or more Assistant Prosecutors to prepare charges and conduct the prosecution for each case before a Commission ("Prosecution"). Prosecutors and Assistant Prosecutors shall be (a) Military Officers who are judge advocates of any United States armed force, or (b) special trial counsel of the Department of Justice who may be made available by the Attorney General of the United States. The duties of the Prosecution are:

(a) To prepare charges for approval and referral by the Appointing Authority;

(b) To conduct the prosecution before the Commission of all cases referred for trial; and

(c) To represent the interests of the Prosecution in any review process.

C. Defense

(1) Office of the Chief Defense Counsel
The Chief Defense Counsel shall be a judge advocate of any United States armed force, shall supervise the overall defense efforts under the President's Military Order, shall ensure proper management of personnel and resources, shall preclude conflicts of interest, and shall facilitate proper representation of all Accused.

(2) Detailed Defense Counsel.
Consistent with any supplementary regulations or instructions issued under Section 7(A), the Chief Defense Counsel shall detail one or more Military Officers who are judge advocates of any United States armed force to conduct the defense for each case before a Commission ("Detailed Defense Counsel"). The duties of the Detailed Defense Counsel are:

(a) To defend the Accused zealously within the bounds of the law without regard to personal opinion as to the guilt of the Accused; and

(b) To represent the interests of the Accused in any review process as provided by this Order.

(3) Choice of Counsel

(a) The Accused may select a Military Officer who is a judge advocate of any United States armed force to replace the Accused's Detailed Defense Counsel, provided that Military Officer has been determined to be available in accordance with any applicable supplementary regulations or instructions issued under Section 7(A).

After such selection of a new Detailed Defense Counsel, the original Detailed Defense Counsel will be relieved of all duties with respect to that case. If requested by the Accused, however, the Appointing Authority may allow the original Detailed Defense Counsel to continue to assist in representation of the Accused as another Detailed Defense Counsel.

(b) The Accused may also retain the services of a civilian attorney of the Accused's own choosing and at no expense to the United States Government ("Civilian Defense Counsel"), provided that attorney: (i) is a United States citizen; (ii) is admitted to the practice of law in a State, district, territory, or possession of the United States, or before a Federal court; (iii) has not been the subject of any sanction or disciplinary action by any court, bar, or other competent governmental authority for relevant misconduct; (iv) has been determined to be eligible for access to information classified at the level SECRET or higher under the authority of and in accordance with the procedures prescribed in reference (c); and (v) has signed a written agreement to comply with all applicable regulations or instructions for counsel, including any rules of court for conduct during the course of proceedings. Civilian attorneys may be prequalified as members of the pool of available attorneys if, at the time of application, they meet the relevant criteria, or they may be qualified on an *ad hoc* basis after being requested by an Accused. Representation by Civilian Defense Counsel will not relieve Detailed Defense Counsel of the duties specified in Section 4(C)(2). The qualification of a Civilian Defense Counsel does not guarantee that person's presence at closed Commission proceedings or that person's access to any information protected under Section 6(D) (5).

(4) Continuity of Representation

The Accused must be represented at all relevant times by Detailed Defense Counsel. Detailed Defense Counsel and Civilian Defense Counsel shall be herein referred to collectively as "Defense Counsel." The Accused and Defense Counsel shall be herein referred to collectively as "the Defense."

D. Other Personnel

Other personnel, such as court reporters, interpreters, security personnel, bailiffs, and clerks may be detailed or employed by the Appointing Authority, as necessary.

5. Procedures Accorded the Accused

The following procedures shall apply with respect to the Accused:

A. The Prosecution shall furnish to the Accused, sufficiently in advance of trial to prepare a defense, a copy of the charges in English and, if appropriate, in another language that the Accused understands.

B. The Accused shall be presumed innocent until proven guilty.

C. A Commission member shall vote for a finding of Guilty as to an offense if and only if that member is convinced beyond a reasonable doubt, based on the evidence admitted at trial, that the Accused is guilty of the offense.

D. At least one Detailed Defense Counsel shall be made available to the Accused suffi-ciently in advance of trial to prepare a defense and until any findings and sentence become final in accordance with Section 6(H)(2).

E. The Prosecution shall provide the Defense with access to evidence the Prosecution in-tends to introduce at trial and with access to evidence known to the Prosecution that tends to exculpate the Accused. Such access shall be consistent with Section 6(D)(5) and subject to Section 9.

F. The Accused shall not be required to testify during trial. A Commission shall draw no adverse inference from an Accused's decision not to testify. This subsection shall not pre-clude admission of evidence of prior statements or conduct of the Accused.

G. If the Accused so elects, the Accused may testify at trial on the Accused's own behalf and shall then be subject to cross-examination.

H. The Accused may obtain witnesses and documents for the Accused's defense, to the extent necessary and reasonably available as determined by the Presiding Officer. Such access shall be consistent with the requirements of Section 6(D)(5) and subject to Section 9. The Appointing Authority shall order that such investigative or other resources be made available to the Defense as the Appointing Authority deems necessary for a full and fair trial.

I. The Accused may have Defense Counsel present evidence at trial in the Accused's de-fense and cross-examine each witness presented by the Prosecution who appears before the Commission.

J. The Prosecution shall ensure that the substance of the charges, the proceedings, and any documentary evidence are provided in English and, if appropriate, in another language that the Accused understands. The Appointing Authority may appoint one or more interpreters to assist the Defense, as necessary.

K. The Accused may be present at every stage of the trial before the Commission, consis-tent with Section 6(B)(3), unless the Accused engages in disruptive conduct that justifies exclusion by the Presiding Officer. Detailed Defense Counsel may not be excluded from any trial proceeding or portion thereof.

L. Except by order of the Commission for good cause shown, the Prosecution shall provide the Defense with access before sentencing proceedings to evidence the Prosecution intends to present in such proceedings. Such access shall be consistent with Section 6(D)(5) and subject to Section 9.

M. The Accused may make a statement during sentencing proceedings.

N. The Accused may have Defense Counsel submit evidence to the Commission during sentencing proceedings.

O. The Accused shall be afforded a trial open to the public (except proceedings closed by the Presiding Officer), consistent with Section 6(B).

P. The Accused shall not again be tried by any Commission for a charge once a Commis-sion's finding on that charge becomes final in accordance with Section 6(H)(2).

6. Conduct of the Trial

A. Pretrial Procedures

(1) Preparation of the Charges
The Prosecution shall prepare charges for approval by the Appointing Authority, as pro-vided in Section 4(B)(2)(a).

(2) Referral to the Commission

The Appointing Authority may approve and refer for trial any charge against an individual or individuals within the jurisdiction of a Commission in accordance with Section 3(A) and alleging an offense within the jurisdiction of a Commission in accordance with Section 3 (B).

(3) Notification of the Accused

The Prosecution shall provide copies of the charges approved by the Appointing Authority to the Accused and Defense Counsel. The Prosecution also shall submit the charges approved by the Appointing Authority to the Presiding Officer of the Commission to which they were referred.

(4) Plea Agreements

The Accused, through Defense Counsel, and the Prosecution may submit for approval to the Appointing Authority a plea agreement mandating a sentence limitation or any other provision in exchange for an agreement to plead guilty, or any other consideration. Any agreement to plead guilty must include a written stipulation of fact, signed by the Accused, that confirms the guilt of the Accused and the voluntary and informed nature of the plea of guilty. If the Appointing Authority approves the plea agreement, the Commission will, after determining the voluntary and informed nature of the plea agreement, admit the plea agreement and stipulation into evidence and be bound to adjudge findings and a sentence pursuant to that plea agreement.

(5) Issuance and Service of Process; Obtaining Evidence

The Commission shall have power to:

(a) Summon witnesses to attend trial and testify;

(b) Administer oaths or affirmations to witnesses and other persons and to question witnesses;

(c) Require the production of documents and other evidentiary material; and

(d) Designate special commissioners to take evidence.

The Presiding Officer shall exercise these powers on behalf of the Commission at the Presiding Officer's own initiative, or at the request of the Prosecution or the Defense, as necessary to ensure a full and fair trial in accordance with the President's Military Order and this Order. The Commission shall issue its process in the name of the Department of Defense over the signature of the Presiding Officer. Such process shall be served as directed by the Presiding Officer in a manner calculated to give reasonable notice to persons required to take action in accordance with that process.

B. Duties of the Commission During Trial

The Commission shall:

(1) Provide a full and fair trial.

(2) Proceed impartially and expeditiously, strictly confining the proceedings to a full and fair trial of the charges, excluding irrelevant evidence, and preventing any unnecessary interference or delay.

(3) Hold open proceedings except where otherwise decided by the Appointing Authority or the Presiding Officer in accordance with the President's Military Order and this Order. Grounds for closure include the protection of information classified or classifiable under reference (d); information protected by law or rule from unauthorized disclosure; the physical safety of participants in Commission proceedings, including prospective witnesses; intelligence and law enforcement sources, methods, or activities; and other national security interests. The Presiding Officer may decide to close all or part of a proceeding on the Presiding Officer's own initiative or based upon a presentation, including an ex *parte, in camera* presentation by either the Prosecution or the Defense. A decision to close a proceeding or portion thereof may include a decision to exclude the Accused, Civilian Defense Counsel, or any other person, but Detailed Defense Counsel may not be excluded from any trial proceeding or portion thereof. Except with the prior authorization of the Presiding Officer and subject to Section 9, Defense Counsel may not disclose any information presented during a closed session to individuals excluded from such proceeding or part thereof. Open proceedings may include, at the discretion of the Appointing Authority, attendance by the public and accredited press, and public release of transcripts at the appropriate time. Proceedings should be open to the maximum extent practicable. Photography, video, or audio broadcasting, or recording of or at Commission proceedings shall be prohibited, except photography, video, and audio recording by the Commission pursuant to the direction of the Presiding Officer as necessary for preservation of the record of trial.

(4) Hold each session at such time and place as may be directed by the Appointing Authority. Members of the Commission may meet in closed conference at any time.

(5) As soon as practicable at the conclusion of a trial, transmit an authenticated copy of the record of trial to the Appointing Authority.

C. Oaths

(1) Members of a Commission, all Prosecutors, all Defense Counsel, all court reporters, all security personnel, and all interpreters shall take an oath to perform their duties faithfully.

(2) Each witness appearing before a Commission shall be examined under oath, as provided in Section 6(D)(2)(b).

(3) An oath includes an affirmation. Any formulation that appeals to the conscience of the person to whom the oath is administered and that binds that person to speak the truth, or, in the case of one other than a witness, properly to perform certain duties, is sufficient.

D. Evidence

(1) Admissibility
Evidence shall be admitted if, in the opinion of the Presiding Officer (or instead, if any other member of the Commission so requests at the time the Presiding Officer renders that opinion, the opinion of the Commission rendered at that time by a majority of the Commission), the evidence would have probative value to a reasonable person.

(2) Witnesses
(a) Production of Witnesses
The Prosecution or the Defense may request that the Commission hear the testimony of any person, and such testimony shall be received if found to be admissible and not cumulative. The Commission may also summon and hear witnesses on its own initiative. The Commission may permit the testimony of witnesses by telephone, audiovisual means, or other means; however, the Commission shall consider the ability to test the veracity of that testimony in evaluating the weight to be given to the testimony of the witness.
(b) Testimony
Testimony of witnesses shall be given under oath or affirmation. The Commission may still hear a witness who refuses to swear an oath or make a solemn undertaking; however, the Commission shall consider the refusal to swear an oath or give an affirmation in evaluating the weight to be given to the testimony of the witness.
(c) Examination of Witnesses
A witness who testifies before the Commission is subject to both direct examination and cross-examination.
The Presiding Officer shall maintain order in the proceedings and shall not permit badgering of witnesses or questions that are not material to the issues before the Commission. Members of the Commission may question witnesses at any time.
(d) Protection of Witnesses
The Presiding Officer shall consider the safety of witnesses and others, as well as the safeguarding of Protected Information as defined in Section 6(D)(5)(a), in determining the appropriate methods of receiving testimony and evidence. The Presiding Officer may hear any presentation by the Prosecution or the Defense, including an *ex parte, in camera* presentation, regarding the safety of potential witnesses before determining the ways in which witnesses and evidence will be protected. The Presiding Officer may authorize any methods appropriate for the protection of witnesses and evidence. Such methods may include, but are not limited to: testimony by telephone, audiovisual means, or other electronic means; closure of the proceedings; introduction of prepared declassified summaries of evidence; and the use of pseudonyms.

(3) Other Evidence
Subject to the requirements of Section 6(D)(1) concerning admissibility, the Commission may consider any other evidence including, but not limited to, testimony from prior trials and proceedings, sworn or unsworn written statements, physical evidence, or scientific or other reports.

(4) Notice
The Commission may, after affording the Prosecution and the Defense an opportunity to be heard, take conclusive notice of facts that are not subject to reasonable dispute either because they are generally known or are capable of determination by resort to sources that cannot reasonably be contested.

(5) Protection of Information
(a) Protective Order
The Presiding Officer may issue protective orders as necessary to carry out the Military Order and this Order, including to safeguard "Protected Information," which includes: (i) information classified or classifiable pursuant to reference (d); (ii) information protected by

law or rule from unauthorized disclosure; (iii) information the disclosure of which may endanger the physical safety of participants in Commission proceedings, including prospective witnesses; (iv) information concerning intelligence and law enforcement sources, methods, or activities; or (v) information concerning other national security interests. As soon as practicable, counsel for either side will notify the Presiding Officer of any intent to offer evidence involving Protected Information.

(b) Limited Disclosure

The Presiding Officer, upon motion of the Prosecution or *sua sponte,* shall, as necessary to protect the interests of the United States and consistent with Section 9, direct (i) the deletion of specified items of Protected Information from documents to be made available to the Accused, Detailed Defense Counsel, or Civilian Defense Counsel; (ii) the substitution of a portion or summary of the information for such Protected Information; or (iii) the substitution of a statement of the relevant facts that the Protected Information would tend to prove. The Prosecution's motion and any materials submitted in support thereof or in response thereto shall, upon request of the Prosecution, be considered by the Presiding Officer *ex parte, in camera,* but no Protected Information shall be admitted into evidence for consideration by the Commission if not presented to Detailed Defense Counsel.

(c) Closure of Proceedings

The Presiding Officer may direct the closure of proceedings in accordance with Section 6 (B)(3).

(d) Protected Information as Part of the Record of Trial

All exhibits admitted as evidence but containing Protected Information shall be sealed and annexed to the record of trial. Additionally, any Protected Information not admitted as evidence but reviewed *in camera* and subsequently withheld from the Defense over Defense objection shall, with the associated motions and responses and any materials submitted in support thereof, be sealed and annexed to the record of trial as additional exhibits. Such sealed material shall be made available to reviewing authorities in closed proceedings.

E. Proceedings During Trial

The proceedings at each trial will be conducted substantially as follows, unless modified by the Presiding Officer to suit the particular circumstances:

(1) Each charge will be read, or its substance communicated, in the presence of the Accused and the Commission.

(2) The Presiding Officer shall ask each Accused whether the Accused pleads "Guilty" or "Not Guilty." Should the Accused refuse to enter a plea, the Presiding Officer shall enter a plea of "Not Guilty" on the Accused's behalf. If the plea to an offense is "Guilty," the Presiding Officer shall enter a finding of Guilty on that offense after conducting sufficient inquiry to form an opinion that the plea is voluntary and informed. Any plea of Guilty that is not determined to be voluntary and informed shall be changed to a plea of Not Guilty. Plea proceedings shall then continue as to the remaining charges. If a plea of "Guilty" is made on all charges, the Commission shall proceed to sentencing proceedings; if not, the Commission shall proceed to trial as to the charges for which a "Not Guilty" plea has been entered.

(3) The Prosecution shall make its opening statement.

(4) The witnesses and other evidence for the Prosecution shall be heard or received.

(5) The Defense may make an opening statement after the Prosecution's opening statement or prior to presenting its case.

(6) The witnesses and other evidence for the Defense shall be heard or received.

(7) Thereafter, the Prosecution and the Defense may introduce evidence in rebuttal and surrebuttal.

(8) The Prosecution shall present argument to the Commission. Defense Counsel shall be permitted to present argument in response, and then the Prosecution may reply in rebuttal.

(9) After the members of the Commission deliberate and vote on findings in closed conference, the Presiding Officer shall announce the Commission's findings in the presence of the Commission, the Prosecution, the Accused, and Defense Counsel. The individual votes of the members of the Commission shall not be disclosed.

(10) In the event a finding of Guilty is entered for an offense, the Prosecution and the Defense may present information to aid the Commission in determining an appropriate sentence. The Accused may testify and shall be subject to crossexamination regarding any such testimony.

(11) The Prosecution and, thereafter, the Defense shall present argument to the Commission regarding sentencing.

(12) After the members of the Commission deliberate and vote on a sentence in closed conference, the Presiding Officer shall announce the Commission's sentence in the presence of the Commission, the Prosecution, the Accused, and Defense Counsel. The individual votes of the members of the Commission shall not be disclosed.

F. Voting

Members of the Commission shall deliberate and vote in closed conference. A Commission member shall vote for a finding of Guilty as to an offense if and only if that member is convinced beyond a reasonable doubt, based on the evidence admitted at trial, that the Accused is guilty of the offense. An affirmative vote of two-thirds of the members is required for a finding of Guilty. When appropriate, the Commission may adjust a charged offense by exceptions and substitutions of language that do not substantially change the nature of the offense or increase its seriousness, or it may vote to convict of a lesser-included offense. An affirmative vote of two-thirds of the members is required to determine a sentence, except that a sentence of death requires a unanimous, affirmative vote of all of the members. Votes on findings and sentences shall be taken by secret, written ballot.

G. Sentence

Upon conviction of an Accused, the Commission shall impose a sentence that is appropriate to the offense or offenses for which there was a finding of Guilty, which sentence may include death, imprisonment for life or for any lesser term, payment of a fine or restitution, or such other lawful punishment or condition of punishment as the Commission shall determine to be proper. Only a Commission of seven members may sentence an Accused to death. A Commission may (subject to rights of third parties) order confiscation of any property of a convicted Accused, deprive that Accused of any stolen property, or order the delivery of such property to the United States for disposition.

H. Post-Trial Procedures

(1) Record of Trial
Each Commission shall make a verbatim transcript of its proceedings, apart from all Commission deliberations, and preserve all evidence admitted in the trial (including any sentencing proceedings) of each case brought before it, which shall constitute the record of trial. The court reporter shall prepare the official record of trial and submit it to the Presiding Officer for authentication upon completion. The Presiding Officer shall transmit the authenticated record of trial to the Appointing Authority. If the Secretary of Defense is serving as the Appointing Authority, the record shall be transmitted to the Review Panel constituted under Section 6(H)(4).

(2) Finality of Findings and Sentence
A Commission finding as to a charge and any sentence of a Commission becomes final when the President or, if designated by the President, the Secretary of Defense makes a final decision thereon pursuant to Section 4(c)(8) of the President's Military Order and in accordance with Section 6(H)(6) of this Order. An authenticated finding of Not Guilty as to a charge shall not be changed to a finding of Guilty. Any sentence made final by action of the President or the Secretary of Defense shall be carried out promptly. Adjudged confinement shall begin immediately following the trial.

(3) Review by the Appointing Authority
If the Secretary of Defense is not the Appointing Authority, the Appointing Authority shall promptly perform an administrative review of the record of trial. If satisfied that the proceedings of the Commission were administratively complete, the Appointing Authority shall transmit the record of trial to the Review Panel constituted under Section 6(H)(4). If not so satisfied, the Appointing Authority shall return the case for any necessary supplementary proceedings.

(4) Review Panel
The Secretary of Defense shall designate a Review Panel consisting of three Military Officers, which may include civilians commissioned pursuant to reference (e). At least one member of each Review Panel shall have experience as a judge. The Review Panel shall review the record of trial and, in its discretion, any written submissions from the Prosecution and the Defense and shall deliberate in closed conference. The Review Panel shall disregard any variance from procedures specified in this Order or elsewhere that would not materially have affected the outcome of the trial before the Commission. Within thirty days

after receipt of the record of trial, the Review Panel shall either (a) forward the case to the Secretary of Defense with a recommendation as to disposition, or (b) return the case to the Appointing Authority for further proceedings, provided that a majority of the Review Panel has formed a definite and firm conviction that a material error of law occurred.

(5) Review by the Secretary of Defense

The Secretary of Defense shall review the record of trial and the recommendation of the Review Panel and either return the case for further proceedings or, unless making the final decision pursuant to a Presidential designation under Section 4(c)(8) of the President's Military Order, forward it to the President with a recommendation as to disposition.

(6) Final Decision

After review by the Secretary of Defense, the record of trial and all recommendations will be forwarded to the President for review and final decision (unless the President has designated the Secretary of Defense to perform this function). If the President has so designated the Secretary of Defense, the Secretary may approve or disapprove findings or change a finding of Guilty to a finding of Guilty to a lesser-included offense, or mitigate, commute, defer, or suspend the sentence imposed or any portion thereof. If the Secretary of Defense is authorized to render the final decision, the review of the Secretary of Defense under Section 6(H)(5) shall constitute the final decision.

7. Regulations

A. Supplementary Regulations and Instructions

The Appointing Authority shall, subject to approval of the General Counsel of the Department of Defense if the Appointing Authority is not the Secretary of Defense, publish such further regulations consistent with the President's Military Order and this Order as are necessary or appropriate for the conduct of proceedings by Commissions under the President's Military Order. The General Counsel shall issue such instructions consistent with the President's Military Order and this Order as the General Counsel deems necessary to facilitate the conduct of proceedings by such Commissions, including those governing the establishment of Commission-related offices and performance evaluation and reporting relationships.

B. Construction

In the event of any inconsistency between the President's Military Order and this Order, including any supplementary regulations or instructions issued under Section 7(A), the provisions of the President's Military Order shall govern. In the event of any inconsistency between this Order and any regulations or instructions issued under Section 7(A), the provisions of this Order shall govern.

8. Authority

Nothing in this Order shall be construed to limit in any way the authority of the President as Commander in Chief of the Armed Forces or the power of the President to grant reprieves and pardons. Nothing in this Order shall affect the authority to constitute military commissions for a purpose not governed by the President's Military Order.

9. Protection of State Secrets

Nothing in this Order shall be construed to authorize disclosure of state secrets to any person not authorized to receive them.

10. Other

This Order is not intended to and does not create any right, benefit, or privilege, substantive or procedural, enforceable by any party, against the United States, its departments, agencies, or other entities, its officers or employees, or any other person. No provision in this Order shall be construed to be a requirement of the United States Constitution. Section and subsection captions in this document are for convenience only and shall not be used in construing the requirements of this Order. Failure to meet a time period specified in this Order, or supplementary regulations or instructions issued under Section 7(A), shall not create a right to relief for the Accused or any other person. Reference (f) shall not apply to this Order or any supplementary regulations or instructions issued under Section 7(A).

11. Amendment

The Secretary of Defense may amend this Order from time to time.

12. Delegation

The authority of the Secretary of Defense to make requests for assistance under Section 5 of the President's Military Order is delegated to the General Counsel of the Department of Defense. The Executive Secretary of the Department of Defense shall provide such assistance to the General Counsel as the General Counsel determines necessary for this purpose.

13. Effective Date

This Order is effective immediately.

Donald H. Rumsfeld
Secretary of Defense

7.2   NATIONAL LAW

☛ **USA: An Act – Making supplemental appropriations for further recovery from and response to terrorist attacks on the United States for the fiscal year ending September 30, 2002, and for other purposes (aka, American Service-members' Protection Act), 23 January 2002**

Be it enacted by the Senate and House of Representatives of the United States of America in Congress assembled, That the following sums are appropriated, out of any money in the Treasury not otherwise appropriated, for the fiscal year ending September 30, 2002, and for other purposes, namely:

Title I—Supplemental Appropriations

TITLE II—American Servicemembers' Protection Act

Sec. 2001. Short Title.

This title may be cited as the 'American Servicemembers' Protection Act of 2002'.
Sec. 2002.

Sec. 2003. Findings

Congress makes the following findings:
(1) On July 17, 1998, the United Nations Diplomatic Conference of Plenipotentiaries on the Establishment of an International Criminal Court, meeting in Rome, Italy, adopted the 'Rome Statute of the International Criminal Court'. The vote on whether to proceed with the statute was 120 in favor to 7 against, with 21 countries abstaining. The United States voted against final adoption of the Rome Statute.
(2) As of April 30, 2001, 139 countries had signed the Rome Statute and 30 had ratified it. Pursuant to Article 126 of the Rome Statute, the statute will enter into force on the first day of the month after the 60th day following the date on which the 60th country deposits an instrument ratifying the statute.
(3) Since adoption of the Rome Statute, a Preparatory Commission for the International Criminal Court has met regularly to draft documents to implement the Rome Statute, including Rules of Procedure and Evidence, Elements of Crimes, and a definition of the Crime of Aggression.
(4) During testimony before the Congress following the adoption of the Rome Statute, the lead United States negotiator, Ambassador David Scheffer stated that the United States could not sign the Rome Statute because certain critical negotiating objectives of the United States had not been achieved. As a result, he stated: 'We are left with consequences that do not serve the cause of international justice.'
(5) Ambassador Scheffer went on to tell the Congress that: 'Multinational peacekeeping forces operating in a country that has joined the treaty can be exposed to the Court's jurisdiction even if the country of the individual peacekeeper has not joined the treaty. Thus, the treaty purports to establish an arrangement whereby United States armed forces operating overseas could be conceivably prosecuted by the international court even if the United States has not agreed to be bound by the treaty. Not only is this contrary to the most fundamental principles of treaty law, it could inhibit the ability of the United States to use its military to meet alliance obligations and participate in multinational operations, including humanitarian interventions to save civilian lives. Other contributors to peacekeeping operations will be similarly exposed.'
(6) Notwithstanding these concerns, President Clinton directed that the United States sign the Rome Statute on December 31, 2000. In a statement issued that day, he stated that in view of the unremedied deficiencies of the Rome Statute, 'I will not, and do not recommend that my successor submit the Treaty to the Senate for advice and consent until our fundamental concerns are satisfied'.
(7) Any American prosecuted by the International Criminal Court will, under the Rome Statute, be denied procedural protections to which all Americans are entitled under the Bill of Rights to the United States Constitution, such as the right to trial by jury.

(8) Members of the Armed Forces of the United States should be free from the risk of prosecution by the International Criminal Court, especially when they are stationed or deployed around the world to protect the vital national interests of the United States. The United States Government has an obligation to protect the members of its Armed Forces, to the maximum extent possible, against criminal prosecutions carried out by the International Criminal Court.

(9) In addition to exposing members of the Armed Forces of the United States to the risk of international criminal prosecution, the Rome Statute creates a risk that the President and other senior elected and appointed officials of the United States Government may be prosecuted by the International Criminal Court. Particularly if the Preparatory Commission agrees on a definition of the Crime of Aggression over United States objections, senior United States officials may be at risk of criminal prosecution for national security decisions involving such matters as responding to acts of terrorism, preventing the proliferation of weapons of mass destruction, and deterring aggression. No less than members of the Armed Forces of the United States, senior officials of the United States Government should be free from the risk of prosecution by the International Criminal Court, especially with respect to official actions taken by them to protect the national interests of the United States.

(10) Any agreement within the Preparatory Commission on a definition of the Crime of Aggression that usurps the prerogative of the United Nations Security Council under Article 39 of the charter of the United Nations to 'determine the existence of any ... act of aggression' would contravene the charter of the United Nations and undermine deterrence.

(11) It is a fundamental principle of international law that a treaty is binding upon its parties only and that it does not create obligations for nonparties without their consent to be bound. The United States is not a party to the Rome Statute and will not be bound by any of its terms. The United States will not recognize the jurisdiction of the International Criminal Court over United States nationals.

Sec. 2003. Waiver and Termination of Prohibitions of this Title

(a) Authority to Initially Waive Sections 5 and 7 – The President is authorized to waive the prohibitions and requirements of sections 2005 and 2007 for a single period of 1 year. A waiver under this subsection may be issued only if the President at least 15 days in advance of exercising such authority –

(1) notifies the appropriate congressional committees of the intention to exercise such authority; and

(2) determines and reports to the appropriate congressional committees that the International Criminal Court has entered into a binding agreement that –

(A) prohibits the International Criminal Court from seeking to exercise jurisdiction over the following persons with respect to actions undertaken by them in an official capacity:

(i) covered United States persons;

(ii) covered allied persons; and

(iii) individuals who were covered United States persons or covered allied persons; and

(B) ensures that no person described in subparagraph (A) will be arrested, detained, prosecuted, or imprisoned by or on behalf of
the International Criminal Court.

(b) Authority to Extend Waiver of Sections 5 and 7 – The President is authorized to waive the prohibitions and requirements of sections 2005 and 2007 for successive periods of 1 year each upon the expiration of a previous waiver pursuant to subsection (a) or this subsection. A waiver under this subsection may be issued only if the President at least 15 days in advance of exercising such authority –

(1) notifies the appropriate congressional committees of the intention to exercise such authority; and

(2) determines and reports to the appropriate congressional committees that the International Criminal Court –

(A) remains party to, and has continued to abide by, a binding agreement that–

(i) prohibits the International Criminal Court from seeking to exercise jurisdiction over the following persons with respect to actions undertaken by them in an official capacity:

(I) covered United States persons;

(II) covered allied persons; and

(III) individuals who were covered United States persons or covered allied persons; and

(ii) ensures that no person described in clause (i) will be arrested, detained, prosecuted, or imprisoned by or on behalf of the International Criminal Court; and

(B) has taken no steps to arrest, detain, prosecute, or imprison any person described in clause (i) of subparagraph (A).

(c) Authority to Waive Sections 4 and 6 With Respect to an Investigation or Prosecution of a Named Individual – The President is authorized to waive the prohibitions and requirements of sections 2004 and 2006 to the degree such prohibitions and requirements would prevent United States cooperation with an investigation or prosecution of a named individual by the International Criminal Court. A waiver under this subsection may be issued only if the President at least 15 days in advance of exercising such authority –

(1) notifies the appropriate congressional committees of the intention to exercise such authority; and

(2) determines and reports to the appropriate congressional committees that –

(A) a waiver pursuant to subsection (a) or (b) of the prohibitions and requirements of sections 2005 and 2007 is in effect;

(B) there is reason to believe that the named individual committed the crime or crimes that are the subject of the International
Criminal Court's investigation or prosecution;

(C) it is in the national interest of the United States for the International Criminal Court's investigation or prosecution of the named individual to proceed; and

(D) in investigating events related to actions by the named individual, none of the following persons will be investigated, arrested, detained, prosecuted, or imprisoned by or on behalf of the International Criminal Court with respect to actions undertaken by them in an official capacity:

(i) Covered United States persons.

(ii) Covered allied persons.

(iii) Individuals who were covered United States persons or covered allied persons.

(d) Termination of Waiver Pursuant to Subsection (c) – Any waiver or waivers exercised pursuant to subsection (c) of the prohibitions and requirements of sections 2004 and 2006 shall terminate at any time that a waiver pursuant to subsection (a) or (b) of the prohibitions and requirements of sections 2005 and 2007 expires and is not extended pursuant to subsection (b).

(e) Termination of Prohibitions of this Title – The prohibitions and requirements of sections 2004, 2005, 2006, and 2007 shall cease to apply, and the authority of section 2008 shall terminate, if the United States becomes a party to the International Criminal Court pursuant to a treaty made under article II, section 2, clause 2 of the Constitution of the United States.

Sec. 2004. Prohibition on Cooperation with the International Criminal Court

(a) Application – The provisions of this section –
(1) apply only to cooperation with the International Criminal Court and shall not apply to cooperation with an ad hoc international criminal tribunal established by the United Nations Security Council before or after the date of the enactment of this Act to investigate and prosecute war crimes committed in a specific country or during a specific conflict; and
(2) shall not prohibit –
(A) any action permitted under section 2008; or
(B) communication by the United States of its policy with respect to a matter.

(b) Prohibition on Responding to Requests for Cooperation – Notwithstanding section 1782 of title 28, United States Code, or any other provision of law, no United States Court, and no agency or entity of any State or local government, including any court, may cooperate with the International Criminal Court in response to a request for cooperation submitted by the International Criminal Court pursuant to the Rome Statute.

(c) Prohibition on Transmittal of Letters Rogatory from the International Criminal Court – Notwithstanding section 1781 of title 28, United States Code, or any other provision of law, no agency of the United States Government may transmit for execution any letter rogatory issued, or other request for cooperation made, by the International Criminal Court to the tribunal, officer, or agency in the United States to whom it is addressed.

(d) Prohibition on Extradition to the International Criminal Court – Notwithstanding any other provision of law, no agency or entity of the United States Government or of any State or local government may extradite any person from the United States to the International Criminal Court, nor support the transfer of any United States citizen or permanent resident alien to the International Criminal Court.

(e) Prohibition on Provision of Support to the International Criminal Court – Notwithstanding any other provision of law, no agency or entity of the United States Government or of any State or local government, including any court, may provide support to the International Criminal Court.

(f) Prohibition on Use of Appropriated Funds to Assist the International Criminal Court – Notwithstanding any other provision of law, no funds appropriated under any provision of law may be used for the purpose of assisting the investigation, arrest, detention, extradition, or prosecution of any United States citizen or permanent resident alien by the International Criminal Court.

(g) Restriction on Assistance Pursuant to Mutual Legal Assistance Treaties – The United States shall exercise its rights to limit the use of assistance provided under all treaties and executive agreements for mutual legal assistance in criminal matters, multilateral conventions with legal assistance provisions, and extradition treaties, to which the United States is a party, and in connection with the execution or issuance of any letter rogatory, to prevent the transfer to, or other use by, the International Criminal Court of any assistance provided by the United States under such treaties and letters rogatory.

(h) Prohibition on Investigative Activities of Agents – No agent of the International Criminal Court may conduct, in the United States or any territory subject to the jurisdiction of the United States, any investigative activity relating to a preliminary inquiry, investigation, prosecution, or other proceeding at the International Criminal Court.

Sec. 2005. Restrictions on United States Participation in Certain United Nations Peacekeeping Operations

(a) Policy – Effective beginning on the date on which the Rome Statute enters into force pursuant to Article 126 of the Rome Statute, the President should use the voice and vote of the United States in the United Nations Security Council to ensure that each resolution of the Security Council authorizing any peacekeeping operation under chapter VI of the charter of the United Nations or peace enforcement operation under chapter VII of the charter of the United Nations permanently exempts, at a minimum, members of the Armed Forces of the United States participating in such operation from criminal prosecution or other assertion of jurisdiction by the International Criminal Court for actions undertaken by such personnel in connection with the operation.

(b) Restriction – Members of the Armed Forces of the United States may not participate in any peacekeeping operation under chapter VI of the charter of the United Nations or peace enforcement operation under chapter VII of the charter of the United Nations, the creation of which is authorized by the United Nations Security Council on or after the date that the Rome Statute enters into effect pursuant to Article 126 of the Rome Statute, unless the President has submitted to the appropriate congressional committees a certification described in subsection (c) with respect to such operation.

(c) Certification – The certification referred to in subsection (b) is a certification by the President that –
(1) members of the Armed Forces of the United States are able to participate in the peacekeeping or peace enforcement operation without risk of criminal prosecution or other assertion of jurisdiction by the International Criminal Court because, in authorizing the operation, the United Nations Security Council permanently exempted, at a minimum, members of the Armed Forces of the United States participating in the operation from criminal prosecution or other assertion of jurisdiction by the International Criminal Court for actions undertaken by them in connection with the operation;
(2) members of the Armed Forces of the United States are able to participate in the peacekeeping or peace enforcement operation without risk of criminal prosecution or other assertion of jurisdiction by the International Criminal Court because each country in which members of the Armed Forces of the United States participating in the operation will be present either is not a party to the International Criminal Court and has not invoked the jurisdiction of the International Criminal Court pursuant to Article 12 of the Rome Statute, or has entered into an agreement in accordance with Article 98 of the Rome Statute pre-

venting the International Criminal Court from proceeding against members of the Armed Forces of the United States present in that country; or

(3) the national interests of the United States justify participation by members of the Armed Forces of the United States in the peacekeeping or peace enforcement operation.

Sec. 2006. Prohibition on Direct or Indirect Transfer of Classified National Security Information and Law Enforcement Information to the International Criminal Court.

(a) In General – Not later than the date on which the Rome Statute enters into force, the President shall ensure that appropriate procedures are in place to prevent the transfer of classified national security information and law enforcement information to the International Criminal Court for the purpose of facilitating an investigation, apprehension, or prosecution.

(b) Indirect Transfer – The procedures adopted pursuant to subsection (a) shall be designed to prevent the transfer to the United Nations and to the government of any country that is party to the International Criminal Court of classified national security information and law enforcement information that specifically relates to matters known to be under investigation or prosecution by the International Criminal Court, except to the degree that satisfactory assurances are received from the United Nations or that government, as the case may be, that such information will not be made available to the International Criminal Court for the purpose of facilitating an investigation, apprehension, or prosecution.

(c) Construction – The provisions of this section shall not be construed to prohibit any action permitted under section 2008.

Sec. 2007. Prohibition of United States Military Assistance to Parties to the International Criminal Court.

(a) Prohibition of Military Assistance – Subject to subsections (b) and (c), and effective 1 year after the date on which the Rome Statute enters into force pursuant to Article 126 of the Rome Statute, no United States military assistance may be provided to the government of a country that is a party to the International Criminal Court.

(b) National Interest Waiver – The President may, without prior notice to Congress, waive the prohibition of subsection (a) with respect to a particular country if he determines and reports to the appropriate congressional committees that it is important to the national interest of the United States to waive such prohibition.

(c) Article 98 Waiver – The President may, without prior notice to Congress, waive the prohibition of subsection (a) with respect to a particular country if he determines and reports to the appropriate congressional committees that such country has entered into an agreement with the United States pursuant to Article 98 of the Rome Statute preventing the International Criminal court from proceeding against United States personnel present in such country.

(d) Exemption – The prohibition of subsection (a) shall not apply to the government of –

(1) a NATO member country;
(2) a major non-NATO ally (including Australia, Egypt, Israel, Japan, Jordan, Argentina, the Republic of Korea, and New Zealand); or
(3) Taiwan.

Sec. 2008. Authority to Free Members of the Armed Forces of the United States and Certain Other Persons Detained or Imprisoned by or on Behalf of the International Criminal Court.

(a) Authority – The President is authorized to use all means necessary and appropriate to bring about the release of any person described in subsection (b) who is being detained or imprisoned by, on behalf of, or at the request of the International Criminal Court.

(b) Persons Authorized to the Freed – The authority of subsection (a) shall extend to the following persons:
(1) Covered United States persons.
(2) Covered allied persons.
(3) Individuals detained or imprisoned for official actions taken while the individual was a covered United States person or a covered allied person, and in the case of a covered allied person, upon the request of such government.

(c) Authorization of Legal Assistance – When any person described in subsection (b) is arrested, detained, investigated, prosecuted, or imprisoned by, on behalf of, or at the request of the International Criminal Court, the President is authorized to direct any agency of the United States Government to provide –
(1) legal representation and other legal assistance to that person (including, in the case of a person entitled to assistance under section 1037 of title 10, United States Code, representation and other assistance in the manner provided in that section);
(2) exculpatory evidence on behalf of that person; and
(3) defense of the interests of the United States through appearance before the International Criminal Court pursuant to Article 18 or 19 of the Rome Statute, or before the courts or tribunals of any country.

(d) Bribes and Other Inducements Not Authorized – This section does not authorize the payment of bribes or the provision of other such incentives to induce the release of a person described in subsection (b).

Sec. 2009. Alliance Command Arrangements.

(a) Report on Alliance Command Arrangements – Not later than 6 months after the date of the enactment of this Act, the President should transmit to the appropriate congressional committees a report with respect to each military alliance to which the United States is party –
(1) describing the degree to which members of the Armed Forces of the United States may, in the context of military operations undertaken by or pursuant to that alliance, be placed under the command or operational control of foreign military officers subject to the jurisdiction of the International Criminal Court because they are nationals of a party to the International Criminal Court; and (2) evaluating the degree to which members of the Armed

Forces of the United States engaged in military operations undertaken by or pursuant to that alliance may be exposed to greater risks as a result of being placed under the command or operational control of foreign military officers subject to the jurisdiction of the International Criminal Court.

(b) Description of Measures to Achieve Enhanced Protection for Members of the Aremd Forces of the United States – Not later than 1 year after the date of the enactment of this Act, the President should transmit to the appropriate congressional committees a description of modifications to command and operational control arrangements within military alliances to which the United States is a party that could be made in order to reduce any risks to members of the Armed Forces of the United States identified pursuant to subsection (a)(2).

(c) Submission in Classified Form – The report under subsection (a), and the description of measures under subsection (b), or appropriate parts thereof, may be submitted in classified form.

Sec. 2010. Withholdings.

Funds withheld from the United States share of assessments to the United Nations or any other international organization during any fiscal year pursuant to section 705 of the Admiral James W. Nance and Meg Donovan Foreign Relations Authorization Act, Fiscal Years 2000 and 2001 (as enacted by section 1000(a)(7) of Public Law 106-113; 113 Stat. 1501A-460), are authorized to be transferred to the Embassy Security, Construction and Maintenance Account of the Department of State.

Sec. 2011. Application of Sections 2004 and 2006 to Exercise of Constitutional Authorities.

(a) In General – Sections 2004 and 2006 shall not apply to any action or actions with respect to a specific matter involving the International Criminal Court taken or directed by the President on a case-by-case basis in the exercise of the President's authority as Commander in Chief of the Armed Forces of the United States under article II, section 2 of the United States Constitution or in the exercise of the executive power under article II, section 1 of the United States Constitution.

(b) Notification to Congress –
(1) In General – Subject to paragraph (2), not later than 15 days after the President takes or directs an action or actions described in subsection (a) that would otherwise be prohibited under section 2004 or 2006, the President shall submit a notification of such action to the appropriate congressional committees. A notification under this paragraph shall include a description of the action, a determination that the action is in the national interest of the United States, and a justification for the action.
(2) Exception – If the President determines that a full notification under paragraph (1) could jeopardize the national security of the United States or compromise a United States law enforcement activity, not later than 15 days after the President takes or directs an action or actions referred to in paragraph (1) the President shall notify the appropriate congressional committees that an action has been taken and a determination has been made pursuant to

this paragraph. The President shall provide a full notification under paragraph (1) not later than 15 days after the reasons for the determination under this paragraph no longer apply.

(c) Construction – Nothing in this section shall be construed as a grant of statutory authority to the President to take any action.

Sec. 2012. Non-Delegation

The authorities vested in the President by sections 2003 and 2011(a) may not be delegated by the President pursuant to section 301 of title 3, United States Code, or any other provision of law. The authority vested in the President by section 2005(c)(3) may not be delegated by the President pursuant to section 301 of title 3, United States Code, or any other provision of law to any official other than the Secretary of Defense, and if so delegated may not be subdelegated.

Sec. 2013. Definitions.

As used in this title and in section 706 of the Admiral James W. Nance and Meg Donovan Foreign Relations Authorization Act, Fiscal Years 2000 and 2001:
(1) Appropriate Congressional Committees – The term 'appropriate congressional committees' means the Committee on International Relations of the House of Representatives and the Committee on Foreign Relations of the Senate.
(2) Classified National Security Information – The term 'classified national security information' means information that is classified or classifiable under Executive Order 12958 or a successor Executive order.
(3) Covered Allied Persons – The term 'covered allied persons' means military personnel, elected or appointed officials, and other persons employed by or working on behalf of the government of a NATO member country, a major non-NATO ally (including Australia, Egypt, Israel, Japan, Jordan, Argentina, the Republic of Korea, and New Zealand), or Taiwan, for so long as that government is not a party to the International Criminal Court and wishes its officials and other persons working on its behalf to be exempted from the jurisdiction of the International Criminal Court.
(4) Covered United States Persons – The term 'covered United States persons' means members of the Armed Forces of the United States, elected or appointed officials of the United States Government, and other persons employed by or working on behalf of the United States Government, for so long as the United States is not a party to the International Criminal Court.
(5) Extradition – The terms 'extradition' and 'extradite' mean the extradition of a person in accordance with the provisions of chapter 209 of title 18, United States Code, (including section 3181(b) of such title) and such terms include both extradition and surrender as those terms are defined in Article 102 of the Rome Statute.
(6) International Criminal Court – The term 'International Criminal Court' means the court established by the Rome Statute.
(7) Major Non-NATO Ally – The term 'major non-NATO ally' means a country that has been so designated in accordance with section 517 of the Foreign Assistance Act of 1961.
(8) Participate in Any United Nations or Peace Enforcement Operation Under Chapter VII of the Charter of the United Nations – The term 'participate in any peacekeeping operation under chapter VI of the charter of the United Nations or peace enforcement operation under

chapter VII of the charter of the United Nations' means to assign members of the Armed Forces of the United States to a United Nations military command structure as part of a peacekeeping operation under chapter VI of the charter of the United Nations or peace enforcement operation under chapter VII of the charter of the United Nations in which those members of the Armed Forces of the United States are subject to the command or operational control of one or more foreign military officers not appointed in conformity with article II, section 2, clause 2 of the Constitution of the United States.

(9) Party to the International Criminal Court – The term 'party to the International Criminal Court' means a government that has deposited an instrument of ratification, acceptance, approval, or accession to the Rome Statute, and has not withdrawn from the Rome Statute pursuant to Article 127 thereof.

(10) Peacekeeping Operation Under Chapter VII of the Charter of the United Nations or Peace Enforcement Operation Under Chapter VII of the Charter of the United Nations – The term 'peacekeeping operation under chapter VI of the charter of the United Nations or peace enforcement operation under chapter VII of the charter of the United Nations' means any military operation to maintain or restore international peace and security that –

(A) is authorized by the United Nations Security Council under chapter VI or VII of the charter of the United Nations; and

(B) is paid for from assessed contributions of United Nations members that are made available for peacekeeping or peace enforcement activities.

(11) Rome Statute – The term 'Rome Statute' means the Rome Statute of the International Criminal Court, adopted by the United Nations Diplomatic Conference of Plenipotentiaries on the Establishment of an International Criminal Court on July 17, 1998.

(12) Support – The term 'support' means assistance of any kind, including financial support, transfer of property or other material support, services, intelligence sharing, law enforcement cooperation, the training or detail of personnel, and the arrest or detention of individuals.

(13) United States Military Assistance – The term 'United States military assistance' means –

(A) assistance provided under chapter 2 or 5 of part II of the Foreign Assistance Act of 1961 (22 U.S.C. 2151 et seq.); or

(B) defense articles or defense services furnished with the financial assistance of the United States Government, including through loans and guarantees, under section 23 of the Arms Export Control Act (22 U.S.C. 2763).

Sec. 2014. Repeal of Limitation.

The Department of Defense Appropriations Act, 2002 (division A of Public Law 107-117) is amended by striking section 8173.

Sec. 2015. Assistance to International Efforts.

Nothing in this title shall prohibit the United States from rendering assistance to international efforts to bring to justice Saddam Hussein, Slobodan Milosovic, Osama bin Laden, other members of Al Queda, leaders of Islamic Jihad, and other foreign nationals accused of genocide, war crimes or crimes against humanity.

TITLE III—Other Matters.

This Act may be cited as the '2002 Supplemental Appropriations Act for Further Recovery From and Response To Terrorist Attacks on the United States'.

7.22   LEGISLATION TO IMPLEMENT OBLIGATIONS *VIS À VIS* THE STATUTE OF THE INTERNATIONAL CRIMINAL COURT AND OTHER INTERNATIONAL CRIMINAL TRIBUNALS AND COURTS

☛ **Germany: Act to Introduce the Code of Crimes against International Law of 26 June 2002**[45]

The Federal Parliament has passed the following Act:

Article 1 – Code of Crimes against International Law (CCAIL)

Part 1
General provisions

Section 1
Scope of application

This Act shall apply to all criminal offences against international law designated under this Act, to serious criminal offences[46] designated therein even when the offence was committed abroad and bears no relation to Germany.

Section 2
Application of the general law

The general criminal law shall apply to offences pursuant to this Act so far as this Act does not make special provision in sections 1 and 3 to 5.

Section 3
Acting upon orders

Whoever commits an offence pursuant to Sections 8 to 14 in execution of a military order or of an order comparable in its actual binding effect shall have acted without guilt so far as the perpetrator does not realise that the order is unlawful and so far as it is also not manifestly unlawful.

---

45.   Translation Brian Duffett; revision by Jan Christoph Nemitz and Steffen Wirth.

46.   [1] In German law the term "serious criminal offence" ("Verbrechen") is used to denote criminal offences ("Straftaten") that are punishable with not less than one year of imprisonment. Mitigating (and aggravating) circumstances – as regulated for instance in section 8 subsection (5) – are to be disregarded in this respect (section 12 German Criminal Code). As a result, all criminal offences in the present Draft Code are "serious criminal offences" ("Verbrechen") with the sole exception of the criminal offences in sections 13 and 14 (see the Explanations: B. Article 1, section 1). Please note that the terminological differentiation between "criminal offences" ("Straftaten") and "serious criminal offence" ("Verbrechen") is, for technical reasons, not reflected everywhere in this translation.

Section 4
Responsibility of military commanders and other superiors

(1) A military commander or civilian superior who omits to prevent his or her subordinate from committing an offence pursuant to this Act shall be punished in the same way as a perpetrator of the offence committed by that subordinate. Section 13 subsection (2) of the Criminal Code shall not apply in this case.

(2) Any person effectively giving orders or exercising command and control in a unit shall be deemed equivalent to a military commander. Any person effectively exercising command and control in a civil organisation or in an enterprise shall be deemed equivalent to a civilian superior.

Section 5
Non-applicability of statute of limitations

The prosecution of serious criminal offencess pursuant to this Act and the execution of sentences imposed on their account shall not be subject to any statute of limitations. ("Straftaten") and "serious criminal offences" ("Verbrechen") is, for technical reasons, not reflected everywhere in this translation.

Part 2
Crimes against International Law

Chapter 1
Genocide and crimes against humanity

Section 6
Genocide

(1) Whoever with the intent of destroying as such, in whole or in part, a national, racial, religious or ethnic group
1. kills a member of the group,
2. causes serious bodily or mental harm to a member of the group, especially of the kind referred to in section 226 of the Criminal Code,
3. inflicts on the group conditions of life calculated to bring about their physical destruction in whole or in part,
4. imposes measures intended to prevent births within the group,
5. forcibly transfers a child of the group to another group
shall be punished with imprisonment for life.
(2) In less serious cases referred to under subsection (1), numbers 2 to 5, the punishment shall be imprisonment for not less than five years.

Section 7
Crimes against humanity

(1) Whoever, as part of a widespread or systematic attack directed against any civilian population,
1. kills a person,

2. inflicts, with the intent of destroying a population in whole or in part, conditions of life on that population or on parts thereof, being conditions calculated to bring about its physical destruction in whole or in part,

3. traffics in persons, particularly in women or children, or whoever enslaves a person in another way and in doing so arrogates to himself a right of ownership over that person,

4. deports or forcibly transfers, by expulsion or other coercive acts, a person lawfully present in an area to another State or another area in contravention of a general rule of international law,

5. tortures a person in his or her custody or otherwise under his or her control by causing that person substantial physical or mental harm or suffering where such harm or suffering does not arise only from sanctions that are compatible with international law,

6. sexually coerces, rapes, forces into prostitution or deprives a person of his or her reproductive capacity, or confines a woman forcibly made pregnant with the intent of affecting the ethnic composition of any population,

7. causes a person's enforced disappearance, with the intention of removing him or her from the protection of the law for a prolonged period of time,

(a) by abducting that person on behalf of or with the approval of a State or a political organisation, or by otherwise severely depriving such person of his or her physical liberty, followed by a failure immediately to give truthful information, upon inquiry, on that person's fate and whereabouts, or

(b) by refusing, on behalf of a State or of a political organisation or in contravention of a legal duty, to give information immediately on the fate and whereabouts of the person deprived of his or her physical liberty under the circumstances referred to under letter (a) above, or by giving false information thereon,

8. causes another person severe physical or mental harm, especially of the kind referred to in section 226 of the Criminal Code,

9. severely deprives, in contravention of a general rule of international law, a person of his or her physical liberty, or

10. persecutes an identifiable group or collectivity by depriving such group or collectivity of fundamental human rights, or by substantially restricting the same, on political, racial, national, ethnic, cultural or religious, gender or other grounds that are recognised as impermissible under the general rules of international law shall be punished, in the cases referred to under numbers 1 and 2, with imprisonment for life, in the cases referred to under numbers 3 to 7, with imprisonment for not less than five years, and, in the cases referred to under numbers 8 to 10, with imprisonment for not less than three years.

(2) In less serious cases under subsection (1), number 2, the punishment shall be imprisonment for not less than five years, in less serious cases under subsection (1), numbers 3 to 7, imprisonment for not less than two years, and in less serious cases under subsection (1), numbers 8 and 9, imprisonment for not less than one year.

(3) Where the perpetrator causes the death of a person through an offence pursuant to subsection (1), numbers 3 to 10, the punishment shall be imprisonment for life or for not less than ten years in cases under subsection (1), numbers 3 to 7, and imprisonment for not less than five years in cases under subsection (1), numbers 8 to 10.

(4) In less serious cases under subsection (3) the punishment for an offence pursuant to subsection (1), numbers 3 to 7, shall be imprisonment for not less than five years, and for an offence pursuant to subsection (1), numbers 8 to 10, imprisonment for not less than three years.

(5) Whoever commits a crime pursuant to subsection (1) with the intention of maintaining an institutionalised regime of systematic oppression and domination by one racial group

over any other shall be punished with imprisonment for not less than five years so far as the offence is not punishable more severely pursuant to subsection (1) or subsection (3). In less serious cases the punishment shall be imprisonment for not less than three years so far as the offence is not punishable more severely pursuant to subsection (2) or subsection (4).

Chapter 2
War crimes

Section 8
War crimes against persons

(1) Whoever in connection with an international armed conflict or with an armed conflict not of an international character
1. kills a person who is to be protected under international humanitarian law,
2. takes hostage a person who is to be protected under international humanitarian law,
3. treats a person who is to be protected under international humanitarian law cruelly or inhumanly by causing him or her substantial physical or mental harm or suffering, especially by torturing or mutilating that person,
4. sexually coerces, rapes, forces into prostitution or deprives a person who is to be protected under international humanitarian law of his or her reproductive capacity, or confines a woman forcibly made pregnant with the intent of affecting the ethnic composition of any population,
5. conscripts children under the age of fifteen years into the armed forces, or enlists them in the armed forces or in armed groups, or uses them to participate actively in hostilities,
6. deports or forcibly transfers, by expulsion or other coercive acts, a person who is to be protected under international humanitarian law and lawfully present in an area to another State or another area in contravention of a general rule of international law,
7. imposes on, or executes a substantial sentence in respect of a person who is to be protected under international humanitarian law, in particular the death penalty or imprisonment, without that person having been sentenced in a fair and regular trial affording the legal guarantees required by international law,
8. exposes a person who is to be protected under international humanitarian law to the risk of death or of serious injury to health
(a) by carrying out experiments on such a person , being a person who has not previously given his or her voluntary and express consent, or where the experiments concerned are neither medically necessary nor carried out in his or her interest,
(b) by taking body tissue or organs from such a person for transplantation purposes so far as it does not constitute removal of blood or skin for therapeutic purposes in conformity with generally recognised medical principles and the person concerned has previously not given his or her voluntary and express consent, or
(c) by using treatment methods that are not medically recognised on such person, without this being necessary from a medical point of view and without the person concerned having previously given his or her voluntary and express consent, or
9. treats a person who is to be protected under international humanitarian law in a gravely humiliating or degrading manner shall be punished, in the cases referred to under number 1, with imprisonment for life,
in the cases referred to under number 2, with imprisonment for not less than five years,

in the cases referred to under numbers 3 to 5, with imprisonment for not less than three years,

in the cases referred to under numbers 6 to 8, with imprisonment for not less than two years, and, in the cases referred to under number 9, with imprisonment for not less than one year.

(2) Whoever in connection with an international armed conflict or with an armed conflict not of an international character, wounds a member of the adverse armed forces or a combatant of the adverse party after the latter has surrendered unconditionally or is otherwise placed hors de combat shall be punished with imprisonment for not less than three years.

(3) Whoever in connection with an international armed conflict

1. unlawfully holds as a prisoner or unjustifiably delays the return home of a protected person within the meaning of subsection (6), number 1,

2. transfers, as a member of an Occupying Power, parts of its own civilian population into the occupied territory,

3. compels a protected person within the meaning of subsection (6), number 1, by force or threat of appreciable harm to serve in the forces of a hostile Power or

4. compels a national of the adverse party by force or threat of appreciable harm to take part in the operations of war directed against his or her own country

shall be punished with imprisonment for not less than two years.

(4) Where the perpetrator causes the death of the victim through an offence pursuant to subsection (1), numbers 2 to 6, the punishment shall, in the cases referred to under subsection (1), number 2, be imprisonment for life or imprisonment for not less than ten years, in the cases referred to under subsection (1), numbers 3 to 5, imprisonment for not less than five years, and, in the cases referred to under subsection (1), number 6, imprisonment for not less than three years. Where an act referred to under subsection (1), number 8, causes death or serious harm to health, the punishment shall be imprisonment for not less than three years.

(5) In less serious cases referred to under subsection (1), number 2, the punishment shall be imprisonment for not less than two years, in less serious cases referred to under subsection (1), numbers 3 and 4, and under subsection (2) the punishment shall be imprisonment for not less than one year, in less serious cases referred to under subsection (1), number 6, and under subsection (3), number 1, the punishment shall be imprisonment from six months to five years.

(6) Persons who are to be protected under international humanitarian law shall be

1. in an international armed conflict: persons protected for the purposes of the Geneva Conventions and of the Protocol Additional to the Geneva Conventions (Protocol I) (annexed to this Act), namely the wounded, the sick, the shipwrecked, prisoners of war and civilians;

2. in an armed conflict not of an international character: the wounded, the sick, the shipwrecked as well as persons taking no active part in the hostilities who are in the power of the adverse party;

3. in an international armed conflict and in an armed conflict not of an international character: members of armed forces and combatants of the adverse party, both of whom have laid down their arms or have no other means of defence.

Section 9
War crimes against property and other rights

(1) Whoever in connection with an international armed conflict or with an armed conflict not of an international character pillages or, unless this is imperatively demanded by the

necessities of the armed conflict, otherwise extensively destroys, appropriates or seizes property of the adverse party contrary to international law, such property being in the power of the perpetrator's party, shall be punished with imprisonment from one to ten years.

(2) Whoever in connection with an international armed conflict and contrary to international law declares the rights and actions of all, or of a substantial proportion of, the nationals of the hostile party abolished, suspended or inadmissible in a court of law shall be punished with imprisonment from one to ten years.

Section 10
War crimes against humanitarian operations and emblems

(1) Whoever in connection with an international armed conflict or with an armed conflict not of an international character
1. directs an attack against personnel, installations, material, units or vehicles involved in a humanitarian assistance or peacekeeping mission in accordance with the Charter of the United Nations, as long as they are entitled to the protection given to civilians or civilian objects under international humanitarian law, or
2. directs an attack against personnel, buildings, material, medical units and transport, using the distinctive emblems of the Geneva Conventions in conformity with international humanitarian law
shall be punished with imprisonment for not less than three years. In less serious cases, particularly where the attack does not take place by military means, the punishment shall be imprisonment for not less than one year.
(2) Whoever in connection with an international armed conflict or with an armed conflict not of an international character makes improper use of the distinctive emblems of the Geneva Conventions, of the flag of truce, of the flag or of the military insignia or of the uniform of the enemy or of the United Nations, thereby causing a person's death or serious personal injury (section 226 of the Criminal Code) shall be punished with imprisonment for not less than five years.

Section 11
War crimes consisting in the use of prohibited methods of warfare

(1) Whoever in connection with an international armed conflict or with an armed conflict not of an international character
1. directs an attack by military means against the civilian population as such or against individual civilians not taking direct part in hostilities,
2. directs an attack by military means against civilian objects, so long as these objects are protected as such by international humanitarian law, namely buildings dedicated to religion, education, art, science or charitable purposes, historic monuments, hospitals and places where the sick and wounded are collected, or against undefended towns, villages, dwellings or buildings, or against demilitarized zones, or against works and installations containing dangerous forces,
3. carries out an attack by military means and definitely anticipates that the attack will cause death or injury to civilians or damage to civilian objects on a scale out of proportion to the concrete and direct overall military advantage anticipated,
4. uses a person who is to be protected under international humanitarian law as a shield to restrain a hostile party from undertaking operations of war against certain targets,

5. uses starvation of civilians as a method of warfare by depriving them of objects indispensable to their survival or impedes relief supplies in contravention of international humanitarian law,

6. orders or threatens, as a commander, that no quarter will be given, or

7. treacherously kills or wounds a member of the hostile armed forces or a combatant of the adverse party

shall be punished with imprisonment for not less than three years. In less serious cases under number 2 the punishment shall be imprisonment for not less than one year.

(2) Where the perpetrator causes the death or serious injury of a civilian (section 226 of the Criminal Code) or of a person who is to be protected under international humanitarian law through an offence pursuant to subsection (1), numbers 1 to 6, he shall be punished with imprisonment for not less than five years. Where the perpetrator intentionally causes death, the punishment shall be imprisonment for life or for not less than ten years.

(3) Whoever in connection with an international armed conflict carries out an attack by military means and definitely anticipates that the attack will cause widespread, long term and severe damage to the natural environment on a scale out of proportion to the concrete and direct overall military advantage anticipated

shall be punished with imprisonment for not less than three years.

Section 12
War crimes consisting in employment of prohibited means of warfare

(1) Whoever in connection with an international armed conflict or with an armed conflict not of an international character

1. employs poison or poisoned weapons,

2. employs biological or chemical weapons or

3. employs bullets which expand or flatten easily in the human body, in particular bullets with a hard envelope which does not entirely cover the core or is pierced with incisions

shall be punished with imprisonment for not less than three years.

(2) Where the perpetrator causes the death or serious injury of a civilian (section 226 of the Criminal Code) or of a person protected under international humanitarian law through an offence pursuant to subsection (1), he shall be punished with imprisonment for not less than five years. Where the perpetrator intentionally causes death, the punishment shall be imprisonment for life or for not less than ten years.

Chapter 3
Other crimes

Section 13
Violation of the duty of supervision

(1) A military commander who intentionally or negligently omits properly to supervise a subordinate under his or her command or under his or her effective control shall be punished for violation of the duty of supervision if the subordinate commits an offence pursuant to this Act, where the imminent commission of such an offence was discernible to the commander and he or she could have prevented it.

(2) A civilian superior who intentionally or negligently omits properly to supervise a subordinate under his or her authority or under his or her effective control shall be punished for

violation of the duty of supervision if the subordinate commits an offence pursuant to this Act, where the imminent commission of such an offence was discernible to the superior without more and he or she could have prevented it.

(3) Section 4 subsection (2) shall apply *mutatis mutandis*.

(4) Intentional violation of the duty of supervision shall be punished with imprisonment for not more than five years, and negligent violation of the duty of supervision shall be punished with imprisonment for not more than three years.

Section 14
Omission to report a crime

(1) A military commander or a civilian superior who omits immediately to draw the attention of the agency responsible for the investigation or prosecution of any offence pursuant to this Act, to such an offence committed by a subordinate, shall be punished with imprisonment for not more than five years.

(2) Section 4 subsection (2) shall apply *mutatis mutandis*.

Annex (to Section 8 subsection (6) number 1)

For the purposes of this Act the term "Geneva Conventions" shall constitute a reference to the following:
— I. Geneva Convention of 12 August 1949 for the Amelioration of the Condition of the Wounded and Sick in Armed Forces in the Field (Federal Law Gazette 1954 II page 781, 783),
— II. Geneva Convention of 12 August 1949 for the Amelioration of the Condition of Wounded, Sick and Shipwrecked Members of Armed Forces at Sea (Federal Law Gazette 1954 II page 781, 813),
— III. Geneva Convention of 12 August 1949 relative to the Treatment of Prisoners of War (Federal Law Gazette 1954 II page 781, 838) and
— IV. Geneva Convention of 12 August 1949 relative to the Protection of Civilian Persons in Time of War (Federal law Gazette 1954 II page 781, 917).
For the purposes of this Act Protocol I shall constitute a reference to the following:
Protocol Additional to the Geneva Conventions of 12 August 1949 and relating to the Protection of Victims of International Armed Conflicts (Protocol I) of 8 June 1977 (Federal Law Gazette 1990 II page 1550, 1551).

Article 2
Amendment to the Criminal Code

The Criminal Code in the version published on 13 November 1998 (Federal Law Gazette I page 3322), as last amended by Article 11, number 13, of the Act of 20 June 2002 (Federal Law Gazette I page 1946*)*, shall be amended as follows:

1. In the Table of Contents the indications in respect of sections 220 and 220a shall be amended as follows:
"Sections 220 and 220a (Deleted)".

2. Section 6, number 1, shall be hereby repealed.

3. In section 78 subsection (2) the words "under Section 220a (genocide) and" shall be deleted.

4. In section 79 subsection (2) the words "punishments for genocide (Section 220a) and of" shall be deleted.

5. In section 126 subsection (1), number 2, the words "murder, manslaughter or genocide (Sections 211, 212 or 220a)" shall be .replaced by the words "murder

(Section 211), manslaughter (Section 212) or genocide (section 6 of the Code of Crimes against International Law) or a crime against humanity (section 7 of the Code of Crimes against International Law) or a war crime (sections 8, 9, 10, 11 or 12 of the Code of Crimes against International Law)".

6. In section 129a subsection (1), number 1, the words "murder, manslaughter or genocide (Sections 211, 212 or 220a)" shall be replaced by the words "murder (Section 211) or manslaughter (Section 212) or genocide (section 6 of the Code of Crimes against International Law) or crimes against humanity (section 7 of the Code of Crimes against International Law) or war crimes (sections 8, 9, 10, 11 or 12 of the Code of Crimes against International Law)".

7. In section 130 subsection (3) the words "Section 220a subsection (1)" shall be replaced by the words "section 6 subsection (1) of the Code of Crimes against International Law".

8. In section 138 subsection (1), number 6, the words "murder, manslaughter or genocide (Sections 211, 212 or 220a)" shall be replaced by the words "murder (Section 211) or manslaughter (Section 212) or genocide (section 6 of the Code of Crimes against International Law) or a crime against humanity (section 7 of the Code of Crimes against International Law) or a war crime (sections 8, 9, 10, 11 or 12 of the Code of Crimes against International Law)".

9. In section 139 subsection (3), number 2, the words "Section 220a subsection (1), number 1," shall be replaced by the words "section 6 subsection (1), number 1, of the Code of Crimes against International Law or a crime against humanity in the cases under section 7 subsection (1), number 1, of the Code of Crimes against International Law or a war crime in the cases under section 8 subsection (1), number 1, of the Code of Crimes against International Law)".

10. Section 220a shall be hereby repealed.

Article 3
Amendment to the Code of Criminal Procedure

The Code of Criminal Procedure in the version published on 7 April 1987 (Federal Law Gazette I page 1074, 1319), as last amended by Article 1 of the Act of 21 June 2002 (Federal Law Gazette I page 2144), shall be amended as follows:

1. In section 100a, first sentence, number 2, the words "murder, manslaughter or genocide (sections 211, 212, 220a Criminal Code)" shall be replaced by the words "murder, manslaughter (sections 211, 212 Criminal Code) or genocide (section 6 Code of Crimes against International Law)".

2. In section 100c subsection (1), number 3 (a), the words "murder, manslaughter or genocide (sections 211, 212 and 220a Criminal Code) shall be replaced by the words "murder, manslaughter (sections 211, 212 Criminal Code) or genocide (section 6 Code of Crimes against International Law)".

3. In section 112 subsection (3) the words "section 6 subsection (1), number 1, of the Code of Crimes against International Law or" shall be inserted after the words "of a criminal offence pursuant to", and the words "section 220a subsection (1), number 1, Sections" shall be deleted.

4. Section 153c shall be amended as follows:
a) Subsection (1) shall be amended as follows:

aa) In number 2 the comma shall be replaced by a full stop.

bb) The following sentence shall be inserted after number 2:

"Section 153f shall apply to offences punishable pursuant to the Code of Crimes against International Law."

cc) The previous number 3 shall become subsection (2), and the words "The public prosecution office may dispense with prosecuting an offence" shall be inserted after the subsection mark.

b) The previous subsections (2) to (4) shall become subsections (3) to (5).

5. The following section 153f shall be inserted after section 153e: "Section 153f

(1) In the cases referred to under Section 153c subsection (1), numbers 1 and 2, the public prosecution office may dispense with prosecuting an offence punishable pursuant to sections 6 to 14 of the Code of Crimes against International Law, if the accused is not present in Germany and such presence is not to be anticipated. If in the cases referred to under Section 153c subsection (1), number 1, the accused is a German, this shall however apply only where the offence is being prosecuted before an international court or by a state on whose territory the offence was committed or whose national was harmed by the offence.

(2) In the cases referred to under Section 153c subsection (1), numbers 1 and 2, the public prosecution office can, in particular, dispense with prosecuting an offence punishable pursuant to sections 6 to 14 of the Code of Crimes against International Law, if

1. there is no suspicion of a German having committed such offence,

2. such offence was not committed against a German,

3. no suspect in respect of such offence is residing in Germany and such residence is not to be anticipated and

4. the offence is being prosecuted before an international court or by a state on whose territory the offence was committed, whose national is suspected of its commission or whose national was harmed by the offence. The same shall apply if a foreigner accused of an offence committed abroad is residing in Germany but the requirements pursuant to the first sentence, numbers 2 and 4, have been fulfilled and transfer to an international court or extradition to the prosecuting state is permissible and is intended.

(3) If in the cases referred to under subsection (1) or (2) public charges have already been preferred, the public prosecution office may withdraw the charges at any stage of the proceedings and terminate the proceedings.

Article 4
Amendment to the Courts Constitution Act

In section 120 subsection (1), number 8, of the Courts Constitution Act in the version published on 9 May 1975 (Federal Law Gazette I page 1077), as last amended by Article 4 of the Act of 21 June 2002 (Federal Law Gazette I page 2144), the words "(section 220a Criminal Code)" shall be replaced by the words "(section 6 Code of Crimes against International Law)".

Article 5
Amendment to the Act Amending the Introductory Act to the Courts Constitution Act

In Article 2 paragraph (1), first sentence, number 1, of the Act Amending the Introductory Act to the Courts Constitution Act of 30 September 1977 (Federal Law Gazette I page 1877), as amended by Article 4 of the Act of 28 March 1980 (Federal Law Gazette I page

373), the words "murder, manslaughter or genocide (sections 211, 212, 220a)" shall be replaced by the words "murder or manslaughter (sections 211, 212) or genocide (section 6 of the Code of Crimes against International Law)".

Article 6
Amendment to the Act on State Security Files of the Former German Democratic Republic

Section 23 subsection (1), first sentence, number 1 (b) of the Act on State Security Files of the Former German Democratic Republic of 20 December 1991 (Federal Law Gazette I page 2272), as last amended by Article 3, number 3, of the Act of 20 December 2001 (Federal Law Gazette I page 3926), shall be amended as follows:
1. The words "or 220a" shall be deleted.
2. The following dash shall precede the first dash:
"– section 6 of the Code of Crimes against International Law,".

Article 7
Repeal of a continuing provision of the Criminal Code of the German Democratic Republic

Section 84 of the Criminal Code of the German Democratic Republic – CC – of 12 January 1986 in the new version of 14 December 1988 (Law Gazette I 1989 Number 3 page 33), as amended by the Sixth Criminal Law Amendment Act of 29 June 1990 (Law Gazette I Number 39 page 526), which, pursuant to Annex II Title III Subject Area C Chapter I Number 1 of the Unification Treaty of 31 August 1990 in conjunction with Article 1 of the Act of 23 September 1990 (Federal Law Gazette 1990 II page 885, 1168) continues in force, shall be hereby repealed.

Article 8
Entry into force

This Act shall enter into force on the day after its promulgation.

The constitutional rights of the Federal Council have been heeded.
The above Act is hereby executed. It is to be promulgated in the Federal Law Gazette.
Berlin, 26 June 2002
For the Federal President
The President of the Federal Council
Klaus Wowereit
The Federal Chancellor
Gerhard Schröder
The Federal Minister of Justice
Däubler-Gmelin

☛ **Sierra Leone: The Special Court Agreement, 2002, Ratification Act, 2002, 7 March 2002**

Bill
Supplement to the Sierra Leone Gazette Vol. CXXX. No II dated 7th March 2002
The Special Court Agreement, 2002, Ratification, 2002

[…]

Whereas the Agreement for the Special Court which was, for the part of the Government of Sierra Leone, signed under the authority of the President and is by the proviso to subsection (4) of section 40 of the Constitution of Sierra Leone, 1991 required to be ratified by an Act of Parliament:

And Whereas it is desirable that provision be also made for the implementation of all elements of the Agreement that are not self-executing as well as those which need to be supplemented:

Now, Therefore, it is enacted by the President and Members of Parliament in this present Parliament assembled as follows: –

PART I – PRELIMINARY

Interpretation

1. In this Act, unless the context otherwise requires –

"Agreement" means the Agreement between the Government of Sierra Leone and the United Nations for the establishment for the establishment of a Special Court, signed on the 16th January, 2002, and set out in the Schedule; "arresting officer" means a person authorised under this Act to arrest another person;

"Attorney-General" means the Attorney-General and Minister of Justice of Sierra Leone;

"Constitution" means the Constitution of Sierra Leone 1991;

"Director of Prisons" has the same meaning as the Prisons Act, 1960;

"indictee" means a person indicted before the Special Court;

"indictment" means an indictment brought before the Special Court;

"Management Committee" means the Management Committee referred to in Article 7 of the Agreement;

"Minister of Internal Affairs" means the Minister for internal affairs of Sierra Leone;

"officer in charge" has the same meaning as in the Prison Act, 1960;

"official" in relation to the Special Court means the Prosecutor, Deputy Prosecutor, Registrar and any other personnel of the Special Court;

"order of the Special Court" means any order, summons, subpoena, warrant, transfer order or any other order issued by a judge of the Special Court;

"prisoner of Sierra Leone" means a person who is in the lawful custody of the Director of Prisons or officer in charge of any prison, whether or not that person has been convicted of an offence;

"prison officer" has the same meaning as in the Prisons Act, 1960;

"Prosecutor" means the Prosecutor of the Special Court;

"Sierra Leone Court" has the same meaning as in the Constitution;

"Sierra Leone prison" or "prison" means a prison as defined in section 2 of the Prisons Act, 1960;

"Sierra Leone sentence" means any sentence of imprisonment imposed by a Sierra Leone court;

"Special Court" means the Special Court established by the Agreement and includes any organ of the Special Court;

"Special Court prisoner" means a person who is for the time being detained under an order of, or sentence imposed by the Special Court.

PART II – ADMINISTRATION OF SPECIAL COURT

Legal capacity of Special Court

2. (1) The Special Court shall have the capacity to do the following acts in Sierra Leone –

(a) contract;

(b) acquire and dispose of moveable and immovable property;

(c) institute legal proceedings;

(d) enter into agreements with States or such other bodies possessing international legal personality as may be necessary for the exercise of its functions and for the furtherance of its operations; and

(e) any other act a company may undertake pursuant to the Companies Act.

(2) The Special Court shall have a common seal, the affixing of which shall be authenticated by the signatures of –

(a) the President of the Court, and the Registrar, or another member of the staff of the Special Court designated in that behalf by the President of the Court after consultation with the Management Committee.

Administration of Special Court

3. The Registrar shall be responsible immediately to the President of the Special Court for –

(a) the servicing of the Chambers of the Special Court and the Office of the Prosecutor;

(b) the recruitment, administration and discipline of the support staff; and

(c) the day-to-day administration of the financial and staff resources of the Special Court.

Application of funds of Special Court

4. The funds of the Special Court shall be applied to meet the expenses of –

(a) servicing the Chambers of the Special Court;

(b) the salaries, allowances and other costs of the support staff;

(c) the administrative costs of the Special Court other than those specified in paragraphs (a) and (b).

Accounts and audit of funds

5. (1) The Special Court shall keep proper books of account and other records in relation to the activities, property and finances of the Special Court and shall prepare in respect of each financial year of the Special Court a statement of accounts in a form designed to ensure the correct use of the finances of the Special Court.

(2) The accounts of the Special Court kept under subsection (1) shall be audited every six months by an auditor appointed by the Management Committee.

Annual report of the Special Court

6. (1) The Registrar shall, within three months after the end of the financial year of the Special Court, submit for the approval of the Management Committee an annual report of the activities, operation, property and finances of the Special Court for that year.

(2) Subject to subsection (1), an annual report shall include –

(a) a copy of the audited accounts of the Special Court together with the audit report thereon;

(b) the semi-annual summary financial reports of the Special Court for the preceding year approved by the Management Committee.

Property of Special Court

7. (1) The property of the Special Court shall be inviolable, whether by executive, administrative, judicial or legislative action.

(2) Without prejudice to the generality of subsection (1), the property of the Special Court shall not be subject to any laws regarding any of the following –

(a) search and seizure;

(b) requisition;

(c) confiscation; or

(d) expropriation.

(3) The Special Court shall exercise exclusive and free enjoyment of its property, in whole or in part and shall not be dispossessed of any real property unless the President of the Special Court gives express consent otherwise.

(4) Without prejudice to the generality of subsection (3), any real property owned or occupied by the Special Court or any of its organs shall not be subject to any laws or executive or administrative action regarding compulsory acquisition of property.

Financial arrangements of Special Court

8. (1) The Special Court, its funds, assets or property, wherever located and by whomsoever held, shall be immune from every form of legal process in Sierra Leone, unless the President of the Special Court expressly waives this immunity.

(2) Notwithstanding an express waiver of immunity, no funds, assets or property of the Special Court may be subject to any measure of execution.

(3) The Special Court shall be exempt from any financial controls, regulations or moratoriums.

(4) Without prejudice to the generality of subsection (3), the Special Court may –

(a) hold and use funds or negotiable instruments of any kind;

(b) maintain and operate accounts in any currency;

(c) convert any currency held by it into any other currency; and

(d) transfer its funds or currency from Sierra Leone, or within Sierra Leone, or

to the United Nations or any other agency, free of any charges or restrictions.

Premises of Special Court

9. The Government shall endeavour to provide to the premises of the Special Court such utilities, facilities and other services as may be necessary for the operation of the Special Court and shall ensure that the Special Court is not dispossessed of all or any part of the premises of the Special Court without the express consent of the President of the Special Court.

PART III – EXERCISE OF JURISDICTION OF SPECIAL COURT

Jurisdiction, procedure and evidence

10. The Special Court shall exercise the jurisdiction and powers conferred upon it by the Agreement in the manner provided in the Rules of Procedure and Evidence of the International Criminal Tribunal for Rwanda in force at the time of the establishment of the Special Court as adapted for the purposes of the Special Court by the judges of the Special Court as a whole.

Special Court may sit in Sierra Leone

11. (1) The Special Court may sit in Sierra Leone in such place as may be determined by the President of the Special Court after consultation with the Attorney-General for the purpose of performing its functions under the Agreement.

(2) The Special Court shall not form part of the Judiciary of Sierra Leone.

Special Court may administer oaths

12. The Special Court may, at any of its sittings, administer an oath or affirmation giving an undertaking as to truthfulness.

Offences before Special Court

13. Offences prosecuted before the Special Court are not prosecuted in the name of the Republic of Sierra Leone.

Request for deferral or discontinuance of proceedings

14. Where, pursuant to Article 8 of the Statute of the Special Court, the Attorney-General receives any request for deferral or discontinuance in respect of any proceedings, he shall grant the request, if in his opinion there are sufficient grounds for him to do so.

PART IV – MUTUAL ASSISTANCE BETWEEN SIERRA LEONE AND SPECIAL COURT

Request to Sierra Leone for assistance

Request by Special Court for assistance

15. (1) The Attorney-General shall, upon receiving from the Special Court a request for assistance, including an urgent request for assistance, consider such request without any undue delay.

(2) A request for assistance made by the Special Court may include, but shall not be limited to –

(a) identification and location of persons;

(b) service of documents;

(c) arrest or detention of persons; and

(d) transfer of an indictee to the Special Court.

(3) Nothing in this Act shall –

(a) limit the type of assistance the Special Court may request under the Agreement; or

(b) prevent co-operation with the Special Court otherwise than pursuant to this Act, including co-operation of an informal nature.

Execution of request for assistance

16. (1) Subject to subsection (2), if the Special Court makes a request for assistance, it shall be dealt with in accordance with the relevant procedure

(2) If the request for assistance specifies that it should be executed in a particular manner or by using a particular procedure that is not prohibited by Sierra Leone law, the Attorney-General shall use his best endeavours to ensure that the request is executed in that manner or using that procedure.

Confidentiality of request

17. A request for assistance and any supporting documents shall be set confidential by the Sierra Leone authorities who deal with any aspect of the request whenever the request includes a stipulation that it shall be kept confidential, except to the extent that disclosure is necessary for execution of the request.

Response to request

18. (1) The Attorney-General shall notify the Special Court, without undue delay, of his response to a request for assistance and the outcome of any action that has been taken in relation to it.

(2) If the Attorney-General decides to refuse or postpone the assistance requested, in whole or in part, he shall notify the Special Court accordingly and shall set out the reasons for that decision.

(3) If the request for assistance cannot be complied with for any other reason, the notification to the Special Court shall set out the reasons for the inability or failure to comply with the request.

(4) If the request for assistance relates to material that may be prejudicial to the national security of the Republic of Sierra Leone, the Attorney-General shall, without undue delay, notify the Special Court of that fact together with the reasons therefor.

(5) If –

(a) the Special Court has been notified pursuant to subsection (4); and

(b) a Judge of the Special Court nevertheless orders disclosure of the material;

that material shall be transferred to the Special Court.

(6) The disclosure of material to the Special Court under subsection (5) shall be deemed to be an authorised disclosure for the purposes of the Treason and State Offences Act, 1963.

Request to Special Court for assistance

Request by Attorney-General for assistance

19. (1) The Attorney-General may make a request for assistance to the Special Court for the purposes of any investigation into or trial in respect of any act or omission that may constitute a crime within the jurisdiction of the Special Court.

(2) A request for assistance by the Attorney-General and Minister of Justice may include, but shall not be limited to –

(a) the transmission of statements, documents or other types of evidence obtained in the course of an investigation or trial conducted by the Special Court; and

(b) the questioning of any person detained by order of the Special Court.

PART V – ORDERS OF SPECIAL COURT

Orders of Special Court

20. For the purposes of execution, an order of the Special Court shall have the same force or effect as if it had been issued by a Judge, Magistrate or Justice of the Peace of a Sierra Leone court.

Execution of orders

21. (1) Any person executing an order of the Special Court shall comply with any direction specified in that order.

(2) Notwithstanding any other law, every natural person, corporation, or other body created by or under Sierra Leone law shall comply with any direction specified in an order of the Special Court.

(3) Without prejudice to the generality of subsection (1), any person executing an order of the Special Court shall deliver forthwith any books, documents, photographs, tangible objects or other physical objects seized during the execution of that order into the custody of the Special Court.

(4) If a person to whom an order of the Special Court is directed is unable to execute that order, he shall report forthwith the inability to the Special Court and give the reasons therefor.

Forfeiture orders of Special Court

22. (1) When a forfeiture order issued by the Special Court is executed and property, proceeds or assets are delivered to the State, the Minister of Internal Affairs shall –

(a) if a use is specified in the forfeiture order, use the property, proceeds or assets according to that use; or

(b) if no use is specified in the order, either –

(i) use the property, proceeds or assets for a purpose aimed at addressing the consequences of the armed conflict in Sierra

Leone between 1991 and 2002; or

(ii) sell such property, proceeds or assets as may be sold and

deposit the amount realised together with any money forfeited

under the forfeiture order into the War Victims Fund

established pursuant to the Lome Agreement.

(2) The Minister of Internal Affairs shall make such regulations as are necessary to give effect to subsection (1).

PART VI—ARREST AND DELIVERY OF PERSONS

Warrant of arrest

23. For the purposes of execution, a warrant of arrest issued by the Special Court shall have the same force or effect as if it had been issued by a Judge, Magistrate or Justice of the Peace of a Sierra Leone court.

Execution of warrant of arrest

24. Where a warrant of arrest issued under section 23 is executed, the arresting officer shall serve on the person against whom the warrant is issued certified copies of –

(a) the warrant of arrest issued by the Special Court;

(b) where appropriate, the indictment;

(c) a statement of the rights of the accused; and

(d) if necessary, a translation thereof into a language understood by the accused.

Delivery of persons arrested

25. Where a warrant of arrest is executed, the person arrested shall be delivered forthwith into the custody of the Special Court.

Detention after delivery

26. Notwithstanding formal delivery of a person into the custody of the Special Court, a Sierra Leone prison may continue to detain that person on behalf of the Special Court if so requested or ordered by the Special Court.

Execution of warrant of arrest

27. (1) Where a warrant of arrest is issued against a prisoner of Sierra Leone, the arresting officer shall present the warrant of arrest to the Director of Prisons or the officer in charge, who shall deliver the prisoner into the custody of the arresting officer.

(2) After delivery of the prisoner of Sierra Leone into the custody of an arresting officer under subsection (1), the arresting officer shall deal with the prisoner in accordance with sections 24 and 25.

Arrest without warrant

28. Where a person against whom a warrant of arrest is issued under section 23 escapes or is unlawfully at large, he may be arrested without warrant by an arresting officer and, if so arrested, shall be delivered into the custody of the Special Court.

Official position of the accused no bar to arrest etc.

29. The existence of an immunity or special procedural rule attaching to the official capacity of any person shall not be a bar to the arrest and delivery of that person into the custody of the Special Court.

PART VII – JUDGEMENTS AND SENTENCES

Judgements

Proof of orders or judgements

30. (1) Any order or judgement of the Special Court purporting to bear the seal of the Special Court, or to be signed by a person in his capacity as a judge or official of the Special Court, shall be deemed to have been duly sealed or signed by that person, as the case may be.

(2) A document, duly authenticated, which purports to be a copy of any order made or judgement given by the Special Court shall be deemed to be a true copy.

Evidence regarding Special Court procedures and orders

31. (1) For the purposes of this Act, a statement contained in a document, duly authenticated, which purports to have been received in evidence or to be a copy of a document so received, or to set out or summarise evidence given, in proceedings before the Special Court is admissible as evidence of any fact stated in it.

(2) Nothing in this section shall be taken to affect the admission of any evidence, whether contained in a document or otherwise, which is admissible apart from this section.

Sentences

Enforcement of sentences of imprisonment

32. (1) Where a sentence of imprisonment imposed by the Special Court is to be served in Sierra Leone, it shall be served in accordance with the terms of the imprisonment.

(2) Subject to subsection (1), the conditions of imprisonment shall be governed by the relevant laws of Sierra Leone.

Modification of sentences

33. (1) The length of a sentence shall only be modified or altered by the Special Court. *Special Court Agreement, 2002 (Ratification) Act, 2002*

(2) If the length of the sentence is modified or altered by the Special Court, upon notification of the modification or alteration to the Director of Prisons, the length of the sentence of a Special Court prisoner serving his sentence in a Sierra Leone prison shall be modified or altered accordingly.

Supervision of sentences

34. (1) The imprisonment being served by a Special Court prisoner in a Sierra Leone prison shall be subject to supervision by the Special Court.

(2) In allowing the Special Court to supervise the conditions of imprisonment, the Director of Prisons shall ensure –

(a) the facilitation of communication between the Special Court prisoner and the Special Court, including the confidentiality of that communication; and

(b) the provision of any information, report or expert opinion as requested by the Special Court about the imprisonment of the Special Court prisoner; and

(c) the access of a judge or other official of the Special Court to a Special Court prisoner without the presence of any other person, except with the consent of the Special Court prisoner.

(3) Nothing in this section shall prevent the Director of Prisons from complying with any other request of the Special Court in relation to the supervision of sentences.

Pardon or commutation of sentences

35. (1) A Special Court prisoner may only be pardoned or have his sentence commuted by order of the Special Court.

(2) If it appears to the President of the Republic of Sierra Leone that a Special Court prisoner is eligible for pardon or commutation of sentence under the relevant laws of Sierra Leone, he shall notify the Special Court of that fact together with the reasons therefor.

Concurrent Sierra Leone sentences

36. (1) Where a Special Court prisoner is also subject to a Sierra Leone sentence imposed before his sentence of imprisonment is imposed by the Special Court, any sentence of imprisonment imposed by the Special Court shall be deemed to run concurrently with the Sierra Leone sentence, unless the Special Court orders otherwise.

(2) Where a Special Court prisoner is also subject to a Sierra Leone sentence imposed after his sentence of imprisonment is imposed by the Special Court, any sentence of imprisonment imposed by the Special Court shall be deemed to run concurrently with the Sierra Leone sentence, unless the Sierra Leone court orders otherwise.

PART VIII – OFFENCES AGAINST ADMINISTRATION OF JUSTICE AND OTHER OFFENCES

Offences against administration of justice
Obstructing justice

37. (1) Any person who wilfully obstructs, perverts or defeats the course of justice in relation to the Special Court commits an offence and shall be liable, on conviction to a fine not

exceeding two million leones or a term of imprisonment not exceeding two years or to both such fine and imprisonment.

(2) Without prejudice to the generality of subsection (1), a person is deemed willfully to obstruct, pervert or defeat the course of justice who, in any existing or proposed proceeding of the Special Court –

(a) dissuades or attempts to dissuade a person by threats, bribes or other corrupt means from giving evidence; or

(b) accepts, obtains, agrees to accept or attempts to obtain a bribe or other corrupt consideration to abstain from giving evidence.

Obstructing officials

38. Any person who resists or wilfully obstructs –

(a) an official of the Special Court in the execution of his duty, or any person lawfully acting in aid of such an official; or

(b) any person executing an order of the Special Court, commits an offence and shall be liable on conviction, to a fine not exceeding two million leones or to a term of imprisonment not exceeding two years or to both such fine and imprisonment.

Bribery of judges and officials

39. Subject to articles 12 and 13 of the Agreement, any person who –

(a) being a judge or an official of the Special Court, corruptly accepts, obtains, agrees to accept or attempts to obtain for himself or any other person any money, valuable consideration, office, place or employment –

(i) in respect of anything done or omitted or to be done in his official capacity; or

(ii) with intent to interfere in any other way with the administration of justice of the Special Court; or

(b) gives or offers, corruptly, to a judge or an official of the Special Court any money, valuable consideration, office, place or employment –

(i) in respect of anything done or omitted or to be done in his or her official capacity; or

(ii) with intent to interfere in any other way with the administration by justice of the Special Court;

commits an offence and shall be liable on conviction to a fine not exceeding thirty millions leones or to a term of imprisonment not exceeding ten years or to both such fine and imprisonment.

Intimidation of officials and witnesses

40. Any person who, wrongfully or without lawful authority, for the purpose of compelling another person to abstain from doing anything that he has a lawful right to do, or to do anything that he has a lawful right to abstain from doing, in relation to a proceeding of the Special Court, causes the other person reasonably, in all the circumstances, to fear for his safety or the safety of any other person commits an offence and shall be liable on conviction to a fine not exceeding two million leones or to a term of imprisonment not exceeding two years or to both such fine and imprisonment.

Fabricating evidence

41. Any person who, with intent to mislead the Special Court in an existing or proposed proceeding, by any means other than perjury or incitement to perjury –

(a) fabricates anything with intent that it be used as evidence before the Special Court; or

(b) knowingly makes use of fabricated evidence;

commits an offence and shall be liable on conviction to a fine not exceeding two million leones or to a term of imprisonment not exceeding two years or to both such fine and imprisonment.

Offences outside Sierra Leone

42. Any person who commits outside Sierra Leone any act or omission in relation to the Special Court that, if committed in Sierra Leone, would be an offence under this Act, may be tried as if he had committed the act or omission in Sierra Leone.

Other offences

Illegal possession of property

43. (1) Any person who possesses any property or any proceeds of property knowing that all or part of the property or proceeds were obtained or derived directly or indirectly as a result of –

(a) any act or omission that constitutes a crime within the jurisdiction of the Special Court; or

(b) the commission of any offence under this Act;

commits an offence and shall be liable on conviction to a fine not exceeding thirty million leones or to a term of imprisonment not exceeding ten years or to both such fine and imprisonment.

(2) A person is not guilty of an offence under this section by reason only that he is in possession of property or the proceeds of property mentioned in subsection (1) for the purpose of –

(a) executing an order of the Special Court;

(b) complying with a request by the Special Court; or

(c) otherwise acting for the purpose of a lawful investigation

Money laundering

44. (1) Any person who –

(a) knowingly uses, transfers the possession of, sends or delivers to another person or to any place, transports, transmits, alters, disposes of or otherwise deals with, in any manner or by any means, any property or any property or any proceeds of property with intent to conceal or convert the property or proceeds; or

(b) knowing or believing that all or part of the property or proceeds was obtained or derived directly or indirectly as a result of –

(i) any act or omission that constitutes a crime within the jurisdiction of the Special Court; or

(ii) the commission of any offence under this Act;

commits an offence and shall be liable on conviction to a fine not exceeding thirty million leones or to a term of imprisonment not exceeding ten years or to both such fine and imprisonment.

(2) A person is not guilty of an offence under this section by reason only that he is in possession of property or the proceeds of property mentioned in subsection (1) for the purpose of—

(a) executing an order of the Special Court;

(b) complying with a request by the Special Court; or

(c) otherwise acting for the purpose of a lawful investigation.

PART IX – MISCELLANEOUS

Compensation of victims

45. Any person who has been a victim of a crime within the jurisdiction of the Special Court, or persons claiming through him, may claim compensation in accordance with the Criminal Procedure Act, 1965 if the Special Court has found a person guilty of that crime.

Obligations imposed by Agreement

46. Unless this Act provides otherwise, for the purposes of any provision of the Agreement that confers a power, or imposes a duty or function on the State, that power, duty or function may be exercised or carried out on behalf of the Government of Sierra Leone by the Attorney-General.

Regulations

47. The Attorney-General may, after consultation with the Special Court, make regulations to give effect to this Act.

SCHEDULE

Agreement Between the United Nations and the Government of Sierra Leone on the Establishment of a Special Court for Sierra Leone

MEMORANDUM OF OBJECTS AND REASONS

The object of this Bill is to make provision for the ratification and implementation of the Agreement between the Government of Sierra Leone and the United Nations signed on 16th January 2002, for the establishment of the Special Court for Sierra Leone.

It is a requirement of the Constitution under the proviso to subsection (4) of section 40 thereof, that an international agreement which, among other things imposes any charge on the finances of the State, i.e. the Consolidated Fund, must be ratified by either an Act of Parliament or by resolution of Parliament supported by a simple majority vote in Parliament. In addition to compliance with the Constitution, ratification by an Act of Parliament also serves the purpose of transforming the Agreement into local statute and therefore directly applicable in Sierra Leone. However, not all the provisions of the Agreement are capable if being implemented either in the form of the substance in which they appear in the Agreement. There are quite a number of those provisions for which supplementary provisions are needed for their implementation. Thus, for instance, Article 25 of the Statute attached to the Agreement provides that the President of the Special Court shall submit an annual report on the operations and activities of the Court to the Secretary-General and to the Government of Sierra Leone. This provision calls for not only operational but also financial accountability on which the Agreement is silent, hence the need for clauses 3 to 5 of the Bill. Similarly, as a corporate body, the Court must have its own common seal for the authentication of its documents and other instruments of process, provision for which is now made clause 2 of the Bill.

Then again, although the Agreement spells out clearly the jurisdiction of the Special Court, the Agreement is almost silent about the manner in which the jurisdiction may be exercised. Much of the Bill, starting from Part III is devoted to providing for the details needed to effectuate the exercise of jurisdiction by the Special Court.

Solomon E. Berewa
Attorney-General and Minister of Justice
Freetown
Sierra Leone
March, 2002

10.1   EUROPEAN

☛ **European Parliament Resolution P5_TA-PROV(2002)0449 on the International Criminal Court (ICC), 26 September 2002**

The European Parliament,

— having regard to its previous resolutions on the International Criminal Court, in particular those of 19 November 1998,[47] 18 January 2001,[48] 28 February 2002,[49] its resolution of 4 July 2002 on the draft American Service Members' Protection Act (ASPA),[50]

— having regard to the Rome Statute of the International Criminal Court and in particular Articles 16, 86 and 98 thereof,

— having regard to the declaration of 1 July 2002 on the International Criminal Court by the Council Presidency on behalf of the EU,

A. whereas a positive development in transatlantic relations could reinforce the convergence between the European Union and the USA as regards the major values and objectives of democracy and the rule of law and should take place in the framework of a strong commitment to a multilateral approach to problems,

B. whereas the Rome Statute makes a decisive contribution to the implementation of international law and justice and can thus be seen as part of the Copenhagen political criteria,

C. regretting UN Security Council Resolution 1422 adopted on 12 July 2002 on operations established or authorised by the United Nations, whereby the ICC shall not commence or proceed with investigation or prosecution of any case of acts or omissions by current or former officials or personnel from a contributing State not a party to the Rome Statute for a twelve-month period starting on 1 July 2002, with the possibility of renewal each 1 July for a further twelve-month period,

D. whereas the current worldwide political pressure being exerted by the government of the United States to persuade States Parties and Signatory States of the Rome Statute, as well as non-signatory states, to enter into bilateral immunity agreements which seek, through mis-

---

47. [1] OJ C 379, 7.12.1998, p. 265.
48. [2] OJ C 262, 18.9.2001, p. 262.
49. [3] P5_TA(2002)0082
50. [4] P5_TA(2002)0367.

use of its Article 98, to prevent US government officials, employees, military personnel or nationals from being surrendered to the International Criminal Court should not succeed with any country, in particular with the Member States, the candidate countries, the countries involved in the Stabilisation and Association Process, the countries associated with the EU in the Euro-Mediterranean partnership, the Mercosur, Andean Pact and San José Process countries or the ACP countries,

E. regretting that the Council and the Commission did not address clear political guidelines in this regard to the candidate countries, as well as to all the other countries associated with the EU under various agreements,

F. deeply disappointed by the decision of the Romanian government to sign an agreement with the United States contradicting the spirit of the status of the ICC and worried that three other candidate countries – the Czech Republic, Lithuania and Malta – have not yet ratified the treaty,

G. taking the view that Turkey's failure even to sign the Treaty is unacceptable,

H. deeply concerned at the approach to the ICC expressed by representatives of some of the governments of Member States during the informal meeting of the EU foreign ministers in Helsingor on 29 and 30 August 2002 and at the lack of clear information on the outcome of the meeting held in New York on 13 September 2002 between the US Administration and the Foreign Affairs Ministers of the Member States,

I. whereas the independent prosecutor may prosecute criminal acts before the ICC which are not prosecuted in the State Party whose national has committed the crime,

J. insisting that the common guidelines that the Council is to adopt on 30 September 2002 should not represent any step backwards in EU support for the full effectiveness of the ICC and should respect the letter and spirit of the EU common position already adopted in this regard,

1. Underlines that no immunity agreement should ever afford the possibility of impunity for any individual accused of war crimes, crimes against humanity or genocide;

2. Underlines the heavy US involvement in peacekeeping operations and considers that the credibility of the EU position vis-à-vis the United States could be strengthened by accepting a proportionate contribution to peacekeeping operations;

3. Firmly believes that the ICC States Parties and Signatory States are obliged under international law not to defeat the object and purpose of the Rome Statute, under which, according to its Preamble, 'the most serious crimes of concern to the international community as a whole must not go unpunished' and that States Parties are obliged to cooperate fully with the Court, in accordance with Article 86 of the Rome Statute, thus preventing them from entering into immunity agreements which remove certain citizens from the States' or the International Criminal Court's jurisdictions, undermining the full effectiveness of the ICC and jeopardising its role as a complementary jurisdiction to the State jurisdictions and a building block in collective global security;

4. Stresses that the Rome Statute was ratified by all Member States as an essential component of the democratic model and values of the European Union and calls upon the Member States to make the Rome Statute a part of the Community acquis;

5. Expects the governments and parliaments of the Member States to refrain from adopting any agreement which undermines the effective implementation of the Rome Statute considers in consequence that ratifying such an agreement is incompatible with membership of the EU;

6. Addresses the same request to the candidate countries, the countries associated with the EU in the Euro-Mediterranean partnership, the Mercosur, Andean Pact and San José Process countries, the countries involved in the Stabilisation and Association Process and the ACP countries which are parties or signatories to the Statute; encourages the parliaments of Romania, Israel, Tajikistan, East Timor, Honduras, India, Uzbekistan, Mauritania, Palau, the Marshall Islands and the Dominican Republic not to ratify the agreements signed by their governments with the United States, under Article 98 of the Rome Statute;

7. Invites all Signatory States to ratify the Statute and calls in particular on the Czech Republic – currently in the chair of the UN General Assembly –, Lithuania and Malta to do so as a matter of the utmost urgency in order to prevent any delay in the ongoing process of EU accession;

8. Is convinced that the Member States and candidate countries should act as a single bloc in the establishment of the ICC in order to commit fully to it and to enable it to succeed in preserving its independence, impartiality and integrity, in particular by:

— reinforcing the EU political dialogue with the United States, inside and outside the Transatlantic Dialogue, with the purpose of persuading its government to change its attitude towards the ICC,

— reinforcing EU financial support for the ICC through the funding of actions under the European Initiative for Human Rights,

— adopting a common approach to the future appointment of its judges, prosecutor and staff; respecting the principles of transparency and full consistency with the criteria of the Rome Statute, in particular on gender equality;

9. Invites the Conference of European Affairs Committees (COSAC) to examine, at its next meeting in October 2002,[51] the current situation regarding the ICC and the possible violation of the Rome Statute by the bilateral agreements proposed by the USA government under its Article 98;

---

51. Under points II 5 and 6 of the Protocol to the Treaty of Amsterdam on the 'role of National Parliaments in the European Union'.

10. Invites the governments and national parliaments of the candidate countries and all other countries associated with the EU under various agreements respectively to sign and ratify the ICC Treaty immediately;

11. Recalls its request to the Council to present to the European Parliament a progress report on the ICC before the next Copenhagen European Council in December 2002; is of the opinion that this report should identify any international agreement related to the ICC and evaluate its compatibility with the Rome Statute, and therefore with the Community acquis;

12. Urges Member States, candidate countries and all other countries associated with the EU under various agreements to undertake an analysis of the legal implications of Security Council Resolution 1422, and calls for strong action against the renewal of the UN Security Council Resolution in July 2003;

13. Reminds Member States of their obligations regarding the prohibition of the death penalty and the European Arrest Warrant, and calls for an in-depth analysis of the legal implications of Article 98 in this area;

14. Instructs its President to forward this resolution to the Council, the Commission, the parliaments of Romania, Israel, Tajikistan and East Timor, Honduras, India, Uzbekistan, Mauritania, Palau, the Marshall Islands and the Dominican Republic the government and Congress of the United States, the UN Secretary-General, COSAC, the national parliaments of the candidate countries and the abovementioned countries associated with the EU under various agreements, and the President of the Assembly of States Parties to the Rome Statute of the ICC.

☞ Council of the European Union Decision of 13 June 2002 Setting up a European Network of Contact Points in Respect of Persons Responsible for Genocide, Crimes against Humanity and War Crimes (2002/494/JHA)

The Council of the European Union,
Having regard to Title VI of the Treaty on European Union, and in particular Article 30 and Article 34(2)(c) thereof,
Having regard to the initiative of the Kingdom of the Netherlands,
Having regard to the opinion of the European Parliament,[52]
Whereas:
(1) The International Criminal Tribunals for the former Yugoslavia and for Rwanda have since 1995 been investigating, prosecuting and bringing to justice violations of laws and customs of war, genocide and crimes against humanity.
(2) The Rome Statute of the International Criminal Court of 17 July 1998 affirms that the most serious crimes of concern to the international community as a whole, in particular genocide, crimes against humanity and war crimes, must not go unpunished and that their effective prosecution must be ensured by taking measures at national level and by enhancing international cooperation.

---

52. [1] OJ C 295, 20.10.2001, p. 7.

(3) The Rome Statute recalls that it is the duty of every State to exercise its criminal jurisdiction over those responsible for such international crimes.

(4) The Rome Statute emphasises that the International Criminal Court established under it
is to be complementary to national criminal jurisdictions.

(5) All Member States of the European Union have either signed or ratified the Rome Statute.

(6) The investigation and prosecution of, and exchange of information on, genocide, crimes
against humanity and war crimes is to remain the responsibility of national authorities, except as affected by international law.

(7) Member States are being confronted with persons who were involved in such crimes
and are seeking refuge within the European Union's frontiers.

(8) The successful outcome of effective investigation and prosecution of such crimes at
national level depends to a high degree on close cooperation between the various authorities involved in combating them.

(9) It is essential that the relevant authorities of the States Parties to the Rome Statute,
including the Member States of the European Union, cooperate closely in this connection.

(10) Close cooperation will be enhanced if the Member States make provision for direct
communication between centralised, specialised contact points.

(11) Close cooperation between such contact points may provide a more complete overview
of persons involved in such crimes, including the question of in which Member States they
are the subject of investigation.

(12) The Member States, in Council Common Position 2001/443/CFSP of 11 June 2001 on
the International Criminal Court,[53] have expressed that the crimes within the jurisdiction of
the International Criminal Court are of concern for all Member States, which are determined to cooperate for the prevention of those crimes and for putting an end to the impunity
of the perpetrators thereof.

(13) This Decision does not affect any convention, agreement or arrangement regarding
mutual assistance in criminal matters between judicial authorities,

Has Decided As Follows:

Article 1

Designation and notification of contact points

1. Each Member State shall designate a contact point for the exchange of information concerning the investigation of genocide, crimes against humanity and war crimes such as
those defined in Articles 6, 7 and 8 of the Rome Statute of the International Criminal Court
of 17 July 1998.

2. Each Member State shall notify the General Secretariat of the Council in writing of its
contact point within the meaning of this Decision. The General Secretariat shall ensure that
this notification is passed on to the Member States, and inform the Member States of any
changes in these notifications.

Article 2

Collection and exchange of information

1. Each contact point's task shall be to provide on request, in accordance with the relevant
arrangements between Member States and applicable national law, any available informa-

---

53. [2] Opinion delivered on 9 April 2002 (not yet published in the Official Journal).

tion that may be relevant in the context of investigations into genocide, crimes against humanity and war crimes as referred to in Article 1(1), or to facilitate cooperation with the competent national authorities.

2. Within the limits of the applicable national law, contact points may exchange information without a request to that effect.

Article 3

Informing the European Parliament

The Council will inform the European Parliament of the functioning and effectiveness of the European network of contact points in the context of the annual debate held by the European Parliament pursuant to Article 39 of the Treaty.

Article 4

Implementation

Member States shall ensure that they are able to cooperate fully in accordance with the provisions of this Decision at the latest one year after this Decision takes effect.

Article 5

Taking effect

This Decision shall take effect on the date of its adoption.

Done at Luxembourg, 13 June 2002.

For the Council
The President
M. Rajoy Brey

☛ **European Parliament Resolution P5_TA-PROV(2002)0521 on the International Criminal Court, 24 October 2002**

European Parliament resolution on the General Affairs Council's position concerning the International Criminal Court

The European Parliament,

– having regard to its previous resolutions on the International Criminal Court, in particular those of 19 November 1998,[54] 18 January 2001,[55] 28 February 2002,[56] its resolution of 4 July 2002 on the draft American Service Members' Protection Act (ASPA)[57] and its resolution of 26 September 2002,[58]

– having regard to the Rome Statute of the International Criminal Court and in particular Articles 16, 86 and 98 thereof,

---

54. [1] OJ C 379, 7.12.1998, p. 265.
55. [2] OJ C 262, 18.9.2001, p. 262.
56. [3] P5_TA(2002)0082
57. [4] P5_TA(2002)0367.
58. [5] P5_TA(2002)0449.

– having regard to the declaration of 1 July 2002 on the International Criminal Court by the Council Presidency on behalf of the EU,

– having regard to the EU Council conclusion on the ICC and its guiding principles adopted on 30 September,

A. whereas all the Member States and most applicant states have ratified the Rome Statute,

B. underlining that the US action from the very beginning was aimed at weakening the credibility of the ICC, exerting pressure on all the signatories and threatening to impose sanctions on states that ratified the Rome Statute in order to prevent its full establishment,

C. highlighting the fact that by supporting the enactment of the American Service Members' Protection Act (ASPA) in 2001 and withdrawing the signature of the US from the Rome Treaty in 2002 the Bush administration has proved openly its hostility to the ICC,

D. whereas the USA seeks to conclude a series of bilateral immunity agreements to prevent its officials, employees, military personnel or nationals from being surrendered to the ICC,

E. whereas the EU Council, at its meeting on 30 September 2002, adopted four 'guiding principles',

1. Is firmly committed to preserving the full integrity of the Rome Statute and the early establishment as an effectively functioning body of the International Criminal Court;

2. Welcomes the initial efforts of the Danish Presidency to preserve a united position of the EU Member States, but regrets that the General Affairs Council, against the clear will of the European Parliament, has not adopted a clear common position in response to the US Administration's efforts to conclude bilateral agreements with individual Member States and by doing this to undermine the universality of the International Criminal Court;

3. Regrets the vague indications contained in the Council's Decision on the ICC and calls on the Council to undertake further efforts to adopt a truly common EU policy on this issue;

4. Reiterates that no immunity agreement should ever create the possibility of impunity of any individual accused of war crimes, crimes against humanity or genocide;

5. Calls on National Parliaments in the EU and in the applicant countries to carefully scrutinise any activity their respective governments may undertake in relation to the Rome Statute of the ICC;

6. Firmly believes that under the Rome Statute ICC State Parties must refrain from undermining the full effectiveness of the Court and jeopardising the Court's role as a complementary jurisdiction to State jurisdictions;

7. Recalls its request to the Council to present to the Parliament a progress report on the ICC before the Copenhagen European Council in December, identifying any international agreement relating to the ICC and evaluating its compatibility with the Rome Statute;

8. Urges the Council to make all efforts to start a frank dialogue with the US Government and Congress in order to stop the pressure and the threat of sanctions against the countries which have ratified the Rome Treaty and encourage the US administration to approach the ICC in a spirit of cooperation;

9. Recalls that it expects the governments and parliaments of the Member States to refrain from adopting any agreement which undermines the effective implementation of the Rome Statute; considers in consequence that ratifying such an agreement is incompatible with membership of the EU;

10. Addresses the same request to the applicant countries, the countries associated with the EU in the Euro-Mediterranean partnership, the Mercosur, Andean Pact and San José Process countries, the countries involved in the Stabilisation and Association Process and the ACP countries which are parties or signatories to the Statute;

11. Instructs its President to forward this resolution to the Council, the Commission, the Government and Congress of the United States, the President of the Assembly of the state parties to the Rome Statute of the ICC and the National Parliaments of applicant countries and countries associated with the EU under various agreements, in particular the ACP Assembly, which will debate this issue at its upcoming meeting.

13.1   JUS AD BELLUM

☛ Georgia: Statement by the Parliament of Georgia on the 23 August 2002 bombing by the Russian Federation, 26 August 2002

The Parliament of Georgia expresses its extreme indignation and protest regarding the violation of the airspace and bombing the territory of Georgia by the Russian Federation on 23 August 2002 intended to bring destabilization to the country that resulted in civilian casualties. The Parliament of Georgia presents condolences to the families of perished.

Despite the repeated protest statements of the Parliament of Georgia, the Russian Federation still continues barefaced military aggression against Georgia. The OSCE observers have also confirmed the fact of violation of Georgian airspace and bombing. Thus, the refusal of this fact on the Russian side is considered as a cynical attitude towards Georgia and the world community.

The Parliament of Georgia considers this barbaric act as the military aggression against sovereignty of Georgia and such assessment can be based on irresponsible and threatening allegations that have been voiced recently by the high-level officials of the Russian Duma, the Ministry of Foreign Affairs and the Ministry of Defense of the Russian Federation and illegal activities carried out by the Russian peacekeeping forces acting under the aegis of the CIS in Abkhazia and the contingent of the Russian peacekeeping forces deployed in the Tskhinvali region.

The Parliament of Georgia believes that the Russian military aggression is an attempt aimed at undermining the anti-criminal operation to be carried out in Pankisi gorge. Such a position of the Russian Federation runs counter to the norms of international law and constitutes vivid example of the double-standard policy – on the one hand, recognition of Georgia's sovereignty and territorial integrity by Russia, and on the other hand, purposeful and permanent aggressive actions aimed to endanger the state sovereignty of Georgia.

As a result of repeated violations of the airspace and bombing of the territory of Georgia by the Russian Federation, as well as negligence of protest statements of Georgia, the Russian-Georgian relations have reached a deadlock, thereby posing a serious threat to the further development of civilized relationship between these countries and stability in the whole region.

☛ USA: Joint Resolution of Congress to authorize the use of United States Armed Forces against Iraq, 10 October 2002

107th Congress
2d Session
H. J. Res. 114

Joint Resolution

To authorize the use of United States Armed Forces against Iraq.

Whereas in 1990 in response to Iraq's war of aggression against and illegal occupation of Kuwait, the United States forged a coalition of nations to liberate Kuwait and its people in order to defend the national security of the United States and enforce United Nations Security Council resolutions relating to Iraq;

Whereas after the liberation of Kuwait in 1991, Iraq entered into a United Nations sponsored cease-fire agreement pursuant to which Iraq unequivocally agreed, among other things, to eliminate its nuclear, biological, and chemical weapons programs and the means to deliver and develop them, and to end its support for international terrorism;

Whereas the efforts of international weapons inspectors, United States intelligence agencies, and Iraqi defectors led to the discovery that Iraq had large stockpiles of chemical weapons and a large scale biological weapons program, and that Iraq had an advanced nuclear weapons development program that was much closer to producing a nuclear weapon than intelligence reporting had previously indicated;

Whereas Iraq, in direct and flagrant violation of the cease-fire, attempted to thwart the efforts of weapons inspectors to identify and destroy Iraq's weapons of mass destruction stockpiles and development capabilities, which finally resulted in the withdrawal of inspectors from Iraq on October 31, 1998;

Whereas in Public Law 105-235 (August 14, 1998), Congress concluded that Iraq's continuing weapons of mass destruction programs threatened vital United States interests and international peace and security, declared Iraq to be in 'material and unacceptable breach of its international obligations' and urged the President 'to take appropriate action, in accordance with the Constitution and relevant laws of the United States, to bring Iraq into compliance with its international obligations';

Whereas Iraq both poses a continuing threat to the national security of the United States and international peace and security in the Persian Gulf region and remains in material and unacceptable breach of its international obligations by, among other things, continuing to possess and develop a significant chemical and biological weapons capability, actively seeking a nuclear weapons capability, and supporting and harboring terrorist organizations;

Whereas Iraq persists in violating resolution of the United Nations Security Council by continuing to engage in brutal repression of its civilian population thereby threatening international peace and security in the region, by refusing to release, repatriate, or account for non-Iraqi citizens wrongfully detained by Iraq, including an American serviceman, and by failing to return property wrongfully seized by Iraq from Kuwait;

Whereas the current Iraqi regime has demonstrated its capability and willingness to use weapons of mass destruction against other nations and its own people;

Whereas the current Iraqi regime has demonstrated its continuing hostility toward, and willingness to attack, the United States, including by attempting in 1993 to assassinate former President Bush and by firing on many thousands of occasions on United States and Coalition Armed Forces engaged in enforcing the resolutions of the United Nations Security Council;

Whereas members of al Qaida, an organization bearing responsibility for attacks on the United States, its citizens, and interests, including the attacks that occurred on September 11, 2001, are known to be in Iraq;

Whereas Iraq continues to aid and harbor other international terrorist organizations, including organizations that threaten the lives and safety of United States citizens;

Whereas the attacks on the United States of September 11, 2001, underscored the gravity of the threat posed by the acquisition of weapons of mass destruction by international terrorist organizations;

Whereas Iraq's demonstrated capability and willingness to use weapons of mass destruction, the risk that the current Iraqi regime will either employ those weapons to launch a surprise attack against the United States or its Armed Forces or provide them to international terrorists who would do so, and the extreme magnitude of harm that would result to the United States and its citizens from such an attack, combine to justify action by the United States to defend itself;

Whereas United Nations Security Council Resolution 678 (1990) authorizes the use of all necessary means to enforce United Nations Security Council Resolution 660 (1990) and subsequent relevant resolutions and to compel Iraq to cease certain activities that threaten international peace and security, including the development of weapons of mass destruction and refusal or obstruction of United Nations weapons inspections in violation of United Nations Security Council Resolution 687 (1991), repression of its civilian population in violation of United Nations Security Council Resolution 688 (1991), and threatening its neighbors or United Nations operations in Iraq in violation of United Nations Security Council Resolution 949 (1994);

Whereas in the Authorization for Use of Military Force Against Iraq Resolution (Public Law 102-1), Congress has authorized the President 'to use United States Armed Forces pursuant to United Nations Security Council Resolution 678 (1990) in order to achieve implementation of Security Council Resolution 660, 661, 662, 664, 665, 666, 667, 669, 670, 674, and 677';

Whereas in December 1991, Congress expressed its sense that it 'supports the use of all necessary means to achieve the goals of United Nations Security Council Resolution 687 as being consistent with the Authorization of Use of Military Force Against Iraq Resolution (Public Law 102-1),' that Iraq's repression of its civilian population violates United Nations Security Council Resolution 688 and 'constitutes a continuing threat to the peace, security, and stability of the Persian Gulf region,' and that Congress, 'supports the use of all necessary means to achieve the goals of United Nations Security Council Resolution 688';

Whereas the Iraq Liberation Act of 1998 (Public Law 105-338) expressed the sense of Congress that it should be the policy of the United States to support efforts to remove from power the current Iraqi regime and promote the emergence of a democratic government to replace that regime;

Whereas on September 12, 2002, President Bush committed the United States to 'work with the United Nations Security Council to meet our common challenge' posed by Iraq and to 'work for the necessary resolutions,' while also making clear that 'the Security Council resolutions will be enforced, and the just demands of peace and security will be met, or action will be unavoidable';

Whereas the United States is determined to prosecute the war on terrorism and Iraq's ongoing support for international terrorist groups combined with its development of weapons of mass destruction in direct violation of its obligations under the 1991 cease-fire and other United Nations Security Council resolutions make clear that it is in the national security interests of the United States and in furtherance of the war on terrorism that all relevant United Nations Security Council resolutions be enforced, including through the use of force if necessary;

Whereas Congress has taken steps to pursue vigorously the war on terrorism through the provision of authorities and funding requested by the President to take the necessary actions against international terrorists and terrorist organizations, including those nations, organizations, or persons who planned, authorized, committed, or aided the terrorist attacks that occurred on September 11, 2001, or harbored such persons or organizations;

Whereas the President and Congress are determined to continue to take all appropriate actions against international terrorists and terrorist organizations, including those nations, organizations, or persons who planned, authorized, committed, or aided the terrorist attacks that occurred on September 11, 2001, or harbored such persons or organizations;

Whereas the President has authority under the Constitution to take action in order to deter and prevent acts of international terrorism against the United States, as Congress recognized in the joint resolution on Authorization for Use of Military Force (Public Law 107-40); and

Whereas it is in the national security interests of the United States to restore international peace and security to the Persian Gulf region: Now, therefore, be it

Resolved by the Senate and House of Representatives of the United States of America in Congress assembled,

Section 1. Short Title.

This joint resolution may be cited as the 'Authorization for Use of Military Force Against Iraq Resolution of 2002'.

Section 2. Support for United States Diplomatic Efforts.

The Congress of the United States supports the efforts by the President to –

(1) strictly enforce through the United Nations Security Council all relevant Security Council resolutions regarding Iraq and encourages him in those efforts; and

(2) obtain prompt and decisive action by the Security Council to ensure that Iraq abandons its strategy of delay, evasion and noncompliance and promptly and strictly complies with all relevant Security Council resolutions regarding Iraq.

Section 3. Authorization for Use of United States Armed Forces.

(a) Authorization – The President is authorized to use the Armed Forces of the United States as he determines to be necessary and appropriate in order to –

(1) defend the national security of the United States against the continuing threat posed by Iraq; and

(2) enforce all relevant United Nations Security Council resolutions regarding Iraq.

(b) Presidential Determination – In connection with the exercise of the authority granted in subsection (a) to use force the President shall, prior to such exercise or as soon thereafter as may be feasible, but no later than 48 hours after exercising such authority, make available to the Speaker of the House of Representatives and the President pro tempore of the Senate his determination that –

(1) reliance by the United States on further diplomatic or other peaceful means alone either (A) will not adequately protect the national security of the United States against the continuing threat posed by Iraq or (B) is not likely to lead to

enforcement of all relevant United Nations Security Council resolutions regarding Iraq ; and

(2) acting pursuant to this joint resolution is consistent with the United States and other countries continuing to take the necessary actions against international terrorist and terrorist organizations, including those nations, organizations, or persons who planned, authorized, committed or aided the terrorist attacks that occurred on September 11, 2001.

(c) War Powers Resolution Requirements –

(1) Specific Statutory Authorization – Consistent with section 8(a)(1) of the War Powers Resolution, the Congress declares that this section is intended to constitute specific statutory authorization within the meaning of section 5(b) of the War Powers Resolution.

(2) Applicability of Other Requirements – Nothing in this joint resolution supersedes any requirement of the War Powers Resolution.

Section 4. Reports to Congress.

(a) Reports – The President shall, at least once every 60 days, submit to the Congress a report on matters relevant to this joint resolution, including actions taken pursuant to the exercise of authority granted in section 3 and the status of planning for efforts that are expected to be required after such actions are completed, including those actions described in section 7 of the Iraq Liberation Act of 1998 (Public Law 105-338).

(b) Single Consolidated Report – To the extent that the submission of any report described in subsection (a) coincides with the submission of any other report on matters relevant to this joint resolution otherwise required to be submitted to Congress pursuant to the reporting requirements of the War Powers Resolution (Public Law 93-148), all such reports may be submitted as a single consolidated report to the Congress.

(c) Rule of Construction – To the extent that the information required by section 3 of the Authorization for Use of Military Force Against Iraq Resolution (Public Law 102-1) is included in the report required by this section, such report shall be considered as meeting the requirements of section 3 of such resolution.

Passed the House of Representatives October 10, 2002.
Attest:
Clerk.

BIBLIOGRAPHY 2001-2002

0.   INTERNATIONAL HUMANITARIAN LAW IN GENERAL

Books
– Bouchet-Saulnier, Françoise, ed., *The Practical Guide to Humanitarian Law*, 1st English language edn. (Lanham, Rowman & Littlefield 2002) 489 pp.
– Cario, Jérôme, *Le droit des conflits armés* (Panazol, Lavauzelle 2002) 192 pp.
– David, Eric, Françoise Tulkens and Damien Vandermeersch, *Code de droit international humanitaire: textes réunis au 1er mars 2002* (Brussels, Bruylant 2002) 750 pp.
– De Keijzer, M., M. Heijmans-van Bruggen and E. Somers, eds., *Onrecht: oorlog en rechtvaardigheid in de twintigste eeuw* (Zutphen, Walburg Pers 2001) 256 pp.
– Deyra, Michel, *L'essentiel du droit des conflits armés* (Paris, Gualino 2002) 130 pp.
– Fernández-Flores y de Funes, José Luis, *El derecho de los conflictos armados: de iure belli, el derecho de la guerra: el derecho internacional humanitario: el derecho humanitario bélico* (Madrid, Ministerio de Defensa 2001) 879 pp.
– Harouel, Véronique, *Grands textes du droit humanitaire, que sais-je?* (Paris, Presses Universitaires de France 2001) 127 pp.
– Kalshoven, Frits and Liesbeth Zegveld, *Constraints on the Waging of War: An Introduction to International Humanitarian Law*, 3rd edn. (Geneva, International Committee of the Red Cross 2001) 223 pp.
– Kolanowski, Stéphane, ed., *Actes du colloque de Bruges: défis contemporains en droit international humanitaire 27-28 octobre 2000 – Proceedings of the Bruges Colloquium: Current Challenges in International Humanitarian Law 27-28 October 2000* (Bruges, Collège d'Europe 2001) 119 pp.
– Ramón Chornet, Consuelo, *El derecho internacional humanitario ante los nuevos conflictos armadas* (Valencia, Tirant lo Blanch) 398 pp.
– Ronzitti, Natalino, *Diritto internazionale dei conflitti armati*, 2nd edn. (Turin, Giappichelli 2001) 364 pp.
– Round Table on Current Problems of International Humanitarian Law (2 September 1998; San Remo) and Round Table on Current Problems of International Humanitarian Law (2 September 1999; San Remo), *Current Problems of International Humanitarian Law: Proceedings* (Milan, Nagard 2001) 206 pp.
– Ruiz Ruiz, Florentino, *Sucesión de estados y salvaguardia de la dignidad humana: la sucesión de estados en los tratados generales sobre protección de los derechos humanos y derecho humanitario* (Burgos, Universidad de Burgos 2001) 204 pp.
– Van der Wolf, René and Willem-Jan F.M. van der Wolf, eds., *Laws of War and International Law*, Vol. 1 (Nijmegen, Wolf Legal Publishers 2002) 402 pp.
– *Yearbook of International Humanitarian Law*, Vol. 3, 2000 (The Hague, T.M.C. Asser Press 2002) 873 pp.

Articles
– Bouchet-Saulnier, Françoise, 'Just War, Unjust Means? International Humanitarian Law After September 11', 58 *The World Today* (2002) pp. 26-28

– Bring, Ove, 'International Humanitarian Law After Kosovo: Is Lex Lata Sufficient?', 71 *Nordic JIL* (2002) pp. 39-54
– Cockayne, James, 'Islam and International Humanitarian Law: From a Clash to a Conversation Between Civilizations', 84 *IRRC* (2002) pp. 597-626
– Desagné, R., 'European Union Practice in the Field of International Humanitarian Law – An Overview', in V. Kronenberger, ed., *The European Union and the International Legal Order: Discord or Harmony?* (The Hague, T.M.C. Asser Press 2001) pp. 455-477
– Ferraro, Tristan, 'International Humanitarian Law in the European Union's Foreign and Common Security Policy', 84 *IRRC* (2002) pp. 435-461
– Gossiaux, Christian, 'Les règles d'engagement norme juridique nouvelle?', 40 *Revue de droit militaire et de droit de guerre* (2001) pp. 159-179
– Kleffner, Jann, 'Improving Compliance with International Humanitarian Law Through the Establishment of an Individual Complaints Procedure', 15 *Leiden JIL* (2002) pp. 237-250
– Kritsiotis, Dino, 'International Humanitarian Law and the Desintegration of States', 30 *Israel YB HR* (2000) pp. 17-35
– Lebrat, Chantal, ed., 'Dossier: droit de la guerre – Le droit des conflits armés à l'épreuve de la réalité', 275 *Armées d'aujourd'hui* (2002) pp. 34-51
– Mani, V.S., 'International Humanitarian Law: An Indo-Asian Perspective', 83 *IRRC* (2001) pp. 59-76
– Mundis, Daryl A., 'New Mechanisms for the Enforcement of International Humanitarian Law', 95 *AJIL* (2001) pp. 934-952
– Pictet, Jean, 'La formation du droit international humanitaire', 84 *IRRC* (2002) pp. 321-344
– Roberts, Adam, 'The Laws of War After Kosovo', 31 *Israel YB HR* (2001) pp. 79-109
– Sassòli, Marco, 'State Responsibility for Violations of International Humanitarian Law', 84 *IRRC* (2002) pp. 401-434

1.12   Hague Law

Articles

– Bugnion, François, 'Droit de Genève et droit de La Haye', 83 *IRRC* (2001) pp. 901-922
– Vöneky, Silja, 'Der Lieber's Code und die Wurzeln des modernen Kriegsvölkerrechts', 62 *ZaöRV* (2002) pp. 423-460

1.13   Geneva Law

Articles

– Boed, Roman, 'Individual Criminal Responsibility for Violations of Article 3 Common to the Geneva Conventions of 1949 and of Additional Protocol II Thereto in the Case Law of the International Criminal Tribunal for Rwanda', 13 *Criminal LF* (2002) pp. 293-322
– Bugnion, François, 'Droit de Genève et droit de La Haye', 83 *IRRC* (2001) pp. 901-922

– Dixit, R.K., 'Special Protection of Children During Armed Conflicts Under the Geneva Conventions Regime', 1 *ISIL Yearbook of International Humanitarian and Refugee Law* (2001) pp. 12-35

– Eiting, R.M., 'Over "de Geneefse Conventie", "unlawful combatants" en de kenbaarheid van het oorlogsrecht', 95 *Militair Rechtelijk Tijdschrift* (2002) pp. 261-271

– Fux, Pierre-Yves and Mirko Zambelli, 'Mise en oeuvre de la Quatrième Convention de Genève dans les territoires palestiniens occupés: historique d'un processus multilatéral (1997-2001)', 84 *IRRC* (2002) pp. 661-695

– Gandhi, M., 'Common Article 3 of Geneva Conventions, 1949 in the Era of International Criminal Tribunals', 1 *ISIL Yearbook of International Humanitarian and Refugee Law* (2001) pp. 207-218

– Hassouna, Hussein A., 'The Enforcement of the Fourth Geneva Convention in the Occupied Palestinian Territory, Including Jerusalem', 7 *ILSA JI & CL* (2001) pp. 461-468

– Kessler, Birgit, 'The Duty to "Ensure Respect" Under Common Article 1 of the Geneva Conventions: Its Implications on International and Non-International Armed Conflicts', 44 *GYIL* (2001) pp. 498-516

– Schotten, Gregor, 'Gewohnheitsrechtliche Kontrollrechte der Konfliktparteien nicht-internationaler bewaffneter Konflikte bei humanitären Hilfslieferungen: aktuelle Entwicklungen im Lichte der Vierten Genfer Konvention', 15 *Humanitäres Völkerrecht* (2002) pp. 17-25

– Wieczorek, Judith, 'Der völkerrechtliche Status der Gefangenen von Guantanamo nach dem III. Genfer Abkommen über die Behandlung der Kriegsgefangenen vom 12. August 1949', 15 *Humanitäres Völkerrecht* (2002) pp. 88-96

1.14 Post-1977 Developments

Articles

– Benvenuti, Paolo, 'The Two Additional Protocols to the Geneva Conventions 25 Years Later: Achievements and Challenges', 57 *La Comunità internazionale* (2002) pp. 347-362

– Boed, Roman, 'Individual Criminal Responsibility for Violations of Article 3 Common to the Geneva Conventions of 1949 and of Additional Protocol II Thereto in the Case Law of the International Criminal Tribunal for Rwanda', 13 *Criminal LF* (2002) pp. 293-322

– Decaux, Emmanuel, 'La ratification par la France du premier Protocole additionnel aux Conventions de Genève de 1949', 13 *Revue trimestrielle des droits de l'homme* (2002) pp. 321-334

– Fischer, Horst, 'The Additional Protocols 25 Years Later: Remarks on a Success Story', 15 *Humanitäres Völkerrecht* (2002) pp. 218-220

– Henckaerts, Jean-Marie, 'De ontwikkeling van het internationaal humanitair recht: 25 jaar Aanvullende Protocollen', 11 *Zoeklicht* (2002) pp. 11-15

– Kalshoven, Frits, 'Wel en wee van de Internationale Feitencommissie van artikel 90, Protocol I', 11 *Zoeklicht* (2002) pp. 20-23

– Laucci, Cyril, 'La France adhère au protocole I relatif à la protection des victimes des conflits armés internationaux', 105 *RGDIP* (2001) pp. 677-704

– Pocar, Fausto, 'Protocol I Additional to the 1949 Geneva Conventions and Customary International Law', 31 *Israel YB HR* (2001) pp. 145-159

1.15   Customary Law

Articles
– Henckaerts, Jean-Marie, 'International Humanitarian Law as Customary International Law', 21 *Refugee Survey Quarterly* (2002) pp. 186-193
– Magenis, Sean D., 'Natural Law as the Customary International Law of Self-Defense', 20 *Boston Univ. ILJ* (2002) pp. 413-435
– Pocar, Fausto, 'Protocol I Additional to the 1949 Geneva Conventions and Customary International Law', 31 *Israel YB HR* (2001) pp. 145-159

1.2   GENERAL PRINCIPLES

Books
– David, Eric, *Principes de droit des conflits armés*, 3rd edn. (Brussels, Bruylant 2002) 994 pp.

1.21   Martens Clause

Books
– Schircks, Rhea, *Die Martens'sche Klausel: Rezeption und Rechtsqualität* (Baden-Baden, Nomos 2002) 197 pp.

1.22   Superfluous Injury and Unnecessary Suffering

Articles
– Sitaropoulos, Nicholas, 'Weapons and Superfluous Injury or Unnecessary Suffering in International Humanitarian Law: Human Pain in Time of War and the Limits of Law', 54 *Revue hellénique de droit international* (2001) pp. 71-108

1.23   Principle of Distinction

Articles
– Bothe, Michael, 'Legal Restraints on Targeting: Protection of Civilian Population and the Changing Faces of Modern Conflicts', 31 *Israel YB HR* (2001) pp. 35-49
– De Mulinen, Frédéric, 'Distinction Between Military and Civilian Objects', in Christian Tomuschat, ed., *Kosovo and the International Community: A Legal Assessment* (The Hague, Kluwer Law International 2002) pp. 103-127
– Dinstein, Yoram, 'Legitimate Military Objectives Under the Current Jus in Bello', 31 *Israel YB HR* (2001) pp. 1-34

— Terry, James P., 'The Lawfulness of Attacking Computer Networks in Armed Conflict and in Selfdefense in Periods Short of Armed Conflict: What Are the Targeting Constraints?', 169 *Mil. LR* (2001) pp. 70-91

1.24   Principle of Proportionality

Books
— Vale Majerus, Isabel, *De quel droit? Le droit international humanitaire et les dommages collatéraux* (Paris, Le serpent à plumes 2002) 228 pp.

Articles
— Bonafede, Michael C., 'Here, There, and Everywhere: Assessing the Proportionality Doctrine and U.S. Uses of Force in Response to Terrorism After the September 11 Attacks', 88 *Cornell LR* (2002) pp. 155-214
— Cannizzaro, Enzo, 'The Role of Proportionality in the Law of International Countermeasures', 12 *EJIL* (2001) pp. 889-916
— Cerna, Christina, 'Bombing for Peace: Collateral Damage and Human Rights', 96 *Proc. ASIL* (2002) pp. 95-108
— Fenrick, W.J., 'Targeting and Proportionality During the NATO Bombing Campaign Against Yugoslavia', 12 *EJIL* (2001) pp. 489-502
— Herold, Marc W., 'Collateral Damage? Civilians and the US Air War in Afghanistan', 20 *Vierteljahresschrift für Sicherheit und Frieden* (2002) pp. 18-26
— Murphy, John F., 'Some Legal (and a Few Ethical) Dimensions of the Collateral Damage Resulting from NATO's Kosovo Campaign', 31 *Israel YB HR* (2001) pp. 51-77
— Parker, Tom, 'The Proportionality Principle in the War on Terror', 15 *Hague YIL* (2002) pp. 3-15
— Wedgwood, Ruth, 'Proportionality, Cyberwar, and the Law of War', in Michael N. Schmitt and Brian T. O'Donnell, eds., *Computer Network Attack and International Law* (Newport, Naval War College 2002) pp. 219-232

2.1   TYPES OF CONFLICTS

Books
— Coker, Christopher, *Waging War Without Warriors? The Changing Culture of Military Conflict* (Boulder, Lynne Rienner 2002) 225 pp.
— McInnes, Colin, *Spectator-Sport War: The West and Contemporary Conflict* (Boulder, Lynne Rienner 2002) 186 pp.

Articles
— Gareis, Sven Bernhard, 'Die Kriege der Zukunft: Charakteristika, Reaktionsweisen und strategische Erfordernisse', 15 *Humanitäres Völkerrecht* (2002) pp. 151-158
— Geeraerts, Gustaaf and Jacobus Delwaide, 'Gewapend conflict na de Koude Oorlog', 11 *Zoeklicht* (2002) pp. 4-7
— Ibanga, Michael, 'Concept of Armed Conflict in Public International Law: Some Reflections', 14 *Sri Lanka JIL* (2002) pp. 107-116

– Sassòli, Marco, 'The Legal Qualification of the Conflicts in the Former Yugoslavia: Double Standards or New Horizons for International Humanitarian Law?', in Sienho Yee and Wang Tieya, eds., *International Law in the Post-Cold War World: Essays in Memory of Li Haopei* (London, Routledge 2001) pp. 307-333
– Seybolt, Taylor B., 'Major Armed Conflicts', *SIPRI Yearbook* (2001) pp. 15-21

2.11   International

Books

– Conflict Research Unit, Netherlands Institute of International Relations Clingendael, *The Role of SNV in Development Countries in International Armed Conflict* (The Hague, Netherlands Institute of International Relations Clingendael 2001) 51 pp. (SNV = Netherlands Development Organization for Technical Assistance to Development Countries)
– Dixit, J.N., *India-Pakistan in War & Peace*, new reprinted edn. (London, Routledge 2002) 514 pp.
– Racine, Jean-Luc, *Cachemire: au péril de la guerre* (Paris, Autrement 2002) 159 pp.
– Vöneky, Silja, *Die Fortgeltung des Umweltvölkerrechts in internationalen bewaffneten Konflikten* (Berlin, Springer 2001) 593 pp.

Articles

– Abou Zahab, Mariam, Isabelle Cordonnier, Jean-Luc Racine and Waheguru Pal Singh Sidnu, 'Inde-Pakistan: guerre improbable, paix impossible?', 67   *Politique étrangère* (2002) pp. 271-333
– Bacik, Gökhan and Havva Karakas-Keles, 'The Iraqi Question in the International Context and Its Domestic Reflections', 32 *Turkish Yearbook of International Relations* (2001) pp. 61-89
– Boelaert-Suominen, Sonja, 'Internationale en interne conflicten voor het Joegoslavië Tribunaal', 11 *Zoeklicht* (2002) pp. 8-10
– Bradford, William C., 'International Legal Regimes and the Incidence of Interstate War in the Twentieth Century: A Cursory Quantitative Assessment of the Associative Relationship', 16 *Amer. Univ. ILR* (2001) pp. 647-741
– Byron, Christine, 'Armed Conflicts: International or Non-International?', 6 *Journal of Conflict and Security Law* (2001) pp. 63-90
– Davies, Graeme A.M., 'Domestic Strife and the Initiation of International Conflicts: A Directed Dyad Analysis, 1950-1982', 46 *Journal of Conflict Resolution* (2002) pp. 672-692
– Dinstein, Yoram, 'Protection of the Environment in International Armed Conflict', 5 *MPYBUNL* (2001) pp. 523-549
– Dinstein, Yoram et al., 'Humanitarian Law on the Conflict in Afghanistan', 96 *Proc. ASIL* (2002) pp. 23-41
– Dörmann, Knut, 'Preparatory Commission for the International Criminal Court: The Elements of War Crimes: Part II: Other Serious Violations of the Laws and Customs Applicable in International and Non-International Armed Conflicts', 83 *IRRC* (2001) pp. 461-487
– Feinstein, Barry A., 'Operation Enduring Freedom: Legal Dimensions of an Infinitely Just Operation', 11 *Journal of Transnational Law & Policy* (2002) pp. 201-295

– Hoffman, Michael H., 'Rights and Duties, as Captives and Captors, of Nonstate Intervenors During International and Internal Armed Conflicts', 96 *Proc. ASIL* (2002) pp. 32-35

– Kelly, Michael J., 'Understanding September 11th – An International Legal Perspective on the War in Afghanistan', 35 *Creighton LR* (2002) pp. 283-293

– Kessler, Birgit. 'The Duty to "Ensure Respect" Under Common Article 1 of the Geneva Conventions: Its Implications on International and Non-International Armed Conflicts', 44 *GYIL* (2001) pp. 498-516

– Kritsiotis, Diro, 'Armed Activities on the Territory of the Congo (Democratic Republic of Congo) v. Uganda: Provisional Measures', 50 *ICLQ* (2001) pp. 662-670

– Mercado Jarrín, Edgardo, 'La guerra en Afganistán: sus primeras lecciones', 51 *Revista peruana de derecho internacional* (2001) pp. 197-203

– Pozo Serrano, Pilar, 'El estatuto jurídico de las personas detenidas durante el conflicto armado internacional en Afganistán', 18 *Anuario de derecho internacional* (2002) pp. 171-204

– Pratap Singh, Ravi, 'The Non-State Actor as the Potent New Enemy in Global Politics: Beginning of the Third Phase in International Relations', 58 *India Quarterly* (2002) pp. 105-118

2.12 Non-International

Books

– Adebajo, Adekeye, *Liberia's Civil War: Nigeria, ECOMOG, and Regional Security in West Africa* (Boulder, Lynne Rienner 2002) 285 pp.

– Bermejo, Romualdo, *El conflicto árabe-israelí en la encrucijada: ¿Es posible la paz?* (Pamplona, Ediciones Universidad de Navarra 2002) 247 pp.

– Biggar, Nigel, ed., *Burying the Past: Making Peace and Doing Justice After Civil Conflict* (Washington, Georgetown University Press 2001) 312 pp.

– Boyce, James K., *Investing in Peace: Aid and Conditionality After Civil Wars* (Oxford, Oxford University Press 2002) 85 pp.

– Delapierre, Fabienne, *L'application du droit international humanitaire au conflit tchétchène* (Geneva, Institut universitaire des hautes études internationales, Université de Genève 2001) 70 pp.

– Ekango, Njoume and Albert Roger, *Innerstaatliche bewaffnete Konflikte und Drittstaaten* (Leipzig, Leipziger Univ.-Verl. 2002) 277 pp.

– Ghavamabadi, Mohammad Hossein Ramazani, *La codification des normes applicables aux conflits armés non internationaux par le CICR* (Paris, Faculté de droit, Université de Paris X–Nanterre 2002) 112 pp.

– Götze, Andreas, *Fragen der Anwendbarkeit des humanitären Völkerrechts unter besonderer Berücksichtigung der sogenannten Nationalen Befreiungskriege* (Frankfurt am Main, Peter Lang 2002) 558 pp.

– Haumann, Mathew, *Sud-Soudan: la longue route vers la paix* (Paris, Karthala 2002) 178 pp.

– Kumar, Krishna, ed., *Women and Civil War: Impact, Organization and Action* (Boulder, Lynne Rienner 2001) 260 pp.

– Moir, Lindsay, *The Law of Internal Armed Conflict* (Cambridge, Cambridge University Press 2002) 306 pp.
– Nojumi, Neamatollah, *The Rise of the Taliban in Afghanistan: Mass Mobilization, Civil War, and the Future of the Region* (New York, Palgrave 2002) 260 pp.
– Ohlson, Thomas and Mimmi Söderberg, *From Intra-State War to Democratic Peace in Weak States* (Uppsala, Uppsala Universitet / Institutionen för Freds- och Konfliktforskning 2002) 35 pp.
– Stedman, Stephen John, Donald Rothchild and Elizabeth M. Cousens, eds., *Ending Civil Wars: The Implementation of Peace Agreements* (Boulder, Lynne Rienner 2002) 729 pp.
– Walter, Barbara F., *Committing to Peace: The Successful Settlement of Civil Wars* (Princeton, Princeton University Press 2002) 200 pp.
– Zegveld, Liesbeth, *The Accountability and Armed Opposition Groups in International Law* (Cambridge, Cambridge University Press 2002) 288 pp.

Articles

– Adejumobi, Said, 'Citizenship, Rights, and the Problem of Conflicts and Civil Wars in Africa', 23 *HRQ* (2001) pp. 148-170
– Arnold, Roberta, 'The Development of the Notion of War Crimes in Non-International Conflicts Through the Jurisprudence of the UN Ad Hoc Tribunals', 15 *Humanitäres Völkerrecht* (2002) pp. 134-142
– Boelaert-Suominen, Sonja, 'Internationale en interne conflicten voor het Joegoslavië Tribunaal', 11 *Zoeklicht* (2002) pp. 8-10
– Bruch, Carl E., 'All's Not Fair in (Civil) War: Criminal Liability for Environmental Damage in Internal Armed Conflict', 25 *Vermont LR* (2001) pp. 695-752
– Byron, Christine, 'Armed Conflicts: International or Non-International?', 6 *Journal of Conflict and Security Law* (2001) pp. 63-90
– Carcione, Massimo Marco, 'Terrorism and Cultural Property: A "Conflict" of a Non-International Character', 10 *Tilburg For. LR* (2002) pp. 82-89
– Collier, Paul and Anke Hoeffler, 'On the Incidence of Civil War in Africa', 46 *Journal of Conflict Resolution* (2002) pp. 13-28
– Collier, Paul and Nicholas Sambanis, 'Understanding Civil War: A New Agenda', 46 *Journal of Conflict Resolution* (2002) pp. 3-12
– Davies, Graeme A.M., 'Domestic Strife and the Initiation of International Conflicts: A Directed Dyad Analysis, 1950-1982', 46 *Journal of Conflict Resolution* (2002) pp. 672-692
– Dörmann, Knut, 'Preparatory Commission for the International Criminal Court: The Elements of War Crimes: Part II: Other Serious Violations of the Laws and Customs Applicable in International and Non-International Armed Conflicts', 83 *IRRC* (2001) pp. 461-487
– Ferencz, Benjamin B., 'International Trials for Internal Armed Conflicts', 95 *Proc. ASIL* (2001) pp. 35-36
– Fleck, Dieter, 'Towards a Code of Conduct for Internal Armed Conflicts: Current Efforts, Problems, and Opportunities', 96 *Proc. ASIL* (2002) pp. 25-32
– Fujita, Hisakazu, 'Application of International Humanitarian Law to Internal Armed Conflicts', in Timothy L.H. McCormack, Michael Tilbury and Gillian D. Triggs, eds., *A Century of War and Peace: Asia-Pacific Perspectives on the Centenary of the 1899 Hague Peace Conference* (The Hague, Kluwer Law International 2001) pp. 139-154

– Ghebaldi, Victor-Yves, 'Remarques politico-historiques sur l'étiologie des guerres civiles', in Laurence Boisson de Chazournes and Vera Gowlland-Debbas, eds., *The International Legal System in Quest of Equity and Universality: Liber Amicorum Georges Abi-Saab* (The Hague, Nijhoff 2001) pp. 463-476

– Hartzell, Caroline, Matthew Hoddie and Donald Rotchild. 'Stabilizing the Peace After Civil War: An Investigation of Some Key Variables', 55 *International Organization* (2001) pp. 183-208

– Hoffman, Michael H., 'Rights and Duties, as Captives and Captors, of Nonstate Intervenors During International and Internal Armed Conflicts', 96 *Proc. ASIL* (2002) pp. 32-35

– Jackson, Richard, 'The State and Internal Conflict', 55 *Australian Journal of International Affairs* (2001) pp. 65-81

– Jaramillo, Daniel García-Peña, 'Humanitarian Protection in Non-International Conflicts: A Case Study of Colombia', 30 *Israel YB HR* (2000) pp. 179-207

– Juma, Laurence, 'The Human Rights Approach to Peace in Sierra Leone: The Analysis of the Peace Process and Human Rights Enforcement in a Civil War Situation', 30 *Denver JIL & Pol.* (2002) pp. 325-376

– Kessler, Birgit, 'The Duty to "Ensure Respect" Under Common Article 1 of the Geneva Conventions: Its Implications on International and Non-International Armed Conflicts', 44 *GYIL* (2001) pp. 498-516

– Kreß, Claus, 'War Crimes Committed in Non-International Armed Conflict and the Emerging System of International Criminal Justice', 30 *Israel YB HR* (2000) pp. 103-177

– Lair, Éric, 'La Colombie entre guerre et paix', 66 *Politique étrangère* (2001) pp. 110-121

– Larson, Geoff, 'The Right of International Intervention in Civil Conflicts: Evolving International Law on State Sovereignty in Observance of Human Rights and Application to the Crisis in Chechnya', 11 *Transn. L & Contemp. Probs.* (2001) pp. 251-275

– Mansoob Murshed, S., ed., Special Issue: Civil War in Developing Countries, 39 *Journal of Peace Research* (2002) pp. 387-511

– Martin, Randolph, 'Sudan's Perfect War', 81 *Foreign Affairs* (2002) pp. 111-127

– Miller, Anja, 'Military Mergers: The Reintegration of Armed Forces After Civil Wars', 25 *The Fletcher Forum of World Affairs* (2001) pp. 129-146

– Momtaz, Djamchid, 'Le droit international humanitaire applicable aux conflits armés non internationaux', 292 *Recueil des Cours* (2001) pp. 9-145

– Murthy, C.S.R., 'United Nations Peacekeeping in Intrastate Conflicts: Emerging Trends', 38 *International Studies* (2001) pp. 207-227

– Newman, Edward and Albrecht Schnabel, 'Recovering from Civil Conflict. Reconciliation, Peace and Development', 9 *International Peacekeeping* (2002) pp. 1-6

– O'Connell, Mary Ellen, 'Humanitarian Assistance in Non-International Armed Conflict: The Fourth Wave of Rights, Duties and Remedies', 31 *Israel YB HR* (2001) pp. 183-217

– Peterson, Alex G., 'Order out of Chaos: Domestic Enforcement of the Law of Internal Armed Conflict', 171 *Mil. LR* (2002) pp. 1-90

– Ramirez, Philippe, 'La guerre populaire au Népal: d'où viennent les maoïstes?', 107 *Hérodote: revue de géographie et de géopolitique* (2002) pp. 47-64

– Regan, Patrick M., 'Third-Party Interventions and the Duration of Intrastate Conflicts', 46 *Journal of Conflict Resolution* (2002) pp. 55-73

– Sambanis, Nicholas, 'Do Ethnic and Nonethnic Civil Wars Have the Same Causes? A Theoretical and Empirical Inquiry (Part 1)', 45 *Journal of Conflict Resolution* (2001) pp. 259-282

– Schotten, Gregor, 'Gewohnheitsrechtliche Kontrollrechte der Konfliktparteien nicht-internationaler bewaffneter Konflikte bei humanitären Hilfslieferungen: aktuelle Entwicklungen im Lichte der Vierten Genfer Konvention', 15 *Humanitäres Völkerrecht* (2002) pp. 17-25
– Veuthey, Michel, 'Remedies to Promote the Respect of Fundamental Human Values in Non-International Armed Conflicts', 30 *Israel YB HR* (2001) pp. 37-77
– Werner, Wouter G., 'Self-Determination and Civil War', 6 *Journal of Conflict & Security Law* (2001) pp. 171-190

2.13   Other

Books

– Alexander, Yonah and Michael S. Swetman, eds., *Cyber Terrorism and Information Warfare: Treats and Responses* (Ardsley, Transnational Publishers 2001) 248 pp.
– Pottier, Johan, *Re-imagining Rwanda Conflict, Survival and Information Warfare* (Cambridge, Cambridge University Press 2002) 224 pp.
– Zawati, Hilmi M., *Is Jihad a Just War? War, Peace, and Human Rights Under Islamic and Public International Law* (Lewiston, Edwin Mellen Press 2002) 244 pp.

Articles

– Arkin, William, 'Cyber Warfare and the Environment', 25 *Vermont LR* (2001) pp. 779-791
– Gross, Oren and Fionnuala Ni Aolain, 'Emergency, War and International Law – Another Perspective', 70 *Nordic JIL* (2001) pp. 29-63
– Grunewald, François and Laurence Tessier, 'Zones grises, crises durables, conflits oubliés: les défis humanitaires', 83 *IRRC* (2001) pp. 323-351
– Haryomataram, G.P.H., 'Internal Disturbances and Tensions: Forgotten Conflicts', in Timothy L.H. McCormack, Michael Tilbury and Gillian D. Triggs, eds., *A Century of War and Peace: Asia-Pacific Perspectives on the Centenary of the 1899 Hague Peace Conference* (The Hague, Kluwer Law International 2001) pp. 155-166
– Hoffmann, Ralf, 'Information War: Tendenzen – Optionen – Perspektiven', 15 *Humanitäres Völkerrecht* (2002) pp. 158-165
– Kadam, Umesh, 'Protection of Human Rights During Emergency Situations: International Standards and the Constitution of India', 41 *Indian JIL* (2001) pp. 601-621
– Newman, David, 'From Peace to War: Relighting the Flames of the Israel – Palestine Conflict', 9 *Boundary and Security Bulletin* (2001) pp. 94-100

2.21   Armed Forces and Combatant Status

Books

– Legault, Albert and Joel Sokolsky, eds., *The Soldier and the State in the Post Cold War Era* (Montreal, l'Institut Québécois des Hautes Études Internationales, Université Laval, l'Université du Québec 2002) 236 pp.

Articles
- Aldrich, George H., 'The Taliban, Al Qaeda and the Determination of Illegal Combatants', 96 *AJIL* (2002) pp. 891-898
- Anderson, Kenneth, 'What to Do with Bin Laden and Al Qaeda Terrorists? A Qualified Defense of Military Commissions and United States Policy on Detainees at Guantanamo Bay Naval Base', 25 *Harvard Journal of Law & Public Policy* (2002) pp. 591-634
- Broomes, John W., 'Maintaining Honor in Troubled Times: Defining the Rights of Terrorism Suspects Detained in Cuba', 42 *Washburn Law Journal* (2002) pp. 107-141
- Brune, Tim and Daniel H. Göbel, 'BGS und Kombattantenstatus', 43 *Neue Zeitschrift für Wehrrecht* (2001) pp. 241-245
- Eiting, R.M., 'Over "de Geneefse Conventie", "unlawful combatants" en de kenbaarheid van het oorlogsrecht', 95 *Militair Rechtelijk Tijdschrift* (2002) pp. 261-271
- Gill, T.D., 'De gedetineerden in Guantánamo en het internationale humanitaire recht', 77 *Nederlands Juristenblad* (2002) pp. 407-408
- Hoffman, Michael H., 'Quelling Unlawful Belligerency: The Judicial Status and Treatment of Terrorists Under the Laws of War', 31 *Israel YB HR* (2001) pp. 161-181
- Hoffman, Michael H., 'Terrorists Are Unlawful Belligerents, Not Unlawful Combatants: A Distinction with Implications for the Future of International Humanitarian Law', 34 *Case Western Reserve JIL* (2002) pp. 227-230
- Kurt, Michael E., 'Der völkerrechtliche Status der Gefangenen von Guantánamo Bay', 35 *Zeitschrift für Rechtspolitik* (2002) pp. 404-407
- Makubuya, Apollo N., 'Women in the Armed Forces in Uganda: Human Rights Issues', in Wolfgang Benedek, Esther M. Kisaakye and Gerd Oberleitner, eds., *The Human Rights of Women: International Instruments and African Experiences* (London, Zed Books 2002) pp. 295-301
- McDonald, Avril, 'Defining the War on Terror and the Status of Detainees: Comments on the Presentation of Judge George Aldrich', 15 *Humanitäres Völkerrecht* (2002) pp. 206-209
- Pérez González, Manuel and José Luis Rodríguez-Villasante y Prieto, 'El caso de los detenidos de Guantánamo ante el derecho internacional humanitario y de los derechos humanos', 54 *Revista española de derecho internacional* (2002) pp. 11-40
- Peterke, Sven, 'Der aktuelle Fall: Mujahir – der "feindliche Kombattant" mit der "schmutzigen (Atom-)Bombe"', 15 *Humanitäres Völkerrecht* (2002) pp. 143-148
- Pozo Serrano, Pilar, 'El estatuto jurídico de las personas detenidas durante el conflicto armado internacional en Afganistán', 18 *Anuario de derecho internacional* (2002) pp. 171-204
- Shelton, Dinah, 'The Legal Status of the Detainees at Guantanamo Bay: Innovative Elements in the Decision of the Inter-American Commission on Human Rights of 12 March 2002', 23 *HRLJ* (2002) pp. 13-14
- Sinha, Manoj Kumar, 'Al-Qaida Prisoners at Guantanamo Bay: An Inquiry', 42 *Indian JIL* (2002) pp. 85-91
- Talsma, H.J.J., 'De status van gevangen genomen Al Qaeda-strijders in het humanitair oorlogsrecht', 95 *Militair Rechtelijk Tijdschrift* (2002) pp. 120-124
- Weckel, Philippe, 'Le statut incertain des détenus sur la base américaine de Guantanamo', 106 *RGDIP* (2002) pp. 329-369
- Wieczorek, Judith, 'Der völkerrechtliche Status der Gefangenen von Guantanamo nach dem III. Genfer Abkommen über die Behandlung der Kriegsgefangenen vom 12. August 1949', 15 *Humanitäres Völkerrecht* (2002) pp. 88-96

2.22   Non-State Actors

Articles
- Hoffman, Michael H., 'Rights and Duties, as Captives and Captors, of Nonstate Intervenors During International and Internal Armed Conflicts', 96 *Proc. ASIL* (2002) pp. 32-35
- Krajewski, Markus, 'Selbstverteidigung gegen bewaffnete Angriffe nicht-staatlicher Organisation – Der 11. September 2001 und seine Folgen', 40 *Archiv des Völkerrechts* (2002) pp. 183-214
- Orrego Vicuña, Francisco, 'Individuals and Non-State Entities Before International Courts and Tribunals', 5 *MPYBUNL* (2001) pp. 53-66
- Paust, Jordan J., 'Sanctions Against Non-State Actors for Violations of International Law', 8 *ILSA JI & CL* (2002) pp. 417-429

2.231   Mercenaries

Books
- United Nations, Commission on Human Rights, *The Impact of Mercenary Activities on the Right of Peoples to Self-Determination* (Geneva, United Nations 2002) 40 pp.

Articles
- Serewicz, Lawrence W., 'Globalization, Sovereignty and the Military Revolution: From Mercenaries to Private International Security Companies', 39 *International Politics* (2002) pp. 75-89

3.12   Prisoners of War

Articles
- Joseph, Jennifer, 'POWs Left in the Cold: Compensation Eludes American WWII Slave Laborers for Private Japanese Companies', 29 *Pepperdine Law Review* (2001) pp. 209-242
- Külpmann, Christoph, 'Entschädigung für die Zwangsarbeit von Kriegsgefangenen im Zweiten Weltkrieg', 54 *Die öffentliche Verwaltung* (2001) pp. 417-422
- Mackinlay, John, 'Prisoners of War: Vulnerable', 58 *World Today* (2002) pp. 15-16
- Morrow, James D., 'The Institutional Features of the Prisoners of War Treaties', 55 *International Organization* (2001) pp. 971-991
- Naqvi, Yasmin, 'Doubtful Prisoner-of-War', 84 *IRRC* (2002) pp. 571-595
- Post, H., 'Al Qaeda- en Talibanstrijders: krijgsgevangenen of niet?', 56 *Internationale Spectator* (2002) pp. 258-259
- Stein, Ralph Michael, '"Artillery Lends Dignity to What Otherwise Would Be a Common Brawl": An Essay on Post-Modern Warfare and the Classification of Captured Adversaries', 14 *Pace ILR* (2002) pp. 133-151

3.131   Civilians Generally

Books
- Chesterman, S., ed., *Civilians in War* (London, Lynne Rienner 2001) 291 pp.
- Human Rights Watch, *Erased in a Moment: Suicide Bombing Attacks Against Israeli Civilians* (New York, Human Rights Watch 2002) 160 pp.
- Le Pape, Marc and Pierre Salignon, eds., *Une guerre contre les civils: réflexions sur les pratiques humanitaires au Congo Brazzaville (1998–2000)* (Paris, Karthala 2001) 176 pp.
- McKeogh, Colm, *Innocent Civilians: The Morality of Killing in War* (Basingstoke, Palgrave 2002) 200 pp.

Articles
- Boot, Machteld, 'Comments on the Presentation of Dr. Hans-Peter Gasser', 15 *Humanitäres Völkerrecht* (2002) pp. 212-213
- Bothe, Michael, 'The Protection of the Civilian Population and NATO Bombing on Yugoslavia: Comments on a Report to the Prosecutor of the ICTY', 12 *EJIL* (2001) pp. 531-535
- Bothe, Michael, 'Legal Restraints on Targeting: Protection of Civilian Population and the Changing Faces of Modern Conflicts', 31 *Israel YB HR* (2001) pp. 35-49
- Elewa, Mohamed S., 'Genocide at the Safe Area of Srebrenica: A Search for a New Strategy for Protecting Civilians in Contemporary Armed Conflict', 10 *Michigan State University, Detroit College of Law Journal of International Law* (2001) pp. 429-463
- Gasser, Hans-Peter, 'New Rules Protecting Civilians in Armed Conflict: Was It Worth the Effort?', 15 *Humanitäres Völkerrecht* (2002) pp. 209-212
- Gross, Emanuel, 'Use of Civilians as a Human Shield: What Legal and Moral Restrictions Pertain to a War Waged by a Democratic State Against Terrorism?', 16 *Emory ILR* (2002) pp. 445-524
- Herby, Peter and Anna R. Nuiten, 'Explosive Remnants of War: Protecting Civilians Through an Additional Protocol to the 1980 Convention on Certain Conventional Weapons', 83 *IRRC* (2001) pp. 195-205
- Lefort, Pascal, 'Congo-Brazzaville: A Civilian Population Held Hostage to Militias', in Action Against Hunger, *The Geopolitics of Hunger, 2000-2001: Hunger and Power* (Boulder, Lynne Rienner 2001) pp. 11-20
- Lippman, Matthew, 'Aerial Attacks on Civilians and the Humanitarian Law of War: Technology and Terror from World War I to Afghanistan', 33 *Calif. Western ILJ* (2002) pp. 1-67
- Reschke, Brigitte, 'Der Bericht des UN-Generalsekretärs über den Schutz von Zivilpersonen in bewaffneten Konflikten: ein Beitrag zur Effektivierung des humanitären Völkerrechts', 14 *Humanitäres Völkerrecht* (2001) pp. 10-19
- Robertson, Kate, 'Protecting Civilians in Conflict and Post-Conflict Reconstruction', in David Barnhizer, ed., *Effective Strategies for Protecting Human Rights: Economic Sanctions, Use of National Courts and International 'Fora' and Coercive Power* (Aldershot, Ashgate 2001) pp. 79-84
- Robinson, Mary, 'Der Schutz der Zivilbevölkerung in bewaffneten Konflikten', *Jahrbuch Menschenrechte* (2002) pp. 123-129

— Slim, Hugo, 'Violence and Humanitarianism: Moral Paradox and the Protection of Civilians', 32 *Security Dialogue* (2001) pp. 325-339
— Voon, Tania, 'Pointing the Finger: Civilian Casualties of NATO Bombing in the Kosovo Conflict', 16 *Amer. Univ. ILR* (2001) pp. 1083-1113

3.132   Women and Children

Books

— Chaponnière, Corinne, ed., *Femmes en guerre, femmes de paix* (Geneva, Atoutexte 2002) 92 pp.
— Goldstein, Joshua S., *War and Gender. How Gender Shapes the War System and Vice Versa* (Cambridge, Cambridge University Press 2001) 544 pp.
— Human Rights Watch, *La guerre dans la guerre: violence sexuelle contre les femmes et les filles dans l'est du Congo* (New York, Human Rights Watch 2002) 62 pp.
— Human Rights Watch, *My Gun Was as Tall as Me: Child Soldiers in Burma* (New York, Human Rights Watch 2002) 213 pp.
— Kumar, Krishna, ed., *Women and Civil War. Impact, Organization and Action* (Boulder, Lynne Rienner 2001) 260 pp.
— Lindsey, Charlotte, *Women Facing War; ICRC Study on the Impact of Armed Conflict on Women* (Geneva, International Committee of the Red Cross 2001) 274 pp.
— Machel, Graça, *The Impact of War on Children: A Review of Progress Since the 1996 United Nations Report on the Impact of Armed Conflict on Children* (London, Hurst 2001) 230 pp.
— Olsson, Louise and Torunn L. Tryggestad, eds., *Women and International Peacekeeping* (London, Frank Cass 2001) 145 pp.
— The Coalition to Stop the Use of Child Soldiers, *Child Soldiers: Global Report on Child Soldiers 2001* (London, The Coalition to Stop the Use of Child Soldiers 2001) 452 pp.
— UNICEF, *Adult Wars, Child Soldiers: Voices of Children Involved in Armed Conflict in the East Asia and Pacific Region* (Bangkok, UNICEF 2002) 81 pp.
— Van Creveld, Martin, *Men, Women and War: Do Women Belong in the Front Line?* (London, Cassell 2001) 287 pp.
— Zermatten, Jean, ed., *L'enfant et la guerre: 7e Séminaire de l'IDE, 16 au 20 octobre 2001* (Sion, Institut Universitaire Kurt Bosch 2002) 162 pp.

Articles

— Alfredson, Lisa, 'Child Soldiers, Displacement and Human Security', 4 *Disarmament Forum* (2002) pp. 17-27
— Amman, Diane Marie, 'Calling Children to Account: The Proposal for a Juvenile Chamber in the Special Court for Sierra Leone', 29 *Pepperdine Law Review* (2001) pp. 167-185
— Askin, Kelly, 'The Rwanda and Yugoslav Tribunals: Revolutionizing the Prosecution of War Crimes Against Women', 2 *Africa Legal aid Quarterly* (2001) pp. 10-13
— Ayissi, Anatole, 'Protecting Children in Armed Conflict: From Commitment to Compliance', 4 *Disarmament Forum* (2002) pp. 5-16
— Brett, Rachel, 'Juvenile Justice, Counter-Terrorism and Children', 4 *Disarmament Forum* (2002) pp. 29-36

— Corriero, Michael A., 'The Involvement and Protection of Children in Truth and Justice-Seeking Processes: The Special Court for Sierra Leone', 18 *New York Law School Journal of Human Rights* (2002) pp. 337-360

— De Berry, Jo, 'Child Soldiers and the Convention on the Rights of the Child', 575 *The Annals of the American Academy of Political and Social Science* (2001) pp. 92-105

— Dixit, R.K., 'Special Protection of Children During Armed Conflicts Under the Geneva Conventions Regime', 1 *ISIL Yearbook of International Humanitarian and Refugee Law* (2001) pp. 12-35

— Durham, Helen, 'Women, Armed Conflict and International Law', 84 *IRRC* (2002) pp. 655-659

— Freedson, Julia, 'The Impact of Conflict on Children: The Role of Small Arms', 4 *Disarmament Forum* (2002) pp. 37-44

— Gallagher, Michael S., 'Soldier Boy Bad: Child Soldiers, Culture and Bars to Asylum', 13 *International Journal of Refugee Law* (2001) pp. 310-362

— Grünfeld, F., 'Child Soldiers', in J.C.M. Willems, ed., *Developmental and Autonomy Rights of Children: Empowering Children, Caregivers and Communities* (Antwerp, Intersentia 2002) pp. 273-316

— Hampson, Françoise, 'Women and Humanitarian Law', in Wolfgang Benedek, Esther M. Kisaakye and Gerd Oberleitner, eds., *The Human Rights of Women: International Instruments and African Experiences* (London, Zed Books 2002) pp. 173-209

— Happold, Matthew, 'Excluding Children from Refugee Status: Child Soldiers and Article 1F of the Refugee Convention', 17 *Amer. Univ. ILR* (2002) pp. 1131-1176

— International Committee of the Red Cross, 'Les enfants et la guerre: une action globale pour répondre à des besoins spécifiques', 83 *IRRC* (2001) pp. 494-504

— Isaksson, Eva, 'Women as Victims', in Ilkka Taipale et al., eds., *War or Health? A Reader* (London, Zed 2002) pp. 274-279

— Jesseman, Christine, 'The Protection and Participation Rights of the Child Soldier: An African and Global Perspective', 1 *African Human Rights Law Journal* (2001) pp. 140-154

— Kaprielian-Churchill, Isabel, 'The Armenian Genocide and the Survival of Children', in Alexandre Kimenyi and Otis L. Scott, eds., *Anatomy of Genocide: State Sponsored Mass-Killings in the Twentieth Century* (Lewiston, The Edwin Mellen Press 2001) pp. 221-258

— Kures, Megan E., 'The Effect of Armed Conflict on Children: The Plight of Unaccompanied Refugee Minors', 25 *Suffolk Transnational Law Review* (2001) pp. 141-163

— La Luz, Dinorah, 'Concerns of Women in Armed Conflict Situations in Latin America', 3 *Women and International Human Rights Law* (2001) pp. 325-363

— Lindsey, Charlotte, 'Women and War: The Detention of Women During Wartime', 83 *IRRC* (2001) pp. 505-520

— Makubuya, Apollo N., 'Women in the Armed Forces in Uganda: Human Rights Issues', in Wolfgang Benedek, Esther M. Kisaakye and Gerd Oberleitner, eds., *The Human Rights of Women: International Instruments and African Experiences* (London, Zed Books 2002) pp. 295-301

— Millard, Ananda S., 'Children in Armed Conflicts: Transcending Legal Responses', 32 *Security Dialogue* (2001) pp. 187-200

— Park, Byoungwook, 'Comfort Women During WWII: Are U.S. Courts a Final Resort for Justice?', 17 *Amer. Univ. ILR* (2001) pp. 403-458

— Parker, Karen, 'Human Rights of Women During Armed Conflict', 3 *Women and International Human Rights Law* (2001) pp. 283-323
— Robinson, J.A., 'International Humanitarian and Human-Rights Law Pertaining to Child Civilians in Armed Conflict: An Overview', 65 *Tydskrif vir hedendaags Romeins-Hollandse reg* (2002) pp. 186-202
— Rossano, Riccardo, 'Il Protocollo opzionale alla Convenzione sui diritti del fanciullo sul coinvolgimento dei bambini nei conflitti armati', 14 *Rivista internazionale dei diritti dell'uomo* (2001) pp. 859-866
— Schimmelpenninck van der Oije, Pita J.C., 'Kindsoldaten: met recht beschermd', 51 *Ars Aequi* (2002) pp. 422-429
— Solantaus, Tytti, 'Children's Responses to the Threat of Nuclear War', in Ilkka Taipale et al., eds., *War or Health? A Reader* (London, Zed 2002) pp. 259-266
— Stohl, Rachel, 'Children in Conflict: Assessing the Optional Protocol', 2 *Journal of Conflict, Security and Development* (2002) pp. 135-140
— Taipale, Vappu, 'Children and War', in Ilkka Taipale et al., eds., *War or Health? A Reader* (London, Zed 2002) pp. 249-258
— Vachachira, Jisha S., 'Report 2002: Implementation of the Optional Protocol to the Convention on the Rights of the Child on the Involvement of Children in Armed Conflict', 18 *New York Law School of Human Rights* (2002) pp. 543-547
— Veerman, Philip and Hephzibah Levine, 'Protecting Palestinian Intifada Children: Peaceful Demonstrators, Child Soldiers or Child Martyrs?', 9 *International Journal of Children's Rights* (2001) pp. 71-88
— Weiner, Justus Reid, 'The Use of Palestinian Children in the Al-Aqsa Intifada: A Legal and Political Analysis', 16 *Temple International and Comparative Law Journal* (2001) pp. 43-92

3.134   Journalists

Articles
— Cooper, Ann, 'Targeting Journalists to Prevent the Dissemination of Knowledge of Human Rights Violations', in David Barnhizer, ed., *Effective Strategies for Protecting Human Rights: Prevention and Intervention, Trade and Education* (Aldershot, Ashgate 2001) pp. 21-28
— Howard, Dylan, 'Remaking the Pen Mightier Than the Sword: An Evaluation of the Growing Need for the International Protection of Journalists', 30 *Georgia Journal of International and Comparative Law* (2002) pp. 505-542

3.21   Internment

Books
— Ng, Wendy, *Japanese American Internment During World War II: A History and Reference Guide* (Westport, Greenwood Press 2002) 204 pp.
— Robinson, Greg, *By Order of the President: FDR and the Internment of Japanese Americans* (Cambridge, Harvard University Press 2001) 322 pp.

Articles
— Branca-Santos, Paula, 'Injustice Ignored: The Internment of Italian-Americans During World War II', 13 *Pace ILR* (2001) pp. 151-182
— Muller, Eric L., 'Apologies or Apologists? Remembering the Japanese American Internment in Wyoming', 1 *Wyoming Law Review* (2001) pp. 473-496
— Tulkens, Françoise, 'Les droits de l'homme en detention', 56 *RSCDPC* (2001) pp. 881-890

3.22   Occupation

Books
— Bishara, Marwan, *Palestine/Israel: Peace or Apartheid: Occupation, Terrorism and the Future*, 2nd updated edn. (London, Zed 2002) 173 pp.
— Eiji, Takemae, *Inside GHQ: The Allied Occupation of Japan and Its Legacy* (London, Continuum 2002) 751 pp.
— Kretzmer, David, *The Occupation of Justice: The Supreme Court of Israel and the Occupied Territories* (Albany, State University of New York Press 2002) 262 pp.
— Renda, Mary A., *Taking Haiti: Military Occupation and the Culture of U.S. Imperialism, 1915-1940* (Chapel Hill, University of North Carolina Press 2001) 414 pp.
— Tarling, Nicholas, *A Sudden Rampage: The Japanese Occupation of Southeast Asia, 1941-1945* (London, Hurst 2001) 286 pp.

Articles
— Acke, Arianne, 'Bezetting, rechten en plichten', 11 *Zoeklicht* (2002) pp. 23-26
— Alnajjar, Ghanim, 'Human Rights in a Crisis Situation: The Case of Kuwait After Occupation', 23 *HRQ* (2001) pp. 188-209
— Amnesty International, '"Israel and the Occupied Territories: State Assassinations and Other Unlawful Killings", London, 21 February 2001 (excerpts)', 30 *Journal of Palestine Studies* (2001) pp. 143-146
— Cohen, Barak, 'Democracy and the Mis-Rule of Law: The Israeli Legal System's Failure to Prevent Torture in the Occupied Territories', 12 *Indiana International & Comparative Law Review* (2001) pp. 75-105
— Domb, Fania, 'Judgments of the Supreme Court of Israel Relating to the Administered Territories', 30 *Israel YB HR* (2000) pp. 305-359
— Fux, Pierre-Yves and Mirko Zambelli, 'Mise en oeuvre de la Quatrième Convention de Genève dans les territoires palestiniens occupés: historique d'un processus multilatéral (1997-2001)', 84 *IRRC* (2002) pp. 661-695
— Hassouna, Hussein A., 'The Enforcement of the Fourth Geneva Convention in the Occupied Palestinian Territory, Including Jerusalem', 7 *ILSA JI & CL* (2001) pp. 461-468
— Howlett, Stacy, 'Palestinian Private Property Rights in Israel and the Occupied Territories', 34 *Vanderbilt JTL* (2001) pp. 117-167
— Irmscher, Tobias H., 'The Legal Framework for the Activities of the United Nations Interim Administration Mission in Kosovo: The Charter, Human Rights, and the Law of Occupation', 44 *GYIL* (2001) pp. 353-395

- Maeda, Mariko D., 'G.I. Joe Meets Geisha Girls: Japan's Postwar Policies of Legalized Prostitution for U.S. Occupation Forces', 29 *Hitotsubashi Journal of Law and Politics* (2001) pp. 41-48
- Marcus, I. Maxine, 'Humanitarian Intervention Without Borders: Belligerent Occupation or Colonization?', 25 *Houston Journal of International Law* (2002) pp. 99-139
- Soto, Jorene, 'The Application of Education Rights in the Occupied Territories', 13 *Florida Journal of International Law* (2001) pp. 211-229

3.24   Prohibition of Deportation and Transfer

Books
- Ziegler, Katja S., *Fluchtverursachung als völkerrechtliches Delikt: die völkerrechtliche Verantwortlichkeit des Herkunftsstaates für die Verursachung von Fluchtbewegungen* (Berlin, Duncker & Humblot 2002) 976 pp.

Articles
- Comins-Richmond, Walter, 'The Karachay Struggle After the Deportation', 22 *Journal of Muslim Minority Affairs* (2002) pp. 63-79
- Eiting, R.M., 'Deportatie en evacuatie. Enkele aantekeningen vanuit oorlogsrechtelijk perspectief', 95 *Militair Rechtelijk Tijdschrift* (2002) pp. 133-136
- Haslam, Emily, 'Unlawful Population Transfer and the Limits of International Criminal Law', 61 *The Cambridge Law Journal* (2001) pp. 66-75
- Lavanchy, Philippe, 'La communauté internationale face aux déplacements forcés de populations', 19 *Arès* (2002) pp. 83-94
- Mälksoo, Lauri, 'Soviet Genocide? Communist Mass Deportations in the Baltic States and International Law', 14 *Leiden JIL* (2001) pp. 757-787
- Mangala, Jack M., 'Prévention des déplacements forcés de population: possibilités et limites', 83 *IRRC* (2001) pp. 1067-1095
- Nilsson, Jonas, 'The Vuckovic Trial in Kosovo: Deportation and Forcible Transfer Under the Definition of Genocide', 71 *Nordic JIL* (2002) pp. 545-555
- Van Baarda, Th.A., 'Deportatie is verboden, evacuatie niet. Maar, wat is het verschil?', 95 *Militair Rechtelijk Tijdschrift* (2002) pp. 61-119

3.25   Reprisals

Articles
- Mitchell, Andrew D., 'Does One Illegality Merit Another? The Law of Belligerent Reprisals in International Law', 170 *Mil. LR* (2001) pp. 155-177

4.1   METHODS AND MEANS OF WARFARE

Books
- Clark, Wesley K., *Waging Modern War: Bosnia, Kosovo, and the Future of Combat* (New York, PublicAffairs 2001) 479 pp.

− Guenivet, Karima, *Violences sexuelles: la nouvelle arme de guerre* (Paris, Editions Michalon 2001) 204 pp.
− Naylor, R.T., *Economic Warfare: Sanctions, Embargo Busting, and Their Human Cost* (Boston, Northeastern University Press 2001) 459 pp.

Articles

− Barkham, Jason, 'Information Warfare and International Law on the Use of Force', 34 *NY Univ. JIL & Pol.* (2001) pp. 57-113
− Bouchet-Saulnier, Françoise, 'Just War, Unjust Means? International Humanitarian Law After September 11', 58 *The World Today* (2002) pp. 26-28
− Coker, Christopher, 'Towards Post-Human Warfare: Ethical Implications of the Revolution in Military Affairs', 77 *Die Friedenswarte* (2002) pp. 399-410
− Daoust, Isabelle, Robin Copland and Rikke Ishoey, 'New Wars, New Weapons? The Obligation of States to Assess the Legality of Means and Methods of Warfare', 84 *IRRC* (2002) pp. 345-363
− Doswald-Beck, Louise, 'Some Thoughts on Computer Network Attack and the International Law of Armed Conflict', 7 *International Law Studies* (2002) pp. 163-185
− Hoffmann, Ralf, 'Information War: Tendenzen − Optionen − Perspektiven', 15 *Humanitäres Völkerrecht* (2002) pp. 158-165
− Joyner, Christopher C. and Catherine Lotrionte, 'Information Warfare as International Coercion: Elements of a Legal Framework', 12 *EJIL* (2001) pp. 825-865
− Schmitt, Michael N., 'Wired Warfare: Computer Network Attack and Jus in Bello', 84 *IRRC* (2002) pp. 365-399
− Stein, Ralph Michael, '"Artillery Lends Dignity to What Otherwise Would Be a Common Brawl": An Essay on Post-Modern Warfare and the Classification of Captured Adversaries', 14 *Pace ILR* (2002) pp. 133-151
− Taylor, Philip M., 'Information Warfare and Information Intervention', in Monroe E. Price and Mark Thompson, eds., *Forging Peace: Intervention, Human Rights and the Management of Media Space* (Edinburgh, Edinburgh University Press 2002) pp. 313-328
− Waldman, Adir, 'Clashing Behavior, Converging Interests: A Legal Convention Regulating a Military Conflict', 27 *Yale JIL* (2002) pp. 249-314

4.1111   Conventional Weapons

Articles

− Hagelin, Björn, 'Transfer of Major Conventional Weapons', in *SIPRI Yearbook* (2001) pp. 323-352
− Herby, Peter and Anna R. Nuiten, 'Explosive Remnants of War: Protecting Civilians Through an Additional Protocol to the 1980 Convention on Certain Conventional Weapons', 83 *IRRC* (2001) pp. 195-205
− Hoyt, Timothy D., 'The Next Strategic Threat: Advanced Conventional Weapons Proliferation', in Henry Sokolski and James M. Ludes, eds., *Twenty-first Century Weapons Proliferation: Are We Ready?* (London, Frank Cass 2001) pp. 33-51
− Kaye, David and Steven A. Solomon, 'The Second Review Conference of the 1980 Convention on Certain Conventional Weapons', 96 *AJIL* (2002) pp. 922-936

— Mathews, Robert J., 'The 1980 Convention on Certain Conventional Weapons: A Useful Framework Despite Earlier Disappointments', 83 *IRRC* (2001) pp. 991-1012
— Parachini, John V., 'Comparing Motives and Outcomes of Mass Casualty Terrorism Involving Conventional and Unconventional Weapons', 24 *Studies in Conflict and Terrorism* (2001) pp. 389-406
— Spear, Joanna, 'Warfare: Conventional Weapons', in P.J. Simmons and Chantal de Jonge Oudraat, eds., *Managing Global Issues: Lessons Learned* (Washington, Carnegie Endowment for International Peace 2001) pp. 564-609

4.11111   Mines

Books
— International Committee of the Red Cross, *Cluster Bombs and Landmines in Kosovo: Explosive Remnants of War*, rev. edn. (Geneva, International Committee of the Red Cross 2001) 42 pp.
— Monin, Lydia and Andrew Gallimore, *The Devil's Gardens: A History of Landmines* (London, Pimlico 2002) 234 pp.

Articles
— Bittner, Gary, 'The Land Mine Debate in the United States', 32 *Peace and Security: The IIP Research Quarterly* (2001) pp. 1-8
— Carrière, Sébastien, 'La Convention d'Ottawa comme réponse au problème des mines antipersonnel: le cas de l'Afrique', 33 *Études internationales* (2002) pp. 527-542
— Kerdoun, Azzouz, 'Les mines antipersonnel et le droit de l'Homme à l'environnement', 56 *Revue juridique et politique* (2002) pp. 174-184
— Rosengard, Ulf, Thomas Dolan, Dmitri Miklush and Massoud Samiei, 'Déminage humanitaire: les techniques nucléaires à l'appui de la recherche de mines', 43 *AIEA Bulletin* (2001) pp. 16-19

4.11112   Small Weapons and Others

Articles
— Batchelor, Peter, 'NGO Perspectives: NGOs and the Small Arms Issue', 4 *Disarmament Forum* (2002) pp. 37-40
— De Alba, Luis Alfonso, 'A Regional Perspective on the Problem of Small Arms and Light Weapons', 4 *Disarmament Forum* (2002) pp. 49-52
— Orlov, Aleksandr, 'Big Troubles from Small Arms', 47 *International Affairs: A Russian Journal* (2001) pp. 29-36
— Waszink, Camilla, 'Kleinwaffen: eine Bedrohung der Menschenrechte', *Jahrbuch Menschenrechte* (2002) pp. 223-233
— Wulf, Herbert, 'Kleinwaffen – die Massenvernichtungsmittel unserer Zeit. Die Bemühungen der Vereinten Nationen um Mikroabrüstung', 49 *Vereinte Nationen* (2001) pp. 174-178

4.1112   Weapons of Mass Destruction

Books
- Butler, Richard, *Saddam Defiant: The Threat of Weapons of Mass Destruction and the Crisis of Global Security* (London, Phoenix 2001) 271 pp.
- Cordesman, Anthony H., *Terrorism, Asymmetric Warfare, and Weapons of Mass Destruction: Defending the U.S. Homeland* (Westport, Praeger 2002) 448 pp.

Articles
- Cornell, Michael L., 'Comment: A Decade of Failure: The Legality and Efficacy of United Nations Actions in the Elimination of Iraqi Weapons of Mass Destruction', 16 *Connecticut Journal of International Law* (2001) pp. 325-368
- Damrosch, Lori F., 'The Permanent Five as Enforcers of Controls on Weapons of Mass Destruction: Building on the Iraq "Precedent"?', 13 *EJIL* (2002) pp. 305-321
- Parachini, John V., 'Comparing Motives and Outcomes of Mass Casualty Terrorism Involving Conventional and Unconventional Weapons', 24 *Studies in Conflict and Terrorism* (2001) pp. 389-406
- Pettitt, Leah, 'Weapons of Mass Destruction Stockpiled in Russia: Should the United States Continue to Implement Programs Designed to Reduce and Safeguard These Weapons?', 16 *The Transnational Lawyer* (2002) pp. 169-214

4.11121   Nuclear Weapons

Books
- Butler, Richard, *Fatal Choice: Nuclear Weapons and the Illusion of Missile Defense* (Boulder, Westview Press 2001) 178 pp.

Articles
- Bernauer, Thomas, 'Warfare, Nuclear, Biological and Chemical Weapons', in P.J. Simmons and Chantal de Jonge Oudraat, eds., *Managing Global Issues: Lessons Learned* (Washington, Carnegie Endowment for International Peace 2001) pp. 610-659
- Biehler, Anke, 'Radioaktive Uranmunition – völkerrechtlich erlaubt?', 6 *Juristische Arbeitsblätter* (2001) pp. 526-528
- Burroughs, John, 'Rescue Operation for Humanity: The Advisory Opinion of the International Court of Justice on the Lgality of Threat or Use of Nuclear Weapons', in ELSA International, ed., *International Law as We Enter the 21st Century: International Focus Programme 1997-1999* (Berlin, Spitz 2001) pp. 53-71
- Dycus, Stephen, 'Nuclear War: Still the Gravest Threat to the Environment', 25 *Vermont LR* (2001) pp. 753-771
- Fahey, Dan, 'The Final Word on Depleted Uranium', 25 *The Fletcher Forum of World Affairs* (2001) pp. 189-201
- Gilinsky, Victor, 'Nuclear Proliferation After the Indian and Pakistani Tests', in Henry Sokolski and James M. Ludes, eds., *Twenty-first Century Weapons Proliferation: Are We Ready?* (London, Frank Cass 2001) pp. 3-13
- Hunt, Gaillard T., 'The World Court and the Bomb: Nuremberg and Babel at The Hague', 8 *ILSA JI & CL* (2001) pp. 151-168

- International Committee of the Red Cross, 'Depleted Uranium Munitions: Comments of the International Committee of the Red Cross', 83 *IRRC* (2001) pp. 543-545
- Kalivretakis, Elaina I., 'Are Nuclear Weapons Above the Law? A Look at the International Criminal Court and the Prohibited Weapons Category', 15 *Emory ILR* (2001) pp. 683-732
- McCarron, Paula B. and Cynthia A. Holt, 'A Faustain Bargain? Nuclear Weapons, Negative Security Assurances, and Belligerent Reprisal', 25 *The Fletcher Forum of World Affairs* (2001) pp. 203-237
- Mohr, Manfred, 'Uranwaffeneinsatz: eine humanitär-völkerrechtliche Standortbestimmung', 14 *Humanitäres Völkerrecht* (2001) pp. 27-34
- Moxley Jr., Charles J., 'The Unlawfulness of the Use or Threat of Use of Nuclear Weapons', 8 *ILSA JI & CL* (2002) pp. 447-472
- Neff, Stephen C., 'International Law and Nuclear Weapons in Scottish Courts', 51 *ICLQ* (2002) pp. 171-176
- Sethi, Manpreet, 'Steps to Devalue/Delegitimize Nuclear Weapons', 39 *International Studies* (2002) pp. 66-78
- Skordas, Achilles, 'Epilegomena to a Silence: Nuclear Weapons, Terrorism and the Moment of Concern', 6 *Journal of Conflict & Security Law* (2001) pp. 191-224
- Turner, Stansfield, 'The Dilemma of Nuclear Weapons in the Twenty-first Century', 54 *Naval War College Review* (2001) pp. 13-23

4.11122   Chemical and Biological Weapons

Books

- Burger, Marléne and Chandré Gould, *Secrets and Lies – Wouter Basson and South Africa's Chemical and Biological Warfare Programme* (Cape Town, Zebra Press 2002) 231 pp.
- Dando, Malcolm, *The New Biological Weapons: Threats, Proliferation and Control* (Boulder, Lynne Rienner 2001) 181 pp.
- Tucker, Jonathan B., ed., *The Chemical Weapons Convention: Implementation, Challenges and Solutions* (Washington, Monterey Institute of International Studies 2001) 72 pp.
- Wright, Susan, ed., *Biological Warfare and Disarmament: New Problems/New Perspectives* (Lanham, Rowman & Littlefield 2002) 458 pp.

Articles

- Beard, Jack M., 'A New Urgency About Anthrax: Recent Efforts to Prevent the Proliferation of Biological Weapons in the Former Soviet Union', 96 *Proc. ASIL* (2002) pp. 275-278
- Bernauer, Thomas, 'Warfare, Nuclear, Biological and Chemical Weapons', in P.J. Simmons and Chantal de Jonge Oudraat, eds., *Managing Global Issues: Lessons Learned* (Washington, Carnegie Endowment for International Peace 2001) pp. 610-659
- Clevenger, Greg, 'And You Thought Getting the Flu Was Bad: Working to Prevent Germ Warfare', 12 *Transn. L & Contemp. Probs.* (2002) pp. 195-216
- Eshbaugh, Megan, 'The Chemical Weapons Convention: With Every Step Forward, We Take Two Steps Back', 18 *Arizona JI & CL* (2001) pp. 209-244

– Gorka, Sebestyèn and Richard Sullivan, 'Biological Toxins: A Bioweapon Threat in the 21st Century', 33 *Security Dialogue* (2002) pp. 141-156
– Guesnier, Francine M., 'World Trade Center Attacks: Fears of Biological Warfare Stand in the Wake', *Colorado Jl Environ. L & Pol.* (2001) pp. 181-190
– Harper, Ernest, 'A Call for a Definition of Method of Warfare in Relation to the Chemical Weapons Convention', 48 *NILR* (2001) pp. 132-160
– Inglesby, Thomas V., 'Medical and Public Health Threats Posed by Biological Weapons', in Yonah Alexander and Stephen D. Prior, eds., *Terrorism and Medical Responses: U.S. Lessons and Policy Implications* (Ardsley, Transnational Publishers 2001) pp. 87-94
– Mäkelä, P. Helena, 'Biological Warfare – How Serious a Threat?', in Ilkka Taipale et al., eds., *War or Health? A Reader* (London, Zed 2002) pp. 127-142
– Manley, Ron G., 'The Role of Governments and Research Institutes in the Implementation of the Chemical Weapons Convention', *OPCW Synthesis* (2001) pp. 15-19
– Metcalfe, Neil, 'A Short History of Biological Warfare', 18 *Medicine, Conflict and Survival* (2002) pp. 271-282
– Paris, Kristen, 'The Expansion of the Biological Weapons Convention: The History and Problems of a Verification Regime', 24 *Houston Journal of International Law* (2002) pp. 509-550
– Robinson, Julian P. Perry, 'Chemical Weapons', in Ilkka Taipale et al., eds., *War or Health? A Reader* (London, Zed 2002) pp. 119-126
– Stokes, Deborah, 'Addressing the Chemical and Biological Weapons Threat', in Timothy L.H. McCormack, Michael Tilbury and Gillian D. Triggs, eds., *A Century of War and Peace: Asia-Pacific Perspectives on the Centenary of the 1899 Hague Peace Conference* (The Hague, Kluwer Law International 2001) pp. 223-231
– Tabassi, Lisa, 'Legal Assistance Under the Chemical Weapons Convention: A Proposal for an Optional Protocol to the Convention?', *OPCW Synthesis* (2001) pp. 20-23
– Zanders, Jean Pascal, 'The Chemical Weapons Convention and Universality: A Question of Quality over Quantity?', 4 *Disarmament Forum* (2002) pp. 23-31

4.112   New Weapons

Articles

– Durieux, Yves, 'L'évaluation juridique de nouveaux systèmes d'armes', 41 *Revue de droit militaire et de droit de guerre* (2002) pp. 179-191

4.14   Protection of Civilian and Other Specified Objects

Articles

– De Mulinen, Frédéric, 'Distinction Between Military and Civilian Objects', in Christian Tomuschat, ed., *Kosovo and the International Community: A Legal Assessment* (The Hague, Kluwer Law International 2002) pp. 103-127
– Jia, Bing Bing, '"Protected Property" and Its Protection in International Humanitarian Law', 15 *Leiden JIL* (2002) pp. 131-153

— Shue, Henry and David Wippman, 'Limiting Attacks on Dual-Use Facilities Performing Indispensable Civilian Functions', 35 *Cornell ILJ* (2002) pp. 559-579

4.142   Cultural Property and Places of Worship

Books

— Dutli, María Teresa et al., eds., *Protection of Cultural Property in the Event of Armed Conflict* (Geneva, International Committee of the Red Cross 2002) 224 pp.
— Micewski, Edwin R. and Gerhard Sladek, eds., *Protection of Cultural Property in the Event of Armed Conflict: A Challenge in Peace Support Operations* (Vienna, Armed Forces Printing Office 2002) 163 pp.

Articles

— Abtahi, Hirad, 'The Protection of Cultural Property in Times of Armed Conflict: The practice of the International Criminal Tribunal for the Former Yugoslavia', 14 *Harvard Human Rights Journal* (2001) pp. 1-32
— Bhat, P. Ishwara, 'Protection of Cultural Property Under International Humanitarian Law: Some Emerging Trends', 1 *ISIL Yearbook of International Humanitarian and Refugee Law* (2001) pp. 47-71
— Carcione, Massimo Marco, 'Terrorism and Cultural Property: A "Conflict" of a Non-International Character', 10 *Tilburg For. LR* (2002) pp. 82-89
— Chadha, Neeru, 'Protection of Cultural Property During Armed Conflict: Recent Developments', 1 *ISIL Yearbook of International Humanitarian and Refugee Law* (2001) pp. 219-229
— Davis, Derek H., 'Destruction and Desecration of Sacred Sites During Wars and Conflicts: A Neglected Travesty', 44 *Journal of Church and State* (2002) pp. 417-424
— Eagen, Sarah, 'Preserving Cultural Property: Our Public Duty: A Look at How and Why We Must Create International Laws That Support International Action', 13 *Pace ILR* (2001) pp. 407-448
— Gioia, Andrea, 'The Development of the International Law Relating to the Protection of Cultural Property in the Event of Armed Conflict: The Second Protocol to the 1954 Hague Convention', 11 *Italian Yearbook of International Law* (2001) pp. 25-57
— Hladík, Jan, 'Protection of Cultural Property During Hostilities: Meeting of Experts in Latin America', 84 *IRRC* (2002) pp. 697-699

4.144   The Natural Environment

Books

— Guruswamy, Lakshman D. and Suzette R. Grillot, eds., *Arms Control and the Environment* (Ardsley, Transnational Publishers 2001) 274 pp.
— Mollard-Bannelier, Karine, *La protection de l'environnement en temps de conflit armé* (Paris, Pedone 2001) 542 pp.
— Vöneky, Silja, *Die Fortgeltung des Umweltvölkerrechts in internationalen bewaffneten Konflikten* (Berlin, Springer 2001) 593 pp.

Articles
- Aznar Gómez, Mariano J., 'Environmental Damages and the 1991 Gulf War: Some Yardsticks Before the UNCC', 14 *Leiden JIL* (2001) pp. 301-334
- Bruch, Carl E., 'All's Not Fair in (Civil) War: Criminal Liability for Environmental Damage in Internal Armed Conflict', 25 *Vermont LR* (2001) pp. 695-752
- Dinstein, Yoram, 'Protection of the Environment in International Armed Conflict', 5 *MPYBUNL* (2001) pp. 523-549
- Dobson, Andrew, 'The Natural Environment and the Balkan Conflict', in Michael Waller, Kyril Drezov and Bülent Gökay, eds., *Kosovo: The Politics of Delusion* (London, Frank Cass 2001) pp. 138-141
- Hourcle, Laurent R., 'Environmental Law of War', 25 *Vermont LR* (2001) pp. 653-693
- Malviya, R. A., 'Laws of Armed Conflict and Environmental Protection: An Analysis of Their Inter-Relationship', 1 *ISIL Yearbook of International Humanitarian and Refugee Law* (2001) pp. 72-93
- Rakate, Phenyo Keiseng and Neil D. McDonald, 'Desperate Measures? The Protection of the Environment Through the Law of Armed Conflict', 26 *South African Yearbook of International Law* (2001) pp. 132-143
- Sinha, Manoj Kumar, 'Protection of the Environment During Armed Conflicts: A Case Study of Kosovo', 1 *ISIL Yearbook of International Humanitarian and Refugee Law* (2001) pp. 230-250

4.145 Localities and Zones

Books
- Nederlands Instituut voor Oorlogsdocumentatie, *Srebrenica, een 'veilig' gebied: reconstructie, achtergronden, gevolgen en analyses van de val van een Safe Area* (Amsterdam, Boom 2002) 3393 pp.

Articles
- Elewa, Mohamed S., 'Genocide at the Safe Area of Srebrenica: A Search for a New Strategy for Protecting Civilians in Contemporary Armed Conflict', 10 *Michigan State University, Detroit College of Law Journal of International Law* (2001) pp. 429-463
- Lopez-Reyes, Ramon, 'Regional Governance, Human Security, and Zones of Peace', 15 *Ocean Yearbook* (2001) pp. 428-441
- Oswald, Bruce M., 'The Creation and Control of Places of Protection During United Nations Peace Operations', 84 *IRRC* (2001) pp. 1013-1035
- Principe, Philippe R., 'Secret Codes, Military Hospitals, and the Law of Armed Conflict: Could Military Medical Facilities' Use of Encrypted Communications Subject Them to Attack Under International Law?', 24 *University of Arkansas at Little Rock Law Review* (2002) pp. 727-750
- Silliman, Scott L., 'The Iraqi Quagmire: Enforcing the No-Fly Zones', 36 *New England LR* (2002) pp. 767-773
- Simon, Annette and Brecht Vandenberghe, 'Der Fall der UN "Safe Area" Srebrenica und die Rolle des niederländischen Batallions Dutchbat – Eine Zusammenfassung der niederländischen Untersuchungen', 61 *ZaöRV* (2001) pp. 681-698

– Spearin, Christopher, 'Private Security Companies and Humanitarians: A Corporate Solution to Securing Humanitarian Spaces?', 8 *International Peacekeeping* (2001) pp. 20-43
– Wills, Siobhán, 'What Price the Right to Remain? An Enquiry into the Use of Safe Havens as a Means of Affording Protection to People Forced to Leave Their Homes as a Result of Persecution in the Context of Intra-State War', 20 *Irish Law Times* (2002) pp. 26-31

4.15   Medical Assistance

Books
– Coupland, Robin M., Asa Molde and John Navein, *Care in the Field for Victims of Weapons of War* (Geneva, International Committee of the Red Cross 2001) 92 pp.

Articles
– Rosén, Gunnar, 'Problems of Assistance and Protection in Modern Conflict', in Ilkka Taipale et al., eds., *War or Health? A Reader* (London, Zed 2002) pp. 42-47

4.16   Humanitarian Assistance Operations

Books
– Danieli, Yael, *Sharing the Front Line and the Bank Hills: International Protectors and Providers: Peacekeepers, Humanitarian Aid Workers and the Media in the Midst of Crisis* (Amityville, Baywood 2002) 429 pp.
– Inter-Agency Standing Committee, *Growing the Sheltering Tree: Protecting Rights Through Humanitarian Action: Programmes and Practices Gathered from the Field* (Geneva, Inter-Agency Standing Committee 2002) 199 pp.
– Macrae, J., *Aiding Recovery? The Crisis of Aid in Chronic Political Emergencies* (London, Overseas Development Institute 2001) 224 pp.
– Macrae, J., *The New Humanitarianisms: A Review of Trends in Global Humanitarian Action* (London, Overseas Development Institute 2002) 67 pp.
– Terry, Fiona, *Condemned to Repeat? The Paradox of Humanitarian Action* (Ithaca, Cornell University Press 2002) 282 pp.

Articles
– Curtet, Charlotte Lindsay, 'Afghanistan: An IRCR Perspective on Bringing Assistance and Protection to Women During the Taliban Regime', 84 *IRRC* (2002) pp. 643-654
– O'Connell, Mary Ellen, 'Humanitarian Assistance in Non-International Armed Conflict: The Fourth Wave of Rights, Duties and Remedies', 31 *Israel YB HR* (2001) pp. 183-217
– Perrin, P. et al., 'Action humanitaire', 62 *Médecine tropicale* (2002) pp. 345-464
– Perrin, P., 'Les relations entre les services de santé militaire et les organisations humanitaires: le point de vue du CICR', 62 *Médecine tropicale* (2002) pp. 414-417
– Rey-Schyrr, Catherine, 'Le CICR et l'assistance aux réfugiés arabes palestiniens (1948-1950)', 83 *IRRC* (2001) pp. 739-761

- Richardson, A., 'Negotiating Humanitarian Access in Angola: 1990-2000', 21 *Refugee Survey Quarterly* (2002) pp. 74-112
- Schotten, Gregor, 'Gewohnheitsrechtliche Kontrollrechte der Konfliktparteien nicht-internationaler bewaffneter Konflikte bei humanitären Hilfslieferungen: aktuelle Entwicklungen im Lichte der Vierten Genfer Konvention', 15 *Humanitäres Völkerrecht* (2002) pp. 17-25
- Verdirame, Guglielmo, 'Testing the Effectiveness of International Norms: UN Humanitarian Assistance and Sexual Apartheid in Afghanistan', 23 *HRQ* (2001) pp. 733-768
- Vuori, Hannu, 'Humanitarian Assistance to Countries at War: An Exercise in Futility?', in Ilkka Taipale et al., eds., *War or Health? A Reader* (London, Zed 2002) pp. 555-566

4.22   Air and Missile Warfare

Books

- Pascallon, Pierre, ed., *La guerre des missiles: missiles et antimissiles tactiques balistiques et non balistiques* (Paris, Harmattan 2001) 255 pp.

Articles

- Bothe, Michael, 'Moderner Luftkrieg und Schutz der Zivilbevölkerung', 15 *Humanitäres Völkerrecht* (2002) pp. 31-34
- Bothe, Michael, 'The Protection of the Civilian Population and NATO Bombing on Yugoslavia: Comments on a Report to the Prosecutor of the ICTY', 12 *EJIL* (2001) pp. 531-535
- Carle, Christophe, 'Fighting Fire with Fire: Missiles Against Missiles', 3 *Disarmament Forum* (2001) pp. 21-29
- Faber, H., 'Considerations of the Law of Armed Conflict (LOAC) in a Modern Air Warfare', 50 *Ars Aequi* (2001) pp. 101-105
- Fenrick, W.J., 'Targeting and Proportionality During the NATO Bombing Campaign Against Yugoslavia', 12 *EJIL* (2001) pp. 489-502
- Herold, Marc W., 'Collateral Damage? Civilians and the US Air War in Afghanistan', 20 *Vierteljahresschrift für Sicherheit und Frieden* (2002) pp. 18-26
- Jenkins, B., 'The NATO Air Campaign in Kosovo: Legal Issues and Dilemmas Posed by Armed Humanitarian Intervention', 17 *Miller Centre Report* (2001) pp. 28-31
- Kirchner, Stefan, 'Der aktuelle Fall: der Einsatz von Bomben des Typs BLU-82 "Daisy Cutter" durch die USA in Afghanistan', 15 *Humanitäres Völkerrecht* (2002) pp. 26-30
- Lippman, Matthew, 'Aerial Attacks on Civilians and the Humanitarian Law of War: Technology and Terror from World War I to Afghanistan', 33 *Calif. Western ILJ* (2002) pp. 1-67
- Quenivet, Noelle, 'Report of the Prosecutor of the ICTY Concerning NATO Bombing Against the FRY: A Comment', 41 *Indian JIL* (2001) pp. 478-494
- Shinoda, H., 'The Politics of Legitimacy in International Society: A Case Study of the Air Strike by NATO in Yugoslavia', 47 *Journal of International Studies* (2001) pp. 1-22
- Singh, Ravi Pratap, 'Rogue Doctrine and Missile Defence: A Prescription for More Aggression, More Intervention', 57 *India Quarterly* (2001) pp. 139-150
- Sprockeels, Jeffrey, 'Een voorbeeld van een nieuwe gevechtsmethode: het bombarderen vanop 15.000 voet', 41 *Revue de droit militaire et de droit de guerre* (2002) pp. 163-178

– Voon, Tania, 'Pointing the Finger: Civilian Casualties of NATO Bombing in the Kosovo Conflict', 16 *Amer. Univ. ILR* (2001) pp. 1083-1113
– Weckel, Philippe, 'Les devoirs de l'attaquant à la lumière de la campagne aérienne en Yougoslavie', in Christian Tomuschat, ed., *Kosovo and the International Community: A Legal Assessment* (The Hague, Kluwer Law International 2002) pp. 129-155
– Wilson, Keith, 'Why Are the Missiles (and Missile Defence) Called Peace-Keepers? Corroding the Concept of Peaceful Use', 14 *Leiden JIL* (2001) pp. 789-828

4.23   Naval Warfare

Articles

– Roach, J. Ashley, 'Legal Aspects of Modern Submarine Warfare', 6 *MPYBUNL* (2002) pp. 367-385

5.1   CEASEFIRE, ARMISTICES AND PEACE AGREEMENTS

Books

– Asselin, Pierre-Yves, *A Bitter Peace: Washington, Hanoi, and the Making of the Paris Agreement* (Chapel Hill, University of North Carolina Press 2002) 272 pp.
– Stedman, Stephen John, Donald Rothchild and Elizabeth M. Cousens, eds., *Ending Civil Wars: The Implementation of Peace Agreements* (Boulder, Lynne Rienner 2002) 729 pp.

Articles

– Ackermann, Alice, 'Macedonia in a Post-Peace Agreement Environment: A Role for Conflict Prevention and Reconciliation', 37 *Internationale Spectator* (2002) pp. 71-82
– Aolain, Fionnuala Ni, 'The Fractured Soul of the Dayton Peace Agreement: A Legal Analysis', in Džemal Sokolović and Florian Bieber, eds., *Reconstructing Multiethnic Societies: The Case of Bosnia-Herzegovina* (Aldershot, Ashgate 2001) pp. 63-94
– Bockel, Alain, 'Le pari perdu d'Oslo: le règlement du conflit israélo-palestinien dans l'impasse', 46 *AFDI* (2001) pp. 131-138
– Chartouni-Dubarry, May, 'L'après-Oslo: paix avortée ou guerre annoncée?', 67 *Politique étrangère* (2002) pp. 574-585
– Chinkin, Christine and Kate Paradine, 'Vision and Reality: Democracy and Citizenship of Women in the Dayton Peace Accords', 26 *Yale JIL* (2001) pp. 103-178
– Eilers, Karolyn A., 'Article 14(b) of the 1951 Treaty of Peace with Japan: Interpretation and Effect on POWs' Claims Against Japanese Corporations', 11 *Transn. L & Contemp. Probs.* (2001) pp. 469-490
– Hara, Kimie, '50 Years from San Francisco: Re-Examining the Peace Treaty and Japan's Territorial Problems', 74 *Pacific Affairs* (2001) pp. 361-382
– Jouannet, Emmanuelle, 'Le règlement de paix entre l'Ethiopie et l'Erythrée: "un succès majeur pour l'ensemble de l'Afrique"?', 105 *RGDIP* (2001) pp. 849-896
– Macaluso, Daniel J., 'Absolute and Free Pardon: The Effect of the Amnesty Provision in the Lomé Peace Agreement on the Jurisdiction of the Special Court for Sierra Leone', 27 *Brooklyn Journal of International Law* (2001) pp. 347-380

— Masenkó-Mavi, Viktor, 'The Dayton Peace Agreement and Human Rights in Bosnia and Herzegovina', 42 *Acta juridica Hungarica* (2001) pp. 53-68
— Quigley, John, 'The Oslo Accords: International Law and the Israeli-Palestinian Peace Agreements', 25 *Suffolk Transnational Law Review* (2001) pp. 73-89
— Schattner, Marius, 'De la paix manquée d'Oslo à la marche vers l'abîme', 67 *Politique étrangère* (2002) pp. 587-600
— Totsuka, Etsuro, 'Peace Treaty and Japan's Wartime Responsibility: Breaking the Treaty Defense', 15 *Humanitäres Völkerrecht* (2002) pp. 43-46

5.3   AMNESTIES, TRUTH AND RECONCILIATION COMMISSIONS

Books

— Centre de Gestion des Conflits, *Les juridictions gacaca et les processus de réconciliation nationale* (Kigali, Université Nationale du Rwanda 2001) 173 pp.
— Chigara, Ben, *Amnesty in International Law: The Legality Under International Law of National Amnesty Laws* (Harlow, Longman 2002) 190 pp.
— Edelstein, Jillian, *Truth & Lies: Stories from the Truth and Reconciliation Commission in South Africa* (New York, New Press 2002) 227 pp.
— Graybill, L.S., *Truth and Reconciliation in South Africa. Miracle or Model?* (Boulder, Lynne Rienner 2002) 230 pp.
— Hayner, Priscilla B., *Unspeakable Truths. Confronting State Terror and Atrocity. How Truth Commissions Around the World Are Challenging the Past and Shaping the Future* (New York, Routledge 2001) 340 pp.
— Hayner, Priscilla B., *Unspeakable Truths: Facing the Challenge of Truth Commissions* (New York, Routledge 2002) 353 pp.
— James, Wilmot and Linda van de Vijver, eds., *After the TRC: Reflections on Truth and Reconciliation in South Africa* (Athens, Ohio University Press 2001) 228 pp.
— Klumpp, Guido, *Vergangenheitsbewältigung durch Wahrheitskommissionen. Das Beispiel Chile* (Berlin, Berlin Verlag 2001) 420 pp.
— Kutz, Florian, *Amnestie für politische Straftäter in Südafrika: von der Sharpeville-Amnestie bis zu den Verfahren der Wahrheits- und Versöhnugskommission* (Berlin, Spitz 2001) 322 pp.
— O'Shea, Andreas, *Amnesty for Crime in International Law and Practice* (The Hague, Kluwer Law International 2002) 376 pp.
— Rigby, A., *Justice and Reconciliation: After the Violence* (Boulder, Lynne Rienner 2001) 207 pp.
— Samaddar, Ranabir and Helmut Reifeld, *Peace as Process: Reconciliation and Conflict Resolution in South Asia* (New Delhi, Manohar 2001) 328 pp.
— Wilson, Richard A., *The Politics of Truth and Reconciliation in South Africa: Legitimizing the Post-Apartheid State* (Cambridge, Cambridge University Press 2001) 271 pp.

Articles

— Ackermann, Alice, 'Macedonia in a Post-Peace Agreement Environment: A Role for Conflict Prevention and Reconciliation', 37 *Internationale Spectator* (2002) pp. 71-82
— Baker, Judith, 'Truth Commissions', 51 *University of Toronto Law Journal* (2001) pp. 309-326

− Bhargava, Anurima, 'Defining Political Crimes: A Case Study of the South African Truth and Reconciliation Commission', 102 *Columbia LR* (2002) pp. 1304-1337
− Brown, Andrew S., 'Adiós Amnesty: Prosecutorial Discretion and Military Trials in Argentina', 37 *Texas ILJ* (2002) pp. 203-225
− Burke-White, William W., 'Reframing Impunity: Applying Liberal International Law Theory to an Analysis of Amnesty Legislation', 42 *Harvard ILJ* (2001) pp. 467-533
− Chapman, Audrey R. and Patrick Ball, 'The Truth of Truth Commissions: Comparative Lessons from Haiti, South Africa, and Guatemala', 23 *HRQ* (2001) pp. 1-43
− Corriero, Michael A., 'The Involvement and Protection of Children in Truth and Justice-Seeking Processes: The Special Court for Sierra Leone', 18 *New York Law School Journal of Human Rights* (2002) pp. 337-360
− Daly, Erin, 'Transformative Justice: Charting a Path to Reconciliation', 12 *International Legal Perspectives* (2001) pp. 73-183
− Drumbl, Mark A., 'The Taliban's "Other" Crimes', 23 *Third World Quarterly* (2002) pp. 1121-1131
− Dugard, John, 'Possible Conflicts of Jurisdiction with Truth Commissions', in Antonio Cassese, Paola Gaeta and John R.W.D. Jones, eds., *The Rome Statute of the International Criminal Court: A Commentary* (Oxford, Oxford University Press 2002) pp. 693-704
− Gavron, Jessica, 'Amnesties in the Light of Developments in International Law and the Establishment of the International Criminal Court', 51 *ICLQ* (2002) pp. 91-117
− Guinchard, Serge, 'La justice pénale internationale entre le devoir d'exister et le droit de pardonner', in Simone Gaboriau and Hélène Pauliat, *La justice pénale internationale: actes du colloque organisé à Limoges les 22-23 novembre 2001* (Limoges, Presses Universitaires de Limoges 2002) pp. 277-295
− Jackson Christensen, Mariah, 'The Promise of Truth Commissions in Times of Transition', 23 *Mich. JIL* (2002) pp. 695-707
− Jenkins, Catherine, 'A Truth Commission for East Timor: Lessons from South Africa?', 7 *Journal of Conflict and Security Law* (2002) pp. 233-251
− Koss, Tama, 'South Africa's Truth and Reconciliation Commission: A Model for the Future', 14 *Florida Journal of International Law* (2002) pp. 517-526
− Kritz, Neil J. and Jacob Finci, 'A Truth and Reconciliation Commission in Bosnia and Herzegovina: An Idea Whose Time Has Come', 3 *Int. LF* (2001) pp. 50-58
− Macaluso, Daniel J., 'Absolute and Free Pardon: The Effect of the Amnesty Provision in the Lomé Peace Agreement on the Jurisdiction of the Special Court for Sierra Leone', 27 *Brooklyn Journal of International Law* (2001) pp. 347-380
− Mattarollo, Rodolfo, 'Truth Commissions', in M. Cherif Bassiouni, ed., *Post-Conflict Justice* (Ardsley, Transnational Publishers 2002) pp. 295-324
− Ntsebeza, Dumisa, 'Truth, Justice and Reconciliation: The Legacy of the South African Truth and Reconciliation Commission', 2 *Africa Legal Aid Quarterly* (2001) pp. 23-24
− Olson, Laura, 'Mechanisms Complementing Prosecution', 84 *IRRC* (2002) pp. 173-189
− Parker, Robert, 'Fighting the Siren's Song: The Problem of Amnesty in Historical and Contemporary Perspective', 42 *Acta juridica Hungarica* (2001) pp. 69-89
− Pejic, Jelena, 'The Yugoslav Truth and Reconciliation Commission: A Shaky Start', 25 *Fordham ILJ* (2001) pp. 1-22
− Poulet-Gibot Leclerc, Nadine, 'Les demarches de pardon: l'exemple de l'Afrique du Sud', in Simone Gaboriau and Hélène Pauliat, *La justice pénale internationale: actes*

du colloque organisé à Limoges les 22-23 novembre 2001 (Limoges, Presses Universitaires de Limoges 2002) pp. 243-256

– Quinn, Joanna R., 'Dealing with a Legacy of Mass Atrocity: Truth Commissions in Uganda and Chile', 19 *NQHR* (2001) pp. 383-402

– Rakate, Phenyo Keiseng, 'The South African Amnesty Process: Is International Law at the Crossroads?', 56 *ZöR* (2001) pp. 97-112

– Rombouts, Heidy and Stephan Parmentier, 'The Role of the Legal Profession in the South African Truth and Reconciliation Commission', 20 *NQHR* (2002) pp. 273-298

– Sachs, Albie, 'South Africa's Truth and Reconciliation Commission', 34 *Connecticut Law Review* (2002) pp. 1037-1047

– Sachs, Albie, 'The South African Truth Commission', 63 *Montana Law Review* (2002) pp. 25-37

– Sarkin, Jeremy, 'The Tension Between Justice and Reconciliation in Rwanda: Politics, Human Rights, Due Process and the Role of the Gacaca Courts in Dealing with the Genocide', 45 *Journal of African Law* (2001) pp. 143-172

– Schiff, Benjamin N., 'Do Truth Commissions Promote Accountability or Impunity? The Case of the South African Truth and Reconciliation Commission', in M. Cherif Bassiouni, ed., *Post-Conflict Justice* (Ardsley, Transnational Publishers 2002) pp. 325-343

– Seils, Paul, 'The Limits of Truth Commissions in the Search for Justice: An Analysis of the Truth Commissions of El Salvador and Guatemala and Their Effect in Achieving Post-Conflict Justice', in M. Cherif Bassiouni, ed., *Post-Conflict Justice* (Ardsley, Transnational Publishers 2002) pp. 775-795

– Slye, Ronald C., 'The Legitimacy of Amnesties Under International Law and General Principles of Anglo-American Law: Is a Legitimate Amnesty Possible?', 43 *Virginia JIL* (2002) pp. 173-247

– Smith, Gregory L., 'Immune to Truth? Latin American Truth Commissions and US Support for Abusive Regimes', 33 *Colum. HRLR* (2001) pp. 241-273

– Stahn, Carsten, 'Accommodating Individual Criminal Responsibility and National Reconciliation: The UN Truth Commission for East Timor', 95 *AJIL* (2001) pp. 952-966

– Stahn, Carsten, 'United Nations Peace-Building, Amnesties and Alternative Forms of Justice: A Change in Practice?', 84 *IRRC* (2002) pp. 191-205

– Stanley, Elizabeth, 'Evaluating the Truth and Reconciliation Commission', 39 *The Journal of Modern African Studies* (2001) pp. 525-546

– Van den Wyngaert, Christine and Tom Ongena, 'Ne Bis in Idem Principle, Including the Issue of Amnesty', in Antonio Cassese, Paola Gaeta and John R.W.D. Jones, eds., *The Rome Statute of the International Criminal Court: A Commentary* (Oxford, Oxford University Press 2002) pp. 705-729

– Van der Merwe, Hugo, 'National and Community Reconciliation: Competing Agendas in the South African Truth and Reconciliation Commission', in Nigel Biggar, ed., *Burying the Past: Making Peace and Doing Justice After Civil Conflict* (Washington, Georgetown University Press 2001) pp. 85-106

– Van der Voort, Karlijn and Marten Zwanenburg, 'From "Raison d'État" to "état de droit international": Amnesties and the French Implementation of the Rome Statute', 1 *International Criminal Law Review* (2001) pp. 315-342

– Van Zyl, Paul, 'Unfinished Business: The Truth and Reconciliation Commission's Contribution to Justice in Post-Apartheid South Africa', in M. Cherif Bassiouni, ed., *Post-Conflict Justice* (Ardsley, Transnational Publishers 2002) pp. 745-760

— Villa-Vicencio, Charles, 'Restorative Justice in Social Context: The South African Truth and Reconciliation Commission', in Nigel Biggar, ed., *Burying the Past: Making Peace and Doing Justice After Civil Conflict* (Washington, Georgetown University Press 2001) pp. 207-222

— Weston, Rose, 'Facing the Past, Facing the Future: Applying the Truth Commission Model to the Historic Treatment of Native Americans in the United States', 18 *Arizona JI & CL* (2001) pp. 1017-1058

— Wilson, Stuart, 'The Myth of Restorative Justice: Truth, Reconciliation and the Ethics of Amnesty', 17 *South African Journal on Human Rights* (2001) pp. 531-562

— Young, Gwen K., 'Amnesty and Accountability', 35 *UC Davis Law Review* (2002) pp. 427-482

5.4   REPARATIONS/COMPENSATION

Books

— Barkan, Elazar, *The Guilt of Nations: Restitution and Negotiating Historical Injustices* (Baltimore, Johns Hopkins University Press 2001) 414 pp.

— Crawford, James, *The International Law Commission's Articles on State Responsibility. Introduction, Text and Commentaries* (Cambridge, Cambridge University Press 2002) 352 pp.

— d'Argent, Pierre, *Les réparations de guerre en droit international public: la responsabilité des états à l'épreuve de la guerre* (Brussels, Bruylant 2002) 902 pp.

— Eichhorst, Markus, *Rechtsprobleme der United Nations Compensation Commission* (Berlin, Duncker & Humblot 2002) 255 pp.

— Kolliopoulos, Alexandros, *La Commission d'indemnisation des Nations Unies et le droit de la responsabilité internationale* (Paris, L.G.D.J. 2001) 483 pp.

— Strang, Heather, *Repair or Revenge: Victims and Restorative Justice* (Oxford, Oxford University Press 2002) 318 pp.

— Zweig, Ronald W., *German Reparations and the Jewish World: A History of the Claims Conference*, 2nd edn. (London, Frank Cass 2001) 232 pp.

Articles

— Adler, Libby and Peer Zumbansen, 'The Forgetfulness of Noblesse: A Critique of the German Foundation Law Compensating Slave and Forced Laborers of the Third Reich', 39 *Harvard Journal on Legislation* (2002) pp. 1-61

— Aznar Gómez, Mariano J., 'Environmental Damages and the 1991 Gulf War: Some Yardsticks Before the UNCC', 14 *Leiden JIL* (2001) pp. 301-334

— Beresford, Stuart, 'Redressing the Wrongs of the International Justice System: Compensation for Persons Erroneously Detained, Prosecuted, or Convicted by the Ad Hoc Tribunals', 96 *AJIL* (2002) pp. 628-646

— Bettauer, Ronald J., 'The Role of the United States Government in Recent Holocaust Claims Resolution', 95 *Proc. ASIL* (2001) pp. 37-41

— Bradley, Curtis A., 'The World War II Compensation and Foreign Relations Federalism', 20 *Berkeley JIL* (2002) pp. 282-295

— Caron, David D. and Brian Morris, 'The UN Compensation Commission: Practical Justice, Not Retribution', 13 *EJIL* (2002) pp. 183-199

– Curran, Vivian Grosswald, 'Competing Frameworks for Assessing Contemporary Holocaust-Era Claims', 25 *Fordham ILJ* (2001) pp. 107-132

– d'Argent, Pierre, 'Les réparations de guerre en droit international public: essai sur les limités de la responsabilité internationale des États et de la mise hors la loi de la guerre', 61 *Annales de droit de Louvain* (2001) pp. 509-518

– Doms, Madeline, 'Compensation for Survivors of Slave and Forced Labor: The Swiss Bank Settlement and the German Foundation Provide Options for Recovery for Holocaust Survivors', 14 *The Transnational Lawyer* (2001) pp. 171-205

– Ellis, Mark S. and Elizabeth Hutton, 'Policy Implications of World War II Reparations as Applied to the Former Yugoslavia', 20 *Berkeley JIL* (2002) pp. 342-354

– Ferstman, Carla, 'The Reparation Regime of the International Criminal Court: Practical Considerations', 15 *Leiden JIL* (2002) pp. 667-686

– Fox, Merritt B., 'Imposing Liability for Losses from Aggressive War: An Economic Analysis of the UN Compensation Commission', 13 *EJIL* (2002) pp. 201-221

– Gattini, Andrea, 'The UN Compensation Commission: Old Rules, New Procedures on War Reparations', 13 *EJIL* (2002) pp. 161-181

– Glauner, Lindsay, 'The Need for Accountability and Reparation: 1830-1976: The United States Government's Role in the Promotion, Implementation, and Execution of the Crime of Genocide Against Native Americans', 51 *DePaul Law Review* (2002) pp. 911-961

– Huber, Thomas, 'Holocaust Compensation Payments and the Global Search for Justice for Victims of Nazi Persecution', 48 *The Australian Journal of Politics and History* (2002) pp. 85-101

– Huston, Meredith DuBarry, 'Wartime Environmental Damages: Financing the Cleanup', 23 *University of Pennsylvania Journal of International Economic Law* (2002) pp. 899-929

– Johnson, Nathalie I., 'Justice for "Comfort Women": Will the Alien Tort Claims Act Bring Them the Remedies They Seek?', 20 *Penn State International Law Review* (2001) pp. 253-300

– Joseph, Jennifer, 'POWs Left in the Cold: Compensation Eludes American WWII Slave Laborers for Private Japanese Companies', 29 *Pepperdine Law Review* (2001) pp. 209-242

– Kamminga, M.T., 'De United Nations Compensation Commission: wonderkind of wangedrocht?', 51 *Ars Aequi* (2002) pp. 580-586

– Külpmann, Christoph, 'Entschädigung für die Zwangsarbeit von Kriegsgefangenen im Zweiten Weltkrieg', 54 *Die öffentliche Verwaltung* (2001) pp. 417-422

– Legg, Michael, 'Indigenous Australians and International Law: Racial Discrimination, Genocide and Reparations', 20 *Berkeley JIL* (2002) pp. 387-435

– Libera, Rosemary E., 'Divide, Conquer, and Pay: Civil Compensation for Wartime Damages', 24 *Boston College Int. & Comp. LR* (2001) pp. 291-312

– Lynk, Michael, 'The Right to Compensation in International Law and the Displaced Palestinians', in Diane Hiscox, ed., *Looking Ahead: International Law in the 21st Century: Proceedings of the 29th Annual Conference of the Canadian Council on International Law, Ottawa, October 26-28, 2000* (The Hague, Kluwer Law International 2002) pp. 235-271

– Mundkur, Ramanand, Michael J. Mucchetti and D. Craig Christensen, 'The Intersection of International Accounting Practices and International Law: The Review of Kuwaiti

Corporate Claims at the United Nations Compensation Commission', 16 *Amer. Univ. ILR* (2001) pp. 1195-1239
— Naldi, Gino, 'Reparations in the Practice of the African Commission on Human and Peoples' Rights', 14 *Leiden JIL* (2001) pp. 681-693
— Neary, Joseph P., 'Seeking Reparations in the New Millennium: Will Japan Compensate the "Comfort Women" of World War II?', 15 *Temple International and Comparative Law Journal* (2001) pp. 121-145
— Park, Byoungwook, 'Comfort Women During WWII: Are U.S. Courts a Final Resort for Justice?', 17 *Amer. Univ. ILR* (2001) pp. 403-458
— Rosensaft, Menachem Z. and Joanna D. Rosensaft, 'The Early History of German-Jewish Reparations', 25 *Fordham ILJ* (2001) pp. 1-45
— Scheiber, Harry N., 'Taking Responsibility: Moral and Historical Perspectives on the Japanese War-Reparations Issues', 20 *Berkeley JIL* (2002) pp. 233-249
— Shelton, Dinah, 'Righting Wrongs: Reparations in the Articles on State Responsibility', 96 *AJIL* (2002) pp. 833-856
— Tomuschat, Christian, 'Reparation for Victims of Grave Human Rights Violations', 10 *Tulane Journal of International and Comparative Law* (2002) pp. 157-184
— Torpey, John, 'Making Whole What Has Been Smashed: Reflections on Reparations', in M. Cherif Bassiouni, ed., *Post-Conflict Justice* (Ardsley, Transnational Publishers 2002) pp. 217-242
— Vagts, Detlev and Peter Murray, 'Litigating the Nazi Labor Claims: The Path Not Taken', 43 *Harvard ILJ* (2002) pp. 503-530
— Van der Auweraert, Peter, 'Holocaust Reparation Claims Fifty Years After: The Swiss Banks Litigation', 71 *Nordic JIL* (2001) pp. 557-583
— Van Dyke, Jon M., 'The Fundamental Human Right to Prosecution and Compensation', 29 *Denver JIL & Pol.* (2001) pp. 77-100
— Yasuaki, Onuma, 'Japanese War Guilt and Postwar Responsibilities of Japan', 20 *Berkeley JIL* (2002) pp. 600-620
— Zappalà, Salvatore, 'Compensation to an Arrested or Convicted Person', in Antonio Cassesse, Paola Gaeta and John R.W.D. Jones, eds., *The Rome Statute of the International Criminal Court: A Commentary* (Oxford, Oxford University Press 2002) pp. 1577-1585

6.   INTERNATIONAL CRIMINAL LAW

Books
— Bantekas, Ilias, Susan Nash and Mark Mackarel, *International Criminal Law* (London, Cavendish 2001) 323 pp.
— Bassiouni, M. Cherif, *Introduction au droit pénal international* (Brussels, Bruylant 2002) 343 pp.
— Kost, I.L., *The International Criminal Court in the Bibliography on International Criminal Law* (The Hague, Peace Palace Library 2002) 69 pp.
— Pisani, Mario, *Temi e casi di procedura penale internazionale* (Milan, LED 2001) 135 pp.
— Roggemann, Herwig and Petar Šarčević, eds., *National Security and International Criminal Justice* (The Hague, Kluwer Law International 2002) 240 pp.

Articles

- Ayat, Mohammed, 'Silence is Golden: The Right to Remain Silent in International Criminal Law', 79 *Revue de droit international, de sciences diplomatiques et politiques* (2001) pp. 303-338
- Bohlander, Michael and Mark Findlay, 'The Use of Domestic Sources as a Basis for International Criminal Law Principles', 2 *The Global Community* (2002) pp. 3-26
- Broomhall, Bruce, 'The Future of Immunities in International Criminal Law', in M. Cherif Bassiouni, ed., *Post-Conflict Justice* (Ardsley, Transnational Publishers 2002) pp. 1007-1025
- Burke-White, William W., 'A Community of Courts: Toward a System of International Criminal Law Enforcement', 24 *Mich. JIL* (2002) pp. 1-101
- Carcano, Andrea, 'Sentencing and the Gravity of the Offence in International Criminal Law', 51 *ICLQ* (2002) pp. 583-609
- Cassese, Antonio, 'Justification and Excuses in International Criminal Law', in Antonio Cassese, Paola Gaeta and John R.W.D. Jones, eds., *The Rome Statute of the International Criminal Court: A Commentary* (Oxford, Oxford University Press 2002) pp. 951-956
- Clark, Roger S., 'The Mental Element in International Criminal Law: The Rome Statute of the International Criminal Court and the Elements of Offences', 12 *Criminal LF* (2001) pp. 291-334
- Danner, Allison Marston, 'Constructing a Hierarchy of Crimes in International Criminal Law Sentencing', 87 *Virginia LR* (2001) pp. 415-501
- Durham, Helen, 'Women and Civil Society: NGOs and International Criminal Law', 3 *Women and International Human Rights Law* (2001) pp. 819-843
- El Zeidy, Mohamed M., 'The Principle of Complementarity: A New Machinery to Implement International Criminal Law', 23 *Mich. JIL* (2002) pp. 869-975
- Jurovics, Yann, 'Le procès international pénal face au temps', 56 *RSCDPC* (2001) pp. 781-797
- Labuschagne, J.M.T., 'Immunity of the Head of State for Human Rights Violations in International Criminal Law', 26 *South African Yearbook of International Law* (2001) pp. 180-191
- Lukashuk, I.I., 'Contemporary International Criminal Law: Concept and General Features', in Roger Clark, Ferdinand Feldbrugge and Stanislaw Pomorski, eds., *International and National Law in Russia and Eastern Europe: Essays in Honor of George Ginsburgs* (The Hague, Nijhoff 2001) pp. 261-275
- Mandel, Michael, 'NATO's Bombing of Kosovo Under International Law: Politics and Human Rights in International Criminal Law: Our Case Against NATO and the Lessons to Be Learned from It', 25 *Fordham ILJ* (2001) pp. 95-128
- Mettraux, Guenael, 'Current Developments', 1 *International Criminal Law Review* (2001) pp. 261-284
- Powell, C.H. and A. Pillay, 'Revisiting Pinochet: The Development of Customary International Criminal Law', 17 *South African Journal on Human Rights* (2001) pp. 477-502
- Stoelting, David, 'International Criminal Law', 36 *The International Lawyer* (2002) pp. 569-587
- Tallgren, Immi, 'The Sensibility and Sense of International Criminal Law', 13 *EJIL* (2002) pp. 561-595

6.1   THE CRIMES

Articles
— Dixon, Rosalind, 'Rape as a Crime in International Humanitarian Law: Where to from Here?', 13 *EJIL* (2002) pp. 697-719

6.11   War Crimes

Books
— Arbour, Louise, *War Crimes and the Culture of Peace* (Toronto, University of Toronto Press 2002) 64 pp.
— Ball, Howard, *War Crimes and Justice: A Reference Handbook* (Santa Barbara, ABC-CLIO 2002) 259 pp.
— Bartov, Omer, Atina Grossmann and Mary Nolan, eds., *Crimes of War: Guilt and Denial in the Twentieth Century* (New York, New Press 2002) 344 pp.
— Beijer, A., A. Klip, M. Oomen and M. van der Spek, *Opsporing van oorlogsmisdrijven: evaluatie van het Nationaal Opsporingsteam Voor Oorlogsmisdrijven: 1998-2001* (Deventer, Kluwer 2002) 98 pp.
— Boot, Machteld, *Nullum Crimen Sine Lege and the Subject Matter Jurisdiction of the International Criminal Court: Genocide, Crimes Against Humanity, War Crimes* (Antwerp, Intersentia 2002) 708 pp.
— Dörmann, Knut, *Elements of War Crimes Under the Rome Statute of the International Criminal Court: Sources and Commentary* (Cambridge, Cambridge University Press 2002) 524 pp.
— Gutman, Roy and David Rieff, eds., *Crimes de guerre: ce que nous devons savoir* (Paris, Autrement 2002) 445 pp.
— Hogg, Peter, *Crimes of War*, 2nd edn. (New York, St. Martin's Press 2001) 229 pp.
— Lamont-Brown, Raymond, *Ships from Hell: Japanese War Crimes on the High Seas* (Stroud, Sutton 2002) 174 pp.
— Maga, Timothy P., *Judgment at Tokyo: The Japanese War Crimes Trials* (Lexington, University Press of Kentucky 2001) 181 pp.
— Paust, Jordan J. et al., *Human Rights Module: On Crimes Against Humanity, Genocide, Other Crimes Against Human Rights and War Crimes: Revised Extracts from International Criminal Law*, 2nd edn. (Durham, Carolina Academic Press 2001) 370 pp.
— Van Dijk, W.A.M. and J.L. Hovens, eds., *Arresting War Criminals* (Nijmegen, Wolf Legal Publishers 2001) 128 pp.
— Williams, Paul R. and Michael P. Scharf, *Peace with Justice? War Crimes and Accountability in the Former Yugoslavia* (Lanham, Rowman & Littlefield 2002) 323 pp.

Articles
— Abi-Saab, Georges, 'The Concept of "War Crimes"', in Sienho Yee and Wang Tieya, eds., *International Law in the Post-Cold War World: Essays in Memory of Li Haopei* (London, Routledge 2001) pp. 99-118
— Arnold, Roberta, 'The Development of the Notion of War Crimes in Non-International Conflicts Through the Jurisprudence of the UN Ad Hoc Tribunals', 15 *Humanitäres Völkerrecht* (2002) pp. 134-142

— Askin, Kelly, 'The Rwanda and Yugoslav Tribunals: Revolutionizing the Prosecution of War Crimes Against Women', 2 *Africa Legal Aid Quarterly* (2001) pp. 10-13

— Bothe, Michael, 'War Crimes', in Antonio Cassese, Paola Gaeta and John R.W.D. Jones, eds., *The Rome Statute of the International Criminal Court: A Commentary* (Oxford, Oxford University Press 2002) pp. 379-425

— Buehler, Carmela, 'War Crimes, Crimes Against Humanity and Genocide: The Crime of Forced Pregnancy in the Nascent System of Supranational Criminal Law', 18 *Nemesis* (2002) pp. 158-167

— Cottier, Michael, 'The Rome Statute and War Crimes', in ELSA International, ed., *International Law as We Enter the 21st Century: International Focus Programme 1997-1999* (Berlin, Spitz 2001) pp. 163-180

— Dörmann, Knut, 'Preparatory Commission for the International Criminal Court: The Elements of War Crimes: Part II: Other Serious Violations of the Laws and Customs Applicable in International and Non-International Armed Conflicts', 83 *IRRC* (2001) pp. 461-487

— Feller, Erica, 'Rape Is a War Crime. How to Support the Survivors? Lessons from Bosnia. Strategies for Kosovo', 21 *Refugee Survey Quarterly* (2002) pp. 35-43

— Frulli, Micaela, 'Are Crimes Against Humanity More Serious Than War Crimes?', 12 *EJIL* (2001) pp. 329-350

— Granados Peña, Jaime Enrique, 'Los crímenes de guerra en el conflicto interno colombiano a la luz de la Corte Penal Internacional', 103 *Universitas* (2002) pp. 95-112

— Herman, David L., 'A Dish Best Not Served at All: How Foreign Military War Crimes Suspects Lack Protection Under United States and International Law', 172 *Mil. LR* (2002) pp. 40-95

— Hoß, Cristina and Russell A. Miller, 'German Federal Constitutional Court and Bosnian War Crimes: Liberalizing Germany's Genocide Jurisprudence', 44 *GYIL* (2001) pp. 576-611

— Kellogg, D.E., 'Jus Post Bellum: The Importance of War Crimes Trials', 32 *Parameters* (2002) pp. 87-100

— Kerr, Rachel, 'Operational Justice: The Reality of War Crimes Prosecution in the International Criminal Tribunal for the Former Yugoslavia', 5 *International Journal of Human Rights* (2001) pp. 110-122

— King, Henry T., 'Universal Jurisdiction: Myths, Realities, Prospects, War Crimes and Crimes Against Humanity: The Nuremberg Precedent', 35 *New England LR* (2001) pp. 281-286

— Kreß, Claus, 'The 1999 Crisis in East Timor and the Threshold of the Law on War Crimes', 13 *Criminal LF* (2002) pp. 409-470

— Kreß, Claus, 'War Crimes Committed in Non-International Armed Conflict and the Emerging System of International Criminal Justice', 30 *Israel YB HR* (2000) pp. 103-177

— McGrath, Raymond, 'Problems of Investigations into War Crimes and Crimes Against Humanity During and After Ethnic Conflicts', in M. Cherif Bassiouni, ed., *Post-Conflict Justice* (Ardsley, Transnational Publishers 2002) pp. 893-909

— Moghalu, Kingsley Chiedu, 'Image and Reality of War Crimes: External Perceptions of the International Criminal Tribunal for Rwanda', 26 *The Fletcher Forum of World Affairs* (2002) pp. 19-44

— Nishigai, Makoto, 'The Comfort Women Case in the United States: A Note on Questions Resolved and Unresolved in Hwang v. Japan, the first Lawsuit Brought by Asian

Women Against Japan for War Crimes', 20 *Wisconsin International Law Journal* (2001-2002) pp. 371-395

- Obote-Odora, Alex, 'Prosecution of War Crimes by the International Criminal Tribunal for Rwanda', 10 *International & Comparative Law Review. University of Miami School of Law* (2001/2002) pp. 43-73
- Paust, Jordan J., 'Content and Contours of Genocide, Crimes Against Humanity and War Crimes', in Sienho Yee and Wang Tieya, eds., *International Law in the Post-Cold War World: Essays in Memory of Li Haopei* (London, Routledge 2001) pp. 289-306
- Reydams, Luc, 'Swiss Military Trial of Former Rwanda Town Mayor Accused of War Crimes for Inciting Murder of Civilians in Rwanda', 96 *AJIL* (2002) pp. 231-236
- Rudolph, Christopher, 'Constructing an Atrocities Regime: The Politics of War Crimes Tribunals', 55 *International Organization* (2001) pp. 655-691
- Sánchez Patrón, José Manuel, 'La distinción entre crímenes de guerra y crímenes contra la humanidad a la luz de la jurisprudencia de los Tribunales penales internacionales para la ex-Yugoslavia y Ruanda', 78 *Revista española de derecho militar* (2001) pp. 53-84
- Sieff, Michelle and Leslie Vinjamuri, 'Prosecuting War Criminals: The Case for Decentralisation', 2 *Journal of Conflict, Security and Development* (2002) pp. 103-113
- Weiß, Norman, 'Vergewaltigung und erzwungene Mutterschaft als Verbrechen gegen die Menschlichkeit, Kriegsverbrechen und Genozid: wie beurteilen sich diese Vorfälle aus der Perspektive der Kinder, die gewaltsam gezeugt wurden?', 6 *MenschenRechtsMagazin* (2001) pp. 132-142
- Werle, Gerhard and Volker Nerlich, 'Die Strafbarkeit von Kriegsverbrechen nach deutschem Recht', 15 *Humanitäres Völkerrecht* (2002) pp. 124-134
- Wilson, Richard J., 'Will History Repeat Itself? Case Studies of Systemic Constraints on Defense Counsel in Historic International War Crimes Trials and the Need for Resource Parity', in David Barnhizer, ed., *Effective Strategies for Protecting Human Rights: Economic Sanctions, Use of National Courts and International 'Fora' and Coercive Power* (Aldershot, Ashgate 2001) pp. 187-216
- Wippman, David, 'Justice: The Past and Future of War Crimes Prosecutions', 5 *International Journal of Human Rights* (2001) pp. 90-109

6.12　　Genocide

Books
- Barnett, Michael N., *Eyewitness to a Genocide: The United Nations and Rwanda* (Ithaca, Cornell University Press 2002) 215 pp.
- Bartov, Omer and Phyllis Mack, eds., *In God's Name: Genocide and Religion in the Twentieth Century* (New York, Berghahn Books 2001) 401 pp.
- Bizimana, Jean Damascène, *L'Église et le génocide au Rwanda: les Pères Blancs et le négationnisme* (Paris, L'Harmattan 2001) 155 pp.
- Boot, Machteld, *Nullum Crimen Sine Lege and the Subject Matter Jurisdiction of the International Criminal Court: Genocide, Crimes Against Humanity, War Crimes* (Antwerp, Intersentia 2002) 708 pp.
- Bulambo Katambu, Ambroise, *Mourir au Kivu: du génocide Tutsi aux massacres dans l'Est du Congo-RDC* (Kinshasa, Trottoir 2001) 180 pp.

– Campbell, Kenneth J., *Genocide and the Global Village* (New York, Palgrave 2001) 178 pp.
– Charney, Israël W., ed., *Le livre noir de l'humanité* (Toulouse, Privat 2001) 718 pp.
– Chirot, Daniel and Martin E.P. Seligman, eds., *Ethnopolitical Warfare: Causes, Consequences, and Possible Solutions* (Washington, America Psychological Association 2002) 379 pp.
– Faber, Mient Jan, *Srebrenica: de genocide die niet werd voorkomen* (The Hague, Interkerkelijk Vredesberaad 2002) 127 pp.
– Gouteux, Jean-Paul, *La nuit rwandaise: l'implication française dans le dernier génocide du siècle* (Paris, Dagorno 2002) 531 pp.
– Heidenrich, John G., *How to Prevent Genocide: A Guide for Policymakers, Scholars, and the Concerned Citizen* (Westport, Praeger 2001) 275 pp.
– Hinton, Alexander Laban, ed., *Annihilating Difference: The Anthropology of Genocide* (Berkeley, University of California Press 2002) 419 pp.
– Horowitz, Irving Louis, *Taking Lives: Genocide and State Power*, 5th edn. (New Brunswick, Transaction Publishers 2001) 447 pp.
– Kalere, Jean Migabo, *Génocide au Congo? Analyse des massacres de populations civiles* (Brussels, Broederlijk Delen 2002) 216 pp.
– Kayimahe, Vénuste, *France-Rwanda: les coulisses d'un génocide: témoignage d'un rescapé* (Paris, Dagorno 2001) 359 pp.
– Kiernan, Ben, *The Pol Pot Regime: Race, Power and Genocide in Cambodia Under the Khmer Rouge, 1975-79*, 2nd edn. (New Haven, Yale University Press 2002) 477 pp.
– Kimenyi, Alexandre and Otis L. Scott, eds., *Anatomy of Genocide: State Sponsored Mass-Killings in the Twentieth Century* (Lewiston, The Edwin Mellen Press 2001) 446 pp.
– Kressel, Neil J., *Mass Hate: The Global Rise of Genocide and Terror*, rev. and updated edn. (New York, Westview Press 2002) 312 pp.
– Kuperman, Alan J., *The Limits of Humanitarian Intervention: Genocide in Rwanda* (Washington, Bookings Institution Press 2001) 162 pp.
– Lorey, David E. and William H. Beezley, eds., *Genocide, Collective Violence, and Popular Memory: The Politics of Remembrance in the Twentieth Century* (Wilmington, Scholarly Resources 2002) 258 pp.
– Mamdani, Mahmood, *When Victims Become Killers: Colonialism, Nativism, and the Genocide in Rwanda* (Princeton, Princeton University Press 2001) 364 pp.
– Power, Samantha, *A Problem from Hell: America and the Age of Genocide* (New York, Basic Books 2002) 610 pp.
– Raimondo, Fabián, *Corte Internacional de Justicia, derecho internacional humanitario y crimen internacional de genocido: el valor de la jurisprudencia de la Corte Internacional de Justicia como verificadora del derecho internacional humanitario y el crimen internacional de genocido* (La Plata, Universidad Nacional de La Plata 2002) 117 pp.
– Ronayne, Peter, *Never Again? The United States and the Prevention and Punishment of Genocide Since the Holocaust* (Lanham, Rowman & Littlefield 2001) 223 pp.
– Scherrer, C.P., *Genocide and Crisis in Central Africa. Conflict Roots, Mass Violence, and Regional War* (Westport, Praeger 2001) 272 pp.

Articles
- Alonzo-Maizlish, David, 'In Whole or in Part: Group Rights, the Intent Element of Genocide, and the "Quantitative Criterion"', 77 *New York University Law Review* (2002) pp. 1369-1403
- Amman, Diane Marie, 'Group Mentality, Expressivism and Genocide', 2 *International Criminal Law Review* (2002) pp. 93-143
- Aptel, Cécile, 'The Intent to Commit Genocide in the Case Law of the International Criminal Tribunal for Rwanda', 13 *Criminal LF* (2002) pp. 273-291
- Bisharat, George E., 'Sanctions as Genocide', 11 *Transn. L & Contemp. Probs.* (2001) pp. 379-425
- Buchanan, David, 'Gendercide and Human Rights', 4 *Journal of Genocide Research* (2002) pp. 95-108
- Buehler, Carmela, 'War Crimes, Crimes Against Humanity and Genocide: The Crime of Forced Pregnancy in the Nascent System of Supranational Criminal Law', 18 *Nemesis* (2002) pp. 158-167
- Cassese, Antonio, 'Genocide', in Antonio Cassese, Paola Gaeta and John R.W.D. Jones, eds., *The Rome Statute of the International Criminal Court: A Commentary* (Oxford, Oxford University Press 2002) pp. 335-351
- Combs, Nancy Amoury, 'Copping a Plea to Genocide: The Plea Bargaining of International Crimes', 151 *University of Pennsylvania Law Review* (2002) pp. 1-157
- Daglish, Kirsten, 'The Crime of Genocide: Nulyarimma v. Thompson', 50 *ICLQ* (2001) pp. 404-411
- Dinstein, Yoram, 'Humanitarian Intervention from Outside, in the Face of Genocide, Is Legitimate Only When Undertaken by the Security Council', 27 *Justice, The International Association of Jewish Lawyers and Jurists* (2001) pp. 4-7
- Dinstein, Yoram, 'The Collective Human Rights of Religious Groups: Genocide and Humanitarian Intervention', 30 *Israel YB HR* (2000) pp. 227-241
- Dragadze, Tamara, 'Comprehending Genocide in Rwanda', 24 *Ethnic and Racial Studies* (2001) pp. 1065-1070
- Drumbl, Mark, 'The (Al)lure of the Genocide Trial: Justice, Reconciliation and Reconstruction in Rwanda', in David Barnhizer, ed., *Effective Strategies for Protecting Human Rights: Economic Sanctions, Use of National Courts and International 'Fora' and Coercive Power* (Aldershot, Ashgate 2001) pp. 217-234
- Elewa, Mohamed S., 'Genocide at the Safe Area of Srebrenica: A Search for a New Strategy for Protecting Civilians in Contemporary Armed Conflict', 10 *Michigan State University, Detroit College of Law Journal of International Law* (2001) pp. 429-463
- Fry, James D., 'Terrorism as a Crime Against Humanity and Genocide: The Backdoor to Universal Jurisdiction', 7 *UCLA Journal of International Law & Foreign Affairs* (2002) pp. 169-199
- Gaparayi, Idi T., 'Justice and Social Reconstruction in the Aftermath of Genocide in Rwanda: An Evaluation of the Possible Role of the Gacaca Tribunals', 1 *African Human Rights Law Journal* (2001) pp. 78-106
- Gaudreault-DesBiens, Jean-François, 'From Sisyphus's Dilemma to Sisyphus's Duty? A Meditation on the Regulation of Hate Propaganda in Relation to Hate Crimes and Genocide', 46 *MacGill Law Journal* (2001) pp. 1117-1137
- Glauner, Lindsay, 'The Need for Accountability and Reparation: 1830-1976: The United States Government's Role in the Promotion, Implementation, and Execution of the

Crime of Genocide Against Native Americans', 51 *DePaul Law Review* (2002) pp. 911-961

— Gopalani, Ameer F., 'The International Standard of Direct and Public Incitement to Commit Genocide: An Obstacle to U.S. Ratification of the International Criminal Court Statute?', 32 *Calif. Western ILJ* (2001) pp. 87-117

— Green, Llezlie L., 'Gender Hate Propaganda and Sexual Violence in the Rwandan Genocide: An Argument for Intersectionality in International Law', 33 *Colum. HRLR* (2002) pp. 733-776

— Guilfoyle, Douglas, 'Nulyarimma v Thompson: Is Genocide a Crime at Common Law in Australia?', 29 *Federal Law Review* (2001) pp. 1-36

— Hilf, Rudolf, 'Legalization of an Act of Genocide by the European Union', 59 *Europa ethnica* (2002) pp. 19-30

— Holter, Oystein Gullvag, 'A Theory of Gendercide', 4 *Journal of Genocide Research* (2002) pp. 11-38

— Hoß, Cristina and Russell A. Miller, 'German Federal Constitutional Court and Bosnian War Crimes: Liberalizing Germany's Genocide Jurisprudence', 44 *GYIL* (2001) pp. 576-611

— Hylan, Heval, 'Genocide in Kurdistan', 34 *Zambia Law Journal* (2002) pp. 66-110

— International Panel of Eminent Personalities, 'Report on the 1994 Genocide in Rwanda and Surrounding Events (Selected Sections) [July 7, 2000]', 40 *ILM* (2001) pp. 143-235

— Jones, Adam, 'Gender and Genocide in Rwanda', 4 *Journal of Genocide Research* (2002) pp. 65-94

— Jørgensen, Nina H.B., 'The Definition of Genocide: Joining the Dots in the Light of Recent Practice', 1 *International Criminal Law Review* (2001) pp. 285-313

— Jørgensen, Nina H.B., 'The Genocide Acquittal in the Sikirica Case Before the International Criminal Tribunal for the Former Yugoslavia and the Coming of Age of the Guilty Plea', 15 *Leiden JIL* (2002) pp. 389-407

— Kamatali, Jean Marie, 'Freedom of Expression and Its Limitations: The Case of the Rwandan Genocide', 38 *Stanford JIL* (2002) pp. 57-77

— Kaprielian-Churchill, Isabel, 'The Armenian Genocide and the Survival of Children', in Alexandre Kimenyi and Otis L. Scott, eds., *Anatomy of Genocide: State Sponsored Mass-Killings in the Twentieth Century* (Lewiston, The Edwin Mellen Press 2001) pp. 221-258

— Kaufmann, C., 'See No Evil: Why America Doesn't Stop Genocide', 81 *Foreign Affairs* (2002) pp. 142-149

— Keeler, Joseph A., 'Genocide: Prevention Through Nonmilitary Measures', 171 *Mil. LR* (2002) pp. 135-191

— Kelly, Michael J., 'Can Sovereigns Be Brought to Justice? The Crime of Genocide's Evolution and the Meaning of the Milošević Trial', 76 *St. John's Law Review* (2002) pp. 257-378

— Kindiki, Kithure, 'Prosecuting the Perpetrators of the 1994 Genocide in Rwanda: Its Basis in International Law and the Implications for the Protection of Human Rights in Africa', 1 *African Human Rights Law Journal* (2001) pp. 64-77

— Legg, Michael, 'Indigenous Australians and International Law: Racial Discrimination, Genocide and Reparations', 20 *Berkeley JIL* (2002) pp. 387-435

— Lippman, Matthew, 'A Road Map to the 1948 Convention on the Prevention and Punishment of the Crime Genocide', 4 *Journal of Genocide Research* (2002) pp. 177-195

– Lippman, Matthew, 'Genocide: The Crime of the Century: The Jurisprudence of Death at the Dawn of the New Millennium', 23 *Houston Journal of International Law* (2001) pp. 467-535

– Lyons, Margaret A., 'Hearing the Cry Without Answering the Call: Rape, Genocide, and the Rwandan Tribunal', 28 *Syracuse Journal of International Law and Commerce* (2001) pp. 99-124

– Makino, Uwe, 'Final Solutions, Crimes Against Mankind: On the Genesis and Criticism of the Concept of Genocide', 3 *Journal of Genocide Research* (2001) pp. 49-73

– Mälksoo, Lauri, 'Soviet Genocide? Communist Mass Deportations in the Baltic States and International Law', 14 *Leiden JIL* (2001) pp. 757-787

– Marchand, Michel, 'La justice internationale face au drame rwandais – la défence de "présumés génocides": le difficile équilibre entre le droit international humanitaire et le respect des droits de la personne', in Martine Hallers, Chantal Joubert and Jan Sjöcrona, eds., *The Position of the Defence at the International Criminal Court and the Role of The Netherlands as the Host State: Including the Proceedings of the Conference Held in The Hague, 3-4 November 2000* (Amsterdam, Rozenberg Publishers 2002) pp. 55-89

– Mendlovitz, Saul and John Fousek, 'A UN Constabulary to Enforce the Law on Genocide and Crimes Against Humanity', in Laurence Boisson de Chazournes and Vera Gowlland-Debbas, eds., *The International Legal System in Quest of Equity and Universality: Liber Amicorum Georges Abi-Saab* (The Hague, Nijhoff 2001) pp. 449-461

– Murray, Rachel, 'The Report of the OAU's International Panel of Eminent Personalities to Investigate the 1994 Genocide in Rwanda and the Surrounding Events', 45 *Journal of African Law* (2001) pp. 123-133

– Nersessian, David L., 'The Contours of Genocidal Intent: Troubling Jurisprudence from the International Criminal Tribunals', 37 *Texas ILJ* (2002) pp. 231-276

– Nilsson, Jonas, 'The Vuckovic Trial in Kosovo: Deportation and Forcible Transfer Under the Definition of Genocide', 71 *Nordic JIL* (2002) pp. 545-555

– Nsereko, Daniel D. Ntanda, 'Genocidal Conflict in Rwanda and the ICTR', 48 *NILR* (2001) pp. 31-65

– Odello, Marco E., 'Genocide en de jurisprudentie van de internationale ad hoc straftribunalen', 94 *Militair Rechtelijk Tijdschrift* (2001) pp. 261-268

– Paust, Jordan J., 'Content and Contours of Genocide, Crimes Against Humanity and War Crimes', in Sienho Yee and Wang Tieya, eds., *International Law in the Post-Cold War World: Essays in Memory of Li Haopei* (London, Routledge 2001) pp. 289-306

– Prunier, Gérard, 'Genocide in Rwanda', in Daniel Chirot and Martin E.P. Seligman, eds., *Ethnopolitical Warfare: Causes, Consequences, and Possible Solutions* (Washington, America Psychological Association 2002) pp. 109-116

– Rubinstein, William D., 'Genocide Surveyed', 5 *International Journal of Human Rights* (2001) pp. 113-129

– Sarkin, Jeremy, 'The Tension Between Justice and Reconciliation in Rwanda: Politics, Human Rights, Due Process and the Role of the Gacaca Courts in Dealing with the Genocide', 45 *Journal of African Law* (2001) pp. 143-172

– Sassòli, Marco, 'Le génocide rwandais, la justice militaire suisse et le droit international', 12 *SZIER/RSDIE* (2002) pp. 151-178

– Saul, Ben, 'Was the Conflict in East Timor "Genocide" and Why Does It Matter?', 2 *Melbourne JIL* (2001) pp. 477-522

– Saura, Jaume, 'Free Determination and Genocide in East Timor', 3 *Human Rights Review* (2002) pp. 34-52

– Saxon, Dan, 'Robbery Against Humanity: The Treatment in International Humanitarian Law of Economic Crime as a Basis for Persecution and Genocide', 2 *Forum on Crime and Society* (2002) pp. 101-108

– Schabas, William A., 'Genocide and Crimes Against Humanity in the Rome Statute', in ELSA International, ed., *International Law as We Enter the 21st Century: International Focus Programme 1997-1999* (Berlin, Spitz 2001) pp. 153-162

– Schabas, William A., 'Problems of International Codification – Were the Atrocities in Cambodia and Kosovo Genocide?', 35 *New England LR* (2001) pp. 287-309

– Schabas, William A., 'Was Genocide Committed in Bosnia and Herzegovina? First Judgments of the International Criminal Tribunal for the Former Yugoslavia', 25 *Fordham ILJ* (2001) pp. 23-53

– Schiessl, Christoph, 'An Element of Genocide: Rape, Total War, and International Law in the Ttwentieth Century', 4 *Journal of Genocide Research* (2002) pp. 197-210

– Shah, Sonali B., 'The Oversight of the Last Great International Institution of the Twentieth Century: The International Criminal Court's Definition of Genocide', 16 *Emory ILR* (2002) pp. 351-389

– Shamsey, John, '80 Years Too Late: The International Criminal Court and the 20th Century's First Genocide', 11 *Journal of Transnational Law and Policy* (2002) pp. 327-383

– Stein, Stuart, 'Geno- and Other Cides: A Cautionary Note on Knowledge Accumulation', 4 *Journal of Genocide Research* (2002) pp. 39-63

– Stern, Brigitte, 'Les questions de succession d'états dans l'affaire relative à l'application de la Convention pour la prévention et la répression du crime de génocide devant la Cour internationale de Justice', in Nisuke Ando, Edward McWhinney, Rudiger Wolfrum and Betsy Baker Röben, eds., *Liber Amicorum Judge Shigeru Oda* (The Hague, Kluwer Law International 2002) pp. 285-305

– Strizek, Helmut. 'Der Völkermord, den man hätte stoppen können: analyse des MASIRE-Berichts über den Genozid in Ruanda und seine Konsequenzen (Juli 2000)', 37 *Internationales Afrikaforum* (2001) pp. 153-167

– Triffterer, Otto, 'Genocide, Its Particular Intent to Destroy in Whole or in Part the Group as Such', 14 *Leiden JIL* (2001) pp. 399-408

– Vandeginste, Stef, 'Rwanda: Dealing with Genocide and Crimes Against Humanity in the Context of Armed Conflict and Failed Political Transition', in Nigel Biggar, ed., *Burying the Past: Making Peace and Doing Justice After Civil Conflict* (Washington, Georgetown University Press 2001) pp. 223-253

– Vullo, Maria T., 'Prosecuting Genocide', 2 *Chicago Journal of International Law* (2001) pp. 495-501

– Wallenstein, Joshua, 'Punishing Words: An Analysis of the Necessity of the Element of Causation in Prosecutions for Incitement to Genocide', 54 *Stanford LR* (2001) pp. 351-398

– Weiß, Norman, 'Vergewaltigung und erzwungene Mutterschaft als Verbrechen gegen die Menschlichkeit, Kriegsverbrechen und Genozid: wie beurteilen sich diese Vorfälle aus der Perspektive der Kinder, die gewaltsam gezeugt wurden?', 6 *MenschenRechtsMagazin* (2001) pp. 132-142

– Wyler, Eric, 'Les rapports entre exceptions préliminaires et fond du litige à la lumière de l'arrêt de la CIJ du 11 juillet 1996 dans l'affaire du génocide', 105 *RGDIP* (2001) pp. 25-54

– Zahar, Alexander, 'Command Responsibility of Civilian Superiors for Genocide', 14 *Leiden JIL* (2001) pp. 591-616

— Zakr, Nasser, 'Analyse spécifique du crime de génocide dans le Tribunal pénal international pour le Rwanda', 56 *RSCDPC* (2001) pp. 263-275

6.13   Crimes Against Humanity

Books

— Boot, Machteld, *Nullum Crimen Sine Lege and the Subject Matter Jurisdiction of the International Criminal Court: Genocide, Crimes Against Humanity, War Crimes* (Antwerp, Intersentia 2002) 708 pp.
— Jurovics, Yann, *Réflexions sur la spécificité du crime contre l'humanité* (Paris, L.G.D.J. 2002) 519 pp.
— Paust, Jordan J. et al., *Human Rights Module: On Crimes Against Humanity, Genocide, Other Crimes Against Human Rights and War Crimes: Revised Extracts from International Criminal Law*, 2nd edn. (Durham, Carolina Academic Press 2001) 370 pp.
— Robertson, Geoffrey, *Crimes Against Humanity: The Struggle for Global Justice*, 2nd edn. (London, Penguin 2002) 657 pp.

Articles

— Ambos, Kai and Steffen Wirth, 'The Current Law of Crimes Against Humanities: An Analysis of UNTAET Regulation 15/2000', 13 *Criminal LF* (2002) pp. 1-90
— Buehler, Carmela, 'War Crimes, Crimes Against Humanity and Genocide: The Crime of Forced Pregnancy in the Nascent System of Supranational Criminal Law', 18 *Nemesis* (2002) pp. 158-167
— Cassese, Antonio, 'Crimes Against Humanity: Comments on Some Problematic Aspects', in Laurence Boisson de Chazournes and Vera Gowlland-Debbas, eds., *The International Legal System in Quest of Equity and Universality: Liber Amicorum Georges Abi-Saab* (The Hague, Nijhoff 2001) pp. 429-447
— Cassese, Antonio, 'Crimes Against Humanity', in Antonio Cassese, Paola Gaeta and John R.W.D. Jones, eds., *The Rome Statute of the International Criminal Court: A Commentary* (Oxford, Oxford University Press 2002) pp. 353-377
— Fenrick, William J., 'The Crime Against Humanity of Persecution in the Jurisprudence of the ICTY', 32 *NYIL* (2001) pp. 81-96
— Frulli, Micaela, 'Are Crimes Against Humanity More Serious Than War Crimes?', 12 *EJIL* (2001) pp. 329-350
— Fry, James D., 'Terrorism as a Crime Against Humanity and Genocide: The Backdoor to Universal Jurisdiction', 7 *UCLA Journal of International Law & Foreign Affairs* (2002) pp. 169-199
— King, Henry T., 'Universal Jurisdiction: Myths, Realities, Prospects, War Crimes and Crimes Against Humanity: The Nuremberg Precedent', 35 *New England LR* (2001) pp. 281-286
— Labuschagne, J.M.T., 'Psychosexual Autonomy, Crimes Against Humanity and the Rome Statute: Remarks on the Process of Internationalisation of Criminal Law', 34 *Comparative and International Law Journal of Southern Africa* (2001) pp. 325-348
— Mallat, Chibli, 'The Original Sin: "Terrorism" or "Crime Against Humanity"?', 34 *Case Western Reserve JIL* (2002) pp. 245-248

— Mattarollo, Rodolfo, 'Recent Argentine Jurisprudence in the Matter of Crimes Against Humanity', 62-63 *The Review – International Commission of Jurists* (2001) pp. 11-46

— McGrath, Raymond, 'Problems of Investigations into War Crimes and Crimes Against Humanity During and After Ethnic Conflicts', in M. Cherif Bassiouni, ed., *Post-Conflict Justice* (Ardsley, Transnational Publishers 2002) pp. 893-909

— Mendlovitz, Saul and John Fousek, 'A UN Constabulary to Enforce the Law on Genocide and Crimes Against Humanity', in Laurence Boisson de Chazournes and Vera Gowlland-Debbas, eds., *The International Legal System in Quest of Equity and Universality: Liber Amicorum Georges Abi-Saab* (The Hague, Nijhoff 2001) pp. 449-461

— Mettraux, Guénaël, 'Crimes Against Humanity in the Jurisprudence of the International Criminal Tribunals for the Former Yugoslavia and for Rwanda', 43 *Harvard ILJ* (2002) pp. 237-316

— Meyer, Carlin, 'Crimes Against Humanity Women: The Uncomfortable Stories of "Comfort Women": A Review Essay', 17 *New York Law School Journal of Human Rights* (2001) pp. 1019-1061

— Sánchez Patrón, José Manuel, 'La distinción entre crímenes de guerra y crímenes contra la humanidad a la luz de la jurisprudencia de los Tribunales penales internacionales para la ex-Yugoslavia y Ruanda', 78 *Revista española de derecho militar* (2001) pp. 53-84

— Schabas, William A., 'Genocide and Crimes Against Humanity in the Rome Statute', in ELSA International, ed., *International Law as We Enter the 21st Century: International Focus Programme 1997-1999* (Berlin, Spitz 2001) pp. 153-162

— Schwarz, Madeleine J., 'Prosecuting Crimes Against Humanity in Canada: What Must Be Proved', 46 *The Criminal Law Quarterly* (2002) pp. 40-88

— Skogly, Sigrun I., 'Crimes Against Humanity – Revisited: Is There a Role for Economic and Social Rights?', 5 *International Journal of Human Rights* (2001) pp. 58-80

— Sugarman, David, 'The Pinochet Case: International Criminal Justice in the Gothic Style?', 64 *MLR* (2001) pp. 933-944

— Vandeginste, Stef, 'Rwanda: Dealing with Genocide and Crimes Against Humanity in the Context of Armed Conflict and Failed Political Transition', in Nigel Biggar, ed., *Burying the Past: Making Peace and Doing Justice After Civil Conflict* (Washington, Georgetown University Press 2001) pp. 223-253

— Weiß, Norman, 'Vergewaltigung und erzwungene Mutterschaft als Verbrechen gegen die Menschlichkeit, Kriegsverbrechen und Genozid: wie beurteilen sich diese Vorfälle aus der Perspektive der Kinder, die gewaltsam gezeugt wurden?', 6 *MenschenRechtsMagazin* (2001) pp. 132-142

— Zakr, Nasser, 'Approche analytique du crime contre l'humanité en droit international', 105 *RGDIP* (2001) pp. 281-306

6.14   Aggression

Books

— Hummrich, Martin, *Der völkerrechtliche Straftatbestand der Aggression: historische Entwicklung, Geltung und Definition im Hinblick auf das Statut des Internationalen Strafgerichtshofes* (Baden-Baden, Nomos 2001) 259 pp.

Articles

- Clark, Roger S., 'Rethinking Aggression as a Crime and Formulating Its Elements: The Final Work-Product of the Preparatory Commission for the International Criminal Court', 15 *Leiden JIL* (2002) pp. 859-890
- Dascalopoulou-Livada, Phani, 'The Crime Aggression: Making Operative the Jurisdiction of the ICC: Tendencies in the PrepCom', 96 *Proc. ASIL* (2002) pp. 185-190
- Fernandéz de Gurmendi, Silvia A., 'The Working Group on Aggression at the Preparatory Commission for the International Criminal Court', 25 *Fordham ILJ* (2002) pp. 589-605
- Fox, Merritt B., 'Imposing Liability for Losses from Aggressive War: An Economic Analysis of the UN Compensation Commission', 13 *EJIL* (2002) pp. 201-221
- Gaja, Giorgio, 'The Long Journey Towards Repressing Aggression', in Antonio Cassese, Paola Gaeta and John R.W.D. Jones, eds., *The Rome Statute of the International Criminal Court: A Commentary* (Oxford, Oxford University Press 2002) pp. 427-441
- Guidon, Patrick, 'Das Verbrechen der Aggression – pièce de résistance des Rom-Statuts', 11 *Aktuelle juristische Praxis* (2002) pp. 1317-1324
- Meron, Theodor, 'Defining Aggression for the International Criminal Court', 25 *Suffolk Transnational Law Review* (2001) pp. 1-15
- Müller-Schieke, Irina Kaye, 'Defining the Crime of Aggression Under the Statute of the International Criminal Court', 14 *Leiden JIL* (2001) pp. 409-430
- Nsereko, Daniel D. Ntanda, 'Aggression Under the Rome Statute of the International Criminal Court', 71 *Nordic JIL* (2002) pp. 497-521
- Reisman, W. Michael et al., 'The Definition of Aggression and the ICC', 96 *Proc. ASIL* (2002) pp. 181-192
- Singh, Ravi Pratap, 'Rogue Doctrine and Missile Defence: A Prescription for More Aggression, More Intervention', 57 *India Quarterly* (2001) pp. 139-150
- Trahan, Jennifer, 'Defining "Aggression": Why the Preparatory Commission for the International Criminal Court Has Faced Such a Conundrum', 24 *Loyola of LA Intern. & Comp. LR* (2002) pp. 439-474

6.21   Nullum Crimen Sine Lege and Nulla Poena Sine Lege

Books

- Boot, Machteld, *Nullum Crimen Sine Lege and the Subject Matter Jurisdiction of the International Criminal Court: Genocide, Crimes Against Humanity, War Crimes* (Antwerp, Intersentia 2002) 708 pp.

Articles

- Endo, Guillaume, 'Nullum Crimen Nulla Poena Sine Lege Principle and the ICTY and ICTR', 15 *RQDI* (2002) pp. 205-220
- Labuschagne, J.M.T., 'The European Court of Human Rights and the Principle of Legality in International Criminal Law: Streletz, Kessler and Krenz v Germany (22 March 2001 (2001) 22 Human Rights Law Journal (HRLJ) 74)', 27 *South African Yearbook of International Law* (2002) pp. 237-247
- Lamb, Susan, 'Nullum Crimen, Nulla Poena Sine Lege in International Criminal Law', in Antonio Cassese, Paola Gaeta and John R.W.D. Jones, eds., *The Rome Statute of the*

International Criminal Court: A Commentary (Oxford, Oxford University Press 2002) pp. 733-766

6.22   Individual Criminal Responsibility

Books
- Osiel, Mark J., *Mass Atrocity, Ordinary Evil, and Hannah Arendt: Criminal Consciousness in Argentina's Dirty War* (New Haven, Yale University Press 2001) 257 pp.

Articles
- Barret, Nicole, 'Holding Individual Leaders Responsible for Violations of Customary International Law: The U.S. Bombardment of Cambodia and Laos', 32 *Colum. HRLR* (2001) pp. 429-476
- Boed, Roman, 'Individual Criminal Responsibility for Violations of Article 3 Common to the Geneva Conventions of 1949 and of Additional Protocol II Thereto in the Case Law of the International Criminal Tribunal for Rwanda', 13 *Criminal LF* (2002) pp. 293-322
- Eser, Albin, 'Individual Criminal Responsibility', in Antonio Cassese, Paola Gaeta and John R.W.D. Jones, eds., *The Rome Statute of the International Criminal Court: A Commentary* (Oxford, Oxford University Press 2002) pp. 767-822
- Guariglia, Fabricio, 'The Rules of Procedure and Evidence for the International Criminal Court: A New Development in International Adjudication of Individual Criminal Responsibility', in Antonio Cassese, Paola Gaeta and John R.W.D. Jones, eds., *The Rome Statute of the International Criminal Court: A Commentary* (Oxford, Oxford University Press 2002) pp. 1111-1133
- Labuschagne, J.M.T., 'Criminal Responsibility of Children in International Human Rights Law', 26 *South African Yearbook of International Law* (2001) pp. 198-202
- Mose, Erik, 'The Criminality Perspective', 15 *Georgetown Immigration Law Journal* (2001) pp. 463-478
- Panken, Heidi, 'Individuele strafrechtelijke aansprakelijkheid naar internationaal recht voor ernstige schendingen van mensenrechten: chronologisch overzicht', in Jan Wouters and Heidi Panken, eds., *De genocidewet in internationaal perspectief* (Ghent, Larcier 2002) pp. 361-364
- Scaliotti, Massimo, 'Defences Before the International Criminal Court: Substantive Grounds for Excluding Criminal Responsibility: Part I', 1 *International Criminal Law Review* (2001) pp. 111-172
- Scaliotti, Massimo, 'Defences Before the International Criminal Court: Substantive Grounds for Excluding Criminal Responsibility: Part II', 2 *International Criminal Law Review* (2002) pp. 1-46
- Spinedi, Marina, 'State Responsibility v. Individual Responsibility for International Crimes: Tertium Non Datur', 13 *EJIL* (2002) pp. 895-899
- Stahn, Carsten, 'Accommodating Individual Criminal Responsibility and National Reconciliation: The UN Truth Commission for East Timor', 95 *AJIL* (2001) pp. 952-966
- Stirling-Zanda, Simonetta, 'The Individual Criminal Responsibility of Judicial Organs in International Law in the Light of International Practice', 48 *NILR* (2001) pp. 67-100

– Vogel, Joachim, 'Individuelle Verantwortlichkeit im Völkerstrafrecht', 114 *Zeitschrift für die gesamte Strafrechtswissenschaft* (2002) pp. 403-436
– Vouilloz, Madeleine, 'L'immunité du chef d'Etat et le principe de la responsabilité pénale internationale', 2 *Revue valaisanne de jurisprudence = Zeitschrift für walliser Rechtsprechung* (2001) pp. 127-142

6.23   Superior/Command Responsibility

Books

– Bantekas, Ilias, *Principles of Direct and Superior Responsibility in International Humanitarian Law* (Manchester, Manchester University Press 2002) 162 pp.
– Savastano, Mona H., *Defining Who Is a Subordinate, Under the International Doctrine of Command Responsibility* (Boston, New England School of Law 2001) 31 pp.

Articles

– Ambos, Kai, 'Superior Responsibility', in Antonio Cassese, Paola Gaeta and John R.W. D. Jones, eds., *The Rome Statute of the International Criminal Court: A Commentary* (Oxford, Oxford University Press 2002) pp. 823-872
– Arnold, Roberta, 'Command Responsibility: A Case Study of Alleged Violations of the Laws of War at Khiam Detention Centre', 7 *Journal of Conflict and Security Law* (2001) pp. 191-231
– Boelaert-Suominen, Sonja, 'Prosecuting Superiors for Crimes Committed by Subordinates: A Discussion of the First Significant Case Law Since the Second World War', 41 *Virginia JIL* (2001) pp. 747-785
– Damaška, Mirjan, 'The Shadow Side of Command Responsibility', 49 *American Journal of Comparative Law* (2001) pp. 455-496
– Henquet, Thomas, 'Convictions for Command Responsibility Under Articles 7(1) and 7 (3) of the Statute of the International Criminal Tribunal for the Former Yugoslavia', 15 *Leiden JIL* (2002) pp. 805-834
– Keijzer, Nico, 'Command Responsibility', 41 *Revue de droit militaire et de droit de guerre* (2002) pp. 193-214
– Keith, Kirsten, 'Superior Responsibility Applied Before the ICTY', 14 *Humanitäres Völkerrecht* (2001) pp. 98-106
– Keith, Kirsten, 'The Mens Rea of Superior Responsibility as Developed by ICTY Jurisprudence', 14 *Leiden JIL* (2001) pp. 617-634
– Sarooshi, Danesh, 'Command Responsibility and the Blaskić Case', 50 *ICLQ* (2001) pp. 452-465
– Shany, Yuval and Keren R Michaeli, 'The Case Against Ariel Sharon: Revisiting the Doctrine of Command Responsibility', 34 *NY Univ. JIL & Pol.* (2002) pp. 797-886
– Triffterer, Otto, 'Causality, a Separate Element of the Doctrine of Superior Responsibility as Expressed in Article 28 Rome Statute?', 15 *Leiden JIL* (2002) pp. 179-205
– Triffterer, Otto, '"Command Responsibility": Grundstrukturen und Anwendungsbereiche von Art. 28 des Rom Statutes – Eignung, auch zur Bekämpfung des internationalen Terrorismus?', in Cornelius Prittwitz, ed., *Festschrift für Klaus Lüderssen* (Baden-Baden, Nomos 2002) pp. 437-462

— United States Air Force Academy, 'Command Responsibility: How Much Should a Commander Be Expected to Know', 11 *Journal of Legal Studies* (2002) pp. 27-82
— Van Sliedregt, E., 'Milošević en Command Responsibility: de strafrechtelijke aansprakelijkheid van een agressor', 50 *Ars Aequi* (2001) pp. 635-638
— Wenqi, Zhu, 'The Doctrine of Command Responsibility as Applied to Civilian Leaders: The ICTR and the "Kayishema" Case', in Sienho Yee and Wang Tieya, eds., *International Law in the Post-Cold War World: Essays in Memory of Li Haopei* (London, Routledge 2001) pp. 373-384
— Williamson, Jamie A., 'Command Responsibility in the Case Law of the International Criminal Tribunal for Rwanda', 13 *Criminal LF* (2002) pp. 365-384
— Zahar, Alexander, 'Command Responsibility of Civilian Superiors for Genocide', 14 *Leiden JIL* (2001) pp. 591-616
— Zakr, Nasser, 'L'imputabilité des faits et actes criminels des subalternes au supérieur hiérarchique devant le Tribunal pénal international pour le Rwanda', 78 *Revue de droit international et de droit comparé* (2001) pp. 51-73
— Zakr, Nasser, 'La responsabilité du supérieur hiérarchique devant les tribunaux pénaux internationaux', 73 *Revue internationale de droit pénal* (2002) pp. 59-80

6.24 Irrelevance of Official Capacity

Articles
— Gaeta, Paola, 'Official Capacity and Immunities', in Antonio Cassese, Paola Gaeta and John R.W.D. Jones, eds., *The Rome Statute of the International Criminal Court: A Commentary* (Oxford, Oxford University Press 2002) pp. 975-974
— Ruffert, Matthias, 'Pinochet Follow Up: The End of Sovereign Immunity?', 48 *NILR* (2001) pp. 171-195

6.27 Grounds for Excluding Criminal Responsibility

Articles
— Ambos, Kai, 'Other Grounds for Excluding Criminal Responsibility', in Antonio Cassese, Paola Gaeta and John R.W.D. Jones, eds., *The Rome Statute of the International Criminal Court: A Commentary* (Oxford, Oxford University Press 2002) pp. 1003-1048
— Cassese, Antonio, 'When May Senior State Officials Be Tried for International Crimes? Some Comments on the Congo v. Belgium Case', 13 *EJIL* (2002) pp. 853-875
— Fenet, Alain, 'La responsabilité pénale internationale du Chef d'État', 32 *Revue générale de droit* (2002) pp. 585-615
— Henzelin, Marc, 'L'immunité pénale des ministres selon la Cour internationale de Justice', 120 *Schweizerische Zeitschrift für Strafrecht* (2002) pp. 249-264
— Jennings, Robert Y., 'Jurisdiction and Immunity in the ICJ Decision in the Yerodia Case', 4 *Int. LF* (2002) pp. 99-103
— Jia, Bing Bing, 'Judicial Decisions as a Source of International Law and the Defence of Duress in Murder or Other Cases Arising from Armed Conflict', in Sienho Yee and Wang Tieya, eds., *International Law in the Post-Cold War World: Essays in Memory of Li Haopei* (London, Routledge 2001) pp. 77-95

− Jonassen, Rebecca, 'The Defence of Superior Orders in New Zealand: A Soldier's Dilemma?', 9 *Auckland University Law Review* (2002) pp. 643-670
− Jones, John R.W.D., 'Immunity and "Double Criminality": General Augusto Pinochet Before the House of Lords', in Sienho Yee and Wang Tieya, eds., *International Law in the Post-Cold War World: Essays in Memory of Li Haopei* (London, Routledge 2001) pp. 254-267
− Kamto, Maurice, 'Une troublante "Immunité totale" du ministre des Affaires étrangères: sur un aspect de l'arrêt du 14 février 2002 dans l'affaire relative au Mandat d'arrêt du 11 avril 2000', 35 *RBDI* (2002) pp. 518-530
− Labuschagne, J.M.T., 'Immunity of the Head of State for Human Rights Violations in International Criminal Law', 26 *South African Yearbook of International Law* (2001) pp. 180-191
− McCoubrey, Hilaire, 'From Nuremberg to Rome: Restoring the Defence of Superior Orders', 50 *ICLQ* (2001) pp. 386-394
− Merkel, Reinhard, 'Gründe für den Ausschluss der Strafbarkeit im Völkerstrafrecht', 114 *Zeitschrift für die gesamte Strafrechtswissenschaft* (2002) pp. 437-454
− Schreuer, Christoph and Stephan Wittich, 'Immunity v. Accountability: The ICJ's Judgment in the Yerodia Case', 4 *Int. LF* (2002) pp. 117-120
− Wirth, Steffen, 'Immunity for Core Crimes? The ICJ's Judgment in the Congo v. Belgium Case', 13 *EJIL* (2002) pp. 877-893

6.3   REPRESSION OF BREACHES

Books

− Beigbeder, Yves, *Judging Criminal Leaders. The Slow Erosion of Impunity* (The Hague, Kluwer Law International 2002) 200 pp.
− Garapon, Antoine, *Des crimes qu'on ne peut ni punir ni pardonner: pour une justice internationale* (Paris, Odile Jacob 2002) 348 pp.
− May, Richard and Marieke Wierda, *International Criminal Evidence* (Ardsley, Transnational Publishers 2002) 369 pp.

Articles

− Anderson, Kent, 'An Asian Pinochet? Not Likely: The Unfulfilled International Law Promise in Japan's Treatment of Former Peruvian President Alberto Fujimori', 38 *Stanford JIL* (2002) pp. 177-206
− Bassiouni, M. Cherif, 'Universal Jurisdiction for International Crimes: Historical Perspectives and Contemporary Practice', 42 *Virginia JIL* (2001) pp. 81-162
− Broomhall, Bruce, 'Towards the Development of an Effective System of Universal Jurisdiction for Crimes Under International Law', 35 *New England LR* (2001) pp. 399-420
− Cifende Kaciko, Moise, 'La répression pénale des violations graves du droit international humanitaire: le case de la République du Congo', 61 *Annales de droit de Louvain* (2001) pp. 477-508
− Degan, Vladimir-Djuro, 'Responsibility of States and Individuals for International Crimes', in Sienho Yee and Wang Tieya, eds., *International Law in the Post-Cold War World: Essays in Memory of Li Haopei* (London, Routledge 2001) pp. 202-223

— Hasson, Adam Isaac, 'Extraterritorial Jurisdiction and Sovereign Immunity on Trial: Noriega, Pinochet, and Milosevic: Trends in Political Accountability and Transnational Criminal Law', 25 *Boston College Int. & Comp. LR* (2002) pp. 125-158
— Haveman, R., 'Nut, noodzaak en nadelen van supranationaal straffen', 56 *Internationale Spectator* (2002) pp. 252-257
— King, Henry T., 'Universal Jurisdiction: Myths, Realities, Prospects, War Crimes and Crimes Against Humanity: The Nuremberg Precedent', 35 *New England LR* (2001) pp. 281-286
— Koskenniemi, Martti, 'Between Impunity and Show Trials', 6 *MPYBUNL* (2002) pp. 1-35
— Martín Martínez, Magdalena M., 'Jurisdicción universal y crímenes internacionales', 9 *International & Comparative Law Review. University of Miami School of Law* (2000/2001) pp. 171-187
— May, Richard, 'Challenges to Indictments in International Criminal Trials', in Sienho Yee and Wang Tieya, eds., *International Law in the Post-Cold War World: Essays in Memory of Li Haopei* (London, Routledge 2001) pp. 433-445
— Pejic, Jelena, 'Accountability for International Crimes: From Conjecture to Reality', 84 *IRRC* (2002) pp. 13-33
— Sharma, Vishnu Dutt, 'International Crimes and Universal Jurisdiction', 42 *Indian JIL* (2002) pp. 139-155
— Stern, Brigitte, 'Les questions de succession d'états dans l'affaire relative à l'application de la Convention pour la prévention et la répression du Crime de génocide devant la Cour internationale de Justice', in Nisuke Ando, Edward McWhinney, Rudiger Wolfrum and Betsy Baker Röben, eds., *Liber Amicorum Judge Shigeru Oda* (The Hague, Kluwer Law International 2002) pp. 285-305
— Vander Beken, Tom, 'De moeilijke zoektocht naar het beste forum voor internationale misdrijven: de ad hoc tribunalen als ideale oplossing?', in Jan Wouters and Heidi Panken, eds., *De genocidewet in internationaal perspectief* (Ghent, Larcier 2002) pp. 117-137

6.31 International and Internationalised Courts

Books

— Dixon, Rodney, Karim Kahn and Judge Richard May, eds., *Archbold: International Criminal Courts: Practice, Procedure and Evidence* (London, Sweet & Maxwell 2002) 1000 pp.
— Knoops, Geert-Jan Alexander, *Surrendering to International Criminal Courts: Contemporary Practice and Procedures* (Ardsley, Transnational Publishers 2002) 350 pp.

Articles

— Ascensio, Hervé and Rafaëlle Maison, 'L'activité des tribunaux pénaux internationaux (2000)', 46 *AFDI* (2000) pp. 285-325
— Bekker, Pieter H.F., Daryl A. Mundis and Mark B. Rees, 'International Courts and Tribunals', 35 *The International Lawyer* (2001) pp. 595-611
— Benison, Audrey I., 'International Criminal Tribunals: Is There a Substantive Limitation on the Treaty Power?', 37 *Stanford JIL* (2001) pp. 75-115

— Bohlander, Michael, 'International Criminal Tribunals and Their Power to Punish Contempt and False Testimony', 12 *Criminal LF* (2001) pp. 91-118

— Bohlander, Michael, 'Possible Conflicts of Jurisdiction with the Ad Hoc International Tribunals', in Antonio Cassese, Paola Gaeta and John R.W.D. Jones, eds., *The Rome Statute of the International Criminal Court: A Commentary* (Oxford, Oxford University Press 2002) pp. 687-691

— Bourwell, Jaime Serenity, 'A Predictive Framework for the Effectiveness of International Criminal Tribunals', 34 *Vanderbilt JTL* (2001) pp. 405-454

— Buergenthal, Thomas, 'International Law and the Proliferation of International Courts', 5 *Cursos Euromediterráneos Bancaja de Derecho Internacional* (2001) pp. 29-43

— Capaldo, Giuliana Ziccardi, 'Decisions of International Courts and Tribunals from January 1998 to June 1999', 1 *The Global Community* (2001) pp. 143-781

— Chinkin, Christine M., 'Women's International Tribunal on Japanese Military Sexual Slavery', 95 *AJIL* (2001) pp. 335-341

— Cogan, Jacob Katz, 'International Criminal Courts and Fair Trials: Difficulties and Prospects', 27 *Yale JIL* (2002) pp. 111-140

— DeFrancia, Cristian, 'Due Process in International Criminal Courts: Why Procedure Matters', 87 *Virginia LR* (2001) pp. 1381-1439

— Dickenson, Laura A., 'Using Legal Process to Fight Terrorism: Detentions, Military Commissions, International Tribunals, and the Rule of Law', 75 *Southern California Law Review* (2002) pp. 1407-1492

— Drumbl, Mark A. and Kenneth S. Gallant, 'Appeals in the Ad Hoc International Criminal Tribunals: Structure, Procedure, and Recent Cases', 3 *Journal of Appelate Practice and Procedure* (2001) pp. 589-659

— Findlay, Mark, 'Synthesis in Trial Procedures? The Experience of International Criminal Tribunals', 50 *ICLQ* (2001) pp. 26-53

— Fleming, Mark C., 'Appellate Review in the International Criminal Tribunals', 37 *Texas ILJ* (2002) pp. 111-155

— Gandhi, M., 'Common Article 3 of Geneva Conventions, 1949 in the Era of International Criminal Tribunals', 1 *ISIL Yearbook of International Humanitarian and Refugee Law* (2001) pp. 207-218

— Griffin, John Blount, 'A Predictive Framework for the Effectiveness of International Criminal Tribunals', 34 *Vanderbilt JTL* (2001) pp. 405-454

— Jacovides, Andrew A., 'International Tribunals: Do They Really Work for Small States', 34 *NY Univ. JIL & Pol.* (2001) pp. 253-261

— Janik Jr., Anton L., 'Prosecuting al Qaeda: America's Human Rights Policy Interests are Best Served by Trying Terrorists Under International Tribunals', 30 *Denver JIL & Pol.* (2002) pp. 498-531

— Jeannet, Stéphane, 'Non-Disclosure of Evidence Before International Criminal Tribunals: Recent Developments Regarding the International Committee of the Red Cross', 50 *ICLQ* (2001) pp. 643-656

— McClelland, Gregory A., 'A Non-Adversary Approach to International Criminal Tribunals', 26 *Suffolk Transnational Law Review* (2002) pp. 1-38

— McDonald, Gabrielle Kirk, 'Contributions of the International Criminal Tribunals to the Development of Substantive International Humanitarian Law', in Sienho Yee and Wang Tieya, eds., *International Law in the Post-Cold War World: Essays in Memory of Li Haopei* (London, Routledge 2001) pp. 446-472

— McDonald, Gabrielle Kirk, 'The International Criminal Tribunals: Crime and Punishment in the International Arena', 7 *ILSA JI & CL* (2001) pp. 667-686
— McDowell, Joshua, 'The International Committee of the Red Cross as a Witness Before International Criminal Tribunals', 1 *Chinese Journal of International Law* (2002) pp. 158-184
— Miller, Nathan, 'An International Jurisprudence? The Operation of "Precedent" Across International Tribunals', 15 *Leiden JIL* (2002) pp. 483-526
— Mundis, Daryl A., 'The Legal Character and Status of the Rules of Procedure and Evidence of the Ad Hoc International Criminal Tribunals', 1 *International Criminal Law Review* (2001) pp. 191-239
— Mundis, Daryl A. and Mark B. Rees, 'International Courts and Tribunals', 36 *The International Lawyer* (2002) pp. 549-567
— Nersessian, David L., 'The Contours of Genocidal Intent: Troubling Jurisprudence from the International Criminal Tribunals', 37 *Texas ILJ* (2002) pp. 231-276
— Oellers-Frahm, Karin, 'Multiplication of International Courts and Tribunals and Conflicting Jurisdiction: Problems and Solutions', 5 *MPYBUNL* (2001) pp. 67-104
— Rakate, Phenyo Keiseng, 'A Tale of Three Cases: UN International Tribunals for Sierra Leone, East Timor and Cambodia', 42 *Codicillus* (2001) pp. 2-7
— Sands, Philippe, 'After Pinochet: The Proper Relationship Between National and International Courts', in Laurence Boisson de Chazournes and Vera Gowlland-Debbas, eds., *The International Legal System in Quest of Equity and Universality: Liber Amicorum Georges Abi-Saab* (The Hague, Nijhoff 2001) pp. 699-715
— Shahabuddeen, Mohamed, 'Consistency in Holdings by International Tribunals', in Nisuke Ando, Edward McWhinney, Rudiger Wolfrum and Betsy Baker Röben, eds., *Liber Amicorum Judge Shigeru Oda* (The Hague, Kluwer Law International 2002) pp. 633-650
— Simbeye, Yitiha, 'International Criminal Courts and Tribunals: Practice and Prospects', 4 *Int. LF* (2002) pp. 82-85
— Sluiter, G., 'Naleving van de rechten van de mens door internationale straftribunalen', 27 *NJCM-bulletin* (2002) pp. 699-713
— Spelliscy, Shane, 'The Proliferation of International Tribunals: A Chink in the Armor', 40 *Columbia JTL* (2001) pp. 143-175
— Stover, Eric and Rachel Shigekane, 'The Missing in the Aftermath of War: When Do the Needs of Victims' Families and International War Crimes Tribunals Clash?', 84 *IRRC* (2002) pp. 823-844
— Tracol, Xavier, 'The Appeals Chambers of the International Criminal Tribunals', 12 *Criminal LF* (2001) pp. 137-165
— Orrego Vicuña, Francisco, 'Individuals and Non-State Entities Before International Courts and Tribunals', 5 *MPYBUNL* (2001) pp. 53-66
— Warioba, Joseph Sinde, 'Monitoring Compliance with and Enforcement of Binding Decisions of International Courts', 5 *MPYBUNL* (2001) pp. 41-52
— Wilson, Richard J., 'Assigned Defense Counsel in Domestic and International War Crimes Tribunals: The Need for a Structural Approach', 2 *International Criminal Law Review* (2002) pp. 145-193
— Zakr, Nasser, 'La responsabilité du supérieur hiérarchique devant les tribunaux pénaux internationaux', 73 *Revue internationale de droit pénal* (2002) pp. 59-80

6.311   Nuremberg and Tokyo

Books
- Overy, Richard J., *De verhoren: de nazi-elite ondervraagd* (Amsterdam, De Bezige Bij 2002) 699 pp.
- Welch, Jeanie M., *The Tokyo Trial: A Bibliographic Guide to English-Language Sources* (Westport, Greenwood Press 2002) 225 pp.

Articles
- Awaya, Kentarô, 'The Tokyo Trials and the BC Class Trials', in Klaus Marxen, Koichi Miyazawa and Gerhard Werle, eds., *Der Umgang mit Kriegs- und Besatzungsunrecht in Japan und Deutschland* (Berlin, Arno Spitz 2001) pp. 39-54
- Bush, Jonathan A., 'Lex Americana: Constitutional Due Process and the Nuremberg Defendants', 45 *Saint Louis University Law Journal* (2001) pp. 515-540
- Cassese, Antonio, 'From Neurenberg to Rome: International Military Tribunals to the International Criminal Court', in Antonio Cassese, Paola Gaeta and John R.W.D. Jones, eds., *The Rome Statute of the International Criminal Court: A Commentary* (Oxford, Oxford University Press 2002) pp. 3-19
- Hunt, Gaillard T., 'The World Court and the Bomb: Nuremberg and Babel at The Hague', 8 *ILSA JI & CL* (2001) pp. 151-168
- Jørgensen, Nina H.B., 'A Reappraisal of the Abandoned Nuremberg Concept of Criminal Organisations in the Context of Justice in Rwanda', 12 *Criminal LF* (2001) pp. 371-406
- King, Henry T., 'Universal Jurisdiction: Myths, Realities, Prospects, War Crimes and Crimes Against Humanity: The Nuremberg Precedent', 35 *New England LR* (2001) pp. 281-286
- McCoubrey, Hilaire, 'From Nuremberg to Rome: Restoring the Defence of Superior Orders', 50 *ICLQ* (2001) pp. 386-394
- Moghalu, Kingsley Chiedu, 'International Humanitarian Law from Nuremberg to Rome: The Weighty Precedents of the International Criminal Tribunal for Rwanda', 14 *Pace ILR* (2002) pp. 273-305
- O'Connor, Michael J., 'Bearing True Faith and Allegiance? Allowing Recovery for Soldiers Under Fire in Military Experiments that Violate the Nuremberg Code', 25 *Suffolk Transnational Law Review* (2002) pp. 649-686
- Rancilio, Peggy E., 'From Nuremberg to Rome: Establishing an International Criminal Court and the Need for U.S. Participation', 78 *University of Detroit Mercy Law Review* (2001) pp. 299-339
- Scheinin, Martin, 'From Nuremberg to the International Criminal Court', in Ilkka Taipale et al., eds., *War or Health? A Reader* (London, Zed 2002) pp. 465-470

6.312   International Criminal Tribunal for the Former Yugoslavia

Books
- Bohlander, Michael, *Gerichtliche Sanktionen gegen Anwälte wegen Mißbrauchs von Verfahrensrechten: eine Studie zum institutionellen Rollenverständnis von Rechtsanwälten gegenüber den Gerichten, unter besonderer Berücksichtigung der USA, der ad hoc-*

Tribunale für Jugoslawien und Ruanda sowie des künftigen Ständigen Internationalen Strafgerichtshofes (Aachen, Shaker 2001) 226 pp.

— International Criminal Tribunal for Rwanda, *ICTR and ICTY Rules: Comparison* (Arusha, International Criminal Tribunal for Rwanda 2001) 199 pp.

— International Criminal Tribunal for the Former Yugoslavia, *Compilation of Articles of the Rules of Procedure and Evidence as Adopted and Amended During the Plenary Session = Compilation des articles du règlement de procédure et de preuve tels qu'adoptés et modifiés lors des sessions plénières* (The Hague, International Criminal Tribunal for the Former Yugoslavia 2001) 326 pp.

— International Criminal Tribunal for the Former Yugoslavia, *Judicial Reports (Recueils judiciaires) 1996 (Volumes I and II)* (The Hague, Kluwer Law International 2002) 1800 pp.

— Klip, André and Göran Sluiter, eds., *Annotated Leading Cases of International Criminal Tribunals, Vol. III: The International Criminal Tribunal for the Former Yugoslavia 1997-1999* (Antwerp, Intersentia 2001) 884 pp.

— Klip, André and Göran Sluiter, eds., *Annotated Leading Cases of International Criminal Tribunals, Vol. IV: The International Criminal Tribunal for the Former Yugoslavia 1999-2000* (Antwerp, Intersentia 2001) 900 pp.

— Stroh, Dagmar P., *Die nationale Zusammenarbeit mit den Internationalen Straftribunalen für das ehemalige Jugoslawien und für Ruanda* (Heidelberg, Springer 2002) 395 pp.

— United Nations, *Basic Documents: International Tribunal for the Former Yugoslavia = Documents de référence: Tribunal International de l'ex-Yugoslavie* (The Hague, International Tribunal for the Former Yugoslavia 2001) 477 pp.

— United Nations, *The Path to The Hague: Selected Documents on the Origins of the ICTY = Le chemin vers La Haye: sélection de documents sur les origines du TPIY* (The Hague, International Tribunal for the Former Yugoslavia 2001) 102 pp.

Articles

— Abtahi, Hirad, 'The Protection of Cultural Property in Times of Armed Conflict: The Practice of the International Criminal Tribunal for the Former Yugoslavia', 14 *Harvard Human Rights Journal* (2001) pp. 1-32

— Askin, Kelly, 'The Rwanda and Yugoslav Tribunals: Revolutionizing the Prosecution of War Crimes Against Women', 2 *Africa Legal Aid Quarterly* (2001) pp. 10-13

— Benvenuti, Paolo, 'The ICTY Prosecutor and the Review of the NATO Bombing Campaign Against the Federal Republic of Yugoslavia', 12 *EJIL* (2001) pp. 503-529

— Beresford, Stuart, 'Unshackling the Paper Tiger – the Sentencing Practices of the Ad Hoc International Criminal Tribunals for the Former Yugoslavia and Rwanda', 1 *International Criminal Law Review* (2001) pp. 33-90

— Boas, Gideon, 'Creating Laws of Evidence for International Criminal Law: The ICTY and the Principle of Flexibility', 12 *Criminal LF* (2001) pp. 41-90

— Boas, Gideon, 'Developments in the Law of Procedure and Evidence at the International Criminal Tribunal for the Former Yugoslavia and the International Criminal Court', 12 *Criminal LF* (2001) pp. 167-183

— Boelaert-Suominen, Sonja, 'De Internationale Tribunalen voor het voormalige Joegoslavië en Ruanda: unieke plaats in de internationale rechtsorde en belangrijke bijdragen tot de ontwikkeling van het internationaal strafrecht', in Jan Wouters and Heidi Panken, eds., *De genocidewet in internationaal perspectief* (Ghent, Larcier 2002) pp. 139-165

- Boelaert-Suominen, Sonja, 'Internationale en interne conflicten voor het Joegoslavië Tribunaal', 11 *Zoeklicht* (2002) pp. 8-10
- Boelaert-Suominen, Sonja, 'The International Criminal Tribunal for the Former Yugoslavia (ICTY) Anno 1999: Its Place in the International Legal System, Mandate and Most Notable Jurisprudence', 24 *Polish Yearbook of International Law* (2001) pp. 95-155
- Bogdan, Attila, 'Cumulative Charges, Convictions and Sentencing at the Ad Hoc International Tribunals for the Former Yugoslavia and Rwanda', 3 *Melbourne JIL* (2002) pp. 1-32
- Caianiello, Michele and Giulio Illuminati, 'From the International Criminal Tribunal for the Former Yugoslavia to the International Criminal Court', 26 *North Carolina Journal of International Law and Commercial Regulation* (2001) pp. 407-455
- Cassese, Antonio, 'The Contribution of the International Criminal Tribunal for the Former Yugoslavia to the Ascertainment of General Principles of Law Recognized by the Community of Nations', in Sienho Yee and Wang Tieya, eds., *International Law in the Post-Cold War World: Essays in Memory of Li Haopei* (London, Routledge 2001) pp. 43-55
- Castellà Surribas, S.J., 'El acuerdo entre España y las Naciones Unidas sobre la ejecución de condenas impuestas por el Tribunal Penal Internacional para la Ex Yugoslavia', 54 *Revista española de derecho internacional* (2002) pp. 506-509
- Davis, Jeffrey W., 'Two Wrongs Do Make a Right: The International Criminal Tribunal for the Former Yugoslavia Was Established Illegally, But It Was the Right Thing to Do... So Who Cares?', 28 *North Carolina Journal of International Law and Commercial Regulation* (2002) pp. 395-419
- De Brouwer, Anne-Marie, 'International Criminal Tribunal for the Former Yugoslavia (ICTY): Kunarac, Kovac and Vuković Case ("Foca")', 9 *Tilburg For. LR* (2001) pp. 221-236
- DeFrank, Matthew M., 'ICTY Provisional Release: Current Practice, a Dissenting Voice, and the Case for a Rule Change', 80 *Texas LR* (2002) pp. 1429-1463
- De Roux, Xavier, 'La défense devant le Tribunal Pénal International pour l'ex-Yougoslavie', in Simone Gaboriau and Hélène Pauliat, *La justice pénale internationale: actes du colloque organisé à Limoges les 22-23 novembre 2001* (Limoges, Presses Universitaires de Limoges 2002) pp. 119-138
- De Waynecourt-Steele, Tiffany, 'The Contribution of the Statute of the International Criminal Court to the Enforcement of International Law in the Light of the Experiences of the ICTY', 27 *South African Yearbook of International Law* (2002) pp. 1-63
- Endo, Guillaume, 'Nullum Crimen Nulla Poena Sine Lege Principle and the ICTY and ICTR', 15 *RQDI* (2002) pp. 205-220
- Fakhreshafaei, Reza, 'Die Rechtsprechung des Internationalen Strafgerichtshofes für das ehemalige Jugoslawien im Jahre 2001', 44 *GYIL* (2001) pp. 661-678
- Fenrick, William J., 'The Crime Against Humanity of Persecution in the Jurisprudence of the ICTY', 32 *NYIL* (2001) pp. 81-96
- Gallmetzer, Reinhold and Kazuna Inomata, 'International Tribunal for the Former Yugoslavia: Introductory Note', 1 *The Global Community* (2001) pp. 493-503
- Henquet, Thomas, 'Convictions for Command Responsibility Under Articles 7(1) and 7(3) of the Statute of the International Criminal Tribunal for the Former Yugoslavia', 15 *Leiden JIL* (2002) pp. 805-834

- Henquet, Thomas, 'The International Criminal Tribunal for the Former Yugoslavia: Ad Hoc Justice?', in ELSA International, ed., *International Law as We Enter the 21st Century: International Focus Programme 1997-1999* (Berlin, Spitz 2001) pp. 91-120
- Holthuis, Hans, 'Operational Aspects of Setting up the International Criminal Court: Building on the Experience of the International Tribunal for the Former Yugoslavia', 25 *Fordham ILJ* (2002) pp. 708-716
- Hoß, Cristina, 'Das Recht auf ein faires Verfahren und der Internationale Strafgerichtshof für das ehemalige Jugoslawien: zwischen Sein und Werden', 62 *ZaöRV* (2002) pp. 809-839
- Ivkovich, Sanja Kutnjak, 'Justice by the International Criminal Tribunal for the Former Yugoslavia', 37 *Stanford JIL* (2001) pp. 255-346
- Jorda, Claude, 'Le TPIY: laisser une trace durable', in Simone Gaboriau and Hélène Pauliat, *La justice pénale internationale: actes du colloque organisé à Limoges les 22-23 novembre 2001* (Limoges, Presses Universitaires de Limoges 2002) pp. 299-301
- Jørgensen, Nina H.B., 'The Genocide Acquittal in the Sikirica Case Before the International Criminal Tribunal for the Former Yugoslavia and the Coming of Age of the Guilty Plea', 15 *Leiden JIL* (2002) pp. 389-407
- Kalinauskas, Mikas, 'The Use of International Military Force in Arresting War Criminals: The Lessons of the International Criminal Tribunal for the Former Yugoslavia', 50 *The University of Kansas Law Review* (2002) pp. 383-429
- Kaszubinski, Megan, 'The International Criminal Tribunal for the Former Yugoslavia', in M. Cherif Bassiouni, ed., *Post-Conflict Justice* (Ardsley, Transnational Publishers 2002) pp. 459-485
- Keith, Kirsten, 'Superior Responsibility Applied Before the ICTY', 14 *Humanitäres Völkerrecht* (2001) pp. 98-106
- Keith, Kirsten, 'The Mens Rea of Superior Responsibility as Developed by ICTY Jurisprudence', 14 *Leiden JIL* (2001) pp. 617-634
- Keller, Andrew N., 'Punishment for Violations of International Criminal Law: An Analysis of Sentencing at the ICTY and ICTR', 12 *Indiana International & Comparative Law Review* (2001) pp. 53-74
- Kerr, Rachel, 'Operational Justice: The Reality of War Crimes Prosecution in the International Criminal Tribunal for the Former Yugoslavia', 5 *International Journal of Human Rights* (2001) pp. 110-122
- Kolb, Robert, 'The Jurisprudence of the Yugoslav and Rwandan Criminal Tribunals on Their Jurisdiction and on International Crimes', 71 *BYIL* (2000) pp. 259-315
- Konstantinow, Georg E., 'Die Anklage gegen Milošević im System des Jugoslawien-Tribunals', 34 *Zeitschrift für Rechtspolitik* (2001) pp. 359-363
- Larkin, Jennifer L., 'The Insanity Defense Founded on Ethnic Oppression: Defending the Accused in the International Criminal Tribunal for the Former Yugoslavia', 21 *New York Law School Journal of International and Comparative Law* (2001) pp. 91-108
- Laursen, Andreas, 'NATO, the War over Kosovo, and the ICTY Investigation', 17 *Amer. Univ. ILR* (2002) pp. 765-814
- Lenzerini, Federico, 'La definizione internazionale di schiavitù secondo il Tribunale per la ex-Iugoslavia: un caso di cosmosi tra consuetudine e norme convenzionali', 84 *RDI* (2001) pp. 1026-1042
- Lundqvist, Ulf S., 'Admitting and Evaluating Evidence in the International Criminal Tribunal for the Former Yugoslavia Appeals Chamber Proceedings. A Few Remarks', 15 *Leiden JIL* (2002) pp. 641-665

– Magliveras, Konstantinos D., 'The Interplay Between the Transfer of Slobodan Miloše-vić to the ICTY and Yugoslav Constitutional Law', 13 *EJIL* (2002) pp. 661-677
– McDonald, Gabrielle Kirk, 'Reflections on the Contributions of the International Criminal Tribunal for the Former Yugoslavia', 24 *Hastings International and Comparative Law Review* (2001) pp. 155-172
– Meernik, James and Kimi Lynn King, 'The Effectiveness of International Law and the ICTY – Preliminary Results of an Empirical Study', 1 *International Criminal Law Review* (2001) pp. 343-372
– Mettraux, Guénaël, 'Crimes Against Humanity in the Jurisprudence of the International Criminal Tribunals for the Former Yugoslavia and for Rwanda', 43 *Harvard ILJ* (2002) pp. 237-316
– Morrison, Howard, 'Practice at the Ad Hoc Tribunals for the Former Yugoslavia and Rwanda', in Martine Hallers, Chantal Joubert and Jan Sjöcrona, eds., *The Position of the Defence at the International Criminal Court and the Role of The Netherlands as the Host State: Including the Proceedings of the Conference Held in The Hague, 3-4 November 2000* (Amsterdam, Rozenberg Publishers 2002) pp. 43-48
– Mundis, Daryl A., 'From "Common Law" Towards "Civil Law"; The Evolution of the ICTY Rules of Procedure and Evidence', 14 *Leiden JIL* (2001) pp. 367-382
– Negri, Stefania, 'International Tribunal for the Former Yugoslavia: Legal Maxims: Summaries and Extracts from Selected Case Law', 1 *The Global Community* (2001) pp. 505-585
– Nollkaemper, A., 'The Legitimacy of International Law in the Case Law of the International Criminal Tribunal for the Former Yugoslavia', in Th.A.J.A. Vandamme and J.H. Reestman, eds., *Ambiguity in the Rule of Law; The Interface Between National and International Legal Systems* (Groningen, Europa Law Publishing 2001) pp. 13-23
– Pauliat, Héléne, 'Le TPIY: un tribunal pour l'histoire? Carnets de voyage à La Haye', in Simone Gaboriau and Hélène Pauliat, *La justice pénale internationale: actes du colloque organisé à Limoges les 22-23 novembre 2001* (Limoges, Presses Universitaires de Limoges 2002) pp. 93-108
– Piliouras, Sophia, 'International Criminal Tribunal for the Former Yugoslavia and Milosevic's Trial', 18 *New York Law School Journal of Human Rights* (2002) pp. 515-525
– Roberts, Ken, 'The Law of Persecution Before the International Criminal Tribunal for the Former Yugoslavia', 15 *Leiden JIL* (2002) pp. 623-639
– Rodrigues, Almiro Simões, 'Le Tribunal Pénal International pour l'ex-Yougoslavie: bilan et perspectives', in Simone Gaboriau and Hélène Pauliat, *La justice pénale internationale: actes du colloque organisé à Limoges les 22-23 novembre 2001* (Limoges, Presses Universitaires de Limoges 2002) pp. 109-118
– Rohde, Christian, 'Defence Related Issues at the Registry of the ICTY', in Martine Hallers, Chantal Joubert and Jan Sjöcrona, eds., *The Position of the Defence at the International Criminal Court and the Role of The Netherlands as the Host State: Including the Proceedings of the Conference Held in The Hague, 3-4 November 2000* (Amsterdam, Rozenberg Publishers 2002) pp. 121-125
– Sánchez Patrón, José Manuel, 'La distinción entre crímenes de guerra y crímenes contra la humanidad a la luz de la jurisprudencia de los Tribunales penales internacionales para la ex-Yugoslavia y Ruanda', 78 *Revista española de derecho militar* (2001) pp. 53-84

– Schabas, William A., 'Was Genocide Committed in Bosnia and Herzegovina? First Judgments of the International Criminal Tribunal for the Former Yugoslavia', 25 *Fordham ILJ* (2001) pp. 23-53

– Shenk, Maury D., Brian J. Newquist, Lesly Stone and Daryl A. Mundis, 'International Criminal Tribunals for the Former Yugoslavia and for Rwanda', 35 *The International Lawyer* (2001) pp. 622-631

– Sluiter, G., 'Het Joegoslavië Tribunaal; enige beschouwingen van procedurele aard', 14 *VN Forum* (2001) pp. 13-22

– Stroh, Dagmar, 'State Cooperation with the International Criminal Tribunals for the Former Yugoslavia and for Rwanda', 5 *MPYBUNL* (2001) pp. 249-283

– Swart, Mia, 'Ad Hoc Rules for Ad Hoc Tribunals? The Rule-Making Power of the Judges of the ICTY and ICTR', 18 *South African Journal on Human Rights* (2002) pp. 570-589

– Tavernier, Paul, 'Responsabilité pénale? L'action du Tribunal pénal international pour l'ex-Yougoslavie', in Christian Tomuschat, ed., *Kosovo and the International Community: A Legal Assessment* (The Hague, Kluwer Law International 2002) pp. 157-179

– Tochilovsky, Vladimir, 'Proceedings in the International Criminal Court: Some Lessons to Learn from ICTY Experience', 10 *Eur. J. Crime, Crim. L & Crim. Jus* (2002) pp. 268-275

– Tolbert, David, 'The International Criminal Tribunal for the Former Yugoslavia: Unforeseen Successes and Foreseeable Shortcomings', 26 *The Fletcher Forum of World Affairs* (2002) pp. 7-19

– Valabhji, Nisha, 'Cumulative Convictions Based on the Same Acts Under the Statute of the I.C.T.Y.', 10 *Tulane Journal of International and Comparative Law* (2002) pp. 185-202

– Wald, Patricia M., 'To "Establish Incredible Events by Credible Evidence": The Use of Affidavit Testimony in Yugoslavia War Crimes Tribunal Proceedings', 42 *Harvard ILJ* (2001) pp. 535-553

6.313   International Criminal Tribunal for Rwanda

Books

– Bohlander, Michael, *Gerichtliche Sanktionen gegen Anwälte wegen Mißbrauchs von Verfahrensrechten: eine Studie zum institutionellen Rollenverständnis von Rechtsanwälten gegenüber den Gerichten, unter besonderer Berücksichtigung der USA, der ad hoc-Tribunale für Jugoslawien und Ruanda sowie des künftigen Ständigen Internationalen Strafgerichtshofes* (Aachen, Shaker 2001) 226 pp.

– International Criminal Tribunal for Rwanda, *ICTR and ICTY Rules: Comparison* (Arusha, International Criminal Tribunal for Rwanda 2001) 199 pp.

– International Criminal Tribunal for Rwanda, *Testifying Before the International Criminal Tribunal for Rwanda* (Arusha, ICTR 2001) 35 pp.

– International Crisis Group, *Tribunal pénal international pour le Rwanda: l'urgence de juger* (Arusha, ICG 2001) 45 pp.

– Klip, André and Göran Sluiter, eds., *Annotated Leading Cases of International Criminal Tribunals: Volume II: The International Criminal Tribunal for Rwanda, 1994-1999* (Antwerp, Intersentia 2001) 847 pp.

— Mégret, Frédéric, *Le Tribunal Pénal International pour le Rwanda* (Paris, Pedone 2002) 249 pp.
— Stroh, Dagmar P., *Die nationale Zusammenarbeit mit den Internationalen Straftribunalen für das ehemalige Jugoslawien und für Ruanda* (Heidelberg, Springer 2002) 395 pp.

Articles
— Aptel, Cécile, 'Overview of the Statute of the ICTR', in Christof Heyns, ed., *Human Rights Law in Africa 1998* (The Hague, Kluwer Law International 2001) pp. 93-96
— Aptel, Cécile, 'The Intent to Commit Genocide in the Case Law of the International Criminal Tribunal for Rwanda', 13 *Criminal LF* (2002) pp. 273-291
— Askin, Kelly, 'The Rwanda and Yugoslav Tribunals: Revolutionizing the Prosecution of War Crimes Against Women', 2 *Africa Legal Aid Quarterly* (2001) pp. 10-13
— Beresford, Stuart, 'Unshackling the Paper Tiger – the Sentencing Practices of the Ad Hoc International Criminal Tribunals for the Former Yugoslavia and Rwanda', 1 *International Criminal Law Review* (2001) pp. 33-90
— Boed, Roman, 'Current Developments in the Jurisprudence of the International Criminal Tribunal for Rwanda', 2 *International Criminal Law Review* (2002) pp. 283-295
— Boed, Roman, 'Individual Criminal Responsibility for Violations of Article 3 Common to the Geneva Conventions of 1949 and of Additional Protocol II Thereto in the Case Law of the International Criminal Tribunal for Rwanda', 13 *Criminal LF* (2002) pp. 293-322
— Boed, Roman, 'The International Criminal Tribunal for Rwanda', in M. Cherif Bassiouni, ed., *Post-Conflict Justice* (Ardsley, Transnational Publishers 2002) pp. 487-498
— Boed, Roman, 'The United Nations International Criminal Tribunal for Rwanda: Its Establishment, Work and Impact on International Criminal Justice', 17 *The Central European Review of International Affairs* (2001/2002) pp. 59-67
— Boelaert-Suominen, Sonja, 'De Internationale Tribunalen voor het voormalige Joegoslavië en Ruanda: unieke plaats in de internationale rechtsorde en belangrijke bijdragen tot de ontwikkeling van het internationaal strafrecht', in Jan Wouters and Heidi Panken, eds., *De genocidewet in internationaal perspectief* (Ghent, Larcier 2002) pp. 139-165
— Bogdan, Attila, 'Cumulative Charges, Convictions and Sentencing at the Ad Hoc International Tribunals for the Former Yugoslavia and Rwanda', 3 *Melbourne JIL* (2002) pp. 1-32
— Dieng, Adama, 'International Criminal Justice: From Paper to Practice – A Contribution from the International Criminal Tribunal for Rwanda to the Establishment of the International Criminal Court', 25 *Fordham ILJ* (2002) pp. 688-707
— Endo, Guillaume, 'Nullum Crimen Nulla Poena Sine Lege Principle and the ICTY and ICTR', 15 *RQDI* (2002) pp. 205-220
— Graybill, Lyn S., 'To Punish or Pardon: A Comparison of the International Criminal Tribunal for Rwanda and the South African Truth and Reconciliation Commission', 2 *Human Rights Review* (2001) pp. 3-18
— Keller, Andrew N., 'Punishment for Violations of International Criminal Law: An Analysis of Sentencing at the ICTY and ICTR', 12 *Indiana International & Comparative Law Review* (2001) pp. 53-74
— Kolb, Robert, 'The Jurisprudence of the Yugoslav and Rwandan Criminal Tribunals on Their Jurisdiction and on International Crimes', 71 *BYIL* (2000) pp. 259-315
— Magnarella, Paul J., 'Recent Developments in the International Law of Genocide: An Anthropological Perspective on the International Criminal Tribunal for Rwanda', in

Alexander Laban Hinton, ed., *Annihilating Difference: The Anthropology of Genocide* (Berkeley, University of California Press 2002) pp. 310-322

— Mettraux, Guénaël, 'Crimes Against Humanity in the Jurisprudence of the International Criminal Tribunals for the Former Yugoslavia and for Rwanda', 43 *Harvard ILJ* (2002) pp. 237-316

— Moghalu, Kingsley Chiedu, 'Image and Reality of War Crimes: External Perceptions of the International Criminal Tribunal for Rwanda', 26 *The Fletcher Forum of World Affairs* (2002) pp. 19-44

— Moghalu, Kingsley Chiedu, 'International Humanitarian Law from Nuremberg to Rome: The Weighty Precedents of the International Criminal Tribunal for Rwanda', 14 *Pace ILR* (2002) pp. 273-305

— Morrison, Howard, 'Practice at the Ad Hoc Tribunals for the Former Yugoslavia and Rwanda', in Martine Hallers, Chantal Joubert and Jan Sjöcrona, eds., *The Position of the Defence at the International Criminal Court and the Role of The Netherlands as the Host State: Including the Proceedings of the Conference Held in The Hague, 3-4 November 2000* (Amsterdam, Rozenberg Publishers 2002) pp. 43-48

— Murungi, Betty, 'Prosecuting Gender Crimes at the International Criminal Tribunal for Rwanda', 2 *Africa Legal Aid Quarterly* (2001) pp. 14-17

— Mutua, Makau Wa, 'The Rwanda Tribunal: A Critical Assessment', 2 *Africa Legal Aid Quarterly* (2001) pp. 6-9

— Nahamya, Elizabeth and Rokhayatou Diarra, 'Disclosure of Evidence Before the International Criminal Tribunal for Rwanda', 13 *Criminal LF* (2002) pp. 339-364

— Negri, Stefania, 'International Criminal Tribunal for Rwanda: Legal Maxims: Summaries and Extracts from Selected Case Law', 1 *The Global Community* (2001) pp. 593-655

— Niang, Mame Mandiaye, 'Les obligations du Procureur face à la défense devant le Tribunal pénal international pour le Rwanda', 56 *RSCDPC* (2001) pp. 277-289

— Niang, Mame Mandiaye, 'The Right to Counsel Before the International Criminal Tribunal for Rwanda', 13 *Criminal LF* (2002) pp. 323-338

— Nsereko, Daniel D. Ntanda, 'Genocidal Conflict in Rwanda and the ICTR', 48 *NILR* (2001) pp. 31-65

— Nsereko, Daniel D. Ntanda, 'The African Great Lakes Region and the International Criminal Tribunal for Rwanda', in ELSA International, ed., *International Law as We Enter the 21st Century: International Focus Programme 1997-1999* (Berlin, Spitz 2001) pp. 73-89

— Obote-Odora, Alex, 'Drafting of Indictments for the International Criminal Tribunal for Rwanda', 12 *Criminal LF* (2001) pp. 335-358

— Sánchez Patrón, José Manuel, 'La distinción entre crímenes de guerra y crímenes contra la humanidad a la luz de la jurisprudencia de los Tribunales penales internacionales para la ex-Yugoslavia y Ruanda', 78 *Revista española de derecho militar* (2001) pp. 53-84

— Schabas, William A., 'International Criminal Tribunal for Rwanda: Introductory Note', 1 *The Global Community* (2001) pp. 589-592

— Shenk, Maury D., Brian J. Newquist, Lesly Stone and Daryl A. Mundis, 'International Criminal Tribunals for the Former Yugoslavia and for Rwanda', 35 *The International Lawyer* (2001) pp. 622-631

— Stroh, Dagmar, 'State Cooperation with the International Criminal Tribunals for the Former Yugoslavia and for Rwanda', 5 *MPYBUNL* (2001) pp. 249-283

— Swart, Mia, 'Ad Hoc Rules for Ad Hoc Tribunals? The Rule-Making Power of the Judges of the ICTY and ICTR', 18 *South African Journal on Human Rights* (2002) pp. 570-589

— Van den Herik, L., 'Het Rwanda-tribunaal: uitdagingen en verworvenheden', 56 *Internationale Spectator* (2002) pp. 246-251

— Wenqi, Zhu, 'The Doctrine of Command Responsibility as Applied to Civilian Leaders: The ICTR and the "Kayishema" Case', in Sienho Yee and Wang Tieya, eds., *International Law in the Post-Cold War World: Essays in Memory of Li Haopei* (London, Routledge 2001) pp. 373-384

— Williamson, Jamie, 'Overview of the Assignment of Defence Counsel for ICTR', in Christof Heyns, ed., *Human Rights Law in Africa 1998* (The Hague, Kluwer Law International 2001) pp. 102-107

— Williamson, Jamie, 'Command Responsibility in the Case Law of the International Criminal Tribunal for Rwanda', 13 *Criminal LF* (2002) pp. 365-384

— Zakr, Nasser, 'Analyse spécifique du crime de génocide dans le Tribunal pénal international pour le Rwanda', 56 *RSCDPC* (2001) pp. 263-275

— Zakr, Nasser, 'L'imputabilité des faits et actes criminels des subalternes au supérieur hiérarchique devant le Tribunal pénal international pour le Rwanda', 78 *Revue de droit international et de droit comparé* (2001) pp. 51-73

— Zakr, Nasser, 'La responsabilité pénale individuelle devant le Tribunal pénal international pour le Rwanda', 82 *RDPC* (2002) pp. 55-74

6.314   International Criminal Court

Books

— Bohlander, Michael, *Gerichtliche Sanktionen gegen Anwälte wegen Mißbrauchs von Verfahrensrechten: eine Studie zum institutionellen Rollenverständnis von Rechtsanwälten gegenüber den Gerichten, unter besonderer Berücksichtigung der USA, der ad hoc-Tribunale für Jugoslawien und Ruanda sowie des künftigen Ständigen Internationalen Strafgerichtshofes* (Aachen, Shaker 2001) 226 pp.

— Bruer-Schäfer, Aline, *Der internationale Strafgerichtshof: die internationale Strafgerichtsbarkeit im Spannungsfeld von Recht und Politik* (Frankfurt aM, Peter Lang 2001) 387 pp.

— Cabezudo Rodríguez, Nicolás, *La Corte Penal Internacional* (Madrid, Dykinson 2002) 171 pp.

— Diaconu, Ion, *International Criminal Court: A New Stage* (Bucharest, IRSI 2002) 390 pp.

— Dörmann, Knut, *Elements of War Crimes Under the Rome Statute of the International Criminal Court: Sources and Commentary* (Cambridge, Cambridge University Press 2002) 524 pp.

— Hummrich, Martin, *Der völkerrechtliche Straftatbestand der Aggression: historische Entwicklung, Geltung und Definition im Hinblick auf das Statut des Internationalen Strafgerichtshofes* (Baden-Baden, Nomos 2001) 259 pp.

— Ingadottir, Thordis, *The International Criminal Court: The Trust Fund for Victims (Article 79 of the Rome Statute): A Discussion Paper* (London, PICT 2001) 43 pp.

— Kost, I.L., *The International Criminal Court in the Bibliography on International Criminal Law* (The Hague, Peace Palace Library 2002) 69 pp.
— Lirola Delgado, Isabel and Magdalena M. Martín Martínez, *La Corte penal internacional: justicia versus impunidad* (Barcelona, Ariel 2001) 307 pp.
— Sadat, Leila Nadya, *The International Criminal Court and the Transformation of International Law: Justice for the New Millennium* (Ardsley, Transnational Publishers 2002) 547 pp.
— Strijards, G.A.M., *Een permanent strafhof in Nederland*, 2nd augmented edn. (Nijmegen, Wolf Legal Publishers 2001) 355 pp.

Articles
— Amann, Diane Marie and M.N.S. Sellers, 'The United States of America and the International Criminal Court', 50 *American Journal of Comparative Law* (2002) pp. 381-404
— Ambos, Kai, 'The Right of Non-Self-Incrimination of Witnesses Before the ICC', 15 *Leiden JIL* (2002) pp. 155-177
— Arbour, Louise, 'Litigation Before the ICC: Not If and When, But How?', 40 *Columbia JTL* (2001) pp. 1-10
— Bassiouni, M. Cherif, 'The Universal Model: The International Criminal Court', in M. Cherif Bassiouni, ed., *Post-Conflict Justice* (Ardsley, Transnational Publishers 2002) pp. 813-825
— Baum, Lynne Miriam, 'Pursuing Justice in a Climate of Moral Outrage: An Evaluation of the Rights of the Accused in the Rome Statute of the International Criminal Court', 19 *Wisconsin International Law Journal* (2000-2001) pp. 197-229
— Bevers, J.A.C., 'The Position of the Defence Counsel in the 6th, 7th and 8th PrepCom Sessions and Further', in Martine Hallers, Chantal Joubert and Jan Sjöcrona, eds., *The Position of the Defence at the International Criminal Court and the Role of The Netherlands as the Host State: Including the Proceedings of the Conference Held in The Hague, 3-4 November 2000* (Amsterdam, Rozenberg Publishers 2002) pp. 165-173
— Bevers, J.A.C., N.M. Blokker and J.F.L. Roording, 'Nederland en het Internationaal Strafhof: over statuutsverplichtingen en goed gastheerschap', 77 *Nederlands Juristenblad* (2002) pp. 1730-1741
— Blumenthal, Daniel A., 'The Politics of Justice: Why Israel Signed the International Criminal Court Statute and What the Signature Means', 30 *Georgia Journal of International and Comparative Law* (2002) pp. 593-615
— Boas, Gideon, 'Developments in the Law of Procedure and Evidence at the International Criminal Tribunal for the Former Yugoslavia and the International Criminal Court', 12 *Criminal LF* (2001) pp. 167-183
— Bolton, John R., 'The Risks and Weaknesses of the International Criminal Court from America's Perspective', 64 *Law and Contemporary Problems* (2001) pp. 167-180
— Boon, Kristen, 'Rape and Forced Pregnancy Under the ICC Statute: Human Dignity, Autonomy, and Consent', 32 *Colum. HRLR* (2001) pp. 625-675
— Bos, A., 'De Verenigde Staten en het Internationale Strafhof', 56 *Internationale Spectator* (2002) pp. 239-245
— Broomhall, Bruce, 'Toward U.S. Acceptance of the International Criminal Court', 64 *Law and Contemporary Problems* (2001) pp. 141-151
— Brown, B.S., 'Unilateralism, Multilateralism and the International Criminal Court', in Stewart Patrick and Shepard Forman, eds., *Multilateralism and U.S. Foreign Policy: Ambivalent Engagement* (Boulder, Lynne Rienner 2001) pp. 494-528

− Buisman, Caroline, 'Discussions on Civil and Common Law', in Martine Hallers, Chantal Joubert and Jan Sjöcrona, eds., *The Position of the Defence at the International Criminal Court and the Role of The Netherlands as the Host State: Including the Proceedings of the Conference Held in The Hague, 3-4 November 2000* (Amsterdam, Rozenberg Publishers 2002) pp. 161-163

− Byron, Christine and David Turns, 'The Preparatory Commission for the International Criminal Court', 50 *ICLQ* (2001) pp. 420-435

− Caflisch, Lucius, 'The Rome Statute and the European Convention on Human Rights', 23 *HRLJ* (2002) pp. 1-12

− Caianiello, Michele and Giulio Illuminati, 'From the International Criminal Tribunal for the Former Yugoslavia to the International Criminal Court', 26 *North Carolina Journal of International Law and Commercial Regulation* (2001) pp. 407-455

− Casey, Lee A., 'The Case Against the International Criminal Court', 25 *Fordham ILJ* (2002) pp. 840-872

− Cassel, Douglass, 'Empowering United States Courts to Hear Crimes Within the Jurisdiction of the International Criminal Court', 35 *New England LR* (2001) pp. 421-449

− Cassese, Antonio, 'From Neurenberg to Rome: International Military Tribunals to the International Criminal Court', in Antonio Cassese, Paola Gaeta and John R.W.D. Jones, eds., *The Rome Statute of the International Criminal Court: A Commentary* (Oxford, Oxford University Press 2002) pp. 3-19

− Chatoor, Delia, 'The Role of Small States in International Diplomacy: CARICOM's Experience in the Negotiations on the Rome Statute of the International Criminal Court', 7 *International Peacekeeping: The Yearbook of International Peace Operations* (2001) pp. 295-310

− Clark, Roger S., 'The Mental Element in International Criminal Law: The Rome Statute of the International Criminal Court and the Elements of Offences', 12 *Criminal LF* (2001) pp. 291-334

− Clark, Roger S., 'Rethinking Aggression as a Crime and Formulating Its Elements: The Final Work-Product of the Preparatory Commission for the International Criminal Court', 15 *Leiden JIL* (2002) pp. 859-890

− Cottier, Michael, 'The Rome Statute and War Crimes', in ELSA International, ed., *International Law as We Enter the 21st Century: International Focus Programme 1997-1999* (Berlin, Spitz 2001) pp. 163-180

− Dascalopoulou-Livada, Phani, 'The Crime Aggression: Making Operative the Jurisdiction of the ICC: Tendencies in the PrepCom', 96 *Proc. ASIL* (2002) pp. 185-190

− De Bertodano, Sylvia, 'Judicial Independence in the International Criminal Court', 15 *Leiden JIL* (2002) pp. 409-430

− Deen-Racsmány, Zsuzsanna, 'The ICC, Peacekeepers and Resolution 1422: Will the Court Defer to the Council?', 49 *NILR* (2002) pp. 353-388

− Degli, Jean Yaovi, 'Egalité des armes?', in Martine Hallers, Chantal Joubert and Jan Sjöcrona, eds., *The Position of the Defence at the International Criminal Court and the Role of The Netherlands as the Host State: Including the Proceedings of the Conference Held in The Hague, 3-4 November 2000* (Amsterdam, Rozenberg Publishers 2002) pp. 91-108

− Della Morte, Gabriele, 'Les frontières de la compétence de la Cour Pénale Internationale: observations critiques', 73 *Revue internationale de droit pénal* (2002) pp. 23-57

– De Waynecourt-Steele, Tiffany, 'The Contribution of the Statute of the International Criminal Court to the Enforcement of International Law in the Light of the Experiences of the ICTY', 27 *South African Yearbook of International Law* (2002) pp. 1-63
– Dieng, Adama, 'International Criminal Justice: From Paper to Practice – A Contribution from the International Criminal Tribunal for Rwanda to the Establishment of the International Criminal Court', 25 *Fordham ILJ* (2002) pp. 688-707
– Dörmann, Knut, 'Preparatory Commission for the International Criminal Court: The Elements of War Crimes: Part II: Other Serious Violations of the Laws and Customs Applicable in International and Non-International Armed Conflicts', 83 *IRRC* (2001) pp. 461-487
– Duffy, Helen, 'National Constitutional Compatibility and the International Criminal Court', 11 *Duke JCIL* (2001) pp. 5-38
– Dunworth, Treasa, 'The International Criminal Court', *New Zealand Law Journal* (2002) pp. 231-232
– Ebdalin, Franklin M., 'The International Criminal Court: An Overview', 46 *Ateneo Law Journal* (2001) pp. 318-331
– Economides, Spyros, 'The International Criminal Court', in Karen E. Smith and Margot Light, eds., *Ethics and Foreign Policy* (Cambridge, Cambridge University Press 2001) pp. 112-128
– Editorial Comments, 'The European Union, the United States and the International Criminal Court', 39 *Common Market Law Review* (2002) pp. 939-944
– Edwards, George E., 'International Human Rights Law Challenges to the New International Criminal Court: The Search and Seizure Right to Privacy', 26 *Yale JIL* (2001) pp. 323-412
– Ellis, Mark S., 'The International Criminal Court and Its Implication for Domestic Law and National Capacity Building', 15 *Florida Journal of International Law* (2002) pp. 215-242
– El Zeidy, Mohamed, 'The United States Dropped the Atomic Bomb of Article 16 of the ICC Statute: Security Council Power of Deferrals and Resolution 1422', 35 *Vanderbilt JTL* (2002) pp. 1503-1544
– England, Joel F., 'The Response of the United States to the International Criminal Court: Rejection, Ratification or Something Else?', 18 *Arizona JI & CL* (2001) pp. 941-977
– Eser, H.C. Mult Albin, 'Towards an International Criminal Court: Genesis and Main Features of the Rome Statute', 20 *University of Tasmania Law Review* (2001) pp. 1-28
– Feehly, Colleen, 'The International Criminal Court: Progress to Date and Prospects for the Future', in Diane Hiscox, ed., *Looking Ahead: International Law in the 21st Century: Proceedings of the 29th Annual Conference of the Canadian Council on International Law, Ottawa, October 26-28, 2000* (The Hague, Kluwer Law International 2002) pp. 1-15
– Fernandéz de Gurmendi, Silvia A., 'The Working Group on Aggression at the Preparatory Commission for the International Criminal Court', 25 *Fordham ILJ* (2002) pp. 589-605
– Ferstman, Carla, 'The Reparation Regime of the International Criminal Court: Practical Considerations', 15 *Leiden JIL* (2002) pp. 667-686
– Gallant, Kenneth, 'Protection of the Rights of the Defence in the Agreement on Privileges and Immunities of the International Criminal Court, with Special Attention to the Needs of the Defence Outside the Host Country', in Martine Hallers, Chantal Joubert and Jan Sjöcrona, eds., *The Position of the Defence at the International Criminal Court*

    and the Role of The Netherlands as the Host State: Including the Proceedings of the Conference Held in The Hague, 3-4 November 2000 (Amsterdam, Rozenberg Publishers 2002) pp. 109-120

— Garcés Lloreda, Maria Teresa and Augusto J. Ibañez Guzman, 'La Corte penal internacional: estatuto de Roma: algunas reflexiones sobre su ratificación, 78 *Revista española de derecho militar* (2001) pp. 129-141

— García Ramírez, Sergio, 'Cuestiones constitucionales a propósito de la Corte Penal Internacional', 6 *Cuestiones constitucionales* (2002) pp. 175-189

— Gavron, Jessica, 'Amnesties in the Light of Developments in International Law and the Establishment of the International Criminal Court', 51 *ICLQ* (2002) pp. 91-117

— Gopalani, Ameer F., 'The International Standard of Direct and Public Incitement to Commit Genocide: An Obstacle to U.S. Ratification of the International Criminal Court Statute?', 32 *Calif. Western ILJ* (2001) pp. 87-117

— Gowland-Debbas, Vera, 'The Relationship Between Political and Judicial Organs of International Organisations: The Role of the Security Council in the New International Criminal Court', in Laurence Boisson de Chazournes, Cesare P.R. Romano and Ruth Mackenzie, eds., *International Organizations and International Dispute Settlement: Trends and Prospects* (Ardsley, Transnational Publishers 2002) pp. 195-219

— Gowland-Debbas, Vera, 'The Role of the Security Council in the New International Criminal Court from a Systematic Perspective', in Laurence Boisson de Chazournes and Vera Gowlland-Debbas, eds., *The International Legal System in Quest of Equity and Universality: Liber Amicorum Georges Abi-Saab* (The Hague, Nijhoff 2001) pp. 629-650

— Granados Peña, Jaime Enrique, 'Los crímenes de guerra en el conflicto interno colombiano a la luz de la Corte Penal Internacional', 103 *Universitas* (2002) pp. 95-112

— Groulx, Elise, 'The Defence Pillar: Making the Defence a Full Partner in the International Criminal Justice System', in Martine Hallers, Chantal Joubert and Jan Sjöcrona, eds., *The Position of the Defence at the International Criminal Court and the Role of The Netherlands as the Host State: Including the Proceedings of the Conference Held in The Hague, 3-4 November 2000* (Amsterdam, Rozenberg Publishers 2002) pp. 17-24

— Guariglia, Fabricio, 'The Rules of Procedure and Evidence for the International Criminal Court: A New Development in International Adjudication of Individual Criminal Responsibility', in Antonio Cassese, Paola Gaeta and John R.W.D. Jones, eds., *The Rome Statute of the International Criminal Court: A Commentary* (Oxford, Oxford University Press 2002) pp. 1111-1133

— Guidon, Patrick, 'Das Verbrechen der Aggression – pièce de résistance des Rom-Statuts', 11 *Aktuelle juristische Praxis* (2002) pp. 1317-1324

— Gurulé, Jimmy, 'United States Opposition to the 1998 Rome Statute Establishing an International Criminal Court: Is the Court's Jurisdiction Truly Complementary to National Criminal Jurisdictions?', 35 *Cornell ILJ* (2002) pp. 1-45

— Gutiérrez Espada, Cesáreo, 'La Corte Penal Internacional (CPI) y las Naciones Unidas: la discutida posición del Consejo de Seguridad', 18 *Anuario de derecho internacional* (2002) pp. 3-61

— Hans, Monica, 'Providing for Uniformity in the Exercise of Universal Jurisdiction: Can Either the Princeton Principles on Universal Jurisdiction or an International Criminal Court Accomplish this Goal?', 15 *Transnational Lawyer* (2002) pp. 357-403

— Herbst, Jochen, 'Immunität von Angehörigen der U.S. Streitkräfte vor der Strafvervolgung durch den IStGH? Zu Resolution 1422 (2002) des UN-Sicherheitsrates vom 12. Juli 2002', 29 *Europäische Grundrechte-Zeitschrift* (2002) pp. 581-588

— Herzer, Eva, 'International Criminal Court Comes into Effect', 87 *Women Lawyers Journal* (2002) pp. 21-23

— Heselhaus, Sebastian, 'Resolution 1422 (2002) des Sicherheitsrates zur Begrenzung der Tätigkeit des Internationalen Strafgerichtshofs', 62 *ZaöRV* (2002) pp. 907-940

— Holcombe, A. Diane, 'The United States Becomes a Signatory to the Rome Treaty Establishing the International Criminal Court: Why Are so Many Concerned by This Action?', 62 *Montana Law Review* (2001) pp. 301-337

— Holthuis, Hans, 'Operational Aspects of Setting Up the International Criminal Court: Building on the Experience of the International Tribunal for the Former Yugoslavia', 25 *Fordham ILJ* (2002) pp. 708-716

— Holthuis, Piet, 'The Need for an International Bar in the ICC Framework', in Martine Hallers, Chantal Joubert and Jan Sjöcrona, eds., *The Position of the Defence at the International Criminal Court and the Role of The Netherlands as the Host State: Including the Proceedings of the Conference Held in The Hague, 3-4 November 2000* (Amsterdam, Rozenberg Publishers 2002) pp. 9-11

— Inazumi, Mitsue, 'The Meaning of the State Consent Precondition in Article 12(2) of the Rome Statute of the International Criminal Court: A Theoretical Analysis of the Source of International Criminal Jurisdiction', 49 *NILR* (2002) pp. 159-193

— Izard, Michel et al., 'Les outils et les conditions de travail de la défense: suggestion du Barreau de Draguignan (La France)', in Martine Hallers, Chantal Joubert and Jan Sjöcrona, eds., *The Position of the Defence at the International Criminal Court and the Role of The Netherlands as the Host State: Including the Proceedings of the Conference Held in The Hague, 3-4 November 2000* (Amsterdam, Rozenberg Publishers 2002) pp. 137-145

— Jäger, Susen and Alexander Roth, 'Der Internationale Strafgerichtshof – Ratifizierung und Umsetzung des Römischen Statuts in Osteuropa', 44 *WGO: Monatshefte für Osteuropäisches Recht* (2002) pp. 185-203

— Jayaraj, C., 'The International Criminal Court and the United States: Recent Legal and Policy Issues', 42 *Indian JIL* (2002) pp. 489-511

— Kalivretakis, Elaina I., 'Are Nuclear Weapons Above the Law? A Look at the International Criminal Court and the Prohibited Weapons Category', 15 *Emory ILR* (2001) pp. 683-732

— Kambale, Pascal K., 'Quelques considérations sur la compatibilité du statut de la Cour Pénale Internationale avec certains principes constitutionnels en Afrique francophone', 6 *Revue de droit africain* (2002) pp. 41-65

— Kaul, Hans-Peter, 'Der Aufbau des Internationalen Strafgerichtshofs', 49 *Vereinte Nationen* (2001) pp. 215-222

— Kirsch, Philippe, 'The International Criminal Court: Current Issues and Perspectives', 64 *Law and Contemporary Problems* (2001) pp. 3-11

— Kirsch, Philippe, 'La Cour pénale internationale face à la souveraineté des États', in Antonio Cassese and Mireille Delmas-Marty, eds., *Crimes internationaux et jurisdictions internationales* (Paris, Presses universitaires de France 2002) pp. 31-37

— Kirsch, Philippe and Valerie Oosterveld, 'Negotiating an Institution for the Twenty-first Century: Multilateral Diplomacy and the International Criminal Court', 46 *MacGill Law Journal* (2001) pp. 1141-1160

− Kirsch, Philippe and Valerie Oosterveld, 'The Preparatory Commission for the International Criminal Court', 25 *Fordham ILJ* (2002) pp. 563-588

− Kleffner, Jann, 'Some Preliminary Thoughts on the Position of the Defence at the New International Criminal Court and the Role of The Netherlands as the Host State', in Martine Hallers, Chantal Joubert and Jan Sjöcrona, eds., *The Position of the Defence at the International Criminal Court and the Role of The Netherlands as the Host State: Including the Proceedings of the Conference Held in The Hague, 3-4 November 2000* (Amsterdam, Rozenberg Publishers 2002) pp. 1-8

− Labuschagne, J.M.T., 'Psychosexual Autonomy, Crimes Against Humanity and the Rome Statute: Remarks on the Process of Internationalisation of Criminal Law', 34 *Comparative and International Law Journal of Southern Africa* (2001) pp. 325-348

− Latore, Roseann M., 'Escape out the Back Door or Charge in the Front Door: U.S. Reactions to the International Criminal Court', 25 *Boston College Int. & Comp. LR* (2002) pp. 159-176

− Lee, Joanne, 'The Ratification Process and the Entry into Force of the International Criminal Court Statute', in ELSA International, ed., *International Law as We Enter the 21st Century: International Focus Programme 1997-1999* (Berlin, Spitz 2001) pp. 121-152

− Lee, Roy, 'An Assessment of the ICC Statute', 25 *Fordham ILJ* (2002) pp. 750-766

− Lee, Roy, 'Statement on the Position of the Defence at the ICC and the Role of the Host State', in Martine Hallers, Chantal Joubert and Jan Sjöcrona, eds., *The Position of the Defence at the International Criminal Court and the Role of The Netherlands as the Host State: Including the Proceedings of the Conference Held in The Hague, 3-4 November 2000* (Amsterdam, Rozenberg Publishers 2002) pp. 35-38

− Leigh, Monroe, 'The United States and the Statute of Rome', 95 *AJIL* (2001) pp. 124-131

− Leurdijk, D.A., 'Amerika en zijn weerzin tegen het Internationale Strafhof', 56 *Internationale Spectator* (2002) pp. 549-554

− Lietzau, William K., 'The United States and the International Criminal Court: International Criminal Law After Rome: Concerns from a U.S. Military Perspective', 64 *Law and Contemporary Problems* (2001) pp. 119-140

− Llewellyn, Jennifer J., 'A Comment on the Complementary Jurisdiction of the International Criminal Court: Adding Insult to Injury in Transitional Contexts?', 24 *Dalhousie LJ* (2001) pp. 192-217

− Lüder, Sascha Rolf, 'The Legal Nature of the International Criminal Court and the Emergence of Supranational Elements in International Criminal Justice', 84 *IRRC* (2002) pp. 79-92

− MacIntire, Alison M., 'Be Careful What You Wish for Because You Just Might Get It: The United States and the International Criminal Court', 25 *Suffolk Transnational Law Review* (2001) pp. 249-274

− Malabat, Valérie, 'La Cour pénale internationale', 76 *La semaine juridique* (2002) pp. 1601-1602

− Martin, Pierre M., 'La signature par les Etats-Unis de la Convention créant la Cour pénale internationale', 177 *Recueil Le Dalloz* (2001) pp. 1256-1258

− Martinez, Lucy, 'Prosecuting Terrorists at the International Criminal Court: Possibilities and Problems', 34 *Rutgers Law Journal* (2002) pp. 1-62

− McCoubrey, Hilaire, 'From Nuremberg to Rome: Restoring the Defence of Superior Orders', 50 *ICLQ* (2001) pp. 386-394

– McNerney, Patricia, 'The International Criminal Court: Issues for Consideration by the United States Senate', 64 *Law and Contemporary Problems* (2001) pp. 181-191

– Mégret, Frédéric, 'Epilogue to an Endless Debate: The International Criminal Court's Third Party Jurisdiction and the Looming Revolution of International Law', 12 *EJIL* (2001) pp. 247-268

– Meron, Theodor, 'Defining Aggression for the International Criminal Court', 25 *Suffolk Transnational Law Review* (2001) pp. 1-15

– Metcalf, Jo, 'International Criminal Court', 10 *Journal of Law & Medicine* (2002) pp. 17-19

– Misetic, Luka, 'Sacrificing the Rights of the Accused for the "Success" of International Criminal Justice', in Martine Hallers, Chantal Joubert and Jan Sjöcrona, eds., *The Position of the Defence at the International Criminal Court and the Role of The Netherlands as the Host State: Including the Proceedings of the Conference Held in The Hague, 3-4 November 2000* (Amsterdam, Rozenberg Publishers 2002) pp. 49-54

– Mochochoko, Phakiso, 'The Agreement of Privileges and Immunities of the International Criminal Court', 25 *Fordham ILJ* (2002) pp. 638-664

– Moghalu, Kingsley Chiedu, 'International Humanitarian Law from Nuremberg to Rome: The Weighty Precedents of the International Criminal Tribunal for Rwanda', 14 *Pace ILR* (2002) pp. 273-305

– Morris, Madeline, 'High Crimes and Misconceptions: The ICC and Non-Party States', 64 *Law and Contemporary Problems* (2001) pp. 13-66

– Müller-Schieke, Irina Kaye, 'Defining the Crime of Aggression Under the Statute of the International Criminal Court', 14 *Leiden JIL* (2001) pp. 409-430

– Murphy, S., 'U.S. Signing of the Statute of the International Criminal Court', 95 *AJIL* (2001) pp. 397-399

– Neier, Aryeh, 'Will the International Criminal Court Make a Difference?', 12 *Helsinki Monitor* (2001) pp. 163-164

– Nsereko, Daniel D. Ntanda, 'Aggression Under the Rome Statute of the International Criminal Court', 71 *Nordic JIL* (2002) pp. 497-521

– Ongena, Tom, 'The Implementation of the Rome Statute in Belgium', in Ernest Krings, *The Belgian Reports at the Congress of Brisbane of the International Academy of Comparative Law = Rapports belges au Congrès de l'Academie Internationale de Droit comparé à Brisbane = De Belgische rapporten voor het Congres van de "Academie Internationale de Droit comparé" te Brisbane* (Brussels, Bruylant 2002) pp. 575-653

– Oosterveld, Valerie, Mike Perry and John McManus, 'The Cooperation of States with the International Criminal Court', 25 *Fordham ILJ* (2002) pp. 767-839

– Ottenhof, Reynald, 'L'Association Internationale de Droit Pénal et la création de la Cour Pénale Internationale: de l'utopie à la réalité', 73 *Revue internationale de droit pénal* (2002) pp. 15-21

– Pejic, Jelena, 'The United States and the International Criminal Court: One Loophole Too Many', 78 *University of Detroit Mercy Law Review* (2001) pp. 267-297

– Pellet, Alain, 'Pour la Cour Pénal Internationale, quand même! – Quelques remarques sur sa compétence et sa saisine', 1 *International Criminal Law Review* (2001) pp. 91-110

– Perrin de Brichambaut, Marc, 'Les tribunaux pénaux internationaux: la Cour Pénale Internationale', in Marc Perrin de Brichambaut, Jean-François Dobelle and Marie-Reine d'Haussy, *Leçons de droit international public* (Paris, Presses de Sciences Po 2002) pp. 343-369

— Popoff, Evo, 'Inconsistency and Impunity in International Human Rights Law: Can the International Criminal Court Solve the Problems Raised by the Rwanda and Augusto Pinochet Cases', 33 *The George Washington International Law Review* (2001) pp. 363-395

— Poppe, Gerd, 'Der Internationale Strafgerichtshof: Instrument zur Ahndung und Prävention schwerster Verbrechen', *Jahrbuch Menschenrechte* (2002) pp. 199-209

— Poupart, Pierre, 'Les outils et les conditions de travail de la défense: réflexions d'un avocat de la défense sur ce qui semble avoir été et sur ce qui doit être', in Martine Hallers, Chantal Joubert and Jan Sjöcrona, eds., *The Position of the Defence at the International Criminal Court and the Role of The Netherlands as the Host State: Including the Proceedings of the Conference Held in The Hague, 3-4 November 2000* (Amsterdam, Rozenberg Publishers 2002) pp. 129-136

— Reisman, W. Michael et al., 'The Definition of Aggression and the ICC', 96 *Proc. ASIL* (2002) pp. 181-192

— Roberts, Guy, 'Assault on Sovereignty: The Clear and Present Danger of the New International Criminal Court', 17 *Amer. Univ. ILR* (2001) pp. 35-77

— Rovine, Arthur W., 'Memorandum to Congress on the ICC from Current and Past Presidents of the ASIL', 95 *AJIL* (2001) pp. 967-969

— Rubin, Alfred P., 'Legal Response to Terror: An International Criminal Court?', 43 *Harvard ILJ* (2002) pp. 65-70

— Rubin, Alfred P., 'The International Criminal Court: Possibilities for Prosecutorial Abuse', 64 *Law and Contemporary Problems* (2001) pp. 153-165

— Ruiz Fabri, Hélène, 'La Convention de Rome créant la Cour pénale internationale: questions de ratification', 54 *Revue internationale de droit comparé* (2002) pp. 441-463

— Sachar, Rajinder, 'International Humanitarian Law with Particular Reference to International Criminal Court', 1 *ISIL Yearbook of International Humanitarian and Refugee Law* (2001) pp. 1-11

— Santulli, Carlo, 'Pourquoi combattre l'impunité dans un cadre international? La Cour pénale internationale: de l'impunité à la répression?', in Simone Gaboriau and Hélène Pauliat, *La justice pénale internationale: actes du colloque organise à Limoges les 22-23 novembre 2001* (Limoges, Presses Universitaires de Limoges 2002) pp. 179-188

— Sarooshi, D., 'Aspects of the Relationship Between the International Criminal Court and the United Nations', 32 *NYIL* (2002) pp. 27-53

— Scaliotti, Massimo, 'Defences Before the International Criminal Court: Substantive Grounds for Excluding Criminal Responsibility: Part I', 1 *International Criminal Law Review* (2001) pp. 111-172

— Scaliotti, Massimo, 'Defences Before the International Criminal Court: Substantive Grounds for Excluding Criminal Responsibility: Part II', 2 *International Criminal Law Review* (2002) pp. 1-46

— Schabas, William A., 'International Criminal Court: The Secret of Its Success', 12 *Criminal LF* (2001) pp. 415-428

— Scharf, Michael P., 'The United States and the International Criminal Court: The ICC's Jurisdiction over the Nationals of Non-Party States: A Critique of the U.S. Position', 64 *Law and Contemporary Problems* (2001) pp. 67-117

— Scheffer, David J., 'Fourteenth Waldemar A. Solf Lecture in International Law: A Negotiator's Perspective on the International Criminal Court', 167 *Mil. LR* (2001) pp. 1-19

— Scheffer, David J., 'Staying the Course with the International Criminal Court', 35 *Cornell ILJ* (2002) pp. 47-100

— Scheinin, Martin, 'From Nuremberg to the International Criminal Court', in Ilkka Taipale et al., eds., *War or Health? A Reader* (London, Zed 2002) pp. 465-470
— Schense, Jennifer, 'Necessary Steps for the Creation of the International Criminal Court', 25 *Fordham ILJ* (2002) pp. 717-736
— Schrag, Minna, 'Substantive Role for ICC Criminal Defence Bar', in Martine Hallers, Chantal Joubert and Jan Sjöcrona, eds., *The Position of the Defence at the International Criminal Court and the Role of The Netherlands as the Host State: Including the Proceedings of the Conference Held in The Hague, 3-4 November 2000* (Amsterdam, Rozenberg Publishers 2002) pp. 39-41
— Shah, Sonali B., 'The Oversight of the Last Great International Institution of the Twentieth Century: The International Criminal Court's Definition of Genocide', 16 *Emory ILR* (2002) pp. 351-389
— Smidt, Michael L., 'The International Criminal Court: An Effective Means of Deterrence?', 167 *Mil. LR* (2001) pp. 156-240
— Smith, Thomas W., 'Moral Hazard and Humanitarian Law: The International Criminal Court and the Limits of Legalism', 39 *International Politics* (2002) pp. 175-192
— Soulez-Larivière, Daniel, 'La déontologie, organisation et contrôle', in Martine Hallers, Chantal Joubert and Jan Sjöcrona, eds., *The Position of the Defence at the International Criminal Court and the Role of The Netherlands as the Host State: Including the Proceedings of the Conference Held in The Hague, 3-4 November 2000* (Amsterdam, Rozenberg Publishers 2002) pp. 147-150
— Steytler, C., 'International Criminal Court', 76 *Australian Law Journal* (2002) pp. 469-473
— Strapatsas, Nicolaos, 'The European Union and Its Contribution to the Development of the International Criminal Court', 33 *Revue de droit / Faculté de droit, Université de Sherbrooke* (2002) pp. 399-425
— Strapatsas, Nicolaos, 'Universal Jurisdiction and the International Criminal Court', 29 *Manitoba Law Journal* (2002) pp. 1-31
— Strijards, G.A.M., 'De United Nations, een internationaal strafhof en zijn gastland: een spannende driehoeksverhouding', 31 *Delikt en delinkwent* (2001) pp. 548-584
— Strydom, Hennie, 'South Africa and the International Criminal Court', 6 *MPYBUNL* (2002) pp. 345-366
— Summers, Mark A., 'A Fresh Look at the Jurisdictional Provisions of the Statute of the International Criminal Court: The Case for Scrapping the Treaty', 20 *Wisconsin International Law Journal* (2001-2002) pp. 57-88
— Sweeney, Joseph C. et al., 'The Eve of the International Criminal Court: Preparations and Commentary', 25 *Fordham ILJ* (2002) pp. 541-562
— Szasz, Paul C. and Thordis Ingadottir, 'The UN and the ICC: The Immunity of the UN and Its Officials', 14 *Leiden JIL* (2001) pp. 867-885
— Tavernier, Paul, 'Comment surmonter les obstacles constitutionnels à la ratification du Statut de Rome de la Cour pénale internationale', 13 *Revue trimestrielle des droits de l'homme* (2002) pp. 545-561
— Tenorio, Pedro J., 'Estatuto de la Corte Penal Internacional y Constitucional', 51 *Revista de derecho político* (2001) pp. 57-103
— Tochilovsky, Vladimir, 'Proceedings in the International Criminal Court: Some Lessons to Learn from ICTY Experience', 10 *Eur. J. Crime, Crim. L & Crim. Jus* (2002) pp. 268-275

— Trahan, Jennifer, 'Defining "Aggression": Why the Preparatory Commission for the International Criminal Court Has Faced Such a Conundrum', 24 *Loyola LA I & Comp. LR* (2002) pp. 439-474

— Triffterer, Otto, 'Causality, a Separate Element of the Doctrine of Superior Responsibility as Expressed in Article 28 Rome Statute?', 15 *Leiden JIL* (2002) pp. 179-205

— Vanchestein, Erick, 'Cour Pénale Internationale: évaluation de la qualification des conseils de la défense', in Martine Hallers, Chantal Joubert and Jan Sjöcrona, eds., *The Position of the Defence at the International Criminal Court and the Role of The Netherlands as the Host State: Including the Proceedings of the Conference Held in The Hague, 3-4 November 2000* (Amsterdam, Rozenberg Publishers 2002) pp. 151-159

— Van Genugten, W.J.M., 'De Verenigde Staten versus het Permanente Internationale Strafhof', 77 *Nederlands Juristenblad* (2002) pp. 356-357

— Verweij, Harry, 'The International Criminal Court: Alive, Soon Kicking!', 25 *Fordham ILJ* (2002) pp. 737-749

— Vigorito, Rosaria, 'The Evolution and Establishment of the International Criminal Court (ICC): A Selected Annotated Bibliography of Secondary Sources', 30 *International Journal of Legal Information* (2002) pp. 92-162

— Ward, Alex, 'Breaking the Sovereignty Barrier: The United States and the International Criminal Court', 41 *Santa Clara Law Review* (2001) pp. 1123-1145

— Washburn, John, 'The International Criminal Court Arrives – The U.S. Position: Status and Prospects', 25 *Fordham ILJ* (2002) pp. 873-883

— Watters, Lawrence, 'Convergence and the Procedures of the International Criminal Court: An International and Comparative Perspective', 40 *Columbia JTL* (2002) pp. 419-430

— Wedgwood, Ruth, 'The Irresolution of Rome', 64 *Law and Contemporary Problems* (2001) pp. 193-214

— Wirth, Steffen, 'Immunities, Related Problems, and Article 98 of the Rome Statute', 12 *Criminal LF* (2001) pp. 429-458

— Yengejeh, Saeid Mirzaee, 'Rules of Procedure of the Assembly of States Parties to the Rome Statute of the International Criminal Court', 25 *Fordham ILJ* (2002) pp. 665-673

— Young, Simon, 'Surrendering the Accused to the International Criminal Court', 71 *BYIL* (2000) pp. 317-356

— Zakr, Nasser, 'Les aspects institutionnels de la Cour pénale internationale', 129 *Journal du droit international* (2002) pp. 449-474

— Zelniker, Lindsay, 'Towards a Functional International Criminal Court: An Argument in Favor of a Strong Privileges and Immunities Agreement', 24 *Fordham ILJ* (2001) pp. 988-1027

— Zimmermann, Andreas and Holger Scheel, 'Zwischen Konfrontation und Kooperation: die Vereinigten Staaten und der Internationale Strafgerichtshof', 50 *Vereinte Nationen* (2002) pp. 137-144

— Zwanenburg, M.C., 'Het Internationaal Strafhof en de bescherming van vredesmachten', 94 *Militair Rechtelijk Tijdschrift* (2001) pp. 177-188

6.315 East Timor's Special Panels for Serious Crimes

Articles

– Linton, S., 'Cambodia, East Timor and Sierra Leone: Experiments in International Justice', 12 *Criminal LF* (2001) pp. 185-246
– Linton, S., 'Prosecuting Atrocities at the District Court of Dili', 2 *Melbourne JIL* (2001) pp. 414-458
– Linton, S., 'New Approaches to International Justice in Cambodia and East Timor', 84 *IRRC* (2002) pp. 93-119
– Strohmeyer, Hansjörg, 'Collapse and Reconstruction of a Judicial System: The United Nations Mission in Kosovo and East Timor', 95 *AJIL* (2001) pp. 46-63
– Tracol, Xavier, 'Justice pour le Timor oriental', 56 *RSCDPC* (2001) pp. 291-306
– Trotter, Peter F., 'Like Lambs to the Slaughter: The Scope of and Liability for International Crimes in East Timor and the Need for an International Criminal Tribunal', 7 *New England International & Comparative Law Annual* (2001) pp. 31-67

6.316 Kosovo's Internationalised Courts

Articles

– Strohmeyer, Hansjörg, 'Collapse and Reconstruction of a Judicial System: The United Nations Mission in Kosovo and East Timor', 95 *AJIL* (2001) pp. 46-63

6.317 Special Court for Sierra Leone

Articles

– Amman, Diane Marie, 'Calling Children to Account: The Proposal for a Juvenile Chamber in the Special Court for Sierra Leone', 29 *Pepperdine Law Review* (2001) pp. 167-185
– Bald, Stephanie H., 'Searching for a Lost Childhood: Will the Special Court of Sierra Leone Find Justice for Its Children?', 18 *Amer. Univ. ILR* (2002) pp. 537-583
– Beresford, Stuart and A.S. Muller, 'The Special Court for Sierra Leone: An Initial Comment', 14 *Leiden JIL* (2001) pp. 635-651
– Cerone, John, 'The Special Court for Sierra Leone: Establishing a New Approach to International Criminal Justice', 8 *ILSA JI & CL* (2002) pp. 379-387
– Corriero, Michael A., 'The Involvement and Protection of Children in Truth and Justice-Seeking Processes: The Special Court for Sierra Leone', 18 *New York Law School Journal of Human Rights* (2002) pp. 337-360
– Crippa, Matteo, 'La Corte Speciale per la Sierra Leone', 15 *Rivista internazionale dei diritti dell'uomo* (2002) pp. 449-473
– Cryer, Robert, 'A "Special Court" for Sierra Leone?', 50 *ICLQ* (2001) pp. 435-446
– Denis, Catherine, 'Le tribunal spécial pour la Sierra Leone: quelques observations', 34 *RBDI* (2001) pp. 236-287
– De Sanctis, Francesco, 'Il processo di istituzione di una Special Court per i crimini della guerra civile in Sierra Leone', 56 *La Comunità internazionale* (2001) pp. 475-497

- Fritz, Nicole and Alison Smith, 'Current Apathy for Coming Anarchy: Building the Special Court for Sierra Leone', 25 *Fordham ILJ* (2001) pp. 391-430
- Linton, S., 'Cambodia, East Timor and Sierra Leone: Experiments in International Justice', 12 *Criminal LF* (2001) pp. 185-246
- Macaluso, Daniel J., 'Absolute and Free Pardon: The Effect of the Amnesty Provision in the Lomé Peace Agreement on the Jurisdiction of the Special Court for Sierra Leone', 27 *Brooklyn Journal of International Law* (2001) pp. 347-380
- McDonald, Avril, 'Sierra Leone's Shoestring Special Court', 84 *IRRC* (2002) pp. 121-143
- Nalin, Egeria, 'La Corte speciale per la Sierra Leone', 57 *La Comunità internazionale* (2002) pp. 363-405
- Picavet, Sofie, 'Een speciaal tribunaal voor Sierra Leone', 10 *Zoeklicht* (2001) pp. 18-20
- Poole, Jennifer L., 'Post-Conflict Justice in Sierra Leone', in M. Cherif Bassiouni, ed., *Post-Conflict Justice* (Ardsley, Transnational Publishers 2002) pp. 563-592
- Schocken, Celina, 'The Special Court for Sierra Leone: Overview and Recommendations', 20 *Berkeley JIL* (2002) pp. 436-461
- Sieff, Michelle, 'War Criminals: Watch Out: Prosecuting War Criminals in Sierra Leone', 57 *The World Today* (2001) pp. 18-20
- Tejan-Cole, Abdul, 'The Special Court for Sierra Leone: Conceptual Concerns and Alternatives', 1 *African Human Rights Law Journal* (2001) pp. 107-126

6.318   Extraordinary Chambers for Cambodia

Articles

- Buckley, Aaron J., 'The Conflict in Cambodia and Post-Conflict Justice', in M. Cherif Bassiouni, ed., *Post-Conflict Justice* (Ardsley, Transnational Publishers 2002) pp. 635-657
- Linton, S., 'Cambodia, East Timor and Sierra Leone: Experiments in International Justice', 12 *Criminal LF* (2001) pp. 185-246
- Linton, S., 'New Approaches to International Justice in Cambodia and East Timor', 84 *IRRC* (2002) pp. 93-119

6.32   National Courts

Books

- Cassese, Antonio and Mireille Delmas-Marty, *Jurisdictions nationales et crimes internationaux* (Paris, Presses Universitaires de France 2002) 673 pp.

Articles

- Cassel, Douglass, 'Empowering United States Courts to Hear Crimes Within the Jurisdiction of the International Criminal Court', 35 *New England LR* (2001) pp. 421-449
- Charney, Jonathan I., 'International Criminal Law and the Role of Domestic Courts', 95 *AJIL* (2001) pp. 120-124

– Erasmus, Gerhard and Gerhard Kemp, 'The Application of International Criminal Law Before Domestic Courts in the Light of Recent Developments in International and Constitutional Law', 27 *South African Yearbook of International Law* (2002) pp. 65-81
– Reydams, Luc, 'Swiss Military Trial of Former Rwanda Town Mayor Accused of War Crimes for Inciting Murder of Civilians in Rwanda', 96 *AJIL* (2002) pp. 231-236
– Roht-Arriaza, Naomi, 'The Pinochet Precedent and Universal Jurisdiction', 35 *New England LR* (2001) pp. 311-319
– Schimmelpenninck van der Oije, Pita J.C., 'A Surinam Crime Before a Dutch Court: Post Colonial Injustice or Universal Jurisdiction?', 14 *Leiden JIL* (2001) pp. 455-476
– Solera, Oscar, 'Complementary Jurisdiction and International Criminal Justice', 84 *IRRC* (2002) pp. 145-171
– Vanderweert, Susan Jenkins, 'Seeking Justice for "Comfort" Women: Without an International Criminal Court, Suits Brought by World War II Sex Slaves of the Japanese Army May Find Their Best Hope of Success in U.S. Federal Courts', 27 *North Carolina Journal of International Law and Commercial Regulation* (2001) pp. 141-183
– Weisburd, Mark and Harold Hongju Koh, '"Vertical" Conflicts Between International and National Tribunals', 96 *Proc. ASIL* (2002) pp. 41-53
– Wickremasinghe, Chanaka, 'Case Concerning the Arrest Warrant of 11 April 2000 (Democratic Republic of Congo v. Belgium)', 50 *ICLQ* (2001) pp. 670-675
– Wilson, Richard J., 'Assigned Defense Counsel in Domestic and International War Crimes Tribunals: The Need for a Structural Approach', 2 *International Criminal Law Review* (2002) pp. 145-193
– Zaid, Mark S., 'Symposium: Universal Jurisdiction: Myths, Realities, and Prospects: Will or Should the United States Ever Prosecute War Criminals? A Need for Greater Expansion in the Area of Both Criminal and Civil Liability', 35 *New England LR* (2001) pp. 1-16
– Zappala, Salvatore, 'Do Heads of State in Office Enjoy Immunity from Jurisdiction for International Crimes? The Ghaddafi Case Before the French Cour de Cassation', 12 *EJIL* (2001) pp. 595-612

7.2   NATIONAL LAW

Books

– International Committee of the Red Cross, *Punishing Violations of International Humanitarian Law at the National Level* (Geneva, International Committee of the Red Cross 2001) 199 pp.
– International Committee of the Red Cross, *National Implementation of International Humanitarian Law: Biennial Report 2000-2001* (Geneva, International Committee of the Red Cross 2002) 111 pp.
– Segall, Anna, *Punishing Violations of International Humanitarian Law at the National Level: A Guide for Common Law States: Drawing in the Proceedings of a Meeting of Experts (Geneva, 11-13 November 1998)* (Geneva, International Committee of the Red Cross 2001) 199 pp.

Articles

– Kadam, Umesh, 'Promoting Humanitarian Law at the National Level: Usefullness of National Bodies', 1 *ISIL Yearbook of International Humanitarian and Refugee Law* (2001) pp. 36-46
– Klip, A.H., 'Komt er een eind aan de nationale strafvervolging van internationale misdrijven?', in Taru Spronken et al., *Iets bijzonders: liber amicorum aangeboden aan Mischa Wladimiroff ter gelegenheid van zijn 30-jarig jubileum als advocaat* (The Hague, SDU 2002) pp. 263-279
– Werle, Gerhard and Volker Nerlich, 'Die Strafbarkeit von Kriegsverbrechen nach deutschem Recht', 15 *Humanitäres Völkerrecht* (2002) pp. 124-134

7.21   Legislation to Implement IHL Treaties

Books

– Bothe, Michael, ed., *Towards a Better Implementation of International Humanitarian Law. Proceedings of an Expert Meeting Organized by the Advisory Committee on International Humanitarian Law of the German Red Cross, Frankfurt am Main, May 28-30, 1999* (Berlin, Berlin Verlag 2002) pp. 149 pp.

Articles

– Hall, Christopher, 'National Implementation of Universal Jurisdiction for International Crimes', 2 *Africa Legal Aid Quarterly* (2001) pp. 27-29
– Peterson, Alex G., 'Order Out of Chaos: Domestic Enforcement of the Law of Internal Armed Conflict', 171 *Mil. LR* (2002) pp. 1-90
– Qiuchao, Shen, 'Implementation of the Law of Armed Conflict by the Chinese People's Liberation Army', 40 *Revue de droit militaire et de droit de guerre* (2001) pp. 49-60
– Vandermeersch, Damien, 'Les poursuites et le jugement des infractions de droit humanitaire en droit belge', 6 *Actualité du droit international humanitaire* (2001) pp. 121-180
– Werle, Gerhard and Florian Jessberger, 'International Criminal Justice Is Coming Home: The New German Code of Crimes Against International Law', 13 *Criminal LF* (2002) pp. 191-223

7.22   Legislation to Implement Obligations *vis-à-vis* the International Criminal Court and International Criminal Tribunals

Books

– Camen, Tony and Réka Varga, eds., *Regional Conference on the Implementation of the Rome Statute of the International Criminal Court: Budapest, 6-8 June 2002* (Geneva, International Committee of the Red Cross 2002) 302 pp.
– Lüder, Sascha Rolf and Thomas Vormbaum, eds., *Materialien zum Völkerstrafgesetzbuch. Dokumentation des Gesetzgebungsverfahrens* (Münster, LIT Verlag 2002) 144 pp.
– Stroh, Dagmar P., *Die nationale Zusammenarbeit mit den Internationalen Straftribunalen für das ehemalige Jugoslawien und für Ruanda* (Heidelberg, Springer 2002) 395 pp.

Articles

- Carlson, Matthew S., 'The International Criminal Court: Selected Considerations for Ratification and National Implementing Legislation', 72 *Revue internationale de droit pénal* (2001) pp. 783-812
- Coolen, G.L., 'Het wetsvoorstel internationale misdrijven', 95 *Militair Rechtelijk Tijdschrift* (2002) pp. 373-384
- Cryer, Robert, 'Implementation of the International Criminal Court Statute in England and Wales', 51 *ICLQ* (2002) pp. 733-743
- De Smet, Leen and Frederik Naert, 'Making or Breaking International Law? An International Law Analysis of Belgium's Act Concerning the Punishment of Grave Breaches of International Humanitarian Law', 35 *RBDI* (2002) pp. 471-511
- Forsythe, David P., 'The United States and International Criminal Justice', 24 *HRQ* (2002) pp. 974-991
- Hartley, James, 'The International Crimes and International Criminal Court Act 2000', 9 *Auckland University Law Review* (2001) pp. 623-632
- Keijzer, N., 'Implementatie van het Statuut van Rome', 95 *Militair Rechtelijk Tijdschrift* (2002) pp. 1-16
- Meißner, Jörg, 'Die Zusammenarbeit Deutschlands mit dem Internationalen Strafgerichtshof: Anmerkungen zum Regierungsentwurf eines IStGH-Gesetzes', 15 *Humanitäres Völkerrecht* (2002) pp. 35-42
- Nemitz, Jan Cristoph, 'Spreading the Good News: The Rome Statute and Its Implementation in Domestic Legislation', 12 *Criminal LF* (2001) pp. 509-515
- Newton, Michael A., 'Comparative Complementarity: Domestic Jurisdiction Consistent with the Rome Statute of the International Criminal Court', 167 *Mil. LR* (2001) pp. 20-73
- Ongena, Tom and Ignace Van Daele, 'Universal Jurisdiction for International Core Crimes: Recent Developments in Belgium', 15 *Leiden JIL* (2002) pp. 687-701
- Satzger, Helmut, 'German Criminal Law and the Rome Statute – A Critical Analysis of the New German Code of Crimes Against International Law', 2 *International Criminal Law Review* (2002) pp. 261-282
- Van Boven, Theo, 'The Principle of Complementarity: The International Criminal Court and National Laws', in Jan Wouters and Heidi Panken, eds., *De genocidewet in internationaal perspectief* (Ghent, Larcier 2002) pp. 65-74
- Van der Voort, Karlijn and Marten Zwanenburg, 'From "Raison d'État" to "État de Droit International": Amnesties and the French Implementation of the Rome Statute', 1 *International Criminal Law Review* (2001) pp. 315-342
- Van Elst, R. and M. Boot-Matthijssen, 'Wetsvoorstel internationale misdrijven: enkele knelpunten en mogelijke verbeteringen', 77 *Nederlands Juristenblad* (2002) pp. 1742-1750
- Wilkitzki, Peter, 'The German Law on Co-operation with the ICC', 2 *International Criminal Law Review* (2002) pp. 195-212

7.23   Military Manuals/National Instructions/Codes of Conduct

Articles
- Fleck, Dieter, 'Towards a Code of Conduct for Internal Armed Conflicts: Current Efforts, Problems, and Opportunities', 96 *Proc. ASIL* (2002) pp. 25-32

7.4   ICRC

Books
- Enzensberger, Hans Magnus, *Krieger ohne Waffen: das Internationale Komitee vom Roten Kreuz* (Frankfurt aM, Eichborn 2001) 347 pp.
- International Committee of the Red Cross, *Humanitarian Action and Armed Conflict: Coping with Stress* (Geneva, International Committee of the Red Cross 2001) 28 pp.
- International Committee of the Red Cross, *Rapport d'activité 2000* (Geneva, International Committee of the Red Cross 2001) 298 pp.
- International Committee of the Red Cross, *Report of the 27th International Conference of the Red Cross and Red Crescent (Geneva, 31 October-6 November 1999)* (Geneva, International Committee of the Red Cross 2002) 165 pp.

Articles
- Blondel, Jean-Luc, 'Rôle du CICR en matière de prévention des conflits armés: possibilités d'action et limites', 83 *IRRC* (2001) pp. 923-945
- Distefano, Giovanni, 'Le CICR et l'immunité de juridiction en droit international contemporain: fragments d'investigation autour d'une notion centrale de l'organisation internationale', 3 *SZIER/RSDIE* (2002) pp. 355-370
- Escorihuela, Alejandro Lorite, 'Le Comité international de la Croix rouge comme organisation sui generis? Remarques sur la personnalité juridique internationale du CICR', 105 *RGDIP* (2001) pp. 581-616
- Fischer, Thomas, 'The ICRC and the 1962 Cuban Missile Crises', 83 *IRRC* (2001) pp. 287-309
- International Committee of the Red Cross, 'Depleted Uranium Munitions: Comments of the International Committee of the Red Cross', 83 *IRRC* (2001) pp. 543-545
- International Committee of the Red Cross, 'Preventive Action: Understanding the Concept and Defining the ICRC's Role in Preventing Armed Conflicts', 84 *IRRC* (2002) pp. 463-466
- International Committee of the Red Cross, 'ICRC Position on Hostage Taking', 84 *IRRC* (2002) pp. 467-474
- McDowell, Joshua, 'The International Committee of the Red Cross as a Witness Before International Criminal Tribunals', 1 *Chinese Journal of International Law* (2002) pp. 158-184
- Rona, Gabor, 'The ICRC Privilege Not to Testify: Confidentiality in Action', 84 *IRRC* (2002) pp. 207-219
- Ryniker, Anne, 'Position du Comité international de la Croix-Rouge sur l'"intervention humanitaire"', 83 *IRRC* (2001) pp. 521-532
- Sassòli, Marco and Marie-Louise Tougas, 'The ICRC and the Missing', 84 *IRRC* (2002) pp. 727-750

– Studer, Meinrad, 'The ICRC and Civil-Military Relations in Armed Conflict', 83 *IRRC* (2001) pp. 367-391
– Young, Kirsten, 'UNHCR and ICRC in the Former Yugoslavia: Bosnia-Herzegovina', 83 *IRRC* (2001) pp. 781-805

7.5 FACT-FINDING, INCLUDING THE INTERNATIONAL FACT-FINDING COMMISSION

Articles

– Ben Mahfoudh, Haykel, 'L'enquête internationale', in Ferhat Horchani, ed., *Règlement pacifique des différends internationaux* (Brussels, Bruylant 2002) pp. 147-168
– Kalshoven, Frits, 'The International Humanitarian Fact-Finding Commission: A Sleeping Beauty?', 15 *Humanitäres Völkerrecht* (2002) pp. 213-216
– Kalshoven, Frits, 'Wel en wee van de Internationale Feitencommissie van artikel 90, Protocol I', 34 *Zoeklicht* (2002) pp. 20-23
– Lenk, Arthur, 'Fact-Finding as a Peace Negotiation Tool: The Mitchell Report and the Israeli-Palestinian Peace Process', 24 *Loyola LA I & CLR* (2002) pp. 289-325
– Murray, Rachel, 'Evidence and Fact-Finding by the African Commission', in Malcolm D. Evans and Rachel Murray, eds., *The African Charter on Human and Peoples' Rights: The System in Practice, 1986-2000* (Cambridge, Cambridge University Press 2002) pp. 100-136
– The Sharm al-Shaykh Fact-Finding Committee, '"The Mitchell Report", 20 May 2001 (excerpts)', 30 *Journal of Palestine Studies* (2001) pp. 146-151

7.6 DISSEMINATION

Articles

– Cooper, Ann, 'Targeting Journalists to Prevent the Dissemination of Knowledge of Human Rights Violations', in David Barnhizer, ed., *Effective Strategies for Protecting Human Rights: Prevention and Intervention, Trade and Education* (Aldershot, Ashgate 2001) pp. 21-28
– Kadam, Umesh, 'Teaching International Humanitarian Law in Academic Institutions in South Asia: An Overview of an ICRC Dissemination Programme', 83 *IRRC* (2001) pp. 167-169
– Shearer, Ivan, 'Teaching the Laws of War: Much Too Important to Be Left to Military Academies?', 7 *ILSA JI & CL* (2001) pp. 441-445

8. THE LAW OF NEUTRALITY

Books

– Chadwick, Elizabeth, *Traditional Neutrality Revisited. Law, Theory and Case Studies* (The Hague, Kluwer Law International 2002) 296 pp.
– Chevallaz, Georges-André, *The Challenge of Neutrality: Diplomacy and the Defense of Switzerland* (Lanham, Lexington Books 2001) 278 pp.

– Gabriel, Jürg Martin, *The American Conception of Neutrality After 1941*, 2nd updated and rev. edn. (Basingstoke, Palgrave 2002) 310 pp.
– Wylie, Neville, *European Neutrals and Non-Belligerents During the Second World War* (Cambridge, Cambridge University Press 2002) 368 pp.

Articles
– Donald, Dominick, 'Neutrality, Impartiality and UN Peacekeeping at the Beginning of the 21st Century', 9 *International Peacekeeping* (2002) pp. 21-38
– Dubrulle, Carole, 'Humanitarianism and the International Criminal Justice System: Abandoning Neutrality and Impartiality?', in Action Against Hunger, *The Geopolitics of Hunger, 2000-2001: Hunger and Power* (Boulder, Lynne Rienner 2001) pp. 215-225
– Greenwood, Christopher, 'The Applicability of International Humanitarian Law and the Law of Neutrality to the Kosovo Campaign', 31 *Israel YB HR* (2001) pp. 111-144
– Hummer, Waldemar, 'Österreichs dauernde Neutralität und die "Gemeinsame Aussen- und Sicherheitspolitik" (GASP) bzw. "Gemeinsame Europäische Sicherheits- und Verteidigungspolitik" (GEVSP) in der Europäische Union', 11 *SZIER/RSDIE* (2001) pp. 443-480
– Marston, John, 'Neutrality and the Negotiation of an Information Order in Cambodia', in Monroe E. Price and Mark Thompson, eds., *Forging Peace: Intervention, Human Rights and the Management of Media Space* (Edinburgh, Edinburgh University Press 2002) pp. 177-200
– Oprescu, Ana, 'European Neutral Countries and NATO', 8 *Romanian Journal of International Affairs* (2002) pp. 283-290

9.1   INTERNATIONAL ORGANISATIONS

Books
– Benchikh, Madjid, ed., *Les organisations internationales et les conflits armés* (Paris, Harmattan 2002) 308 pp.
– Boisson de Chazournes, Laurence, Cesare P.R. Romano and Ruth Mackenzie, eds., *International Organizations and International Dispute Settlement: Trends and Prospects* (Ardsley, Transnational Publishers 2002) 283 pp.
– Coicaud, Jean-Marc and Veijo Heiskanen, eds., *The Legitimacy of International Organizations* (Tokyo, United Nations University Press 2001) 578 pp.
– Ölz, Martin, *Die NGO's im Recht des internationalen Menschenrechtsschutzes* (Vienna, Verlag Österreich 2002) 436 pp.
– Strauss, Ekkehard, *Prävention von Menschenrechtsverletzungen als Aufgabe internationaler Organisationen. Rechtsgrundlagen und inhaltliche Ansätze* (Berlin, Berlin Verlag 2001) 354 pp.

Articles
– Pemmaraju, Sreenivasa Rao, 'International Organizations and Use of Force', in Nisuke Ando, Edward McWhinney, Rudiger Wolfrum and Betsy Baker Röben, eds., *Liber Amicorum Judge Shigeru Oda* (The Hague, Kluwer Law International 2002) pp. 1575-1608
– Remacle, Eric, 'The Co-operation Between International Organisations in the Management of the Third Yugoslav War', in Victor Yves Ghebali and Daniel Warner, eds., *The*

Operational Role of the OSCE in Southeastern Europe: Contributing to Regional Stability in the Balkans (Aldershot, Ashgate 2001) pp. 69-76
- Romano, Cesare P.R., 'International Organizations and the International Judicial Process', in Laurence Boisson de Chazournes, Cesare P.R. Romano and Ruth Mackenzie, eds., *International Organizations and International Dispute Settlement: Trends and Prospects* (Ardsley, Transnational Publishers 2002) pp. 3-36
- Ziemele, Ineta, 'The Role of International Organisations in Strengthening Human Rights Performances in the Baltic Sea Region', 43 *GYIL* (2000) pp. 9-37

9.11 United Nations Organization

Books
- Azimi, Nassrine and Chang Li Lin, *The Reform Process of United Nations Peace Operations: Debriefing and Lessons: Report of the 2001 Singapore Conference* (The Hague, Kluwer Law International 2001) 313 pp.
- Barnett, Michael N., *Eyewitness to a Genocide: The United Nations and Rwanda* (Ithaca, Cornell University Press 2002) 215 pp.
- Bassiouni, M. Cherif, *International Terrorism: A Compilation of U.N. Documents (1972-2001)*, Vol. I (Ardsley, Transnational Publishers 2002) 891 pp.
- Bassiouni, M. Cherif, *International Terrorism: A Compilation of U.N. Documents (1972-2001)*, Vol. II (Ardsley, Transnational Publishers 2002) 942 pp.
- Boulden, J., *Peace Enforcement. The United Nations Experience in Congo, Somalia, and Bosnia* (Westport, Praeger 2001) 176 pp.
- Chevallier, Eric, *L'ONU au Kosovo. Leçons de la première MINUK* (Paris, European Union Institute for Security Studies 2002) 32 pp.
- Connolly, Sean, *United Nations Keeping the Peace* (Oxford, Heinemann Library 2001) 64 pp.
- Cortright, David, George A. Lopez and Linda Gerber, *Sanctions and the Search for Security: Challenges to UN Action* (Boulder, Lynne Rienner 2002) 249 pp.
- Eichhorst, Markus, *Rechtsprobleme der United Nations Compensation Commission* (Berlin, Duncker & Humblot 2002) 255 pp.
- Findlay, Trevor, *The Use of Force in UN Peace Operations* (Oxford, Oxford University Press 2002) 486 pp.
- Hampson, Fen Osler and David M. Malone, eds., *From Reaction to Conflict Prevention: Opportunities for the UN System* (Boulder, Lynne Rienner 2002) 431 pp.
- Katayanagi, Mari, *Human Rights Functions of United Nations Peacekeeping Operation* (The Hague, Nijhoff 2002) 316 pp.
- Kern, Reiner, *Global governance durch UN und Regionalorganisationen: OAU und OSZE als Partner der Weltorganisation beim Konfliktmanagement* (Baden-Baden, Nomos 2002) 360 pp.
- Kolliopoulos, Alexandros, *La Commission d'indemnisation des Nations Unies et le droit de la responsabilité internationale* (Paris, L.G.D.J. 2001) 483 pp.
- MacQueen, Norrie, *United Nations Peacekeeping in Africa Since 1960* (London, Longman 2002) 308 pp.
- Martin, Ian, *Self-Determination in East Timor: The United Nations, the Ballot and International Intervention* (Boulder, Lynne Rienner 2001) 171 pp.

— Nations Unies, Division des droits des palestiniens, *Réunion internationale des Nations Unies sur la question de Palestine: thème: "La route vers la paix israélo-palestinienne": Madrid, 17 et 18 juillet 2001* (Geneva, Nations Unies 2001) 30 pp.

— Newman, Edward and Oliver P. Richmond, eds., *The United Nations and Human Security* (New York, Palgrave 2001) 231 pp.

— Osman, Mohamed Awad, *The United Nations and Peace Enforcement: Wars, Terrorism and Democracy* (Aldershot, Ashgate 2002) 224 pp.

— Rao, Vinayak, *International Negotiation: The United Nations in Afghanistan and Cambodia* (New Delhi, Manak 2001) 296 pp.

— Rittberger, Volker, *Global Governance and the United Nations System* (Tokyo, United Nations University Press 2001) 252 pp.

— Schweigman, David, *The Authority of the Security Council Under Chapter VII of the UN Charter: Legal Limits and the Role of the International Court of Justice* (The Hague, Kluwer Law International 2001) 354 pp.

— Sinha, Manoj Kumar, *Humanitarian Intervention by the United Nations* (New Delhi, Manak Publications 2002) 134 pp.

— Thakur, Ramesh and Albrecht Schnabel, eds., *United Nations Peacekeeping Operations: Ad Hoc Missions, Permanent Engagement* (Tokyo, United Nations University Press 2001) 267 pp.

— United Nations Institute for Disarmament Research, *Disarmament as Humanitarian Action: A Discussion on the Occasion of the 20th Anniversary of the United Nations Institute for Disarmament Research* (Geneva, United Nations Institute for Disarmament Research 2001) 19 pp.

— Wellens, Karel, ed., *Resolutions and Statements of the United Nations Security Council (1946-2000): A Thematic Guide* (The Hague, Kluwer Academic Publishers 2001) 193 pp.

— Zambelli, Mirko, *La constatation des situations de l'article 39 de la Charte des Nations Unies par le Conseil de Sécurité: le champ d'application des pouvoirs prévus au chapitre VII de la Charte des Nations Unies* (Geneva, Helbing & Lichtenhahn 2002) 517 pp.

Articles

— Andersson, Andreas, 'United Nations Intervention by United Democracies? State Commitment to UN Interventions 1991-99', 37 *Cooperation and Conflict: Nordic Journal of International Studies* (2002) pp. 363-386

— Andreu-Guzmán, Federico, 'Le Groupe de travail sur les disparitions forcées des Nations Unies', 84 *IRRC* (2002) pp. 803-818

— Arcari, Maurizio, 'Quelques remarques à propos de l'action du Conseil de Sécurité dans le domaine de la justice pénale internationale', 18 *Anuario de derecho internacional* (2002) pp. 207-228

— Arend, Anthony Clark, 'International Law and Rogue States: The Failure of the Charter Framework', 36 *New England LR* (2002) pp. 735-753

— Baros, Miroslav, 'The UN's Response to the Yugoslav Crisis: Turning the UN Charter on Its Head', 8 *International Peacekeeping* (2001) pp. 44-63

— Bassiouni, M. Cherif, 'The United Nations Commission of Experts Established Pursuant to Security Council Resolution 780 (1992) to Investigate Violations of International Humanitarian Law in the Former Yugoslavia', in M. Cherif Bassiouni, ed., *Post-Conflict Justice* (Ardsley, Transnational Publishers 2002) pp. 429-485

- Bayaoui, Besma, 'Le rôle de l'Assemblée générale en matière de règlement pacifique des différends internationaux', in Ferhat Horchani, ed., *Règlement pacifique des différends internationaux* (Brussels, Bruylant 2002) pp. 225-240
- Bayaoui, Besma, 'Le rôle du Secrétaire général en matière de règlement pacifique des différends internationaux', in Ferhat Horchani, ed., *Règlement pacifique des différends internationaux* (Brussels, Bruylant 2002) pp. 241-264
- Bongiorno, Carla, 'A Culture of Impunity: Applying International Human Rights Law to the United Nations in East Timor', 33 *Colum. HRLR* (2002) pp. 623-692
- Brand, Marcus G., 'Institution-Building and Human Rights Protection in Kosovo in the Light of UNMIK Legislation', 70 *Nordic JIL* (2001) pp. 461-488
- Buo, Sammy Kum, 'Reflections on United Nations Peace Operations in Africa: Responsibility of African States', 3 *Int. LF* (2001) pp. 87-94
- Caccese, Gina, 'The United Nations and Terrorism: The Response to September 11th and Mayor Giuliani's Address to the General Assembly', 18 *New York Law School Journal of Human Rights* (2002) pp. 461-466
- Carpentier, Chantal, 'Conflit israélo-palestinien: l'ONU se discrédite-t-elle?', 58 *Défense nationale* (2002) pp. 77-88
- Catena, Marina, 'La missione ONU in Kosovo: mantenere o fare la pace?', 56 *La Comunità internazionale* (2001) pp. 579-593
- Cellamare, Giovanni, 'Caratteri della missione delle Nazioni Unite in Etiopia ed Eritrea (UNMEE)', 57 *La Comunità internazionale* (2002) pp. 3-17
- Chandler, David, 'The People-Centred Approach to Peace Operations: The New UN Agenda', 8 *International Peacekeeping* (2001) pp. 1-19
- Chesterman, Simon, 'East Timor in Transition: Self-Determination, State-Building and the United Nations', 9 *International Peacekeeping* (2002) pp. 45-76
- Chesterman, Simon, 'Walking Softly in Afghanistan: The Future of UN State-Building', 44 *Survival* (2002) pp. 37-46
- Dale, Alexander C., 'Countering Hate Messages That Lead to Violence: The United Nation's Chapter VII Authority to Use Radio Jamming to Halt Incendiary Broadcasts', 11 *Duke JCIL* (2001) pp. 109-131
- Datan, Merav, 'The United Nations and Civil Society', 4 *Disarmament Forum* (2002) pp. 41-44
- Debiel, Tobias, 'Friedenseinsätze der UN in Afrika: Bilanz, Lehren und (mangelnde) Konsequenzen', 50 *Vereinte Nationen* (2002) pp. 57-61
- De Hoogh, André, 'Attribution or Delegation of (Legislative) Power by the Security Council? The Case of the United Nations Transitional Administration in East Timor (UNTAET)', 7 *International Peacekeeping: The Yearbook of International Peace Operations* (2001) pp. 1-41
- De Wet, Erika, 'The Relationship Between the Security Council and Regional Organizations During Enforcement Action Under Chapter VII of the United Nations Charter', 71 *Nordic JIL* (2002) pp. 1-37
- Donald, Dominick, 'Neutrality, Impartiality and UN Peacekeeping at the Beginning of the 21st Century', 9 *International Peacekeeping* (2002) pp. 21-38
- Dorigo, Stefano, 'Imputazione e responsabilità internazionale per l'attività delle forze di Peacekeeping delle Nazioni Unite', 85 *RDI* (2002) pp. 903-945
- Eide, Asbjørn, 'Minorities, Indigenous Peoples and the Prevention of Conflicts: The Role of the United Nations Sub-Commission on the Promotion and Protection of Human Rights', 14 *International Geneva Yearbook* (2000-2001) pp. 35-45

— Fassbender, Bardo, 'Uncertain Steps into a Post-Cold War World: The Role and Functioning of the UN Security Council After a Decade of Measures Against Iraq', 13 *EJIL* (2002) pp. 273-303

— Flinterman, Cees and Berber Hettinga, 'Irak, de VS, de VN en het internationale recht', 77 *Nederlands Juristenblad* (2002) pp. 1799-1800

— Fröhlich, Manuel, 'Keeping Track of UN-Peacekeeping: Suez, Srebrenica, Rwanda and the Brahimi Report', 5 *MPYBUNL* (2001) pp. 185-248

— Goldstone, Richard, 'The Role of the United Nations in the Prosecution of International War Criminals', 5 *Washington University Journal of Law and Policy* (2001) pp. 119-127

— Gowland-Debbas, Vera, 'The Role of the Security Council in the New International Criminal Court from a Systematic Perspective', in Laurence Boisson de Chazournes and Vera Gowlland-Debbas, eds., *The International Legal System in Quest of Equity and Universality: Liber Amicorum Georges Abi-Saab* (The Hague, Nijhoff 2001) pp. 629-650

— Gowland-Debbas, Vera, 'The Relationship Between Political and Judicial Organs of International Organisations: The Role of the Security Council in the New International Criminal Court', in Laurence Boisson de Chazournes, Cesare P.R. Romano and Ruth Mackenzie, eds., *International Organizations and International Dispute Settlement: Trends and Prospects* (Ardsley, Transnational Publishers 2002) pp. 195-219

— Griep, Ekkehard, 'Neue Maßstäbe für UN-Friedensmissionen', 50 *Vereinte Nationen* (2002) pp. 61-66

— Guéhenno, Jean-Marie, 'Konfliktverhütung und Friedenssicherung: für eine Bündelung der Interessen von EU und UN', 57 *Internationale Politik* (2002) pp. 11-24

— Guéhenno, Jean-Marie, 'On the Challenges and Achievements of Reforming UN Peace Operations', 9 *International Peacekeeping* (2002) pp. 69-80

— Gutiérrez Espada, Cesáreo, 'La Corte Penal Internacional (CPI) y las Naciones Unidas: la discutida posición del Consejo de Seguridad', 18 *Anuario de derecho internacional* (2002) pp. 3-61

— Hatzenbichler, Gerald, 'Civil-Military Cooperation in UN Peace Operations Designed by SHIRBRIG', 8 *International Peacekeeping* (2001) pp. 117-121

— Hendrickson, Ryan C., 'Article 51 and the Clinton Presidency: Military Strikes and the U.N. Charter', 19 *Boston Univ. ILJ* (2001) pp. 207-230

— Hughes, Ann, '"Impartiality" and the UN Observation Group in Lebanon', 9 *International Peacekeeping* (2002) pp. 1-20

— Irmscher, Tobias H., 'The Legal Framework for the Activities of the United Nations Interim Administration Mission in Kosovo: The Charter, Human Rights, and the Law of Occupation', 44 *GYIL* (2001) pp. 353-395

— Isselé, Pierre, 'La métamorphose des opérations de maintien de la paix des Nations Unies', in Laurence Boisson de Chazournes and Vera Gowlland-Debbas, eds., *The International Legal System in Quest of Equity and Universality: Liber Amicorum Georges Abi-Saab* (The Hague, Nijhoff 2001) pp. 777-796

— Jakobsen, Peter Viggo, 'The Transformation of United Nations Peace Operations in the 1990's: Adding Globalization to the Conventional "End of the Cold War Explanation"', 37 *Cooperation and Conflict: Nordic Journal of International Studies* (2002) pp. 267-282

— Jakobsen, Peter Viggo, 'UN Peace Operations in Africa Today and Tomorrow', 7 *International Peacekeeping: The Yearbook of International Peace Operations* (2001) pp. 153-180

− Kamminga, M.T., 'De United Nations Compensation Commission: wonderkind of wangedrocht?', 51 *Ars Aequi* (2002) pp. 580-586

− Kamto, Maurice, 'Le cadre juridique des opérations de maintien de la paix des Nations Unies', 3 *Int. LF* (2001) pp. 95-104

− Kane, Angela, 'United Nations and UN System in the Service of Peace and Security', 8 *Romanian Journal of International Affairs* (2002) pp. 108-114

− Koivusalo, Meri, 'The Role of International Organizations: Does the United Nations Still Matter?', in Ilkka Taipale et al., eds., *War or Health? A Reader* (London, Zed 2002) pp. 530-540

− Kondoch, Boris, 'The United Nations Administration of East Timor', 6 *Journal of Conflict & Security Law* (2001) pp. 245-265

− Kramer, Callie, 'Kofi Annan and United Nations Win the 2001 Nobel Peace Prize', 18 *New York Law School Journal of Human Rights* (2002) pp. 475-480

− Lewis, Patricia, 'From UNSCOM to UNMOVIC: The United Nations and Iraq', 3 *Disarmament Forum* (2001) pp. 63-68

− MacCullough, H.B., 'A Critique of the Report of the Panel on United Nations Peace Operations', 29 *Pepperdine Law Review* (2001) pp. 15-32

− Manusama, Kenneth M., 'Terrorisme en zelfverdediging in de Veiligheidsraad', 30 *Vrede en veiligheid* (2001) pp. 481-499

− Matheson, Michael J., 'United Nations Governance of Post Conflict Societies', 95 *AJIL* (2001) pp. 76-85

− Matheson, Michael J., 'United Nations Governance of Post-Conflict Societies: East Timor and Kosovo', in M. Cherif Bassiouni, ed., *Post-Conflict Justice* (Ardsley, Transnational Publishers 2002) pp. 523-536

− Morrow, Jonathan and Rachel White, 'The United Nations in Transitional East Timor: International Standards and the Reality of Governance', 22 *Australian YIL* (2002) pp. 1-45

− Mundkur, Ramanand, Michael J. Mucchetti and D. Craig Christensen, 'The Intersection of International Accounting Practices and International Law: The Review of Kuwaiti Corporate Claims at the United Nations Compensation Commission', 16 *Amer. Univ. ILR* (2001) pp. 1195-1239

− Murthy, C.S.R., 'United Nations Peacekeeping in Intrastate Conflicts: Emerging Trends', 38 *International Studies* (2001) pp. 207-227

− Neisse, Frank, 'Le règlement du conflit du Sahara Occidental en l'ONU: "pour quelle troisième voie"?', 3 *Annuaire français de relations internationales* (2002) pp. 700-710

− Oswald, Bruce M., 'The Creation and Control of Places of Protection During United Nations Peace Operations', 84 *IRRC* (2001) pp. 1013-1035

− Othman, Mohamed, 'Peacekeeping Operations in Asia: Justice and UNTAET', 3 *Int. LF* (2001) pp. 114-126

− Panel on United Nations Peace Operations, 'Report', 62 *ZaöRV* (2002) pp. 607-640

− Pauwels, A., 'De VN-operatie in Kosovo. De ultieme "test-case" voor de nieuwe generatie VN-vredesoperaties?', 171 *Militaire Spectator* (2002) pp. 465-477

− Pauwels, A., 'Een nieuwe generatie VN-vredesoperaties. Mythe of realiteit?', 33 *Vrede en Veiligheid* (2002) pp. 33-53

− Péchoux, Pierre-Yves, 'La zone tampon ou Buffer zone des Nations Unies à Chypre', 51 *Guerres mondiales et conflits contemporains* (2001) pp. 97-118

– Peterke, Sven, 'Die Bekämpfung der Terrorismusfinanzierung unter Kapitel VII der UN-Charta: die Resolution 1373 (2001) des UN-Sicherheitsrats', 14 *Humanitäres Völkerrecht* (2001) pp. 217-221

– Poltak, Celeste, 'Humanitarian Intervention: A Contemporary Interpretation of the Charter of the United Nations', 60 *University of Toronto Faculty of Law Review* (2002) pp. 1-38

– Pradetto, August, 'Die Vereinten Nationen nach den Terroranschlägen vom 11. September 2001: Anhängsel der USA?', 20 *Vierteljahresschrift für Sicherheit und Frieden* (2002) pp. 9-18

– Pritchard, Sarah, 'United Nations Involvement in Post-Conflict Reconstruction Efforts: New and Continuing Challenges in the Case of East Timor', 24 *University of New South Wales Law Journal* (2001) pp. 183-190

– Rawski, Frederick, 'To Waive or Not to Waive: Immunity and Accountability in U.N. Peacekeeping Operations', 18 *Connecticut Journal of International Law* (2002) pp. 103-132

– Reinisch, August, 'Developing Human Rights and Humanitarian Law Accountability of the Security Council for the Imposition on Economic Sanctions', 95 *AJIL* (2001) pp. 851-872

– Ricca, Michele, 'Human Rights and the UN Special Rapporteurs' System: Tendencies in Reporting on Conflict Areas', 15 *Humanitäres Völkerrecht* (2002) pp. 165-174

– Richmond, Oliver P., 'The Limits of UN Multidimensional Peace Operations', in Edward Newman and Oliver P. Richmond, eds., *The United Nations and Human Security* (New York, Palgrave 2001) pp. 31-46

– Saada, Riadh, 'Le Conseil de Sécurité et le règlement pacifique des différends internationaux', in Ferhat Horchani, ed., *Règlement pacifique des différends internationaux* (Brussels, Bruylant 2002) pp. 183-223

– Samuilov, Sergei, 'The United Nations, the United States, and the War on Terrorism', 40 *Russian Politics and Law* (2002) pp. 28-46

– Sarooshi, D., 'Aspects of the Relationship Between the International Criminal Court and the United Nations', 32 *NYIL* (2002) pp. 27-53

– Schrijver, N., 'Irak en de Veiligheidsraad: is een oorlog voorkomen?', 77 *Nederlands Juristenblad* (2002) pp. 2094-2095

– Sicilianos, Linos-Alexandre, 'L'autorisation par le Conseil de sécurité de recourir à la force: une tentative d'évalation', 106 *RGDIP* (2002) pp. 5-50

– Sinjela, Mpazi, 'The United Nations and Internal/International Conflicts in Africa: A Documentary Survey', 9 *African Yearbook of International Law* (2001) pp. 391-433

– Solomon, Andrew, 'United Nations Observer Mission in Georgia: Keeping the Peace and Observing the Peacekeepers', 7 *International Peacekeeping: The Yearbook of International Peace Operations* (2001) pp. 197-235

– Stahn, Carsten, 'United Nations Peace-Building, Amnesties and Alternative Forms of Justice: A Change in Practice?', 84 *IRRC* (2002) pp. 191-205

– Strijards, G.A.M., 'De United Nations, een internationaal strafhof en zijn gastland: een spannende driehoeksverhouding', 31 *Delikt en delinkwent* (2001) pp. 548-584

– Strohmeyer, Hansjörg, 'Collapse and Reconstruction of a Judicial System: The United Nations Mission in Kosovo and East Timor', 95 *AJIL* (2001) pp. 46-63

– Strydom, Hennie, 'United Nations Sanctions and Africa's Wars of Enrichment', 26 *South African Yearbook of International Law* (2001) pp. 41-61

– Sybesma-Knol, Neri, 'Palestine and the United Nations', in Sanford R. Silverbug, ed., *Palestine and International Law: Essays on Politics and Economics* (Jefferson, McFarland 2001) pp. 271-298
– Szasz, Paul C. and Thordis Ingadottir, 'The UN and the ICC: The Immunity of the UN and Its Officials', 14 *Leiden JIL* (2001) pp. 867-885
– Tönnies, Sibylle, 'Weltfrieden und Völkerrecht – Made in the USA oder Aufgabe der UNO?', 46 *Blätter für deutsche und internationale Politik* (2001) pp. 829-836
– Van Heusden, Alfons, 'De toepassing van het internationaal humanitair recht op militaire operaties van de Verenigde Naties', 40 *Revue de droit militaire et de droit de guerre* (2001) pp. 13-46
– Vieira de Mello, Sergio, 'United Nations Transnational Authority in East Timor', in Nassrine Azimi and Chang Li Lin, *The Reform Process of United Nations Peace Operations: Debriefing and Lessons: Report of the 2001 Singapore Conference* (The Hague, Kluwer Law International 2001) pp. 93-99
– Villani, Ugo, 'Les rapports entre l'ONU et les organisations régionales dans le domaine du maintien de la paix', 290 *Recueil des Cours* (2001) pp. 225-436
– Villani, Ugo, 'The Security Council's Authorization of Enforcement Action by Regional Organizations', 6 *MPYBUNL* (2002) pp. 535-557
– Weller, Marc, 'Undoing the Global Constitution: UN Security Council Action on the International Criminal Court', 78 *International Affairs* (2002) pp. 693-712
– White, Nigel D., 'Commentary on the Report of the Panel on United Nations Peace Operations (The Brahimi Report)', 6 *Journal of Conflict and Security Law* (2001) pp. 127-146
– Young, Kirsten, 'UNHCR and ICRC in the Former Yugoslavia: Bosnia-Herzegovina', 83 *IRRC* (2001) pp. 781-805

9.12   Other

Books

– Dauvin, Pascal and Johanna Siméant, *Le travail humanitaire: les acteurs des ONG, du siège au terrain* (Paris, Presses de Science Po 2002) 443 pp.
– Ghandour, Abdel-Rahman, *Jihad humanitaire: enquête sur les ONG islamiques* (Paris, Flammarion 2002) 346 pp.
– Herrero Ansola, J.-L., I. Besheri, T. Bernstein et al., *International Organizations in Kosovo: Finding the Path Through the Maze: The UN, the OSCE, and the EU: Structures, Experiences, Prospects* (Vienna, Diplomatische Akademie 2001) 100 pp.
– International Council on Human Rights Policy, *Human Rights Crises: NGO Responses to Military Interventions* (Versoix, International Council on Human Rights Policy 2002) 66 pp.
– Kaufman, Joyce P., *NATO and the Former Yugoslavia. Crisis, Conflict, and the Atlantic Alliance* (Lanham, Rowman and Littlefield 2002) 248 pp.
– Kern, Reiner, *Global Governance durch UN und Regionalorganisationen: OAU und OSZE als Partner der Weltorganisation beim Konfliktmanagement* (Baden-Baden, Nomos 2002) 360 pp.

Articles

- Abass, Ademola, 'The Implementation of ECOWAS' New Protocol and Security Council Resolution 1270 in Sierra Leone: New Developments in Regional Intervention', 10 *International & Comparative Law Review. University of Miami School of Law* (2001/2002) pp. 177-216
- Asseburg, Muriel, 'Der Nahost-Friedensprozess und der Beitrag der EU: Bilanz und Perspektiven','76 *Die Friedenswarte* (2001) pp. 257-288
- Bloed, Arie, 'The OSCE Involvement in the Deteriorating Conflict in Kosovo', 12 *Helsinki Monitor* (2001) pp. 136-138
- Bloed, Arie, 'The OSCE and the War Against Terror', 12 *Helsinki Monitor* (2001) pp. 313-317
- Fornasier, Matteo and Jens-Uwe Franck, 'Die NATO-Luftangriffe auf die Bundesrepublik Jugoslawien (BRJ) und das völkerrechtliche Gewaltverbot', 24 *Jura* (2002) pp. 520-526
- Gazzini, Tarcisio, 'NATO Coercive Military Activities in the Yugoslav Crisis (1992-1999)', 12 *EJIL* (2001) pp. 391-436
- Geiger, Gunnar, 'Die völker- und verfassungsrechtliche wirksame Erweiterung des Aufgabenspektrums von NATO und WEU um Kriesenmanagementaufgaben', 43 *Neue Zeitschrift für Wehrrecht* (2001) pp. 133-150
- Ghebali, Victor Yves, 'The Role of the OSCE in Conflict Management. Some Reflections on the Case of "Frozen Conflicts"', in Daniel Warner and Valérie Clerc, eds., *Challenges Faced by the OSCE During 2001* (Geneva, The Graduate Institute of International Studies 2002) pp. 27-45
- Homan, C., 'De tweede uitbreiding van de NAVO; op weg naar een OVSE met militaire tanden?', 55 *Internationale Spectator* (2001) pp. 493-497
- Korte, Werner, 'Kriegspartei oder Friedensstifter. ECOMOG in Liberia', 21 *Peripherie* (2001) pp. 48-69
- Lüder, Sascha Rolf, 'Die völkerrechtliche Verantwortlichkeit der Nortatlantikvertrags-Organisation bei der militärischen Absicherung der Friedensvereinbarung von Dayton', 43 *Neue Zeitschrift für Wehrrecht* (2001) pp. 107-117
- Rollins, J.W., 'Civil-Military Cooperation (CIMIC) in Crisis Response Operations: The Implications for NATO', 8 *International Peacekeeping* (2001) pp. 122-129
- Van Baarda, Ted A., 'A Legal Perspective of Cooperation Between Military and Humanitarian Organizations in Peace Support Organizations', 8 *International Peacekeeping* (2001) pp. 99-116
- Werner, W.G., 'Artikel 5 van het NAVO-verdrag', 94 *Militair Rechtelijk Tijdschrift* (2001) pp. 373-377

9.2   INTERNATIONAL ACTIONS

Books

- Bernecker, Arabelle, *Internationales Konfliktmanagement am Beispiel des Krieges um Bosnien, 1992-1995* (Frankfurt am Main, Peter Lang 2001) 129 pp.

Articles
- Heinrich, Hans Georg, 'Konfliktmanagement durch die OSZE in Georgien: der politische Kontext', 7 *OSZE-Jahrbuch* (2001) pp. 229-234
- Hermann, Rainer, 'Konfliktkostellationen in Zentralasien: Herausforderungen für die OSZE', 7 *OSZE-Jahrbuch* (2001) pp. 199-216
- Olson, Gorm Rye, 'The EU and Conflict Management in African Emergencies', 9 *International Peacekeeping* (2002) pp. 87-102
- Said Ali, Ali, 'Globalization and the Future of Humanitarian Action: New Priorities for the International Red Cross and Red Crescent Movement?', 83 *IRRC* (2001) pp. 841-846

9.21   Peacekeeping

Books
- Azimi, Nassrine and Chang Li Lin, *The Reform Process of United Nations Peace Operations: Debriefing and Lessons: Report of the 2001 Singapore Conference* (The Hague, Kluwer Law International 2001) 313 pp.
- Byman, Daniel L., *Keeping the Peace: Lasting Solutions to Ethnic Conflicts* (Baltimore, John Hopkins University Press 2002) 280 pp.
- Connolly, Sean, *United Nations Keeping the Peace* (Oxford, Heinemann Library 2001) 64 pp.
- Danieli, Yael, *Sharing the Front Line and the Bank Hills: International Protectors and Providers: Peacekeepers, Humanitarian Aid Workers and the Media in the Midst of Crisis* (Amityville, Baywood 2002) 429 pp.
- Fleitz Jr., Frederick H., *Peacekeeping Fiascoes of the 1990s: Causes, Solutions, and U.S. Interests* (Westport, Prager 2002) 224 pp.
- Gammer, Nicholas, *From Peacekeeping to Peacemaking: Canada's Response to the Yugoslav Crisis* (Montreal, McGill-Queen's University Press 2001) 243 pp.
- Gordon, D.S. and F.H. Toase, eds., *Aspects of Peacekeeping* (London, Frank Cass 2001) 286 pp.
- James, Alan, *Keeping the Peace in the Cyprus Crisis of 1963-64* (Basingstoke, Palgrave 2002) 241 pp.
- Jett, Dennis C., *Why Peacekeeping Fails* (New York, Palgrave 2001) 236 pp.
- Katayanagi, Mari, *Human Rights Functions of United Nations Peacekeeping Operation* (The Hague, Nijhoff 2002) 316 pp.
- Laremont, R.R., ed., *The Causes of War and the Consequences of Peacekeeping in Africa* (Portsmouth, Heinemann 2001) 344 pp.
- MacQueen, Norrie, *United Nations Peacekeeping in Africa Since 1960* (London, Longman 2002) 308 pp.
- Malan, Mark, Phenyo Keiseng Rakate and Angela McIntyre, *Peacekeeping in Sierra Leone. UNAMSIL Hits the Home Straight* (Pretoria, Institute for Security Studies 2002) 126 pp.
- Marchal, Luc, *Rwanda: La descente aux enfers: témoignage d'un Peacekeeper: décembre 1993-avril 1994* (Brussels, Éditions Labor 2001) 335 pp.
- Olsson, Louise and Torunn L. Tryggestad, eds., *Women and International Peacekeeping* (London, Frank Cass 2001) 145 pp.

- Smith, Michael G. and Moreen Dee, *Peacekeeping in East Timor: The Path to Independence* (Boulder, Lynne Rienner 2002) 200 pp.
- Thakur, Ramesh and Albrecht Schnabel, eds., *United Nations Peacekeeping Operations: Ad Hoc Missions, Permanent Engagement* (Tokyo, United Nations University Press 2001) 267 pp.

Articles
- Adjovi, Roland, 'Maintien de la paix et recours à la force en Afrique: le cas de la République centrafricaine', 6 *Revue de droit africain* (2002) pp. 241-253
- Bratt, Duane, 'Blue Condoms: The Use of International Peacekeepers in the Fight Against AIDS', 9 *International Peacekeeping* (2002) pp. 67-86
- Bullion, Alan, 'India in Sierra Leone: A Case of Muscular Peacekeeping?', 8 *International Peacekeeping* (2001) pp. 77-91
- Deen-Racsmány, Zsuzsanna, 'The ICC, Peacekeepers and Resolution 1422: Will the Court Defer to the Council?', 49 *NILR* (2002) pp. 353-388
- DeGroot, Gerard J., 'A Few Good Women: Gender Stereotypes, the Military and Peacekeeping', 8 *International Peacekeeping* (2001) pp. 23-38
- Diehl, Paul F., 'Forks in the Road: Theoretical and Policy Concerns for 21st Century Peacekeeping', in Paul F. Diehl, ed., *The Politics of Global Governance: International Organizations in an Interdependent World* (Boulder, Lynne Rienner 2001) pp. 202-228
- Donald, Dominick, 'Neutrality, Impartiality and UN Peacekeeping at the Beginning of the 21st Century', 9 *International Peacekeeping* (2002) pp. 21-38
- Dorigo, Stefano, 'Imputazione e responsabilità internazionale per l'attività delle forze di Peacekeeping delle Nazioni Unite', 85 *RDI* (2002) pp. 903-945
- Fox, Mary-Jane, 'The Idea of Women in Peacekeeping: Lysistrata and Antigone', 8 *International Peacekeeping* (2001) pp. 9-22
- Fröhlich, Manuel, 'Keeping Track of UN-Peacekeeping: Suez, Srebrenica, Rwanda and the Brahimi Report', 5 *MPYBUNL* (2001) pp. 185-248
- Frulli, M., 'Le operazioni di "peacekeeping" delle Nazioni Unite e l'uso della forza', 84 *RDI* (2001) pp. 347-392
- Gómez-Robledo Verduzco, Alonso, 'Consideraciones en torno a las "operaciones para el mantenimiento de la paz"', 35 *Boletín mexicano de derecho comparado* (2002) pp. 99-114
- Gray, Christine, 'Peacekeeping After the Brahimi Report: Is There a Crisis of Credibility for the UN?', 6 *Journal of Conflict & Security Law* (2001) pp. 267-288
- Horvat, S., 'Causes of Violence Against Local Populations by Western Soldiers on Peace Keeping Operations', 40 *Revue de droit militaire et de droit de la guerre* (2001) pp. 87-113
- Horvat, S., 'Geweld door peace-keepers: een Belgisch etiologisch onderzoek', 94 *Militair Rechtelijk Tijdschrift* (2001) pp. 133-148
- Isselé, Jean-Pierre, 'La métamorphose des opérations de maintien de la paix des Nations Unies', in Laurence Boisson de Chazournes and Vera Gowlland-Debbas, eds., *The International Legal System in Quest of Equity and Universality: Liber Amicorum Georges Abi-Saab* (The Hague, Nijhoff 2001) pp. 777-796
- Johansson, Eva and Gerry Larsson, 'Swedish Peacekeepers in Bosnia and Herzegovina: A Quantitative Analysis', 8 *International Peacekeeping* (2001) pp. 64-76
- Júnior, Domício Proença, 'O enquadramento das Missões de Paz (PKO) nas teorias da guerra e de polícia', 45 *Revista brasileira de política internacional* (2002) pp. 147-197

− Kamto, Maurice, 'Le cadre juridique des opérations de maintien de la paix des Nations Unies', 3 *Int. LF* (2001) pp. 95-104
− Krishnasamy, Kabilan, '"Recognition" for Third World Peacekeepers: India and Pakistan', 8 *International Peacekeeping* (2001) pp. 56-76
− Krishnasamy, Kabilan, 'Pakistan's Peacekeeping Experiences', 9 *International Peacekeeping* (2002) pp. 103-120
− Lee, Roy S., 'Panel on Peacekeeping: Legal and Political Issues', 8 *ILSA JI & CL* (2002) pp. 431-446
− Lewis, Flora, 'Problems of UN Peacekeepings', 3 *Int. LF* (2001) pp. 80-86
− Ocran, T. Mobido, 'The Doctrine of Humanitarian Intervention in Light of Robust Peacekeeping', 25 *Boston College Int. & Comp. LR* (2002) pp. 1-58
− O'Shea, Brendan, 'The Future of UN Peacekeeping', 25 *Studies in Conflict and Terrorism* (2002) pp. 145-148
− Othman, Mohamed, 'Peacekeeping Operations in Asia: Justice and UNTAET', 3 *Int. LF* (2001) pp. 114-126
− Paris, Roland, 'Echoes of the "Mission Civilisatrice": Peacekeeping in the Post-Cold War era', in Edward Newman and Oliver P. Richmond, eds., *The United Nations and Human Security* (New York, Palgrave 2001) pp. 100-118
− Peou, Sorpong, 'The UN, Peacekeeping, and Collective Human Security: From an Agenda for Peace to the Brahimi Report', 9 *International Peacekeeping* (2002) pp. 51-68
− Rawski, Frederick, 'To Waive or Not to Waive: Immunity and Accountability in U.N. Peacekeeping Operations', 18 *Connecticut Journal of International Law* (2002) pp. 103-132
− Reno, William S.K., 'War and the Failure of Peacekeeping in Sierra Leone', *SIPRI Yearbook* (2001) pp. 149-161
− Richardson, Henry J., 'Peacemaking Practices "From the South": Africa's Influence: African Contributions to the Law of Peacekeeping', 96 *Proc. ASIL* (2002) pp. 135-136
− Sitkowski, Andrzej, 'Reflections on the Peacekeeping Doctrine', 7 *International Peacekeeping: The Yearbook of International Peace Operations* (2001) pp. 181-196
− Solomon, Andrew, 'United Nations Observer Mission in Georgia: Keeping the Peace and Observing the Peacekeepers', 7 *International Peacekeeping: The Yearbook of International Peace Operations* (2001) pp. 197-235
− Sorel, Jean-Marc, 'La responsabilité des Nations Unies dans les opérations de maintien de la paix', 3 *Int. LF* (2001) pp. 127-138
− Stahn, Carsten, 'NGO's and International Peacekeeping: Issues, Prospects and Lessons Learned', 61 *ZaöRV* (2001) pp. 379-401
− Stiehm, Judith Hicks, 'Women, Peacekeeping and Peacemaking: Gender Balance and Mainstreaming', 8 *International Peacekeeping* (2001) pp. 39-48
− Timmermans, J., 'Intelligence Gathering in the Context of Peace Keeping Activities', in Brice De Ruyver, Gert Vermeulen and Tom Vander Beken, eds., *Strategies of the EU and the US in Combating Transnational Organized Crime* (Antwerp, Maklu 2002) pp. 255-258
− Villani, Ugo, 'Les rapports entre l'ONU et les organisations régionales dans le domaine du maintien de la paix', 290 *Recueil des Cours* (2001) pp. 225-436
− Wallenius, Claes, Curt R. Johansson and Gerry Larsson, 'Reactions and Performance of Swedish Peacekeepers in Life-Threatening Situations', 9 *International Peacekeeping* (2002) pp. 133-152

− Wilson, Keith, 'Why Are the Missiles (and Missile Defence) Called Peace-Keepers? Corroding the Concept of Peaceful Use', 14 *Leiden JIL* (2001) pp. 789-828

9.22　　Peace Enforcement and Peace Building

Books
− Adebajo, A., *Building Peace in West Africa: Liberia, Sierra Leone, and Guinea Bissau* (London, Lynne Rienner 2002) 150 pp.
− Azimi, Nassrine and Chang Li Lin, *The Reform Process of United Nations Peace Operations: Debriefing and Lessons: Report of the 2001 Singapore Conference* (The Hague, Kluwer Law International 2001) 313 pp.
− Boulden, J., *Peace Enforcement. The United Nations Experience in Congo, Somalia, and Bosnia* (Westport, Praeger 2001) 176 pp.
− Cousens, Elizabeth M., Chetan Kumar and Karin Wermester, eds., *Peacebuilding as Politics: Cultivating Peace in Fragile Societies* (Boulder, Lynne Rienner 2001) 248 pp.
− De Klerk, Cecilia and Johannes Sifoleni, *Report on the Seminar on Peace-Building, Governance and Civil Society in the SADC Region: November 5-November 24, 2000: Culture and Congress Center Midgard, Namibia* (Stadtschlaining, Peace Center Burg Schlaining 2001) 41 pp.
− Galama, Anneke and Paul van Tongeren, eds., *Towards Better Peacebuilding Practice: On Lessons Learned, Evaluation Practices and Aid & Conflict* (Utrecht, European Centre for Conflict Prevention 2002) 278 pp.
− Gammer, Nicholas, *From Peacekeeping to Peacemaking: Canada's Response to the Yugoslav Crisis* (Montreal, McGill-Queen's University Press 2001) 243 pp.
− Goodhand, Jonathan and Philippa Atkinson, *Conflict and Aid: Enhancing the Peacebuilding Impact of International Engagement: A Synthesis of Findings from Afghanistan, Liberia and Sri Lanka* (London, International Alert 2001) 49 pp.
− Hansen, Annika S., *From Congo to Kosovo: Civilian Police in Peace Operations* (Oxford, Oxford University Press 2002) 118 pp.
− Hawk, Kathleen Hill, *Constructing the Stable State: Goals for Intervention and Peacebuilding* (Westport, Praeger 2002) 162 pp.
− Herz, M. and J. Pontes Nogueira, *Ecuador vs. Peru. Peacemaking Amid Rivalry* (London, Lynne Rienner 2002) 120 pp.
− Jeong, Ho-Won, ed., *Approaches to Peacebuilding* (Basingstoke, Palgrave 2002) 203 pp.
− Kievelitz, Uwe and Tara Polzer, *Nepal Country Study on Conflict Transformation and Peace Building* (Eschborn, Deutsche Gesellschaft für Technische Zusammenarbeit 2002) 126 pp.
− Lederach, John Paul and Janice Moomaw Jenner, eds., *A Handbook of International Peacebuilding: Into the Eye of the Storm* (San Francisco, Jossey-Bass 2002) 336 pp.
− Mekenkamp, Monique et al., eds., *Searching for Peace in Central and South Asia: An Overview of Conflict Prevention and Peacebuilding Activities* (Boulder, Lynne Rienner 2002) 665 pp.
− Osman, Mohamed Awad, *The United Nations and Peace Enforcement: Wars, Terrorism and Democracy* (Aldershot, Ashgate 2002) 224 pp.

– Reychler, Luc and Thania Paffenholz, eds., *Peacebuilding: A Field Guide* (Boulder, Lynne Rienner 2001) 573 pp.
– Tebtebba Foundation, *Highlights of the International Conference on Conflict Resolution, Peace Building, Sustainable Development and Indigenous Peoples: December 6-8, 2000, Philippines* (Baguio City, Tebtebba Foundation 2001) 93 pp.
– Van Tongeren, Paul et al., eds., *Searching for Peace in Europe and Eurasia: An Overview of Conflict Prevention and Peacebuilding Activities* (Boulder, Lynne Rienner 2002) 831 pp.

Articles
– Batista, Guilherme, Sean Byrne, Karin Jenkins and Gabriel Posadas, 'Early Warning and Contingency Approaches: Shaping a Multi-Dimensional Peacebuilding System Within Ethnic Conflicts', 13 *Sri Lanka JIL* (2001) pp. 203-242
– Bojicic-Dzelilovic, Vesna, 'World Bank, NGOs and the Private Sector in Post-War Reconstruction', 9 *International Peacekeeping* (2002) pp. 81-98
– Chimni, B.S., 'Refugees and Post-Conflict Reconstruction: A Critical Perspective', 9 *International Peacekeeping* (2002) pp. 163-180
– David, Charles-Philippe, 'Alice in Wonderland meets Frankenstein: constructivism, realism and Peacebuilding in Bosnia', 22 *Contemporary Security Policy* (2001) pp. 1-30
– Ducasse-Rogier, Marianne, 'The Operational Role of the OSCE in the Field of Peace-Building: The Case of Bosnia and Herzegovina', in Victor Yves Ghebali and Daniel Warner, eds., *The Operational Role of the OSCE in Southeastern Europe* (Aldershot, Ashgate 2001) pp. 24-29
– Gerson, Allan, 'Peace Building: The Private Sector's Role', 95 *AJIL* (2001) pp. 102-119
– Gillard, Steve, 'Winning the Peace: Youth, Identity and Peacebuilding in Bosnia and Herzegovina', 8 *International Peacekeeping* (2001) pp. 77-98
– Ginifer, Jeremy, 'Peacebuilding in the Congo: Mission Impossible?', 9 *International Peacekeeping* (2002) pp. 121-128
– Juergensen, O.T., 'Repatriation as Peacebuilding and Reconstruction: The Case of Northern Mozambique, 1992-1995', 21 *Refugee Survey Quarterly* (2002) pp. 160-200
– Kingma, Kees, 'Demobilization, Reintegration and Peacebuilding in Africa', 9 *International Peacekeeping* (2002) pp. 181-201
– Lambourne, Wendy, 'Justice and Reconciliation: Postconflict Peacebuilding in Cambodia and Rwanda', in Mohammed Abu-Nimer, ed., *Reconciliation, Justice and Coexistence: Theory & Practice* (Lanham, Lexington Books 2001) pp. 311-337
– Matheson, Michael J., 'United Nations Governance of Post Conflict Societies', 95 *AJIL* (2001) pp. 76-85
– Okuizumi, Kaoru, 'Peacebuilding Mission: Lessons from the UN Mission in Bosnia and Herzegovina', 24 *HRQ* (2002) pp. 721-735
– Paris, Roland, 'International Peacebuilding and the "Mission Civilisatrice"', 28 *Review of International Studies* (2002) pp. 637-656
– Paris, Roland, 'Peacebuilding in Central America: Reproducing the Sources of Conflict?', 9 *International Peacekeeping* (2002) pp. 39-68
– Pouligny, Béatrice, 'Building Peace After Mass Crimes', 9 *International Peacekeeping* (2002) pp. 202-221
– Poulton, Robin Edward, 'Micro-Disarmament and Peace-Building: The European Union's ASAC Programme in Cambodia', 3 *Disarmament Forum* (2001) pp. 77-82

– Schnabel, Albrecht, 'Post-Conflict Peacebuilding and Second-Generation Preventive Action', 9 *International Peacekeeping* (2002) pp. 7-30
– Stahn, Carsten, 'United Nations Peace-Building, Amnesties and Alternative Forms of Justice: A Change in Practice?', 84 *IRRC* (2002) pp. 191-205
– Strohmeyer, Hansjörg, 'Collapse and Reconstruction of a Judicial System: The United Nations Mission in Kosovo and East Timor', 95 *AJIL* (2001) pp. 46-63

9.23   Fact-Finding and Monitoring

Books

– Deaver, Michael V., *Disarming Iraq: Monitoring Power and Resistance* (Westport, Praeger 2001) 151 pp.
– Rai, Rahul, *Monitoring International Human Rights* (Delhi, Authorspress 2002) 304 pp.

Articles

– Clay, Jason W., 'Investigating Human Rights Violations: Some Lessons from the Field', in David Barnhizer, ed., *Effective Strategies for Protecting Human Rights: Prevention and Intervention, Trade and Education* (Aldershot, Ashgate 2001) pp. 29-37
– Grist, Ryan, 'More than Eunuchs at the Orgy: Observation and Monitoring Reconsidered', 8 *International Peacekeeping* (2001) pp. 59-78
– Leaning, Jennifer, Jonathan Fine and Richard Garfield, 'Conflict Monitoring', in Ilkka Taipale et al., eds., *War or Health? A Reader* (London, Zed 2002) pp. 510-519
– Takirambudde, Peter, 'Building the Record of Human Rights Violations in Africa: The Functions of Monitoring, Investigation and Advocacy', in David Barnhizer, ed., *Effective Strategies for Protecting Human Rights: Prevention and Intervention, Trade and Education* (Aldershot, Ashgate 2001) pp. 11-19

9.24   Humanitarian and Other Interventions

Books

– Aklilu, Yakob and Mike Wekesa, *Drought, Livestock and Livelihoods: Lessons from the 1999-2001 Emergency Response in the Pastoral Sector in Kenya* (London, Overseas Development Institute 2002) 40 pp.
– Allin, Dana H., *NATO's Balkan Interventions* (London, International Institute for Strategic Studies 2002) 112 pp.
– Barnhizer, David, ed., *Effective Strategies for Protecting Human Rights: Prevention and Intervention, Trade and Education* (Aldershot, Ashgate 2001) 250 pp.
– Barry, J. and A. Jefferys, *A Bridge Too Far: Aid Agencies and the Military in Humanitarian Response* (London, Overseas Development Institute 2002) 36 pp.
– Borton, John and Kate Robertson, eds., *ALNAP Annual Review 2002: Humanitarian Action: Improving Performance Through Improved Learning* (London, Overseas Development Institute 2002) 190 pp.
– Bose, Sumantra, *Bosnia After Dayton: Nationalist Partition and International Intervention* (London, Hurst 2002) 295 pp.

− Buzzi, Alessandro, *L'intervention armée de l'OTAN en République fédérale de Yougo-slavie* (Paris, Pedone 2001) 277 pp.
− Callaghy, Thomas M., Robert Latham and Ronald Kassimir, eds., *Intervention and Transnationalism in Africa: Global-Local Networks of Power* (Cambridge, Cambridge University Press 2001) 322 pp.
− Chandler, David, *From Kosovo to Kabul: Human Rights and International Intervention* (London, Pluto Press 2002) 268 pp.
− Chesterman, Simon, *Just War or Just Peace? Humanitarian Intervention and Interna-tional Law* (Oxford, Oxford University Press 2002) 326 pp.
− Conoir, Yvan and Gérard Verna, eds., *L'action humanitaire du Canada: histoire, con-cepts, politiques et pratiques du terrain* (Sainte-Foy, Presses de l'Université Laval 2002) 615 pp.
− Crawford, Neta C., *Argument and Change in World Politics. Ethics, Decolonization, and Humanitarian Intervention* (Cambridge, Cambridge University Press 2002) 360 pp.
− DiPrizio, Robert C., *Armed Humanitarians: U.S. Interventions from Northern Iraq to Kosovo* (Baltimore, John Hopkins University Press 2002) 234 pp.
− Escudero Espinosa, Juan Francisco, *Aproximación histórica a la noción de intervención humanitaria en el derecho internacional* (Léon, Universidad de León 2002) 431 pp.
− Furley, Oliver and Roy May, eds., *African Interventionist States* (Aldershot, Ashgate 2001) 286 pp.
− Glennon, Michael J., *Limits of Law, Prerogatives of Power: Interventionism After Koso-vo* (New York, Palgrave 2001) 250 pp.
− Hawk, Kathleen Hill, *Constructing the Stable State: Goals for Intervention and Peace-building* (Westport, Praeger 2002) 162 pp.
− International Commission on Intervention and State Sovereignty, *The Responsibility to Protect: Report on the International Commission on Intervention and State Sovereignty* (Ottawa, International Development Research Centre 2001) 108 pp.
− Keren, Michael and Donald A. Sylvan, eds., *International Intervention: Sovereignty versus Responsibility* (London, Frank Cass 2002) 191 pp.
− Kuperman, Alan J., *The Limits of Humanitarian Intervention: Genocide in Rwanda* (Washington, Bookings Institution Press 2001) 162 pp.
− Langley, Lester D., *The Banana Wars: United States Intervention in the Caribbean, 1898-1934*, 3rd rev. edn. (Wilmington, SR Books 2002) 265 pp.
− Lepard, Brian D., *Rethinking Humanitarian Intervention: A Fresh Legal Approach Based on Fundamental Ethical Principles in International Law and World Religions* (University Park, The Pennsylvania State University 2002) 496 pp.
− MacFarlane, S. Neil, *Intervention in Contemporary World Politics* (Oxford, Oxford University Press 2002) 95 pp.
− Martin, Ian, *Self-Determination in East Timor: The United Nations, the Ballot and Inter-national Intervention* (Boulder, Lynne Rienner 2001) 171 pp.
− Massenet, Michel, *Les guerriers humanitaires: de l'humanitarisme à la guerre* (Paris, De Guibert 2001) 170 pp.
− McInnes, Colin and Nicholas J. Wheeler, eds., *Dimensions of Western Military Interven-tion* (London, Frank Cass 2002) 202 pp.
− Mills, Nicolaus and Kira Brunner, eds., *The New Killing Fields: Massacre and the Pol-itics of Intervention* (New York, Basic Books 2002) 276 pp.
− Moseley, Alexander and Richard Norman, eds., *Human Rights and Military Intervention* (Aldershot, Ashgate 2002) 283 pp.

— Muggah, R. and M. Griffiths, *Reconsidering the Tools of War: Small Arms and Humanitarian Action* (London, Overseas Development Institute 2002) 40 pp.

— Österdahl, Inger, ed., *Is Intervention Humanitarian? Protecting Human Rights and Democracy Abroad* (Uppsala, Department for Peace and Conflict Research 2002) 98 pp.

— Price, Monroe E. and Mark Thompson, eds., *Forging Peace: Intervention, Human Rights and the Management of Media Space* (Edinburgh, Edinburgh University Press 2002) 408 pp.

— Rezac, David, *Militärische Intervention als Problem des Völkerrechts: eine Untersuchung bewaffneten Eingreifens in innerstaatliche Konflikte anhand des Kosovo-Krieges* (Vienna, Landesverteidungsakademie 2002) 168 pp.

— Sinha, Manoj Kumar, *Humanitarian Intervention by the United Nations* (New Delhi, Manak Publications 2002) 134 pp.

— Terry, Fiona, *Condemned to Repeat? The Paradox of Humanitarian Action* (Ithaca, Cornell University Press 2002) 282 pp.

— Tomuschat, Christian, ed., *Kosovo and the International Community: A Legal Assessment* (The Hague, Kluwer Law International 2001) 368 pp.

— Wellhausen, Malte, *Humanitäre Intervention: Probleme der Anerkennung des Rechtsinstituts unter besonderer Berücksichtigung des Kosovo-Konflikts* (Baden-Baden, Nomos 2002) 261 pp.

— Wheeler, Nicholas J., *Saving Strangers: Humanitarian Intervention in International Society* (Oxford, Oxford University Press 2001) 352 pp.

— Wood, Adrian, Raymond Apthorpe and John Borton, eds., *Evaluating International Humanitarian Action: Reflections from Practitioners* (London, Zed Books 2001) 222 pp.

Articles

— Abass, Ademola, 'The Implementation of ECOWAS' New Protocol and Security Council Resolution 1270 in Sierra Leone: New Developments in Regional Intervention', 10 *International & Comparative Law Review. University of Miami School of Law* (2001/2002) pp. 177-216

— Adjovi, Roland and Matthieu Monin, 'Commission Internationale de l'Intervention et de la Souveraineté des États (CIISE): de la responsabilité de protéger: étude critique', 6 *Revue de droit africain: doctrine & jurisprudence* (2002) pp. 377-399

— Andersson, Andreas, 'United Nations Intervention by United Democracies? State Commitment to UN Interventions 1991-99', 37 *Cooperation and Conflict: Nordic Journal of International Studies* (2002) pp. 363-386

— Ankenbrand, Birthe, 'Kriterien einer humanitären Intervention', in Erwin Müller, Patricia Schneider and Kristina Thony, eds., *Menschenrechtsschutz: politische Maßnahmen, zivilgesellschaftliche Strategien, humanitäre Interventionen* (Baden-Baden, Nomos 2002) pp. 185-199

— Ayoob, M. 'Humanitarian Intervention and State Sovereignty', 6 *International Journal of Human Rights* (2002) pp. 81-102

— Barutciski, Michael, 'Peut-on justifier l'intervention de l'OTAN au Kosovo sur le plan humanitaire? Analyse de la politique occidentale et ses conséquences en Macédoine', 38 *Canadian YIL* (2001) pp. 121-154

— Bishai, Linda S., 'Intervention in Law and Politics', 36 *Cooperation and Conflict: Nordic Journal of International Studies* (2001) pp. 415-424

− Blinderman, Eric, 'International Law and Information Intervention', in Monroe E. Price and Mark Thompson, eds., *Forging Peace: Intervention, Human Rights and the Management of Media Space* (Edinburgh, Edinburgh University Press 2002) pp. 104-138

− Brown, Chris, 'A Qualified Defence of the Use of Force for "Humanitarian" Reasons', in Ken Booth, ed., *The Kosovo Tragedy: The Human Rights Dimensions* (London, Frank Cass 2001) pp. 283-288

− Cahin, Gérard, 'L'action internationale au Timor oriental', 46 *AFDI* (2000) pp. 139-175

− Carlson, Scott, 'Humanitäre Intervention in Kosovo, die Auswertung der Daten über Menschenrechtsverletzungen und die Lektionen daraus', 47 *Osteuropa-Recht* (2001) pp. 197-199

− Cetinyan, Rupen, 'Ethnic Bargaining in the Shadow of Third-Party Intervention', 56 *International Organization* (2002) pp. 645-677

− Chandler, D. 'The Road to Military Humanitarianism: How the Human Rights NGOs Shaped a New Humanitarian Agenda', 23 *HRQ* (2001) pp. 678-700

− Chesterman, Simon et al., 'Ethics of Humanitarian Intervention', 33 *Security Dialogue* (2002) pp. 261-340

− Chimni, B.S., 'A New Humanitarian Council for Humanitarian Interventions', 6 *International Journal of Human Rights* (2002) pp. 103-112

− Clark, John F., 'Explaining Ugandan Intervention in Congo: Evidence and Interpretations', 39 *The Journal of Modern African Studies* (2001) pp. 261-287

− Cotton, James, 'Against the Grain: The East Timor Intervention', 43 *Survival* (2001) pp. 127-142

− Darbishire, Helen, 'Non-Governmental Perspectives: Media Freedom Versus Information Intervention', in Monroe E. Price and Mark Thompson, eds., *Forging Peace: Intervention, Human Rights and the Management of Media Space* (Edinburgh, Edinburgh University Press 2002) pp. 329-364

− Dekker, Ige F., 'Illegality and Legitimacy of Humanitarian Intervention: Synopsis of and Comments on a Dutch Report', 6 *Journal of Conflict and Security Law* (2001) pp. 115-126

− Delwaide, Jacobus, 'Voor vrijheid en recht? De legitimiteit van humanitaire interventie', 30 *Vrede en Veiligheid* (2001) pp. 327-344

− Dinstein, Yoram, 'Humanitarian Intervention from Outside, in the Face of Genocide, Is Legitimate Only When Undertaken by the Security Council', 27 *Justice, The International Association of Jewish Lawyers and Jurists* (2001) pp. 4-7

− Dinstein, Yoram, 'The Collective Human Rights of Religious Groups: Genocide and Humanitarian Intervention', 30 *Israel YB HR* (2000) pp. 227-241

− Doyle, Michael W., 'UN Intervention and National Sovereignty', in Wolfgang Danspeckgruber, ed., *The Self-Determination of Peoples: Community, Nation and State in an Interdependent World* (Boulder, Lynne Rienner 2002) pp. 67-100

− Dreist, Peter, 'Humanitäre Intervention: zur Rechtmäßigkeit der NATO-Operation ALLIED FORCE', 15 *Humanitäres Völkerrecht* (2002) pp. 68-77

− Dupont, Pascal, 'La Somalie, de la guerre de l'Ogaden à l'intervention de l'ONU', 58 *Défense nationale* (2002) pp. 119-131

− Egan, Patrick T., 'The Kosovo Intervention and Collective Self-Defence', 8 *International Peacekeeping* (2001) pp. 39-58

− Elshtain, Jean Bethke, 'The Third Annual Grotius Lecture: Just War and Humanitarian Intervention', 17 *Amer. Univ. ILR* (2001) pp. 1-25

− Falk, Richard, 'Humanitarian Intervention After Kosovo', in Laurence Boisson de Cha-zournes and Vera Gowlland-Debbas, eds., *The International Legal System in Quest of Equity and Universality: Liber Amicorum Georges Abi-Saab* (The Hague, Nijhoff 2001) pp. 177-198

− Fischer, Horst, 'Die Amnesty-NATO-Debatte über den Kosovo-Krieg: ein Beitrag zum Schutz der Zivilbevölkerung in "humanitären" Kriegen?', *Jahrbuch Menschenrechte* (2002) pp. 113-122

− Flauss, Jean-François, 'La primauté des droits de la personne: licéité ou illicéité de l'intervention humanitaire?', in Christian Tomuschat, ed., *Kosovo and the International Community: A Legal Assessment* (The Hague, Kluwer Law International 2002) pp. 87-102

− Gasiokwu, Martin Uzo, 'ECOWAS Intervention in Liberia and Sierra-Leone: A New Dimension in Regional Security System', 24 *Polish Yearbook of International Law* (2001) pp. 157-168

− Gill, T.D., 'Humanitaire interventie: rechtmatigheid, rechtvaardigheid, en legitimiteit nader bekeken', 94 *Militair-rechtelijk tijdschrift* (2001) pp. 221-241

− Gnaedinger, Angelo, 'Security Challenges for Humanitarian Action', 83 *IRRC* (2001) pp. 171-182

− Greenwood, Christopher, 'Humanitarian Intervention: The Case of Kosovo', 10 *Finnish Yearbook of International Law* (1999) pp. 141-175

− Hillgruber, Christian, 'Humanitäre Intervention, Grossmachtpolitik und Völkerrecht', 40 *Der Staat* (2001) pp. 165-191

− Howe, Brendan, 'The Case for the Offense: Legality, Legitimacy and Military Intervention', 30 *Korean Journal of International and Comparative Law* (2002) pp. 113-135

− Jenkins, B., 'The NATO Air Campaign in Kosovo: Legal Issues and Dilemmas Posed by Armed Humanitarian Intervention', 17 *Miller Centre Report* (2001) pp. 28-31

− Joyner, Daniel H., 'The Kosovo Intervention: Legal Analysis and a More Persuasive Paradigm', 13 *EJIL* (2002) pp. 597-619

− Kdhir, Moncef, 'Pour le respect des droit de l'homme sans droit d'ingérence', 13 *Revue trimestrielle des droits de l'homme* (2002) pp. 901-923

− Kelly, Michael J., Timothy L.H. McCormack, Paul Muggleton et al., 'Legal Aspects of Australia's Involvement in the International Force for East Timor', 83 *IRRC* (2001) pp. 101-138

− Krug, Peter and Monroe E. Price, 'A Module for Media Intervention: Content Regulation in Post-Conflict Zones', in Monroe E. Price and Mark Thompson, eds., *Forging Peace: Intervention, Human Rights and the Management of Media Space* (Edinburgh, Edinburgh University Press 2002) pp. 148-174

− Larson, Geoff, 'The Right of International Intervention in Civil Conflicts: Evolving International Law on State Sovereignty in Observance of Human Rights and Application to the Crisis in Chechnya', 11 *Transn. L & Contemp. Probs.* (2001) pp. 251-275

− Leutheusser-Schnarrenberger, Sabine, 'Mit (aller) Gewalt zum Frieden? Militärische Interventionen der Vereinten Nationen zwischen Moralität und Legalität', *Jahrbuch Menschenrechte* (2002) pp. 87-104

− Levitt, Jeremy, 'The Evolving Intervention Regime in Africa: From Basket Case to Market Place?', 96 *Proc. ASIL* (2002) pp. 136-143

− Lindgren, R. V., 'When Foreign Intervention Is Justified: Women Under the Taliban', 62 *The Humanist* (2002) pp. 21-25

– MacGregor, Lorna, 'Military and Judicial Intervention: The Way Forward in Human Rights Enforcement?', 12 *Indiana International & Comparative Law Review* (2001) pp. 107-124

– Maxine Marcus, I., 'Humanitarian Intervention Without Borders: Belligerent Occupation or Colonization?', 25 *Houston Journal of International Law* (2002) pp. 99-139

– Merrills, J.G., 'Sovereignty over Pulau Ligatan and Pulau Sipadan (Indonesia v Malaysia): The Philippines' Intervention', 51 *ICLQ* (2002) pp. 718-722

– Mertus, Julie, 'Note on Legality of Information Intervention', in Monroe E. Price and Mark Thompson, eds., *Forging Peace: Intervention, Human Rights and the Management of Media Space* (Edinburgh, Edinburgh University Press 2002) pp. 139-147

– Moorman, William, 'Humanitarian Intervention and International Law in the Case of Kosovo', 36 *New England LR* (2001) pp. 775-784

– Ocran, T. Mobido, 'The Doctrine of Humanitarian Intervention in Light of Robust Peacekeeping', 25 *Boston College Int. & Comp. LR* (2002) pp. 1-58

– Pasquier, André, 'Action humanitaire: une légitimité en question?', 83 *IRRC* (2001) pp. 311-321

– Peters, A., 'Le droit d'ingérence et le devoir d'ingérence – vers une responsabilité de protéger', 79 *Revue de droit international et de droit comparé* (2001) pp. 290-308

– Poltak, Celeste, 'Humanitarian Intervention: A Contemporary Interpretation of the Charter of the United Nations', 60 *University of Toronto Faculty of Law Review* (2002) pp. 1-38

– Posteraro, Christopher Clarke, 'Intervention in Iraq: Towards a Doctrine of Anticipatory Counter-Terrorism, Counterproliferation Intervention', 15 *Florida Journal of International Law* (2002) pp. 151-213

– Regan, Patrick M., 'Third-Party Interventions and the Duration of Intrastate Conflicts', 46 *Journal of Conflict Resolution* (2002) pp. 55-73

– Rich, Paul B., 'Warlordism, Complex Emergencies and the Search for a Doctrine of Humanitarian Intervention', in D.S. Gordon and F.H. Toase, eds., *Aspects of Peacekeeping* (London, Frank Cass 2001) pp. 253-273

– Ruiz Ruiz, Florentino, 'Democratic Intervention: A Legal Analysis of Its Lawfulness', 41 *Indian JIL* (2001) pp. 377-417

– Ryniker, Anne, 'Position du Comité international de la Croix-Rouge sur "l'intervention humanitaire"', 83 *IRRC* (2001) pp. 521-532

– Schaller, Christan, 'Massenvernichtungswaffen und Präventivkrieg – Möglichkeiten der Rechtfertigung einer militärischen Intervention im Irak aus völkerrechtlicher Sicht', 62 *ZaöRV* (2002) pp. 641-668

– Schermers, Henry G., 'International Humanitarian Intervention', in ELSA International, ed., *International Law as We Enter the 21st Century: International Focus Programme 1997-1999* (Berlin, Spitz 2001) pp. 25-31

– Schüßler, Rudolf, 'Die humanitäre Intervention in der Doktrin des gerechten Krieges', in Erwin Müller, Patricia Schneider and Kristina Thony, eds., *Menschenrechtsschutz: politische Maßnahmen, zivilgesellschaftliche Strategien, humanitäre Interventionen* (Baden-Baden, Nomos 2002) pp. 200-217

– Spiermann, Ole, 'Humanitarian Intervention as a Necessity and the Threat or Use of Jus Cogens', 71 *Nordic JIL* (2002) pp. 523-543

– Stannard, Robert W., 'The Laws of War: An Examination of the Legality of NATO's Intervention in the Former Yugoslavia and the Role of the European Court of Human

Rights in Redressing Claims for Civilian Casualties in War', 30 *Georgia Journal of International and Comparative Law* (2002) pp. 617-637
- Strohmeyer, Hansjörg, 'Making Multilateral Interventions Work: The U.N. and the Creation of Transitional Justice Systems in Kosovo and East Timor', 25 *The Fletcher Forum of World Affairs* (2001) pp. 107-128
- Taylor, Philip M., 'Information Warfare and Information Intervention', in Monroe E. Price and Mark Thompson, eds., *Forging Peace: Intervention, Human Rights and the Management of Media Space* (Edinburgh, Edinburgh University Press 2002) pp. 313-328
- Thompson, Mark and Dan De Luce, 'Escalating to Success? The Media Intervention in Bosnia and Herzegovina', in Monroe E. Price and Mark Thompson, eds., *Forging Peace: Intervention, Human Rights and the Management of Media Space* (Edinburgh, Edinburgh University Press 2002) pp. 201-235
- Thürer, Daniel, 'Die NATO-Intervention im Kosovo und das humanitäre Völkerrecht', 22 *Liechtensteinische Juristen-Zeitung* (2001) pp. 36-41
- Uerpmann, Robert, 'La primauté des droits de l'homme: licéité ou illicéité de l'intervention humanitaire', in Christian Tomuschat, ed., *Kosovo and the International Community: A Legal Assessment* (The Hague, Kluwer Law International 2002) pp. 65-86
- Van Wielink, Joost P.J., 'Kosovo Revisited: The (Il)legality of NATO's Military Intervention in the Federal Republic of Yugoslavia', 9 *Tilburg For. LR* (2001) pp. 133-161
- Walker, George K., 'Principles for Collective Humanitarian Intervention to Succor Other Countries' Imperiled Indigenous Nationals', 18 *Amer. Univ. ILR* (2002) pp. 35-162
- Walther, Manfred, 'Intervention in die "inneren Angelegenheiten" souveräner Staaten zum Schutz der Menschenrechte – Überlegungen zur Vollzugslücke im gegenwärtigen Völkerrecht aus Anlaß des Kosovo Krieges: ein Kommentar zu Michael Bothe', in Karl Graf Ballestrem, ed., *Internationale Gerechtigkeit* (Opladen, Leske and Budrich 2001) pp. 236-254
- Warner, Daniel, 'Ethics, Law and Unethical Compassion in the Kosovo Intervention', in Laurence Boisson de Chazournes and Vera Gowlland-Debbas, eds., *The International Legal System in Quest of Equity and Universality: Liber Amicorum Georges Abi-Saab* (The Hague, Nijhoff 2001) pp. 199-217
- Wheeler, N. J., 'Reflections on the Legality and Legitimacy of Nato's Intervention in Kosovo', in Ken Booth, ed., *The Kosovo Tragedy: The Human Rights Dimensions* (London, Frank Cass 2001) pp. 145-163
- Williams, Ian, 'Righting the Wrongs of Past Interventions: A Review of the International Commission on Intervention and State Sovereignty', 6 *International Journal of Human Rights* (2002) p. 103-113
- Williams, Paul, 'Fighting for Freedom: British Military Intervention in Sierra Leone', 22 *Contemporary Security Policy* (2001) pp. 140-168
- Wippman, David, 'Pro-Democratic Intervention in Africa', 96 *Proc. ASIL* (2002) pp. 143-145
- Zemanek, Karl, 'Intervention in the 21st Century', 5 *Cursos Euromediterráneos Bancaja de Derecho Internacional* (2001) pp. 613-666

9.25   Sanctions

Books

— Barnhizer, David, ed., *Effective Strategies for Protecting Human Rights: Economic Sanctions, Use of National Courts and International 'Fora' and Coercive Power* (Aldershot, Ashgate 2001) 278 pp.
— Brzoska, Michael, ed., *Design and Implementation of Arms Embargoes and Travel and Aviation Related Sanctions: Results of the 'Bonn-Berlin-Process'* (Bonn, Bonn International Center for Conversion 2001) 129 pp.
— Brzoska, Michael, ed., *Smart Sanctions: The Next Steps: The Debate on Arms Embargoes and Travel Sanctions Within the 'Bonn Berlin Process'* (Baden-Baden, Nomos 2001) 316 pp.
— Cortright, David, George A. Lopez and Linda Gerber, *Sanctions and the Search for Security: Challenges to UN Action* (Boulder, Lynne Rienner 2002) 249 pp.
— Cortright, David and George A. Lopez, eds., *Smart Sanctions: Targeting Economic Statecraft* (Lanham, Rowan & Littlefield 2002) 259 pp.
— Naylor, R.T., *Economic Warfare: Sanctions, Embargo Busting, and Their Human Cost* (Boston, Northeastern University Press 2001) 459 pp.
— Niblock, Tim, *'Pariah States' & Sanctions in the Middle East: Iraq, Libya, Sudan* (Boulder, Lynne Rienner 2001) 241 pp.
— Simons, Geoff, *Targeting Iraq: Sanctions and Bombing in US Policy* (London, Saqi Books 2002) 274 pp.
— Speier, Richard H., Brian G. Chow and S. Rae Starr, *Nonproliferation Sanctions* (Santa Monica, Rand 2001) 279 pp.

Articles

— Babić, Jovan and Aleksandar Jokić, 'Economic Sanctions, Morality and Escalation of
· Demands on Yugoslavia', 9 *International Peacekeeping* (2002) pp. 119-126
— Bisharat, George E., 'Sanctions as Genocide', 11 *Transn. L & Contemp. Probs.* (2001) pp. 379-425
— Boersma, Michael Eric, 'Analysis of the Application of Economic Coercion to Correct Breaches of International Obligations: The Use of Force by the United States to Correct Cuba's Breaches of Its International Obligations', 10 *JIL & Prac.* (2001) pp. 281-317
— Byers, Michael, 'The Shifting Foundations of International Law: A Decade of Forceful Measures Against Iraq', 13 *EJIL* (2002) pp. 21-41
— Craven, Matthew, 'Humanitarianism and the Quest for Smarter Sanctions', 13 *EJIL* (2002) pp. 43-61
— Das, Himamauli, 'The United States Sanctions Response to the Attacks of September 11, 2001: A Synopsis of Remarks at the NESL Rogue Regimes Conference', 36 *New England LR* (2002) pp. 943-955
— De Wet, Erika, 'Human Rights Limitations to Economic Enforcement Measures Under Article 41 of the United Nations Charter and the Iraqi Sanctions Regime', 14 *Leiden JIL* (2001) pp. 277-300
— Dordevic, Bratislav and Duško Lopandic, 'Introduction of Sanctions Against the FR of Yugoslavia and Their Lifting, 1991-2001', 42 *Yugoslav Survey* (2001) pp. 25-40
— Fassbender, Bardo, 'Uncertain Steps into a Post-Cold War World: The Role and Functioning of the UN Security Council After a Decade of Measures Against Iraq', 13 *EJIL* (2002) pp. 273-303

– Fitzgerald, Peter L., 'Managing "Smart Sanctions" Against Terrorism Wisely', 36 *New England LR* (2002) pp. 957-983

– Garfield, Richard, 'Health and Well-Being in Iraq: Sanctions and the Impact of the Oil for Food Program', 11 *Transn. L & Contemp. Probs.* (2001) pp. 277-298

– Heine-Ellison, Sofia, 'The Impact and Effectiveness of Multilateral Economic Sanctions: A Comparative Study', 5 *International Journal of Human Rights* (2001) pp. 81-112

– Hulsroj, Peter, 'Unsanctioned Sanctions', 43 *GYIL* (2000) pp. 239-252

– Kondoch, Boris, 'The Limits of Economic Sanctions Under International Law: The Case of Iraq', 7 *International Peacekeeping: The Yearbook of International Peace Operations* (2001) pp. 267-294.

– LaRae-Perez, Cassandra, 'Economic Sanctions as a Use of Force: Reevaluating the Legality of Sanctions from an Effects-Based Perspective', 20 *Boston Univ. ILJ* (2002) pp. 161-188

– Mesa Delmonte, Luis, 'Economic Sanctions, Iraq, and U.S. Foreign Policy', 11 *Transn. L & Contemp. Probs.* (2001) pp. 345-377

– Normand, Roger and Christoph Wilcke, 'Human Rights, Sanctions, and Terrorist Threats: The United Nations Sanctions Against Iraq', 11 *Transn. L & Contemp. Probs.* (2001) pp. 299-343

– O'Connell, Mary Ellen, 'Debating the Law of Sanctions', 13 *EJIL* (2002) pp. 63-79

– Oette, Lutz, 'A Decade of Sanctions Against Iraq: Never Again! The End of Unlimited Sanctions in the Recent Practice of the UN Security Council', 13 *EJIL* (2002) pp. 93-103

– Österdahl, Inger, 'FN-sanktioner och mänskliga rättigheter eller Hur kunde det bli på detta viset?', 10 *Svensk juristtidning* (2002) pp. 894-916

– Paust, Jordan J., 'Sanctions Against Non-State Actors for Violations of International Law', 8 *ILSA JI & CL* (2002) pp. 417-429

– Petman, Jarna, 'Fighting the Evil with International Economic Sanctions', 10 *Finnish Yearbook of International Law* (1999) pp. 209-230

– Reinisch, August, 'Developing Human Rights and Humanitarian Law Accountability of the Security Council for the Imposition of Economic Sanctions', 95 *AJIL* (2001) pp. 851-872

– Schuette, Sarah P., 'U.S. Economic Sanctions Regarding the Proliferation of Nuclear Weapons: A Call for Reform of the Arms Export Control Act Sanctions', 35 *Cornell ILJ* (2002) pp. 231-262

– Spinellis, Calliope D. and Dionysios Spinellis, 'Sanctions Imposed, Sanctions Executed: Who Benefits from the Discrepancy?', 55 *Revue hellénique de droit international* (2002) pp. 311-345

– Sponeck, H.C. Graf, 'Sanctions and Humanitarian Exemptions: A Practitioner's Commentary', 13 *EJIL* (2002) pp. 81-87

11.   ARMS CONTROL AND DISARMAMENT

Books
– Anthony, Ian and Adam Daniel Rotfeld, eds., *A Future Arms Control Agenda: Proceedings of Nobel Symposium 118, 1999* (Oxford, Oxford University Press 2001) 371 pp.

— Deaver, Michael V., *Disarming Iraq: Monitoring Power and Resistance* (Westport, Praeger 2001) 151 pp.

— Den Bakker, Guido, *The Law of Arms Control: International Supervision and Enforcement* (The Hague, Nijhoff 2001) 404 pp.

— Dhanapala, Jayantha et al., *Terrorism and Disarmament* (New York, United Nations Department for Disarmament Affairs 2001) 63 pp.

— Goldblat, Jozef, *Arms Control: The New Guide to Negotiations and Agreements*, 2nd rev. and updated edn. (London, Sage 2002) 396 pp.

— Graham Jr., Thomas, *Disarmament Sketches: Three Decades of Arms Control and International Law* (Seattle, Institute for Global and Regional Security Studies 2002) 362 pp.

— Guruswamy, Lakshman D. and Suzette R. Grillot, eds., *Arms Control and the Environment* (Ardsley, Transnational Publishers 2001) 274 pp.

— Larsen, Jeffrey A., ed., *Arms Control: Cooperative Security in a Changing Environment* (Boulder, Lynne Rienner 2002) 375 pp.

— Tulliu, Steve and Thomas Schmalberger, *Coming to Terms with Security: A Lexicon for Arms Control, Disarmament and Confidence-Building* (Geneva, United Nations Institute for Disarmament Research 2001) 246 pp.

— United Nations Department for Disarmament Affairs, *A Disarmament Agenda for the Twenty-first Century: UN-China Disarmament Conference, Beijing, China, 2-4 April 2002* (New York, United Nations Department for Disarmament Affairs 2002) 195 pp.

— United Nations Institute for Disarmament Research, *Disarmament as Humanitarian Action: A Discussion on the Occasion of the 20th Anniversary of the United Nations Institute for Disarmament Research* (Geneva, United Nations Institute for Disarmament Research 2001) 19 pp.

— United Nations Institute for Disarmament Research, *Missile Defence, Deterrence and Arms Control: Contradictory Aims or Compatible Goals?* (Geneva, United Nations Institute for Disarmament Research 2002) 38 pp.

— Willett, Susan, *Costs of Disarmament: Rethinking the Price Tag: A Methodological Inquiry into the Costs and Benefits of Arms Control* (Geneva, United Nations Institute for Disarmament Research 2002) 75 pp.

Articles

— Anthony, Ian, 'European Union Approaches to Arms Control, Non-Proliferation and Disarmament', *SIPRI Yearbook* (2001) pp. 599-614

— Biad, Abdelwahab, 'Face à la perspective d'un bouclier antimissile: l'architecture de l'arms control et du désarmement en question', 46 *AFDI* (2000) pp. 221-241

— Blix, Hans, 'Arms Control and Disarmament: One of the Main Themes of The Hague Peace Conference of 1899', in Timothy L.H. McCormack, Michael Tilbury and Gillian D. Triggs, eds., *A Century of War and Peace: Asia-Pacific Perspectives on the Centenary of the 1899 Hague Peace Conference* (The Hague, Kluwer Law International 2001) pp. 169-178

— Burroughs, John R., 'Arms Control and National Security', 36 *The International Lawyer* (2002) pp. 471-505

— Downer, Alexander, 'Approaches to Disarmament, the Peaceful Settlement of Disputes and International Humanitarian Law', in Timothy L.H. McCormack, Michael Tilbury and Gillian D. Triggs, eds., *A Century of War and Peace: Asia-Pacific Perspectives on the Centenary of the 1899 Hague Peace Conference* (The Hague, Kluwer Law International 2001) pp. 17-27

— Feaver, Peter D., 'Proliferation Theory and Nonproliferation Practice', in Henry Sokolski and James M. Ludes, eds., *Twenty-first Century Weapons Proliferation: Are We Ready?* (London, Frank Cass 2001) pp. 168-181
— Fleck, Dieter, 'Developments of the Law of Arms Control as a Result of the Iraq-Kuwait Conflict', 13 *EJIL* (2002) pp. 105-119
— Harrington, John A., 'Arms Control and Disarmament', 35 *The International Lawyer* (2001) pp. 579-593
— Lysenko, Mikhail, 'Conference on Prohibiting Arms in Space', 47 *International Affairs: A Russian Journal* (2001) pp. 78-82
— O'Donnell, Joshua P., 'The Anti-Ballistic Missile Treaty Debate: Time for Some Clarification of the President's Authority to Terminate a Treaty', 35 *Vanderbilt JTL* (2002) pp. 1601-1636
— Perez, Antonio F., 'The Adequacy of International Law for Arms Control, Post-September 11: Arms Control and Nonproliferation', 96 *Proc. ASIL* (2002) pp. 273-275
— Wilkinson, Paul, 'Disarmament and Terrorism', *OPCW synthesis* (2001) pp. 12-17
— Wisnumurti, Nugroho, 'Arms Control and Disarmament: The Development of Approaches in the Asia-Pacific Region', in Timothy L.H. McCormack, Michael Tilbury and Gillian D. Triggs, eds., *A Century of War and Peace: Asia-Pacific Perspectives on the Centenary of the 1899 Hague Peace Conference* (The Hague, Kluwer Law International 2001) pp. 179-199

11.1   CONVENTIONAL WEAPONS

Articles

— Lachowski, Zdzislaw, 'Conventional Arms Control', *SIPRI Yearbook* (2001) pp. 549-577

11.11   Mines

Books

— Dörmann, Knut, *Völkerrechtliche Probleme des Landmineneinsatzes: Weiterentwicklung des geltenden Vertragsrechts durch das geänderte Minenprotokoll vom 3. Mai 1996 zum UN-Waffenübereinkommen von 1980* (Berlin, Berliner Wissenschafts-Verlag 2002) 531 pp.
— International Campaign to Ban Landmines, *ICBL Report on Activities During the Third Meeting of States Parties to the 1997 Convention on the Prohibition of the Use, Stockpiling, Production and Transfer of Anti-Personnel Mines and on Their Destruction: 18-21 September 2001, Managua, Nicaragua* (Washington, International Campaign to Ban Landmines 2002) 236 pp.

Articles

— Brem, Stefan, 'Walking Together or Divided Agenda? Comparing Landmines and Small-Arms Campaigns', 32 *Security Dialogue* (2001) pp. 169-186
— Kitchen, Veronica, 'From Rhetoric to Reality: Canada, the United States, and the Ottawa Process to Ban Landmines', 57 *International Journal* (2002) pp. 37-55

− Polkinghorne, Michael and James Cockayne, 'Dealing with the Risks and Responsibilities of Landmines and Their Clearance', 25 *Fordham ILJ* (2002) pp. 1187-1204

11.12   Small Weapons and Others

Articles
− Brem, Stefan, 'Walking Together or Divided Agenda? Comparing Landmines and Small-Arms Campaigns', 32 *Security Dialogue* (2001) pp. 169-186
− Ewing, James E., 'The 1972 U.S.-Soviet ABM Treaty: Cornerstone of Stability or Relic of the Cold War?', 43 *William and Mary Law Review* (2001) pp. 787-818
− Müllerson, Rein, 'The ABM Treaty: Changed Circumstances, Extraordinary Events, Supreme Interests and International Law', 50 *ICLQ* (2001) pp. 509-539
− Rhinelander, John B., 'The ABM Treaty: Past, Present and Future (Part III)', 6 *Journal of Conflict & Security Law* (2001) pp. 225-243
− Smith, Hillary A., 'Is Honesty Still the Best Policy: Considering Legal Options for Missile Defense and the Antiballistic Missile Treaty', 31 *Georgia Journal of International and Comparative Law* (2002) pp. 199-223
− Turner, Robert F., 'National Missile Defense and the 1972 ABM Treaty', 36 *New England LR* (2002) pp. 807-813

11.2   WEAPONS OF MASS DESTRUCTION

Books
− Barnaby, Frank, *Waiting for Terror: How Realistic is the Biological, Chemical and Nuclear Threat?* (Oxford, Oxford Research Group 2001) 27 pp.
− Cirincione, Joseph, Jon B. Wolfsthal and Miriam Rajkumar, *Deadly Arsenals: Tracking Weapons of Mass Destruction* (Washington, Carnegie Endowment for International Peace 2002) 465 pp.
− Höhl, K., H. Müller and A. Schaper, *Die Rolle der Europäischen Union in der Abrüstung von Russischen Massenvernichtungswaffen: eine Bestandsaufnahme* (Frankfurt am Main, Hessische Stiftung Friedens- und Konfliktforschung 2002) 50 pp.

11.21   Nuclear Weapons

Books
− Khan, Saira, *Nuclear Proliferation Dynamics in Protracted Conflict Regions: A Comparative Study of South Asia and the Middle East* (Aldershot, Ashgate 2002) 316 pp.
− Thomson, David B., *A Guide to the Nuclear Arms Control Treaties* (Los Alamos, Los Alamos Historical Society 2001) 332 pp.
− Ungerer, Carl and Marianne Hanson, eds., *The Politics of Nuclear Non-Proliferation* (St. Leonards, Allen & Unwin 2001) 218 pp.

Articles
- Blix, Hans, 'Nuclear Non-Proliferation Efforts in the Asia-Pacific Region', in Timothy L.H. McCormack, Michael Tilbury and Gillian D. Triggs, eds., *A Century of War and Peace: Asia-Pacific Perspectives on the Centenary of the 1899 Hague Peace Conference* (The Hague, Kluwer Law International 2001) pp. 213-221
- Datan, Merav, Brian Rawson and Lars Pohlmeier, 'Elimination of Nuclear Weapons: Strategies for Overcoming the Political Deadlock', in Ilkka Taipale et al., eds., *War or Health? A Reader* (London, Zed 2002) pp. 482-496
- Dembinski, Ludwik, 'Nuclear Disarmament at the UN: Mechanisms, Achievements, Prospects', 14 *International Geneva Yearbook* (2000-2001) pp. 1-23
- Den Dekker, G., 'Nieuwe strategische kernwapenbeheersing: meer dan een voetnoot in de geschiedenis?', 33 *Vrede en Veiligheid* (2002) pp. 149-153
- Dhanapala, Jayantha, 'Prospects for Nuclear Disarmament', in Timothy L.H. McCormack, Michael Tilbury and Gillian D. Triggs, eds., *A Century of War and Peace: Asia-Pacific Perspectives on the Centenary of the 1899 Hague Peace Conference* (The Hague, Kluwer Law International 2001) pp. 201-212
- Kile, Shannon, 'Nuclear Arms Control and Ballistic Missile Defence', *SIPRI Yearbook* (2001) pp. 423-456
- Schuette, Sarah P., 'U.S. Economic Sanctions Regarding the Proliferation of Nuclear Weapons: A Call for Reform of the Arms Export Control Act Sanctions', 35 *Cornell ILJ* (2002) pp. 231-262

11.22   Chemical and Biological Weapons

Books
- Carus, W.S., *Bioterrorism and Biocrimes: The Illicit Use of Biological Agents Since 1900*, rev. edn. (Washington, Center for Counterproliferation Research 2001) 209 pp.
- Nair, Roshila, ed., *Chemical and Biological Warfare: Non-Proliferation and the Ethics of Science* (Cape Town, University of Cape Town, Centre for Conflict Resolution 2001) 60 pp.
- Sims, Nicholas A., *The Evolution of Biological Disarmament* (Oxford, Oxford University Press 2001) 203 pp.
- Wright, Susan, ed., *Biological Warfare and Disarmament: New Problems/New Perspectives* (Lanham, Rowman & Littlefield 2002) 458 pp.
- Yepes-Enríquez, Rodrigo and Lisa Tabassi, *Treaty Enforcement and International Cooperation in Criminal Matters; With Special Reference to the Chemical Weapons Convention* (The Hague, T.M.C. Asser Press 2002) 656 pp.

Articles
- Dando, Malcolm, 'Scientific and Technological Change and the Future of the CWC: The Problem of Non-Lethal Weapons', 4 *Disarmament Forum* (2002) pp. 33-44
- Feakes, Daniel, 'Evaluating the CWC Verification System', 4 *Disarmament Forum* (2002) pp. 11-21
- Guesnier, Francine M., 'World Trade Center Attacks: Fears of Biological Warfare Stand in the Wake', *Colorado Jl Environ. L & Pol.* (2001) pp. 181-190

- Kelle, Alexander, 'The First CWC Review Conference: Taking Stock and Paving the Way Ahead', 4 *Disarmament Forum* (2002) pp. 3-9
- Kervers, Onno, 'Strengthening Compliance with the Biological Weapons Convention: The Protocol Negotiations', 7 *Journal of Conflict and Security Law* (2002) pp. 275-292
- Kraatz-Wadsack, Gabriele, 'Die Verifikation biologischer Waffen: Abrüstung und Rüstungskontrolle in Irak', 57 *Internationale Politik* (2002) pp. 25-30
- Krutzsch, Walter and Adolf von Wagner, 'Die Verifizierung des Chemiewaffenverbots', 57 *Internationale Politik* (2002) pp. 55-60
- Pearson, Graham S., 'The Biological and Toxin Weapons Convention: Report from Geneva', 54 *The CBW Conventions Bulletin* (2001) pp. 13-26
- Rosenau, William, 'Aum Shinrikyo's Biological Weapons Program: Why Did It Fail?', 24 *Studies in Conflict and Terrorism* (2001) pp. 289-301
- Schaller, Christan, 'Massenvernichtungswaffen und Präventivkrieg – Möglichkeiten der Rechtfertigung einer militärischen Intervention im Irak aus völkerrechtlicher Sicht', 62 *ZaöRV* (2002) pp. 641-668
- Zanders, Jean Pascal, 'Chemical and Biological Weapon Developments and Arms Control', *SIPRI Yearbook* (2001) pp. 513-548
- Zanders, Jean Pascal, 'The Chemical Weapons Convention and Universality: A Question of Quality over Quantity?', 4 *Disarmament Forum* (2002) pp. 23-31

12.1   CONFLICT PREVENTION

Books

- Adebajo, A. and C.L. Sriram, eds., *Managing Armed Conflicts in the 21st Century* (London, Frank Cass 2001) 221 pp.
- Ango-Ela, Paul, ed., *La prévention des conflits en Afrique centrale: prospective pour une culture de la paix* (Paris, Karthala 2001) 218 pp.
- Atlantische Commissie, *NMD: The End of Deterrence? American and European Perspectives on Missile Defence: Report of a Seminar in The Hague: 29 June 2001* (The Hague, Atlantische Commissie 2001) 55 pp.
- Campbell, Kurt M. and Michèle A. Flournoy, *To Prevail: An American Strategy for the Campaign Against Terrorism* (Washington, Center for Strategic and International Studies 2001) 399 pp.
- Economic Commission for Europe, *The Role of the Economic Dimension in Conflict Prevention: A UNECE-OSCE Colloquium with the Participation of Experts from NATO on the Role of the Economic Dimension in Conflict Prevention in Europe: Proceedings, Villars, Switzerland, 19-20 November 2001* (New York, United Nations Economic Commission for Europe 2002) 54 pp.
- García Izquierdo, Bernardo, *Una nueva oportunidad para la prevención de conflictos: análisis comparativo de las políticas de Estados Unidos y de la Unión Europea sobre la prevención de conflictos violentos* (Bilbao, Universidad de Deusto 2002) 89 pp.
- Hamburg, David A., *No More Killing Fields: Preventing Deadly Conflict* (Lanham, Rowman & Littlefield 2002) 365 pp.
- Hampson, Fen Osler and David M. Malone, eds., *From Reaction to Conflict Prevention: Opportunities for the UN System* (Boulder, Lynne Rienner 2002) 431 pp.

— Krummenacher, Heinz, *Conflict Prevention and Power Politics: Central Asia as a Show Case* (Berne, Schweizerische Friedensstiftung: Institut für Konfliktlösung 2001) 24 pp.
— Krummenacher, Heinz and Susanne Schmeidl, *Practical Challenges in Predicting Violent Conflict FAST: An Example of a Comprehensive Early-Warning Methodology* (Berne, Swiss Peace Foundation, Institute for Conflict Resolution 2001) 22 pp.
— Mekenkamp, Monique et al., eds., *Searching for Peace in Central and South Asia: An Overview of Conflict Prevention and Peacebuilding Activities* (Boulder, Lynne Rienner 2002) 665 pp.
— Meyer, E.C., *Balkans 2010: Report of an Independent Task Force* (New York, Council on Foreign Relations 2002) 120 pp.
— Muscat, Robert J., *Investing in Peace: How Development Aid Can Prevent or Promote Conflict* (Armonk, Sharpe 2002) 265 pp.
— Organisation for Economic Co-operation and Development, *Helping Prevent Violent Conflict: The DAC Guidelines* (Paris, Organisation for Economic Co-operation and Development 2001) 155 pp.
— Retiere, Alain and Heinz Schurmann-Zeggel, *Conflict Prevention and Peace Consolidation in the South Pacific: Papua New Guinea, Solomon Islands, Fiji Islands* (Brussels, European Commission Conflict Prevention and Crisis Management Unit 2002) 62 pp.
— Van de Goor, Luc, ed., *Mainstreaming Conflict Prevention: Concept and Practice* (Baden-Baden: Nomos 2002) 274 pp.
— Van der Stoel, M., *Conflictpreventie: de lessen van Kosovo en Macedonië* (Tilburg, Catholic University of Brabant 2002) 32 pp.
— Van Tongeren, Paul et al., eds., *Searching for Peace in Europe and Eurasia: An Overview of Conflict Prevention and Peacebuilding Activities* (Boulder, Lynne Rienner 2002) 831 pp.
— Wallensteen, Peter et al., *Conflict Prevention Through Development Co-operation: An Inventory of Recent Research Findings – With Implications for International Development Co-operation* (Uppsala, Department of Peace and Conflict Research 2001) 60 pp.

Articles
— Dwan, Renata, 'Armed Conflict Prevention, Management and Resolution', *SIPRI Yearbook* (2001) pp. 69-127
— Evans, Gareth, 'Conflict Prevention with Regard to Inter-Ethnic Issues, Including the Role of Third Parties: Experiences and Challenges from the Asian-Pacific Region', 8 *International Journal on Minority and Group Rights* (2001) pp. 31-38
— Levitt, Jeremy, 'Conflict Prevention, Management, and Resolution: Africa – Regional Strategies for the Prevention of Displacement and Protection of Displaced Persons: The Cases of the OAU, ECOWAS, SADC, and IGAD', 11 *Duke JCIL* (2001) pp. 39-79
— Murray, Rachel, 'Preventing Conflicts in Africa: The Need for a Wider Perspective', 45 *Journal of African Law* (2001) pp. 13-24
— Palma Valderrama, Hugo E., 'Paz, seguridad humana y prevención de conflictos en América Latina y el Caribe', 51 *Revista peruana de derecho internacional* (2001) pp. 205-218
— Rogier, Emeric, 'The Operational Role of the OSCE in the Field of Conflict Prevention: An Assessment of the Spillover Monitor Mission to Skopje (Macedonia)', in Victor Yves Ghebali and Daniel Warner, eds., *The Operational Role of the OSCE in Southeastern Europe: Contributing to Regional Stability in the Balkans* (Aldershot, Ashgate 2001) pp. 47-51

- Shoemaker, Jolynn, 'In War and Peace: Women and Conflict Prevention', 5 *Civil Wars* (2002) pp. 27-54
- Spehar, Elizabeth, 'The Role of the Organization of American States in Conflict Prevention', 8 *International Journal on Minority and Group Rights* (2001) pp. 61-70

12.2   CONFLICT RESOLUTION

Books
- Evangelista, Matthew, *The Chechen Wars: Will Russia Go the Way of the Soviet Union?* (Washington, Brookings Institution 2002) 244 pp.
- Fitzduff, Mari, *Beyond Violence: Conflict Resolution Process in Northern Ireland* (Tokyo, United Nations University Press 2002) 252 pp.
- Gerson, Allan and Nat J. Colletta, *Privatizing Peace: From Conflict to Security* (Ardsley, Transnational Publishers 2002) 207 pp.
- Hauss, Charles, *International Conflict Resolution* (London, Continuum 2001) 244 pp.
- Höglund, Kristine, *Violence – Catalyst or Obstacle to Conflict Resolution? Seven Steps Propositions Concerning the Effect of Violence on Peace Negotiations* (Uppsala, Uppsala University, Department of Peace and Conflict Research 2001) 21 pp.
- Rogers, Paul and Scilla Elworthy, *The United States, Europe and the Majority World After 11 September* (Oxford, Oxford Research Group 2001) 13 pp.
- Said, Abdul Aziz et al., eds., *Peace and Conflict Resolution in Islam: Precept and Practice* (Lanham, University Press of America 2001) 298 pp.
- Samaddar, Ranabir and Helmut Reifeld, eds., *Peace as Process: Reconciliation and Conflict Resolution in South Asia* (New Delhi, Manohar 2001) 328 pp.
- Väyrynen, Tarja, *Culture and International Conflict Resolution: A Critical Analysis of the Work of John Burton* (Manchester, Manchester University 2001) 164 pp.

Articles
- Bukurura, Sufian Hemed, 'Traditional Institutions and Conflict Resolution in Swaziland: Some Observations on Recent Events', 17 *South African Journal on Human Rights* (2001) pp. 421-434
- Nagan, Winston P. and Lucie Atkins, 'Conflict Resolution and Democratic Transformation: Confronting the Shameful Past: Prescribing a Human Future', 119 *The South African Law Journal* (2002) pp. 174-214
- Yasuaki, Onuma, 'The ICJ: An Emperor Without Clothes? International Conflict Resolution, Article 38 of the ICJ Statute and the Sources of International Law', in Nisuke Ando, Edward McWhinney, Rudiger Wolfrum and Betsy Baker Röben, eds., *Liber Amicorum Judge Shigeru Oda* (The Hague, Kluwer Law International 2002) pp. 191-212
- Zegs, Zegbe, 'Le recours à la force en Afrique: un moyen éfficace pour résoudre les conflits armés entre les états?', 18 *Revue de droit Africain: doctrine & jurisprudence* (2001) pp. 171-206

12.3   THE PEACE MOVEMENT

Books

— Alatas, Ali, *A Voice for a Just Peace: A Collection of Speeches* (Jakarta, Gramedia Pustaka Utama 2001) 616 pp.
— Ango-Ela, Paul, ed., *La prévention des conflits en Afrique centrale: prospective pour une culture de la paix* (Paris, Karthala 2001) 218 pp.
— Ayissi, Anatole, ed., *Cooperating for Peace in West Africa: An Agenda for the 21st Century* (Geneva, United Nations Institute for Disarmament Research 2001) 154 pp.
— Biggar, Nigel, ed., *Burying the Past: Making Peace and Doing Justice After Civil Conflict* (Washington, Georgetown University Press 2001) 312 pp.
— Boutros-Ghali, Boutros, *Paix, développement, démocratie: trois agendas pour gérer la planète* (Paris, Pedone 2002) 235 pp.
— Boyce, James K., *Investing in Peace: Aid and Conditionality After Civil Wars* (Oxford, Oxford University Press 2002) 85 pp.
— Darby, John, *The Effects of Violence on Peace Processes* (Washington, United States Institute of Peace Press 2001) 153 pp.
— Enderlin, Charles, *Le rêve brisé: histoire de l'échec du processsus de paix au Proche-Orient (1995-2002)* (Paris, Fayard 2002) 396 pp.
— Englund, Harri, *From War to Peace on the Mozambique-Malawi Borderland* (Edinburgh, Edinburgh University Press 2002) 217 pp.
— Jones, Dorothy V., *Toward a Just World: The Critical Years in the Search for International Justice* (Chicago, University of Chicago Press 2002) 270 pp.
— McCormack, Timothy L.H., Michael Tilbury and Gillian D. Triggs, eds., *A Century of War and Peace: Asia-Pacific Perspectives on the Centenary of the 1899 Hague Peace Conference* (The Hague, Kluwer Law International 2001) 292 pp.
— Nagel, Stuart S., *Promoting Peace: Via Legal and International Policy* (Lanham, Lexington Books 2001) 329 pp.
— Price, Monroe E. and Mark Thompson, eds., *Forging Peace: Intervention, Human Rights and the Management of Media Space* (Edinburgh, Edinburgh University Press 2002) 408 pp.
— Williams, Paul R. and Michael P. Scharf, *Peace with Justice? War Crimes and Accountability in the Former Yugoslavia* (Lanham, Rowman & Littlefield 2002) 323 pp.

Articles

— Albright, Madeleine and B. Joseph White, 'Interview: The Business of Peace', 35 *Vanderbilt JTL* (2002) pp. 697-701
— Bisharat, George E., 'Peace and the Political Imperative of Legal Reform in Palestine', in Sanford R. Silverbug, ed., *Palestine and International Law: Essays on Politics and Economics* (Jefferson, McFarland 2001) pp. 214-250
— Caflisch, L., 'Cent ans de règlement pacifique des différends interétatiques', 288 *Recueil des Cours* (2001) pp. 245-468
— Cardenas, Maria Cristina, 'Colombia's Peace Process: The Continuous Search for Peace', 15 *Florida Journal of International Law* (2002) pp. 273-297
— Cederman, Lars-Erik, 'Modeling the Democratic Peace as a Kantian Selection Process', 45 *Journal of Conflict Resolution* (2001) pp. 470-502
— Chi, Bongdo, 'Friedenspolitik in und für Korea – eine völkerrechtliche Perspektive', 34 *Verfassung und Recht in Übersee* (2001) pp. 241-252

– Cornell, Timothy and Lance Salisbury, 'The Importance of Civil Law in the Transition to Peace: Lessons from the Human Rights Chamber for Bosnia and Herzegovina', 35 *Cornell ILJ* (2002) pp. 389-426

– Ellis, Mark S., 'International Legal Assistance', in M. Cherif Bassiouni, ed., *Post-Conflict Justice* (Ardsley, Transnational Publishers 2002) pp. 921-943

– Esquirol, Jorge L., 'Can International Law Help? An Anlaysis of the Colombian Peace Process', 13 *Hague YIL* (2000) pp. 50-56

– Evans, Gareth, 'Achieving Peace in Cambodia', in Timothy L.H. McCormack, Michael Tilbury and Gillian D. Triggs, eds., *A Century of War and Peace: Asia-Pacific Perspectives on the Centenary of the 1899 Hague Peace Conference* (The Hague, Kluwer Law International 2001) pp. 235-246

– Fort, Timothy L. and Cindy A. Schipani, 'The Role of the Corporation in Fostering Sustainable Peace', 35 *Vanderbilt JTL* (2002) pp. 389-436

– Gries, Tobias, 'A Right to Peace?', in ELSA International, ed., *International Law as We Enter the 21st Century: International Focus Programme 1997-1999* (Berlin, Spitz 2001) pp. 213-228

– Juma, Laurence, 'The Human Rights Approach to Peace in Sierra Leone: The Analysis of the Peace Process and Human Rights Enforcement in a Civil War Situation', 30 *Denver JIL & Pol.* (2002) pp. 325-376

– Kramer, Callie, 'Kofi Anan and United Nations Win the 2001 Nobel Peace Prize', 18 *New York Law School Journal of Human Rights* (2002) pp. 475-480

– Lalor, Paul, 'The Palestinian-Israeli Peace Process in 2000', *SIPRI Yearbook* (2001) pp. 162-173

– Lenk, Arthur, 'Fact-Finding as a Peace Negotiation Tool: The Mitchell Report and the Israeli-Palestinian Peace Process', 24 *Loyola LA I & Comp.LR* (2002) pp. 289-325

– Meier, Benjamin M., 'Reunification of Cyprus: The Possibility of Peace in the Wake of Past Failure', 34 *Cornell ILJ* (2001) pp. 455-480

– Mitchell, George J., 'Negotiating for Peace in Northern Ireland', 37 *Stanford JIL* (2001) pp. 163-169

– Morris, Madeline, 'Lacking a Leviathan: The Quandaries of Peace and Accountability', in M. Cherif Bassiouni, ed., *Post-Conflict Justice* (Ardsley, Transnational Publishers 2002) pp. 135-153

– Nesteruk, Jeffrey, 'Conceptions of the Corporation and the Prospects of Sustainable Peace', 35 *Vanderbilt JTL* (2002) pp. 437-456

– Nobel, Peter, 'Alfred Bernhard Nobel and the Peace Prize', 83 *IRRC* (2001) pp. 259-273

– Palmer, Laura R., 'A Very Clear and Present Danger: Hate Speech, Media Reform and Post-Conflict Democratization in Kosovo', 26 *Yale JIL* (2001) pp. 179-218

– Przetacznik, Frank, 'The Concept of a Genuine and Just Peace', 24 *Polish Yearbook of International Law* 1999-(2000) pp. 9-45

– Tönnies, Sibylle, 'Weltfrieden und Völkerrecht – Made in the USA oder Aufgabe der UNO?', 46 *Blätter für deutsche und internationale Politik* (2001) pp. 829-836

– Williams, Paul R., 'The Role of Justice in Peace Negotiations', in M. Cherif Bassiouni, ed., *Post-Conflict Justice* (Ardsley, Transnational Publishers 2002) pp. 115-133

13.1   JUS AD BELLUM

Books
- Everts, Philip and Pierangelo Isernia, eds., *Public Opinion and the International Use of Force* (London, Routledge 2001) 293 pp.
- Findlay, Trevor, *The Use of Force in UN Peace Operations* (Oxford, Oxford University Press 2002) 486 pp.
- Franck, Thomas M., *Recourse to Force: State Action Against Threats and Armed Attacks* (Cambridge, Cambridge University Press 2002) 205 pp.
- Jaberg, Sabine, *Kants Friedensschrift und die Idee kollektiver Sicherheit. Eine Rechtfertigungsgrundlage für den Kosovo-Krieg der NATO?* (Hamburg, Institut für Friedensforschung und Sicherheitspolitik 2002) 66 pp.
- Krisch, Nico, *Selbstverteidigung und kollektive Sicherheit* (Berlin, Springer 2001) 449 pp.
- Prittwitz, Cornelius, 'Krieg als Strafe – Strafrecht als Krieg: wird nach dem "11. September" nichts mehr sein wie es War?', in Cornelius Prittwitz, ed., *Festschrift für Klaus Lüderssen* (Baden-Baden, Nomos 2002) pp. 499-514
- Rodin, David, *War and Self-Defense* (Oxford, Clarendon Press 2002) 213 pp.
- Sur, S., *The Use of Force in the Kosovo Affair and International Law* (Paris, Institut français des relations internationals 2001) 43 pp.
- Zambelli, Mirko, *La constatation des situations de l'article 39 de la Charte des Nations Unies par le Conseil de sécurité: le champ d'application des pouvoirs prévus au chapitre VII de la Charte des Nations Unies* (Geneva, Helbing & Lichtenhahn 2002) 517 pp.

Articles
- Abraham, Garth and Kevin Hopkins, 'Bombing for Humanity: The American Response to the 11 September Attacks and the Plea of Self-Defence', 119 *The South African Law Journal* (2002) pp. 783-801
- Abramowitz, David, 'The President, the Congress, and Use of Force: Legal and Political Considerations in Authorizing Use of Force Against International Terrorism', 43 *Harvard ILJ* (2002) pp. 71-103
- Arai-Takahashi, Yutaka, 'Shifting Boundaries of the Right of Self-Defence – Appraising the Impact of the September 11 Attacks on Jus ad Bellum', 36 *International Lawyer* (2002) pp. 1081-1102
- Barkham, Jason, 'Information Warfare and International Law on the Use of Force', 34 *NY Univ. JIL & Pol.* (2001) pp. 57-113
- Beard, Jack M., 'America's New War on Terror: The Case for Self-Defense Under International Law', 25 *Harvard Journal of Law & Public Policy* (2002) pp. 559-590
- Bonafede, Michael C., 'Here, There, and Everywhere: Assessing the Proportionality Doctrine and U.S. Uses of Force in Response to Terrorism After the September 11 Attacks', 88 *Cornell LR* (2002) pp. 155-214
- Bouchet-Saulnier, Françoise, 'Just War, Unjust Means? International Humanitarian Law After September 11', 58 *The World Today* (2002) pp. 26-28
- Brown, Chris, 'A Qualified Defence of the Use of Force for "Humanitarian" Reasons', in Ken Booth, ed., *The Kosovo Tragedy: The Human Rights Dimensions* (London, Frank Cass 2001) pp. 283-288
- Brownlie, Ian, 'International Law and the Use of Force by States Revisited', 21 *Australian YIL* (2001) pp. 21-37

– Bruha, Thomas, 'Gewaltverbot und humanitäres Völkerrecht nach dem 11. September 2001', 40 *Archiv des Völkerrechts* (2002) pp. 383-421

– Bruha, Thomas and Matthias Bortfeld, 'Terrorismus und Selbstverteidugung: Voraussetzungen und Umfang erlaubter Selbstverteidigungsmaßnahmen nach den Anschlägen vom 11. September 2001', 49 *Vereinte Nationen* (2001) pp. 161-163

– Bugnion, François, 'Guerre juste, guerre d'agression et droit International humanitaire', 84 *IRRC* (2002) pp. 523-546

– Bush, Jonathan A., '"The Supreme...Crime" and Its Origins: The Lost Legislative History of the Crime of Aggressive War', 102 *Columbia LR* (2002) pp. 2324-2423

– Byers, Michael, 'Terrorism, the Use of Force and International Law After 11 September 2001', 51 *ICLQ* (2002) pp. 401-414

– Ceulemans, C., 'Operatie Allied Force versus operatie Enduring Freedom. Een vergelijkende bellum-justum-analyse', 33 *Vrede en Veiligheid* (2002) pp. 9-32

– Charney, Jonathan I., 'The Use of Force Against Terrorism and International Law', 95 *AJIL* (2001) pp. 835-839

– Davis, Edward B., Sheila M. Davis and Terry Mays, 'The Legitimate Use of Force', 40 *Revue de droit militaire et de droit de la guerre* (2001) pp. 61-85

– Delbrück, Jost, 'The Fight Against Global Terrorism: Self-Defense or Collective Security as International Police Action? Some Comments on the International Legal Implications of the "War Against Terrorism"', 44 *GYIL* (2001) pp. 9-24

– Ducheine, P.A.L., 'The sky is the limit? Legitimiteit van interstatelijk geweld gebruik', 171 *Militaire Spectator* (2002) pp. 370-374

– Duursma, J., 'Preventing and Solving Wars of Seccession: Recent Unorthodox Views on the Use of Force', in G.P.H. Kreijen, M.M.T.A. Brus, A.E. de Vos, C.J.R. Dugard and J. Duursma, eds., *State, Sovereignty, and International Governance* (Oxford, Oxford University Press 2002) pp. 349-372

– Egan, Patrick T., 'The Kosovo Intervention and Collective Self-Defence', 8 *International Peacekeeping* (2001) pp. 39-58

– Fernández Tomás, Antonio Francisco, 'El recurso al artículo del Tratado de Washington tras los acontecimientos del 11 septiembre: mucho ruido y pocas nueces', 53 *Revista española de derecho internacional* (2001) pp. 205-226

– Fornasier, Matteo and Jens-Uwe Franck, 'Die NATO-Luftangriffe auf die Bundesrepublik Jugoslawien (BRJ) und das völkerrechtliche Gewaltverbot', 24 *Jura* (2002) pp 520-525

– Franck, Thomas M., 'Terrorism and the Right of Self-Defense', 95 *AJIL* (2001) pp. 839-843

– Frost, Mervyn, 'War, Policing or Global Civil Defence? The Justified Use of Violence in Contemporary International Relations', 10 *WeltTrends* (2002) pp. 35-48

– Frulli, M., 'Le operazioni di "peacekeeping" delle Nazioni Unite e l'uso della forza', 84 *RDI* (2001) pp. 347-392

– González Vega, Javier A., 'Los atentados del 11 de septiembre, la operación "Libertad Duradera" y el derecho de legítima defensa', 53 *Revista española de derecho internacional* (2001) pp. 247-271

– Gray, Christine, 'The US National Security Strategy and the New "Bush Doctrine" on Preemptive Self-Defense', 1 *Chinese Journal of International Law* (2002) pp. 437-447

– Gray, Christine, 'From Unity to Polarization: International Law and the Use of Force Against Iraq', 13 *EJIL* (2002) pp. 1-19

– Griffiths, Richard L., 'International Law, the Crime of Aggression and the Ius ad Bellum', 2 *International Criminal Law Review* (2002) pp. 301-373
– Gross, Emanuel, 'Thwarting Terrorist Acts by Attacking the Perpetrators or Their Commanders as an Act of Self-Defense: Human Rights Versus the State's Duty to Protect Its Citizens', 15 *Temple International & Comparative Law Journal* (2001) pp. 195-246
– Holcomb, M. Scott, 'Operation Enduring Freedom: The Use of Force in Self-Defense Against Al Qaida and the Taliban', 40 *Revue de droit militaire et de droit de la guerre* (2001) pp. 115-145
– Jensen, Eric Talbot, 'Computer Attacks on Critical National Infrastructure: A Use of Force Invoking the Right of Self-Defense', 38 *Stanford JIL* (2002) pp. 207-240
– Juan, Michelle Ann U., 'Testing the Legality of the Attack on Afghanistan', 47 *Ateneo Law Journal* (2002) pp. 499-551
– Krajewski, Markus, 'Terroranschläge in den USA und Krieg gegen Afghanistan: welche Antworten gibt das Völkerrecht?', 34 *Kritische Justiz* (2001) pp. 363-383
– Krajewski, Markus, 'Selbstverteidigung gegen bewaffnete Angriffe nicht-staatlicher Organisation – Der 11. September 2001 und seine Folgen', 40 *Archiv des Völkerrechts* (2002) pp. 183-214
– Kritsiotis, Dino, 'On the Jus ad Bellum and Jus in Bello of Operation Enduring Freedom', 96 *Proc. ASIL* (2002) pp. 35-41
– Leaning, J., 'Was the Afghan Conflict a Just War? An Analysis of the "Just War" Theory Poses Questions About US Action in Afghanistan', 324 *British Medical Journal* (2002) pp. 353-356
– Magenis, Sean D., 'Natural Law as the Customary International Law of Self-Defense', 20 *Boston Univ. ILJ* (2002) pp. 413-435
– Manusama, Kenneth M., 'Terrorisme en zelfverdediging in de Veiligheidsraad', 30 *Vrede en Veiligheid* (2001) pp. 481-499
– Martin, Francisco Forrest, 'Using International Human Rights Law for Establishing a Unified Use of Force Rule in the Law of Armed Conflict', 64 *Saskatchean Law Review* (2001) pp. 347-396
– Miller, Judith, 'NATO's Use of Force in the Balkans', 45 *New York Law School Law Review* (2001) pp. 91-100
– Miller, Judith, 'Comments on the Use of Force in Afghanistan', 35 *Cornell ILJ* (2002) pp. 605-610
– Müllerson, Rein, 'Jus ad bellum: plus ça change (le monde) plus c'est la même chose (le droit)?', 7 *Journal of Conflict & Security Law* (2002) pp. 149-189
– Murase, Shinya, 'The Relationship Between the UN Charter and General International Law Regarding Non-Use of Force: The Case of NATO's Air Campaign in the Kosovo Crisis of 1999', in Nisuke Ando, Edward McWhinney, Rudiger Wolfrum and Betsy Baker Röben, eds., *Liber Amicorum Judge Shigeru Oda* (The Hague, Kluwer Law International 2002) pp. 1543-1554
– Myjer, Eric P.J. and Nigel D. White, 'The Twin Towers Attack: An Unlimited Right to Self-Defence?', 7 *Journal of Conflict & Security Law* (2002) pp. 5-17
– O'Connell, Mary Ellen, 'American Exceptionalism and the International Law of Self-Defense', 31 *Denver JIL & Pol.* (2002) pp. 43-57
– Pails, Rodney, 'Self-Determination, the Use of Force and International Law: An Analytical Framework', 20 *University of Tasmania Law Review* (2001) pp. 70-97

– Pemmaraju, Sreenivasa Rao, 'International Organizations and Use of Force', in Nisuke Ando, Edward McWhinney, Rudiger Wolfrum and Betsy Baker Röben, eds., *Liber Amicorum Judge Shigeru Oda* (The Hague, Kluwer Law International 2002) pp. 1575-1608

– Perrin de Brichambaut, Marc, 'Le recours à la force et l'emploi de la force: le cas du Kosovo et celui de l'Afghanistan', in Marc Perrin de Brichambaut, Jean-François Dobelle and Marie-Reine d'Haussy, *Leçons de droit international public* (Paris, Presses de Sciences Po 2002) pp. 281-310

– Petras, Christopher M., 'The Use of Force in Response to Cyber-Attack on Commercial Space Systems: Reexamining "Self-Defense" in Outer Space in Light of the Convergence of U.S. Military and Commercial Space Activities', 67 *Journal of Air Law and Commerce* (2002) pp. 1213-1268

– Raines, Joshua, 'Osama, Augustine, and Assassination: The Just War Doctrine and Targeted Killings', 12 *Transn. L & Contemp. Probs.* (2002) pp. 217-243

– Ratner, Steven R., 'Jus ad Bellum and Jus in Bello After September 11', 96 *AJIL* (2002) pp. 905-921

– Sadat M., S.H., 'An Agenda for War: The Law of Self-Defence in the Light of the 11 September Terrorist Attacks', 10 *Tilburg For. LR* (2002) pp. 76-81

– Saito, Natsu Taylor, 'Will Force Trump Legality After September 11? American Jurisprudence Confronts the Rule of Law', 17 *Georgetown Immigration Law Journal* (2002) pp. 1-62

– Schaller, Christan, 'Massenvernichtungswaffen und Präventivkrieg – Möglichkeiten der Rechtfertigung einer militärischen Intervention im Irak aus völkerrechtlicher Sicht', 62 *ZaöRV* (2002) pp. 641-668

– Schreuer, Christoph, 'Is There a Legal Basis for the Air Strikes Against Iraq?', 3 *Int. LF* (2001) pp. 72-75

– Schüßler, Rudolf, 'Humanitäre Intervention und gerechter Krieg', 19 *Vierteljahresschrift für Sicherheit und Frieden* (2001) pp. 138-145

– Schüßler, Rudolf, 'Die humanitäre Intervention in der Doktrin des gerechten Krieges', in Erwin Müller, Patricia Schneider and Kristina Thony, eds., *Menschenrechtsschutz: politische Maßnahmen, zivilgesellschaftliche Strategien, humanitäre Interventionen* (Baden-Baden, Nomos 2002) pp. 200-217

– Singh, Ravi Pratap, 'Rogue Doctrine and Missile Defence: A Prescription for More Aggression, More Intervention', 57 *India Quarterly* (2001) pp. 139-150

– Stahn, Carsten, 'Collective Security and Self-Defence After the September 11 Attacks', 10 *Tilburg For. LR* (2002) pp. 10-42

– Van Schooten, Hanneke and Wouter G. Werner, 'Democratic Control on the Use of Force Under the Dutch Constitution', 10 *Tilburg For. LR* (2002) pp. 43-62

– Weigel, George, 'Pope John XXIII Lecture. The Just War Tradition and the World After September 11', 51 *Catholic University Law Review* (2002) pp. 689-714

– Wielink, J.P.J. and M. Zieck, 'Veiligheidsraad-resolutie 1441 en de vraag naar de rechtmatigheid van unilateraal militair geweld tegen Irak', 77 *Nederlands Juristenblad* (2002) pp. 2240-2241

– Wingfield, Thomas C., 'Chivalry in the Use of Force', 32 *The University of Toledo Law Review* (2001) pp. 111-136

– Yee, Sienho, 'The Potential Impact of the Possible US Responses to the 9-11 Atrocities on the Law Regarding the Use of Force and Self-Defence', 1 *Chinese Journal of International Law* (2002) pp. 287-293

— Zacher, Mark W., 'The Territorial Integrity Norm: International Boundaries and the Use of Force', 55 *International Organization* (2001) pp. 215-250

13.2   THE LAW RELATING TO TERRORISM AND COUNTER-TERRORISM

Books

— Alexander, Yonah, ed., *Combating Terrorism: Strategies of Ten Countries* (Michigan, University of Michigan Press 2002) 426 pp.
— Alexander, Yonah and Edgar H. Brenner, eds., *Terrorism and the Law* (Ardsley, Transnational Publishers 2001) 175 pp.
— Bassiouni, M. Cherif, *International Terrorism: Multilateral Conventions (1937-2001)* (Ardsley, Transnational Publishers 2001) 608 pp.
— Bishara, Marwan, *Palestine/Israel: Peace or Apartheid: Occupation, Terrorism and the Future*, 2nd updated edn. (London, Zed 2002) 173 pp.
— Bribosia, Emmanuelle and Anne Weyembergh, eds., *Lutte contre le terrorisme et droits fondamentaux* (Brussels, Bruylant 2002) 305 pp.
— Brouwers, A., *Met vereende kracht: Europa en de oorlog tegen (Amerika) terrorisme* (The Hague, Atlantische Commissie 2002) 46 pp.
— Cappè, Francesco, ed., *International Terrorism Prevention Strategies* (Turin, United Nations Interregional Crime & Justice Research Institute 2002) 127 pp.
— Corten, Olivier, ed., *Le droit international face au terrorisme: après le 11 septembre 2001* (Paris, Pedone 2002) 356 pp.
— Dhanapala, Jayantha et al., *Terrorism and Disarmament* (New York, United Nations Department for Disarmament Affairs 2001) 63 pp.
— Donohue, Laura K., *Counter-Terrorist Law and Emergency Powers in the United Kingdom, 1922-2000* (Dublin, Irish Academic Press 2001) 422 pp.
— Gill, T.D., *The 11th September and the International Law of Military Operations* (Amsterdam, Vossiuspers UvA 2002) 43 pp.
— Heisbourg, François and la Fondation pour la Recherche Stratégique, *Hyperterrorisme: la nouvelle guerre* (Paris, Odile Jacob 2001) 270 pp.
— Klugmann, Marcel, *Europäische Menschenrechtskonvention und antiterroristische Maßnahmen: eine Untersuchung der Rechtsprechung des Europäischen Gerichtshofes für Menschenrechte am Beispiel des Nordirland- und des Kurdenkonfliktes* (Frankfurt am Main, Peter Lang 2002) 178 pp.
— Strawson, John, *Law After Ground Zero* (London, Cavendish Publishing 2002) 242 pp.
— United Nations, *International Instruments Related to the Prevention and Suppression of International Terrorism* (New York, United Nations 2001) 266 pp.
— Van Krieken, Peter J., *Terrorism and the International Legal Order: With Special Reference to the UN, the EU and Cross-Border Aspects* (The Hague, T.M.C. Asser Press 2002) 482 pp.
— Walker, Clive, *Blackstone's Guide to the Anti-Terrorism Legislation* (Oxford, Oxford University Press 2002) 569 pp.

Articles

— Abi-Saab, Georges, 'The Proper Role of International Law in Combating Terrorism', 1 *Chinese Journal of International Law* (2002) pp. 305-327

— Abramowitz, David, 'The President, the Congress, and Use of Force: Legal and Political Considerations in Authorizing Use of Force Against International Terrorism', 43 *Harvard ILJ* (2002) pp. 71-103

— Anderson, Kenneth, 'What to Do with Bin Laden and Al Qaeda Terrorists? A Qualified Defense of Military Commissions and United States Policy on Detainees at Guantanamo Bay Naval Base', 25 *Harvard Journal of Law & Public Policy* (2002) pp. 591-634

— Anderson, Malcolm and Joanna Apap, 'What Future for Counter-Terrorism as an Objective of European Police Co-operation?', in Malcolm Anderson and Joanna Apap, eds., *Police and Justice Co-operation and the New European Borders* (The Hague, Kluwer Law International 2002) pp. 227-240

— Aust, Anthony, 'Counter-Terrorism: A New Approach: The International Convention for the Suppression of the Financing of Terrorism', 5 *MPYBUNL* (2001) pp. 285-306

— Ayers, Andrew, 'The Financial Action Task Force: The War on Terrorism Will Not Be Fought on the Battlefield', 18 *New York Law School Journal of Human Rights* (2002) 449-459

— Bâli, Asli, 'Stretching the Limits of International Law: The Challenge of Terrorism', 8 *ILSA JI & CL* (2002) pp. 403-416

— Bassiouni, M. Cherif, 'Legal Control of International Terrorism: A Policy-Oriented Assessment', 43 *Harvard ILJ* (2002) pp. 83-103

— Bayefsky, Anne F., 'Panel on the Responses to the Recent Terrorist Attacks on the U.S.', 8 *ILSA JI & CL* (2002) pp. 349-352

— Beard, Jack M., 'America's New War on Terror: The Case for Self-Defense Under International Law', 25 *Harvard Journal of Law & Public Policy* (2002) pp. 559-590

— Benoit, Loïck, 'La lutte contre le terrorisme dans le cadre du deuxième pilier: un nouveau volet des relations extérieurs de l'Union européenne', 3 *Revue du droit de l'Union européenne* (2002) pp. 283-313

— Biggio, Frank A., 'Neutralizing the Threat: Reconsidering Existing Doctrines in the Emerging War on Terrorism', 34 *Case Western Reserve JIL* (2002) pp. 1-43

— Binning, Peter, 'In Safe Hands? Striking the Balance Between Privacy and Security: Anti-Terrorist Finance Measures', 6 *European Human Rights Law Review* (2002) pp. 737-749

— Black-Branch, Jonathan L., 'Powers of Detention of Suspected International Terrorists Under the United Kingdom Anti-Terrorism, Crime and Security Act 2001: Dismantling the Cornerstones of a Civil Society', 27 *European Law Review* (2002) pp. 19-32

— Bloed, Arie, 'The OSCE and the War Against Terror', 12 *Helsinki monitor* (2001) pp. 313-317

— Bonafede, Michael C., 'Here, There, and Everywhere: Assessing the Proportionality Doctrine and U.S. Uses of Force in Response to Terrorism After the September 11 Attacks', 88 *Cornell LR* (2002) pp. 155-214

— Bonner, David, 'Managing Terrorism While Respecting Human Rights? European Aspects of the Anti-Terrorism Crime and Security Act 2001', 8 *European Public Law* (2002) pp. 497-524

— Bruha, Thomas and Matthias Bortfeld, 'Terrorismus und Selbstverteidigung: Voraussetzungen und Umfang erlaubter Selbstverteidigungsmaßnahmen nach den Anschlägen vom 11. September 2001', 49 *Vereinte Nationen* (2001) pp. 161-163

– Bruin, R. and K. Wouters, 'Terrorisme en refoulement, De invloed van de strijd tegen het terrorisme op het absolute karakter van het refoulementverbod', 18 *Nieuwsbrief Asiel- en Vluchtelingenrecht* (2002) pp. 428-438

– Bulterman, Mielle, 'De financiële strijd tegen het terrorisme en de mensenrechten', 27 *NJCM-bulletin* (2002) pp. 834-848

– Byers, Michael, 'Terror and the Future of International Law', in Ken Booth and Tim Dunne, eds., *Worlds in Collision: Terror and the Future of Global Order* (Basingstoke, Palgrave 2002) pp. 118-127

– Byers, Michael, 'Terrorism, the Use of Force and International Law After 11 September 2001', 51 *ICLQ* (2002) pp. 401-414

– Caccese, Gina, 'The United Nations and Terrorism: The Response to September 11th and Mayor Giuliani's Address to the General Assembly', 18 *New York Law School Journal of Human Rights* (2002) pp. 461-466

– Carcione, Massimo Marco, 'Terrorism and Cultural Property: A "Conflict" of a Non-International Character', 10 *Tilburg For. LR* (2002) pp. 82-89

– Cassese, Antonio, 'Terrorism Is Also Disrupting Some Crucial Legal Categories of International Law', 12 *EJIL* (2001) pp. 993-1001

– Charney, Jonathan I., 'The Use of Force Against Terrorism and International Law', 95 *AJIL* (2001) pp. 835-839

– Cohan, John Alan, 'Formulation of a State's Response to Terrorism and State-Sponsored Terrorism', 14 *Pace ILR* (2002) pp. 77-119

– Cohn, M., 'Understanding, Responding to, and Preventing Terrorism', 24 *Arab Studies Quarterly* (2002) pp. 25-30

– Condorelli, Luigi, 'Les attentats du 11 septembre et leurs suites: où va le droit international?', 105 *RGDIP* (2001) pp. 829-848

– Corten, Olivier and François Dubuisson, 'La guerre "antiterroriste" engagée par les Etats-Unis a-t-elle été autorisée par le Conseil de Sécurité?', 120 *Journal des tribunaux* (2001) pp. 889-895

– Das, Himamauli, 'The United States Sanctions Response to the Attacks of September 11, 2001: A Synopsis of Remarks at the NESL Rogue Regimes Conference', 36 *New England LR* (2002) pp. 943-955

– Delbrück, Jost, 'The Fight Against Global Terrorism: Self-Defense or Collective Security as International Police Action? Some Comments on the International Legal Implications of the "War Against Terrorism"', 44 *GYIL* (2001) pp. 9-24

– DeRose, Claudio, 'Lotta al terrorismo e par la pace nel rispetto dei diritti dell'uomo: un messaggio dall'Europa Unita', 53 *Il Consiglio di Stato* (2002) pp. 1243-1253

– De Schutter, Olivier, 'La Convention européenne des droits de l'homme à l'épreuve de la lutte contre le terrorisme', 13 *Revue universelle des droits de l'homme* (2001) pp. 185-207

– Dickenson, Laura A., 'Using Legal Process to Fight Terrorism: Detentions, Military Commissions, International Tribunals, and the Rule of Law', 75 *Southern California Law Review* (2002) pp. 1407-1492

– Dörenberg, A.J.T., 'International Society for Military Law and the Law of War: Seminar on Military Jurisdiction', 94 *Militair Rechtelijk Tijdschrift* (2001) pp. 378-381

– Drumbl, Mark A., 'Terrorist Crime, Taliban Guilt, Western Victims, and International Law', 31 *Denver JIL & Pol.* (2002) pp. 69-79

– Drumbl, Mark A., 'Judging the 11 September Terrorist Attack', 24 *HRQ* (2002) pp. 323-360

– Drumbl, Mark A., 'Victimhood in Our Neighborhood: Terrorist Crime, Taliban Guilt, and the Asymmetries of the International Legal Order', 81 *North Carolina Law Review* (2002) pp. 1-113

– Ecobescu, Nicolae, 'A New Phase in Fighting Terrorism', 8 *Romanian Journal of International Affairs* (2002) pp. 170-198

– Evans, Christopher M., 'Terrorism on Trial: The President's Constitutional Authority to Order the Prosecution of Suspected Terrorists by Military Commission', 51 *Duke Law Journal* (2002) pp. 1831-1856

– Fidler, David P., 'Bioterrorism, Public Health, and International Law', 3 *Chicago Journal of International Law* (2002) pp. 7-26

– Fijnaut, C., 'De aanslagen van 11 september 2001 en de reactie van de Europese Unie', 28 *Justitiële Verkenningen* (2002) pp. 26-44

– Fitzpatrick, Joan, 'Jurisdiction of Military Commissions and the Ambiguous War on Terrorism', 96 *AJIL* (2002) pp. 345-354

– Fitzgerald, Peter L., 'Managing "Smart Sanctions" Against Terrorism Wisely', 36 *New England LR* (2002) pp. 957-983

– Franck, Thomas M., 'Terrorism and the Right of Self-Defense', 95 *AJIL* (2001) pp. 839-843

– Frank, Jonathan A., 'A Return to Lockerbie and the Montreal Convention in the Wake of the September 11th Terrorist Attacks', 30 *Denver JIL & Pol.* (2002) pp. 532-546

– Frowein, Jochen Abr., 'Der Terrorismus als Herausforderung für das Völkerrecht', 62 *ZaöRV* (2002) pp. 879-905

– Fry, James D., 'Terrorism as a Crime Against Humanity and Genocide: The Backdoor to Universal Jurisdiction', 7 *UCLA Journal of International Law & Foreign Affairs* (2002) pp. 169-199

– Ganeles, Cheri, 'Technological Advancements and the Evolution of Terrorism', 8 *ILSA JI & CL* (2002) pp. 617-661

– Gasser, Hans-Peter, 'Acts of Terror, "Terrorism" and International Humanitarian Law', 84 *IRRC* (2002) pp. 547-570

– Geraghty, Thomas, 'The Criminal-Enemy Distinction: Prosecuting a Limited War Against Terrorism Following the September 11, 2001 Terrorist Attacks', 33 *McGeorge Law Review* (2002) pp. 551-591

– Ghatate, N.M., 'Combating International Terrorism: A Perspective', 42 *Indian JIL* (2002) pp. 194-198

– Giuliani, Rudolph, 'Combating Terrorism', 16 *Notre Dame Journal of Law, Ethics, and Public Policy* (2002) pp. 57-63

– Greenwood, Christopher, 'International Law and the "War Against Terrorism"', 78 *International Affairs* (2002) pp. 301-317

– Gross, Emanuel, 'Thwarting Terrorist Acts by Attacking the Perpetrators or Their Commanders as an Act of Self-Defense: Human Rights Versus the State's Duty to Protect Its Citizens', 15 *Temple International & Comparative Law Journal* (2001) pp. 195-246

– Gross, Emanuel, 'Legal Aspects of Tackling Terrorism: The Balance Between the Right of a Democracy to Defend Itself and the Protection of Human Rights', 6 *UCLA Journal of International Law & Foreign Affairs* (2001) pp. 89-169

– Gross, Emanuel, 'Use of Civilians as a Human Shield: What Legal and Moral Restrictions Pertain to a War Waged by a Democratic State Against Terrorism?', 16 *Emory ILR* (2002) pp. 445-524

— Gross, Emanuel, 'Democracy's Struggle Against Terrorism: The Powers of Military Commanders to Decide upon the Demolition of Houses, the Imposition of Curfews, Blockades, Encirclements and the Declaration of an Area as a Closed Military Area', 30 *Georgia Journal of International & Comparative Law* (2002) pp. 165-231

— Gross, Emanuel, 'Trying Terrorists – Justification for Differing Trial Rules: The Balance Between Security Considerations and Human Rights', 13 *Indiana International & Comparative Law Review* (2002) pp. 1-97

— Gross, Emanuel, 'Democracy in the War Against Terrorism: The Israeli Experience', 35 *Loyola of Los Angeles Law Review* (2002) pp. 1161-1216

— Gross, Emanuel, 'The Influence of Terrorist Attacks on Human Rights in the United States: The Aftermath of September 11, 2001', 28 *North Carolina Journal of International Law and Commercial Regulation* (2002) pp. 1-101

— Häußler, Ulf, 'Der Schutz der Rechtsidee: zur Notwendigkeit effektiver Terrorismusbekämpfung nach geltendem Völkerrecht', 34 *Zeitschrift für Rechtspolitik* (2001) pp. 537-541

— Henning, Virginia Helen, 'Anti-Terrorism, Crime and Security Act 2001: Has the United Kingdom Made a Valid Derogation from the European Convention on Human Rights?', 17 *Amer. Univ. ILR* (2002) pp. 1263-1297

— Hoffman, Michael H., 'Terrorists Are Unlawful Belligerents, Not Unlawful Combatants: A Distinction with Implications for the Future of International Humanitarian Law', 34 *Case Western Reserve JIL* (2002) pp. 227-230

— Hoffman, Michael H., 'Quelling Unlawful Belligerency: The Judicial Status and Treatment of Terrorists Under the Laws of War', 31 *Israel YB HR* (2001) pp. 161-181

— Hoye, William P., 'Fighting Fire with…Mire? Civil Remedies and the New War on State-Sponsored Terrorism', 12 *Duke JC & IL* (2002) pp. 105-152

— Hugues, Eric, 'La notion de terrorisme en droit international: en quête d'une définition juridique', 129 *Journal du droit international* (2002) pp. 753-771

— Janik Jr., Anton L., 'Prosecuting Al Qaeda: America's Human Rights Policy Interests Are Best Served by Trying Terrorists Under International Tribunals', 30 *Denver JIL & Pol.* (2002) pp. 498-531

— Jinks, Derek, 'International Human Rights Law and the War on Terrorism', 31 *Denver JIL & Pol.* (2002) pp. 58-68

— Johnson, Larry D., 'The Threat of Nuclear Terrorism and September 11th: Wake Up Call to Get the Treaties Right', 31 *Denver JIL & Pol.* (2002) pp. 80-86

— Kapur, Ratna, 'Un-Veiling Women's Rights in the "War on Terrorism"', 9 *Duke Journal of Gender Law & Policy* (2002) pp. 211-225

— Karber, Phillip A., 'Re-Constructing Global Aviation in an Era of the "Civil Aircraft as a Weapon of Destruction"', 25 *Harvard Journal of Law & Public Policy* (2002) pp. 781-814

— Kellman, Barry, 'An International Criminal Law Approach to Bioterrorism', 25 *Harvard Journal of Law & Public Policy* (2002) pp. 721-742

— Khan, Rahmatullah, 'The U.S. Military Tribunals to Try Terrorists', 62 *ZaöRV* (2002) pp. 293-316

— Kotzur, Markus, '"Krieg gegen den Terrorismus": politische Rhetorik oder neue Konturen des "Kriegsbegriffs" im Völkerrecht?', 40 *Archiv des Völkerrechts* (2002) pp. 454-479

— Krajewski, Markus, 'Terroranschläge in den USA und Krieg gegen Afghanistan: welche Antworten gibt das Völkerrecht?', 34 *Kritische Justiz* (2001) pp. 363-383

− Kumar, Nilendra, 'Prosecuting Terrorists: A Case for Use of Military Justice Apparatus', 42 *Indian JIL* (2002) pp. 187-193
− Lehrer, Rudolph, 'Unbalancing the Terrorists' Checkbook: Analysis of U.S. Policy in Its Economic War on International Terrorism', 10 *Tulane Journal of International and Comparative Law* (2002) pp. 333-360
− Leurdijk, Dick A., 'De strijd tegen het internationale Terrorisme en het recht op zelfverdediging', 56 *Internationale Spectator* (2002) pp. 12-14
− Levenson, Laurie L., 'Detention, Material Witnesses & the War on Terrorism', 35 *Loyola of Los Angeles Law Review* (2002) pp. 1217-1226
− Love, Maryann Cusimano, 'Globalization, Ethics, and the War on Terrorism', 16 *Notre Dame Journal of Law, Ethics, and Public Policy* (2002) pp. 65-80
− Maddox, Heather Anne, 'After the Dust Settles: Military Tribunal Justice for Terrorists After September 11, 2001', 28 *North Carolina Journal of International Law & Commercial Regulation* (2002) pp. 421-476
− Mallat, Chibli, 'The Original Sin: "Terrorism" or "Crime Against Humanity"?', 34 *Case Western Reserve JIL* (2002) pp. 245-248
− Malzahn, Scott M., 'State Sponsorship and Support of International Terrorism: Customary Norms of State Responsibility', 26 *Hastings International and Comparative Law Review* (2002) pp. 83-114
− Martinez, Lucy, 'Prosecuting Terrorists at the International Criminal Court: Possibilities and Problems', 34 *Rutgers Law Journal* (2002) pp. 1-62
− Masterton, R. Peter, 'Military Commissions and the War on Terrorism', 36 *The International Lawyer* (2002) pp. 1165-1172
− McWhinney, Edward, 'International Law-Based Responses to the September 11 International Terrorist Attacks', 1 *Chinese Journal of International Law* (2002) pp. 280-286
− Mégret, Frédéric, '"Krieg"? Völkerrechtssemantik und der Kampf gegen den Terrorismus', 35 *Kritische Justiz* (2002) pp. 157-179
− Mellor, Justin S.C., 'Missing the Boat: The Legal and Practical Problems of the Prevention of Maritime Terrorism', 18 *Amer. Univ. ILR* (2002) pp. 341-397
− Moyano Bonilla, César, 'La represión del terrorismo mediante el derecho internacional', 102 *Universitas* (2001) pp. 107-161
− Muguruza, Cristina Churruca, 'The European Union's Reaction to the Terrorist Attacks on the United States', 14 *Humanitäres Völkerrecht* (2001) pp. 234-243
− Mundis, Daryl A., 'The Use of Military Commissions to Prosecute Individuals Accused of Terrorist Acts', 96 *AJIL* (2002) pp. 320-327
− Murphy, Sean D., 'Terrorism and the Concept of "Armed Attack" in Article 51 of the U.N. Charter', 43 *Harvard ILJ* (2002) pp. 41-51
− Normand, Roger and Christoph Wilcke, 'Human Rights, Sanctions, and Terrorist Threats: The United Nations Sanctions Against Iraq', 11 *Transn. L & Contemp. Probs.* (2001) pp. 299-343
− Note, 'Responding to Terrorism: Crime, Punishment, and War', 115 *Harvard Law Review* (2002) pp. 1217-1238
− Oeter, Stefan, 'Terrorismus – ein völkerrechtliches Verbrechen? Zur Frage der Unterstellung terroristischer Akte unter die internationale Strafgerichtsbarkeit', 76 *Die Friedenswarte* (2001) pp. 11-31
− Oeter, Stefan, 'Terrorismus und Menschenrechte', 40 *Archiv des Völkerrechts* (2002) pp. 422-453

− Orentlicher Diane F. and Robert Kogod Goldman, 'When Justice Goes to War: Prosecuting Terrorists Before Military Commissions', 25 *Harvard Journal of Law & Public Policy* (2002) pp. 653-663

− Parker, Tom, 'The Proportionality Principle in the War on Terror', 15 *Hague YIL* (2002) pp. 3-15

− Paust, Jordan J., 'Use of Armed Force Against Terrorists in Afghanistan, Iraq, and Beyond', 35 *Cornell ILJ* (2002) pp. 533-557

− Paust, Jordan J., 'Antiterrorism Military Commissions: The Ad Hoc DOD Rules of Procedure', 23 *Mich. JIL* (2002) pp. 677-694

− Peterke, Sven, 'Die Bekämpfung der Terrorismusfinanzierung unter Kapitel VII der UN-Charta: die Resolution 1373 (2001) des UN-Sicherheitsrats', 14 *Humanitäres Völkerrecht* (2001) pp. 217-221

− Petit, Françoise Camille, 'Terrorisme et droit international humanitaire: quelles leçons tirer du statut controversé des prisonniers de Guantanamo?', 3 *Droit et défense: revue générale du droit de la sécurité et de la défense* (2002) pp. 25-32

− Posteraro, Christopher Clarke, 'Intervention in Iraq: Towards a Doctrine of Anticipatory Counter-Terrorism, Counterproliferation Intervention', 15 *Florida Journal of International Law* (2002) pp. 151-213

− Prakken, E., 'Voorzichtig met Europese strafrechtelijke terrorismebestrijding', 76 *Nederlands Juristenblad* (2001) pp. 1879-1882

− Ramón Chornet, Consuelo, 'La lucha contra el terrorismo internacional después del 11 de septiembre de 2001', 53 *Revista española de derecho internacional* (2001) pp. 273-288

− Remiro Brotóns, Antonio, 'Terrorismo, mantenimiento de la paz y nuevo orden', 53 *Revista española de derecho internacional* (2001) pp. 125-171

− Roberts, Adam, 'Counter-Terrorism, Armed Force and the Laws of War', 44 *Survival* (2002) pp. 7-32

− Rostow, Nicholas, 'Before and After: The Changed UN Response to Terrorism Since September 11th, 35 *Cornell ILJ* (2002) pp. 475-490

− Roth, Brad R. et al., 'Terror Symposium: Journal of International Law Symposium: War on Terrorism and the Responses in the United States and Abroad', 10 *Michigan State University. Detroit College of Law Journal of International Law* (2001) pp. 539-672

− Rubin, Alfred P., 'Legal Response to Terror: An International Criminal Court?', 43 *Harvard ILJ* (2002) pp. 65-70

− Ruffert, Matthias, 'Terrorismusbekämpfung zwischen Selbstverteidigung und kollektiver Sicherheit', 35 *Zeitschrift für Rechtspolitik* (2002) 247-252

− Sadat M., S.H., 'An Agenda for War: The Law of Self-Defence in the Light of the 11 September Terrorist Attacks', 10 *Tilburg For. LR* (2002) pp. 76-81

− Samuilov, Sergei, 'The United Nations, the United States, and the War on Terrorism', 40 *Russian Politics and Law* (2002) pp. 28-46

− Sandoz, Yves, 'Lutte contre le terrorisme et droit international: risques et opportunités', 12 *SZIER/RSDIE* (2002) pp. 319-354

− Scharf, Michael P., 'The Broader Meaning of the Lockerbie Trial and the Future of International Counter-Terrorism', 29 *Syracuse Journal of International Law and Commerce* (2001) pp. 50-64

− Scharf, Michael P., 'The Case for an International Trial of the Al-Qaeda and Taliban Perpetrators of the 9/11 Attacks', 36 *New England LR* (2002) pp. 911-917

– Schmahl, Stefanie and Andreas Haratsch, 'Internationaler Terrorismus als Herausforderung an das Völkerrecht', 32 *WeltTrends* (2001) pp. 111-117
– Schneider, Michaela, 'Der 11. September und die militärischen Reaktionen: Anwend-
barkeit des humanitären Völkerrechts?', 14 *Humanitäres Völkerrecht* (2001) pp. 222-
226
– Schrijver, Nico, 'Responding to International Terrorism: Moving the Frontiers of Inter-
national Law for "Enduring Freedom"?', 48 *NILR* (2001) pp. 271-291
– Sofaer, Abraham D., 'Terrorism as War', 96 *Proc. ASIL* (2002) pp. 254-259
– Stahn, Carsten, 'International Law at a Crossroads? The Impact of September 11', 62
ZaöRV (2002) pp. 183-255
– Subedi, Surya P., 'The UN Resolution to International Terrorism in the Aftermath of the
Terrorist Attack in America and the Problem of the Definition of Terrorism in Interna-
tional Law', 4 *Int. LF* (2002) pp. 159-169
– Sucharitkul, Sompng, 'Jurisdiction, Terrorism and the Rule of International Law', 32
Golden Gate University Law Review (2002) pp. 311-323
– Tietje, Christian and Karsten Nowrot, 'Völkerrechtliche Aspekte militärischer Maßnah-
men gegen den internationalen Terrorismus', 44 *Neue Zeitschrift für Wehrrecht* (2002)
pp. 1-18
– Tomuschat, Christian, 'Der 11. September 2001 und seine rechtlichen Konsequenzen',
28 *Europäische Grundrechte-Zeitschrift* (2001) pp. 535-545
– Trahan, Jennifer, 'Trying a Bin Laden and Others: Evaluating the Options for Terrorist
Trials', 24 *Houston Journal of International Law* (2002) pp. 475-508
– Valki, László, 'The 11 September Terrorist Attacks and the Rules of International Law',
41 *Revue de droit militaire et de droit de guerre* (2002) pp. 111-127
– Vogelson, Jay M., 'Multinational Approaches to Eradicating International Terrorism', 36
The International Lawyer (2002) pp. 67-76
– Von Bubnoff, Eckhart, 'Terrorismusbekämpfung – eine weltweite Herausforderung', 55
Neue juristische Wochenschrift (2002) pp. 2672-2676
– Warbrick, Colin, 'The Principles of the European Convention on Human Rights and the
Response of States to Terrorism', 3 *European Human Rights Law Review* (2002)
pp. 287-314
– Wilkinson, Paul, 'Disarmament and Terrorism', *OPCW Synthesis* (2001) pp. 12-17
– Wolf, Joachim, 'Terrorismusbekämpfung unter Beweisnot: völkerrechtliche Informa-
tionsanforderungen im bewaffneten Konflikt', 14 *Humanitäres Völkerrecht* (2001)
pp. 204-215
– Zelman, Joshua D., 'Recent Developments in International Law: Anti-Terrorism Legislation – Part One: An Overview', 11 *Journal of Transnational Law and Policy* (2001)
pp. 183-200
– Zelman, Joshua D., 'Recent Developments in International Law: Anti-Terrorism Legislation – Part Two: The Impact and Consequences', 11 *Journal of Transnational Law and
Policy* (2002) pp. 421-441

13.3   MILITARY LAW

Books
- Belknap, Michal R., *The Vietnam War on Trial: The My Lai Massacre and the Court-martial of Lieutenant Calley* (Lawrence, University Press of Kansas 2002) 298 pp.
- Borch, Frederic L., *Judge Advocates in Combat: Army Lawyers in Military Operations from Vietnam to Haiti* (Washington, Office of the Judge Advocate General 2001) 413 pp.
- Brunelli, David and Giuseppe Mazzi, *Diritto penale militare*, 3rd edn. (Milan, Giuffrè 2002) 552 pp.
- Fidell, Eugene R. and Dwight H. Sullivan, eds., *Evolving Military Justice* (Annapolis, Naval Institute Press 2002) 362 pp.

Articles
- Anderson, Kenneth, 'What to Do with Bin Laden and Al Qaeda Terrorists? A Qualified Defense of Military Commissions and United States Policy on Detainees at Guantanamo Bay Naval Base', 25 *Harvard Journal of Law & Public Policy* (2002) pp. 591-634
- Bartolini, Giulio, 'Le modifiche al codice penale militare di guerra a seguito della missione italiana in Afghanistan', 57 *La Comunità internazionale* (2002) pp. 171-199
- Beery, Ryan H., 'Modern Use of Military Tribunals: A Legal "Can" and a Political "Should"?', 28 *Ohio Northern University Law Review* (2002) pp. 789-813
- De Andrade, Aurélie, 'Une particularité de la procédure pénale applicable aux militaires: l'avis du ministre de la défense', 57 *RSCDPC* (2002) pp. 71-80
- Dickenson, Laura A., 'Using Legal Process to Fight Terrorism: Detentions, Military Commissions, International Tribunals, and the Rule of Law', 75 *Southern California Law Review* (2002) pp. 1407-1492
- Evans, Christopher M., 'Terrorism on Trial: The President's Constitutional Authority to Order the Prosecution of Suspected Terrorists by Military Commission', 51 *Duke Law Journal* (2002) pp. 1831-1856
- Fitzpatrick, Joan, 'Jurisdiction of Military Commissions and the Ambiguous War on Terrorism', 96 *AJIL* (2002) pp. 345-354
- French, Anne English, 'Trials in Times of War: Do the Bush Military Commissions Sacrifice Our Freedoms?', 63 *Ohio State Law Journal* (2002) pp. 1225-1283
- Khan, Rahmatullah, 'The U.S. Military Tribunals to Try Terrorists', 62 *ZaöRV* (2002) pp. 293-316
- Koh, Harold Hongju, 'The Case Against Military Commissions', 96 *AJIL* (2002) pp. 337-349
- Kumar, Nilendra, 'Prosecuting Terrorists: A Case for Use of Military Justice Apparatus', 42 *Indian JIL* (2002) pp. 187-193
- Kumar Katyal, Neal and Laurence H. Tribe, 'Waging War. Deciding Guilt: Trying the Military Tribunals', 111 *Yale LJ* (2002) pp. 1259-1310
- Maddox, Heather Anne, 'After the Dust Settles: Military Tribunal Justice for Terrorists After September 11, 2001', 28 *North Carolina Journal of International Law & Commercial Regulation* (2002) pp. 421-476
- Masterton, R. Peter, 'Military Commissions and the War on Terrorism', 36 *The International Lawyer* (2002) pp. 1165-1172
- Matheson, Michael J., 'U.S. Military Commissions: One of Several Options', 96 *AJIL* (2002) pp. 354-358

− Mundis, Daryl A., 'The Use of Military Commissions to Prosecute Individuals Accused of Terrorist Acts', 96 *AJIL* (2002) pp. 320-327

− Noone, Gregory P., 'President Bush's Military Order: Detention, Treatment, and Trial of Certain Non-Citizens in the War Against Terrorism: Essay', 34 *Case Western Reserve JIL* (2002) pp. 253-257

− Orentlicher Diane F. and Robert Kogod Goldman, 'When Justice Goes to War: Prosecuting Terrorists Before Military Commissions', 25 *Harvard Journal of Law & Public Policy* (2002) pp. 653-663

− Paust, Jordan J., 'Antiterrorism Military Commissions: Courting Illegality', 23 *Mich. JIL* (2001) pp. 1-29

− Paust, Jordan J., 'Antiterrorism Military Commissions: The Ad Hoc DOD Rules of Procedure', 23 *Mich. JIL* (2002) pp. 677-694

− Reydams, Luc, 'Swiss Military Trial of Former Rwanda Town Mayor Accused of War Crimes for Inciting Murder of Civilians in Rwanda', 96 *AJIL* (2002) pp. 231-236

− Rogers, A.P.V., 'The Use of Military Courts to Try Suspects', 51 *ICLQ* (2002) pp. 967-979

− Sharfstein, Daniel J., 'Human Rights Beyond the War on Terrorism: Extradition Defenses Based on Prison Conditions in the United States', 42 *Santa Clara Law Review* (2002) pp. 1137-1157

− Van Baarda, Ted and Fred van Iersel, 'The Uneasy Relationship Between Conscience and Military Law: The Brahimi Report's Unresolved Dilemma', 9 *International Peacekeeping* (2002) pp. 25-50

− Wedgwood, Ruth, 'Al Qaeda, Terrorism, and Military Commissions', 96 *AJIL* (2002) pp. 328-337

13.4   HUMAN RIGHTS LAW

Books

− Buchbender, Ortwin, ed., *Kämpfen für die Menschenrechte: der Kosovo-Konflikt im Spiegel der Friedensethik*, Vol. 1 (Baden-Baden, Nomos 2002) 398 pp.

− Chakrabarty, Manik, *Human Rights and Refugees: Problems, Laws and Practices* (New Delhi, Deep & Deep 2001) 271 pp.

− Human Rights Watch, *Playing with Fire: Weapons Proliferation, Political Violence, and Human Rights in Kenya* (New York, Human Rights Watch 2002) 119 pp.

− Katayanagi, Mari, *Human Rights Functions of United Nations Peacekeeping Operation* (The Hague, Nijhoff 2002) 316 pp.

− Matláry, Janne Haaland, *Intervention for Human Rights in Europe* (Basingstoke, Palgrave 2002) 286 pp.

− Moseley, Alexander and Richard Norman, eds., *Human Rights and Military Intervention* (Aldershot, Ashgate 2002) 283 pp.

− Müller, Erwin, Patricia Schneider and Kristina Thony, eds., *Menschenrechtsschutz: politische Maßnahmen, zivilgesellschaftliche Strategien, humanitäre Interventionen* (Baden-Baden, Nomos 2002) 387 pp.

− Ölz, Martin, *Die NGOs im Recht des internationalen Menschenrechtsschutzes* (Vienna, Verlag Österreich 2002) 436 pp.

- Provost, René, *International Human Rights and Humanitarian Law* (Cambridge, Cambridge University Press 2002) 418 pp.
- Ramcharan, Bertrand G., *Human Rights and Human Security* (The Hague, Kluwer Law International 2002) 250 pp.
- Von Sternberg, Mark R., *The Grounds of Refugee Protection in the Context of International Human Rights and Humanitarian Law: Canadian and United States Case Law Compared* (The Hague, Nijhoff 2002) 334 pp.
- Wodarz, Katharina, *Gewaltverbot, Menschenrechtsschutz und Selbstbestimmungsrecht im Kosovo-Konflikt* (Frankfurt am Main, Peter Lang 2002) 253 pp.
- Zawati, Hilmi M., *Is Jihad a Just War? War, Peace, and Human Rights Under Islamic and Public International Law* (Lewiston, Edwin Mellen Press 2002) 244 pp.

Articles
- Bassiouni, M. Cherif, 'Accountability for Violations of International Humanitarian Law and Other Serious Violations of Human Rights', 1 *The Global Community* (2001) pp. 3-51
- Bennoune, Karima, '"Sovereignty vs. Suffering"? Re-Examining Sovereignty and Human Rights Through the Lens of Iraq', 13 *EJIL* (2002) pp. 243-262
- Böhme, Jörn, 'Kein Frieden ohne Menschenrechte – keine Menschenrechte ohne Frieden: Menschenrechte und der israelisch-palestinensische Konflikt', *Jahrbuch Menschenrechte* (2002) pp. 145-157
- Boot, M., 'Mensenrechten en oorlogsmisdadigers: het recht op een eerlijk proces in internationale strafrechtspraak', 50 *Ars Aequi* (2001) pp. 443-448
- Bruscoli, Francesco, 'The Rights of Individuals in Times of Armed Conflict', 6 *International Journal of Human Rights* (2002) pp. 45-60
- Buchanan, David, 'Gendercide and Human Rights', 4 *Journal of Genocide Research* (2002) pp. 95-108
- Burr, Sherri L., 'From Noriega to Pinochet: Is There an International Moral and Legal Right to Kidnap Individuals Accused of Gross Human Rights Violations?', 29 *Denver JIL & Pol.* (2001) pp. 101-114
- Cerone, John, 'Legal Constraints on the International Community's Responses to Gross Violations of Human Rights and Humanitarian Law in Kosovo, East Timor, and Chechnya', 2 *Human Rights Review* (2001) pp. 19-53
- Clapham, Andrew and Scott Jerbi, 'Categories of Complicity in Human Rights Abuses', 24 *Hasting International and Comparative Law Review* (2001) pp. 339-349
- De Wet, Erika, 'Human Rights Limitations to Economic Enforcement Measures Under Article 41 of the United Nations Charter and the Iraqi Sanctions Regime', 14 *Leiden JIL* (2001) pp. 277-300
- Edwards, George E., 'International Human Rights Law Challenges to the New International Criminal Court: The Search and Seizure Right to Privacy', 26 *Yale JIL* (2001) pp. 323-412
- Eide, Asbjørn, 'Minorities, Indigenous Peoples and the Prevention of Conflicts: The Role of the United Nations Sub-Commission on the Promotion and Protection of Human Rights', 14 *International Geneva Yearbook* (2000-2001) pp. 35-45
- Greenberg, Jason S., 'Torture of Terrorists in Israel: The United Nations and the Supreme Court of Israel Pave the Way for Human Rights to Trump Communitarianism', 7 *ILSA JI & CL* (2001) pp. 539-552

– Gross, Emanuel, 'Trying Terrorists – Justification for Differing Trial Rules: The Balance Between Security Considerations and Human Rights', 13 *Indiana International & Comparative Law Review* (2002) pp. 1-97

– Jinks, Derek, 'International Human Rights Law and the War on Terrorism', 31 *Denver JIL & Pol.* (2002) pp. 58-68

– Juma, Laurence, 'The Human Rights Approach to Peace in Sierra Leone: The Analysis of the Peace Process and Human Rights Enforcement in a Civil War Situation', 30 *Denver JIL & Pol.* (2002) pp. 325-376

– Kamali, Maryam, 'Accountability for Human Rights Violations: A Comparison of Transitional Justice in East Germany and South Africa', 40 *Colum. JTL* (2001) pp. 89-141

– Latore, Roseann M., 'Coming Out of the Dark: Achieving Justice for Victims of Human Rights Violations by South American Military Regimes', 25 *Boston College Int. & Comp. LR* (2002) pp. 419-448

– Lediakh, Irina A., 'Protecting the Right to Life During Armed Conflicts', in Roger Clark, Ferdinand Feldbrugge and Stanislaw Pomorski, eds., *International and National Law in Russia and Eastern Europe: Essays in Honor of George Ginsburgs* (The Hague, Nijhoff 2001) pp. 207-224

– Martin, Francisco Forrest, 'Using International Human Rights Law for Establishing a Unified Use of Force Rule in the Law of Armed Conflict', 64 *Saskatchean Law Review* (2001) pp. 347-396

– Mutua, Makau, 'Terrorism and Human Rights: Power, Culture, and Subordination', 8 *Buffalo Human Rights Law Review* (2002) pp. 1-13

– Normand, Roger and Christoph Wilcke, 'Human Rights, Sanctions, and Terrorist Threats: The United Nations Sanctions Against Iraq', 11 *Transn. L & Contemp. Probs.* (2001) pp. 299-343

– Opie, Rachel, 'International Human Rights Promotion and Protection Through Peace Operations: A Strong Mechanism?', 7 *International Peacekeeping: The Yearbook of International Peace Operations* (2001) pp. 99-151

– Österdahl, Inger, 'FN-sanktioner och mänskliga rättigheter eller Hur kunde det bli på detta viset?', 87 *Svensk juristtidning* (2002) pp. 894-916

– Parker, Karen, 'Human Rights of Women During Armed Conflict', 3 *Women and International Human Rights Law* (2001) pp. 283-323

– Pejic, Jelena, 'Non-Discrimination and Armed Conflict', 83 *IRRC* (2001) pp. 183-194

– Pejic, Jelena, 'The Right to Food in Situations of Armed Conflict: The Legal Framework', 83 *IRRC* (2001) pp. 1097-1109

– Reinisch, August, 'Developing Human Rights and Humanitarian Law Accountability of the Security Council for the Imposition on Economic Sanctions', 95 *AJIL* (2001) pp. 851-872

– Ricca, Michele, 'Human Rights and the UN Special Rapporteurs' System: Tendencies in Reporting on Conflict Areas', 15 *Humanitäres Völkerrecht* (2002) pp. 165-174

– Robinson, J.A., 'International Humanitarian and Human-Rights Law Pertaining to Child Civilians in Armed Conflict: An Overview', 65 *Tydskrif vir hedendaags Romeins-Hollandse reg* (2002) pp. 186-202

– Van Alebeek, Rosanne, 'The Pinochet Case: International Human Rights Law on Trial', 71 *BYIL* (2000) pp. 29-70

13.5   REFUGEE LAW

Books
- Chetail, Vincent, ed., *La Convention de Genève du 28 juillet 1951 relative au statut des réfugiés 50 ans après: bilan et perspectives* (Brussels, Bruylant 2001) 456 pp.
- Helton, Arthur C., *The Price of Indifference: Refugees and Humanitarian Action in the New Century* (Oxford, Oxford University Press 2002) 314 pp.
- Von Sternberg, Mark R., *The Grounds of Refugee Protection in the Context of International Human Rights and Humanitarian Law: Canadian and United States Case Law Compared* (The Hague, Nijhoff 2002) 334 pp.

Articles
- Chimni, B.S., 'Refugees and Post-Conflict Reconstruction: A Critical Perspective', 9 *International Peacekeeping* (2002) pp. 163-180
- Happold, Matthew, 'Excluding Children from Refugee Status: Child Soldiers and Article 1F of the Refugee Convention', 17 *Amer. Univ. ILR* (2002) pp. 1131-1176
- Hart, Barry, 'Refugee Return in Bosnia and Herzegovina: Coexistence Before Reconciliation', in Mohammed Abu-Nimer, ed., *Reconciliation, Justice and Coexistence: Theory & Practice* (Lanham, Lexington Books 2001) pp. 291-310
- Heintze, Hans-Joachim, 'Flüchtlingsrechtliche Aspekte der Afghanistankrise', 40 = 49 *AWR bulletin* (2002) pp. 8-20
- Hickel, Marguerite Contat, 'Protection of Internally Displaced Persons Affected by Armed Conflict: Concept and Challenges', 83 *IRRC* (2001) pp. 699-711
- Kälin, Walter, 'Flight in Times of War', 83 *IRRC* (2001) pp. 629-650
- Kures, Megan E., 'The Effect of Armed Conflict on Children: The Plight of Unaccompanied Refugee Minors', 25 *Suffolk Transnational Law Review* (2001) pp. 141-163
- Storey, Hugo and Rebecca Wallace, 'War and Peace in Refugee Law Jurisprudence', 95 *AJIL* (2001) pp. 349-366
- Whitman, Jim, 'The Kosovo Refugee Crisis: NATO's Humanitarianism Versus Human Rights', in Ken Booth, ed., *The Kosovo Tragedy: The Human Rights Dimensions* (London, Frank Cass 2001) pp. 164-183

TABLE OF CASES[*]

INTERNATIONAL

---

[*] The Table of Cases was compiled by Mrs. B.M. Hall, Elie, UK.

NATIONAL

INDEX

The index contains references to all matters of substance dealt with in the text of the articles. Detailed references to cases dealt with will be found in the accompanying Table of Cases. Multilateral agreements are indexed under Agreements, multilateral, classified by subject. The section on Correspondents' Reports is also indexed, but for information on the practice of individual states regarding detailed aspects of international humanitarian law the reader should consult the index under the states concerned. The index does contain, however, references to material from this section and the Documentation section which relate to the major topics of discussion in the present volume. Footnotes containing substantive material are also indexed, as are references to the work of scholars the first time such work is listed.

The index was compiled by Mrs. B.M. Hall, Elie, UK

Abbreviations frequently used

g.r.	general references
ICC	International Criminal Court
ICJ	International Court of Justice
ICTR	International Criminal Tribunal for Rwanda
ICTY	International Criminal Tribunal for the Former Yugoslavia
IHL	International humanitarian law
p.a.r.	parties, accessions, ratifications
UN	United Nations Organisation
US	United States of America